Financial Accounting Standards Board

Current Text

2002/2003 Edition

Accounting Standards

as of June 1, 2002

Volume I

General Standards
Topical Index

JOHN WILEY & SONS, INC.
New York • Chichester • Brisbane • Toronto • Singapore

Published by the
Financial Accounting Standards Board

The materials in this volume have been prepared and compiled by the staff of the Financial Accounting Standards Board and have not been reviewed or approved by the Board.

NOTICE TO USERS OF THE *CURRENT TEXT*

This year's edition of the Financial Accounting Standard Board's (FASB) *Current Text* has been revised and updated as follows:

New Pronouncements

The *Current Text* has been updated to include the following new pronouncements:

FAS141: Business Combinations

Section B51, "Business Combinations (FAS 141)," has been added to reflect the issuance of Statement 141 and to replace Section B50, "Business Combinations (APB 16)." Statement 141, issued in June 2001, addresses financial accounting and reporting for business combinations and supersedes APB Opinion No. 16, *Business Combinations,* and FASB Statement No. 38, *Accounting for Preacquisition Contingencies of Purchased Enterprises.* Statement 141 improves the transparency of the accounting and reporting for business combinations by requiring that all business combinations be accounted for under a single method—the purchase method. Use of the pooling-of-interests method is no longer permitted.

Statement 141 requires that the purchase method be used for business combinations initiated after June 30, 2001. Statement 141 does not apply, however, to combinations of two or more not-for-profit organizations, the acquisition of a for-profit organization by a not-for-profit organization, and combinations of two or more mutual enterprises. Due to the previously mentioned fact, Section B50 has been moved to Appendix E for continued reference by users.

FAS142: Goodwill and Other Intangible Assets

Section G40, "Goodwill and Other Intangible Assets," has been added to reflect the issuance of Statement 142 and replaces Section I60, "Intangible Assets." Statement 142 supersedes APB Opinion No. 17, *Intangible Assets*. This Statement addresses the financial accounting and reporting for acquired goodwill and other intangible assets. It addresses how intangible assets that are acquired individually or with a group of other assets (but not those acquired in a business combination) should be accounted for in financial statements upon their acquisition. This Statement also addresses how goodwill and other intangible assets should be accounted for after they have been initially recognized in the financial statements.

Statement 142 provides that both goodwill and intangible assets that have indefinite useful lives will not be amortized but will be tested at least annually for impairment. Intangible assets that have finite useful lives will continue to be amortized over their useful lives.

The provisions of Statement 142 are required to be applied starting with fiscal years beginning after December 15, 2001. Because of the delayed effective date, Section I60 has been moved to Appendix E for continued reference by users.

FAS143: Accounting for Asset Retirement Obligations

Section A50, "Asset Retirement Obligations," has been added to reflect the issuance of Statement 143. This Statement addresses financial accounting and reporting for obligations associated with the retirement of tangible long-lived assets and the associated asset retirement costs and applies to all entities. Statement 143 applies to legal obligations associated with the retirement of long-lived assets that result from the acquisition, construction, development, and (or) the normal operation of a long-lived asset, except for certain obligations of lessees.

Statement 143 requires that the fair value of a liability for an asset retirement obligation be recognized in the period in which it is incurred if a reasonable estimate of fair value can be made. The associated asset retirement cost is capitalized as part of the carrying amount of the long-lived asset. Since the liability for an asset retirement obligation is recorded at its fair value, accretion expense shall be recognized each period using the credit-adjusted risk-free interest rate in effect when the liability was initially recognized. The capitalized asset retirement cost is allocated to expense using a systematic and rational method over its useful life.

FAS144: Accounting for the Impairment or Disposal of Long-Lived Assets

The latter half of Section I08, "Impairment," has been revised and Section D60, "Disposal of Long-Lived Assets," has been added to reflect the issuance of Statement 144. Statement 144, issued in August 2001, addresses financial accounting and reporting for the impairment of long-lived assets and for long-lived assets to be disposed of. Statement 144 replaces FASB Statement 121, *Accounting for the Impairment of Long-Lived Assets and for Long-Lived Assets to Be Disposed Of,* and institutes one accounting model, based on the framework established in Statement 121, for long-lived assets to be disposed of. This model applies to all long-lived assets to be disposed of, including discontinued operations, and replaces the provisions of APB Opinion 30, *Reporting the Results of Operations—Reporting the Effects of Disposal of a Segment of a Business, and Extraordinary, Unusual and Infrequently Occurring Events and Transactions,* for the disposal of components of an entity. Section I14, "Income Statement Presentation: Discontinued Operations (FAS 144)," has been added to reflect the issuance of Statement 144 and to replace Section I13, "Income Statement Presentation: Discontinued Operations (APB 30)."

Statement 144 requires that long-lived assets to be disposed of by sale be measured at the lower of carrying amount or fair value less cost to sell, whether reported in continuing operations or in discontinued operations. Therefore, discontinued operations will no longer be measured at net realizable value or include amounts for operating losses that have not yet occurred. Statement 144 also broadens the reporting of discontinued operations to include all components of an entity with operations that can be distinguished from the rest of the entity and that will be eliminated from the ongoing operations of the entity in a disposal transaction.

Section I13 and a portion of Section I08 have been moved to Appendix E for continued reference by users who have not yet adopted the new standard.

FAS145: Rescission of FASB Statements No. 4, 44, and 64, Amendment of FASB Statement No. 13, and Technical Corrections

Section I17, "Income Statement Presentation: Extraordinary Items," Section L10, "Leases," and Section L35, "Liabilities: Extinguishments," have been revised to reflect the issuance of Statement 145. Statement 145, issued in April 2002, rescinds FASB Statement 4, *Reporting Gains and Losses from Extinguishment of Debt,* FASB Statement 44, *Accounting for Intangible Assets of Motor Carriers,* and FASB Statement 64, *Extinguishments of Debt Made to Satisfy Sinking-Fund Requirements.* Statement 145 also amends FASB Statement 13, *Accounting for Leases.*

Statement 4 required all gains and losses from extinguishment of debt to be aggregated and, if material, classified as an extraordinary item, net of related income tax effect. As a result of the issuance of Statement 145, the criteria in APB Opinion 30, *Reporting the Results of Operations—Reporting the Effects of Disposal of a Segment of a Business, and Extraordinary, Unusual and Infrequently Occurring Events and Transactions,* will now be used to classify those gains and losses.

Statement 44 was issued to establish accounting requirements for the effects of the transition to the provisions of the Motor Carrier Act of 1980 (Public Law 96-296, 96th Congress, July 1, 1980). Those transitions are completed; therefore, Statement 44 is no longer necessary.

Statement 145 amends Statement 13 to require that certain lease modifications that have economic effects similar to sale-leaseback transactions be accounted for in the same manner as sale-leaseback transactions. This Statement also makes various technical corrections to existing pronouncements. Those corrections are not substantive in nature.

Statement 145 also makes various technical corrections to existing authoritative literature. Many of those corrections previously had been incorporated into the *Current Text*. Where necessary, those corrections have been made in this edition.

FTB01-1: Effective Date for Certain Financial Institutions of Certain Provisions of Statement 140 Related to the Isolation of Transferred Financial Assets

Section F39, "Financial Instruments: Transfers," has been updated to reflect the issuance of Technical Bulletin 01-1. Technical Bulletin 01-1 defers the effective date for certain provisions of FASB Statement No. 140, *Accounting for Transfers and Servicing of Financial Assets and Extinguishments of Liabilities,* for certain banks and other financial institutions and provides additional transition time for voluntary transfers to certain transferees (for example, certain master trusts).

ADDITIONAL MATERIAL

A new appendix, Appendix H, "Excerpts from FASB Concepts Statement 7," has been added. Some sections such as A50, "Asset Retirement Obligations," and G40, "Goodwill and Other Intangible Assets," refer to various paragraphs of FASB Concepts Statement 7, *Using Cash Flow Information and Present Value in Accounting Measurements*. Those paragraphs are reproduced in this appendix for the convenience of the user.

AN INTRODUCTION TO THE CURRENT TEXT

Material Disclosed in the *Current Text*

The FASB *Current Text* is an integration of currently effective accounting and reporting standards. Material in the *Current Text* is drawn from AICPA Accounting Research Bulletins, APB Opinions, FASB Statements of Financial Accounting Standards, and FASB Interpretations. Those pronouncements are covered by Rule 203 of the AICPA Code of Professional Conduct, which states:

> *Rule 203—Accounting principles.* A member shall not (1) express an opinion or state affirmatively that the financial statements or other financial data of any entity are presented in conformity with generally accepted accounting principles or (2) state that he or she is not aware of any material modifications that should be made to such statements or data in order for them to be in conformity with generally accepted accounting principles, if such statements or data contain any departure from an accounting principle promulgated by bodies designated by Council to establish such principles that has a material effect on the statements or data taken as a whole. If, however, the statements or data contain such a departure and the member can demonstrate that due to unusual circumstances the financial statements or data would otherwise have been misleading, the member can comply with the rule by describing the departure, its approximate effects, if practicable, and the reasons why compliance with the principle would result in a misleading statement.

Interpretation No. 2 of Rule 203 states:

> *Status of FASB, GASB and FASAB interpretations.* Council is authorized under Rule 203 to designate bodies to establish accounting principles. Council has designated the Financial Accounting Standards Board (FASB) as such body and has resolved that FASB Statements of Financial Accounting Standards, together with those Accounting Research Bulletins and APB Opinions which are not superseded by action of the FASB, constitute accounting principles as contemplated in Rule 203. . . .
>
> In determining the existence of a departure from an accounting principle established by a Statement of Financial Accounting Standards, Accounting Research Bulletin or APB Opinion encompassed by Rule 203 . . . , the division of professional ethics will construe such Statements, Bulletin or Opinion in the light of any interpretations thereof issued by the FASB. . . .

The *Current Text* also incorporates the supplemental guidance provided by FASB Technical Bulletins and AICPA Accounting Interpretations.

The *Current Text* does not in any way supersede, change, or otherwise affect the pronouncements from which it is drawn. Although edited by the FASB staff, the abridged text has not been subjected to the FASB's due process procedures used for issuing FASB Statements. The authority of the *Current Text* is derived from the underlying pronouncements, which remain in force.

Material Excluded from the *Current Text*

The *Current Text* does not include FASB Statements of Financial Accounting Concepts. The concepts Statements may be found in *Original Pronouncements,* the companion publication to the *Current Text,* and in the separate publication, *Statements of Financial Accounting Concepts*. The *Current Text* also does not include FASB Special Reports in question-and-answer format (Q&As) which are available individually and in the annual bound volume, *FASB Staff Implementation Guides*.

Although the *Current Text* does not include the Issues discussed by the FASB Emerging Issues Task Force (EITF), where applicable, a list of specific EITF Issues is included in *Current Text* sections to alert the reader to additional guidance provided by the EITF on various topics. In addition, specific paragraphs in the *Current Text* have been linked to EITF Issues that provide interpretive guidance on those paragraphs. The text of the EITF Issues are contained in the FASB's *EITF Abstracts.* References to EITF Issues and the accounting literature referred to in the above paragraph are included in the *Current Text* topical index. (See the introduction to the topical index, page INTRO-1, for order information for *EITF Abstracts* and the Q&As.)

The *Current Text* also does not include AICPA audit and accounting Guides, Statements of Position, or Practice Bulletins, except insofar as specialized principles in them have been extracted and issued in FASB Statements. All of those documents, however, are available from the American Institute of Certified Public Accountants, Order Department, P.O. Box 2209, Jersey City, NJ 07303-2209 or Customer Service at (888) 777-7077.

The *Current Text* is a condensed version of original pronouncements. Descriptive material, such as information about Exposure Drafts, respondents' comments, background information, and reasons for conclusions and dissents, is generally excluded. However, certain material contained in other than the standards section of an original pronouncement is included to help the reader understand or implement the *Current Text.* Readers wishing to better understand the rationale behind a pronouncement or seeking background information should refer to the original pronouncement from which the related *Current Text* material is drawn. This is easy to do because each paragraph in the *Current Text* contains a source reference to the original pronouncement.

Organization of Text

The *Current Text* integrates financial accounting and reporting standards according to the major subject areas to which they apply. The subjects are arranged alphabetically in sections that are grouped into two volumes. Volume I (General Standards) contains those standards that are generally applicable to all enterprises; Volume II (Industry Standards) contains specialized standards that are applicable to not-for-profit organizations and enterprises operating in specific industries. A comprehensive topical index and various appendixes are included in the *Current Text.* (Refer to the introduction to the topical index for detailed information about the contents and use of the index.) The *Current Text* includes an appendix (G) showing where material from each paragraph of each original pronouncement is located in the *Current Text* or the reason why it is not included.

Each **section** is identified by an alpha-numeric code. (The numeric part has been arbitrarily selected to allow space for future additions.) The alpha-numeric code in the General Standards follows an alpha-numeric-numeric pattern (for example, A99), and the code in the Industry Standards follows an alpha-alpha-numeric pattern (for example, Aa9).

Paragraphs within each section are numbered consecutively, according to the following numeric format:

- Paragraphs .101 - .399: Standards
- Paragraphs .401 - .499: Glossary
- Paragraphs .501 - .999: Supplemental guidance (not covered by Rule 203)
- Paragraph .1000 and higher: List of EITF Issues that provide supplemental guidance.

All **section-paragraph references** are made in the following form: B05.127 or In6.102. For example, B05.127 refers to Section B05, "Balance Sheet Classification: Current Assets and Current Liabilities," paragraph .127, and In6.102 refers to Section In6, "Insurance Industry," paragraph .102.

Terms defined in the **Glossary** for a section are in boldface type the first time they appear in that section.

Source references are provided to indicate the original pronouncements from which material in each paragraph and footnote is derived. They appear in brackets and use the following abbreviations:

FAS	FASB Statement of Financial Accounting Standards
FIN	FASB Interpretation
FTB	FASB Technical Bulletin
CON	FASB Statement of Financial Accounting Concepts
APB	AICPA Accounting Principles Board Opinion
ARB	AICPA Accounting Research Bulletin
AIN	AICPA Accounting Interpretation
ch	chapter
fn	footnote

For example, the source reference [FIN21, ¶15, fn3] indicates footnote 3 to paragraph 15 of FASB Interpretation No. 21, *Accounting for Leases in a Business Combination.* Similarly, the source reference [AIN-APB18, #2] indicates the second AICPA Accounting Interpretation of APB Opinion No. 18, *The Equity Method of Accounting for Investments in Common Stock.*

Transitional language and editorial changes that *add* wording to an original pronouncement to maintain a consistent editorial style within the volumes appear in brackets. If an original pronouncement *deletes* wording from a previous pronouncement and it does not provide substitute wording, the amending pronouncement is not included in the source reference described in the preceding paragraph. Only the source reference for the earlier pronouncement is noted. However, Appendix B identifies the sources for all such deletions. Certain editorial deletions have been made to original pronouncements either to maintain a consistent editorial style or for clarity. Those deletions also are not noted. However, in such cases the deletions have not affected the substance of the text. Other changes, which are not presented in brackets, have been made to conform format (for example, "iii" may have been changed to "c"), to provide paragraph and exhibit headings, or to conform terminology, as follows:

Term in *Original Pronouncement*	**Term in *Current Text***
should (meaning *must*)	shall
see (in making a reference)	refer to
which (in a restrictive clause)	that
where (not location)	if
when (not specific timing)	if
entity (if used broadly)	enterprise
company	enterprise
corporation	enterprise
earned surplus	retained earnings
capital surplus	additional paid-in capital
additional paid-in surplus	additional paid-in capital

Effective Dates and Transition Provisions of Underlying Pronouncements

The effective dates of FASB Statements of Financial Accounting Standards, FASB Interpretations, APB Opinions, and Accounting Research Bulletins, and the issue dates of AICPA Accounting Interpretations and FASB Technical Bulletins are summarized in Appendix C. That appendix also presents the transition paragraphs of more recent pronouncements whose effective dates and transition provisions are such that they might be initially applied in annual financial statements issued on or after June 1, 2002.

If an entire section of the *Current Text* is superseded by a recently issued pronouncement that has a significantly delayed effective date, that superseded section is retained in the *Current Text* in a separate appendix (E) for the benefit of those enterprises that have not yet adopted the new standard. To indicate that its material is superseded, the entire appendix is shaded.

Users may need to refer to Appendix C to determine if the requirements of recently issued pronouncements that do not affect entire sections are effective in their particular circumstances. Users concerned with accounting and reporting standards for financial statements of prior years also may need to refer to the original pronouncements that were effective for those years. Appendix B lists changes to original pronouncements as the result of subsequent pronouncements.

Appendix H, "Excerpts from Concepts Statement 7"

Some sections such as A50, "Asset Retirement Obligations," and G40, "Goodwill and Other Intangible Assets," refer to various paragraphs of FASB Concepts Statement 7, *Using Cash Flow Information and Present Value in Accounting Measurements.* Those paragraphs are reproduced in this appendix for the convenience of the user.

FASB Emerging Issues Task Force

The Emerging Issues Task Force (EITF) was established in 1984 to aid the FASB in identifying implementation and emerging issues that may ultimately require action by the FASB. Make-up of the Task Force is designed to include persons in a position to be aware of emerging issues before they become widespread and before divergent practices regarding them become entrenched. After discussing the issues and the relevant accounting pronouncements, the group sometimes can reach a consensus on an issue, in which case no action by the FASB is usually needed. Because the application of EITF consensuses is mandatory under AICPA Statement on Auditing Standards (SAS) No. 69 (see Appendix A), a listing of all Issues discussed to date and their current status is presented in Appendix D and references to those Issues are included in the comprehensive topical index. In addition, where applicable, a list of specific EITF Issues that provide supplemental guidance for a *Current Text* section is included in paragraph .1000 of that section.

The FASB publishes a summary of the proceedings of the Task Force in a loose-leaf service, *EITF Abstracts.* A separate Abstract is presented for each Issue considered by the Task Force since its inception in 1984. A comprehensive topical index is included to facilitate quick identification of relevant Issues that have been addressed by the Task Force. *EITF Abstracts* is also published annually in a bound version.

Copies of *EITF Abstracts,* the Issue Summary packages, and related meeting minutes can be obtained from the FASB Order Department. For information on prices and discounts, call 1-800-748-0659.

Volume I

GENERAL STANDARDS
TABLE OF CONTENTS

Table of Contents

Table of Contents

(Refer to Volume II of the *Current Text*
for the appendixes and topical index.)

Volume II

INDUSTRY STANDARDS TABLE OF CONTENTS

(A Companion Volume)

Table of Contents

(The next page is 251.)

ACCOUNTING CHANGES SECTION A06

Sources: APB Opinion 20; FASB Statement 63; FASB Statement 73;
FASB Statement 95; FASB Statement 111; FASB Statement 128;
FASB Interpretation 1; FASB Interpretation 20

[**Note:** A list of Issues discussed by the Emerging Issues Task Force (EITF) that provide supplemental guidance for this section is presented in paragraph .1000.]

Summary

There is a presumption in preparing financial statements that an accounting principle once adopted should not be changed in accounting for events and transactions of a similar type. That presumption may be overcome only if the enterprise justifies the use of an alternative acceptable accounting principle on the basis that it is preferable.

Except for changes in certain specified accounting principles that are made by retroactive restatement, the cumulative effect of a change in an accounting principle shall be included in net income of the period of the change and presented in the income statement net of related tax effects after extraordinary items.

A change in accounting estimate shall be accounted for in the period of change if the change affects that period only or in the period of change and future periods if the change affects both. The change shall not be accounted for by restating amounts reported in financial statements of prior periods or by reporting pro forma amounts for prior periods. This section does not apply to accounting changes made in conformity with FASB Statements, Interpretations, and Technical Bulletins, AICPA Accounting Research Bulletins, APB Opinions, Industry Guides, Statements of Position, and Practice Bulletins, or EITF consensuses issued in the past or in the future.

Applicability and Scope

.101 This section defines various types of **accounting changes** and establishes guides for determining the manner of reporting each type. [APB20, ¶2]

.102 This section applies to financial statements that purport to present financial position, [APB20, ¶3] cash flows, [FAS95, ¶152(a)] and results of operations in conformity with generally accepted accounting principles. The guides in this section also may be appropriate in presenting financial information in other forms or for special purposes. [APB20, ¶3]

.103 Each FASB Statement and Interpretation, APB Opinion, and AICPA Accounting Research Bulletin specifies its effective date and manner of reporting a change to conform with the conclusions of that pronouncement. Other pronouncements of the FASB or other designated bodies as described in categories *(b)-(d)* of AICPA Statement on Auditing Standards (SAS) No. 69, *The Meaning of "Present Fairly in Conformity with Generally Accepted Accounting Principles" in the Independent Auditor's Report,* may also prescribe the manner of reporting a change in accounting principle. [FAS111, ¶7] [Refer to Appendix A for a current list of AICPA documents in categories *(b)-(d)* and for a more detailed explanation of SAS 69.] This section does not apply to [accounting] changes made in conformity with such pronouncements issued in the past or in the future. [APB20, ¶4]

Types of Accounting Changes

.104 The term *accounting change* in this section means a change in (a) an **accounting principle,** (b) an accounting estimate, or (c) the reporting enterprise (which is a special type of change in accounting principle [discussed in Section A35, "Adjustments of Financial Statements for Prior Periods," paragraphs .112 and .113]). The correction of an error in previously issued financial statements is not deemed to be an accounting change. [APB20, ¶6]

Change in Accounting Principle

.105 A change in accounting principle results from adoption of a generally accepted accounting principle different from the one used previously for reporting purposes. The term *accounting principle* includes not only accounting principles and practices but also the methods of applying them. [APB20, ¶7] [Refer to paragraph .1001 for an EITF Issue that provides interpretive guidance on this paragraph.]

.106 A characteristic of a change in accounting principle is that it concerns a choice from among two or more generally accepted accounting principles. However, neither (a) initial adoption of an accounting principle in recognition of events or transactions occurring for the first time or that previously were immaterial in their effect, nor (b) adoption or modification of an accounting principle necessitated by transactions or events that are clearly different in substance from those previously occurring is a change in accounting principle. [APB20, ¶8]

.107 Changes in accounting principle are numerous and varied. They include, for example, a change in the method of inventory pricing, such as from the last-in, first-out (LIFO) method to the first-in, first-out (FIFO) method; a change in depreciation method for previously recorded assets, such as from the double-declining-balance method to the straight-line method;[1] and a change in the method of accounting for long-term construction-type contracts, such as from the completed-contract method to the percentage-of-completion method. (Paragraph .110 covers a change in accounting principle to effect a change in estimate.) [APB20, ¶9]

.108 A change in composition of the elements of costs included in inventory also is an accounting change. An enterprise that makes such a change for financial reporting shall conform to the requirements of this section, including justifying the change on the basis of preferability as specified by paragraph .112. In applying this section, preferability among accounting principles shall be determined on the basis of whether the new principle constitutes an improvement in financial reporting and not on the basis of the income tax effect alone. [FIN1, ¶5]

Change in Accounting Estimate

.109 Changes in estimates used in accounting are necessary consequences of periodic presentations of financial statements. Preparing financial statements requires estimating the effects of future events. Examples of items for which estimates are necessary are uncollectible receivables, inventory obsolescence, service lives and salvage values of depreciable assets, warranty costs, periods benefited by a deferred cost, and recoverable mineral reserves. Future events and their effects cannot be perceived with certainty; estimating, therefore, requires the exercise of judgment. Thus, accounting estimates change as new events occur, as more experience is acquired, or as additional information is obtained. [APB20, ¶10]

Change in Estimate Effected by a Change in Accounting Principle

.110 Distinguishing between a change in an accounting principle and a change in an accounting estimate is sometimes difficult. For example, an enterprise may change from deferring and amortizing a cost to recording it as an expense when incurred because future benefits of the cost have become doubtful. The new accounting method is adopted, therefore, in partial or complete recognition of the change in estimated future benefits. The effect of the change in accounting principle is inseparable from the effect of the change in accounting estimate. Changes of this type are often related to the continuing process of obtaining additional information and revising estimates and are therefore considered as changes in estimates for purposes of applying this section. [APB20, ¶11]

---

[1] A change to the straight-line method at a specific point in the service life of an asset may be planned at the time the accelerated depreciation method is adopted to fully depreciate the cost over the estimated life of the asset. Consistent application of such a policy does not constitute a change in accounting principle for purposes of applying this section. [APB20, ¶9, fn3]

Justification for a Change in Accounting Principle

.111 In the preparation of financial statements, there is a presumption that an accounting principle once adopted should not be changed in accounting for events and transactions of a similar type. Consistent use of accounting principles from one accounting period to another enhances the utility of financial statements to users by facilitating analysis and understanding of comparative accounting data. [APB20, ¶15]

.112 The presumption that an enterprise should not change an accounting principle may be overcome only if the enterprise justifies the use of an alternative acceptable accounting principle on the basis that it is preferable. However, a method of accounting that was previously adopted for a type of transaction or event that is being terminated or that was a single, nonrecurring event in the past shall not be changed. For example, the method of accounting shall not be changed for a tax or tax credit that is being discontinued or for preoperating costs relating to a specific plant. [That is not intended] to imply, however, that a change in the estimated period to be benefited for a deferred cost (if justified by the facts) should not be recognized as a change in accounting estimate. [APB20, ¶16] The issuance of a new pronouncement by the FASB or by other designated bodies as described in categories *(a)-(d)* of SAS 69 that creates a new accounting principle, interprets an existing principle, expresses a preference for an accounting principle, or rejects a specific principle *may require* an entity to adopt a change in accounting principle. The issuance of such a pronouncement is considered to constitute sufficient support for making a change in accounting principle provided that the hierarchy established by SAS 69 is followed. [FAS111, ¶7(b)] [SAS 69 requires that] if there is a conflict between accounting principles relevant to the circumstances from one or more sources in category *(b), (c),* or *(d),* the enterprise should follow the treatment specified by the source in the higher category—for example, follow category *(b)* treatment over category *(c)*. [FAS111, ¶17] The burden of justifying other changes rests with the enterprise proposing the change. [APB20, ¶16] [Refer to paragraph .1001 for an EITF Issue that provides interpretive guidance on this paragraph.]

Exhibit 112A

[Deleted 11/92 because of FASB Statement 111, *Rescission of FASB Statement No. 32 and Technical Corrections.*]

[[1a]Deleted 2/92 because of FASB Statement 109, *Accounting for Income Taxes.*]

[[1b through 1d]Deleted 11/92 because of Statement 111.]

General Disclosure—A Change in Accounting Principle

.113 The nature of and justification for a change in accounting principle and its effect on income shall be disclosed in the financial statements of the period in which the change is made. The justification for the change shall explain clearly why the newly adopted accounting principle is preferable. [APB20, ¶17]

Reporting a Change in Accounting Principle

.114 Although they conflict, both (a) the potential dilution of public confidence in financial statements resulting from restating financial statements of prior periods and (b) consistent application of accounting principles in comparative statements are important factors in reporting a change in accounting principles. Most changes in accounting shall be recognized by including the cumulative effect, based on a retroactive computation, of changing to a new accounting principle in net income of the period of the change (refer to paragraphs .115 through .122) but a few specific changes in accounting principles shall be reported by restating the financial statements of prior periods (refer to paragraphs .123 through .126 and to Section A35, paragraphs .112 and .113, regarding a change in entity). [APB20, ¶18]

.115 For all changes in accounting principle except those described in paragraphs .123 through .128 and Section A35, paragraphs .112 and .113, regarding a change in entity:

a. Financial statements for prior periods included for comparative purposes shall be presented as previously reported.
b. The cumulative effect of changing to a new accounting principle on the amount of retained earnings at the beginning of the period in which the change is made shall be included in net income of the period of the change (refer to paragraph .116).
c. The effect of adopting the new accounting principle on income before extraordinary items and on net income (and on the related per share amounts) of the period of the change shall be disclosed.
d. Income before extraordinary items and net income computed on a pro forma basis[2] shall be shown on the face of the income statements for all periods presented as if the newly adopted accounting principle had been applied during all periods affected (refer to paragraph .117).

---

[2]The pro forma amounts include both (a) the direct effects of a change and (b) nondiscretionary adjustments in items based on income before taxes or net income, such as profit sharing expense and certain royalties, that would have been recognized if the newly adopted accounting principle had been followed in prior periods: related income tax effects shall be recognized for both (a) and (b). Direct effects are limited to those adjustments that would have been recorded to restate the financial statements of prior periods to apply the change retroactively. The nondiscretionary adjustments described in (b) shall not therefore be recognized in computing the adjustment for the cumulative effect of the change described in paragraph .116 unless nondiscretionary adjustments of the prior periods are actually recorded. [APB20, ¶19, fn6]

Thus, income before extraordinary items and net income (exclusive of the cumulative adjustment) for the period of the change shall be reported on the basis of the newly adopted accounting principle. The conclusions in this paragraph are modified for various special situations that are described in paragraphs .119 through .128. [APB20, ¶19]

Cumulative Effect of a Change in Accounting Principle

.116 The amount shown in the income statement for the cumulative effect of changing to a new accounting principle is the difference between (a) the amount of retained earnings at the beginning of the period of a change and (b) the amount of retained earnings that would have been reported at that date if the new accounting principle had been applied retroactively for all prior periods that would have been affected and by recognizing only the direct effects of the change and related income tax effect.[3] The amount of the cumulative effect shall be shown in the income statement between the captions "extraordinary items" and "net income." The cumulative effect is not an extraordinary item but shall be reported in a manner similar to an extraordinary item. [APB20, ¶20] Presentation of per-share amounts for the cumulative effect of an accounting change shall be made either on the face of the income statement or in the related notes. [FAS128, ¶163(a)]

Pro Forma Effects of Retroactive Application

.117 Pro forma effects of retroactive application (refer to paragraph .115(d) including footnote 2) shall be shown on the face of the income statement for income before extraordinary items and net income. The earnings per share amounts [APB20, ¶21] (basic and diluted, as appropriate under Section E11, "Earnings per Share") [FAS128, ¶163(b)] for income before extraordinary items and net income computed on a pro forma basis shall be shown on the face of the income statement. If space does not permit, such per share amounts may be disclosed prominently in a separate schedule or in tabular form in the notes to the financial statements with appropriate cross-reference; if this is done, the actual per share amounts shall be repeated for comparative purposes. Pro forma amounts

[3]Refer to footnote 2. [APB20, ¶20, fn7]

shall be shown in both current and future reports for all periods presented that are prior to the change and that would have been affected. Paragraphs .135 through .138 illustrate the manner of reporting a change in accounting principle. If an income statement is presented for the current period only, the actual and the pro forma amounts (and related per share data) for the immediately preceding period shall be disclosed. [APB20, ¶21]

.118 The principal steps in computing and reporting the cumulative effect and the pro forma amounts of a change in accounting principle may be illustrated by a change in depreciation method for previously recorded assets as follows:

a. The class or classes of depreciable assets to which the change applies shall be identified. (A *class of assets* relates to general physical characteristics.)
b. The amount of accumulated depreciation on recorded assets at the beginning of the period of the change shall be recomputed on the basis of applying retroactively the new depreciation method. Accumulated depreciation shall be adjusted for the difference between the recomputed amount and the recorded amount. Deferred taxes shall be adjusted for the related income tax effects.
c. The cumulative effect on the amount of retained earnings at the beginning of the period of the change resulting from the adjustments referred to in (b) above shall be shown in the income statement of the period of the change.
d. The pro forma amounts shall give effect to the pro forma provisions for depreciation of each prior period presented and to the pro forma adjustments of nondiscretionary items,[4] computed on the assumption of retroactive application of the newly adopted method to all prior periods and adjusted for the related income tax effects.

[APB20, ¶22]

Change in Method of Amortization and Related Disclosure

.119 Accounting for the costs of long-lived assets requires adopting a systematic pattern of charging those costs to expense. Those patterns are referred to as depreciation, depletion, or amortization methods (all of which are referred to in this section as *methods of amortization*). Various patterns of charging costs to expenses are acceptable for depreciable assets; fewer patterns are acceptable for other long-lived assets. [APB20, ¶23]

.120 Various factors are considered in selecting an amortization method for identifiable assets, and those factors may change, even for similar assets. For example, an enterprise may adopt a new method of amortization for newly acquired, identifiable, long-lived

[4]Refer to footnote 2. [APB20, ¶22, fn8]

assets and use that method for all additional new assets of the same class but continue to use the previous method for existing balances of previously recorded assets of that class. For that type of change in accounting principle, there is no adjustment of the type outlined in paragraphs .115 through .118, but a description of the nature of the change in method and its effect on income before extraordinary items and net income of the period of the change, together with the related per share amounts, shall be disclosed. If the new method of amortization is, however, applied to previously recorded assets of that class, the change in accounting principle requires an adjustment for the cumulative effect of the change and the provisions of paragraphs .111 through .118 shall be applied. [APB20, ¶24]

Pro Forma Amounts Not Determinable

.121 In rare situations, the pro forma amounts described in paragraph .117 cannot be computed or reasonably estimated for individual prior periods, although the cumulative effect on retained earnings at the beginning of the period of change can be determined. The cumulative effect shall then be reported in the income statement of the period of change in the manner described in paragraph .116. The reason for not showing the pro forma amounts by periods shall be explained because disclosing those amounts is otherwise required and is expected by users of financial statements. [APB20, ¶25]

Cumulative Effect Not Determinable

.122 Computing the effect on retained earnings at the beginning of the period in which a change in accounting principle is made may sometimes be impossible. In those rare situations, disclosure will be limited to showing the effect of the change on the results of operations of the period of change (including per share data) and to explaining the reason for omitting accounting for the cumulative effect and disclosure of pro forma amounts for prior years. The principle example of this type of accounting change is a change in inventory pricing method from FIFO to LIFO. [APB20, ¶26]

Special Changes in Accounting Principle Reported by Applying Retroactively the New Method in Restatements of Prior Periods

.123 Certain changes in accounting principle are such that the advantages of retroactive treatment in prior period reports outweigh the disadvantages. Accordingly, for those few changes, the financial statements of all prior periods presented shall be restated. The changes that shall be accorded that treatment are: (a) a change from the LIFO method of inventory pricing to another method, (b) a change in the method of accounting for long-term construction-type contracts, and (c) a change to or from the *full cost* method of accounting that is used in the extractive industries [APB20, ¶27] , [and] (d) a change from retirement-replacement-betterment accounting[5] to depreciation accounting. [FAS73, ¶2]

.124 The nature of and justification for a change in accounting principle described in paragraph .123 shall be disclosed in the financial statements for the period the change was adopted. In addition, the effect of the change on income before extraordinary items, net income, and the related per share amounts shall be disclosed for all periods presented. That disclosure may be on the face of the income statement or in the notes. Paragraphs .139 through .142 illustrate the manner of reporting a change in accounting principle retroactively by restating the statements of those prior periods affected. Financial statements of subsequent periods need not repeat the disclosures. [APB20, ¶28]

Special Exemption for an Initial Public Distribution

.125 In one specific situation, the application of the foregoing provisions of this section may result in financial statement presentations of results of operations that are not of maximum usefulness to intended users. For example, an enterprise owned by a few individuals may decide to change from one acceptable accounting principle to another acceptable principle in connection with a forthcoming public offering of shares of its equity securities. The potential investors may be better served by statements of income for a period of years reflecting the use of the newly adopted accounting principles because they will be the same as those expected to be used in future periods. In recognition of that situation, financial statements for all prior periods presented may be restated retroactively when an enterprise first issues its financial statements for any one of the following purposes: (a) obtaining additional equity capital from investors, (b) effecting a business combination, or (c) registering securities. This exemption is available only once for changes made at thetime an enterprise's financial statements are first used for any of those purposes and is not available to enterprises whose securities currently are widely held. [APB20, ¶29]

---

[5]On February 17, 1983, the Interstate Commerce Commission (ICC) ruled that railroads must use depreciation accounting for railroad track structures in reports to the ICC. The ruling is effective for 1983 annual filings, 1984 quarterly filings, and all filings thereafter with the ICC. The ICC previously had required RRB [(retirement-replacement-betterment)] for railroad track structures in reports to the ICC. [FAS73, ¶5] Under RRB, the initial costs of installing track are capitalized, not depreciated, and remain capitalized until the track is retired. The costs of replacing track are expensed unless a betterment (for example, replacing a 110-lb. rail with a 132-lb. rail) occurs. In that case, the amount by which the cost of the new part exceeds the current cost of the part replaced is considered a betterment and is capitalized but not depreciated, and the current cost of the part replaced is expensed. Railroads generally have used RRB for financial reporting. [FAS73, ¶6] The ICC ruling does not apply to financial reporting by railroads, but [if a] railroad adopts depreciation accounting for financial reporting, [the] change from RRB to depreciation accounting would be a change in accounting principle under this section. [FAS73, ¶7]

.126 The enterprise shall disclose in financial statements issued under the circumstances described in paragraph .125 the nature of the change in accounting principle and the justification for it (refer to paragraph .113). [APB20, ¶30]

Reporting Accounting Changes under AICPA Statements of Position and Practice Bulletins, FASB Technical Bulletins, or EITF Consensuses

.127 For purposes of applying this section, an enterprise making a change in accounting principle to conform with the recommendations of an AICPA statement of position [FIN20, ¶5] or practice bulletin, an FASB technical bulletin, or a consensus of the FASB Emerging Issues Task Force (EITF) [FAS111, ¶10] shall report the change as specified in the [FIN20, ¶5] pronouncement. If the pronouncement does not specify the manner of reporting a change in accounting principle to conform with its recommendations, an enterprise making a change in accounting principle to conform with the recommendations of the pronouncement shall report the change as specified by this section, except that EITF consensuses may be applied prospectively to future transactions unless otherwise stated.[6] [FAS111, ¶10]

.128 [Deleted 12/90 because of FASB Statement 106, *Employers' Accounting for Postretirement Benefits Other Than Pensions.*]

Reporting Accounting Changes in Interim Financial Statements

.129 [The reporting of accounting changes in interim financial statements is indicated in Section I73, "Interim Financial Reporting," paragraphs .131 through .142.]

Reporting a Change in Accounting Estimate

.130 The effect of a change in accounting estimate shall be accounted for in (a) the period of change if the change affects that period only or (b) the period of change and future periods if the change affects both. A change in an estimate shall not be accounted for by restating amounts reported in financial statements of prior periods or by reporting pro forma amounts for prior periods. [APB20, ¶31]

.131 A change in accounting estimate that is recognized in whole or in part by a change in accounting principle shall be reported as a change in an estimate because the cumulative effect attributable to the change in accounting principle cannot be separated from the current or future effects of the change in estimate (refer to paragraph .110). Although that type of accounting change is somewhat similar to a change in method of amortiza-

[6]Unless a consensus specifies the manner of reporting a change in accounting principle, an enterprise making a change in accounting principle to conform with an EITF consensus may apply the consensus prospectively to future transactions or may apply the provisions of this section to prior transactions. [FAS111, ¶27]

tion (refer to paragraphs .119 and .120), the accounting effect of a change in a method of amortization can be separated from the effect of a change in the estimate of periods of benefit or service and residual values of assets. A change in method of amortization for previously recorded assets therefore shall be treated as a change in accounting principle, whereas a change in the estimated period of benefit or residual value shall be treated as a change in accounting estimate. [APB20, ¶32]

Disclosure

.132 The effect on income before extraordinary items, net income and related per share amounts of the current period shall be disclosed for a change in estimate that affects several future periods, such as a change in service lives of depreciable assets or actuarial assumptions affecting pension costs. Disclosure of the effect on those income statement amounts is not necessary for estimates made each period in the ordinary course of accounting for items such as uncollectible accounts or inventory obsolescence; however, disclosure is recommended if the effect of a change in the estimate is material. [APB20, ¶33]

Materiality

.133 A number of factors are relevant to the materiality of accounting changes contemplated in this section in determining both the accounting treatment of those items and the necessity for disclosure. Materiality shall be considered in relation to both the effects of each change separately and the combined effect of all changes. If a change has a material effect on income before extraordinary items or on net income of the current period before the effect of the change, the treatments and disclosures described in this section shall be followed. Furthermore, if a change has a material effect on the trend of earnings, the same treatments and disclosures are required. A change that does not have a material effect in the period of change but is reasonably certain to have a material effect in later periods shall be disclosed whenever the financial statements of the period of change are presented. [APB20, ¶38]

Historical Summaries of Financial Information

.134 Summaries of financial information for a number of periods are commonly included in financial reports. The summaries often show condensed income statements, including related earnings per share amounts, for five years or more. In many annual reports to stockholders, the financial highlights present similar information in capsule form. That information shall be prepared in the same manner (including the presentation of pro forma amounts) as that prescribed in this section for primary financial statements (refer to paragraphs .111 through .128 and .130 through .133) because the summaries include financial data based on the primary financial statements. In a summary of financial information that includes an accounting period in which a change in accounting principle was made, the amount of the cumulative effect of the change that was included in net income of the period of the change shall be shown separately along with the net income and related per share amounts of that period and shall not be disclosed only by a note or parenthetical notation. [APB20, ¶39]

An Illustration of Reporting a Change in Accounting Principle

.135 ABC Company decides in 19X5 to adopt the straight-line method of depreciation for plant equipment. The straight-line method will be used for new acquisitions as well as for previously acquired plant equipment for which depreciation had been provided on an accelerated method. [APB20, ¶41]

.136 This illustration assumes that the direct effects are limited to the effect on depreciation and related income tax provisions and that the direct effect on inventories is not material. The pro forma amounts have been adjusted for the hypothetical effects of the change in the provisions for incentive compensation. The per share amounts are computed assuming that 1,000,000 shares of common stock are issued and outstanding, that 100,000 additional shares would be issued if all outstanding bonds are converted, and that the annual interest expense, less taxes, for the convertible bonds is $25,000. Other data assumed for this illustration are as follows:

Year	Excess of Accelerated Depreciation over Straight-Line Depreciation	Effects of Change: Direct, Less Tax Effect	Effects of Change: Pro Forma (Note A)
Prior to 19X1	$ 20,000	$ 10,000	$ 9,000
19X1	80,000	40,000	36,000
19X2	70,000	35,000	31,500
19X3	50,000	25,000	22,500
19X4	30,000	15,000	13,500
Total at beginning of 19X5	$250,000	$125,000	$112,500

[APB20, ¶42]

.137 The manner of reporting the change in two-year comparative statements is [presented in Exhibit 137A]. [APB20, ¶43]

Exhibit 137A

Two-Year Illustration of Reporting a Change in Accounting Principle

	19X5	**19X4**
Income before extraordinary item and cumulative effect of a change in accounting principle	$1,200,000	$1,100,000
Extraordinary item (description)	(35,000)	100,000
Cumulative effect on prior years (to December 31, 19X4) of changing to a different depreciation method (Note A)	125,000	
Net income	$1,290,000	$1,200,000
Per share amounts:		
Earnings per common share—assuming no dilution:		
Income before extraordinary item and cumulative effect of a change in accounting principle	$1.20	$1.10
Extraordinary item	(0.04)	0.10
Cumulative effect on prior years (to December 31, 19X4) of changing to a different depreciation method	0.13	
Net income	$1.29	$1.20
Earnings per common share—assuming dilution:		
Income before extraordinary item and cumulative effect of a change in accounting principle	$1.11	$1.02
Extraordinary item	(0.03)	0.09
Cumulative effect on prior years (to December 31, 19X4) of changing to a different depreciation method	0.11	
Net income	$1.19	$1.11
Pro forma amounts assuming the new depreciation method is applied retroactively:		
Income before extraordinary item	$1,200,000	$1,113,500
Earnings per common share—assuming no dilution	$1.20	$1.11
Earnings per common share—assuming dilution	$1.11	$1.04
Net income	$1,165,000	$1,213,500
Earnings per common share—assuming no dilution	$1.16	$1.21
Earnings per common share—assuming dilution	$1.08	$1.13

(Refer to accompanying note to the financial statements.)

Exhibit 137A (continued)

Note A—Change in Depreciation Method for Plant Equipment

Depreciation of plant equipment has been computed by the straight-line method in 19X5. Depreciation of plant equipment in prior years, beginning in 19WW, was computed by the sum-of-the-years' digits method. The new method of depreciation was adopted to recognize . . . (state justification for change of depreciation method) . . . and has been applied retroactively to equipment acquisitions of prior years. The effect of the change in 19X5 was to increase income before extraordinary item by approximately $10,000 (or 1 cent per share). The adjustment of $125,000 (after reduction for income taxes of $125,000) to apply retroactively the new method is included in income of 19X5. The pro forma amounts shown on the income statement have been adjusted for the effect of retroactive application on depreciation, the change in provisions for incentive compensation that would have been made had the new method been in effect, and the related income taxes. [APB20, ¶43]

.138 The manner of reporting the change in five-year comparative statements is [presented in Exhibit 138A].

(This page intentionally left blank.)

Exhibit 138A

Five-Year Illustration of Reporting a Change in Accounting Principle

	19X5	19X4	19X3	19X2	19X1
Income before extraordinary item and cumulative effect of a change in accounting principle	$1,200,000	$1,100,000	$1,300,000	$1,000,000	$800,000
Extraordinary item	(35,000)	100,000		40,000	
Cumulative effect on prior years (to December 31, 19X4) of changing to a different depreciation method (Note A)	125,000				
Net income	$1,290,000	$1,200,000	$1,300,000	$1,040,000	$800,000
Earnings per common share—assuming no dilution:					
Income before extraordinary item and cumulative effect of change in accounting principle	$1.20	$1.10	$1.30	$1.00	$0.80
Extraordinary item	(0.04)	0.10		0.04	
Cumulative effect on prior years (to December 31, 19X4) of changing to a different depreciation method	0.13				
Net income	$1.29	$1.20	$1.30	$1.04	$0.80

Earnings per common share—assuming dilution:					
Income before extraordinary item and cumulative effect of change in accounting principle	$1.11	$1.02	$1.20	$0.93	$0.75
Extraordinary item	(0.03)	0.09		0.04	
Cumulative effect on prior years (to December 31, 19X4) of changing to a different depreciation method	0.11				
Net income	$1.19	$1.11	$1.20	$0.97	$0.75
Pro forma amounts assuming the new depreciation method is applied retroactively:					
Income before extraordinary item	$1,200,000	$1,113,500	$1,322,500	$1,031,500	$ 836,000
Earnings per common share—assuming no dilution	$1.20	$1.11	$1.32	$1.03	$0.84
Earnings per common share—assuming dilution	$1.11	$1.04	$1.23	$0.96	$0.78
Net income	$1,165,000	$1,213,500	$1,322,500	$1,071,500	$836,000
Earnings per common share—assuming no dilution	$1.16	$1.21	$1.32	$1.07	$0.84
Earnings per common share—assuming dilution	$1.08	$1.13	$1.23	$1.00	$0.78

A note similar to Note A of Exhibit 137A shall accompany the five-year comparative income statement. [APB20, ¶44]

An Illustration of Reporting a Special Change in Accounting Principle by Restating Prior Period Financial Statements

.139 XYZ Company decides in 19X5 to adopt the percentage-of-completion method in accounting for all of its long-term construction contracts. The enterprise had used in prior years the completed-contract method and had maintained records that are adequate to apply retroactively the percentage-of-completion method. The change in accounting principle is to be reported in the manner described in paragraphs .123 and .124. [APB20, ¶45]

.140 The direct effect of the change in accounting principle and other data assumed for this illustration are as follows:

	Pretax Income Reported by		Difference in Income	
Year	Percentage-of-Completion Method	Completed-Contract Method	Direct	Less Tax Effect
Prior to 19X1	$1,800,000	$1,300,000	$ 500,000	$ 250,000
19X1	900,000	800,000	100,000	50,000
19X2	700,000	1,000,000	(300,000)	(150,000)
19X3	800,000	600,000	200,000	100,000
19X4	1,000,000	1,100,000	(100,000)	(50,000)
Total at beginning of 19X5	5,200,000	4,800,000	400,000	200,000
19X5	1,100,000	900,000	200,000	100,000
Total	$6,300,000	$5,700,000	$ 600,000	$ 300,000

The per share amounts are computed assuming that 1,000,000 shares of common stock are issued and outstanding, that 100,000 additional shares would be issued if all outstanding bonds are converted, and that the annual interest expense, less taxes, for the convertible bonds is $25,000. [APB20, ¶46]

.141 The manner of reporting the change in two-year comparative statements is presented in Exhibit 141A. [APB20, ¶47]

Exhibit 141A

Two-Year Illustration of an Accounting Change with Restatement of Prior Period Financial Statements

	19X5	19X4 as adjusted (Note A)
Income Statement		
Income before extraordinary item	$ 550,000	$ 500,000
Extraordinary item (description)		(80,000)
Net income	$ 550,000	$ 420,000
Per share amounts:		
Earnings per common share—assuming no dilution:		
Income before extraordinary item	$0.55	$0.50
Extraordinary item		(.08)
Net income	$0.55	$0.42
Earnings per common share—assuming dilution:		
Income before extraordinary item	$0.52	$0.47
Extraordinary item		(.07)
Net income	$0.52	$0.40
Statement of Retained Earnings		
Balance at beginning of year, as previously reported	$17,800,000	$17,330,000
Add adjustment for the cumulative effect on prior years of applying retroactively the new method of accounting for long-term contracts (Note A)	200,000	250,000
Balance at beginning of year, as adjusted	18,000,000	17,580,000
Net income	550,000	420,000
Balance at end of year	$18,550,000	$18,000,000

(Refer to accompanying note to the financial statements.)

Note A—Change in Method of Accounting for Long-Term Contracts

The enterprise has accounted for revenue and costs for long-term construction contracts by the percentage-of-completion method in 19X5, whereas in all prior years revenue and costs were determined by the completed-contract method. The new method of accounting for long-term contracts was adopted to recognize . . . (state justification for change in accounting principle) . . . and financial statements of prior years have been restated to apply the new method retroactively. For income tax purposes, the completed-contract method has been continued. The effect of the accounting change on income of 19X5 and on income as previously reported for 19X4 is—

	Increase	**(Decrease)**
	19X5	**19X4**
Effect on—		
Income before extraordinary item and net income	$100,000	$(50,000)
Earnings per common share—assuming no dilution	$0.10	$(0.05)
Earnings per common share—assuming dilution	$0.09	$(0.05)

The balances of retained earnings for 19X4 and 19X5 have been adjusted for the effect (net of income taxes) of applying retroactively the new method of accounting. [APB20, ¶47]

.142 A note to a five-year summary of financial statements should disclose the effect of the change on net income and related per share amounts for the periods affected in the manner illustrated in Exhibit 142A. [APB20, ¶48]

Exhibit 142A

Illustrative Note for a Five-Year Illustration of an Accounting Change with Restatement of Prior Period Financial Statements

Note A—Change in Method of Accounting for Long-Term Contracts

The enterprise has accounted for revenue and costs for long-term construction contracts by the percentage-of-completion method in 19X5, whereas in all prior years rev-

Exhibit 142A (continued)

enue and costs were determined by the completed-contract method. The new method of accounting for long-term contracts was adopted to recognize . . . (state justification for change in accounting principle) . . . and financial statements of prior years have been restated to apply the new method retroactively. For income tax purposes, the completed-contract method has been continued. The effect of the accounting change on net income as previously reported for 19X4 and prior years is:

	19X4	**19X3**	**19X2**	**19X1**
Net income as previously reported	$470,000	$300,000	$ 500,000	$ 400,00
Adjustment for effect of a change in accounting principle that is applied retroactively	(50,000)	100,000	(150,000)	50,000
Net income as adjusted	$420,000	$500,000	$ 350,000	$450,000
Per share amounts:				
Earnings per common share—assuming no dilution:				
Net income as previously reported	$0.47	$0.30	$0.50	$0.40
Adjustment for effect of a change in accounting principle that is applied retroactively	(0.05)	0.10	0.15	0.05
Net income as adjusted	$0.42	$0.40	$0.35	$0.45
Earnings per common share—assuming dilution:				
Net income as previously reported	$0.45	$0.30	$0.47	$0.38
Adjustment for effect of a change in accounting principle that is applied retroactively	(0.05)	0.09	(0.13)	0.05
Net income as adjusted	$0.40	$0.39	$0.34	$0.43

[APB20, ¶48]

Glossary

.401 **Accounting change.** A change in (a) an accounting principle, (b) an accounting estimate, or (c) the reporting enterprise (which is a special type of change in accounting principle [discussed in Section A35, paragraphs .112 and .113]). The correction of an error in previously issued financial statements is not deemed to be an accounting change. [APB20, ¶6]

.402 **Accounting principle.** The term includes not only accounting principles and practices but also the methods of applying them. [APB20, ¶7]

Supplemental Guidance: Emerging Issues Task Force (EITF) Issues

.1000 [Listed below are EITF Issues that provide supplemental guidance for this section. These Issues may be either interpretive of or related by topic to the guidance in this section.

EITF Issue No. 84-9, "Deposit Float of Banks"
EITF Issue No. 84-10, "LIFO Conformity of Companies Relying on *Insilco* Tax Court Decision"
EITF Topic No. D-1, "Implications and Implementation of an EITF Consensus"
EITF Topic No. D-74, "Issues Concerning the Scope of the AICPA Guide on Investment Companies"]

.1001 [Listed below is an EITF Issue that provides interpretive guidance on specific material in this section.

Paragraph .105 (APB 20, ¶7)—EITF Issue No. 84-9
Paragraph .112 (APB 20, ¶16)—EITF Issue No. 84-9]

(The next page is 421.)

ACCOUNTING POLICIES SECTION A10

Sources: APB Opinion 22; FASB Statement 95; FASB Interpretation 40

[**Note:** A list of Issues discussed by the Emerging Issues Task Force (EITF) that provide supplemental guidance for this section is presented in paragraph .1000.]

Summary

All significant accounting policies followed by an enterprise shall be disclosed in its financial statements. The format and the location of the disclosure are flexible, although preference is given to the use of a separate summary preceding the notes to the financial statements or to presentation as the first note.

.101 The **accounting policies** of a reporting enterprise are the specific accounting principles and the methods of applying those principles that are judged by the management of the enterprise to be the most appropriate in the circumstances to present fairly financial position, [APB22, ¶6] cash flows, [FAS95, ¶152(b)] and results of operations in accordance with generally accepted accounting principles and that accordingly have been adopted for preparing the financial statements. [APB22, ¶6]

Applicability

.102 Information about the accounting policies adopted by a reporting enterprise is essential for financial statement users. When financial statements are issued purporting to present fairly financial position, [APB22, ¶8] cash flows, [FAS95, ¶152(b)] and results of operations in accordance with generally accepted accounting principles, a description of all significant accounting policies of the reporting enterprise shall be included as an integral part of the financial statements. If one or more of the basic financial statements [are issued] without the others and purport to present fairly the information given in accordance with generally accepted accounting principles, the statements so presented shall also include disclosure of the pertinent accounting policies. [APB22, ¶8]

.102A All business enterprises are required to provide disclosures about significant accounting policies used to prepare financial statements that are intended to be in conformity with generally accepted accounting principles. This section provides guidance on the content of those disclosures, which shall include [those described in paragraph .105]. [FIN40, ¶5]

.103 Information about the accounting policies adopted and followed by not-for-profit enterprises shall be presented as an integral part of their financial statements. [APB22, ¶9]

.104 The provisions of paragraphs .102 and .103 are not intended to apply to unaudited financial statements issued as of a date between annual reporting dates (for example, each quarter) if the reporting enterprise has not changed its accounting policies since the end of its preceding fiscal year.[1] [APB22, ¶10]

Disclosure

.105 Disclosure of accounting policies shall identify and describe the accounting principles followed by the reporting enterprise and the methods of applying those principles that materially affect the determination of financial position, [APB22, ¶12] cash flows, [FAS95, ¶152(b)] or results of operations. In general, the disclosure shall encompass important judgments as to appropriateness of principles relating to recognition of revenue and allocation of asset costs to current and future periods; in particular, it shall encompass those accounting principles and methods that involve any of the following:

a. A selection from existing acceptable alternatives;
b. Principles and methods peculiar to the industry in which the reporting enterprise operates, even if such principles and methods are predominantly followed in that industry;
c. Unusual or innovative applications of generally accepted accounting principles (and, as applicable, of principles and methods peculiar to the industry in which the reporting enterprise operates). [APB22, ¶12]

.106 Examples of disclosures by a business enterprise commonly required with respect to accounting policies include those relating to basis of consolidation, depreciation methods, amortization of intangibles, inventory pricing, and recognition of profit on long-term construction-type contracts. This list of examples is not all-inclusive. [APB22, ¶13]

.107 Financial statement disclosure of accounting policies shall not duplicate details (for example, composition of inventories or of plant assets) presented elsewhere as part of the financial statements. In some cases, the disclosure of accounting policies shall refer to related details presented elsewhere as part of the financial statements; for example, changes in accounting policies during the period shall be described with cross-reference to the disclosure required by Section A06, "Accounting Changes," of the current effect of the change and of the pro forma effect of retroactive application. [APB22, ¶14]

---

[1] It may be appropriate to omit disclosure of accounting policies in some other circumstances; for example, from certain special reports in which incomplete or no financial presentations are made. [APB22, ¶10, fn2]

Presentation

.108 Provided that the enterprise identifies and describes its significant accounting policies as an integral part of its financial statements in accordance with paragraph .105, [the format (including location) for disclosing those policies is flexible. Preference is given to disclosing accounting policies] in a separate "Summary of Significant Accounting Policies" [or a similar title] preceding the notes to financial statements or as the initial note. [APB22, ¶15]

Glossary

.401 **Accounting policies.** The specific accounting principles and the methods of applying those principles that are judged by the management of the enterprise to be the most appropriate in the circumstances. [APB22, ¶6]

Supplemental Guidance: Emerging Issues Task Force (EITF) Issues

.1000 [Listed below are EITF Issues that provide supplemental guidance for this section. These Issues are related by topic to the guidance in this section.

EITF Issue No. 00-10, "Accounting for Shipping and Handling Fees and Costs"
EITF Issue No. 01-14, "Income Statement Characterization of Reimbursements Received for 'Out-of-Pocket' Expenses Incurred"]

(The next page is 1303.)

ADDITIONAL PAID-IN CAPITAL SECTION A31

Source: ARB 43, Chapter 1A

Summary

Items that would normally be charged to expense in the current or future years should not be charged against additional paid-in capital. The only exception to this rule may occur when an enterprise undergoes a reorganization or a quasi reorganization, in which the shareholders have been fully informed and have approved the action.

.101 Additional paid-in capital, however created, shall not be used to relieve income of the current or future years of charges which would otherwise be made against [income]. This rule might be subject to the exception that where, upon reorganization, a reorganized enterprise would be relieved of charges that would be made against income if the existing enterprise were continued, it might be regarded as permissible to accomplish the same result without reorganization provided the facts were as fully revealed to and the action as formally approved by the shareholders as in reorganization. [ARB43, ch1A, ¶2] [For discussion of quasi reorganizations including disclosure requirements, refer to Section Q15, "Quasi Reorganizations."]

.102 [Section C08, "Capital Stock: Capital Transactions," paragraph .102, requires disclosure of changes in the separate accounts, such as additional paid-in capital, comprising stockholders' equity.]

(The next page is 1471.)

ADJUSTMENTS OF FINANCIAL STATEMENTS FOR PRIOR PERIODS — SECTION A35

Sources: APB Opinion 9; APB Opinion 20; FASB Statement 16; FASB Statement 58; FASB Statement 73; FASB Statement 109; FASB Statement 111; FASB Statement 141

Summary

Adjustments of previously issued financial statements are required if there is a correction of an error in the financial statements of a prior period, a change in certain accounting principles, or an adjustment related to prior interim statements of the current fiscal period or if an enterprise realizes the income tax benefits of a preacquisition loss carryforward of a purchased subsidiary. All other revenues, expenses, gains, and losses recognized during a period shall be included in the net income of that period.

Applicability

.101 This section does not affect the manner of reporting accounting changes required or permitted by other sections. [FAS16, ¶12]

Prior-Period Adjustments

.102 Except as specified in paragraph .103 and in paragraphs .109 and .110 with respect to prior interim periods of the current year, all items of profit and loss recognized during a period,[2] including accruals of estimated losses from loss contingencies, shall be included in the determination of net income for that period. [FAS16, ¶10]

.103 An item of profit and loss related to the correction of an error in the financial statements of a prior period [(as discussed in paragraph .104)] shall be accounted for and reported as a prior-period adjustment [(as described in paragraphs .106 and .107)] and excluded from the determination of net income for the current period. [FAS109, ¶288(n)]

---

[1][Deleted 6/01 because of FASB Statement 141, *Business Combinations.*]

[2]As used in this section, the term *period* refers to both annual and interim reporting periods. [FAS16, ¶10, fn1]

[3][Deleted 2/92 because of FASB Statement 109, *Accounting for Income Taxes.*]

.104 Errors[4] in financial statements result from mathematical mistakes, mistakes in the application of accounting principles, or oversight or misuse of facts that existed at the time the financial statements were prepared. In contrast, a change in accounting estimate results from new information or subsequent developments and accordingly from better insight or improved judgment. Thus, an error is distinguishable from a change in estimate. A change from an accounting principle that is not generally accepted to one that is generally accepted is a correction of an error for purposes of applying this section. [APB20, ¶13]

.105 The nature of an error in previously issued financial statements and the effect of its correction on income before extraordinary items, net income, and the related per share amounts shall be disclosed in the period in which the error was discovered and corrected. Financial statements of subsequent periods need not repeat the disclosures. [APB20, ¶37]

.106 Those items that are reported as prior-period adjustments shall, in single period statements, be reflected as adjustments of the opening balance of retained earnings. [FAS16, ¶16(a)] When comparative statements are presented, corresponding adjustments shall be made of the amounts of net income, its components, retained earnings balances, and other affected balances for all of the periods presented to reflect the retroactive application of the prior-period adjustments. [APB9, ¶18]

.107 If prior-period adjustments are recorded, the resulting effects (both gross and net of applicable income tax) on the net income of prior periods shall be disclosed in the annual report for the year in which the adjustments are made. If financial statements for a single period only are presented, this disclosure shall indicate the effects of such restatement on the balance of retained earnings at the beginning of the period and on the net income of the immediately preceding period. If financial statements for more than one period are presented, which is ordinarily the preferable procedure,[5] the disclosure shall include the effects for each of the periods included in the statements. Such disclosures shall include the amounts of income tax applicable to the prior-period adjustments. Disclosure of restatements in annual reports issued subsequent to the first such post-revision disclosure would ordinarily not be required. [APB9, ¶26]

---

[4]Section 561 of Statement on Auditing Standards No. 1, *Codification of Auditing Standards and Procedures,* [FAS111, ¶9(a)] discusses other aspects of errors in previously issued financial statements. [APB20, ¶13, fn4]

[5]Refer to Section F43, "Financial Statements: Comparative Financial Statements." [APB9, ¶26, fn4]

Historical Summaries of Financial Data

.108 It has become customary for business enterprises to present historical statistical-type summaries of financial data for a number of periods—commonly 5 or 10 years. [If] prior-period adjustments have been recorded during any of the periods [presented], the reported amounts of net income, its components, and other affected items, shall be appropriately restated, with disclosure, in the first summary published after the adjustments. [APB9, ¶27]

Adjustments Related to Prior Interim Periods of the Current Fiscal Year

.109 For purposes of this section, an *adjustment related to prior interim periods of the current fiscal year* is an adjustment or settlement of litigation or similar claims, of income taxes [FAS16, ¶13] (except for the effects of retroactive tax legislation) [FAS109, ¶288(n)], of renegotiation proceedings, or of utility revenue under rate-making processes provided that the adjustment or settlement meets each of the following criteria:

a. The effect of the adjustment or settlement is material in relation to income from continuing operations of the current fiscal year or in relation to the trend of income from continuing operations or is material by other appropriate criteria.
b. All or part of the adjustment or settlement can be specifically identified with and is directly related to business activities of specific prior interim periods of the current fiscal year.
c. The amount of the adjustment or settlement could not be reasonably estimated prior to the current interim period but becomes reasonably estimable in the current interim period.

Criterion (b) above is not met solely because of incidental effects such as interest on a settlement. Criterion (c) would be met by the occurrence of an event with currently measurable effects such as a final decision on a rate order. Treatment as adjustments related to prior interim periods of the current fiscal year shall not be applied to the normal recurring corrections and adjustments that are the result of the use of estimates inherent in the accounting process. Changes in provisions for doubtful accounts shall not be considered to be adjustments related to prior interim periods of the current fiscal year even though the changes result from litigation or similar claims. [FAS16, ¶13]

.110 If an item of profit or loss occurs in *other than the first* interim period of the enterprise's fiscal year and all or a part of the item of profit or loss is an adjustment related to prior interim periods of the current fiscal year,[5a] as defined in paragraph .109, the item shall be reported as follows:

a. The portion of the item that is directly related to business activities of the enterprise during the current interim period, if any, shall be included in the determination of net income for that period.
b. Prior interim periods of the current fiscal year shall be restated to include the portion of the item that is directly related to business activities of the enterprise during each prior interim period in the determination of net income for that period.
c. The portion of the item that is directly related to business activities of the enterprise during prior fiscal years, if any, shall be included in the determination of net income of the first interim period of the current fiscal year.

[FAS16, ¶14]

.111 The following disclosures shall be made in interim financial reports about an adjustment related to prior interim periods of the current fiscal year. In financial reports for the interim period in which the adjustment occurs, disclosure shall be made of (a) the effect on income from continuing operations, net income, and related per share amounts for each prior interim period of the current fiscal year and (b) income from continuing operations, net income, and related per share amounts for each prior interim period restated in accordance with paragraph .110. [FAS16, ¶15]

Changes in Accounting Principles

Change in Reporting Entity

.112 Accounting changes that result in financial statements that are in effect the statements of a different reporting entity shall be reported by restating the financial statements of all prior periods presented in order to show financial information for the new reporting entity for all periods.[6] [APB20, ¶34] This type [of accounting change] is limited mainly to (a) presenting consolidated or combined statements in place of statements of individual enterprises, (b) changing specific subsidiaries comprising the group of enterprises for which consolidated financial statements are presented, and (c) changing the enterprises included in combined financial statements. A different group of entities comprise the reporting entity after each change. [APB20, ¶12]

[[5a]Deleted 2/92 because of FASB Statement 109.]

[6]The amount of interest cost capitalized through application of Section I67, "Interest: Capitalization of Interest Costs," shall not be changed when restating financial statements of prior periods [for a change in the reporting entity]. [FAS58, ¶8]

.113 The financial statements of the period of a change in reporting entity shall describe the nature of the change and the reason for it. In addition, the effect of the change on income before extraordinary items, net income, and related per share amounts shall be disclosed for all periods presented. Financial statements of subsequent periods need not repeat the disclosures. [APB20, ¶35] (Section B51, paragraphs .164 through .171 [FAS141, ¶E2(b)] describe the manner of reporting and the disclosures required for a change in reporting entity that occurs because of a business combination.) [APB20, ¶35]

Other Changes in Accounting Principles

.114 Certain changes in accounting principle are such that the advantages of retroactive treatment in prior period reports outweigh the disadvantages. Accordingly, for those few changes, the financial statements of all prior periods presented shall be restated. The changes that shall be accorded this treatment are:

a. A change from the LIFO method of inventory pricing to another method
b. A change in the method of accounting for long-term construction-type contracts
c. A change to or from the "full cost" method of accounting that is used in the extractive industries [APB20, ¶27]
d. A change from retirement-replacement-betterment accounting[7] to depreciation accounting. [FAS73, ¶2]

[This treatment also can be used for] a change from one acceptable accounting principle to another acceptable principle in connection with a forthcoming public offering when an enterprise first issues its financial statements for any one of the following purposes: (1) obtaining additional equity capital from investors, (2) effecting a business combination, [or] (3) registering securities. [Such restatement is a special exemption (refer to Section A06, "Accounting Changes," paragraph .125) that] is available only once for changes made at the time an enterprise's financial statements are first used for any of those purposes and is not available to enterprises whose securities currently are widely held. [APB20, ¶29]

---

[7]On February 17, 1983, the Interstate Commerce Commission (ICC) ruled that railroads must use depreciation accounting for railroad track structures in reports to the ICC. The ruling is effective for 1983 annual filings, 1984 quarterly filings, and all filings thereafter with the ICC. The ICC previously had required RRB [(retirement-replacement-betterment)] for railroad track structures in reports to the ICC. [FAS73, ¶5] Under RRB, the initial costs of installing track are capitalized, not depreciated, and remain capitalized until the track is retired. The costs of replacing track are expensed unless a betterment (for example, replacing a 110-lb rail with a 132 lb. rail) occurs. In that case, the amount by which the cost of the new part exceeds the current cost of the part replaced is considered a betterment and is capitalized but not depreciated, and the current cost of the part replaced is expensed. Railroads generally have used RRB for financial reporting. [FAS73, ¶6] The ICC ruling does not apply to financial reporting by railroads, but [if a] railroad adopts depreciation accounting for financial reporting, [the] change from RRB to depreciation accounting would be a change in accounting principle under this section. [FAS73, ¶7]

.115 The nature of and justification for a change in accounting principle described in paragraph .114 shall be disclosed in the financial statements for the period the change was adopted. In addition, [for accounting changes described in subparagraphs .114(a) through .114(c),] the effect of the change on income before extraordinary items, net income, and the related per share amounts shall be disclosed for all periods presented. This disclosure may be on the face of the income statement or in the notes. Paragraphs .116 through .119 illustrate the manner of reporting a change in accounting principle retroactively by restating the statements of those prior periods affected. Financial statements of subsequent periods need not repeat the disclosures. [APB20, ¶28]

An Illustration of Reporting a Special Change in Accounting Principle by Restating Prior Period Financial Statements

.116 XYZ Company decides in 19X5 to adopt the percentage-of-completion method in accounting for all of its long-term construction contracts. The enterprise had used the completed-contract method in prior years and had maintained records that are adequate to apply retroactively the percentage-of-completion method. The change in accounting principle is to be reported in the manner described in paragraphs .114 and .115. [APB20, ¶45]

.117 The direct effect of the change in accounting principle and other data assumed for this illustration are:

	Pretax Income Reported by		Difference in Income	
Year	Percentage-of-Completion Method	Completed-Contract Method	Direct	Less Tax Effect
Prior to 19X1	$1,800,000	$1,300,000	$ 500,000	$ 250,000
19X1	900,000	800,000	100,000	50,000
19X2	700,000	1,000,000	(300,000)	(150,000)
19X3	800,000	600,000	200,000	100,000
19X4	1,000,000	1,100,000	(100,000)	(50,000)
Total at beginning of 19X5	5,200,000	4,800,000	400,000	200,000
19X5	1,100,000	900,000	200,000	100,000
Total	$6,300,000	$5,700,000	$ 600,000	$ 300,000

The per share amounts are computed assuming that 1,000,000 shares of common stock are issued and outstanding, that 100,000 additional shares would be issued if all outstanding bonds are converted, and that the annual interest expense, less taxes, for the convertible bonds is $25,000. [APB20, ¶46]

.118 The manner of reporting the change in two-year comparative statements is [presented in Exhibit 118A]. [APB20, ¶47]

Exhibit 118A

Two-Year Illustration of an Accounting Change with Restatement of Prior Period Financial Statements

Income Statement

	19X5	19X4 as Adjusted (Note A)
Income before extraordinary item	$550,000	$500,000
Extraordinary item (description)		(80,000)
Net income	$550,000	$420,000
Per share amounts:		
Earnings per common share—assuming no dilution:		
Income before extraordinary item	$ 0.55	$ 0.50
Extraordinary item		(.08)
Net income	$ 0.55	$ 0.42
Earnings per common share—assuming dilution:		
Income before extraordinary item	$ 0.52	$ 0.47
Extraordinary item		(.07)
Net income	$ 0.52	$ 0.40

Statement of Retained Earnings

	19X5	**19X4 as Adjusted (Note A)**
Balance at beginning of year, as previously reported	$17,800,000	$17,330,000
Add adjustment for the cumulative effect on prior years of applying retroactively the new method of accounting for long-term contracts (Note A)	200,000	250,000
Balance at beginning of year, as adjusted	$18,000,000	$17,580,000
Net income	550,000	420,000
Balance at end of year	$18,550,000	$18,000,000

(Refer to accompanying note to the financial statements.)

Note A—Change in Method of Accounting for Long-Term Contracts

The enterprise has accounted for revenue and costs for long-term construction contracts by the percentage-of-completion method in 19X5, whereas in all prior years revenue and costs were determined by the completed-contract method. The new method of accounting for long-term contracts was adopted to recognize . . . (state justification for change in accounting principle) . . . and financial statements of prior years have been restated to apply the new method retroactively. For income tax purposes, the completed-contract method has been continued. The effect of the accounting change on income of 19X5 and on income as previously reported for 19X4 is:

	Increase 19X5	**(Decrease) 19X4**
Effect on:		
Income before extraordinary item and net income	$100,000	$(50,000)
Earnings per common share—assuming no dilution	$0.10	$(0.05)
Earnings per common share—assuming dilution	$0.09	$(0.05)

The balances of retained earnings for 19X4 and 19X5 have been adjusted for the effect (net of income taxes) of applying retroactively the new method of accounting. [APB20, ¶47]

.119 A note to a five-year summary of financial statements should disclose the effect of the change on net income and related per share amounts for the periods affected in the manner [illustrated in Exhibit 119A].

Exhibit 119A

Illustrative Note for a Five-Year Illustration of an Accounting Change with Restatement of Prior Period Financial Statements

Note A—Change in Method of Accounting for Long-Term Contracts

The enterprise has accounted for revenue and costs for long-term construction contracts by the percentage-of-completion method in 19X5, whereas in all prior years revenue and costs were determined by the completed-contract method. The new method of accounting for long-term contracts was adopted to recognize . . . (state justification for change in accounting principle) . . . and financial statements of prior years have been restated to apply the new method retroactively. For income tax purposes, the completed-contract method has been continued. The effect of the accounting change on net income as previously reported for 19X4 and prior years is:

Exhibit 119A (continued)

	19X4	19X3	19X2	19X1
Net income as previously reported	$470,000	$300,000	$ 500,000	$400,000
Adjustment for effect of a change in accounting principle that is applied retroactively	(50,000)	100,000	(150,000)	50,000
Net income as adjusted	$420,000	$400,000	$ 350,000	$450,000
Per share amounts:				
Earnings per common share—assuming no dilution:				
Net income as previously reported	$ 0.47	$ 0.30	$ 0.50	$ 0.40
Adjustment for effect of a change in accounting principle that is applied retroactively	(0.05)	0.10	(0.15)	0.05
Net income as adjusted	$ 0.42	$ 0.40	$ 0.35	$ 0.45
Earnings per common share—assuming dilution:				
Net income as previously reported	$ 0.45	$ 0.30	$ 0.47	$ 0.38
Adjustment for effect of a change in accounting principle that is applied retroactively	(0.05)	0.09	(0.13)	0.05
Net income as adjusted	$ 0.40	$ 0.39	$ 0.34	$ 0.43

[APB20, ¶48]

(The next page is 3201.)

ASSET RETIREMENT OBLIGATIONS SECTION A50

Sources: FASB Statement 143; FASB Statement 144

[**Note:** A list of Issues discussed by the Emerging Issues Task Force (EITF) that provide supplemental guidance for this section is presented in paragraph .1000.]

Summary

This section addresses financial accounting and reporting for obligations associated with the retirement of tangible long-lived assets and the associated asset retirement costs. This section applies to all entities. It applies to legal obligations associated with the retirement of long-lived assets that result from the acquisition, construction, development and (or) the normal operation of a long-lived asset, except for certain obligations of lessees. As used in this section, a legal obligation is an obligation that a party is required to settle as a result of an existing or enacted law, statute, ordinance, or written or oral contract or by legal construction of a contract under the doctrine of promissory estoppel.

This section requires that the fair value of a liability for an asset retirement obligation be recognized in the period in which it is incurred if a reasonable estimate of fair value can be made. The associated asset retirement costs are capitalized as part of the carrying amount of the long-lived asset. Accretion expense is recorded in each subsequent period to recognize the changes in the liability for an asset retirement obligation resulting from the passage of time. Changes resulting from revisions to the original estimate of the fair value of the liability are recognized as an increase or a decrease in the carrying amount of the liability and the related asset retirement costs capitalized as part of the carrying amount of the related long-lived asset. The capitalized asset retirement cost is allocated to expense using a systematic and rational method over its useful life.

This section contains disclosure requirements that provide descriptions of asset retirement obligations and reconciliations of changes in the components of those obligations.

Introduction

.101 This section establishes accounting standards for recognition and measurement of a liability for an asset retirement obligation and the associated asset retirement cost.[1] [FAS143, ¶1]

Scope

.102 This section applies to all entities. This section applies to legal obligations associated with the *retirement* [2] of a tangible long-lived asset that result from the acquisition, construction, or development and (or) the normal operation of a long-lived asset, except as explained in paragraph .117 for certain obligations of lessees. As used in this section, a legal obligation is an obligation that a party is required to settle as a result of an existing or enacted law, statute, ordinance, or written or oral contract or by legal construction of a contract under the doctrine of promissory estoppel.[3] [FAS143, ¶2] This section does not apply to obligations that arise solely from a plan to sell or otherwise dispose of a long-lived asset covered by Section I08, "Impairment." [FAS144, ¶C18(a)] An obligation that results from the improper operation of an asset also is not within the scope of this section but may be subject to the provisions of AICPA Statement of Position 96-1, *Environmental Remediation Liabilities.* [FAS143, ¶2]

Initial Recognition and Measurement of a Liability for an Asset Retirement Obligation

.103 An entity shall recognize the fair value of a liability for an asset retirement obligation in the period in which it is incurred if a reasonable estimate of fair value can be

---

[1]The term *asset retirement obligation* refers to an obligation associated with the retirement of a tangible long-lived asset. The term *asset retirement cost* refers to the amount capitalized that increases the carrying amount of the long-lived asset when a liability for an asset retirement obligation is recognized. [FAS143, ¶1, fn1]

[2]In this section, the term *retirement* is defined as the other-than-temporary removal of a long-lived asset from service. That term encompasses sale, abandonment, recycling, or disposal in some other manner. However, it does not encompass the temporary idling of a long-lived asset. [FAS143, ¶2, fn2]

[3]*Black's Law Dictionary,* seventh edition, defines *promissory estoppel* as, "The principle that a promise made without consideration may nonetheless be enforced to prevent injustice if the promisor should have reasonably expected the promisee to rely on the promise and if the promisee did actually rely on the promise to his or her detriment." [FAS143, ¶2, fn3]

made.[4] If a reasonable estimate of fair value cannot be made in the period the asset retirement obligation is incurred, the liability shall be recognized when a reasonable estimate of fair value can be made. [FAS143, ¶3]

.104 Paragraph 35 of FASB Concepts Statement 6, *Elements of Financial Statements,* defines a liability as follows:

> Liabilities are probable[21] future sacrifices of economic benefits arising from present obligations of a particular entity to transfer assets or provide services to other entities in the future as a result of past transactions or events. [Footnote 22 omitted.]
>
> [21] *Probable* is used with its usual general meaning, rather than in a specific accounting or technical sense (such as that in Section C59, "Contingencies," paragraph .104), and refers to that which can reasonably be expected or believed on the basis of available evidence or logic but is neither certain nor proved (*Webster's New World Dictionary,* p. 1132). Its inclusion in the definition is intended to acknowledge that business and other economic activities occur in an environment characterized by uncertainty in which few outcomes are certain (paragraphs 44–48).

[FAS143, ¶4]

.105 As stated in the above footnote, the definition of a liability in Concepts Statement 6 uses the term *probable* in a different sense than it is used in Section C59, "Contingencies." As used in Section C59, probable requires a high degree of expectation. The term probable in the definition of a liability, however, is intended to acknowledge that business and other economic activities occur in an environment in which few outcomes are certain. [FAS143, ¶5]

.106 Section C59 and FASB Concepts Statement 7, *Using Cash Flow Information and Present Value in Accounting Measurements,* deal with uncertainty in different ways. Section C59 deals with uncertainty about whether a loss has been incurred by setting forth criteria to determine when to *recognize* a loss contingency. Concepts Statement 7 ad-

[4] If a tangible long-lived asset with an existing asset retirement obligation is acquired, a liability for that obligation shall be recognized at the asset's acquisition date as if that obligation were incurred on that date. [FAS143, ¶3, fn4]

dresses measurement of liabilities and provides a *measurement* technique to deal with uncertainties about the amount and timing of the future cash flows necessary to settle the liability. Paragraphs 55 through 61 of Concepts Statement 7[5] discuss, in detail, the relationship between the fair value measurement objective and expected cash flow approach that is articulated in Concepts Statement 7 and accounting for contingencies under Section C59. The guidance in Section C59 is not applicable to a liability for which the objective is to measure that liability at fair value. That is because in Section C59 uncertainty is used to decide whether to recognize a liability, whereas in Concepts Statement 7 uncertainties in the amount and timing of settlement are incorporated into the fair value measurement of the recognized liability. This section requires that all asset retirement obligations within the scope of this section be recognized when a reasonable estimate of fair value can be made. [FAS143, ¶6]

.107 The fair value of a liability for an asset retirement obligation is the amount at which that liability could be settled in a current transaction between willing parties, that is, other than in a forced or liquidation transaction. Quoted market prices in active markets are the best evidence of fair value and shall be used as the basis for the measurement, if available. If quoted market prices are not available, the estimate of fair value shall be based on the best information available in the circumstances, including prices for similar liabilities and the results of present value (or other valuation) techniques. [FAS143, ¶7]

.108 A present value technique[6] is often the best available technique with which to estimate the fair value of a liability. If a present value technique is used to estimate fair value, estimates of future cash flows used in that technique shall be consistent with the objective of measuring fair value.[7] Concepts Statement 7 discusses two present value techniques: a traditional approach, in which a single set of estimated cash flows and a single interest rate (a rate commensurate with the risk) are used to estimate fair value, and an expected cash flow approach, in which multiple cash flow scenarios that reflect the range of possible outcomes and a credit-adjusted risk-free rate are used to estimate fair value. Although either present value technique could theoretically be used for a fair value measurement, the expected cash flow approach will usually be the only appropriate technique for an asset retirement obligation. As discussed in paragraph 44 of Concepts Statement 7, proper application of a traditional approach entails analysis of at least two liabilities—one that exists in the marketplace and has an observable interest rate and

[5][In the *Current Text,*] Appendix H, "Excerpts from Concepts Statement 7," incorporates those paragraphs. [FAS143, ¶6, fn5]

[6]Appendix H incorporates paragraphs 39 through 54 and 75 through 88 of Concepts Statement 7 that discuss present value techniques. [FAS143, ¶8, fn6]

[7]Appendix H incorporates paragraph 23 of Concepts Statement 7 that discusses the essential elements of a fair value measurement. [FAS143, ¶8, fn7]

the liability being measured. The appropriate rate of interest for the cash flows being measured must be inferred from the observable rate of interest of some other liability, and to draw that inference the characteristics of the cash flows must be similar to those of the liability being measured. It would be rare, if ever, that there would be an observable rate of interest for a liability that has cash flows similar to an asset retirement obligation being measured. In addition, an asset retirement obligation will usually have uncertainties in both timing and amount. In that circumstance, employing a traditional present value technique, where uncertainty is incorporated into the rate, will be difficult, if not impossible. [FAS143, ¶8]

.109 The cash flows used in estimates of fair value shall incorporate assumptions that marketplace participants would use in their estimates of fair value whenever that information is available without undue cost and effort. Otherwise, an entity may use its own assumptions.[8] Those estimates shall be based on reasonable and supportable assumptions and shall consider all available evidence. The weight given to the evidence shall be commensurate with the extent to which the evidence can be verified objectively. If a range is estimated for the timing or the amount of possible cash flows, the likelihood of possible outcomes shall be considered. An entity, when using the expected cash flow technique, shall discount the estimated cash flows using a credit-adjusted risk-free rate. Thus, the effect of the entity's credit standing is reflected in the discount rate rather than in the estimated cash flows. [FAS143, ¶9]

.110 A liability for an asset retirement obligation may be incurred over more than one reporting period if the events that create the obligation occur over more than one reporting period. Any incremental liability incurred in a subsequent reporting period shall be considered to be an additional layer of the original liability. Each layer shall be initially measured at fair value. For example, the liability for decommissioning a nuclear power plant is incurred as contamination occurs. Each period, as contamination increases, a separate layer shall be measured and recognized. [FAS143, ¶10]

Recognition and Allocation of an Asset Retirement Cost

.111 Upon initial recognition of a liability for an asset retirement obligation, an entity shall capitalize an asset retirement cost by increasing the carrying amount of the related long-lived asset by the same amount as the liability.[9] An entity shall subsequently allocate that asset retirement cost to expense using a systematic and rational method over its

[8]Paragraph 32 of Concepts Statement 7 (included in Appendix H) provides reasons why an entity's assumptions may differ from those expected by others in the marketplace. [FAS143, ¶9, fn8]

[9]Capitalized asset retirement costs do not qualify as *expenditures* for purposes of paragraph .113 of Section I67, "Interest: Capitalization of Interest Costs." [FAS143, ¶11, fn9]

useful life. Application of a systematic and rational allocation method does not preclude an entity from capitalizing an amount of asset retirement cost and allocating an equal amount to expense in the same accounting period.[10] [FAS143, ¶11]

Asset Impairment

.112 In applying the provisions of Section I08, the carrying amount of the asset being tested for impairment shall include amounts of capitalized asset retirement costs. Estimated future cash flows related to the liability for an asset retirement obligation that has been recognized in the financial statements shall be excluded from (a) the undiscounted cash flows used to test the asset for recoverability and (b) the discounted cash flows used to measure the asset's fair value. If the fair value of the asset is based on a quoted market price and that price considers the costs that will be incurred in retiring that asset, the quoted market price shall be increased by the fair value of the asset retirement obligation for purposes of measuring impairment. [FAS143, ¶12]

Subsequent Recognition and Measurement

.113 In periods subsequent to initial measurement, an entity shall recognize period-to-period changes in the liability for an asset retirement obligation resulting from (a) the passage of time and (b) revisions to either the timing or the amount of the original estimate of undiscounted cash flows. An entity shall measure and incorporate changes due to the passage of time into the carrying amount of the liability before measuring changes resulting from a revision to either the timing or the amount of estimated cash flows. [FAS143, ¶13]

.114 An entity shall measure changes in the liability for an asset retirement obligation due to passage of time by applying an interest method of allocation to the amount of the liability at the beginning of the period.[11] The interest rate used to measure that change shall be the credit-adjusted risk-free rate that existed when the liability, or portion thereof, was initially measured. That amount shall be recognized as an increase in the carrying

[10]For example, assume an entity acquires a long-lived asset with an estimated life of 10 years. As that asset is operated, the entity incurs one-tenth of the liability for an asset retirement obligation each year. Application of a systematic and rational allocation method would not preclude that entity from capitalizing and then expensing one-tenth of the asset retirement costs each year. [FAS143, ¶11, fn10]

[11]The subsequent measurement provisions require an entity to identify undiscounted estimated cash flows associated with the initial measurement of a liability. Therefore, an entity that obtains an initial measurement of fair value from a market price or from a technique other than the expected cash flow approach described in Concepts Statement 7 must determine the undiscounted cash flows and estimated timing of those cash flows that are embodied in that fair value amount for purposes of applying the subsequent measurement provisions. Paragraph .163 includes an example of the subsequent measurement of a liability that is initially obtained from a market price. [FAS143, ¶14, fn12]

amount of the liability and as an expense classified as an operating item in the statement of income, hereinafter referred to as *accretion expense*.[12] Accretion expense shall not be considered to be interest cost for purposes of applying Section I67, "Interest: Capitalization of Interest Costs." [FAS143, ¶14]

.115 Changes resulting from revisions to the timing or the amount of the original estimate of undiscounted cash flows shall be recognized as an increase or a decrease in (a) the carrying amount of the liability for an asset retirement obligation and (b) the related asset retirement cost capitalized as part of the carrying amount of the related long-lived asset. Upward revisions in the amount of undiscounted estimated cash flows shall be discounted using the current credit-adjusted risk-free rate. Downward revisions in the amount of undiscounted estimated cash flows shall be discounted using the credit-adjusted risk-free rate that existed when the original liability was recognized. If an entity cannot identify the prior period to which the downward revision relates, it may use a weighted-average credit-adjusted risk-free rate to discount the downward revision to estimated future cash flows. When asset retirement costs change as a result of a revision to estimated cash flows, an entity shall adjust the amount of asset retirement cost allocated to expense in the period of change if the change affects that period only or in the period of change and future periods if the change affects more than one period as required by paragraph .130 of Section A06, "Accounting Changes," for a change in estimate. [FAS143, ¶15]

Effects of Funding and Assurance Provisions

.116 Providing assurance that an entity will be able to satisfy its asset retirement obligation does not satisfy or extinguish the related liability. Methods of providing assurance include surety bonds, insurance policies, letters of credit, guarantees by other entities, and establishment of trust funds or identification of other assets dedicated to satisfy the asset retirement obligation.[[13]] The existence of funding and assurance provisions may affect the determination of the credit-adjusted risk-free rate. For a previously recognized asset retirement obligation, changes in funding and assurance provisions have no effect on the initial measurement or accretion of that liability, but may affect the credit-adjusted risk-free rate used to discount upward revisions in undiscounted cash flows for

---

[12] An entity may use any descriptor for accretion expense so long as it conveys the underlying nature of the expense. [FAS143, ¶14, fn13]

[[13]] The effect of surety bonds, letters of credit, and guarantees is to provide assurance that third parties will provide amounts to satisfy the asset retirement obligations if the entity that has primary responsibility (the obligor) to do so cannot or does not fulfill its obligations. The possibility that a third party will satisfy the asset retirement obligations does not relieve the obligor from its primary responsibility for those obligations. If a third party is required to satisfy asset retirement obligations due to the failure or inability of the obligor to do so directly, the obligor would then have a liability to the third party. [FAS143, ¶B60]

that obligation. Costs associated with complying with funding or assurance provisions are accounted for separately from the asset retirement obligation. [FAS143, ¶16]

Leasing Transactions

.117 This section does not apply to obligations of a lessee in connection with leased property, whether imposed by a lease agreement or by a party other than the lessor, that meet the definition of either minimum lease payments or contingent rentals in paragraphs .417 and .404 of Section L10, "Leases."[14] Those obligations shall be accounted for by the lessee in accordance with the requirements of Section L10. However, if obligations of a lessee in connection with leased property, whether imposed by a lease agreement or by a party other than the lessor, meet the provisions in paragraph .102 of this section but do not meet the definition of either minimum lease payments or contingent rentals in paragraphs .417 and .404 of Section L10, those obligations shall be accounted for by the lessee in accordance with the requirements of this section. [FAS143, ¶17]

.118 Obligations of a lessor in connection with leased property that meet the provisions in paragraph .102 of this section shall be accounted for by the lessor in accordance with the requirements of this section. [FAS143, ¶18]

Rate-Regulated Entities

.119 This section applies to rate-regulated entities that meet the criteria for application of Section Re6, "Regulated Operations," as provided in paragraph .115 of that section. Paragraphs .119 and .121 of Section Re6 provide specific conditions that must be met to recognize a regulatory asset and a regulatory liability, respectively. [FAS143, ¶19]

.120 Many rate-regulated entities currently provide for the costs related to the retirement of certain long-lived assets in their financial statements and recover those amounts in rates charged to their customers. Some of those costs result from asset retirement obligations within the scope of this section; others result from costs that are not within the scope of this section. The amounts charged to customers for the costs related to the retirement of long-lived assets may differ from the period costs recognized in accordance with this section and, therefore, may result in a difference in the timing of recognition of period costs for financial reporting and rate-making purposes. An additional recognition timing difference may exist when the costs related to the retirement of long-lived assets are included in amounts charged to customers but liabilities are not recognized in the

[14]Paragraph .101 of Section L10 provides that Section L10 does not apply to lease agreements concerning the rights to explore for or to exploit natural resources such as oil, gas, minerals, and timber. [FAS143, ¶17, fn14]

financial statements. If the requirements of Section Re6 are met, a regulated entity also shall recognize a regulatory asset or liability for differences in the timing of recognition of the period costs associated with asset retirement obligations for financial reporting pursuant to this section and rate-making purposes. [FAS143, ¶20]

.121 The capitalized amount of an asset retirement cost shall be included in the assessment of impairment of long-lived assets of a rate-regulated entity just as that cost is included in the assessment of impairment of long-lived assets of any other entity. Section Re6, paragraph .127A, applies to the asset retirement cost related to a long-lived asset of a rate-regulated entity that has been closed or abandoned. [FAS143, ¶21]

Disclosures

.122 An entity shall disclose the following information about its asset retirement obligations:

a. A general description of the asset retirement obligations and the associated long-lived assets
b. The fair value of assets that are legally restricted for purposes of settling asset retirement obligations
c. A reconciliation of the beginning and ending aggregate carrying amount of asset retirement obligations showing separately the changes attributable to (1) liabilities incurred in the current period, (2) liabilities settled in the current period, (3) accretion expense, and (4) revisions in estimated cash flows, whenever there is a significant change in one or more of those four components during the reporting period.

If the fair value of an asset retirement obligation cannot be reasonably estimated, that fact and the reasons therefor shall be disclosed. [FAS143, ¶22]

Implementation Guidance

.123 Paragraphs .124 through .150 describe certain provisions of this section in more detail and explain how they apply to certain situations. Facts and circumstances need to be considered carefully in applying this section. Paragraphs .124 through .150 are an integral part of this section. [FAS143, ¶A1]

Scope

Legal Obligation

.124 This section applies to legal obligations associated with the retirement of a tangible long-lived asset. For purposes of this section, a legal obligation can result from (a) a government action, such as a law, statute, or ordinance, (b) an agreement between entities, such as a written or oral contract, or (c) a promise conveyed to a third party that imposes a reasonable expectation of performance upon the promisor under the doctrine of promissory estoppel. *Black's Law Dictionary,* seventh edition, defines *promissory estoppel* as, "The principle that a promise made without consideration may nonetheless be enforced to prevent injustice if the promisor should have reasonably expected the promisee to rely on the promise and if the promisee did actually rely on the promise to his or her detriment." [FAS143, ¶A2]

.125 In most cases involving an asset retirement obligation, the determination of whether a legal obligation exists should be unambiguous. However, in situations in which no law, statute, ordinance, or contract exists but an entity makes a promise to a third party (which may include the public at large) about its intention to perform retirement activities, facts and circumstances need to be considered carefully in determining whether that promise has imposed a legal obligation upon the promisor under the doctrine of promissory estoppel. A legal obligation may exist even though no party has taken any formal action. In assessing whether a legal obligation exists, an entity is not permitted to forecast changes in the law or changes in the interpretation of existing laws and regulations. Preparers and their legal advisors are required to evaluate current circumstances to determine whether a legal obligation exists. [FAS143, ¶A3]

.126 For example, assume a company operates a manufacturing facility and has plans to retire it within five years. Members of the local press have begun to publicize the fact that when the company ceases operations at the plant, it plans to abandon the site without demolishing the building and restoring the underlying land. Due to the significant negative publicity and demands by the public that the company commit to dismantling the plant upon retirement, the company's chief executive officer holds a press conference at city hall to announce that the company will demolish the building and restore the underlying land when the company ceases operations at the plant. Although no law, statute, ordinance, or written contract exists requiring the company to perform any demolition or restoration activities, the promise made by the company's chief executive officer may have created a legal obligation under the doctrine of promissory estoppel. In that circumstance, the company's management (and legal counsel, if necessary) would have to evaluate the particular facts and circumstances to determine whether a legal obligation exists. [FAS143, ¶A4]

.127 Contracts between entities may contain an option or a provision that requires one party to the contract to perform retirement activities when an asset is retired. The other party may decide in the future not to exercise the option or to waive the provision to perform retirement activities, or that party may have a history of waiving similar provisions in other contracts. Even if there is an expectation of a waiver or nonenforcement, the contract still imposes a legal obligation. That obligation is included in the scope of this section. The likelihood of a waiver or nonenforcement will affect the measurement of the liability. [FAS143, ¶A5]

Issues Associated with the Retirement of a Tangible Long-Lived Asset

.128 In this section, the term *retirement* is defined as the other-than-temporary removal of a long-lived asset from service. As used in this section, that term encompasses sale, abandonment, or disposal in some other manner. However, it does not encompass the temporary idling of a long-lived asset. After an entity retires an asset, that asset is no longer under the control of that entity, no longer in existence, or no longer capable of being used in the manner for which the asset was originally acquired, constructed, or developed. Activities necessary to prepare an asset for an alternative use are not associated with the retirement of the asset and are not within the scope of this section. [FAS143, ¶A6]

.129 Typically, settlement of an asset retirement obligation is not required until the associated asset is retired. However, certain circumstances may exist in which partial settlement of an asset retirement obligation is required or performed before the asset is fully retired. [FAS143, ¶A7] The nature of asset retirement obligations in various industries is such that the obligations are not necessarily satisfied when the current operation or use of the asset ceases and, in fact, can be settled during operation of the asset or after the operations cease. The timing of the ultimate settlement of a liability [is] unrelated to and should not affect its initial recognition in the financial statements provided the obligation is associated with the retirement of a tangible long-lived asset. [FAS143, ¶B14] The fact that partial settlement of an obligation is required or performed prior to full retirement of an asset does not remove that obligation from the scope of this section. [FAS143, ¶A7]

.130 For example, consider an entity that owns and operates a landfill. Regulations require that that entity perform capping, closure, and post-closure activities. Capping activities involve covering the land with topsoil and planting vegetation. Closure activities include drainage, engineering, and demolition and must be performed prior to commencing the post-closure activities. Post-closure activities, the final retirement activities, include maintaining the landfill once final certification of closure has been received and monitoring the ground and surface water, gas emissions, and air quality. Closure and post-closure activities are performed after the entire landfill ceases receiving waste (that is, after the landfill is retired). However, capping activities are performed as sections of the landfill become full and are effectively retired. The fact that some of the capping activities are performed while the landfill continues to accept waste does not remove the obligation to perform those intermediate capping activities from the scope of this section. [FAS143, ¶A8]

.131 Obligations associated with maintenance, rather than retirement, of a long-lived asset are excluded from the scope of this section. The cost of a replacement part that is a component of a long-lived asset is not within the scope of this section. Any legal obligations that require disposal of the replaced part are within the scope of this section. [FAS143, ¶A9]

Obligations Resulting from the Acquisition, Construction, or Development and (or) Normal Operation of an Asset

.132 Paragraph .102 of this section limits its scope to those legal obligations that result from the acquisition, construction, or development and (or) the normal operation of a long-lived asset. [FAS143, ¶A10]

.133 Identifying the obligating event is often difficult, especially in situations that involve the occurrence of a series of transactions or other events or circumstances affecting the entity. For example, in the case of an asset retirement obligation, a law or an entity's promise may create a duty or responsibility, but that law or promise in and of itself may not be the obligating event that results in an entity's having little or no discretion to avoid a future transfer or use of assets. An entity must look to the nature of the duty or responsibility to assess whether the obligating event has occurred. For example, in the case of a nuclear power facility, an entity assumes responsibility for decontamination of that facility upon receipt of the license to operate it. However, no obligation to decontaminate exists until the facility is operated and contamination occurs. Therefore, the contamination, not the receipt of the license, constitutes the obligating event. [FAS143, ¶B31]

.134 Whether an obligation results from the acquisition, construction, or development of a long-lived asset should, in most circumstances, be clear. For example, if an entity acquires a landfill that is already in operation, an obligation to perform capping, closure, and post-closure activities results from the acquisition and assumption of obligations related to past normal operations of the landfill. Additional obligations will be incurred as a result of future operations of the landfill. [FAS143, ¶A11]

.135 Whether an obligation results from the normal operation of a long-lived asset may require judgment. Obligations that result from the normal operation of an asset should be predictable and likely of occurring. For example, consider a company that owns and operates a nuclear power plant. That company has a legal obligation to perform decontamination activities when the plant ceases operations. Contamination, which gives rise to the obligation, is predictable and likely of occurring and is unavoidable as a result of operating the plant. Therefore, the obligation to perform decontamination activities at that plant results from the normal operation of the plant. [FAS143, ¶A12]

.136 An environmental remediation liability that results from the improper operation of a long-lived asset does not fall within the scope of this section. Obligations resulting from improper operations do not represent costs that are an integral part of the tangible long-lived asset and therefore should not be accounted for as part of the cost basis of the asset. For example, a certain amount of spillage may be inherent in the normal operations of a fuel storage facility, but a catastrophic accident caused by noncompliance with a company's safety procedures is not. The obligation to clean up after the catastrophic accident does not result from the normal operation of the facility and is not within the scope of this section. An environmental remediation liability that results from the normal operation of a long-lived asset and that is associated with the retirement of that asset shall be accounted for under the provisions of this section.[15] [FAS143, ¶A13]

Asset Retirement Obligations with Indeterminate Settlement Dates

.137 An asset retirement obligation may result from the acquisition, construction, or development and (or) normal operation of a long-lived asset that has an indeterminate useful life and thereby an indeterminate settlement date for the asset retirement obligation. Uncertainty about the timing of settlement of the asset retirement obligation does not remove that obligation from the scope of this section but will affect the measurement of a liability for that obligation (refer to paragraph .139). [FAS143, ¶A14]

Asset Retirement Obligations Related to Component Parts of Larger Systems

.138 An asset retirement obligation may exist for component parts of a larger system. In some circumstances, the retirement of the component parts may be required before the retirement of the larger system to which the component parts belong. [FAS143, ¶A15] There is no conceptual difference between interim property retirements and replacements and those retirements that occur in circumstances in which the retired asset is not replaced. Therefore, any asset retirement obligation associated with the retirement of or

[15]SOP 96-1 applies to environmental remediation liabilities that relate to pollution arising from some past act, generally as a result of the provision of Superfund, the corrective action provisions of the Resource Conservation and Recovery Act of 1976, or analogous state and non-U.S. laws and regulations. An environmental remediation liability that results from other than the normal operation of a long-lived asset probably falls within the scope of SOP 96-1. [FAS143, ¶B20]

the retirement and replacement of a component part of a larger system qualifies for recognition provided that the obligation meets the definition of a liability.[16] [FAS143, ¶B17] For example, consider an aluminum smelter that owns and operates several kilns lined with a special type of brick. The kilns have a long useful life, but the bricks wear out after approximately five years of use and are replaced on a periodic basis to maintain optimal efficiency of the kilns. Because the bricks become contaminated with hazardous chemicals while in the kiln, a state law requires that when the bricks are removed, they must be disposed of at a special hazardous waste site. The obligation to dispose of those bricks is within the scope of this section. The cost of the replacement bricks and their installation are not part of that obligation. [FAS143, ¶A15]

Liability Recognition—Asset Retirement Obligations with Indeterminate Settlement Dates

.139 Instances may occur in which insufficient information to estimate the fair value of an asset retirement obligation is available. For example, if an asset has an indeterminate useful life, sufficient information to estimate a range of potential settlement dates for the obligation might not be available. In such cases, the liability would be initially recognized in the period in which sufficient information exists to estimate a range of potential settlement dates that is needed to employ a present value technique to estimate fair value. [FAS143, ¶A16]

Liability Recognition—Conditional Obligations

.140 A conditional obligation to perform a retirement activity is within the scope of this section. For example, if a governmental unit retains the right (an option) to decide whether to require a retirement activity, there is some uncertainty about whether those retirement activities will be required or waived. Regardless of the uncertainty attributable to the option, a legal obligation to stand ready to perform retirement activities still exists, and the governmental unit might require them to be performed. Uncertainty about whether performance will be required does not defer the recognition of a retirement obligation; rather, that uncertainty is factored into the measurement of the fair value of the liability through assignment of probabilities to cash flows. Uncertainty about performance of conditional obligations shall not prevent the determination of a reasonable estimate of fair value. [FAS143, ¶A17]

---

[16]Examples of interim property retirement and replacements for component parts of larger systems are components of transmission and distribution systems (utility poles), railroad ties, a single oil well that is part of a larger oil field, and aircraft engines. The assets in those examples may or may not have associated retirement obligations. [FAS143, ¶B17, fn22]

.141 A past history of nonenforcement of an unambiguous obligation does not defer recognition of a liability, but its measurement is affected by the uncertainty over the requirement to perform retirement activities. Uncertainty about the requirement to perform retirement activities shall not prevent the determination of a reasonable estimate of fair value. Guidance on how to estimate a liability in the presence of uncertainty about a requirement to perform retirement activities is provided in paragraphs .151 through .162. [FAS143, ¶A18]

Initial Measurement of a Liability for an Asset Retirement Obligation

.142 The objective of the initial measurement of a liability for an asset retirement obligation shall be fair value. Quoted market prices are the best representation of fair value. When market prices are not available, the amount of the liability must be estimated using some other measurement technique. The use of an expected present value technique in measuring the fair value of a liability is discussed in Concepts Statement 7. [FAS143, ¶A19]

.143 In estimating the fair value of a liability for an asset retirement obligation using an expected present value technique, an entity shall begin by estimating cash flows that reflect, to the extent possible, a marketplace assessment of the cost and timing of performing the required retirement activities. The measurement objective is to determine the amount a third party[17] would demand to assume the obligation. Considerations in estimating those cash flows include developing and incorporating explicit assumptions, to the extent possible, about all of the following:

a. The costs that a third party would incur in performing the tasks necessary to retire the asset
b. Other amounts that a third party would include in determining the price of settlement, including, for example, inflation, overhead, equipment charges, profit margin, and advances in technology
c. The extent to which the amount of a third party's costs or the timing of its costs would vary under different future scenarios and the relative probabilities of those scenarios
d. The price that a third party would demand and could expect to receive for bearing the uncertainties and unforeseeable circumstances inherent in the obligation, sometimes referred to as a market-risk premium.

[17] In this context, a third party is meant to encompass participants (or hypothetical participants) that provide settlement of asset retirement obligations in a market. [FAS143, ¶A20, fn17]

It is expected that uncertainties about the amount and timing of future cash flows can be accommodated by using the expected cash flow technique and therefore will not prevent the determination of a reasonable estimate of fair value. [FAS143, ¶A20]

.144 An entity shall discount estimates of future cash flows using an interest rate that equates to a risk-free interest rate adjusted for the effect of its credit standing (a credit-adjusted risk-free rate).[18] The risk-free interest rate is the interest rate on monetary assets that are essentially risk free and that have maturity dates that coincide with the expected timing of the estimated cash flows required to satisfy the asset retirement obligation.[19] Concepts Statement 7 illustrates an adjustment to the risk-free interest rate to reflect the credit standing of the entity, but acknowledges that adjustments for default risk can be reflected in either the discount rate or the estimated cash flows. In most situations, an entity will know the adjustment required to the risk-free interest rate to reflect its credit standing. Consequently, it would be easier and less complex to reflect that adjustment in the discount rate. In addition, because of the requirements in paragraph .115 relating to upward and downward adjustments in cash flow estimates, it is essential to the operationality of this section that the credit standing of the entity be reflected in the interest rate. For those reasons, the risk-free rate [is] required [to] be adjusted for the credit standing of the entity to determine the discount rate. [FAS143, ¶A21]

.145 Where assets with asset retirement obligations are components of a larger group of assets (for example, a number of oil wells that make up an entire oil field operation), aggregation techniques may be necessary to derive a collective asset retirement obligation. This section does not preclude the use of estimates and computational shortcuts that are consistent with the fair value measurement objective when computing an aggregate asset retirement obligation for assets that are components of a larger group of assets. [FAS143, ¶A22]

.146 This section requires recognition of the fair value of a conditional asset retirement obligation before the event that either requires or waives performance occurs. Uncertainty surrounding conditional performance of the retirement obligation is factored into its measurement by assessing the likelihood that performance will be required. In situations in which the conditional aspect has only 2 outcomes and there is no information about which outcome is more probable, a 50 percent likelihood for each outcome shall be used until additional information is available. As the time for notification approaches, more information

---

[18]In determining the adjustment for the effect of its credit standing, an entity should consider the effects of all terms, collateral, and existing guarantees that would affect the amount required to settle the liability. [FAS143, ¶A21, fn18]

[19]In the United States, the risk-free rate is the rate for zero-coupon U.S. Treasury instruments. [FAS143, ¶A21, fn19]

and a better perspective about the ultimate outcome will likely be obtained. Consequently, reassessment of the timing, amount, and probabilities associated with the expected cash flows may change the amount of the liability recognized. If, as time progresses, it becomes apparent that retirement activities will not be required, the liability and the remaining unamortized asset retirement cost are reduced to zero. [FAS143, ¶A23]

.147 In summary, an unambiguous requirement that gives rise to an asset retirement obligation coupled with a low likelihood of required performance still requires recognition of a liability. Uncertainty about the conditional outcome of the obligation is incorporated into the measurement of the fair value of that liability, not the recognition decision. [FAS143, ¶A24]

Subsequent Recognition and Measurement

.148 In periods subsequent to initial measurement, an entity recognizes the effect of the passage of time on the amount of a liability for an asset retirement obligation. A period-to-period increase in the carrying amount of the liability shall be recognized as an operating item (accretion expense) in the statement of income. An equivalent amount is added to the carrying amount of the liability. To calculate accretion expense, an entity shall multiply the beginning of the period liability balance by the credit-adjusted risk-free rate that existed when the liability was initially measured. The liability shall be adjusted for accretion prior to adjusting for revisions in estimated cash flows. [FAS143, ¶A25]

.149 Revisions to a previously recorded asset retirement obligation will result from changes in the assumptions used to estimate the cash flows required to settle the asset retirement obligation, including changes in estimated probabilities, amounts, and timing of the settlement of the asset retirement obligation, as well as changes in the legal requirements of an obligation. Any changes that result in upward revisions to the undiscounted estimated cash flows shall be treated as a new liability and discounted at the current rate. Any downward revisions to the undiscounted estimated cash flows will result in a reduction of the asset retirement obligation. For downward revisions, the amount of the liability to be removed from the existing accrual shall be discounted at the rate that was used at the time the obligation to which the downward revision relates was originally recorded (or the historical weighted-average rate if the year(s) to which the downward revision applies cannot be determined). [FAS143, ¶A26]

.150 Revisions to the asset retirement obligation result in adjustments of capitalized asset retirement costs and will affect subsequent depreciation of the related asset. Such adjustments are depreciated on a prospective basis. [FAS143, ¶A27]

Illustrative Examples—Recognition and Measurement Provisions

.151 Paragraphs .153 through .162 include four examples that illustrate the recognition and measurement provisions of this section. Example 1 illustrates (a) initial measurement of a liability for an asset retirement obligation using an expected present value technique, (b) subsequent measurement assuming that there are no changes in estimated cash flows, and (c) settlement of the asset retirement obligation liability (ARO liability) at the end of its term. Example 2 is similar to Example 1. However, Example 2 illustrates subsequent measurement of an ARO liability after a change in estimated cash flows. Example 3 highlights the recognition and measurement provisions of this Statement for an ARO liability that is incurred over more than one reporting period. Example 4 illustrates accounting for asset retirement obligations that are conditional and that have a low likelihood of enforcement. [FAS143, ¶C1]

.152 The examples in paragraphs .153 through .164 incorporate simplified assumptions to provide guidance in implementing this section. For instance, Examples 1 and 2 relate to the asset retirement obligation associated with an offshore production platform that also would likely have individual wells and production facilities that would have separate asset retirement obligations. Those examples also assume straight-line depreciation, even though, in practice, depreciation would likely be applied using a units-of-production method. Other simplifying assumptions are used throughout the examples. [FAS143, ¶C2]

Example 1

.153 Example 1 depicts an entity that completes construction of and places into service an offshore oil platform on January 1, 2003. The entity is legally required to dismantle and remove the platform at the end of its useful life, which is estimated to be 10 years. Based on the requirements of this section, on January 1, 2003, the entity recognizes a liability for an asset retirement obligation and capitalizes an amount for an asset retirement cost. The entity estimates the initial fair value of the liability using an expected present value technique. The significant assumptions used in that estimate of fair value are as follows:

a. Labor costs are based on current marketplace wages required to hire contractors to dismantle and remove offshore oil platforms. The entity assigns probability assessments to a range of cash flow estimates as follows:

Cash Flow Estimate	Probability Assessment	Expected Cash Flows
$100,000	25%	$ 25,000
125,000	50	62,500
175,000	25	43,750
		$131,250

b. The entity estimates allocated overhead and equipment charges using the rate it applies to labor costs for transfer pricing (80 percent). The entity has no reason to believe that its overhead rate differs from those used by contractors in the industry.

c. A contractor typically adds a markup on labor and allocated internal costs to provide a profit margin on the job. The rate used (20 percent) represents the entity's understanding of the profit that contractors in the industry generally earn to dismantle and remove offshore oil platforms.

d. A contractor would typically demand and receive a premium (market risk premium) for bearing the uncertainty and unforeseeable circumstances inherent in "locking in" today's price for a project that will not occur for 10 years. The entity estimates the amount of that premium to be 5 percent of the estimated inflation-adjusted cash flows.

e. The risk-free rate of interest on January 1, 2003, is 5 percent. The entity adjusts that rate by 3.5 percent to reflect the effect of its credit standing. Therefore, the credit-adjusted risk-free rate used to compute expected present value is 8.5 percent.

f. The entity assumes a rate of inflation of 4 percent over the 10-year period.

[FAS143, ¶C3]

.154 On December 31, 2012, the entity settles its asset retirement obligation by using its internal workforce at a cost of $351,000. Assuming no changes during the 10-year period in the cash flows used to estimate the obligation, the entity would recognize a gain of $89,619 on settlement of the obligation [as shown in Exhibits .154A through .154E].

[FAS143, ¶C4]

Exhibit 154A

Gain on the Settlement of the ARO

Labor	$195,000
Allocated overhead and equipment charges (80 percent of labor)	156,000
Total costs incurred	351,000
ARO liability	440,619
Gain on settlement of obligation	$ 89,619

[FAS143, ¶C4]

Exhibit 154B

Initial Measurement of the ARO Liability at January 1, 2003

	Expected Cash Flows 1/1/03
Expected labor costs	$131,250
Allocated overhead and equipment charges (.80 × $131,250)	105,000
Contractor's markup [.20 × ($131,250 + $105,000)]	47,250
Expected cash flows before inflation adjustment	283,500
Inflation factor assuming 4 percent rate for 10 years	1.4802
Expected cash flows adjusted for inflation	419,637
Market-risk premium (.05 × $419,637)	20,982
Expected cash flows adjusted for market risk	$440,619
Present value using credit-adjusted risk-free rate of 8.5 percent for 10 years	$194,879

[FAS143, ¶C4]

Exhibit 154C

Interest Method of Allocation

Year	Liability Balance 1/1	Accretion	Liability Balance 12/31
2003	$194,879	$16,565	$211,444
2004	211,444	17,973	229,417
2005	229,417	19,500	248,917
2006	248,917	21,158	270,075
2007	270,075	22,956	293,031
2008	293,031	24,908	317,939
2009	317,939	27,025	344,964
2010	344,964	29,322	374,286
2011	374,286	31,814	406,100
2012	406,100	34,519	440,619

[FAS143, ¶C4]

Exhibit 154D

Schedule of Expenses

Year-End	Accretion Expense	Depreciation Expense	Total Expense
2003	$16,565	$19,488	$36,053
2004	17,973	19,488	37,461
2005	19,500	19,488	38,988
2006	21,158	19,488	40,646
2007	22,956	19,488	42,444
2008	24,908	19,488	44,396
2009	27,025	19,488	46,513
2010	29,322	19,488	48,810
2011	31,814	19,488	51,302
2012	34,519	19,488	54,007

[FAS143, ¶C4]

Exhibit 154E

Journal Entries

January 1, 2003:		
Long-lived asset (asset retirement cost)	194,879	
ARO liability		194,879
To record the initial fair value of the ARO liability		
December 31, 2003–2012:		
Depreciation expense (asset retirement cost)	19,488	
Accumulated depreciation		19,488
To record straight-line depreciation on the asset retirement cost		
Accretion expense	Per schedule	
ARO liability		Per schedule
To record accretion expense on the ARO liability		
December 31, 2012:		
ARO liability	440,619	
Wages payable		195,000
Allocated overhead and equipment charges (.80 × $195,000)		156,000
Gain on settlement of ARO liability		89,619
To record settlement of the ARO liability		

[FAS143, ¶C4]

Example 2

.155 Example 2 is the same as Example 1 with respect to initial measurement of the ARO liability. In this example, the entity's credit standing improves over time, causing the credit-adjusted risk-free rate to decrease by .5 percent to 8 percent at December 31, 2004. [FAS143, ¶C5]

.156 On December 31, 2004, the entity revises its estimate of labor costs to reflect an increase of 10 percent in the marketplace. In addition, it revises the probability assessments related to those labor costs. The change in labor costs results in an upward revision to the undiscounted cash flows; consequently, the incremental cash flows are discounted at the current rate of 8 percent. All other assumptions remain unchanged. The revised estimate of expected cash flows for labor costs is as follows:

Cash Flow Estimate	Probability Assessment	Expected Cash Flows
$110,000	30%	$ 33,000
137,500	45	61,875
192,500	25	48,125
		$143,000

[FAS143, ¶C6]

.157 On December 31, 2012, the entity settles its asset retirement obligation by using an outside contractor. It incurs costs of $463,000, resulting in the recognition of a $14,091 gain on settlement of the obligation [as shown in Exhibits 157A through 157F]. [FAS143, ¶C7]

Exhibit 157A

Gain on the Settlement of the ARO

ARO liability	$477,091
Outside contractor	463,000
Gain on settlement of obligation	$ 14,091

[FAS143, ¶C7]

Exhibit 157B

Initial Measurement of the ARO Liability at January 1, 2003

	Expected Cash Flows 1/1/03
Expected labor costs	$131,250
Allocated overhead and equipment charges (.80 × $131,250)	105,000
Contractor's markup [.20 × ($131,250 + $105,000)]	47,250
Expected cash flows before inflation adjustment	283,500
Inflation factor assuming 4 percent rate for 10 years	1.4802
Expected cash flows adjusted for inflation	419,637
Market-risk premium (.05 × $419,637)	20,982
Expected cash flows for market risk	$440,619
Present value using credit-adjusted risk-free rate of 8.5 percent for 10 years	$194,879

[FAS143, ¶C7]

Exhibit 157C

Subsequent Measurement of the ARO Liability Reflecting a Change in Labor Cost Estimate as of December 31, 2004

	Revised Expected Cash Flows 12/31/04
Incremental expected labor costs ($143,000 – $131,250)	$11,750
Allocated overhead and equipment charges (.80 × $11,750)	9,400
Contractor's markup [.20 × ($11,750 + $9,400)]	4,230
Expected cash flows before inflation adjustment	25,380
Inflation factor assuming 4 percent rate for 8 years	1.3686
Expected cash flows adjusted for inflation	34,735
Market-risk premium (.05 × $34,735)	1,737
Expected cash flows adjusted for market risk	$36,472
Present value of incremental liability using credit-adjusted risk-free rate of 8 percent for 8 years	$19,704

[FAS143, ¶C7]

Exhibit 157D

Interest Method of Allocation

Year	Liability Balance 1/1	Accretion	Change in Cash Flow Estimate	Liability Balance 12/31
2003	$194,879	$16,565		$211,444
2004	211,444	17,973	$19,704	249,121*
2005	249,121	21,078		270,199
2006	270,199	22,862		293,061
2007	293,061	24,796		317,857
2008	317,857	26,894		344,751
2009	344,751	29,170		373,921
2010	373,921	31,638		405,559
2011	405,559	34,315		439,874
2012	439,874	37,217		477,091

*The remainder of this table is an aggregation of two layers: the original liability, which is accreted at a rate of 8.5%, and the new incremental liability, which is accreted at a rate of 8.0%.

[FAS143, ¶C7]

Exhibit 157E

Schedule of Expenses

Year-End	Accretion Expense	Depreciation Expense	Total Expense
2003	$16,565	$19,488	$36,053
2004	17,973	19,488	37,461
2005	21,078	21,951	43,029
2006	22,862	21,951	44,813
2007	24,796	21,951	46,747
2008	26,894	21,951	48,845
2009	29,170	21,951	51,121
2010	31,638	21,951	53,589
2011	34,315	21,951	56,266
2012	37,217	21,951	59,168

[FAS143, ¶C7]

Exhibit 157F

Journal Entries

January 1, 2003:		
Long-lived asset (asset retirement cost)	194,879	
ARO liability		194,879
To record the initial fair value of the ARO liability		
December 31, 2003:		
Depreciation expense (asset retirement cost)	19,488	
Accumulated depreciation		19,488
To record straight-line depreciation on the asset retirement cost		
Accretion expense	16,565	
ARO liability		16,565
To record accretion expense on the ARO liability		
December 31, 2004:		
Depreciation expense (asset retirement cost)	19,488	
Accumulated depreciation		19,488
To record straight-line depreciation on the asset retirement cost		
Accretion expense	17,973	
ARO liability		17,973
To record accretion expense on the ARO liability		
Long-lived asset (asset retirement cost)	19,704	
ARO liability		19,704
To record the change in estimated cash flows		
December 31, 2005–2012:		
Depreciation expense (asset retirement cost)	21,951	
Accumulated depreciation		21,951
To record straight-line depreciation on the asset retirement cost adjusted for the change in cash flow estimate		
Accretion expense	Per schedule	
ARO liability		Per schedule
To record accretion expense on the ARO liability		
December 31, 2012:		
ARO liability	477,091	
Gain on settlement of ARO liability		14,091
Accounts payable (outside contractor)		463,000
To record settlement of the ARO liability		

[FAS143, ¶C7]

Example 3

.158 Example 3 depicts an entity that places a nuclear utility plant into service on December 31, 2003. The entity is legally required to decommission the plant at the end of its useful life, which is estimated to be 20 years. Based on the requirements of this section, the entity recognizes a liability for an asset retirement obligation and capitalizes an amount for an asset retirement cost over the life of the plant as contamination occurs. The following schedule reflects the undiscounted expected cash flows and respective credit-adjusted risk-free rates used to measure each portion of the liability through December 31, 2005, at which time the plant is 90 percent contaminated.

Date	Undiscounted Expected Cash Flows	Credit-Adjusted Risk-Free Rate
12/31/03	$23,000	9.0%
12/31/04	1,150	8.5
12/31/05	1,900	9.2

[FAS143, ¶C8]

.159 On December 31, 2005, the entity increases by 10 percent its estimate of undiscounted expected cash flows that were used to measure those portions of the liability recognized on December 31, 2003, and December 31, 2004. Because the change results in an upward revision to the undiscounted estimated cash flows, the incremental estimated cash flow is discounted at the current credit-adjusted risk-free rate of 9.2 percent. As a result, $2,300 (10 percent of $23,000) plus $115 (10 percent of $1,150) plus $1,900 (resulting from contamination in 2005), which totals $4,315 of incremental undiscounted cash flows are discounted at the then current credit-adjusted risk-free rate of 9.2 percent and recorded as a liability on December 31, 2005 [as shown in Exhibits 159A and 159B].

	Date Incurred		
	12/31/03	12/31/04	12/31/05
Initial measurement of the ARO liability:			
Expected cash flows adjusted for market risk	$23,000	$1,150	$1,900
Credit-adjusted risk-free rate	9.00%	8.50%	9.20%
Discount period in years	20	19	18
Expected present value	$4,104	$244	$390
Measurement of revision in expected cash flows occurring on December 31, 2005:			
Revision in expected cash flows (increase of 10 percent) [($23,000 × 10%) + ($1,150 × 10%)]			$2,415
Credit-adjusted risk-free rate at December 31, 2005			9.20%
Discount period remaining in years			18
Expected present value			$495

[FAS143, ¶C9]

Exhibit 159A

Carrying Amount of Total ARO Liability

Carrying Amount of Liability Incurred in 2003

Year	Liability Balance 1/1	Accretion (9.0%)	New Liability	Liability Balance 12/31
2003			$4,104	$4,104
2004	$4,104	$369		4,473
2005	4,473	403		4,876

Carrying Amount of Liability Incurred in 2004

Year	Liability Balance 1/1	Accretion (8.5%)	New Liability	Liability Balance 12/31
2004			$244	$244
2005	$244	$21		265

Exhibit 159A (continued)

Carrying Amount of Liability Incurred in 2005 Plus Effect of Change in Estimated Cash Flows

Year	Liability Balance 1/1	Accretion (9.2%)	Change in Cash Flow Estimate	New Liability	Liability Balance 12/31
2005			$495	$390	$885

Carrying Amount of Total Liability

Year	Liability Balance 1/1	Accretion	Change in Cash Flow Estimate	New Liability	Total Carrying Amount 12/31
2003				$4,104	$4,104
2004	$4,104	$369		244	4,717
2005	4,717	424	$495	390	6,026

[FAS143, ¶C9]

Exhibit 159B

Journal Entries

December 31, 2003:		
Long-lived asset (asset retirement cost)	4,104	
ARO liability		4,104
To record the initial fair value of the ARO liability incurred this period		
December 31, 2004:		
Depreciation expense ($4,104 ÷ 20)	205	
Accumulated depreciation		205
To record straight-line depreciation on the asset retirement cost		
Accretion expense	369	
ARO liability		369
To record accretion expense on the ARO liability		
Long-lived asset (asset retirement cost)	244	
ARO liability		244
To record the initial fair value of the ARO liability incurred this period		
December 31, 2005:		
Depreciation expense [($4,104 ÷ 20) + ($244 ÷ 19)]	218	
Accumulated depreciation		218
To record straight-line depreciation on the asset retirement cost		
Accretion expense	424	
ARO liability		424
To record accretion expense on the ARO liability		
Long-lived asset (asset retirement cost)	495	
ARO liability		495
To record the change in liability resulting from a revision in expected cash flows		
Long-lived asset (asset retirement cost)	390	
ARO liability		390
To record the initial fair value of the ARO liability incurred this period		

[FAS143, ¶C9]

Example 4

.160 Example 4 illustrates a timber lease[20] wherein the lessor has an option to require the lessee to settle an asset retirement obligation. Assume an entity enters into a five-year lease agreement that grants it the right to harvest timber on a tract of land and that agreement grants the lessor an option to require that the lessee reforest the underlying land at the end of the lease term. Based on past history, the lessee believes that the likelihood that the lessor will exercise that option is low. Rather, at the end of the lease, the lessor will likely accept the land without requiring reforestation. The lessee estimates that there is only a 10 percent probability that the lessor will elect to enforce reforestation. [FAS143, ¶C10]

.161 At the end of the first year, 20 percent of the timber has been harvested. The lessee estimates that the fair value of performing reforestation activities in 4 years for the portion of the land that has been harvested will be $300,000. When estimating the fair value of the ARO liability to be recorded, the lessee incorporates the probability that the restoration provisions will not be enforced:

	Cash Flow Estimate	Probability Assessment	Expected Cash Flows
	$300,000	10%	$30,000
	0	90	0
			$30,000
Present value using credit-adjusted risk-free rate of 8.5 percent for 4 years			$21,647

[FAS143, ¶C11]

.162 During the term of the lease, the lessee should reassess the likelihood that the lessor will require reforestation. For example, if the lessee subsequently determines that the likelihood of the lessor electing the reforestation option has increased, that change will result in a change in the estimate of future cash flows and be accounted for as illustrated in Example 2. [FAS143, ¶C12]

[20]Section L10 excludes from its scope "lease agreements concerning the rights to explore for or to exploit natural resources such as oil, gas, minerals, and timber" (paragraph .101). [FAS143, ¶C10, fn26]

Illustrative Example—Subsequent Measurement of a Liability Obtained from a Market Price

.163 Subsequent to initial measurement, an entity is required to recognize period-to-period changes in an ARO liability resulting from (a) the passage of time (accretion expense) and (b) revisions in cash flow estimates. To apply the subsequent measurement provisions of this section, an entity must identify undiscounted cash flows related to an ARO liability irrespective of how the liability was initially measured. Therefore, if an entity obtains the initial fair value from a market price, it must impute undiscounted cash flows from that price. [FAS143, ¶E1]

.164 Exhibits 164A and 164B include an example that illustrates the subsequent measurement of a liability in situations where the initial liability is based on a market price. The example assumes that the liability is initially recognized at the end of period 0 when the market price is $300,000 and the entity's credit-adjusted risk-free rate is 8 percent. As required by this section, revisions in the timing or the amount of estimated cash flows are assumed to occur at the end of the period after accretion on the beginning balance of the liability is calculated. At the end of each period, the following procedure is used to impute cash flows from the end of period market price, compute the change in that price attributable to revisions in estimated cash flows, and calculate accretion expense.

a. The market price and the credit-adjusted risk-free interest rate are used to impute the undiscounted cash flows embedded in the market price.
b. The undiscounted cash flows from (a) are discounted at the initial credit-adjusted risk-free rate of 8 percent to arrive at the ending balance of the ARO liability per the provisions of this section.
c. The beginning balance of the ARO liability is multiplied by the initial credit-adjusted risk-free rate of 8 percent to arrive at the amount of accretion expense per the provisions of this section.
d. The difference between the undiscounted cash flows at the beginning of the period and the undiscounted cash flows at the end of the period represents the revision in cash flow estimates that occurred during the period. If that change is an upward revision to the undiscounted estimated cash flows, it is discounted at the current credit-adjusted risk-free rate. If that change is a downward revision, it is discounted at the historical weighted-average rate because it is not practicable to separately identify the period to which the downward revision relates.

[FAS143, ¶E2]

Exhibit 164A

Subsequent Measurement of an ARO Liability Obtained from a Market Price

	End of Period			
	0	**1**	**2**	**3**
Market assumptions:				
Market price (includes market risk premium)	$300,000	$400,000	$350,000	$380,000
Current risk-free rate adjusted for entity's credit standing	8.00%	7.00%	7.50%	7.50%
Time period remaining	3	2	1	0
Imputed undiscounted cash flows (market price discounted at market rate)	$377,914	$457,960	$376,250	$380,000
Change in undiscounted cash flows	377,914	80,046	(81,710)	3,750
Discount rate:				
Current credit-adjusted risk-free rate (for upward revisions)	8.00%	7.00%		
Historical weighted-average credit-adjusted risk-free rate (for downward revisions)			7.83%	
Change in undiscounted cash flows discounted at credit-adjusted risk-free rate (current rate for upward revisions and historical rate for downward revisions)	$300,000	$69,916	$(75,777)	$3,750

[FAS143, ¶E2]

Exhibit 164B

Measurement of Liability under Provisions of ARO Section

Period	Beginning Balance	Accretion (8.0%)	Change in Cash Flows	Ending Balance
0			$300,000	$300,000
1	$300,000	$24,000		324,000
2	324,000	25,920		349,920
3	349,920	27,994		377,914

Period	Beginning Balance	Accretion (7.0%)	Change in Cash Flows	Ending Balance
0				
1			$69,916	$69,916
2	$69,916	$4,894		74,810
3	74,810	5,236		80,046

Period	Beginning Balance	Accretion (7.83%)	Change in Cash Flows	Ending Balance
0				
1				
2			$(75,777)	$(75,777)
3	$(75,777)	$(5,933)		(81,710)

Period	Beginning Balance	Accretion	Change in Cash Flows	Ending Balance
0				
1				
2				
3			$3,750	$3,750

Period	Beginning Balance	Total Accretion Expense	Change in Cash Flows	Ending Balance
0			$300,000	$300,000
1	$300,000	$24,000	69,916	393,916
2	393,916	30,814	(75,777)	348,953
3	348,953	27,297	3,750	380,000

[FAS143, ¶E2]

Supplemental Guidance: Emerging Issues Task Force (EITF) Issues

.1000 [Listed below are EITF Issues that provide supplemental guidance for this section. These Issues are related by topic to the guidance in this section.

EITF Issue No. 89-13, "Accounting for the Cost of Asbestos Removal"
EITF Issue No. 90-8, " Capitalization of Costs to Treat Environmental Contamination"
EITF Issue No. 95-23, "The Treatment of Certain Site Restoration/Environmental Exit Costs When Testing a Long-Lived Asset for Impairment"
EITF Issue No. 02-6, "Classification in the Statement of Cash Flows of Payments Made to Settle an Asset Retirement Obligation within the Scope of FASB Statement No. 143"]

(The next page is 4471.)

Supplemental Guidance: Emerging Issues Task Force (EITF) Issues

[illegible] EITF issues [illegible]. [illegible] related EITF issues [illegible] guidance in this section.

EITF Issue No. 89-13, Accounting for the Cost of Asbestos Removal
EITF Issue No. 90-8, Capitalization of Costs to Treat Environmental Contamination
EITF Issue No. 95-23, The Treatment of Certain Site Restoration/Environmental Exit Costs When Testing a Long-Lived Asset for Impairment
EITF Issue No. [illegible], [illegible] in the [illegible] Useful Life of [illegible] Asset Retirement Obligation within the scope of FASB Statement No. 143

BALANCE SHEET CLASSIFICATION: CURRENT ASSETS AND CURRENT LIABILITIES

SECTION B05

Sources: ARB 43, Chapter 3A; APB Opinion 6; FASB Statement 6; FASB Statement 78; FASB Statement 115; FASB Interpretation 8; FASB Technical Bulletin 79-3

[**Note:** A list of Issues discussed by the Emerging Issues Task Force (EITF) that provide supplemental guidance for this section is presented in paragraph .1000.]

Summary

An enterprise preparing a classified balance sheet shall segregate current assets and current liabilities separately from other assets and liabilities. The current classification applies to those assets which will be realized in cash, sold or consumed within one year (or operating cycle, if longer), and those liabilities that will be discharged by use of current assets or the creation of other current liabilities within one year (or operating cycle, if longer). The current liability classification is also intended to include obligations that, by their terms, are due on demand or will be due on demand within one year (or operating cycle, if longer) from the balance sheet date, even though liquidation may not be expected within that period. It is also intended to include long-term obligations that are or will be callable by the creditor either because the debtor's violation of a provision of the debt agreement at the balance sheet date makes the obligation callable or because the violation, if not cured within a specified grace period, will make the obligation callable. Such callable obligations are to be classified as current liabilities unless one of the following conditions is met:

a. The creditor has waived or subsequently lost the right to demand repayment for more than one year (or operating cycle, if longer) from the balance sheet date.
b. For long-term obligations containing a grace period within which the debtor may cure the violation, it is probable that the violation will be cured within that period, thus preventing the obligation from becoming callable.

Short-term obligations expected to be refinanced on a long-term basis, including those callable obligations discussed above, shall be excluded from current liabilities only if the enterprise intends to refinance the obligation on a long-term basis and has the demonstrated ability to consummate the refinancing.

.101 [Editorial deletion.]

.102 The balance sheets of most enterprises show separate classifications of **current assets** and **current liabilities** (commonly referred to as classified balance sheets) permitting ready determination of **working capital.** Enterprises in several specialized industries (including broker-dealers and finance, real estate, and stock life insurance enterprises) for which the current/noncurrent distinction is deemed in practice to have little or no relevance prepare unclassified balance sheets. The standards established in paragraphs .110 through .137 apply only when an enterprise is preparing a classified balance sheet for financial accounting and reporting purposes. [FAS6, ¶7]

.103 Financial statements of a going concern are prepared on the assumption that the enterprise will continue in business. Accordingly, this section represents a departure from any narrow definition or strict *one-year* interpretation of either current assets or current liabilities; the objective is to relate the criteria developed to the **operating cycle** of a business. [ARB43, ch3A, ¶2]

.104 Financial position is revealed in a presentation of the assets and liabilities of the enterprise. Generally [these assets and liabilities] are classified and segregated; summations or totals of the current assets and current liabilities will permit the ready determination of *working capital. Working capital,* sometimes called *net working capital,* is represented by the excess of current assets over current liabilities and identifies the relatively liquid portion of total enterprise capital that constitutes a margin or buffer for meeting obligations within the ordinary operating cycle of the business. It is recognized that there may be exceptions, in special cases, to certain of the inclusions and exclusions as set forth in this section. When such exceptions occur they should be accorded the treatment merited in the particular circumstances under the general principles outlined herein. [ARB43, ch3A, ¶3]

Current Assets

.105 For accounting purposes, the term *current assets* is used to designate cash and other assets or resources commonly identified as those that are reasonably expected to be realized in cash or sold or consumed during the normal operating cycle of the business. Thus the term comprehends in general such resources as (a) cash available for current operations and items that are the equivalent of cash; (b) inventories of merchandise, raw materials, goods in process, finished goods, operating supplies, and ordinary maintenance material and parts; (c) trade accounts, notes, and acceptances receivable; (d) receivables from officers, employees, affiliates, and others, if collectible in the ordinary course of business within a year; (e) installment or deferred accounts and notes receivable if they conform generally to normal trade practices and terms within the business;

(f) marketable securities representing the investment of cash available for current operations [ARB43, ch3A, ¶4], including investments in debt and equity securities classified as trading securities under Section I80, "Investments: Debt and Equity Securities"; [FAS115, ¶125] and (g) prepaid expenses such as insurance, interest, rents, taxes, unused royalties, current paid advertising service not yet received, and operating supplies. Prepaid expenses are current assets not in the sense that they will be converted into cash but in the sense that, if not paid in advance, they would require the use of current assets during the operating cycle. [ARB43, ch3A, ¶4]

.106 The ordinary operations of a business involve a circulation of capital within the current asset group. Cash is expended for materials, finished parts, operating supplies, labor, and other factory services, and such expenditures are accumulated as inventory cost. Inventory costs, upon sale of the products to which such costs attach, are converted into trade receivables and ultimately into cash again. The average time intervening between the acquisition of materials or services entering this process and the final cash realization constitutes an *operating cycle*. A one-year time period is to be used as a basis for the segregation of current assets in cases where there are several operating cycles occurring within a year. However, where the period of the operating cycle is more than 12 months, as in, for instance, the tobacco, distillery, and lumber businesses, the longer period shall be used. Where a particular business has no clearly defined operating cycle, the one-year rule shall govern.[1] [ARB43, ch3A, ¶5]

.107 This concept of the nature of current assets contemplates the exclusion from that classification of such resources as: (a) cash and claims to cash that are restricted as to withdrawal or use for other than current operations, are designated for expenditure in the acquisition or construction of noncurrent assets, or are segregated[2] for the liquidation of long-term debts; (b) investments in securities (whether marketable or not) or advances that have been made for the purposes of control, affiliation, or other continuing business advantage; (c) receivables arising from unusual transactions (such as the sale of capital assets, or loans or advances to affiliates, officers, or employees) that are not expected to be collected within 12 months; (d) cash surrender value of life insurance policies; (e) land and other natural resources; (f) depreciable assets; and (g) long-term prepayments that are fairly chargeable to the operations of several years, or deferred charges

---

[[1]The criteria for classifying deferred income tax assets as current assets are described in Section I27, "Income Taxes," paragraph .140.]

[2]Even though not actually set aside in special accounts, funds that are clearly to be used in the near future for the liquidation of long-term debts, payments to sinking funds, or for similar purposes should also, under this concept, be excluded from current assets. However, where such funds are considered to offset maturing debt that has properly been set up as a current liability, they may be included within the current asset classification. [ARB43, ch3A, ¶6, fn1]

such as bonus payments under a long-term lease, costs of rearrangement of factory layout, or removal to a new location. [ARB43, ch3A, ¶6]

.107A The amounts at which various current assets are carried do not always represent their present realizable cash values. Accounts receivable net of allowances for uncollectible accounts, and for unearned discounts where unearned discounts are considered, are effectively stated at the amount of cash estimated as realizable.[3] [ARB43, ch3A, ¶9] [Refer to Section I78, "Inventory," for disclosure requirements for inventory.]

Current Liabilities

.108 The term *current liabilities* is used principally to designate obligations whose liquidation is reasonably expected to require the use of existing resources properly classifiable as current assets, or the creation of other current liabilities. As a balance sheet category, the classification is intended to include obligations for items that have entered into the operating cycle, such as payables incurred in the acquisition of materials and supplies to be used in the production of goods or in providing services to be offered for sale; collections received in advance of the delivery of goods or performance of services;[4] and debts that arise from operations directly related to the operating cycle, such as accruals for wages, salaries, commissions, rentals, royalties, and income and other taxes. Other liabilities whose regular and ordinary liquidation is expected to occur within a relatively short period of time, usually 12 months, are also intended for inclusion,[5] such as short-term debts arising from the acquisition of capital assets, serial maturities of **long-term obligations,** amounts required to be expended within 1 year under sinking

[3]Unearned discounts (other than cash or quantity discounts and the like), finance charges, and interest included in the face amount of receivables shall be shown as a deduction from the related receivables. [APB6, ¶14]

[4]Examples of such current liabilities are obligations resulting from advance collections on ticket sales, which will normally be liquidated in the ordinary course of business by the delivery of services. On the contrary, obligations representing long-term deferments of the delivery of goods or services would not be shown as current liabilities. Examples of the latter are the issuance of a long-term warranty or the advance receipt by a lessor of rental for the final period of a 10-year [operating] lease as a condition to execution of the lease agreement. [ARB43, ch3A, ¶7, fn2]

[[5]The criteria for classifying deferred income tax liabilities as current liabilities are described in Section I27, paragraph .140.]

fund provisions, and agency obligations arising from the collection or acceptance of cash or other assets for the account of third persons.[6] [ARB43, ch3A, ¶7] [Refer to paragraph .1001 for EITF Issues that provide interpretive guidance on this paragraph.]

.109 This concept of current liabilities would include estimated or accrued amounts that are expected to be required to cover expenditures within the year for known obligations (a) the amount of which can be determined only approximately (as in the case of provisions for accruing bonus payments) or (b) where the specific person or persons to whom payment will be made cannot as yet be designated (as in the case of estimated costs to be incurred in connection with guaranteed servicing or repair of products already sold). The current liability classification, however, is not intended to include debts to be liquidated by funds that have been accumulated in accounts of a type not properly classified as current assets, or long-term obligations incurred to provide increased amounts of working capital for long periods. When the amounts of the periodic payments of an obligation are, by contract, measured by current transactions, as for example by rents or revenues received in the case of equipment trust certificates or by the depletion of natural resources in the case of property obligations, the portion of the total obligation to be included as a current liability shall be that representing the amount accrued at the balance sheet date. [ARB43, ch3A, ¶8]

.109A The current liability classification is also intended to include obligations that, by their terms, are due on demand or will be due on demand within one year (or operating cycle, if longer) from the balance sheet date, even though liquidation may not be expected within that period. It is also intended to include long-term obligations that are or will be **callable** by the creditor either because the debtor's violation of a provision[6a] of the debt agreement at the balance sheet date makes the obligation callable or because the

---

[6]Loans accompanied by pledge of life insurance policies would be classified as current liabilities when, by their terms or by intent, they are to be repaid within 12 months. The pledging of life insurance policies does not affect the classification of the asset any more than does the pledging of receivables, inventories, real estate, or other assets as collateral for a short-term loan. However, when a loan on a life insurance policy is obtained from the insurance enterprise with the intent that it will not be paid but will be liquidated by deduction from the proceeds of the policy upon maturity or cancellation, the obligation shall be excluded from current liabilities. [ARB43, ch3A, ¶7, fn3]

[6a]A *violation of a provision* is the failure to meet a condition in a debt agreement or a breach of a provision in the agreement for which compliance is objectively determinable, whether or not a grace period is allowed or the creditor is required to give notice of its intention to demand repayment. [FAS78, ¶1, fn2] Drawing a distinction between significant violations of critical conditions and technical violations is not practicable. A violation that a debtor considers to be technical may be considered critical by the creditor. Furthermore, a creditor may choose to use a technical violation as a means to withdraw from its lending relationship with the debtor. If the violation is considered insignificant by the creditor, then the debtor should be able to obtain a waiver as discussed in (a) of this paragraph. [FAS78, ¶16] The effect of a violation of a debt agreement that occurs between the balance sheet date and the date the financial statements are issued [is not addressed by paragraph .109A]. [FAS78, ¶17]

violation, if not cured within a specified grace period, will make the obligation callable. Accordingly, such callable obligations shall be classified as current liabilities unless one of the following conditions is met:

a. The creditor has waived[6b] or subsequently lost[6c] the right to demand repayment for more than one year (or operating cycle, if longer) from the balance sheet date.
b. For long-term obligations containing a grace period within which the debtor may cure the violation, it is probable[6d] that the violation will be cured within that period, thus preventing the obligation from becoming callable.

Short-term obligations that are expected to be refinanced on a long-term basis, including those callable obligations discussed herein, shall be classified in accordance with paragraphs .110 through .118 of this section. [FAS78, ¶5] [Refer to paragraph .1001 for EITF Issues that provide interpretive guidance on this paragraph.]

.109B [The] general principle [underlying paragraph .109A is that] classification of debt in a debtor's balance sheet should be based on facts existing at the balance sheet date rather than on expectations. If the creditor has at that date, or will have within one year (or operating cycle, if longer) from that date, the unilateral right to demand immediate repayment of the debt under any provision of the debt agreement, the obligation shall be classified as a current liability unless (a) one of the conditions in paragraph .109A is met or (b) the obligation is expected to be refinanced on a long-term basis and the provisions of paragraphs .110 through .118 are met. [FAS78, ¶13]

Classification of Short-Term Obligations Expected to Be Refinanced

.110 Some **short-term obligations** are expected to be refinanced on a long-term basis and, therefore, are not expected to require the use of enterprise working capital during the ensuing fiscal year. Examples include commercial paper, construction loans, and the currently maturing portion of long-term debt. [FAS6, ¶1]

.111 For purposes of this section, *short-term obligations* are those that are scheduled to mature within one year after the date of an enterprise's balance sheet or, for those enterprises that use the operating cycle concept of working capital described in paragraphs .106 and .108, within an enterprise's operating cycle that is longer than one year.

[6b]If the obligation is callable because of violations of certain provisions of the debt agreement, the creditor needs to waive its right with regard only to those violations. [FAS78, ¶5, fn*]

[6c]For example, the debtor has cured the violation after the balance sheet date and the obligation is not callable at the time the financial statements are issued. [FAS78, ¶5, fn†]

[6d]*Probable* is defined in Section C59, "Contingencies," paragraph .104(a), as "likely to occur" and is used in the same sense in this paragraph. [FAS78, ¶5, fn‡]

Long-term obligations are those scheduled to mature beyond one year (or the operating cycle, if applicable) from the date of an enterprise's balance sheet. *Refinancing a short-term obligation on a long-term basis* means either replacing it with a long-term obligation or with equity securities or renewing, extending, or replacing it with short-term obligations for an uninterrupted period extending beyond one year (or the operating cycle, if applicable) from the date of an enterprise's balance sheet. Accordingly, despite the fact the short-term obligation is scheduled to mature during the ensuing fiscal year (or the operating cycle, if applicable), it will not require the use of working capital during that period. [FAS6, ¶2]

.112 Short-term obligations arising from transactions in the normal course of business that are due in customary terms [(refer to paragraph .108)[7]] shall be classified as current liabilities. [FAS6, ¶8] [Refer to paragraph .1001 for EITF Issues that provide interpretive guidance on this paragraph.]

.113 A short-term obligation other than one classified as a current liability in accordance with paragraph .112 shall be excluded from current liabilities only if[8] [FAS6, ¶9] the enterprise intends to *refinance the obligation on a long-term basis* (refer to paragraph .111) [FAS6, ¶10] [and such] intent is supported by an ability to consummate the refinancing demonstrated in either of the following ways:

a. *Post-balance-sheet-date issuance of a long-term obligation or equity securities.* After the date of an enterprise's balance sheet but before that balance sheet is issued, a long-term obligation or equity securities[9] have been issued for the purpose of refinancing the short-term obligation on a long-term basis.

[[7]Paragraph .112 does not apply to] short-term obligations arising from the acquisition or construction of noncurrent assets [or to those] not directly related to the operating cycle (for example, a note given to a supplier to replace an account payable that originally arose in the normal course of business and had been due in customary terms) [(refer to paragraph .113)]. [FAS6, ¶20]

[8]Paragraph .109 describes a circumstance, unaffected by paragraph .113, in which obligations maturing within one year would be excluded from current liabilities as follows: "The current liability classification, however, is not intended to include debts to be liquidated by funds that have been accumulated in accounts of a type not properly classified as current assets. . . ." Footnote 2 describes another circumstance, also unaffected by paragraph .113: ". . . Funds that are clearly to be used in the near future for the liquidation of long-term debts, payments to sinking funds, or for similar purposes should also . . . be excluded from current assets. However, if such funds are considered to offset maturing debt that has properly been set up as a current liability, they may be included within the current asset classification." Accordingly, funds obtained on a long-term basis prior to the balance sheet date would be excluded from current assets if the obligation to be liquidated is excluded from current liabilities. [FAS6, ¶9, fn1]

[9]If equity securities have been issued, the short-term obligation, although excluded from current liabilities, shall not be included in owners' equity. [FAS6, ¶11, fn2]

b. *Financing agreement.* Before the balance sheet is issued, the enterprise has entered into a financing agreement that clearly permits the enterprise to refinance the short-term obligation on a long-term basis on terms that are readily determinable, and all of the following conditions are met:

(1) The agreement does not expire within one year (or operating cycle—refer to paragraph .111) from the date of the enterprise's balance sheet and during that period the agreement is not cancelable by the lender or the prospective lender or investor (and obligations incurred under the agreement are not callable during that period) except for violation of a provision[10] with which compliance is objectively[[11]] determinable or measurable.[12]

(2) No violation of any provision in the financing agreement exists at the balance sheet date and no available information indicates that a violation has occurred thereafter but prior to the issuance of the balance sheet, or, if one exists at the balance sheet date or has occurred thereafter, a waiver has been obtained.

(3) The lender or the prospective lender or investor with which the enterprise has entered into the financing agreement is expected to be financially capable of honoring the agreement.

[FAS6, ¶11] [Refer to paragraph .1001 for EITF Issues that provide interpretive guidance on this paragraph.]

.114 If an enterprise's ability to consummate an intended refinancing of a short-term obligation on a long-term basis is demonstrated by post-balance-sheet-date issuance of a long-term obligation or equity securities (refer to paragraph .113(a)), the amount of the short-term obligation to be excluded from current liabilities shall not exceed the proceeds of the new long-term obligation or the equity securities issued. If ability to refinance is demonstrated by the existence of a financing agreement (refer to paragraph .113(b)), the amount of the short-term obligation to be excluded from current liabilities shall be reduced to the amount available for refinancing under the agreement when the amount available is less than the amount of the short-term obligation. The amount to be excluded shall be reduced further if information (such as restrictions in other agreements or restrictions as to transferability of funds) indicates that funds obtainable under the agreement will not be available to liquidate the short-term obligation. Further, if amounts

[10]For purposes of this section, *violation of a provision* means failure to meet a condition set forth in the agreement or breach or violation of a provision such as a restrictive covenant, representation, or warranty, whether or not a grace period is allowed or the lender is required to give notice. [FAS6, ¶11, fn3]

[[11]Refer to paragraphs .501 through .503 for guidance regarding classification of long-term debt agreements with **subjective acceleration clauses.**]

[12]Financing agreements cancelable for violation of a provision that can be evaluated differently by the parties to the agreement (such as *a material adverse change* or *failure to maintain satisfactory operations*) do not comply with this condition. [FAS6, ¶11, fn4]

that could be obtained under the financing agreement fluctuate (for example, in relation to the enterprise's needs, in proportion to the value of collateral, or in accordance with other terms of the agreement), the amount to be excluded from current liabilities shall be limited to a reasonable estimate of the minimum amount expected to be available at any date from the scheduled maturity of the short-term obligation to the end of the fiscal year (or operating cycle—refer to paragraph .111). If no reasonable estimate can be made, the entire outstanding short-term obligation shall be included in current liabilities. [FAS6, ¶12]

.115 The enterprise may intend to seek an alternative source of financing rather than to exercise its rights under the existing agreement when the short-term obligation becomes due. The enterprise must intend to exercise its rights under the existing agreement, however, if that other source does not become available.[13] [FAS6, ¶13]

.116 Replacement of a short-term obligation with another short-term obligation after the date of the balance sheet but before the balance sheet is issued is not, by itself, sufficient to demonstrate an enterprise's ability to refinance the short-term obligation on a long-term basis. If, for example, the replacement is made under the terms of a revolving credit agreement that provides for renewal or extension of the short-term obligation for an uninterrupted period extending beyond one year (or operating cycle—refer to paragraph .111) from the date of the balance sheet, the revolving credit agreement must meet the conditions in paragraph .113(b) to justify excluding the short-term obligation from current liabilities. Similarly, if the replacement is a rollover of commercial paper accompanied by a *standby* credit agreement, the standby agreement must meet the conditions in paragraph .113(b) to justify excluding the short-term obligation from current liabilities. [FAS6, ¶14]

.117 Repayment of a short-term obligation *before* funds are obtained through a long-term refinancing requires the use of current assets. Therefore, if a short-term obligation is repaid after the balance sheet date and subsequently a long-term obligation or equity securities are issued whose proceeds are used to replenish current assets before the balance sheet is issued, the short-term obligation shall not be excluded from current liabilities at the balance sheet date. [(Refer to paragraphs .138 and .139 for an example of applying this paragraph.)] [FIN8, ¶3]

---

[13]The intent to exercise may not be present if the terms of the agreement contain conditions or permit the prospective lender or investor to establish conditions, such as interest rates or collateral requirements, that are unreasonable to the enterprise. [FAS6, ¶13, fn5]

Disclosure

.118 A total of current liabilities[13a] shall be presented in classified balance sheets. If a short-term obligation is excluded from current liabilities pursuant to the provisions of this section, the notes to the financial statements shall include a general description of the financing agreement and the terms of any new obligation incurred or expected to be incurred or equity securities issued or expected to be issued as a result of a refinancing. [FAS6, ¶15] If an obligation under paragraph .109A(b) is classified as a long-term liability (or, in the case of an unclassified balance sheet, is included as a long-term liability in the disclosure of debt maturities), the circumstances shall be disclosed. [The requirements of Section C32, "Commitments: Long-Term Obligations," may also apply.] [FAS78, ¶5] [Refer to paragraph .1001 for EITF Issues that provide interpretive guidance on this paragraph.]

Examples of Classifying Obligations

.119 The following examples provide guidance for applying this section. It should be recognized that these examples do not comprehend all possible circumstances and do not include all the disclosures that would typically be made regarding long-term debt or current liabilities. [FAS6, ¶32]

General Assumptions

.120 The assumptions on which examples [1 through 7] are based are:

a. ABC Company's fiscal year-end is December 31, 19X5.
b. The date of issuance of the December 31, 19X5 financial statements is March 31, 19X6; the Company's practice is to issue a classified balance sheet.
c. At December 31, 19X5, short-term obligations include $5,000,000 representing the portion of 6 percent long-term debt maturing in February 19X6 and $3,000,000 of 9 percent notes payable issued in November 19X5 and maturing in July 19X6.
d. The Company intends to refinance on a long-term basis both the current maturity of long-term debt and the 9 percent notes payable.
e. Accounts other than the long-term debt maturing in February 19X6 and the notes payable maturing in July 19X6 are:

Current assets	$30,000,000
Other assets	$50,000,000
Accounts payable and accruals	$10,000,000
Other long-term debt	$25,000,000
Shareholders' equity	$37,000,000

[13aB05.104 addresses the need to present a total of current assets.]

f. Unless otherwise indicated, the examples also assume that the lender or prospective lender is expected to be capable of honoring the agreement, that there is no evidence of a violation of any provision, and that the terms of borrowings available under the agreement are readily determinable. [FAS6, ¶33]

Example 1—Financing Agreement Used to Refinance Existing Obligation

.121 The Company negotiates a financing agreement with a commercial bank in December 19X5 for a maximum borrowing of $8,000,000 at any time through 19X7 with the following terms:

a. Borrowings are available at ABC Company's request for such purposes as it deems appropriate and will mature three years from the date of borrowing.
b. Amounts borrowed will bear interest at the bank's prime rate.
c. An annual commitment fee of ½ of 1 percent is payable on the difference between the amount borrowed and $8,000,000.
d. The agreement is cancelable by the lender only if:
   (1) The Company's working capital, excluding borrowings under the agreement, falls below $10,000,000.
   (2) The Company becomes obligated under lease agreements to pay an annual rental in excess of $1,000,000.
   (3) Treasury stock is acquired without the prior approval of the prospective lender.
   (4) The Company guarantees indebtedness of unaffiliated persons in excess of $500,000. [FAS6, ¶34]

.122 The enterprise's intention to refinance meets the condition specified by paragraph .113. Compliance with the provisions listed in paragraph .121(d) is objectively determinable or measurable; therefore, the condition specified by paragraph .113(b)(1) is met. The proceeds of borrowings under the agreement are clearly available for the liquidation of the 9 percent notes payable and the long-term debt maturing in February 19X6. Both obligations, therefore, would be classified as other than current liabilities. [FAS6, ¶35]

.123 Following are the liability section of ABC Company's balance sheet at December 31, 19X5 and the related footnote disclosures required by this section, based on the information in paragraphs .120 and .121. Because the balance sheet is issued subsequent to the February 19X6 maturity of the long-term debt, the footnote describes the refinancing of that obligation.

	December 31, 19X5
Current Liabilities:	
Accounts payable and accruals	$10,000,000
Total Current Liabilities	10,000,000
Long-Term Debt:	
9% notes payable (Note A)	3,000,000*
6% debt due February 19X6 (Note A)	5,000,000*
Other long-term debt	25,000,000
Total Long-Term Debt	33,000,000
Total Liabilities	$43,000,000

*These obligations may also be shown in captions distinct from both current liabilities and long-term debt, such as "Interim Debt," "Short-Term Debt Expected to Be Refinanced," and "Intermediate Debt."

Note A—The Company has entered into a financing agreement with a commercial bank that permits the Company to borrow at any time through 19X7 up to $8,000,000 at the bank's prime rate of interest. The Company must pay an annual commitment fee of ½ of 1 percent of the unused portion of the commitment. Borrowings under the financing agreement mature three years after the date of the loan. Among other things, the agreement prohibits the acquisition of treasury stock without prior approval by the bank, requires maintenance of working capital of $10,000,000 exclusive of borrowings under the agreement, and limits the annual rental under lease agreements to $1,000,000. In February 19X6, the Company borrowed $5,000,000 at 8 percent and liquidated the 6 percent long-term debt, and it intends to borrow additional funds available under the agreement to refinance the 9 percent notes payable maturing in July 19X6. [FAS6, ¶36]

Example 2—Effect of Restriction on Transferring Funds to Be Obtained from Financing Agreement by Foreign Subsidiary

.124 A foreign subsidiary of the enterprise negotiates a financing agreement with its local bank in December 19X5. Funds are available to the subsidiary for its unrestricted use, including loans to affiliated companies; other terms are identical to those cited in paragraph .121. Local laws prohibit the transfer of funds outside the country. [FAS6, ¶37]

.125 The requirement of paragraph .113(b)(1) is met because compliance with the provisions of the agreement is objectively determinable or measurable. Because of the laws prohibiting the transfer of funds, however, the proceeds from borrowings under the agreement are not available for liquidation of the debt maturing in February and July 19X6. Accordingly, both the 6 percent debt maturing in February 19X6 and the 9 percent notes payable maturing in July 19X6 would be classified as current liabilities. [FAS6, ¶38]

Example 3—Refinancing through Post-Balance-Sheet-Date Issuance of Long-Term Obligations or Equity Securities

.126 Assume that instead of utilizing the agreement cited in paragraph .121, the Company issues $8,000,000 of 10-year debentures to the public in January 19X6. The Company intends to use the proceeds to liquidate the $5,000,000 debt maturing February 19X6 and the $3,000,000 of 9 percent notes payable maturing July 19X6. In addition, assume the debt maturing February 19X6 is paid prior to the issuance of the balance sheet, and the remaining proceeds from the sale of debentures are invested in a U.S. Treasury note maturing the same day as the 9 percent notes payable. [FAS6, ¶39]

.127 Since the Company refinanced the long-term debt maturing in February 19X6 in a manner that meets the conditions set forth in paragraph .113, that obligation would be excluded from current liabilities. In addition, the 9 percent notes payable maturing in July 19X6 would also be excluded because the Company has obtained funds expressly intended to be used to liquidate those notes and not intended to be used in current operations. In balance sheets after the date of sale of the debentures and before the maturity date of the notes payable, the Company would exclude the notes payable from current liabilities if the U.S. Treasury note is excluded from current assets (refer to paragraph .107). [FAS6, ¶40]

.128 If the debentures had been sold prior to January 1, 19X6, the $8,000,000 of obligations to be paid would be excluded from current liabilities in the balance sheet at that date if the $8,000,000 in funds were excluded from current assets. [FAS6, ¶41]

.129 If, instead of issuing the 10-year debentures, the Company had issued $8,000,000 of equity securities and all other facts in this example remained unchanged, both the 6 percent debt due February 19X6 and the 9 percent notes payable due July 19X6 would be classified as liabilities other than current liabilities, such as "Indebtedness Due in 19X6 Refinanced in January 19X6." [FAS6, ¶42]

Example 4—Use of Revolving Credit Agreement

.130 In December 19X5 the Company negotiates a revolving credit agreement providing for unrestricted borrowings up to $10,000,000. Borrowings will bear interest at 1 percent over the prevailing prime rate of the bank with which the agreement is arranged but in any event not less than 8 percent, will have stated maturities of 90 days, and will be continuously renewable for 90-day periods at the Company's option for 3 years provided there is compliance with the terms of the agreement. Provisions of the agreement are similar to those cited in paragraph .121(d). Further, the enterprise intends to renew obligations incurred under the agreement for a period extending beyond one year from the balance sheet date. There are no outstanding borrowings under the agreement at December 31, 19X5. [FAS6, ¶43]

.131 In this instance, the long-term debt maturing in February 19X6 and the 9 percent notes payable maturing in July 19X6 would be excluded from current liabilities because the Company consummated a financing agreement meeting the conditions set forth in paragraph .113(b) prior to the issuance of the balance sheet. [FAS6, ¶44]

Example 5—Financing Agreement with Fluctuating Maximum Borrowings

.132 Assume that the agreement cited in Example 4 above included an additional provision limiting the amount to be borrowed by the Company to the amount of its inventory, which is pledged as collateral and is expected to range between a high of $8,000,000 during the second quarter of 19X6 and a low of $4,000,000 during the fourth quarter of 19X6. [FAS6, ¶45]

.133 The terms of the agreement comply with the conditions required by this section; however, because the minimum amount expected to be available from February to December 19X6 is $4,000,000, only that amount of short-term obligations can be excluded from current liabilities (refer to paragraph .114). Whether the obligation to be excluded is a portion of the currently maturing long-term debt or some portions of both it and the 9 percent notes payable depends on the intended timing of the borrowing. [FAS6, ¶46]

.134 If the Company intended to refinance only the 9 percent notes payable due July 19X6 and the amount of its inventory is expected to reach a low of approximately $2,000,000 during the second quarter of 19X6 but be at least $3,000,000 in July 19X6 and thereafter during 19X6, the $3,000,000 [of] 9 percent notes payable would be excluded from current liabilities at December 31, 19X5 (refer to paragraph .114). [FAS6, ¶47]

Example 6—Classifying Obligations Related to Acquisition of Noncurrent Assets

.135 In lieu of the facts given in paragraphs .120(c) and .120(d), assume that during 19X5 the Company entered into a contract to have a warehouse built. The warehouse is expected to be financed by issuance of the Company's commercial paper. In addition, the Company negotiated a standby agreement with a commercial bank that provides for maximum borrowings equal to the expected cost of the warehouse, which will be pledged as collateral. The agreement also requires that the proceeds from the sale of commercial paper be used to pay construction costs. Borrowings may be made under the agreement only if the Company is unable to issue new commercial paper. The proceeds of borrowings must be used to retire outstanding commercial paper and to liquidate additional liabilities incurred in the construction of the warehouse. At December 31, 19X5 the Company has $7,000,000 of commercial paper outstanding and $1,000,000 of unpaid construction costs resulting from a progress billing through December 31. [FAS6, ¶48]

.136 Because the commercial paper will be refinanced on a long-term basis, either by uninterrupted renewal or, failing that, by a borrowing under the agreement, the commercial paper would be excluded from current liabilities. The $1,000,000 liability for the unpaid progress billing results from the construction of a noncurrent asset and will be refinanced on the same basis as the commercial paper and, therefore, it would also be excluded from current liabilities (refer to footnote 7 of this section). [FAS6, ¶49]

Example 7—Reporting Obligations That Are Expected to Be Refinanced But Do Not Meet Criteria in Paragraph .113

.137 Following are two methods of presenting liabilities in ABC Company's balance sheet at December 31, 19X5 assuming the Company intends to refinance the 6 percent debt maturing in February 19X6 and the 9 percent notes payable maturing in July 19X6 but has not met the conditions required by this section to exclude those obligations from current liabilities.

Alternative 1

	December 31, 19X5
Current Liabilities:	
Accounts payable and accruals	$10,000,000
Notes payable due July 19X6	3,000,000
6% debt due February 19X6	5,000,000
Total Current Liabilities	18,000,000
Long-Term Debt	25,000,000
Total Liabilities	$43,000,000

Alternative 2

		December 31, 19X5
Current Liabilities:		
Accounts payable and accruals		$10,000,000
Short-term debt expected to be refinanced:		
Notes payable due July 19X6	$3,000,000	
6% debt due February 19X6	5,000,000	8,000,000
Total Current Liabilities		18,000,000
Long-Term Debt		25,000,000
Total Liabilities		$43,000,000

[FAS6, ¶50]

Example 8—Classifying Short-Term Obligations Repaid Prior to Being Replaced by a Long-Term Security

.138 Assume that an enterprise has issued $3,000,000 of short-term commercial paper during the year to finance construction of a plant. At June 30, 19X6, the enterprise's fiscal year-end, the enterprise intends to refinance the commercial paper by issuing long-term debt. However, because the enterprise temporarily has excess cash, in July 19X6 it liquidates $1,000,000 of the commercial paper as the paper matures. In August 19X6, the enterprise completes a $6,000,000 long-term debt offering. Later during the month of August, it issues its June 30, 19X6 financial statements. The proceeds of the long-term debt offering are to be used to replenish $1,000,000 in working capital, to pay $2,000,000 of commercial paper as it matures in September 19X6, and to pay $3,000,000 of construction costs expected to be incurred later that year to complete the plant. [FIN8, ¶2]

.139 In the example described in paragraph .138, the $1,000,000 of commercial paper liquidated in July would be classified as a current liability in the enterprise's balance sheet at June 30, 19X6. The $2,000,000 of commercial paper liquidated in September 19X6 but refinanced by the long-term debt offering in August 19X6 would be excluded from current liabilities in balance sheets at the end of June 19X6, July 19X6, and August 19X6.[14] It should be noted that the existence of a financing agreement at the date of issuance of the financial statements rather than a completed financing at that date would not change these classifications. [FIN8, ¶4]

[14]At the end of August 19X6, $2,000,000 of cash would be excluded from current assets or if included in current assets, a like amount of debt would be classified as a current liability [(refer to footnote 8 and paragraph .127)]. [FIN8, ¶4, fn1]

Glossary

.400 **Callable.** An obligation is *callable* at a given date if the creditor has the right at that date to demand, or to give notice of its intention to demand, repayment of the obligation owed to it by the debtor. [FAS78, ¶1, fn1]

.401 **Current assets.** [Those assets that] are reasonably expected to be realized in cash or sold or consumed during the normal operating cycle of the business. [ARB43, ch3A, ¶4]

.402 **Current liabilities.** [Those] obligations whose liquidation is reasonably expected to require the use of existing resources properly classifiable as current assets or the creation of other current liabilities. [ARB43, ch3A, ¶7]

.403 **Long-term obligations.** Those [obligations] scheduled to mature beyond one year (or the operating cycle, if applicable) from the date of an enterprise's balance sheet. [FAS6, ¶2]

.404 **Operating cycle.** The average time intervening between the acquisition of materials or services and the final cash realization [from the sale of products or services (refer to paragraph .106)]. [ARB43, ch3A, ¶5]

.405 **Short-term obligations.** Those [obligations] that are scheduled to mature within one year after the date of an enterprise's balance sheet or, for those enterprises that use the operating cycle concept of working capital, within an enterprise's operating cycle that is longer than one year. [FAS6, ¶2]

.405A **Subjective acceleration clause.** A provision in a debt agreement that states that the creditor may accelerate the scheduled maturities of the obligation under conditions that are not objectively determinable (for example, "if the debtor fails to maintain satisfactory operations" or "if a material adverse change occurs"). [FAS78, ¶10, fn3]

.406 **Working capital.** The excess of current assets over current liabilities. [ARB43, ch3A, ¶3]

Supplemental Guidance

Subjective Acceleration Clauses in Long-Term Debt Agreements

.501 *Question*—Should long-term debt be classified as a current liability if the long-term debt agreement contains a subjective clause that may accelerate the due date? [FTB79-3, ¶1]

.502 *Background*—Paragraph .113 indicates that a subjective acceleration clause contained in a financing agreement that would otherwise permit a short-term obligation to be refinanced on a long-term basis would preclude that short-term obligation from being classified as long-term. That paragraph does not address financing agreements other than those related to short-term obligations. [FTB79-3, ¶2]

.503 *Response*—In some situations, the circumstances (for example, recurring losses or liquidity problems) would indicate that long-term debt subject to a subjective acceleration clause should be classified as a current liability. Other situations would indicate only disclosure of the existence of such clauses. It would seem that neither reclassification nor disclosure would be required if the likelihood of the acceleration of the due date were remote, such as when the lender historically has not accelerated due dates of loans containing similar clauses and the financial condition of the borrower is strong and its prospects bright. [The requirements of this paragraph are not modified by the requirements of paragraphs .109A and .109B.] [FTB79-3, ¶3] [Refer to paragraph .1001 for EITF Issues that provide interpretive guidance on this paragraph.]

Supplemental Guidance: Emerging Issues Task Force (EITF) Issues

.1000 [Listed below are EITF Issues that provide supplemental guidance for this section. These Issues are grouped by subject matter and may be either interpretive of or related by topic to the guidance in this section.

Debt Classification

EITF Issue No. 86-5, "Classifying Demand Notes with Repayment Terms"
EITF Issue No. 86-30, "Classification of Obligations When a Violation Is Waived by the Creditor"
EITF Issue No. 95-22, "Balance Sheet Classification of Borrowings Outstanding under Revolving Credit Agreements That Include both a Subjective Acceleration Clause and a Lock-Box Arrangement"
EITF Topic No. D-23, "Subjective Acceleration Clauses and Debt Classification"
EITF Topic No. D-61, "Classification by the Issuer of Redeemable Instruments That Are Subject to Remarketing Agreements"

Other

EITF Issue No. 86-15, "Increasing-Rate Debt"
EITF Issue No. 87-30, "Sale of a Short-Term Loan Made under a Long-Term Credit Commitment"]

.1001 [Listed below are those EITF Issues that provide interpretive guidance on specific material in this section.

Paragraph .108 (ARB 43, Ch. 3A, ¶7)—EITF Issues No. 86-5 and 86-30
Paragraph .109A (FAS 78, ¶5)—EITF Issues No. 86-5 and 86-30
Paragraph .112 (FAS 6, ¶8)—EITF Issues No. 87-30 and 95-22
Paragraph .113 (FAS 6, ¶9)—EITF Issues No. 86-30 and 95-22 and Topic No. D-23
Paragraph .113 (FAS 6, ¶10-11)—EITF Issue No. 86-30
Paragraph .118 (FAS 78, ¶5)—EITF Issues No. 86-5 and 86-30
Paragraph .503 (FTB 79-3, ¶3)—EITF Issues No. 86-5 and 95-22 and Topic No. D-23]

(The next page is 4521.)

Supplemental Guidance: Emerging Issues Task Force (EITF) Issues

[illegible]

Debt Classification

[illegible]

Other

[illegible]

BALANCE SHEET DISPLAY: OFFSETTING

Sources: APB Opinion 10; FASB Statement 135; FASB Interpretation 39; FASB Interpretation 41

[**Note:** A list of Issues discussed by the Emerging Issues Task Force (EITF) that provide supplemental guidance for this section is presented in paragraph .1000.]

Summary

The offsetting of related assets and liabilities in the statement of financial position (balance sheet) is permitted only when there is a right of setoff. This section presents the criteria for determining when a right of setoff exists.

The offset of cash or other assets against the tax liability or other amounts owing to governmental bodies is not acceptable except in limited circumstances described in this section. This section also addresses the applicability of the general principle on offsetting to forward, interest rate swap, currency swap, option, and other conditional or exchange contracts and clarifies the circumstances in which it is appropriate to offset amounts recognized for those contracts in the statement of financial position. The conditions required to offset payables and receivables that represent repurchase agreements and reverse repurchase agreements are also described in this section.

General Principle on Offsetting

.101 It is a general principle of accounting that the offsetting of assets and liabilities in the [statement of financial position] is improper except when a **right of setoff** exists. [APB10, ¶7(1)]

.101A A *right of setoff* is a debtor's legal right, by contract or otherwise, to discharge all or a portion of the debt owed to another party by applying against the debt an amount that the other party owes to the debtor.[1] A right of setoff exists when all of the following conditions are met:

a. Each of *two* parties[2] owes the other determinable amounts.[3]

---

[1]For purposes of this section, cash on deposit at a financial institution is to be considered by the depositor as cash rather than as an amount owed to the depositor. [FIN39, ¶5, fn2]

[2]A right of setoff involves only two parties. [FIN39, ¶43]

[3]If the parties meet the other criteria specified in the definition, [it] is unnecessary [that] those amounts be in the same currency and bear the same interest rate. However, if maturities differ, only the party with the nearer maturity could offset because the party with the longer term maturity must settle in the manner that the other party selects at the earlier maturity date. [FIN39, ¶44]

b. The reporting party has the right to set off the amount owed with the amount owed by the other party.
c. The reporting party intends to set off.[4]
d. The right of setoff is enforceable at law. [5]

A debtor having a valid right of setoff may offset the related asset and liability and report the net amount.[6] [FIN39, ¶5]

.101B Generally, debts may be set off if they exist between mutual debtors each acting in its capacity as both debtor and creditor. In particular cases, however, state laws about the right of setoff may provide results different from those normally provided by contract or as a matter of common law. Similarly, the U.S. Bankruptcy Code imposes restrictions on or prohibitions against the right of setoff in bankruptcy under certain circumstances. Legal constraints shall be considered to determine whether the right of setoff is enforceable. [FIN39, ¶6] [Refer to paragraph .1001 for an EITF Issue that provides interpretive guidance on this paragraph.]

Offsetting Securities against Taxes Payable

.102 The offset of cash or other assets against the tax liability or other amounts owing to governmental bodies is not acceptable except in the circumstances described in paragraph .103. [APB10, ¶7(1)] Most securities now issued by governments are not by their terms designed specifically for the payment of taxes and, accordingly, shall not be deducted from taxes payable on the [statement of financial position]. [APB10, ¶7(2)] [Refer to paragraph .1001 for an EITF Issue that provides interpretive guidance on paragraphs .102 and .103.]

.103 [Regarding the offsetting of assets against the tax liability] the only exception to the general principle [in paragraph .101] occurs when it is clear that a purchase of securities (acceptable for the payment of taxes) is in substance an advance payment of taxes that will be payable in the relatively near future, so that in the special circumstances the purchase is tantamount to the prepayment of taxes. This occurs at times, for example, as

[4]Acknowledgment of the intent to set off by the reporting party and, if applicable, demonstration of the execution of the setoff in similar situations meet the criterion of intent. [FIN39, ¶45]

[5][The phrase] *enforceable at law* includes those situations in which the right of setoff is enforceable because of regulatory procedures or as part of normal business practice [even if] not specifically included in contractual agreements. [FIN39, ¶47]

[6]This section does not address derecognition or nonrecognition of assets and liabilities. Derecognition by sale of an asset or extinguishment of a liability results in removal of a recognized asset or liability and generally results in the recognition of gain or loss. Although conceptually different, offsetting that results in a net amount of zero and derecognition with no gain or loss are indistinguishable in their effects on the statement of financial position. Likewise, not recognizing assets and liabilities of the same amount in financial statements achieves similar reported results. [FIN39, ¶5, fn3]

an accommodation to a local government and in some instances when governments issue securities that are specifically designated as being acceptable for the payment of taxes of those governments. [APB10, ¶7(3)]

Offsetting Forward, Interest Rate Swap, Currency Swap, Option, and Other Conditional or Exchange Contracts

.104 Unless the conditions in paragraph .101A are met, the *fair value* of **[conditional or exchange] contracts**[7] in a loss position shall not be offset against the fair value of contracts in a gain position. [Refer to paragraph .115A of Section F25, "Financial Instruments: Disclosure," for the definition of fair value.] Similarly, amounts recognized as accrued receivables shall not be offset against amounts recognized as accrued payables unless a right of setoff exists. [FIN39, ¶8]

.105 When fair value or an amount receivable or payable related to conditional or exchange contracts of the reporting entity are recognized in the statement of financial position, the amount recognized represents an asset or a liability. The fair value of a contract in a gain position or an amount accrued as a receivable represents a probable future economic benefit controlled by the reporting entity under the contract. The fair value of a contract in a loss position or an amount accrued as a payable represents a probable future sacrifice of economic benefits arising from the reporting entity's present obligations to transfer assets under the contract. [FIN39, ¶9]

.106 Without regard to the condition in paragraph .101A(c), fair value amounts[8,][9] recognized for forward, interest rate swap, currency swap, option, and other conditional or exchange contracts executed with the same counterparty under a **master netting**

[7]*Conditional contracts* are those whose obligations or rights depend on the occurrence of some specified future event that is not certain to occur and that could change the timing of the amounts or of the instruments to be received, delivered, or exchanged. *Exchange contracts* are those that require a future exchange of assets or liabilities rather than a one-way transfer of assets. [FIN39, ¶3]

[8]The fair value recognized for some contracts may include an accrual component for the periodic unconditional receivables and payables that result from the contract; the accrual component included therein may also be offset for contracts executed with the same counterparty under a master netting arrangement. [FIN39, ¶10, fn4]

[9]This paragraph applies only to fair value amounts recognized for conditional or exchange contracts executed with the same counterparty under a master netting arrangement. It does not apply to other amounts recognized for other types of contracts executed under a master netting arrangement; however, those amounts could otherwise meet the conditions of paragraph .101A for a right of setoff. For example, unless the conditions in paragraph .101A are met, the amount recognized under a repurchase agreement may not be offset against the amount recognized under a reverse repurchase agreement solely because the agreements are executed with the same counterparty under a master netting arrangement, nor may an accrued receivable be offset against an accrued payable on interest rate swaps that are not recognized at fair value solely because the swaps are executed with the same counterparty under a master netting arrangement. [FIN39, ¶22]

arrangement may be offset. The reporting entity's choice to offset or not must be applied consistently. A master netting arrangement exists if the reporting entity has multiple contracts, whether for the same type of conditional or exchange contract or for different types of contracts, with a single counterparty that are subject to a contractual agreement that provides for the net settlement of all contracts through a single payment in a single currency in the event of default on or termination of any one contract. Offsetting the fair values recognized for forward, interest rate swap, currency swap, option, and other conditional or exchange contracts outstanding with a single counterparty results in the net fair value of the position between the two counterparties being reported as an asset or a liability in the statement of financial position. [FIN39, ¶10]

Offsetting Payables and Receivables under Repurchase and Reverse Repurchase Agreements

.106A Notwithstanding the condition in paragraph .101A(c), an enterprise may, but is not required to, offset amounts recognized as payables under **repurchase agreements**[10] and amounts recognized as receivables under **reverse repurchase agreements**[11] if all of the following conditions are met:[12]

a. The repurchase and reverse repurchase agreements are executed with the same counterparty.
b. The repurchase and reverse repurchase agreements have the same explicit settlement date specified at the inception of the agreement.

---

[10]For purposes of this section, a repurchase agreement (repo) refers to a transaction that is accounted for as a collateralized borrowing in which a seller-borrower of securities sells those securities to a buyer-lender with an agreement to repurchase them at a stated price plus interest at a specified date or in specified circumstances. The "payable" under a repurchase agreement refers to the amount of the seller-borrower's obligation recognized for the future repurchase of the securities from the buyer-lender. In certain industries, the terminology is reversed; that is, entities in those industries refer to this type of agreement as a "reverse repo." [FIN41, ¶1, fn1]

[11]For purposes of this section, a reverse repurchase agreement (reverse repo) refers to a transaction that is accounted for as a collateralized lending in which a buyer-lender buys securities with an agreement to resell them to the seller-borrower at a stated price plus interest at a specified date or in specified circumstances. The "receivable" under a reverse repurchase agreement refers to the amount due from the seller-borrower for the repurchase of the securities from the buyer-lender. In certain industries, the terminology is reversed; that is, entities in those industries refer to this type of agreement as a "repo." [FIN41, ¶1, fn2]

[12]Paragraph .106A does not apply to amounts recognized for other types of repurchase and reverse repurchase agreements executed under a master netting arrangement; however, those amounts could otherwise meet the conditions of paragraph .101A for a right of setoff. Therefore, unless all conditions in paragraph .101A are met, the amount recognized under a repurchase agreement that does not settle in accordance with the conditions of paragraphs .106A and .106B may not be offset against the amount recognized under a reverse repurchase agreement merely because the agreements are executed with the same counterparty under a master netting arrangement. [FIN41, ¶14]

c. The repurchase and reverse repurchase agreements are executed in accordance with a master netting arrangement. [Refer to paragraph .106.]
d. The securities underlying the repurchase and reverse repurchase agreements exist in "book entry" form and can be transferred only by means of entries in the records of the transfer system operator or securities custodian.[13]
e. The repurchase and reverse repurchase agreements will be settled on a securities transfer system that operates in the manner described in paragraph .106B, and the enterprise must have associated banking arrangements in place as described in paragraph .106B. Cash settlements for securities transferred are made under established banking arrangements that provide that the enterprise will need available cash on deposit only for any net amounts that are due at the end of the business day. It must be *probable*[14] that the associated banking arrangements will provide sufficient **daylight overdraft or other intraday credit**[15] at the settlement date for each of the parties.
f. The enterprise intends to use the same account at the clearing bank or other financial institution at the settlement date in transacting both (1) the cash inflows resulting from the settlement of the reverse repurchase agreement and (2) the cash outflows in settlement of the offsetting repurchase agreement.

The enterprise's choice to offset or not must be applied consistently. Net receivables resulting from the application of this section should not be offset against net payables resulting from the application of this section in the statement of financial position. [FIN41, ¶3]

.106B In a securities transfer system for repurchase and reverse repurchase agreements that meets the requirements of paragraph .106A(e), cash transfers are initiated by notification from the owner of record of the securities to its securities custodian[16] to transfer

[13]**"Book entry" securities** meeting the criterion in paragraph .106A(d) exist only as items in accounting records maintained by a transfer system operator. This requirement does not preclude offsetting of securities held in "book entry" form solely because other securities of the same issue exist in other forms. [FIN41, ¶3, fn4]

[14]The term *probable* is used in this section consistent with its use in paragraph .104(a) of Section C59, "Contingencies," to mean that a transaction or event is likely to occur. [FIN41, ¶3, fn5]

[15]*Daylight overdraft or other intraday credit* refers to the accommodation in the banking arrangements that allows transactions to be completed even if there is insufficient cash on deposit during the day provided there is sufficient cash to cover the net cash requirement at the end of the day. That accommodation may be through a credit facility, including a credit facility for which a fee is charged, or from a deposit of collateral. [FIN41, ¶3, fn6]

[16]The securities custodian for a securities transfer system may be the bank or financial institution that executes securities transfers over the securities transfer system, and "book entry" securities exist only in electronic form on the records of the transfer system operator for each entity that has a security account with the transfer system operator. "Book entry" securities exist only as items of account on the "controlling" records of the transfer system operator. Banks or other financial institutions may maintain "subsidiary" records of "book entry" securities. "Book entry" securities may be transferred on the subsidiary records of a bank or financial institution but, for entities that have a security account with the transfer system operator, may be transferred from the account of such an entity only through the transfer system operator. [FIN41, ¶4, fn7]

those securities to the counterparty to the agreement. Under associated banking arrangements, each party to a same-day settlement of both a repurchase agreement and a reverse repurchase agreement would be obligated to pay a gross amount of cash for the securities transferred from its counterparty but would be able to reduce that gross obligation by notifying its securities custodian to transfer other securities to that counterparty the same day. Thus, each party is responsible for maintaining available cash on deposit only for the amount of any net payable unless it fails to instruct its securities custodian to transfer securities to its counterparty.[17] If both parties transfer the appropriate securities in settlement of the repurchase and reverse repurchase agreements, the party with a net receivable will not need any cash to facilitate the settlement, while the party with a net payable will need only to have available the required net amount due at the end of the business day. [FIN41, ¶4]

Special Applications

.107 Various other sections and AICPA Audit and Accounting Guides, Industry Audit Guides, and Statements of Position specify accounting treatments in circumstances that result in offsetting or in a presentation in a statement of financial position that is similar to the effect of offsetting. This section does not modify the accounting treatment in the particular circumstances prescribed by any other sections or AICPA Guides or Statements of Position. Examples of those other sections and AICPA Guides are:

a. Section L10, "Leases" (leveraged leases, paragraphs .144 through .149)
b. [Deleted 12/92 because of FASB Statement 113, *Accounting and Reporting for Reinsurance of Short-Duration and Long-Duration Contracts.*]
c. Section P16, "Pension Costs" (accounting for pension plan assets and liabilities)
d. Section P40, "Postretirement Benefits Other Than Pensions" (accounting for plan assets and liabilities)
e. Section I27, "Income Taxes" (net tax asset or liability amounts reported)
f. [Deleted 8/01 because of FASB Statement 144, *Accounting for the Impairment or Disposal of Long-Lived Assets.*]
g. AICPA Audit and Accounting Guides, *Audits of Brokers and Dealers in Securities* (trade date accounting for trading portfolio positions), and *Construction Contractors* and *Audits of Federal Government Contractors* (advances received on construction contracts)
h. AICPA [FIN39, ¶7] Audit and Accounting Guide, *Banks and Savings Institutions,* [FAS135, ¶5(d)] (reciprocal balances with other banks).

[17]Failure by either party to instruct its securities custodian to transfer securities owned of record would result in that party's failing to receive cash from the counterparty and, thereby, would require that party to have available cash on deposit for the gross payable due for securities transferred to it. The failure also should be an event of default under the master netting arrangement required by paragraph .106A(c). The event of default, in turn, should entitle the other party to terminate the arrangement and demand the immediate net settlement of all contracts. [FIN41, ¶4, fn8]

Glossary

.401 **"Book entry" securities.** Exist only as items in accounting records maintained by a [securities] transfer system operator. [FIN41, ¶3, fn4]

.402 **Conditional contracts.** Those [contracts] whose obligations or rights depend on the occurrence of some specified future event that is not certain to occur and that could change the timing of the amounts or of the instruments to be received, delivered, or exchanged. [FIN39, ¶3]

.403 **Daylight overdraft or other intraday credit.** Refers to the accommodation in banking arrangements that allows transactions to be completed even if there is insufficient cash on deposit during the day provided there is sufficient cash to cover the net cash requirement at the end of the day. [FIN41, ¶3, fn6]

.404 **Exchange contracts.** Those [contracts] that require a future exchange of assets or liabilities rather than a one-way transfer of assets. [FIN39, ¶3]

.405 **Master netting arrangement.** Exists if the reporting entity has multiple contracts, whether for the same type of conditional or exchange contract or for different types of contracts, with a single counterparty that are subject to a contractual agreement that provides for the net settlement of all contracts through a single payment in a single currency in the event of default on or termination of any one contract. [FIN39, ¶10]

.406 **Repurchase agreement (repo).** Refers to a transaction that is accounted for as a collateralized borrowing in which a seller-borrower of securities sells those securities to a buyer-lender with an agreement to repurchase them at a stated price plus interest at a specified date or in specified circumstances. [FIN41, ¶1, fn1]

.407 **Reverse repurchase agreement (reverse repo).** Refers to a transaction that is accounted for as a collateralized lending in which a buyer-lender buys securities with an agreement to resell them to the seller-borrower at a stated price plus interest at a specified date or in specified circumstances. [FIN41, ¶1, fn2]

.408 **Right of setoff.** A debtor's legal right, by contract or otherwise, to discharge all or a portion of the debt owed to another party by applying against the debt an amount that the other party owes to the debtor. [FIN39, ¶5]

Supplemental Guidance

.501-.504 [Deleted 3/92 because of FASB Interpretation 39, *Offsetting of Amounts Related to Certain Contracts.*]

[501-505][Deleted 3/92 because of FASB Interpretation 39.]

Supplemental Guidance: Emerging Issues Task Force (EITF) Issues

.1000 [Listed below are EITF Issues that provide supplemental guidance for this section. These Issues may be either interpretive of or related by topic to the guidance in this section.

EITF Issue No. 86-25, "Offsetting Foreign Currency Swaps"
EITF Issue No. 92-2, "Measuring Loss Accruals by Transferors for Transfers of Receivables with Recourse"
EITF Issue No. 97-14, "Accounting for Deferred Compensation Arrangements Where Amounts Earned Are Held in a Rabbi Trust and Invested"
EITF Topic No. D-43, "Assurance That a Right of Setoff Is Enforceable in a Bankruptcy under FASB Interpretation No. 39"
EITF Topic No. D-79, "Accounting for Retroactive Insurance Contracts Purchased by Entities Other Than Insurance Enterprises"]

.1001 [Listed below is an EITF Issue that provides interpretive guidance on specific material in this section.

Paragraph .101B (FIN 39, ¶6)—EITF Topic No. D-43
Paragraphs .102 and .103 (APB 10, ¶7)—EITF Topic No. D-43]

(The next page is 4801.)

BUSINESS COMBINATIONS (APB 16) SECTION B50

The material in this section has been superseded by FASB Statement 141, *Business Combinations*. Due to the delayed effective date of Statement 141 and the prohibition of early or retroactive application, this section has been moved to Appendix E for continued reference by users. For business combinations initiated on or before June 30, 2001, Section B50 must be applied. Section B50 must also be applied to combinations of two or more not-for-profit organizations, the acquisition of a for-profit business enterprise by a not-for-profit organization, and combinations of two or more mutual enterprises. (Refer to Appendix C, "Effective Dates of Pronouncements," for details of the effective date and transition provisions of Statement 141.)

BUSINESS COMBINATIONS (FAS141) SECTION B51

Sources: ARB 43, Chapter 1A; ARB 51; FASB Statement 72; FASB Statement 87; FASB Statement 106; FASB Statement 109; FASB Statement 121; FASB Statement 141; FASB Statement 142; FASB Statement 145; FASB Interpretation 4; FASB Interpretation 9; FASB Technical Bulletin 85-5

[**Note:** A list of Issues discussed by the Emerging Issues Task Force (EITF) that provide supplemental guidance for this section is presented in paragraph .1000.]

Summary

This section addresses financial accounting and reporting for business combinations. All business combinations in the scope of this section are to be accounted for using one method—the purchase method.

The provisions of this section reflect a fundamentally different approach to accounting for business combinations than previously allowed. The single-method approach used in this section reflects the conclusion that virtually all business combinations are acquisitions and, thus, all business combinations should be accounted for in the same way that other asset acquisitions are accounted for—based on the values exchanged.

This section changes the accounting for business combinations in the following significant respects:

- This section requires that all business combinations be accounted for by a single method—the purchase method.
- This section requires that intangible assets that can be identified and named be recognized as assets apart from goodwill if they meet one of two criteria—the contractual-legal criterion or the separability criterion. To assist in identifying acquired intangible assets, this section also provides an illustrative list of intangible assets that meet either of those criteria.
- Disclosure is now required of the primary reasons for a business combination and the allocation of the purchase price paid to the assets acquired and liabilities assumed by major balance sheet caption. When the amounts of goodwill and intangible assets acquired are significant in relation to the purchase price paid, disclosure of other information about those assets is required, such as the amount of goodwill by reportable segment and the amount of the purchase price assigned to each major intangible asset class.

This section does not apply, however, to combinations of two or more not-for-profit organizations, the acquisition of a for-profit business entity by a not-for-profit organization, and combinations of two or more mutual enterprises.

Introduction

.101 This section addresses financial accounting and reporting for business combinations. [FAS141, ¶1] Paragraphs .175 through .200 of this section provide implementation guidance on the application of the purchase method of accounting for a business combination and are an integral part of the standards provided in this section. Paragraphs .173 and .174 provide illustrations of some of the financial statement disclosures that this section requires. [FAS141, ¶2]

Accounting for Asset Acquisitions—General Concepts

.102 The accounting for a business combination follows the concepts normally applicable to the initial recognition and measurement of assets acquired, liabilities assumed or incurred, and equity shares issued, as well as to the subsequent accounting for those items. Those concepts are set forth in paragraphs .103 through .107. The standards of accounting and reporting for a business combination by the purchase method, which are based on those concepts, are set forth in paragraphs .108 through .143 and .156 through .171. [FAS141, ¶3]

.103 *Initial recognition.* Assets are commonly acquired in exchange transactions that trigger the initial recognition of the assets acquired and any liabilities assumed. If the consideration given in exchange for the asset (or net assets) acquired is in the form of assets surrendered (such as cash), the assets surrendered are derecognized at the date of acquisition. If the consideration given is in the form of liabilities incurred or equity interests issued, the liabilities incurred and equity interests issued are initially recognized at the date of acquisition. [FAS141, ¶4] [Refer to paragraph .1001 for an EITF Issue that provides interpretive guidance on paragraphs .103 through .106.]

.104 *Initial measurement.* Like other exchange transactions generally, acquisitions are measured on the basis of the **fair values** exchanged. In exchange transactions, the fair values of the net assets acquired and the consideration paid are assumed to be equal, absent evidence to the contrary. Thus, the "cost"[1] of an acquisition to the acquiring entity is equal to the fair values exchanged and no gain or loss is generally recognized. Exceptions to that general condition include (a) the gain or loss that is recognized if the fair value of noncash assets given as consideration differs from their carrying amounts on the acquiring entity's books and (b) the extraordinary gain that is sometimes recognized by the acquiring entity if the fair value of the net assets acquired in a business combination exceeds the cost of the acquired entity (refer to paragraphs .158 and .159). [FAS141, ¶5]

.105 Exchange transactions in which the consideration given is cash are measured by the amount of cash paid. However, if the consideration given is not in the form of cash (that is, in the form of noncash assets, liabilities incurred, or equity interests issued), measurement is based on the fair value of the consideration given or the fair value of the asset (or net assets) acquired, whichever is more clearly evident and, thus, more reliably measurable. [FAS141, ¶6]

.106 *Allocating cost.* Acquiring assets in groups requires not only ascertaining the cost of the asset (or net asset) group but also allocating that cost to the individual assets (or individual assets and liabilities) that make up the group. The cost of such a group is determined using the concepts described in paragraphs .104 and .105. A portion of the cost of the group is then assigned to each individual asset (or individual assets and liabilities) acquired on the basis of its fair value. In a business combination, an excess of the cost of the group over the sum of the amounts assigned to the tangible assets, **financial assets,** and separately recognized **intangible assets** acquired less liabilities assumed is evidence of an unidentified intangible asset or assets. [FAS141, ¶7]

.107 *Accounting after acquisition.* The nature of an asset and not the manner of its acquisition determines an acquiring entity's subsequent accounting for the asset. The basis for measuring the asset acquired—whether the amount of cash paid, the fair value of an asset received or given up, the fair value of a liability incurred, or the fair value of equity shares issued—has no effect on the subsequent accounting for the asset. [FAS141, ¶8]

[1]Cost is a term that is often used to refer to the amount at which an entity initially recognizes an asset at the date it is acquired, whatever the manner of acquisition. [FAS141, ¶5, fn2]

Accounting for Business Combinations

Scope

.108 For purposes of applying this section, a *business combination* occurs when an entity[2] acquires net assets that constitute a business[3] or acquires equity interests of one or more other entities and obtains control[4] over that entity or entities. This section does not address transactions in which control is obtained through means other than an acquisition of net assets or equity interests. For purposes of this section, the formation of a joint venture is not a business combination.[5] [FAS141, ¶9]

.109 This section applies to combinations involving either incorporated or unincorporated entities. The provisions of this section apply equally to a business combination in which (a) one or more entities are merged or become subsidiaries, (b) one entity transfers net assets or its owners transfer their equity interests to another, or (c) all entities transfer net assets or the owners of those entities transfer their equity interests to a newly formed entity (some of which are referred to as roll-up or put-together transactions). All those transactions are business combinations regardless of whether the form of consideration given is cash, other assets, a business or a subsidiary of the entity, debt, common or preferred shares or other equity interests, or a combination of those forms and regardless of whether the former owners of one of the combining entities as a group retain or receive a majority of the voting rights of the combined entity. An exchange of a business for a business also is a business combination. [FAS141, ¶10]

.110 The acquisition of some or all of the noncontrolling interests in a subsidiary is not a business combination. However, paragraph .113 of this section specifies the method of accounting for those transactions. The term *business combination* as used in this section

---

[2]This section applies to a business enterprise, a new entity formed to complete a business combination, or a **mutual enterprise,** each of which is referred to herein as an *entity*. That term can refer to any of the various forms in which the participants in a business combination may exist. However, a new entity formed to complete a business combination would not necessarily be the acquiring entity (refer to paragraph .118). [FAS141, ¶9, fn3]

[3]EITF Issue No. 98-3, "Determining Whether a Nonmonetary Transaction Involves Receipt of Productive Assets or of a Business," provides guidance on determining whether an asset group constitutes a business. [FAS141, ¶9, fn4]

[4]Control is generally indicated by "ownership by one company, directly or indirectly, of over fifty percent of the outstanding voting shares of another company" (Section C51, "Consolidation," paragraph .102), although control may exist in other circumstances. [FAS141, ¶9, fn5]

[5]The Board intends to address the accounting for other events or transactions that are similar to a business combination but do not meet this section's definition of a business combination and the accounting for joint venture formations in another project. [FAS141, ¶9, fn6]

also excludes transfers of net assets or exchanges of equity interests between entities under common control. Paragraphs .201 through .208 provide examples of those transactions and accounting guidance for them. [FAS141, ¶11]

.111 This section does not apply to combinations between **not-for-profit organizations,** nor does it apply to the acquisition of a for-profit business entity by a not-for-profit organization.[6] [FAS141, ¶12] [Refer to Section B50, "Business Combinations," in Appendix E, "*Current Text* Sections That Are Superseded by Pronouncements with Delayed Effective Dates," for accounting guidance for these transactions.]

Method of Accounting

.112 All business combinations in the scope of this section shall be accounted for using the purchase method as described in this section and other sections. [FAS141, ¶13] Guidance in those sections, which are listed below, shall be considered when applying the provisions of this section.

a. Section C47, "Compensation to Employees: Stock Purchase and Option Plans" (paragraphs .228 through .230)
b. Section L10, "Leases" (paragraphs .137 through .142)
c. Section Bt7, "Banking and Thrift Industries" [FAS141, ¶A3]

.113 The acquisition of some or all of the noncontrolling equity interests in a subsidiary—whether acquired by the parent, the subsidiary itself, or another affiliate—shall be accounted for using the purchase method. Paragraphs .177 through .179 provide additional accounting guidance for those transactions. [FAS141, ¶14]

Application of the Purchase Method

Identifying the Acquiring Entity

.114 Application of the purchase method requires the identification of the acquiring entity. All business combinations in the scope of this section shall be accounted for using the purchase method. Thus, the acquiring entity shall be identified in all business combinations. [FAS141, ¶15]

---

[6]The Board intends to address issues related to the accounting for combinations between not-for-profit organizations and issues related to the accounting for the acquisition of a for-profit business entity by a not-for-profit organization in another project. [FAS141, ¶12, fn7]

.115 In a business combination effected solely through the distribution of cash or other assets or by incurring liabilities, the entity that distributes cash or other assets or incurs liabilities is generally the acquiring entity. [FAS141, ¶16] [Refer to paragraph .1001 for an EITF Issue that provides interpretive guidance on paragraphs .115 through .117.]

.116 In a business combination effected through an exchange of equity interests, the entity that issues the equity interests is generally the acquiring entity. In some business combinations (commonly referred to as reverse acquisitions), however, the acquired entity issues the equity interests. Commonly, the acquiring entity is the larger entity. However, the facts and circumstances surrounding a business combination sometimes indicate that a smaller entity acquires a larger one. In some business combinations, the combined entity assumes the name of the acquired entity. Thus, in identifying the acquiring entity in a combination effected through an exchange of equity interests, all pertinent facts and circumstances shall be considered, in particular:

a. The relative voting rights in the combined entity after the combination—all else being equal, the acquiring entity is the combining entity whose owners as a group retained or received the larger portion of the voting rights in the combined entity. In determining which group of owners retained or received the larger portion of the voting rights, consideration shall be given to the existence of any unusual or special voting arrangements and options, warrants, or convertible securities.
b. The existence of a large minority voting interest in the combined entity when no other owner or organized group of owners has a significant voting interest—all else being equal, the acquiring entity is the combining entity whose single owner or organized group of owners holds the large minority voting interest in the combined entity.
c. The composition of the governing body of the combined entity—all else being equal, the acquiring entity is the combining entity whose owners or governing body has the ability to elect or appoint a voting majority of the governing body of the combined entity.
d. The composition of the senior management of the combined entity—all else being equal, the acquiring entity is the combining entity whose senior management dominates that of the combined entity. Senior management generally consists of the chairman of the board, chief executive officer, chief operating officer, chief financial officer, and those divisional heads reporting directly to them, or the executive committee if one exists.

e. The terms of the exchange of equity securities—all else being equal, the acquiring entity is the combining entity that pays a premium over the market value of the equity securities of the other combining entity or entities.[7]

[FAS141, ¶17]

.117 Some business combinations involve more than two entities. In identifying the acquiring entity in those cases, consideration also shall be given to which combining entity initiated the combination and whether the assets, revenues, and earnings of one of the combining entities significantly exceed those of the others. [FAS141, ¶18]

.118 If a new entity is formed to issue equity interests to effect a business combination, one of the existing combining entities shall be determined to be the acquiring entity on the basis of the evidence available. The guidance in paragraphs .115 through .117 shall be used in making that determination. [FAS141, ¶19]

Determining the Cost of the Acquired Entity

.119 The same accounting principles shall apply in determining the cost of assets acquired individually, those acquired in a group, and those acquired in a business combination. A cash payment by an acquiring entity shall be used to measure the cost of an acquired entity. Similarly, the fair values of other assets distributed as consideration, such as marketable securities or properties, and the fair values of liabilities incurred by an acquiring entity shall be used to measure the cost of an acquired entity. [FAS141, ¶20] [Refer to paragraph .1001 for EITF Issues that provide interpretive guidance on this paragraph.]

.120 The distinctive characteristics of preferred shares make some preferred share issues similar to debt securities, while others are similar to common shares, with many gradations in between. Those characteristics may affect the determination of the cost of an acquired entity. For example, the fair value of nonvoting, nonconvertible preferred shares that lack characteristics of common shares may be determined by comparing the specified dividend and redemption terms with those of comparable securities and by assessing market factors. Thus, although the principle of recording the fair value of consideration received for shares issued applies to all equity securities, senior as well as common shares, the cost of an entity acquired by issuing senior equity securities may be determined in practice on the same

[7]This criterion shall apply only if the equity securities exchanged in a business combination are traded in a public market on either (a) a stock exchange (domestic or foreign) or (b) in an over-the-counter market (including securities quoted only locally or regionally). [FAS141, ¶17, fn9]

basis as for debt securities. [FAS141, ¶21] [Refer to paragraph .1001 for an EITF Issue that provides interpretive guidance on this paragraph.]

.121 The fair value of securities traded in the market is generally more clearly evident than the fair value of an acquired entity (paragraph .105). Thus, the quoted market price of an equity security issued to effect a business combination generally should be used to estimate the fair value of an acquired entity after recognizing possible effects of price fluctuations, quantities traded, issue costs, and the like. The market price for a reasonable period before and after the date that the terms of the acquisition are agreed to and announced shall be considered in determining the fair value of securities issued. [FAS141, ¶22] [Refer to paragraph .1001 for EITF Issues that provide interpretive guidance on this paragraph.]

.122 If the quoted market price is not the fair value of the equity securities, either preferred or common, the consideration received shall be estimated even though measuring directly the fair values of net assets received is difficult. Both the net assets received, including **goodwill,** and the extent of the adjustment of the quoted market price of the shares issued shall be weighed to determine the amount to be recorded. All aspects of the acquisition, including the negotiations, shall be studied, and independent appraisals may be used as an aid in determining the fair value of securities issued. Consideration other than equity shares distributed to effect an acquisition may provide evidence of the total fair value received. [FAS141, ¶23] [Refer to paragraph .1001 for an EITF Issue that provides interpretive guidance on paragraphs .122 and .123.]

Costs of the business combination

.123 The cost of an entity acquired in a business combination includes the direct costs of the business combination. Costs of registering and issuing equity securities shall be recognized as a reduction of the otherwise determinable fair value of the securities. However, indirect and general expenses related to business combinations shall be expensed as incurred. [FAS141, ¶24]

Contingent consideration

.124 A business combination agreement may provide for the issuance of additional shares of a security or the transfer of cash or other consideration contingent on specified events or transactions in the future. Some agreements provide that a portion of the consideration be placed in escrow to be distributed or returned to the transferor when specified events occur. Either debt or equity securities may be placed in escrow, and amounts equal to interest or dividends on the securities during the contingency period may be paid to the escrow agent or to the potential security holder. [FAS141, ¶25] [Refer to paragraph .1001 for EITF Issues that provide interpretive guidance on paragraphs .124 through .126.]

.125 Cash and other assets distributed, securities issued unconditionally, and amounts of contingent consideration that are determinable at the date of acquisition shall be included in determining the cost of an acquired entity and recorded at that date. Consideration that is issued or issuable at the expiration of the contingency period or that is held in escrow pending the outcome of the contingency shall be disclosed but not recorded as a liability or shown as outstanding securities unless the outcome of the contingency is determinable beyond a reasonable doubt. [FAS141, ¶26]

.126 The contingent consideration usually should be recorded when the contingency is resolved and consideration is issued or becomes issuable. In general, the issuance of additional securities or distribution of other consideration at resolution of contingencies based on earnings shall result in an additional element of cost of an acquired entity. In contrast, the issuance of additional securities or distribution of other consideration at resolution of contingencies based on security prices shall not change the recorded cost of an acquired entity. [FAS141, ¶27]

Contingency based on earnings

.127 Additional consideration may be contingent on maintaining or achieving specified earnings levels in future periods. When the contingency is resolved and additional consideration is distributable, the acquiring entity shall record the fair value of the consideration issued or issuable as an additional cost of the acquired entity.[8] [FAS141, ¶28] [Refer to paragraph .1001 for EITF Issues that provide interpretive guidance on this paragraph.]

Contingency based on security prices

.128 Additional consideration may be contingent on the market price of a specified security issued to effect a business combination. Unless the price of the security at least equals the specified amount on a specified date or dates, the acquiring entity is required to issue additional equity or debt securities or transfer cash or other assets sufficient to make the current value of the total consideration equal to the specified amount. The securities issued unconditionally at the date the combination is consummated shall be

[8]Paragraph .159 provides guidance on accounting for contingent consideration in a business combination if the fair value of the net assets acquired exceeds the cost of the acquired entity. [FAS141, ¶28, fn10]

recorded at that date at the specified amount. [FAS141, ¶29] [Refer to paragraph .1001 for an EITF Issue that provides interpretive guidance on paragraphs .128 through .130.]

.129 The issuance of additional securities or distribution of other consideration upon resolution of a contingency based on security prices shall not affect the cost of the acquired entity, regardless of whether the amount specified is a security price to be maintained or a higher security price to be achieved. When the contingency is resolved and additional consideration is distributable, the acquiring entity shall record the current fair value of the additional consideration issued or issuable. However, the amount previously recorded for securities issued at the date of acquisition shall be simultaneously reduced to the lower current value of those securities. Reducing the value of debt securities previously issued to their later fair value results in recording a discount on debt securities. That discount shall be amortized from the date the additional securities are issued. [FAS141, ¶30]

.130 Accounting for contingent consideration based on conditions other than those described shall be inferred from the procedures outlined. For example, if the consideration contingently issuable depends on both future earnings and future security prices, an additional cost of the acquired entity shall be recorded for the additional consideration contingent on earnings, and previously recorded consideration shall be reduced to the current value of the consideration contingent on security prices. Similarly, if the consideration contingently issuable depends on later settlement of a contingency, an increase in the cost of acquired assets, if any, shall be amortized, if applicable, over the remaining useful life of the assets.[9] [FAS141, ¶31]

Interest or dividends during contingency period

.131 Amounts paid to an escrow agent representing interest and dividends on securities held in escrow shall be accounted for according to the accounting for the securities. That is, until the disposition of the securities in escrow is resolved, payments to the escrow agent shall not be recorded as interest expense or dividend distributions. An amount equal to interest and dividends later distributed by the escrow agent to the former shareholders shall be added to the cost of the acquired assets at the date distributed. [FAS141, ¶32]

---

[9]Whether an increase in the cost of the acquired assets will be amortized depends on the nature of the asset. Guidance on the subsequent accounting for goodwill and other intangible assets acquired in a business combination is provided in Section G40, "Goodwill and Other Intangible Assets." [FAS141, ¶31, fn11]

Tax effect of imputed interest

.132 A tax reduction resulting from imputed interest on contingently issuable shares reduces the fair value recorded for contingent consideration based on earnings and increases additional capital recorded for contingent consideration based on security prices. [FAS141, ¶33]

Compensation in contingent agreements

.133 If the substance of the agreement for contingent consideration is to provide compensation for services or use of property or profit sharing, the additional consideration given shall be recognized as an expense of the appropriate periods. [FAS141, ¶34] [Refer to paragraph .1001 for an EITF Issue that provides interpretive guidance on this paragraph.]

Allocating the Cost of an Acquired Entity to Assets Acquired and Liabilities Assumed

.134 Following the process described in paragraphs .135 through .145 and .156 through .159 (commonly referred to as the purchase price allocation), an acquiring entity shall allocate the cost of an acquired entity to the assets acquired and liabilities assumed based on their estimated fair values at date of acquisition (refer to paragraph .161). Prior to that allocation, the acquiring entity shall (a) review the purchase consideration if other than cash to ensure that it has been valued in accordance with the requirements in paragraphs .119 through .122 and (b) identify all of the assets acquired and liabilities assumed, including intangible assets that meet the recognition criteria in paragraph .138, regardless of whether they had been recorded in the financial statements of the acquired entity. [FAS141, ¶35]

.135 Among other sources of relevant information, independent appraisals and actuarial or other valuations may be used as an aid in determining the estimated fair values of assets acquired and liabilities assumed. The tax basis of an asset or liability shall not be a factor in determining its estimated fair value. [FAS141, ¶36] [Refer to paragraph .1001 for EITF Issues that provide interpretive guidance on this paragraph.]

Assets acquired and liabilities assumed, except goodwill

.136 The following is general guidance for assigning amounts to assets acquired and liabilities assumed, except goodwill:

a. Marketable securities at fair values

b. Receivables at present values of amounts to be received determined at appropriate current interest rates, less allowances for uncollectibility and collection costs, if necessary
c. Inventories
   (1) Finished goods and merchandise at estimated selling prices less the sum of (a) costs of disposal and (b) a reasonable profit allowance for the selling effort of the acquiring entity
   (2) Work in process at estimated selling prices of finished goods less the sum of (a) costs to complete, (b) costs of disposal, and (c) a reasonable profit allowance for the completing and selling effort of the acquiring entity based on profit for similar finished goods
   (3) Raw materials at current replacement costs
d. Plant and equipment
   (1) To be used, at the current replacement cost for similar capacity[10] unless the expected future use of the assets indicates a lower value to the acquiring entity
   (2) To be sold, at fair value less cost to sell
e. Intangible assets that meet the criteria in paragraph .138 at estimated fair values[[11]]
f. Other assets, including land, natural resources, and nonmarketable securities, at appraised values
g. Accounts and notes payable, long-term debt, and other claims payable, at present values of amounts to be paid determined at appropriate current interest rates
h. A liability for the projected benefit obligation in excess of plan assets or an asset for plan assets in excess of the projected benefit obligation of a single-employer defined benefit pension plan, at amounts determined in accordance with paragraph .139
i. A liability for the accumulated postretirement benefit obligation in excess of the fair value of plan assets or an asset for the fair value of the plan assets in excess of the

---

[10] Replacement cost may be determined directly if a used-asset market exists for the assets acquired. Otherwise, the replacement cost should be estimated from the replacement cost new less estimated accumulated depreciation. [FAS141, ¶37, fn12]

[[11]] For example, the fair value of an order backlog would represent the amount a buyer would be willing to pay to acquire the future cash flows expected to arise from that order backlog. [FAS141, ¶B172] The amount by which the terms of a contract are favorable relative to market prices would not necessarily represent the fair value of that contract. [FAS141, ¶B173] While many contracts or other rights (including customer contracts) are fixed in duration, past history (and industry practice) often provides evidence that the contracts or rights are generally renewed without substantial cost and effort. For example, although contracts to manage investments of mutual funds are often short-term contracts (one year or less), in many (if not most) cases, those contracts are continuously renewed. [In addition,] while some legal rights such as trademarks and broadcast licenses have finite legal lives, those rights are renewable and are often renewed without challenge. In cases such as those, estimates of future cash flows used in measuring the fair value of the acquired intangible asset likely would reflect cash flows for periods that extend beyond the remaining term of the acquired contract or legal right. [FAS141, ¶B174]

accumulated postretirement benefit obligation of a single-employer defined benefit postretirement plan at amounts determined in accordance with paragraphs .140 and .141

j. Liabilities and accruals—such as accruals for warranties, vacation pay, and deferred compensation—at present values of amounts to be paid determined at appropriate current interest rates [Refer to paragraph .1001 for an EITF Issue that provides interpretive guidance on this subparagraph.]

k. Other liabilities and commitments—such as unfavorable leases, contracts, and commitments and plant closing expense incident to the acquisition—at present values of amounts to be paid determined at appropriate current interest rates

l. **Preacquisition contingencies** at amounts determined in accordance with paragraph .142.

[FAS141, ¶37] [Refer to paragraph .1001 for EITF Issues that provide interpretive guidance on this paragraph.]

.137 An acquiring entity shall not recognize the goodwill previously recorded by an acquired entity, nor shall it recognize the deferred income taxes recorded by an acquired entity before its acquisition. A deferred tax liability or asset shall be recognized for differences between the assigned values and the tax bases of the recognized assets acquired and liabilities assumed in a business combination in accordance with paragraph .129 of Section I27, "Income Taxes." [FAS141, ¶38]

Intangible assets

.138 An intangible asset shall be recognized as an asset apart from goodwill if it arises from contractual or other legal rights (regardless of whether those rights are transferable or separable from the acquired entity or from other rights and obligations). If an intangible asset does not arise from contractual or other legal rights, it shall be recognized as an asset apart from goodwill only if it is separable, that is, it is capable of being separated or divided from the acquired entity and sold, transferred, licensed, rented, or exchanged (regardless of whether there is an intent to do so). For purposes of this section, however, an intangible asset that cannot be sold, transferred, licensed, rented, or exchanged individually is considered separable if it can be sold, transferred, licensed, rented, or exchanged in combination with a related contract, asset, or liability. For purposes of this section, an assembled workforce shall not be recognized as an intangible asset apart from goodwill. Paragraphs .176 through .200 provide additional guidance relating to the recognition of acquired intangible assets apart from goodwill, including an illustrative list of intangible assets that meet the recognition criteria in this paragraph. [FAS141, ¶39]

Defined benefit pension plan assets

.139 When an employer is acquired in a business combination and that employer sponsors a single-employer defined benefit pension plan, the assignment of the purchase price to individual assets acquired and liabilities assumed shall include a liability for the projected benefit obligation in excess of plan assets or an asset for plan assets in excess of the projected benefit obligation, thereby eliminating any previously existing unrecognized net gain or loss, unrecognized prior service cost, or unrecognized net obligation or net asset existing at the date of initial application of Section P16, "Pension Costs." Subsequently, to the extent that those amounts are considered in determining the amounts of contributions, differences between the purchaser's net pension cost and amounts contributed will reduce the liability or asset recognized at the date of the combination. If it is expected that the plan will be terminated or curtailed, the effects of those actions shall be considered in measuring the projected benefit obligation. [FAS87, ¶74] [For an employer that participates in a multi-employer pension plan] no recognition of [a] withdrawal liability is probable. [FAS87, ¶253]

Defined benefit postretirement plan assets

.140 When an employer is acquired in a business combination and that employer sponsors a single-employer defined benefit postretirement plan [other than a pension plan], the assignment of the purchase price to individual assets acquired and liabilities assumed shall include a liability for the accumulated postretirement benefit obligation in excess of the fair value of the plan assets or an asset for the fair value of the plan assets in excess of the accumulated postretirement benefit obligation. The accumulated postretirement benefit obligation assumed shall be measured based on the benefits attributed by the acquired entity to employee service prior to the date the business combination is consummated, adjusted to reflect (a) any changes in assumptions based on the purchaser's assessment of relevant future events (as discussed in paragraphs .116 through .137 of Section P40, "Postretirement Benefits Other Than Pensions") and (b) the terms of the substantive plan (as discussed in paragraphs .116 through .121 of Section P40) to be provided by the purchaser to the extent they differ from the terms of the acquired entity's substantive plan. [FAS106, ¶86] [For an employer that participates in a multi-employer postretirement benefit plan] no recognition of [an] additional liability [is] required under this section unless conditions exist that make an additional liability probable. [FAS106, ¶387]

.141 If the postretirement benefit plan of the acquired entity is amended as a condition of the business combination (for example, if the change is required by the seller as part of the consummation of the acquisition), the effects of any improvements attributed to services rendered by the participants of the acquired entity's plan prior to the date of the business combination shall be accounted for as part of the accumulated postretirement benefit obligation of the acquired entity. Otherwise, if improvements to the postretirement benefit plan of the acquired entity are not a condition of the business combination, credit granted for prior service shall be recognized as a plan amendment. If it is expected that the plan will be terminated or curtailed, the effects of those actions shall be considered in measuring the accumulated postretirement benefit obligation. Otherwise, no future changes to the plan shall be anticipated. [FAS106, ¶87] Subsequently, to the extent that the net obligation assumed or net assets acquired are considered in determining the amounts of contributions to the plan, differences between the purchaser's net periodic postretirement benefit cost and amounts it contributes will reduce the liability or asset recognized at the date of the combination. [FAS106, ¶88]

Preacquisition contingencies

.142 A preacquisition contingency other than the potential tax effects of (a) temporary differences and carryforwards of an acquired entity that exist at the acquisition date and (b) income tax uncertainties related to the acquisition (for example, an uncertainty related to the tax basis of an acquired asset that will ultimately be agreed to by the taxing authority)[12] shall be included in the purchase price allocation based on an amount determined as follows:

a. If the fair value of the preacquisition contingency can be determined during the **allocation period,** that preacquisition contingency shall be included in the allocation of the purchase price based on that fair value.[13]
b. If the fair value of the preacquisition contingency cannot be determined during the allocation period, that preacquisition contingency shall be included in the allocation of the purchase price based on an amount determined in accordance with the following criteria:
   (1) Information available prior to the end of the allocation period indicates that it is probable that an asset existed, a liability had been incurred, or an asset had been impaired at the consummation of the business combination. It is implicit in this condition that it must be probable that one or more future events will occur confirming the existence of the asset, liability, or impairment.
   (2) The amount of the asset or liability can be reasonably estimated.

[12]Those potential income tax effects shall be accounted for in accordance with the provisions of Section I27. [FAS141, ¶40, fn13]

[13]For example, if it can be demonstrated that the parties to a business combination agreed to adjust the total consideration by an amount because of a contingency, that amount would be a determined fair value of that contingency. [FAS141, ¶40, fn14]

The criteria of this subparagraph shall be applied using the guidance provided in Section C59, "Contingencies."[14]

[FAS141, ¶40] [Refer to paragraph .1001 for EITF Issues that provide interpretive guidance on this paragraph.]

.143 After the end of the allocation period, an adjustment that results from a preacquisition contingency other than a loss carryforward[15] shall be included in the determination of net income in the period in which the adjustment is determined. [FAS141, ¶41]

Research and development assets acquired

.144 Costs shall be assigned to all identifiable tangible and intangible assets, including any *resulting from* research and development activities of the acquired enterprise or *to be used in* research and development activities of the combined enterprise. Identifiable assets *resulting from* research and development activities of the acquired enterprise might include, for example, patents received or applied for, blueprints, formulas, and specifications or designs for new products or processes. Identifiable assets *to be used in* research and development activities of the combined enterprise might include, for example, materials and supplies, equipment and facilities, and perhaps even a specific research project in process. In either case, the costs to be assigned are determined from the amount paid by the acquiring enterprise and *not* from the original cost to the acquired enterprise. [FIN4, ¶4]

.145 The subsequent accounting by the combined enterprise for the costs allocated to assets *to be used in* research and development activities shall be determined by reference to Section R50, "Research and Development." Accordingly, costs assigned to assets to be used in a particular research and development project and that have no alternative future use (refer to Section R50, paragraph .107) shall be charged to expense at the date of consummation of the combination. Therefore, the accounting for the cost of an item to be used in research and development activities is the same under paragraphs .107 and .108 of Section R50 whether the item is purchased singly, or as part of a group of assets, or as part of an entire enterprise in a business combination. [FIN4, ¶5] [Refer to paragraph .1001 for an EITF Issue that provides interpretive guidance on this paragraph.]

---

[14]Section C59 specifies the amount to be accrued if the reasonable estimate of the amount is a range. If some amount within the range appears at the time to be a better estimate than any other amount within the range, that amount is accrued. If no amount within the range is a better estimate than any other amount, however, the minimum amount in the range is accrued. [FAS141, ¶40, fn15]

[15]Refer to footnote 12. [FAS141, ¶41, fn16]

Acquisition of a banking or thrift institution

.146 [In applying this section to] the acquisition of a [banking or thrift institution][16] [FIN9, ¶1] the net-spread method[[17]] [is inappropriate] because [that] method ignores fair value of individual assets and liabilities or types of assets and liabilities. [FIN9, ¶4]

.147 Ascertaining appropriate current interest rates (and the periods over which the receivables [refer to paragraph .136(b)]) are to be discounted requires an analysis of the many factors that determine the fair values of the portfolio of loans acquired. [FIN9, ¶5] As described in paragraph .136(e), acquired intangible assets that meet the criteria in paragraph .138 shall be assigned an amount based on their estimated fair values. [FAS141, ¶E20(c)]

.148 [The] present value of savings deposits due on demand [refer to paragraph .136(g)] is their face amount plus interest accrued or accruable as of the date of acquisition. [The] present value for other liabilities assumed, for example, time savings deposits, borrowings from a Federal Home Loan Bank, or other borrowings, shall be determined by using prevailing interest rates for similar liabilities at the acquisition date. [FIN9, ¶7]

Recognized intangible assets

.149 In a business combination involving the acquisition of a banking or thrift institution, intangible assets acquired that meet the criteria in paragraph .138 of this section shall be recognized as assets apart from goodwill. [FAS141, ¶E11(a)] [For example], the purchase price paid for a [banking or thrift institution] may include an amount for one or more factors, such as the following:

---

[16]Paragraphs .147 through .155 apply not only in the case of the acquisition of a savings and loan association but also in the case of the acquisition of a savings and loan association holding company, [FIN9, ¶1, fn1] a commercial bank, a mutual savings bank, a credit union, [or] other depository institutions having assets and liabilities of the same types as those institutions, and branches of such enterprises. [FAS72, ¶2]

[[17]]Under the net-spread method, the acquisition of a savings and loan association is viewed as the acquisition of a leveraged whole rather than the acquisition of the separate assets and liabilities of the association. Therefore, if the spread between the rates of interest received on mortgage loans and the rates of interest (often called *dividends* in the industry) paid on savings accounts is normal for the particular market area, the acquired savings and loan association's principal assets and liabilities, i.e., its mortgage loan portfolio and savings accounts, are brought forward at the carrying amounts shown in the financial statements of the acquired association. [FIN9, ¶2] In contrast, under the separate-valuation method, each of the identifiable assets and liabilities [assumed] of the acquired savings and loan association is accounted for in the consolidated financial statements at an amount based on fair value at the date of acquisition, either individually or by types of assets and types of liabilities. [FIN9, ¶3]

a. Capacity of existing savings accounts and loan accounts to generate future income
b. Capacity of existing savings accounts and loan accounts to generate additional business or new business
c. Nature of territory served. [FIN9, ¶8]

If any of those factors meet the criteria in paragraph .138, the fair value of that factor shall be recognized as an asset apart from goodwill. [FAS141, ¶E20(e)] An acquired intangible asset that does not meet the criteria in paragraph .138 shall be included in the amount recorded as goodwill. [FAS141, ¶E20(e)] The fair values of [FAS72, ¶4] separately recognized intangible assets [FAS141, ¶E20(e)] that relate to depositor or borrower relationships ([such as] (a) and (b) [above]) shall be based on the estimated benefits attributable to the relationships that *exist* at the date of acquisition without regard to new depositors or borrowers that may replace them. [FAS72, ¶4] [Refer to paragraph .156 of Section G40 for guidance on accounting for those intangible assets.] The [FIN9, ¶8] fair value for [other] separately recognized intangible asset[s] [FAS141, ¶E20(e)] shall be recorded as the cost of the intangible [asset] and [FIN9, ¶8] accounted for in accordance with the provisions of [paragraphs .109 through .115 of] Section G40. [FAS142, ¶D11(a)]

Unidentifiable intangible asset

.150 If, in a combination [involving a banking or thrift institution], the fair value of liabilities assumed exceeds the fair value of tangible and identified intangible assets acquired, that excess constitutes an unidentifiable intangible asset. [FAS72, ¶5] [Section G40, paragraphs .157 through .159 describe appropriate accounting for such intangible assets.] [Refer to paragraph .1001 for EITF Issues that provide interpretive guidance on this paragraph.]

Regulatory-assisted combinations

.151 The provisions of paragraphs .152 through .155, which relate to the reporting of regulatory financial assistance, apply to all acquisitions of banking or thrift institutions. [It is] understood that regulatory financial assistance agreements are not standardized and that the conditions under which assistance will be granted vary widely. As a result, this section does not specifically address all forms of regulatory financial assistance, but its provisions should serve as a general guide. [FAS72, ¶3]

.152 In connection with a business combination [involving a banking or thrift institution], a regulatory authority may agree to pay amounts by which future interest received or receivable on the interest-bearing assets acquired is less than the interest cost of carrying those assets for a period by a stated margin. In such a case, the projected assistance, computed as of the date of acquisition based on the interest-rate margin existing at that date, shall be considered as additional interest on the interest-bearing assets acquired in determining their fair values for purposes of applying the purchase method [FAS72, ¶8] (refer to paragraphs .134 and .138). [FAS141, ¶E11(b)] The carrying amount of those interest-bearing assets shall not be adjusted for subsequent changes in the estimated amount of assistance to be received. Actual assistance shall be reported in income of the period in which it accrues. Notwithstanding the above provisions, if an enterprise intends to sell all or a portion of the interest-bearing assets acquired, those assets shall not be stated at amounts in excess of their current market values. [FAS72, ¶8]

.153 Other forms of financial assistance may be granted to a combining enterprise or the combined enterprise by a regulatory authority in connection with a business combination. If receipt of the assistance is probable and the amount is reasonably estimable, that portion of the cost of the acquired enterprise shall be assigned to such assistance. Assets and liabilities that have been or will be transferred to or assumed by a regulatory authority shall not be recognized in the acquisition. If receipt of the assistance is not probable or the amount is not reasonably estimable, any assistance subsequently recognized in the financial statements shall be reported as a reduction of the unidentifiable intangible asset, described in paragraph .150, that was recognized in the acquisition. Subsequent amortization shall be adjusted proportionally. Assistance recognized in excess of that intangible asset shall be reported in income. [FAS72, ¶9]

.154 Under certain forms of assistance granted in connection with a business combination, the combined enterprise may agree to repay all or a portion of the assistance if certain criteria related to the level of future revenues, expenses, or profits are met. Such a repayment obligation shall be recognized as a liability and as a charge to income at the time the conditions in Section C59, paragraph .105, are met. This paragraph does not address repayments of assistance granted in exchange for debt or equity instruments. [FAS72, ¶10]

Disclosures

.155 The nature and amounts of any regulatory financial assistance granted to or recognized by an enterprise during a period in connection with the acquisition of a banking or thrift institution shall be disclosed. [FAS72, ¶11]

Excess of cost over the fair value of acquired net assets (goodwill)

.156 The excess of the cost of an acquired entity over the net of the amounts assigned to assets acquired and liabilities assumed shall be recognized as an asset referred to as goodwill.[18] An acquired intangible asset that does not meet the criteria in paragraph .138 shall be included in the amount recognized as goodwill. [FAS141, ¶43]

Excess of fair value of acquired net assets over cost

.157 In some cases, the sum of the amounts assigned to assets acquired and liabilities assumed will exceed the cost of the acquired entity *(excess over cost* or *excess).* That excess shall be allocated as a pro rata reduction of the amounts that otherwise would have been assigned to all of the acquired assets[19] except (a) financial assets other than investments accounted for by the equity method, (b) assets to be disposed of by sale,[20] (c) deferred tax assets, (d) prepaid assets relating to pension or other postretirement benefit plans, and (e) any other current assets.[21] [FAS141, ¶44]

.158 If any excess remains after reducing to zero the amounts that otherwise would have been assigned to those assets, that remaining excess shall be recognized as an extraordinary gain as described in paragraph .102 of Section I17, "Income Statement Presentation: Extraordinary Items." The extraordinary gain shall be recognized in the period in which the business combination is completed unless the combination involves contingent consideration that, if paid or issued, would be recognized as an additional element of cost of the acquired entity (refer to paragraph .159). If an extraordinary gain is recognized before the end of the period, any subsequent adjustments to that extraordinary gain that result from changes to the purchase price allocation shall be recognized as an extraordinary item. [FAS141, ¶45]

.159 If a business combination involves a contingent consideration agreement that might result in recognition of an additional element of cost of the acquired entity when the contingency is resolved (a contingency based on earnings), an amount equal to the lesser of the maximum amount of contingent consideration or the excess [FAS141, ¶46] prior to the pro rata allocation required by paragraph .157 [FAS145, ¶9(l)] shall be recognized

[18]Acquiring entities should make every effort (a) to measure the purchase consideration accurately, (b) to record the fair values rather than the book values of net assets acquired, and (c) to ensure that all intangible assets not previously recorded are recorded so that those items are not included in what is recognized as goodwill. [FAS141, ¶B146]

[19]The acquired assets include research and development assets acquired and charged to expense in accordance with paragraph .145. [FAS141, ¶44, fn17]

[20][Deleted 8/01 because of FASB Statement 144, *Accounting for the Impairment or Disposal of Long-Lived Assets.*]

[21]Prior to allocation of the excess, if any, the acquiring entity shall reassess whether all acquired assets and assumed liabilities have been identified and recognized and perform remeasurements to verify that the consideration paid, assets acquired, and liabilities assumed have been properly valued (refer to paragraph .134). [FAS141, ¶44, fn19]

as if it was a liability. When the contingency is resolved and the consideration is issued or becomes issuable, any excess of the fair value of the contingent consideration issued or issuable over the amount that was recognized as if it was a liability shall be recognized as an additional cost of the acquired entity. If the amount initially recognized as if it was a liability exceeds the fair value of the consideration issued or issuable, that excess shall be allocated as a pro rata reduction of the amounts assigned to assets acquired in accordance with paragraph .157. Any amount that remains after reducing those assets to zero shall be recognized as an extraordinary gain in accordance with paragraph .158. [FAS141, ¶46]

Accounting for Goodwill and Other Intangible Assets Acquired

.160 After initial recognition, goodwill and other intangible assets acquired in a business combination shall be accounted for in accordance with the provisions of Section G40.[22] [FAS141, ¶47]

Date of Acquisition

.161 The date of acquisition (also referred to as the acquisition date) ordinarily is the date assets are received and other assets are given, liabilities are assumed or incurred, or equity interests are issued. However, the parties may, for convenience, designate as the effective date the end of an accounting period between the dates a business combination is initiated and consummated. The designated date should ordinarily be the acquisition date for accounting purposes if a written agreement provides that effective control of the acquired entity is transferred to the acquiring entity on that date without restrictions except those required to protect the shareholders or other owners of the acquired entity, such as restrictions on significant changes in the operations, permission to pay dividends equal to those regularly paid before the effective date, and the like. Designating an effective date other than the date assets or equity interests are transferred or liabilities are assumed or incurred requires adjusting the cost of an acquired entity and net income otherwise reported to compensate for recognizing income before consideration is transferred. The cost of an acquired entity and net income shall therefore be reduced by imputed interest at an appropriate current rate on assets given, liabilities assumed or incurred, or preferred shares distributed as of the transfer date to acquire the entity. [FAS141, ¶48]

.162 The cost of an acquired entity and the amounts assigned to the assets acquired and liabilities assumed shall be determined as of the date of acquisition. The statement of

[22] As stated in paragraph .106 of Section G40, the accounting for some acquired intangible assets after initial recognition is prescribed by [guidance] other than [that in] Section G40. [FAS141, ¶47, fn20]

income of an acquiring entity for the period in which a business combination occurs shall include the income of the acquired entity after the date of acquisition by including the revenue and expenses of the acquired entity based on the cost to the acquiring entity. [FAS141, ¶49] Any dividend declared out of [an acquired enterprise's retained earnings created prior to acquisition shall not be included in income of the acquiring enterprise]. [ARB43, ch1A, ¶3] The retained earnings or deficit of [an acquired enterprise] at the date of acquisition shall not be included in consolidated retained earnings. [ARB51, ¶9] [Refer to paragraph .1001 for an EITF Issue that provides interpretive guidance on this paragraph.]

Documentation at Date of Acquisition

.163 The provisions of Section G40 require that the assets acquired and liabilities assumed in a business combination that meet certain criteria, including goodwill, be assigned to a **reporting unit** as of the date of acquisition. For use in making those assignments, the basis for and method of determining the purchase price of an acquired entity and other related factors (such as the underlying reasons for the acquisition and management's expectations related to dilution, synergies, and other financial measurements) shall be documented at the date of acquisition. [FAS141, ¶50]

Disclosures in Financial Statements

.164 The notes to the financial statements of a combined entity shall disclose the following information in the period in which a material business combination is completed:

a. The name and a brief description of the acquired entity and the percentage of voting equity interests acquired
b. The primary reasons for the acquisition, including a description of the factors that contributed to a purchase price that results in recognition of goodwill
c. The period for which the results of operations of the acquired entity are included in the income statement of the combined entity
d. The cost of the acquired entity and, if applicable, the number of shares of equity interests (such as common shares, preferred shares, or partnership interests) issued or issuable, the value assigned to those interests, and the basis for determining that value
e. A condensed balance sheet disclosing the amount assigned to each major asset and liability caption of the acquired entity at the acquisition date
f. Contingent payments, options, or commitments specified in the acquisition agreement and the accounting treatment that will be followed should any such contingency occur

g. The amount of purchased research and development assets acquired and written off in the period (refer to paragraph .145) and the line item in the income statement in which the amounts written off are aggregated
h. For any purchase price allocation that has not been finalized, that fact and the reasons therefor. In subsequent periods, the nature and amount of any material adjustments made to the initial allocation of the purchase price shall be disclosed.

[FAS141, ¶51]

.165 The notes to the financial statements also shall disclose the following information in the period in which a material business combination is completed if the amounts assigned to goodwill or to other intangible assets acquired are significant in relation to the total cost of the acquired entity:

a. For intangible assets subject to amortization:[23]
   (1) The total amount assigned and the amount assigned to any major **intangible asset class**
   (2) The amount of any significant **residual value,** in total and by major intangible asset class
   (3) The weighted-average amortization period, in total and by major intangible asset class
b. For intangible assets *not* subject to amortization,[24] the total amount assigned and the amount assigned to any major intangible asset class
c. For goodwill:
   (1) The total amount of goodwill and the amount that is expected to be deductible for tax purposes
   (2) The amount of goodwill by reportable segment (if the combined entity is required to disclose segment information in accordance with Section S30, "Segment Disclosures and Related Information"), unless not practicable.[25]

An example of the disclosure requirements in this paragraph and paragraph .164 is provided in Illustration 1 in paragraph .173. [FAS141, ¶52]

---

[23]Section G40 provides guidance for determining whether an intangible asset is subject to amortization. [FAS141, ¶52, fn21]

[24]Refer to footnote 23. [FAS141, ¶52, fn22]

[25]For example, it would not be practicable to disclose this information if the assignment of goodwill to reporting units (as required by Section G40) has not been completed as of the date the financial statements are issued. [FAS141, ¶52, fn23]

.166 The notes to the financial statements shall disclose the following information if a series of individually immaterial business combinations completed during the period are material in the aggregate:

a. The number of entities acquired and a brief description of those entities
b. The aggregate cost of the acquired entities, the number of equity interests (such as common shares, preferred shares, or partnership interests) issued or issuable, and the value assigned to those interests
c. The aggregate amount of any contingent payments, options, or commitments and the accounting treatment that will be followed should any such contingency occur (if potentially significant in relation to the aggregate cost of the acquired entities)
d. The information described in paragraph .165 if the aggregate amount assigned to goodwill or to other intangible assets acquired is significant in relation to the aggregate cost of the acquired entities.

An example of those disclosure requirements is provided in Illustration 2 in paragraph .174. [FAS141, ¶53]

.167 If the combined entity is a **public business enterprise,** the notes to the financial statements shall include the following supplemental information on a pro forma basis for the period in which a material business combination occurs (or for the period in which a series of individually immaterial business combinations occur that are material in the aggregate):

a. Results of operations for the current period as though the business combination or combinations had been completed at the beginning of the period, unless the acquisition was at or near the beginning of the period
b. Results of operations for the comparable prior period as though the business combination or combinations had been completed at the beginning of that period if comparative financial statements are presented. [FAS141, ¶54]

.168 At a minimum, the supplemental pro forma information shall display revenue, income before extraordinary items and the cumulative effect of accounting changes, net income, and earnings per share. In determining the pro forma amounts, income taxes, interest expense, preferred share dividends, and depreciation and amortization of assets shall be adjusted to the accounting base recognized for each in recording the combination. Pro forma information related to results of operations of periods prior to the combination shall be limited to the results of operations for the immediately preceding period. Disclosure also shall be made of the nature and amount of any material, nonrecurring items included in the reported pro forma results of operations. [FAS141, ¶55]

.169 In the period in which an extraordinary gain is recognized related to a business combination (paragraphs .158 and .159), the notes to the financial statements shall disclose the information required by paragraph .102 of Section I17. [FAS141, ¶56]

.170 The notes to the financial statements also shall disclose the information required by paragraphs .164 and .165 if a material business combination is completed after the balance sheet date but before the financial statements are issued (unless not practicable). [FAS141, ¶57]

Disclosures in Interim Financial Information

.171 The summarized interim financial information of a public business enterprise shall disclose the following information if a material business combination is completed during the current year up to the date of the most recent interim statement of financial position presented:

a. The information described in paragraph .164(a)–(d).
b. Supplemental pro forma information that discloses the results of operations for the current interim period and the current year up to the date of the most recent interim statement of financial position presented (and for the corresponding periods in the preceding year) as though the business combination had been completed as of the beginning of the period being reported on. That pro forma information shall display, at a minimum, revenue, income before extraordinary items and the cumulative effect of accounting changes (including those on an interim basis), net income, and earnings per share.
c. The nature and amount of any material, nonrecurring items included in the reported pro forma results of operations. [FAS141, ¶58]

Illustrations of Disclosure Requirements

.172 Paragraphs .173 and .174 provide illustrations of some of the disclosure requirements of this section. The information is presented for illustrative purposes only and, therefore, may not be representative of actual transactions. [FAS141, ¶C1]

Illustration 1—Disclosure of a Material Business Combination in the Year of Acquisition

.173 Exhibit 173A illustrates the disclosures required if a material business combination is completed during the reporting period (paragraphs .164 and .165). [FAS141, ¶C2]

Exhibit 173A

Required Disclosures for a Material Business Combination in the Year of Acquisition

Footnote C: Acquisitions (dollars in thousands)

On June 30, 20X2, Alpha acquired 100 percent of the outstanding common shares of Beta. The results of Beta's operations have been included in the consolidated financial statements since that date. Beta is a provider of data networking products and services in Canada and Mexico. As a result of the acquisition, Alpha is expected to be the leading provider of data networking products and services in those markets. It also expects to reduce costs through economies of scale.

The aggregate purchase price was $9,400, including $7,000 of cash and common stock valued at $2,400. The value of the 100,000 common shares issued was determined based on the average market price of Alpha's common shares over the 2-day period before and after the terms of the acquisition were agreed to and announced.

The following table summarizes the estimated fair values of the assets acquired and liabilities assumed at the date of acquisition. Alpha is in the process of obtaining third-party valuations of certain intangible assets; thus, the allocation of the purchase price is subject to refinement.

At June 30, 20X2
($000s)

Current assets	$ 2,400
Property, plant, and equipment	1,500
Intangible assets	4,900
Goodwill	2,200
Total assets acquired	11,000
Current liabilities	(500)
Long-term debt	(1,100)
Total liabilities assumed	(1,600)
Net assets acquired	$ 9,400

Exhibit 173A (continued)

Of the $4,900 of acquired intangible assets, $1,400 was assigned to registered trademarks that are not subject to amortization and $1,000 was assigned to research and development assets that were written off at the date of acquisition in accordance with paragraph .145. Those write-offs are included in general and administrative expenses. The remaining $2,500 of acquired intangible assets have a weighted-average useful life of approximately 4 years. The intangible assets that make up that amount include computer software of $1,500 (3-year weighted-average useful life), patents of $800 (7-year weighted-average useful life), and other assets of $200 (5-year weighted-average useful life).

The $2,200 of goodwill was assigned to the technology and communications segments in the amounts of $1,300 and $900, respectively. Of that total amount, $250 is expected to be deductible for tax purposes.

[FAS141, ¶C2]

Illustration 2—Disclosures in Year of Acquisition of Several Individually Immaterial Business Combinations That Are Material in the Aggregate

.174 Exhibit 174A illustrates the disclosures required if a series of individually immaterial business combinations are completed during a period that are material in the aggregate (paragraph .166). The illustration assumes that Alpha completed four business combinations, one during each quarter of its fiscal year ending December 31, 20X3. [FAS141, ¶C3]

Exhibit 174A

Required Disclosures if a Series of Immaterial Business Combinations That are Material in the Aggregate are Completed During a Period

Footnote C: Acquisitions (dollars in thousands)

In 20X3, Alpha acquired the following 4 entities for a total cost of $1,000, which was paid primarily in cash:

- Omega Consulting, based in Zurich, Switzerland, a leading provider of telecommunications consulting services

Exhibit 174A (continued)

- Nittany Systems, based in Toronto, Canada, a producer of digital networking technology
- Sherman Communications, Inc., based in Portland, Oregon, a start-up data networking company
- Blue and White Networks, Inc., based in Atlanta, Georgia, a designer and manufacturer of wireless communications networks.

Goodwill recognized in those transactions amounted to $300, and that amount is expected to be fully deductible for tax purposes. Goodwill was assigned to the communication and technology segments in the amounts of $120 and $180, respectively.

[FAS141, ¶C3]

Implementation Guidance

.175 Paragraphs .176 through .200 provide guidance to assist entities in the application of certain provisions of this section and are therefore an integral part of the standards provided in this section. Paragraphs .176 through .200 discuss generalized situations. The facts and circumstances of each business combination should be considered carefully in applying this section. [FAS141, ¶A1]

.176 This section requires that intangible assets that meet the criteria in paragraph .138 be recognized as assets apart from goodwill. Paragraphs .182 through .185 provide examples that illustrate how the guidance in paragraph .138 should be applied to certain generalized situations. Paragraph .186 includes a non-inclusive list of intangible assets that meet the criteria for recognition apart from goodwill.[26] Paragraphs .187 through .200 describe some of the intangible assets included on that list and explain how the criteria in paragraph .138 generally apply to them. [FAS141, ¶A4]

[26]As described in paragraph .190, some of the intangible assets identified on that list as meeting the separability criterion should not be recognized apart from goodwill if terms of confidentiality or other agreements prohibit the acquiring entity from selling, leasing, or otherwise exchanging the asset. [FAS141, ¶A4, fn27]

Application of Paragraph .113—Accounting for the Acquisition of Some or All of the Noncontrolling Equity Interests in a Subsidiary

.177 Paragraph .113 continues the practice of accounting for the acquisition of noncontrolling equity interests of a subsidiary (commonly referred to as a minority interest) using the purchase method. [Paragraphs .178 and .179 contain additional guidance for the application of paragraph .113.] [FAS141, ¶A5]

.178 Examples of the types of transactions that constitute the acquisition of a minority interest include the following: (a) a parent exchanges its common stock or assets or debt for common stock held by minority stockholders of its subsidiary, (b) the subsidiary buys as treasury stock the common stock held by minority stockholders, or (c) another subsidiary of the parent exchanges its common stock or assets or debt for common stock held by the minority stockholders of an affiliated subsidiary. [FAS141, ¶A6]

.179 Another type of transaction that constitutes the acquisition of a minority interest is a transaction in which a subsidiary exchanges its common stock for the outstanding voting common stock of its parent (usually referred to as a downstream merger). Those transactions shall be accounted for as if the parent had exchanged its common stock for common stock held by minority stockholders of its subsidiary. Whether a parent acquires the minority or a subsidiary acquires its parent, the result is a single stockholder group, including the former minority stockholders, owning the consolidated net assets. The same would be true if a new corporation exchanged its common stock for the common stock of the parent and the common stock of the subsidiary held by minority stockholders. [FAS141, ¶A7]

Application of Paragraph .123—Costs of the Business Combination

.180 Paragraph .123 states that the cost of an acquired entity includes the direct costs of the business combination. Those direct costs include "out-of-pocket" or incremental costs directly related to a business combination such as a finder's fee and fees paid to outside consultants for accounting, legal, or engineering investigations or for appraisals. Internal costs associated with a business combination (whether one-time costs or recurring in nature) shall be expensed as incurred. In addition, costs related to unsuccessful negotiations also shall be expensed as incurred. [FAS141, ¶A8]

.181 Paragraph .123 also states that costs of registering and issuing equity securities shall be recognized as a reduction of the otherwise determinable fair value of the securities. A publicly held company issuing *unregistered* equity securities in a business combination with an agreement for subsequent registration shall record those securities at the fair value of its registered securities less an estimate of the related registration costs. A liability shall be recognized at the date of acquisition in the amount of the present value of the estimated costs of registration. Any difference between the actual costs of registration and the recorded liability (including imputed interest) shall be recognized as an adjustment to the carrying amount of goodwill. If the securities issued in the business combination are to be included in the registration of a planned future offering of other securities (piggyback registration), only the incremental costs of registering the equity securities issued shall be recognized as a liability at the acquisition date. [FAS141, ¶A9]

Application of Paragraph .138—Recognition of Intangible Assets Apart from Goodwill

.182 Paragraph .138 states that an acquired intangible asset shall be recognized as an asset apart from goodwill if it arises from contractual or other legal rights (the contractual-legal criterion). Intangible assets that meet that criterion shall be recognized apart from goodwill even if the asset is not transferable or separable from the acquired entity or from other rights and obligations. For example:

a. An acquired entity leases a manufacturing facility under an operating lease that has terms that are favorable relative to market prices.[27] The lease terms explicitly prohibit transfer of the lease (through either sale or sublease). The value arising from that operating lease contract is an intangible asset that meets the contractual-legal criterion for recognition apart from goodwill, even though the lease contract cannot be sold or otherwise transferred.
b. An acquired entity owns and operates a nuclear power plant. The license to operate that power plant is an intangible asset that meets the contractual-legal criterion for recognition apart from goodwill, even if it cannot be sold or transferred apart from the acquired power plant. This section does not preclude an acquiring entity from recognizing the fair value of the operating license and the fair value of the power plant as a single asset for financial reporting purposes if the useful lives of those assets are similar.
c. An acquired entity owns a technology patent. It has licensed that patent to others for their exclusive use outside the United States in exchange for which the entity receives a specified percentage of future non-U.S. revenue. Both the technology patent and the related license agreement meet the contractual-legal criterion for recognition apart from goodwill even if it would not be practical to sell or exchange the patent and the related license agreement apart from one another.

[FAS141, ¶A10]

[27] In some cases, the terms of an operating lease might be unfavorable relative to market prices. Paragraph .136(k) of this section states that a portion of the purchase price be assigned to such as unfavorable leases. [FAS141, ¶A10, fn28]

.183 If an acquired intangible asset does *not* arise from contractual or other legal rights, paragraph .138 requires that it be recognized as an asset apart from goodwill only if it is separable—that is, it is capable of being separated or divided from the acquired entity and sold, transferred, licensed, rented, or exchanged (the separability criterion). Exchange transactions provide evidence that an intangible asset is separable from the acquired entity and might provide information that can be used to estimate its fair value. An acquired intangible asset meets the separability criterion if there is evidence of exchange transactions for that type of asset or an asset of a similar type (even if those exchange transactions are infrequent and regardless of whether the acquiring entity is involved in them). For example, customer and subscriber lists are frequently leased and thus meet the separability criterion. Even if an entity believes its customer lists have different characteristics than other customer lists, the fact that customer lists are frequently leased generally means that the acquired entity's customer list meets the separability criterion. Title plant assets also are bought and sold in exchange transactions (either in whole or in part) or are leased, although less frequently than customer lists. Title plant assets also would meet the separability criterion. [FAS141, ¶A11]

.184 An intangible asset that meets the separability criterion shall be recognized apart from goodwill even if the acquiring entity does not intend to sell, lease, or otherwise exchange that asset. The separability criterion is met because the asset is capable of being separated from the acquired entity and sold, transferred, licensed, rented, or otherwise exchanged for something else of value. For example, because an acquired customer list is generally capable of being rented, it meets the separability criterion regardless of whether the acquiring entity intends to rent it. [FAS141, ¶A12]

.185 As stated in paragraph .138, an intangible asset that is not separable from the entity individually still meets the separability criterion if it is separable from the acquired entity in combination with a related contract, asset, or liability. For example:

a. Deposit liabilities and related depositor relationship intangible assets are exchanged in observable exchange transactions. Therefore, the depositor relationship intangible asset shall be recognized apart from goodwill.
b. An acquired entity owns a registered trademark, a related secret formula, and unpatented technical expertise used to manufacture the trademarked product. To transfer ownership of a trademark in the United States, the owner is also required to transfer everything else necessary for the new owner to produce a product or service indistinguishable from that produced by the former owner. Because the unpatented technical expertise must be separated from the entity and sold if the related trademark is sold, it meets the separability criterion.

[FAS141, ¶A13]

Examples of Intangible Assets That Meet the Criteria for Recognition Apart from Goodwill

.186 The following are examples of intangible assets that meet the criteria for recognition as an asset apart from goodwill. The following illustrative list is not intended to be all-inclusive, thus, an acquired intangible asset might meet the recognition criteria of this section but not be included on that list. Assets designated by the symbol (†) are those that would be recognized apart from goodwill because they meet the contractual-legal criterion.[28] Assets designated by the symbol (▲) do not arise from contractual or other legal rights, but shall nonetheless be recognized apart from goodwill because they meet the separability criterion. The determination of whether a specific acquired intangible asset meets the criteria in this section for recognition apart from goodwill shall be based on the facts and circumstances of each individual business combination.[29]

a. Marketing-related intangible assets
   (1) Trademarks, tradenames†
   (2) Service marks, collective marks, certification marks†
   (3) Trade dress (unique color, shape, or package design)†
   (4) Newspaper mastheads†
   (5) Internet domain names†
   (6) Noncompetition agreements†
b. Customer-related intangible assets
   (1) Customer lists▲
   (2) Order or production backlog†
   (3) Customer contracts and related **customer relationships**†
   (4) Noncontractual customer relationships▲
c. Artistic-related intangible assets
   (1) Plays, operas, ballets†
   (2) Books, magazines, newspapers, other literary works†
   (3) Musical works such as compositions, song lyrics, advertising jingles†

[28] The intangible assets designated by the symbol (†) also might meet the separability criterion. However, separability is not a necessary condition for an asset to meet the contractual-legal criterion. [FAS141, ¶A14, fn29]

[29] A customer base [is viewed] as a group of customers that are not known or identifiable to the entity (such as customers of a fast-food franchise). A customer base does not meet the criteria for recognition apart from goodwill. Other intangible assets [that] would not generally meet the recognition criteria in this section include customer service capability, presence in geographic markets or locations, nonunion status or strong labor relations, ongoing training or recruiting programs, outstanding credit ratings and access to capital markets, and favorable government relations. [FAS141, ¶B165]

(4) Pictures, photographs†

(5) Video and audiovisual material, including motion pictures, music videos, television programs†

d. Contract-based intangible assets

(1) Licensing, royalty, standstill agreements†

(2) Advertising, construction, management, service or supply contracts†

(3) Lease agreements†

(4) Construction permits†

(5) Franchise agreements†

(6) Operating and broadcast rights†

(7) Use rights such as drilling, water, air, mineral, timber cutting, and route authorities†

(8) Servicing contracts such as mortgage servicing contracts†

(9) Employment contracts†

e. Technology-based intangible assets

(1) Patented technology†

(2) Computer software and mask works†

(3) Unpatented technology▲

(4) Databases, including title plants▲

(5) Trade secrets, such as secret formulas, processes, recipes.†

[FAS141, ¶A14]

Marketing-Related Intangible Assets

.187 Marketing-related intangible assets are those assets that are primarily used in the marketing or promotion of products or services. Trademarks are words, names, symbols, or other devices used in trade to indicate the source of the product and to distinguish it from the products of others. A service mark identifies and distinguishes the source of a service rather than a product. Collective marks are used to identify the goods or services of members of a group, and certification marks are used to certify the geographic origin or other characteristics of a good or service. In the United States and other countries, trademarks, service marks, collective marks, and certification marks may be protected legally through registration with governmental agencies, continuous use in commerce, or by other means. If registered or otherwise provided legal protection, a trademark or other mark is an intangible asset that meets the contractual-legal criterion for recognition apart from goodwill. Otherwise, a trademark or other mark shall be recognized apart from goodwill only if the separability criterion is met, which would normally be the case. [FAS141, ¶A15]

.188 The terms *brand* and *brand name* often are used as synonyms for trademarks and tradenames. However, the former are general marketing terms that are typically used to refer to a group of complementary assets such as the trademark (or service mark) and its related tradename, formulas, recipes, and technological expertise (which may or may not be patented). This section does not preclude an entity from recognizing, as a single asset apart from goodwill, a group of complementary intangible assets commonly referred to as a brand if the assets that make up that group have similar useful lives. [FAS141, ¶A16]

.189 An Internet domain name is a unique alphanumeric name that is used to identify a particular numeric Internet address. Registration of a domain name associates the name with a designated computer on the Internet for the period the registration is in effect. Those registrations are renewable. Registered domain names shall be recognized as an intangible asset apart from goodwill because they meet the contractual-legal criterion. [FAS141, ¶A17]

Customer-related intangible assets

Customer lists

.190 A customer list consists of information about customers such as their name and contact information. A customer list also may be in the form of a database that includes other information about the customers such as their order history and demographic information. A customer list does not generally arise from contractual or other legal rights. However, customer lists are valuable and are frequently leased or exchanged. Therefore, an acquired customer list would meet the separability criterion for recognition apart from goodwill. An acquired customer list would *not* meet that criterion, however, if the terms of confidentiality or other agreements prohibit an entity from selling, leasing, or otherwise exchanging information about its customers. [FAS141, ¶A18]

Order or production backlog

.191 If an acquired order or production backlog arises from contracts such as purchase or sales orders, it meets the contractual-legal criterion for recognition apart from goodwill (even if the purchase or sales orders were cancelable). [FAS141, ¶A19]

Customer contracts and related customer relationships

.192 If an entity establishes relationships with its customers through contracts, those customer relationships would arise from contractual rights. Therefore, customer contracts and the related customer relationships are intangible assets that meet the contractual-legal criterion. This section requires that those intangible assets be recognized as assets apart from goodwill even if confidentiality or other contractual terms prohibit the sale or transfer of the contract separately from the acquired entity. [FAS141, ¶A20]

Noncontractual customer relationships

.193 If a customer relationship does not arise from a contract, this section requires that the relationship be recognized as an intangible asset apart from goodwill if it meets the separability criterion. Exchange transactions for the same asset or a similar type of asset provide evidence of separability of a noncontractual customer relationship and might also provide information about exchange prices that should be considered when estimating its fair value. For example, relationships with depositors are frequently exchanged with the related deposits and, thus, meet the criteria for recognition as an intangible asset apart from goodwill. [FAS141, ¶A21]

Artistic-related intangible assets

.194 Artistic-related intangible assets meet the criteria for recognition apart from goodwill if the assets arise from contractual rights or legal rights such as those provided by copyright. In the United States for example, copyrights are granted by the government for the life of the creator plus 50 years. Copyrights can be transferred either in whole through assignments or in part through licensing agreements. In determining the fair value of an intangible asset protected by copyright, consideration shall be given to the existence of any assignments or licenses of the acquired copyrights. This section does not preclude an acquiring entity from recognizing a copyright intangible asset and any related assignments or license agreements as a single intangible asset for financial reporting purposes if their useful lives are similar. [FAS141, ¶A22]

Contract-based intangible assets

.195 Contract-based intangible assets represent the value of rights that arise from contractual arrangements. Customer contracts (refer to paragraph .192) are one particular type of contract-based intangible asset. Contracts to service financial assets are another. While servicing is inherent in all financial assets, it becomes a distinct asset or liability only when (a) contractually separated from the underlying financial assets by sale or securitization of the assets with servicing retained or (b) through the separate purchase and assumption of the servicing. If mortgage loans, credit card receivables, or other financial assets are acquired in a business combination with servicing retained, this section does not require recognition of the inherent servicing rights as an intangible asset because the fair value of the servicing intangible asset is considered in the measurement of the fair value of the acquired financial asset. However, a contract representing an acquired **servicing asset** is an intangible asset that shall be recognized apart from goodwill. [FAS141, ¶A23]

.196 If the terms of a contract give rise to a liability or commitment (which might be the case if the terms of an operating lease or customer contract are unfavorable relative to market prices), that liability or commitment shall be recognized as required by paragraph .136(k) of this section. [FAS141, ¶A24]

Technology-based intangible assets

.197 Technology-based intangible assets relate to innovations or technological advances. As stated in paragraphs .198 through .200, the future economic benefits of those assets are often protected through contractual or other legal rights. Thus, many technology-based intangible assets meet the contractual-legal criterion for recognition apart from goodwill. [FAS141, ¶A25]

Computer software and mask works

.198 If computer software and program formats are protected legally such as by patent or copyright, they meet the contractual-legal criterion for recognition apart from goodwill. Mask works are software permanently stored on a read-only memory chip as a series of stencils or integrated circuitry. Mask works may be provided legal protection; for example, in the United States mask works qualify for protection under the Semiconductor Chip Protection Act of 1984. Acquired mask works protected under the provisions of that Act or other similar laws or regulations also meet the contractual-legal criterion for recognition apart from goodwill. [FAS141, ¶A26]

Databases, including title plants

.199 Databases are collections of information, often stored in electronic form (such as on computer disks or files). An acquired database that includes original works of authorship is entitled to copyright protection and, if so protected, meets the contractual-legal criterion for recognition apart from goodwill. However, a database often includes information created as a consequence of an entity's normal operations, such as a customer list or specialized information such as a title plant, scientific data, and credit information. Databases that are not protected by copyright can be (and often are) exchanged in their entirety or in part. Alternatively, they can be (and often are) licensed or leased to others. Thus, even if the future economic benefit of a database does not arise from legal rights, it meets the separability criterion for recognition as an asset apart from goodwill. [FAS141, ¶A27]

Trade secrets, such as secret formulas, processes, recipes

.200 A trade secret is "information, including a formula, pattern, compilation, program, device, method, technique, or process, that (1) derives independent economic value, actual or potential, from not being generally known . . . and (2) is the subject of efforts that are reasonable under the circumstances to maintain its secrecy."[30] If the future economic benefit of an acquired trade secret is protected legally, such as by the Uniform Trade Secrets Act or other laws and regulations, that asset meets the contractual-legal criterion for recognition as an asset apart from goodwill. Otherwise, a trade secret would be recognized as an asset apart from goodwill only if the separability criterion was met, which is likely to be the case. [FAS141, ¶A28]

Transactions between Entities under Common Control

.201 Paragraph .110 of this section states that the term *business combination* excludes transfers of net assets or exchanges of shares between entities under common control. The following are examples of those types of transactions:

a. An entity charters a newly formed entity and then transfers some or all of its net assets to that newly chartered entity.
b. A parent company transfers the net assets of a wholly owned subsidiary into the parent company and liquidates the subsidiary. That transaction is a change in legal organization but not a change in the reporting entity.
c. A parent company transfers its interest in several partially owned subsidiaries to a new wholly owned subsidiary. That also is a change in legal organization but not in the reporting entity.
d. A parent company exchanges its ownership interests or the net assets of a wholly owned subsidiary for additional shares issued by the parent's partially owned subsidiary, thereby increasing the parent's percentage of ownership in the partially owned subsidiary but leaving all of the existing minority interest outstanding.

[FAS141, ¶D11]

.202 When accounting for a transfer of assets or exchange of shares between entities under common control, the entity that receives the net assets or the equity interests shall initially recognize the assets and liabilities transferred at their carrying amounts in the accounts of the transferring entity at the date of transfer. [FAS141, ¶D12]

.203 The purchase method of accounting shall be applied if the effect of the transfer or exchange described in paragraph .201 is the acquisition of all or a part of the noncontrolling equity interests in a subsidiary (refer to paragraph .113). [FAS141, ¶D13]

---

[30] Melvin Simensky and Lanning Bryer, *The New Role of Intellectual Property in Commercial Transactions* (New York: John Wiley & Sons, 1998), page 293. [FAS141, ¶A28, fn30]

Procedural Guidance

.204 Some transfers of net assets or exchanges of shares between entities under common control result in a change in the reporting entity. In practice, the method that many entities have used to account for those transactions is similar to the pooling method. Paragraphs .205 through .208 provide procedural guidance that should be considered when preparing financial statements and related disclosures for the entity that receives the net assets. [FAS141, ¶D14]

.205 In some instances, the entity that receives the net assets or equity interests (the receiving entity) and the entity that transferred the net assets or equity interests (the transferring entity) may account for similar assets and liabilities using different accounting methods. In such circumstances, the carrying values of the assets and liabilities transferred may be adjusted to the basis of accounting used by the receiving entity if the change would otherwise have been appropriate. Any such change in accounting method should be applied retroactively, and financial statements presented for prior periods should be restated. [FAS141, ¶D15]

.206 The financial statements of the receiving entity should report results of operations for the period in which the transfer occurs as though the transfer of net assets or exchange of equity interests had occurred at the beginning of the period. Results of operations for that period will thus comprise those of the previously separate entities combined from the beginning of the period to the date the transfer is completed and those of the combined operations from that date to the end of the period. By eliminating the effects of intercompany transactions in determining the results of operations for the period before the combination, those results will be on substantially the same basis as the results of operations for the period after the date of combination. The effects of intercompany transactions on current assets, current liabilities, revenue, and cost of sales for periods presented and on retained earnings at the beginning of the periods presented should be eliminated to the extent possible. The nature of and effects on earnings per share of nonrecurring intercompany transactions involving long-term assets and liabilities need not be eliminated but should be disclosed. [FAS141, ¶D16]

.207 Similarly, the receiving entity should present the statement of financial position and other financial information as of the beginning of the period as though the assets and liabilities had been transferred at that date. Financial statements and financial information presented for prior years should also be restated to furnish comparative information. All restated financial statements and financial summaries should indicate clearly that financial data of previously separate entities are combined. [FAS141, ¶D17]

.208 Notes to financial statements of the receiving entity should disclose the following for the period in which the transfer of assets and liabilities or exchange of equity interests occurred:

a. The name and brief description of the entity included in the reporting entity as a result of the net asset transfer or exchange of equity interests
b. The method of accounting for the transfer of net assets or exchange of equity interests.

[FAS141, ¶D18]

Transitional Guidance

Disposition of Assets after a Combination Accounted for Using the Pooling Method

.209 Following a business combination accounted for by the pooling method, the combined entity might dispose of assets of the previously separate entities. Unless those disposals are part of customary business activities of the combined entity, any gain or loss recognized resulting from that disposition might require recognition as an extraordinary item. Recognition as an extraordinary item is warranted because the pooling method of accounting would have been inappropriate if the combined entity had made a commitment or had planned to dispose of a significant part of the assets of one of the combining entities. [FAS141, ¶D9]

.210 The combined entity should recognize the gain or loss resulting from the disposal of a significant part of the assets or a separable segment of the previously separate entities, less applicable income tax effect, as an extraordinary item if (a) the gain or loss is material in relation to the net income of the combined entity and (b) the disposition is within two years after the combination is consummated. [FAS141, ¶D10] [illegible] and [illegible] the [illegible] [illegible] [illegible] or exchange [illegible]

[illegible] portion of the [illegible] [illegible]

[illegible]

Transitional Guidance

[illegible] Accounting for Derivatives [illegible]

[illegible]

[illegible]

Glossary

.401 **Allocation period.** The period that is required to identify and measure the fair value of the assets acquired and the liabilities assumed in a business combination. The allocation period ends when the acquiring entity is no longer waiting for information that it has arranged to obtain and that is known to be available or obtainable. Thus, the existence of a preacquisition contingency for which an asset, a liability, or an impairment of an asset cannot be estimated does not, of itself, extend the allocation period. Although the time required will vary with circumstances, the allocation period should usually not exceed one year from the consummation of a business combination. [FAS141, ¶F1]

.402 **Customer relationship.** For purposes of this section, a customer relationship exists between an entity and its customer if (a) the entity has information about the customer and has regular contact with the customer and (b) the customer has the ability to make direct contact with the entity. Relationships may arise from contracts (such as supplier contracts and service contracts). However, customer relationships may arise through means other than contracts, such as through regular contact by sales or service representatives. [FAS141, ¶F1]

.403 **Fair value.** The amount at which an asset (or liability) could be bought (or incurred) or sold (or settled) in a current transaction between willing parties, that is, other than in a forced or liquidation sale. [FAS141, ¶F1]

.404 **Financial asset.** Cash, evidence of an ownership interest in an entity, or a contract that conveys to a second entity a contractual right (a) to receive cash or another financial instrument from a first entity or (b) to exchange other financial instruments on potentially favorable terms with the first entity (Section F25, "Financial Instruments: Disclosures," paragraph .106(b)). [FAS141, ¶F1]

.405 **Goodwill.** The excess of the cost of an acquired entity over the net of the amounts assigned to assets acquired and liabilities assumed. The amount recognized as goodwill includes acquired intangible assets that do not meet the criteria in paragraph .138 for recognition as assets apart from goodwill. [FAS141, ¶F1]

.406 **Intangible assets.** Assets (not including financial assets) that lack physical substance. [FAS141, ¶F1]

.407 **Intangible asset class.** A group of intangible assets that are similar, either by their nature or by their use in the operations of an entity. [FAS141, ¶F1]

.408 **Mutual enterprise.** An entity other than an investor-owned entity that provides dividends, lower costs, or other economic benefits directly and proportionately to its owners, members, or participants. Mutual insurance companies, credit unions, and farm and rural electric cooperatives are examples of mutual enterprises (FASB Concepts Statement 4, *Objectives of Financial Reporting by Nonbusiness Organizations,* paragraph 7). [FAS141, ¶F1]

.409 **Not-for-profit organization.** An entity that possesses the following characteristics that distinguish it from a business enterprise: (a) contributions of significant amounts of resources from resource providers who do not expect commensurate or proportionate pecuniary return, (b) operating purposes other than to provide goods or services at a profit, and (c) absence of ownership interests like those of business enterprises. Not-for-profit organizations have those characteristics in varying degrees (Concepts Statement 4, paragraph 6). Entities that clearly fall outside this definition include all investor-owned entities and mutual enterprises. [FAS141, ¶F1]

.410 **Pooling-of-interests method.** A method of accounting for business combinations that was required to be used in certain circumstances [under prior guidance]. Under the pooling-of-interests method, the carrying amount of assets and liabilities recognized in the statements of financial position of each combining entity are carried forward to the statement of financial position of the combined entity. No other assets or liabilities are recognized as a result of the combination, and thus the excess of the purchase price over the book value of the net assets acquired (the purchase premium) is not recognized. The income statement of the combined entity for the year of the combination is presented as if the entities had been combined for the full year; all comparative financial statements are presented as if the entities had previously been combined. [FAS141, ¶F1]

.411 **Preacquisition contingency.** A contingency of an entity that is acquired in a business combination that is in existence before the consummation of the combination. A preacquisition contingency can be a contingent asset, a contingent liability, or a contingent impairment of an asset. [FAS141, ¶F1] [Refer to paragraph .1001 for an EITF Issue that provides interpretive guidance on this paragraph.]

.412 **Public business enterprise.** An enterprise that has issued debt or equity securities that are traded in a public market (a domestic or foreign stock exchange or an over-the-counter market, including local or regional markets), that is required to file financial statements with the Securities and Exchange Commission, or that provides financial statements for the purpose of issuing any class of securities in a public market (Section S30, paragraph .108). [FAS141, ¶F1]

.413 **Reporting unit.** The level of reporting at which goodwill is tested for impairment. A reporting unit is an operating segment or one level below an operating segment (as that term is defined in paragraph .109 of Section S30). [FAS141, ¶F1]

.414 **Residual value.** The estimated fair value of an intangible asset at the end of its useful life to the entity, less any disposal costs. [FAS141, ¶F1]

.415 **Servicing asset.** A contract to service financial assets under which the estimated future revenues from contractually specified servicing fees, late charges, and other ancillary revenues are expected to more than adequately compensate the servicer for performing the servicing. A servicing contract is either (a) undertaken in conjunction with selling or securitizing the financial assets being serviced or (b) purchased or assumed separately (Section F39, "Financial Instruments: Transfers," paragraph .423). [FAS141, ¶F1]

Supplemental Guidance

Costs of Closing Duplicate Facilities of an Acquirer

.501 *Question*—Are the costs incurred to close duplicate facilities of an acquiring enterprise recognized as part of the cost of acquisition in a business combination? [FTB85-5, ¶1]

.502 *Response*—No. Only the direct costs of an acquisition should be included in the cost of a purchased enterprise in a business combination. Indirect expenses of an acquiring enterprise, including costs incurred when the acquiring enterprise closes some of its facilities because they duplicate facilities acquired in a business combination, should be charged to expense in determining net income. Therefore, the disposition of the acquiring enterprise's assets do not affect the accounting for assets acquired and liabilities assumed of the acquired enterprise, and any gain or loss on disposal or other cost associated with the disposition of an existing asset of the acquiring enterprise should be charged to income. [Refer also to paragraph .123.] [FTB85-5, ¶2] [Refer to paragraph .1001 for an EITF Issue that provides interpretive guidance on this paragraph.]

Stock Transactions between Enterprises under Common Control

.503 *Question*—How should a parent enterprise account for minority interest in an exchange of stock between two of its subsidiaries if one or both of the subsidiaries are partially owned? [FTB85-5, ¶5]

.504 *Response*—The accounting depends on whether the minority shareholders are party to the exchange of shares. If some or all of the shares owned by minority shareholders are exchanged for shares of ownership in another subsidiary of the parent (or a new subsidiary formed by combining two or more subsidiaries of the parent), then the transaction is recognized by the parent enterprise as the acquisition of shares from the minority interest, which according to [FTB85-5, ¶6] paragraph .113 of this section [FAS141, ¶E24(e)] should be accounted for by the purchase method, that is, based on fair value. The original minority interest effectively is purchased, and a new minority interest in a different subsidiary is created. However, if the exchange lacks substance, it is not a purchase event and should be accounted for based on existing carrying amounts. That is, if the minority interest does not change and if in substance the only assets of the combined entity after the exchange are those of the partially owned subsidiary prior to the exchange, a change in ownership has not taken place, and the exchange should be accounted for based on the carrying amounts of the partially owned subsidiary's assets and liabilities. [FTB85-5, ¶6] [Refer to paragraph .1001 for an EITF Issue that provides interpretive guidance on this paragraph.]

.505 If, however, minority shareholders are not party to an exchange of shares between two subsidiaries of the same parent (a partially owned subsidiary issues its shares in exchange for shares of another subsidiary previously owned by the same parent), the minority interest in the issuing subsidiary remains outstanding, and the transaction is an exchange of stock between enterprises under common control. In contrast to the acquisition of a minority interest, this transaction leaves all of the issuing subsidiary's minority interest outstanding, although the minority stockholders' interest in the net assets has changed in each case. [FTB85-5, ¶7] Paragraph .202 [FAS141, ¶E24(f)] of this section indicates that the assets and liabilities transferred in such an exchange of shares should be accounted for at existing carrying amounts. [FTB85-5, ¶7]

.506 Some transactions involve both an effective acquisition of a minority interest and an exchange of stock between enterprises under common control, which usually are accounted for differently. In those cases, the accounting depends on whether the minority shareholders are party to the exchange of shares. The accounting for the above types of transactions depends on the nature of the exchange that takes place, not the apparent similarity of the results of different transactions. [FTB85-5, ¶12]

Supplemental Guidance: Emerging Issues Task Force (EITF) Issues

.1000 [Listed below are EITF Issues that provide supplemental guidance for this section. These Issues are grouped by subject matter and may be either interpretive of or related by topic to the guidance in this section.

Banking and Thrift Institutions

EITF Issue No. 85-8, "Amortization of Thrift Intangibles"

EITF Issue No. 85-41, "Accounting for Savings and Loan Associations under FSLIC Management Consignment Program"

EITF Issue No. 85-42, "Amortization of Goodwill Resulting from Recording Time Savings Deposits at Fair Values"

EITF Issue No. 88-19, "FSLIC-Assisted Acquisitions of Thrifts"

Contingent Consideration

EITF Issue No. 95-8, "Accounting for Contingent Consideration Paid to the Shareholders for an Acquired Enterprise in a Purchase Business Combination"

EITF Issue No. 97-8, "Accounting for Contingent Consideration Issued in a Purchase Business Combination"

EITF Issue No. 97-15, "Accounting for Contingency Arrangements Based on Security Prices in a Purchase Business Combination"

Exchange Transactions

EITF Issue No. 84-39, "Transfers of Monetary and Nonmonetary Assets among Individuals and Entities under Common Control"

EITF Issue No. 90-5, "Exchanges of Ownership Interests between Entities under Common Control"

EITF Issue No. 91-5, "Nonmonetary Exchange of Cost-Method Investments"

EITF Issue No. 98-3, "Determining Whether a Nonmonetary Transaction Involves Receipt of Productive Assets or of a Business"

EITF Issue No. 01-2, "Interpretations of APB Opinion No. 29"

EITF Issue No. 02-5, "Definition of 'Common Control' in Relation to FASB Statement No. 141"

Leveraged Buyouts

EITF Issue No. 85-11, "Use of an Employee Stock Ownership Plan in a Leveraged Buyout"

EITF Issue No. 88-16, "Basis in Leveraged Buyout Transactions"

EITF Issue No. 90-12, "Allocating Basis to Individual Assets and Liabilities for Transactions within the Scope of Issue No. 88-16"

Measurement Date

EITF Issue No. 99-12, "Determination of the Measurement Date for the Market Price of Acquirer Securities Issued in a Purchase Business Combination"
EITF Topic No. D-87, "Determination of the Measurement Date for Consideration Given by the Acquirer in a Business Combination When That Consideration Is Securities Other Than Those Issued by the Acquirer"

Partnerships

EITF Issue No. 85-46, "Partnership's Purchase of Withdrawing Partner's Equity"
EITF Issue No. 87-21, "Change of Accounting Basis in Master Limited Partnership Transactions"

Push-Down Accounting

EITF Issue No. 86-9, "IRC Section 338 and Push-Down Accounting"
EITF Topic No. D-97, "Push-Down Accounting"

Real Estate Investment Trusts

EITF Issue No. 94-2, "Treatment of Minority Interests in Certain Real Estate Investment Trusts"
EITF Issue No. 95-7, "Implementation Issues Related to the Treatment of Minority Interests in Certain Real Estate Investment Trusts"

Recognition of Liabilities

EITF Issue No. 84-35, "Business Combinations: Sale of Duplicate Facilities and Accrual of Liabilities"
EITF Issue No. 95-3, "Recognition of Liabilities in Connection with a Purchase Business Combination"
EITF Issue No. 95-14, "Recognition of Liabilities in Anticipation of a Business Combination"
EITF Issue No. 96-5, "Recognition of Liabilities for Contractual Termination Benefits or Changing Benefit Plan Assumptions in Anticipation of a Business Combination"

Research and Development Activities

EITF Issue No. 86-14, "Purchased Research and Development Projects in a Business Combination"
EITF Issue No. 96-7, "Accounting for Deferred Taxes on In-Process Research and Development Activities Acquired in a Purchase Business Combination"

Taxes

EITF Issue No. 93-7, "Uncertainties Related to Income Taxes in a Purchase Business Combination"

EITF Issue No. 99-15, "Accounting for Decreases in Deferred Tax Asset Valuation Allowances Established in a Purchase Business Combination As a Result of a Change in Tax Regulations"

Other

EITF Issue No. 85-45, "Business Combinations: Settlement of Stock Options and Awards"

EITF Issue No. 87-11, "Allocation of Purchase Price to Assets to Be Sold"

EITF Issue No. 90-6, "Accounting for Certain Events Not Addressed in Issue No. 87-11 Relating to an Acquired Operating Unit to Be Sold"

EITF Issue No. 90-13, "Accounting for Simultaneous Common Control Mergers"

EITF Issue No. 92-9, "Accounting for the Present Value of Future Profits Resulting from the Acquisition of a Life Insurance Company"

EITF Issue No. 97-2, "Application of FASB Statement No. 94 and APB Opinion No. 16 to Physician Practice Management Entities and Certain Other Entities with Contractual Management Arrangements"

EITF Issue No. 98-1, "Valuation of Debt Assumed in a Purchase Business Combination"

EITF Issue No. 98-4, "Accounting by a Joint Venture for Businesses Received at Its Formation"

EITF Issue No. 99-7, "Accounting for an Accelerated Share Repurchase Program"

EITF Issue No. 00-6, "Accounting for Freestanding Derivative Financial Instruments Indexed to, and Potentially Settled in, the Stock of a Consolidated Subsidiary"

EITF Issue No. 00-23, "Issues Related to the Accounting for Stock Compensation under APB Opinion No. 25 and FASB Interpretation No. 44"

EITF Issue No. 01-3, "Accounting in a Purchase Business Combination for Deferred Revenue of an Acquiree"

EITF Topic No. D-54, "Accounting by the Purchaser for a Seller's Guarantee of the Adequacy of Liabilities for Losses and Loss Adjustment Expenses of an Insurance Enterprise Acquired in a Purchase Business Combination"

EITF Topic No. D-84, "Accounting for Subsequent Investments in an Investee After Suspension of Equity Method Loss Recognition When an Investor Increases Its Ownership Interest from Significant Influence to Control through a Market Purchase of Voting Securities"

EITF Topic No. D-100, "Clarification of Paragraph 61(b) of FASB Statement No. 141 and Paragraph 49(b) of FASB Statement No. 142"]

.1001 [Listed below are those EITF Issues that provide interpretive guidance on specific material in this section.

Paragraphs .103 through .106 (FAS 141, ¶4-7)—EITF Issue No. 90-13
Paragraphs .115 through .117 (FAS 141, ¶16-18)—EITF Issue No. 90-13
Paragraph .119 (FAS 141, ¶20)—EITF Issues No. 88-16 and 95-3
Paragraph .120 (FAS 141, ¶21)—EITF Issue No. 88-16
Paragraph .121 (FAS 141, ¶22)—EITF Issues No. 88-16 and 99-12
Paragraphs .122 and .123 (FAS 141, ¶23-24)—EITF Issue No. 88-16
Paragraphs .124 through .126 (FAS 141, ¶25-27)—EITF Issues No. 97-8 and 97-15
Paragraph .127 (FAS 141, ¶28)—EITF Issues No. 95-8 and 97-15
Paragraphs .128 through .130 (FAS 141, ¶29-31)—EITF Issue No. 97-15
Paragraph .133 (FAS 141, ¶34)—EITF Issue No. 95-8
Paragraph .135 (FAS 141, ¶36)—EITF Issues No. 85-41, 87-11, 90-6, 90-12, 95-3, and 98-1
Paragraph .136 (FAS 141, ¶37)—EITF Issues No. 85-41, 88-19, 90-12, 95-3, and 98-1
Paragraph .136(j) (FAS 141, ¶37(j))—EITF Issue No. 85-45
Paragraph .142 (FAS 141, ¶40)—EITF Issues No. 90-6 and 93-7
Paragraph .145 (FIN 4, ¶5)—EITF Issue No. 96-7
Paragraph .150 (FAS 72, ¶5)—EITF Issues No. 85-8, 85-42, and 88-19
Paragraph .162 (FAS 141, ¶49)—EITF Topic No. D-87
Paragraph .411 (FAS 141, ¶F1)—EITF Issue No. 95-3
Paragraph .502 (FTB 85-5, ¶2)—EITF Issue No. 95-3
Paragraph .504 (FTB 85-5, ¶6)—EITF Issue No. 90-5]

(The next page is 5329.)

CAPITAL STOCK: CAPITAL TRANSACTIONS SECTION C08

Sources: ARB 43, Chapter 1A; APB Opinion 9; APB Opinion 12;
APB Opinion 14

[**Note:** A list of Issues discussed by the Emerging Issues Task Force (EITF) that provide supplemental guidance for this section is presented in paragraph .1000.]

Summary

Capital transactions shall generally be excluded from the determination of income but shall be adequately disclosed in the financial statements.

Capital Transactions Are Excluded from Income

.101 The following [capital transactions] shall be excluded from the determination of net income or the results of operations under all circumstances:

a. Adjustments or charges or credits resulting from transactions in the enterprise's own capital stock [(refer to Section C23, "Capital Stock: Treasury Stock," paragraphs .102 through .104)]
b. Transfers to and from accounts properly designated as appropriated retained earnings (such as general purpose contingency reserves or provisions for replacement costs of fixed assets) [(refer to Section C59, "Contingencies," paragraph .117)]
c. Adjustments made pursuant to a quasi reorganization [(refer to Section Q15, "Quasi Reorganizations," paragraphs .104 through .109)]

[APB9, ¶28]

Disclosure of Changes in Capital Accounts

.102 When both financial position and results of operations are presented, disclosure of changes in the separate accounts comprising stockholders' equity (in addition to retained earnings) and of the changes in the number of shares of equity securities during at least the most recent annual fiscal period and any subsequent interim period presented is required. Disclosure of such changes may take the form of separate statements or maybe made in the basic financial statements or notes thereto. [APB12, ¶10]

Disclosures about Capital Structure

.102A [All entities, public and nonpublic, that have issued securities, including options, warrants, debt, and stock, must comply with the disclosure requirements of Section C24, "Capital Structure: Disclosures."]

Stock Issued for Property and Subsequently Contributed Back to Enterprise

.103 If capital stock is issued nominally for the acquisition of property and it appears that at about the same time, and pursuant to a previous agreement or understanding, some portion of the stock so issued is donated to the enterprise, the par value of the stock nominally issued for the property [shall not be treated] as the cost of that property. If stock so donated is subsequently sold, the proceeds [shall not be treated] as a credit to additional paid-in capital of the enterprise. [ARB43, ch1A, ¶6]

Detachable Stock Purchase Warrants Issued in Connection with Debt

.104 The portion of the proceeds of debt securities issued with detachable stock purchase warrants that is allocable to the warrants shall be accounted for as additional paid-in capital. [(For further information refer to Section D10, "Debt: Convertible Debt, Conversion of Convertible Debt, and Debt with Stock Purchase Warrants," paragraphs .104 through .106.)] [APB14, ¶16] [Refer to paragraph .1001 for an EITF Issue that provides interpretive guidance on this paragraph.]

Supplemental Guidance: Emerging Issues Task Force (EITF) Issues

.1000 [Listed below are EITF Issues that provide supplemental guidance for this section. These Issues may be either interpretive of or related by topic to the guidance in this section.

EITF Issue No. 88-9, "Put Warrants"

EITF Issue No. 98-2, "Accounting by a Subsidiary or Joint Venture for an Investment in the Stock of Its Parent Company or Joint Venture Partner"

EITF Issue No. 98-12, "Application of Issue No. 00-19 to Forward Equity Sales Transactions"

EITF Issue No. 00-19, "Accounting for Derivative Financial Instruments Indexed to, and Potentially Settled in, a Company's Own Stock"

EITF Topic No. D-98, "Classification and Measurement of Redeemable Securities"]

.1001 [Listed below is an EITF Issue that provides interpretive guidance on specific material in this section.

Paragraph .104 (APB 14, ¶16)—EITF Issue No. 88-9]

(The next page is 5529.)

CAPITAL STOCK: DIVIDENDS-IN-KIND SECTION C11

Source: APB Opinion 29

Summary

Dividends-in-kind are recorded at the fair value of the assets transferred.

.101 [This section does not apply to] a transfer of nonmonetary assets solely between enterprises or persons under common control, such as between a parent company and its subsidiaries or between two subsidiary corporations of the same parent, or between a corporate joint venture and its owners. [APB29, ¶4(b)] [The distribution of nonmonetary assets, other than an enterprise's own capital stock, to stockholders as dividends is generally referred to as a *dividend-in-kind,* and is considered a nonreciprocal transfer. A dividend-in-kind] shall be recorded at the fair value of the asset transferred, and a gain or loss shall be recognized [by the enterprise] on the disposition of the asset. [APB29, ¶18]

.102 [The issuer of a dividend-in-kind] shall disclose in financial statements for the period the nature of the transaction, the basis of accounting for the assets transferred, and the gains and losses recognized. [APB29, ¶28] Paragraph .113 of Section C51, "Consolidation," includes additional disclosures that are preferred if a parent company disposes of a subsidiary during the year. [APB29, ¶28, fn7]

(The next page is 5859.)

CAPITAL STOCK: DIVIDENDS IN KIND — SECTION C11

Sources: APB Opinion 29

Summary

Dividends in kind are recorded at the fair value of the assets transferred.

[illegible]

[illegible]

CAPITAL STOCK: PREFERRED STOCK SECTION C16

Source: FASB Statement 129

[**Note:** A list of Issues discussed by the Emerging Issues Task Force (EITF) that provide supplemental guidance for this section is presented in paragraph .1000.]

Summary

Enterprises shall disclose the aggregate liquidation preference of its outstanding preferred stock and the price at which the preferred stock may be called or redeemed. Enterprises shall also disclose the aggregate and per-share amounts of cumulative preferred dividends in arrears.

.101 All entities, public and nonpublic, [FAS129, ¶3] that issue preferred stock (or other senior stock) that has a preference in involuntary liquidation considerably in excess of the par or stated value of the shares shall disclose the liquidation preference of the stock (the relationship between the preference in liquidation and the par or stated value of the shares). That disclosure shall be made in the equity section of the statement of financial position in the aggregate, either parenthetically or "in short," rather than on a per-share basis or through disclosure in the notes. [FAS129,¶6]

.102 In addition, [all entities] shall disclose within their financial statements (either on the face of the statement of financial position or in the notes thereto):

a. The aggregate or per-share amounts at which preferred stock may be called or is subject to redemption through sinking-fund operations or otherwise; and
b. The aggregate and per-share amounts of arrearages in cumulative preferred dividends.

[FAS129, ¶7]

Supplemental Guidance: Emerging Issues Task Force (EITF) Issues

.1000 [Listed below are EITF Issues that provide supplemental guidance for this section. These Issues are related by topic to the guidance in this section.

EITF Issue No. 86-32, "Early Extinguishment of a Subsidiary's Mandatorily Redeemable Preferred Stock"
EITF Topic No. D-82, "Effect of Preferred Stock Dividends Payable in Common Shares on Computation of Income Available to Common Stockholders"
EITF Topic No. D-98, "Classification and Measurement of Redeemable Securities"]

(The next page is 5923.)

CAPITAL STOCK: STOCK DIVIDENDS AND STOCK SPLITS SECTION C20

Sources: ARB 43, Chapter 7B; ARB 51

[**Note:** A list of Issues discussed by the Emerging Issues Task Force (EITF) that provide supplemental guidance for this section is presented in paragraph .1000.]

Summary

An enterprise issuing a stock dividend shall capitalize retained earnings in an amount equal to the fair value of the additional shares issued. On the other hand, an enterpise effecting a stock split shall capitalize retained earnings only to the extent required by law. Stock distributions involving issuance of additional shares of more than 25 percent of the number previously outstanding are generally accounted for as stock splits.

.101 [This section presents the accounting for **stock dividends** and **stock splits** (also called stock split-ups).] It is not concerned with the accounting for a distribution or issuance to shareholders of (a) shares of another enterprise theretofore held as an investment or (b) shares of a different class or (c) rights to subscribe for additional shares or (d) shares of the same class in cases where each shareholder is given an election to receive cash or shares. [ARB43, ch7B, ¶3]

Accounting by the Recipient

.102 Since a shareholder's interest in the enterprise remains unchanged by a stock dividend or split except as to the number of share units constituting such interest, the cost of the shares previously held shall be allocated equitably to the total shares held after receipt of the stock dividend or split. When any shares are later disposed of, a gain or loss shall be determined on the basis of the adjusted cost per share. [ARB43, ch7B, ¶9]

Accounting by the Issuer

Stock Dividends

.103 A stock dividend does not give rise to any change in either the enterprise's assets or its respective shareholders' proportionate interests therein. However, merely as a consequence of the expressed purpose of the transaction and its characterization as a *dividend* in related notices to shareholders and the public at large, many recipients of stock dividends look upon them as distributions of corporate earnings and usually in an amount equivalent to the fair value of the additional shares received. Furthermore, when issuances [of stock dividends] are small in comparison with the shares previously outstanding, they do not have any apparent effect upon the share market value. Therefore, where these circumstances exist, the enterprise shall account for [stock dividends] by transferring from retained earnings to the category of permanent capitalization (represented by the capital stock and additional paid-in capital accounts) an amount equal to the fair value of the additional shares issued. [ARB43, ch7B, ¶10]

.104 When the number of additional shares issued as a stock dividend is so great that it has, or may reasonably be expected to have, the effect of materially reducing the share market value, the transaction partakes of the nature of a stock split. Consequently, under such circumstances there is no need to capitalize retained earnings, other than to the extent occasioned by legal requirements. It is recommended, however, that in such instances every effort be made to avoid the use of the word *dividend* in related corporate resolutions, notices, and announcements and that, in those cases where because of legal requirements this cannot be done, the transaction be described, for example, as a *[stock] split effected in the form of a dividend.* [ARB43, ch7B, ¶11]

.105 In closely held enterprises, the intimate knowledge of the enterprises' affairs possessed by their shareholders would preclude implications [that the stock dividends are distributions of corporate earnings]. In such cases, there is no need to capitalize retained earnings other than to meet legal requirements. [ARB43, ch7B, ¶12]

.106 The point at which the relative size of the additional shares issued becomes large enough to materially influence the unit market price of the stock will vary with individual enterprises and under differing market conditions and, hence, no single percentage can be laid down as a standard for determining when capitalization of retained earnings in excess of legal requirements is called for and when it is not. However, it would appear that there would be few instances involving the issuance of additional shares of less than, say, 20 percent or 25 percent of the number previously outstanding where the effect would not be such as to call for the procedure referred to in paragraph .103, [that is, the capitalization of retained earnings in an amount equal to the fair value of the shares issued]. [ARB43, ch7B, ¶13]

.107 The accounting recommended in paragraph .103 will in many cases, probably the majority, result in the capitalization of retained earnings in an amount in excess of that called for by the laws of the state of incorporation; such laws generally require the capitalization only of the par value of the shares issued, or, in the case of shares without par value, an amount usually within the discretion of the board of directors. However, these legal requirements are, in effect, minimum requirements and do not prevent the capitalization of a larger amount per share. [ARB43, ch7B, ¶14]

Stock Splits

.108 When a stock split is clearly for the purpose of effecting a reduction in the unit market price of shares of the class issued and, thus, of obtaining wider distribution and improved marketability of the shares, no transfer from retained earnings to the additional paid-in capital or capital stock account is called for, other than to the extent occasioned by legal requirements. However, few cases will arise where the aforementioned purpose can be accomplished through an issuance of shares which is less than, say, 20 percent or 25 percent of the previously outstanding shares. [ARB43, ch7B, ¶15]

.109 An enterprise's representations to its shareholders as to the nature of the issuance is one of the principal considerations in determining whether it should be recorded as a stock dividend or a [stock] split. Nevertheless, the issuance of new shares in ratios of less than, say, 20 percent or 25 percent of the previously outstanding shares, or the frequent recurrence of issuances of shares, would destroy the presumption that transactions represented to be [stock] splits should be recorded as [stock] splits. [ARB43, ch7B, ¶16]

Stock Dividends of Subsidiaries

.110 Occasionally, subsidiary enterprises capitalize retained earnings arising since acquisition, by means of a stock dividend or otherwise. This does not require a transfer to additional paid-in capital on consolidation, inasmuch as the retained earnings in the consolidated financial statements should reflect the accumulated earnings of the consolidated group not distributed to the shareholders of, or capitalized by, the parent company. [ARB51, ¶18]

Glossary

.401 **Stock dividend.** An issuance by an enterprise of its own common shares to its common shareholders without consideration and under conditions indicating that such action is prompted mainly by a desire to give the recipient shareholders some ostensibly separate evidence of a part of their respective interests in accumulated corporate earnings without distribution of cash or other property which the board of directors deems necessary or desirable to retain in the business. [ARB43, ch7B, ¶1]

.402 **Stock split.** An issuance by an enterprise of its own common shares to its common shareholders without consideration and under conditions indicating that such action is prompted mainly by a desire to increase the number of outstanding shares for the purpose of effecting a reduction in their unit market price, and, thereby, of obtaining wider distribution and improved marketability of the shares. [ARB43, ch7B, ¶2]

Supplemental Guidance: Emerging Issues Task Force (EITF) Issues

.1000 [Listed below is an EITF Issue that provides supplemental guidance for this section. This Issue is related by topic to the guidance in this section.

EITF Topic No. D-82, "Effect of Preferred Stock Dividends Payable in Common Shares on Computation of Income Available to Common Stockholders"]

(The next page is 6125.)

CAPITAL STOCK: TREASURY STOCK SECTION C23

Sources: ARB 43, Chapter 1B; APB Opinion 6; FASB Technical Bulletin 85-6

[**Note:** A list of Issues discussed by the Emerging Issues Task Force (EITF) that provide supplemental guidance for this section is presented in paragraph .1000.]

Summary

If an enterprise acquires shares of its own capital stock, the cost of the acquired shares shall generally be shown as a deduction from capital. Dividends on such shares held in the enterprise's treasury (treasury stock) shall not be credited to income. Gains and losses on sales of treasury stock shall be accounted for as adjustments to capital and not as part of income.

If the price paid for the shares is significantly in excess of current market price, that may indicate that the price paid may include consideration for other factors such as stated or unstated rights, privileges, or agreements in addition to the capital stock. In such cases, the excess should be attributed to the other factors.

Dividends on Treasury Stock

.101 [The dividends on treasury stock shall not be treated as a credit to the income account of the enterprise.]

Retirement of Treasury Stock

.102 If an enterprise's [capital] stock is retired, or purchased for constructive retirement (with or without an intention to retire the stock formally in accordance with applicable laws):[a]

a. *An excess of purchase price over par or stated value* may be allocated between additional paid-in capital and retained earnings. The portion of the excess allocated to additional paid-in capital shall be limited to the sum of (1) all additional paid-in capi-

[[a]Refer to paragraphs .501 through .503 for guidance regarding accounting for a purchase of treasury shares at a price significantly in excess of the current market price of the shares.]

tal arising from previous retirements and net "gains" on sales of treasury stock of the same issue and (2) the pro rata portion of additional paid-in capital, voluntary transfers of retained earnings, capitalization of stock dividends, etc., on the same issue. For this purpose, any remaining additional paid-in capital applicable to issues fully retired (formal or constructive) is deemed to be applicable pro rata to shares of common stock. Alternatively, the excess may be charged entirely to retained earnings in recognition of the fact that an enterprise can always capitalize or allocate retained earnings for such purposes [APB6, ¶12(a)] or may be reflected [entirely as a deduction from] additional paid-in capital. [ARB43, ch1B, ¶7]

b. *An excess of par or stated value over purchase price* shall be credited to additional paid-in capital. [APB6, ¶12(a)]

.103 If an enterprise's stock is acquired for purposes other than retirement (formal or constructive), or if ultimate disposition has not yet been decided, the cost[1] of acquired stock may be shown separately as a deduction from the total of capital stock, additional paid-in capital, and retained earnings, or may be accorded the accounting treatment appropriate for retired stock. "Gains" on sales of treasury stock not previously accounted for as constructively retired shall be credited to additional paid-in capital;[2] "losses" may be charged to additional paid-in capital to the extent that previous net "gains" from sales or retirements of the same class of stock are included therein, otherwise to retained earnings.[3] [APB6, ¶12(b)]

.104 Laws of some states govern the circumstances under which an enterprise may acquire its own stock and prescribe the accounting treatment therefor. If such requirements are at variance with paragraphs .102 and .103, the accounting shall conform to the applicable law. If state laws relating to acquisition of stock restrict the availability of retained earnings for payment of dividends or have other effects of a significant nature, these facts shall be disclosed. [APB6, ¶13]

[[1]Refer to Section N35, "Nonmonetary Transactions," paragraph .105, for guidance regarding the cost of stock acquired in a nonmonetary transaction.]

[2]Although there may be cases where the transactions involved are so inconsequential as to be immaterial, [ARB43, ch1B, ¶10] [accounting treatment different from that specified in paragraph .102] shall not be applied to any transaction that, although in itself inconsiderable in amount, is a part of a series of transactions that in the aggregate are of substantial importance. [ARB43, ch1B, ¶11]

[[3]Refer to paragraphs .501 through .503 for guidance regarding accounting for a purchase of treasury shares at a stated price significantly in excess of the current market price of the shares.]

Supplemental Guidance

Accounting for a Purchase of Treasury Shares at a Price Significantly in Excess of the Current Market Price of the Shares

.501 *Question*—How should an enterprise account for a purchase of treasury shares at a stated price significantly in excess of the current market price of the shares? [FTB85-6, ¶1]

.502 *Response*—An agreement to purchase shares from a shareholder may also involve the receipt or payment of consideration in exchange for stated or unstated rights or privileges that should be identified to allocate properly the purchase price. [FTB85-6, ¶2]

.503 An enterprise offering to repurchase shares only from a specific shareholder (or group of shareholders) suggests that the repurchase may involve more than the purchase of treasury shares. [FTB85-6, ¶14] [Also,] a purchase of shares at a price significantly in excess of the current market price creates a presumption that the purchase price includes amounts attributable to items other than the shares purchased. For example, the selling shareholder may agree to abandon certain acquisition plans, forego other planned transactions, settle litigation, settle employment contracts, or restrict voluntarily the ability to purchase shares of the enterprise or its affiliates within a stated time period. If the purchase of treasury shares includes the receipt of stated or unstated rights, privileges, or agreements in addition to the capital stock, only the amount representing the fair value of the treasury shares at the date the major terms of the agreement to purchase the shares are reached should be accounted for as the cost of the shares acquired. The price paid in excess of the amount accounted for as the cost of treasury shares should be attributed to the other elements of the transaction and accounted for according to their substance. If the fair value of those other elements of the transaction is more clearly evident, for example, because an enterprise's shares are not publicly traded, that amount should be assigned to those elements and the difference recorded as the cost of treasury shares. If no stated or unstated consideration in addition to the capital stock can be identified, the entire purchase price should be accounted for as the cost of treasury shares. The allocation of amounts paid and the accounting treatment for such amounts should be disclosed. [FTB85-6, ¶3] The allocation of amounts described in this paragraph requires significant judgment and consideration of many factors that can significantly affect amounts recognized in the financial statements. [FTB85-6, ¶16]

.504 Transactions do arise, however, in which an acquisition of an enterprise's stock may take place at prices different from routine transactions in the open market. For example, to obtain the desired number of shares in a tender offer to all or most shareholders, the offer may need to be at a price in excess of the current market price. In addition, a block of shares representing a controlling interest will generally trade at a price in excess of market, and a large block of shares may trade at a price above or below the current market price depending on whether the buyer or seller initiates the transaction. An enterprise's acquisition of its shares in those circumstances is solely a treasury stock transaction properly accounted for at the purchase price of the treasury shares. Therefore, in the absence of the receipt of stated or unstated consideration in addition to the capital stock, the entire purchase price should be accounted for as the cost of treasury shares. [FTB85-6, ¶15]

Supplemental Guidance: Emerging Issues Task Force (EITF) Issues

.1000 [Listed below are EITF Issues that provide supplemental guidance for this section. These Issues are related by topic to the guidance in this section.

EITF Issue No. 85-2, "Classification of Costs Incurred in a Takeover Defense"
EITF Issue No. 85-46, "Partnership's Purchase of Withdrawing Partner's Equity"
EITF Issue No. 97-14, "Accounting for Deferred Compensation Arrangements Where Amounts Earned Are Held in a Rabbi Trust and Invested"]

(The next page is 6179.)

CAPITAL STRUCTURE: DISCLOSURES SECTION C24

Source: FASB Statement No. 129

[**Note:** A list of Issues discussed by the Emerging Issues Task Force (EITF) that provide supplemental guidance for this section is presented in paragraph .1000.]

Summary

This section presents standards for disclosing information about an entity's capital structure. It applies to all entities. This section continues previous requirements to disclose certain information about an entity's capital structure.

Scope

.101 This section applies to all entities, public and nonpublic, that have issued **securities** addressed by this section. [FAS129, ¶3] The scope of this section is unchanged from that of the prior standards that previously contained its disclosure requirements except for the elimination of the exemption of nonpublic entities from the provisions in paragraphs .102 and .103. [FAS129, ¶16]

Information about Securities

.102 An entity shall explain, in summary form within its financial statements, the pertinent rights and privileges of the various securities outstanding. Examples of information that shall be disclosed are dividend and liquidation preferences, **participation rights,** call prices and dates, conversion or exercise prices or rates and pertinent dates, sinking-fund requirements, unusual voting rights, and significant terms of contracts to issue additional shares. [FAS129, ¶4] [Refer to paragraph .1001 for an EITF Issue that provides interpretive guidance on this paragraph.]

.103 An entity shall disclose within its financial statements the number of shares issued upon conversion, exercise, or satisfaction of required conditions during at least the most recent annual fiscal period and any subsequent interim period presented.[1] [FAS129, ¶5]

---

[1][Refer to] Section C08, "Capital Stock: Capital Transactions," paragraph .102. That paragraph requires, among other things, disclosure of the changes in the number of shares of equity securities during at least the most recent annual fiscal period and any subsequent interim period presented to make the financial statements sufficiently informative. The disclosure required by paragraph .103 above meets that requirement. [FAS129, ¶5, fn2]

Liquidation Preference of Preferred Stock

.104 An entity that issues **preferred stock** (or other senior stock) that has a preference in involuntary liquidation considerably in excess of the par or stated value of the shares shall disclose the liquidation preference of the stock (the relationship between the preference in liquidation and the par or stated value of the shares). That disclosure shall be made in the equity section of the statement of financial position in the aggregate, either parenthetically or "in short," rather than on a per-share basis or through disclosure in the notes. [FAS129, ¶6]

.105 In addition, an entity shall disclose within its financial statements (either on the face of the statement of financial position or in the notes thereto):

a. The aggregate or per-share amounts at which preferred stock may be called or is subject to redemption through sinking-fund operations or otherwise; and
b. The aggregate and per-share amounts of arrearages in cumulative preferred dividends.

[FAS129, ¶7]

Redeemable Stock

.106 An entity that issues redeemable stock shall disclose the amount of redemption requirements, separately by issue or combined, for all issues of capital stock that are redeemable at fixed or determinable prices on fixed or determinable dates in each of the five years following the date of the latest statement of financial position presented. [FAS129, ¶8] [Refer to paragraph .1001 for an EITF Issue that provides interpretive guidance on this paragraph.]

Glossary

.401 **Participation rights.** Contractual rights of security holders to receive dividends or returns from the security issuer's profits, cash flows, or returns on investments. [FAS129, ¶2(b)]

.402 **Preferred stock.** A security that has preferential rights compared to common stock. [FAS129, ¶2(c)]

.403 **Securities.** The evidence of debt or ownership or a related right. For purposes of this section, the term *securities* includes options and warrants as well as debt and stock. [FAS129, ¶2(a)]

Supplemental Guidance: Emerging Issues Task Force (EITF) Issues

.1000 [Listed below are EITF Issues that provide supplemental guidance for this section. These Issues may be either interpretive of or related by topic to the guidance in this section.

EITF Issue No. 86-32, "Early Extinguishment of a Subsidiary's Mandatorily Redeemable Preferred Stock"
EITF Issue No. 98-5, "Accounting for Convertible Securities with Beneficial Conversion Features or Contingently Adjustable Conversion Ratios"
EITF Issue No. 00-19, "Accounting for Derivative Financial Instruments Indexed to, and Potentially Settled in, a Company's Own Stock"
EITF Issue No. 00-27, "Application of Issue No. 98-5 to Certain Convertible Instruments"]

.1001 [Listed below is an EITF Issue that provides interpretive guidance on specific material in this section.

Paragraph .102 (FAS 129, ¶4)—EITF Issue No. 00-19
Paragraph .106 (FAS 129, ¶8)—EITF Issue No. 00-19]

(The next page is 6251.)

[illegible]

[illegible] Issue [illegible] Accounting [illegible] Contracts [illegible] Hedged [illegible]

CASH FLOWS STATEMENT SECTION C25

Sources: FASB Statement 95; FASB Statement 102; FASB Statement 104; FASB Statement 115; FASB Statement 117; FASB Statement 133; FASB Statement 135; FASB Statement 141; FASB Statement 145

[**Note:** A list of Issues discussed by the Emerging Issues Task Force (EITF) that provide supplemental guidance for this section is presented in paragraph .1000.]

Summary

This section presents standards for cash flow reporting. A statement of cash flows is required as part of a full set of financial statements for all business enterprises and not-for-profit organizations other than defined benefit pension plans and certain other employee benefit plans and highly liquid investment companies that meet specified conditions.

A statement of cash flows shall classify cash receipts and payments according to whether they stem from operating, investing, or financing activities. This section provides definitions of each category.

Generally, cash flow information about the gross amounts of cash receipts and cash payments during a period is more relevant than information about net amounts of cash receipts and payments. However, because the net amount of related receipts and payments provides sufficient information when the turnover is quick, the amounts are large, and the maturities are short, the reporting of net cash flows for certain items with those characteristics is permitted. Additionally, certain investing and financing activities of banks, savings institutions, and credit unions may be reported as net cash flows.

Enterprises are encouraged to report cash flows from operating activities directly by showing major classes of operating cash receipts and payments (the direct method). Enterprises that choose not to show operating cash receipts and payments are required to report the same amount of net cash flow from operating activities indirectly by adjusting net income of a business enterprise or change in net assets of a not-for-profit organization to reconcile it to net cash flow from operating activities (the indirect or reconciliation method). If the direct method is used, a reconciliation of net income of a business enterprise or change in net assets of a not-for-profit organization and net cash flow from operating activities is required to be provided in a separate schedule.

A statement of cash flows shall report the reporting currency equivalent of foreign currency cash flows, using the current exchange rate at the time of the cash flows. The effect of the exchange rate changes on cash held in foreign currencies is reported as a separate item in the reconciliation of beginning and ending balances of cash and cash equivalents.

Information about investing and financing activities not resulting in cash receipts or payments in the period shall be provided separately.

Scope

.101 This section [presents] standards for providing a statement of cash flows in general-purpose financial statements. [FAS95, ¶1] A business enterprise [FAS95, ¶3] or not-for-profit organization [FAS117, ¶30(a)] that provides a set of financial statements that reports both financial position and results of operations shall also provide a statement of cash flows for each period for which results of operations are provided. [FAS95, ¶3] In this section, *enterprise* encompasses both business enterprises and not-for-profit organizations, and the phrase *investors, creditors, and others* encompasses donors. The terms *income statement* and *net income* apply to a business enterprise; the terms *statement of activities* and *change in net assets* apply to a not-for-profit organization. [FAS117, ¶30(b)] [However,] a statement of cash flows is not required for defined benefit pension plans and certain other employee benefit plans or for certain investment companies as provided by paragraphs .135A through .135C. [FAS102, ¶10(a)]

Purpose of a Statement of Cash Flows

.102 The primary purpose of a statement of cash flows is to provide relevant information about the cash receipts and cash payments of an enterprise during a period. [FAS95, ¶4]

.103 The information provided in a statement of cash flows, if used with related disclosures and information in the other financial statements, should help investors, creditors, and others to (a) assess the enterprise's ability to generate positive future net cash flows; (b) assess the enterprise's ability to meet its obligations, its ability to pay dividends, and its needs for external financing; (c) assess the reasons for differences between net income and associated cash receipts and payments; and (d) assess the effects on an enterprise's financial position of both its cash and noncash investing and financing transactions during the period. [FAS95, ¶5]

[[1]Editorial deletion, 6/93.]

.104 To achieve its purpose of providing information to help investors, creditors, and others in making those assessments, a statement of cash flows should report the cash effects during a period of an enterprise's operations, its investing transactions, and its financing transactions. Related disclosures should report the effects of investing and financing transactions that affect an enterprise's financial position but do not directly affect cash flows during the period. A reconciliation of net income and net cash flow from operating activities, which generally provides information about the net effects of operating transactions and other events that affect net income and operating cash flows in different periods, also should be provided. [FAS95, ¶6]

Focus on Cash and Cash Equivalents

.105 A statement of cash flows shall explain the change during the period in cash[2] and cash equivalents. The statement shall use descriptive terms such as *cash* or *cash and cash equivalents* rather than ambiguous terms such as *funds*. The total amounts of cash and cash equivalents at the beginning and end of the period shown in the statement of cash flows shall be the same amounts as similarly titled line items or subtotals shown in the statements of financial position as of those dates. [FAS95, ¶7]

.106 For purposes of this section, cash equivalents are short-term, highly liquid investments that are both:

a. Readily convertible to known amounts of cash
b. So near their maturity that they present insignificant risk of changes in value because of changes in interest rates.

Generally, only investments with original maturities[3] of three months or less qualify under that definition. [FAS95, ¶8]

---

[2]Consistent with common usage, *cash* includes not only currency on hand but demand deposits with banks or other financial institutions. *Cash* also includes other kinds of accounts that have the general characteristics of demand deposits in that the customer may deposit additional funds at any time and also effectively may withdraw funds at any time without prior notice or penalty. All charges and credits to those accounts are cash receipts or payments to both the entity owning the account and the bank holding it. For example, a bank's granting of a loan by crediting the proceeds to a customer's demand deposit account is a cash payment by the bank and a cash receipt of the customer when the entry is made. [FAS95, ¶7, fn1]

[3]*Original maturity* [in this paragraph] means original maturity to the entity holding the investment. For example, both a three-month U.S. Treasury bill and a three-year Treasury note purchased three months from maturity qualify as cash equivalents. However, a Treasury note purchased three years ago does not become a cash equivalent when its remaining maturity is three months. [FAS95, ¶8, fn2]

.107 Examples of items commonly considered to be cash equivalents are Treasury bills, commercial paper, money market funds, and federal funds sold (for an enterprise with banking operations). Cash purchases and sales of those investments generally are part of the enterprise's cash management activities rather than part of its operating, investing, and financing activities, and details of those transactions need not be reported in a statement of cash flows. [FAS95, ¶9]

.108 Not all investments that qualify [as cash equivalents under paragraph .106] are required to be treated as cash equivalents [in the statement of cash flows]. An enterprise shall establish a policy concerning which short-term, highly liquid investments that satisfy the definition in paragraph .106 are treated as cash equivalents. For example, an enterprise having banking operations might decide that all investments that qualify except for those purchased for its trading account will be treated as cash equivalents, while an enterprise whose operations consist largely of investing in short-term, highly liquid investments might decide that all those items will be treated as investments rather than cash equivalents. An enterprise shall disclose its policy for determining which items are treated as cash equivalents [in the statement of cash flows]. Any change to that policy is a change in accounting principle that shall be effected by restating financial statements for earlier years presented for comparative purposes. [FAS95, ¶10]

Gross and Net Cash Flows

.109 Generally, information about the gross amounts of cash receipts and cash payments during a period is more relevant than information about the net amounts of cash receipts and payments. However, the net amount of related receipts and payments provides sufficient information not only for cash equivalents, as noted in paragraph .107, but also for certain other classes of cash flows specified in paragraphs .110, .111, [.111A], and .126. [FAS95, ¶11]

.110 For certain items, the turnover is quick, the amounts are large, and the maturities are short. For certain other items, such as demand deposits of a bank and customer accounts payable of a broker-dealer, the enterprise is substantively holding or disbursing cash on behalf of its customers. Only the net changes during the period in assets and liabilities with those characteristics need be reported because knowledge of the gross cash receipts and payments related to them may not be necessary to understand the enterprise's operating, investing, and financing activities. [FAS95, ¶12]

.111 Items that qualify for net reporting because their turnover is quick, their amounts are large, and their maturities are short are cash receipts and payments pertaining to

(a) investments (other than cash equivalents), (b) loans receivable, and (c) debt, providing that the original maturity of the asset or liability is three months or less.[4] [FAS95, ¶13]

.111A Banks, savings institutions, and credit unions are not required to report gross amounts of cash receipts and cash payments for (a) deposits placed with other financial institutions and withdrawals of deposits, (b) time deposits accepted and repayments of deposits, and (c) loans made to customers and principal collections of loans. When those enterprises constitute part of a consolidated enterprise, net amounts of cash receipts and cash payments for deposit or lending activities of those enterprises shall be reported separate from gross amounts of cash receipts and cash payments for other investing and financing activities of the consolidated enterprise, including those of a subsidiary of a bank, savings institution, or credit union that is not itself a bank, savings institution, or credit union. [FAS104, ¶7(a)]

Classification of Cash Receipts and Cash Payments

.112 A statement of cash flows shall classify cash receipts and cash payments as resulting from investing, financing, or operating activities.[5] [FAS95, ¶14]

Cash Flows from Investing Activities

.113 Investing activities include making and collecting loans and acquiring and disposing of debt or equity instruments and property, plant, and equipment and other productive assets, that is, assets held for or used in the production of goods or services by the enterprise (other than materials that are part of the enterprise's inventory). [FAS95, ¶15]

---

[4]For this purpose, amounts due on demand are considered to have maturities of three months or less. For convenience, credit card receivables of financial services operations—generally, receivables resulting from cardholder charges that may, at the cardholder's option, be paid in full when first billed, usually within one month, without incurring interest charges and that do not stem from the enterprise's sale of goods or services—also are considered to be loans with original maturities of three months or less. [FAS95, ¶13, fn3]

[5]Generally, each cash receipt or payment is to be classified according to its nature without regard to whether it stems from an item intended as a hedge of another item. For example, the proceeds of a borrowing are a financing cash inflow even though the debt is intended as a hedge of an investment, and the purchase or sale of a futures contract is an investing activity even though the contract is intended as a hedge of a firm commitment to purchase inventory. However, cash flows from [FAS104, ¶7(b)] derivative instruments that are accounted for as fair value hedges or cash flow hedges under Section D50, "Derivative Instruments and Hedging Activities," [FAS133, ¶530] may be classified in the same category as the cash flows from the items being hedged provided that accounting policy is disclosed. If for any reason hedge accounting for an instrument that hedges an [FAS104, ¶7(b)] asset, liability, firm commitment, or forecasted transaction [FAS133, ¶530] is discontinued, then any cash flows subsequent to the date of discontinuance shall be classified consistent with the nature of the instrument. [FAS104, ¶7(b)]

Investing activities exclude acquiring and disposing of certain loans or other debt or equity instruments that are acquired specifically for resale, as discussed in paragraphs .122A through .122B, [FAS102, ¶10(b)] and securities that are classified as trading securities as discussed in paragraph .109 of Section I80, "Investments: Debt and Equity Securities." [FAS145, ¶9(f)]

.114 Cash inflows from investing activities are:[6]

a. Receipts from collections or sales of loans made by the enterprise and of other entities' debt instruments [FAS95, ¶16] (other than cash equivalents, certain debt instruments that are acquired specifically for resale as discussed in paragraph .122B of this section and securities classified as trading securities as discussed in paragraph .109 of Section I80) [FAS145, ¶9(f)] that were purchased by the enterprise
b. Receipts from sales of equity instruments of other enterprises [FAS95, ¶16] (other than certain equity instruments carried in a trading account as described in paragraph .122A of this section and certain securities classified as trading securities as discussed in paragraph .109 of Section I80) [FAS145, ¶9(f)] and from returns *of* investment in those instruments
c. Receipts from sales of property, plant, and equipment and other productive assets. [FAS95, ¶16]

.115 Cash outflows for investing activities are:

a. Disbursements for loans made by the enterprise and payments to acquire debt instruments of other entities [FAS95, ¶17] (other than cash equivalents, certain debt instruments that are acquired specifically for resale as discussed in paragraph .122B of this section and securities classified as trading securities as discussed in paragraph .109 of Section I80) [FAS145, ¶9(f)]
b. Payments to acquire equity instruments of other enterprises [FAS95, ¶17] (other than certain equity instruments carried in a trading account as described in paragraph .122A of this section and certain securities classified as trading securities as discussed in paragraph .109 of Section I80) [FAS145, ¶9(f)]

[6]Receipts from disposing of loans, debt or equity instruments [FAS95, ¶16, fn5] (other than cash equivalents, certain debt instruments that are acquired specifically for resale as discussed in paragraph .122B of this section, and securities classified as trading securities as discussed in paragraph .109 of Section I80), [FAS145, ¶9(f)] or property, plant, and equipment include directly related proceeds of insurance settlements, such as the proceeds of insurance on a building that is damaged or destroyed. [FAS95, ¶16, fn5]

c. Payments at the time of purchase or soon before or after purchase[7] to acquire property, plant, and equipment and other productive assets.[8] [FAS95, ¶17]

Cash Flows from Financing Activities

.116 Financing activities include obtaining resources from owners and providing them with a return on, and a return of, their investment; [FAS95, ¶18] receiving restricted resources that by donor stipulation must be used for long-term purposes; [FAS117, ¶30(c)] borrowing money and repaying amounts borrowed, or otherwise settling the obligation; and obtaining and paying for other resources obtained from creditors on long-term credit. [FAS95, ¶18]

.117 Cash inflows from financing activities are:

a. Proceeds from issuing equity instruments
b. Proceeds from issuing bonds, mortgages, notes, and from other short- or long-term borrowing [FAS95, ¶19]
c. Receipts from contributions and investment income that by donor stipulation are restricted for the purposes of acquiring, constructing, or improving property, plant, equipment, or other long-lived assets or establishing or increasing a permanent endowment or term endowment. [FAS117, ¶30(d)]

.118 Cash outflows for financing activities are:

a. Payments of dividends or other distributions to owners, including outlays to reacquire the enterprise's equity instruments
b. Repayments of amounts borrowed
c. Other principal payments to creditors who have extended long-term credit.[9]

[FAS95, ¶20] [Refer to paragraph .1001 for an EITF Issue that provides interpretive guidance on this paragraph.]

[7] Generally, only advance payments, the down payment, or other amounts paid at the time of purchase or soon before or after purchase of property, plant, and equipment and other productive assets are investing cash outflows. Incurring directly related debt [payable] to the seller is a financing transaction, and subsequent payments of principal on that debt thus are financing cash outflows. [FAS95, ¶17, fn6]

[8] Enterprises [are not] required to distinguish between expenditures for maintenance and those for expansion. [FAS95, ¶99] Payments to acquire productive assets include interest capitalized as part of the cost of those assets. [FAS95, ¶17, fn7]

[9] Refer to footnote 7, which indicates that most principal payments on seller-financed debt directly related to a purchase of property, plant, and equipment or other productive assets are financing cash outflows. [FAS95, ¶20, fn8]

Cash Flows from Operating Activities

.119 Operating activities include all transactions and other events that are not defined as investing or financing activities in paragraphs .113 through .118. Operating activities generally involve producing and delivering goods and providing services. Cash flows from operating activities are generally the cash effects of transactions and other events that enter into the determination of net income. [Refer to paragraphs .122A and .122B for guidance on reporting cash flows from assets in trading accounts and from loans acquired for resale.] [FAS95, ¶21]

.120 Cash inflows from operating activities are:

a. Cash receipts from sales of goods[9a] or services, including receipts from collection or sale of accounts and both short- and long-term notes receivable from customers arising from those sales
b. Cash receipts from returns *on* loans, other debt instruments of other entities, and equity securities—interest and dividends
c. All other cash receipts that do not stem from transactions defined as investing or financing activities, such as amounts received to settle lawsuits; proceeds of insurance settlements except for those that are directly related to investing or financing activities, such as from destruction of a building; and refunds from suppliers.

[FAS95, ¶22]

.121 Cash outflows for operating activities are:

a. Cash payments to acquire materials for manufacture or goods[9b] for resale, including principal payments on accounts and both short- and long-term notes payable to suppliers for those materials or goods
b. Cash payments to other suppliers and employees for other goods or services
c. Cash payments to governments for taxes, duties, fines, and other fees or penalties
d. Cash payments to lenders and other creditors for interest
e. All other cash payments that do not stem from transactions defined as investing or financing activities, such as payments to settle lawsuits, cash contributions to charities, and cash refunds to customers.

[FAS95, ¶23]

[9a]The term *goods* includes certain loans and other debt and equity instruments of other enterprises that are acquired specifically for resale, as discussed in paragraph .122B, [FAS102, ¶10(e)] and securities that are classified as trading securities as discussed in paragraph .109 of Section I80. [FAS145, ¶9(f)]

[9b][Refer to footnote 9a.] [FAS102, ¶10(e)]

.122 Certain cash receipts and payments may have aspects of more than one class of cash flows. For example, a cash payment may pertain to an item that could be considered either inventory or a productive asset. If so, the appropriate classification shall depend on the activity that is likely to be the predominant source of cash flows for the item. For example, the acquisition and sale of equipment to be used by the enterprise or rented to others generally are investing activities. However, equipment sometimes is acquired or produced to be used by the enterprise or rented to others for a short period and then sold. In those circumstances, the acquisition or production and subsequent sale of those assets shall be considered operating activities. [FAS95, ¶24] [Similarly,] real estate generally is considered a productive asset, and a cash payment to purchase real estate generally is an investing cash outflow. However, if real estate is acquired by a real estate developer to be subdivided, improved, and sold in individual lots, then the cash payment to purchase that real estate would be classified as an operating cash flow because the real estate is acquired specifically for resale and is similar to inventory in other businesses. [FAS102, ¶25]

Classification of Cash Flows from Acquisitions and Sales of Certain Securities and Other Assets

.122A Banks, brokers and dealers in securities, and other enterprises may carry securities and other assets in a trading account.[9c] [FAS102, ¶8] Cash receipts and cash payments resulting from purchases and sales of securities classified as trading securities as discussed in paragraph .109 of Section I80 shall be classified as operating cash flows. [FAS145, ¶9(g)] Cash receipts and cash payments resulting from purchases and sales of [FAS102, ¶8] other [FAS145, ¶9(g)] securities and other assets shall be classified as operating cash flows if those assets are acquired specifically for resale and are carried at market value in a trading account. [FAS102, ¶8] Cash flows from purchases, sales, and maturities of available-for-sale securities shall be classified as cash flows from investing activities and reported gross in the statement of cash flows. [FAS115, ¶132(a)]

.122B Some loans are similar to securities in a trading account in that they are originated or purchased specifically for resale and are held for short periods of time. Cash receipts and cash payments resulting from acquisitions and sales of loans also shall be classified as operating cash flows if those loans are acquired specifically for resale and are carried at market value or at the lower of cost or market value.[9d] Cash receipts re-

[9c]Characteristics of trading account activities are described in Section C28, "Changing Prices: Reporting Their Effects in Financial Reporting," paragraphs .192 and .193, and in the AICPA [FAS102, ¶8, fn3] Audit and Accounting Guides, *Banks and Savings Institutions,* [FAS135, ¶5(b)] and *Audits of Brokers and Dealers in Securities.* [FAS102, ¶8, fn3]

[9d]Mortgage loans held for sale are required to be reported at the lower of cost or market value in accordance with Section Mo4, "Mortgage Banking Activities," paragraph .105. [FAS102, ¶9, fn4]

sulting from sales of loans that were not specifically acquired for resale shall be classified as investing cash inflows. That is, if loans were acquired as investments, cash receipts from sales of those loans shall be classified as investing cash inflows regardless of a change in the purpose for holding those loans. [FAS102, ¶9]

Foreign Currency Cash Flows

.123 A statement of cash flows of an enterprise with foreign currency transactions or foreign operations shall report the reporting currency equivalent of foreign currency cash flows using the exchange rates in effect at the time of the cash flows. An appropriately weighted average exchange rate for the period may be used for translation if the result is substantially the same as if the rates at the dates of the cash flows were used.[10] The statement shall report the effect of exchange rate changes on cash balances held in foreign currencies as a separate part of the reconciliation of the change in cash and cash equivalents during the period. [FAS95, ¶25]

Content and Form of the Statement of Cash Flows

.124 A statement of cash flows for a period shall report net cash provided or used by operating, investing, and financing activities[11] and the net effect of those flows on cash and cash equivalents during the period in a manner that reconciles beginning and ending cash and cash equivalents. [FAS95, ¶26]

.125 In reporting cash flows from operating activities, enterprises are encouraged to report major classes of gross cash receipts and gross cash payments and their arithmetic sum—the net cash flow from operating activities (the direct method). Enterprises that do so should, at a minimum, separately report the following classes of operating cash receipts and payments:[12]

a. Cash collected from customers, including lessees, licensees, and the like

---

[10]Paragraph .118 of Section F60, "Foreign Currency Translation," recognizes the general impracticality of translating revenues, expenses, gains, and losses at the exchange rates on dates they are recognized and permits an appropriately weighted average exchange rate for the period to be used to translate those elements. This section applies that provision to cash receipts and cash payments. [FAS95, ¶25, fn9]

[11]Separate disclosure of cash flows pertaining to extraordinary items or discontinued operations reflected in those categories is not required. An enterprise that nevertheless chooses to report separately operating cash flows of discontinued operations shall do so consistently for all periods affected, which may include periods long after sale or liquidation of the operation. [FAS95, ¶26, fn10]

[12]Paragraphs .130 through .133 and paragraph .141, respectively, discuss and illustrate a method by which those major classes of gross operating cash receipts and payments generally may be determined indirectly. [FAS95, ¶27, fn11]

b. Interest and dividends received[12a]
c. Other operating cash receipts, if any
d. Cash paid to employees and other suppliers of goods or services, including suppliers of insurance, advertising, and the like
e. Interest paid
f. Income taxes paid
g. Other operating cash payments, if any.

Enterprises are encouraged to provide further breakdowns of operating cash receipts and payments that they consider meaningful and feasible. For example, a retailer or manufacturer might decide to further divide cash paid to employees and suppliers (category (d) above) into payments for costs of inventory and payments for selling, general, and administrative expenses. [FAS95, ¶27]

.126 Enterprises that choose not to provide information about major classes of operating cash receipts and payments by the direct method as encouraged in paragraph .125 shall determine and report the same amount for net cash flow from operating activities indirectly by adjusting net income [FAS95, ¶28] of a business enterprise or change in net assets of a not-for-profit organization [FAS117, ¶30(f)] to reconcile it to net cash flow from operating activities (the indirect or reconciliation method). That requires adjusting net income [FAS95, ¶28] of a business enterprise or change in net assets of a not-for-profit organization [FAS117, ¶30(f)] to remove (a) the effects of all deferrals of past operating cash receipts and payments, such as changes during the period in inventory, deferred income, and the like, and all accruals of expected future operating cash receipts and payments, such as changes during the period in receivables and payables,[13] and (b) the effects of all items whose cash effects are investing or financing cash flows, such as depreciation, amortization of goodwill, and gains or losses on sales of property, plant, and equipment and discontinued operations (which relate to investing activities), and gains or losses on extinguishment of debt (which is a financing activity). [FAS95, ¶28]

[12a]Interest and dividends that are donor restricted for long-term purposes as noted in paragraphs .116 and .117(c) are not part of operating cash receipts. [FAS117, ¶30(e)]

[13]Adjustments to net income [FAS95, ¶28, fn12] of a business enterprise or change in net assets of a not-for-profit organization [FAS117, ¶30(f)] to determine net cash flow from operating activities shall reflect accruals for interest earned but not received and interest incurred but not paid. Those accruals may be reflected in the statement of financial position in changes in assets and liabilities that relate to investing or financing activities, such as loans or deposits. However, interest credited directly to a deposit account that has the general characteristics described in paragraph .105, footnote 2, is a cash outflow of the payor and a cash inflow of the payee when the entry is made. [FAS95, ¶28, fn12]

.127 The reconciliation of net income [FAS95, ¶29] of a business enterprise or change in net assets of a not-for-profit organization [FAS117, ¶30(f)] to net cash flow from operating activities described in paragraph .126 shall be provided regardless of whether the direct or indirect method of reporting net cash flow from operating activities is used. That reconciliation shall separately report all major classes of reconciling items. For example, major classes of deferrals of past operating cash receipts and payments and accruals of expected future operating cash receipts and payments, including at a minimum changes during the period in receivables pertaining to operating activities, in inventory, and in payables pertaining to operating activities, shall be separately reported. Enterprises are encouraged to provide further breakdowns of those categories that they consider meaningful. For example, changes in receivables from customers for an enterprise's sale of goods or services might be reported separately from changes in other operating receivables. In addition, if the indirect method is used, amounts of interest paid (net of amounts capitalized) and income taxes paid during the period shall be provided in related disclosures. [FAS95, ¶29]

.128 If the direct method of reporting net cash flow from operating activities is used, the reconciliation of net income [FAS95, ¶30] of a business enterprise or change in net assets of a not-for-profit orgnization [FAS117, ¶30(f)] to net cash flow from operating activities shall be provided in a separate schedule. If the indirect method is used, the reconciliation may be either reported within the statement of cash flows or provided in a separate schedule, with the statement of cash flows reporting only the net cash flow from operating activities. If the reconciliation is presented in the statement of cash flows, all adjustments to net income [FAS95, ¶30] of a business enterprise or change in net assets of a not-for-profit organization [FAS117, ¶30(f)] to determine net cash flow from operating activities shall be clearly identified as reconciling items. [FAS95, ¶30]

.129 Except for items described in paragraphs .110 and .111, both investing cash inflows and outflows and financing cash inflows and outflows shall be reported separately in a statement of cash flows—for example, outlays for acquisitions of property, plant, and equipment shall be reported separately from proceeds from sales of property, plant, and equipment; proceeds of borrowings shall be reported separately from repayments of debt; and proceeds from issuing stock shall be reported separately from outlays to reaquire the enterprise's stock. [FAS95, ¶31]

Indirectly Determining Amounts of Operating Cash Receipts and Payments

.130 Given sufficiently detailed information, major classes of operating cash receipts and payments may be determined indirectly by adjusting revenue and expense amounts for the change during the period in related asset and liability accounts. For example, cash collected from customers may be determined indirectly by adjusting sales for the change during the period in receivables from customers for the enterprise's delivery of goods or services. Likewise, cash paid to suppliers and employees may be determined indirectly by adjusting cost of sales and expenses (exclusive of depreciation, interest, and income taxes) for the change during the period in inventories and payables for operating items. That procedure, of course, requires the availability of information concerning the change during the period in the appropriate classes of receivables and payables.[14] The more detailed the categories of operating cash receipts and payments to be reported, the more complex the procedure for determining them. [FAS95, ¶115]

.131 It seems likely that amounts of operating cash receipts and payments at the minimum level of detail specified in paragraph .125 often may be determined indirectly without incurring unduly burdensome costs over those involved in appropriately applying the indirect method. For example, determining net cash flow from operating activities by the indirect method requires the availability of the total amount of operating receivables. That is, any receivables for investing or financing items must be segregated. Within the total amount of operating receivables, information on receivables from customers for an enterprise's delivery of goods or services may well be available separately from those for interest and dividends. Thus, it may be possible to determine indirectly cash collected from customers and interest and dividends received using much the same information needed to determine net cash flow from operating activities using the indirect method. [FAS95, ¶116]

.132 The same procedure may be used to determine cash paid to suppliers and employees. Determining net cash flow from operating activities by the direct method requires the availability of the total amount of payables pertaining to operating activities. Within that amount, payables to suppliers and employees may well be available separately from those for interest and taxes. [FAS95, ¶117]

.133 Many enterprises may well be able to determine amounts of operating cash receipts and payments at the minimum level of detail that this section encourages (refer to paragraph .125) indirectly at reasonable cost by the procedure discussed in the foregoing paragraphs. The degree of difficulty encountered in applying it undoubtedly would vary depending on the nature of an enterprise's operations and the features of its current accounting system. [FAS95, ¶118]

---

[14]For the resulting operating cash receipts and payments to be accurate, the effects of all noncash entries to accounts receivable and payable, inventory, and other balance sheet accounts used in the calculation must be eliminated. For example, the change in accounts receivable would have to be determined exclusive of any bad debt write-offs and other noncash charges and credits to customer accounts during the period. [FAS95, ¶115, fn17]

Information about Noncash Investing and Financing Activities

.134 Information about all investing and financing activities of an enterprise during a period that affect recognized assets or liabilities but that do not result in cash receipts or cash payments in the period shall be reported in related disclosures. Those disclosures may be either narrative or summarized in a schedule. [FAS95, ¶32] If there are only a few such transactions, it may be convenient to include them on the same page as the statement of cash flows. Otherwise, the transactions may be reported elsewhere in the financial statements, clearly referenced to the statement of cash flows. [FAS95, ¶74] [The disclosures] shall clearly relate the cash and noncash aspects of transactions involving similar items. Examples of noncash investing and financing transactions are converting debt to equity; acquiring assets by assuming directly related liabilities, such as purchasing a building by incurring a mortgage to the seller; obtaining an asset by entering into a capital lease; [FAS95, ¶32] obtaining a building or investment asset by receiving a gift; [FAS117, ¶30(g)] and exchanging noncash assets or liabilities for other noncash assets or liabilities. Some transactions are part cash and part noncash; only the cash portion shall be reported in the statement of cash flows. [FAS95, ¶32]

Cash Flow per Share

.135 Financial statements shall not report an amount of cash flow per share. Neither cash flow nor any component of it is an alternative to net income as an indicator of an enterprise's performance, as reporting per share amounts might imply.[15] [FAS95, ¶33]

Exemptions from the Requirement to Provide a Statement of Cash Flows

Employee Benefit Plans

.135A A statement of cash flows is not required to be provided by a defined benefit pension plan that presents financial information in accordance with the provisions of Section Pe5, "Pension Funds: Accounting and Reporting by Defined Benefit Pension Plans."[16] Other employee benefit plans that present financial information similar to that required by Section Pe5 (including the presentation of plan investments at fair value)

---

[15]Reporting a contractually determined per unit amount, [such as a] per unit amount of cash flow distributable under the terms of a partnership agreement or other agreement between an enterprise and its owners, is not the same as reporting a cash flow per share amount intended to provide information useful to all investors and creditors and thus is not precluded by this section. [FAS95, ¶125]

[16]Paragraph .105 of Section Pe5 presents a comprehensive list of the basic financial statements that defined benefit pension plans are required to provide, although additional financial information may be provided. This section [does not] modify the reporting requirements for [defined benefit pension] plans. [FAS102, ¶15]

also are not required to provide a statement of cash flows. Employee benefit plans are encouraged to include a statement of cash flows with their annual financial statements when that statement would provide relevant information about the ability of the plan to meet future obligations (for example, when the plan invests in assets that are not highly liquid or obtains financing for investments). [FAS102, ¶5]

Investment Companies

.135B Provided that the conditions in paragraph .135C are met, a statement of cash flows is not required to be provided by (a) an investment company that is subject to the registration and regulatory requirements of the Investment Company Act of 1940 (1940 Act),[17] (b) an investment enterprise that has essentially the same characteristics as those subject to the 1940 Act,[18] or (c) a common trust fund, variable annuity account, or similar fund maintained by a bank, insurance company, or other enterprise in its capacity as a trustee, administrator, or guardian for the collective investment and reinvestment of moneys. [FAS102, ¶6]

.135C For an investment enterprise specified in paragraph .135B to be exempt from the requirement to provide a statement of cash flows, all of the following conditions must be met:

a. During the period, substantially all of the enterprise's investments were highly liquid (for example, marketable securities and other assets for which a market is readily available).[19]
b. Substantially all of the enterprise's investments are carried at market value.[20]

---

[17]Investment companies that are subject to the reporting requirements of the 1940 Act are required to provide a statement of changes in net assets. Net assets and changes in those net assets are relevant because net asset value per share is used by many investment companies to determine the price of shares redeemed and sold. [FAS102, ¶21]

[18]Certain investment enterprises have essentially the same characteristics as investment companies that are subject to the requirements of the 1940 Act [but] may not be subject to the registration requirements of the 1940 Act either because the number of stockholders is limited or because they are otherwise exempted from the 1940 Act (for example, offshore funds, commodity pools, certain common trust funds of banks, or variable annuity accounts of life insurance companies). [FAS102, ¶22]

[19]For highly liquid investment companies that do not finance investments with debt, the financial statements other than a statement of cash flows generally provide sufficient information for users to assess the enterprises' liquidity, financial flexibility, profitability, and risk. [FAS102, ¶20]

[20]Securities for which market value is determined using matrix pricing techniques, which are described in the AICPA Audit and Accounting Guide, *Audits of Investment Companies* [3d ed. (1987)], would meet this condition. Other securities for which market value is not readily determinable and for which fair value must be determined in good faith by the board of directors would not. [FAS102, ¶7, fn1]

c. The enterprise had little or no debt, based on average debt outstanding[21] during the period, in relation to average total assets.
d. The enterprise provides a statement of changes in net assets.[22]

[FAS102, ¶7]

Illustrative Examples

.136 Paragraphs .137 through .155 provide illustrations for the preparation of statements of cash flows [FAS95, ¶130] of business enterprises. Paragraph .136 of Section No5, "Not-for-Profit Organizations," provides illustrations for the preparation of statements of cash flows for a not-for-profit organization. [FAS117, ¶ 30(h)] Example 1 (paragraphs .137 through .141) illustrates a statement of cash flows under both the direct method and the indirect method for a domestic manufacturing company. Example 2 (paragraphs .142 through .152) illustrates a statement of cash flows under the direct method for a manufacturing company with foreign operations. Example 3 (paragraphs .153 through .155) illustrates a statement of cash flows under the direct method for a financial institution. These illustrations are intended as examples only. Also, the illustrations of the reconciliation of net income to net cash provided by operating activities may provide detailed information in excess of that required for a meaningful presentation. Other formats or levels of detail may be appropriate for particular circumstances. [FAS95, ¶130]

Example 1

.137 [Exhibits 137A, 137B, and 137C] present a statement of cash flows [and related schedule and disclosures] for the year ended December 31, 19X1 for Company M, a U.S. corporation engaged principally in manufacturing activities. This statement of cash flows illustrates the direct method of presenting cash flows from operating activities, as encouraged in paragraph .125 of this section. [FAS95, ¶131]

---

[21]For the purpose of determining average debt outstanding, obligations resulting from redemptions of shares by the enterprise, from unsettled purchases of securities or similar assets, or from covered options written generally may be excluded. However, any extension of credit by the seller that is not in accordance with standard industry practices for redeeming shares or for settling purchases of investments shall be included in average debt outstanding. [FAS102, ¶7, fn2]

[22]Although the purpose and format of a statement of changes in net assets are different from those of a statement of cash flows, much of the information contained in those statements is similar. [FAS102, ¶21]

(This page intentionally left blank.)

Exhibit 137A

Company M
Consolidated Statement of Cash Flows
For the Year Ended December 31, 19X1

Cash flows from operating activities:		
Cash received from customers	$ 13,850	
Cash paid to suppliers and employees	(12,000)	
Dividend received from affiliate	20	
Interest received	55	
Interest paid (net of amount capitalized)	(220)	
Income taxes paid	(325)	
Insurance proceeds received	15	
Cash paid to settle lawsuit for patent infringement	(30)	
Net cash provided by operating activities		$ 1,365
Cash flows from investing activities:		
Proceeds from sale of facility	600	
Payment received on note for sale of plant	150	
Capital expenditures	(1,000)	
Payment for purchase of Company S, net of cash acquired	(925)	
Net cash used in investing activities		(1,175)
Cash flows from financing activities:		
Net borrowings under line-of-credit agreement	300	
Principal payments under capital lease obligation	(125)	
Proceeds from issuance of long-term debt	400	
Proceeds from issuance of common stock	500	
Dividends paid	(200)	
Net cash provided by financing activities		875
Net increase in cash and cash equivalents		1,065
Cash and cash equivalents at beginning of year		600
Cash and cash equivalents at end of year		$ 1,665

[FAS95, ¶131]

Exhibit 137B

Reconciliation of Net Income to Net Cash Provided by Operating Activities

Net income		$ 760
Adjustments to reconcile net income to net cash provided by operating activities:		
Depreciation and amortization	$ 445	
Provision for losses on accounts receivable	200	
Gain on sale of facility	(80)	
Undistributed earnings of affiliate	(25)	
Payment received on installment note receivable for sale of inventory	100	
Change in assets and liabilities net of effects from purchase of Company S:		
Increase in accounts receivable	(215)	
Decrease in inventory	205	
Increase in prepaid expenses	(25)	
Decrease in accounts payable and accrued expenses	(250)	
Increase in interest and income taxes payable	50	
Increase in deferred taxes	150	
Increase in other liabilities	50	
Total adjustments		605
Net cash provided by operating activities		$1,365

[FAS95, ¶131]

Exhibit 137C

Disclosures in Financial Statements

Supplemental Schedule of Noncash Investing and Financing Activities

The Company purchased all of the capital stock of Company S for $950. In conjunction with the acquisition, liabilities were assumed as follows:

Fair value of assets acquired	$1,580
Cash paid for the capital stock	(950)
Liabilities assumed	$ 630

A capital lease obligation of $850 was incurred when the Company entered into a lease for new equipment.

Additional common stock was issued upon the conversion of $500 of long-term debt.

Disclosure of Accounting Policy

For purposes of the statement of cash flows, the Company considers all highly liquid debt instruments purchased with a maturity of three months or less to be cash equivalents.

[FAS95, ¶131]

.138 [Exhibits 138A and 138B] present Company M's statement of cash flows [and the related disclosures] for the year ended December 31, 19X1 prepared using the indirect method, as described in paragraph .126 of this section. [FAS95, ¶132]

.139 [Exhibits 139A and 139B] summarize financial information for the current year for Company M, which provides the basis for the statements of cash flows presented in Exhibits 137A and 138A. [FAS95, ¶133]

Exhibit 138A

Company M
Consolidated Statement of Cash Flows
For the Year Ended December 31, 19X1

Cash flows from operating activities:		
Net income		$ 760
Adjustments to reconcile net income to net cash provided by operating activities:		
Depreciation and amortization	$ 445	
Provision for losses on accounts receivable	200	
Gain on sale of facility	(80)	
Undistributed earnings of affiliate	(25)	
Payment received on installment note receivable for sale of inventory	100	
Change in assets and liabilities net of effects from purchase of Company S:		
Increase in accounts receivable	(215)	
Decrease in inventory	205	
Increase in prepaid expenses	(25)	
Decrease in accounts payable and accrued expenses	(250)	
Increase in interest and income taxes payable	50	
Increase in deferred taxes	150	
Increase in other liabilities	50	
Total adjustments		605
Net cash provided by operating activities		1,365
Cash flows from investing activities:		
Proceeds from sale of facility	600	
Payment received on note for sale of plant	150	
Capital expenditures	(1,000)	
Payment for purchase of Company S, net of cash acquired	(925)	
Net cash used in investing activities		(1,175)
Cash flows from financing activities:		
Net borrowings under line-of-credit agreement	300	
Principal payments under capital lease obligation	(125)	
Proceeds from issuance of long-term debt	400	
Proceeds from issuance of common stock	500	
Dividends paid	(200)	
Net cash provided by financing activities		875
Net increase in cash and cash equivalents		1,065
Cash and cash equivalents at beginning of year		600
Cash and cash equivalents at end of year		$ 1,665

[FAS95, ¶132]

Exhibit 138B

Disclosures in Financial Statements

Supplemental Disclosures of Cash Flow Information

Cash paid during the year for:	
Interest (net of amount capitalized)	$220
Income taxes	325

Supplemental Schedule of Noncash Investing and Financing Activities

The Company purchased all of the capital stock of Company S for $950. In conjunction with the acquisition, liabilities were assumed as follows:

Fair value of assets acquired	$1,580
Cash paid for the capital stock	(950)
Liabilities assumed	$ 630

A capital lease obligation of $850 was incurred when the Company entered into a lease for new equipment.

Additional common stock was issued upon the conversion of $500 of long-term debt.

Disclosure of Accounting Policy

For purposes of the statement of cash flows, the Company considers all highly liquid debt instruments purchased with a maturity of three months or less to be cash equivalents.

[FAS95, ¶132]

Exhibit 139A

Company M
[Comparative] Consolidated Statements of Financial Position
[January 1 and December 31, 19X1]

	1/1/X1	12/31/X1	Change
Assets:			
Cash and cash equivalents	$ 600	$ 1,665	$1,065
Accounts receivable (net of allowance for losses of $600 and $450)	1,770	1,940	170
Notes receivable	400	150	(250)
Inventory	1,230	1,375	145
Prepaid expenses	110	135	25
Investments	250	275	25
Property, plant, and equipment:			
Cost	6,460	8,460	2,000
Accumulated depreciation	(2,100)	(2,300)	(200)
Property, plant, and equipment, net	4,360	6,160	1,800
Intangible assets	40	175	135
Total assets	$ 8,760	$11,875	$3,115
Liabilities:			
Accounts payable and accrued expenses	$ 1,085	$ 1,090	$ 5
Interest payable	30	45	15
Income taxes payable	50	85	35
Short-term debt	450	750	300
Lease obligation	–	725	725
Long-term debt	2,150	2,425	275
Deferred taxes	375	525	150
Other liabilities	225	275	50
Total liabilities	4,365	5,920	1,555
Stockholders' equity:			
Capital stock	2,000	3,000	1,000
Retained earnings	2,395	2,955	560
Total stockholders' equity	4,395	5,955	1,560
Total liabilities and stockholders' equity	$ 8,760	$11,875	$3,115

[FAS95, ¶133]

Exhibit 139B

Company M
Consolidated Statement of Income
For the Year Ended December 31, 19X1

Sales	$ 13,965
Cost of sales	(10,290)
Depreciation and amortization	(445)
Selling, general, and administrative expenses	(1,890)
Interest expense	(235)
Equity in earnings of affiliate	45
Gain on sale of facility	80
Interest income	55
Insurance proceeds	15
Loss from patent infringement lawsuit	(30)
Income before income taxes	1,270
Provision for income taxes	(510)
Net income	$ 760

[FAS95, ¶133]

.140 The following transactions were entered into by Company M during 19X1 and are reflected in the above financial statements:

a. Company M wrote off $350 of accounts receivable when a customer filed for bankruptcy. A provision for losses on accounts receivable of $200 was included in Company M's selling, general, and administrative expenses.
b. Company M collected the third and final annual installment payment of $100 on a note receivable for the sale of inventory and collected the third of four annual installment payments of $150 each on a note receivable for the sale of a plant. Interest on these notes through December 31 totaling $55 was also collected.
c. Company M received a dividend of $20 from an affiliate accounted for under the equity method of accounting.
d. Company M sold a facility with a book value of $520 and an original cost of $750 for $600 cash.
e. Company M constructed a new facility for its own use and placed it in service. Accumulated expenditures during the year of $1,000 included capitalized interest of $10.

f. Company M entered into a capital lease for new equipment with a fair value of $850. Principal payments under the lease obligation totaled $125.

g. Company M purchased all of the capital stock of Company S for $950 [FAS95, ¶134] in a business combination. [FAS141, ¶E13(a)] The fair values of Company S's assets and liabilities at the date of acquisition are presented below:

Cash	$ 25
Accounts receivable	155
Inventory	350
Property, plant, and equipment	900
Patents	80
Goodwill	70
Accounts payable and accrued expenses	(255)
Long-term note payable	(375)
Net assets acquired	$ 950

h. Company M borrowed and repaid various amounts under a line-of-credit agreement in which borrowings are payable 30 days after demand. The net increase during the year in the amount borrowed against the line-of-credit totaled $300.

i. Company M issued $400 of long-term debt securities.

j. Company M's provision for income taxes included a deferred provision of $150.

k. Company M's depreciation totaled $430, and amortization of intangible assets totaled $15.

l. Company M's selling, general, and administrative expenses included an accrual for incentive compensation of $50 that has been deferred by executives until their retirement. The related obligation was included in other liabilities.

m. Company M collected insurance proceeds of $15 from a business interruption claim that resulted when a storm precluded shipment of inventory for one week.

n. Company M paid $30 to settle a lawsuit for patent infringement.

o. Company M issued $1,000 of additional common stock of which $500 was issued for cash and $500 was issued upon conversion of long-term debt.

p. Company M paid dividends of $200. [FAS95, ¶134]

.141 Based on the financial data from the preceding example, the following computations [in Exhibit 141A] illustrate a method of indirectly determining cash received from customers and cash paid to suppliers and employees for use in a statement of cash flows under the direct method. [FAS95, ¶135]

Exhibit 141A

Computation of Cash Received from Customers and Cash Paid to Suppliers and Employees

Cash received from customers during the year:

Customer sales		$13,965
Collection of installment payment for sale of inventory		100
Gross accounts receivable at beginning of year	$ 2,370	
Accounts receivable acquired in purchase of Company S	155	
Accounts receivable written off	(350)	
Gross accounts receivable at end of year	(2,390)	
Excess of new accounts receivable over collections from customers		(215)
Cash received from customers during the year		$13,850

Exhibit 141A (continued)

Cash paid to suppliers and employees during the year:			
Cost of sales			$10,290
General and administrative expenses		$ 1,890	
Expenses not requiring cash outlay (provision for uncollectible accounts receivable)		(200)	
Net expenses requiring cash payments			1,690
Inventory at beginning of year		(1,230)	
Inventory acquired in purchase of Company S		(350)	
Inventory at end of year		1,375	
Net decrease in inventory from Company M's operations			(205)
Adjustments for changes in related accruals:			
Account balances at beginning of year:			
Accounts payable and accrued expenses	$1,085		
Other liabilities	225		
Prepaid expenses	(110)		
Total		1,200	
Accounts payable and accrued expenses acquired in purchase of Company S		255	
Account balances at end of year:			
Accounts payable and accrued expenses	1,090		
Other liabilities	275		
Prepaid expenses	(135)		
Total		(1,230)	
Additional cash payments not included in expense			225
Cash paid to suppliers and employees during the year			$12,000

[FAS95, ¶135]

Example 2

.142 [Exhibits 142A, 142B, and 142C] present a consolidating statement of cash flows [and the related disclosures] for the year ended December 31, 19X1 for Company F, a multinational U.S. corporation engaged principally in manufacturing activities, which has two wholly owned foreign subsidiaries—Subsidiary A and Subsidiary B. For Subsidiary A, the local currency is the functional currency. For Subsidiary B, which operates in a highly inflationary economy, the U.S. dollar is the functional currency. [FAS95, ¶136]

Exhibit 142A

Company F
Consolidating Statement of Cash Flows
For the Year Ended December 31, 19X1

	Parent Company	Subsidiary A	Subsidiary B	Eliminations	Consolidated
Cash flows from operating activities:					
Cash received from customers	$ 4,610[a]	$ 888[a]	$ 561[a]	$(430)	$ 5,629
Cash paid to suppliers and employees	(3,756)[a]	(806)[a]	(370)[a]	430	(4,502)
Interest paid	(170)	(86)	(135)	–	(391)
Income taxes paid	(158)	(25)	(21)	–	(204)
Interest and dividends received	57	–	–	(22)	35
Miscellaneous cash received (paid)	–	45	(5)	–	40
Net cash provided by operating activities	583	16	30	(22)	607
Cash flows from investing activities:					
Proceeds from sale of equipment	150	116	14	–	280
Payments for purchase of equipment	(450)	(258)	(15)	–	(723)
Net cash used in investing activities	(300)	(142)	(1)	–	(443)

Cash flows from financing activities:					
Proceeds from issuance of short-term debt	20	75	–	–	95
Intercompany loan	(15)	–	15	–	–
Proceeds from issuance of long-term debt	–	165	–	–	165
Repayment of long-term debt	(200)	(105)	(35)	–	(340)
Payment of dividends	(120)	(22)	–	22	(120)
Net cash provided by (used in) financing activities	(315)	113	(20)	22	(200)
Effect of exchange rate changes on cash	–	9[b]	(5)[b]	–	4
Net change in cash and cash equivalents	(32)	(4)	4	–	(32)
Cash and cash equivalents at beginning of year	255	15	5	–	275
Cash and cash equivalents at end of year	$ 223	$ 11	$ 9	$ –	$ 243

[a]The computation of this amount is provided in paragraph .151.

[b]The computation of this amount is provided in paragraph .152.

[FAS95, ¶136]

Exhibit 142B

Reconciliation of Net Income to Net Cash Provided by Operating Activities

	Parent Company	Subsidiary A	Subsidiary B	Eliminations	Consolidated
Net income	$ 417	$ 50	$ (66)	$(37)	$ 364
Adjustment to reconcile net income to net cash provided by operating activities:					
Depreciation and amortization	350	85	90	–	525
(Gain) loss on sale of equipment	(115)	–	25	–	(90)
Writedown of facility to net realizable value	50	–	–	–	50
Exchange gain	–	–	(115)	–	(115)
Provision for deferred taxes	90	–	–	–	90
Increase in accounts receivable	(85)	(37)	(9)	–	(131)
(Increase) decrease in inventory	(80)	(97)	107	15	(55)
Increase (decrease) in accounts payable and accrued expenses	(41)	16	(6)	–	(31)
Increase (decrease) in interest and taxes payable	(3)	(1)	4	–	–
Net cash provided by operating activities	$ 583	$ 16	$ 30	$(22)	$ 607

[FAS95, ¶136]

Exhibit 142C

Disclosure of Accounting Policy

Cash in excess of daily requirements is invested in marketable securities consisting of Treasury bills with maturities of three months or less. Such investments are deemed to be cash equivalents for purposes of the statement of cash flows.

[FAS95, ¶136]

.143 [Exhibits 143A and 143B] summarize financial information for the current year for Company F, which provides the basis for the statement of cash flows presented in paragraph .142. [FAS95, ¶137]

.144 The U.S. dollar equivalents of one unit of local currency applicable to Subsidiary A and to Subsidiary B are as follows:

	Subsidiary A	Subsidiary B
1/1/X1	.40	.05
Weighted average	.43	.03
12/31/X1	.45	.02

The computation of the weighted-average exchange rate for Subsidiary A excludes the effect of Subsidiary A's sale of inventory to the parent company at the beginning of the year discussed in paragraph .148(a). [FAS95, ¶138]

.145 Comparative statements of financial position for the parent company and for each of the foreign subsidiaries are presented [in Exhibit 145A]. [FAS95, ¶139]

Exhibit 143A

Company F
Consolidating Statement of Financial Position
December 31, 19X1

	Parent Company	Subsidiary A	Subsidiary B	Eliminations	Consolidated
Assets:					
Cash and cash equivalents	$ 223	$ 11	$ 9	$ –	$ 243
Accounts receivable	725	95	20	–	840
Intercompany loan receivable	15	–	–	(15)	–
Inventory	630	281	96	(15)	992
Investments	730	–	–	(730)	–
Property, plant, and equipment, net	3,305	1,441	816	–	5,562
Other assets	160	11	–	–	171
Total assets	$5,788	$1,839	$941	$(760)	$7,808
Liabilities:					
Accounts payable and accrued expenses	$ 529	$ 135	$ 38	$ –	$ 702
Interest payable	35	11	4	–	50
Taxes payable	45	5	2	–	52
Short-term debt	160	135	–	–	295
Intercompany debt	–	–	15	(15)	–
Long-term debt	1,100	315	40	–	1,455
Deferred taxes	342	–	–	–	342
Total liabilities	2,211	601	99	(15)	2,896
Stockholders' equity:					
Capital stock	550	455	275	(730)	550
Retained earnings	3,027	554	567	(15)	4,133
Cumulative translation adjustment	–	229	–	–	229
Total stockholders' equity	3,577	1,238	842	(745)	4,912
Total liabilities and stockholders' equity	$5,788	$1,839	$941	$(760)	$7,808

[FAS95, ¶137]

Exhibit 143B

Company F
Consolidating Statement of Income
For the Year Ended December 31, 19X1

	Parent Company	Subsidiary A	Subsidiary B	Eliminations	Consolidated
Revenues	$ 4,695	$ 925	$ 570	$(430)	$ 5,760
Cost of sales	(3,210)	(615)	(406)	415	(3,816)
Depreciation and amortization	(350)	(85)	(90)	–	(525)
General and administrative expenses	(425)	(110)	(65)	–	(600)
Interest expense	(165)	(90)	(135)	–	(390)
Interest and dividend income	57	–	–	(22)	35
Gain (loss) on sale of equipment	115	–	(25)	–	90
Miscellaneous income (expense)	(50)	45	(5)	–	(10)
Exchange gain	–	–	115	–	115
Income before income taxes	667	70	(41)	(37)	659
Provision for income taxes	(250)	(20)	(25)	–	(295)
Net income	$ 417	$ 50	$ (66)	$ (37)	$ 364

[FAS95, ¶137]

Exhibit 145A

Comparative Statements of Financial Position

	Parent Company			Subsidiary A Local Currency		
	1/1/X1	12/31/X1	Change	1/1/X1	12/31/X1	Change
Assets:						
Cash and cash equivalents	$ 255	$ 223	$ (32)	LC 38	LC 25	LC (13)
Accounts receivables	640	725	85	125	210	85
Intercompany loan receivable	–	15	15	–	–	–
Inventory	550	630	80	400	625	225
Investments	730	730	–	–	–	–
Property, plant, and equipment, net	3,280	3,305	25	3,075	3,202	127
Other assets	170	160	(10)	25	25	–
Total assets	$5,625	$5,788	$ 163	LC3,663	LC4,087	LC 424
Liabilities:						
Accounts payable and accrued expenses	$ 570	$ 529	$ (41)	LC 263	LC 300	LC 37
Interest payable	40	35	(5)	15	24	9
Taxes payable	43	45	2	25	12	(13)
Short-term debt	140	160	20	125	300	175
Intercompany debt	–	–	–	–	–	–
Long-term debt	1,300	1,100	(200)	550	700	150
Deferred taxes	252	342	90	–	–	–
Total liabilities	2,345	2,211	(134)	978	1,336	358
Stockholders' equity:						
Capital stock	550	550	–	1,300	1,300	–
Retained earnings	2,730	3,027	297	1,385	1,451	66
Cumulative translation adjustment	–	–	–	–	–	–
Total stockholders' equity	3,280	3,577	297	2,685	2,751	66
Total liabilities and stockholders' equity	$5,625	$5,788	$ 163	LC3,663	LC4,087	LC 424

[FAS95, ¶139]

Subsidiary A			Subsidiary B			Subsidiary B		
U.S. Dollars			Local Currency			U.S. Dollars		
1/1/X1	12/31/X1	Change	1/1/X1	12/31/X1	Change	1/1/X1	12/31/X1	Change
$ 15	$ 11	$ (4)	LC 100	LC 449	LC 349	$ 5	$ 9	$ 4
50	95	45	700	1,000	300	35	20	(15)
–	–	–	–	–	–	–	–	–
160	281	121	2,900	3,200	300	203	96	(107)
–	–	–	–	–	–	–	–	–
1,230	1,441	211	6,200	5,900	(300)	930	816	(114)
10	11	1	–	–	–	–	–	–
$1,465	$1,839	$374	LC9,900	LC10,549	LC 649	$1,173	$941	$(232)
$ 105	$ 135	$ 30	LC2,100	LC 1,900	LC (200)	$ 105	$ 38	$ (67)
6	11	5	200	200	–	10	4	(6)
10	5	(5)	–	120	120	–	2	2
50	135	85	–	–	–	–	–	–
–	–	–	–	500	500	–	15	15
220	315	95	3,000	2,000	(1,000)	150	40	(110)
–	–	–	–	–	–	–	–	–
391	601	210	5,300	4,720	(580)	265	99	(166)
455	455	–	1,375	1,375	–	275	275	–
526	554	28	3,225	4,454	1,229	633	567	(66)
93	229	136	–	–	–	–	–	–
1,074	1,238	164	4,600	5,829	1,229	908	842	(66)
$1,465	$1,839	$374	LC9,900	LC10,549	LC 649	$1,173	$941	$(232)

.146 Statements of income in local currency and U.S. dollars for each of the foreign subsidiaries are presented [in Exhibit 146A]. [FAS95, ¶140]

Exhibit 146A

Statements of Income
For the Year Ended December 31, 19X1

	Subsidiary A		Subsidiary B	
	Local Currency	U.S. Dollars	Local Currency	U.S. Dollars
Revenues	LC2,179	$ 925[a]	LC19,000	$ 570
Cost of sales	(1,458)	(615)[b]	(9,667)	(406)
Depreciation and amortization	(198)	(85)	(600)	(90)
General and administrative expenses	(256)	(110)	(2,167)	(65)
Interest expense	(209)	(90)	(4,500)	(135)
Gain (loss) on sale of equipment	–	–	150	(25)
Miscellaneous income (expense)	105	45	(167)	(5)
Exchange gain	–	–	–	115
Income before income taxes	163	70	2,049	(41)
Provision for income taxes	(47)	(20)	(820)	(25)
Net income	LC 116	$ 50	LC 1,229	$ (66)

[a]This amount was computed as follows:

Sale to parent company at beginning of year	LC 400 @ .40 =	$160
Sales to customers	LC1,779 @ .43 =	765
Total sales in U.S. dollars		$925

[b]This amount was computed as follows:

Cost of sale to parent company at beginning of year	LC 400 @ .40 =	$160
Cost of sales to customers	LC1,058 @ .43 =	455
Total cost of sales in U.S. dollars		$615

[FAS95, ¶140]

.147 The following transactions were entered into during the year by the parent company and are reflected in the above financial statements:

a. The parent company invested cash in excess of daily requirements in Treasury bills. Interest earned on such investments totaled $35.
b. The parent company sold excess property with a net book value of $35 for $150.
c. The parent company's capital expenditures totaled $450.
d. The parent company wrote down to its estimated net realizable value of $25 a facility with a net book value of $75.
e. The parent company's short-term debt consisted of commercial paper with maturities not exceeding 60 days.
f. The parent company repaid long-term notes of $200.
g. The parent company's depreciation totaled $340, and amortization of intangible assets totaled $10.
h. The parent company's provision for income taxes included deferred taxes of $90.
i. Because of a change in product design, the parent company purchased all of Subsidiary A's beginning inventory for its book value of $160. All of the inventory was subsequently sold by the parent company.
j. The parent company received a dividend of $22 from Subsidiary A. The dividend was credited to the parent company's income.
k. The parent company purchased from Subsidiary B $270 of merchandise of which $45 remained in the parent company's inventory at year-end. Intercompany profit on the remaining inventory totaled $15.
l. The parent company loaned $15, payable in U.S. dollars, to Subsidiary B.
m. Company F paid dividends totaling $120 to shareholders.

[FAS95, ¶141]

.148 The following transactions were entered into during the year by Subsidiary A and are reflected in the above financial statements. The U.S. dollar equivalent of the local currency amount based on the exchange rate at the date of each transaction is included. Except for the sale of inventory to the parent company (transaction (a) below), Subsidiary A's sales and purchases and operating cash receipts and payments occurred evenly throughout the year.

a. Because of a change in product design, Subsidiary A sold all of its beginning inventory to the parent company for its book value of LC400 ($160).
b. Subsidiary A sold equipment for its book value of LC275 ($116) and purchased new equipment at a cost of LC600 ($258).
c. Subsidiary A issued an additional LC175 ($75) of 30-day notes and renewed the notes at each maturity date.

d. Subsidiary A issued long-term debt of LC400 ($165) and repaid long-term debt of LC250 ($105).
e. Subsidiary A paid a dividend to the parent company of LC50 ($22).

[FAS95, ¶142]

.149 The following transactions were entered into during the year by Subsidiary B and are reflected in the above financial statements. The U.S. dollar equivalent of the local currency amount based on the exchange rate at the date of each transaction is included. Subsidiary B's sales and operating cash receipts and payments occurred evenly throughout the year. For convenience, all purchases of inventory were based on the weighted-average exchange rate for the year. Subsidiary B uses the FIFO method of inventory valuation.

a. Subsidiary B had sales to the parent company as follows:

	Local Currency	**U.S. Dollars**
Intercompany sales	LC 9,000	$ 270
Cost of sales	(4,500)	(180)
Gross profit	LC 4,500	$ 90

b. Subsidiary B sold equipment with a net book value of LC200 ($39) for LC350 ($14). New equipment was purchased at a cost of LC500 ($15).
c. Subsidiary B borrowed $15 (LC500), payable in U.S. dollars, from the parent company.
d. Subsidiary B repaid LC1,000 ($35) of long-term debt. [FAS95, ¶143]

.150 Statements of cash flows in the local currency and in U.S. dollars for Subsidiary A and Subsidiary B, [and related reconciliation of net cash provided by operating activities,] are presented [in Exhibits 150A and 150B]. [FAS95, ¶144]

(This page intentionally left blank.)

Exhibit 150A

Statement of Cash Flows
For the Year Ended December 31, 19X1

	Subsidiary A		Subsidiary B	
	Local Currency	U.S. Dollars	Local Currency	U.S. Dollars
Cash flows from operating activities:				
Cash received from customers	LC2,094[a]	$ 888[a]	LC18,700[a]	$ 561[a]
Cash paid to suppliers and employees	(1,902)[a]	(806)[a]	(12,334)[a]	(370)[a]
Interest paid	(200)	(86)[b]	(4,500)	(135)[b]
Income taxes paid	(60)	(25)[b]	(700)	(21)[b]
Miscellaneous receipts (payments)	105	45[b]	(167)	(5)[b]
Net cash provided by operating activities	37	16	999	30
Cash flows from investing activities:				
Proceeds from sale of equipment	275	116[c]	350	14[c]
Payments for purchase of equipment	(600)	(258)[c]	(500)	(15)[c]
Net cash used in investing activities	(325)	(142)	(150)	(1)
Cash flows from financing activities:				
Net increase in short-term debt	175	75[c]	–	–
Proceeds from intercompany loan	–	–	500	15[c]
Proceeds from issuance of long-term debt	400	165[c]	–	–
Repayment of long-term debt	(250)	(105)[c]	(1,000)	(35)[c]
Payment of dividends	(50)	(22)[c]	–	–
Net cash provided by (used in) financing activities	275	113	(500)	(20)
Effect of exchange rate changes on cash	–	9[d]	–	(5)[d]
Net increase (decrease) in cash	(13)	(4)	349	4
Cash at beginning of year	38	15	100	5
Cash at end of year	LC 25	$ 11	LC 449	$ 9

[a]The computation of this amount is provided in paragraph .151.

[b]This amount represents the U.S. dollar equivalent of the foreign currency cash flow based on the weighted-average exchange rate for the year.

[c]This amount represents the U.S. dollar equivalent of the foreign currency cash flow based on the exchange rate in effect at the time of the cash flow.

[d]The computation of this amount is provided in paragraph .152.

[FAS95, ¶144]

Exhibit 150B

Reconciliation of Net Income to Net Cash Provided by Operating Activities

	Subsidiary A		Subsidiary B	
	Local Currency	U.S. Dollars	Local Currency	U.S. Dollars
Net income	LC116	$ 50	LC1,229	$ (66)
Adjustments to reconcile net income to net cash provided by operating activities:				
Depreciation and amortization	198	85[a]	600	90[b]
(Gain) loss on sale of equipment	–	–	(150)	25[b]
Exchange gain	–	–	–	(115)[c]
Increase in accounts receivable	(85)	(37)[a]	(300)	(9)[a]
(Increase) decrease in inventory	(225)	(97)[a]	(300)	107[d]
Increase (decrease) in accounts payable and accrued expenses	37	16[a]	(200)	(6)[a]
Increase (decrease) in interest and taxes payable	(4)	(1)[a]	120	4[a]
Net cash provided by operating activities	LC 37	$ 16	LC 999	$ 30

[a]This amount represents the U.S. dollar equivalent of the foreign currency amount based on the weighted-average exchange rate for the year.

[b]This amount represents the U.S. dollar equivalent of the foreign currency amount based on historical exchange rates.

[c]This amount represents the exchange gain included in net income as a result of remeasuring Subsidiary B's financial statements from the local currency to U.S. dollars.

[d]This amount represents the difference between beginning and ending inventory after remeasurement into U.S. dollars based on historical exchange rates.

[FAS95, ¶144]

.151 Exhibit 151A presents the computation of cash received from customers and cash paid to suppliers and employees as reported in the consolidating statement of cash flows for Company F appearing in paragraph .142. [FAS95, ¶145]

.152 [Exhibit 152A] presents the computation of the effect of exchange rate changes on cash for Subsidiary A and Subsidiary B. [FAS95, ¶146]

Exhibit 151A

Computation of Cash Received from Customers and Cash Paid to Suppliers and Employees

	Parent	Subsidiary A		Subsidiary B	
	Company	Local Currency	U.S. Dollars	Local Currency	U.S. Dollars
Cash received from customers during the year:					
Revenues	$4,695	LC2,179	$925	LC19,000	$ 570
Increase in accounts receivable	(85)	(85)	(37)	(300)	(9)
Cash received from customers	$4,610	LC2,094	$888	LC18,700	$ 561
Cash paid to suppliers and employees during the year:					
Cost of sales	$3,210	LC1,458	$615	L C9,667	$ 406
Effect of exchange rate changes on cost of sales	–	–	–	–	(116)[a]
General and administrative expenses	425	256	110	2,167	65
Total operating expenses requiring cash payments	3,635	1,714	725	11,834	355
Increase in inventory	80	225	97	300	9
Decrease (increase) in accounts payable and accrued expenses	41	(37)	(16)	200	6
Cash paid to suppliers and employees	$3,756	LC1,902	$806	LC12,334	$ 370

[a]This adjustment represents the difference between cost of sales remeasured at historical exchange rates ($406) and cost of sales translated based on the weighted-average exchange rate for the year ($290). The adjustment is necessary because cash payments for inventory, which were made evenly throughout the year, were based on the weighted-average exchange rate for the year.

[FAS95, ¶145]

Exhibit 152A

Computation of the Effect of Exchange Rate Changes on Cash

	Subsidiary A		**Subsidiary B**	
Effect on beginning cash balance:				
Beginning cash balance in local currency	LC 38		LC 100	
Net change in exchange rate during the year	× .05		× (.03)	
Effect on beginning cash balance		$ 2		$ (3)
Effect from operating activities during the year:				
Cash provided by operating activities in local currency	LC 37		LC 999	
Year-end exchange rate	× 45		× .02	
Operating cash flows based on year-end exchange rate	$ 16[a]		$ 20	
Operating cash flows reported in the statement of cash flows	16		30	
Effect from operating activities during the year		0		(10)
Effect from investing activities during the year:				
Cash used in investing activities in local currency	LC(325)		LC(150)	
Year-end exchange rate	× .45		× .02	
Investing cash flows based on year-end exchange rate	$ (146)		$ (3)	
Investing cash flows reported in the statement of cash flows	(142)		(1)	
Effect from investing activities during the year		(4)		(2)
Effect from financing activities during the year:				
Cash provided by (used in) financing activities in local currency	LC 275		LC(500)	
Year-end exchange rate	× .45		× .02	
Financing cash flows based on year-end exchange rate	$ 124		$ (10)	
Financing cash flows reported in the statement of cash flows	113		(20)	
Effect from financing activities during the year		11		10
Effect of exchange rate changes on cash		$ 9		$ (5)

[a]This amount includes the effect of rounding.

[FAS95, ¶146]

Example 3

.153 [Exhibits 153A, 153B, and 153C] present a statement of cash flows [and related schedule and disclosures] for Financial Institution, Inc., a U.S. corporation that provides a broad range of financial services. This statement of cash flows illustrates the direct method of presenting cash flows from operating activities, as encouraged in paragraph .125 of this section. [FAS95, ¶147]

.154 [Exhibits 154A and 154B] summarize financial information for the current year for Financial Institution, Inc., which provides the basis for the statement of cash flows presented in paragraph .153. [FAS95, ¶148]

(This page intentionally left blank.)

Exhibit 153A

Financial Institution, Inc.
Statement of Cash Flows
For the Year Ended December 31, 19X1

Cash flows from operating activities:		
Interest received	$ 5,350	
Fees and commissions received	1,320	
Proceeds from sales of trading securities	20,550	
Purchase of trading securities	(21,075)	
Financing revenue received under leases	60	
Interest paid	(3,925)	
Cash paid to suppliers and employees	(795)	
Income taxes paid	(471)	
Net cash provided by operating activities		$ 1,014
Cash flows from investing activities:		
Proceeds from sales of investment securities	2,225	
Purchase of investment securities	(4,000)	
Net increase in credit card receivables	(1,300)	
Net decrease in customer loans with maturities of 3 months or less	2,250	
Principal collected on longer term loans	26,550	
Longer term loans made to customers	(36,300)	
Purchase of assets to be leased	(1,500)	
Principal payments received under leases	107	
Capital expenditures	(450)	
Proceeds from sale of property, plant, and equipment	260	
Net cash used in investing activities		(12,158)
Cash flows from financing activities:		
Net increase in demand deposits, NOW accounts, and savings accounts	3,000	
Proceeds from sales of certificates of deposit	63,000	
Payments for maturing certificates of deposit	(61,000)	
Net increase in federal funds purchased	4,500	
Net increase in 90-day borrowings	50	
Proceeds from issuance of nonrecourse debt	600	
Principal payment on nonrecourse debt	(20)	
Proceeds from issuance of 6-month note	100	
Proceeds from issuance of long-term debt	1,000	
Repayment of long-term debt	(200)	
Proceeds from issuance of common stock	350	
Payments to acquire treasury stock	(175)	
Dividends paid	(240)	
Net cash provided by financing activities		10,965
Net decrease in cash and cash equivalents		(179)
Cash and cash equivalents at beginning of year		6,700
Cash and cash equivalents at end of year		$ 6,521

[FAS102, ¶30]

Exhibit 153B

Reconciliation of Net Income to Net Cash Provided by Operating Activities

Net income		$1,056
Adjustments to reconcile net income to net cash provided by operating activities:		
Depreciation	$ 100	
Provision for probable credit losses	300	
Provision for deferred taxes	58	
Loss on sales of investment securities	75	
Gain on sale of equipment	(50)	
Increase in trading securities (including unrealized appreciation of $25)	(700)	
Increase in taxes payable	175	
Increase in interest receivable	(150)	
Increase in interest payable	75	
Decrease in fees and commissions receivable	20	
Increase in accrued expenses	55	
Total adjustments		(42)
Net cash provided by operating activities		$1,014

[FAS102, ¶30]

Exhibit 153C

Disclosures in Financial Statements

Supplemental Schedule of Noncash Investing and Financing Activities

Conversion of long-term debt to common stock	$500

Disclosure of Accounting Policy

For purposes of reporting cash flows, cash and cash equivalents include cash on hand, amounts due from banks, and federal funds sold. Generally, federal funds are purchased and sold for one-day periods. [FAS95, ¶147]

Exhibit 154A

Financial Institution, Inc.
[Comparative] Statements of Financial Position
[January 1 and December 31, 19X1]

	1/1/X1	12/31/X1	Change
Assets:			
Cash and due from banks	$ 4,400	$ 3,121	$ (1,279)
Federal funds sold	2,300	3,400	1,100
Total cash and cash equivalents	6,700	6,521	(179)
Trading securities	4,000	4,700	700
Investment securities	5,000	6,700	1,700
Credit card receivables	8,500	9,800	1,300
Loans	28,000	35,250	7,250
Allowance for credit losses	(800)	(850)	(50)
Interest receivable	600	750	150
Fees and commissions receivable	60	40	(20)
Investment in direct financing lease	–	421	421
Investment in leveraged lease	–	392	392
Property, plant, and equipment, net	525	665	140
Total assets	$52,585	$64,389	$11,804
Liabilities:			
Deposits	$38,000	$43,000	$ 5,000
Federal funds purchased	7,500	12,000	4,500
Short-term borrowings	1,200	1,350	150
Interest payable	350	425	75
Accrued expenses	275	330	55
Taxes payable	75	250	175
Dividends payable	–	80	80
Long-term debt	2,000	2,300	300
Deferred taxes	–	58	58
Total liabilities	49,400	59,793	10,393
Stockholders' equity:			
Common stock	1,250	2,100	850
Treasury stock	–	(175)	(175)
Retained earnings	1,935	2,671	736
Total stockholders' equity	3,185	4,596	1,411
Total liabilities and stockholders' equity	$52,585	$64,389	$11,804

[FAS102, ¶31]

Exhibit 154B

Financial Institution, Inc.
Statement of Income
For the Year Ended December 31, 19X1

Revenues:		
Interest income	$5,500	
Fees and commissions	1,300	
Net gain on sales of trading and investment securities	75	
Unrealized appreciation of trading securities	25	
Lease income	60	
Gain on sale of equipment	50	
Total revenues		$7,010
Expenses:		
Interest expense	4,000	
Provision for probable credit losses	300	
Operating expenses	850	
Depreciation	100	
Total expenses		5,250
Income before income taxes		1,760
Provision for income taxes		704
Net income		$1,056

[FAS102, ¶31]

.155 The following transactions were entered into by Financial Institution, Inc., during 19X1 and are reflected in the above financial statements [FAS95, ¶149]:

a. Financial Institution sold trading securities with a carrying value of $20,400 for $20,550 and purchased trading securities for $21,075. Financial Institution recorded unrealized appreciation of trading securities of $25. Financial Institution also sold investment securities with a carrying value of $2,300 for $2,225 and purchased investment securities for $4,000. [FAS102, ¶32]
b. Financial Institution had a net decrease in short-term loans receivable (those with original maturities of 3 months or less) of $2,250. Financial Institution made longer term loans of $36,300 and collected $26,550 on those loans. Financial Institution wrote off $250 of loans as uncollectible.

c. Financial Institution purchased property for $500 to be leased under a direct financing lease. The first annual rental payment of $131 was collected. The portion of the rental payment representing interest income totaled $52.

d. Financial Institution purchased equipment for $1,000 to be leased under a leveraged lease. The cost of the leased asset was financed by an equity investment of $400 and a long-term nonrecourse bank loan of $600. The first annual rental payment of $90, of which $28 represented principal, was collected and the first annual loan installment of $74, of which $20 represented principal, was paid. Pretax income of $8 was recorded.

e. Financial Institution purchased new property, plant, and equipment for $450 and sold property, plant, and equipment with a book value of $210 for $260.

f. Customer deposits with Financial Institution consisted of the following:

	1/1/X1	12/31/X1	Increase
Demand deposits	$ 8,000	$ 8,600	$ 600
NOW accounts and savings accounts	15,200	17,600	2,400
Certificates of deposit	14,800	16,800	2,000
Total deposits	$38,000	$43,000	$5,000

Sales of certificates of deposit during the year totaled $63,000; certificates of deposit with principal amounts totaling $61,000 matured. For presentation in the statement of cash flows, Financial Institution chose to report gross cash receipts and payments for both certificates of deposit with maturities of three months or less and those with maturities of more than three months.

g. Short-term borrowing activity for Financial Institution consisted of repayment of a $200 90-day note and issuance of a 90-day note for $250 and a 6-month note for $100.

h. Financial Institution repaid $200 of long-term debt and issued 5-year notes for $600 and 10-year notes for $400.

i. Financial Institution issued $850 of common stock, $500 of which was issued upon conversion of long-term debt and $350 of which was issued for cash.

j. Financial Institution acquired $175 of treasury stock.

k. Financial Institution declared dividends of $320. The fourth quarter dividend of $80 was payable the following January.

l. Financial Institution's provision for income taxes included a deferred provision of $58.

m. In accordance with paragraph .105, footnote 2, of this section, interest paid includes amounts credited directly to demand deposit, NOW, and savings accounts.

[FAS95, ¶149]

Supplemental Guidance: Emerging Issues Task Force (EITF) Issues

.1000 [Listed below are EITF Issues that provide supplemental guidance for this section. These Issues may be either interpretive of or related by topic to the guidance in this section.

EITF Issue No. 95-13, "Classification of Debt Issue Costs in the Statement of Cash Flows"
EITF Issue No. 00-15, "Classification in the Statement of Cash Flows of the Income Tax Benefit Received by a Company upon Exercise of a Nonqualified Employee Stock Option"
EITF Issue No. 02-6, "Classification in the Statement of Cash Flows of Payments Made to Settle an Asset Retirement Obligation within the Scope of FASB Statement No. 143"]

.1001 [Listed below is an EITF Issue that provides interpretive guidance on specific material in this section.

Paragraph .118 (FAS 95, ¶20)—EITF Issue No. 95-13]

(The next page is 6601.)

CHANGING PRICES: REPORTING THEIR EFFECTS IN FINANCIAL REPORTS — SECTION C28

Sources: FASB Statement 89; FASB Statement 109; FASB Statement 135; FASB Statement 139

[**Note:** A list of Issues discussed by the Emerging Issues Task Force (EITF) that provide supplemental guidance for this section is presented in paragraph .1000.]

Summary

This section encourages supplementary disclosure of current cost/constant purchasing power information.

Disclosure

.101 A business enterprise that prepares its financial statements in U.S. dollars and in accordance with U.S. generally accepted accounting principles is encouraged, but not required, to disclose supplementary information on the effects of changing prices. This section provides measurement and presentation guidelines for disclosure. Entities are not discouraged from experimenting with other forms of disclosure. [FAS89, ¶3]

.102 [The following paragraphs present guidance for the presentation and measurement of supplementary information on effects of changing prices:]

[FAS89, Appendix A]

Presentation

Five-Year Summary of Selected Financial Data

.103 An enterprise shall[1] disclose the following information[2] for each of the five most recent years[3] (paragraphs .132 and .133):

a. Net sales and other operating revenues
b. **Income from continuing operations** on a current cost basis (paragraphs .128 and .129)
c. **Purchasing power gain or loss** on net monetary items (paragraphs .136 through .139)
d. Increase or decrease in the current cost or lower **recoverable amount** of inventory and property, plant, and equipment,[4] net of inflation (paragraphs .130 and .131)
e. The aggregate foreign currency **translation adjustment** on a current cost basis, if applicable (paragraphs .105, .134, and .135)
f. Net assets at year-end on a current cost basis (paragraphs .123 and .124)
g. Income per common share from continuing operations on a current cost basis
h. Cash dividends declared per common share
i. Market price per common share at year-end.

[FAS89, ¶7]

[[1]This section uses the word] "shall" even though the presentations and measurements described are now voluntary. [FAS89, ¶5, fn1]

[2]An enterprise that presents consolidated financial statements shall present the information required by this section on the same consolidated basis. The information required by this section need not be presented for a parent company, an investee company, or other enterprise in a financial report that includes the results for that enterprise in consolidated financial statements. [FAS89, ¶7, fn2]

[3]The information required by this section shall be presented as supplementary information in any published annual report that contains the primary financial statements of the enterprise except that the information need not be presented in an interim financial report. The information required by this section need not be presented for segments of a business enterprise although such presentations are encouraged. [FAS89, ¶7, fn3]

[4]For the purposes of this section, except where otherwise provided, "inventory" and "property, plant, and equipment" shall include land and other natural resources and capitalized leasehold interests but *not* goodwill or other intangible assets. [FAS89, ¶7, fn5]

.104 The information presented in the five-year summary shall be stated as either of the following:

a. In average-for-the-year or end-of-year units of constant purchasing power
b. In dollars[5] having a purchasing power equal to that of dollars of the base period used by the Bureau of Labor Statistics in calculating the Consumer Price Index for All Urban Consumers (CPI-U)[6] [FAS89, ¶8] (currently 1982–1984). [FAS135, ¶4(q)]

An enterprise shall disclose the level of the CPI-U used for each of the five most recent years. [FAS89, ¶8]

.105 If the enterprise has a significant foreign operation measured in a functional currency other than the U.S. dollar (dollar), it shall disclose whether adjustments to the current cost information to reflect the effects of general inflation are based on the U.S. general price level index (the **translate-restate** method, paragraph .134) or on a functional currency general price level index (the **restate-translate** method, paragraph .135). [FAS89, ¶9]

.106 The enterprise shall provide an explanation of the disclosures required by this section and a discussion of their significance in the circumstances of the enterprise. Disclosure and discussion of additional information to help users of the financial report understand the effects of changing prices on the activities of the enterprise are encouraged. [FAS89, ¶10]

Additional Disclosures for the Current Year

.107 In addition to the information required by paragraphs .103 through .106, an enterprise shall provide the information specified in paragraphs .108 and .109 if income from continuing operations on a **current cost/constant purchasing power** basis would differ significantly from income from continuing operations in the primary financial statements. [FAS89, ¶11]

---

[5]As a practical matter, this option is not available to enterprises that measure a significant part of their operations in one or more functional currencies other than the U.S. dollar and that elect to use the restate-translate method (paragraph .135) for measuring inflation-adjusted current cost information. [FAS89, ¶8, fn6]

[6][Refer to paragraph .204.] The index is [available on the Department of Labor, Bureau of Labor Statistics web site at http://stats.bls.gov/cpihome.htm and is published in the *CPI Detailed Report*]. If the level of the Consumer Price Index at the end of the year and the data required to compute the average level of the index over the year have not been published in time for preparation of the annual report, they may be estimated by referring to published forecasts based on economic statistics or by extrapolation based on recently reported changes in the index. [FAS89, ¶8, fn7]

.108 An enterprise shall disclose certain components of income from continuing operations for the current year on a current cost basis (paragraphs .128 and .129) applying the same constant purchasing power option used for presentation of the five-year summary. The information may be presented in a *statement format* (disclosing revenues, expenses, gains, and losses), in a *reconciliation format* (disclosing adjustments to the income from continuing operations that is shown in the primary income statement), or in notes to the five-year summary required by paragraph .103. Formats for presenting the supplementary information are illustrated in paragraph .140. Whichever format is used, the presentation shall disclose (for example, in a reconciliation format) or allow the reader to determine (for example, in a statement format) the difference between the amount in the primary statements and the current cost amount of the following items: cost of goods sold and depreciation, depletion, and amortization expense. If depreciation has been allocated among various expense categories in the supplementary computations of income from continuing operations (for example, among cost of goods sold and other functional expenses), the aggregate amount of depreciation on a current cost basis shall be included in the notes to the supplementary information. In addition to information about income from continuing operations, the enterprise may include the following items in a schedule of current year information: (a) the purchasing power gain or loss on net monetary items, (b) the increase or decrease in the current cost or lower recoverable amount of inventory and property, plant, and equipment, net of inflation, and (c) the translation adjustment. As illustrated in paragraph .140 and defined in the glossary in paragraph .405, income from continuing operations does not include items (a), (b), or (c). [FAS89, ¶12]

.109 An enterprise shall also disclose:

a. Separate amounts for the current cost or lower recoverable amount at the end of the current year of inventory and property, plant, and equipment (paragraphs .112 through .122 and .125 through .127)
b. The increase or decrease in current cost or lower recoverable amount before and after adjusting for the effects of inflation of inventory and property, plant, and equipment for the current year (paragraphs .130 and .131)
c. The principal types of information used to calculate the current cost of inventory; property, plant, and equipment; cost of goods sold; and depreciation, depletion, and amortization expense (paragraphs .115 through .122)
d. Any differences between (1) the depreciation methods, estimates of useful lives, and salvage values of assets used for calculations of current cost/constant purchasing power depreciation and (2) the methods and estimates used for calculations of depreciation in the primary financial statements (paragraph .118).

[FAS89, ¶13]

Additional Disclosures by Enterprises with Mineral Resource Assets

.110 For its mineral reserves other than oil and gas, an enterprise shall disclose the following additional information for each of its five most recent fiscal years:

a. Estimates of significant quantities of **proved mineral reserves** or proved and **probable mineral reserves** (whichever is used for cost amortization purposes) at the end of the year or at the most recent date during the year for which estimates can be made (If estimates are not made as of the end of the year, the disclosures shall indicate the dates of the estimates.)
b. The estimated quantity, expressed in physical units or in percentages of reserves, of each mineral product that is recoverable in significant commercial quantities if the mineral reserves included under subparagraph (a) include deposits containing one or more significant mineral products
c. The quantities of each significant mineral produced during the year (If the mineral reserves included under subparagraph (a) are ones that are milled or similarly processed, the quantity of each significant mineral product produced by the milling or similar process shall also be disclosed.)
d. The quantity of significant proved, or proved and probable, mineral reserves purchased or sold in place during the year
e. For each significant mineral product, the average market price or, for mineral products transferred within the enterprise, the equivalent market price prior to use in a manufacturing process.

[FAS89, ¶14]

.111 In determining the quantities to be reported in conformity with paragraph .110:

a. If the enterprise issues consolidated financial statements, 100 percent of the quantities attributable to the parent company and 100 percent of the quantities attributable to its consolidated subsidiaries (whether or not wholly owned) shall be included.
b. If the enterprise's financial statements include investments that are proportionately consolidated, the enterprise's quantities shall include its proportionate share of the investee's quantities.
c. If the enterprise's financial statements include investments that are accounted for by the equity method, the investee's quantities shall not be included in the disclosures of the enterprise's quantities. However, the enterprise's (investor's) share of the investee's quantities of reserves shall be reported separately, if significant.

[FAS89, ¶15]

Measurement

Inventory and Property, Plant, and Equipment

.112 Current cost amounts of inventory and property, plant, and equipment are measured as follows:

a. Inventory at current cost or lower recoverable amount at the measurement date
b. Property, plant, and equipment at the current cost or lower recoverable amount of the assets' remaining service potential at the measurement date
c. Resources used on a partly completed contract at current cost or lower recoverable amount at the date of use on or commitment to the contract.

[FAS89, ¶16]

.113 The current cost of inventory owned by an enterprise is the current cost of purchasing the goods concerned or the current cost of the resources required to produce the goods concerned (including an allowance for the current overhead costs according to the allocation bases used under generally accepted accounting principles), whichever would be applicable in the circumstances of the enterprise. [FAS89, ¶17]

.114 The current cost of property, plant, and equipment owned by an enterprise is the current cost of acquiring the same service potential (indicated by operating costs and physical output capacity) as embodied by the asset owned; the information used to measure current cost reflects whatever method of acquisition would currently be appropriate in the circumstances of the enterprise. The current cost of a used asset may be calculated:

a. By measuring the current cost of a new asset that has the same service potential as the used asset had when it was new (the current cost of the asset as if it were new) and deducting an allowance for depreciation
b. By measuring the current cost of a used asset of the same age and in the same condition as the asset owned
c. By measuring the current cost of a new asset with a different service potential and adjusting that cost for the value of the difference in service potential due to differences in life, output capacity, nature of service, and operating costs.

[FAS89, ¶18]

.115 Various types of information may be used in the measurement methods described in paragraphs .113 and .114 to determine the current cost of inventory; property, plant, and equipment; cost of goods sold;[7] and depreciation, depletion, and amortization expense. The information may be applied to single items or broad categories, as appropriate in the circumstances. The following types of information are listed as examples of the information that may be used but are *not* listed in any order of preferability. The enterprise is expected to select types of information appropriate to its particular circumstances, giving due consideration to their availability, reliability, and cost:

a. Indexation
   (1) Externally generated price indexes for the class of goods or services being measured
   (2) Internally generated price indexes for the class of goods or services being measured
b. Direct pricing
   (1) Current invoice prices
   (2) Vendors' price lists or other quotations or estimates
   (3) Standard manufacturing costs that reflect current costs.

[FAS89, ¶19]

.116 An enterprise may substitute **historical cost** amounts adjusted by an externally generated price index of a broad-based measure of general purchasing power (that is, **historical cost/constant purchasing power** amounts) for current cost amounts if that substitution would not result in a significantly different number for income from continuing operations than other means of estimating current cost amounts described in this section. For example, an enterprise with small amounts of inventory and property, plant, and equipment apart from certain specialized assets (paragraphs .119 through .122) may be able to report historical cost/constant purchasing power information. In such circumstances, disclosure of the increase or decrease in the current cost or lower recoverable amount of inventory and property, plant, and equipment, net of inflation (paragraphs .103(d) and .109(b)), is not required, but the discussions described in paragraphs .106 and .109(a), (c), and (d) are required. [FAS89, ¶20]

.117 Current cost measurements are to be based on production or purchase of the asset in whatever location or market would minimize total cost including transportation cost. For a U.S. operation, either (a) the purchase would be made in the United States and current cost would be estimated directly in dollars or (b) the purchase would be made in

[7]If turnover is rapid and material amounts of depreciation are not allocated to inventory, cost of goods sold measured on a Last-In, First-Out (LIFO) basis may provide an acceptable approximation of cost of goods sold, measured at current cost, provided that the effect of any LIFO inventory liquidations (that is, any decreases in earlier years' LIFO layers) is excluded. [FAS89, ¶19, fn8]

a foreign market and the current cost in that market would be translated into dollars at the current exchange rate. An enterprise may need to measure the current cost of inventory and property, plant, and equipment located outside the United States. That may be difficult depending upon the availability of information in the country concerned, and, accordingly, reasonable approximations are acceptable. If a foreign operation first measures current cost in a currency other than its functional currency, that amount is then translated into the functional currency at the current exchange rate. [FAS89, ¶21]

.118 There is a presumption that depreciation methods, estimates of useful lives, and salvage values of assets for purposes of the supplementary information are the same as the methods and estimates used for calculations in the primary financial statements. However, if the primary financial statements are based on methods and estimates that partly allow for price changes, different methods and estimates may be used for purposes of the supplementary information. [FAS89, ¶22]

Specialized Assets

.119 The current cost of **mineral resource assets** is determined by current market buying prices or by the current cost of finding and developing mineral reserves. [It is recognized] that no generally accepted approach exists for measuring the current finding cost of mineral reserves. To indicate the effects of changes in current costs, it may be impracticable to do more than adjust historical costs by an index of the changes in specific prices of the inputs concerned. That approach may fail to yield a close approximation of the current cost of finding and developing new reserves. In recognition of that difficulty, the requirements of this section are flexible regarding the approach used to measure current cost of mineral resource assets. The approach may include use of specific price indexes, direct information about market buying prices, and other statistical evidence of the cost of acquisitions. [FAS89, ¶23]

.120 Because Section Oi5, "Oil and Gas Producing Activities," requires an enterprise to disclose a standardized measure of discounted future net cash flows relating to proved oil and gas reserve quantities, the enterprise may follow the approach in paragraph .119 or in paragraph .121 for its oil and gas mineral resource assets. Paragraph .109(c) requires disclosure of the types of information that have been used to measure current costs. [FAS89, ¶24]

.121 Timberlands and growing timber, **income-producing real estate,** and **motion picture films** have certain special features that raise doubts about the applicability of the current cost measurement methods required for other assets. Accordingly, an enterprise may disclose historical cost amounts adjusted by an externally generated index of a broad-based measure of general purchasing power as substitutes for current cost amounts for such assets and their related expenses. [FAS89, ¶25]

.122 If an enterprise estimates the current cost of growing timber and timber harvested by adjusting historical cost for the changes in specific prices, those historical costs may either (a) be limited to the costs that are capitalized in the primary financial statements or (b) include all costs that are directly related to reforestation and forest management, such as planting, fertilization, fire protection, property taxes, and nursery stock, whether or not those costs are capitalized in the primary financial statements. [FAS89, ¶26]

Net Assets

.123 If the enterprise presents the minimum information required by this section, the amount of net assets (that is, shareholders' equity) is the amount of net assets reported in the primary financial statements, adjusted for the difference between the historical cost amounts and the current cost or lower recoverable amounts of inventory and property, plant, and equipment. [FAS89, ¶27]

.124 If the enterprise elects to present comprehensive current cost/constant purchasing power financial statements as supplementary information, the amount of net assets in the five-year summary is the amount reported in the supplementary balance sheet. [FAS89, ¶28]

Recoverable Amount

.125 Recoverable amount is the current worth of the net amount of cash expected to be recoverable from the use or sale of an asset. It may be measured by considering the **value in use** or **current market value** of the asset concerned. Value in use is used to determine recoverable amount of an asset if immediate sale of the asset is not intended. Current market value is used to determine recoverable amount only if the asset is about to be sold. [FAS89, ¶29]

.126 If the recoverable amount for a group of assets is judged to be materially and permanently lower than the current cost amount, the *recoverable amount* is used as a measure of the assets and of the expense associated with the use or sale of the assets. Decisions on the measurement of assets at their recoverable amounts need not be made by considering assets individually unless they are used independently of other assets. [FAS89, ¶30]

.127 An enterprise that is subject to rate regulation or another form of price control may be limited to a maximum recovery through its selling prices, based on the nominal currency amount of the historical cost of its assets. In that situation, historical costs measured in nominal currency may represent an appropriate basis for the measurement of the recoverable amounts associated with those assets. Recoverable amounts may also be lower than historical costs. Nevertheless, cost of goods sold and depreciation, depletion, and amortization expense are to be measured at current cost/constant purchasing power amounts provided that replacement of the service potential of the related assets would be undertaken, if necessary, in current economic conditions; if replacement would not be undertaken, those expenses are to be measured at recoverable amounts. [FAS89, ¶31]

Income from Continuing Operations

.128 An enterprise that presents the minimum information required by this section shall measure income from continuing operations on a current cost basis as follows:

a. Cost of goods sold at current cost or lower recoverable amount at the date of sale or at the date on which resources are used on or committed to a specific contract
b. Depreciation, depletion, and amortization expense of property, plant, and equipment on the basis of the average current cost of the assets' service potential or lower recoverable amount during the period of use.

Other revenues, expenses, gains, and losses may be measured at the amounts included in the primary income statement. (Refer to paragraphs .112 through .122 and .125 through .127 for discussions of current cost or lower recoverable amount measurements.) [FAS89, ¶32]

.129 The amount of income tax expense in computations of current cost/constant purchasing power income from continuing operations is the same as the amount of income tax expense charged against income from continuing operations in the primary financial statements. No adjustments are to be made to income tax expense for any [FAS89, ¶33] temporary differences [FAS109, ¶287] that might be deemed to arise as a result of the use of current cost accounting methods. Income tax expense is not to be allocated between income from continuing operations and the increases or decreases in current cost amounts of inventory and property, plant, and equipment. [FAS89, ¶33]

Increase or Decrease in the Current Cost Amounts of Inventory and Property, Plant, and Equipment, Net of Inflation

.130 The increase or decrease in the current cost amounts of inventory and property, plant, and equipment represents the difference between the measures of the assets at their *entry dates* for the year and the measures of the assets at their *exit dates* for the year. *Entry dates* means the beginning of the year or the dates of acquisition, whichever is applicable; *exit dates* means the end of the year or the dates of use, sale, or commitment to a specific contract, whichever is applicable. For the purposes of this paragraph, assets are measured in accordance with the provisions of paragraphs .112 through .122 and .125 through .127. [FAS89, ¶34]

.131 For the current year, the increase or decrease in current cost amounts of inventory and property, plant, and equipment is reported both before and after eliminating the effects of general inflation (paragraph .109(b)). In the five-year summary, the increase or decrease is reported after elimination of the effects of each year's general inflation (paragraph .103(d)). An acceptable approximate method of calculating the increase or decrease in current cost amounts and the inflation adjustment is illustrated in paragraphs .162 through .165. [FAS89, ¶35]

Restatement of Current Cost Information into Units of Constant Purchasing Power

.132 Enterprises that do not have significant foreign operations or that use the dollar as the functional currency for all significant foreign operations are to use the CPI-U to restate current costs into units of constant purchasing power. Acceptable approximate methods are illustrated in paragraph .177. [FAS89, ¶36]

.133 The effects of general inflation on current cost information for operations measured in a foreign functional currency are measured either (a) after translation and based upon the CPI-U (the translate-restate method) or (b) before translation and based on a broad-based measure of the change in the general purchasing power of the functional currency (the restate-translate method).[8] The same method is to be used for all operations measured in functional currencies other than the dollar and for all periods presented. Acceptable approximate methods are illustrated in paragraphs .177, .178, .185, and .186. [FAS89, ¶37]

Translation Adjustment

.134 If current cost information for operations measured in functional currencies other than the dollar is based on the translate-restate method, the aggregate translation adjustment on the current cost basis is stated net of any income taxes allocated to the aggregate translation adjustment in the primary financial statements (Section F60, "Foreign Currency Translation," paragraph .141(c)). [FAS89, ¶38]

---

[8] The choice of a measure of functional currency purchasing power should take into account the availability, reliability, and timeliness of a general price level index and the frequency with which it is adjusted. It is anticipated that an appropriate index of the change in the general price level will be available for most functional currencies. Indexes are published in most countries, and some indexes are published periodically by organizations such as the International Monetary Fund, the Organisation for Economic Co-Operation and Development, and the United Nations. However, in some cases indexes may not be available on a timely basis or may not be sufficiently reliable. In those circumstances, management should estimate the change in the general price level. [FAS89, ¶37, fn9]

.135 If current cost information for operations measured in functional currencies other than the dollar is based on the restate-translate method, the aggregate translation adjustment on the current cost basis is stated net of both any income taxes allocated to the aggregate translation adjustment in the primary financial statements and the aggregate **parity adjustment.** The parity adjustment is the amount needed to measure end-of-year net assets in (a) average-for-the-year dollars, if income from continuing operations is measured in average-for-the-year functional currency units, or (b) end-of-year dollars, if income from continuing operations is measured in end-of-year functional currency units. [FAS89, ¶39]

Purchasing Power Gain or Loss on Net Monetary Items

.136 The purchasing power gain or loss on net monetary items is the net gain or loss determined by restating in units of constant purchasing power the opening and closing balances of, and transactions in, **monetary assets** and **monetary liabilities.** Acceptable approximate methods of calculating the purchasing power gain or loss on net monetary items are illustrated in paragraphs .161, .178, and .185. [FAS89, ¶40]

.137 The economic significance of monetary assets and liabilities depends heavily on the general purchasing power of money, although other factors, such as creditworthiness of debtors, may affect their significance. The economic significance of nonmonetary items depends heavily on the value of specific goods and services. Nonmonetary assets include (a) goods held primarily for resale or assets held primarily for direct use in providing services for the business of the enterprise, (b) claims to cash in amounts dependent on future prices of specific goods or services, and (c) residual rights such as goodwill or equity interests. Nonmonetary liabilities include (a) obligations to furnish goods or services in quantities that are fixed or determinable without reference to changes in prices and (b) obligations to pay cash in amounts dependent on future prices of specific goods or services. Guidance on the classification of balance sheet items as monetary or nonmonetary is set forth in paragraphs .191 through .203. [FAS89, ¶41]

.138 If inflation-adjusted current cost information is based on the translate-restate method, the purchasing power gain or loss on net monetary items is equal to the net gain or loss determined by restating the opening and closing balances of, and transactions in, monetary assets and liabilities in units of constant purchasing power as measured by the CPI-U. [FAS89, ¶42]

.139 If inflation-adjusted current cost information is based on the restate-translate method, the purchasing power gain or loss on net monetary items is equal to the net gain or loss determined by restating the opening and closing balances of, and transactions in, monetary assets and liabilities in units of constant purchasing power as measured by the change in the general purchasing power of the functional currency. The purchasing power gain or loss computed in that manner is translated into its dollar equivalent at the average exchange rate for the period. [FAS89, ¶43]

Illustrations of Disclosures

.140 This paragraph illustrates formats that may be used to disclose the information required by this section for a manufacturing enterprise. An enterprise may choose to disclose the information required by paragraphs .103 through .109 of this section (a) in a schedule of annual information (for example, Exhibit 140A or Exhibit 140B), in a five-year summary (for example, Exhibit 140C or Exhibit 140D), and notes to those schedules or (b) in a five-year summary and notes to that summary (for example, Exhibit 140E). Many enterprises have included amounts reported in the primary statements alongside current cost/constant purchasing power amounts in the five-year summary. Enterprises [are encouraged] to continue to adapt the disclosure formats to enhance such comparisons. Exhibit 140D illustrates a five-year summary with comparative data from the primary financial statements. Enterprises [also are encouraged] to provide more detailed discussions than the illustrative notes in this paragraph—especially discussion of the significance of the information in the circumstances of the enterprise (required by paragraph .106) and the principal types of information used to calculate current cost amounts (required by paragraph .109(c)). Illustrative calculations are given in paragraphs .141 through .190. In the exhibits that follow, the CPI-U is expressed in average dollars. [FAS89, ¶45]

Exhibit 140A

Statement of Income from Continuing Operations Adjusted for Changing Prices[a]
For the Year Ended December 31, 19X6
In Thousands of Average 19X6 Dollars

Income from continuing operations, as reported in the primary income statement	$22,995
Adjustments to reflect current costs	
Cost of goods sold	(8,408)
Depreciation expense	(9,748)
Income from continuing operations adjusted for changes in specific prices	$ 4,839
Gain from decline in purchasing power of net amounts owed[b]	$ 2,449
Increase in specific prices (current cost) of inventory and property, plant, and equipment held during the year[c]	$25,846
Effect of increase in general price level	5,388
Excess of increase in specific prices over increase in the general price level	$20,458
Foreign currency translation adjustment[d]	$ (624)

[a]The condensed financial information in this exhibit compares selected information from the primary financial statements with information that reflects effects of changes in the specific prices (current cost) of inventory and property, plant, and equipment expressed in units of constant purchasing power. The current cost amounts for inventory and cost of goods sold reflect actual manufacturing costs incurred in 19X6. The current cost amounts for major components of property, plant, and equipment were determined by applying specific price indexes to the applicable historical costs. For assets used in U.S. operations, Producer Price Indexes and Factory Mutual Building Indexes were used; for assets used in foreign operations, appropriate indexes for each country were used. The current cost information is expressed in average 19X6 dollars as measured by the CPI-U.

[b]The purchasing power gain on net amounts owed is an economic benefit to the enterprise that results from being able to repay those amounts with cheaper dollars.

[c]During 19X6, the specific prices (current cost) of inventory increased by $9,108 and of property, plant, and equipment by $16,738. The total increase of $25,846 exceeded the increase necessary to keep pace with general inflation. At December 31, 19X6, the current cost of inventory was $65,700 and of property, plant, and equipment, net of accumulated depreciation, was $89,335 (both measured in December 31, 19X6 units of purchasing power). Those amounts are higher than the amounts in the primary statements of $63,000 for inventory and $45,750 for property, plant, and equipment, net of accumulated depreciation; therefore, it is reasonable to expect income from continuing operations on a current cost basis for 19X7 to remain significantly below that reported in the primary statements.

[d]Current cost amounts for foreign operations are measured in their functional currencies, translated into dollar equivalents using the average exchange rate for the year, and restated into constant units of purchasing power using the CPI-U. Essentially, the foreign currency translation adjustment is the effect of changes in exchange rates during the year on shareholders' equity. The negative translation adjustment indicates that, overall, the dollar has increased in value relative to the functional currencies used to measure the foreign operations of the enterprise.

[FAS89, ¶45]

Exhibit 140B

Statement of Income from Continuing Operations Adjusted for Changing Prices[a]

For the Year Ended December 31, 19X6
In Thousands of Dollars

	As Reported in the Primary Statements	Adjusted for Changes in Specific Prices (Current Cost)
Net sales and other operating revenues	$275,500	$275,500
Cost of goods sold	197,000	205,408
Depreciation expense	10,275	20,023
Other operating expenses	14,685	14,685
Interest expense	7,550	7,550
Income tax expense	22,995	22,995
[Total expenses]	252,505	270,661
Income from continuing operations	$ 22,995	$ 4,839
Gain from decline in purchasing power of net amounts owed[b]		$ 2,449
Increase in specific prices (current cost) of inventory and property, plant, and equipment held during the year[c]		$ 25,846
Effect of increase in general price level		5,388
Excess of increase in specific prices over increase in the general price level		$ 20,458
Foreign currency translation adjustment[d]	$ (295)	$ (624)

(Footnotes are on the following page.)

[a]The condensed financial information in this exhibit compares selected information from the primary financial statements with information that reflects effects of changes in the specific prices (current cost) of inventory and property, plant, and equipment expressed in units of constant purchasing power. The current cost amounts for inventory and cost of goods sold reflect actual manufacturing costs incurred in 19X6. The current cost amounts for major components of property, plant, and equipment were determined by applying specific price indexes to the applicable historical costs. For assets used in U.S. operations, Producer Price Indexes and Factory Mutual Building Indexes were used; for assets used in foreign operations, appropriate indexes for each country were used. The current cost information is expressed in average 19X6 dollars as measured by the CPI-U.

[b]The purchasing power gain on net amounts owed is an economic benefit to the enterprise that results from being able to repay those amounts with cheaper dollars.

[c]During 19X6, the specific prices (current cost) of inventory increased by $9,108 and of property, plant, and equipment by $16,738. The total increase of $25,846 exceeded the increase necessary to keep pace with general inflation. At December 31, 19X6, the current cost of inventory was $65,700 and of property, plant, and equipment, net of accumulated depreciation, was $89,335 (both measured in December 31, 19X6 units of purchasing power). Those amounts are higher than the amounts in the primary statements of $63,000 for inventory and $45,750 for property, plant, and equipment, net of accumulated depreciation; therefore, it is reasonable to expect income from continuing operations on a current cost basis for 19X7 to remain significantly below that reported in the primary statements.

[d]Current cost amounts for foreign operations are measured in their functional currencies, translated into dollar equivalents using the average exchange rate for the year, and restated into constant units of purchasing power using the CPI-U. Essentially, the foreign currency translation adjustment is the effect of changes in exchange rates during the year on shareholders' equity. The negative translation adjustment indicates that, overall, the dollar has increased in value relative to the functional currencies used to measure the foreign operations of the enterprise.

[FAS89, ¶45]

Exhibit 140C

Five-Year Comparison of Selected
Financial Data Adjusted for Effects of Changing Prices

In Thousands of Average 19X6 Dollars,
except for Per Share Amounts

	Year Ended December 31,				
	19X6	**19X5**	**19X4**	**19X3**	**19X2**
Net sales and other operating revenues	$275,500	$247,500	$240,000	$235,500	$265,000
Income (loss) from continuing operations	4,839	1,660	(2,102)	(4,663)	1,261
Gain from decline in purchasing power of net amounts owed	2,449	7,027	5,432	1,247	6,375
Excess of increase in specific prices of inventory and property, plant, and equipment over increase in the general price level	20,458	2,292	3,853	8,597	3,777
Foreign currency translation adjustment	(624)	(386)	(454)	(293)	127
Net assets at year-end[a]	92,027	67,905	60,409	56,966	55,705
Per share information:					
Income (loss) from continuing operations	$ 3.23	$ 1.11	$ (1.40)	$ (3.11)	$ .84
Cash dividends declared	2.00	2.06	2.19	2.42	2.75
Market price at year-end	35	39	43	27	32
Average consumer price index[b]	298.4	289.1	272.4	246.8	217.4

---

[a]Net assets include inventory and property, plant, and equipment at current cost and all other items as they are reported in the primary financial statements. No adjustment has been made for the lower tax basis applicable to the current cost amounts included in net assets.

[b]For purposes of this exhibit, although the years for which information has been provided are nonspecific, the actual 1979-1983 average index numbers have been applied.

[FAS89, ¶45]

Exhibit 140D

Five-Year Comparison of Selected Financial Data

In Thousands of Dollars, except for Per Share Amounts

	Year Ended December 31,				
	19X6	19X5	19X4	19X3	19X2
Total revenue					
As reported	$275,500	$239,800	$219,100	$194,800	$193,100
Adjusted for general inflation[a]	275,500	247,500	240,000	235,500	265,000
Income (loss) from operations					
As reported	22,995	11,097	4,756	9,977	11,847
Adjusted for specific price changes[a]	4,839	1,660	(2,102)	(4,663)	1,261
Purchasing power gain from holding net monetary liabilities[a]	2,449	7,027	5,432	1,247	6,375
Excess of increase in specific prices of assets over increase in the general price level[a]	20,458	2,292	3,853	8,597	3,777
Foreign currency translation adjustment					
As reported	(295)	(276)	(396)	(138)	76
Adjusted for specific price changes[a]	(624)	(386)	(454)	(293)	127
Net assets at year-end					
As reported	47,700	28,000	20,179	18,819	11,980
Adjusted for specific price changes[b]	92,027	67,905	60,409	56,966	55,705

Per share information:					
Income (loss) from operations					
As reported	$15.33	$ 7.40	$ 3.17	$ 6.65	$ 7.90
Adjusted for specific price changes[a]	3.23	1.11	(1.40)	(3.11)	.84
Cash dividends declared					
As reported	2.00	2.00	2.00	2.00	2.00
Adjusted for general inflation[a]	2.00	2.06	2.19	2.42	2.75
Market price at year-end					
As reported	36	38	41	23	25
Adjusted for general inflation[a]	35	39	43	27	32
Average consumer price index[c]	298.4	289.1	272.4	246.8	217.4

---

[a]In average 19X6 dollars.

[b]Net assets adjusted for specific price changes include inventory and property, plant, and equipment at current cost and all other items as they are reported in the primary financial statements. No adjustment has been made for the lower tax basis applicable to the current cost amounts included in net assets.

[c]For purposes of this exhibit, although the years for which information has been provided are nonspecific, the actual 1979-1983 average index numbers have been applied.

[FAS89, ¶45]

Exhibit 140E

Five-Year Comparison of Selected Financial Data Adjusted for Effects of Changing Prices[a]

In Thousands of Average 19X6 Dollars, except for Per Share Amounts

	Year Ended December 31,				
	19X6	19X5	19X4	19X3	19X2
Net sales and other operating revenues	$275,500	$247,500	$240,000	$235,500	$265,000
Income (loss) from continuing operations[b]	4,839	1,660	(2,102)	(4,663)	1,261
Gain from decline in purchasing power of net amounts owed[c]	2,449	7,027	5,432	1,247	6,375
Increase in specific prices of inventory and property, plant, and equipment[d]	20,458	2,292	3,853	8,597	3,777
Foreign currency translation adjustment[e]	(624)	(386)	(454)	(293)	127
Net assets at year-end[d]	92,027	67,905	60,409	56,966	55,705
Per share information:					
Income (loss) from continuing operations	$ 3.23	$ 1.11	$ (1.40)	$ (3.11)	$ .84
Cash dividends declared	2.00	2.06	2.19	2.42	2.75
Market price at year-end	35	39	43	27	32
Average consumer price index[f]	298.4	289.1	272.4	246.8	217.4

[a]The condensed financial information in this exhibit presents selected information that reflects effects of changes in the specific prices (current cost) of inventory and property, plant, and equipment expressed in units of constant purchasing power. The current cost amounts for inventory and cost of goods sold reflect actual manufacturing costs incurred in 19X6. The current cost amounts for major components of property, plant, and equipment were determined by applying specific price indexes to the applicable historical costs. For assets used in U.S. operations, Producer Price Indexes and Factory Mutual Building Indexes were used; for assets used in foreign operations, appropriate indexes for each country were used. The current cost information is expressed in average 19X6 dollars as measured by the CPI-U.

[b]Income from continuing operations reported in the primary financial statements was $22,995 for 19X6. Current cost income reported in the five-year summary was only $4,839 because depreciation expense on a current cost basis exceeded depreciation expense in the primary statements by $9,748 and current cost of goods sold was $8,408 greater than the amount reported in the primary statements.

[c]The purchasing power gain on net amounts owed is an economic benefit to the enterprise that results from being able to repay those amounts with cheaper dollars.

[d]During 19X6, the specific prices (current cost) of inventory increased by $9,108 and of property, plant, and equipment by $16,738. The total increase exceeded the increase necessary to keep pace with general inflation by $20,458. Net assets include inventory and property, plant, and equipment at current cost and all other items as reported in the primary financial statements (restated into average-for-19X6 dollars). No adjustment has been made for the lower tax basis applicable to the current cost amounts included in net assets. At December 31, 19X6, the current cost of inventory was $65,700 and of property, plant, and equipment, net of accumulated depreciation, was $89,335 (both measured in December 31, 19X6 units of purchasing power). Those amounts are higher than the amounts in the primary statements of $63,000 for inventory and $45,750 for property, plant, and equipment, net of accumulated depreciation; therefore, it is reasonable to expect income from continuing operations on a current cost basis for 19X7 to remain significantly below that reported in the primary statements.

[e]Current cost amounts for foreign operations are measured in their functional currencies, translated into dollar equivalents using the average exchange rate for the year, and restated into constant units of purchasing power using the CPI-U. Essentially, the foreign currency translation adjustment is the effect of changes in exchange rates during the year on shareholders' equity. A negative (positive) translation adjustment indicates that, overall, the dollar increased (decreased) in value relative to the functional currencies used to measure the foreign operations of the enterprise.

[f]For purposes of this exhibit, although the years for which information has been provided are nonspecific, the actual 1979-1983 average index numbers have been applied.

[FAS89, ¶45]

Illustrative Calculations of Current Cost/Constant Purchasing Power Information

Introduction

.141 Paragraphs .142 through .190 illustrate the methodology that might be used in calculating the disclosures in paragraph .140. [FAS89, ¶46]

.142 Computation of current cost information should be based on a detailed analysis of all transactions; however, the costs of preparing the information can be reduced with little loss of usefulness by simplifying the methods of calculation. Therefore, only cost of sales and depreciation expense need to be adjusted from the amounts shown in the primary income statement. Revenues, other expenses, and gains and losses need not be adjusted. Approximate methods of computation are acceptable for adjusting cost of sales and depreciation expense. The *measurement* of current cost is not illustrated. [FAS89, ¶47]

.143 The objective in making these calculations is to obtain a *reasonable degree* of accuracy—complete precision is not required. Preparers are encouraged to devise short-cut methods of calculation, appropriate to their individual circumstances. [FAS89, ¶48]

.144 If inventories and cost of sales are accounted for under the LIFO method in the primary financial statements, the only adjustment normally required in computing income from continuing operations would be to eliminate the effect of changing prices on any prior-period LIFO layer liquidation. [FAS89, ¶49]

.145 Seven basic steps to restate historical cost information into current cost/constant purchasing power information are illustrated in paragraphs .142 through .190:

a. Analyze inventory (at the beginning and end of the year) and cost of goods sold to determine when the costs were incurred
b. Restate inventory and cost of goods sold into current cost
c. Analyze property, plant, and equipment to determine when the related assets were acquired
d. Restate property, plant, and equipment and depreciation, depletion, and amortization expense into current cost
e. Identify the amount of net monetary items (paragraphs .191 through .203) at the beginning and end of the period and changes during the period
f. Compute the purchasing power gain or loss on net monetary items
g. Compute the change in current cost of inventory and property, plant, and equipment and the related effect of the increase in the general price level.

[FAS89, ¶50]

.146 The methodology illustrated in paragraphs .142 through .190 has been developed for the hypothetical enterprise, Parent Company. Parent Company has a wholly owned foreign subsidiary, Sub Company. Sub Company measures its operations in a functional currency other than the dollar. The changing prices disclosures for Parent Company and Sub Company are developed separately. Merging the amounts calculated for each entity results in a consolidated disclosure:

a. Paragraphs .154 through .166 illustrate the minimum recommended calculations for the domestic operations of Parent Company. A method of checking the arithmetic accuracy of the calculations is included in paragraph .167.
b. Paragraphs .174 through .181 illustrate the translate-restate method for Sub Company, a foreign subsidiary that does not use the dollar as a functional currency. A method of checking the arithmetic accuracy of the calculations is included in paragraph .179.
c. The results of the calculations described in (a) and (b) are summarized in paragraph .182 and are reflected in the illustrative disclosures in paragraph .140.

[FAS89, ¶51]

.147 Paragraphs .183 through .190 illustrate the restate-translate method for Sub Company. A method of checking the arithmetic accuracy of the calculations is included in paragraphs .187 and .188. [FAS89, ¶52]

.148 Throughout this section, $ indicates nominal dollars, C$ indicates average 19X6 constant dollars, FC indicates nominal functional currency, C$E indicates dollar equivalents of FC amounts using the translate-restate method, CFC indicates average 19X6 constant functional currency, and CFC$ indicates the translated dollar equivalents of CFC amounts using the restate-translate method. [FAS89, ¶53]

Parent Company Information

.149 The historical cost/nominal dollar financial statements [are presented below] :

Parent Company
Balance Sheet (Unconsolidated)
As of December 31, 19X6 and 19X5
(000s)

	19X6	19X5		19X6	19X5
Current assets:			Current liabilities:		
Cash	$ 1,000	$ 2,000	Accounts payable and accrued expenses	$ 47,000	$ 32,000
Accounts receivable	36,000	16,500	Income taxes payable	6,000	6,000
Inventories, at FIFO cost	63,000	56,000	Current portion of long-term debt	5,000	5,000
Total current assets	100,000	74,500	Total current liabilities	58,000	43,000
Property, plant, and equipment, at cost	100,000	85,000	Deferred income taxes	6,000	5,000
Less accumulated depreciation	56,000	46,000	Long-term debt	34,000	39,000
	44,000	39,000	Total liabilities	98,000	87,000
Investment in Sub Company*	1,500	1,500	Capital stock†	10,000	10,000
			Retained earnings	37,500	18,000
	$145,500	$115,000		$145,500	$115,000

* Investment in Sub Company is recorded at cost and is eliminated in consolidation. Parent Company does not issue separate unconsolidated statements.

† 1,500,000 shares outstanding.

Parent Company (Unconsolidated)
Statement of Earnings and Retained Earnings
For the Year Ended December 31, 19X6

	(000s)
Sales	$270,000
Cost of goods sold, exclusive of depreciation	197,000
Selling, general, and administrative expenses	10,835
Depreciation	10,000
Interest	7,165
[Total expenses]	225,000
Earnings before taxes	45,000
Income taxes	22,500
Net income	22,500
Retained earnings at beginning of year	18,000
	40,500
Dividends	3,000
Retained earnings at end of year	$ 37,500
Net income per share	$ 15

[FAS89, ¶54]

.150 Inventory and production [information is as follows]:

a. Inventory is accounted for on a first-in, first-out (FIFO) basis and turns over four times per year. There is no significant amount of work in progress or raw materials.
b. At December 31, 19X6 and 19X5 inventory consisted of 900,000 units and 1,000,000 units respectively—representing production of the immediately preceding quarter. Management has measured the current cost of inventory at $73 per unit at December 31, 19X6 ($65,700,000) and $58 per unit at December 31, 19X5 ($58,000,000).
c. Costs were incurred and goods produced as follows:

(000s)

	19X5	19X6				
	4th	1st	2nd	3rd	4th	Total
Historical costs	$56,000	$39,560	$59,400	$42,040	$63,000	$204,000
Units produced	1,000	618	900	618	900	3,036
Units sold		1,000	618	900	618	3,136

d. At December 31, 19X6 the selling price per unit was $85.
e. There were no write-downs or disposals of inventory.

[FAS89, ¶55]

.151 Property, plant, and equipment [information is as follows]:

a. Details of fixed assets at December 31, 19X6 are as follows:

Date Acquired	Percent Depreciated	Historical Cost (000s)	Accumulated Depreciation (000s)
19W9	80	$ 50,000	$40,000
19X0	70	5,000	3,500
19X1	60	5,000	3,000
19X2	50	5,000	2,500
19X3	40	5,000	2,000
19X4	30	5,000	1,500
19X5	20	10,000	2,000
19X6	10	15,000	1,500
		$100,000	$56,000

b. Depreciation is calculated at 10 percent per annum, straight line. A full year's depreciation is charged in the year of acquisition.
c. There were no disposals.
d. Management has measured the current cost of property, plant, and equipment at December 31, 19X6 and 19X5 as follows:

	(000s)			
	December 31, 19X6		December 31, 19X5	
Date Acquired	Current Cost	Accumulated Depreciation	Current Cost	Accumulated Depreciation
19W9	$120,000	$ 96,000	$110,000	$77,000
19X0	10,000	7,000	6,000	3,600
19X1	15,000	9,000	7,000	3,500
19X2	18,000	9,000	12,000	4,800
19X3	12,000	4,800	10,000	3,000
19X4	17,000	5,100	15,000	3,000
19X5	12,000	2,400	10,000	1,000
19X6	16,000	1,600	—	—
	220,000	$134,900	170,000	$95,900
Accumulated depreciation	134,900		95,900	
Net current cost	$ 85,100		$ 74,100	

e. The recoverable amount has been determined by management to be in excess of current cost, net of accumulated depreciation.

[FAS89, ¶56]

.152 Dividends were paid at the rate of $750,000 per quarter. [FAS89, ¶57]

.153 Consumer Price Index for All Urban Consumers (from the *Survey of Current Business,* U.S. Department of Commerce, Bureau of Economic Analysis) [is as follows]:

December 19X5	292.4
Average 19X6	298.4
December 19X6	303.5

[FAS89, ¶58]

Parent Company Calculations

.154 The objective is to express the supplementary information in average 19X6 dollars. As indicated in paragraph .123, nominal dollar measurements may be used for all elements of net assets other than inventory and property, plant, and equipment. As indicated in paragraph .128, nominal dollar measurements may be used for all elements of income from continuing operations other than cost of sales and depreciation. [FAS89, ¶59]

Step 1: Analysis of Inventory and Cost of Goods Sold

.155 Inventory is assumed to turn over four times per year. Therefore, inventory with a historical cost of $63,000,000 at December 31, 19X6 is assumed to have been acquired during the fourth quarter of 19X6, and inventory with a historical cost of $56,000,000 at December 31, 19X5 is assumed to have been acquired in the fourth quarter of 19X5. [FAS89, ¶60]

Step 2: Current Cost of Inventory and Cost of Goods Sold

.156 Cost of goods sold, current cost, [data is as follows]:

Current cost at the beginning of year	$ 58/unit
Current cost at the end of year	73/unit
	$ 131/unit
Average current cost ($131 ÷ 2)	$ 65.5/unit
Units sold during the year (000s) (par. .150(c))	× 3,136
Average current cost of goods sold (000s)	$205,408

[FAS89, ¶61]

.157 The current cost amounts should be compared with the recoverable amount. This is illustrated below:

Market price per unit at end of year	$85
Current cost per unit of inventory on hand at end of year	73
Excess—no write-down required	$12

[FAS89, ¶62]

Step 3: Analysis of Property, Plant, and Equipment and Depreciation

.158 An analysis of property, plant, and equipment was given in paragraph .151. [FAS89, ¶63]

Step 4: Current Cost of Property, Plant, and Equipment and Depreciation

.159 It will usually be appropriate to calculate current cost depreciation, depletion, and amortization expense by reference to average current cost of the related assets (current cost of assets at beginning of year + current cost of assets at end of year ÷ 2).

	(000s) Current Cost
Current cost—12/31/X5 (par. .151(d))	$170,000
Current cost—12/31/X6 (par. .151(d))	220,000
	390,000
	÷ 2
Average current cost	$195,000
Current cost depreciation: 10%, straight line	$ 19,500

In this example, management has determined that the recoverable amount is greater than net current cost of property, plant, and equipment and there is no write-down. [FAS89, ¶64]

Step 5: Identification of Net Monetary Items

.160 Net monetary items (refer to paragraph .149) [are as follows]:

	(000s)	
	Dec. 31, 19X6	**Dec. 31, 19X5**
Cash	$ 1,000	$ 2,000
Accounts receivable	36,000	16,500
Accounts payable and accrued expenses	(47,000)	(32,000)
Income taxes payable	(6,000)	(6,000)
Current portion of long-term debt	(5,000)	(5,000)
Deferred income taxes	(6,000)	(5,000)
Long-term debt	(34,000)	(39,000)
Net monetary liabilities	$(61,000)	$(68,500)

[FAS89, ¶65]

Step 6: Computation of the Purchasing Power Gain or Loss on Net Monetary Items

.161 The amount of net monetary items at the beginning of the year, changes in the net monetary items, and the amount at the end of the year are restated into average 19X6 dollars. The purchasing power gain or loss on net monetary items is then the balancing item as illustrated below:

	(000s) Nominal Dollars	Conversion Factor	(000s) Avg. 19X6 Dollars
Balance—1/1/X6	$68,500	298.4 (avg. 19X6) / 292.4 (Dec. 19X5)	C$69,906
Decrease in net monetary liabilities during the year	(7,500)	*	(7,500)
Balance—12/31/X6	$61,000	298.4 (avg. 19X6) / 303.5 (Dec. 19X6)	(59,975)
Purchasing power gain on net monetary items			C$ 2,431

* Assumed to be in average 19X6 dollars.

[FAS89, ¶66]

Step 7: Computation of the Change in Current Cost of Inventory and Property, Plant, and Equipment and the Effect of General Price-Level Changes

.162 The increase in current cost of inventories [is as follows]:

	(000s) Current Cost/ Nominal Dollars	Conversion Factor	(000s) Current Cost/ Average 19X6 Dollars
Balance—1/1/X6 (par. .150(b))	$ 58,000	298.4 (avg. 19X6) / 292.4 (Dec. 19X5)	C$59,190
Production (par. .150(c))	204,000	*	204,000
Cost of goods sold (par. .156)	(205,408)	*	(205,408)
Balance—12/31/X6 (par. .150(b))	(65,700)	298.4 (avg. 19X6) / 303.5 (Dec. 19X6)	(64,596)
Increase in current cost of inventories	$ 9,108		C$ 6,814

*Assumed to be in average 19X6 dollars.

[FAS89, ¶67]

.163 The inflation component of the increase in current cost amount is the difference between the nominal dollar and constant dollar measures. Using the numbers from paragraph .162, [the inflation component is]:

	(000s)
Increase in current cost (nominal dollars)	$9,108
Increase in current cost (constant dollars)	C$6,814
Inflation component	2,294

[FAS89, ¶68]

.164 The increase in current cost of property, plant, and equipment [is as follows]:

	(000s) Current Cost/ Nominal Dollars	Conversion Factor	(000s) Current Cost/ Average 19X6 Dollars
Balance—1/1/X6 (par. .151(d))	$ 74,100	298.4 (avg. 19X6) / 292.4 (Dec. 19X5)	C$75,621
Additions (par. .151(a))	15,000	*	15,000
Depreciation (par. .159)	(19,500)	*	(19,500)
Balance—12/31/X6 (par. .151(d))	(85,100)	298.4 (avg. 19X6) / 303.5 (Dec. 19X6)	(83,670)
Increase in current cost of property, plant, and equipment	$ 15,500		C$12,549

*Assumed to be in average 19X6 dollars.

[FAS89, ¶69]

.165 The inflation component of the increase in current cost amount is the difference between the nominal dollar and constant dollar measures. Using the numbers from paragraph .164, [the inflation component is]:

	(000s)
Increase in current cost (nominal dollars)	$15,500
Increase in current cost (constant dollars)	C$12,549
Inflation component	2,951

[FAS89, ¶70]

Summary of Increase in Current Cost Amounts

.166 [The following summarizes] paragraphs .163 and .165 above:

	(000s) Increase in Current Cost	Inflation Component	Increase Net of Inflation
Inventory	$ 9,108	2,294	C$ 6,814
Property, plant, and equipment	15,500	2,951	12,549
Total	$24,608	5,245	C$19,363

[FAS89, ¶71]

Check of Calculations

.167 A reconciliation of shareholders' equity[9] (net assets) on a current cost/constant purchasing power basis acts as a check on the arithmetic accuracy of the calculations. Changes in shareholders' equity during 19X6 in average 19X6 dollars appear below:

	Source Paragraph	(000s) Current Cost/ Average 19X6 Dollars
Equity at January 1, 19X6		
Inventory	.162	C$59,190
Property, plant, and equipment—net	.164	75,621
Net monetary items	.161	(69,906)
		64,905
Income from continuing operations	.182	4,592
Dividends	.152	(3,000)
Gain from decline in purchasing power of net monetary liabilities	.161	2,431
Excess of increase in specific prices over increase in the general price level	.166	19,363
		C$88,291
Equity at December 31, 19X6		
Inventory	.162	C$64,596
Property, plant, and equipment—net	.164	83,670
Net monetary items	.161	(59,975)
		C$88,291

[FAS89, ¶72]

[9]To facilitate the illustration of consolidated amounts in paragraph .182, investment in Sub Company has been excluded from net assets of Parent Company in this paragraph. [FAS89, ¶72, fn10]

Sub Company Information

.168 The functional currency financial statements of Sub Company[10] [are presented] below:

Sub Company
Historical Cost/Nominal FC Balance Sheets
As of December 31, 19X6 and 19X5
(000s)

	19X6	19X5
Cash	FC2,550	FC1,250
Equipment	2,500	2,500
Accumulated depreciation	750	500
Net equipment	1,750	2,000
Total assets	FC4,300	FC3,250
Accounts payable	FC 600	FC 500
Long-term debt	2,000	1,500
Total liabilities	2,600	2,000
Capital stock	500	500
Retained earnings	1,200	750
Total equity	1,700	1,250
Total liabilities and equity	FC4,300	FC3,250

Sub Company
Historical Cost/Nominal FC Statement of Income and Retained Earnings
For the Year Ended December 31, 19X6

	(000s)
Revenue	FC5,000
General and administrative expenses	3,500
Depreciation	250
Interest	350
[Total expenses]	4,100
Income before taxes	900
Income taxes	450
Net income	450
Retained earnings—beginning of year	750
Retained earnings—end of year	FC1,200

[FAS89, ¶73]

[10] For simplicity, Sub Company is assumed to have a fixed asset but no inventory. The mechanics of restating inventory and cost of goods sold on a current cost basis are essentially the same as those illustrated for property, plant, and equipment. [FAS89, ¶73, fn11]

.169 The fixed asset was acquired on December 31, 19X4. It is depreciated on a straight-line basis over 10 years and is expected to have no salvage value. There were no acquisitions or disposals of assets during the year. [FAS89, ¶74]

.170 Exchange rates between the functional currency and the dollar are:

December 31, 19X5	FC1 = $1.20
Average 19X6	FC1 = $1.10
December 31, 19X6	FC1 = $1.00

[FAS89, ¶75]

.171 Management has measured the current cost of equipment at December 31, 19X6 and 19X5 as follows:

	(000s)	
	19X6	**19X5**
Current cost	FC5,500	FC4,000
Accumulated depreciation	(1,650)	(800)
Net current cost	FC3,850	FC3,200

The recoverable amount has been determined to be in excess of net current cost at both dates. [FAS89, ¶76]

.172 Current cost equity in nominal FC at the beginning and end of the year may be computed by adding net monetary items and net property, plant, and equipment at current cost. To determine current cost equity in nominal dollars, those FC amounts are translated at the appropriate exchange rate:

	December 31,					
	19X6			19X5		
	(000s) FC	Exchange Rate	(000s) $	(000s) FC	Exchange Rate	(000s) $
Monetary items (par. .168):						
Cash	FC2,550	$1	$ 2,550	FC1,250	$1.20	$ 1,500
Current liabilities	(600)	$1	(600)	(500)	$1.20	(600)
Long-term debt	(2,000)	$1	(2,000)	(1,500)	$1.20	(1,800)
Net monetary liabilities	FC (50)		$ (50)	FC (750)		$ (900)
Equipment—net (par. .171)	FC3,850	$1	$ 3,850	FC3,200	$1.20	$ 3,840
Equity at current cost	FC3,800		$ 3,800	FC2,450		$ 2,940

[FAS89, ¶77]

.173 The U.S. and local general price level indexes are:

	Local	U.S.
December 19X5	144	292.4
Average 19X6	158	298.4
December 19X6	173	303.5

[FAS89, ¶78]

Sub Company Calculations: Translate-Restate Method

.174 To apply the translate-restate method, amounts measured in nominal FC are first translated into their dollar equivalents. Changes in those dollar equivalent amounts are then restated to reflect the effects of U.S. inflation. [FAS89, ¶79]

Current Cost Depreciation and Income from Continuing Operations

.175 The first step is to determine current cost depreciation for the year as follows:

	(000s)
Current cost—beginning of year (par. .171)	FC4,000
Current cost—end of year (par. .171)	5,500
	9,500
	÷ 2
Average current cost, gross	FC4,750

Current cost depreciation expense for the year is FC475,000 (FC4,750,000 × 10%). Computation of current cost depreciation and income from continuing operations does not involve use of a general price level index if measurements are made in average-for-the-year currency units. Accordingly, reported current cost depreciation under the translate-restate method is C$E523,000 (FC475,000 × $1.10). [FAS89, ¶80]

.176 Income from continuing operations on a current cost basis is computed by simply replacing historical cost depreciation in income from continuing operations in the primary financial statements with the current cost amount. Accordingly, current cost income from continuing operations is:

Net income + historical cost depreciation – current cost depreciation
= FC450,000 (par. .168) + FC250,000 (par. .168) – FC475,000
(par. .175) = FC225,000.

Reported current cost income from continuing operations under the translate-restate method is C$E247,000[11] (FC225,000 × $1.10). [FAS89, ¶81]

[11]Current cost income has been rounded down from $247,500 to $247,000. This is necessary because current cost depreciation was rounded up to $523,000 from $522,500 and current cost income is a remainder of this number. [FAS89, ¶81, fn12]

Excess of Increase in Specific Prices over Increase in General Price Level

.177 The second step is to compute the change in the current cost of equipment and the effect of the increase in the general price level. To measure the increase in current cost of equipment in nominal FC dollar equivalents, the effect of the exchange rate change must be excluded. One way to accomplish this is to translate the December 31, 19X5 and 19X6 FC current cost amounts to dollar equivalents at the average exchange rate and then restate those dollar amounts to average 19X6 constant dollar equivalents:

	(000s) Current Cost/FC	Exchange Rate	(000s) Current Cost/$	Conversion Factor	(000s) Current Cost/C$E
Current cost, net—12/31/X5 (par. .171)	FC3,200	$1.10	$ 3,520	298.4 (avg. 19X6) / 292.4 (Dec. 19X5)	C$E3,592
Depreciation (par. .175)	(475)	$1.10	(523)	*	(523)
Current cost, net—12/31/X6 (par. .171)	(3,850)	$1.10	(4,235)	298.4 (avg. 19X6) / 303.5 (Dec. 19X6)	(4,164)
Increase in current cost	FC1,125		$ 1,238		C$E1,095

* Assumed to be in average 19X6 C$E.

The inflation component of the increase in current cost amount is the difference between the nominal dollar and the constant dollar equivalent amounts:

	(000s)
Increase in current cost (nominal dollars)	$1,238
Increase in current cost (constant dollars)	C$E1,095
Inflation component	143

[FAS89, ¶82]

Purchasing Power Gain or Loss on Net Monetary Items

.178 The third step is to compute the purchasing power gain or loss on net monetary items. Under the translate-restate method, the translated beginning and ending net monetary liabilities are restated to average 19X6 dollars. The U.S. purchasing power gain is then the balancing amount:

	(000s) FC	Exchange Rate	(000s) $
Net monetary liabilities—12/31/X5 (par. .172)	FC750	$1.20	$900
Net monetary liabilities—12/31/X6 (par. .172)	50	$1.00	50
Decrease during the year	FC700		$850

	(000s) $	Conversion Factor	(000s) C$E
Net monetary liabilities—12/31/X5	$ 900	298.4 (avg. 19X6) / 292.4 (Dec. 19X5)	C$E918
Decrease during the year	(850)	*	(850)
Net monetary liabilities—12/31/X6	$ 50	298.4 (avg. 19X6) / 303.5 (Dec. 19X6)	(49)
Purchasing power gain			C$E 19

*Assumed to be in average 19X6 C$E.

In some circumstances, the above procedure will include a part of the effect of exchange rate changes on net monetary items in the purchasing power gain or loss. A more precise computation that would completely exclude the effect of exchange rate changes would be to compute a separate purchasing power gain or loss for each functional currency operation in a manner similar to that illustrated in paragraph .177 for the increase in specific prices. For Sub Company, that alternative method produces a purchasing power gain of C$E18:

	(000s) FC	Average Exchange Rate	(000s) $	Conversion Factor	(000s) C$E
Net monetary liabilities—12/31/X5 (par. .172)	FC750	$1.10	$ 825	298.4 (avg. 19X6) / 292.4 (Dec. 19X5)	C$E842
Decrease during the year	(700)	$1.10	(770)	*	(770)
Net monetary liabilities—12/31/X6 (par. .172)	FC50	$1.10	$ 55	298.4 (avg. 19X6) / 303.5 (Dec. 19X6)	(54)
Purchasing power gain					C$E 18

* Assumed to be in average 19X6 C$E.

The first procedure illustrated is less costly because it can be applied on a consolidated basis, and it generally provides a reasonable approximation. Accordingly, that method is acceptable. For this exercise, the more precise computation is used. [FAS89, ¶83]

Check of Calculations

.179 A reconciliation of equity serves as a check of the calculations and is a convenient way to compute the translation adjustment:

	(000s)	
Equity at 12/31/X5 in average 19X6 C$—$2,940 (par. .172) × 298.4/292.4		C$3,000
Income from continuing operations (par. .176)	C$E247	
Purchasing power gain (par. .178)	18	
Excess of increase in specific prices over increase in general price level (par. .177)	1095	
Translation adjustment (par. .180)	(624)	
Increase in equity in terms of U.S. purchasing power		736
		C$3,736
Equity at 12/31/X6 in average 19X6 C$—$3,800 (par. .172) × 298.4/303.5		C$3,736

[FAS89, ¶84]

Translation Adjustment

.180 The preceding paragraph shows that the translation adjustment is the amount needed to balance the reconciliation of equity. The translation adjustment may be checked by computing the effect of changes in the exchange rate on beginning-of-year equity and on the increase or decrease in equity during the year. To check the translation adjustment determined under the translate-restate method: (a) translate the beginning- and end-of-year equity on a C$ basis into FC amounts and (b) use those FC amounts to compute the effect on equity of changes in the exchange rate.

	(000s) C$	Exchange Rate	(000s) FC
Equity at 12/31/X5 in average 19X6 C$ (par. .179)	C$3,000	$0.833*	FC2,499
Equity at 12/31/X6 in average 19X6 C$ (par. .179)	3,736	$ 1.00	3,736
Increase in equity	C$ 736		FC1,237

	(000s)	
Beginning-of-year equity	FC2,499	
Exchange rate change during 19X6 ($1.20 – $1.00)	× (.20)	$(500)
Increase in equity	FC1,237	
Difference between ending exchange rate and average rate for 19X6 ($1.10 – $1.00)	× (.10)	
		$(124)
Translation adjustment		$(624)

*FC1 – $1.20 = $0.833

If the short-cut method for determining the purchasing power gain or loss described in paragraph .178 were followed, the translation adjustment would be $(625). [FAS89, ¶85]

Consolidation: Translate-Restate Method

.181 Parent Company prepares its changing prices disclosures on a consolidated basis and complies with the minimum requirements in determining current cost income from continuing operations (paragraph .128). Accordingly, revenue, general and administrative expenses, interest, and income taxes (paragraph .129) are shown at amounts reported in the historical cost financial statements. For Sub Company, those amounts are translated into dollars as follows:

	(000s) FC Amount (Par. .168)	Exchange Rate	(000s) U.S. Dollars
Revenue	FC5,000	1.10	$5,500
General and administrative expenses	FC3,500	1.10	$3,850
Interest	FC 350	1.10	$ 385
Income taxes	FC 450	1.10	$ 495

[FAS89, ¶86]

.182 The "Total" column of the following schedule provides the figures in Exhibit 140B, "Illustrations of Disclosures."

	Source Par.	(000s) Parent Company	Source Par.	(000s) Sub Company	Total
Average 19X6 Units of Purchasing Power					
Net sales & other revenues	.149	$270,000	.181	$5,500	$275,500
Cost of goods sold	.156	205,408			205,408
Depreciation expense	.159	19,500	.175	523	20,023
Selling, general, and administrative expenses	.149	10,835	.181	3,850	14,685
Interest expense	.149	7,165	.181	385	7,550
Provision for taxes	.149	22,500	.181	495	22,995
		265,408		5,253	270,661
Income (loss) from operations		$ 4,592		$ 247	$ 4,839
Purchasing power gain (loss)	.161	$ 2,431	.178	$ 18	$ 2,449
Increase in specific prices					
Inventory	.166	$ 9,108			$ 9,108
Property, plant, and equipment	.166	15,500	.177	$1,238	16,738
		24,608		1,238	25,846
Effect of increase in general price level	.166	5,245	.177	143	$ 5,388
Increase in specific prices—net of inflation	.166	$ 19,363	.177	$1,095	$ 20,458
Translation adjustment			.180	$ (624)	$ (624)
Net assets	.167	$ 88,291	.179	$3,736	$ 92,027
December 31, 19X6 Units of Purchasing Power					
Inventory	.150	$ 65,700			$ 65,700
Property, plant, and equipment—net of accumulated depreciation	.151(d)	$ 85,100	.177	$4,235	$ 89,335

[FAS89, ¶87]

Sub Company Calculations: Restate-Translate Method

.183 To apply the restate-translate method, the steps illustrated in paragraphs .174 through .180 are followed except that all restatements to reflect the effects of general inflation are made using the local general price level index before translation to dollar equivalents. [FAS89, ¶88]

Current Cost Depreciation and Income from Continuing Operations

.184 Current cost depreciation and income from continuing operations are FC475,000 and FC225,000, respectively, as determined in paragraphs .175 and .176. [FAS89, ¶89]

Purchasing Power Gain or Loss on Net Monetary Items

.185 To apply the restate-translate method, the FC amount of net monetary items at the beginning of the year, changes in the net monetary items, and the amount at the end of the year are restated into average 19X6 CFC. The purchasing power gain or loss on net monetary items is then the balancing item:

	(000s) FC	Conversion Factor	(000s) CFC
Net monetary liabilities— 12/31/X5 (par. .172)	FC750	158 (avg. 19X6) / 144 (Dec. 19X5)	CFC823
Decrease during the year	(700)	*	(700)
Net monetary liabilities— 12/31/X6 (par. .172)	FC 50	158 (avg. 19X6) / 173 (Dec. 19X6)	(46)
Purchasing power gain			CFC 77

*Assumed to be in average 19X6 C$E.

[FAS89, ¶90]

Excess of Increase in Specific Prices over Increase in General Price Level

.186 Under the restate-translate method, the local index is used to restate the beginning and ending current cost FC amounts into average 19X6 CFC:

	(000s) Current Cost/FC	Conversion Factor	(000s) Current Cost/CFC
Current cost, net— 12/31/X5 (par. .171)	FC3,200	158 (avg. 19X6) / 144 (Dec. 19X5)	CFC3,511
Depreciation (par. .184)	(475)	*	(475)
Current cost, net— 12/31/X6 (par. 171)	(3,850)	158 (avg. 19X6) / 173 (Dec. 19X6)	(3,516)
Increase in current cost	FC1,125		CFC 480

*Assumed to be in average 19X6 C$E.

The inflation component of the increase in current cost amount is the difference between the nominal functional currency and constant functional currency amounts:

	(000s)
Increase in current cost (FC)	FC1,125
Increase in current cost (CFC)	CFC 480
Inflation component	645

[FAS89, ¶91]

Check of Calculations

.187 As with the translate-restate method, a reconciliation of equity acts as a check of the calculations. A reconciliation of equity also is a convenient point at which to translate the functional currency amounts determined in the preceding paragraphs into dollar equivalents and is a convenient way to compute the translation and parity adjustments. [FAS89, ¶92]

.188 If beginning and ending equity are restated to average 19X6 CFC using the local index, the reconciliation of equity under the restate-translate method would be:

	(000s) CFC	Exchange Rate	(000s) CFC$
Equity at 12/31/X5 in average 19X6 CFC (FC2,450 (par. .172) × 158/144)	CFC2,688	1.20	CFC$3,226
Income from continuing operations (par. .184)	225	1.10	247
Purchasing power gain (par. .185)	77	1.10	85
Excess of increase in specific prices over increase in general price level (par. .186)	480	1.10	528
Translation adjustment (par. .189)			(616)
	CFC3,470		CFC$3,470
Equity at 12/31/X6 in average 19X6 CFC (FC3,800 (par. .172) × 158/173)	CFC3,470	1.00	CFC$3,470

[FAS89, ¶93]

Translation Adjustment

.189 The translation adjustment is the amount needed to balance the CFC$ reconciliation of equity. The adjustment may be computed as (a) the change in exchange rates during the period multiplied by the restated amount of net assets at the beginning of the period plus (b) the difference between the average exchange rate for the period and the end-of-period exchange rate multiplied by the increase or decrease in restated net assets for the period. Accordingly, the translation adjustment under the restate-translate method is:

	(000s)	
Beginning-of-year equity (par. .188)	CFC2,688	
Exchange rate change during 19X6 ($1.20 – $1.00)	× .20	
		$(538)
Increase in equity (3,470 – 2,688)	CFC 782	
Difference between ending exchange rate and average rate for 19X6 ($1.10 – $1.00)	× .10	
		(78)
Translation adjustment		$(616)

[FAS89, ¶94]

Parity Adjustment

.190 The reconciliation of equity in paragraph .188, in which beginning-of-year and end-of-year equity are stated in average 19X6 CFC, is needed to calculate the translation adjustment in CFC$. However, beginning- and end-of-year equity and the increase in equity must be stated in average 19X6 constant dollars in the supplementary current cost information. Beginning- and end-of-year equity in average 19X6 constant dollars are C$3,000,000 and C$3,736,000, respectively, as computed in paragraph .179. Thus, the overall increase in U.S. purchasing power for the year is C$3,736,000 – C$3,000,000 = C$736,000. However, the reconciliation of equity in paragraph .188 indicates that the increase in equity for the year is CFC$244,000 (CFC$3,470,000 – CFC$3,226,000). The difference between C$736,000 and CFC$244,000 is the parity adjustment needed to adjust the ending net investment and the increase in the net investment to measures in average 19X6 constant dollars. Accordingly, the parity adjustment is C$736,000 – CFC$244,000 = $492,000. That amount represents (a) the effect of the difference between local and U.S. inflation from December 31, 19X5 average for 19X6 on the restatement of opening equity to average units plus (b) the effect of the difference between local and U.S. inflation from average for 19X6 to December 31, 19X6 the restatement of ending nominal dollar equity to average units:

	(000s)	
Beginning-of-year equity (par. .172)	$ 2,940	
Difference between local and U.S. inflation from 12/31/X5 to average 19X6 (158/144 – 298.4/292.4)	× 0.0767	
		$225
Equity at 12/31/X6 (par. .172)	3,800	
Difference between local and U.S. inflation from average 19X6 to 12/31/X6 (158/173 – 298.4/303.5)	× 0.0699	
		266
		491
Rounding difference		1
Parity adjustment		$492

For display purposes, the parity adjustment [is]combined with the $(616,000) translation adjustment (paragraph .189). Accordingly, the net translation adjustment disclosed in the supplementary current cost information prepared using the restate-translate method would be \$(616,000) + \$492,000 = \$(124,000). The components of current cost information based on the restate-translate method thus would be:

	(000s)	
Beginning-of-year equity— \$2,940 (par. .172) × 298.4/292.4		C\$3,000
Income from continuing operations— CFC225 (par. .184) × 1.10	CFC\$ 247	
Purchasing power gain— CFC77 (par. .185) × 1.10	85	
Excess of increase in specific prices over increase in general price level—CFC480 (par. .186) × 1.10	528	
Translation and parity adjustments	(124)	
Increase in equity in terms of U.S. purchasing power		736
End-of-year equity—\$3,800 (par. .172) × 298.4/303.5		C\$3,736

[FAS89, ¶95]

Monetary and Nonmonetary Items

.191 Paragraphs .191 through .203 provide guidance on the interpretation of paragraphs .136 through .139 for the classification of certain asset and liability items as monetary or nonmonetary. The following table illustrates the application of the definitions to common cases under typical circumstances. In other circumstances the classification should be resolved by reference to the definitions. Paragraphs .191 through .203 are not intended to provide answers that should be followed regardless of the circumstances of the case. (Footnote reference is at the end of the table.)

	Monetary	Nonmonetary
Assets		
Cash on hand and demand bank deposits (dollars)	X	
Time deposits (dollars)	X	
Foreign currency on hand and claims to foreign currency[a]	X	
Securities:		
Common stocks (not accounted for on the equity method)		X
Common stocks represent residual interests in the underlying net assets and earnings of the issuer.		

<table>
<tr><th></th><th>Monetary</th><th>Nonmonetary</th></tr>
<tr><td>Assets</td><td></td><td></td></tr>
<tr><td>Preferred stock (convertible or participating)</td><td colspan="2">Circumstances may indicate that such stock is either monetary or nonmonetary. Refer to convertible bonds.</td></tr>
<tr><td>Preferred stock (nonconvertible, nonparticipating)
Future cash receipts are likely to be substantially unaffected by changes in specific prices.</td><td>X</td><td></td></tr>
<tr><td>Convertible bonds</td><td colspan="2">If the market values the security primarily as a bond, it is monetary, if it values the security primarily as stock, it is nonmonetary.</td></tr>
<tr><td>Bonds (other than convertibles)</td><td>X</td><td></td></tr>
<tr><td>Trading account investments in fixed-income securities owned by banks, investment brokers, and others (paragraphs .192 and .193)</td><td></td><td>X</td></tr>
<tr><td>Accounts and notes receivable</td><td>X</td><td></td></tr>
<tr><td>Allowance for doubtful accounts and notes receivable</td><td>X</td><td></td></tr>
<tr><td>Variable-rate mortgage loans
The terms of such loans do not link them directly to the rate of inflation. Also, there are practical reasons for classifying all loans as monetary.</td><td>X</td><td></td></tr>
<tr><td>Inventories used on contracts</td><td colspan="2">They are, in substance, rights to receive sums of money if the future cash receipts on the contracts will not vary due to future changes in specific prices. Goods used on contracts to be priced at market upon delivery are nonmonetary.</td></tr>
</table>

	Monetary	Nonmonetary
Assets		
Inventories (other than inventories used on contracts) and commodity inventories (other than those described below)		X
Commodity inventories whose values are hedged by futures contracts whose contract amounts have not been recorded in the financial statements	Refer to paragraphs .194 and .195.	
Loans to employees	X	
Prepaid insurance, advertising, rent, and other prepayments	Claims to future services are nonmonetary. Prepayments that are deposits, advance payments, or receivables are monetary because the prepayment does not obtain a given quantity of future services, but rather is a fixed-money offset.	
Long-term receivables	X	
Refundable deposits	X	
Advances to unconsolidated subsidiaries	X	
Equity investment in unconsolidated subsidiaries or other investees		X
Pension, sinking, and other funds under an enterprise's control	The specific assets in the fund should be classified as monetary or nonmonetary. Refer to listings under securities above.	
Property, plant, and equipment		X
Accumulated depreciation of property, plant, and equipment		X
The unguaranteed residual value of property owned by a lessor and leased under direct financing, sales-type, and leveraged leases	Refer to paragraphs .196 and .197.	

	Monetary	Nonmonetary
Assets		
Investment tax credits that are deferred by a lessor as part of the unearned income of a leveraged lease	Refer to paragraphs .198 and .199.	
Portion of the carrying amount of lessors' assets leased under noncancellable operating leases that represent claims to fixed sums of money (paragraphs .200 and .201)		X
Cash surrender value of life insurance	X	
Purchase commitments—portion paid on fixed-price contracts An advance on a fixed-price contract is the portion of the purchaser's claim to nonmonetary goods or services that is recognized in the accounts; it is not a right to receive money.		X
Advances to supplier—not on a fixed-price contract Such advances are rights to receive credit for a sum of money, not claims to a specified quantity of goods or services. [FAS89, ¶96]	X	
Deferred tax assets[a] [FAS109, ¶288(w)]	X	
Patents, trademarks, licenses, and formulas		X
Goodwill		X
Deferred life insurance policy acquisition costs[a] Such costs represent the portion of future cash receipts for premiums that is recognized in the accounts and are sometimes viewed as an offset to the policy reserve.	X	
Deferred property and casualty insurance policy acquisition costs related to unearned premiums		X
Other intangible assets and deferred charges		X

	Monetary	Nonmonetary
Liabilities		
Accounts and notes payable	X	
Accrued expenses payable (wages and so forth)	X	
Accrued vacation pay	If to be paid at the wage rates as of the vacation dates and if those rates may vary, accrued vacation pay is nonmonetary.	
Cash dividends payable	X	
Obligations payable in foreign currency	X	
Sales commitments—portion collected on fixed-price contracts An advance received on a fixed-price contract is the portion of the seller's obligation to deliver goods or services that is recognized in the accounts; it is not an obligation to pay money.		X
Advances from customers—not on a fixed-price contract Such advances are equivalent to loans from customers and are not obligations to furnish specified quantities of goods or services.	X	
Accrued losses on firm purchase commitments In essence, these are accounts payable.	X	
Deferred revenue	If an obligation to furnish goods or services is involved, deferred revenue is nonmonetary. Certain "deferred income" items of savings and loan associations are monetary.	
Refundable deposits	X	
Bonds payable and other long-term debt	X	

	Monetary	Nonmonetary
Liabilities		
Unamortized premium or discount and prepaid interest on bonds or notes payable Such items are inseparable from the debt to which they relate—a monetary item.	X	
Convertible bonds payable Until converted, these are obligations to pay sums of money.	X	
Accrued pension obligations	Fixed amounts payable to a fund are monetary; all other amounts are nonmonetary.	
Obligations under warranties These are nonmonetary because they oblige the enterprise to furnish goods or services or their future price. [FAS89, ¶96]		X
Deferred tax liabilities[a] [FAS109, ¶288(w)]	X	
Deferred investment tax credits These are not to be settled by payment of cash and are related to nonmonetary assets.		X
Life insurance policy reserves These represent portions of policies' face values that are now deemed liabilities.	X	
Property and casualty insurance loss reserves	X	
Unearned property and casualty insurance premiums These are nonmonetary because they are principally obligations to furnish insurance coverage. The dollar amount of payments to be made under that coverage might vary materially due to changes in specific prices.		X
Deposit liabilities of financial institutions	X	
Minority interests in consolidated subsidiaries (paragraph .202)		X

	Monetary	Nonmonetary
Equity		
Capital stock of the enterprise or of its consolidated subsidiaries subject to mandatory redemption at fixed amounts (paragraph .203)	X	

[a]Although classification of this item as nonmonetary may be technically preferable, the monetary classification provides a more practical solution for the purposes of computing the purchasing power gain or loss on a consolidated basis.

[FAS89, ¶96]

.192 *Trading account investments in fixed-income securities owned by banks, investment brokers, and others.* Trading account securities are securities of all types carried in a dealer trading account that are held principally for resale to customers. The predominant practice by banks is to carry these securities at market value. Trading account investments include both fixed-income securities (for example, nonconvertible preferred stock, convertible bonds, and other bonds) and other securities (for example, common stock). Usually, trading account securities are held for extremely short periods of time—sometimes for only a few hours. Frequently, the enterprise buys and sells the securities expecting to make a profit on the difference between dealer and retail, or bid and ask, prices rather than on price changes during the period securities are held. However, the prices of the securities change with market forces. [FAS89, ¶97]

.193 Trading account investments in fixed-income securities are not claims to receive sums of money that are fixed or determinable. The market prices of the securities might and frequently do change while the securities are held. Generally, nonconvertible and nonparticipating preferred stock, convertible bonds that the market values primarily as bonds rather than as stocks, and nonconvertible bonds should be classified as monetary items. However, those classifications are based, in part, on the assumption that those securities would be held for long periods, if not to maturity. Trading account investments, on the other hand, are held for shorter periods and their value depends much less heavily on the general purchasing power of money and more on the specific values of the securities. Therefore, trading account investments in fixed-income securities should be classified as nonmonetary. [FAS89, ¶98]

.194 *Commodity inventories whose values are hedged by futures contracts.* Many enterprises hedge commodity inventories (such as grain or metals). *Short hedges* are designed to provide a degree of assurance that a decline in the price of the commodity would be offset by an increase in the value of the hedge contract. Short hedges thus tend to reduce the effects of price changes on the inventory that is hedged. [FAS89, ¶99]

.195 There are certain similarities between inventories that are hedged and inventories that are used on or committed to a fixed-price contract. In each case, the risk of gain or loss due to price changes before the inventory is sold is largely or entirely eliminated. To the extent that hedges fix the value of an inventory in dollars (or units of foreign functional currency, if appropriate), the inventory effectively becomes a monetary item. [FAS89, ¶100]

.196 *The unguaranteed residual value of property owned by a lessor and leased under direct financing, sales-type, and leveraged leases.* The unguaranteed residual value is included with the minimum lease payments, at present value, in the net investment in the lease. [FAS89, ¶101]

.197 The minimum lease payments are monetary items because they are claims to fixed sums of money. The residual value is not a claim to a fixed sum of money, so it is a nonmonetary item. Some assets and liabilities, of which the net investment in the lease is a good example, are combinations of claims to (or obligations of) fixed amounts and claims to (or obligations of) variable amounts. Ideally, those claims should be separated for purposes of classifying them as monetary and nonmonetary. However, if the information necessary to make the separation is not available or is impracticable to obtain, such items need not be divided into monetary and nonmonetary components and would be classified according to their dominant element. If the net investment in leases is principally claims to fixed amounts, it would be classified as monetary; it would be classified as nonmonetary if it is principally claims to residuals. [FAS89, ¶102]

.198 *Investment tax credits that are deferred by a lessor as part of the unearned income of a leveraged lease.* Under Section L10, "Leases," the deferred investment tax credit related to the leased asset is subtracted from rentals receivable and estimated residual value as part of the calculation of the lessor's investment in the leveraged lease. The investment, including the deferred investment tax credit related to the leveraged lease, is presented as one amount in the balance sheet. As indicated in paragraph .197, the investment in a leveraged lease would be classified as monetary or nonmonetary according to its dominant element. [FAS89, ¶103]

.199 As indicated in the table in paragraph .191, a deferred investment tax credit should be classified as nonmonetary but, if it is part of an investment in a leveraged lease and if the information necessary to separate its elements is not available or is impracticable to obtain, the investment would be classified according to its dominant element. [FAS89, ¶104]

.200 *Portion of the carrying amount of lessors' assets leased under noncancellable operating leases that represent claims to fixed sums of money.* These assets are carried at depreciated historical cost under generally accepted accounting principles and are classified with or near property, plant, and equipment, which are nonmonetary. [FAS89, ¶105]

.201 The classification of a lease as an operating lease under Section L10 indicates that the lease has not transferred substantially all of the benefits and risks incident to ownership to the lessee. Thus, the economic significance of the asset continues to depend heavily on the value of the future lease rentals, residual values, and associated costs. Therefore, an asset subject to an operating lease should be classified as nonmonetary. [FAS89, ¶106]

.202 *Minority interests in consolidated subsidiaries.* The interests of minority shareholders in the earnings and equity of subsidiaries are, from the consolidated entity's point of view, claims that are not fixed. Rather, they are residuals that will vary based on the subsidiary's earnings, dividends, and other transactions affecting its equity and so are nonmonetary. (Refer to paragraph .203 as to classification of capital stock of the enterprise or of its consolidated subsidiaries subject to mandatory redemption at fixed amounts.) [FAS89, ¶107]

.203 *Capital stock of the enterprise or of its consolidated subsidiaries subject to mandatory redemption at fixed amounts.* Such securities are claims of the stockholders to a fixed sum of money and therefore are monetary. Classification as a monetary item called for in paragraphs .191 through .203 is only for purposes of determining a purchasing power gain or loss. Paragraphs .191 through .203 do not address how such securities should be classified in balance sheets or the accounting for dividends on those securities. [FAS89, ¶108]

The Consumer Price Index

.204 [The table in Exhibit 204A is the offical Department of Labor Consumer Price Index—CPI(U), U.S. City Average, All Items (1982–1984 = 100). This table includes monthly indexes and the average index for the year from 1913. Monthly updates to the table and historical data are available on the Bureau of Labor Statistics web site at http://stats.bls.gov/cpihome.htm and are published in the *CPI Detailed Report.*]

[Exhibit 204A

Consumer Price Index
All Urban Consumers—(CPI-U)
U.S. City Average
All Items
(1982–1984 = 100)

Year	Jan.	Feb.	Mar.	Apr.	May	June	July	Aug.	Sept.	Oct.	Nov.	Dec.	Avg.
1913	9.8	9.8	9.8	9.8	9.7	9.8	9.9	9.9	10.0	10.0	10.1	10.0	9.9
1914	10.0	9.9	9.9	9.8	9.9	9.9	10.0	10.2	10.2	10.1	10.2	10.1	10.0
1915	10.1	10.0	9.9	10.0	10.1	10.1	10.1	10.1	10.1	10.2	10.3	10.3	10.1
1916	10.4	10.4	10.5	10.6	10.7	10.8	10.8	10.9	11.1	11.3	11.5	11.6	10.9
1917	11.7	12.0	12.0	12.6	12.8	13.0	12.8	13.0	13.3	13.5	13.5	13.7	12.8
1918	14.0	14.1	14.0	14.2	14.5	14.7	15.1	15.4	15.7	16.0	16.3	16.5	15.1
1919	16.5	16.2	16.4	16.7	16.9	16.9	17.4	17.7	17.8	18.1	18.5	18.9	17.3
1920	19.3	19.5	19.7	20.3	20.6	20.9	20.8	20.3	20.0	19.9	19.8	19.4	20.0
1921	19.0	18.4	18.3	18.1	17.7	17.6	17.7	17.7	17.5	17.5	17.4	17.3	17.9
1922	16.9	16.9	16.7	16.7	16.7	16.7	16.8	16.6	16.6	16.7	16.8	16.9	16.8
1923	16.8	16.8	16.8	16.9	16.9	17.0	17.2	17.1	17.2	17.3	17.3	17.3	17.1
1924	17.3	17.2	17.1	17.0	17.0	17.0	17.1	17.0	17.1	17.2	17.2	17.3	17.1
1925	17.3	17.2	17.3	17.2	17.3	17.5	17.7	17.7	17.7	17.7	18.0	17.9	17.5
1926	17.9	17.9	17.8	17.9	17.8	17.7	17.5	17.4	17.5	17.6	17.7	17.7	17.7
1927	17.5	17.4	17.3	17.3	17.4	17.6	17.3	17.2	17.3	17.4	17.3	17.3	17.4
1928	17.3	17.1	17.1	17.1	17.2	17.1	17.1	17.1	17.3	17.2	17.2	17.1	17.1
1929	17.1	17.1	17.0	16.9	17.0	17.1	17.3	17.3	17.3	17.3	17.3	17.2	17.1
1930	17.1	17.0	16.9	17.0	16.9	16.8	16.6	16.5	16.6	16.5	16.4	16.1	16.7

1931	15.9	15.7	15.6	15.5	15.3	15.1	15.1	15.1	15.0	14.9	14.7	14.6	15.2
1932	14.3	14.1	14.0	13.9	13.7	13.6	13.6	13.5	13.4	13.3	13.2	13.1	13.7
1933	12.9	12.7	12.6	12.6	12.6	12.7	13.1	13.2	13.2	13.2	13.2	13.2	13.0
1934	13.2	13.3	13.3	13.3	13.3	13.4	13.4	13.4	13.6	13.5	13.5	13.4	13.4
1935	13.6	13.7	13.7	13.8	13.8	13.7	13.7	13.7	13.7	13.7	13.8	13.8	13.7
1936	13.8	13.8	13.7	13.7	13.7	13.8	13.9	14.0	14.0	14.0	14.0	14.0	13.9
1937	14.1	14.1	14.2	14.3	14.4	14.4	14.5	14.5	14.6	14.6	14.5	14.4	14.4
1938	14.2	14.1	14.1	14.2	14.1	14.1	14.1	14.1	14.1	14.0	14.0	14.0	14.1
1939	14.0	13.9	13.9	13.8	13.8	13.8	13.8	13.8	14.1	14.0	14.0	14.0	13.9
1940	13.9	14.0	14.0	14.0	14.0	14.1	14.0	14.0	14.0	14.0	14.0	14.1	14.0
1941	14.1	14.1	14.2	14.3	14.4	14.7	14.7	14.9	15.1	15.3	15.4	15.5	14.7
1942	15.7	15.8	16.0	16.1	16.3	16.3	16.4	16.5	16.5	16.7	16.8	16.9	16.3
1943	16.9	16.9	17.2	17.4	17.5	17.5	17.4	17.3	17.4	17.4	17.4	17.4	17.3
1944	17.4	17.4	17.4	17.5	17.5	17.6	17.7	17.7	17.7	17.7	17.7	17.8	17.6
1945	17.8	17.8	17.8	17.8	17.9	18.1	18.1	18.1	18.1	18.1	18.1	18.2	18.0
1946	18.2	18.1	18.3	18.4	18.5	18.7	19.8	20.2	20.4	20.8	21.3	21.5	19.5
1947	21.5	21.5	21.9	21.9	21.9	22.0	22.2	22.5	23.0	23.0	23.1	23.4	22.3
1948	23.7	23.5	23.4	23.8	23.9	24.1	24.4	24.5	24.5	24.4	24.2	24.1	24.1
1949	24.0	23.8	23.8	23.9	23.8	23.9	23.7	23.8	23.9	23.7	23.8	23.6	23.8
1950	23.5	23.5	23.6	23.6	23.7	23.8	24.1	24.3	24.4	24.6	24.7	25.0	24.1
1951	25.4	25.7	25.8	25.8	25.9	25.9	25.9	25.9	26.1	26.2	26.4	26.5	26.0
1952	26.5	26.3	26.3	26.4	26.4	26.5	26.7	26.7	26.7	26.7	26.7	26.7	26.5
1953	26.6	26.5	26.6	26.6	26.7	26.8	26.8	26.9	26.9	27.0	26.9	26.9	26.7
1954	26.9	26.9	26.9	26.8	26.9	26.9	26.9	26.9	26.8	26.8	26.8	26.7	26.9
1955	26.7	26.7	26.7	26.7	26.7	26.7	26.8	26.8	26.9	26.9	26.9	26.8	26.8

Exhibit 204A (continued)

Year	Jan.	Feb.	Mar.	Apr.	May	June	July	Aug.	Sept.	Oct.	Nov.	Dec.	Avg.
1956	26.8	26.8	26.8	26.9	27.0	27.2	27.4	27.3	27.4	27.5	27.5	27.6	27.2
1957	27.6	27.7	27.8	27.9	28.0	28.1	28.3	28.3	28.3	28.3	28.4	28.4	28.1
1958	28.6	28.6	28.8	28.9	28.9	28.9	29.0	28.9	28.9	28.9	29.0	28.9	28.9
1959	29.0	28.9	28.9	29.0	29.0	29.1	29.2	29.2	29.3	29.4	29.4	29.4	29.1
1960	29.3	29.4	29.4	29.5	29.5	29.6	29.6	29.6	29.6	29.8	29.8	29.8	29.6
1961	29.8	29.8	29.8	29.8	29.8	29.8	30.0	29.9	30.0	30.0	30.0	30.0	29.9
1962	30.0	30.1	30.1	30.2	30.2	30.2	30.3	30.3	30.4	30.4	30.4	30.4	30.2
1963	30.4	30.4	30.5	30.5	30.5	30.6	30.7	30.7	30.7	30.8	30.8	30.9	30.6
1964	30.9	30.9	30.9	30.9	30.9	31.0	31.1	31.0	31.1	31.1	31.2	31.2	31.0
1965	31.2	31.2	31.3	31.4	31.4	31.6	31.6	31.6	31.6	31.7	31.7	31.8	31.5
1966	31.8	32.0	32.1	32.3	32.3	32.4	32.5	32.7	32.7	32.9	32.9	32.9	32.4
1967	32.9	32.9	33.0	33.1	33.2	33.3	33.4	33.5	33.6	33.7	33.8	33.9	33.4
1968	34.1	34.2	34.3	34.4	34.5	34.7	34.9	35.0	35.1	35.3	35.4	35.5	34.8
1969	35.6	35.8	36.1	36.3	36.4	36.6	36.8	37.0	37.1	37.3	37.5	37.7	36.7
1970	37.8	38.0	38.2	38.5	38.6	38.8	39.0	39.0	39.2	39.4	39.6	39.8	38.8
1971	39.8	39.9	40.0	40.1	40.3	40.6	40.7	40.8	40.8	40.9	40.9	41.1	40.5
1972	41.1	41.3	41.4	41.5	41.6	41.7	41.9	42.0	42.1	42.3	42.4	42.5	41.8
1973	42.6	42.9	43.3	43.6	43.9	44.2	44.3	45.1	45.2	45.6	45.9	46.2	44.4
1974	46.6	47.2	47.8	48.0	48.6	49.0	49.4	50.0	50.6	51.1	51.5	51.9	49.3
1975	52.1	52.5	52.7	52.9	53.2	53.6	54.2	54.3	54.6	54.9	55.3	55.5	53.8
1976	55.6	55.8	55.9	56.1	56.5	56.8	57.1	57.4	57.6	57.9	58.0	58.2	56.9
1977	58.5	59.1	59.5	60.0	60.3	60.7	61.0	61.2	61.4	61.6	61.9	62.1	60.6
1978	62.5	62.9	63.4	63.9	64.5	65.2	65.7	66.0	66.5	67.1	67.4	67.7	65.2
1979	68.3	69.1	69.8	70.6	71.5	72.3	73.1	73.8	74.6	75.2	75.9	76.7	72.6
1980	77.8	78.9	80.1	81.0	81.8	82.7	82.7	83.3	84.0	84.8	85.5	86.3	82.4

1981	87.0	87.9	88.5	89.1	89.8	90.6	91.6	92.3	93.2	93.4	93.7	94.0	90.9
1982	94.3	94.6	94.5	94.9	95.8	97.0	97.5	97.7	97.9	98.2	98.0	97.6	96.5
1983	97.8	97.9	97.9	98.6	99.2	99.5	99.9	100.2	100.7	101.0	101.2	101.3	99.6
1984	101.9	102.4	102.6	103.1	103.4	103.7	104.1	104.5	105.0	105.3	105.3	105.3	103.9
1985	105.5	106.0	106.4	106.9	107.3	107.6	107.8	108.0	108.3	108.7	109.0	109.3	107.6
1986	109.6	109.3	108.8	108.6	108.9	109.5	109.5	109.7	110.2	110.3	110.4	110.5	109.6
1987	111.2	111.6	112.1	112.7	113.1	113.5	113.8	114.4	115.0	115.3	115.4	115.4	113.6
1988	115.7	116.0	116.5	117.1	117.5	118.0	118.5	119.0	119.8	120.2	120.3	120.5	118.3
1989	121.1	121.6	122.3	123.1	123.8	124.1	124.4	124.6	125.0	125.6	125.9	126.1	124.0
1990	127.4	128.0	128.7	128.9	129.2	129.9	130.4	131.6	132.7	133.5	133.8	133.8	130.7
1991	134.6	134.8	135.0	135.2	135.6	136.0	136.2	136.6	137.2	137.4	137.8	137.9	136.2
1992	138.1	138.6	139.3	139.5	139.7	140.2	140.5	140.9	141.3	141.8	142.0	141.9	140.3
1993	142.6	143.1	143.6	144.0	144.2	144.4	144.4	144.8	145.1	145.7	145.8	145.8	144.5
1994	146.2	146.7	147.2	147.4	147.5	148.0	148.4	149.0	149.4	149.5	149.7	149.7	148.2
1995	150.3	150.9	151.4	151.9	152.2	152.5	152.5	152.9	153.2	153.7	153.6	153.5	152.4
1996	154.4	154.9	155.7	156.3	156.6	156.7	157.0	157.3	157.8	158.3	158.6	158.6	156.9
1997	159.1	159.6	160.0	160.2	160.1	160.3	160.5	160.8	161.2	161.6	161.5	161.3	160.5
1998	161.6	161.9	162.2	162.5	162.8	163.0	163.2	163.4	163.6	164.0	164.0	163.9	163.0
1999	164.3	164.5	165.0	166.2	166.2	166.2	166.7	167.1	167.9	168.2	168.3	168.3	166.6
2000	168.7	169.7	171.1	171.2	171.3	171.5	172.4	172.8	173.7	174.0	174.1	174.0	172.2
2001	175.1	175.8	176.2	176.9	177.7	178.0	177.5	177.5	178.3	177.7	177.4	176.7	177.1
2002	177.1	177.8	178.8	179.8	179.8								

Source: U.S. Department of Labor, Room 1539, Bureau of Labor Statistics, Washington, D.C. 20212. The CPI Detailed Report may be ordered from the Superintendent of Documents, U.S. Government Printing Office, Washington, D.C. 20402. The Library of Congress Catalog number is 74-647019.]

Glossary

.401 **Current cost/constant purchasing power** accounting. A method of accounting based on measures of current cost or lower recoverable amount in units of currency, each of which has the same general purchasing power. For operations in which the dollar is the functional currency, the general purchasing power of the dollar is used and the CPI-U is the required measure of purchasing power (paragraph .132). For operations in which the functional currency is other than the dollar, the general purchasing power of either the dollar or the functional currency is used (paragraph .133). [FAS89, ¶44]

.402 **Current market value.** The amount of cash, or its equivalent, expected to be derived from the sale of an asset net of costs required to be incurred as a result of the sale. [FAS89, ¶44]

.403 **Historical cost** accounting. The generally accepted method of accounting used in the primary financial statements that is based on measures of historical prices without restatement into units, each of which has the same general purchasing power. [FAS89, ¶44]

.404 **Historical cost/constant purchasing power** accounting. A method of accounting based on measures of historical prices in units of a currency, each of which has the same general purchasing power. [FAS89, ¶44]

.405 **Income from continuing operations.** Income after applicable income taxes but excluding the results of discontinued operations, extraordinary items, the cumulative effect of accounting changes, translation adjustments, purchasing power gains and losses on monetary items, and increases and decreases in the current cost or lower recoverable amount of nonmonetary assets and liabilities. [FAS89, ¶44]

.406 **Income-producing real estate.** Properties that meet all of the following criteria:

a. Cash flows can be directly associated with a long-term leasing agreement with unaffiliated parties.
b. The property is being operated. (It is not in a construction phase.)
c. Future cash flows from the property are reasonably estimable.
d. Ancillary services are not a significant part of the lease agreement.

Hotels, which have occupancy rates and related cash flows that may fluctuate to a relatively large extent, do not meet the criteria for income-producing real estate. [FAS89, ¶44]

.407 **Mineral resource assets.** Assets that are directly associated with and derive value from all minerals that are extracted from the earth. Such minerals include oil and gas, ores containing ferrous and nonferrous metals, coal, shale, geothermal steam, sulphur, salt, stone, phosphate, sand, and gravel. Mineral resource assets include mineral interests in properties, completed and uncompleted wells, and related equipment and facilities and other facilities required for purposes of extraction (Section Oi5, paragraph .103). This definition does not cover support equipment because that equipment is included in the property, plant, and equipment for which current cost measurements are required by this section. [FAS89, ¶44]

.408 **Monetary asset.** Money or a claim to receive a sum of money the amount of which is fixed or determinable without reference to future prices of specific goods or services. [FAS89, ¶44]

.409 **Monetary liability.** An obligation to pay a sum of money the amount of which is fixed or determinable without reference to future prices of specific goods and services. [FAS89, ¶44]

.410 **Motion picture films.** All types of film, including feature films, television specials, television series, or similar products (including animated films and television programming) that are sold, licensed, or exhibited, whether produced on film, video tape, digital, or other video recording format. [FAS139, ¶6]

.411 **Parity adjustment.** The effect of the difference between local and U.S. inflation for the year on net assets (that is, shareholders' equity) measured in nominal dollars. If only the differential rates of U.S. and local inflation are reflected in the exchange rates (parity), the parity adjustment and the translation adjustment net to zero. Therefore, the sum of the parity adjustment and the translation adjustment represents the effect of exchange rate changes in excess of (or less than) that needed to maintain purchasing power parity between the functional currency and the dollar. [FAS89, ¶44]

.412 **Probable mineral reserves.** In extractive industries other than oil and gas, the estimated quantities of commercially recoverable reserves that are less well defined than proved. [FAS89, ¶44]

.413 **Proved mineral reserves.** In extractive industries other than oil and gas, the estimated quantities of commercially recoverable reserves that, on the basis of geological, geophysical, and engineering data, can be demonstrated with a reasonably high degree of certainty to be recoverable in the future from known mineral deposits by either primary or improved recovery methods. [FAS89, ¶44]

.414 **Purchasing power gain or loss** on net monetary items. The net gain or loss determined by restating in units of constant purchasing power the opening and closing balances of, and transactions in, monetary assets and liabilities. [FAS89, ¶44]

.415 **Recoverable amount.** Current worth of the net amount of cash expected to be recoverable from the use or sale of an asset (paragraphs .125 through .127). [FAS89, ¶44]

.416 **Restate-translate.** An approach to converting current cost/nominal functional currency data of a foreign operation into units of constant purchasing power expressed in dollars. Using this approach, the current cost/nominal functional currency data are restated into units of constant purchasing power using a general price index for the foreign currency. After restatement into units of constant functional currency purchasing power, the current cost data are translated into dollars. This approach often necessitates a parity adjustment. [FAS89, ¶44]

.417 **Translate-restate.** An approach to converting current cost/nominal functional currency data of a foreign operation into units of constant purchasing power expressed in dollars. Using this approach, the current cost/nominal functional currency data are first translated into dollars and then restated into units of constant purchasing power using the CPI-U. [FAS89, ¶44]

.418 **Translation adjustment.** The effect that results from the process of translating an entity's financial statements from its functional currency into the dollar (paragraphs .134 and .135). [FAS89, ¶44]

.419 **Value in use.** The amount determined by discounting the future cash flows (including the ultimate proceeds of disposal) expected to be derived from the use of an asset at an appropriate rate that allows for the risk of the activities concerned. [FAS89, ¶44]

Supplemental Guidance: Emerging Issues Task Force (EITF) Issues

.1000 [Listed below is an EITF Issue that provides supplemental guidance for this section. This Issue is related by topic to the guidance in this section.

EITF Issue No. 93-9, "Application of FASB Statement No. 109 in Foreign Financial Statements Restated for General Price-Level Changes"]

(The next page is 6985.)

COMMITMENTS: LONG-TERM OBLIGATIONS SECTION C32

Sources: FASB Statement 47; FASB Statement 129

[**Note:** A list of Issues discussed by the Emerging Issues Task Force (EITF) that provide supplemental guidance for this section is presented in paragraph .1000.]

Summary

An enterprise shall disclose its commitments under unconditional purchase obligations that are associated with suppliers' financing arrangements. Such obligations often are in the form of take-or-pay contracts and throughput contracts. Future payments on long-term borrowings and redeemable stock also shall be disclosed. For long-term unconditional purchase obligations that are associated with suppliers' financing and are not recognized on purchasers' balance sheets, the disclosures include the nature of the obligation, the amount of the fixed and determinable obligation in the aggregate and for each of the next five years, a description of any portion of the obligation that is variable, and the purchases in each year for which an income statement is presented. For long-term unconditional purchase obligations that are associated with suppliers' financing and are recognized on purchasers' balance sheets, payments for each of the next five years shall be disclosed. For long-term borrowings and redeemable stock, the disclosures include maturities and sinking fund requirements (if any) for each of the next five years and redemption requirements for each of the next five years, respectively.

Definition and Scope

.101 [This section specifies disclosures relating to] unconditional purchase obligations typically associated with **project financing arrangements.** [FAS47, ¶1] An unconditional purchase obligation is an obligation to transfer funds in the future for fixed or minimum amounts or quantities of goods or services at fixed or minimum prices (for example, as in **take-or-pay contracts** or **throughput contracts**). An unconditional purchase obligation that has all of the following characteristics shall be disclosed in accordance with paragraph .102 (if not recorded on the purchaser's balance sheet) or in accordance with paragraph .105(a) (if recorded on the purchaser's balance sheet):

a. Is noncancelable, or cancelable only
   (1) Upon the occurrence of some remote contingency or
   (2) With the permission of the other party or

(3) If a replacement agreement is signed between the same parties or

(4) Upon payment of a penalty in an amount such that continuation of the agreement appears reasonably assured

b. Was negotiated as part of arranging financing for the facilities that will provide the contracted goods or services or for costs related to those goods or services (for example, carrying costs for contracted goods)[1]

c. Has a remaining term in excess of one year.

Future minimum lease payments under leases that have those characteristics need not be disclosed in accordance with this section if they are disclosed in accordance with Section L10, "Leases." [FAS47, ¶6]

Unrecorded Obligations

.102 A purchaser shall disclose unconditional purchase obligations that meet the criteria of paragraph .101 and that have not been recognized on its balance sheet. The disclosures shall include:

a. The nature and term of the obligation(s)

b. The amount of the fixed and determinable portion of the obligation(s) as of the date of the latest balance sheet presented in the aggregate and, if determinable, for each of the five succeeding fiscal years (refer to paragraph .103)

c. The nature of any variable components of the obligation(s)

d. The amounts purchased under the obligation(s) (for example, the take-or-pay or throughput contract) for each period for which an income statement is presented.

Disclosures of similar or related unconditional purchase obligations may be combined. Those disclosures may be omitted only if the aggregate commitment for all such obligations not disclosed is immaterial. [Disclosures about unconditional purchase obligations that are not subject to the requirements of this section may be required by the provisions in Section F25, "Financial Instruments: Disclosure."] [FAS47, ¶7]

.103 Disclosure of the amount of imputed interest necessary to reduce the unconditional purchase obligation(s) to present value is encouraged but not required. The discount rate shall be the effective initial interest rate of the borrowings that financed the facility (or facilities) that will provide the contracted goods or services, if known by the purchaser. If not, the discount rate shall be the **purchaser's incremental borrowing rate** at the date the obligation is entered into. [FAS47, ¶8]

---

[1] A purchaser [is not required] to investigate whether a supplier used an unconditional purchase obligation to help secure financing, if the purchaser would otherwise be unaware of that fact. [FAS47, ¶17]

Recorded Obligations and Redeemable Stock

.104 Certain unconditional purchase obligations are presently recorded as liabilities on purchasers' balance sheets with the related assets also recognized. This section does not alter that accounting treatment or the treatment of future unconditional purchase obligations that are substantially the same as those obligations already recorded as liabilities with related assets, nor does it suggest that disclosure is an appropriate substitute for accounting recognition if the substance of an arrangement is the acquisition of an asset and incurrence of a liability. [FAS47, ¶9]

.105 The following information shall be disclosed for each of the five years following the date of the latest balance sheet presented:

a. The aggregate amount of payments for unconditional purchase obligations that meet the criteria of paragraph .101 and that have been recognized on the purchaser's balance sheet
b. The combined aggregate amount of maturities and sinking fund requirements for all long-term borrowings [FAS47, ¶10]
c. The amount of redemption requirements, separately by issue or combined, for all issues of capital stock that are redeemable at fixed or determinable prices on fixed or determinable dates in each of the five years following the date of the latest statement of financial position presented. [FAS129, ¶8]

Illustrations of the Application of This Section to Common Arrangements

Example 1

.106 B Company has entered into a throughput agreement with a manufacturing plant providing that B will submit specified quantities of a chemical (representing a portion of plant capacity) for processing through the plant each period while the debt used to finance the plant remains outstanding. B's processing charges are intended to be sufficient to cover a proportional share of fixed and variable operating expenses and debt service of the plant. If, however, the processing charges do not cover such operating expenses and debt service, B must advance additional funds to cover a specified percentage of operating expenses and debt service. Such additional funds are considered advance payments for future throughput. [FAS47, ¶24]

.107 B's unconditional obligation to pay a specified percentage of the plant's fixed operating expenses and debt service is fixed and determinable, while the amount of variable operating expenses that B is obligated to pay will vary depending on plant operations and economic conditions. [FAS47, ¶25]

.108 B's disclosure might be as follows:

> To secure access to facilities to process chemical X, the company has signed a processing agreement with a chemical company allowing B Company to submit 100,000 tons for processing annually for 20 years. Under the terms of the agreement, B Company may be required to advance funds against future processing charges if the chemical company is unable to meet its financial obligations. The aggregate amount of required payments at December 31, 19X1 is as follows (in thousands):

19X2	$ 10,000
19X3	10,000
19X4	9,000
19X5	8,000
19X6	8,000
Later years	100,000
Total	145,000
Less: Amount representing interest	(45,000)
Total at present value	$100,000

> In addition, the company is required to pay a proportional share of the variable operating expenses of the plant. The company's total processing charges under the agreement in each of the past 3 years have been $12 million. [FAS47, ¶26]

Example 2

.109 C Company has entered into a throughput agreement with a natural gas pipeline providing that C will provide specified quantities of natural gas (representing a portion of capacity) for transportation through the pipeline each period while the debt used to finance the pipeline remains outstanding. The tariff approved by the Federal Energy Regulatory Commission contains two portions, a demand charge and a commodity charge. The demand charge is computed to cover debt service, depreciation, and certain expected expenses. The commodity charge is intended to cover other expenses and provide a return on the pipeline enterprise's investment. C Company must pay the demand charge based on the contracted quantity regardless of actual quantities shipped, while the commodity charge is applied to actual quantities shipped. Accordingly, the demand charge multiplied by the contracted quantity represents a fixed and determinable payment. [FAS47, ¶27]

.110 C's disclosure might be as follows:

> C Company has signed an agreement providing for the availability of needed pipeline transportation capacity through 1990. Under that agreement, the enterprise must make specified minimum payments monthly. The aggregate amount of such required payments at December 31, 19X1 is as follows (in thousands):
>
> | | |
> |---|---|
> | 19X2 | $ 5,000 |
> | 19X3 | 5,000 |
> | 19X4 | 5,000 |
> | 19X5 | 4,000 |
> | 19X6 | 4,000 |
> | Later years | 26,000 |
> | Total | 49,000 |
> | Less: Amount representing interest | (9,000) |
> | Total at present value | $40,000 |
>
> In addition, the enterprise is required to pay additional amounts depending on actual quantities shipped under the agreement. The enterprise's total payments under the agreement were (in thousands) $6,000 in 19W9 and $5,500 both in 19X0 and in 19X1. [FAS47, ¶28]

Example 3

.111 A subsidiary of F Company has entered into a take-or-pay contract with an ammonia plant. F's subsidiary is obligated to purchase 50 percent of the planned capacity production of the plant each period while the debt used to finance the plant remains outstanding. The monthly payment equals the sum of 50 percent of raw material costs, operating expenses, depreciation, interest on the debt used to finance the plant, and a return on the owner's equity investment. [FAS47, ¶29]

.112 F's disclosure might be as follows:

> To assure a long-term supply, one of the enterprise's subsidiaries has contracted to purchase half the output of an ammonia plant through the year

2005 and to make minimum annual payments as follows, whether or not it is able to take delivery (in thousands):

19X2 through 19X6 ($6,000 per annum)	$ 30,000
Later years	120,000
Total	150,000
Less: Amount representing interest	(65,000)
Total at present value	$ 85,000

In addition, the subsidiary must reimburse the owner of the plant for a proportional share of raw material costs and operating expenses of the plant. The subsidiary's total purchases under the agreement were (in thousands) $7,000, $7,100, and $7,200 in 19W9, 19X0, and 19X1, respectively. [FAS47, ¶30]

Example 4

.113 D Company has outstanding two long-term borrowings and one issue of preferred stock with mandatory redemption requirements. The first borrowing is a $100 million sinking fund debenture with annual sinking fund payments of $10 million in 19X2, 19X3, and 19X4, $15 million in 19X5 and 19X6, and $20 million in 19X7 and 19X8. The second borrowing is a $50 million note due in 19X5. The $30 million issue of preferred stock requires a 5 percent annual cumulative sinking fund payment of $1.5 million until retired. [FAS47, ¶31]

.114 D's disclosures might be as follows:

Maturities and sinking fund requirements on long-term debt and sinking fund requirements on preferred stock subject to mandatory redemption are as follows (in thousands):

	Long-Term Debt	Preferred Stock
19X2	$10,000	$1,500
19X3	10,000	1,500
19X4	10,000	1,500
19X5	65,000	1,500
19X6	15,000	1,500

[FAS47, ¶32]

Glossary

.401 **Project financing arrangement.** The financing of a major capital project in which the lender looks principally to the cash flows and earnings of the project as the source of funds for repayment and to the assets of the project as collateral for the loan. The general credit of the project entity is usually not a significant factor, either because the entity is an enterprise without other assets or because the financing is without direct recourse to the owner(s) of the enterprise. [FAS47, ¶23]

.402 **Purchaser's incremental borrowing rate.** The rate that, at the inception of an unconditional purchase obligation, the purchaser would have incurred to borrow over a similar term the funds necessary to discharge the obligation. [FAS47, ¶23]

.403 **Take-or-pay contract.** An agreement between a purchaser and a seller that provides for the purchaser to pay specified amounts periodically in return for products or services. The purchaser must make specified minimum payments even if it does not take delivery of the contracted products or services. [FAS47, ¶23]

.404 **Throughput contract.** An agreement between a shipper (processor) and the owner of a transportation facility (such as an oil or natural gas pipeline or a ship) or a manufacturing facility that provides for the shipper (processor) to pay specified amounts periodically in return for the transportation (processing) of a product. The shipper (processor) is obligated to provide specified minimum quantities to be transported (processed) in each period and is required to make cash payments even if it does not provide the contracted quantities. [FAS47, ¶23]

Supplemental Guidance: Emerging Issues Task Force (EITF) Issues

.1000 [Listed below are EITF Issues that provide supplemental guidance for this section. These Issues are related by topic to the guidance in this section.

EITF Issue No. 91-6, "Revenue Recognition of Long-Term Power Sales Contracts"
EITF Issue No. 96-17, "Revenue Recognition under Long-Term Power Sales Contracts That Contain both Fixed and Variable Pricing Terms"]

(The next page is 7051.)

COMPENSATION: STOCK-BASED SECTION C36

Sources: FASB Statement 123; FASB Statement 128; FASB Statement 135; FASB Statement 144; FASB Technical Bulletin 97-1

[**Note:** A list of Issues discussed by the Emerging Issues Task Force (EITF) that provide supplemental guidance for this section is presented in paragraph .1000.]

Summary

This section establishes financial accounting and reporting standards for stock-based employee compensation plans. Those plans include all arrangements by which employees receive shares of stock or other equity instruments of the employer or the employer incurs liabilities to employees in amounts based on the price of the employer's stock. Examples are stock purchase plans, stock options, restricted stock, and stock appreciation rights.

This section also applies to transactions in which an entity issues its equity instruments to acquire goods or services from nonemployees. Those transactions must be accounted for based on the fair value of the consideration received or the fair value of the equity instruments issued, whichever is more reliably measurable.

This section defines a *fair value based method* of accounting for an employee stock option or similar equity instrument and encourages all entities to adopt that method of accounting for all of their employee stock compensation plans. However, it also allows an entity to continue to measure compensation cost for those plans using the *intrinsic value based method* of accounting prescribed by Section C47, "Compensation to Employees: Stock Purchase and Option Plans." The fair value based method is preferable to the method prescribed in Section C47 for purposes of justifying a change in accounting principle under Section A06, "Accounting Changes." Entities electing to remain with the accounting in Section C47 must make pro forma disclosures of net income and, if presented, earnings per share, as if the fair value based method of accounting defined in this section had been applied.

Under the fair value based method, compensation cost is measured at the grant date based on the value of the award and is recognized over the service period, which is usually the vesting period. Under the intrinsic value based method, compensation cost is the excess, if any, of the quoted market price of the stock at grant date or other measurement date over the amount an employee must pay to acquire the stock.

Most fixed stock option plans—the most common type of stock compensation plan—have no intrinsic value at grant date, and under the provisions of Section C47 no compensation cost is recognized for them. Compensation cost is recognized for other types of stock-based compensation plans under the provisions of Section C47, including plans with variable, usually performance-based, features.

For stock options, fair value is determined using an option-pricing model that takes into account the stock price at the grant date, the exercise price, the expected life of the option, the volatility of the underlying stock and the expected dividends on it, and the risk-free interest rate over the expected life of the option. Nonpublic entities are permitted to exclude the volatility factor in estimating the value of their stock options, which results in measurement at *minimum value.* The fair value of an option estimated at the grant date is not subsequently adjusted for changes in the price of the underlying stock or its volatility, the life of the option, dividends on the stock, or the risk-free interest rate.

The fair value of a share of nonvested stock (usually referred to as restricted stock) awarded to an employee is measured at the market price of a share of a nonrestricted stock on the grant date unless a restriction will be imposed after the employee has a vested right to it, in which case fair value is estimated taking that restriction into account.

This section requires that an employer's financial statements include certain disclosures about stock-based employee compensation arrangements regardless of the method used to account for them.

The pro forma amounts required to be disclosed by an employer that continues to apply the accounting provisions of Section C47 will reflect the difference between compensation cost, if any, included in net income and the related cost measured by the fair value based method defined in this section, including tax effects, if any, that would have been recognized in the income statement if the fair value based method had been used. The required pro forma amounts will not reflect any other adjustments to reported net income or, if presented, earnings per share.

Introduction

.101 This section establishes a **fair value** based method of accounting for **stock-based compensation plans.** Entities are encouraged to adopt that method in place of the provisions of Section C47, "Compensation to Employees: Stock Purchase and Option Plans," for all arrangements under which employees receive shares of stock or other equity instruments of the employer or the employer incurs liabilities to employees in amounts based on the price of its stock. [FAS123, ¶1]

.102 This section also establishes fair value as the measurement basis for transactions in which an entity acquires goods or services from nonemployees in exchange for equity instruments. This section uses the term *compensation* in its broadest sense to refer to the consideration paid for goods or services, regardless of whether the supplier is an employee or not. For example, employee compensation includes both cash salaries or wages and other consideration that may be thought of more as means of attracting, retaining, and motivating employees than as direct payment for services rendered. [FAS123, ¶2]

.103 Section C47 requires compensation cost[1] for stock-based employee compensation plans to be recognized based on the difference, if any, between the quoted market price of the stock and the amount an employee must pay to acquire the stock. Section C47 specifies different dates for the pertinent quoted market price of the stock used in measuring compensation cost, depending on whether the terms of an award[2] are fixed or variable, as those terms are defined in Section C47. [FAS123, ¶3]

.104 This section permits an entity in determining its net income to continue to apply the accounting provisions of Section C47 to its stock-based employee compensation arrangements. An entity that continues to apply Section C47 must comply with the disclosure requirements of this section. [FAS123, ¶5]

Scope and Alternative Accounting Methods

.105 This section applies to all transactions in which an entity acquires goods or services by issuing equity instruments[3] or by incurring liabilities to the supplier in amounts based

[1]This section refers to recognizing *compensation cost* rather than *compensation expense* because part of the amount recognized in a period may be capitalized as part of the cost to acquire an asset, such as inventory. [FAS123, ¶3, fn2]

[2]This section uses the term *award* as the collective noun for multiple instruments with the same terms granted at the same time either to a single employee or to a group of employees. An award may specify multiple vesting dates, referred to as graded vesting, and different parts of an award may have different expected lives. [FAS123, ¶3, fn3]

[3]An entity may conditionally transfer an equity instrument to another party under an arrangement that permits that party to choose at a later date or for a specified time whether to deliver the consideration for it or to forfeit the right to the conditionally transferred instrument with no further obligation. In that situation, the equity instrument is not *issued* until the issuing entity has received the consideration, such as cash, an enforceable right to receive cash, other financial instruments, goods, or services, agreed to by the parties to the transaction. For that reason, this section does not use the term *issued* for the grant of stock options or other equity instruments subject to service or performance conditions (or both) for vesting. [FAS123, ¶6, fn4]

on the price of the entity's common stock or other equity instruments. Therefore, it applies to all transactions in which an entity grants shares of its common stock, **stock options,** or other equity instruments to its employees, except for equity instruments held by an employee stock ownership plan.[4] [FAS123, ¶6]

.106 The accounting for all stock-based compensation arrangements with employees or others shall reflect the inherent rights and obligations, regardless of how those arrangements are described. For example, the rights and obligations embodied in a transfer of stock to an employee for consideration of a nonrecourse note are substantially the same as if the transaction were structured as the grant of a stock option, and the transaction shall be accounted for as such. The terms of the arrangement may affect the fair value of the stock options or other equity instruments and shall be appropriately reflected in determining that value. For example, whether an employee who is granted an implicit option structured as the exchange of shares of stock for a nonrecourse note is required to pay nonrefundable interest on the note affects the fair value of the implicit option. [FAS123, ¶7]

Accounting for Transactions with Other Than Employees

.107 Except for transactions with employees that are within the scope of Section C47, all transactions in which goods or services are the consideration received for the **issuance of equity instruments** shall be accounted for based on the fair value of the consideration received or the fair value of the equity instruments issued, whichever is more reliably measurable. The fair value of goods or services received from suppliers other than employees frequently is reliably measurable and therefore indicates the fair value of the equity instruments issued. The fair value of the equity instruments issued shall be used to measure the transaction if that value is more reliably measurable than the fair value of the consideration received.[5] A common example of the latter situation is the use of the fair value of tradable equity instruments issued in a business combination to measure the transaction because the value of the equity instruments issued is more reliably measurable than the value of the business acquired. [FAS123, ¶8] [Refer to paragraph .1001 for EITF Issues that provide interpretive guidance on this paragraph.]

.108 This section uses the term *fair value* for assets and financial instruments, including both liability and equity instruments, [FAS123, ¶9] to refer to [FAS144, ¶C15(a)] the amount

[4]AICPA Statement of Position No. 93-6, *Employers' Accounting for Employee Stock Ownership Plans,* specifies the accounting by employers for employee stock ownership plans. [FAS123, ¶6, fn5]

[5]The consideration received for issuing equity instruments, like the consideration involved in a repurchase of treasury shares, may include intangible rights. Section C23, "Capital Stock: Treasury Stock," paragraphs .501 through .504, Section G40, "Goodwill and Other Intangible Assets," paragraphs .501 and .502, and Section I17, "Income Statement: Extraordinary Items," paragraphs .509 and .510 provide pertinent guidance. [FAS123, ¶8, fn6]

at which the asset could be bought or sold in a current transaction between willing parties, that is, other than in a forced or liquidation sale. Quoted market prices in active markets are the best evidence of fair value and shall be used as the basis for the measurement, if available. If quoted market prices are not available, the estimate of fair value shall be based on the best information available in the circumstances. The estimate of fair value shall consider prices for similar assets and the results of valuation techniques to the extent available in the circumstances. Examples of valuation techniques include the present value of estimated expected future cash flows using a discount rate commensurate with the risks involved, option-pricing models, matrix pricing, option-adjusted spread models, and fundamental analysis. [FAS123, ¶9] [Refer to paragraph .1001 for an EITF Issue that provides interpretive guidance on paragraphs .108 and .109.]

.109 If the fair value of the goods or services received is not reliably measurable, paragraph .107 of this section requires that the measure of the cost of goods or services acquired in a transaction with other than an employee be based on the fair value of the equity instruments issued. However, this section does not prescribe the **measurement date,** that is, the date of the stock price on which the fair value of the equity instrument is based, for a transaction with a nonemployee. [FAS123, ¶10]

Accounting for Transactions with Employees

.110 This section provides a choice of accounting methods for transactions with employees that are within the scope of Section C47. Paragraphs .115 through .143 of this section describe a method of accounting based on the fair value, rather than the **intrinsic value,** of an employee stock option or a similar equity instrument. Entities are encouraged to adopt the fair value based method of accounting,[6] which is preferable to the Section C47 method for purposes of justifying a change in accounting principle under Section A06, "Accounting Changes."[7] However, an entity may continue to apply Section C47 in accounting for its stock-based employee compensation arrangements. An entity that does so shall disclose pro forma net income and, if presented, earnings per share, determined as if the

---

[6]Regardless of when an entity initially adopts the [recognition] provisions of this section, they shall be applied to all awards granted after the beginning of the fiscal year in which the recognition provisions are first applied. The recognition provisions shall not be applied to awards granted in fiscal years before the year of initial adoption except to the extent that prior years' awards are modified or settled in cash after the beginning of the fiscal year in which the entity adopts the recognition provisions [of this section]. Accounting for modifications and settlements of awards initially accounted for in accordance with Section C47 is discussed and illustrated in paragraphs .205 through .210 of this section. [FAS123, ¶52]

[7]Section A06, paragraph .106, provides that initial adoption of an accounting principle for a transaction that the entity has not previously had to account for is not a change in accounting principle. [FAS123, ¶11, fn7]

fair value based method had been applied in measuring compensation cost (paragraph .144).[8] [FAS123, ¶11] [Refer to paragraph .1001 for an EITF Issue that provides interpretive guidance on this paragraph.]

.111 The fair value based method described in paragraphs .115 through .143 of this section applies for (a) measuring stock-based employee compensation cost by an entity that adopts that method for accounting purposes and (b) determining the pro forma disclosures required of an entity that measures stock-based employee compensation cost in accordance with the intrinsic value based method in Section C47. Neither those paragraphs (.115 through .143) nor subsequent paragraphs (.144 through .149) of this section affect application of the *accounting* provisions of Section C47 by an entity that continues to apply it in determining reported net income. [FAS123, ¶12]

.112 For convenience, in describing the fair value based method, paragraphs .115 through .143 of this section refer only to *recognition* or *accounting* requirements. However, those provisions apply equally in determining the pro forma amounts that must be disclosed if an entity continues to apply Section C47. [FAS123, ¶13]

.113 An entity shall apply the same accounting method—either the fair value based method described in this section or the intrinsic value based method in Section C47—in accounting for all of its stock-based employee compensation arrangements. Once an entity adopts the fair value based method for those arrangements, that election shall not be reversed.[9] [FAS123, ¶14]

.114 Equity instruments granted or otherwise transferred directly to an employee by a **principal stockholder** are stock-based employee compensation to be accounted for by the entity under either Section C47 or this section, whichever method the entity is applying, unless the transfer clearly is for a purpose other than compensation. [See paragraphs .501 through .506 of Section C47.] The substance of a transaction in which a principal stockholder directly transfers equity instruments to an employee as compensation is that the prin-

[8]An entity that has disclosed the pro forma effects of adopting [the recognition provisions of] this section for several years may choose to adopt the cost recognition method in this section. In that situation, subsequent modifications of awards for which pro forma disclosures were made should be accounted for as if cost had been recognized under the fair value based method as shown in the illustrations for modifications of awards granted after adoption of [the recognition provisions of] this section (paragraphs .198 through .204). Doing so will make the financial statements for periods after adoption more consistent for comparative purposes with the pro forma disclosures made for any prior years presented. [FAS123, ¶195]

[9]Section A10, "Accounting Policies," requires an entity to include a description of all significant accounting policies as an integral part of the financial statements. The method used to account for stock-based employee compensation arrangements is an accounting policy to be included in that description. [FAS123, ¶14, fn8]

cipal stockholder makes a capital contribution to the entity and the entity awards equity instruments to its employee. An example of a situation in which a direct transfer of equity instruments to an employee from a principal stockholder is not compensation cost is a transfer to settle an obligation of the principal stockholder unrelated to employment by the reporting entity. [FAS123, ¶15]

Valuation of Equity Instruments Issued for Employee Services

Measurement Basis

.115 Frequently, part or all of the consideration received for equity instruments issued to employees is past or future employee services. Equity instruments issued to employees and the cost of the services received as consideration shall be measured and recognized based on the fair value of the equity instruments issued. The portion of the fair value of an equity instrument attributed to employee services is net of the amount, if any, that employees pay for the instrument when it is granted. Paragraphs .116 through .124 provide guidance on how to measure the fair value of stock-based employee compensation. Paragraphs .125 through .132 provide guidance on how to attribute compensation cost to the periods in which employees render the related services. Paragraphs .150 through .243 provide additional guidance on both measurement and attribution of employee compensation cost. [FAS123, ¶16]

Measurement Objective and Date

.116 The objective of the measurement process is to estimate the fair value, based on the stock price at the **grant date,** of stock options or other equity instruments to which employees become entitled when they have rendered the requisite service and satisfied any other conditions necessary to earn the right to benefit from the instruments (for example, to exercise stock options or to sell shares of stock). Restrictions that continue in effect after employees have earned the rights to benefit from their instruments, such as the inability to transfer[10] **vested** employee stock options to third parties, affect the value of the instruments actually issued and therefore are reflected in estimating their fair value. However, restrictions that stem directly from the forfeitability of instruments to which employees have not yet earned the right, such as the inability either to exercise a nonvested option or to sell **nonvested stock,** do not affect the value of the instruments issued at the vesting date, and their effect therefore is not included in that value. Instead, no value is attributed

[10]Some employees may be permitted to place their nontransferable options in a trust for the benefit of family members or otherwise to transfer vested options to family members. However, the options remain nontransferable in the hands of the trust or family member. The transfer thus does not affect the value of the option—both the option holder and the option writer (the employer) know it may be economically advantageous for the holder to exercise the options before maturity because exercise remains the only available means to terminate exposure to future price changes. [FAS123, ¶169, fn17]

to instruments that employees forfeit because they fail to satisfy specified service- or performance-related conditions. [FAS123, ¶17]

Measurement Methods

Awards That Call for Settlement by Issuing Equity Instruments

.117 The fair value of a share of nonvested stock awarded to an employee shall be measured at the market price (or estimated market price, if the stock is not publicly traded) of a share of the same stock as if it were vested and issued on the grant date. Nonvested stock granted to employees usually is referred to as **restricted stock,** but this section reserves that term for shares whose sale is contractually or governmentally restricted after the shares are vested and fully outstanding. The fair value of a share of restricted stock awarded to an employee, that is, a share that will be restricted after the employee has a vested right to it, shall be measured at its fair value, which is the same amount as a share of similarly restricted stock issued to nonemployees. [FAS123, ¶18]

.118 The fair value of a stock option (or its equivalent) granted by a **public entity** shall be estimated using an option-pricing model (for example, the Black-Scholes or a binomial model) that takes into account as of the grant date the exercise price and expected life[11] of the option, the current price of the underlying stock and its expected **volatility,** expected dividends on the stock (except as provided in paragraphs .131 and .132), and the risk-free interest rate for the expected term of the option. For options that a U.S. entity grants on its own stock, the risk-free interest rate used shall be the rate currently available on zero-coupon U.S. government issues with a remaining term equal to the ex-

[11]To reflect the effect of employees' inability to sell their vested options, this section requires that the value of an employee stock option be based on its expected life rather than its maximum term. [FAS123, ¶169] For example, a 10-year option with an exercise price of $50 on a stock with a market price of $50 might be valued at $25.89, assuming that the stock's volatility is 30 percent, it pays a dividend of 1 percent, and the risk-free interest rate is 7.5 percent. After 5 years, when the stock price has risen to $75, an option holder might wish to realize the gain on the option, thereby terminating exposure to future price changes. The fair value of a 5-year option with an intrinsic value of $25 ($75 – $50) on the same stock is $39.86, assuming that the stock's volatility is now 35 percent, the dividend yield remains at 1 percent, and the current risk-free rate for 5-year maturities is 7 percent. If the option is transferable, the holder could sell it for $39.86 rather than exercise it and receive only the intrinsic value of $25. An employee who does not wish to remain exposed to future price changes in the underlying stock after 5 years can only exercise the option and sell the stock obtained upon exercise—realizing only the gain of $25 in intrinsic value. The employee is unable to realize the option's remaining time value of $14.86 ($39.86 – $25) because of its nontransferability. In other words, an employee who exercises an option with a contractual term of 10 years after only 5 years receives the benefit of only a 5-year option. Because the economic effect of holding a nontransferable rather than a transferable option is to make early exercise significantly more likely, estimating the fair value of an employee stock option based on its expected life, later adjusted to actual life, rather than its maximum term is a logical and practical means of reducing the option's value to reflect its nontransferability. [FAS123, ¶170]

pected life of the options. Guidance on selecting other assumptions is provided in paragraphs .152 through .166. The fair value of an option estimated at the grant date shall not be subsequently adjusted for changes in the price of the underlying stock or its volatility, the life of the option, dividends on the stock, or the risk-free interest rate. [FAS123, ¶19]

.119 A **nonpublic entity**[12] shall estimate the value of its options based on the factors described in the preceding paragraph, except that a nonpublic entity need not consider the expected volatility of its stock over the expected life of the option.[13] The result of excluding volatility in estimating an option's value is an amount commonly termed **minimum value.** [FAS123, ¶20]

.120 It should be possible to reasonably estimate the fair value of most stock options and other equity instruments at the date they are granted. Paragraphs .150 through .243 illustrate techniques for estimating the fair values of several options with complicated features. However, in unusual circumstances, the terms of a stock option or other equity instrument may make it virtually impossible to reasonably estimate the instrument's fair value at the date it is granted. For example, it may be extremely difficult, if not impossible, to reasonably estimate the fair value of a stock option whose exercise price decreases (or increases) by a specified amount with specified changes in the price of the underlying stock. Similarly, it may not be possible to reasonably estimate the value of a convertible instrument if the conversion ratio depends on the outcome of future events. [FAS123, ¶21]

.121 If it is not possible to reasonably estimate the fair value of an option or other equity instrument at the grant date, the final measure of compensation cost shall be the fair value based on the stock price and other pertinent factors at the first date at which it is possible to reasonably estimate that value. Generally, that is likely to be the date at which the number of shares to which an employee is entitled and the exercise price are determinable. Estimates of compensation cost for periods during which it is not possible to determine fair value shall be based on the current intrinsic value of the award, determined in accordance with the terms that would apply if the option or similar instrument had been currently exercised. [FAS123, ¶22]

Employee Stock Purchase Plans

.122 If an employee stock purchase plan satisfies all of the following criteria, the plan is not compensatory. Therefore, the discount from market price merely reduces the proceeds from issuing the related shares of stock.

---

[12]Public or nonpublic status [should be determined] based on an entity's characteristics at the date an award is granted. [FAS123, ¶181]

[13]A nonpublic entity may incorporate [expected] volatility if it desires to do so. [FAS123, ¶175]

a. The plan incorporates no option features other than the following, which may be incorporated:
   (1) Employees are permitted a short period of time—not exceeding 31 days—after the purchase price has been fixed to enroll in the plan.
   (2) The purchase price is based solely on the stock's market price at date of purchase, and employees are permitted to cancel participation before the purchase date and obtain a refund of amounts previously paid (such as those paid by payroll withholdings).
b. The discount from the market price does not exceed the greater of (1) a per-share discount that would be reasonable in a recurring offer of stock to stockholders or others or (2) the per-share amount of stock issuance costs avoided by not having to raise a significant amount of capital by a public offering. A discount of 5 percent or less from the market price shall be considered to comply with this criterion without further justification.
c. Substantially all full-time employees that meet limited employment qualifications may participate on an equitable basis.

[FAS123, ¶23]

.123 A plan provision that establishes the purchase price as an amount based on the lesser of the stock's market price at date of grant or its market price at date of purchase is, for example, an option feature that causes the plan to be compensatory. Similarly, a plan in which the purchase price is based on the stock's market price at date of grant and that permits a participating employee to cancel participation before the purchase date and obtain a refund of amounts previously paid is a compensatory plan. [FAS123, ¶24]

Awards That Call for Settlement in Cash

.124 Some awards of stock-based compensation result in the entity's incurring a liability because employees can compel the entity to settle the award by transferring its cash or other assets to employees rather than by issuing equity instruments. For example, an entity may incur a liability to pay an employee either on demand or at a specified date an amount to be determined by the increase in the entity's stock price from a specified level. The amount of the liability for such an award shall be measured each period based on the current stock price. The effects of changes in the stock price during the **service period** are recognized as compensation cost over the service period in accordance with the method illustrated in paragraphs .119 through .122 of Section C47. Changes in the amount of the liability due to stock price changes after the service period are compensation cost of the period in which the changes occur. [FAS123, ¶25]

Recognition of Compensation Cost

.125 The total amount of compensation cost recognized for an award of stock-based employee compensation shall be based on the number of instruments that eventually vest. No compensation cost is recognized for awards that employees forfeit either because they fail to satisfy a service requirement for vesting, such as for a **fixed award,** or because the entity does not achieve a **performance condition,** unless the condition is a target stock price or specified amount of intrinsic value on which vesting or exercisability is conditioned. For awards with the latter condition, compensation cost shall be recognized for awards to employees who remain in service for the requisite period regardless of whether the target stock price or amount of intrinsic value is reached.[14] Previously recognized compensation cost shall not be reversed if a vested employee stock option expires unexercised. [FAS123, ¶26]

.126 For purposes of this section, a stock-based employee compensation award becomes vested when an employee's right to receive or retain shares of stock or cash under the award is not contingent on the performance of additional services. Typically, an employee stock option that is vested also is immediately exercisable. However, if performance conditions affect either the exercise price or the exercisability date, the service period used for attribution purposes shall be consistent with the assumptions used in estimating the fair value of the award. Paragraphs .188 and .189 illustrate how to account for an option whose exercise price depends on a performance condition. [FAS123, ¶27]

.127 An entity may choose at the grant date to base accruals of compensation cost on the best available estimate of the number of options or other equity instruments that are expected to vest and to revise that estimate, if necessary, if subsequent information indicates that actual forfeitures are likely to differ from initial estimates. Alternatively, an entity may begin accruing compensation cost as if all instruments granted that are subject only to a service requirement are expected to vest. The effect of actual forfeitures would then be recognized as they occur. Initial accruals of compensation cost for an award with a performance condition that will determine the number of options or shares to which all employees receiving the award will be entitled shall be based on the best estimate of the outcome of the performance condition, although forfeitures by individual employees may either be estimated at the grant date or recognized only as they occur.[15] [FAS123, ¶28]

---

[14] The existence of a target stock price that must be achieved to make an option exercisable generally affects the value of the option. Option-pricing models have been adapted to value many of those *path-dependent* options. [FAS123, ¶26, fn10]

[15] For convenience, the remainder of this section refers to options or shares *expected to vest* because referring specifically to both acceptable methods of accounting for forfeitures by individual employees each time the point is mentioned would be too unwieldy. [FAS123, ¶28, fn11]

.128 Compensation cost estimated at the grant date for the number of instruments that are expected to vest based on performance-related conditions, as well as those in which vesting is contingent only on future service for which the entity chooses to estimate forfeitures[16] at the grant date pursuant to paragraph .127, shall be adjusted for subsequent changes in the expected or actual outcome of service- and performance-related conditions until the vesting date. The effect of a change in the estimated number of shares or options expected to vest is a change in an estimate, and the cumulative effect of the change on current and prior periods shall be recognized in the period of the change. [FAS123, ¶29]

.129 The compensation cost for an award of equity instruments to employees shall be recognized over the period(s) in which the related employee services are rendered by a charge to compensation cost and a corresponding credit to equity (paid-in capital) if the award is for future service. If the service period is not defined as an earlier or shorter period, the service period shall be presumed to be the period from the grant date to the date that the award is vested and its exercisability does not depend on continued employee service (paragraph .126). If an award is for past services, the related compensation cost shall be recognized in the period in which it is granted. [FAS123, ¶30]

.130 Compensation cost for an award with a graded vesting schedule shall be recognized in accordance with the method described in paragraphs .119 through .122 of Section C47 if the fair value of the award is determined based on different expected lives for the options that vest each year, as it would be if the award is viewed as several separate awards, each with a different vesting date.[17] If the expected life or lives of the award is determined in another manner, the related compensation cost may be recognized on a straight-line basis. However, the amount of compensation cost recognized at any date must at least equal the value of the vested portion of the award at that date. Paragraphs .179 through .184 of this section illustrate application of both attribution methods to an award accounted for by the fair value based method. [FAS123, ¶31]

.131 Dividends or dividend equivalents paid to employees on the portion of an award of stock or other equity instruments that vests shall be charged to retained earnings. Nonforfeitable dividends or dividend equivalents paid on shares of stock that do not vest shall be

[16]The term *forfeiture* refers only to an employee's failure to earn a vested right to a stock-based compensation award because the specified vesting requirements are not satisfied. In other words, a vested award is no longer subject to forfeiture as this section uses that term, although the term of a vested award may be truncated by termination of service. [FAS123, ¶166]

[17]That method attributes a higher percentage of the reported cost to the earlier years than to the later years of the service period because the early years of service are part of the vesting period for later awards in the series. For example, cost attributed to the first year of service includes not only the amount that vests in that year but also one-half of the award that vests in the second year, one-third of the award that vests in the third year, and so on. [FAS123, ¶201]

recognized as additional compensation cost. The choice of whether to estimate forfeitures at the grant date or to recognize the effect of forfeitures as they occur described in paragraph .127 also applies to recognition of nonforfeitable dividends paid on shares that do not vest. [FAS123, ¶32]

.132 If employees receive only the dividends declared on the class of stock granted to them after the stock becomes vested, the value of the award at the grant date shall be reduced by the present value of dividends expected to be paid on the stock during the vesting period, discounted at the appropriate risk-free interest rate. The fair value of an award of stock options on which dividend equivalents are paid to employees or are applied to reduce the exercise price pursuant to antidilution provisions shall be estimated based on a dividend payment of zero. [FAS123, ¶33]

Additional Awards and Modifications of Outstanding Awards

.133 The fair value of each award of equity instruments, including an award of **reload options,** shall be measured separately based on its terms and the current stock price and related factors at the date it is granted. [FAS123, ¶34]

.134 A modification of the terms of an award that makes it more valuable shall be treated as an exchange of the original award for a new award. In substance, the entity repurchases the original instrument by issuing a new instrument of greater value, incurring additional compensation cost for that incremental value. The incremental value shall be measured by the difference between (a) the fair value of the modified option determined in accordance with the provisions of this section and (b) the value of the old option immediately before its terms are modified, determined based on the shorter of (1) its remaining expected life or (2) the expected life of the modified option. Paragraphs .198 through .210 provide further guidance on and illustrate the accounting for modifications of both vested and nonvested options. [FAS123, ¶35]

.135 Exchanges of options or changes to their terms in conjunction with business combinations, spinoffs, or other equity restructurings are modifications for purposes of this section. However, a change to the terms of an award in accordance with antidilution provisions that are designed, for example, to equalize an option's value before and after a stock split or a stock dividend is not a modification of an award for purposes of this section. [FAS123, ¶36]

Settlements of Awards

.136 An entity occasionally may repurchase equity instruments issued to employees after the employees have vested rights to them. The amount of cash or other assets paid (or liabilities incurred) to repurchase an equity instrument shall be charged to equity, provided that the amount paid does not exceed the value of the instruments repurchased. For example, an entity that repurchases for $10 a share of stock on the date it becomes vested does not incur additional compensation cost if the market price of the stock is $10 at that date. However, if the market price of the stock is only $8 at that date, the entity incurs an additional $2 ($10 – $8) of cost. An entity that settles a nonvested award for cash has, in effect, vested the award, and the amount of compensation cost measured at the grant date but not yet recognized shall be recognized at the date of repurchase. [FAS123, ¶37]

.137 For employee stock options, the incremental amount, if any, to be recognized as additional compensation cost upon cash settlement shall be determined based on a comparison of the amount paid with the value of the option repurchased, determined based on the remainder of its original expected life at that date. As indicated in paragraph .136, if stock options are repurchased before they become vested, the amount of unrecognized compensation cost shall be recognized at the date of the repurchase. [FAS123, ¶38]

.138 The accounting shall reflect the terms of a stock-based compensation plan as those terms are mutually understood by the employer and the employees who receive awards under the plan. Generally, the written plan provides the best evidence of its terms. However, an entity's past practice may indicate that the **substantive terms** of a plan differ from its written terms. For example, an entity that grants a **tandem award** consisting of either a stock option or a cash stock appreciation right (SAR) is obligated to pay cash on demand if the choice is the employee's, and the entity thus incurs a liability to the employee. In contrast, if the choice is the entity's, it can avoid transferring its assets by choosing to settle in stock, and the award qualifies as an equity instrument. However, if an entity that nominally has the choice of settling awards by issuing stock generally settles in cash, or if the entity generally settles in cash whenever an employee asks for cash settlement, the entity probably is settling a substantive liability rather than repurchasing an equity instrument. The substantive terms shall be the basis for the accounting. [FAS123, ¶39]

.139 To restrict control to a limited group, for example, the members of a particular family, a nonpublic entity may obligate itself to repurchase its equity instruments for their fair value at the date of repurchase. In practice, such an obligation is not deemed to convert the stock to a liability. This section is not intended to change that view of the effect of a fair value repurchase agreement for a nonpublic entity. Thus, a nonpublic entity may grant or otherwise issue to employees equity instruments subject to such a repurchase agreement. The repurchase agreement does not convert those equity instruments to liabilities, provided that the repurchase price is the fair value of the stock at the date of repurchase. [FAS123, ¶40]

Accounting for Tax Consequences of Equity Instruments Awarded to Employees

.140 Income tax regulations specify allowable tax deductions for stock-based employee compensation arrangements in determining an entity's income tax liability. Compensation cost recognized under this section is measured based on the fair value of an award to an employee. Under existing U.S. tax law, allowable tax deductions are generally measured at a specified date as the excess of the market price of the related stock over the amount the employee is required to pay for the stock (that is, at intrinsic value). The **time value** component of the fair value of an option is not tax deductible. Therefore, tax deductions generally will arise in different amounts and in different periods from compensation cost recognized in financial statements. [FAS123, ¶41]

.141 The cumulative amount of compensation cost recognized for a stock-based award that ordinarily results in a future tax deduction under existing tax law shall be considered to be a deductible temporary difference in applying Section I27, "Income Taxes." The deferred tax benefit (or expense) that results from increases (or decreases) in that temporary difference, for example, as additional service is rendered and the related cost is recognized, shall be recognized in the income statement. Recognition of compensation cost for an award that ordinarily does not result in tax deductions under existing tax law shall not be considered to result in a deductible temporary difference in applying Section I27. A future event, such as an employee's disqualifying disposition of stock under existing U.S. tax law, can give rise to a tax deduction for an award that ordinarily does not result in a tax deduction. The tax effects of such an event shall be recognized only when it occurs. [FAS123, ¶42]

.142 Section I27 requires a deferred tax asset to be evaluated for future realization and to be reduced by a valuation allowance if, based on the weight of the available evidence, it is more likely than not that some portion or all of the deferred tax asset will not be realized. Differences between (a) the deductible temporary difference computed pursuant to paragraph .141 and (b) the tax deduction inherent in the current fair value of the entity's stock shall not be considered in measuring either the gross deferred tax asset or the need for a valuation allowance for a deferred tax asset recognized under this section. [FAS123, ¶43]

.143 If a deduction reported on a tax return for a stock-based award exceeds the cumulative compensation cost for that award recognized for financial reporting, the tax benefit for that excess deduction shall be recognized as additional paid-in capital. If the deduction reported on a tax return is less than the cumulative compensation cost recognized for financial reporting, the write-off of a related deferred tax asset in excess of the benefits of the tax deduction, net of the related valuation allowance, if any, shall be recognized in the income statement except to the extent that there is remaining additional paid-in capital from excess tax deductions from previous stock-based employee compensation awards accounted for in accordance with the fair value based method in this section. In that situation, the amount of the write-off shall be charged against that additional paid-in capital. [FAS123, ¶44]

Disclosures

.144 Regardless of the method used to account for stock-based employee compensation arrangements, the financial statements of an entity shall include the disclosures specified in paragraphs .145 through .147.[18] In addition, an entity that continues to apply Section C47 shall disclose for each year for which an income statement is provided the pro forma net income and, if earnings per share is presented, pro forma earnings per share, as if the fair value based accounting method in this section had been used to account for stock-based compensation cost. Those pro forma amounts shall reflect the difference between compensation cost, if any, included in net income in accordance with Section C47 and the related cost measured by the fair value based method, as well as additional tax effects, if any, that would have been recognized in the income statement if the fair value based method had been used. The required pro forma amounts shall reflect no other adjustments to reported net income or earnings per share. [FAS123, ¶45] [Furthermore, all entities, public and nonpublic, subject to the provisions of this section must comply with the requirements of Section C24, "Capital Structure: Disclosures."]

.145 An entity with one or more stock-based compensation plans shall provide a description of the plan(s), including the general terms of awards under the plan(s), such as vesting requirements, the maximum term of options granted, and the number of shares authorized for grants of options or other equity instruments. An entity that uses equity instruments to acquire goods or services other than employee services shall provide disclosures similar to those required by this paragraph and paragraphs .146 and .147 to the extent that those disclosures are important in understanding the effects of those transactions on the financial statements. [FAS123, ¶46]

.146 The following information shall be disclosed for each year[19] for which an income statement is provided:

a. The number and weighted-average exercise prices of options for each of the following groups of options: (1) those outstanding at the beginning of the year, (2) those outstanding at the end of the year, (3) those exercisable at the end of the year, and those (4) granted, (5) exercised, (6) forfeited, or (7) expired during the year.

---

[18]General guidance provided at the end of each FASB pronouncement states "The provisions of this pronouncement need not be applied to immaterial items." That] general guidance applies to both accounting and disclosure requirements. An entity can best determine the materiality of the disclosures in its individual circumstances. Different percentage criteria likely would be needed for different disclosures, for example, the materiality of some items might be best evaluated in terms of the effect on reported net income, while the materiality of other items might be better evaluated in the context of number of shares outstanding. [FAS123, ¶244]

[19]The disclosure requirements need not be applied in an interim report unless a complete set of financial statements is presented for that period. [FAS123, ¶53]

b. The weighted-average grant-date fair value of options granted during the year. If the exercise prices of some options differ from the market price of the stock on the grant date, weighted-average exercise prices and weighted-average fair values of options shall be disclosed separately for options whose exercise price (1) equals, (2) exceeds, or (3) is less than the market price of the stock on the grant date.
c. The number and weighted-average grant-date fair value of equity instruments other than options, for example, shares of nonvested stock, granted during the year.
d. A description of the method and significant assumptions used during the year to estimate the fair values of options, including the following weighted-average information: (1) risk-free interest rate, (2) expected life, (3) expected volatility, and (4) expected dividends.
e. Total compensation cost recognized in income for stock-based employee compensation awards.
f. The terms of significant modifications of outstanding awards.

An entity that grants options under multiple stock-based employee compensation plans shall provide the foregoing information separately for different types of awards to the extent that the differences in the characteristics of the awards make separate disclosure important to an understanding of the entity's use of stock-based compensation. For example, separate disclosure of weighted-average exercise prices at the end of the year for options with a fixed exercise price and those with an indexed exercise price is likely to be important, as would segregating the number of options not yet exercisable into those that will become exercisable based solely on employees' rendering additional service and those for which an additional condition must be met for the options to become exercisable. [FAS123, ¶47]

.147 For options outstanding at the date of the latest statement of financial position presented, the range of exercise prices (as well as the weighted-average exercise price) and the weighted-average remaining contractual life shall be disclosed. If the range of exercise prices is wide (for example, the highest exercise price exceeds approximately 150 percent of the lowest exercise price), the exercise prices shall be segregated into ranges that are meaningful for assessing the number and timing of additional shares that may be issued and the cash that may be received as a result of option exercises.[20] The following information shall be disclosed for each range:

a. The number, weighted-average exercise price, and weighted-average remaining contractual life of options outstanding
b. The number and weighted-average exercise price of options currently exercisable.

[FAS123, ¶48]

[[20]This section does not] specify strict criteria for when further segregation should be required. The 150 percent example is meant to be a guideline. An entity should exercise its judgement in providing the most meaningful disclosures. [FAS123, ¶249]

Earnings per Share Implications

.148 Section E11, "Earnings per Share," requires that employee stock options, nonvested stock, and similar equity instruments granted to employees be treated as potential common shares in computing diluted earnings per share. Diluted earnings per share shall be based on the actual number of options or shares granted and not yet forfeited, unless doing so would be antidilutive. If vesting is contingent upon factors other than continued service, such as the level of future earnings, the shares or options shall be treated as contingently issuable shares in accordance with paragraphs .125 through .130 of Section E11. If stock options or other equity instruments are granted [FAS128, ¶167(a)] or forfeited [FAS135, ¶4(u)] during a period, the shares issuable shall be weighted to reflect the portion of the period during which the equity instruments were outstanding. [FAS128, ¶167(a)]

.149 In applying the treasury stock method of [FAS123, ¶50] Section E11, [FAS128, ¶167(b)] the assumed proceeds shall be the sum of (a) the amount, if any, the employee must pay, (b) the amount of compensation cost attributed to future services and not yet recognized, and (c) the amount of tax benefits, if any, that would be credited to additional paid-in capital. [FAS123, ¶50] Paragraphs .168 through .170 of Section E11 [FAS128, ¶167(b)] provide detailed examples of the treatment of stock compensation plans accounted for under Section C47 in earnings per share computations. Although the related cost and tax amounts will differ if the fair value based accounting method in this section is applied, the principles in [FAS123, ¶50] paragraphs .115 through .117 of Section E11 [FAS128, ¶167(b)] remain applicable. [FAS123, ¶50]

Illustrative Guidance for Applying This Section

Introduction

.150 Paragraphs .150 through .243, which are an integral part of the requirements of this section, discuss further the fair value based method of accounting for stock-based employee compensation and illustrate its application to specific awards. The examples and related assumptions in paragraphs .152 through .243 are illustrative only; they may not represent actual situations. [FAS123, ¶271]

.151 The guidance in paragraphs .152 through .166 on selecting assumptions for use in an option-pricing model applies equally to (a) an entity that applies the fair value based method in accounting for its stock-based employee compensation cost and (b) an entity that accounts for its stock-based employee compensation in accordance with Section C47 and discloses the pro forma information required by paragraph .144. Except where noted, the illustrations in paragraphs .167 through .235 assume that the reporting entity had adopted the fair value based method of accounting for compensation cost before the transactions illustrated. However, had the entity continued to account for its stock-based employee compensation cost in accordance with Section C47, it would follow the same procedures in preparing the pro forma disclosures required by this section. [FAS123, ¶272]

CONTENTS

Selecting Assumptions for Use in an Option-Pricing Model

.152 This section requires a public entity to estimate the fair value of an employee stock option using a pricing model that takes into account the exercise price and expected life of the option, the current price of the underlying stock, its expected volatility, the expected dividends on the stock, and the current risk-free interest rate for the expected life of the option. As indicated in paragraph .118, a U.S. entity issuing an option on its own stock must use as the risk-free interest rate the implied yield currently available on zero-coupon U.S. government issues with a remaining term equal to the expected life of the option that is being valued. Guidance on selecting the other assumptions listed in paragraph .118 is provided in the following paragraphs. [FAS123, ¶273]

.153 In estimating the expected volatility of and dividends on the underlying stock, the objective is to approximate the expectations that likely would be reflected in a current market or negotiated exchange price for the option. Similarly, the objective in estimating the expected lives of employee stock options is to approximate the expectations that an outside party with access to detailed information about employees' exercise behavior likely would develop based on information available at the grant date. [FAS123, ¶274]

.154 In most circumstances there is likely to be a range of reasonable expectations about future volatility, dividends, and option life. If one amount within the range is a better estimate than any other amount, that amount should be used. If no amount within the range is a better estimate than any other amount, it is appropriate to use an estimate at the *low* end of the range for expected volatility and expected option life, and an estimate at the *high* end of the range for expected dividends. (Computed option value varies directly with expected volatility and life, but it varies inversely with expected dividends.) That approach is similar to the one used in paragraphs .106 and .107 and .124 through .127 of Section C59, "Contingencies," which require accrual of the minimum amount in a range of reasonable estimates of the amount of a loss if no amount within the range is a better estimate than any other amount. [FAS123, ¶275]

.155 Expectations about the future generally are based on past experience, modified to reflect ways in which currently available information indicates that the future is reasonably expected to differ from the past. In some circumstances, identifiable factors may indicate that unadjusted historical experience is a relatively poor predictor of future experience. For example, if an entity with two distinctly different lines of business disposes of the one that was significantly less volatile and generated more cash than the other, historical volatility, dividends, and perhaps lives of stock options from the predisposition period are not likely to be the best information on which to base reasonable expectations for the future. [FAS123, ¶276]

.156 In other circumstances, historical information may not be available. For example, an entity whose common stock has only recently become publicly traded will have little, if any, historical data on the volatility of its own stock. In that situation, expected volatility may be based on the average volatilities of similar entities for an appropriate period following their going public. Similarly, an entity whose common stock has been publicly traded for only a few years and has generally become less volatile as more trading experience has been gained might appropriately place more weight on the more recent experience. It also might consider the stock price volatilities of similar entities. [FAS123, ¶277]

.157 Not all of the general guidance on selecting assumptions provided in paragraphs .152 through .156 is repeated in the following discussion of factors to be considered in selecting specific assumptions. However, the general guidance is intended to apply to each individual assumption. [It is] *not* intended [that] an entity base option values on historical average option lives, stock volatility, or dividends (whether stated as a yield or a dollar amount) without considering the extent to which historical experience reasonably predicts future experience. [FAS123, ¶278]

Expected Lives of Employee Stock Options

.158 The value of an award of employee stock options may be based either on an appropriately weighted average expected life for the entire award or on appropriately weighted lives for subgroups of the award based on more detailed data about employees' exercise behavior. Paragraphs .160 and .161 each discuss a different way to incorporate a range of expected lives in estimating option value rather than effectively assuming that all employees hold their options for the weighted-average life. [FAS123, ¶279]

.159 Factors to consider in estimating the expected life of an award of stock options include:

a. The vesting period of the grant. The expected life must at least include the vesting period. In addition, if all other factors are equal, the length of time employees hold options after they first become exercisable may vary inversely with the length of the vesting period. For example, employees may be more likely to exercise options shortly after the options vest if the vesting period is four years than if the vesting period is only two years.
b. The average length of time similar grants have remained outstanding in the past.
c. Expected volatility of the underlying stock. On average, employees may tend to exercise options on highly volatile stocks earlier than on stocks with low volatility.

[FAS123, ¶280]

.160 Segregating options into groups for employees with relatively homogeneous exercise behavior may also be important. Option value is not a linear function of option term; value increases at a decreasing rate as the term lengthens. For example, a two-year option is worth less than twice as much as a one-year option if all other assumptions are equal. That means that calculating estimated option value based on a single weighted-average life that includes widely differing individual lives will overstate the value of the entire award. Segregating options granted into several groups, each of which has a relatively narrow range of lives included in its weighted-average life, reduces that overstatement. For example, the experience of an entity that grants options broadly to all levels of employees might indicate that top-level executives tend to hold their options longer than middle-management employees hold theirs and that hourly employees tend to exercise their options earlier than any other group. In addition, employees who are encouraged or required to hold a minimum amount of their employer's equity instruments, including options, might on average exercise options later than employees not subject to that provision. In those situations, segregating options by groups of recipients with relatively homogeneous exercise behavior and determining the related option values based on appropriate weighted-average expected lives for each group will result in an improved estimate of the fair value of the total award. [FAS123, ¶281]

.161 Rather than estimating expected life directly, an entity may wish to estimate it indirectly, using an option-pricing model that has been modified to compute an option value using an assumed stock price at which the options would be expected to be exercised. For example, an entity's experience might show a large increase in option exercises when the stock price first reaches 200 percent of the exercise price. If so, that entity might compute an option value using a pricing model that implicitly determines a weighted-average life based on exercise at an assumed price of 200 percent of the exercise price. The model would assume exercise of the option at each point on the inherent probability distribution of possible stock prices at which the expected price at exercise is first reached. On branches of the binomial tree on which the stock price does not reach 200 percent of the exercise price but is in-the-money at the end of the contractual term, the model would assume exercise at that date. The expected life is then computed as the weighted-average life of the resulting binomial tree. That method recognizes that employees' exercise behavior is related to the path of the stock price. [FAS123, ¶282]

.162 Segregating options into groups based on the exercise behavior of the recipients also may be important if the technique in paragraph .161 is used. For example, an employer's experience might indicate that hourly employees tend to exercise for a smaller percentage gain than do more highly compensated employees. [FAS123, ¶283]

Expected Volatility

.163 Volatility is a measure of the amount by which a price has fluctuated or is expected to fluctuate during a period. The measure of volatility used in the Black-Scholes option-pricing model is the annualized standard deviation of the continuously compounded rates of return on the stock over a period of time. Generally, at least 20 to 30 price observations made at regular intervals are needed to compute a statistically valid standard deviation. For long-term options, historical volatility generally should be calculated based on more—probably many more—than 30 observations. The concept of volatility is defined more fully in paragraph .424. One method of calculating historical average annualized volatility based on weekly price observations is illustrated in paragraphs .244 through .260. As discussed further in the following paragraph, an entity may need to adjust historical average annualized volatility to estimate a reasonable expected volatility over the expected life of an option. [FAS123, ¶284]

.164 Factors to consider in estimating expected volatility include:

a. The historical volatility of the stock over the most recent period that is generally commensurate with the expected option life.
b. The length of time an entity's stock has been publicly traded. If that period is shorter than the expected life of the option, historical volatility should be computed for the longest period for which trading activity is available. A newly public entity also should consider the historical volatility of similar entities following a comparable period in their lives. For example, an entity that has been publicly traded for only one year that grants options with an average expected life of five years might consider the pattern and level of historical volatility of more mature entities in the same industry for the first six years the stocks of those entities were publicly traded.
c. The mean-reversion tendency of volatilities. For example, an entity with insufficient trading history on which to base an estimate of historical volatility might take into account mean-reversion tendencies (sometimes called *shrinkage*). A newly public entity with a trading history of only 1 year might have a historical volatility of 60 percent, while the mean volatility of an appropriate peer group is only 35 percent. Until a longer series of historical data is available, the entity might use an expected volatility of approximately 47.5 percent [(.60 + .35) ÷ 2]. A more mature entity also should consider mean-reversion tendencies and other reasons for which expected future volatility may differ from past volatility. For example, if an entity's stock was extraordinarily volatile for some identifiable period of time because of a failed takeover bid or a major restructuring, that period might be disregarded in computing historical average annual volatility.
d. Appropriate and regular intervals for price observations. In general, weekly price observations should be sufficient for computing long-term historical volatility. The price

observations should be consistent from period to period. For example, an entity might use the closing price for each week or the highest price for the week, but it should not use the closing price for some weeks and the highest price for other weeks.

[FAS123, ¶285]

Expected Dividends

.165 Standard option-pricing models generally call for expected dividend yield. However, the models may be modified to use an expected dividend amount rather than a yield. An entity may use either its expected yield or its expected payments. If the latter, the entity's historical pattern of increases in dividends should be considered. For example, if an entity's policy generally has been to increase dividends by approximately 3 percent per year, its estimated option value should not assume a fixed dividend amount throughout the expected life unless there is evidence that supports that assumption. [FAS123, ¶286]

.166 Generally, the assumption about expected dividends should be based on publicly available information. An entity that does not pay dividends and has no plans to do so would assume an expected dividend yield of zero. However, an emerging entity with no history of paying dividends might expect to begin paying dividends during the expected lives of its employee stock options. Those entities may use an average of their past dividend yield (zero) and the mean dividend yield of an appropriately comparable peer group. For example, it would not be appropriate for a young, rapidly growing entity to base its expected dividend yield on the average dividend yield of the entities in the Standard & Poor's 500 Index. [FAS123, ¶287]

Illustrative Computations

Illustration 1—Fixed Stock Option

.167 Company S, a public entity, grants options with a maximum term of 10 years to its employees. The exercise price of each option equals the market price of its stock on the grant date. All options vest at the end of three years (cliff vesting). The options do not qualify for tax purposes as incentive stock options. The corporate tax rate is 34 percent. [FAS123, ¶288]

.168 The following table shows assumptions and information about options granted on January 1, 20Y0.

Options granted	900,000
Employees granted options	3,000
Expected forfeitures per year	3%
Stock price	$50
Exercise price	$50
Expected life of options	6 years
Risk-free interest rate	7.5%
Expected volatility	30%
Expected dividend yield	2.5%

[FAS123, ¶289]

.169 Using as inputs the last 6 items from the table above, the Black-Scholes option-pricing model modified for dividends determines a fair value of $17.15 for each option. Using the same assumptions, a binomial model produces a value of $17.26. A difference between a Black-Scholes model and a binomial model grant-date valuation of an option generally arises from the binomial model's fully reflecting the benefit in limited circumstances of being able to exercise an option on a dividend-paying stock before its expiration date when it is economic to do so. (If Company S paid no dividends, both the Black-Scholes and the binomial models would determine a fair value of $22.80, holding other assumptions constant.) Although some available software modifies the Black-Scholes model to attempt to take that benefit into account, the result may not be exactly the same as a binomial model. The following illustrations use a fair value of $17.15, but $17.26 is equally acceptable. [FAS123, ¶290]

.170 Total compensation cost recognized over the vesting period will be the fair value of all options that actually vest, determined based on the stock price at the grant date. This section allows an entity either to estimate at the grant date the number of options expected to vest or to recognize compensation cost each period based on the number of options not yet forfeited. An adjustment to eliminate compensation cost previously recognized for options that were subsequently forfeited is recognized when the forfeitures occur. This example assumes that Company S estimates at the grant date the number of options that will vest and subsequently adjusts compensation cost for changes in the assumed rate of forfeitures and differences between expectations and actual experience. None of the compensation cost is capitalized as part of the cost to produce inventory or other assets. [FAS123, ¶291]

.171 The estimate of the expected number of forfeitures considers historical employee turnover rates and expectations about the future. Company S has experienced historical turnover rates of approximately 3 percent per year for employees at the grantees' level having nonvested options, and it expects that rate to continue. Therefore, Company S estimates the total value of the award at the grant date based on an expected forfeiture rate of 3 percent per year. Actual forfeitures are 5 percent in 20Y0, but no adjustments to cost are recognized in 20Y0 because Company S still expects actual forfeitures to average 3 percent per year over the 3-year vesting period. During 20Y1, however, management decides that the rate of forfeitures is likely to continue to increase through 20Y2, and the assumed forfeiture rate for the entire award is changed to 6 percent per year. Adjustments to cumulative cost to reflect the higher forfeiture rate are made at the end of 20Y1. At the end of 20Y2 when the award becomes vested, actual forfeitures have averaged 6 percent per year, and no further adjustment is necessary. [FAS123, ¶292]

Cliff vesting

.172 The first set of calculations illustrates the accounting for the award of options on January 1, 20Y0, assuming that the entire award vests at the end of three years, that is, the award provides for cliff vesting rather than graded vesting. (Paragraphs .177 through .184 illustrate the accounting for an award assuming graded vesting in which a specified portion of the award vests at the end of each year.) The number of options expected to vest is estimated at the grant date to be 821,406 (900,000 × .97 × .97 × .97). Thus, as shown in Exhibit 173A, the estimated value of the award at January 1, 20Y0 is $14,087,113 (821,406 × $17.15), and the compensation cost to be recognized during each year of the 3-year vesting period is $4,695,704 ($14,087,113 ÷ 3). The journal entries to recognize compensation cost follow.

For 20Y0:

Compensation cost	4,695,704	
Additional paid-in capital—stock options		4,695,704

To recognize compensation cost.

Deferred tax asset	1,596,539	
Deferred tax expense		1,596,539

To recognize the deferred tax asset for the temporary difference related to compensation cost ($4,695,704 × .34 = $1,596,539).

The net after-tax effect on income of recognizing compensation cost for 20Y0 is $3,099,165 ($4,695,704 – $1,596,539). [FAS123, ¶293]

.173 In the absence of a change in estimate or experience different from that initially assumed, the same journal entries would be made to recognize compensation cost and related tax effects for 20Y1 and 20Y2, resulting in a net after-tax cost for each year of $3,099,165. However, at the end of 20Y1, management changes its estimated employee forfeiture rate from 3 percent to 6 percent per year. The revised number of options expected to vest is 747,526 (900,000 × .94 × .94 × .94). Accordingly, the revised total compensation cost to be recognized by the end of 20Y2 is $12,820,071 (747,526 × $17.15). The cumulative adjustment to reflect the effect of adjusting the forfeiture rate is the difference between two-thirds of the revised cost of the award and the cost already recognized for 20Y0 and 20Y1. The related journal entries and the computations follow.

At December 31, 20Y1 to adjust for new forfeiture rate:

Revised total compensation cost	$12,820,071
Revised cumulative cost as of 12/31/Y1 ($12,820,071 × $\frac{2}{3}$)	$ 8,546,714
Cost already recognized in 20Y0 and 20Y1 ($4,695,704 × 2)	9,391,408
Adjustment to cost at 12/31/Y1	$ (844,694)

The related journal entries are:

Additional paid-in capital—stock options	844,694	
Compensation cost		844,694

To adjust compensation cost and equity already recognized to reflect a higher estimated forfeiture rate.

Deferred tax expense	287,196	
Deferred tax asset		287,196

To adjust the deferred tax accounts to reflect the tax effect of increasing the estimated forfeiture rate ($844,694 × .34 = $287,196).

For 20Y2:

Compensation cost	4,273,357	
Additional paid-in capital—stock options		4,273,357

To recognize compensation cost ($12,820,071 ÷ 3 = $4,273,357).

Deferred tax asset	1,452,941	
Deferred tax expense		1,452,941

To recognize the deferred tax asset for additional compensation cost ($4,273,357 × .34 = $1,452,941).

At December 31, 20Y2, the entity would examine its actual forfeitures and make any necessary adjustments to reflect compensation cost for the number of shares that actually vested. [FAS123, ¶294]

Exhibit 173A

Fixed Stock Option—Cliff Vesting

Year	Total Value of Award	Pretax Cost for Year	Cumulative Pretax Cost
20Y0	\$14,087,113 (821,406 × \$17.15)	\$4,695,704 (\$14,087,113 ÷ 3)	\$4,695,704
20Y1	\$12,820,071 (747,526 × \$17.15)	\$3,851,010 [(\$12,820,071 × $\frac{2}{3}$) – \$4,695,704]	\$8,546,714
20Y2	\$12,820,071 (747,526 × \$17.15)	\$4,273,357 (\$12,820,071 ÷ 3)	\$12,820,071

[FAS123, ¶294]

.174 For simplicity, the illustration assumes that all of the options are exercised on the same day and that Company S has already recognized its income tax expense for the year without regard to the effects of the exercise of the employee stock options. In other words, current tax expense and current taxes payable were recognized based on income and deductions before consideration of additional deductions from exercise of the employee stock options. The amount credited to common stock (or other appropriate equity account) for the exercise of the options is the sum of (a) the cash proceeds received and (b) the amounts credited to additional paid-in capital for services received earlier that were charged to compensation cost. At exercise, the stock price is assumed to be \$70.

At exercise:

Cash (747,526 × \$50)	37,376,300	
Additional paid-in capital—stock options	12,820,071	
Common stock		50,196,371

To recognize the issuance of stock upon exercise of options. [FAS123, ¶295]

.175 The difference between the market price of the stock and the exercise price on the date of exercise is deductible for tax purposes because the options do not qualify as incentive stock options. The benefit of tax return deductions in excess of compensation cost recognized results in a credit to additional paid-in capital. Tax return deductions that are less than compensation cost recognized result in a debit to additional paid-in capital to the extent that the benefit of tax deductions from stock-based compensation awards in excess of compensation cost recognized based on the fair value method have been previously credited to capital. To the extent that insufficient credits are available in additional paid-in capital, a charge is made to income tax expense in the period of exercise (paragraph .143). With the stock price at $70 at exercise, the deductible amount is $14,950,520 [747,526 × ($70 – $50)]. The entity has sufficient taxable income, and the tax benefit realized is $5,083,177 ($14,950,520 × .34).

At exercise:

Deferred tax expense	4,358,824	
Deferred tax asset		4,358,824

To write off deferred tax asset related to deductible stock options at exercise ($12,820,071 × .34 = $4,358,824).[21]

Current taxes payable	5,083,177	
Current tax expense		4,358,824
Additional paid-in capital—stock options		724,353

To adjust current tax expense and current taxes payable to recognize the current tax benefit from deductible compensation cost upon exercise of options. The credit to additional paid-in capital is the tax benefit of the excess of the deductible amount over the compensation cost recognized: [($14,950,520 – $12,820,071) × .34 = $724,353]. [FAS123, ¶296]

.176 If instead the options had expired unexercised, the additional paid-in capital—stock options account would have been closed to other paid-in capital. Previously recognized compensation cost would not be reversed. Similar to the adjustment for the actual tax deduction realized described in paragraph .175, whether part or all of the deferred tax asset of $4,358,824 is charged to additional paid-in capital or to income tax expense is determined by applying paragraph .143. [FAS123, ¶297]

Graded vesting

.177 Paragraph .130 of this section provides for use of either the attribution method described in paragraphs .119 through .122 of Section C47 or a straight-line method for awards with graded vesting depending on the approach used to estimate the value of the option award. Both methods are illustrated and use the same assumptions that follow. Company S awards 900,000 options on January 1, 20Y0, that vest according to a graded schedule of 25 percent for the first year of service, 25 percent for the second year, and the remaining 50 percent for the third year. Each employee is granted 300 options. [FAS123, ¶298]

---

[21] Individual entries to the deferred tax asset account do not add to $4,358,824 due to rounding differences. [FAS123, ¶296, fn19]

.178 Exhibit 178A shows the calculation of the number of employees and the related number of options expected to vest. Using the expected 3 percent annual forfeiture rate, 90 employees are expected to terminate during 20Y0 without having vested in any portion of the award, leaving 2,910 employees to vest in 25 percent of the award. During 20Y1, 87 employees are expected to terminate, leaving 2,823 to vest in the second 25 percent of the award. During 20Y2, 85 employees are expected to terminate, leaving 2,738 employees to vest in the last 50 percent of the award. That results in a total of 840,675 options expected to vest from the award of 900,000 options with graded vesting. As provided in paragraph .127, Company S could have chosen to recognize cost based on the number of options granted and recognized forfeitures as they occur; that method is not illustrated. [FAS123, ¶299]

Exhibit 178A

Fixed Stock Option—Graded Vesting—Expected Amounts

Year	Number of Employees		Number of Vested Options	
	Total at date of grant	3,000		
20Y0	3,000 – 90 (3,000 × .03) =	2,910	2,910 × 75 (300 × 25%) =	218,250
20Y1	2,910 – 87 (2,910 × .03) =	2,823	2,823 × 75 (300 × 25%) =	211,725
20Y2	2,823 – 85 (2,823 × .03) =	2,738	2,738 × 150 (300 × 50%) =	410,700
			Total vested options	840,675

[FAS123, ¶299]

Circumstances in which the attribution method from Section C47, paragraphs .119 through .122 is required

.179 If the value of the options that vest over the three-year period is estimated by separating the total award into three groups according to the year in which they vest because the expected life for each group differs significantly, the fair value of the award and its attribution would be determined as follows. (Paragraphs .160 and .162 discuss segregation of options into groups that vest.) The estimated weighted-average expected life of the options that vest in 20Y0 is assumed to be 2.5 years, resulting in a value of $11.33

per option.[22] The estimated weighted-average expected life of the options that vest in 20Y1 is assumed to be 4 years, resulting in a value of $14.32 per option. The estimated weighted-average expected life of the options that vest in 20Y2 is assumed to be 5.5 years, resulting in a value of $16.54 per option. Exhibit 179A shows the estimated compensation cost for the options expected to vest. [FAS123, ¶300]

Exhibit 179A

Fixed Stock Option—Graded Vesting—Expected Cost

Year	Vested Options	Expected Life	Value per Option	Compensation Cost
20Y0	218,250	2.5 years	$11.33	$ 2,472,773
20Y1	211,725	4.0 years	14.32	3,031,902
20Y2	410,700	5.5 years	16.54	6,792,978
	840,675			$12,297,653

[FAS123, ¶300]

.180 Compensation cost is recognized over the periods of service during which each group of options is earned. Thus, the $2,472,773 cost attributable to the 218,250 options that vest in 20Y0 is allocated to the year 20Y0. The $3,031,902 cost attributable to the 211,725 options that vest at the end of 20Y1 is allocated over their 2-year vesting period (20Y0 and 20Y1). The $6,792,978 cost attributable to the 410,700 options that vest at the end of 20Y2 is allocated over their 3-year vesting period (20Y0, 20Y1, and 20Y2). [FAS123, ¶301]

.181 Exhibit 181A shows how the $12,297,653 expected amount of compensation cost determined at the grant date is attributed to the years 20Y0, 20Y1, and 20Y2. [FAS123, ¶302]

[22] To simplify the illustration, the fair value of each of the 3 groups of options is based on the same assumptions about expected volatility, expected dividend yield, and the risk-free interest rate used to determine the value of $17.15 for the cliff-vesting options (paragraph .169). In practice, each of those assumptions would be related to the expected life of the group of options being valued, which means that at least the risk-free interest rate and perhaps all three assumptions would differ for each group. [FAS123, ¶300, fn20]

Exhibit 181A

Fixed Stock Option—Graded Vesting—Computation of Expected Cost

	Pretax Cost to Be Recognized		
	20Y0	**20Y1**	**20Y2**
Options vesting in 20Y0	$2,472,773		
Options vesting in 20Y1	1,515,951	$ 1,515,951	
Options vesting in 20Y2	2,264,326	2,264,326	$ 2,264,326
Cost for the year	$6,253,050	$ 3,780,277	$ 2,264,326
Cumulative cost	$6,253,050	$10,033,327	$12,297,653

[FAS123, ¶302]

Circumstances in which straight-line attribution is permitted

.182 Company S assumes a single weighted-average expected life of five years for the entire award of graded vesting options because the expected lives of each group of options that vest are not expected to be significantly different. Other assumptions except for expected life are the same as in the previous illustration. Company S elects to recognize compensation cost on a straight-line basis. [FAS123, ¶303]

.183 Using an estimated weighted-average expected life of 5 years results in a value of $15.87 per option. The same number of options are expected to vest as shown in the previous illustration, 840,675, based on estimated forfeitures. Total compensation cost to be attributed in a straight-line pattern over the 3-year vesting period is $13,341,512 (840,675 × $15.87). Compensation cost recognized at any date must be at least equal to the amount attributable to options that are vested at that date. For example, if this same option award vested 50 percent in the first year of the 3-year vesting period, at least $6,670,756 ($13,341,512 × 50%) would be recognized in the first year. [FAS123, ¶304]

.184 The estimated value of the award is adjusted to reflect differences between expected and actual forfeitures as illustrated for the cliff-vesting options, regardless of which method described in paragraph .130 is used to estimate value and attribute cost for the graded vesting options. For example, if the actual forfeiture rate is 5 percent rather than 3 percent in 20Y0, the compensation cost for the options that vest in 20Y0 (attributed under the method in paragraphs .119 through .122 of Section C47) is adjusted to $2,421,788 (2,850 × 75 × $11.33), reflecting the reduction in the number of employees

[2,850 = 3,000 – (3,000 × .05)] whose first 75 options became vested at December 31, 20Y0. Compensation cost for the options expected to vest in 20Y1 and 20Y2 also is recomputed to reflect the actual forfeitures in 20Y0. Similar adjustments are made to reflect differences, if any, between expected and actual forfeitures in those years. Total compensation cost at the end of 20Y2 reflects the number of vested options at that date. [FAS123, ¶305]

Illustration 2—Performance-Based Stock Option

Illustration 2(a)—Option award under which the number of options to be earned varies

.185 Illustration 2(a) shows the computation of compensation cost if Company S grants a performance-based stock option award instead of a fixed stock option award. Under the plan, employees vest in differing numbers of options depending on the increase in market share of one of Company S's products over a three-year period. On January 1, 20Y0, Company S grants to each of 1,000 employees an award of up to 300 10-year options on shares of its common stock. If by December 31, 20Y2, market share increases by at least 5 percentage points, each employee vests in at least 100 options at that date. If market share increases by at least 10 percentage points, another 100 options vest, for a total of 200. If market share increases by more than 20 percentage points, each employee vests in 300 options. Company S's stock price on January 1, 20Y0, is $50, and other assumptions are the same as in Illustration 1. The fair value at the grant date of an option expected to vest is $17.15. The estimated fair value of the entire performance-based award depends on the number of options that are expected to be earned during the vesting period. Accruals of cost are based on the best estimate of market share growth over the three-year vesting period, and adjusted for subsequent changes in the expected or actual market share growth. Paragraph .127 requires accruals of cost to be based on the best estimate of the outcome of the performance condition. Therefore, Company S is not permitted to estimate a percentage likelihood of achieving a performance condition and base accruals on an amount that is not a possible outcome. [FAS123, ¶306]

.186 Exhibit 187A shows the compensation cost recognized in 20Y0, 20Y1, and 20Y2 if Company S estimates at the grant date that it is probable that market share will increase between 10 and 20 percentage points. That estimate remains reasonable until the end of 20Y2, when Company S's market share has increased over the 3-year period by more than 20 percentage points. Thus, each employee vests in options on 300 shares. [FAS123, ¶307]

.187 As in Illustration 1, Company S experiences actual forfeiture rates of 5 percent in 20Y0, and in 20Y1 changes its estimate of forfeitures for the entire award from 3 percent to 6 percent per year. In 20Y1, cumulative compensation cost is adjusted to reflect the higher forfeiture rate. By the end of 20Y2, a 6 percent forfeiture rate has been experienced, and no further adjustments for forfeitures are necessary. Through 20Y0, Company S estimates that 913 employees (1,000 × .97 × .97 × .97) will remain in service until the vesting date. At the end of 20Y1, the number of employees estimated to vest is adjusted for the higher forfeiture rate, and the number of employees expected to vest in the award is 831 (1,000 × .94 × .94 × .94). The value of the award is estimated initially based on the number of options expected to vest, which in turn is based on the expected level of performance, and the fair value of each option. Compensation cost is initially recognized ratably over the three-year vesting period, with one-third of the value of the award recognized each year, adjusted as needed for changes in the estimated and actual forfeiture rates and for differences between estimated and actual market share growth. [FAS123, ¶308]

Exhibit 187A

Performance-Based Stock Option—Number of Options Varies

Year	Total Value of Award	Pretax Cost for Year	Cumulative Pretax Cost
20Y0	\$3,131,590 (\$17.15 × 200 × 913)	\$1,043,863 (\$3,131,590 ÷ 3)	\$1,043,863
20Y1	\$2,850,330 (\$17.15 × 200 × 831)	\$856,357 [(\$2,850,330 × $\frac{2}{3}$) – \$1,043,863]	\$1,900,220
20Y2	\$4,275,495 (\$17.15 × 300 × 831)	\$2,375,275 (\$4,275,495 – \$1,900,220)	\$4,275,495

[FAS123, ¶308]

Illustration 2(b)—Option award under which the exercise price varies

.188 Illustration 2(b) shows the computation of compensation cost if Company S grants a performance-based stock option award under which the exercise price, rather than the number of shares, varies depending on the level of performance achieved. On January 1, 20Y0, Company S grants to its chief executive officer (CEO) 10-year options on 10,000 shares of its common stock, which are immediately exercisable. The stock price at the grant date is \$50, and the initial exercise price also is \$50. However, that price decreases to

$30 if the market share of Company S's products increases by at least 10 percentage points by December 31, 20Y1, and provided that the CEO continues to be employed by Company S. [FAS123, ¶309]

.189 Company S estimates at the grant date the expected level of market share growth, the exercise price of the options, and the expected life of the options. Other assumptions, including the risk-free interest rate and the service period over which the cost is attributed, need to be consistent with those estimates. Company S estimates at the grant date that its market share growth will be at least 10 percentage points over the 2-year performance period, which means that the expected exercise price of the options is $30, resulting in an estimated option value of $22.64.[23] Compensation cost of $226,400 (10,000 × $22.64) would be accrued over the expected 2-year service period. Paragraph .118 of this section requires the value of both fixed and performance awards to be estimated as of the date of grant. Paragraph .125, however, calls for recognition of cost for the number of instruments that actually vest. For this performance award, Company S also selects the expected assumptions at the grant date if the performance goal is not met. If market share growth is not at least 10 percentage points over the 2-year period, Company S estimates that the CEO will exercise the options with a $50 exercise price in 5 years. All other assumptions would need to be consistent, resulting in an estimated option value of $15.87.[24] (For convenience, the illustration assumes that all options are expected to be exercised on the same date.) Total compensation cost to be recognized if the performance goal is not met would be $158,700 (10,000 × $15.87). During the two-year service period, adjustments to expected amounts for changes in estimates or actual experience are made and cost recognized by the end of that period reflects whether the performance goal was met. [FAS123, ¶310]

Illustration 3—Stock Option with Indexed Exercise Price

.190 Company S instead might have granted stock options whose exercise price varies with an index of the stock prices of a group of entities in the same industry. Assume that on January 1, 20Y0, Company S grants 100 options on its stock with a base exercise price of $50 to each of 1,000 employees. The options have a maximum term of 10 years. The exercise price of the options increases or decreases on December 31 of each year by the same percentage that the index has increased or decreased during the year. For ex-

[23]Option value is determined using a $50 stock price, $30 exercise price, 3-year expected life, 6.5 percent risk-free interest rate, 2.5 percent dividend yield, and .30 volatility. [FAS123, ¶310, fn21]

[24]Option value is determined using a $50 stock price, $50 exercise price, 5-year expected life, 7.5 percent risk-free interest rate, 2.5 percent dividend yield, and .30 volatility. [FAS123, ¶310, fn22]

ample, if the peer group index increases by 10 percent in 20Y0, the exercise price of the options during 20Y1 increases to $55 ($50 × 1.10). The assumptions about the risk-free interest rate and expected life, dividends, volatility, and forfeiture rates are the same as in Illustration 1. On January 1, 20Y0, the peer group index is assumed to be 400. The dividend yield on the index is assumed to be 1.25 percent. [FAS123, ¶311]

.191 Each indexed option may be analyzed as an option to exchange 0.1250 (50 ÷ 400) "shares" of the peer group index for a share of Company S stock, that is, to exchange one noncash asset for another noncash asset. An option to purchase stock for cash also can be thought of as an option to exchange one asset (cash in the amount of the exercise price) for another (the share of stock). The gain on a cash option equals the difference between the price of the stock upon exercise and the amount—the "price"—of the cash exchanged for the stock. The gain on an option to exchange 0.1250 "shares" of the peer group index for a share of Company S stock also equals the difference between the prices of the 2 assets exchanged. [FAS123, ¶312]

.192 To illustrate the equivalence of an indexed option and the option above, assume that an employee exercises the indexed option when Company S's stock price has increased 100 percent to $100 and the peer group index has increased 75 percent, from 400 to 700. The exercise price of the indexed option thus is $87.50 ($50 × 1.75). The employee's realized gain is $12.50.

Price of Company S stock	$100.00
Less: Exercise price of option	87.50
Gain on indexed option	$ 12.50

That is the same as the gain on an option to exchange 0.1250 "shares" of the index for one share of Company S stock:

Price of Company S stock	$100.00
Less: Price of a "share" of the peer group index (.1250 × $700)	87.50
Gain on exchange	$ 12.50

[FAS123, ¶313]

.193 The Black-Scholes or binomial option-pricing models can be extended to value an option to exchange one asset for another. The principal extension is that the volatility of an option to exchange two noncash assets is based on the relationship between the volatilities of the prices of the assets to be exchanged—their **cross-volatility.** In a cash option, the amount of cash to be paid involves no risk, that is, it is not volatile, so that only the volatility of the stock needs to be considered in estimating the option's value. In contrast, the value of an option to exchange two noncash assets depends on possible movements in the prices of both assets—in this example, a "share" of the peer group index and a share of Company S stock. Historical cross-volatility can be computed directly by measuring the stock price in "shares" of the peer group index. For example, the stock price was 0.1250 "shares" at the grant date and 0.1429 (100 ÷ 700) "shares" at the exercise date. Those share amounts then are used to compute cross-volatility. Cross-volatility also can be computed indirectly based on the respective volatilities of Company S stock and the peer group index and the correlation between them. The cross-volatility between Company S stock and the peer group index is assumed to be 26.5 percent. [FAS123, ¶314]

.194 In a cash option, the assumed risk-free interest rate (discount rate) represents the return on the cash that will not be paid until exercise. In this example, an equivalent "share" of the index, rather than cash, is what will not be "paid" until exercise. The dividend yield on the peer group index of 1.25 percent therefore is used in place of the risk-free interest rate as an input to the Black-Scholes model. [FAS123, ¶315]

.195 The exercise price for the indexed option is the value of an equivalent "share" of the peer group index, which is $50 (0.1250 × 400). The fair value of each option granted is $9.78 based on the following inputs:

Stock price	$50
Exercise price	$50
Dividend yield	2.50%
Discount rate	1.25%
Volatility	26.5%
Expected life	6 years

The value of the entire award would be based on the number of options expected to vest. That cost would be recognized over the service period as shown in Illustration 1. [FAS123, ¶316]

Illustration 4—Option with Exercise Price That Increases by a Fixed Amount or a Fixed Percentage

.196 Some entities grant options with exercise prices that increase by a fixed amount or a constant percentage periodically rather than by the percentage change in an index. For example, the exercise price of the options in Illustration 1 might increase by a fixed amount of $2.50 per year. Binomial option-pricing models can be adapted to accommodate exercise prices that change over time. [FAS123, ¶317]

.197 Options with exercise prices that increase by a constant percentage also can be valued using an option-pricing model that accommodates changes in exercise prices. Alternatively, those options can be valued by deducting from the discount rate the annual percentage increase in the exercise price. That method works because a decrease in the risk-free interest rate and an increase in the exercise price have a similar effect—both reduce the option value. For example, the exercise price of the options in Illustration 1 might increase at the rate of 5 percent annually. For that example, Company S's options would be valued based on a risk-free interest rate of 2.5 percent (7.5% – 5%). Holding all other assumptions constant from Illustration 1, the value of each option granted by Company S would be $12.34. [FAS123, ¶318]

Illustration 5—Modifications and Cash Settlements

Illustration 5(a)—Modification of vested options granted after adoption of the recognition provisions of this section

.198 The following examples of accounting for modifications of the terms of an award are based on Illustration 1, in which Company S granted its employees 900,000 options with an exercise price of $50 on January 1, 20Y0. At January 1, 20Y4, after the options have vested, the market price of Company S stock has declined to $40 per share, and Company S decides to reduce the exercise price of the outstanding options to $40. In effect, Company S issues new options with an exercise price of $40 and a contractual term equal to the remaining contractual term of the original January 1, 20Y0, options, which is 6 years, in exchange for the original vested options. Company S incurs additional compensation cost for the excess of the fair value of the modified options issued over the value of the original options at the date of the exchange measured as shown in paragraph .200. The modified options are immediately vested, and the additional compensation cost is recognized in the period the modification occurs. [FAS123, ¶319]

.199 The fair value on January 1, 20Y4, of the modified award, based on a 3-year expected life, $40 current stock price, $40 exercise price, 7 percent risk-free interest rate, 35 percent volatility, and a 2.5 percent dividend yield, is $10.82. To determine the amount of additional compensation cost arising from the modification, the value of the original vested options assumed to be repurchased is computed based on the shorter of (a) the remaining expected life of the original options or (b) the expected life of the modified options. In this example, the remaining expected life of the original options is two years, which is shorter than the expected life of the modified options (three years). The resulting computed value at January 1, 20Y4, of the original options based on a $40 current stock price, a $50 exercise price, a risk-free interest rate of 7 percent, expected volatility of 35 percent, and a 2.5 percent dividend yield is $5.54 per option. Thus, the additional compensation cost stemming from the modification is $5.28 per option, determined as follows:

Fair value of modified option at January 1, 20Y4	$10.82
Less: Value of original option at January 1, 20Y4	5.54
Additional compensation cost to be recognized	$ 5.28

Compensation cost already recognized during the vesting period of the original award is $12,820,071 for 747,526 vested options (refer to Illustration 1). For simplicity, it is assumed that no options were exercised before the modification. Previously recognized cost is not adjusted. Additional compensation cost of $3,946,937 (747,526 vested options × $5.28) is recognized on January 1, 20Y4, because the modified options are fully vested. [FAS123, ¶320]

Illustration 5(b)—Cash settlement of vested options granted after adoption of the recognition provisions of this section

.200 Rather than modify the option terms, Company S offers to settle the original January 1, 20Y0 options for cash at January 1, 20Y4. The value of each option is estimated in the same way as illustrated in the preceding example, resulting in a value of $5.54. Company S recognizes the settlement as the repurchase of an outstanding equity instrument, and no additional compensation cost is recognized at the date of settlement unless the cash payment exceeds $5.54. Previously recognized compensation cost for the fair value of the original options is not adjusted. [FAS123, ¶321]

Illustration 5(c)—Modification of nonvested options granted after adoption of the recognition provisions of this section

.201 This example assumes that Company S granted its employees 900,000 options with an exercise price of $50, as in Illustration 1. At January 1, 20Y1, 1 year into the 3-year vesting period, the market price of Company S stock has declined to $40 per share, and Company S decides to reduce the exercise price of the options to $40. The 3-year cliff-vesting requirement is not changed. In effect, Company S grants new options with an exercise price of $40 and a contractual term equal to the 9-year remaining contractual term of the options granted on January 1, 20Y0, in exchange for the original nonvested options. The expected life of the repriced options is five years. Company S incurs additional compensation cost for the excess of the fair value of the modified options issued over the value of the original options at the date of the exchange determined in the manner set forth in paragraph .199. Company S adds that incremental amount to the remaining unrecognized compensation cost for the original options at the date of modification and recognizes the total amount over the remaining two years of the three-year vesting period. [FAS123, ¶322]

.202 The fair value at January 1, 20Y1, of the modified options, based on a 5-year expected life, $40 current stock price, $40 exercise price, 7 percent risk-free interest rate, 35 percent volatility, and a 2.5 percent dividend yield, is $13.60 per option. The computed value of the original options at the date of modification used to measure additional compensation cost is based on an expected life of five years because the remaining expected life of the original options and the expected life of the modified options both are five years. The resulting value of the original options, based on a current stock price of $40 and an exercise price of $50, with other assumptions the same as those used to determine the fair value of the modified options, is $10.77. Thus, the additional compensation cost stemming from the modification is $2.83, determined as follows:

Fair value of modified option at January 1, 20Y1	$13.60
Less: Value of original option at January 1, 20Y1	10.77
Incremental value of modified January 1, 20Y1, option	$ 2.83

[FAS123, ¶323]

.203 On January 1, 20Y1, the remaining balance of unrecognized compensation cost for the original options is $11.43 per option.[25] The total compensation cost for each modified option that is expected to vest is $14.26, determined as follows:

Incremental value of modified option	$ 2.83
Unrecognized compensation cost for original option	11.43
Total compensation cost to be recognized	$14.26

That amount is recognized during 20Y1 and 20Y2, which are the two remaining years of the service period. [FAS123, ¶324]

Illustration 5(d)—Cash settlement of nonvested options granted after adoption of the recognition provisions of this section

.204 Rather than modify the option terms, Company S offers to settle the original January 1, 20Y0 grant of options for cash at January 1, 20Y1. Because the stock price decreased from $50 at the grant date to $40 at the date of settlement, the estimated fair value

[25]Using a value of $17.15 for the original option as in Illustration 1 results in recognition of $5.72 ($17.15 ÷ 3) per year. The unrecognized balance at January 1, 20Y1 is $11.43 ($17.15 – $5.72) per option. [FAS123, ¶324, fn23]

of each option is the same as in Illustration 5(c), $10.77. If Company S pays $10.77 per option, it would recognize that cash settlement as the repurchase of an outstanding equity instrument and total compensation cost would not be remeasured. However, the cash payment for the options effectively vests them. Therefore, the remaining unrecognized compensation cost of $11.43 per option also would be recognized at the date of settlement. [FAS123, ¶325]

Illustration 5(e)—Modification of vested options granted before adoption of the recognition provisions of this section

.205 This example assumes that a modification similar to Illustration 5(a) above occurred on January 1, 20X8, and that the original award was granted before Company S adopted this section.[26] Thus, Company S recognized no compensation cost for the original options accounted for in accordance with Section C47 because the exercise price equaled the stock price at the measurement (grant) date. To better illustrate the accounting distinction, all other assumptions are the same as in Illustration 5(a). Therefore, the fair value of the modified option is assumed to be $10.82, as determined in paragraph .199. [FAS123, ¶326]

.206 Because no compensation cost was recognized for the original options, the modified options are treated as a new grant. Compensation cost of $10.82 is recognized for each outstanding option at the date of the modification. However, if immediately before their terms were modified, the original options had been in-the-money and thus had intrinsic value at the date of modification, that intrinsic value would be excluded from the amount of compensation cost recognized. For example, if a modification of terms occurred in conjunction with a spinoff, the original options might have intrinsic value of, say, $2 each, just before their terms are modified. In that situation, if the fair value of a modified option is $16.50, only $14.50 ($16.50 – $2) of compensation cost would be recognized at the date of the modification. The intrinsic value is excluded from compensation cost because the employees could have exercised their options immediately before the modification and received the intrinsic value without affecting the amount of compensation cost recognized. Only the time value of the modified options is additional compensation cost. [FAS123, ¶327]

[26]For purposes of the pro forma disclosures required by paragraph .144 of this section, the method in Illustrations 5(e) through 5(g) applies only to modifications and cash settlements of awards granted before the beginning of the fiscal year for which that paragraph is initially applied. A modification or cash settlement of an award for which compensation cost has been included in pro forma disclosures since it was granted would be treated in the pro forma disclosures in the same manner as in Illustrations 5(a) through 5(d). [FAS123, ¶326, fn24]

Illustration 5(f)—Modification of nonvested options granted before adoption of the recognition provisions of this section

.207 This example of a modification of an option assumes that an award originally accounted for according to Section C47 is not yet vested when it is modified. Company S grants an option with an exercise price of $47 when the stock price is $50 and the option cliff-vests after 3 years. Section C47 requires compensation cost of $3 ($50 – $47) to be recognized over the vesting period at the rate of $1 per year. After two years of that three-year cliff-vesting period, Company S adopts the accounting method for cost recognition encouraged by this section. It also decides to reduce the exercise price of the options to $40, which is the current price of the stock. For convenience, the value of the modified option on the date of the modification is again assumed to be $10.82 (paragraph .199), which consists entirely of time value. [FAS123, ¶328]

.208 Company S had recognized compensation cost of $2 under Section C47 at the date of modification for each option that had not been forfeited. After the modification, the remaining amount of compensation cost to be recognized during the final year of the 3-year service period is $9.17 for each option that vests, determined as follows:

Fair value of modified option	$10.82
Less: Value of original option, based on 1-year remaining life[27]	2.65
Incremental value of modified option	8.17
Plus: Remaining unrecognized cost for original option	1.00
Compensation cost to be recognized	$ 9.17

The value of the original option deducted from the fair value of the modified option to determine the amount of compensation cost to recognize is based on a one-year life because that is the remaining term of the vesting period. To maintain consistency with (a) the requirements of this section for accounting for plan modifications and (b) the principal difference between this section and Section C47—accounting for the time value of an option—the vesting period is used as the expected life of the original option. The life of an option beyond the vesting period is not pertinent to the accounting under Section C47. [FAS123, ¶329]

[27]Other assumptions are $40 stock price, $47 exercise price, expected volatility of 30 percent, risk-free interest rate of 5 percent, and dividend yield of 2.5 percent. [FAS123, ¶329, fn25]

Illustration 5(g)—Cash settlement of vested options granted before adoption of the recognition provisions of this section

.209 This example assumes that a cash settlement of the options described in Illustration 5(a) above occurred on January 1, 20X8, and that the original options were granted before Company S adopted the accounting method for cost recognition encouraged by this section. Thus, Company S recognized no compensation cost for the original award accounted for in accordance with Section C47 because the exercise price equaled the stock price at the measurement (grant) date. All other assumptions are the same as in Illustration 5(a). Therefore, the amount of the cash payment and the fair value of the out-of-the-money option at the date of cash settlement are $10.82, as determined in paragraph .199. [FAS123, ¶330]

.210 Because no cost was recognized for the original award, the cash settlement of the out-of-the-money options for $10.82 each is treated as a new grant. Compensation cost of $10.82 is recognized for each outstanding option at the date of settlement. However, if the original options had been in-the-money and thus had intrinsic value immediately before the settlement, that intrinsic value would be excluded from the amount of compensation cost recognized for the reasons cited in Illustration 5(e), paragraph .206. [FAS123, ¶331]

Illustration 6—Options Granted by a Nonpublic Entity

.211 Company P, a nonpublic entity, grants 100 stock options on its stock to each of its 100 employees. The options cliff-vest after three years. The fair value of the stock and the exercise price of the options is $5, the expected life of the options is 8 years, and the risk-free interest rate is 7.5 percent. Company P calculates a *minimum value* for each option. The so-called minimum value does not take into account the expected volatility of the underlying stock.

Fair value of stock	$5.00
Present value of exercise price (compounded daily)	2.74
Minimum value of each option	$2.26

[FAS123, ¶332]

.212 An option-pricing model can also be used to compute the minimum value of Company P's options if the volatility assumption is set to near zero (say, 0.001), resulting in the same $2.26. If Company P expected to pay dividends, the minimum value of the options would be further reduced to reflect the present value of the expected dividends that the option holder will not receive. Assuming a 1 percent dividend yield over the 8-year expected life of the options, an option-pricing model results in a minimum value of $1.87. [FAS123, ¶333]

.213 Alternatively, the present value of the expected dividends would be computed as $.30, using 32 quarterly (8-year expected life) payments of $.0125 [($5.00 × .01) ÷ 4], and a quarterly interest rate of 1.875 percent (7.5 percent annual rate). That amount would be deducted from the minimum value of an option on a stock that pays no dividends computed in paragraph .211, resulting in a minimum value of $1.96 ($2.26 – $.30). The $0.39 present value of the dividends computed using the option-pricing model ($2.26 – $1.87) differs from the $0.30 present value computed by directly discounting dividend payments because the option-pricing model assumes that dividends will grow with increases in the stock price (if the dividend assumption is stated as a constant yield). The assumed growth rate is the difference between the risk-free interest rate and the dividend rate. In this example, that difference is 6.5 percent (7.5% – 1%). Either method of computing minimum value is acceptable in applying this section. [FAS123, ¶334]

Illustration 7—Tandem Plan—Stock Options or Cash SARs

.214 A plan in which employees are granted awards with two separate components, in which exercise of one component cancels the other, is referred to as a tandem plan. In contrast, a **combination plan** is an award with two separate components, both of which can be exercised. [FAS123, ¶335]

.215 The following illustrates the accounting for a tandem plan in which employees have a choice of either stock options or cash SARs. Company S grants to its employees an award of 900,000 stock options or 900,000 cash SARs on January 1, 20Y0. The award vests on December 31, 20Y2, and has a contractual life of 10 years. If an employee exercises the SARs, the related stock options are canceled. Conversely, if an employee exercises the options, the related SARs are canceled. [FAS123, ¶336]

.216 The tandem award results in Company S's incurring a liability because the employees can demand settlement in cash, and Company S therefore is obligated to pay cash upon demand. If Company S could choose whether to settle the award in cash or by issuing stock, the award would be an equity instrument because Company S would have the discretion to avoid transferring its assets to employees (unless Company S's past practice is to settle most awards in cash, indicating that Company S has incurred a substantive liability as indicated in paragraph .138). In this illustration, however, Company S incurs a liability to pay cash, which it will recognize over the service period. The amount of the liability will be adjusted each year to reflect the current stock price. If employees choose to exercise the options rather than the SARs, the liability is settled by issuing stock. [FAS123, ¶337]

.217 In concept, the fair value of the expected liability at the grant date is $14,087,113 as computed in Illustration 1 because the value of the SARs and the value of the stock options are equal. However, this section does not require accounting for the time value of the cash SARs at the grant date because the compensation cost stemming from the award must be finally measured as the intrinsic value of the SARs at the exercise (or expiration) date. Accordingly, at the end of 20Y0, when the stock price is $55, the amount of the liability is $4,107,030 (821,406 cash SARs expected to vest × $5 increase in stock price). One-third of that amount, $1,369,010, is recognized as compensation cost for 20Y0. At the end of each year during the vesting period, the expected liability is remeasured based on the current stock price. As provided in paragraph .127, Company S has the choice of estimating forfeitures at the grant date or accruing cost for the total grant and adjusting for forfeitures as they occur. After the vesting period, the expected liability is remeasured for all outstanding vested awards. [FAS123, ¶338]

Illustration 8—Tandem Plan—Phantom Shares or Stock Options

.218 The illustration that follows is for a tandem plan in which the components have different values after the grant date, depending on the movement in the price of the entity's stock. The employee's choice of which component to exercise will depend on the relative values of the components when the award is exercised. [FAS123, ¶339]

.219 Company S grants to its CEO an immediately vested award consisting of two measurable parts:

a. 1,000 phantom stock units (units) whose value is always equal to the value of 1,000 shares of Company S's common stock.
b. Options on 3,000 shares of Company S stock with an exercise price of $50 per share.

At the grant date, Company S's stock price is $50 per share. The CEO may choose whether to exercise the options or to cash in the units at any time during the next five years. Exercise of all of the options cancels all of the units, and cashing in all of the units cancels all of the options. The cash value of the units will be paid to the CEO at the end of five years if the option component of the tandem award is not exercised before then. [FAS123, ¶340]

.220 With a 3-to-1 ratio of options to units, exercise of 3 options will produce a higher gain than receipt of cash equal to the value of 1 share of stock if the stock price appreciates from the grant date by more than 50 percent. Below that point, one unit is more valuable than the gain on three options. To illustrate that relationship, the results if the stock price increases 50 percent to $75 are:

	Units		Exercise of Options	
Market value	$75,000	($75 × 1,000)	$225,000	($75 × 3,000)
Purchase price	0		150,000	($50 × 3,000)
Net cash value	$75,000		$ 75,000	

[FAS123, ¶341]

.221 If the price of Company S's common stock increases from $50 to $75, each part of the tandem grant will produce the same net cash inflow (ignoring transaction costs) to the CEO. If the price increases only to $74, the value of 1 share of stock exceeds the gain on exercising 3 options, which would be $72 [3 × ($74 – $50)]. But if the price increases to $76, the gain on exercising 3 options, $78 [3 × ($76 – $50)], exceeds the value of 1 share of stock. [FAS123, ¶342]

.222 At the grant date, the CEO could take $50,000 cash for the units and forfeit the options. Therefore, the total value of the award at the grant date must exceed $50,000 because at stock prices above $75, the CEO receives a higher amount than would the holder of 1 share of stock. To exercise the 3,000 options, the CEO must forfeit the equivalent of 1,000 shares of stock, in addition to paying the total exercise price of $150,000 (3,000 × $50). In effect, the CEO receives only 2,000 shares of Company S stock upon exercise. That is the same as if the option component of the tandem award consisted of options to purchase 2,000 shares of stock for $75 per share. [FAS123, ¶343]

.223 The cash payment obligated by the units qualifies the award as a liability of Company S. The maximum amount of the cash liability, which is indexed to the price of Company S's common stock, is $75,000 because at stock prices above $75, the CEO will exercise the options. [FAS123, ¶344]

.224 In measuring compensation cost, the award may be thought of as a *combination*—not tandem—grant of (a) 1,000 units with a value at grant of $50,000 and (b) 2,000 options with a strike price of $75 per share. Compensation cost is measured as the combined value of the two parts. [FAS123, ¶345]

.225 The expected volatility of Company S stock is assumed to be 30 percent, the risk-free interest rate is 7 percent, Company S stock pays no dividend, and the expected life of the options is 5 years. Using those assumptions, the fair value of an option with an exercise price of $75 is $12.13 when the price of Company S's stock price is $50. Therefore, the total value of the award at the grant date is:

Units (1,000 × $50)	$50,000
Options (2,000 × $12.13)	24,260
Value of award	$74,260

[FAS123, ¶346]

.226 Compensation cost recognized at the date of grant (the award is immediately vested) therefore would be $74,260. That amount is more than either of the components by itself, but less than the total cost that would be computed if both components (1,000 units and 3,000 options with an exercise price of $50) were exercisable. Because granting the units creates a liability, changes in the liability that result from increases or decreases in the price of Company S's stock price would be recognized each period until exercise, except that the amount of the liability would not exceed $75,000. [FAS123, ¶347]

Illustration 9—"Look-Back" Options

.227 Some entities offer options to employees under Section 423 of the Internal Revenue Code, which provides that employees will not be immediately taxed on the difference between the market price of the stock and a discounted purchase price if several requirements are met. One requirement is that the option price may not be less than the smaller of (a) 85 percent of the market price when the option is granted or (b) 85 percent of the price at exercise. An option that provides the employee the choice of (a) or (b) may not have a term in excess of 27 months. Options that provide for the more favorable of two (or more) exercise prices are referred to as "look-back" options. A look-back option with a 15 percent discount from the market price at either grant or exercise is worth more than a fixed option to purchase stock at 85 percent of the current market price because the holder of the look-back option cannot lose. If the price rises, the holder benefits to the same extent as if the exercise price were fixed at the grant date. If the stock price falls, the holder still receives the benefit of purchasing the stock at a 15 percent discount from its price at the date of exercise. [FAS123, ¶348] [Refer to paragraphs .501 through .519 for additional guidance on employee stock purchase plans with a look-back option.]

.228 For example, on January 1, 20Y0, when its stock price is $50, Company S offers its employees the opportunity to sign up for a payroll deduction to purchase its stock at either 85 percent of the stock's current price or 85 percent of the price at the end of the year when the options expire, whichever is lower. The exercise price of the options is the lesser of (a) $42.50 ($50 × .85) or (b) 85 percent of the stock price at the end of the year when the option is exercised. For simplicity, the first set of calculations assumes that

Company S pays no dividends, its expected volatility is .30, and the risk-free interest rate available for the next 12 months is 6.8 percent. [FAS123, ¶349]

.229 The value of that look-back option can be estimated at the grant date by breaking it into its components and valuing the option as a combination position. In this situation, the components are:

- 0.15 of a share of nonvested stock
- 0.85 of a 1-year call option held with an exercise price of $50.

Supporting analysis for the two components is discussed below. [FAS123, ¶350]

.230 Beginning with the first component, an option with an exercise price that equals 85 percent of the value of the stock at the exercise date will always be worth 15 percent (100% – 85%) of the stock price upon exercise. For a stock that pays no dividends, that option is the equivalent of 15 percent of a share of the stock. The holder of the look-back option will receive *at least* the equivalent of 0.15 of a share of stock upon exercise, regardless of the stock price at that date. For example, if the stock price falls to $40, the exercise price of the option will be $34 ($40 × .85), and the holder will benefit by $6 ($40 – $34), which is the same as receiving 0.15 of a share of stock for each option. [FAS123, ¶351]

.231 If the stock price upon exercise is more than $50, the holder of the look-back option receives a benefit that is worth more than 15 percent of a share of stock. At prices of $50 or more, the holder receives a benefit for the difference between the stock price upon exercise and $42.50—the exercise price of the option (.85 × $50). If the stock price is $60, the holder benefits by $17.50 ($60 – $42.50). However, the holder cannot receive *both* the $17.50 value of an option with an exercise price of $42.50 *and* 0.15 of a share of stock. In effect, the holder gives up 0.15 of a share of stock worth $7.50 ($50 × .15) if the stock price is above $50 at exercise. The result is the same as if the exercise price of the option were $50 ($42.50 + $7.50), and the holder of the look-back option held 85 percent of a 1-year call option with an exercise price of $50 in addition to 0.15 of a share of stock that will be received if the stock price is $50 or less upon exercise. [FAS123, ¶352]

.232 A standard option-pricing model can be used to value the 1-year call option on 0.85 of a share of stock represented by the second component. Therefore, the compensation cost for the look-back option at the grant date is:

• 0.15 of a share of nonvested stock ($50 × 0.15)	$ 7.50
• Call on 0.85 of a share of stock, exercise price of $50 ($7.56 × .85)	6.43
Total grant date value	$13.93

[FAS123, ¶353]

.233 For a look-back option on a dividend-paying stock, both the value of the nonvested stock component and the value of the option component would be adjusted to reflect the effect of the dividends that the employee does not receive during the life of the option. The present value of the dividends expected to be paid on the stock during the life of the option, which is one year in the example, would be deducted from the value of a share that receives dividends. One way to accomplish that is to base the value calculation on shares of stock rather than dollars by assuming that the dividends are reinvested in the stock. [FAS123, ¶354]

.234 For example, if Company S pays a quarterly dividend of 0.625 percent (2.5% ÷ 4) of the current stock price, 1 share of stock would grow to 1.0252 (the future value of 1 using a return of 0.625 percent for 4 periods) shares at the end of the year if all dividends are reinvested. Therefore, the present value of 1 share of stock to be received in 1 year is only 0.9754 of a share today (again applying conventional compound interest formulas compounded quarterly) if the holder does not receive the dividends paid during the year. [FAS123, ¶355]

.235 The value of the option component is easier to compute; the appropriate dividend assumption is used in the option-pricing model in determining the value of an option on a whole share of stock. Thus, the compensation cost for the look-back option if Company S pays quarterly dividends at the annual rate of 2.5 percent is:

• 0.15 of a share of nonvested stock ($50 × 0.15 × 0.9754)	$ 7.32
• Call on 0.85 of a share of stock, $50 exercise price, 2.5% dividend yield ($6.78 × 0.85)	5.76
Total grant date value	$13.08

The first component, which is worth $7.32 at the grant date, is the minimum amount the holder benefits regardless of the price of the stock at the exercise date. The second component, worth $5.76 at the grant date, represents the additional benefit to the holder if the stock price is above $50 at the exercise date. [FAS123, ¶356]

Illustration of the Earnings per Share Computation

.236 An illustration of the computation of earnings per share follows. [FAS123, ¶357] Under Section E11 [FAS128, ¶167(c)] stock options, stock appreciation rights, and other awards to be settled in stock are [FAS123, ¶357] potential common shares [FAS128, ¶167(c)] for purposes of computing earnings per share. In applying the treasury stock method, all dilutive [FAS123, ¶357] potential common shares, [FAS128, ¶167(c)] regardless of whether they are exercisable, are treated as if they had been exercised. The treasury stock method assumes that the proceeds upon exercise are used to repurchase the entity's stock, reducing the number of shares to be added to outstanding common stock in computing earnings per share. The proceeds assumed to be received upon exercise include the exercise price that the employee pays, the amount of compensation cost measured and attributed to future services but not yet recognized, and the amount of any tax benefits upon assumed exercise that would be credited to additional paid-in capital. The assumed proceeds exclude any future tax benefits related to compensation cost to be recognized in income. [FAS123, ¶357]

.237 Under paragraph .127 of this section, an entity has the choice of estimating forfeitures in advance or recognizing forfeitures as they occur. However, the weighted-average number of options outstanding, rather than the number of options expected to vest, would be used in computing the diluted EPS. In addition, the average net unrecognized compensation cost would include the options not expected to vest. [FAS135, ¶4(u)] For this illustration, a total of 4,600,000 options are assumed to be outstanding from current year's and prior years' grants. The weighted-average exercise price of outstanding options is assumed to be $40. The average stock price during 20Y0 is assumed to be $52. To simplify the illustration, it is assumed that (a) all outstanding options are the type that upon exercise give rise to deductible compensation cost for income tax purposes and (b) no tax benefit upon exercise would be credited to additional paid-in capital; that is, the tax deduction based on current intrinsic value is less than the amount of cost recognized for financial statement purposes. [FAS123, ¶358]

.238 [The] computation of assumed proceeds for diluted earnings per share [is as follows]:

• Amount employees would pay if [FAS128, ¶167(e)] the weighted-average number of [FAS135, ¶4(u)] options outstanding were exercised using the weighted-average exercise price (4,600,000 × $40)	$184,000,000
• Average unrecognized compensation balance during year[28]	17,700,000
Assumed proceeds	$201,700,000

[FAS128, ¶167(e)]

.239 [The] assumed repurchase of shares [is computed as follows]:

• Repurchase shares at average market price during the year ($201,700,000 ÷ $52)	3,878,846
• Incremental shares to be added (4,600,000 – 3,878,846)	721,154

The number of shares to be added to outstanding shares for purposes of the diluted earnings per share calculation is 721,154.

[FAS128, ¶167(f)]

.240 [Deleted 1/98 because of FASB Statement 128, *Earnings per Share.*]

Illustrative Disclosures

.241 Exhibit 241A illustrates disclosures of an entity's compensation plans. The illustration assumes that compensation cost has been recognized in accordance with the provisions of this section for several years. The amount of compensation cost recognized each year includes both costs from that year's grants and from prior years' grants. The number of options outstanding, exercised, forfeited, and expired each year includes options granted in prior years. The additional disclosures that would be required if the entity had elected to continue to recognize compensation cost in accordance with Section C47 are presented in paragraph .242. [FAS123, ¶362]

[28]Average unrecognized compensation balance is determined by averaging the beginning-of-the-year balance of cost measured and unrecognized and the end-of-year balance of cost measured and unrecognized. The assumed amount is $17,700,000 based on ongoing cost recognition for stock options granted in the current year and prior years. [FAS128, ¶167(e)]

Exhibit 241A

Illustration of Disclosures

Stock Compensation Plans

At December 31, 20Y6, the Company has four stock-based compensation plans, which are described below. The Company accounts for the fair value of its grants under those plans in accordance with FASB Statement 123, *Accounting for Stock-Based Compensation.* The compensation cost that has been charged against income for those plans was $23.3 million, $28.7 million, and $29.4 million for 20Y4, 20Y5, and 20Y6, respectively.

Fixed Stock Option Plans

The Company has two fixed option plans. Under the 20X9 Employee Stock Option Plan, the Company may grant options to its employees for up to 8 million shares of common stock. Under the 20Y4 Managers' Incentive Stock Option Plan, the Company may grant options to its management personnel for up to 5 million shares of common stock. Under both plans, the exercise price of each option equals the market price of the Company's stock on the date of grant and an option's maximum term is 10 years. Options are granted on January 1 and vest at the end of the third year under the 20X9 Plan and at the end of the second year under the 20Y4 Plan.

The fair value of each option grant is estimated on the date of grant using the Black-Scholes option-pricing model with the following weighted-average assumptions used for grants in 20Y4, 20Y5, and 20Y6, respectively: dividend yield of 1.5 percent for all years; expected volatility of 24, 26, and 29 percent, risk-free interest rates of 6.5, 7.5, and 7 percent for the 20X9 Plan options and 6.4, 7.4, and 6.8 percent for the 20Y4 Plan options; and expected lives of 6, 5, and 5 years for the 20X9 Plan options and 5, 4, and 4 years for the 20Y4 Plan options.

A summary of the status of the Company's two fixed stock option plans as of December 31, 20Y4, 20Y5, and 20Y6, and changes during the years ending on those dates is presented below:

Fixed Options	20Y4 Shares (000)	20Y4 Weighted-Average Exercise Price	20Y5 Shares (000)	20Y5 Weighted-Average Exercise Price	20Y6 Shares (000)	20Y6 Weighted-Average Exercise Price
Outstanding at beginning of year	4,500	$34	4,600	$38	4,660	$42
Granted	900	50	1,000	55	950	60
Exercised	(700)	27	(850)	34	(800)	36
Forfeited	(100)	46	(90)	51	(80)	59
Outstanding at end of year	4,600	38	4,660	42	4,730	47
Options exercisable at year-end	2,924		2,873		3,159	
Weighted-average fair value of options granted during the year	$15.90		$17.46		$19.57	

The following table summarizes information about fixed stock options outstanding at December 31, 20Y6:

	Options Outstanding			Options Exercisable	
Range of Exercise Prices	Number Outstanding at 12/31/Y6	Weighted-Average Remaining Contractual Life	Weighted-Average Exercise Price	Number Exercisable at 12/31/Y6	Weighted-Average Exercise Price
$25 to 33	1,107,000	3.6 years	$29	1,107,000	$29
39 to 41	467,000	5.0	40	467,000	40
46 to 50	1,326,000	6.6	48	1,326,000	48
55 to 60	1,830,000	8.5	57	259,000	55
$25 to 60	4,730,000	6.5	47	3,159,000	41

Performance-Based Stock Option Plan

Under its Goals 20Z0 Stock Option Plan adopted in 20Y2, each January 1 the Company grants selected executives and other key employees stock option awards whose vesting is contingent upon increases in the Company's market share for its principal product. If at the end of 3 years market share has increased by at least 5 percentage points from the date of grant, one-third of the options under the award vest to active employees. However, if at that date market share has increased by at least 10 percentage points, two-thirds of the options under the award vest, and if market share has increased by 20 percentage points or more, all of the options under the award vest. The number of shares subject to options under this plan cannot exceed 5 million. The exercise price of each option, which has a 10-year life, is equal to the market price of the Company's stock on the date of grant.

The fair value of each option grant was estimated on the date of grant using the Black-Scholes option-pricing model with the following assumptions for 20Y4, 20Y5, and 20Y6, respectively: risk-free interest rates of 6.5, 7.6, and 7.4 percent; dividend yield of 1.5 percent for all years; expected lives of 6, 6, and 7 years; and volatility of 24, 26, and 29 percent.

A summary of the status of the Company's performance-based stock option plan as of December 31, 20Y4, 20Y5, and 20Y6, and changes during the years ending on those dates is presented below:

Performance Options	20Y4 Shares (000)	20Y4 Weighted-Average Exercise Price	20Y5 Shares (000)	20Y5 Weighted-Average Exercise Price	20Y6 Shares (000)	20Y6 Weighted-Average Exercise Price
Outstanding at beginning of year	830	$46	1,635	$48	2,533	$51
Granted	850	50	980	55	995	60
Exercised	0		0		(100)	46
Forfeited	(45)	48	(82)	50	(604)	51
Outstanding at end of year	1,635	48	2,533	51	2,824	55
Options exercisable at year-end	0		780	46	936	47
Weighted-average fair value of options granted during the year	$16.25		$19.97		$24.32	

As of December 31, 20Y6, the 2.8 million performance options outstanding under the Plan have exercise prices between $46 and $60 and a weighted-average remaining contractual life of 7.7 years. The Company expects that approximately one-third of the nonvested awards at December 31, 20Y6, will eventually vest based on projected market share.

Employee Stock Purchase Plan

Under the 20W7 Employee Stock Purchase Plan, the Company is authorized to issue up to 10 million shares of common stock to its full-time employees, nearly all of whom are eligible to participate. Under the terms of the Plan, employees can choose each year to have up to 6 percent of their annual base earnings withheld to purchase the Company's common stock. The purchase price of the stock is 85 percent of the lower of its beginning-of-year or end-of-year market price. Approximately 75 to 80 percent of eligible employees have participated in the Plan in the last 3 years. Under the Plan, the Company sold 456,000 shares, 481,000 shares, and 503,000 shares to employees in 20Y4, 20Y5, and 20Y6, respectively. Compensation cost is recognized for the fair value of the employees' purchase rights, which was estimated using the Black-Scholes model with the following assumptions for 20Y4, 20Y5, and 20Y6, respectively: dividend yield of 1.5 percent for all years; an expected life of 1 year for all years; expected volatility of 22, 24, and 26 percent; and risk-free interest rates of 5.9, 6.9, and 6.7 percent. The weighted-average fair value of those purchase rights granted in 20Y4, 20Y5, and 20Y6 was $11.95, $13.73, and $15.30, respectively. [FAS123, ¶362]

.242 If compensation cost has been determined by applying Section C47 as permitted by this section (paragraph .104), the total compensation cost disclosed in the first paragraph of the illustrative disclosures [in Exhibit 241A] would need to be revised to reflect the cost recognized under Section C47. The following paragraph in Exhibit 242A would replace that paragraph; all other disclosures about the plans and related assumptions would be required. [FAS123, ¶363]

Exhibit 242A

Illustrative Pro Forma Disclosures

At December 31, 20Y6, the Company has four stock-based compensation plans, which are described below. The Company applies APB Opinion 25, *Accounting for Stock Issued to Employees,* and related Interpretations in accounting for its plans. Accordingly, no compensation cost has been recognized for its fixed stock option plans and its stock purchase plan. The compensation cost that has been charged against income for its performance-based plan was $6.7 million, $9.4 million, and $0.7 million for 20Y4, 20Y5, and 20Y6, respectively. Had compensation cost for the Company's four stock-based compensation plans been determined based on the fair value at the grant dates for awards under those plans consistent with the method of FASB Statement 123, *Accounting for*

Stock-Based Compensation, the Company's net income and earnings per share would have been reduced to the pro forma amounts indicated below:

		20Y4	20Y5	20Y6
Net income	As reported	$347,790	$407,300	$479,300
	Pro forma	$336,828	$394,553	$460,398
Primary earnings per share	As reported	$1.97	$2.29	$2.66
	Pro forma	$1.91	$2.22	$2.56
Fully diluted earnings per share	As reported	$1.49	$1.73	$2.02
	Pro forma	$1.44	$1.68	$1.94

[FAS123, ¶363]

Supplemental Disclosures

.243 In addition to the information required by this section, an entity may disclose supplemental information that it believes would be useful to investors and creditors, such as a range of values calculated on the basis of different assumptions, provided that the supplemental information is reasonable and does not discredit the information required by this section. The alternative assumptions should be described to enable users of the financial statements to understand the basis for the supplemental information. For example, if in the previous example the Company estimated in 20Y4 that its expected stock price volatility over the next 6 years was within a range of 24 to 32 percent in which no amount was a better estimate than any other amount, its use of a 24 percent volatility assumption is consistent with paragraph .154, which indicates that using an estimate at the low end of the range for expected volatility is appropriate in that circumstance. The Company could, however, choose to disclose supplementally the weighted-average fair value of stock options granted during the year (and related effect on the pro forma disclosures) based on the midpoint or the high end of the range of expected volatility. However, presenting supplemental disclosures based on, for example, an expected volatility assumption of 18 percent would not be appropriate because the Company had already concluded in making its calculations that an 18 percent assumption is below the range of reasonable assumptions. Presenting supplemental disclosures of the value of stock options based on an approach contrary to the methodology specified in this section, such as reflecting an additional discount related to the nontransferability of nonvested stock options, is similarly inappropriate. However, the Company's supplemental disclosures could include the intrinsic value of stock options exercised during the year. [FAS123, ¶364]

Calculating Historical Volatility

Introduction

.244 [The following paragraphs are intended to help the user understand the notion of volatility and to illustrate how to compute historical volatility.]

.245 As discussed in paragraphs .152 through .157, estimating expected long-term future volatility generally begins with calculating historical volatility for a similar long-term period and then considering the effects of ways in which the future is reasonably expected to differ from the past. For some mature entities, unadjusted long-term historical volatility may be the best available predictor of future long-term volatility. However, paragraphs .245 through .260 should be read in the context of paragraphs .163 and .164, which mention factors that should be considered in determining whether historical volatility is a reasonable indicator of expected future volatility. [FAS123, ¶396]

.246 The concept of volatility and the reason that it is an important factor in estimating the fair value of an option is well explained in various texts on option-pricing models and the use of derivative financial instruments. However, those texts are generally directed more at mathematicians than at accountants, and one without an extensive background in statistics and mathematics may find them difficult to understand. [FAS123, ¶397]

.247 The goal of paragraphs .249 through .260 is not to explain the development of traditional option-pricing models and why they are valid. Sources for that information are available. Several currently available articles and texts that explain option-pricing models and the place of volatility in option value are listed in paragraph .260. Paragraphs .249 through .260 are intended to help someone familiar with the use of electronic spreadsheets to compute historical volatility in three common situations. The illustrations do not provide a rigorous explanation of the mathematical concepts underlying the computations. In addition, the illustrations do not illustrate the only possible way of calculating historical volatility; for example, observations at daily or monthly, rather than weekly, intervals might have been used. [FAS123, ¶398]

.248 Paragraphs .249 through .260 also are not intended to deemphasize the importance of adjusting historical volatility, however computed, to reflect ways in which future volatility is reasonably expected to differ from historical volatility for entity-specific reasons. [FAS123, ¶399]

Volatility Is a Standard Deviation

.249 The needed assumption about expected volatility for use in the traditional Black-Scholes and binomial option-pricing models is the *annualized* standard deviation of the differences in the natural logarithms of the possible future stock prices. Natural logarithms are needed to compute the continuous rate of return reflected in the change from one stock price to another, plus dividends, if any. A standard deviation is a statistical method used to convert a series of natural logarithms of stock price changes into a single, usable statistic—volatility. Like rates of return, volatility can be measured over any time period. For convenience and consistency, volatility is generally expressed on an annual basis even if the measurement period is longer or shorter than one year. [FAS123, ¶400]

Computing Historical Volatility for a Stock That Pays No Dividends

.250 The first step in computing historical volatility is to gather the necessary stock prices. The expected lives of employee stock options generally are several years long, so weekly (perhaps even monthly) stock price observations generally should be sufficient. (Volatility estimates for shorter-term options, such as 30-, 60-, or 90-day options commonly traded on exchanges, generally rely on daily, or even more frequent, stock price observations.) The consistency of the time intervals between observations is critical—determining the frequency of the observations is not as critical, although the frequency of observations likely will affect the computed volatility. The time intervals between price observations should be as uniform as possible; for example, the weekly stock closing price could be used for all observations. It would not be appropriate to use the weekly closing price for some observations and, for example, the average weekly price for other observations in the same calculation. [FAS123, ¶401]

.251 [It is not known that there is] any research that demonstrates conclusively how long the historical period used to estimate expected long-term future volatility should be. However, informal tests and preliminary research tend to confirm the intuitive expectation that long-term historical volatility generally predicts long-term future volatility better than short-term historical volatility predicts long-term future volatility. Paragraph .164 of this section says that estimates of expected future long-term volatility should be based on historical volatility for a period that approximates the expected life of the option being valued. For example, if the expected life of an employee stock option is three years, historical volatility might be based on weekly closing stock prices for the most recent three years. In that situation, approximately 157 weekly stock price observations would be needed (52 observations per year for 3 years plus the initial observation). [FAS123, ¶402]

.252 For convenience, the illustrative calculations are based on only 20 price observations, which is generally considered to be the minimum number of sample observations necessary to compute a statistically valid estimate of standard deviation. Therefore, Exhibit 253A shows the calculation of the annualized historical volatility based on 19 weeks of stock price activity. More than 20 price observations would be necessary for long-term employee stock options; more observations also would improve the statistical validity of the estimate of expected volatility. [FAS123, ¶403]

.253 In Exhibit 253A column B contains the 20 stock price observations for the 19-week period. Each cell in column C contains the ratio of the stock price at the end of that week to the stock price at the end of the preceding week. That is designated by the symbol P_n/P_{n-1}. For example, in week 4, the number in column C is computed as the week 4 stock closing price ($48.50) divided by the week 3 stock closing price ($51.00), or 0.95098. Column D is the natural logarithm (the mathematical expression *Ln*) of the amount computed in column C. The weekly volatility estimate is the standard deviation of the amounts shown in column D. Most, if not all, electronic spreadsheets include a standard deviation function that will automatically compute the standard deviation of a series of amounts. [FAS123, ¶404]

Exhibit 253A

Calculation of Annualized Historical Volatility

A	B	C	D
Date	Stock Price	P_n/P_{n-1}	$Ln(P_n/P_{n-1})$
Week 0	$50.00		
Week 1	51.50	1.030000	0.029559
Week 2	52.00	1.009709	0.009662
Week 3	51.00	0.980769	-0.019418
Week 4	48.50	0.950980	-0.050262
Week 5	46.50	0.958763	-0.042111
Week 6	45.75	0.983871	-0.016261
Week 7	50.50	1.103825	0.098782
Week 8	53.50	1.059406	0.057708
Week 9	51.75	0.967290	-0.033257
Week 10	53.25	1.028986	0.028573
Week 11	54.50	1.023474	0.023203
Week 12	56.00	1.027523	0.027151
Week 13	53.50	0.955357	-0.045670
Week 14	52.00	0.971963	-0.028438
Week 15	55.00	1.057692	0.056089
Week 16	56.25	1.022727	0.022473
Week 17	58.00	1.031111	0.030637
Week 18	55.50	0.956897	-0.044060
Week 19	56.00	1.009009	0.008969
Weekly Volatility			**0.041516**
Annualized Volatility	$0.041516\sqrt{52}$		**0.299**

[FAS123, ¶404]

.254 Weekly volatility must be converted to an annualized measure of volatility before it can be used in most option-pricing models. To convert from periodic to annualized volatility, the periodic volatility is multiplied by the square root of the number of periods in a year. In this example, weekly observations are used. There are 52 weeks in a year, so weekly volatility is multiplied by the square root of 52 to convert it to annualized volatility. If monthly stock price observations were used, the monthly volatility would be multiplied by the square root of 12 to convert to annualized volatility. Likewise, daily volatility would be multiplied by the square root of the number of trading days in the year to compute annualized volatility (about 260). The annualization calculation is independent of the number of observations used to compute the periodic historical volatility. For example, whether 20 or 157 weeks of data are used to compute weekly volatility, that weekly volatility must be multiplied by the square root of 52 to convert it to annual volatility. [FAS123, ¶405]

Computing Historical Volatility for a Dividend-Paying Stock

.255 Computing volatility for a dividend-paying stock is very similar to computing volatility for a stock that does not pay dividends. The only difference is an adjustment for dividends paid. Because volatility is defined as the standard deviation of the total return on a stock, dividend payments, which are part of the total return, affect the computation. The price change resulting solely from the effect of dividend payment on the stock price must be removed from the price observations used to calculate volatility. [FAS123, ¶406]

.256 As discussed in paragraph .250, stock price observations used in the calculations should be separated by uniform time periods. When gathering data, it is important to observe the payment of dividends. If an ex-dividend date occurs between two price observations, the per-share dollar amount of the dividends should be noted. For example, if the ex-dividend date for a dividend of one dollar occurs between the third and fourth weekly price observations, that payment should be noted when gathering stock price observations. In computing historical volatility, dividends must be added to the stock price after the ex-dividend date before the ratio in column C (the price after the dividend to the price before the dividend) is computed [because] the market reflects the effect on the stock price of a [declared] dividend payment on the ex-dividend date, not the date of the cash distribution. [FAS123, ¶407]

.257 Exhibit 257A illustrates the computation of historical volatility based on weekly stock closing prices for a company that pays a dividend of $1 between both the week 3 and week 4 price observations and the week 15 and week 16 price observations. [FAS123, ¶408]

Exhibit 257A

Computation of Historical Volatility Based on Weekly Stock Closing Prices

A	B	C	D
Date	**Stock Price**	P_n/P_{n-1}	$Ln(P_n/P_{n-1})$
Week 0	$50.00		
Week 1	51.50	1.030000	0.029559
Week 2	52.00	1.009709	0.009662
Week 3	51.00	0.980769	-0.019418
Week 4	48.50		
Dividend Adjusted	49.50	0.970588	-0.029853
Week 5	46.50	0.958763	-0.042111
Week 6	45.75	0.983871	-0.016261
Week 7	50.50	1.103825	0.098782
Week 8	53.50	1.059406	0.057708
Week 9	51.75	0.967290	-0.033257
Week 10	53.25	1.028986	0.028573
Week 11	54.50	1.023474	0.023203
Week 12	56.00	1.027523	0.027151
Week 13	53.50	0.955357	-0.045670
Week 14	52.00	0.971963	-0.028438
Week 15	55.00	1.057692	0.056089
Week 16	56.25		
Dividend Adjusted	57.25	1.040909	0.040094
Week 17	58.00	1.031111	0.030637
Week 18	55.50	0.956897	-0.044060
Week 19	56.00	1.009009	0.008969
Weekly Volatility			**0.040799**
Annualized Volatility	$.040799\sqrt{52}$		**0.294**

[FAS123, ¶408]

.258 The only difference between Exhibit 257A and Exhibit 253A is the necessary adjustment in Exhibit 257A for the dividend payments made between the week 3 and week 4 observations and between the week 15 and week 16 observations. In each case, the ratio of the current period stock price to the prior period stock price must be adjusted for the dividend payment. For example, the pre-dividend week 3 observation is used in the ratio of the week 3 stock price to the week 2 stock price. Then, the post-dividend week 4 stock price must be adjusted by the amount of the dividend payment before the ratio of the week 4 stock price to the week 3 stock price is computed in column C (both stock prices in the ratio must be either pre-dividend or post-dividend). That adjustment is necessary to isolate the price change effect in the change from week 3 to week 4 that is independent from the stock price decrease caused by the dividend payment. [FAS123, ¶409]

Computing Historical Volatility for a Stock That Has Split

.259 If a stock split occurs during the historical period over which volatility is to be calculated, an adjustment much like the one for a dividend payment is required for that split. For computing the ratio of the stock prices around the period of the split, the prices must be shown in consistent form, that is, either pre-split or post-split. For example, in Exhibit 257A, if a stock split had occurred between the week 16 and week 17 stock price observations, the price observed in week 17 would be $29 instead of the $58 shown in the table. For computing column B, the ratio of the week 16 stock price to the week 15 stock price would be unchanged, but the ratio of the week 17 to the week 16 price would need adjustment. The split-adjusted week 17 stock price of $29 should be divided by the split-adjusted week 16 stock price, which is $28.125. After the adjustment is made for the stock split, the calculation of historical volatility is the same as in Exhibit 257A. If the only difference from the Exhibit 257A stock price changes is the stock split, the historical volatility would be the same as the volatility computed in Exhibit 257A because the stock split would not alter the relative size of the random stock price changes that volatility measures. [FAS123, ¶410]

Sources for Further Information about Option-Pricing Models and Volatility

.260 The following sources provide further information on option-pricing models and the relationship of volatility to option value:

- Black, Fischer, and Myron Scholes. "The Pricing of Options and Corporate Liabilities." *The Journal of Political Economy 81,* 3 (May-June 1973): 637-654.
- Cox, John C., and Mark Rubinstein. *Option Markets.* Englewood Cliffs, N.J.: Prentice-Hall, Inc., 1985.
- Figlewski, Stephen, William L. Silber, and Marti G. Subrahmanyam, eds. *Financial Options: From Theory to Practice.* New York: New York University, Business One Irwin, 1990.
- Hull, John C. *Options, Futures, and Other Derivative Securities.* Englewood Cliffs, N.J.: Prentice-Hall, Inc., 1993.
- Smithson, Charles W., Clifford W. Smith, Jr., and D. Sykes Wilford. *Managing Financial Risk.* New York: Richard D. Irwin, Inc., 1995.

Those sources include the classic works in which the Black-Scholes and binomial option-pricing models were first developed and other sources that may be useful. [FAS123, ¶411]

Glossary

.401 **Combination plan.** An award with two (or more) separate components, all of which can be exercised. Each part of the award is actually a separate grant, and compensation cost is measured and recognized for each grant. [FAS123, ¶395]

.402 **Cross-volatility.** A measure of the relationship between the volatilities of the prices of two assets taking into account the correlation between price movements in the assets. [FAS123, ¶395]

.403 **Fair value.** The amount at which an asset could be bought or sold in a current transaction between willing parties, that is, other than in a forced or liquidation sale. Quoted market prices in active markets are the best evidence of fair value and are to be used as the basis for measurement, if available. If quoted market prices are not available, the estimate of fair value is based on the best information available in the circumstances. The estimate of fair value considers prices for similar assets and the results of valuation techniques to the extent available in the circumstances. Examples of valuation techniques include the present value of estimated expected future cash flows using a discount rate commensurate with the risks involved, option-pricing models, matrix pricing, option-adjusted spread models, and fundamental analysis. [FAS123, ¶395]

.404 **Fixed award.** An award of stock-based employee compensation for which vesting is based solely on an employee's continuing to render service to the employer for a specified period of time, that is, an award that does not specify a performance condition for vesting. This section uses the term *fixed award* in a somewhat different sense than Section C47 uses the same or similar terms because Section C47 distinguishes between fixed awards and variable awards, while this section only distinguishes between fixed awards and performance awards. For example, Section C47 does not consider stock appreciation rights (SARs), regardless of whether they call for settlement in stock or in cash, to be fixed awards because the number of shares to which an employee is entitled is not known until the exercise date. This section considers an SAR that calls for settlement in stock to be substantially the same as a fixed stock option. A cash SAR is an indexed liability pursuant to this section, and the measurement date is the settlement (exercise) date because that is consistent with accounting for similar liabilities—not because a cash SAR is a variable award. [FAS123, ¶395]

.405 **Grant date.** The date at which an employer and an employee have a mutual understanding of the terms of a stock-based compensation award. The employer becomes contingently obligated on the grant date to issue equity instruments or transfer assets to employees who fulfill vesting requirements. Awards made under a plan that is subject to shareholder approval are not deemed to be granted until that approval is obtained unless approval is essentially a formality, for example, management and the members of the board of directors control enough votes to approve the plan. The grant date of an award for current service may be the end of a fiscal period instead of a subsequent date when an award is made to an individual employee if (a) the award is provided for by the terms of an established formal plan, (b) the plan designates the factors that determine the total dollar amount of awards to employees for that period (for example, a percentage of net income), and (c) the award is attributable to the employee's service during that period. [FAS123, ¶395]

.406 **Intrinsic value.** The amount by which the market price of the underlying stock exceeds the exercise price of an option. For example, an option with an exercise price of $20 on a stock whose current market price is $25 has an intrinsic value of $5. [FAS123, ¶395]

.407 **Issuance of an equity instrument.** An equity instrument is issued when the issuing entity receives the agreed-upon consideration, which may be cash, an enforceable right to receive cash or another financial instrument, goods, or services. An entity may conditionally transfer an equity instrument to another party under an arrangement that permits that party to choose at a later date or for a specified time whether to deliver the consideration or to forfeit the right to the conditionally transferred instrument with no further obligation. In that situation, the equity instrument is not *issued* until the issuing entity has received the consideration. For that reason, this section does not use the term *issued* for the grant of stock options or other equity instruments subject to service or performance conditions (or both) for vesting. [FAS123, ¶395]

.408 **Measurement date.** The date at which the stock price that enters into measurement of the fair value of an award of employee stock-based compensation is fixed. [FAS123, ¶395]

.409 **Minimum value.** An amount attributed to an option that is calculated without considering the expected volatility of the underlying stock. Minimum value may be computed using a standard option-pricing model and a volatility of effectively zero. It also may be computed as (a) the current price of the stock reduced to exclude the present value of any expected dividends during the option's life minus (b) the present value of the exercise price. Different methods of reducing the current price of the stock for the present value of the expected dividends, if any, may result in different computed minimum values. [FAS123, ¶395]

.410 **Nonpublic entity.** Any entity other than one (a) whose equity securities trade in a public market either on a stock exchange (domestic or foreign) or in the over-the-counter market, including securities quoted only locally or regionally, (b) that makes a filing with a regulatory agency in preparation for the sale of any class of equity securities in a public market, or (c) that is controlled by an entity covered by (a) or (b). [FAS123, ¶395]

.411 **Nonvested stock.** Shares of stock that cannot currently be sold because the employee to whom the shares were granted has not yet satisfied the vesting requirements necessary to earn the right to the shares. The restriction on sale of nonvested stock is due to the forfeitability of the shares. A share of nonvested stock also can be described as a nonvested employee stock option with a cash exercise price of zero—employee services are the only consideration the employer has received for the stock when the option is "exercised," and the employer issues vested, unrestricted shares to the employee. [FAS123, ¶395]

.412 **Performance condition or performance award.** An award of stock-based employee compensation for which vesting depends on both (a) an employee's rendering service to the employer for a specified period of time and (b) the achievement of a specified performance target, for example, attaining a specified growth rate in return on assets or a specified percentage increase in market share for a specified product. A performance condition might pertain either to the performance of the enterprise as a whole or to some part of the enterprise, such as a division. [FAS123, ¶395]

.413 **Principal stockholder.** One who either owns 10 percent or more of an entity's common stock or has the ability, directly or indirectly, to control or significantly influence the entity. [FAS123, ¶395]

.414 **Public entity.** Any entity (a) whose equity securities trade in a public market either on a stock exchange (domestic or foreign) or in the over-the-counter market, including securities quoted only locally or regionally, (b) that makes a filing with a regulatory agency in preparation for the sale of any class of equity securities in a public market, or (c) that is controlled by an entity covered by (a) or (b). [FAS123, ¶395]

.415 **Reload option and option granted with a reload feature.** An option with a reload feature is one that provides for automatic grants of additional options whenever an employee exercises previously granted options using shares of stock, rather than cash, to satisfy the exercise price. At the time of exercise using shares, the employee is automatically granted a new option, called a *reload option* for the same number of shares used to exercise the previous option. The number of reload options granted is the number of shares tendered, and the exercise price of the reload option is the market price of the stock on the date the reload option is granted. All terms of the reload option, such as expiration date and vesting status, are the same as the terms of the previous option. [FAS123, ¶395]

.416 **Restricted stock.** Shares of stock for which sale is contractually or governmentally restricted for a given period of time. Most stock grants to employees are better termed *nonvested stock* because the limitation on sale stems solely from the forfeitability of the shares before employees have satisfied the necessary service or performance requirements to earn the rights to the shares. Restricted stock issued for consideration other than employee services, on the other hand, is fully paid for immediately, that is, there is no period analogous to a vesting period during which the issuer is unilaterally obligated to issue the stock when the purchaser pays for it, but the purchaser is not obligated to buy the stock. This section uses the term *restricted stock* to refer only to fully vested and outstanding stock whose sale is contractually or governmentally restricted. (Refer to the definition of *nonvested stock*.) [FAS123, ¶395]

.417 **Service period.** The period or periods during which the employee performs the service in exchange for stock options or similar awards. If the service period is not defined as an earlier or shorter period, the service period is presumed to be the vesting period. However, if performance conditions affect either the exercise price or the exercisability date, this section requires that the service period over which compensation cost is attributed be consistent with the related assumption used in estimating the fair value of the award. Doing so will require estimates at the grant date, which will be subsequently adjusted as necessary to reflect experience that differs from initial expectations. [FAS123, ¶395]

.418 **Stock option.** A contract that gives the holder the right, but not the obligation, either to purchase or to sell a certain number of shares of stock at a predetermined price for a specified period of time. [FAS123, ¶395]

.419 **Stock-based compensation plan.** A compensation arrangement under which one or more employees receive shares of stock, stock options, or other equity instruments, or the employer incurs a liability(ies) to the employee(s) in amounts based on the price of the employer's stock. [FAS123, ¶395]

.420 **Substantive terms.** The terms of a stock-based compensation plan as those terms are mutually understood by the employer and the employee who receives a stock-based award under the plan. Although the written terms of a stock-based compensation plan usually provide the best evidence of the plan's terms, an entity's past practice may indicate that some aspects of the substantive terms differ from the written terms. [FAS123, ¶395]

.421 **Tandem plan.** An award with two (or more) components in which exercise of one part cancels the other(s). [FAS123, ¶395]

.422 **Time value.** The portion of the fair value of an option that exceeds its intrinsic value. For example, an option with an exercise price of $20 on a stock whose current market price is $25 has intrinsic value of $5. If the fair value of that option is $7, the time value of the option is $2 ($7 – $5). [FAS123, ¶395]

.423 **Vest or Vested.** To earn the rights to. An employee's award of stock-based compensation becomes vested at the date that the employee's right to receive or retain shares of stock or cash under the award is no longer contingent on remaining in the service of the employer or the achievement of a performance condition (other than the achievement of a target stock price or specified amount of intrinsic value). Typically, an employee stock option that is vested also is immediately exercisable. [FAS123, ¶395]

.424 **Volatility.** A measure of the amount by which a price has fluctuated (historical volatility) or is expected to fluctuate (expected volatility) during a period. The volatility of a stock is the standard deviation of the continuously compounded rates of return on the stock over a specified period. That is the same as the standard deviation of the differences in the natural logarithms of the stock prices plus dividends, if any, over the period. The higher the volatility, the more the returns on the stock can be expected to vary—up or down. Volatility is typically expressed in annualized terms that are comparable regardless of the time period used in the calculation, for example, daily, weekly, or monthly price observations.

The *rate of return* (which may be positive or negative) on a stock for a period measures how much a stockholder has benefited from dividends and appreciation (or depreciation) of the share price. Return on a stated rate increases as compounding becomes more frequent, approaching e^{rate} as a limit as the frequency of compounding approaches continuous. For example, the continuously compounded return on a stated rate of 9 percent is $e^{(.09)}$. (The base of the natural logarithm system is *e*, which is a constant, transcendental number, the first 5 digits of which are 2.7183.) Stock price changes are log-normally distributed, but continuously compounded rates of return on stocks are normally distributed.

The expected annualized volatility of a stock is the range within which the continuously compounded annual rate of return is expected to fall roughly two-thirds of the time. For example, to say that a stock with an expected continuously compounded rate of return of 12 percent has a volatility of 30 percent means that the probability that the rate of return on the stock for 1 year will fall between -18 percent (12% – 30%) and 42 percent (12% + 30%) is approximately two-thirds. If the stock price is $100 at the beginning of the year and it does not pay dividends, the year-end price would be expected to fall between $83.53 ($100 $\times$ $e^{(-.18)}$) and $152.20 ($100 $\times$ $e^{(.42)}$) approximately two-thirds of the time.

For the convenience of those who are not familiar with the concept of volatility, paragraphs .244 through .260 provide more information on volatility and show one way in which an electronic spreadsheet may be used to calculate historical volatility based on weekly price observations. [FAS123, ¶395]

[illegible] price. Vesting period: [illegible] the employee [illegible] employee [illegible] the service [illegible] of a [illegible] condition [illegible] or specified amount [illegible] vesting [illegible]

Volatility: A measure of the amount by which a price has fluctuated (historical volatility) or is expected to fluctuate (expected volatility) during a period. The volatility of a stock is the standard deviation of the continuously compounded rates of return on the stock over a specified period. That is the same as the standard deviation of the differences in the natural logarithms of the stock prices plus dividends, if any, over the period. The higher the volatility, the more the returns on the stock can be expected to vary—up or down. Volatility is typically expressed in annualized terms that are comparable regardless of the time period used in the calculation (for example, daily, weekly, or monthly price observations).

The rate of return (which may be positive or negative) on a stock for a period measures how much a stockholder has benefited from dividends and appreciation (or depreciation) in the share price. [illegible] continuously compounded [illegible] (The base of the natural logarithm [illegible]) [illegible] normally distributed.

The expected annualized volatility of a stock is the range within which the continuously compounded annual rate of return is expected to fall approximately two-thirds of the time. For example, to say that a stock with an expected continuously compounded rate of return of 12 percent has a volatility of 30 percent means that the probability that the rate of return on the stock for 1 year will fall between [illegible] (12% − 30%) and [illegible] (12% + 30%) is approximately two-thirds. [illegible] the year-end [illegible] would be expected to fall between [illegible] and [illegible] approximately two-thirds of the time.

[illegible] of the volatility [illegible] with the [illegible] information [illegible] may be used [illegible]

Supplemental Guidance

Accounting for Certain Employee Stock Purchase Plans with a Look-Back Option

.501 *Question*—Illustration 9 of this section provides the only specific guidance on measuring the compensation cost associated with an award under a compensatory employee stock purchase plan (ESPP) with a look-back option (paragraphs .227 through .232). Does the fair value measurement technique specifically described in paragraphs .227 through .232 appropriately value awards under all types of ESPPs with a look-back option? [FTB97-1, ¶5] [Refer to paragraph .503 for a description of all types of ESPPs with a look-back option.]

.502 *Response*—No. The measurement approach described in paragraphs .227 through .232[501] of this section was developed to illustrate how the fair value of an award under a basic type of ESPP with a look-back option could be determined at the grant date by focusing on the substance of the arrangement and valuing separately each feature of the award. Although that general technique of valuing an award as the sum of the values of its separate components applies to all types of ESPPs with a look-back option, the fundamental components of an award may differ from plan to plan thus affecting the individual calculations. For example, the measurement approach described in paragraphs .227 through .232 assumes that the maximum number of shares that an employee may purchase is fixed at the grant date based on the grant date stock price and the employee's elected withholdings (that is, the Type A plan described in paragraph .503 of this section). That approach needs to be modified to appropriately determine the fair value of awards under the other types of plans described in paragraph .503, including a Type B plan, that do not fix the number of shares that an employee is permitted to purchase. [FTB97-1, ¶6]

.503 *Background*—The following are examples of some of the more common types of ESPPs with a look-back option that currently exist and the features that differentiate each type:

a. *Maximum number of shares:* This type of plan permits an employee to have withheld a fixed amount of dollars from the employee's salary (or a stated percentage of the employee's salary) over a one-year period to purchase stock. At the end of the one-

[501] The examples in this section [that illustrate how the fair value of an award under an ESPP with a look-back option could be determined] illustrate the use of the Black-Scholes option pricing model. It also may be acceptable to use a binomial option pricing model to value an award under an ESPP with a look-back option. [FTB97-1, ¶6, fn2]

year period, the employee may purchase stock at 85 percent of the lower of the grant date stock price or the exercise date stock price. If the exercise date stock price is lower than the grant date stock price, the employee may *not* purchase additional shares (that is, the maximum number of shares that may be purchased by an employee is established at the grant date based on the stock price at that date and the employee's elected withholdings); any excess cash is refunded to the employee. This is the basic type of ESPP illustrated in paragraphs .227 through .232 and is referred to as the Type A plan for purposes of paragraphs .501 through .519.

b. *Variable number of shares:* This type of plan is the same as the Type A plan except that the employee may purchase as many shares as the full amount of the employee's withholdings will permit, regardless of whether the exercise date stock price is lower than the grant date stock price. (Type B plan)

c. *Multiple purchase periods:* This type of plan permits an employee to have withheld a fixed amount of dollars from the employee's salary (or a stated percentage of the employee's salary) over a two-year period to purchase stock. At the end of each six-month period, the employee may purchase stock at 85 percent of the lower of the grant date stock price or the exercise date stock price based on the amount of dollars withheld during that period. (Type C plan)

d. *Multiple purchase periods with a reset mechanism:* This type of plan is the same as the Type C plan except that the plan contains a "reset" feature if the market price of the stock at the end of any six-month purchase period is lower than the stock price at the original grant date. In that case, the plan "resets" so that during the next purchase period an employee may purchase stock at 85 percent of the lower of the stock price at (1) the beginning of the purchase period (rather than the original grant date price) or (2) the exercise date. (Type D plan)

e. *Multiple purchase periods with a rollover mechanism:* This type of plan is the same as the Type C plan except that the plan contains a "rollover" feature if the market price of the stock at the end of any six-month purchase period is lower than the stock price at the original grant date. In that case, the plan is immediately canceled after that purchase date, and a new two-year plan is established using the then-current stock price as the base purchase price. (Type E plan)

f. *Multiple purchase periods with semifixed withholdings:* This type of plan is the same as the Type C plan except that the amount (or percentage) that the employee may elect to have withheld is not fixed and may be changed (increased or decreased) at the employee's election immediately after each six-month purchase date for purposes of all future withholdings under the plan. (Type F plan)

g. *Single purchase period with variable withholdings:* This type of plan permits an employee to have withheld an amount of dollars from the employee's salary (or a stated percentage of the employee's salary) over a one-year period to purchase stock. That amount (or percentage) is not fixed and may be changed (increased or decreased) at the employee's election at any time during the term of the plan for purposes of all future withholdings under the plan. At the end of the one-year period, the employee may purchase stock at 85 percent of the lower of the grant date stock price or the exercise date stock price. (Type G plan)

h. *Multiple purchase periods with variable withholdings:* This type of plan combines the characteristics of the Type C and Type G plans in that there are multiple purchase periods over the term of the plan and an employee is permitted to change (increase or decrease) withholding amounts (or percentages) at any time during the term of the plan for purposes of all future withholdings under the plan. (Type H plan)
i. *Single purchase period with variable withholdings and cash infusions:* This type of plan is the same as the Type G plan except that an employee is permitted to remit "catch-up" amounts to the company when (and if) the employee increases withholding amounts (or percentages). The objective of the cash infusion feature is to permit an employee to increase withholding amounts (or percentages) during the term of the plan and remit an amount to the company such that, on the exercise date, it appears that the employee had participated at the new higher amount (or percentage) during the entire term of the plan. (Type I plan)

The distinguishing characteristic between the Type A plan and the Type B plan is whether the maximum number of shares that an employee is permitted to purchase is fixed at the grant date based on the stock price at that date and the expected withholdings. Each of the remaining plans described above (Type C through Type I plans) incorporates the features of either a Type A plan or a Type B plan. The above descriptions are intended to be representative of the types of features commonly found in many existing plans. The accounting guidance in paragraphs .502 and .505 through .519 should be applied to all plans with characteristics similar to those described above. [FTB97-1, ¶4]

.504 Although many ESPPs with a look-back option initially limit the maximum number of shares of stock that the employee is permitted to purchase under the plan (Type A plans), other ESPPs (Type B plans) do not fix the number of shares that the employee is permitted to purchase if the exercise date stock price is lower than the grant date stock price. In effect, an ESPP that does not fix the number of shares that may be purchased has guaranteed that the employee can always receive the value associated with *at least* 15 percent of the stock price at the grant date (the employee can receive much more than 15 percent of the grant date value of the stock if the stock appreciates during the look-back period). That provision provides the employee with the equivalent of a put option on 15 percent of the shares with an exercise price equal to the stock price at the grant date. In contrast, an employee who participates in a Type A plan is only guaranteed 15 percent of *the lower of* the stock price as of the grant date or the exercise date, which is the equivalent of a call option on 85 percent of the shares (as described more fully in paragraph .231 of this section). A participant in a Type B plan receives the equivalent of both a put option and a call option. [FTB97-1, ¶7]

Measurement Approach for Type B ESPP

.505 *Question*—How should the measurement approach in paragraphs .227 through .232 be modified to determine the fair value of an award under an ESPP with a look-back option that does not fix the number of shares that an employee is permitted to purchase (that is, a Type B plan)? [FTB97-1, ¶9]

.506 *Response*—Using the component measurement approach described in paragraphs .227 through .232 as the base, the additional feature associated with a Type B plan that should be included in the fair value calculation is 15 percent of a put option on the employer's stock (valued by use of a standard option-pricing model, using the same measurement assumptions that were used to value the 85 percent of a call option). If the plan in paragraph .228[502] had the provisions of a Type B plan (that is, a plan that does not fix the number of shares that may be purchased), the fair value of the award would be calculated at the grant date as follows:

• 0.15 of a share of nonvested stock ($50 × 0.15)	$ 7.50
• One-year call on 0.85 of a share of stock, exercise price of $50 ($7.56 × 0.85)	6.43
• One-year put on 0.15 of a share of stock, exercise price of $50 ($4.27 × 0.15)[503]	0.64
Total grant date fair value	$14.57

[FTB97-1, ¶10]

.507 In each of the examples in paragraphs .501 through .519, total compensation cost would be measured at the grant date based on the number of shares that can be purchased using the estimated total withholdings and market price of the stock as of the grant date, and not based on the potentially greater number of shares that may ultimately be purchased if the market price declines. In other words, assume that on January 1, 20X0, Employee A elects to have $850 withheld from his pay for the year to purchase

[502]The fair value of the Type A ESPP award described in paragraphs .227 through .232 is determined as follows:

• 0.15 of a share of nonvested stock ($50 × 0.15)	$ 7.50
• One-year call on 0.85 of a share of stock, exercise price of $50 ($7.56 × 0.85)	6.43
Total grant date fair value	$13.93

[FTB97-1, ¶10, fn7]

[503]Other assumptions are the same as those used to value the call option; $50 stock price, an expected life of 1 year, expected volatility of 30 percent, risk-free interest rate of 6.8 percent, and a zero dividend yield. [FTB97-1, ¶10, fn8]

stock. Total compensation cost for the Type B plan award to Employee A would be $291 ($14.57 × 20 grant-date-based shares [$850/$42.50[504]]). [FTB97-1, ¶11]

.508 Paragraphs .227 through .232 of this section do not take into consideration the effect of interest forgone by the employee on the fair value of an award for which the exercise price is paid over time (for instance, through payroll withholdings). Awards for which part or all of the exercise price is paid before the exercise date are less valuable than awards for which the exercise price is paid at the exercise date, and it is appropriate to recognize that difference in applying this section. However, for simplicity and to be consistent with paragraphs .227 through .232, the effect of forgone interest is not reflected in the fair value calculations for the examples in paragraphs .501 through .519. [FTB97-1, ¶12]

Measurement Approach for Types C, D, E, F, G, H, and I ESPPs

.509 *Question*—As noted in paragraph .503, the characteristics associated with either a Type A plan or a Type B plan are incorporated in other ESPPs with a look-back option. The measurement approach described in paragraphs .227 through .232 of this section (for the Type A plan) as modified in paragraph .506 (for the Type B plan) forms the basis for determining the fair value of awards under the other types of ESPPs with a look-back option. What additional modifications are necessary to determine the fair value of awards under the other types of ESPPs described in paragraph .503? [FTB97-1, ¶13]

.510 *Response (Type C Plan)*—In substance, an ESPP with multiple purchase periods (a Type C plan) is a series of linked awards, similar in nature to how some view a graded vesting stock option plan. Accordingly, the fair value of an award under an ESPP with multiple purchase periods should be determined at the grant date in the same manner as an award under a graded vesting stock option plan. Under the graded vesting approach, awards under a two-year plan with purchase periods at the end of each year would be valued as having two separate option tranches both starting on the initial grant date (using the approach in paragraphs .227 through .232 if the plan has the characteristics of a Type A plan or using the approach in paragraph .505 [which modifies the approach used in paragraphs .227 through .232] if the plan has the characteristics of a Type B plan) but with different lives of 12 and 24 months, respectively. All other measurement assumptions would need to be consistent with the separate lives of each tranche. [FTB97-1, ¶14]

---

[504]For purposes of determining the number of shares on which to measure compensation cost, the stock price as of the grant date less the discount, or $50 × 85 percent, is used. [FTB97-1, ¶11, fn9].

.511 For example, if the plan in paragraph .228 was a two-year Type C plan with purchase periods at the end of each year, the fair value of each tranche of the award would be calculated at the grant date as follows:

Tranche No. 1:

• 0.15 of a share of nonvested stock ($50 × 0.15)	$ 7.50
• One-year call on 0.85 of a share of stock, exercise price of $50 ($7.56 × 0.85)[505]	6.43
Total grant date fair value of the first tranche	$13.93

Tranche No. 2:

• 0.15 of a share of nonvested stock ($50 × 0.15)	$ 7.50
• Two-year call on 0.85 of a share of stock, exercise price of $50 ($11.44 × 0.85)[506]	9.72
Total grant date fair value of the second tranche	$17.22

[FTB97-1, ¶15]

.512 *Response (Types D, E, F, G, and H Plans)*—The basic measurement approach described above for a Type C plan also should be used to value awards under ESPPs with multiple purchase periods that incorporate reset or rollover mechanisms (that is, Type D and Type E plans). The fair value of those awards initially can be determined at the grant date using the graded vesting measurement approach. However, at the date that the reset or rollover mechanism becomes effective, the terms of the award have been modified (the exercise price has been decreased and, for a grant under a Type E plan, the term of the award has been extended) which, in substance, is similar to an exchange of the original award for a new award with different terms. [The] modification accounting [prescribed in this section] should be applied at the date that the reset or rollover mechanism becomes effective to determine the amount of any incremental fair value associated with the modified grant. [FTB97-1, ¶16]

.513 Likewise, although not a change to the terms of the ESPP, an election by an employee to increase withholding amounts (or percentages) for future services (Type F through Type H plans) is a modification of the terms of the award to that employee, which, in substance, is similar to an exchange of the original award for a new award with different

[505]The other assumptions are $50 stock price, an expected life of 1 year, expected volatility of 30 percent, risk-free interest rate of 6.8 percent, and a zero dividend yield (same assumptions as in footnote 503). To simplify the illustration, the fair value of each of the tranches is based on the same assumptions about volatility, the risk-free interest rate, and expected dividend yield. In practice, each of those assumptions would be related to the expected life of the respective tranche, which means that at least the risk-free interest rate, and perhaps all three assumptions, would differ for each tranche. [FTB97-1, ¶15, fn10]

[506]Refer to footnote 505. [FTB97-1, ¶15, fn11]

terms. Accordingly, the fair value of an award under an ESPP with variable withholdings should be determined at the grant date (using the Type A, Type B, or Type C measurement approach, as applicable) based on the estimated amounts (or percentages) that a participating employee initially elects to withhold under the terms of the plan. Subsequent to the grant date (except as noted in paragraph .518), any increases in withholding amounts (or percentages) for future services should be accounted for as a plan modification in accordance with the guidance in paragraph .134 of this section. [FTB97-1, ¶17]

.514 To illustrate, if the plan described in paragraph .511 allowed an employee to elect to change withholdings at the end of the first year, modification accounting would be applied at the date the employee elected to increase withholdings to determine the amount, if any, of incremental compensation cost. Assume that on January 1, 20X0, Employee A initially elected to have $850 per year withheld from his pay for each purchase period. However, at the end of year 1 when the stock price is $60 (and assume that no other factors have changed), Employee A elects to have a total of $1,275 withheld for the second purchase period. At that date, $1,275 is equivalent to 30 shares eligible for purchase at the end of the second year ($1,275/$42.50). At the date Employee A elects to increase withholdings, modification accounting should be applied to determine the amount of any incremental fair value associated with the modified award as follows:[507]

Fair value of the old option (Tranche No. 2) before modification:	
• 0.15 of a share of nonvested stock ($60 × 0.15)	$ 9.00
• One-year call on 0.85 of a share of stock, exercise price of $50 ($15.10 × 0.85)	12.84
Total fair value of each option	$21.84
Number of grant date shares ($850/$42.50)	× 20
Total fair value	$ 437
Fair value of the new option after modification:	
• 0.15 of a share of nonvested stock ($60 × 0.15)	$ 9.00
• One-year call on 0.85 of a share of stock, exercise price of $50 ($15.10 × 0.85)	12.84
Total fair value of each option	$21.84
Number of modification date shares ($1,275/$42.50)	× 30
Total fair value	$ 655
Incremental compensation	$ 218

[FTB97-1, ¶19]

[507]Determined based on the fair value measurements at the date of the modification using the then-current stock price. To simplify the illustration, the fair value at the modification date is based on the same assumptions about volatility, the risk-free interest rate, and expected dividend yield as at the grant date. [FTB97-1, ¶19, fn12]

.515 Any decreases in the withholding amounts (or percentages) should be disregarded for purposes of recognizing compensation cost unless the employee services that were valued at the grant date will no longer be provided to the employer due to a termination. However, no compensation cost should be recognized for awards that an employee forfeits because of failure to satisfy a service requirement for vesting. The accounting for decreases in withholdings is consistent with the requirement in paragraph .125 of this section that the total amount of compensation cost that must be recognized for an award is based on the number of instruments that vest rather than the number of instruments that are either granted or exercised. [FTB97-1, ¶20]

.516 *Response (Type I Plan)*—As with all ESPPs, the objective of the measurement process for ESPPs with a look-back option is to reasonably measure the fair value of the award at the grant date. Unlike Type F through Type H plans, which permit an employee to increase withholding amounts (or percentages) only prospectively, the Type I plan permits an employee to make a retroactive election to increase withholdings. Under a Type I plan, an employee may elect not to participate (or to participate at a minimal level) in the plan until just before the exercise date, thus making it difficult to determine when there truly is a mutual understanding of the terms of the award, and thus the date at which the grant occurs. For example, assume that the Type A ESPP in paragraph .228 permits an employee to remit "catch-up" amounts (up to a maximum aggregate withholding of 15 percent of annual salary) to Company S at any time during the term of the plan. On January 1, 20X0, Employee A elects to participate in the plan by having $100 (0.04 percent) of her $250,000 salary withheld monthly from her pay over the year. On December 20, 20X0, when the stock price is $65, Employee A elects to remit a check to Company S for $36,300, which, together with the $1,200 withheld during the year, represents 15 percent of her salary. [FTB97-1, ¶21]

.517 In that situation, December 20, 20X0 is the date at which Company S and Employee A have a mutual understanding of the terms of the award in exchange for the services already rendered and Company S becomes contingently obligated to issue equity instruments to Employee A upon the fulfillment of vesting requirements. The fair value of the entire award to Employee A is therefore measured as of December 20, 20X0. [FTB97-1, ¶22]

.518 *Response (Other Plan Features)*—Changes in total employee withholdings during a purchase period that occur solely as a result of salary increases, commissions, or bonus payments are not plan modifications if they do not represent changes to the terms of the award that was offered by the employer and initially agreed to by the employee at the grant (or measurement) date. Under those circumstances, the only incremental compensation cost is that which results from the additional shares that may be purchased with the additional amounts withheld (using the fair value calculated at the grant date). For example, an employee may elect to participate in the plan on the grant date by requesting that 5 percent of the employee's annual salary be withheld for future purchases of stock. If the employee receives an increase in salary during the term of the award, the base salary on which the 5 percent withholding amount is applied will increase, thus increasing the total amount withheld for future share purchases. That increase in withholdings as a result of the salary increase is not considered a plan modification and thus only increases the total compensation cost associated with the award by the grant date fair value associated with the incremental number of shares that may be purchased with the additional withholdings during the period. The incremental number of shares that may be purchased is calculated by dividing the incremental amount withheld by the exercise price as of the grant date (85 percent of the grant date stock price). [FTB97-1, ¶23]

.519 In some circumstances, applying the measurement approaches described in paragraphs .501 through .519 at the grant date may not be practicable for certain types of ESPPs. For example, an entity may not have access at a reasonable cost to the modeling capabilities needed to determine the fair value of plans with features in addition to or different from those described in paragraphs .501 through .519. If it is *not practicable* to reasonably estimate fair value at the grant date, the guidance in paragraph .121 of this section would apply.[508] [FTB97-1, ¶24]

[508]Paragraph .121 of this section addresses circumstances in which the characteristics of the instrument prevent grant date measurement using available option pricing models rather than circumstances in which an entity considers the amount of recordkeeping involved to be excessive. [FTB97-1, ¶24, fn13]

example, an employee may elect to participate in the plan on an annual [illegible] price of the employer [illegible] the purchase [illegible] increases [illegible] during the term of the [illegible] [illegible]

[illegible]

[illegible]

Supplemental Guidance: Emerging Issues Task Force (EITF) Issues

.1000 [Listed below are EITF Issues that provide supplemental guidance for this section. These Issues are grouped by subject matter and may be either interpretive of or related by topic to the guidance in this section.

Tax Issues

EITF Issue No. 00-15, "Classification in the Statement of Cash Flows of the Income Tax Benefit Received by a Company upon Exercise of a Nonqualified Employee StockOption"
EITF Issue No. 00-16, "Recognition and Measurement of Employer Payroll Taxes on Employee Stock-Based Compensation"
EITF Topic No. D-83, "Accounting for Payroll Taxes Associated with Stock Option Exercises"

Transactions with Nonemployees

EITF Issue No. 84-8, "Variable Stock Purchase Warrants Given by Suppliers to Customers"
EITF Issue No. 96-18, "Accounting for Equity Instruments That Are Issued to Other Than Employees for Acquiring, or in Conjunction with Selling, Goods or Services"
EITF Issue No. 00-8, "Accounting by a Grantee for an Equity Instrument to Be Received in Conjunction with Providing Goods or Services"
EITF Issue No. 00-12, "Accounting by an Investor for Stock-Based Compensation Granted to Employees of an Equity Method Investee"
EITF Issue No. 00-18, "Accounting Recognition for Certain Transactions involving Equity Instruments Granted to Other Than Employees"
EITF Issue No. 01-1, "Accounting for a Convertible Instrument Granted or Issued to a Nonemployee for Goods or Services or a Combination of Goods or Services and Cash"
EITF Topic No. D-90, "Grantor Balance Sheet Presentation of Unvested, Forfeitable Equity Instruments Granted to a Nonemployee"

Other

EITF Issue No. 97-2, "Application of FASB Statement No. 94 and APB Opinion No. 16 to Physician Practice Management Entities and Certain Other Entities with Contractual Management Arrangements"
EITF Issue No. 97-12, "Accounting for Increased Share Authorizations in an IRS Section 423 Employee Stock Purchase Plan under APB Opinion No. 25"
EITF Topic No. D-93, "Accounting for the Rescission of the Exercise of Employee Stock Options"]

.1001 [Listed below are those EITF Issues that provide interpretive guidance on specific material in this section.

Paragraph .107 (FAS 123, ¶8)—EITF Issues No. 96-18 and 97-2
Paragraphs .108 and .109 (FAS 123, ¶9-10)—EITF Issue No. 96-18
Paragraph .110 (FAS 123, ¶11)—EITF Issue No. 97-2]

(The next page is 7301.)

COMPENSATION TO EMPLOYEES: DEFERRED COMPENSATION AGREEMENTS — SECTION C38

Sources: APB Opinion 12; FASB Statement 106; FASB Statement 111

[**Note:** A list of Issues discussed by the Emerging Issues Task Force (EITF) that provide supplemental guidance for this section is presented in paragraph .1000.]

Summary

Estimated amounts to be paid under a deferred compensation contract that is not equivalent to a pension plan or a postretirement health or welfare benefit plan shall be accrued over the period of an employee's active employment from the time the contract is signed to the employee's full eligibility date.

.101 Section P16, "Pension Costs," or Section P40, "Postretirement Benefits Other Than Pensions," applies to deferred compensation contracts with individual employees if those contracts, taken together, are equivalent to a postretirement income plan or a postretirement health or welfare benefit plan, respectively. [FAS106, ¶13]

Individual Deferred Compensation Contracts

.101A Deferred compensation contracts shall be accounted for individually on an accrual basis in accordance with the terms of the underlying contract. To the extent the terms of the contract attribute all or a portion of the expected future benefits to an individual year of the employee's service, the cost of those benefits shall be recognized in that year. To the extent the terms of the contract attribute all or a portion of the expected future benefits to a period of service greater than one year, the cost of those benefits shall be accrued over that period of the employee's service in a systematic and rational manner. At the end of that period the aggregate amount accrued shall equal the then present value of the benefits expected to be provided to the employee, any beneficiaries, and covered dependents in exchange for the employee's service to that date.[1] [FAS106, ¶13] If elements of both current and future services are present, only the portion applicable to the current services shall be accrued. [APB12, ¶6]

---

[1]The amounts to be accrued periodically shall result in an accrued amount at the full eligibility date (as defined in Section P40) equal to the then present value of all of the future benefits expected to be paid. Paragraphs [.104] through .106 illustrate application of this paragraph. [FAS106, ¶13]

.102 Some deferred compensation contracts provide for periodic payments to employees or their surviving spouses for life with provisions for a minimum lump-sum settlement in the event of the early death of one or all of the beneficiaries. The estimated amount[1a] of future payments to be made under those contracts shall be accrued over the period of active employment from the time the contract is entered into. The estimated amount shall be based on the life expectancy of each individual concerned (based on the most recent mortality tables available) or on the estimated cost of an annuity contract rather than on the minimum payable in the event of early death. [APB12, ¶7]

Illustrations

.103 Paragraphs .104 through .106 illustrate the application of paragraph .101A for individual deferred compensation contracts. [FAS106, ¶413]

Contract Provides Only Prospective Benefits

.104 A company enters into a deferred compensation contract with an employee at the date of hire. The contract provides for a payment of $150,000 upon termination of employment following a minimum 3-year service period. The contract provides for a compensation adjustment for each year of service after the third year determined by multiplying $150,000 by the company's return on equity for the year. Also, each year after the third year of service, interest at 10 percent per year is credited on the amount due under the contract at the beginning of that year. Accordingly, a liability of $150,000 is accrued in a systematic and rational manner over the employee's first 3 years of service. Following the third year of service, the accrued liability is adjusted annually for accrued interest and the increased or decreased compensation based on the company's return on equity for that year. At the end of the third year and each subsequent year of the employee's service, the amount accrued equals the then present value of the benefit expected to be paid in exchange for the employee's service rendered to that date. [FAS106, ¶414]

Contract Provides Retroactive Benefits

.105 A company enters into a contract with a 55-year-old employee who has worked 5 years for the company. The contract states that in exchange for past and future services and for serving as a consultant for 2 years after the employee retires, the company will pay an annual pension of $20,000 to the employee, commencing immediately upon the employee's retirement. It is expected that the future benefits to the employer from the consulting services will be minimal. Consequently, the actuarial present value of a lifetime annuity of $20,000 that begins at the employee's expected retirement date is

---

[1a][Refer to footnote 1.] [FAS111, ¶8(f)]

accrued at the date the contract is entered into because the employee is fully eligible for the pension benefit at that date. [FAS106, ¶415]

.106 If the terms of the contract described in paragraph .105 had stated that the employee is entitled to the pension benefit only if the sum of the employee's age and years of service equal 70 or more at the date of retirement, the employee would be fully eligible for the pension benefit at age 60, after rendering 5 more years of service. The actuarial present value of a lifetime annuity of $20,000 that begins at the expected retirement date would be accrued in a systematic and rational manner over the 5-year period from the date the contract is entered into to the date the employee is fully eligible for the pension benefit. [FAS106, ¶416]

Supplemental Guidance: Emerging Issues Task Force (EITF) Issues

.1000 [Listed below are EITF Issues that provide supplemental guidance for this section. These Issues are related by topic to the guidance in this section.

EITF Issue No. 88-23, "Lump-Sum Payments under Union Contracts"
EITF Issue No. 96-5, "Recognition of Liabilities for Contractual Termination Benefits or Changing Benefit Plan Assumptions in Anticipation of a Business Combination"
EITF Issue No. 97-14, "Accounting for Deferred Compensation Arrangements Where Amounts Earned Are Held in a Rabbi Trust and Invested"]

(The next page is 7477.)

COMPENSATION TO EMPLOYEES: PAID ABSENCES

SECTION C44

Sources: FASB Statement 43; FASB Statement 112; FASB Statement 123

Summary

An employer is required to accrue a liability for employees' rights to receive compensation for future absences and for postemployment benefits provided to former or inactive employees, their beneficiaries, and covered dependents when certain conditions are met. For example, a liability shall be accrued for vacation benefits that employees have earned but have not yet taken and for benefits provided as a result of disability or layoff; however, a liability is generally not required to be accrued for future sick pay benefits, holidays, and similar compensated absences until employees are actually absent.

.101 [This section describes the conditions under which an employer is required to accrue a liability for **compensated absences.** Compensated absences are defined, for purposes of this section, as] employee absences, such as vacation, illness, and holidays, for which it is expected that employees will be paid. [FAS43, ¶1] This section also applies to all forms of postemployment benefits as defined in Section P32, "Postemployment Benefits," that meet the conditions in paragraph .104, except as noted in paragraph .102. Postemployment benefits that do not meet the conditions in paragraph .104 shall be accounted for in accordance with Section C59, "Contingencies." This section does not address the accounting for benefits paid to active employees other than compensated absences. [FAS112, ¶8]

.102 This section does not apply to:

a. Postemployment benefits provided through a pension or postretirement benefit plan (Sections P16, "Pensions," and P40, "Postretirement Benefits Other Than Pensions," specify the accounting for those costs.)
b. Individual deferred compensation arrangements that are addressed by Section C38, "Compensation to Employees: Deferred Compensation Agreements"
c. Special or contractual termination benefits covered by Sections P16 and P40
d. Stock compensation plans that are addressed by [FAS112, ¶9] Section C36, "Compensation: Stock-Based." [FAS123, ¶387]

This section does not address the allocation of costs of compensated absences to interim periods. [FAS112, ¶9]

.103 [This section does not present standards for] how an employer should estimate its liability for compensated absences. [Guidance is not provided on measurement issues such as] (a) whether the liability should be based on current or on future rates of pay, (b) whether it should be discounted, and (c) when the effect of scheduled increases should be accrued. [FAS43, ¶20]

Conditions for Accrual

.104 An employer shall accrue a liability for employees' compensation for future absences if *all* of the following conditions are met:[1]

a. The employer's obligation relating to employees' rights to receive compensation for future absences is attributable to employees' services already rendered.
b. The obligation relates to rights that [eventually] vest[2] or accumulate.[3]
c. Payment of the compensation is probable.
d. The amount can be reasonably estimated.

If an employer meets conditions (a), (b), and (c) and does not accrue a liability because condition (d) is not met, that fact shall be disclosed. [FAS43, ¶6]

.105 [The belief] that a liability for amounts to be paid as a result of employees' rights to compensated absences should be accrued, considering anticipated forfeitures, in the year in which earned [is based on the definition of a liability in FASB Concepts Statement No. 6, *Elements of Financial Statements,* paragraph 35.] For example, if new employees receive vested rights to two weeks' paid vacation at the beginning of their second year of employment with no pro rata payment in the event of termination during the first year, the two weeks' vacation would be considered to be earned by work performed

[[1]An exemption to this requirement is discussed in paragraph .108.]

[2]In this section, *vested rights* are those for which the employer has an obligation to make payment even if an employee terminates; thus, they are not contingent on an employee's future service. [FAS43, ¶6, fn1]

[3]For purposes of this section, *accumulate* means that earned but unused rights to compensated absences may be carried forward to one or more periods subsequent to that in which they are earned, even though there may be a limit to the amount that can be carried forward. [FAS43, ¶6, fn2]

in the first year and an accrual for vacation pay would be required for new employees during their first year of service, allowing for estimated forfeitures due to turnover. [FAS43, ¶12]

.106 Furthermore, the definition of a liability [in Concepts Statement 6] does not limit an employer's liability for compensated absences solely to rights to compensation for those absences that eventually vest. The definition also encompasses a constructive obligation for reasonably estimable compensation for past services that, based on the employer's past practices, probably will be paid and can be reasonably estimated. Individual facts and circumstances must be considered in determining when nonvesting rights to compensated absences are earned by services rendered. [FAS43,¶12] [For example,] the appropriate accounting for a sabbatical leave depends on the purpose of the leave. If a sabbatical leave is granted only to perform research or public service to enhance the reputation of or otherwise benefit the employer, the compensation is not attributable to services already rendered (refer to paragraph .104(a)); a liability should not be accrued in advance of the employee's service during such leave. If the leave is granted to provide compensated unrestricted time off for past service and the other conditions for accrual are met, a liability for sabbatical leave should be accrued. [FAS43, ¶18]

.107 The requirement to accrue a liability for nonvesting rights to compensated absences [also] depends on whether the unused rights (a) expire at the end of the year in which earned or (b) accumulate and are carried forward to succeeding years, thereby increasing the benefits that would otherwise be available in those later years. If the rights expire, a liability for future absences should not be accrued at year-end because the benefits to be paid in subsequent years would not be attributable to employee services rendered in prior years. (Jury duty and military leave benefits generally do not accumulate if unused and, unless they accumulate, a liability for those benefits would not be accrued at year-end.) On the other hand, if unused rights do accumulate and increase the benefits otherwise available in subsequent years, a liability should be accrued at year-end to the extent that it is probable that employees will be paid in subsequent years for the increased benefits attributable to the accumulated rights and the amount can be reasonably estimated. [FAS43, ¶13]

.108 Notwithstanding the conditions specified in paragraph .104, an employer is not required to accrue a liability for nonvesting accumulating rights to receive sick pay benefits (that is, compensation for an employee's absence due to illness). [FAS43, ¶7] On the other hand, this section does not prohibit an employer from accruing a liability for such nonvesting accumulating sick pay benefits, providing the criteria of paragraph .104 are met. [FAS43, ¶15]

.109 In accounting for compensated absences, the form of an employer's policy for compensated absences should not prevail over actual practices. For example, if employees are customarily paid "sick pay" benefits even though their absences from work are not actually the result of illness or if employees are routinely allowed to take compensated "terminal leave" for [nonvesting] accumulated unused sick pay benefits prior to retirement, such benefits shall not be considered sick pay benefits for purposes of applying the provisions of paragraph .108 but rather should be accounted for in accordance with paragraph .104. [FAS43, ¶7, fn3]

Glossary

.401 **Compensated absences.** Employee absences, such as vacation, illness, and holidays, for which it is expected that [active] employees will be paid. [FAS43, ¶1]

(The next page is 7675.)

COMPENSATION TO EMPLOYEES: STOCK PURCHASE AND OPTION PLANS — SECTION C47

Sources: ARB 43, Chapter 13B; APB Opinion 25;
AICPA Interpretation of APB Opinion 25; FASB Statement 109;
FASB Statement 123; FASB Statement 128; FASB Statement 141;
FASB Interpretation 28; FASB Interpretation 38; FASB Interpretation 44

[**Note:** A list of Issues discussed by the Emerging Issues Task Force (EITF) that provide supplemental guidance for this section is presented in paragraph .1000.]

Summary

An employer shall measure compensation costs for stock granted through nonvariable employee stock option, purchase, and award plans as the difference between the quoted market price of the stock at the measurement date (ordinarily the date of grant or award) less the amount, if any, the employee is required to pay. That cost shall be charged to expense over the periods in which the employee performs the related services. Some plans, referred to as noncompensatory plans, involve no compensation expense because the employees' purchase price is not set lower than would reasonably be required in an offer of shares to all shareholders for the purpose of raising an equivalent amount of capital.

The measurement date for stock appreciation rights and other variable stock option and award plans typically is not the date of grant or award. Compensation relating to such variable plans shall be measured at the end of each period as the amount by which the quoted market value of the shares of the employer's stock covered by a grant exceeds the option price or value specified under the plan and shall be charged to expense over the periods the employee performs the related services.

The measurement date for grants under stock option, purchase, and award plans involving junior stock is the first date on which are known both the number of shares of the employer's regular common stock that an employee is entitled to receive in exchange for the junior stock and the option or purchase price, if any. Generally, total compensation cost shall be the amount by which the market price at the measurement date of the employer's regular common stock that an employee is entitled to receive exceeds the amount that the employee paid or will pay for the junior stock. If the performance goals to which the junior stock award relates will probably be achieved, compensation cost shall be charged to expense over the periods the employee performs the related services.

Changes in the quoted market value shall be reflected as an adjustment of accrued compensation and compensation expense in the periods in which the changes occur until the date the number of shares and purchase price, if any, are both known.

[**Note:** Section C36, "Compensation: Stock-Based," establishes a fair value based method of accounting for stock-based employee compensation plans. An entity may continue to account for awards granted to employees under the provisions of Section C47; however, the fair value based method in Section C36 is preferable for purposes of justifying a change in accounting principle under Section A06, "Accounting Changes." Entities electing to retain the accounting in Section C47 must make pro forma disclosures of net income and, if presented, earnings per share, as if the fair value based method of accounting defined in Section C36 had been applied.]

Applicability and Scope

.101 Many employers have adopted various **plans,** contracts, and agreements to compensate officers and other employees by issuing to them stock of the employer. Under traditional stock option and stock purchase plans an employer grants options to purchase a fixed number of shares of stock of the employer at a stated price during a specified period or grants rights to purchase shares of stock of the employer at a stated price, often at a discount from the market price of the stock at the date the rights are granted. Stock options and purchase rights are normally granted for future services of employees. [APB25, ¶1]

.102 Some employers have replaced or supplemented traditional plans with more complex plans, contracts, and agreements for issuing stock. [Those latter] arrangements may be based on variable factors that depend on future events; for example, an employer may award a variable number of shares of stock or may grant a stock option with a variable option price. Other arrangements combine the characteristics of two or more types of plans, and some give an employee an election. [APB25, ¶2]

.103 Paragraphs .106 through .118 [discuss] some aspects of accounting for stock issued to employees through both noncompensatory and compensatory plans. [Those paragraphs discuss] (a) plans in which the number of shares of stock that may be acquired by or awarded to an employee and the option or purchase price, if any, are known or determinable at the date of grant or award, (b) plans in which either the number of shares of stock or the option or purchase price depends on future events, and (c) income tax benefits related to stock issued to employees through stock option, purchase, and award plans. Paragraphs .124 through .135 and .136 and .137 illustrate measuring and accounting for compensation under typical plans. [APB25, ¶4] [Paragraphs .119 through .122 provide further guidance in accounting for **stock appreciation rights** and other **variable stock option, purchase, and award plans.** Paragraphs .138 through .144 illustrate accounting for those plans. Paragraphs .135A through .135E provide guidance in accounting for stock option, purchase, and award plans involving **junior stock.** Paragraphs .147 through .292 provide interpretive guidance and illustrations of the guidance in this section.] Section C36, "Compensation: Stock-Based," specifies a fair value based method of accounting for stock-based compensation plans [FAS123, ¶382(a)] (including those that involve variable award plans) [FAS123, ¶392] and encourages entities to adopt that method in place of the provisions of this section for all arrangements under which employees receive shares of stock or other equity instruments of the employer or the employer incurs liabilities to employees in amounts based on the price of the employer's stock. Section C36 permits an entity in determining its net income to continue to apply the accounting provisions of this section [FAS123, ¶382(a)] to all its stock-based employee compensation arrangements. [FAS123, ¶381(a)] If an entity elects to apply Section C36, that election shall not be reversed. [FAS123, ¶382(a)] Paragraph .114 of Section C36 adopts the substance of paragraphs .501 through .506 of this section regardless of the method chosen to account for stock-based compensation. [FAS123, ¶384] Entities that continue to apply [the accounting provisions of] this section shall comply with the disclosure requirements of Section C36. [FAS123, ¶382(a)] [Refer to paragraph .1001 for an EITF Issue that provides interpretive guidance on this paragraph.]

Noncompensatory Plans

.104 Stock option plans in many cases may be intended not primarily as a special form of compensation but rather as an important means of raising capital, or as an inducement to obtain greater or more widespread ownership of the employer's stock among its officers and other employees. In general, the terms under which stock options are granted, including any conditions as to exercise of the options or disposal of the stock acquired, are the most significant evidence ordinarily available as to the nature and purpose of a particular stock option or stock option plan. It is often apparent that a particular option or plan involves elements of two or more of the above purposes. If the inducements are not larger per share than would reasonably be required in an offer of shares to all shareholders for the purpose of raising an equivalent amount of capital, those plans shall be considered noncompensatory. [ARB43, ch13B, ¶4]

.105 Stock purchase plans also are frequently an integral part of an employer's program to secure equity capital or to obtain widespread ownership among employees, or both.

Those [plans shall be considered noncompensatory] if the purchase price is not lower than is reasonably required to interest employees generally or to secure the contemplated funds. [ARB43, ch13B, ¶5]

.106 An employer shall recognize no compensation [expense] for services in [accounting for] consideration received for stock that is issued through noncompensatory plans. Four characteristics are essential in a noncompensatory plan: (a) substantially all full-time employees meeting limited employment qualifications may participate (employees owning a specified percent of the outstanding stock and executives may be excluded), (b) stock is offered to eligible employees equally or based on a uniform percentage of salary or wages (the plan may limit the number of shares of stock that an employee may purchase through the plan), (c) the time permitted for exercise of an option or purchase right is limited to a reasonable period, and (d) the discount from the market price of the stock is no greater than would be reasonable in an offer of stock to stockholders or others. An example of a noncompensatory plan is the "statutory" employee stock purchase plan that qualifies under Section 423 of the Internal Revenue Code. [APB25, ¶7] [Refer to paragraph .1001 for an EITF Issue that provides interpretive guidance on this paragraph.]

Compensatory Plans

.107 Stock options involving an element of compensation usually arise out of an offer or agreement by an employer to issue shares of its capital stock to one or more officers or other employees (referred to in this section as *grantees*) at a stated price. The grantees are accorded the right to require issuance of the shares either at a specified time or during some determinable period. In some cases, the grantees' options are exercisable only if at the time of exercise certain conditions exist, such as that the grantee is then or until a specified date has been an employee. In other cases, the grantees may have undertaken certain obligations, such as to remain in the employment of the employer for at least a specified period, or to take the shares only for investment purposes and not for resale. [ARB43, ch13B, ¶3]

.108 Plans that do not possess the four characteristics of noncompensatory plans [described in paragraph .106] are classified as compensatory plans. Classification as a compensatory plan does not necessarily require that compensation cost be recognized.[1] [APB25, ¶8]

---

[1]All compensation arrangements involving stock, regardless of the name given, shall be accounted for according to their substance. For example, an arrangement in which the consideration for stock issued to an employee is a nonrecourse note secured by the stock issued may be in substance the same as the grant of a stock option and shall be accounted for accordingly. The note shall be classified as a reduction of stockholders' equity rather than as an asset. [APB25, ¶8, fn2] [Refer to paragraph .1001 for an EITF Issue that provides interpretive guidance on this footnote.]

Services as Consideration for Stock Issued

.109 The consideration that an employer receives for stock issued through a stock option, purchase, or award plan consists of cash or other assets, if any, plus services received from the employee. [APB25, ¶9] On exercise of an option, the sum of the cash received and the amount of compensation charged to income shall be accounted for as the consideration received on the issuance of the stock. [ARB43, ch13B, ¶14]

Measuring Compensation for Services

.110 Compensation for services that an employer receives as consideration for stock issued through employee stock option, purchase, and award plans shall be measured by the quoted market price of the stock at the **measurement date** less the amount, if any, that the employee is required to pay.

a. The unadjusted *quoted market price* of a share of stock of the same class that trades freely in an established market shall be used in measuring compensation. If a quoted market price is unavailable, the best estimate of the market value of the stock shall be used to measure compensation.
b. The *measurement date* for determining compensation cost in stock option, purchase, and award plans is the first date on which are known both (1) the number of shares that an individual employee is entitled to receive and (2) the option or purchase price, if any. That date for many or most plans is the date an option or purchase right is granted or stock is awarded to an individual employee. However, the measurement date may be later than the date of grant or award in plans with variable terms that depend on events after date of grant or award. [Refer to paragraph .1001 for EITF Issues that provide interpretive guidance on this subparagraph.]

Thus, an employer recognizes compensation cost for stock issued through compensatory plans unless the employee pays an amount that is at least equal to the quoted market price of the stock at the measurement date. [APB25, ¶10]

Applying the Measurement Principle

.111 The following supplements paragraph .110 for special situations in some plans:

a. Measuring compensation by the cost to an employer of reacquired (treasury) stock that is distributed through a stock option, purchase, or award plan is not acceptable practice. The only exception is that compensation cost under a plan with all the provisions described in paragraph .111(c) may be measured by the cost of stock that the employer (1) reacquires during the fiscal period for which the stock is to be awarded and (2) awards shortly thereafter to employees for services during that period.

b. The measurement date is not changed from the grant or award date to a later date solely by provisions that termination of employment reduces the number of shares of stock that may be issued to an employee.

c. The measurement date of an award of stock for current service may be the end of the fiscal period, which is normally the effective date of the award, instead of the date that the award to an employee is determined if (1) the award is provided for by the terms of an established formal plan; (2) the plan designates the factors that determine the total dollar amount of awards to employees for the period (for example, a percentage of income), although the total amount or the individual awards may not be known at the end of the period; and (3) the award pertains to current service of the employee for the period.

d. Renewing a stock option or purchase right or extending its period establishes a new measurement date as if the right were newly granted. [Refer to paragraph .1001 for an EITF Issue that provides interpretive guidance on this subparagraph.]

e. Transferring stock or assets to a trustee, agent, or other third party for distribution of stock to employees under the terms of an option, purchase, or award plan does not change the measurement date from a later date to the date of transfer unless the terms of the transfer provide that the stock (1) will not revert to the employer, (2) will not be granted or awarded later to the same employee on terms different from or for services other than those specified in the original grant or award, and (3) will not be granted or awarded later to another employee.

f. The measurement date for a grant or award of convertible stock (or stock that is otherwise exchangeable for other securities of the employer) is the date on which the ratio of conversion (or exchange) is known unless other terms are variable at that date (refer to paragraph .110(b)). The higher of the quoted market price at the measurement date of (1) the convertible stock granted or awarded or (2) the securities into which the original grant or award is convertible shall be used to measure compensation. [Refer to paragraphs .135A through .135E for guidance on accounting for stock option, purchase, and award plans involving junior stock.]

g. Cash paid to an employee to settle an earlier award of stock or to settle a grant of option to the employee shall determine compensation cost. If the cash payment differs from the earlier measure of the award of stock or grant of option, compensation cost shall be adjusted (refer to paragraph .115). The amount that an employer pays to an employee to purchase stock previously issued to the employee through a compensation plan is *cash paid to an employee to settle an earlier award of stock or to settle a grant of option* if stock is reacquired shortly after issuance. Cash proceeds that an employer receives from sale of awarded stock or stock issued on exercise of an option and remits to the taxing authorities to cover required withholding of income taxes on an award is not *cash paid to an employee to settle an earlier award of stock or to settle a grant of option* in measuring compensation cost. [Refer to paragraph .1001 for EITF Issues that provide interpretive guidance on this subparagraph.]

h. Some plans are a combination of two or more types of plans. An employer may need to measure compensation for the separate parts. Compensation cost for a combination plan permitting an employee to elect one part shall be measured according to the terms that an employee is most likely to elect based on the facts available each period.

[APB25, ¶11] [Refer to paragraph .1001 for an EITF Issue that provides interpretive guidance on this paragraph.]

Accruing Compensation Cost

.112 Compensation cost in stock option, purchase, and award plans shall be recognized as an expense of one or more periods in which an employee performs services and also as part or all of the consideration received for stock issued to the employee through a plan. The grant or award may specify the period or periods during which the employee performs services, or the period or periods may be inferred from the terms or from the past pattern of grants or awards (refer to Section C38, "Compensation to Employees: Deferred Compensation Agreements," paragraph .101). [APB25, ¶12]

.113 An employee may perform services in several periods before an employer issues stock to him for those services. The employer shall accrue compensation expense in each period in which the services are performed. If the measurement date is later than the date of grant or award, an employer shall record the compensation expense each period from date of grant or award to date of measurement based on the quoted market price of the stock at the end of each period. [APB25, ¶13]

.114 If stock is issued in a plan before some or all of the services are performed,[2] part of the consideration recorded for the stock issued is unearned compensation and shall be shown as a separate reduction of stockholders' equity. The unearned compensation shall be accounted for as expense of the period or periods in which the employee performs service. [APB25, ¶14]

.115 Accruing compensation expense may require estimates, and adjustment of those estimates in later periods may be necessary (refer to Section A06, "Accounting Changes," paragraphs .130 through .132). For example, if a stock option is not exercised (or awarded

[2]State law governs the issuance of an employer's stock including the acceptability of issuing stock for future services. [APB25, ¶14, fn3]

stock is returned to the employer) because an employee fails to fulfill an obligation, the estimate of compensation expense recorded in previous periods shall be adjusted by decreasing compensation expense in the period of forfeiture. [APB25, ¶15]

Accounting for Income Tax Benefits

.116 An employer may obtain an income tax benefit related to stock issued to an employee through a stock option, purchase, or award plan. An employer is usually entitled to a deduction for income tax purposes of the amount that an employee reports as ordinary income, and the deduction is allowable to the employer in the year in which the amount is includable in the gross income of the employee. Thus, a deduction for income tax purposes may differ from the related compensation expense that the employer recognizes,[3] and the deduction may be allowable in a period that differs from the one in which the employer recognizes compensation expense in measuring net income. [APB25, ¶16]

.117 An employer shall reduce income tax expense for a period by no more of a tax reduction under a stock option, purchase, or award plan than the proportion of the tax reduction that is related to the compensation expense for the period. Compensation expenses that are deductible in a tax return in a period different from the one in which they are reported as expenses in measuring net income [APB25,¶17] result in temporary differences [FAS109, ¶288(g)], and deferred taxes shall be recorded [APB25, ¶17] in accordance with the provisions of Section I27. [FAS109, ¶288(g)] The remainder of the tax reduction, if any, is related to an amount that is deductible for income tax purposes but does not affect net income. The remainder of the tax reduction shall not be included in income but shall be added to capital in addition to par or stated value of capital stock in the period of the tax reduction. Conversely, a tax reduction may be less than if recorded compensation expenses were deductible for income tax purposes. If so, the employer may deduct the difference from additional capital in the period of the tax reduction to the extent that tax reductions under the same or similar compensatory stock option, purchase, or award plans have been included in additional capital. [APB25, ¶17]

.118 An employer may, either by cash payment or otherwise—for example, by allowing a reduction in the purchase price of stock—reimburse an employee for his action related to a stock option, purchase, or award plan that results in a reduction of income taxes of the employer. The employer shall include the reimbursement in income as an expense. [APB25, ¶18]

[3] An employer may be entitled to a deduction for income tax purposes even though it recognizes no compensation expense in measuring net income. [APB25, ¶16, fn4]

Stock Appreciation Rights and Other Variable Stock Option or Award Plans

.119 When stock appreciation rights[4] or other variable plan awards[5] are granted, an employer shall measure compensation as the amount by which the quoted market value of the shares of the employer's stock covered by the grant exceeds the option price or value specified, by reference to a market price or otherwise, subject to any appreciation limitations under the plan. Changes, either increases or decreases, in the quoted market value of those shares between the date of grant and the measurement date result in a change in the measure of compensation for the right or award. [FIN28, ¶2] [Refer to paragraph .1001 for an EITF Issue that provides interpretive guidance on this paragraph.]

.120 Compensation determined in accordance with paragraph .119 shall be accrued as a charge to expense over the period or periods the employee performs the related services (referred to in this section as the **service period**). If the stock appreciation rights or other variable plan awards are granted for past services, compensation shall be accrued as a charge to expense of the period in which the rights or awards are granted. If the service period is not defined in the plan or some other agreement, such as an employment agreement, as a shorter or previous period, the service period shall be presumed to be the vesting period.[6] [FIN28, ¶3]

---

[4]Stock appreciation rights are awards entitling employees to receive cash, stock, or a combination of cash and stock in an amount equivalent to any excess of the market value of a stated number of shares of the employer's stock over a stated price. The form of payment may be specified when the rights are granted or may be determined when they are exercised; in some plans the employee may choose the form of payment. [FIN28, ¶9]

[5]Plans for which (a) the number of shares of stock that may be acquired by or awarded to an employee or (b) the price or (c) both are not specified or determinable until after the date of grant or award are referred to in this section as *variable plan* awards. However, plans described in paragraph .111(c) and book value stock option, purchase, or award plans are not covered by paragraphs .119 through .122. Plans under which an employee may receive cash in lieu of stock or additional cash upon the exercise of a stock option are variable plans for purposes of this section if the amount is contingent on the occurrence of future events. [FIN28, ¶2, fn1] Even though junior stock possesses certain features of equity securities, the substance of junior stock plans is that they are compensation plans with the junior stock being a means for an employee ultimately to acquire regular common stock. Because the conversion of junior stock to regular common stock is contingent on certain performance goals being achieved or on certain transactions occurring, the number of shares of regular common stock that an employee is entitled to receive is not known until those future events occur. The number of shares of regular common stock that an employee is entitled to receive depends on events occurring after the date of grant of junior stock, thereby causing the plan to be variable under the provisions of paragraph .110(b). [FIN38, ¶22]

[6]For purposes of this section, stock appreciation rights and other variable plan awards become vested when the employee's right to receive or retain shares or cash under the rights or awards is not contingent upon the performance of additional services. Frequently, the vesting period is the period from the date of grant to the date the rights or awards become exercisable. [FIN28, ¶3, fn3]

.121 Compensation accrued during the service period in accordance with paragraph .120 shall be adjusted in subsequent periods up to the measurement date for changes, either increases or decreases, in the quoted market value of the shares of the employer's stock covered by the grant but shall not be adjusted below zero. The offsetting adjustment shall be made to compensation expense of the period in which changes in the market value occur. Except as provided in paragraph .122, the accrued compensation for a right that is forfeited or canceled shall be adjusted by decreasing compensation expense in the period of forfeiture in accordance with paragraph .115. [FIN28, ¶4]

.122 For purposes of applying paragraph .111(h), compensation expense for a combination plan[7] involving stock appreciation rights or other variable plan awards (including those that are granted after the date of grant of related stock options) shall be measured according to the terms the employee is most likely to elect based on the facts available each period. An employer shall presume that the employee will elect to exercise the stock appreciation rights or other variable plan awards, but the presumption may be overcome if past experience or the terms of a combination plan that limit the market appreciation available to the employee in the stock appreciation rights or other variable plan awards provide evidence that the employee will elect to exercise the related stock option. If an employer has been accruing compensation for a stock appreciation right or other variable plan award and a change in circumstances provides evidence that the employee will likely elect to exercise the related stock option, accrued compensation recorded for the right or award shall *not* be adjusted.[8] If the employee elects to exercise the stock option, the accrued compensation recorded for the right or award shall be recognized as a consideration for the stock issue. If all parts of the grant or award (for example, both the option and the right or award) are forfeited or canceled, accrued compensation shall be adjusted by decreasing compensation expense in that period. [FIN28, ¶5] [Refer to paragraph .1001 for an EITF Issue that provides interpretive guidance on this paragraph.]

---

[7]Stock appreciation rights are usually granted in combination with compensatory stock options but also may be granted separately. Combination plans usually provide that the rights are exercisable for the same period as the companion stock options and that the exercise of either cancels the other. In some combination plans, the employer may grant stock appreciation rights either when the options are granted or at a later date. In some cases, the holder of stock options may apply to receive share appreciation in cash or stock with the approval of the employer in lieu of exercising the options. [FIN28, ¶10]

[8]A change in the circumstances may be indicated by market appreciation in excess of any appreciation limitations under the plan or the cancellation or forfeiture of the stock appreciation right or other variable plan award without a concurrent cancellation or forfeiture of the related stock option. A subsequent decrease in market value that reduces the appreciation to a level below the limitations under the plan would require adjustment of accrued compensation in accordance with paragraph .121 if evidence then indicates that the employee will elect to exercise the stock appreciation right or other variable plan award. [FIN28, ¶5, fn7]

.122A Stock appreciation rights and other variable plan awards are included in the computation of diluted earnings per share pursuant to the provisions of paragraphs .115 through .118 of Section E11, "Earnings per Share." [FAS128, ¶168]

Disclosure

.123 Paragraphs .144 through .147 of Section C36 specify the disclosures related to stock-based employee compensation arrangements that shall be made in the financial statements. [FAS123, ¶382(b)][8a] [In addition, all entities, public and nonpublic, that have issued securities, including options, warrants, debt, and stock, must comply with the requirements of Section C24, "Capital Structure: Disclosures."]

Measuring and Accounting for Compensation under Typical Plans

.124 Enterprises issue stock to officers and other employees through plans with a variety of names and a multiplicity of terms. Plans in which employees pay cash, either directly or through payroll withholding, as all or a significant part of the consideration for stock they receive, are commonly designated by names such as stock option, stock purchase, or stock thrift or savings plans. Plans in which employees receive stock for current or future services without paying cash (or with a nominal payment) are commonly designated by names such as stock bonus or stock award plans. Stock bonus and award plans are invariably compensatory. Stock thrift and savings plans are compensatory to the extent of contributions of an employer. Stock option and purchase plans may be either compensatory or noncompensatory. The combination of terms in some plans tend to make various types of plans shade into one another, and an assigned name may not describe the nature of a plan. [APB25, ¶21]

.125 Paragraphs .126 through .137 are organized according to the most vital distinction in this section—compensatory plans are divided between plans in which the cost of compensation is measured at the date of grant or award and those in which the cost of compensation depends on events after the date of grant or award. Combination plans are also described briefly. [APB25, ¶22]

[8aDeleted 10/95 because of FASB Statement 123, *Accounting for Stock-Based Compensation.*]

Compensation Cost Measured at Date of Grant or Award

Accounting

.126 Total compensation cost is measured by the difference between the quoted market price of the stock at the date of grant or award and the price, if any, to be paid by an employee and is recognized as expense over the period the employee performs related services. The sum of compensation and cash paid by the employee is the consideration received for the stock issued. Compensation cost related to an award of stock may be adjusted for a later cash settlement (refer to paragraph .111(g)). [APB25, ¶23]

Typical Plans with Fixed and Determinable Terms

.127 The characteristic that identifies plans in this group is that the terms fix and provide means for determining at the date of grant or award both the number of shares of stock that may be acquired by or awarded to an employee and the cash, if any, to be paid by the employee. Plans usually presume or provide that the employee perform current or future services. The right to transfer stock received is sometimes restricted for a specified period. [APB25, ¶24]

Stock Option and Stock Purchase Plans

.128 Typical terms provide for an employer to grant to an employee the right to purchase a fixed number of shares of stock of the employer at a stated price during a specified period. [APB25, ¶25]

Stock Bonus or Award Plans

.129 Typical terms provide for an employer to award to an employee a fixed number of shares of stock of the employer without a cash payment (or with a nominal cash payment) by the employee. Often the award is specified as a fixed dollar amount but is distributable in stock with the number of shares determined by the quoted market price of the stock at the date of award, the effective date of award (refer to paragraph .111(c)), or the date treasury stock is acquired (refer to paragraph .111(a)). [APB25, ¶26]

Compensation Cost Measured at Other Than Date of Grant or Award

Accounting

.130 Compensation cost is accounted for the same as for plans in the first group with one exception. The quoted market price used in the measurement is not the price at date of grant or award but the price at the date on which both the number of shares of stock that may be acquired by or awarded to an individual employee and the option or purchase price are known. Total compensation cost is measured by the difference between that quoted market price of the stock and the amount, if any, to be paid by an employee and is recognized as expense over the period the employee performs related services. The sum of compensation and cash paid by the employee is the consideration received for the stock issued. Compensation cost related to an award of stock may be adjusted for a later cash settlement (refer to paragraph .111(g)). [APB25, ¶27]

.131 Estimates of compensation cost are recorded before the measurement date based on the quoted market price of the stock at intervening dates. Recorded compensation expense between the date of grant or award and the measurement date may either increase or decrease because changes in quoted market price of the stock require recomputations of the estimated compensation cost. [APB25, ¶28]

Typical Plans with Variable Terms

.132 The characteristic that identifies plans in this group is that the terms prevent determining at the date of grant or award either the number of shares of stock that may be acquired by or awarded to an employee or the price to be paid by the employee, or both. The indeterminate factors usually depend on events that are not known or determinable at the date of grant or award. Plans usually presume or provide that the employee perform current or future services. The right to transfer stock received is sometimes restricted for a specified period. [APB25, ¶29]

Stock Option and Stock Purchase Plans

.133 Some terms provide for an employer to grant to an employee the right to purchase shares of stock of the employer during a specified period. The number of shares of stock, the option or purchase price, or both may vary depending on various factors during a specified period, such as market performance of the stock, equivalents of dividends distributed, or level of earnings of the employer. [APB25, ¶30]

Stock Bonus or Award Plans

.134 Some terms provide for an employer to award to an employee the right to receive shares of stock of the employer but the number of shares is not determinable at the date of award. Often the award is specified as a fixed dollar amount but is distributable in stock with the number of shares of stock determined by the market price of the stock at the date distributed, or the award may be of an undesignated number of shares of stock and that number is to be determined by variable factors during a specified period. [APB25, ¶31]

.135 The terms of some plans, often called *phantom stock* or *shadow stock* plans, base the obligations for compensation on increases in market price of or dividends distributed on a specified or variable number of shares of stock of the employer but provide for settlement of the obligation to the employee in cash, in stock of the employer, or a combination of cash and stock. [APB25, ¶32]

Stock Option, Purchase, and Award Plans Involving Junior Stock

.135A Stock option, purchase, and award plans involving junior stock are designed to provide that an employer ultimately will issue shares of regular common stock to employees. Those plans are variable plans because the number of shares of regular common stock that an individual employee is entitled to receive is not known until certain performance goals are achieved or certain transactions occur. For purposes of measuring compensation cost, the measurement date for grants under stock option, purchase, and award plans involving junior stock is the first date on which are known both the number of shares of the employer's regular common stock that an employee is entitled to receive in exchange for the junior stock and the option or purchase price, if any. [FIN38, ¶2]

.135B Paragraph .111(f) of this section indicates that the measurement date for a grant or award of convertible stock is the date on which the ratio of conversion is known, unless other terms are variable at that date. Because conversion of junior stock to regular common stock generally is contingent on achieving certain performance goals or on certain transactions occurring, the conversion ratio[9] is not known with certainty until those future events occur. After those goals are achieved or those transactions occur, the conversion ratio is determinable and, accordingly, the number of shares of regular common stock that an individual is entitled to receive is known. [FIN38, ¶3]

.135C Compensation cost for stock option, purchase, and award plans involving junior stock shall be accrued according to the provisions of paragraphs .119 through .121 and paragraph .111. However, the provisions of paragraph .119 shall be applied only when it

[9]If junior stock becomes convertible only to an equal number of shares of regular common stock upon achieving certain performance goals, the conversion ratio is either one-to-zero or one-to-one; some junior stock plans provide for different ratios of conversion depending on the level of performance attained. [FIN38, ¶3, fn2]

becomes probable[10] that certain performance goals will be achieved or certain transactions will occur; that probability may or may not be present at the date junior stock is issued. [FIN38, ¶4]

.135D Stock option, purchase, and award plans involving junior stock generally are based on certain performance goals being achieved or certain transactions occurring within specific periods. Some plans, however, do not specify a period during which those future events must occur. If it is probable that the future event will occur at some time, compensation cost shall be charged to expense over the period from the date the future event becomes probable to the date the future event is most likely to occur or the end of any required service period. Other plans provide for different ratios of conversion of junior stock to regular common stock within a specific period based on variable performance goals. If achieving more than one performance goal is probable, compensation cost shall be based on the highest ratio of conversion of junior stock to regular common stock attributable to those goals whose achievement is probable. However, the final measure of compensation cost shall be based on the ratio of conversion attributable to the performance goal achieved at the measurement date. For all plans, total compensation shall be based on the market price of the regular common stock as of the date compensation cost is determined. [FIN38, ¶5]

.135E Total compensation cost shall be the amount by which the market price at the measurement date of the employer's regular common stock that an employee is entitled to receive exceeds the amount that the employee paid or will pay for the junior stock. If vesting provisions cause junior stock to become convertible to regular common stock after the measurement date, compensation cost shall be recognized during the period from (a) the first date that it becomes probable that the future events will occur or the date the events have occurred to (b) the date that junior stock becomes convertible or the end of the service period, whichever occurs first. If junior stock does not become convertible to regular common stock but cash is paid to an employee to purchase previously issued junior stock, total compensation cost is the amount by which cash paid to the employee exceeds the amount initially paid by the employee for the junior stock. [FIN38, ¶6]

.135F Paragraphs .115 through .118 of Section E11 provide guidance on when and how junior stock plans should be reflected in the diluted earnings per share computation. [FAS128, ¶169]

---

[10]*Probable* is used here, consistent with its use in Section C59, "Contingencies," to mean that it is likely that certain performance goals will be achieved or certain transactions will occur. [FIN38, ¶4, fn3]

Combination and Elective Plans

Accounting

.136 In general, compensation is measured for the separate parts of combination or elective plans. Compensation expense is the sum of the parts that apply. An employer may need to measure compensation at various dates as the terms of separate parts become known. For example, if an employee is entitled to dividend equivalents, compensation cost is the sum of the costs measured at the dates the dividends are credited to the employee in accordance with the terms of the plan. If an employee may choose between alternatives, compensation expense is accrued for the alternative that the employee is most likely to elect based on the facts available at the date of accrual. [APB25, ¶33]

Typical Combination and Elective Plans

.137 Some plans provide for an employer to grant or award to an employee rights with more than one set of terms. Often an employee may elect the right to be exercised. The combination of rights may be granted or awarded simultaneously or an employee who holds a right may subsequently be granted or awarded a second but different right. The rights may run concurrently or for different periods. An illustration is: An employee holding an option to purchase a fixed number of shares of stock at a fixed price during a specified period is granted an alternative option to purchase the same number of shares at a different price or during a different specified period. Instead of a second option, the award may be the right to elect to receive cash or shares of stock without paying cash. Often the election to acquire or receive stock under either right decreases the other right. Plans combining rights are often called *tandem stock* or *alternate stock* plans; the second right may be of the type that is sometimes called a *phantom stock* plan. [APB25, ¶34]

Illustrations of the Accounting for Stock Appreciation Rights and Other Variable Stock Option or Award Plans

.138 Paragraphs .139 through .144 illustrate applications of this section in accounting for stock appreciation rights and other variable stock option or award plans when the service period is presumed to be the vesting period. The examples do not comprehend all possible combinations of circumstances nor do the examples illustrate the computation of deferred income taxes. [FIN28, ¶19]

Example 1

.139 Provisions of the agreements [are as follows]:

Stock appreciation rights are granted in tandem with stock options for market value appreciation in excess of the option price. Exercise of the rights cancels the option for an equal number of shares and vice versa. Share appreciation is payable in stock, cash, or a combination of stock and cash at the employer's election.

Date of grant	January 1, 19X9
Expiration date	December 31, 19Y8
Vesting	100% at the end of 19Y2
Number of shares under option	1,000
Option price	$10 per share
Quoted market price at date of grant	$10 per share

[FIN28, ¶20]

.140 Market price assumptions [are as follows]:

Quoted market price per share at December 31 of subsequent years:

19X9 –$11
19Y0 – 12
19Y1 – 15
19Y2 – 14
19Y3 – 15
19Y4 – 18

[FIN28, ¶21]

.141 Exhibit 141A illustrates the annual computation of compensation expense for the above described stock appreciation right plan. [FIN28, ¶22]

Exhibit 141A

Illustration of Compensation Expense by Year for a Stock Appreciation Right Plan with Complete Vesting at End of Four-Year Period

		Compensation				Accrual of Expense by Year (3)					
Date	Market Price	Per Share	Aggregate (1)	Percentage Accrued (2)	Compensation Accrued to Date	19X9	19Y0	19Y1	19Y2	19Y3	19Y4
12/31/X9	$11	$1	$1,000	25%	$ 250	$250					
					750		$750				
12/31/Y0	12	2	2,000	50	1,000						
					2,750			$2,750			
12/31/Y1	15	5	5,000	75	3,750						
					250				$250		
12/31/Y2	14	4	4,000	100	4,000						
					1,000					$1,000	
12/31/Y3	15	5	5,000	100	5,000						
					3,000						$3,000
12/31/Y4	18	8	8,000	100	$8,000						

Notes:

(1) Aggregate compensation for unexercised shares to be allocated to periods service performed.
(2) The percentage accrued is based upon the four-year vesting period.
(3) A similar computation would be made for interim reporting periods.

[FIN28, ¶22]

Example 2

.142 If the stock appreciation rights vested 25 percent per year commencing in 19X9, the computation of compensation expense in the preceding example would change as illustrated in the following paragraphs. [FIN28, ¶23]

.143 Because 25 percent of the rights vest each year commencing in 19X9, the service period over which compensation is accrued as a charge to expense is determined separately for each 25 percent portion. For example, the services for the 25 percent portion of the rights vesting in 19Y0 are performed in both 19X9 and 19Y0 and the related compensation is accrued proportionately as a charge to expense in each year. Similarly, compensation for rights vesting in 19Y1 is proportionately accrued as a charge to expense in 19X9, 19Y0, and 19Y1. In this way, compensation related to the portion of the rights vesting in 19X9 is recognized in 19X9, compensation related to the portion of the rights vesting in 19Y0 is recognized in 19X9 and 19Y0, and so forth. The following schedule indicates the service period for each 25 percent portion of the rights and the computation of the aggregate percentage of compensation accrued by the end of each year of service (the vesting period). A similar computation would be made for interim reporting periods.

		Aggregate Percentage of Compensation Accrued by the End of Each Year of Service			
For Rights Vesting in	**Service Period**	**19X9**	**19Y0**	**19Y1**	**19Y2**
19X9	1 year	25.00%	25.00%	25.00%	25%
19Y0	2 years	12.50	25.00	25.00	25
19Y1	3 years	8.33	16.67	25.00	25
19Y2	4 years	6.25	12.50	18.75	25
Aggregate percentage accrued at the end of each year		52.08%	79.17%	93.75%	100%
Rounded for purposes of Examples 2 and 3		52%	79%	94%	100%

For periods ending after 19Y2, 100 percent of the aggregate compensation shall be accrued. [FIN28, ¶24]

.144 Additional assumptions [are as follows]:

a. On December 31, 19Y1, the employee exercises the right to receive share appreciation on 300 shares.
b. On March 15, 19Y2, the employee exercises the right to receive share appreciation on 100 shares; quoted market price $15 per share.
c. On June 15, 19Y3, the employee exercises the right to receive share appreciation on 100 shares; quoted market price $16 per share.
d. On December 31, 19Y3, the employee exercises the right to receive share appreciation on 300 shares.
e. On December 31, 19Y4, the employee exercises the right to receive share appreciation on 200 shares.

[FIN28, ¶25]

[Exhibit 144A illustrates the annual computation of compensation expense for the above described stock appreciation right plan.]

Exhibit 144A

Illustration of Compensation Expense by Year for a Stock Appreciation Right Plan with Progressive Vesting over a Four-Year Period

		Number		Compensation					Accrual of Expense by Year (3)					
Date	Transaction	of Shares	Market Price	Per Share	Aggregate (1)	Percentage Accrued (2)	Compensation Accrued to Date	19X9	19Y0	19Y1	19Y2	19Y3	19Y4
12/31/X9	A		$11	$1	$ 1,000	52%	$ 520	$520					
	A						1,060		$1,060				
12/31/Y0			12	2	2,000	79	1,580						
	A						3,120			$3,120			
12/31/Y1			15	5	5,000	94	4,700						
12/31/Y1	E	300	15	5	(1,500)	–	(1,500)						
							3,200						
3/15/Y2	E	100	15	5	(500)	–	(500)						
							2,700						
	A						(300)				$(300)		
12/31/Y2			14	4	2,400	100	2,400						
6/15/Y3	E	100	16	6	(600)	–	(400)					$200	
							2,000						
	A						500					500	
12/31/Y3			15	5	2,500	100	2,500						
12/31/Y3	E	300	15	5	(1,500)	–	(1,500)						
							1,000						
	A						600						$600
12/31/Y4			18	8	1,600	100	1,600						
12/31/Y4	E	200	18	8	(1,600)	–	(1,600)						
							$ –						

Transaction Codes:

A—Adjustment for changes in the market price of stock.
E—Exercise of a stock appreciation right.

Notes:

(1) Aggregate compensation for unexercised shares to be allocated to periods service performed.
(2) Refer to the schedule in paragraph .143.
(3) A similar computation would be made for interim reporting periods.

[FIN28, ¶25]

Example 3

.145 If the plan limits the amount of share appreciation that the employee can receive to $5, the computation of compensation expense in Example 2 would change as illustrated in Exhibit 145A. [FIN28, ¶26]

.146 When the quoted market price exceeds the appreciation limitation, the employee is more likely to exercise the related stock option rather than the stock appreciation right. Therefore, accrued compensation is *not* adjusted for changes in the quoted market price of the stock. The assumptions stated in paragraph .144 are changed to the extent that on June 15, 19Y3 and December 31, 19Y4 the employee exercises the related stock option instead of the stock appreciation right. Accordingly, accrued compensation for the equivalent number of rights is recognized as part or all of the consideration for the stock issued in accordance with paragraph .122. [FIN28, ¶27]

Exhibit 145A

Illustration of Compensation Expense by Year for a Stock Appreciation Right Plan That Limits Appreciation per Share

		Number		Compensation					Accrual of Expense by Year (3)				
Date	Transaction	of Shares	Market Price	Per Share	Aggregate (1)	Percentage Accrued (2)	Compensation Accrued to Date	19X9	19Y0	19Y1	19Y2	19Y3	19Y4
12/31/X9	A		$11	$1	$ 1,000	52%	$ 520	$520					
	A						1,060		$1,060				
12/31/Y0			12	2	2,000	79	1,580						
	A						3,120			$3,120			
12/31/Y1			15	5	5,000	94	4,700						
12/31/Y1	E	300	15	5	(1,500)	–	(1,500)						
							3,200						
3/15/Y2	E	100	15	5	(500)	–	(500)						
							2,700						
	A						(300)				$(300)		
12/31/Y2			14	4	2,400	100	2,400						
6/15/Y3	O	100	16	5	(500)	–	(400)					$100	
							2,000						
	A						500					500	
12/31/Y3			15	5	2,500	100	2,500						
12/31/Y3	E	300	15	5	(1,500)	–	(1,500)						
							1,000						
	NA						–						$ –
12/31/Y4			18	5	1,000	100	1,000						
12/31/Y4	O	200	18	5	(1,000)	–	(1,000)						
							$ –						

Transaction Codes:
A—Adjustment for changes in the market price of stock.
NA—No adjustment required because the market price exceeds the appreciation limitation.
E—Exercise of a stock appreciation right.
O—Exercise of the related stock option.

Notes:
(1) Aggregate compensation for unexercised shares to be allocated to periods service performed.
(2) Refer to the schedule in paragraph .143.
(3) A similar computation would be made for interim reporting periods.

[FIN28, ¶27]

Interpretive Guidance on This Section

Scope

.147 *Question 1(a)*—Does this section apply to the accounting by a grantor for stock compensation granted to independent contractors or other service providers who are not employees of the grantor? [FIN44, ¶2]

.148 *Interpretation*—No. This section applies only to the accounting by an employer corporation for stock compensation based on the employer's stock granted to individuals who meet the definition of *employee* under this section as discussed further in Question 1(b) (paragraphs .149 through .151). Paragraph .103 states, "Paragraphs .106 through .118 [discuss] some aspects of accounting for stock issued to employees. . . ." This section does not apply to stock compensation granted to individuals who are either independent contractors or other service providers who are not employees of the grantor. [FIN44, ¶3]

.149 *Question 1(b)*—What is the definition of *employee* for purposes of applying this section? [FIN44, ¶4]

.150 *Interpretation*—A grantee is an employee if the grantor exercises or has the right to exercise sufficient control over that individual to establish an employer-employee relationship.[11] That relationship shall be determined based on common law as illustrated in case law and currently [in the United States] under U.S. Internal Revenue Service Revenue Ruling 87-41. Accordingly, for purposes of applying this section, a grantee meets the definition of an employee if the grantor consistently represents that individual to be an employee under common law. The definition of an employee for payroll tax purposes under the U.S. Internal Revenue Code includes common law employees. Accordingly, a grantor that classifies a grantee potentially subject to U.S. payroll taxes as an employee under this section must also (except as provided in paragraph .151) represent that individual as an employee for payroll tax purposes. A grantee does not meet the definition of an employee under this section solely because the grantor represents that individual as an employee for some, but not all, purposes. For example, a requirement or decision to classify a grantee as an employee for U.S. payroll tax purposes does not, by itself, indicate that the grantee is an employee for purposes of this section because the grantee must also be an employee of the grantor under common law. [FIN44, ¶5]

---

[11]The task of determining whether an individual service provider is an employee under this section requires judgment. The common law definition of *employee* represents the best available means for evaluating whether an employee-employer relationship exists between a service provider and an entity. This would be the case particularly with non-U.S. entities affiliated with U.S. companies. [FIN44, ¶102]

.151 A grantor may grant stock compensation to an individual who provides services to the grantor pursuant to a lease or co-employment agreement between the grantor and another entity under which the grantor is not the employer of record for payroll tax purposes. In this situation, whether the grantor-lessee classifies the grantee as an employee for payroll tax purposes is not relevant to determining whether the grantee is an employee under this section. A leased individual is deemed to be an employee of the lessee under this section if all of the following requirements are met:

a. The leased individual qualifies as a common law employee of the lessee, and the lessor is contractually required to remit payroll taxes on the compensation paid to the leased individual for the services provided to the lessee.
b. The lessor and lessee agree in writing to all of the following conditions related to the leased individual:
   (1) The lessee has the exclusive right to grant stock compensation to the individual for the employee service to the lessee.
   (2) The lessee has a right to hire, fire, and control the activities of the individual. (The lessor also may have that right.)
   (3) The lessee has the exclusive right to determine the economic value of the services performed by the individual (including wages and the number of units and value of stock compensation granted).
   (4) The individual has the ability to participate in the lessee's employee benefit plans, if any, on the same basis as other comparable employees of the lessee.
   (5) The lessee agrees to and remits funds sufficient to cover the complete compensation, including all payroll taxes, of the individual on or before a contractually agreed upon date or dates to the lessor.

[FIN44, ¶6]

.152 *Question 2*—Does this section apply to stock compensation granted to nonemployee members of the grantor's board of directors? [FIN44, ¶7]

.153 *Interpretation*—A nonemployee member of an entity's board of directors does not meet the definition of an employee in Question 1(b) (paragraphs .149 through .151). However, an exception is made to require the application of this section to stock compensation granted to a nonemployee member of the grantor's board of directors for services provided as a director if the nonemployee director (a) was elected by the grantor's shareholders or (b) was appointed to a board position that will be filled by shareholder election when the existing term expires. This section does not apply to awards granted to individuals for advisory or consulting services in a nonelected capacity or to nonemployee directors for services outside their role as a director, such as legal advice, investment banking advice, or loan guarantees. [FIN44, ¶8]

Awards Granted to Employees of Another Entity

.154 *Question 3*—Does this section apply to the accounting by a grantor for stock compensation granted to a nonemployee for employee services the grantee provides to another entity? [FIN44, ¶9]

.155 *Interpretation*—No. This section applies only to the accounting by a grantor for stock compensation granted to its employees as defined in Question 1(b) (paragraphs .149 through .151). Except for certain awards to nonemployee directors discussed in Question 2 (paragraphs .152 and .153), this section does not apply to the accounting by a grantor for stock compensation granted to nonemployees. For example, this section does not apply to the accounting by a corporate investor of an unconsolidated investee (or a joint venture owner) for stock options or awards granted by the investor (owner) to employees of the investee (joint venture) accounted for under the equity method because the grantees are not employees of the grantor. [FIN44, ¶10] An investor's accounting for costs incurred on behalf of an unconsolidated investee is an issue that is outside the scope of this section. [FIN44, ¶111]

.156 *Consolidated Financial Statements.* In consolidated financial statements, the evaluation of whether a grantee is an employee under this section is made at the consolidated group level and stock compensation based on the stock of a subsidiary is deemed to be stock compensation based on the stock of the consolidated group (the employer). Therefore, in the consolidated financial statements, stock compensation granted based on the stock of any consolidated group member shall be accounted for under this section if the grantee meets the definition of an employee for any entity in the consolidated group. For example, this section applies to the accounting in the consolidated financial statements for awards based on parent stock granted to employees of a (consolidated) subsidiary and to awards in stock of a (consolidated) subsidiary granted to employees of the parent. Also, this section applies to the accounting in the consolidated financial statements for awards based on a subsidiary's stock granted to the employees of another subsidiary. [The] guidance [in this paragraph] applies only to consolidated financial statements. Paragraph .159 addresses the scope of this section as it relates to separate financial statements of subsidiaries. [FIN44, ¶11]

Awards Granted to Employees Based on the Stock of Another Entity

.157 *Question 4*—Does this section apply to the accounting by an employer for stock compensation granted to its employees (a) by another entity based on that entity's stock (for example, an investee's accounting for investor stock awards granted by the investor to the investee's employees) or (b) by the employer based on the stock of another entity? [FIN44, ¶12]

.158 *Interpretation*—No. This section applies only to the accounting by an employer for stock compensation based on the stock of the employer granted to employees of that entity as defined in Question 1(b) (paragraphs .149 through .151).[12] Accordingly, this section does not apply to the accounting by an employer for awards based on stock of an entity other than the employer granted to employees, whether granted by the employer or another entity, such as a corporate investor. [FIN44, ¶13]

.159 *Separate Financial Statements of Subsidiaries.* Under the approach described in paragraph .158, this section does not apply to awards based on the stock of a parent company granted to an employee of a subsidiary for purposes of reporting in the separate financial statements of that subsidiary because parent-company stock is not stock of the subsidiary (employer). However, an exception is made to require the application of this section to stock compensation based on stock of the parent company granted to employees of a consolidated subsidiary for purposes of reporting in the separate financial statements of that subsidiary. The exception applies only to stock compensation based on stock of the parent company (accounted for under this section in the consolidated financial statements) granted to employees of an entity that is part of the consolidated group. This section does not apply in the separate financial statements of a subsidiary to the accounting for stock compensation granted (a) to the subsidiary's employees based on the stock of another subsidiary in the consolidated group or (b) by the subsidiary to employees of the parent or another subsidiary. [FIN44, ¶14]

Changes in Grantee Status

.160 *Question 5(a)*—What is the accounting consequence to a grantor if a grantee (who continues to provide services) changes status to or from that of an employee under this section and an outstanding stock option or award is retained by the grantee without a modification to the award's terms? [FIN44, ¶15]

---

[12]Paragraphs .501 through .506 of this section and paragraph .114 of Section C36 address the accounting by an employer for awards granted (in the stock of the employer) by a principal stockholder. [FIN44, ¶13, fn1]

.161 *Interpretation*—A change in status[13] may not be accompanied by a modification to the terms of an outstanding award that is retained by the grantee after the change in status. That is, the change in status does not result in forfeiture of the award (under the original terms), and no other modification is made to change or provide for a change to the life, the exercise or purchase price, or the number of shares (Question 9—paragraphs .175 and .176). If no modification is made to the terms of an outstanding stock option or award as a result of a change in status, compensation cost shall be measured under the appropriate method of accounting (that is, either the intrinsic value method under paragraphs .124 through .135 for employees or the fair value method under Section C36 for nonemployees) as if the outstanding award was newly granted at the date of the change in status. However, only that portion of the newly measured cost attributable to the remaining vesting (service) period shall be recognized as compensation cost prospectively from the date of the change in status. No adjustment shall be made to any compensation cost recognized by the grantor prior to the change in status unless the award is forfeited unvested because the grantee fails to fulfill an obligation. There is no accounting consequence if no modification is made to the award's terms as a result of the change in status and the retained award is a vested award. [FIN44, ¶16]

.162 For example, assume an entity grants an independent contractor (nonemployee) an option award that cliff-vests five years from the date of grant if the contractor continues as a service provider to the grantor through that date. At the end of the second year of the vesting period, the independent contractor becomes an employee and continues to provide similar services. The change in status does not result in forfeiture of the award under the original terms and no other modification is made. Assume the option award qualifies as a fixed award under this section at the date of the change in status. A new measurement date is required under the intrinsic value method at the date the independent contractor becomes an employee. However, only the portion of the newly measured compensation cost attributable to the remaining service period of 3 years (60 percent of the total vesting period of 5 years) is recognized over the remaining service period. In other words, if the compensation cost measured under the intrinsic value method at the date of the change in status is \$100, only \$60 of that cost is recognized over the remaining 3-year vesting (service) period. The remaining compensation cost measured under the intrinsic value method of this section at the date of the change in status is deemed to relate to services

[13]A grantee change in status from (to) an employee under this section to (from) a nonemployee can arise from a direct change in the relationship between the grantor and the grantee. A common example is an employer corporation that grants stock options to an employee and, at a later date, the grantee transfers to become an employee of an unconsolidated investee, such as a joint venture. Alternatively, a grantee change in status can arise from a transaction that involves the grantor and indirectly causes a change in the status of the grantee relative to the grantor. A common example is a parent company that grants stock options to an employee of a (consolidated) subsidiary. Subsequently, the parent disposes of a portion of its investment in the subsidiary such that it no longer consolidates the former subsidiary. [FIN44, ¶16, fn2]

previously rendered by the grantee as a nonemployee. The compensation cost that was recognized during the first two years of the vesting period (under the fair value method of Section C36) is not adjusted. However, if the individual terminates employment in year four (prior to vesting), the cumulative estimate of compensation cost recorded in the previous periods (under the fair value and intrinsic value methods) would be reduced to zero by decreasing compensation cost in the period of forfeiture. [FIN44, ¶17]

.163 *Question 5(b)*—What is the accounting consequence to a grantor if a grantee (who continues to provide services) changes status to or from that of an employee under this section and the change in status is accompanied by a modification to a stock option or award that is retained by the grantee? [FIN44, ¶18]

.164 *Interpretation*—If the change in status is accompanied by a modification to a stock option or award to change or provide for a change to the life, the exercise or purchase price, or the number of shares, the modified award shall be accounted for as a new award under the method of accounting appropriate for the new status of the grantee. In that case, any compensation cost measured is fully recognized over the remaining vesting (service) period, if any. The appropriate method of accounting (that is, either the fair value method under Section C36 for nonemployees or the intrinsic value method under paragraphs .124 through .135 for employees) shall be used to measure and fully recognize compensation cost on a prospective basis as if the award was newly granted at the date of the change in status. [FIN44, ¶19]

.165 A modification to an award has been made if the terms of the award or plan would have required the award to be forfeited upon the change in status and those terms are then modified to continue the award. In effect, the modification to the terms in connection with the change in status reinstates or extends the life of the award as a new award to the grantee immediately after the status change. Similarly, a modification, and an effective reinstatement of the award, has been made if the terms of an award (or underlying plan) provide for the award to continue at the discretion of the grantor and the grantee retains the award after the change in status. [FIN44, ¶20]

.166 For example, assume an entity grants an option award to an employee. Subsequently, the grantee becomes an employee of an unconsolidated investee. The terms of the award state that the award is forfeited upon termination of employment with the grantor entity (or a consolidated subsidiary). If the grantor modifies the terms of the award such that the award continues when the grantee transfers to the unconsolidated investee, the modified award is, in effect, the cancellation of the original award and the issuance of a new award to a nonemployee. Pursuant to Questions 1(a) and 3 (paragraphs .147, .148, and .154 through .156), this section does not apply to the accounting for the new award. Compensation cost previously recognized for the forfeited award, if any, would be adjusted to zero in the period of forfeiture. The (modified) new award would be accounted for under the fair value method of Section C36. [FIN44, ¶21]

.167 *Question 5(c)*—What is the accounting consequence to a grantor of a change in status of a grantee from that of an employee to a nonemployee as a result of a spinoff transaction? [FIN44, ¶22]

.168 *Interpretation*—A change in grantee status from that of an employee under this section to that of a nonemployee as a direct result of a spinoff transaction does not change the grantor's accounting method from [the method described in] this section to the fair value method for stock options or awards previously granted to the grantee as an employee.[14] Under this exception, compensation cost under this section, if any, would continue to be reported by the grantor as if the grantee was an employee without regard to the change in status. A change in status of the grantee in the consolidated financial reporting of the grantor occurs because, pursuant to Question 3 (paragraphs .154 through .156), a grantee employed by a spun-off entity ceases to be an employee of the grantor at the date of a spinoff transaction. This exception applies only to changes in status occurring as a result of a spinoff transaction (that is, a pro rata distribution to owners of an entity of shares of a subsidiary) such that the entity will no longer consolidate the former subsidiary and only to awards that were granted and outstanding, including adjustments to those awards in accordance with the guidance in Question 11(c) (paragraphs .197 through .199), at the date of the transaction. New awards granted by the grantor to a nonemployee grantee after the date of the spinoff transaction shall be accounted for under the fair value method. Questions 5(a) and 5(b) (paragraphs .160 through .166) apply to all grantee changes in status other than those caused by a spinoff transaction. For example, this exception does not apply to changes in status of a grantee that occur as a result of an exchange transaction, such as the sale by a parent company of a large enough percentage of the shares of a subsidiary such that the parent will no longer consolidate the former subsidiary. [FIN44, ¶23]

Noncompensatory Plans

.169 *Question 6*—Paragraph .106(d) of this section provides as one criterion for determining whether a plan is noncompensatory that "the discount from the market price of the stock is no greater than would be reasonable in an offer of stock to stockholders or others." Does a purchase discount of up to 15 percent meet that criterion? [FIN44, ¶24]

---

[14]Question 11(c) (paragraphs .197 through .199) addresses the accounting consequence of a change to the number of shares, the exercise price, or both, as a result of an equity restructuring, including a spinoff transaction. [FIN44, ¶23, fn3]

.170 *Interpretation*—Yes. This section refers to a plan that qualifies under Section 423 of the U.S. Internal Revenue Code as an example of a noncompensatory plan. Section 423 (which has not changed significantly since the issuance [in 1972] of the guidance in paragraph .106) permits discounts of up to 15 percent for a qualified employee stock purchase plan. [FIN44, ¶25]

.171 *Question 7*—In determining whether a plan is noncompensatory, may the stock price at the date of grant of a stock option be used as the basis for determining whether "the discount from the market price of the stock is no greater than would be reasonable in an offer of stock to stockholders or others"? [FIN44, ¶26]

.172 *Interpretation*—Yes. A noncompensatory plan may be in the form of a stock option with an exercise price that is fixed at the date of grant. Provided that the exercise price on the grant date of the option is no less than 85 percent of the stock price on that date, the discount is considered reasonable for purposes of determining whether the plan is noncompensatory. [FIN44, ¶27]

.173 *Question 8*—May a plan with a *look-back option* qualify as a noncompensatory plan? [FIN44, ¶28]

.174 *Interpretation*—Yes. An example of a look-back option is a provision in an employee stock purchase plan that establishes the purchase price as an amount based on the lesser of the stock's market price at the grant date or its market price at the exercise (purchase) date. This section states that an example of a noncompensatory plan is one that qualifies under Section 423 of the U.S. Internal Revenue Code. Section 423 permits a qualified employee stock purchase plan to contain a look-back option. Consequently, this section permits a plan with a look-back option to qualify as a noncompensatory plan. [FIN44, ¶29]

Modifications to a Fixed Stock Option or Award

.175 *Question 9*—Is there an accounting consequence under this section if the terms of a fixed stock option or award are modified after the original measurement date? [FIN44, ¶30]

.176 *Interpretation*—An accounting consequence occurs under this section if a modification[15] to the terms of a fixed stock option or award changes or, if certain specified future events occur, provides for a change to (a) the life of the award through an extension of the exercise period or a renewal, (b) the exercise or purchase price of the award,

[15]If the terms of an entire plan are modified, the new terms are considered part of an award's original terms only for any stock option or award granted after the plan modification date. [FIN44, ¶31, fn4]

or (c) the number of shares the grantee is entitled to receive. The nature of the accounting consequence depends on the type of modification. A modification to a fixed stock option or award that does not affect the life of the award, the exercise price, or the number of shares to be issued has no accounting consequence. Paragraphs .177 through .204 provide guidance on the accounting consequence under this section for the following types of modifications to a fixed stock option or award:

a. A modification that renews or extends the life of an award (for example, acceleration of vesting) or provides for an extension or renewal if a specified future separation from employment occurs (Question 10—paragraphs .177 through .182)
b. A modification that reduces the exercise price of an award (Question 11—paragraphs .183 through .199)
c. A modification that increases the number of shares to be issued under an award, including the addition of a reload feature (Question 12—paragraphs .200 through .204).

[FIN44, ¶31]

Modifications That Renew or Increase Life

.177 *Question 10*—What is the accounting consequence of a modification that renews or extends the life of a fixed award (for example, acceleration of vesting) or provides for an extension or renewal if a specified future separation from employment occurs? [FIN44, ¶32]

.178 *Interpretation*—Consistent with paragraph .111(d) of this section, a modification that either renews a fixed award or extends the award's period (life) results in a new measurement of compensation cost as if the award were newly granted. [FIN44, ¶33]

.179 A modification, including a modification contingent upon a future separation from employment, that extends the maximum contractual life of an award results in a new measurement of compensation cost at the date of the modification. Any intrinsic value at the modification date in excess of the amount measured at the original measurement date shall be recognized as compensation cost over the remaining future service period if the award is unvested, or immediately if the award is vested, for any employee who could benefit from the modification. [FIN44, ¶34]

.180 A modification to increase the life of an option award upon separation from employment, but not beyond the original maximum contractual life, results in an extension of that award at the date the separation event occurs and the life of the option award is extended. Accordingly, (a) the intrinsic value of the option award shall be measured at the date of the modification and (b) any intrinsic value in excess of the amount measured at the original measurement date shall be recognized as compensation cost if the separation event occurs. If the option award vests and is exercised prior to the separation event, any incremental intrinsic value at the date of the modification is not recognized because the life of the option award has not been extended. Attribution of any additional compensation cost may require estimates, and adjustment of those estimates in later periods may be necessary. [FIN44, ¶35]

.181 A modification to accelerate the vesting of a fixed award effectively results in the renewal of that award if, after the modification, an employee is able to exercise (vest in) an award that, under the original terms, would have expired unexercisable (unvested). A modification may provide for an acceleration of vesting if certain specified future events occur. The modification effectively results in a renewal of the award if the event occurs, vesting accelerates, and the employee is able to exercise (vest in) an award that otherwise would have expired unexercisable (unvested) pursuant to the award's original terms. [FIN44, ¶36] However, if an employee continues to provide service and would have vested in the award under its original vesting provisions, the modification does not cause an effective renewal of the award and, accordingly, any incremental compensation cost measured as of the modification date should not be recognized. [FIN44, ¶126] Accordingly, (a) the intrinsic value of the award shall be measured at the date of the modification and (b) any intrinsic value in excess of the amount measured at the original measurement date shall be recognized as compensation cost if, absent the acceleration, the award would have been forfeited unexercisable (unvested) pursuant to the original terms. Attribution of any additional compensation cost may require estimates, and adjustments of those estimates in later periods may be necessary. [FIN44, ¶36]

.182 If vesting is accelerated based on the occurrence of a specific event or condition in accordance with the original terms of the award, a modification has not been made and, therefore, no new measurement of compensation cost is required.[16] That would be the case if, for example, the original terms of an award specify that vesting is accelerated upon retirement, death, or disability and one of those events occurs in the future. [FIN44, ¶37]

Modifications That Reduce Exercise Price

.183 *Question 11(a)*—What is the accounting consequence of a modification that reduces the exercise price of a fixed stock option award (commonly referred to as repricing)? [FIN44, ¶38]

[16]If the original terms of the award provide for vesting to be accelerated at the discretion of the entity (or on some other discretionary basis), subsequent acceleration of vesting is a modification. [FIN44, ¶37, fn5]

.184 *Interpretation*—If the exercise price of a fixed stock option award is reduced,[17] the award shall be accounted for as variable from the date of the modification to the date the award is exercised, is forfeited, or expires unexercised. The exercise price of an option award has been reduced if the fair value of the consideration required to be remitted by the grantee upon exercise is less than or potentially less than the fair value of the consideration that was required to be remitted pursuant to the award's original terms.[18] [FIN44, ¶39]

.185 A grantor can indirectly reduce the exercise price of an option award without revising the stated terms of the award. For example, a grantor can provide the grantee with a cash bonus arrangement that vests (is paid) only if the option award is exercised, or a grantor can permit the grantee to exercise the option award with a full-recourse note that does not bear a market interest rate. In those cases, the grantor has indirectly reduced the exercise price of the award based on the fair value of the overall consideration that the grantor will receive upon exercise, even though the stated exercise price of the option award itself is unchanged. The guidance in Question 20 (paragraphs .235 through .237) about when stock awards and cash bonus arrangements should be accounted for as combined awards shall be applied to determine when the exercise price of a stock option award has been indirectly reduced by the addition of a cash bonus arrangement. [FIN44, ¶40]

.186 A grantor can directly or indirectly reduce the exercise price of an award contingent upon the occurrence of a specified future event or condition. For example, a grantor can directly modify an award to provide that the exercise price will be reduced if a certain earnings target or stock price is achieved in the future. If a fixed stock option award is modified to provide for a reduction to the award's exercise price if specified future events or conditions occur, variable accounting shall be required for the award from the date of the modification to the date the award is exercised, is forfeited, or expires unexercised, *regardless of whether the triggering event occurs or the contingency provision expires*. In other words, a direct or indirect modification to a fixed option award to provide for a contingent reduction to the exercise price causes the award to be variable for the remainder of its outstanding life. [FIN44, ¶41]

---

[17]It is not practical to address every potential set of facts or sequence of actions that could cause an effective reduction to the exercise price of a stock option award. Any modification or sequence of actions by a grantor to directly or effectively reduce the exercise price of an option award causes variable accounting for the repriced (replacement) award for the remainder of the award's life. [FIN44, ¶131]

[18]Because the price has been changed once, there is no practical way to ascertain whether the price is fixed or whether further reductions to the exercise price will occur in the future. Consequently, the substantive terms of the award prevent the exercise price from being determined until the option award is exercised, is forfeited, or expires unexercised. [FIN44, ¶128] Variable accounting applies only to the individual option awards that are repriced. [FIN44, ¶129]

.187 In contrast, if the original terms of a stock option award provide for a reduction to the award's exercise price if a specified future event or condition occurs, variable accounting would be required from the date of grant. However, a measurement date would occur and variable accounting would cease at the date the contingency is resolved or the contingency provision expires. [FIN44, ¶42]

.188 A grantor can indirectly reduce the exercise price of a fixed stock option award by (a) canceling (paragraph .189 provides guidance on effective cancellations) or settling for cash or other consideration an outstanding option award and (b) granting a replacement award at a lower exercise price, either before or after the cancellation (settlement). If the cancellation (settlement) of a fixed stock option award is combined with the grant of another option award at a lower exercise price, the guidance in paragraphs .190 through .192 requires variable accounting for the replacement award until that award is exercised, is forfeited, or expires unexercised. [FIN44, ¶43]

.189 A grantor can, in effect, cancel an option award in various ways. For example, an option award can be, in effect, canceled by modifying its terms to reduce or eliminate the likelihood that the grantee will exercise that option. Any modification to the terms of an option award to reduce the likelihood of exercise by the grantee shall be considered a cancellation of that award. For example, any increase in the exercise price or any curtailment of the remaining life of an option award shall be considered a cancellation. [FIN44, ¶44]

.190 An option award cancellation (settlement) shall be combined with another option award and results in an indirect reduction to the exercise price of the combined award if another option with a lower exercise price than the canceled (settled) option is granted to the individual within the following periods:

a. The period prior to the date of the cancellation (settlement) that is the shorter of (1) six months or (2) the period from the date of grant of the canceled or settled option
b. The period ending six months after the date of the cancellation (settlement).

[FIN44, ¶45]

.191 For purposes of identifying the replacement award (the combined award) that becomes subject to variable accounting upon the cancellation (settlement) of an award, the grantor shall first look back in the period prior to the cancellation (settlement) described in paragraph .190(a). If an award was granted during that period with an exercise price below that of the canceled award, that award and the canceled award shall be combined. If canceled options remain that were not combined with a replacement award in the look-back period, the grantor shall then look forward to the period described in paragraph .190(b). If an award is granted during that period at a price below that of the canceled award, that award and the canceled award shall be combined. When looking back and then forward, options granted at dates in closest proximity to the date of the cancellation (settlement) shall be the first to be identified as the replacement award. If the replacement option award is identified in the look-back period, variable accounting for that award shall commence at the cancellation date. That is, prior-period financial statements shall not be restated if the award was accounted for as a fixed award in those financial statements. [FIN44, ¶46]

.192 Notwithstanding the guidance above, any oral or written agreement or implied promise by a grantor to compensate the grantee for any increases in the market price of the stock after a cancellation (settlement), but prior to grant of a replacement award, shall require variable accounting for the replacement award irrespective of the period of time elapsed between the cancellation (settlement) and a replacement grant. Any agreement between a grantor and grantee at the time an option award is granted to cancel or settle at a future date another outstanding option award shall require variable accounting for the newly granted award from the date of grant. [FIN44, ¶47]

.193 The guidance in paragraphs .190 though .192 also shall apply to the cancellation (settlement)[19] of an option award that has been accounted for as variable as a result of a reduction to that award's exercise price through a prior modification. However, any option award granted during the look-back and look-forward periods in paragraph .190, regardless of whether the replacement award has a higher, equivalent, or lower exercise price, shall be eligible to be the replacement award. That is, any replacement of a modified award that has been accounted for as a variable award retains that variable status. [FIN44, ¶48]

.194 *Question 11(b)*—What is the accounting consequence of a cancellation (settlement) of a fixed stock option award and the grant of stock? [FIN44, ¶49]

.195 *Interpretation*—If a grantor cancels or settles a fixed stock option award and replaces that award with stock, a new measurement of compensation cost shall be required for the stock award pursuant to the guidance in Question 13 (paragraphs .205 through .209). The exercise price of the original option award has effectively been reduced to zero, and future reductions to the exercise price of the replacement stock award are not possible; therefore, variable accounting shall not apply to the replacement stock award. [FIN44, ¶50]

[19]If the settlement of an option award and the grant of another award are combined according to guidance in paragraphs .190 through .192, the settlement consideration is an additional element of compensation, and variable accounting is required for the replacement award. [FIN44, ¶134]

.196 Any excess of the number of shares underlying a fixed stock option award that is canceled over the number of shares of the replacement stock award shall be subject to the guidance in Question 11(a) (paragraphs .183 through .193). For example, assume a grantor cancels a fixed stock option award for 100 shares. At the date of the cancellation the grantor issues the employee a stock award for 75 shares. A new measurement of compensation cost is required for the stock award. Seventy-five of the 100 canceled options are considered to be replaced by the 75 shares granted in the stock award. The remaining 25 canceled options are then subject to the cancellation guidance in Question 11(a) (paragraphs .183 through .193). [FIN44, ¶51]

.197 *Question 11(c)*—What is the accounting consequence of a change to the exercise price, the number of shares, or both, of a fixed stock option or award that occurs as a direct result of an equity restructuring? [FIN44, ¶52]

.198 *Interpretation*—Adjustments may be made to the exercise price, the number of shares, or both, of outstanding stock options or awards as a result of an equity restructuring transaction. An equity restructuring is a nonreciprocal transaction between an entity and its shareholders, such as a stock dividend, spinoff, stock split, rights offering, or recapitalization through a special, large nonrecurring dividend that causes the market value per share of the stock underlying the option or award to decrease.[20] At the time of an equity restructuring transaction, the exercise price may be reduced, the number of shares under the award increased, or both, to offset the decrease in the per-share price of the stock underlying the award. There shall be no accounting consequence for changes made to the exercise price, the number of shares, or both, of an outstanding fixed award as a result of an equity restructuring if both of the following criteria are met:

a. The aggregate intrinsic value of the award immediately after the change is not greater than the aggregate intrinsic value of the award immediately before the change.
b. The ratio of the exercise price per share to the market value per share is not reduced.

[FIN44, ¶53]

.199 If the criteria above are not met, the modified award shall be accounted for under this section as variable from the date of the modification to the date the award is exercised, is forfeited, or expires unexercised. If the two criteria above are met but the terms of the original award have also been modified to either accelerate the vesting or extend the life of the modified award, the guidance in Question 10 (paragraphs .177 through .182) shall be applied. Cash or other consideration provided to restore the economic position of the grantee as a result of an equity restructuring transaction shall be

[20] Ordinary cash dividends or distributions shall not be considered an equity restructuring for the purposes of applying this guidance. [FIN44, ¶53, fn6]

recognized as compensation cost. The guidance above shall be applied without regard to whether or not the provisions of the stock option or award provide for adjustments to the terms in the event of an equity restructuring. [FIN44, ¶54]

Modifications That Increase the Number of Shares to Be Issued

.200 *Question 12(a)*—What is the accounting consequence of a modification that increases the number of shares to be issued under a fixed stock option award? [FIN44, ¶55]

.201 *Interpretation*—If a grantor increases the number of shares to be issued under a fixed stock option award, the award shall be accounted for as variable from the date of the modification to the date the award is exercised, is forfeited, or expires unexercised. [FIN44, ¶56]

.202 *Question 12(b)*—What is the accounting consequence of a modification to a fixed stock option award to add a reload feature? [FIN44, ¶57]

.203 *Interpretation*—A reload feature provides for the grant of a new option award upon the exercise of an existing award if specified conditions are met. Consistent with Question 12(a) (paragraphs .200 and .201), if a grantor modifies a fixed stock option award to add a reload feature, variable accounting shall be required for the modified award from the date of the modification to the date the award is exercised, is forfeited, or expires unexercised.[21] If the reload feature provides for multiple subsequent grants through further reloads, variable accounting shall be required for each additional grant that includes that reload feature. [FIN44, ¶58]

.204 A common reload feature provides for the automatic grant of a new option at the then-current market price in exchange for each previously owned share tendered by an employee in a stock-for-stock exercise. However, if a fixed stock option award is modified to add any feature that provides for the grant of a new option award if the existing award is exercised, the modified award shall be accounted for as variable, regardless of the method used to determine the terms (exercise price, number of shares, and life) of the reload grant. [FIN44, ¶59]

---

[21]EITF Issue No. 90-7, "Accounting for a Reload Stock Option," has been consistently applied in practice for the limited fact pattern that it addresses (a reload feature that provides for the automatic grant of a new option at the then-current market price in exchange for each previously owned share tendered by an employee in a stock-for-stock exercise). Therefore, [a decision was made] not to overturn at this time the consensus in Issue 90-7 for the specific fact pattern addressed by that consensus. [FIN44, ¶143]

Recognition and Measurement of Compensation Cost

.205 *Question 13*—How should compensation cost be measured and recognized if a fixed stock option or award is canceled or if a new measurement of compensation cost or variable accounting is required as a result of a modification to the award? [FIN44, ¶60]

.206 *Interpretation*—If a fixed stock option or award is canceled or modified such that a new measurement of compensation cost or variable accounting is required, total compensation cost shall be measured as the sum of the following:

a. The intrinsic value of the award (if any) at the original measurement date
b. The intrinsic value of the modified (or variable) award that exceeds the lesser of the intrinsic value of the original award (1) at the original measurement date or (2) immediately prior to the modification.

[FIN44, ¶61]

.207 If a stock option or award is modified such that a new measurement of compensation cost or variable accounting is required, the remaining unrecognized original intrinsic value, if any, plus any additional compensation cost measured under paragraph .206(b) shall be recognized over the remaining vesting (service) period, if any. If the modified award is fully vested at the date of the modification, any additional compensation cost to be recognized shall be recognized immediately. Recognized compensation cost for an award that is forfeited as a result of an employee's failure to fulfill an obligation shall be reduced to zero by decreasing compensation cost in the period of forfeiture, pursuant to paragraph .115 of this section. [FIN44, ¶62]

.208 For modifications to accelerate vesting or to extend the life of an award upon a specified future separation from employment (but not beyond the award's original maximum contractual life), additional compensation cost measured as of the modification date shall be recognized for all awards for which the modification results in an effective term extension or an effective renewal pursuant to the guidance in Question 10 (paragraphs .177 through .182). Attribution of additional compensation cost may require estimates and adjustments of those estimates in later periods. [FIN44, ¶63]

.209 If a modification (including a modification through a cancellation and a replacement grant) requires variable accounting for the modified (replacement) award, compensation cost shall be adjusted for increases or decreases in the intrinsic value of the modified (replacement) award in subsequent periods until that award is exercised, is forfeited, or expires unexercised. However, compensation cost shall not be adjusted below the intrinsic value (if any) of the modified stock option or award at the original measurement date unless the award is forfeited because the employee fails to fulfill an obligation. [FIN44, ¶64]

.210 *Question 14*—How should compensation cost be measured if cash is paid to settle a stock option or (unvested) stock award or to repurchase shares within six months after option exercise or issuance of the repurchased shares? [FIN44, ¶65]

.211 *Interpretation*—If cash is paid to an employee to settle an outstanding stock option, to settle an earlier grant of a stock award within six months after vesting, or to repurchase shares within six months after exercise of an option or issuance, total compensation cost shall be measured as the sum of:

a. The intrinsic value of the stock option or award (if any) at the original measurement date
b. The amount of cash paid to the employee (reduced by any amount paid by the employee to acquire the shares) that exceeds the lesser of the intrinsic value (if any) of the award (1) at the original measurement date or (2) immediately prior to the cash settlement.

[FIN44, ¶66]

Share Repurchase (and Tax-Withholding) Features

.212 *Question 15(a)*—Is variable accounting required for a stock option or award with a share repurchase feature (for example, a put, call, or right of first refusal)? [FIN44, ¶67]

.213 *Interpretation*—For *public entities,* except for repurchases for tax withholding pursuant to Question 15(c) (paragraphs .220 and .221), variable accounting is required for a stock option or award with a share repurchase feature if the shares are expected to be repurchased within six months after option exercise or issuance of those shares. If the repurchase feature is a right held by the employee to sell those shares back to the entity, variable accounting shall be required for the award if that right can be exercised within six months of issuance of the shares. After an option is exercised, the employee bears the risks and rewards of ownership with respect to those shares.[22] Consequently, a subsequent repurchase of the shares by the entity (except within six months after option exercise or share issuance) represents a separate transaction to acquire treasury stock that shall be accounted for apart from the original stock option or award. [FIN44, ¶68]

---

[22]Pursuant to footnote 1 of this section, if the consideration for the exercise is a nonrecourse note, the substance is the same as a stock option and the employee does not bear any risks and rewards of ownership in the shares received. [FIN44, ¶68, fn7]

.214 If an entity repurchases shares within six months of issuance or option exercise and the repurchase was not expected by the entity prior to the date of the repurchase, the entity shall follow the guidance in Question 14 (paragraphs .210 and .211) for cash settlement of an earlier award. [FIN44, ¶69]

.215 If a share repurchase feature gives the employee the right to sell the shares back to the entity (after option exercise or share issuance) for a premium (that is not fixed and determinable) over the then-current stock price, that share repurchase feature creates an arrangement that requires variable accounting even if the shares cannot be sold back to the entity within six months after option exercise or issuance. If a share repurchase feature gives the employee the right to sell shares back to the entity for a fixed dollar amount over the stock price (but not within six months of issuance of those shares), the fixed premium shall be recognized as additional compensation cost over the vesting (service) period. [FIN44, ¶70] [Refer to paragraph .1001 for an EITF Issue that provides interpretive guidance on this paragraph.]

.216 For *nonpublic entities,* variable accounting shall not be required for a stock option or award with the following share repurchase features:

a. The stated share repurchase price is equal to the fair value of the shares at the date of repurchase, the employee cannot require the entity to repurchase the shares within six months of option exercise or share issuance, and the shares are not expected to be repurchased within six months after exercise or share issuance.
b. The stated share repurchase price is other than the fair value of the shares at the date of repurchase (for example, under a book value plan), but the employee has made a substantial investment and must bear risks and rewards normally associated with share ownership for a reasonable period (at least six months).
c. Shares are repurchased for tax-withholding purposes pursuant to Question 15(c) (paragraphs .220 and .221).

[FIN44, ¶71]

.217 For purposes of this section, a public entity includes any entity (a) whose securities trade in a public market either on a stock exchange (domestic or foreign) or in an over-the-counter market, including securities quoted only locally or regionally, (b) that makes a filing with a regulatory agency in preparation for the sale of any class of equity securities in a public market, or (c) that is controlled by an entity that meets the criterion of (a) or (b). A subsidiary of a public entity or a public entity with thinly traded stock shall follow the accounting prescribed for a public entity. However, an entity with publicly traded debt but no publicly traded equity securities shall follow the accounting prescribed for a nonpublic entity. [FIN44, ¶72]

.218 *Question 15(b)*—For nonpublic entities with awards containing repurchase features at other than fair value, such as a book value stock purchase plan, when is an employee considered to have made a substantial investment? [FIN44, ¶73]

.219 *Interpretation*—For purposes of an award that contains a repurchase feature at other than fair value, a substantial investment has been made when the employee invests (in a form other than services rendered to the entity) an amount equal to 100 percent of the stated share repurchase price calculated at the date of grant. Accordingly, if the award is an option, a substantial investment cannot exist prior to exercise of that option. Compensation cost shall be recognized (as the award is variable) for any intrinsic value of the option from the date of grant to the date a substantial investment has been made. [FIN44, ¶74]

.220 *Question 15(c)*—Consistent with paragraph .111(g) of this section, for public and nonpublic entities, variable accounting is not required for shares expected to be repurchased (at fair value) upon option exercise or share issuance only to meet required tax withholding. What is the definition of required tax withholding? [FIN44, ¶75]

.221 *Interpretation*—Required tax withholding is the *employer's* minimum statutory withholding (based on minimum statutory withholding rates for federal and state tax purposes, including payroll taxes, that are applicable to such supplemental taxable income). Withheld amounts in excess of that rate do not represent the *employer's required tax withholding* for purposes of this section. Refer to Question 15(d) (paragraphs .222 through .225). [FIN44, ¶76]

.222 *Question 15(d)*—Is variable accounting required for stock options granted with terms in the award or plan that permit share repurchases upon exercise in excess of the number necessary to satisfy the employer's required tax withholding? [FIN44, ¶77]

.223 *Interpretation*—If the election is at the discretion of the employee, variable accounting is required from the date the award is granted to the date the award is exercised, is forfeited, or expires unexercised. [FIN44, ¶78]

.224 If the terms of an award or plan are silent with respect to tax withholding or if the repurchase of shares for tax withholding in excess of the number necessary to satisfy the employer's required tax withholding is at the discretion of the employer, variable accounting shall not be required. However, in either circumstance, if the employer exhibits a pattern of consistently approving repurchases of excess shares, variable accounting shall be required from the date of grant for all awards under the plan. [FIN44, ¶79]

.225 If shares are repurchased upon exercise of a fixed option award in excess of the number necessary to satisfy the employer's required tax withholding, a new measurement of compensation cost shall be required for the entire award. [FIN44, ¶80]

Business Combinations

.226–.227 [Deleted 6/01 because of FASB Statement 141, *Business Combinations.*]

.228 *Question 17*—Should an exchange of employee stock options or awards in a business combination be accounted for by the acquirer under this section as employee stock compensation or under [FIN44, ¶83] Section B51, "Business Combinations," [FAS141, ¶E22(b)] as part of the consideration paid for the acquiree? [FIN44, ¶83]

.229 *Interpretation—Vested Options.* In a business combination, vested stock options or awards issued by an acquirer in exchange for outstanding awards held by employees of the acquiree shall be considered to be part of the purchase price paid by the acquirer for the acquiree and accounted for under [FIN44, ¶84] Section B51. [FAS141, ¶E22(c)] Accordingly, the fair value of the new (acquirer) awards shall be included as part of the purchase price. [FIN44, ¶84]

.230 *Unvested Options.* Unvested stock options or awards granted by an acquirer in exchange for stock options or awards held by employees of the acquiree shall be considered to be part of the purchase price for the acquiree, and the fair value of the new (acquirer) awards shall be included in the purchase price. However, to the extent that service is required subsequent to the consummation date of the acquisition in order to vest in the replacement awards, a portion of the intrinsic value (if any) of the unvested awards shall be allocated to unearned compensation and recognized as compensation cost over the remaining future vesting (service) period. The amount allocated to unearned compensation cost shall be based on the portion of the intrinsic value at the consummation date related to the future vesting (service) period. That amount shall be calculated as the intrinsic value of the replacement awards at the consummation date multiplied by the fraction that is the remaining future vesting (service) period divided by the total vesting (service) period (the vesting period prior to the consummation date plus the remaining future period required to vest in the replacement award). Any intrinsic value of the replacement awards that is allocated to unearned compensation cost shall be deducted from the fair value of the awards for purposes of the allocation of the purchase price to the other assets acquired. [FIN44, ¶85]

[[23]Editorial deletion, 6/01.]

Other Issues

Grant Date

.231 *Question 18*—If a plan is subject to shareholder approval, can the grant date ever be deemed to occur prior to obtaining that approval? [FIN44, ¶86]

.232 *Interpretation*—Generally, awards granted under a plan that is subject to shareholder approval shall not be deemed granted (and, therefore, no measurement date can occur) until that approval is obtained. However, if management and the members of the board of directors control sufficient votes to approve the plan, a grant date (and a measurement date) may be deemed to occur prior to shareholder approval because such approval is essentially a formality. Consequently, in most cases, required shareholder approval must be obtained in order to conclude that a grant (and a measurement) date for an award has occurred under this section. [FIN44, ¶87]

Deferred Tax Assets

.233 *Question 19*—Should the carrying amount of a deferred tax asset recognized for a temporary difference related to a stock option or award accounted for under this section be adjusted for a subsequent decline in the stock price? [FIN44, ¶88]

.234 *Interpretation*—No. Deferred tax assets shall be determined by the compensation expense recognized for financial reporting rather than by reference to the expected future tax deduction (which would be estimated using the current intrinsic value of the award). A valuation allowance to reduce the carrying amount of those deferred tax assets shall be established only if the entity expects future taxable income to be insufficient to recover the deferred tax assets in the periods in which the deduction would otherwise be recognized for tax purposes. [FIN44, ¶89]

Cash Bonus Plan Linked to a Stock Compensation Award

.235 *Question 20*—When should a cash bonus and a stock option or award be accounted for under this section as a combined award? [FIN44, ¶90]

.236 *Interpretation*—A cash bonus and a stock option award shall be accounted for as a combined award if payment (by the entity) or refund (by the employee) of the cash bonus is contingent upon exercise of the option award. A cash bonus that is not fixed and that is contingent upon exercise of an option award shall be accounted for as a combined variable award. A fixed cash bonus that is contingent upon exercise of a fixed option award shall be accounted for as a combined fixed award with the cash bonus reducing the stated exercise price of the option award. [FIN44, ¶91]

.237 A cash bonus, whether fixed or variable, that is contingent upon vesting of a stock option or award shall be accounted for as compensation cost separate from the stock option or award. [FIN44, ¶92]

Examples Illustrating Application of Paragraphs .147 through .237

.238 Paragraphs .239 through .292 illustrate the application of certain provisions in paragraphs .147 through .237. The examples and related assumptions in paragraphs .239 through .292 are illustrative only. These paragraphs are a supplement to paragraphs .147 through .237. They should not be interpreted to alter any requirements of paragraphs .147 through .237, nor should they be considered a substitute for the requirements. The examples do not comprehend all possible combinations of circumstances. [FIN44, ¶154]

Illustration 1—Definition of an Employee

.239 Company A issues options to members of its Advisory Board. Members of the Advisory Board have specific knowledge and expertise within Company A's industry and are granted stock options as compensation for advising Company A on such matters as policy development, strategic planning, and product development. The Advisory Board members are appointed for two-year terms and meet twice a year for one day. Members receive a fixed number of options for each meeting. Based on an evaluation of the relationship between Company A and the Advisory Board members, Company A concludes that the Advisory Board members do not meet the common law definition of an employee. Accordingly, the awards to the Advisory Board members are outside the scope of this section. Additionally, the exception in Question 2 (paragraphs .152 and .153) applies only to stock options or awards granted to nonemployee members of an entity's board of directors for their services as directors. Therefore, awards to those service providers do not meet the criteria for that exception. [FIN44, ¶155]

Illustration 2—Accounting for a Change in Grantee Status

.240 Company S grants 100,000 fixed options to an employee on January 1, 20X1. Company S measures stock compensation to employees under paragraphs .124 through .135 using the intrinsic value method. The exercise price of each option equals the quoted market price of Company S's stock on the grant (measurement) date. All options cliff-vest at the end of four years. The grantee subsequently changes status on January 1, 20X3 to that of a non-employee service provider. According to the terms under which the options were granted, the grantee does not forfeit the options upon termination as an employee if the grantee continues to provide services as a consultant or other nonemployee service provider. The fair value on January 1 of Company S stock and each option is:

	Stock	Option
20X1	$10	$ 3.00
20X2	15	7.50
20X3	20	12.25
20X4	25	17.50
20X5	30	22.75

[FIN44, ¶156]

.241 Company S has compensation cost of zero for 20X1 and 20X2, because the grantee is an employee and compensation cost is measured at the grant date under the intrinsic value method. For 20X3 and 20X4, compensation cost is measured and recognized under the fair value method[24] (the grantee is now a nonemployee) as follows:

Year Ended	A = Fair Value of Options	B = % Vesting Period Remaining after Change in Status	C = (A * B) Amount of Compensation Cost under the Fair Value Method Attributable to Remaining Vesting	D = % of Nonemployee Service Rendered	E = Nonemployee Cost Previously Recognized	F = (C * D − E) Current Year Cost
20X3	$1,750,000	50%	$875,000	50%	$0	$437,500
20X4	$2,275,000	50%	$1,137,500	100%	$437,500	$700,000

[FIN44, ¶157]

---

[24]The measurement date for equity instruments issued to nonemployees is addressed in EITF Issue No. 96-18, "Accounting for Equity Instruments That Are Issued to Other Than Employees for Acquiring, or in Conjunction with Selling, Goods or Services." This example assumes that a measurement date as defined in Issue 96-18 does not occur until performance is complete. [FIN44, ¶157, fn8]

Illustration 3—Modifications and Cash Settlements

.242 The following examples illustrate application of paragraphs .147 through .237 in measuring and recognizing compensation cost for fixed award modifications and cash settlements. [FIN44, ¶158]

Illustration 3(a)—Modification to Accelerate Vesting of a Fixed Stock Option Award

.243 Company R grants 100 fixed stock options with an exercise price equal to the quoted market price of the stock at the date of grant to each of its 200 employees. The options cliff-vest at the end of five years. Two years after the grant date, Company R modifies the awards to immediately vest the options. At the modification date, each option has an intrinsic value of $40. Based on historical employee turnover rates and Company R's best estimate of future employee separation, Company R estimates that 70 employees will terminate employment prior to the date that vesting in the option awards would have occurred absent the modification. [FIN44, ¶159]

.244 At the modification date, Company R recognizes as compensation cost the intrinsic value measured at the modification date ($40) in excess of the original intrinsic value ($0) for the estimated number of awards that, absent the modification, would have expired unexercisable. Compensation cost is recognized immediately as future vesting has been eliminated. Accordingly, $280,000 of compensation cost is recognized at the modification date based on Company R's estimate of employee turnover in the next 3 years (70 employees, 100 options per employee with incremental intrinsic value of $40 each). The estimate of $280,000 will require adjustment in future periods for actual experience. For example, assume 1 year after the modification, 50 employees with modified awards have terminated employment and Company R now estimates that an additional 50 employees will terminate in the next 2 years (that is, before the original 5-year cliff-vesting date). Company R recognizes an additional $120,000 of compensation cost as an adjustment to the earlier estimate. [FIN44, ¶160]

Illustration 3(b)—Modification to Extend the Maximum Contractual Life of a Fixed Stock Option Award

.245 On January 1, 20X4, Company W grants 100 fixed stock options each to Employee A and Employee B. The options have an exercise price equal to the market price at the date of grant and a 10-year life. Under the original terms of the plan, if an employee retires after reaching age 65, the employee has the lesser of 90 days or the remaining period of the 10-year life to exercise vested options. [FIN44, ¶161]

.246 On January 1, 20X7, Company W modifies the awards to provide that upon retirement after age 65, a retiree will have 2 years to exercise vested options, not limited by the original 10-year option life. At the date of the modification, the intrinsic value is $15 per option. As a result of the modification, the maximum contractual life of an option has been extended beyond 10 years for any employee eligible for retirement at age 65 within the original 10-year option life. [FIN44, ¶162]

.247 At January 1, 20X7, Employee A is 30 years old and Employee B is 61 years old. The effects of the modification on each employee's option award are as follows:

> Employee A: No effect, because Employee A is not eligible for retirement (as defined in the option agreement) within the remaining period of the 10-year option life and, accordingly, Employee A cannot benefit from the modification.
>
> Employee B: The maximum contractual life of Employee B's options has been extended to 12 years (if Employee B retires at the end of the original 10-year option life) because Employee B will be eligible to retire within the remaining life of the options and receive the extended exercise period. Regardless of when in the future Employee B retires, Company W must measure and recognize (over any future vesting period, or immediately if the options are vested) compensation cost of $1,500, representing the additional intrinsic value of the options at the modification date.

[FIN44, ¶163]

Illustration 3(c)—Modification That Does Not Extend the Maximum Contractual Life of a Fixed Stock Option Award

.248 Assume the same facts as in Illustration 3(b) except that on January 1, 20X7, Company W modifies the awards to provide that if an employee retires after reaching age 65, the retiree will have the lesser of 2 years or the remaining period of the 10-year option life to exercise vested awards. [FIN44, ¶164]

.249 In this case, the modification does not extend the maximum contractual life of the awards beyond 10 years. However, the modification results in an extension of the life of any award at the date an employee retires and obtains, as a result of the modification, a remaining exercise period for that award in excess of the 90 days provided in the original terms of the award. Therefore, Company W must measure additional compensation cost equal to the intrinsic value of the modified option awards held by Employee B at the date of the modification and will recognize that compensation cost if Employee B retires and receives, as a result of the modification, a period in excess of 90 days to exercise the awards. (Assuming that Company W is unable to estimate whether Employee B will retire and receive an extension of the award's life as a result of the modification, no estimate of additional compensation cost would be recognized prior to Employee B's retirement.) [FIN44, ¶165]

Illustration 3(d)—Modification to Reduce the Exercise Price of a Fixed Stock Option Award (Exercise Price Equals the Quoted Market Price of the Stock at the Original Measurement Date)

.250 Company M grants fixed stock options to employees on January 1, 20X3. Relevant information on those awards is as follows:

Options granted	10,000
Expiration	10 years from the date of grant
Vesting	100 percent at the end of 20X6 (4-year cliff-vesting)
Stock price at the date of grant	$10
Option exercise price	$10

[FIN44, ¶166]

.251 The quoted market price per share of Company M's stock at December 31 of subsequent years is:

20X3	$14
20X4	6
20X5	20
20X6	10
20X7	15
20X8	18

[FIN44, ¶167]

.252 On December 31, 20X4, Company M reduces the exercise price of the options to $4, which is $2 less than the quoted market price of the stock at that date. As a result of modifying the awards to reduce the exercise price, the option awards are subject to variable accounting from the date of the modification. [FIN44, ¶168]

.253 Exhibit 253A illustrates the annual computation of compensation cost for the options from the date of grant through year six of the life of the options. The exhibit assumes that no options are exercised or forfeited during that period. Compensation cost would continue to be adjusted for increases or decreases in intrinsic value following year six until the options are exercised, are forfeited, or expire unexercised. [FIN44, ¶169]

Exhibit 253A

Annual Computation of Compensation Cost

		Compensation				Recognized to Date		Recognition of Total Compensation Cost by Year					
Date	Market Price	Original Intrinsic Value (1)	Additional Intrinsic Value (2)	Percentage Recognized (3)		Original Intrinsic Value	Additional Intrinsic Value	20X3	20X4	20X5	20X6	20X7	20X8
12/31/X3	$14	$0	$ 0	25%	0%	$0	$ 0	$0					
X4 Activity						0	0		$0				
12/31/X4	6	0	2	50	0	0	0						
X5 Activity						0	80,000			$80,000			
12/31/X5	20	0	16	75	50	0	80,000						
X6 Activity						0	(20,000)				$(20,000)		
12/31/X6	10	0	6	100	100	0	60,000						
X7 Activity						0	50,000					$50,000	
12/31/X7	15	0	11	100	100	0	110,000						
X8 Activity						0	30,000						$30,000
12/31/X8	18	0	14	100	100	$0	$140,000						

Notes:

(1) Prior to the modification, the awards were accounted for as fixed, and compensation cost was based on intrinsic value at the original measurement date (in this case, zero).

(2) In this exhibit, as the original award had no intrinsic value, subsequent to the modification date additional compensation cost equals the intrinsic value of the modified (variable) awards.

(3) The percentage recognized is based on the vesting period. Any original intrinsic value (none in this exhibit) is recognized over the four-year vesting period. Additional compensation cost, during the remaining vesting period after the awards become variable, is recognized over the period from the date of the modification to the date the awards vest. Additional compensation cost after the awards are modified is adjusted in subsequent periods for changes in intrinsic value. After the awards vest, adjustment to additional compensation cost for changes in intrinsic value is recognized immediately.

[FIN44, ¶169]

Illustration 3(e)—Replacement of a Fixed Stock Option Award with Stock (Exercise Price of Option Award Equals the Quoted Market Price of the Stock at the Original Measurement Date)

.254 Using the same facts as in Illustration 3(d), rather than modifying the exercise price of the original January 1, 20X3 grant of options, on December 31, 20X4, Company M replaces the option awards with stock on the basis of one-third of a share of stock for each outstanding option. A new measurement of compensation cost is required and equals $2 per replaced option ($6 intrinsic value per share of restricted stock multiplied by 1/3 of a share granted for each option). The stock will vest pursuant to the original vesting provisions in the options. The total compensation cost for each modified (replaced) award is $2, determined as:

Incremental intrinsic value of the replacement award	$2
Unrecognized original intrinsic value	0
Total remaining compensation cost to be recognized	$2

That amount ($2 per option or $20,000) is recognized during 20X5 and 20X6, the 2 remaining years of the service (vesting) period. [FIN44, ¶170]

Illustration 3(f)—Cash Settlement of a Fixed Stock Option Award (Exercise Price Equals the Quoted Market Price of the Stock at the Original Measurement Date)

.255 Using the same facts as in Illustration 3(d), rather than modifying the exercise price, Company M settles the original January 1, 20X3 grant of options for cash at December 31, 20X4. Company M pays $2 per option and recognizes additional compensation cost for the cash settlement pursuant to Question 14 (paragraphs .210 and .211). As the original intrinsic value of the option awards was zero, $2 of compensation cost per option ($20,000) is recognized at the date of the cash settlement. [FIN44, ¶171]

Illustration 3(g)—Modification to Reduce the Exercise Price of a Fixed Stock Option Award (Exercise Price Is Less Than the Quoted Market Price of the Stock at the Original Measurement Date)

.256 Company A grants fixed stock options to employees on January 1, 20X3. Relevant information on those awards is as follows:

Options granted	1,000
Expiration	10 years from the date of grant
Vesting	100 percent at the end of 20X6 (4-year cliff-vesting)
Stock price at the date of grant	$100
Option exercise price	$60

[FIN44, ¶172]

.257 The quoted market price per share of Company A's stock at December 31 of subsequent years is:

20X3	$ 70
20X4	25
20X5	75
20X6	100
20X7	80
20X8	18

[FIN44, ¶173]

.258 On December 31, 20X3, Company A modifies the options to reduce the exercise price of each option to $35, which is $35 less than the market price of the stock at that date. As a result of the modification to reduce the exercise price, variable accounting is required for the options from the modification date. [FIN44, ¶174]

.259 Exhibit 259A illustrates the annual computation of compensation cost for the options from the date of grant through year six of the life of the options. The exhibit assumes that no options are exercised or forfeited during that period. Compensation cost would continue to be adjusted for increases or decreases in intrinsic value following year six until the options are exercised, are forfeited, or expire unexercised. [FIN44, ¶175]

Exhibit 259A

Annual Computation of Compensation Cost

Date	Market Price	Compensation: Original Intrinsic Value (1)	Compensation: Additional Intrinsic Value (2)	Percentage Recognized (3)		Recognized to Date: Original Intrinsic Value	Recognized to Date: Additional Intrinsic Value	Recognition of Total Compensation Cost by Year: 20X3	20X4	20X5	20X6	20X7	20X8
12/31/X3	$ 70	$40	$25	25%	0%	$10,000	$ 0	$10,000					
X4 Activity						10,000	0		$10,000				
12/31/X4	25	40	0	50	$33\frac{1}{3}$	20,000	0						
X5 Activity						10,000	20,000			$30,000			
12/31/X5	75	40	30	75	$66\frac{2}{3}$	30,000	20,000						
X6 Activity						10,000	35,000				$45,000		
12/31/X6	100	40	55	100	100	40,000	55,000						
X7 Activity						0	(20,000)					$(20,000)	
12/31/X7	80	40	35	100	100	40,000	35,000						
X8 Activity						0	(35,000)						$(35,000)
12/31/X8	18	40	0	100	100	$40,000	$ 0						

Notes:

(1) Prior to the modification, the awards were accounted for as fixed, and compensation cost based on intrinsic value at the original measurement date was $40. This amount continues to be recognized as compensation cost subsequent to the modification.

(2) Subsequent to the modification, additional compensation cost is measured as the intrinsic value of the modified (variable) awards, to the extent that intrinsic value exceeds $10 (the lesser of (a) the original intrinsic value of $40 or (b) the intrinsic value immediately before the modification of $10). For example, at 12/31/X3, additional compensation cost per option equals $25 (intrinsic value of each modified option of $35 less $10), and at 12/31/X6, additional compensation cost per option equals $55 (intrinsic value of each modified option of $65 less $10).

(3) The percentage recognized is based on the vesting period. The original intrinsic value is recognized over the four-year vesting period. Additional compensation cost, during the remaining vesting period after the awards become variable, is recognized over the period from the date of the modification to the date the awards vest. After the awards vest, adjustments to additional compensation cost for changes in intrinsic value are recognized immediately. Additional compensation cost after the awards are modified is adjusted in subsequent periods for changes in intrinsic value.

[FIN44, ¶175]

Illustration 3(h)—Replacement of a Fixed Stock Option Award with Stock (Exercise Price Is Less Than the Quoted Market Price of the Stock at the Original Measurement Date)

.260 Using the same facts as in Illustration 3(g), rather than modifying the exercise price of the original January 1, 20X3 grant of options, on December 31, 20X3, Company A issues one-half of a share of stock for each outstanding option. A new measurement of compensation cost is required and results in additional compensation cost of $25 on a per-option basis ([$70 intrinsic value per share of stock multiplied by 1/2 share granted for each option] less $10 intrinsic value per option [the lesser of the original intrinsic value or the current intrinsic value of an option immediately prior to modification]). The stock is unvested and subject to the remaining vesting period of the options. [FIN44, ¶176]

.261 On January 1, 20X4, the remaining unrecognized compensation cost for the originally measured intrinsic value is $30 per option. The total compensation cost remaining to be recognized on a per-option basis is $55, determined as follows:

Additional compensation cost	$25
Unrecognized compensation cost for the original intrinsic value	30
Total remaining compensation cost to be recognized	$55

That amount is recognized during 20X4, 20X5, and 20X6, the three remaining years of vesting (service). [FIN44, ¶177]

Illustration 3(i)—Cash Settlement of a Fixed Stock Option Award (Exercise Price Is Less Than the Quoted Market Price of the Stock at the Original Measurement Date)

.262 Using the same facts as in Illustration 3(g), rather than modifying the exercise price, Company A settles the January 1, 20X3 grant of options for cash on December 31, 20X3. Company A pays $35 per option and measures additional compensation cost of $25 as a result of the cash settlement, determined as follows:

Cash paid to settle the award	$35
Less: Intrinsic value of original award at the modification date	10
Additional compensation cost	$25

The remaining unrecognized compensation cost for the originally measured intrinsic value of $30 per option and the $25 additional compensation cost (total remaining compensation cost of $55 per option) is recognized on December 31, 20X3, the date of the cash settlement. [FIN44, ¶178]

Illustration 4—Identifying Changes to the Exercise Price of Fixed Options

.263 The following examples illustrate application of the guidance in Question 11(a) (paragraphs .183 through .193) on the types of direct and indirect modifications made to reduce the exercise price of a fixed option award. The examples do not comprehend all possible combinations of circumstances that may represent a reduction to the exercise price of an award. [FIN44, ¶179]

Illustration 4(a)—Direct Reduction of the Exercise Price of a Fixed Stock Option Award

.264 Company S grants fixed stock options to its employees. The exercise price of each option equals the quoted market price of the stock on the grant date. All options cliff-vest at the end of 4 years and have a maximum life of 10 years. Information about the stock options granted to Employee A on January 1, 20X0, follows:

Options granted	1,000
Stock price	$20 per share
Exercise price	$20 per option

[FIN44, ¶180]

.265 On January 1, 20X2, the quoted market price of Company S's stock has decreased to $15 per share. Company S modifies the award held by Employee A to reduce the award's exercise price to $15 per option. Variable accounting is required for the 1,000 options from January 1, 20X2 (the date of the modification), until the date the options are exercised, are forfeited, or expire unexercised. [FIN44, ¶181]

Illustration 4(b)—Indirect Reduction of the Exercise Price of a Fixed Stock Option Award through a Cash Bonus Arrangement

.266 Assume the same facts as in Illustration 4(a) except that on January 1, 20X2, instead of directly reducing the award's exercise price, Company S enters into a cash bonus arrangement for $5,000 (or $5 per option) with Employee A that will vest (be paid) if the 1,000 options granted on January 1, 20X0, are exercised. [FIN44, ¶182]

.267 Because receipt of the cash bonus is contingent upon exercise of the options, the fair value of the consideration required to be remitted by Employee A upon exercise is different from the fair value required to be remitted pursuant to the award's original terms. Before the cash bonus arrangement, Employee A was required to remit a total of $20,000 to exercise the 1,000 options. After the cash bonus arrangement, Employee A is required to remit only $15,000 ($20,000 stated exercise price less the $5,000 cash bonus that will be paid upon exercise of the 1,000 options). The cash bonus indirectly reduces the stated exercise price of the options from $20 to $15 per option. [FIN44, ¶183]

.268 Company S has indirectly reduced the exercise price of the stock options granted to Employee A. Company S accounts for the 1,000 options and the cash bonus as a combined variable award from the date the cash bonus arrangement is granted (January 1, 20X2) until the date the options are exercised, are forfeited, or expire unexercised. [FIN44, ¶184]

Illustration 4(c)—Indirect Reduction of the Exercise Price of a Fixed Stock Option Award through a Below-Market Recourse Note Arrangement

.269 Assume the same facts as in Illustration 4(a) except that on January 1, 20X2, Company S modifies the option award to permit exercise upon vesting with a five-year, full-recourse note that bears no interest. Assume that the market interest rate for notes of similar risk is 10 percent compounded annually. [FIN44, ¶185]

.270 Company S has changed the fair value of the consideration Employee A is required to remit upon exercise of the award. Before the modification, Employee A was required to remit a total of $20,000 to exercise the 1,000 options. After the modification, Employee A is permitted to exercise the options with a full-recourse note with a fair value of only $12,418 (calculated as the present value of a payment of $20,000 in 5 years, discounted at 10 percent). [FIN44, ¶186]

.271 Regardless of the date on which Employee A exercises the award, Company S has reduced the exercise price of the option award because the market interest rate at any future date will exceed the zero interest rate on the full-recourse note. Company S accounts for the option award as variable from the date of the modification to the date the options are exercised, are forfeited, or expire unexercised. At any future exercise date, the final measurement of compensation cost should equal the difference between the then-market price of Company S stock issued upon exercise and the fair value of the non-interest-bearing note. [FIN44, ¶187]

.272 If Company S had modified the award to permit exercise with a full-recourse note at a market interest rate (at the exercise date), variable accounting would not have been required because Company S would not have changed the fair value of the consideration required to be remitted by Employee A upon exercise. [FIN44, ¶188]

Illustration 4(d)—Reduction of the Exercise Price of a Fixed Stock Option Award through Cash Settlement and Grant of a Replacement Award

.273 Company N grants fixed options to its employees. The exercise price of each option equals the quoted market price of the stock on the grant date. All options cliff-vest at the end of 4 years and have a 10-year life. Information about option awards granted to Employee A is as follows:

Grant Date	Options Granted	Stock Price at Grant Date	Exercise Price
January 1, 20X0	1,000	$20 per share	$20 per option
October 1, 20X0	750	15 per share	15 per option
March 1, 20X1	500	17 per share	17 per option

[FIN44, ¶189]

.274 On January 1, 20X1, the market price of Company N's stock is $15 per share. Company N settles the option award for 1,000 shares granted on January 1, 20X0, by paying cash equal to the fair value of the 1,000 options. Company N recognizes compensation cost at the settlement date equal to the cash paid. [FIN44, ¶190]

.275 According to the guidance in Question 11(a) (paragraphs .183 through .193), Company N must potentially identify 1,000 options as replacement awards and account for those options as variable. First, Company N looks back 6 months from the date of settling the 1,000 options for cash. Accordingly, Company N looks back from January 1, 20X1, to July 1, 20X0. Since 750 options were granted on October 1, 20X0, with a lower exercise price per option than the settled award, those 750 options are accounted for as variable from January 1, 20X1, until the date that those options are exercised, are forfeited, or expire unexercised. [FIN44, ¶191]

.276 Because Company N settled 1,000 options and has only identified 750 options as replacement (variable) awards, it must potentially identify an additional 250 options as replacement awards and account for those options as variable. Company N looks forward six months from the date of settlement. Accordingly, Company N looks forward from January 1, 20X1, to July 1, 20X1. Since 500 options were granted on March 1, 20X1, with a lower exercise price per option than the settled options, 250 of those 500 options are accounted for as variable from March 1, 20X1, until the date those options are exercised, are forfeited, or expire unexercised. The remaining 250 options granted on March 1, 20X1, qualify for fixed accounting, assuming those options meet the requirements for a fixed award under this section. [FIN44, ¶192]

.277 In determining whether variable accounting is required for the replacement award(s), identical guidance applies if the 1,000 options had been canceled outright with no consideration or had been effectively canceled, for example, by a change to the terms to reduce the likelihood of exercise by Employee A. [FIN44, ¶193]

Illustration 4(e)—Cancellation of a Fixed Stock Option Award That Is Not Combined with a Past Grant or a Future Grant

.278 Company P grants fixed stock options to its employees. The exercise price of each option equals the quoted market price of the stock on the grant date. All options cliff-vest at the end of 4 years and have a life of 10 years. Information about options granted to Employee A is as follows:

Grant Date	Options Granted	Stock Price at Grant Date	Exercise Price
January 1, 20X0	1,000	$10 per share	$10 per option
January 3, 20X1	1,200	12 per share	12 per option
January 2, 20X2	1,400	25 per share	25 per option
January 5, 20X3	1,700	17 per share	17 per option

[FIN44, ¶194]

.279 On July 4, 20X2, the market price of Company P stock is $15 per share. Company P cancels the award for 1,400 options previously granted on January 2, 20X2. Company P reaches an agreement with Employee A to grant at least 1,400 stock options on or after January 5, 20X3, at an exercise price per option equal to the market price per share of Company P stock at that future date. No other agreement exists between Company P and Employee A to compensate Employee A for increases in the market value of Company P's stock. [FIN44, ¶195]

.280 According to the guidance in Question 11(a) (paragraphs .183 through .193), Company P must potentially identify 1,400 options as replacement awards and account for those options as variable. First, Company P looks back six months from the date the award is canceled. Accordingly, Company P looks back from July 4, 20X2, to January 4, 20X2. No awards were granted with a lower exercise price per option than the canceled award. Company P looks forward six months from the date the award was canceled. Accordingly, Company P looks forward from July 4, 20X2, to January 4, 20X3. No awards for which a measurement date occurred or that provide the grantee with a participation in stock price increases during the six months from the date the award was canceled are granted during that period. [FIN44, ¶196]

.281 Because Company P did not compensate or agree to compensate Employee A for increases in the market price of the stock between the date the award was canceled and January 4, 20X3, and no options were granted with a lower exercise price than the canceled options, the cancellation of the award on July 4, 20X2, is not combined with any past or future awards. The award of 1,700 options granted on January 5, 20X3, qualifies for fixed accounting, assuming it meets the requirements for a fixed award under this section. [FIN44, ¶197]

Illustration 5—Modifications for Equity Restructurings

.282 The following examples of accounting for modifications as a result of an equity restructuring are based on the assumptions below. Certain examples may also have other specific assumptions. Immediately prior to the equity restructuring:

a. The employee holds 100 options in Company A.
b. The exercise price is $10 per share.
c. The market value of Company A is $30 per share.
d. Compensation cost was zero at the original grant (measurement) date.

Company A has an equity restructuring that reduces the market value of Company A stock to $25 per share (a decrease of $5 per share). No other modifications are made to the terms of the previously fixed stock options. [FIN44, ¶198]

Illustration 5(a)—Stapled Options in a Spinoff

.283 Company A spins off Company B. Shareholders receive one share of Company B for each share of Company A held. Option holders retain options previously held in Company A and receive one option in Company B for each option of Company A held. The options cannot be separately exercised. There is no change in the exercise price for an option in Company A, but the holder is now entitled to one share of Company A and one share of Company B when the option is exercised. The market value of a Company B share immediately after the spinoff is $5.

	Market Price	Exercise Price	Number of Options	Aggregate Intrinsic Value	Ratio (Exercise/ Market)
Before:					
Company A	$30	$10	100	$2,000	.33
Company B	—	—	—	—	—
Combined	$30	$10	100	$2,000	.33
After:					
Company A	$25	—	—	—	—
Company B	$5	—	—	—	—
Combined	$30	$10	100	$2,000	.33
Evaluation:					
Criterion A:	Aggregate intrinsic value			Same	
Criterion B:	Ratio (exercise/market)				Same

[FIN44, ¶199]

.284 Because the two criteria of Question 11(c) (paragraph .198) are met, there is no accounting consequence of the modifications to the options. [FIN44, ¶200]

Illustration 5(b)—Nonstapled Options in a Spinoff

.285 Company A spins off Company B. Shareholders receive one share of Company B for each share of Company A held. Option holders retain options previously held in Company A and receive one option in Company B for each option of Company A held. The options can be separately exercised. The market value of a Company B share immediately after the spinoff is $5 per share. The exercise prices of Company A and Company B options are $7 and $3, respectively.

	Market Price	Exercise Price	Number of Options	Aggregate Intrinsic Value	Ratio (Exercise/ Market)
Before:					
Company A	$30	$10	100	$2,000	.33
Company B	—	—	—	—	—
Combined	$30	$10	100	$2,000	.33
After:					
Company A	$25	$7	100	$1,800	.28
Company B	$5	$3	100	$200	.60
Combined	$30	$10	100	$2,000	.33
Evaluation:					
Criterion A:	Aggregate intrinsic value (combined)			Same	
Criterion B:	Ratio (exercise/market): Company A				Reduced
	Ratio (exercise/market): Company B				Increased

[FIN44, ¶201]

.286 Because the ratio of exercise price per award to the market value per share is reduced, variable accounting for both Company A options and Company B options is required as a result of the modifications. If the ratio for each of Company A options and Company B options had been maintained (exercise price of $8.33 and $1.67 for Company A and Company B options, respectively), there would have been no accounting consequence because the two criteria of Question 11(c) (paragraph .198) would have been met. [FIN44, ¶202]

Illustration 5(c)—Reduced Exercise Price

.287 Situation 1: Company A spins off Company B. The exercise price for Company A options is reduced by $5 per option, an amount equal to the decline in market value per share of Company A as a result of the spinoff of Company B. [FIN44, ¶203]

.288 Situation 2: Company A declares a special, nonrecurring dividend of $5 per share for shareholders. The exercise price for Company A options is reduced by $5 per option, an amount equal to the special, nonrecurring dividend paid to shareholders.

	Market Price	**Exercise Price**	**Number of Options**	**Aggregate Intrinsic Value**	**Ratio (Exercise/ Market)**
Before:					
Company A	$30	$10	100	$2,000	.33
After:					
Company A	$25	$5	100	$2,000	.20
Evaluation:					
Criterion A:	Aggregate intrinsic value			Same	
Criterion B:	Ratio (exercise/market)				Reduced

[FIN44, ¶204]

.289 Variable accounting results from the modifications to the options because the second criterion of Question 11(c) (paragraph .198) is not met. If the exercise price for Company A options had been reduced by $1.67 to $8.33 per option (rather than by $5 to $5 per option) so that the ratio of exercise price per share to market value per share was the same before and after the modification to the stock options, there would have been no accounting consequence. Note that, in this case, the number of shares could also be adjusted provided that the aggregate intrinsic value of the modified awards did not exceed $2,000. [FIN44, ¶205]

Illustration 5(d)—Exchange of Options in Company A for Options in Company B

.290 Company A spins off Company B. Employees who previously worked for Company A and now work for Company B are allowed to exchange options held in Company A for options in Company B and maintain the same aggregate intrinsic value. The market value of Company B shares immediately after the spinoff is $5 per share. The employees are given 600 options (100 × $30 ÷ $5) in Company B at an exercise price of $1.67 per share ($10 × $5 ÷ $30). There is no accounting consequence as a result of the modifications because the two criteria of Question 11(c) (paragraph .198) are met.

	Market Price	Exercise Price	Number of Options	Aggregate Intrinsic Value	Ratio (Exercise/ Market)
Before:					
Company A	$30	$10	100	$2,000	.33
Company B	—	—	—	—	—
After:					
Company A	—	—	—	—	—
Company B	$5	$1.67	600	$2,000	.33
Evaluation:					
Criterion A:	Aggregate intrinsic value			Same	
Criterion B:	Ratio (exercise/market)				Same

[FIN44, ¶206]

Illustration 6—Options Exchanged in a Purchase Business Combination

.291 On July 1, 20X6, Company A acquires Company B in a purchase business combination. In the business combination, Company A exchanges 10,000 options with a fair value of $100,000 for 5,000 options held by the employees of Company B prior to the exchange. The options held by Company B employees prior to the exchange were granted on June 30, 20X2, and provided for cliff-vesting on June 30, 20X7. Company A options granted in the exchange vest according to the vesting schedule of the previous Company B options (cliff-vest on June 30, 20X7). The intrinsic value of the Company A options granted at the date of the exchange is $4 per option. [FIN44, ¶207]

.292 The $100,000 fair value of the options granted in the exchange is part of the purchase price paid for Company B. However, $8,000 is allocated to unearned compensation and is deducted from the cost of Company B in allocating the purchase price to the other assets acquired. The unearned compensation ($8,000) is determined as the total intrinsic value of the granted awards of $40,000 ($4 × 10,000) multiplied by the fraction (1/5) that is the remaining vesting period over the total vesting period. [FIN44, ¶208]

Glossary

[Refer to the Glossary of Section C36, "Compensation: Stock-Based," paragraphs .401 through .424, for other defined terms that may be relevant.]

.400 **Junior stock.** A specific type of stock issued to employees that generally is subordinate to an employer's regular common stock with respect to voting, liquidation, and dividend rights and is convertible into regular common stock if certain performance goals are achieved or if certain transactions occur. Junior stock generally is not transferable, except back to the issuing enterprise, and has a fair value lower than regular common stock because of its subordinate rights and the uncertainty of conversion to regular common stock. [FIN38, ¶1] Junior stock that is not convertible per se but that has restrictions that lapse (such as restrictions that lapse when certain performance goals are achieved) so that it ultimately becomes regular common stock is considered to be convertible. [FIN38, ¶1, fn1]

.401 **Measurement date.** The first date on which are known both (a) the number of shares that an individual employee is entitled to receive and (b) the option or purchase price, if any [(refer to paragraphs .110 and .111)]. [APB25, ¶10]

.402 **Plan.** Any arrangement to issue stock to officers and employees, as a group or individually. [APB25, ¶4]

.402A **Service period.** The period or periods the employee performs the related services. If the service period is not defined in the plan or some other agreement, such as an employment agreement, as a shorter or previous period, the service period shall be presumed to be the vesting period [of the plan]. [FIN28, ¶3]

.403 **Stock appreciation rights.** Awards entitling employees to receive cash, stock, or a combination of cash and stock in an amount equivalent to any excess of the market value of a stated number of shares of the employer's stock over a stated price. The form of payment may be specified when the rights are granted or may be determined when they are exercised; in some plans the employee may choose the form of payment. [FIN28, ¶9]

.404 [Editorial Deletion.]

.405 **[Variable stock option, purchase, and award plans.]** The characteristic that identifies [these] plans is that the terms prevent determining at the date of grant or award either the number of shares of stock that may be acquired by or awarded to an employee or the price to be paid by the employee, or both. [APB25, ¶29]

Supplemental Guidance

Stock Plans Established by a Principal Stockholder

.501 *Question*—Accounting for compensatory and noncompensatory stock option, purchase, and award plans adopted by an employer is discussed in this section. Should an employer account for plans or transactions *(plans),* if they have characteristics otherwise similar to compensatory plans adopted by employers, that are established or financed by a principal stockholder (that is, one who either owns 10 percent or more of the employer's common stock or has the ability, directly or indirectly, to control or significantly influence the employer)? [AIN-APB25, #1]

.502 *Interpretation*—It is difficult to evaluate a principal stockholder's intent when he establishes or finances a plan with characteristics otherwise similar to compensatory plans generally adopted by employers. A principal stockholder may be satisfying his generous nature, settling a moral obligation, or attempting to increase or maintain the value of his own investment. If a principal stockholder's intention is to enhance or maintain the value of his investment by entering into such an arrangement, the employer is implicitly benefiting from the plan by retention of, and possibly improved performance by, the employee. In that case, the benefits to a principal stockholder and to the employer are generally impossible to separate. Similarly, it is virtually impossible to separate a principal stockholder's personal satisfaction from the benefit to the employer. APB Statement No. 4, *Basic Concepts and Accounting Principles Underlying Financial Statements of Business Enterprises,* paragraph 127, states that "Financial accounting emphasizes the economic substance of events even though the legal form may differ from the economic substance and suggest different treatment." [AIN-APB25, #1]

.503 The economic substance of this type of plan is substantially the same for the employer and the employee, whether the plan is adopted by the employer or a principal stockholder. Consequently, the employer should account for this type of plan when one is established or financed by a principal stockholder unless (a) the relationship between the stockholder and the employer's employee is one that would normally result in generosity (that is, an immediate family relationship), (b) the stockholder has an obligation to the employee that is completely unrelated to the latter's employment (for example, the stockholder transfers shares to the employee because of personal business relationships in the past, unrelated to the present employment situation), or (c) the employer clearly does not benefit from the transaction (for example, the stockholder transfers shares to a minor employee with whom he has had a close relationship over a number of years). [AIN-APB25, #1]

.504 This type of plan should be treated as a contribution to capital by the principal stockholder with the offsetting charge accounted for in the same manner as compensatory plans adopted by employers. [AIN-APB25, #1]

.505 Compensation cost should be recognized as an expense of one or more periods in accordance with the provisions of paragraphs .112 through .115. [AIN-APB25, #1]

.506 The employer should account for tax benefits, if any, from this type of plan in accordance with the provisions of paragraphs .116 through .118. If the employer receives no tax benefit from this type of plan, but would have received the benefit had the plan been adopted by the employer, the absence of the tax benefit is one of the variables in estimating the plan's cost to the employer. [AIN-APB25, #1]

.507-.516 [Deleted 10/95 because of FASB Statement 123, *Accounting for Stock-Based Compensation.*]

Supplemental Guidance: Emerging Issues Task Force (EITF) Issues

.1000 [Listed below are EITF Issues that provide supplemental guidance for this section. These Issues are grouped by subject matter and may be either interpretive of or related by topic to the guidance in this section.

Book Value Stock Plans

EITF Issue No. 87-23, "Book Value Stock Purchase Plans"
EITF Issue No. 88-6, "Book Value Stock Plans in an Initial Public Offering"

Business Combinations

EITF Issue No. 84-13, "Purchase of Stock Options and Stock Appreciation Rights in a Leveraged Buyout"
EITF Issue No. 85-45, "Business Combinations: Settlement of Stock Options and Awards"

Deferred Receipt of Awards

EITF Issue No. 97-5, "Accounting for the Delayed Receipt of Option Shares upon Exercise under APB Opinion No. 25"
EITF Issue No. 97-14, "Accounting for Deferred Compensation Arrangements Where Amounts Earned Are Held in a Rabbi Trust and Invested"

Tax Issues

EITF Issue No. 00-15, "Classification in the Statement of Cash Flows of the Income Tax Benefit Received by a Company upon Exercise of a Nonqualified Employee Stock Option"
EITF Issue No. 00-16, "Recognition and Measurement of Employer Payroll Taxes on Employee Stock-Based Compensation"
EITF Topic No. D-83, "Accounting for Payroll Taxes Associated with Stock Option Exercises"

Other

EITF Issue No. 84-18, "Stock Option Pyramiding"
EITF Issue No. 84-34, "Permanent Discount Restricted Stock Purchase Plans"
EITF Issue No. 90-7, "Accounting for a Reload Stock Option"
EITF Issue No. 95-16, "Accounting for Stock Compensation Arrangements with Employer Loan Features under APB Opinion No. 25"

EITF Issue No. 97-12, "Accounting for Increased Share Authorizations in an IRS Section 423 Employee Stock Purchase Plan under APB Opinion No. 25"

EITF Issue No. 00-12, "Accounting by an Investor for Stock-Based Compensation Granted to Employees of an Equity Method Investee"

EITF Issue No. 00-23, "Issues Related to the Accounting for Stock Compensation under APB Opinion No. 25 and FASB Interpretation No. 44"

EITF Issue No. 02-8, "Accounting for Options Granted to Employees in Unrestricted, Publicly Traded Shares of an Unrelated Entity"

EITF Topic No. D-18, "Accounting for Compensation Expense If Stock Appreciation Rights Are Cancelled"

EITF Topic No. D-91, "Application of APB Opinion No. 25 and FASB Interpretation No. 44 to an Indirect Repricing of a Stock Option"

EITF Topic No. D-93, "Accounting for the Rescission of the Exercise of Employee Stock Options"]

.1001 [Listed below are those EITF Issues that provide interpretive guidance on specific material in this section.

Paragraph .103 (APB 25, ¶4)—EITF Issue No. 97-2

Paragraph .106 (APB 25, ¶7)—EITF Issue No. 97-12

Paragraph .108, footnote 1 (APB 25, fn2)—EITF Issue No. 95-16

Paragraph .110(b) (APB 25, ¶10(b))—EITF Issues No. 84-18, 90-7, and 95-16 and Topic No. D-93

Paragraph .111 (APB 25, ¶11)—EITF Issue No. 90-7

Paragraph .111(d) (APB 25, ¶11(d))—EITF Issue No. 95-16

Paragraph .111(g) (APB 25, ¶11(g))—EITF Issues No. 84-13 and 85-45 and Topic No. D-93

Paragraph .119 (FIN 28, ¶2)—EITF Issue No. 84 -18

Paragraph .122 (FIN 28, ¶5)—EITF Topic No. D-18

Paragraph .215 (FIN 44, ¶70)—EITF Topic No. D-93]

(The next page is 7775.)

COMPREHENSIVE INCOME: FINANCIAL STATEMENT PRESENTATION

SECTION C49

Source: FASB Statement 130

Summary

This section presents standards for reporting and display of comprehensive income and its components (revenues, expenses, gains, and losses) in a full set of general-purpose financial statements. This section requires that all items that are required to be recognized under accounting standards as components of comprehensive income be reported in a financial statement that is displayed with the same prominence as other financial statements. This section does not require a specific format for that financial statement but requires that an enterprise display an amount representing total comprehensive income for the period in that financial statement.

This section requires that an enterprise (a) classify items of other comprehensive income by their nature in a financial statement and (b) display the accumulated balance of other comprehensive income separately from retained earnings and additional paid-in capital in the equity section of a statement of financial position.

Introduction and Scope

.101 This section establishes standards for reporting and display of comprehensive income and its components in a full set of general-purpose financial statements. It does not address issues of recognition[1] or measurement for comprehensive income and its components. [FAS130, ¶1]

---

[1]Recognition is the process of formally recording or incorporating an item in the financial statements of an entity. Thus, an asset, liability, revenue, expense, gain, or loss may be recognized (recorded) or unrecognized (unrecorded). *Realization* and *recognition* are not used as synonyms, as they sometimes are in accounting and financial literature (FASB Concepts Statement No. 6, *Elements of Financial Statements,* paragraph 143). [FAS130, ¶1, fn1]

.102 This section applies to all enterprises that provide a full set of financial statements that report financial position, results of operations, and cash flows.[2] This section does not apply to an enterprise that has no items of other comprehensive income in any period presented or to a not-for-profit organization that is required to follow the provisions of Section No5, "Not-for-Profit Organizations." [FAS130, ¶6]

.103 This section discusses how to report and display comprehensive income and its components. However, it does not specify when to recognize or how to measure the items that make up comprehensive income. Other sections provide guidance on items that are to be included in comprehensive income and its components. [FAS130, ¶7]

Definition of Comprehensive Income

.104 Comprehensive income is defined as the change in equity [net assets] of a business enterprise during a period from transactions and other events and circumstances from nonowner sources. It includes all changes in equity during a period except those resulting from investments by owners and distributions to owners (FASB Concepts Statement No. 6, *Elements of Financial Statements*, paragraph 70). [FAS130, ¶8]

.105 [It is held] that a full set of financial statements for a period should show financial position at the end of the period, earnings (net income) for the period, comprehensive income (total nonowner changes in equity) for the period, cash flows during the period, and investments by and distributions to owners during the period (FASB Concepts Statement No. 5, *Recognition and Measurement in Financial Statements of Business Enterprises*, paragraph 13). [FAS130, ¶9]

Comprehensive Income and Other Comprehensive Income

.106 This section uses the term *comprehensive income* to describe the total of all components of comprehensive income, including net income.[3] This section uses the term *other comprehensive income* to refer to revenues, expenses, gains, and losses that under generally accepted accounting principles are included in comprehensive income but excluded from net income. This section does not require that an enterprise use the terms *comprehensive income* or *other comprehensive income* in its financial statements, even

---

[2]Investment companies, defined benefit pension plans, and other employee benefit plans that are exempt from the requirement to provide a statement of cash flows by Section C25, "Cash Flows Statement," are not exempt from the requirements of this section if they otherwise apply. [FAS130, ¶6, fn3]

[3]This section uses the term *net income* to describe a measure of financial performance resulting from the aggregation of revenues, expenses, gains, and losses that are not items of other comprehensive income as identified in this section. A variety of other terms such as *net earnings* or *earnings* may be used to describe that measure. [FAS130, ¶10, fn4]

though those terms are used throughout this section.[4] [FAS130, ¶10] [Under current accounting standards] items [of other comprehensive income] are:

a. Foreign currency translation adjustments (Section F60, "Foreign Currency Translation," paragraph .119)
b. Gains and losses on foreign currency transactions that are designated as, and are effective as, economic hedges of a net investment in a foreign entity, commencing as of the designation date (Section F60, paragraph .127(a))
c. Gains and losses on intercompany foreign currency transactions that are of a long-term-investment nature (that is, settlement is not planned or anticipated in the foreseeable future), when the entities to the transaction are consolidated, combined, or accounted for by the equity method in the reporting enterprise's financial statements (Section F60, paragraph .127(b))
d. [A change in the fair value of a derivative instrument that qualifies as the hedging instrument in a cash flow hedge pursuant to Section D50, "Derivative Instruments and Hedging Activities" (Section D50, paragraph .115(c))]
e. A net loss recognized pursuant to Section P16, "Pension Costs," as an additional pension liability not yet recognized as net periodic pension cost (Section P16, paragraph .131)
f. Unrealized holding gains and losses on available-for-sale securities (Section I80, "Investments: Debt and Equity Securities," paragraph .110)
g. Unrealized holding gains and losses that result from a debt security being transferred into the available-for-sale category from the held-to-maturity category (Section I80, paragraph .114(c))
h. Subsequent decreases (if not an other-than-temporary impairment) or increases in the fair value of available-for-sale securities previously written down as impaired (Section I80, paragraph .115). [FAS130, ¶39]

[4]Just as a variety of terms are used for net income in present practice, [it is] anticipated that total nonowner changes in equity, comprehensive loss, and other equivalent terms will be used in future financial statements as names for comprehensive income (Concepts Statement 5, paragraph 40). [FAS130, ¶10, fn5]

Items required by accounting standards to be reported as direct adjustments to paid-in capital, retained earnings, or other nonincome equity accounts are not to be included as components of comprehensive income.[5] [FAS130, ¶5]

Purpose of Reporting Comprehensive Income

.107 The purpose of reporting comprehensive income is to report a measure of all changes in equity of an enterprise that result from recognized transactions and other economic events of the period other than transactions with owners in their capacity as owners. Prior to the [addition] of this section, some of those changes in equity were displayed in a statement that reports the results of operations, while others were included directly in balances within a separate component of equity in a statement of financial position. [FAS130, ¶11]

Reporting and Display of Comprehensive Income

.108 All components of comprehensive income shall be reported in the financial statements in the period in which they are recognized. A total amount for comprehensive income shall be displayed in the financial statement where the components of other comprehensive income are reported. [FAS130, ¶14]

Classifications within Comprehensive Income

.109 This section divides comprehensive income into net income and other comprehensive income. An enterprise shall continue to display an amount for net income. An enterprise that has no items of other comprehensive income in any period presented is not required to report comprehensive income. [FAS130, ¶15]

Classifications within Net Income

.110 Items included in net income are displayed in various classifications. Those classifications can include income from continuing operations, discontinued operations,

[5Some examples of these items are] unearned or deferred compensation expense, which is shown as a separate reduction of shareholders' equity pursuant to Section C47, "Compensation to Employees: Stock Purchase and Stock Option Plans," [FAS130, ¶109] reductions of shareholders' equity related to employee stock ownership plans (ESOPs), [FAS130, ¶110] credits to paid-in capital resulting from taxes not payable in cash, [FAS130, ¶115] [and] net cash settlements resulting from changes in value of contracts that give [a] company a choice of net cash settlement or settlement in its own shares. [FAS130, ¶118] Transactions [such as these] that [are] required by generally accepted accounting principles to be recognized in paid-in capital or other similar nonincome equity accounts are not to be displayed as other comprehensive income. [FAS130, ¶119]

extraordinary items, and cumulative effects of changes in accounting principle. This section does not change those classifications or other requirements for reporting results of operations. [FAS130, ¶16]

Classifications within Other Comprehensive Income

.111 Items included in other comprehensive income shall be classified based on their nature. For example, under existing accounting standards, other comprehensive income shall be classified separately into foreign currency items, minimum pension liability adjustments, and unrealized gains and losses on certain investments in debt and equity securities. Additional classifications or additional items within current classifications may result from future accounting standards. [FAS130, ¶17]

Reclassification adjustments

.112 Adjustments shall be made to avoid double counting in comprehensive income items that are displayed as part of net income for a period that also had been displayed as part of other comprehensive income in that period or earlier periods. For example, gains on investment securities that were realized and included in net income of the current period that also had been included in other comprehensive income as unrealized holding gains in the period in which they arose must be deducted through other comprehensive income of the period in which they are included in net income to avoid including them in comprehensive income twice. Those adjustments are referred to in this section as *reclassification adjustments*. [FAS130, ¶18]

.113 An enterprise shall determine reclassification adjustments for each classification of other comprehensive income, except minimum pension liability adjustments.[6] The requirement for a reclassification adjustment for foreign currency translation adjustments [as described in] Section F60 is limited to translation gains and losses realized upon sale or upon complete or substantially complete liquidation of an investment in a foreign entity. [FAS130, ¶19]

.114 An enterprise may display reclassification adjustments on the face of the financial statement in which comprehensive income is reported, or it may disclose reclassification adjustments in the notes to the financial statements. Therefore, for all classifications of other comprehensive income other than minimum pension liability adjustments, an enterprise may use either (a) a gross display on the face of the financial statement

---

[6It is noted] that it should be practicable for an enterprise to calculate reclassification adjustments for securities and other financial instruments and for foreign currency translation items but that it is not practicable for an enterprise to calculate reclassification adjustments for minimum pension liability adjustments. [FAS130, ¶91]

or (b) a net display on the face of the financial statement and disclose the gross change in the notes to the financial statements.[7] Gross and net displays are illustrated in Exhibits 124A through 124D. An example of the calculation of reclassification adjustments for available-for-sale securities [as described in] Section I80 is included in paragraphs .131 through .135. [FAS130, ¶20]

.115 An enterprise shall not determine a reclassification adjustment for minimum pension liability adjustments. Therefore, an enterprise shall use a net display for that classification. [FAS130, ¶21]

Alternative Formats for Reporting Comprehensive Income

.116 An enterprise shall display comprehensive income and its components in a financial statement that is displayed with the same prominence as other financial statements that constitute a full set of financial statements. This section does not require a specific format for that financial statement but requires that an enterprise display net income as a component of comprehensive income in that financial statement.[8] Exhibits 124A through 124D provide illustrations of the components of other comprehensive income and total comprehensive income being reported below the total for net income in a statement that reports results of operations, in a separate statement of comprehensive income that begins with net income, and in a statement of changes in equity. [FAS130, ¶22]

.117 Although this section does not require a specific format for displaying comprehensive income and its components, an enterprise [is] encouraged[9] to display the compo-

[7]If displayed gross, reclassification adjustments are reported separately from other changes in the respective balance; thus, the total change is reported as two amounts. If displayed net, reclassification adjustments are combined with other changes in the balance; thus, the total change is reported as a single amount. [FAS130, ¶20, fn6]

[8]Under Section I82, "Investments: Equity Method," an investor records its proportionate share of the investee's net income (net loss) as investment income along with a corresponding increase (decrease) to the investment account. [FAS130, ¶120] The format in which an investee displays other comprehensive income should not impact how an investor displays its proportionate share of those amounts. Therefore, regardless of how an investee chooses to display other comprehensive income, an investor should be permitted to combine its proportionate share of those amounts with its own other comprehensive income items and display the aggregate of those amounts in an income-statement-type format or in a statement of changes in equity. [FAS130, ¶122]

[[9]It is believed that] displaying comprehensive income in an income-statement format is conceptually superior to displaying it in a statement of changes in equity. That type of display also is consistent with the all-inclusive income concept. Furthermore, display of comprehensive income in an income-statement-type format provides the most transparency for its components. [FAS130, ¶67]

nents of other comprehensive income and total comprehensive income below the total for net income in a statement that reports results of operations or in a separate statement of comprehensive income that begins with net income. [FAS130, ¶23]

.118 An enterprise may display components of other comprehensive income either (a) net of related tax effects or (b) before related tax effects with one amount shown for the aggregate income tax expense or benefit related to the total of other comprehensive income items. [FAS130, ¶24]

.119 An enterprise shall disclose the amount of income tax expense or benefit allocated to each component of other comprehensive income, including reclassification adjustments, either on the face of the statement in which those components are displayed or in the notes to the financial statements. Alternative formats for disclosing the tax effects related to the components of other comprehensive income are illustrated in Exhibits 124A and 124B and Exhibit 125A. [FAS130, ¶25]

Reporting Other Comprehensive Income in the Equity Section of a Statement of Financial Position

.120 The total of other comprehensive income for a period shall be transferred to a component of equity that is displayed separately from retained earnings and additional paid-in capital in a statement of financial position at the end of an accounting period. A descriptive title such as *accumulated other comprehensive income* shall be used for that component of equity. An enterprise shall disclose accumulated balances for each classification in that separate component of equity on the face of a statement of financial position, in a statement of changes in equity, or in notes to the financial statements. The classifications shall correspond to classifications used elsewhere in the same set of financial statements for components of other comprehensive income. [FAS130, ¶26]

Interim-Period Reporting

.121 Section I73, "Interim Financial Reporting," clarifies the application of accounting principles and reporting practices to interim financial information, including interim financial statements and summarized interim financial data of publicly traded companies issued for external reporting purposes. An enterprise shall report a total for comprehensive income in condensed financial statements of interim periods. [FAS130, ¶27]

Illustrative Examples of Reporting Formats

.122 Exhibits 124A through 124D, and Exhibits 125A through 127A provide illustrations of reporting formats for comprehensive income, required disclosures, and a corresponding statement of financial position. The illustrations are intended as examples only; they illustrate some recommended formats. Other formats or levels of detail may be appropriate for certain circumstances. An enterprise is encouraged to provide information in ways that are most understandable to investors, creditors, and other external users of financial statements. For simplicity, the illustrations provide information only for a single period; however, most enterprises are required to provide comparative financial statements. [FAS130, ¶129]

.123 Brackets are used to highlight certain basic totals that must be displayed in financial statements to comply with the provisions of this section. This section requires not only displaying those certain basic totals but also reporting components of those aggregates. For example, it requires reporting information about unrealized gains and losses on available-for-sale securities, foreign currency items, and minimum pension liability adjustments. [FAS130, ¶130]

.124 The illustrations use the term *comprehensive income* to label the total of all components of comprehensive income, including net income. The illustrations use the term *other comprehensive income* to label revenues, expenses, gains, and losses that are included in comprehensive income but excluded from net income. This section does not require that an enterprise use those terms in its financial statements. Other equivalent terms, such as *total nonowner changes in equity,* can be used as labels for what this section refers to as comprehensive income. [FAS130, ¶131]

Exhibit 124A

Format A: One-Statement Approach

Enterprise
Statement of Income and Comprehensive Income
Year Ended December 31, 19X9

Revenues		$140,000
Expenses		(25,000)
Other gains and losses		8,000
Gain on sale of securities		2,000
Income from operations before tax		125,000
Income tax expense		(31,250)
Income before extraordinary item and cumulative effect of accounting change		93,750
Extraordinary item, net of tax		(28,000)
Income before cumulative effect of accounting change		65,750
Cumulative effect of accounting change, net of tax		(2,500)
[Net income		63,250]
Other comprehensive income, net of tax:		
Foreign currency translation adjustments[a]		8,000
Unrealized gains on securities:[b]		
Unrealized holding gains arising during period	$13,000	
Less: reclassification adjustment for gains included in net income	(1,500)	11,500
Minimum pension liability adjustment[c]		(2,500)
Other comprehensive income		17,000
[Comprehensive income		$ 80,250]

Alternatively, components of other comprehensive income could be displayed before tax with one amount shown for the aggregate income tax expense or benefit:

Other comprehensive income, before tax:		
Foreign currency translation adjustments[a]		$10,666
Unrealized gains on securities:[b]		
Unrealized holding gains arising during period	$17,333	
Less: reclassification adjustment for gains included in net income	(2,000)	15,333
Minimum pension liability adjustment[c]		(3,333)
Other comprehensive income, before tax		22,666
[Income tax expense related to items of other comprehensive income		(5,666)]
Other comprehensive income, net of tax		$17,000

[a]It is assumed that there was no sale or liquidation of an investment in a foreign entity. Therefore, there is no reclassification adjustment for this period.

[b]This illustrates the gross display. Alternatively, a net display can be used, with disclosure of the gross amounts (current-period gain and reclassification adjustment) in the notes to the financial statements.

[c]This illustrates the required net display for this classification.

[FAS130, ¶131]

Exhibit 124B

Format B: Two-Statement Approach

Enterprise
Statement of Income
Year Ended December 31, 19X9

Revenues	$140,000
Expenses	(25,000)
Other gains and losses	8,000
Gain on sale of securities	2,000
Income from operations before tax	125,000
Income tax expense	(31,250)
Income before extraordinary item and cumulative effect of accounting change	93,750
Extraordinary item, net of tax	(28,000)
Income before cumulative effect of accounting change	65,750
Cumulative effect of accounting change, net of tax	(2,500)
[Net income	$ 63,250]

Enterprise
Statement of Comprehensive Income
Year Ended December 31, 19X9

[Net income		$63,250]
Other comprehensive income, net of tax:		
Foreign currency translation adjustments[a]		8,000
Unrealized gains on securities:[b]		
Unrealized holding gains arising during period	$13,000	
Less: reclassification adjustment for gains included in net income	(1,500)	11,500
Minimum pension liability adjustment[c]		(2,500)
Other comprehensive income		17,000
[Comprehensive income		$80,250]

Alternatively, components of other comprehensive income could be displayed before tax with one amount shown for the aggregate income tax expense or benefit as illustrated in Exhibit 124A.

[a]It is assumed that there was no sale or liquidation of an investment in a foreign entity. Therefore, there is no reclassification adjustment for this period.

[b]This illustrates the gross display. Alternatively, a net display can be used, with disclosure of the gross amounts (current-period gain and reclassification adjustment) in the notes to the financial statements.

[c]This illustrates the required net display for this classification.

[FAS130, ¶131]

Exhibit 124C

Format C: Statement-of-Changes-in-Equity Approach (Alternative 1)

Enterprise
Statement of Changes in Equity
Year Ended December 31, 19X9

	Total	Comprehensive Income[a]	Retained Earnings	Accumulated Other Comprehensive Income	Common Stock	Paid-in Capital
Beginning balance	$563,500		$ 88,500	$25,000	$150,000	$300,000
Comprehensive income						
Net income	63,250	$63,250	63,250			
Other comprehensive income, net of tax						
Unrealized gains on securities, net of reclassification adjustment (see disclosure)	11,500	11,500				
Foreign currency translation adjustments	8,000	8,000				
Minimum pension liability adjustment	(2,500)	(2,500)				
Other comprehensive income		17,000		17,000		
Comprehensive income		$80,250				
Common stock issued	150,000				50,000	100,000
Dividends declared on common stock	(10,000)		(10,000)			
Ending balance	$783,750		$141,750	$42,000	$200,000	$400,000

Disclosure of reclassification amount:[b]

Unrealized holding gains arising during period	$13,000
Less: reclassification adjustment for gains included in net income	(1,500)
Net unrealized gains on securities	$11,500

[a]Alternatively, an enterprise can omit the separate column labeled "Comprehensive Income" by displaying an aggregate amount for comprehensive income ($80,250) in the "Total" column.

[b]It is assumed that there was no sale or liquidation of an investment in a foreign entity. Therefore, there is no reclassification adjustment for this period.

[FAS130, ¶131]

Exhibit 124D

Format D: Statement-of-Changes-in-Equity Approach (Alternative 2)

Enterprise
Statement of Changes in Equity
Year Ended December 31, 19X9

Retained earnings		
Balance at January 1	$ 88,500	
Net income	63,250	[$ 63,250]
Dividends declared on common stock	(10,000)	
Balance at December 31	141,750	
Accumulated other comprehensive income[a]		
Balance at January 1	25,000	
Unrealized gains on securities, net of reclassification adjustment (see disclosure)		11,500
Foreign currency translation adjustments		8,000
Minimum pension liability adjustment		(2,500)
Other comprehensive income	17,000	17,000
Comprehensive income		[$ 80,250]
Balance at December 31	42,000	
Common stock		
Balance at January 1	150,000	
Shares issued	50,000	
Balance at December 31	200,000	
Paid-in capital		
Balance at January 1	300,000	
Common stock issued	100,000	
Balance at December 31	400,000	
Total equity	$783,750	

Disclosure of reclassification amount:[b]

Unrealized holding gains arising during period	$ 13,000
Less: reclassification adjustment for gains included in net income	(1,500)
Net unrealized gains on securities	$ 11,500

[a]All items of other comprehensive income are displayed net of tax.

[b]It is assumed that there was no sale or liquidation of an investment in a foreign entity. Therefore, there is no reclassification adjustment for this period.

[FAS130, ¶131]

.125 [Exhibit 125A illustrates the disclosure required by paragraph .119 of the amount of income tax expense or benefit allocated to each component of other comprehensive income, including reclassification adjustments (illustrated in Exhibits 124A through 124D).] Alternatively, [as discussed in paragraph .119,] the tax amounts for each component can be displayed parenthetically on the face of the financial statement in which comprehensive income is reported. [FAS130, ¶131]

Exhibit 125A

Enterprise
Notes to Financial Statements
Year Ended December 31, 19X9

	Before-Tax Amount	Tax (Expense) or Benefit	Net-of-Tax Amount
Foreign currency translation adjustments	$10,666	$(2,666)	$ 8,000
Unrealized gains on securities:			
Unrealized holding gains arising during period	17,333	(4,333)	13,000
Less: reclassification adjustment for gains realized in net income	(2,000)	500	(1,500)
Net unrealized gains	15,333	(3,833)	11,500
Minimum pension liability adjustment	(3,333)	833	(2,500)
Other comprehensive income	$22,666	$(5,666)	$17,000

[FAS130, ¶131]

.126 [Exhibit 126A illustrates the requirement that the total of accumulated other comprehensive income be displayed separately as a component of equity in a statement of financial position.]

Exhibit 126A

Enterprise
Statement of Financial Position
December 31, 19X9

Assets:	
Cash	$ 150,000
Accounts receivable	175,000
Available-for-sale securities	112,000
Plant and equipment	985,000
Total assets	$1,422,000
Liabilities:	
Accounts payable	$ 112,500
Accrued liabilities	79,250
Pension liability	128,000
Notes payable	318,500
Total liabilities	$ 638,250
Equity:	
Common stock	$ 200,000
Paid-in capital	400,000
Retained earnings	141,750
[Accumulated other comprehensive income	42,000]
Total equity	783,750
Total liabilities and equity	$1,422,000

[FAS130, ¶131]

.127 [Exhibit 127A illustrates the disclosure required in paragraph .120 of the accumulated balances for each classification within the amount of accumulated other comprehensive income displayed in the equity section of the statement of financial position.] Alternatively, the balances of each classification within accumulated other comprehensive income can be displayed in a statement of changes in equity or in a statement of financial position. [FAS130, ¶131]

Exhibit 127A

Enterprise
Notes to Financial Statements
Year Ended December 31, 19X9

	Foreign Currency Items	Unrealized Gains on Securities	Minimum Pension Liability Adjustment	Accumulated Other Comprehensive Income
Beginning balance	$ (500)	$25,500	$ 0	$25,000
Current-period change	8,000	11,500	(2,500)	17,000
Ending balance	$7,500	$37,000	$(2,500)	$42,000

[FAS130, ¶131]

Illustrative Examples of the Determination of Reclassification Adjustments

.128 This section requires that an enterprise determine reclassification adjustments for each classification of other comprehensive income, except minimum pension liability adjustments. An enterprise may display reclassification adjustments on the face of the financial statement in which comprehensive income is reported, or it may disclose reclassification adjustments in the notes to the financial statements. [FAS130, ¶132]

.129 Paragraphs .131 through .135 provide illustrations of the calculation of reclassification adjustments for available-for-sale securities [as described in] Section I80. Illustration 1 is of available-for-sale equity securities, and Illustration 2 is of available-for-sale debt securities. The illustrations are intended as examples only; they do not represent actual situations. [FAS130, ¶133]

.130 Illustrations 1 and 2 involve a nonpublic enterprise that follows the practice of recognizing all unrealized gains and losses on available-for-sale securities in other comprehensive income before recognizing them as realized gains and losses in net income. Therefore, the before-tax amount of the reclassification adjustment recognized in other comprehensive income is equal to, but opposite in sign from, the amount of the realized gain or loss recognized in net income. [FAS130, ¶134]

Illustration 1: Available-for-Sale Equity Securities

.131 In this illustration the equity securities [that are classified as] available for sale [under Section I80] appreciate in fair value. On December 31, 19X7, Enterprise purchased 1,000 shares of equity securities at $10 per share, which it classified as available for sale. The fair value of the securities at December 31, 19X8 and December 31, 19X9 was $12 and $15, respectively. There were no dividends declared on the securities that were sold on December 31, 19X9. A tax rate of 30 percent is assumed.

Calculation of Holding Gains

	Before Tax	Income Tax	Net of Tax
Holding gains recognized in other comprehensive income:			
Year ended December 31, 19X8	$2,000	$ 600	$1,400
Year ended December 31, 19X9	3,000	900	2,100
Total gain	$5,000	$1,500	$3,500

Amounts Reported in Net Income and Other Comprehensive Income for the Years Ended December 31, 19X8 and December 31, 19X9

	19X8	19X9
Net income:		
Gain on sale of securities		$ 5,000
Income tax expense		(1,500)
Net gain realized in net income		3,500
Other comprehensive income:		
Holding gain arising during period, net of tax	$1,400	2,100
Reclassification adjustment, net of tax	0	(3,500)
Net gain (loss) recognized in other comprehensive income	1,400	(1,400)
Total impact on comprehensive income	$1,400	$ 2,100

[FAS130, ¶135]

Illustration 2: Available-for-Sale Debt Securities

.132 In this illustration the interest-bearing debt securities (bonds) [that are classified as] available for sale [under Section I80] were purchased at a premium to yield 6.5 percent. Interest income is included in net income based on the historical yield, and the bonds decline in fair value during the first two years in which they are held. [FAS130, ¶136]

.133 On December 31, 19X5, registration of Company A's 8-year, 8 percent debentures, interest payable annually, became effective and the entire issue of $10,000,000 was sold at par. At the end of each of the next four years, the closing prices and the related market interest rates to maturity were as follows:

December 31	Price ($000)	Yield (%)
19X6	$102.6	7.5
19X7	107.3	6.5
19X8	96.1	9.0
19X9	92.2	10.5

[FAS130, ¶137]

.134 On December 31, 19X7, Enterprise purchased $1,000,000 of Company A's bonds on the open market at 107.3 and classified them as available for sale. Enterprise continued to hold the bonds until December 31, 19X9, at which time they were sold at 92.2. Enterprise prepared the following schedules in relation to the bonds:

Cost-Based Carrying Amount, Interest Income, and Premium Amortization

Year	(a) Beginning Carrying Value	(b) Cash Interest Received [8% × par]	(c) Interest Income [(a) × 6.5%]	(d) Premium Amortization [(b) – (c)]	(e) Ending Carrying Value [(a) – (d)]
19X7					$1,073,000
19X8	$1,073,000	$80,000	$69,745	$10,255	1,062,745
19X9	1,062,745	80,000	69,078	10,922	1,051,823

Calculation of Before-Tax Holding Loss

Year Ended 12/31	(a) Ending Carrying Value	(b) Ending Fair Value	(c) Change in Fair Value	(d) Premium Amortization	(e) Holding Loss [(c) + (d)]
19X7	$1,073,000	$1,073,000	$ 0		
19X8	1,062,745	961,000	(112,000)	$10,255	$(101,745)
19X9	1,051,823	922,000	(39,000)	10,922	(28,078)

Net-of-Tax Holding Losses (Assume a Tax Rate of 30 Percent)

	Before Tax	Income Tax	Net of Tax
Holding losses recognized in other comprehensive income:			
Year ended December 31, 19X8	$(101,745)	$30,523	$(71,222)
Year ended December 31, 19X9	(28,078)	8,423	(19,655)
Total loss	$(129,823)	$38,946	$(90,877)

Amounts Reported in Net Income and Other Comprehensive Income for the Years Ended December 31, 19X8 and December 31, 19X9

	19X8	19X9
Net income:		
Interest income	$ 69,745	$ 69,078
Loss on sale of bonds		(129,823)
Income tax (expense) benefit	(20,923)	18,223
Amounts realized in net income	48,822	(42,522)
Other comprehensive income (OCI):		
Holding loss arising during period, net of tax	(71,222)	(19,655)
Reclassification adjustment, net of tax		90,877
Net (loss) gain recognized in other comprehensive income	(71,222)	71,222
Total impact on comprehensive income	$(22,400)	$ 28,700

[FAS130, ¶138]

.135 The following before-tax entries would be made to record the purchase, accrue interest (using the effective interest method based on cost), recognize the change in fair value, and record the sale:

December 31, 19X7:

Investment in bonds	$1,073,000	
Cash		$1,073,000
To record purchase of bond		

December 31, 19X8:

Cash	80,000	
Investment in bonds		10,255
Interest income (to earnings)		69,745
To record interest income on the bond, amortize the premium, and record cash received		
Unrealized holding loss (to OCI)	101,745	
Investment in bonds		101,745
To adjust carrying amount of bond to fair value		
Accumulated OCI	101,745	
Unrealized holding loss		101,745
Interest income	69,745	
Retained earnings		69,745
To close nominal accounts to real accounts at year-end		

December 31, 19X9:

Cash	80,000	
Investment in bonds		10,922
Interest income (to earnings)		69,078
To record interest income on the bond, amortize the premium, and record cash received		
Unrealized holding loss (to OCI)	28,078	
Investment in bonds		28,078
To adjust carrying amount of bond to fair value		

Accumulated OCI	28,078	
Unrealized holding loss		28,078
To close nominal account to real account at year-end		
Cash	922,000	
Loss on sale of securities (to earnings)	129,823	
Investment in bonds		922,000
Reclassification adjustment (to OCI)		129,823
To record sale of bond		
Reclassification adjustment	129,823	
Accumulated OCI		129,823
Retained earnings	60,745	
Interest income	69,078	
Loss on sale of securities		129,823
To close nominal accounts to real accounts at year-end		

[FAS130, ¶139]

(The next page is 7873.)

CONSOLIDATION SECTION C51

Sources: ARB 51; FASB Statement 13; FASB Statement 58; FASB Statement 94; FASB Statement 109; FASB Statement 131; FASB Statement 140

[**Note:** A list of Issues discussed by the Emerging Issues Task Force (EITF) that provide supplemental guidance for this section is presented in paragraph .1000.]

Summary

Consolidated financial statements present the results of operations, financial position, and cash flows of a parent and its subsidiaries as if the group were a single enterprise. This section provides that consolidated financial statements generally shall include enterprises in which the parent has a controlling financial interest (usually, majority voting interest). This section also describes consolidation accounting procedures, such as elimination of intercompany profit and treatment of minority interests.

Consolidation Policy

.101 The purpose of **consolidated statements** is to present, primarily for the benefit of the shareholders and creditors of the parent company, the results of operations and the financial position of a parent company and its subsidiaries essentially as if the group were a single enterprise with one or more branches or divisions. There is a presumption that consolidated statements are more meaningful than separate statements and that they are usually necessary for a fair presentation when one of the enterprises in the group directly or indirectly has a controlling financial interest in the other enterprises. [ARB51, ¶1] If an enterprise has one or more subsidiaries, consolidated [statements] rather than parent-company financial statements are the appropriate general purpose financial statements. [FAS94, ¶61]

.102 The usual condition for a controlling financial interest is ownership of a majority voting interest, and, therefore, as a general rule ownership by one enterprise, directly or indirectly, of over fifty percent of the outstanding voting shares of another enterprise is a condition pointing toward consolidation. However, there are exceptions to this general rule.[a] A majority-owned subsidiary shall not be consolidated if control does not rest with the majority owner (as, for instance, if the subsidiary is in legal reorganization or in bankruptcy or operates under foreign exchange restrictions, controls, or other governmentally imposed uncertainties so severe that they cast significant doubt on the parent's ability to control the subsidiary). [FAS94, ¶13] A qualifying SPE shall not be consolidated in the financial statements of a transferor or its affiliates. [FAS140, ¶46] [Refer to paragraph .1001 for EITF Issues that provide interpretive guidance on paragraphs .102 and .103.]

.103 All majority-owned subsidiaries—all companies in which a parent has a controlling financial interest through direct or indirect ownership of a majority voting interest—shall be consolidated except those described in the last sentence of paragraph .102. [FAS94, ¶13]

.104-.106 [Deleted 11/87 because of FASB Statement 94, *Consolidation of All Majority-Owned Subsidiaries*.]

.107 A difference in fiscal periods of a parent and subsidiary does not of itself justify the exclusion of the subsidiary from consolidation. It ordinarily is feasible for the subsidiary to prepare, for consolidation purposes, statements for a period that corresponds with or closely approaches the fiscal period of the parent. However, if the difference is not more than about three months, it usually is acceptable to use, for consolidation purposes, the subsidiary's statements for its fiscal period; when this is done, recognition shall be given by disclosure or otherwise to the effect of intervening events that materially affect the financial position or results of operations.[2] [ARB51, ¶4]

Disclosure

.108 Consolidated statements shall disclose the consolidation policy that is being followed. In most cases this can be made apparent by the headings or other information in the statements, but in other cases a footnote is required. [ARB51, ¶5]

.108A An entity that is a member of a group that files a consolidated tax return shall disclose in its separately issued financial statements:

[[a]These exceptions] relate to the concept of control and its place in consolidation policy [and] are part of a broader FASB project on the reporting entity, including consolidations and the equity method. Similarly, consolidation of subsidiaries controlled by means other than ownership of a majority voting interest—control by significant minority ownership, by contract, lease, or agreement with other stockholders, by court decree, or otherwise—[is also] part of the project on the reporting entity. [FAS94,¶10]

[1][Deleted 11/87 because of FASB Statement 94.]

[[2]Editorial deletion, 5/93.]

a. The aggregate amount of current and deferred tax expense for each statement of earnings presented and the amount of any tax-related balances due to or from affiliates as of the date of each statement of financial position presented
b. The principal provisions of the method by which the consolidated amount of current and deferred tax expense is allocated to members of the group and the nature and effect of any changes in that method (and in determining related balances to or from affiliates) during the years for which the disclosures in (a) above are presented.

[FAS109, ¶49]

Consolidation Procedure Generally

.109 In the preparation of consolidated statements, intercompany balances and transactions shall be eliminated. This includes intercompany open account balances, security holdings, sales and purchases, interest, dividends, etc. As consolidated statements are based on the assumption that they represent the financial position and operating results of a single business enterprise, such statements shall not include gain or loss on transactions among the enterprises in the group. Accordingly, any intercompany profit or loss on assets remaining within the group shall be eliminated; the concept usually applied for this purpose is gross profit or loss (refer to paragraph .110). [ARB51, ¶6] [Refer to paragraph .1001 for an EITF Issue that provides interpretive guidance on this paragraph.]

.110 If income taxes have been paid on intercompany profits on assets remaining within the group, such taxes should be deferred or the intercompany profits to be eliminated in consolidation should be appropriately reduced. [ARB51, ¶17]

.111 If one enterprise purchases two or more blocks of stock of another enterprise at various dates and eventually obtains control of the other enterprise, the date of acquisition (for the purpose of preparing consolidated statements) depends on the circumstances. If two or more purchases are made over a period of time, the retained earnings of the subsidiary at acquisition shall generally be determined on a step-by-step basis; however, if small purchases are made over a period of time and then a purchase is made that results in control, the date of the latest purchase, as a matter of convenience, may be considered as the date of acquisition. Thus, there would generally be included in consolidated income for the year in which control is obtained the postacquisition income for that year, and in consolidated retained earnings the postacquisition income of prior years attributable to each block previously acquired [if not previously recognized by accounting for the investment by the equity method]. For example, if a 45 percent interest was acquired on October 1, 19X7 and a further 30 percent interest was acquired on

---

[2a][Deleted 2/92 because of FASB Statement 109, *Accounting for Income Taxes.*]

April 1, 19X8, it would be appropriate to include in consolidated income for the year ended December 31, 19X8, 45 percent of the earnings of the subsidiary for the 3 months ended March 31, and 75 percent of the earnings for the 9 months ended December 31, and to credit consolidated retained earnings in 19X8 with 45 percent of the undistributed earnings of the subsidiary for the 3 months ended December 31, 19X7 [if the investor's equity in those undistributed earnings had not been recognized previously].[3] [ARB51, ¶10] [Refer to paragraph .1001 for EITF Issues that provide interpretive guidance on this paragraph.]

.112 If a subsidiary is purchased during the year, there are alternative ways of dealing with the results of its operations in the consolidated income statement. One method, which usually is preferable, especially if there are several dates of acquisition of blocks of shares, is to include the subsidiary in the consolidation as though it had been acquired at the beginning of the year, and to deduct at the bottom of the consolidated income statement the preacquisition earnings applicable to each block of stock. This method presents results that are more indicative of the current status of the group, and facilitates future comparison with subsequent years. Another method of prorating income is to include in the consolidated statement only the subsidiary's revenue and expenses subsequent to the date of acquisition. [ARB51, ¶11]

.113 [Deleted 8/01 because of FASB Statement 144, *Accounting for the Impairment or Disposal of Long-Lived Assets.*]

.114 Shares of the parent held by a subsidiary shall not be treated as outstanding stock in the consolidated balance sheet. [ARB51, ¶13]

Minority Interests

.115 The amount of intercompany profit or loss to be eliminated in accordance with paragraph .109 is not affected by the existence of a minority interest. The complete elimination of the intercompany profit or loss is consistent with the underlying assumption that consolidated statements represent the financial position and operating results of a single business enterprise. The elimination of the intercompany profit or loss may be allocated proportionately between the majority and minority interests. [ARB51, ¶14] [Refer to paragraph .1001 for EITF Issues that provide interpretive guidance on paragraphs .115 and .116.]

---

[3]The amount of interest cost capitalized through application of Section I67, "Interest: Capitalization of Interest Costs," shall not be changed when restating financial statements of prior periods [to account for acquiring a subsidiary on a step-by-step basis]. [FAS58, ¶8]

.116 In the unusual case in which losses applicable to the minority interest in a subsidiary exceed the minority interest in the equity capital of the subsidiary, such excess and any further losses applicable to the minority interest shall be charged against the majority interest, as there is no obligation of the minority interest to make good such losses. However, if future earnings do materialize, the majority interest shall be credited to the extent of such losses previously absorbed. [ARB51, ¶15]

Stock Dividends of Subsidiaries

.117 Occasionally, subsidiary enterprises capitalize retained earnings arising since acquisition, by means of a stock dividend or otherwise. This does not require a transfer to capital surplus on consolidation, inasmuch as the retained earnings in the consolidated financial statements shall reflect the accumulated earnings of the consolidated group not distributed to the shareholders of, or capitalized by, the parent company. [ARB51, ¶18]

Unconsolidated Subsidiaries in Consolidated Statements

.118 [Section I82, "Investments: Equity Method," describes when investments in unconsolidated subsidiaries shall be accounted for by the equity method in consolidated financial statements. The limitations on consolidation described in paragraphs .102 and .103 of this section also are limitations on use of the equity method; a subsidiary affected by those limitations shall be accounted for by the cost method.]

.119-.120 [Deleted 11/87 because of FASB Statement 94.]

.120A [Deleted 6/97 because of FASB Statement 131, *Disclosures about Segments of an Enterprise and Related Information.*]

Combined Statements

.121 To justify the preparation of consolidated statements, the controlling financial interest shall rest directly or indirectly in one of the enterprises included in the consolidation. There are circumstances, however, where combined financial statements (as distinguished from consolidated statements) of commonly controlled enterprises are likely to be more meaningful than their separate statements. For example, combined financial statements would be useful if one individual owns a controlling interest in several enterprises that are related in their operations. Combined statements also would be used to present the financial position and the results of operations of a group of unconsolidated subsid-

---

[[3a]Editorial deletion, 6/97.]

iaries. [(Refer to paragraph .102 for rules requiring consolidation of majority-owned subsidiaries.)] They also might be used to combine the financial statements of enterprises under common management. [ARB51, ¶22]

.122 If combined statements are prepared for a group of related enterprises, such as a group of unconsolidated subsidiaries [(refer to paragraph .102 for rules requiring consolidation of majority-owned subsidiaries)] or a group of commonly controlled enterprises, intercompany transactions and profits or losses shall be eliminated, and if there are problems in connection with such matters as minority interests, foreign operations, different fiscal periods, or income taxes, they shall be treated in the same manner as in consolidated statements. [ARB51, ¶23]

Parent Company Statements

.123 In some cases parent company statements may be needed, in addition to consolidated statements, to indicate adequately the position of bondholders and other creditors or preferred stockholders of the parent. Consolidated statements, in which one column is used for the parent company and other columns for particular subsidiaries or groups of subsidiaries, often are an effective means of presenting the pertinent information. [ARB51, ¶24]

Glossary

.401 **Consolidated statements.** Consolidated statements present, primarily for the benefit of the shareholders and creditors of the parent company, the results of operations and the financial position of a parent company and its subsidiaries essentially as if the group were a single enterprise with one or more branches or divisions. [ARB51, ¶1]

Supplemental Guidance: Emerging Issues Task Force (EITF) Issues

.1000 [Listed below are EITF Issues that provide supplemental guidance for this section. These Issues are grouped by subject matter and may be either interpretive of or related by topic to the guidance in this section.

Minority Interests in Certain Real Estate Investment Trusts (REIT)

EITF Issue No. 94-2, "Treatment of Minority Interests in Certain Real Estate Investment Trusts"

EITF Issue No. 95-7, "Implementation Issues Related to the Treatment of Minority Interests in Certain Real Estate Investment Trusts"

New Basis of Accounting

EITF Issue No. 84-23, "Leveraged Buyout Holding Company Debt"

EITF Issue No. 84-42, "Push-Down of Parent Company Debt to a Subsidiary"

EITF Issue No. 85-21, "Changes of Ownership Resulting in a New Basis of Accounting"

EITF Issue No. 88-16, "Basis in Leveraged Buyout Transactions"

EITF Issue No. 90-12, "Allocating Basis to Individual Assets and Liabilities for Transactions within the Scope of Issue No. 88-16"

EITF Topic No. D-97, "Push-Down Accounting"

Special-Purpose Entities

EITF Issue No. 84-15, "Grantor Trusts Consolidation"

EITF Issue No. 84-30, "Sales of Loans to Special-Purpose Entities"

EITF Issue No. 90-15, "Impact of Nonsubstantive Lessors, Residual Value Guarantees, and Other Provisions in Leasing Transactions"

EITF Issue No. 96-20, "Impact of FASB Statement No. 125 on Consolidation of Special-Purpose Entities"

EITF Issue No. 97-1, "Implementation Issues in Accounting for Lease Transactions, including Those involving Special-Purpose Entities"

EITF Issue No. 97-6, "Application of Issue No. 96-20 to Qualifying Special-Purpose Entities Receiving Transferred Financial Assets Prior to the Effective Date of FASB Statement No. 125"

EITF Topic No. D-14, "Transactions involving Special-Purpose Entities"

Other

EITF Issue No. 84-33, "Acquisition of a Tax Loss Carryforward—Temporary Parent-Subsidiary Relationship"

EITF Issue No. 84-40, "Long-Term Debt Repayable by a Capital Stock Transaction"

EITF Issue No. 85-12, "Retention of Specialized Accounting for Investments in Consolidation"

EITF Issue No. 88-15, "Classification of Subsidiary's Loan Payable in Consolidated Balance Sheet When Subsidiary's and Parent's Fiscal Years Differ"

EITF Issue No. 96-16, "Investor's Accounting for an Investee When the Investor Owns a Majority of the Voting Stock but the Minority Shareholder or Shareholders Have Certain Approval or Veto Rights"

EITF Issue No. 97-2, "Application of FASB Statement No. 94 and APB Opinion No. 16 to Physician Practice Management Entities and Certain Other Entities with Contractual Management Arrangements"

EITF Issue No. 98-2, "Accounting by a Subsidiary or Joint Venture for an Investment in the Stock of Its Parent Company or Joint Venture Partner"

EITF Issue No. 98-6, "Investor's Accounting for an Investment in a Limited Partnership When the Investor Is the Sole General Partner and the Limited Partners Have Certain Approval or Veto Rights"

EITF Topic No. D-74, "Issues Concerning the Scope of the AICPA Guide on Investment Companies"

EITF Topic No. D-105, "Accounting in Consolidation for Energy Trading Contracts between Affiliated Entities When the Activities of One but Not Both Affiliates Are within the Scope of Issue No. 98-10"]

.1001 [Listed below are those EITF Issues that provide interpretive guidance on specific material in this section.

Paragraphs .102 and .103 (FAS 94, ¶13)—EITF Issues No. 90-15 and 97-2
Paragraph .109 (ARB 51, ¶6)—EITF Topic No. D-105
Paragraph .111 (ARB 51, ¶10)—EITF Issues No. 88-16 and 90-12
Paragraphs .115 and .116 (ARB 51, ¶14-15)—EITF Issues No. 94-2 and 95-7]

(The next page is 8301.)

CONTINGENCIES SECTION C59

Sources: APB Opinion 16; FASB Statement 5; FASB Statement 16; FASB Statement 38; FASB Statement 87; FASB Statement 109; FASB Statement 112; FASB Statement 113; FASB Statement 114; FASB Statement 123; FASB Statement 141; FASB Interpretation 14; FASB Interpretation 34

[**Note:** A list of Issues discussed by the Emerging Issues Task Force (EITF) that provide supplemental guidance for this section is presented in paragraph .1000.]

Summary

An estimated loss from a loss contingency shall be charged to income if (a) it is probable that an asset had been impaired or a liability had been incurred at the date of the financial statements and (b) the amount of the loss can be reasonably estimated. Disclosure is required for loss contingencies not meeting both those conditions if there is a reasonable possibility that a loss may have been incurred. Gain contingencies shall not be credited to income because to do so would recognize income prior to realization.

.101 For purposes of this section, a **contingency** is defined as an existing condition, situation, or set of circumstances involving uncertainty as to possible gain (hereinafter a *gain contingency*) or loss (hereinafter a *loss contingency*) to an enterprise that will ultimately be resolved when one or more future events occur or fail to occur.[1] Resolution of the uncertainty may confirm the acquisition of an asset or the reduction of a liability or the loss or impairment of an asset or the incurrence of a liability. [FAS5, ¶1] The term *loss* is used in this section to include many charges against income that are commonly referred to as *expenses* and others that are commonly referred to as *losses.* [FAS5, ¶1, fn1]

Scope

.102 This section [presents] standards of financial accounting and reporting for loss contingencies and gain contingencies. [FAS5, ¶6] [However, accounting for pension costs, for vacation pay,] and for deferred compensation contracts and stock issued to employees are excluded from the scope of this section. Those matters are covered in [Sec-

[1Refer to paragraphs .121 and .122 for further discussion and examples of loss contingencies.]

tion P16, "Pension Costs," Section C44, "Compensation to Employees: Paid Absences,"] Section C38, "Compensation to Employees: Deferred Compensation Agreements," [FAS5, ¶7] and Section C36, "Compensation: Stock-Based," [FAS123, ¶385] [respectively.] Accounting for other employment-related costs is also excluded from the scope of this section except for postemployment benefits that become subject to [the provisions of] this section through application of paragraph .103 of Section P32, "Postemployment Benefits." [FAS112, ¶10] [Further,] this section does not change [prescribed] accounting practices for life insurance enterprises [FAS5, ¶102] [in Section In6, "Insurance Industry." As discussed in paragraph .137, this section does not address the question of whether] it is appropriate to write down the carrying amount of an operating asset to an amount expected to be recoverable through future operations. [FAS5, ¶31]

.103 Examples of application of the conditions for accrual of loss contingencies in paragraph .105 and the disclosure requirements in paragraphs .108 through .114 are presented in paragraphs .124 through .151. [FAS5, ¶16]

Probability Classifications for Loss Contingencies

.104 When a loss contingency exists, the likelihood that the future event or events will confirm the loss or impairment of an asset or the incurrence of a liability can range from probable to remote. This section uses the terms **probable, reasonably possible,** and **remote** to identify three areas within that range, as follows:

a. *Probable.* The future event or events are likely to occur.
b. *Reasonably possible.* The chance of the future event or events occuring is more than remote but less than likely.
c. *Remote.* The chance of the future event or events occurring is slight.

[FAS5, ¶3]

Accrual of Loss Contingencies

.105 An estimated loss from a loss contingency (as defined in paragraph .101) shall be accrued by a charge to income if *both* of the following conditions are met:

a. Information available prior to issuance of the financial statements indicates that it is probable[2] that an asset had been impaired or a liability had been incurred at the date of the financial statements.[3] It is implicit in this condition that it must be probable that one or more future events will occur confirming the fact of the loss.

[2]Virtual certainty [is not required] before a loss is accrued. [FAS5, ¶84]

[3]*Date of the financial statements* means the end of the most recent accounting period for which financial statements are being presented. [FAS5, ¶8, fn4]

b. The amount of loss can be reasonably estimated.[4]

[FAS5, ¶8] [Refer to paragraph .1001 for EITF Issues that provide interpretive guidance on this paragraph.]

.106 Condition (b) in paragraph .105 does not delay accrual of a loss until only a single amount can be reasonably estimated. To the contrary, if condition (a) in paragraph .105 is met and information available indicates that the estimated amount of loss is within a range of amounts, it follows that some amount of loss has occurred and can be reasonably estimated. [FIN14, ¶2] [Refer to paragraph .1001 for an EITF Issue that provides interpretive guidance on this paragraph.]

.107 If condition (a) in paragraph .105 is met with respect to a particular loss contingency and the reasonable estimate of the loss is a range, condition (b) in paragraph .105 is met and an amount shall be accrued for the loss. If some amount within the range appears at the time to be a better estimate than any other amount within the range, that amount shall be accrued. If no amount within the range is a better estimate than any other amount, however, the minimum amount in the range shall be accrued. [FIN14, ¶3] (Even though the minimum amount in the range is not necessarily the amount of loss that will be ultimately determined, it is not likely that the ultimate loss will be less than the minimum amount.) [FIN14, ¶3, fn1]

Disclosure of Loss Contingencies

.108 Disclosure of the nature of an accrual made pursuant to the provisions of paragraph .105, and in some circumstances the amount accrued, may be necessary for the financial statements not to be misleading. [FAS5, ¶9] (Terminology used shall be descriptive of the nature of the accrual.) [FAS5, ¶9, fn5]

.109 If no accrual is made for a loss contingency because one or both of the conditions in paragraph .105 are not met, or if an exposure to loss exists in excess of the amount accrued pursuant to the provisions of paragraph .105, disclosure of the contingency shall be made when there is at least a reasonable possibility that a loss or an additional loss may have been incurred. The disclosure shall indicate the nature of the contingency and shall give an estimate of the possible loss or range of loss or state that such an estimate cannot be made.[5] [FAS5, ¶10]

[4]If a loss cannot be accrued in the period when it is probable that an asset had been impaired or a liability had been incurred because the amount of loss cannot be reasonably estimated, the loss shall be charged to the income [of the period] when the amount of the loss can be reasonably estimated [and not] be charged retroactively to an earlier period. [FAS16, ¶37] [Refer to Section A35, "Adjustments of Financial Statements for Prior Periods," paragraph .102.]

[5]Disclosure is not required for uninsured risks. However, disclosure in appropriate circumstances is not discouraged. [FAS5, ¶103]

.110 For example, disclosure shall be made of any loss contingency that meets the condition in paragraph .105(a) but that is not accrued because the amount of loss cannot be reasonably estimated (refer to paragraph .105(b)). Disclosure is also required of some loss contingencies that do not meet the condition in paragraph .105(a)—namely, those contingencies for which there is a *reasonable possibility* that a loss may have been incurred even though information may not indicate that it is *probable* that an asset had been impaired or a liability had been incurred at the date of the financial statements. [FAS5, ¶10, fn6]

.111 Disclosure is not required of a loss contingency involving an unasserted claim or assessment if there has been no manifestation by a potential claimant of an awareness of a possible claim or assessment unless it is considered probable that a claim will be asserted and there is a reasonable possibility that the outcome will be unfavorable. [FAS5, ¶10]

.112 After the date of an enterprise's financial statements but before those financial statements are issued, information may become available indicating that an asset was impaired or a liability was incurred after the date of the financial statements or that there is at least a reasonable possibility that an asset was impaired or a liability was incurred after that date. The information may relate to a loss contingency that existed at the date of the financial statements, that is, an asset that was not insured at the date of the financial statements. On the other hand, the information may relate to a loss contingency that did not exist at the date of the financial statements, that is, threat of expropriation of assets after the date of financial statements or the filing for bankruptcy by an enterprise whose debt was guaranteed after the date of the financial statements. In none of the cases cited in this paragraph was an asset impaired or a liability incurred at the date of the financial statements, and the condition for accrual in paragraph .105(a) is, therefore, not met. Disclosure of those kinds of losses or loss contingencies may be necessary, however, to keep the financial statements from being misleading. If disclosure is deemed necessary, the financial statements shall indicate the nature of the loss or loss contingency and give an estimate of the amount or range of loss or possible loss or state that such an estimate cannot be made. Occasionally, in the case of a loss arising after the date of the financial statements where the amount of asset impairment or liability incurrence can be reasonably estimated, disclosure may best be made by supplementing the historical financial statements with pro forma financial data giving effect to the loss as if it had occurred at the date of the financial statements. It may be desirable to present pro forma statements, usually a balance sheet only, in columnar form on the face of the historical financial statements. [FAS5, ¶11]

.113 Certain loss contingencies are presently being disclosed in financial statements even though the possibility of loss may be remote. The common characteristic of those contingencies is a guarantee, normally with a right to proceed against an outside party in the event that the guarantor is called upon to satisfy the guarantee. Examples include (a) guarantees of indebtedness of others, (b) obligations of commercial banks under standby letters of credit, and (c) guarantees to repurchase receivables (or, in some cases, to repurchase the related property) that have been sold or otherwise assigned. Disclosure of those loss contingencies, and others that in substance have the same characteristic, shall be continued. The disclosure shall include the nature and amount of the guarantee. Consideration should be given to disclosing, if estimable, the value of any recovery that could be expected to result, such as from the guarantor's right to proceed against an outside party. [FAS5, ¶12]

.114 The term *guarantees of indebtedness of others* in paragraph .113 includes **indirect guarantees of indebtedness of others.** [FIN34, ¶3] An indirect guarantee of another arises under an agreement that obligates one enterprise to transfer funds to a second enterprise upon occurrence of specified events, under conditions whereby (a) the funds are legally available to creditors of the second enterprise and (b) those creditors may enforce the second enterprise's claims against the first enterprise under the agreement. Examples of indirect guarantees include agreements to advance funds if a second enterprise's income, coverage of fixed charges, or working capital falls below a specified minimum.[6] [FIN34, ¶2]

.115 [Deleted 12/82 because of FASB Statement 71, *Accounting for the Effects of Certain Types of Regulation.*]

General or Unspecified Business Risks

.116 Some enterprises have in the past accrued so-called reserves for general contingencies. General or unspecified business risks do not meet the conditions for accrual in paragraph .105 and no accrual for loss shall be made. No disclosure about them is required by this section. [FAS5, ¶14]

Appropriation of Retained Earnings

.117 Some enterprises have classified a portion of retained earnings as *appropriated* for loss contingencies. In some cases, the appropriation has been shown outside the stockholders' equity section of the balance sheet. Appropriation of retained earnings is not prohibited by this section provided that it is shown within the stockholders' equity section of the balance sheet and is clearly identified as an appropriation of retained earn-

[6]Disclosure of an indirect guarantee is not required if it is otherwise disclosed in an entity's financial statements. [FIN34, ¶2, fn1]

ings. Costs or losses shall not be charged to an appropriation of retained earnings, and no part of the appropriation shall be transferred to income. [FAS5, ¶15]

Gain Contingencies

.118 Contingencies that might result in gains usually are not reflected in the accounts since to do so might be to recognize revenue prior to its realization. Adequate disclosure shall be made of contingencies that might result in gains, but care shall be exercised to avoid misleading implications as to the likelihood of realization. [FAS5, ¶17]

Contingencies Related to Business Combinations

.119 A business combination agreement may provide for the issuance of additional shares of a security or the transfer of cash or other consideration contingent on specified events or transactions in the future. [FAS141, ¶25] [The accounting for such contingent consideration is discussed in Section B51, "Business Combinations," paragraphs .124 through .133. Similarly, Section B51, paragraphs .142 and .143, discuss the accounting for preacquisition contingencies.] A preacquisition contingency [is] a contingency of an entity that is acquired in a business combination that is in existence before the consummation of the combination. A preacquisition contingency can be a contingent asset, a contingent liability, or a contingent impairment of an asset. [FAS141, ¶F1]

Other Disclosures

.120 Unused letters of credit, assets pledged as security for loans, and commitments, such as those for plant acquisition or an obligation to reduce debts, maintain working capital, or restrict dividends, [FAS5, ¶18] shall be disclosed in financial statements. This section does not alter the present disclosure requirements with respect to those items. [Refer to Section F25, "Financial Instruments: Disclosure," for guidance on possible additional disclosure requirements.] [FAS5, ¶19]

Examples of Loss Contingencies

.121 Not all uncertainties[6a] inherent in the accounting process give rise to *contingencies* as that term is used in this section. Estimates are required in financial statements for many ongoing and recurring activities of an enterprise. The mere fact that an estimate is involved does not of itself constitute the type of uncertainty referred to in the definition

[6a]The possibility of a change in the tax law in some future year is not an *uncertainty* as that term is used in this section. [FAS109, ¶172]

in paragraph .101. For example, the fact that estimates are used to allocate the known cost of a depreciable asset over the period of use by an enterprise does not make depreciation a contingency; the eventual expiration of the utility of the asset is not uncertain. Thus, depreciation of assets is not a contingency as defined in paragraph .101, nor are such matters as recurring repairs, maintenance, and overhauls, which interrelate with depreciation. Also, amounts owed for services received, such as advertising and utilities, are not contingencies even though the accrued amounts may have been estimated; there is nothing uncertain about the fact that those obligations have been incurred. [FAS5, ¶2]

.122 Examples of loss contingencies include:

a. Collectibility of receivables
b. Obligations related to product warranties and product defects
c. Risk of loss or damage of enterprise property by fire, explosion, or other hazards
d. Threat of expropriation of assets
e. Pending or threatened litigation
f. Actual or possible claims and assessments
g. Risk of loss from catastrophes assumed by property and casualty insurance enterprises including reinsurance enterprises
h. Guarantees of indebtedness of others
i. Obligations of commercial banks under standby letters of credit[7]
j. Agreements to repurchase receivables (or to repurchase the related property) that have been sold [FAS5, ¶4]
[k. Withdrawal from a multiemployer plan.[7a]]

[7]As defined by the Federal Reserve Board, *standby letters of credit* include "every letter of credit (or similar arrangement however named or designated) which represents an obligation to the beneficiary on the part of the issuer (1) to repay money borrowed by or advanced to or for the account of the account party or (2) to make payment on account of any evidence of indebtedness undertaken by the account party or (3) to make payment on account of any default by the account party in the performance of an obligation." A note to that definition states that "as defined, 'standby letters of credit' would not include (1) commercial letters of credit and similar instruments where the issuing bank expects the beneficiary to draw upon the issuer and which do not 'guaranty' payment of a money obligation or (2) a guaranty or similar obligation issued by a foreign branch in accordance with and subject to the limitations of Regulation M [of the Federal Reserve Board]." Regulations of the Comptroller of the Currency and the Federal Deposit Insurance Corporation contain similar definitions. [FAS5, ¶4, fn2]

[7a]In some situations, withdrawal from a multiemployer plan may result in an employer's having an obligation to the plan for a portion of its unfunded benefit obligations. If withdrawal under circumstances that would give rise to an obligation is either probable or reasonably possible, the provisions of this section shall apply. [FAS87, ¶70]

Examples of Application of the Conditions for Accrual and Disclosure of Loss Contingencies

.123 Paragraphs .124 through .151 contain examples of application of the conditions for accrual of loss contingencies in paragraph .105 and of the disclosure requirements in paragraphs .108 through .114. It should be recognized that no set of examples can encompass all possible contingencies or circumstances. Accordingly, accrual and disclosure of loss contingencies should be based on an evaluation of the facts in each particular case. [FAS5, ¶21]

Estimation of a Loss within a Range of Amounts

.124 Assume that an enterprise is involved in litigation at the close of its fiscal year ending December 31, 19X6 and information available indicates that an unfavorable outcome is probable. Subsequently, after a trial on the issues, a verdict unfavorable to the enterprise is handed down, but the amount of damages remains unresolved at the time the financial statements are issued. Although the enterprise is unable to estimate the exact amount of loss, its reasonable estimate at the time is that the judgment will be for not less than $3 million or more than $9 million. No amount in that range appears at the time to be a better estimate than any other amount. This section requires accrual of the $3 million at December 31, 19X6, disclosure of the nature of the contingency and the exposure to an additional amount of loss of up to $6 million, and possibly disclosure of the amount of the accrual. [FIN14, ¶4]

.125 The same answer would result under the example in paragraph .124 if it is probable that a verdict will be unfavorable even though the trial has not been completed before the financial statements are issued. In that situation, condition (a) in paragraph .105 would be met because information available to the enterprise indicates that an unfavorable verdict is probable. An assessment that the range of loss is between $3 million and $9 million would meet condition (b) in paragraph .105. If no single amount in that range is a better estimate than any other amount, this section requires accrual of $3 million at December 31, 19X6, disclosure of the nature of the contingency and the exposure to an additional amount of loss of up to $6 million, and possibly disclosure of the amount of the accrual. Note, however, that if the enterprise had assessed the verdict differently (that is, that an unfavorable verdict was *not* probable but was only reasonably possible), condition (a) in paragraph .105 would not have been met and no amount of loss would be accrued but the nature of the contingency and any amount of loss that is reasonably possible would be disclosed. [FIN14, ¶5]

.126 Assume that in the examples given in paragraphs .124 and .125 condition (a) in paragraph .105 has been met and a reasonable estimate of loss is a range between

$3 million and $9 million but a loss of $4 million is a better estimate than any other amount in that range. In that situation, this section requires accrual of $4 million, disclosure of the nature of the contingency and the exposure to an additional amount of loss of up to $5 million, and possibly disclosure of the amount of the accrual. [FIN14, ¶6]

.127 As a further example, assume that at December 31, 19X6 an enterprise has an investment of $1,000,000 in the securities of another enterprise that has declared bankruptcy, and there is no quoted market price for the securities. Condition (a) in paragraph .105 has been met because information available indicates that the value of the investment has been impaired, and a reasonable estimate of loss is a range between $300,000 and $600,000. No amount of loss in that range appears at the time to be a better estimate of loss than any other amount. This section requires accrual of the $300,000 loss at December 31, 19X6, disclosure of the nature of the contingency and the exposure to an additional amount of loss of up to $300,000, and possibly disclosure of the amount of the accrual. [FIN14, ¶7]

Collectibility of Receivables

.128 The assets of an enterprise may include receivables that arose from credit sales, loans, or other transactions. The conditions under which receivables exist usually involve some degree of uncertainty about their collectibility, in which case a contingency exists as defined in paragraph .101. Losses from uncollectible receivables shall be accrued when both conditions in paragraph .105 are met. Those conditions may be considered in relation to individual receivables or in relation to groups of similar types of receivables. If the conditions are met, accrual shall be made even though the particular receivables that are uncollectible may not be identifiable. [FAS5, ¶22]

.129 If, based on current information and events, it is probable that the enterprise will be unable to collect all amounts due according to the contractual terms of the receivable, the condition in paragraph .105(a) is met. As used here, *all amounts due according to the contractual terms* means that both the contractual interest payments and the contractual principal payments will be collected as scheduled according to the receivable's contractual terms. However, a creditor need not consider an insignificant delay or insignificant shortfall in amount of payments as meeting the condition in paragraph .105(a). [FAS114, ¶21] Whether the amount of loss can be reasonably estimated (the condition in paragraph .105(b)) will normally depend on, among other things, the experience of the enterprise, information about the ability of individual debtors to pay, and appraisal of the receivables in light of the current economic environment. In the case of an enterprise that has no experience of its own, reference to the experience of other enterprises in the same business may be appropriate. Inability to make a reasonable estimate of the amount of loss from uncollectible receivables (that is, failure to satisfy the condition in paragraph .105(b)) precludes accrual and may, if there is significant uncertainty as to collection, suggest that the installment method, the cost recovery method, or some other method of revenue recognition be used [(refer to Section R75, "Revenue Recognition")]; in addition, the disclosures called for by paragraph .109 should be made. [FAS5, ¶23]

Obligations Related to Product Warranties and Product Defects

.130 A warranty is an obligation incurred in connection with the sale of goods or services that may require further performance by the seller after the sale has taken place. Because of the uncertainty surrounding claims that may be made under warranties, warranty obligations fall within the definition of a contingency in paragraph .101. Losses from warranty obligations shall be accrued when the conditions in paragraph .105 are met. Those conditions may be considered in relation to individual sales made with warranties or in relation to groups of similar types of sales made with warranties. If the conditions are met, accrual shall be made even though the particular parties that will make claims under warranties may not be identifiable. [FAS5, ¶24] [Refer to Section R75, paragraphs .501 through .505, for guidance on recognition of revenues and costs from separately priced extended warranty and product maintenance contracts.]

.131 If, based on available information, it is probable that customers will make claims under warranties relating to goods or services that have been sold, the condition in paragraph .105(a) is met at the date of an enterprise's financial statements because it is probable that a liability has been incurred. Satisfaction of the condition in paragraph .105(b) will normally depend on the experience of an enterprise or other information. In the case of an enterprise that has no experience of its own, reference to the experience of other enterprises in the same business may be appropriate. Inability to make a reasonable estimate of the amount of a warranty obligation at the time of sale because of significant uncertainty about possible claims (that is, failure to satisfy the condition in paragraph .105(b)) precludes accrual and, if the range of possible loss is wide, may raise a question about whether a sale should be recorded prior to expiration of the warranty period or until sufficient experience has been gained to permit a reasonable estimate of the obligation; in addition, the disclosures called for by paragraph .109 should be made. [FAS5, ¶25]

.132 Obligations other than warranties may arise with respect to products or services that have been sold, for example, claims resulting from injury or damage caused by product defects. If it is probable that claims will arise with respect to products or services that have been sold, accrual for losses may be appropriate. The condition in paragraph .105(a) would be met, for instance, with respect to a drug product or toys that have been sold if a health or safety hazard related to those products is discovered and as a result it is considered probable that liabilities have been incurred. The condition in paragraph .105(b) would be met if experience or other information enables the enterprise to make a reasonable estimate of the loss with respect to the drug product or the toys. [FAS5, ¶26]

Risk of Loss or Damage of Enterprise Property

.133 At the date of an enterprise's financial statements, it may not be insured against risk of future loss or damage to its property by fire, explosion, or other hazards. The absence of insurance against losses from risks of those types constitutes an existing condition involving uncertainty about the amount and timing of any losses that may occur, in which case a contingency exists as defined in paragraph .101. Uninsured risks may arise in a number of ways, including (a) noninsurance of certain risks or coinsurance or deductible clauses in an insurance contract or (b) insurance through a subsidiary or investee[8] to the extent not reinsured with an independent insurer. Some risks, for all practical purposes, may be noninsurable, and the self-assumption of those risks is mandatory. [FAS5, ¶27]

.134 The absence of insurance does not mean that an asset has been impaired or a liability has been incurred at the date of an enterprise's financial statements. Fires, explosions, and other similar events that may cause loss or damage of an enterprise's property are random in their occurrence.[9] With respect to events of that type, the condition for accrual in paragraph .105(a) is not satisfied prior to the occurrence of the event because until that time there is no diminution in the value of the property. There is no relationship of those events to the activities of the enterprise prior to their occurrence, and no asset is impaired prior to their occurrence. Further, unlike an insurance enterprise, which has a contractual obligation under policies in force to reimburse insureds for losses, an enterprise can have no such obligation to itself and, hence, no liability. [FAS5, ¶28]

Risk of Loss from Future Injury to Others, Damage to the Property of Others, and Business Interruption

.135 An enterprise may choose not to purchase insurance against risk of loss that may result from injury to others, damage to the property of others, or interruption of its busi-

[8]The effects of transactions between a parent or other investor and a subsidiary or investee insurance enterprise shall be eliminated from an enterprise's financial statements (refer to Section C51, "Consolidation," and Section I82, "Investments: Equity Method"). [FAS5, ¶27, fn7]

[9]Experience regarding loss or damage to depreciable assets is in some cases one of the factors considered in estimating the depreciable lives of a group of depreciable assets, along with such other factors as wear and tear, obsolescence, and maintenance and replacement policies. This section is not intended to alter present depreciation practices (refer to paragraph .121). [FAS5, ¶28, fn8]

ness operations.[10] Exposure to risks of those types constitutes an existing condition involving uncertainty about the amount and timing of any losses that may occur, in which case a contingency exists as defined in paragraph .101. [FAS5, ¶29]

.136 Mere exposure to risks of those types, however, does not mean that an asset has been impaired or a liability has been incurred. The condition for accrual in paragraph .105(a) is not met with respect to loss that may result from injury to others, damage to the property of others, or business interruption that may occur after the date of an enterprise's financial statements. Losses of those types do not relate to the current or a prior period but rather to the *future* period in which they occur. Thus, for example, an enterprise with a fleet of vehicles should not accrue for injury to others or damage to the property of others that may be caused by those vehicles in the future even if the amount of those losses may be reasonably estimable. On the other hand, the conditions in paragraph .105 would be met with respect to uninsured losses resulting from injury to others or damage to the property of others that took place prior to the date of the financial statements, even though the enterprise may not become aware of those matters until after that date, if the experience of the enterprise or other information enables it to make a reasonable estimate of the loss that was incurred prior to the date of its financial statements. [FAS5, ¶30]

Write-Down of Operating Assets

.137 In some cases, the carrying amount of an operating asset not intended for disposal may exceed the amount expected to be recoverable through future use of that asset even though there has been no physical loss or damage of the asset or threat of such loss or damage. For example, changed economic conditions may have made recovery of the carrying amount of a productive facility doubtful. The question of whether, in those cases, it is appropriate to write down the carrying amount of the asset to an amount expected to be recoverable through future operations is not covered by this section. [FAS5, ¶31]

Threat of Expropriation

.138 The threat of expropriation of assets is a contingency within the definition of paragraph .101 because of the uncertainty about its outcome and effect. If information indicates that expropriation is imminent and compensation will be less than the carrying amount of the assets, the condition for accrual in paragraph .105(a) is met. Imminence may be indicated, for example, by public or private declarations of intent by a government to expropriate assets of the enterprise or actual expropriation of assets of other enterprises.

---

[10] As to injury or damage resulting from products that have been sold, refer to paragraph .132. [FAS5, ¶29, fn9]

Paragraph .105(b) requires that accrual be made only if the amount of loss can be reasonably estimated. If the conditions for accrual are not met, the disclosures specified in paragraph .109 would be made when there is at least a reasonable possibility that an asset has been impaired. [FAS5, ¶32]

Litigation, Claims, and Assessments

.139 The following factors, among others, must be considered in determining whether accrual and disclosure, or both, are required with respect to pending or threatened litigation and actual or possible claims and assessments:

a. The period in which the underlying cause (that is, the cause for action) of the pending or threatened litigation or of the actual or possible claim or assessment occurred
b. The degree of probability of an unfavorable outcome
c. The ability to make a reasonable estimate of the amount of loss.

[FAS5, ¶33]

.140 As a condition for accrual of a loss contingency, paragraph .105(a) requires that information available prior to the issuance of financial statements indicates that it is probable that an asset had been impaired or a liability had been incurred at the date of the financial statements. Accordingly, accrual would clearly be inappropriate for litigation, claims, or assessments whose underlying cause is an event or condition occurring after the date of financial statements but before those financial statements are issued, for example, a suit for damages alleged to have been suffered as a result of an accident that occurred after the date of the financial statements. Disclosure may be required, however, by paragraph .112. [FAS5, ¶34]

.141 On the other hand, accrual may be appropriate for litigation, claims, or assessments whose underlying cause is an event occurring on or before the date of an enterprise's financial statements even if the enterprise does not become aware of the existence or possibility of the lawsuit, claim, or assessment until after the date of the financial statements. If those financial statements have not been issued, accrual of a loss related to the litigation, claim, or assessment would be required if the probability of loss is such that the condition in paragraph .105(a) is met and the amount of loss can be reasonably estimated. [FAS5, ¶35]

.142 If the underlying cause of the litigation, claim, or assessment is an event occurring before the date of an enterprise's financial statements, the probability of an outcome unfavorable to the enterprise must be assessed to determine whether the condition in paragraph .105(a) is met. Among the factors that should be considered are the nature of the litigation, claim, or assessment; the progress of the case (including progress after the date of the financial statements but before those statements are issued); the opinions or views of legal counsel and other advisers; the experience of the enterprise in similar cases; the experience of other enterprises; and any decision of the enterprise's management as to how the enterprise intends to respond to the lawsuit, claim, or assessment (for example, a decision to contest the case vigorously or a decision to seek an out-of-court settlement). The fact that legal counsel is unable to express an opinion that the outcome will be favorable to the enterprise should not necessarily be interpreted to mean that the condition for accrual of a loss in paragraph .105(a) is met. [FAS5, ¶36]

.143 The filing of a suit or formal assertion of a claim or assessment does not automatically indicate that accrual of a loss may be appropriate. The degree of probability of an unfavorable outcome must be assessed. The condition for accrual in paragraph .105(a) would be met if an unfavorable outcome is determined to be probable. If an unfavorable outcome is determined to be reasonably possible but not probable, or if the amount of loss cannot be reasonably estimated, accrual would be inappropriate, but disclosure would be required by paragraph .109. [FAS5, ¶37]

.144 With respect to unasserted claims and assessments, an enterprise must determine the degree of probability that a suit may be filed or a claim or assessment may be asserted and the possibility of an unfavorable outcome. For example, a catastrophe, accident, or other similar physical occurrence predictably engenders claims for redress, and in such circumstances their assertion may be probable; similarly, an investigation of an enterprise by a governmental agency, if enforcement proceedings have been or are likely to be instituted, is often followed by private claims for redress, and the probability of their assertion and the possibility of loss should be considered in each case. By way of further example, an enterprise may believe there is a possibility that it has infringed on another enterprise's patent rights, but the enterprise owning the patent rights has not indicated an intention to take any action and has not even indicated an awareness of the possible infringement. In that case, a judgment must first be made as to whether the assertion of a claim is probable. If the judgment is that assertion is not probable, no accrual or disclosure would be required. On the other hand, if the judgment is that assertion is probable, then a second judgment must be made as to the degree of probability of an unfavorable outcome. If an unfavorable outcome is probable and the amount of loss can be reasonably estimated, accrual of a loss is required by paragraph .105. If an unfavorable outcome is probable but the amount of loss cannot be reasonably estimated, accrual would not be appropriate, but disclosure would be required by paragraph .109. If an unfavorable outcome is reasonably possible but not probable, disclosure would be required by paragraph .109. [FAS5, ¶38]

.145 As a condition for accrual of a loss contingency, paragraph .105(b) requires that the amount of loss can be reasonably estimated. In some cases, it may be determined that a loss was incurred because an unfavorable outcome of the litigation, claim, or assessment is probable (thus satisfying the condition in paragraph .105(a)), but the range of possible loss is wide. For example, an enterprise may be litigating an income tax matter. In preparation for the trial, it may determine that, based on recent decisions involving one aspect of the litigation, it is probable that it will have to pay additional taxes of $2 million. Another aspect of the litigation may, however, be open to considerable interpretation, and depending on the interpretation by the court the enterprise may have to pay taxes of $8 million over and above the $2 million. In that case, paragraph .105 requires accrual of the $2 million if that is considered a reasonable estimate of the loss. Paragraph .109 requires disclosure of the additional exposure to loss if there is a reasonable possibility that additional taxes will be paid. Depending on the circumstances, paragraph .108 may require disclosure of the $2 million that was accrued. [FAS5, ¶39]

Catastrophe Losses of Property and Casualty Insurance Enterprises

.146 At the time that a property and casualty insurance enterprise or reinsurance enterprise issues an insurance policy covering risk of loss from catastrophes, a contingency arises. The contingency is the risk of loss *assumed* by the insurance enterprise, that is, the risk of loss from catastrophes that may occur *during the term of the policy.* The insurance enterprise has not assumed risk of loss for catastrophes that may occur *beyond* the term of the policy. Clearly, therefore, no asset has been impaired or liability incurred with respect to catastrophes that may occur beyond the terms of policies in force. [FAS5, ¶40]

.147 The conditions in paragraph .105 should be considered with respect to the risk of loss assumed by an insurance enterprise for catastrophes that may occur during the terms of policies in force to determine whether accrual of a loss is appropriate. To satisfy the condition in paragraph .105(a) that it be probable that a liability has been incurred to existing policyholders, the occurrence of catastrophes (that is, the confirming future events) would have to be reasonably predictable within the terms of policies in force. Further, to satisfy the condition in paragraph .105(b), the amounts of losses therefrom would have to be reasonably estimable. Actuarial techniques are employed by insurance enterprises to predict the rate of occurrence of and amounts of losses from catastrophes over long periods of time for insurance rate-setting purposes. Predictions over relatively short periods of time, such as an individual accounting period or the terms of a large number of existing insurance policies in force, are subject to substantial deviations. Consequently, assumption of risk of loss from catastrophes by property and casualty insurance enterprises and reinsurance enterprises fails to satisfy the conditions for accrual in paragraph .105. [FAS5, ¶41]

.148 Although some property and casualty insurance enterprises have accrued an estimated amount for catastrophe losses, other insurance enterprises have accomplished the same objective by deferring a portion of the premium income. Deferral of any portion of premium income *beyond the terms of policies in force* is, in substance, similar to premature accrual of catastrophe losses and, therefore, also does not meet the conditions of paragraph .105. [FAS5, ¶42]

.149 The conditions for accrual in paragraph .105 do not prohibit a property and casualty insurance enterprise from accruing probable catastrophe losses that have been incurred on or before the date of its financial statements but that have not been reported by its policyholders as of that date. If the amount of loss can be reasonably estimated, paragraph .105 requires accrual of those incurred-but-not-reported losses. [FAS5, ¶43]

Payments to Insurance Enterprises That May Not Involve Transfer of Risk

.150 To the extent that an insurance contract or reinsurance contract does not, despite its form, provide for indemnification of the insured or the ceding enterprise by the insurer or reinsurer against loss or liability, the premium paid less the amount of the premium to be retained by the insurer or reinsurer shall be accounted for as a deposit by the insured or the ceding enterprise. Those contracts may be structured in various ways, but if, regardless of form, their substance is that all or part of the premium paid by the insured or the ceding enterprise is a deposit, it shall be accounted for as such.[11] [FAS5, ¶44] [Refer to paragraph .1001 for an EITF Issue that provides interpretive guidance on this paragraph.]

.151 Operations in certain industries may be subject to such high risks that insurance is unavailable or is available only at what is considered to be a prohibitively high cost. Some enterprises in those industries have "pooled" their risks by forming a mutual insurance enterprise in which they retain an equity interest and to which they pay insurance premiums. For example, some electric enterprises have formed such a mutual insurance enterprise to insure risks related to nuclear power plants, and some oil enterprises have formed an enterprise to insure against risks associated with petroleum exploration and production. Whether the premium paid represents a payment for the transfer of risk or whether it represents merely a deposit will depend on the circumstances surrounding each enterprise's interest in and insurance arrangement with the mutual insurance enterprise. An analysis of the contract is required to determine whether risk has been transferred and to what extent. [FAS5, ¶45] [Refer to paragraph .1001 for an EITF Issue that provides interpretive guidance on this paragraph.]

---

[11]Paragraphs .171 through .177 of Section In6 identify conditions that are required for a reinsurance contract to indemnify the ceding enterprise against loss or liability and to be accounted for as reinsurance. Any transaction between enterprises to which Section In6 applies must meet those conditions to be accounted for as reinsurance. [FAS113, ¶30]

Glossary

.401 **Contingency.** An existing condition, situation, or set of circumstances involving uncertainty as to possible gain (a *gain contingency*) or loss (a *loss contingency*) to an enterprise that will ultimately be resolved when one or more future events occur or fail to occur. [FAS5, ¶1]

.402 **Indirect guarantee of indebtedness of others.** A guarantee under an agreement that obligates one enterprise to transfer funds to a second enterprise upon occurrence of specified events under conditions whereby (a) the funds are legally available to creditors of the second enterprise and (b) those creditors may enforce the second enterprise's claims against the first enterprise under the agreement. [FIN34, ¶2]

.403 **Probable.** [A probability classification for loss contingencies—when] the future event or events are likely to occur. [FAS5, ¶3]

.404 **Reasonably possible.** [A probability classification for loss contingencies—when] the chance of the future event or events occurring is more than remote but less than likely. [FAS5, ¶3]

.405 **Remote.** [A probability classification for loss contingencies—when] the chance of the future event or events occurring is slight. [FAS5, ¶3]

[**Note:** Additional guidance with respect to implementing Section C59 is presented in FASB *Viewpoints,* "Application of FASB Statements 5 and 114 to a Loan Portfolio," April 12, 1999. This article addresses 31 questions and was written by FASB staff members Sean Leonard, Tim Lucas, and Leslie Seidman. This article is available from the Order Department, Financial Accounting Standards Board, 401 Merritt 7, P.O. Box 5116, Norwalk, CT 06856-5116, telephone 800-748-0659.]

Supplemental Guidance: Emerging Issues Task Force (EITF) Issues

.1000 [Listed below are EITF Issues that provide supplemental guidance for this section. These Issues are grouped by subject matter and may be either interpretive of or related by topic to the guidance in this section.

Banking and Thrift Industries

EITF Issue No. 87-22, "Prepayments to the Secondary Reserve of the FSLIC"
EITF Topic No. D-47, "Accounting for the Refund of Bank Insurance Fund and Savings Association Insurance Fund Premiums"
EITF Topic No. D-57, "Accounting Issues Related to the Deposit Insurance Funds Act of 1996"

Business Combinations

EITF Issue No. 94-3, "Liability Recognition for Certain Employee Termination Benefits and Other Costs to Exit an Activity (including Certain Costs Incurred in a Restructuring)"
EITF Issue No. 95-14, "Recognition of Liabilities in Anticipation of a Business Combination"

Executory Contracts

EITF Issue No. 99-14, "Recognition by a Purchaser of Losses on Firmly Committed Executory Contracts"
EITF Issue No. 00-26, "Recognition by a Seller of Losses on Firmly Committed Executory Contracts"

Insurance Industry

EITF Issue No. 86-12, "Accounting by Insureds for Claims-Made Insurance Policies"
EITF Issue No. 93-6, "Accounting for Multiple-Year Retrospectively Rated Contracts by Ceding and Assuming Enterprises"
EITF Issue No. 93-14, "Accounting for Multiple-Year Retrospectively Rated Insurance Contracts by Insurance Enterprises and Other Enterprises"
EITF Topic No. D-35, "FASB Staff Views on Issue No. 93-6, 'Accounting for Multiple-Year Retrospectively Rated Contracts by Ceding and Assuming Enterprises'"
EITF Topic No. D-79, "Accounting for Retroactive Insurance Contracts Purchased by Entities Other Than Insurance Enterprises"

Revenue Recognition

EITF Issue No. 98-9, "Accounting for Contingent Rent"
EITF Issue No. 00-22, "Accounting for 'Points' and Certain Other Time-Based or Volume-Based Sales Incentive Offers, and Offers for Free Products or Services to Be Delivered in the Future"
EITF Issue No. 01-9, "Accounting for Consideration Given by a Vendor to a Customer (Including a Reseller of the Vendor's Products)"

Other

EITF Issue No. 91-10, "Accounting for Special Assessments and Tax Increment Financing Entities (TIFEs)"
EITF Issue No. 92-13, "Accounting for Estimated Payments in Connection with the Coal Industry Retiree Health Benefit Act of 1992"
EITF Issue No. 97-1, "Implementation Issues in Accounting for Lease Transactions, including Those involving Special-Purpose Entities"
EITF Issue No. 99-20, "Recognition of Interest Income and Impairment on Purchased and Retained Beneficial Interests in Securitized Financial Assets"
EITF Issue No. 01-10, "Accounting for the Impact of the Terrorist Attacks of September 11, 2001"
EITF Topic No. D-77, "Accounting for Legal Costs Expected to Be Incurred in Connection with a Loss Contingency"
EITF Topic No. D-80, "Application of FASB Statements No. 5 and No. 114 to a Loan Portfolio"
EITF Topic No. D-89, "Accounting for Costs of Future Medicare Compliance Audits"]

.1001 [Listed below are those EITF Issues that provide interpretive guidance on specific material in this section.

Paragraph .105 (FAS 5, ¶8)—EITF Issues No. 87-22 and 92-13 and Topics No. D-47 and D-57
Paragraph .106 (FAS 5, ¶9)—EITF Issue No. 92-13
Paragraph .150 (FAS 5, ¶44)—EITF Topic No. D-79
Paragraph .151 (FAS 5, ¶45)—EITF Issue No. 93-14]

(The next page is 9051.)

CONTRIBUTIONS SECTION C67

Sources: FASB Statement 116; FASB Statement 136; FASB Statement 140

Summary

This section presents standards for contributions and applies to all entities that receive or make contributions. Generally, contributions received, including unconditional promises to give, are recognized as revenues in the period received at their fair values. Contributions made, including unconditional promises to give, are recognized as expenses in the period made at their fair values. Conditional promises to give, whether received or made, are recognized when they become unconditional, that is, when the conditions are substantially met.

Certain exceptions are allowed for contributions of services and works of art, historical treasures, and similar assets. Contributions of services are recognized only if the services received (a) create or enhance nonfinancial assets or (b) require specialized skills, are provided by individuals possessing those skills, and would typically need to be purchased if not provided by donation. Contributions of works of art, historical treasures, and similar assets need not be recognized as revenues and capitalized if the donated items are added to collections held for public exhibition, education, or research in furtherance of public service rather than financial gain. Certain disclosures are required for collection items not capitalized and for receipts of contributed services and promises to give.

This section also clarifies that an organization that receives assets acts as a donee and donor, rather than as an agent, trustee, or intermediary, if a resource provider specifies a third-party beneficiary and explicitly grants the recipient organization variance power.

This section also presents standards for transactions in which an entity—the *donor*—makes a contribution by transferring assets to a not-for-profit organization or charitable trust—the *recipient organization*—that accepts the assets from the donor and agrees to use those assets on behalf of or transfer those assets, the return on investment of those assets, or both to another entity—the *beneficiary*—that is specified by the donor. It also establishes standards for transactions that take place in a similar manner but are not contributions because the transfers are revocable, repayable, or reciprocal.

[**Note:** Not-for-profit organizations should refer to Section No5, "Not-for-Profit Organizations," for guidance on reporting information about donor-imposed restrictions on contributions received and recognition of the expiration of those restrictions and for disclosure requirements for transfers of assets made to a recipient organization when a not-for-profit organization specifies itself or its affiliate as the beneficiary of the transfer.]

.101 This section establishes standards of financial accounting and reporting for **contributions** received and contributions made. Accounting for contributions is an issue primarily for **not-for-profit organizations** because contributions are a significant source of revenues for many of those organizations. However, this section applies to all entities (not-for-profit organizations and business enterprises) that receive or make contributions. [Not-for-profit organizations should refer to paragraphs .143 through .147 of Section No5, "Not-for-Profit Organizations," for guidance on reporting information about donor-imposed restrictions on contributions received and recognition of the expiration of those restrictions.] This section also establishes standards for accounting for **collections** of works of art, historical treasures, and similar assets acquired by contribution or by other means. [FAS116, ¶1] [This section also provides guidance for all entities on accounting for transfers of assets in which a not-for-profit organization acts as an agent, trustee, or intermediary between a resource provider (donor) and a specified beneficiary.[a] Not-for-profit organizations should refer to paragraphs .176 and .177 of Section No5 for disclosure requirements for transfers of assets made to a recipient organization when a not-for-profit organization specifies itself or its affiliate as the beneficiary of the transfer, and to paragraphs .142A and .142B of Section No5 for examples of possible financial statement presentation of fundraising revenues and expenses.]

---

[a]The recipient of assets who is an agent or trustee has little or no discretion in determining how the transferred assets will be used. [FAS116, ¶53] Discretion to determine the timing of the distribution to the specified beneficiary, by itself, [does not] give the recipient organization discretion sufficient to recognize a contribution. [FAS136, ¶72] An organization has discretion sufficient to recognize a contribution received if it can choose the beneficiaries of the assets. [FAS136, ¶69] The recipient organization has the ability to choose the beneficiaries if neither the language used by the donor nor the representations of the recipient organization cause the donor to believe that it can direct the gift to a specified beneficiary. [FAS136, ¶70] If the resource provider allows the recipient to establish, define, and carry out the programs that disburse the cash, products, or services to the recipient's beneficiaries, the recipient generally is involved in receiving and making contributions. [FAS116, ¶54] For example, a recipient organization might request that a donor indicate an organization that best serves the needs of the community and tell the donor that the information will be considered by the allocation committee when it makes its distributions to community organizations. If that request is conveyed in a manner that leads a donor to reasonably conclude that its role is merely to propose a possible allocation, the recipient organization has the discretion to choose the beneficiary of the assets. [FAS136, ¶70] Conversely, if that request is conveyed in a manner that creates a donor's reasonable expectation that the gift will be used for the benefit of or will be transferred to the indicated beneficiary, the recipient organization does not have discretion to choose the beneficiary unless the donor explicitly grants variance power. [FAS136, ¶71]

Scope

.102 This section (paragraphs .104 through .160) applies to contributions[1] of cash and other assets, including **promises to give.** It does not apply to transfers of assets that are in substance purchases of goods or services—exchange transactions in which each party receives and sacrifices commensurate value. However, if an entity voluntarily transfers assets to another or performs services for another in exchange for assets of substantially lower value and no unstated rights or privileges are involved, the contribution inherent in that transaction is within the scope of this section. [FAS116, ¶3] Because some exchange transactions may appear to be much like contributions, a careful assessment of the characteristics of the transaction is required to determine whether the recipient of a transfer of assets has given up an asset or incurred a liability of commensurate value. Assessing the characteristics of transactions from the perspectives of both the resource provider and the recipient [may be] necessary to determine whether a contribution has occurred.[2] [FAS116, ¶49]

.102A This section (paragraphs .161 through .169) applies to transactions in which an entity—the *donor*—makes a contribution by transferring assets to a not-for-profit organization or charitable trust[2a]—the *recipient organization*—that accepts the assets from the donor and agrees to use those assets on behalf of or transfer those assets, the return

[1]This section also uses terms such as *gift* and *donation* to refer to a contribution; however, it generally avoids terms such as *awards, grants, sponsorships,* and *appropriations* that often are more broadly used to refer not only to contributions but also to assets transferred in exchange transactions in which the *grantor, sponsor,* or *appropriator* expects to receive commensurate value. [FAS116, ¶3, fn3]

[2]For example, a resource provider may sponsor research and development activities at a research university and retain proprietary rights or other privileges, such as patents, copyrights, or advance and exclusive knowledge of the research outcomes. The research outcomes may be intangible, uncertain, or difficult to measure, and may be perceived by the university as a sacrifice of little or no value; however, their value often is commensurate with the value that a resource provider expects in exchange. Similarly, a resource provider may sponsor research and development activities and specify the protocol of the testing so the research outcomes are particularly valuable to the resource provider. Those transactions are not contributions if their potential public benefits are secondary to the potential proprietary benefits to the resource providers. [FAS116, ¶50] Moreover, a single transaction may be in part an exchange and in part a contribution. For example, if a donor transfers a building to an entity at a price significantly lower than its market value and no unstated rights or privileges are involved, the transaction is in part an exchange of assets and in part a contribution to be accounted for as required by this section. [FAS116, ¶51]

[2a]In some states, not-for-profit organizations are organized under trust law rather than as corporations. Those organizations are not trustees as described in paragraph .162 of this section because, under those statutes, they hold assets "in trust" for the community or some other broadly described group, rather than for a specific beneficiary. Thus, those organizations are included within the scope of this section. [FAS136, ¶81]

on investment of those assets, or both to an unaffiliated[2b] entity—the *beneficiary*—that is specified[[2c]] by the donor.[2d] [FAS136, ¶3]

.102B This section (paragraphs .170 and .171) applies to transactions that take place in a similar manner but are not contributions for one of the following reasons:

a. The entity that transfers the assets to the recipient organization—the *resource provider*[2e]—is related to the beneficiary in a way that causes the transfer to be reciprocal.
b. Conditions imposed by the resource provider or the relationships between the parties make the transfer of assets to the recipient organization revocable or repayable.

[FAS136, ¶4]

.102C This section (paragraphs .161 through .208) applies to transfers of cash and other assets, including the assets described in paragraph .104 of this section. [FAS136, ¶6]

.103 This section does not apply to tax exemptions, tax incentives, or tax abatements, or to transfers of assets from governmental units to business enterprises. [FAS116, ¶4]

.103A [Deleted 6/99 because of FASB Statement 136, *Transfers of Assets to a Not-for-Profit Organization or Charitable Trust That Raises or Holds Contributions for Others.*]

[2b]Section R36, "Related Parties," defines *affiliate* as "a party that, directly or indirectly through one or more intermediaries, controls, is controlled by, or is under common control with an enterprise" (paragraph .401). Thus, an *unaffiliated* beneficiary is a beneficiary other than the donor or its affiliate. [FAS136, ¶3, fn1]

[[2c]]A donor may specify the beneficiary (a) by name, (b) by stating that all entities that meet a set of donor-defined criteria are beneficiaries, or (c) by actions surrounding the transfer that make clear the identity of the beneficiary, such as by responding to a request from an organization that exists to raise assets for the beneficiary. [FAS136, ¶68] If a donor uses broad generalizations to describe beneficiaries or to indicate a field of interest, such as Midwestern flood victims, homeless individuals, or teenaged children, the recipient organization has the ability to choose the beneficiaries of the assets and is a donee. [FAS136, ¶69]

[2d]In some cases, the donor, recipient organization, or beneficiary is a governmental entity. Paragraphs .161 through .208 of this section (FASB Statement 136, *Transfers of Assets to a Not-for-Profit Organization or Charitable Trust That Raises or Holds Contributions for Others*) and other pronouncements of the Financial Accounting Standards Board do not apply to governmental entities unless the Governmental Accounting Standards Board issues a pronouncement that makes them applicable. [FAS136, ¶3, fn2]

[2e]If the transfer of assets is not a contribution or not yet a contribution, paragraphs .161 through .208 of this section use the term resource provider rather than the term donor to refer to the entity that transfers the assets to the recipient organization. [FAS136, ¶4, fn3]

[[3-3b]Deleted 6/99 because of FASB Statement 136, *Transfers of Assets to a Not-for-Profit Organization or Charitable Trust That Raises or Holds Contributions for Others.*]

Definitions

.104 A contribution is an unconditional transfer of cash or other assets to an entity or a settlement or cancellation of its liabilities in a voluntary **nonreciprocal transfer** by another entity acting other than as an owner. Other assets include securities, land, buildings, use of facilities or utilities, materials and supplies, intangible assets, services, and **unconditional promises to give** those items in the future. [FAS116, ¶5]

.105 A promise to give is a written or oral agreement to contribute cash or other assets to another entity; however, to be recognized in financial statements there must be sufficient evidence in the form of verifiable documentation that a promise was made and received. A communication that does not indicate clearly whether it is a promise is considered an unconditional promise to give if it indicates an unconditional intention to give that is legally enforceable.[4] [FAS116, ¶6]

.106 A **donor-imposed condition** on a transfer of assets or a promise to give specifies a future and uncertain event whose occurrence or failure to occur gives the promisor a right of return of the assets transferred or releases the promisor from its obligation to transfer assets promised. [FAS116, ¶7] Imposing a condition creates a barrier that must be overcome before the recipient of the transferred assets has an unconditional right to retain those promised assets. For example, a transfer of cash with a promise to contribute that cash if a like amount of new gifts are raised from others within 30 days and a provision that the cash be returned if the gifts are not raised imposes a condition on which a promised gift depends. [FAS116, ¶60]

.107 In contrast, a **donor-imposed restriction** limits the use of contributed assets; it specifies a use that is more specific than broad limits resulting from the nature of the organization, the environment in which it operates, and the purposes specified in its articles of incorporation or bylaws or comparable documents for an unincorporated association. [FAS116, ¶7] Failures to comply with donors' restrictions, although rare, do occur, sometimes as a result of events occurring subsequent to receiving a contribution. [FAS116, ¶65] [Refer to] Section C59, "Contingencies," paragraph .105 if a subsequent event raises the possibility that an organization may not satisfy a restriction. [FAS116, ¶66]

Contributions Received

.108 Except as provided in paragraphs .109 and .111, contributions received shall be recognized as revenues or gains in the period received and as assets, decreases of liabili-

[4Legal enforceability refers to] the *availability* of legal remedies, [not] the intent to use them. [FAS116, ¶108]

ties, or expenses depending on the form of the benefits received. Contributions received shall be measured at their fair values. Contributions received by not-for-profit organizations shall be reported as **restricted support** or **unrestricted support** as provided in Section No5, paragraphs .143 through .145. [FAS116, ¶8]

Contributed Services

.109 Contributions of services shall be recognized if the services received (a) create or enhance nonfinancial assets or (b) require specialized skills, are provided by individuals possessing those skills, and would typically need to be purchased if not provided by donation. Services requiring specialized skills are provided by accountants, architects, carpenters, doctors, electricians, lawyers, nurses, plumbers, teachers, and other professionals and craftsmen. Contributed services and promises to give services that do not meet the above criteria shall not be recognized. [FAS116, ¶9]

.110 An entity that receives contributed services shall describe the programs or activities for which those services were used, including the nature and extent[5] of contributed services received for the period and the amount recognized as revenues for the period. Entities are encouraged to disclose the fair value of contributed services received but not recognized as revenues if that is practicable. [FAS116, ¶10]

Contributed Collection Items

.111 An entity need not recognize contributions of works of art, historical treasures, and similar assets if the donated items are added to collections[6] that meet all of the following conditions:

a. Are held for public exhibition, education, or research in furtherance of public service rather than financial gain
b. Are protected, kept unencumbered, cared for, and preserved
c. Are subject to an organizational policy that requires the proceeds from sales of collection items to be used to acquire other items for collections.

[FAS116, ¶11]

[5The nature and extent can be described by] nonmonetary information, such as the number and trends of donated hours received or service outputs provided by volunteer efforts, [or] other monetary information such as the dollar amount of contributions raised by volunteers. [FAS116, ¶123]

[6]Collections, as used in this section, generally are held by museums, botanical gardens, libraries, aquariums, arboretums, historic sites, planetariums, zoos, art galleries, nature, science and technology centers, and similar educational, research, and public service organizations that have those divisions; however, the definition is not limited to those entities nor does it apply to all items held by those entities. [FAS116, ¶128]

.112 Works of art, historical treasures, and similar items that are not part of a collection shall be recognized as assets in financial statements. Some entities that hold these items do not espouse the mission of public education, exhibition, and research and the attendant responsibilities to protect, keep unencumbered, care for, and preserve the items, and some entities that do maintain collections have some items that are not part of their collections [and, thus, are not exempted from recognition as assets]. [FAS116, ¶135]

.113 Contributed collection items shall be recognized as revenues or gains if collections are capitalized and shall not be recognized as revenues or gains if collections are not capitalized. An entity that does not recognize and capitalize its collections or that capitalizes collections prospectively shall disclose the additional information required by paragraphs .123 and .124. [FAS116, ¶13] Capitalization of selected collections or items is precluded. [FAS116, ¶12]

Contributions Made

.114 Contributions made shall be recognized as expenses in the period made and as decreases of assets or increases of liabilities depending on the form of the benefits given. For example, gifts of items from inventory held for sale are recognized as decreases of inventory[7] and contribution expenses, and unconditional promises to give cash are recognized as payables and contribution expenses. Contributions made shall be measured at the fair values of the assets given or, if made in the form of a settlement or cancellation of a donee's liabilities, at the fair value of the liabilities canceled. [FAS116, ¶18]

Measurement at Fair Value

.115 Quoted market prices, if available, are the best evidence of the fair value of monetary and nonmonetary assets, including services. If quoted market prices are not available, fair value may be estimated based on quoted market prices for similar assets, independent appraisals, or valuation techniques, such as the present value of estimated future cash flows. Contributions of services that create or enhance nonfinancial assets may be measured by referring to either the fair value of the services received or the fair value of

[7] If the fair value of an asset transferred differs from its carrying amount, a gain or loss should be recognized on the disposition of the asset. (Refer to Section N35, "Nonmonetary Transactions," paragraph .105.) [FAS116, ¶18, fn6]

the asset or of the asset enhancement resulting from the services. A major uncertainty about the existence of value may indicate that an item received or given should not be recognized.[8] [FAS116, ¶19]

.116 The present value of estimated future cash flows using a discount rate commensurate with the risks involved is an appropriate measure of fair value of unconditional promises to give cash.[9] Subsequent accruals of the interest element shall be accounted for as contribution income by donees and contribution expense by donors. [FAS116, ¶20]

.117 Unconditional promises to give that are expected to be collected or paid in less than one year may be measured at net realizable value (net settlement value) because that amount, although not equivalent to the present value of estimated future cash flows, results in a reasonable estimate of fair value. [FAS116, ¶21]

Conditional Promises to Give

.118 **Conditional promises to give,** which depend on the occurrence of a specified future and uncertain event to bind the promisor, shall be recognized when the conditions on which they depend are substantially met, that is, when the conditional promise becomes unconditional. A conditional promise to give is considered unconditional if the possibility that the condition will not be met is remote. For example, a stipulation that an annual report must be provided by the donee to receive subsequent annual payments on a multiyear promise is not a condition if the possibility of not meeting that administrative requirement is remote. [FAS116, ¶22]

.119 A transfer of assets with a conditional promise to contribute them shall be accounted for as a refundable advance until the conditions have been substantially met. [FAS116, ¶22] [Some entities] transfer cash or other assets with both donor-imposed restrictions and stipulations that impose a condition on which a gift depends. If a restric-

---

[8]Contributed tangible property worth accepting generally possesses the common characteristic of all assets—future economic benefit or service potential. The future economic benefit or service potential of a tangible item usually can be obtained by exchanging it for cash or by using it to produce goods or services. However, if an item is accepted solely to be saved for its potential future use in scientific or educational research and has no alternative use, it may have uncertain value, or perhaps no value, and should not be recognized. [FAS116, ¶19, fn7]

[9]An entity may estimate the future cash flows of a portfolio of short-term promises resulting from a mass fund-raising appeal by using experience it gained from similar appeals. [FAS116, ¶20, fn8]

tion and a condition exist, the transfer shall be accounted for as a refundable advance until the condition on which it depends is substantially met.[10] [FAS116, ¶63]

.120 Determining whether a promise is conditional or unconditional can be difficult if it contains donor stipulations that do not clearly state whether the right to receive payment or delivery of the promised assets depends on meeting those stipulations. It may be difficult to determine whether those stipulations are conditions or restrictions. In cases of ambiguous donor stipulations, a promise containing stipulations that are not clearly unconditional shall be presumed to be a conditional promise. [FAS116, ¶23]

Disclosures of Promises to Give

.121 Recipients of unconditional promises to give shall disclose the following:

a. The amounts of promises receivable in less than one year, in one to five years, and in more than five years
b. The amount of the allowance for uncollectible promises receivable.

[FAS116, ¶24]

.122 Recipients of conditional promises to give shall disclose the following:

a. The total of the amounts promised
b. A description and amount for each group of promises having similar characteristics, such as amounts of promises conditioned on establishing new programs, completing a new building, and raising matching gifts by a specified date.[11]

[FAS116, ¶25]

[10]A change in the original conditions of the agreement between promisor and promisee shall not be implied without an explicit waiver. A transfer of assets after a conditional promise to give is made and before the conditions are met is the same as a transfer of assets with a conditional promise to contribute those assets. [FAS116, ¶81]

[11]This section neither requires nor precludes disclosures for intentions to give. [FAS116, ¶117]

Financial Statement Presentation and Disclosure for Collections

.123 An entity that does not recognize and capitalize its collections shall report the following on the face of its statement of activities [or income statement for business enterprises], separately from revenues, expenses, gains, and losses:

a. Costs of collection items purchased as a decrease in the appropriate class of net assets [or equity]
b. Proceeds from sale of collection items as an increase in the appropriate class of net assets [or equity]
c. Proceeds from insurance recoveries of lost or destroyed collection items as an increase in the appropriate class of net assets [or equity].

Similarly, an entity that capitalizes its collections prospectively shall report proceeds from sales and insurance recoveries of items not previously capitalized separately from revenues, expenses, gains, and losses. [FAS116, ¶26] [Not-for-profit organizations should refer to paragraph .142, Exhibit 142A of Section No5 for an example of a possible format for these disclosures.]

.124 An entity that does not recognize and capitalize its collections or that capitalizes collections prospectively shall describe its collections, including their relative significance, and its accounting and stewardship policies for collections. If collection items not capitalized are deaccessed during the period, it also shall (a) describe the items given away, damaged, destroyed, lost, or otherwise deaccessed during the period or (b) disclose their fair value. In addition, a line item shall be shown on the face of the statement of financial position that refers to the disclosures required by this paragraph. That line item shall be dated if collections are capitalized prospectively, for example, "Collections acquired since January 1, 1995 (Note X)." [FAS116, ¶27]

Examples of the Application of This Section to Specific Situations

.125 Paragraphs .126 through .160 provide additional discussion and examples that illustrate application of this section to some specific situations. The examples do not address all possible applications of this section and assume that all items addressed are material. [FAS116, ¶173]

Scope and Definition

.126 Some transfers of assets that are exchange transactions may appear to be contributions if the services or other assets given in exchange are perceived to be a sacrifice of little value and the exchanges are compatible with the recipient's mission. Furthermore, a single transaction may be in part an exchange and in part a contribution. A careful assessment of the characteristics of the transaction, from the perspectives of both the resource provider and the recipient, is necessary to determine whether a contribution has occurred. Examples 1 and 2 illustrate the need to assess the relevant facts and circumstances to distinguish between the receipt of resources in an exchange and the receipt of resources in a contribution. [FAS116, ¶174]

.127 A transfer of assets also may appear to be a contribution when a donor uses an agent, a trustee, or an intermediary to transfer assets to a donee. Receipts of resources as an agent, trustee, or intermediary of a donor are not contributions received to the agent. Deliveries of resources as an agent, trustee, or intermediary of a donor are not contributions made by the agent. Similarly, contributions of services (time, skills, or expertise) between donors and donees that are facilitated by an intermediary are not contributions received or contributions made by the intermediary. Examples 3 through 5 illustrate the need to assess the relevant facts and circumstances to distinguish between the receipt of resources as a donee and the receipt of resources as an agent, a trustee, or an intermediary organization. [FAS116, ¶175]

Example 1—Receipt of Resources in an Exchange

.128 University A, a large research university with a cancer research center, regularly conducts research to discover more effective methods of treating cancer and often receives contributions to support its efforts. University A receives resources from a pharmaceutical company to finance the costs of a clinical trial of an experimental cancer drug the company developed. The pharmaceutical company specifies the protocol of the testing, including the number of participants to be tested, the dosages to be administered, and the frequency and nature of follow-up examinations. The pharmaceutical company requires a detailed report of the test outcome within two months of the test's conclusion. Because the results of the clinical trial have particular commercial value for the pharmaceutical company, receipt of the resources is not a contribution received by University A, nor is the disbursement of the resources a contribution made by the pharmaceutical company. [FAS116, ¶176]

Example 2—Receipt of Resources Partially in Exchange and Partially as a Contribution

.129 Organization B receives $100,000 in cash from a donor under a charitable remainder annuity trust agreement designating Organization B as the trustee and charitable remainder beneficiary—a donee. The terms of the trust agreement require that Organization B, as trustee, invest the trust assets and pay $5,000 each year to an annuitant (an income beneficiary specified by the donor) for the remainder of the annuitant's life. Upon death of the annuitant, Organization B may use its remainder interest for any purpose consistent with its mission. [FAS116, ¶177]

.130 Organization B, as a donee, would recognize the contribution received as revenue in the period the trust is established. The transfer is partially an exchange transaction—an agreement for annuity payments to a beneficiary over time—and partially a contribution. The contribution received by Organization B is the unconditional right to receive the remainder interest of the annuity trust. The amount of the contribution received by Organization B is the fair value of the trust assets ($100,000 cash transferred) less the fair value of the estimated annuity payments (the present value of $5,000 to be paid annually over the expected life of the annuitant). Because Organization B must invest the underlying donated assets until the annuitant's death, [if Organization B is a not-for-profit organization,] the revenue recognized [is] temporarily restricted support [and] shall be distinguished from revenues from gifts that are either unrestricted or permanently restricted (paragraph .143 of Section No5). The death of the annuitant determines when the required annuity payments cease and when the trust expires and effectively removes all restrictions on the net assets of Organization B. If [Organization B is a not-for-profit organization and] the terms of this agreement had specified that upon death of the annuitant Organization B is to use its remainder interest to establish a permanent endowment, the revenue would be recognized as permanently restricted support rather than temporarily restricted support. [FAS116, ¶178]

Example 3—Receipt of Resources as an Agent Rather Than as a Donee

.131 Organization C receives relief supplies from Individual D with instructions to deliver the supplies to specified third-party beneficiaries. Organization C accepts responsibility for delivering those supplies because it has a distribution network and a mutual interest in serving the needs of the specified beneficiaries. Organization C has no discretion in determining the parties to be benefited; it must deliver the resources to the specified beneficiaries. Receipt of those goods is not a contribution received to Organization C, nor is the delivery of those goods to the beneficiaries a contribution made by Organization C. Rather, a contribution of goods is made by Individual D and received by the third-party beneficiaries. [FAS116, ¶179]

Example 4—Intermediary between Donor and Donee

.132 Organization E develops and maintains a list of lawyers and law firms that are interested in providing services without charge to charitable organizations and certain individuals. Organization E encourages individuals in need of free legal services to contact Organization E for referral to lawyers in the individual's community that may be willing to serve them. The decision about whether and how to serve a specific individual rests with the lawyer. Under those circumstances, Organization E merely acts as an intermediary in bringing together a willing donor and donee. The free legal services are not a contribution received by Organization E. [FAS116, ¶180]

Example 5—Intermediary between Government Provider and Its Beneficiary

.133 Hospital F provides health care services to patients that are entitled to Medicaid assistance under a joint federal and state program. The program sets forth various administrative and technical requirements covering provider participation, payment mechanisms, and individual eligibility and benefit provisions. Medicaid payments made to Hospital F on behalf of the program beneficiaries are third-party payments for patient services rendered. Hospital F provides patient care for a fee—an exchange transaction—and acts as an intermediary between the government provider of assistance and the eligible beneficiary. The Medicaid payments are not contributions to Hospital F. [FAS116, ¶181]

Contributions Received

.134 Contributions are received in several different forms. Most often the item contributed is an asset, but it also can be forgiveness of a liability. The types of assets commonly contributed include cash, marketable securities, land, buildings, use of facilities or utilities, materials and supplies, other goods or services, and unconditional promises to give those items in the future. This section requires entities receiving contributions to recognize them at the fair values of the assets received. However, recognition of contributions of works of art, historical treasures, and similar assets is not required if the donated items are added to collections (paragraph .111). Recognition of contributions of services is required for those contributed services received that meet one of the specified conditions of paragraph .109 of this section and is precluded for contributed services that do not. Examples 6 through 16 illustrate application of the recognition and measurement principles in this section. [FAS116, ¶182]

Example 6—Contribution of Real Property

.135 Organization G receives a building (including the land on which it was constructed) as a gift from a local corporation with the understanding that the building will be used principally as an education and training center for organization members or for any other purpose consistent with the organization's mission. Educating and training its members is an important activity of the organization. [FAS116, ¶183]

.136 Organization G would recognize the contributed property as an asset and as support and measure that property at its fair value (paragraph .108). Information necessary to estimate the fair value of that property could be obtained from various sources, including (a) amounts recently paid for similar properties in the locality, (b) estimates of the market value of the property by local appraisers or real estate brokers, (c) an estimate of the fair value of the property by the local tax assessor's office, or (d) estimates of its replacement cost (paragraph .115). [If Organization G is a not-for-profit organization,] this contribution is unrestricted support because the donated assets may be used for any purpose and Organization G does not have a policy of implying time restrictions on gifts of long-lived assets (paragraph .145 of Section No5). If Organization G's policy is to imply a time restriction, the contribution is temporarily restricted support and the restriction expires over the useful life of the building. [FAS116, ¶184]

Example 7—Contribution of a Work of Art

.137 Museum H, which preserves its collections as described in paragraph .111, receives a gift of a valuable painting from a donor. The donor obtained an independent appraisal of the fair value of the painting for tax purposes and furnished a copy to the museum. The museum staff evaluated the painting to determine its authenticity and worthiness for addition to the museum's collection. The staff recommended that the gift be accepted, adding that it was not aware of any evidence contradicting the fair value provided by the donor and the donor's appraiser. [FAS116, ¶185]

.138 If Museum H capitalizes its collections, Museum H would recognize the fair value of the contributed work of art received as revenue and capitalize it as an asset at its fair value (paragraphs .113 and .115). The staff of Museum H is qualified to estimate the fair value of the contributed painting and evidence of its fair value exists. If Museum H does not capitalize its collections, Museum H is precluded from recognizing the contribution (paragraph .113) and would provide the information required by paragraphs .123 and .124. [FAS116, ¶186]

.139 If Museum H [is a not-for-profit organization and] accepted the painting with the donor's understanding that it would be sold rather than added to its collection, Museum H would recognize the contribution of the painting received as unrestricted revenue and as an asset at its fair value (paragraph .108 and paragraph .145 of Section No5). [FAS116, ¶187]

Example 8—Contribution of Historical Objects

.140 Historical Society I receives several old photographs as a gift from a long-time local resident. The photographs depict a particular area as it was 75 years ago. After evaluating whether the photographs were worthy of addition to the historical society's collection, the staff concluded the photographs should be accepted solely because of their potential historical and educational use; that is, the photographs may be of interest to future researchers, historians, or others interested in studying the area. The photographs are not suitable for display and no alternative use exists. [FAS116, ¶188]

.141 Regardless of whether Historical Society I capitalizes its collections, Historical Society I would not recognize the contributed photographs in this example as assets because there is major uncertainty about the existence of value and no alternative use exists (paragraph .115). [FAS116, ¶189]

Example 9—Contribution of Utilities

.142 Organization J operates from a building it owns in City K. The holding company of a local utility has been contributing electricity on a continuous basis subject to the donor's cancellation. [FAS116, ¶190]

.143 The simultaneous receipt and use of electricity or other utilities is a form of contributed assets and not services. Organization J would recognize the fair value of the contributed electricity as both revenue and expense in the period it is received and used (paragraph .108). Organization J could estimate the fair value of the electricity received by using rates normally charged to a consumer of similar usage requirements. [FAS116, ¶191]

Example 10—Contribution of Use of Property

.144 Organization L receives the free use of 10,000 square feet of prime office space provided by a local company. The local company has informed Organization L that it intends to continue providing the space as long as it is available, and although it expects it would be able to give the organization 30 days advance notice, it may discontinue providing the space at any time. The local company normally rents similar space for $14 to $16 annually per square foot, the going market rate for office space in the area. Organization L decides to accept this gift—the free use of office space—to conduct its daily central administrative activities. [FAS116, ¶192]

.145 The simultaneous receipt and use of facilities is a form of contributed assets and not services. Organization L would recognize the fair value of the contributed use of facilities as both revenue and expense in the period it is received and used (paragraph .108). [FAS116, ¶193]

.146 If the local company explicitly and unconditionally promises the use of the facility for a specified period of time (for example, five years), the promise would be an unconditional promise to give. In that case, Organization L would recognize the receipt of the unconditional promise as a receivable and [if Organization L is a not-for-profit organization it would recognize the unconditional promise] as restricted support at its fair value. The donor would recognize the unconditional promise when made as a payable and an expense at its fair value (paragraph .114). [FAS116, ¶194]

Example 11—Contribution of Services

.147 Organization M decides to construct a building on its property. It obtains the necessary architectural plans and specifications and purchases the necessary continuing architectural services, materials, permits, and so forth at a total cost of $400,000. A local construction company contributes the necessary labor and equipment. An independent appraisal of the building (exclusive of land), obtained for insurance purposes, estimates its fair value at $725,000. [FAS116, ¶195]

.148 Organization M would recognize the services contributed by the construction company because the contributed services received meet condition (a)—the services received create or enhance nonfinancial assets—or because the services meet condition (b)—the services require specialized skills, are provided by individuals possessing those skills, and would typically need to be purchased if not provided by donation (paragraph .109). Contributions of services that create or enhance nonfinancial assets may be measured by referring to either the fair value of the services received or the fair value of the asset or of the asset enhancement resulting from the services (paragraph .115). In this example, the fair value of the contributed services received could be determined by subtracting the cost of the purchased services, materials, and permits ($400,000) from the fair value of the asset created ($725,000), which results in contributed services received of $325,000. Alternatively, the amount the construction company would have charged could be used if more readily available. [FAS116, ¶196]

.149 If some of the labor did not require specialized skills and was provided by volunteers, those services still would be recognized because they meet condition (a). [FAS116, ¶197]

Example 12—Contribution of Services

.150 Faculty salaries are a major expense of University N. The faculty includes both compensated faculty members (approximately 80 percent) and uncompensated faculty members (approximately 20 percent) who are associated with religious orders and contribute their services to the university. The performance of both compensated and uncompensated faculty members is regularly and similarly evaluated; both must meet the university's standards and both provide services in the same way. [FAS116, ¶198]

.151 University N would recognize both revenue and expense for the services contributed by the uncompensated faculty members because the contribution meets condition (b) of paragraph .109. Teaching requires specialized skills; the religious personnel are qualified and trained to provide those skills; and University N typically would hire paid instructors if the religious personnel did not donate their services. University N could refer to the salaries it pays similarly qualified compensated faculty members to determine fair value of the services received. [FAS116, ¶199]

.152 Similarly, if the uncompensated faculty members in this example were given a nominal stipend to help defray certain of their out-of-pocket expenses, University N still would recognize both revenue and expense for the services contributed. The contribution received would be measured at the fair value of the services received less the amount of the nominal stipend paid. [FAS116, ¶200]

Example 13—Contribution of Services

.153 A member of the Board of Trustees of Organization O is a lawyer and from time to time in the capacity of a trustee provides advice on general business matters, including questions about business opportunities and risks and ethical, moral, and legal matters. The advice provided on legal matters is provided as a trustee in the role of a trustee, not as a lawyer, and the opinions generally are limited to routine matters. Generally, the lawyer suggests that Organization O seek the opinion of its attorneys on substantive or complex legal questions. All of the organization's trustees serve without compensation, and most trustees have specialized expertise (for example, a chief executive officer, a minister, a physician, a professor, and a public accountant) that makes their advice valuable to Organization O. The trustee-lawyer also serves without compensation as a trustee for two other organizations. [FAS116, ¶201]

.154 Organization O would be precluded from recognizing the contributed services it receives from its trustee-lawyer or its other trustees because the services contributed do not meet either of the conditions of paragraph .109. Condition (a) is not relevant. The trustee-lawyer's services do not meet condition (b) because the substantive or complex legal questions that require the specialized skills of a lawyer are referred to the organization's attorneys or because the advice provided by trustees typically would not be purchased if not provided by donation. [FAS116, ¶202]

Example 14—Contribution of Services

.155 Hospital P provides short-term inpatient and outpatient care and also provides long-term care for the elderly. As part of the long-term care program, the hospital has organized a program whereby local high school students may contribute a minimum of 10 hours a week, from 3:00 p.m. to 6:00 p.m., to the hospital. These students are assigned various duties, such as visiting and talking with the patients, distributing books and magazines, reading, playing chess, and similar activities. The hospital does not pay for these services or similar services. The services are accepted as a way of enhancing or supplementing the quality of care and comfort provided to the elderly long-term care patients. [FAS116, ¶203]

.156 Hospital P would be precluded from recognizing the contributed services because the services contributed do not meet either of the conditions of paragraph .109. Condition (a) is not relevant. Condition (b) has not been met because the services the students provide do not require specialized skills nor would they typically need to be purchased if not provided by donation. [FAS116, ¶204]

Example 15—Contribution of Services

.157 School Q conducts an annual fund-raising campaign to solicit contributions from its alumni. In prior years, School Q recruited unpaid student volunteers to make phone calls to its alumni. This year, a telemarketing company, whose president is an alumnus of School Q, contributed its services to School Q for the annual alumni fund-raising campaign. The company normally provides telemarketing services to a variety of clients on a fee basis. School Q provided the company with a list of 10,000 alumni, several copies of a typed appeal to be read over the phone, and blank contribution forms to record pledges received. The company contacted most of the 10,000 alumni. [FAS116, ¶205]

.158 School Q would be precluded from recognizing the contributed services of the telemarketing company. Condition (a) of paragraph .109 is not relevant. Condition (b) has not been met because the services do not require specialized skills or because School Q typically would not need to purchase the services if they were not provided by donation. School Q normally conducts its campaign with untrained students in a manner similar to the manner used by the telemarketing firm. [FAS116, ¶206]

Example 16—Contribution of an Interest in an Estate

.159 In 19X0, Individual R notifies Organization S that she has remembered the organization in her will and provides a written copy of the will. In 19X5, Individual R dies. In 19X6, Individual R's last will and testament enters probate and the probate court declares the will valid. The executor informs Organization S that the will has been declared valid and that it will receive 10 percent of Individual R's estate, after satisfying the estate's liabilities and certain specific bequests. The executor provides an estimate of the estate's assets and liabilities and the expected amount and time for payment of Organization S's interest in the estate. [FAS116, ¶207]

.160 The 19X0 communication between Individual R and Organization S specified an intention to give. The ability to modify a will at any time prior to death is well established; thus, in 19X0 Organization S did not receive a promise to give and did not recognize a contribution received. When the probate court declares the will valid, Organization S would recognize a receivable and revenue for an unconditional promise to give at the fair value of its interest in the estate (paragraphs .108 and .115 through .117). If the promise to give contained in the valid will was instead conditioned on a future and uncertain event, Organization S would recognize the contribution when the condition was substantially met. A conditional promise in a valid will would be disclosed in notes to financial statements (paragraph .122). [FAS116, ¶208]

Transfers of Assets to a Not-for-Profit Organization or Charitable Trust That Raises or Holds Contributions for Others

Intermediary

.161 Although in general usage the term *intermediary* encompasses a broad range of situations in which an organization acts between two or more other parties, use of the term in paragraph .101 of this section is more narrow and specific. The term is used to refer to situations in which a recipient organization acts as a facilitator for the transfer of assets between a potential donor and a potential beneficiary (donee) but is neither an agent or trustee nor a donee and donor as contemplated by this section. [The example in paragraph .132 of this section illustrates the use of the term intermediary.] If an intermediary receives cash or other financial assets,[12] it shall recognize its liability to the specified beneficiary concurrent with its recognition of the assets received from the donor. Both the liability and the assets shall be measured at the fair value of the assets received. If an intermediary receives nonfinancial assets,[13] it is permitted, but not required, to recognize its liability and those assets provided that the intermediary reports consistently from period to period and discloses its accounting policy. [FAS136, ¶8]

[12]Section F39, "Financial Instruments: Transfers," [FAS140, ¶354] defines *financial asset* as "cash, evidence of an ownership interest in an entity, or a contract that conveys to a second entity a contractual right (a) to receive cash or another financial instrument from a first entity or (b) to exchange other financial instruments on potentially favorable terms with the first entity" [FAS136, ¶8, fn5] (paragraph .413). [FAS140, ¶354]

[[13]Examples of] nonfinancial assets [are] land, buildings, use of facilities or utilities, materials and supplies, intangible assets, or services. [FAS136, ¶78]

Trustee

.162 A recipient organization acts as a *trustee* if it has a duty to hold and manage assets for the benefit of a specified beneficiary in accordance with a charitable trust agreement. This section does not establish standards for a trustee's reporting of assets held on behalf of a specified beneficiary, but paragraphs .168 and .169 establish standards for the beneficiary's reporting of its rights to trust assets—its beneficial interest in the charitable trust. [FAS136, ¶9]

Agent

.163 An *agent* acts for and on behalf of another. Although the term *agency* has a legal definition, the term is used in paragraphs .161 through .208 with a broader meaning to encompass not only legal agency, but also the relationships described in those paragraphs. A recipient organization acts as an agent for and on behalf of a donor if it receives assets from the donor and agrees to use those assets on behalf of or transfer those assets, the return on investment of those assets, or both to a specified beneficiary. A recipient organization acts as an agent for and on behalf of a beneficiary if it agrees to solicit assets from potential donors specifically for the beneficiary's use and to distribute those assets to the beneficiary. A recipient organization also acts as an agent if a beneficiary can compel the organization to make distributions to it or on its behalf. [FAS136, ¶10]

.164 Except as described in paragraphs .165 and .167 of this section, a recipient organization that accepts assets from a donor and agrees to use those assets on behalf of or transfer those assets, the return on investment of those assets, or both to a specified beneficiary is not a donee. It shall recognize its liability to the specified beneficiary concurrent with its recognition of cash or other financial assets received from the donor. Both the liability and the assets shall be measured at the fair value of the assets received. Except as described in paragraphs .165 and .167 of this section, a recipient organization that receives nonfinancial assets is permitted, but not required, to recognize its liability and those assets provided that the organization reports consistently from period to period and discloses its accounting policy. [FAS136, ¶11]

.165 A recipient organization that is directed by a donor to distribute the transferred assets, the return on investment of those assets, or both to a specified unaffiliated beneficiary acts as a donee, rather than an agent, trustee, or intermediary, if the donor explicitly grants the recipient organization variance power[14]—that is, the unilateral power to redirect the use of the transferred assets to another beneficiary. In that situation, *explicitly grants* means that the recipient organization's unilateral power to redirect the use of the assets is explicitly referred to in the instrument transferring the assets, and *unilateral power* means that the recipient organization can override the donor's instructions without approval from the donor, specified beneficiary, or any other interested party. [FAS136, ¶12]

Financially Interrelated Organizations

.166 The recipient organization and the specified beneficiary are *financially interrelated organizations* if the relationship between them has both of the following characteristics:

a. One organization has the ability to influence the operating and financial decisions of the other. The ability to exercise that influence may be demonstrated in several ways:
   (1) The organizations are affiliates.
   (2) One organization has considerable representation on the governing board of the other organization.
   (3) The charter or bylaws of one organization limit its activities to those that are beneficial to the other organization.
   (4) An agreement between the organizations allows one organization to actively participate in policymaking processes of the other, such as setting organizational priorities, budgets, and management compensation.
b. One organization has an ongoing economic interest in the net assets of the other. If the specified beneficiary has an ongoing economic interest in the net assets of the recipient organization, the beneficiary's rights to the assets held by the recipient organization are residual rights; that is, the value of those rights increases or decreases

[14]A recipient organization may obtain the power to redirect the use of assets transferred to it through various means, including standard provisions in donor-choice forms or explicit donor stipulation in gift instruments. For example, community foundations may obtain the unilateral power to redirect the use of assets transferred to them through explicit reference to the variance power granted to them by donors in written gift instruments. The variance power may be explicitly referred to in the terms of the gift instrument and further explained in the community foundation's declaration of trust, articles of incorporation, or governing instruments. Variance power, required by the U.S. Treasury Regulations for trust-form community foundations, is described in those regulations as the power to

> . . . modify any restriction or condition on the distribution of funds for any specified charitable purpose or to specified organizations if in the sole judgement of the governing body (without the necessity of the approval of any participating trustee, custodian, or agent), such restriction or condition becomes, in effect, unnecessary, incapable of fulfillment, or inconsistent with the charitable needs of the community or area served.

[FAS136, ¶84]

as a result of the investment, fundraising, operating, and other activities of the recipient organization. Alternatively, but less common, a recipient organization may have an ongoing economic interest in the net assets of the specified beneficiary. If so, the recipient organization's rights are residual rights, and their value changes as a result of the operations of the beneficiary.

[FAS136, ¶13]

.167 If a recipient organization and a specified beneficiary are financially interrelated organizations and the recipient organization is not a trustee, the recipient organization shall recognize a contribution received when it receives assets (financial or nonfinancial) from the donor that are specified for the beneficiary. For example, a foundation that exists to raise, hold, and invest assets for the specified beneficiary or for a group of affiliates of which the specified beneficiary is a member generally is financially interrelated with the organization or organizations it supports and recognizes contribution revenue when it receives assets from the donor. [FAS136, ¶14]

Beneficiary

.168 A specified beneficiary shall recognize its rights to the assets (financial or nonfinancial) held by a recipient organization as an asset unless the recipient organization is explicitly granted variance power. Those rights are either an interest in the net assets of the recipient organization, a beneficial interest, or a receivable. If the beneficiary and the recipient organization are financially interrelated organizations, the beneficiary shall recognize its interest in the net assets of the recipient organization and adjust that interest for its share of the change in net assets of the recipient organization.[15] If the beneficiary has an unconditional right to receive all or a portion of the specified cash flows from a charitable trust or other identifiable pool of assets, the beneficiary shall recognize that beneficial interest, measuring and subsequently remeasuring it at fair value, using a valuation technique such as the present value of the estimated expected future cash flows. In all other cases, a beneficiary shall recognize its rights to the assets held by a recipient

---

[15]Recognizing an interest in the net assets of the recipient organization and adjusting that interest for a share of the change in net assets of the recipient organization is similar to the equity method, which is described in Section I82, "Investments: Equity Method." If the beneficiary and the recipient organization are included in consolidated financial statements, the beneficiary's interest in the net assets of the recipient organization would be eliminated in accordance with paragraph .109 of Section C51, "Consolidations." [FAS136, ¶15, fn6]

organization as a receivable and contribution revenue in accordance with the provisions for unconditional promises to give.[16] [FAS136, ¶15]

.169 If the donor explicitly grants a recipient organization variance power, the specified unaffiliated beneficiary shall not recognize its potential for future distributions from the assets held by the recipient organization. [FAS136, ¶16]

Transfers of Assets That Are Not Contributions

.170 A transfer of assets to a recipient organization is not a contribution[17] and shall be accounted for as an asset by the resource provider and as a liability by the recipient organization if one or more of the following conditions is present:

a. The transfer is subject to the resource provider's unilateral right to redirect the use of the assets to another beneficiary.
b. The transfer is accompanied by the resource provider's conditional promise to give or is otherwise revocable or repayable.
c. The resource provider controls[18] the recipient organization and specifies an unaffiliated beneficiary.
d. The resource provider specifies itself or its affiliate as the beneficiary and the transfer is not an equity transaction (paragraph .171).

[FAS136, ¶17]

---

[16]For an unconditional promise to give to be recognized in financial statements, paragraph .105 of this section states, ". . . there must be sufficient evidence in the form of verifiable documentation that a promise was made and received." Paragraph .144 of Section No5 states, "Receipts of unconditional promises to give with payments due in future periods shall be reported as restricted support unless explicit donor stipulations or circumstances surrounding the receipt of a promise make clear that the donor intended it to be used to support activities of the current period." Paragraph .116 of this section states, "The present value of estimated future cash flows using a discount rate commensurate with the risks involved is an appropriate measure of fair value of unconditional promises to give cash" (footnote reference omitted). [FAS136, ¶15, fn7]

[17]In some agency and some trustee arrangements, a resource provider has not made a gift because it can derive future economic benefit from the transferred assets. [FAS136, ¶68]

[18]Several definitions of control exist. For the purposes of Section R36, control is defined as "the possession, direct or indirect, of the power to direct or cause the direction of the management and policies of an enterprise through ownership, by contract, or otherwise" (paragraph .402). AICPA Statement of Position 94-3, *Reporting of Related Entities by Not-for-Profit Organizations,* has a similar definition; it defines control as "the direct or indirect ability to determine the direction of management and policies through ownership, contract, or otherwise" (glossary). The guidance in those documents should be considered when determining whether one entity controls another. [FAS136, ¶93]

.171 A transfer of assets to a recipient organization is an equity transaction if all of the following conditions are present:

a. The resource provider specifies itself or its affiliate as the beneficiary.
b. The resource provider and the recipient organization are financially interrelated organizations.
c. Neither the resource provider nor its affiliate expects payment of the transferred assets, although payment of investment return on the transferred assets may be expected.

If a resource provider specifies itself as beneficiary, it shall report an equity transaction as an interest in the net assets of the recipient organization (or as an increase in a previously recognized interest). If a resource provider specifies an affiliate as beneficiary, the resource provider shall report an equity transaction as a separate line in its statement of activities, and the affiliate named as beneficiary shall report an interest in the net assets of the recipient organization. A recipient organization shall report an equity transaction as a separate line item in its statement of activities. [FAS136, ¶18]

Illustrative Guidance

.172 Paragraphs .173 through .208 provide a diagram to assist entities in the application of paragraphs .161 through .171 and examples that illustrate the application of those paragraphs in specific situations. The diagram is a visual supplement. It should not be interpreted to alter any requirements of paragraphs .161 through .171, nor should it be considered a substitute for those requirements. The relevant paragraphs of this section are identified in the parenthetical notes. The examples do not address all possible situations or applications of these paragraphs. [FAS136, ¶23]

Diagram

.173 The diagram in Exhibit 173A depicts the process for determining the appropriate accounting for a transfer of assets from a donor to a recipient organization that accepts the assets and agrees to use those assets on behalf of a beneficiary specified by the donor or transfer those assets, the return on investment of those assets, or both to a beneficiary specified by the donor. The diagram also depicts the process for determining the appropriate accounting for a transfer from a resource provider that takes place in a similar manner but is not a contribution because the transfer is revocable, repayable, or reciprocal. [FAS136, ¶24]

Exhibit 173A

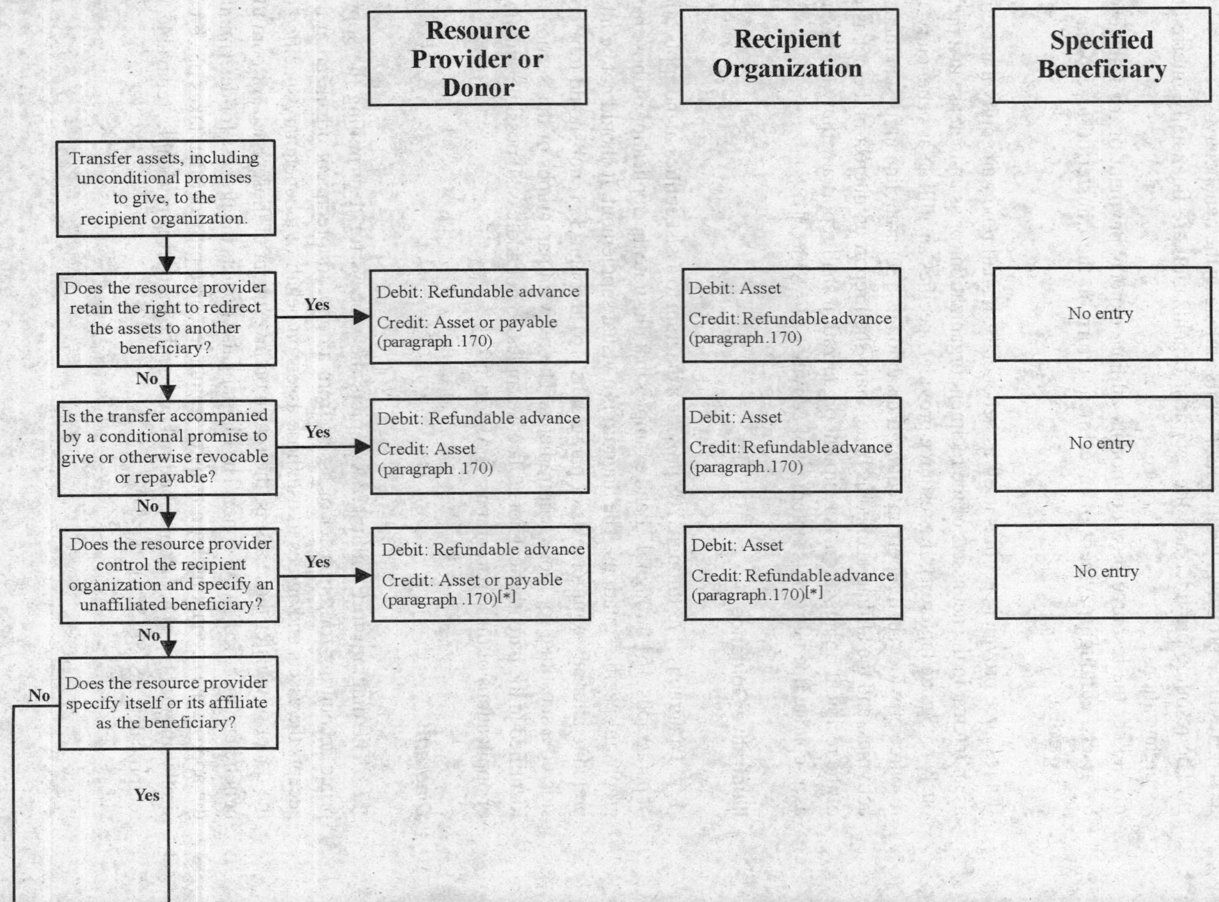

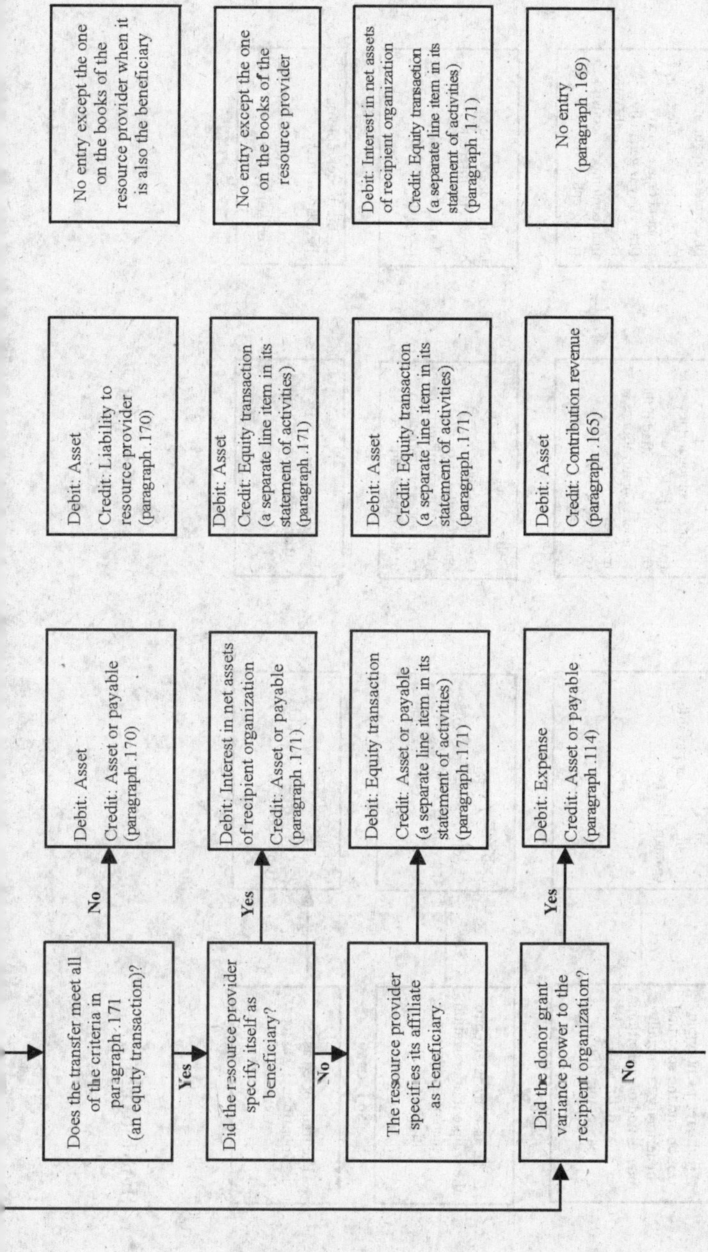

[*]Until the transferred assets are beyond the control of the resource provider, the transaction should be reported as an asset by the resource provider and a liability by the recipient organization. [FAS136, ¶92]

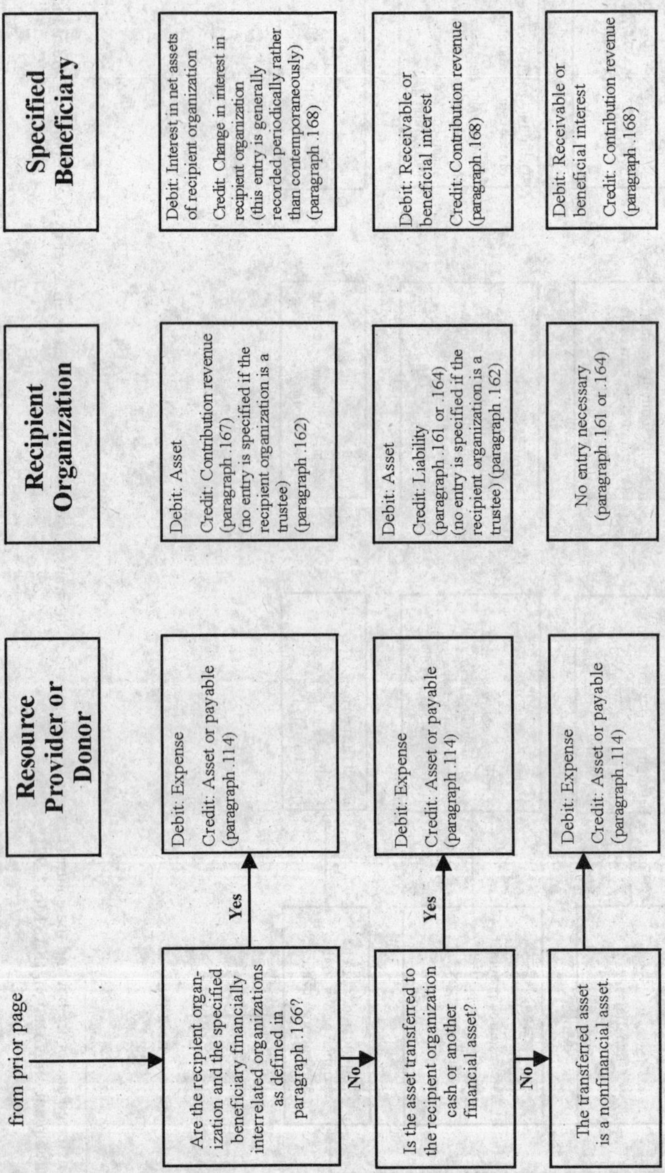
from prior page
Resource Provider or Donor
Recipient Organization
Specified Beneficiary
Are the recipient organization and the specified beneficiary financially interrelated organizations as defined in paragraph .166?
Yes
Debit: Expense
Credit: Asset or payable (paragraph .114)
Debit: Asset
Credit: Contribution revenue (paragraph .167)
(no entry is specified if the recipient organization is a trustee)
(paragraph .162)
Debit: Interest in net assets of recipient organization
Credit: Change in interest in recipient organization
(this entry is generally recorded periodically rather than contemporaneously)
(paragraph .168)
No
Is the asset transferred to the recipient organization cash or another financial asset?
Yes
Debit: Expense
Credit: Asset or payable (paragraph .114)
Debit: Asset
Credit: Liability (paragraph .161 or .164)
(no entry is specified if the recipient organization is a trustee) (paragraph .162)
Debit: Receivable or beneficial interest
Credit: Contribution revenue (paragraph .168)
No
The transferred asset is a nonfinancial asset.
Debit: Expense
Credit: Asset or payable (paragraph .114)
No entry necessary (paragraph .161 or .164)
Debit: Receivable or beneficial interest
Credit: Contribution revenue (paragraph .168)

[FAS136, ¶24]

Example 1—Gifts to a Federated Fundraising Organization

.174 Federated Fundraising Organization provides three choices to donors in its annual workplace campaign. Donors can give without restriction, direct their gifts to one of four community needs identified by Federated Fundraising Organization, or specify that their gifts be transferred to an organization of their choice. The campaign literature informs donors that if they choose to specify an organization to which their gift should be transferred, the organization must be a social welfare organization within the community that has tax-exempt status under Internal Revenue Code Section 501(c)(3). The campaign literature also provides a schedule of the administrative fees that will be deducted from all gifts that are to be transferred to the donor's chosen organization. [FAS136, ¶25]

.175 Federated Fundraising Organization would recognize the fair values of the unrestricted gifts as contribution revenue that increases unrestricted net assets. It would recognize the fair values of the gifts targeted to the four specified community needs as contribution revenue that increases temporarily restricted net assets. It would recognize the fair values of gifts that are to be transferred to organizations chosen by the donors as increases in its assets and as liabilities to those specified beneficiaries (paragraph .164). However, if some of the gifts that are intended for specified beneficiaries are gifts of nonfinancial assets, Federated Fundraising Organization would recognize those nonfinancial assets and its liability to transfer them to the specified beneficiaries if that were its policy; otherwise, it would recognize neither the nonfinancial assets nor a liability (paragraph .164). Federated Fundraising Organization would recognize as revenue the administrative fees withheld from amounts to be transferred to the donors' chosen organizations. [FAS136, ¶26]

.176 The organizations chosen by the donors would recognize the fair value of the transferred assets as contribution revenue in accordance with the provisions of this section for unconditional promises to give (paragraph .168). Thus, the revenue would increase temporarily restricted net assets unless the donor specified a permanent restriction or it was clear that the donor intended the gift to support activities of the current period (paragraph .144 of Section No5). In accordance with paragraph .121 of Section No5, the beneficiaries would report the gross amounts of the gifts as contribution revenue and the administrative fees withheld by Federated Fundraising Organization as expenses. The net amount would be recognized as a receivable (paragraph .168). [FAS136, ¶27]

.177 Instead of conducting the campaign as described above, Federated Fundraising Organization's campaign literature, including the form that donors use to specify a beneficiary, clearly states that if donors choose to give and specify a beneficiary, the allocation committee has the authority to redirect their gifts if the committee perceives needs elsewhere in the community that are greater. By giving under those terms, donors explicitly grant Federated Fundraising Organization variance power. Thus, Federated Fundraising Organization would recognize an unrestricted contribution (paragraph .165), and the specified beneficiaries would be precluded from recognizing their potential for future distributions from the assets (paragraph .169). [FAS136, ¶28]

Example 2—Gifts to a Community Foundation for the Benefit of a Not-for-Profit Organization

.178 The governing board of City Botanical Society decides to raise funds to build an endowment. The governing board signs an agreement to establish a fund at Community Foundation. Community Foundation and City Botanical Society are not financially interrelated organizations. City Botanical Society solicits gifts to the fund. The campaign materials inform donors that the endowment will be owned and held by Community Foundation. The materials explain that the gifts will be invested and that the return from their investment will be distributed to City Botanical Society, subject to Community Foundation's spending policy and to Community Foundation's right to redirect the return to another beneficiary without the approval of the donor, City Botanical Society, or any other party if distributions to City Botanical Society become unnecessary, impossible, or inconsistent with the needs of the community. The donor-response card also clearly describes Community Foundation's right to redirect the return of the fund. The campaign materials indicate that donors should send their contributions to Community Foundation using a preaddressed envelope included for that purpose. [FAS136, ¶29]

.179 Community Foundation would recognize the fair value of gifts received as assets and as contribution revenue. The donors explicitly granted variance power by using a donor-response card that clearly states that gifts are subject to Community Foundation's unilateral power to redirect the return to another beneficiary (paragraph .165). [FAS136, ¶30]

.180 City Botanical Society is precluded from recognizing its potential rights to the assets held by Community Foundation because the donors explicitly granted variance power (paragraph .169). City Botanical Society would recognize only its annual grants from Community Foundation as contributions. [FAS136, ¶31]

.181 Whether a donor intended to make a contribution to Community Foundation may not be clear if the donor responds to the campaign materials by sending a contribution and the donor-response card directly to City Botanical Society. City Botanical Society could resolve the ambiguity by a review of the facts and circumstances surrounding the gift, communications with the donor, or both. If it is ultimately determined that the donor intended to make a gift to the fund owned and held by Community Foundation and to explicitly grant variance power, City Botanical Society would be an agent responsible for transferring that gift to Community Foundation (paragraph .164). [FAS136, ¶32]

Example 3—Cash Transfer from a Not-for-Profit Organization to Another Not-for-Profit Organization for the Benefit of an Individual

.182 Local Church transfers cash to Seminary and instructs Seminary to use the money to grant a scholarship to Individual, who is a parishioner of Local Church. [FAS136, ¶33]

.183 Seminary would recognize the cash and a liability to Individual in the same amount because it merely is facilitating the cash transfer from Local Church to Individual (paragraph .161). [FAS136, ¶34]

Example 4—Assets Transferred from an Individual to a Bank to Establish a Charitable Trust for the Benefit of a Not-for-Profit Organization

.184 Individual transfers assets to National Bank to establish an irrevocable charitable trust for the sole benefit of Museum. National Bank will serve as trustee. Individual sets forth in the trust agreement the policies that direct the economic activities of the trust. The trust term is five years. Each year, the income received on the investments of the trust will be distributed to Museum. At the end of year 5, the corpus of the trust (original assets and net appreciation on those assets) will be paid to Museum. [FAS136, ¶35]

.185 This section does not establish standards for the trustee, National Bank (paragraph .162). Because Museum is unable to influence the operating or financial decisions of the trustee, Museum and National Bank are not financially interrelated organizations (paragraph .166(a)). Therefore, Museum would recognize its asset (a beneficial interest in the trust) and contribution revenue that increases temporarily restricted net assets (paragraph .168). Museum would measure its beneficial interest at fair value, using a valuation technique such as the present value of the estimated expected future cash receipts from the trust's assets (paragraph .168). That value generally can be measured by the fair value of the assets contributed to the trust. [FAS136, ¶36]

Example 5—Gift of Nonfinancial Assets to an Institutionally Related Foundation

.186 Corporation sends dental supplies to University Foundation to be used by students in University's dental clinic. University Foundation's bylaws state that it is organized for the purpose of stimulating voluntary financial support from alumni and other donors for the benefit of University, especially for addressing the long-term academic priorities of University. As with most gifts it receives, University Foundation can choose the timing of the distribution to University and can place additional limitations on the distribution if those limitations are consistent with Corporation's restrictions. University does not control University Foundation. [FAS136, ¶37]

.187 University Foundation recognizes the fair value of the dental supplies (nonfinancial assets) as an increase in assets and as contribution revenue that increases temporarily restricted net assets because University and University Foundation are financially interrelated organizations (paragraph .167). University can influence the financial and operating decisions of University Foundation because the bylaws of University Foundation limit its activities to those that benefit University (paragraph .166(a)). University has an ongoing economic interest in the net assets of University Foundation because the results of University Foundation's activities accrue to the benefit of University (paragraph .166(b)). When University Foundation distributes the dental supplies to University, it reduces its assets and recognizes an expense and the expiration of the restriction. [FAS136, ¶38]

.188 Periodically, in conjunction with preparing its financial statements, University recognizes the change in its interest in the net assets of University Foundation, which would include the gift of nonfinancial assets received by the foundation (paragraph .168). Because payments from University Foundation are due in future periods, the increase (or decrease) in University's interest would be classified as a change in temporarily restricted net assets unless donors placed permanent restrictions on their gifts (footnote 17 to paragraph .168). When the dental supplies and other assets are distributed to it, University would recognize the assets received and decrease its interest in the net assets of University Foundation.[19] [FAS136, ¶39]

.189 If, instead, University controlled University Foundation, University would be able to access at will any assets held by University Foundation. Implying a time restriction on the gifts held by University Foundation would be inappropriate. When recognizing the change in its interest in University Foundation, University would report the resulting net assets in the same net asset classifications as University Foundation. [FAS136, ¶40]

Example 6—Cash Gift to a Healthcare Foundation That Supports Three Affiliated Organizations

.190 Corporation transfers cash to Healthcare Foundation and requests that Healthcare Foundation use the gift to provide healthcare benefits to the community. Healthcare Foundation's bylaws state that it is organized for the purpose of stimulating voluntary financial support from donors for the benefit of Hospital, Nursing Home, and Walk-in Clinic, all of which are located in the community. Hospital, Nursing Home, Walk-in Clinic, and Healthcare Foundation are affiliates that are controlled by Healthcare System. [FAS136, ¶41]

[19]The provisions of this section do not apply to University if University is a governmental entity. The Governmental Accounting Standards Board sets standards for those entities. [FAS136, ¶39, fn8]

.191 Healthcare Foundation would recognize cash and contribution revenue that increases unrestricted net assets because Corporation did not specify a beneficiary for its gift. Healthcare Foundation can choose how to distribute the gift among the three affiliates (footnote 2a to paragraph .102A). [FAS136, ¶42]

.192 Periodically, in conjunction with preparing their financial statements, Hospital, Nursing Home, and Walk-in Clinic recognize the changes in their interests in the net assets of Healthcare Foundation (paragraph .168). When measuring its interest in Healthcare Foundation, each affiliate would include only the net assets of Healthcare Foundation that are restricted to that affiliate's use. None of them would include in their individual interest the net assets resulting from the gift received from Corporation because Healthcare Foundation can choose how to distribute the gift among the three affiliates. Healthcare System would include the net assets resulting from the gift received from Corporation, as well as other changes in the net assets of Healthcare Foundation, in its interest in the net assets of the foundation.[20] [FAS136, ¶43]

.193 If Healthcare Foundation, Hospital, Nursing Home, and Walk-in Clinic entered into an agreement that specified how unrestricted gifts to Healthcare Foundation should be divided, each affiliate would also include its share of Healthcare Foundation's unrestricted net assets, computed in accordance with that agreement, when it measured its interest in Healthcare Foundation. Similarly, if Healthcare System directed that unrestricted gifts to Healthcare Foundation be distributed to the three affiliates in accordance with a specified formula, each affiliate would include its share of unrestricted net assets, computed in accordance with that formula, when it measured its interest in Healthcare Foundation. [FAS136, ¶44]

.194 If Corporation had specified that its gift be used for the benefit of Walk-in Clinic rather than giving without restriction, Healthcare Foundation would recognize contribution revenue that increases temporarily restricted net assets because Hospital, Nursing Home, Walk-in Clinic, and Healthcare Foundation are financially interrelated organizations (paragraph .167). Their relationship meets both requirements of paragraph .166. Hospital, Nursing Home, and Walk-in Clinic can influence the financial and operating decisions of Healthcare Foundation because all four organizations are under common control and the bylaws of Healthcare Foundation limit its activities to support of its three affiliates (paragraph .166(a)). Hospital, Nursing Home, and Walk-in Clinic each have an ongoing economic interest in the net assets of Healthcare Foundation because their rights to the assets held by Healthcare Foundation are residual rights in an ongoing relation-

[20]An interest in the net assets of an affiliate would be eliminated if that affiliate were included in the consolidated financial statements of the interest holder. [FAS136, ¶43, fn9]

ship (paragraph .166(b)). Walk-in Clinic would include the net assets resulting from the gift received from Corporation in its interest in the net assets of Healthcare Foundation. [FAS136, ¶45]

Example 7—Cash Gift to a Foundation That Supports Two Unaffiliated Not-for-Profit Organizations

.195 Individual transfers cash to Arts Foundation and specifies that the money be used to support the expenses of the ballet. Arts Foundation's bylaws state that it is organized for the purpose of stimulating voluntary financial support from donors for the benefit of Community Ballet and Community Theater. At the time Arts Foundation was created, the three organizations entered into an agreement that specifies that if a donor does not specify the organization to which the gift should be transferred, the gift will be split equally between Community Ballet and Community Theater. The agreement also specifies that (a) representatives from the three organizations will meet annually and determine campaign priorities for the next year and (b) the costs of operating Arts Foundation will be equally split between Community Ballet and Community Theater. Arts Foundation is not controlled by Community Ballet, Community Theater, or Individual. [FAS136, ¶46]

.196 Arts Foundation would report assets and contribution revenue that increases temporarily restricted net assets because Community Ballet and Arts Foundation are financially interrelated organizations (paragraph .167). Community Ballet has the ability to influence the operating and financial decisions of Arts Foundation because the agreement allows Community Ballet to participate in the policymaking processes of Arts Foundation (paragraph .166(a)). The agreement also establishes Community Ballet's rights as residual rights because it specifies how the revenues and expenses of Arts Foundation will be shared (paragraph .166(b)). When Arts Foundation distributes assets to Community Ballet, it reduces its assets and recognizes an expense. [FAS136, ¶47]

.197 Periodically, in conjunction with preparing their financial statements, Community Ballet and Community Theater recognize the changes in their interests in the net assets of Arts Foundation (paragraph .168). Community Ballet would include the net assets resulting from the gift received from Individual in its interest in the net assets of Arts Foundation because Individual specified that the gift be used to support the ballet and Arts Foundation's bylaws limit it to supporting Community Ballet. Community Ballet would also include in its interest all other gifts restricted to its benefit and its share of unrestricted net assets. Because payments from Arts Foundation are due in future periods, the increase (or decrease) in Community Ballet's interest would be classified as a change in temporarily restricted net assets unless donors placed permanent restrictions on their gifts (footnote 16 to paragraph .168). When assets are distributed to Community Ballet, it recognizes the assets received and decreases its interest in the net assets of Arts Foundation. [FAS136, ¶48]

.198 In contrast to this example, some foundations and associations raise contributions for a large number of unaffiliated not-for-profit organizations (often referred to as member organizations). By virtue of their numbers, those member organizations generally do not individually influence the operating and financial decisions of the foundation (or association). Thus, any one member organization and the foundation (or association) are not financially interrelated organizations (paragraph .166(a)). Because the organizations are not financially interrelated, the foundation (or association) recognizes a liability if a donor to the foundation (or association) specifies that the gift should be transferred to a particular member organization (paragraph .164). The specified member organization would recognize a receivable and contribution revenue that increases temporarily restricted net assets unless the donor specified a permanent restriction or it was clear that the donor intended the gift to support activities of the current period (paragraph .168 and footnote 16). [FAS136, ¶49]

Example 8—Gift of a Nonfinancial Asset to a Federated Fundraising Organization for Transfer to Another Not-for-Profit Organization

.199 Individual transfers a car to Federated Fundraising Organization and requests that the car be transferred to Local Daycare Center. Individual specifies that Federated Fundraising Organization may use the car for one year before transferring it to Local Daycare Center. Local Daycare Center is a member organization of Federated Fundraising Organization, but that status does not confer any ability to actively participate in the policymaking processes of Federated Fundraising Organization. [FAS136, ¶50]

.200 Because Federated Fundraising Organization and Local Daycare Center are not financially interrelated organizations, Federated Fundraising Organization would recognize the car as an asset and a liability to Local Daycare Center if its policy were to recognize nonfinancial assets; otherwise, it would recognize neither the nonfinancial assets nor a liability (paragraph .164). If, instead of refusing the gift of the use of the car, Federated Fundraising Organization decides to use it for a year before transferring it to Local Daycare Center, Federated Fundraising Organization would recognize the fair value of the gift of one-year's use of the car in accordance with paragraph .108 of this section. (The use of a car is a contributed asset and not a contributed service.) [FAS136, ¶51]

.201 Local Daycare Center would recognize a receivable and contribution revenue that increases temporarily restricted net assets (paragraph .168). It would measure the contribution received at the fair value of the car; however, if Federated Fundraising Organization chooses to use the car for a year before transferring it, the fair value would be reduced accordingly. [FAS136, ¶52]

Example 9—Transfer of Assets from a Not-for-Profit Organization to a Community Foundation to Establish an Endowment for the Benefit of the Not-for-Profit Organization

.202 Symphony Orchestra receives a large unrestricted gift of securities from Individual. Because it has no investment expertise, Symphony Orchestra transfers the securities to Community Foundation to establish an endowment fund. The agreement between Symphony Orchestra and Community Foundation states that the transfer is irrevocable and that the transferred assets will not be returned to Symphony Orchestra. However, Community Foundation will make annual distributions of the income earned on the endowment fund, subject to Community Foundation's spending policy. The agreement also permits Community Foundation to substitute another beneficiary in the place of Symphony Orchestra if Symphony Orchestra ceases to exist or if the governing board of Community Foundation votes that support of Symphony Orchestra (a) is no longer necessary or (b) is inconsistent with the needs of the community. (That is, Symphony Orchestra explicitly grants variance power to Community Foundation.) The agreement does not permit either organization to appoint members to the other organization's governing board or otherwise participate in the policymaking processes of the other. [FAS136, ¶53]

.203 Community Foundation would recognize the fair value of the transferred securities as an increase in investments and a liability to Symphony Orchestra because Symphony Orchestra transferred assets to Community Foundation and specified itself as beneficiary (paragraph .170(d)). The transfer is not an equity transaction because Community Foundation and Symphony Orchestra are not financially interrelated organizations (paragraph .171(b)). Symphony Orchestra is unable to influence the operating or financial decisions of Community Foundation (paragraph .166(a)). [FAS136, ¶54]

.204 Symphony Orchestra would recognize the fair value of the gift of securities from Individual as contribution revenue. When it transfers the securities to Community Foundation, it would recognize the transfer as a decrease in investments and an increase in an asset, for example, as a beneficial interest in assets held by Community Foundation (paragraph .170(d)). Also, Symphony Orchestra would disclose in its financial statements the identity of Community Foundation, the terms under which Community Foundation will distribute amounts to Symphony Orchestra, a description of the variance power granted to Community Foundation, and the aggregate amount reported in the statement of financial position and how that amount is described (paragraph .177 of Section No5). [FAS136, ¶55]

.205 In this example, Symphony Orchestra would recognize an asset and Community Foundation would recognize a liability because the transaction is deemed to be reciprocal.[21] Symphony Orchestra transfers its securities to Community Foundation in exchange for future distributions. Community Foundation, by its acceptance of the transfer, agrees that at the time of the transfer distributions to Symphony Orchestra are capable of fulfillment and consistent with the foundation's mission. Although the value of those future distributions may not be commensurate with the value of the securities given up (because Symphony Orchestra is at risk of cessation of the distributions), the transaction is accounted for as though those values are commensurate. In comparison, the donors to Community Foundation in Example 2 (paragraphs .178 through .181) explicitly grant variance power to Community Foundation in a nonreciprocal transfer. In that example, it is clear that the donors have made a contribution because they retain no beneficial interests in the transferred assets. Because the donors in Example 2 explicitly grant variance power to Community Foundation, it, rather than City Botanical Society, is the recipient of that contribution. [FAS136, ¶56]

Example 10—Transfer of Investments from a Not-for-Profit Organization to a Foundation It Creates to Hold Those Assets

.206 The governing board of Private Elementary School creates a foundation to hold and manage the school's investments. It transfers its investment portfolio to the newly created PES Foundation. An agreement between Private Elementary School and PES Foundation allows the school to request distributions from both the original investments and the return on those investments, subject to approval by the governing board of PES Foundation, which will not be unreasonably withheld. The agreement also permits Private Elementary School to transfer additional investments in the future. [FAS136, ¶57]

.207 PES Foundation would recognize the fair value of the investments as assets and a liability to Private Elementary School because Private Elementary School transferred assets to PES Foundation and specified itself as beneficiary (paragraph .170(d)). The transfer of assets is not an equity transaction because Private Elementary School expects repayment of the transferred assets, and thus the transaction does not meet the criterion in paragraph .171(c). [FAS136, ¶58]

.208 Private Elementary School would decrease its investments and recognize another asset, for example, a beneficial interest in assets held by PES Foundation (paragraph .170(d)). Also, Private Elementary School would disclose in its financial state-

[21]If a resource provider transfers assets to a recipient organization and specifies itself or its affiliate as the beneficiary, a presumption that the transfer is reciprocal, and therefore not a contribution, is necessary even if the resource provider explicitly grants the recipient organization variance power. [FAS136, ¶96]

ments the identity of PES Foundation, the terms of the agreement under which it can receive future distributions, including the fact that the distributions are not subject to variance power, and the aggregate amount reported in the statement of financial position and how that amount is described (paragraph .177 of Section No5). [FAS136, ¶59]

[**Note:** Additional guidance with respect to implementing Section C67 is presented in FASB Highlights, "Time for a Change—Implementing FASB Statements 116 and 117," in FASB *Status Report,* January 6, 1995. The article addresses 18 questions and was written by FASB staff member Karen F. Berk. This publication is available from the Order Department, Financial Accounting Standards Board, 401 Merritt 7, P.O. Box 5116, Norwalk, CT 06856-5116, telephone (203) 847-0700, extension 555.]

Glossary

.400 **Agent.** [Refer to paragraph .163.]

.401 **Collections.** Works of art, historical treasures, or similar assets that are (a) held for public exhibition, education, or research in furtherance of public service rather than financial gain, (b) protected, kept unencumbered, cared for, and preserved, and (c) subject to an organizational policy that requires the proceeds of items that are sold to be used to acquire other items for collections. [FAS116, ¶209]

.402 **Conditional promise to give.** A promise to give that depends on the occurrence of a specified future and uncertain event to bind the promisor. [FAS116, ¶209]

.403 **Contribution.** An unconditional transfer of cash or other assets to an entity or a settlement or cancellation of its liabilities in a voluntary nonreciprocal transfer by another entity acting other than as an owner. [FAS116, ¶209]

.404 **Donor-imposed condition.** A donor stipulation that specifies a future and uncertain event whose occurrence or failure to occur gives the promisor a right of return of the assets it has transferred or releases the promisor from its obligation to transfer its assets. [FAS116, ¶209]

.405 **Donor-imposed restriction.** A donor stipulation that specifies a use for the contributed asset that is more specific than broad limits resulting from the nature of the organization, the environment in which it operates, and the purposes specified in its articles of incorporation or bylaws or comparable documents for an unincorporated association. A restriction on an organization's use of the asset contributed may be temporary or permanent. [FAS116, ¶209]

.405A **Financially interrelated organizations.** [Refer to paragraph .166.]

.405B **Intermediary.** A recipient organization that acts as a facilitator for the transfer of assets between a potential donor and a potential beneficiary (donee) but is neither an agent [nor] trustee. [FAS136, ¶8]

.406 **Nonreciprocal transfer.** A transaction in which an entity incurs a liability or transfers an asset to another entity (or receives an asset or cancellation of a liability) without directly receiving (or giving) value in exchange. [FAS116, ¶209]

.407 **Not-for-profit organization.** An entity that possesses the following characteristics that distinguish it from a business enterprise: (a) contributions of significant amounts of resources from resource providers who do not expect commensurate or proportionate pecuniary return, (b) operating purposes other than to provide goods or services at a profit, and (c) absence of ownership interests like those of business enterprises. Not-for-profit organizations have those characteristics in varying degrees (FASB Concepts Statement 4, *Objectives of Financial Reporting by Nonbusiness Organizations,* paragraph 6). Organizations that clearly fall outside this definition include all investor-owned enterprises and entities that provide dividends, lower costs, or other economic benefits directly and proportionately to their owners, members, or participants, such as mutual insurance companies, credit unions, farm and rural electric cooperatives, and employee benefit plans (Concepts Statement 4, paragraph 7). [FAS116, ¶209]

.408 **Promise to give.** A written or oral agreement to contribute cash or other assets to another entity. A promise to give may be either conditional or unconditional. [FAS116, ¶209]

.409 **Restricted support.** Donor-restricted revenues or gains from contributions that increase either temporarily restricted net assets or permanently restricted net assets. Also refer to **Unrestricted support.** [FAS116, ¶209]

.409A **Trustee.** A recipient organization [that] has a duty to hold and manage assets for the benefit of a specified beneficiary in accordance with a charitable trust agreement. [FAS136, ¶9]

.410 **Unconditional promise to give.** A promise to give that depends only on passage of time or demand by the promisee for performance. [FAS116, ¶209]

.411 **Unrestricted support.** Revenues or gains from contributions that are not restricted by donors. Also refer to **Restricted support.** [FAS116, ¶209]

.412 **Variance power.** The unilateral power to redirect the use of transferred assets to a beneficiary [other than the unaffiliated beneficiary specified by the resource provider] is referred to as variance power. Unilateral power means that the recipient organization can override the donor's instructions without approval from the donor, specified beneficiary, or any other interested party. [FAS136, ¶12]

(The next page is 9501.)

Source: EITF Issues

Scope

.101 [This section lists EITF Issues that provide supplemental guidance on the general topic of debt. Accounting and reporting standards on specific debt-related topics can be found in other *Current Text* sections, including Sections D10, "Debt: Convertible Debt, Conversion of Convertible Debt, and Debt with Stock Purchase Warrants," D18, "Debt: Product Financing Arrangements," D22, "Debt: Restructurings," and L35, "Liabilities: Extinguishments."]

Supplemental Guidance: Emerging Issues Task Force (EITF) Issues

.1000 [Listed below are EITF Issues that provide supplemental guidance on the general topic of accounting for debt. EITF Issues that relate to specific aspects of the accounting for debt are referenced in their respective sections. For example, Issues that relate to convertible debt are included in Section D10, "Debt: Convertible Debt, Conversion of Convertible Debt, and Debt with Stock Purchase Warrants."

Debt Classification

EITF Issue No. 86-5, "Classifying Demand Notes with Repayment Terms"
EITF Issue No. 86-30, "Classification of Obligations When a Violation Is Waived by the Creditor"
EITF Issue No. 88-15, "Classification of Subsidiary's Loan Payable in Consolidated Balance Sheet When Subsidiary's and Parent's Fiscal Years Differ"
EITF Issue No. 95-22, "Balance Sheet Classification of Borrowings Outstanding under Revolving Credit Agreements That Include both a Subjective Acceleration Clause and a Lock-Box Arrangement"
EITF Topic No. D-23, "Subjective Acceleration Clauses and Debt Classification"
EITF Topic No. D-61, "Classification by the Issuer of Redeemable Instruments That Are Subject to Remarketing Agreements"

Employee Stock Ownership Plans (ESOPs)

EITF Issue No. 89-8, "Expense Recognition for Employee Stock Ownership Plans"
EITF Issue No. 89-10, "Sponsor's Recognition of Employee Stock Ownership Plan Debt"

Modification or Exchange of Debt Instruments

EITF Issue No. 96-19, "Debtor's Accounting for a Modification or Exchange of Debt Instruments"
EITF Issue No. 01-7, "Creditor's Accounting for a Modification or Exchange of Debt Instruments"

Other

EITF Issue No. 84-15, "Grantor Trusts Consolidation"
EITF Issue No. 84-23, "Leveraged Buyout Holding Company Debt"
EITF Issue No. 84-40, "Long-Term Debt Repayable by a Capital Stock Transaction"
EITF Issue No. 84-42, "Push-Down of Parent Company Debt to a Subsidiary"
EITF Issue No. 85-18, "Earnings-per-Share Effect of Equity Commitment Notes"

EITF Issue No. 86-15, "Increasing-Rate Debt"
EITF Issue No. 86-25, "Offsetting Foreign Currency Swaps"
EITF Issue No. 87-12, "Foreign Debt-for-Equity Swaps"
EITF Issue No. 91-10, "Accounting for Special Assessments and Tax Increment Financing Entities (TIFEs)"
EITF Issue No. 98-1, "Valuation of Debt Assumed in a Purchase Business Combination"
EITF Issue No. 98-14, "Debtor's Accounting for Changes in Line-of-Credit or Revolving-Debt Arrangements"]

(The next page is 11421.)

DEBT: CONVERTIBLE DEBT, CONVERSION OF CONVERTIBLE DEBT, AND DEBT WITH STOCK PURCHASE WARRANTS

SECTION D10

Sources: APB Opinion 14; AICPA Interpretation of APB Opinion 26; FASB Statement 84

[**Note:** A list of Issues discussed by the Emerging Issues Task Force (EITF) that provide supplemental guidance for this section is presented in paragraph .1000.]

Summary

The proceeds from issuance of debt securities with detachable warrants shall be allocated between the warrants and the debt securities based on their relative fair values at time of issuance; the portion allocable to the warrants shall be accounted for as additional paid-in capital. No similar allocation shall be made for the issuance of either convertible debt or debt securities with nondetachable warrants.

When a debtor induces conversion of convertible debt by issuing additional securities or paying other consideration to convertible debt holders, there shall be recognition of an expense equal to the fair value of the additional securities or other consideration issued to induce conversion.

Convertible Debt

.101 Convertible debt securities discussed in this section are those debt securities that are convertible into common stock of the issuer or an affiliated enterprise at a specified price at the option of the holder and that are sold at a price or have a value at issuance not significantly in excess of the face amount. The terms of such securities generally include (a) an interest rate that is lower than the issuer could establish for nonconvertible debt, (b) an initial conversion price that is greater than the market value of the common stock at time of issuance, and (c) a conversion price that does not decrease except pursuant to antidilution provisions. In most cases such securities also are callable at the option of the issuer and are subordinated to nonconvertible debt. [APB14, ¶3]

.102 A convertible debt security is an instrument bearing an option, the alternative choices of which are mutually exclusive; they cannot both be consummated. Thus, the security will either be converted into common stock or be redeemed for cash. The holder cannot exercise the option to convert unless he foregoes the right to redemption, and vice versa. [APB14, ¶7] If the market value of the underlying common stock increases sufficiently in the future, the issuer [of a convertible debt security] can [effectively] force conversion of the convertible debt into common stock by calling the issue for redemption. [APB14, ¶4]

.103 No portion of the proceeds from the issuance of convertible debt securities shall be accounted for as attributable to the conversion feature. [APB14, ¶12] [Refer to paragraph .1001 for an EITF Issue that provides interpretive guidance on this paragraph.]

Conversion of Debt

Scope

.103A [Paragraphs .103A through .103D] apply to conversions[1] of convertible debt to equity securities pursuant to terms that reflect changes made by the debtor to the conversion privileges provided in the terms of the debt at issuance (including changes that involve the payment of consideration) for the purpose of inducing conversion. [The paragraphs apply] only to conversions[2] that both (a) occur pursuant to changed conversion privileges that are exercisable only for a limited period of time and (b) include the issuance of all of the equity securities issuable pursuant to conversion privileges included in the terms of the debt at issuance for each debt instrument that is converted.[3] The changed terms may involve reduction of the original conversion price thereby resulting in the issuance of additional shares of stock, issuance of warrants or other securities not provided for in the original conversion terms, or payment of cash or other consideration to those debt holders who convert during the specified time period. [Paragraphs .103A through .103D do] not apply to conversions pursuant to other changes in conversion privileges or to changes in terms of convertible debt instruments that are different from those described in this paragraph. [FAS84, ¶2]

.103B [Paragraphs .103A through .103D] require no recognition of gain or loss with respect to the shares issuable pursuant to the original conversion privileges of the convertible debt when additional securities or assets are transferred to a debt holder to induce

[1]A conversion includes an exchange of a convertible debt instrument for equity securities or a combination of equity securities and other consideration, whether or not the exchange involves legal exercise of the contractual conversion privileges included in terms of debt. [FAS84, ¶2, fn2]

[2]Some convertible debt instruments include provisions allowing the debtor to alter terms of the debt to the benefit of debt holders in a manner similar to transactions described in this paragraph. Such provisions may be general in nature, permitting the debtor or trustee to take actions to protect the interests of the debt holders, or they may be specific, for example, specifically authorizing the debtor to temporarily reduce the conversion price for the purpose of inducing conversion. Conversions pursuant to amended or altered conversion privileges on such instruments, even though they are literally "provided in the terms of the debt at issuance," should be included within the scope of [paragraphs .103A through .103D]. [FAS84, ¶29]

[3]A transaction that does not include the issuance of all of the equity securities issuable pursuant to the conversion privileges should not be characterized as a conversion transaction. [FAS84, ¶33]

prompt conversion of the debt to equity securities. [FAS84, ¶22] In a conversion pursuant to original conversion terms, debt is extinguished in exchange for equity pursuant to a preexisting contract that is already recognized in the financial statements, and no gain or loss is recognized upon conversion. [FAS84, ¶23]

Recognition of Expense upon Conversion

.103C When convertible debt is converted to equity securities of the debtor pursuant to an inducement offer described in paragraph .103A, the debtor enterprise shall recognize an expense equal to the fair value of all securities and other consideration transferred in the transaction in excess of the fair value of securities issuable pursuant to the original conversion terms. The expense shall not be reported as an extraordinary item. [FAS84, ¶3]

.103D The fair value of the securities or other consideration shall be measured as of the date the inducement offer is accepted by the convertible debt holder. Normally this will be the date the debt holder converts the convertible debt into equity securities or enters into a binding agreement to do so. [FAS84, ¶4] The transaction should not be recognized until the inducement offer has been accepted by the debt holder. [FAS84, ¶30]

Debt with Stock Purchase Warrants

.104 Unlike convertible debt, debt with detachable warrants to purchase stock is usually issued with the expectation that the debt will be repaid when it matures. Detachable warrants often trade separately from the debt instrument. Thus, the two elements of the security exist independently and may be treated as separate securities. [APB14, ¶13]

.105 The portion of the proceeds of debt securities issued with detachable stock purchase warrants that is allocable to the warrants shall be accounted for as additional paid-in capital. The allocation shall be based on the relative fair values of the two securities at time of issuance.[4] Any resulting discount or premium on the debt securities shall be accounted for as such.[5] The same accounting treatment applies to issues of debt securities (issued with detachable warrants) that may be surrendered in settlement of the exercise price of the warrant. However, if stock purchase warrants are not detachable from the debt and the debt security must be surrendered in order to exercise the warrant, the two securities taken together are substantially equivalent to convertible debt and the account-

[4]The time of issuance generally is the date when agreement as to terms has been reached and announced, even though the agreement is subject to certain further actions, such as directors' or stockholders' approval. [APB14, ¶16, fn2]

[5][Refer to Section I69, "Interest: Imputation of an Interest Cost," paragraph .108, footnote 4, for guidance regarding the amortization of debt discount and premium.]

ing specified in paragraph .103 shall apply. [APB14, ¶16] [Refer to paragraph .1001 for an EITF Issue that provides interpretive guidance on this paragraph.]

.106 If detachable warrants are issued in conjunction with debt as consideration in purchase transactions, the amounts attributable to each class of security issued shall be determined separately, based on values at the time of issuance.[6] The debt discount or premium is obtained by comparing the value attributed to the debt securities with the face amount thereof. [APB14, ¶17]

Other Types of Debt Securities

.107 It is not practicable in this section to discuss all possible types of debt with conversion features, debt issued with stock purchase warrants, or debt securities with a combination of such features. Securities not explicitly discussed in this section shall be dealt with in accordance with the substance of the transaction. For example, when convertible debt is issued at a substantial premium, there is a presumption that such premium represents additional paid-in capital. [APB14, ¶18]

Disclosures about Capital Structure

.107A [All entities, public and nonpublic, that have issued securities, including options, warrants, debt, and stock, must comply with the disclosure requirements of Section C24, "Capital Structure: Disclosures."]

Examples of Accounting for Conversion of Debt

.108 Paragraphs .109 to .114 present examples that illustrate application of [the requirements of paragraphs .103A through .103D]. The facts assumed are illustrative only and are not intended to modify or limit in any way the provisions of [these paragraphs]. For simplicity, the face amount of each security is assumed to be equal to its carrying amount in the financial statements (that is, no original issue premium or discount exists). [FAS84, ¶7]

Example 1

.109 On January 1, 19X4, Company A issues a $1,000 face amount 10 percent convertible bond maturing December 31, 20X3. The carrying amount of the bond in the financial statements of Company A is $1,000, and it is convertible into common shares of

[6][See footnote 4.]

Company A at a conversion price of $25 per share. On January 1, 19X6, the convertible bond has a market value of $1,700. To induce convertible bondholders to convert their bonds promptly, Company A reduces the conversion price to $20 for bondholders who convert prior to February 29, 19X6 (within 60 days). [FAS84, ¶8]

.110 Assuming the market price of Company A's common stock on the date of conversion is $40 per share, the fair value of the incremental consideration paid by Company A upon conversion is calculated as follows for each $1,000 bond that is converted prior to February 29, 19X6:

Value of securities issued[a]	$2,000
Value of securities issuable pursuant to original conversion privileges[b]	$1,600
Fair value of incremental consideration	$ 400

---

[a]Value of securities issued to debt holders is computed as follows:

Face amount		$1,000	
÷ New conversion price	÷	$ 20	per share
Number of common shares issued upon conversion		50	shares
× Price per common share	×	$ 40	per share
Value of securities issued		$2,000	

[b]Value of securities issuable pursuant to original conversion privileges is computed as follows:

Face amount		$1,000	
÷ Original conversion price	÷	$ 25	per share
Number of common shares issuable pursuant to original conversion privileges		40	shares
× Price per common share	×	$ 40	per share
Value of securities issuable pursuant to original conversion privileges		$1,600	

[FAS84, ¶9]

.111 Therefore, Company A records debt conversion expense equal to the fair value of the incremental consideration paid as follows:

	Debit	Credit
Convertible debt	1,000	
Debt conversion expense	400	
Common stock		1,400

[FAS84, ¶10]

Example 2

.112 On January 1, 19X1, Company B issues a $1,000 face amount 4 percent convertible bond maturing December 31, 20X0. The carrying amount of the bond in the financial statements of Company B is $1,000, and it is convertible into common shares of Company B at a conversion price of $25. On June 1, 19X4, the convertible bond has a market value of $500. To induce convertible bondholders to convert their bonds promptly, Company B reduces the conversion price to $20 for bondholders who convert prior to July 1, 19X4 (within 30 days). [FAS84, ¶11]

.113 Assuming the market price of Company B's common stock on the date of conversion is $12 per share, the fair value of the incremental consideration paid by Company B upon conversion is calculated as follows for each $1,000 bond that is converted prior to July 1, 19X4:

Value of securities issued[a]	$600
Value of securities issuable pursuant to original conversion privileges[b]	$480
Fair value of incremental consideration	$120

[a]Value of securities issued to debt holders is computed as follows:

Face amount		$1,000	
÷ New conversion price	÷	$ 20	per share
Number of common shares issued upon conversion		50	shares
× Price per common share	×	$ 12	per share
Value of securities issued		$ 600	

[b]Value of securities issuable pursuant to original conversion privileges is computed as follows:

Face amount		$1,000	
÷ Original conversion price	÷	$ 25	per share
Number of common shares issuable pursuant to original conversion privileges		40	shares
× Price per common share	×	$ 12	per share
Value of securities issuable pursuant to original conversion privileges		$ 480	

[FAS84, ¶12]

.114 Therefore, Company B records debt conversion expense equal to the fair value of the incremental consideration paid as follows:

	Debit	Credit
Convertible debt	1,000	
Debt conversion expense	120	
Common stock		1,120

The same accounting would apply if, instead of reducing the conversion price, Company B issued shares pursuant to a tender offer of 50 shares of its common stock for each $1,000 bond surrendered to the company before July 1, 19X4. Refer to paragraph .103A of this section. [FAS84, ¶13]

Supplemental Guidance

Accounting for the Conversion of Debt Pursuant to Original Conversion Terms

.501 In practice, the carrying amount of the debt, including any unamortized premium or discount, is credited to the capital accounts upon conversion to reflect the stock issued and no gain or loss is recognized. [AIN-APB26, #1]

Supplemental Guidance

Accounting for [illegible] Pursuant to Original Conversion Terms

[illegible]

Supplemental Guidance: Emerging Issues Task Force (EITF) Issues

.1000 [Listed below are EITF Issues that provide supplemental guidance for this section. These Issues are grouped by subject matter and may be either interpretive of or related by topic to the guidance in this section.

Convertible Debt with Warrants and Put Options

EITF Issue No. 85-9, "Revenue Recognition on Options to Purchase Stock of Another Entity"
EITF Issue No. 85-29, "Convertible Bonds with a 'Premium Put'"
EITF Issue No. 88-9, "Put Warrants"
EITF Topic No. D-60, "Accounting for the Issuance of Convertible Preferred Stock and Debt Securities with a Nondetachable Conversion Feature"

Other

EITF Issue No. 85-17, "Accrued Interest upon Conversion of Convertible Debt"
EITF Issue No. 86-28, "Accounting Implications of Indexed Debt Instruments"
EITF Issue No. 90-19, "Convertible Bonds with Issuer Option to Settle for Cash upon Conversion"
EITF Issue No. 98-5, "Accounting for Convertible Securities with Beneficial Conversion Features or Contingently Adjustable Conversion Ratios"
EITF Issue No. 99-1, "Accounting for Debt Convertible into the Stock of a Consolidated Subsidiary"
EITF Issue No. 00-19, "Accounting for Derivative Financial Instruments Indexed to, and Potentially Settled in, a Company's Own Stock"
EITF Issue No. 00-27, "Application of Issue No. 98-5 to Certain Convertible Instruments"
EITF Issue No. 01-1, "Accounting for a Convertible Instrument Granted or Issued to a Nonemployee for Goods or Services or a Combination of Goods or Services and Cash"
EITF Topic No. D-95, "Effect of Participating Convertible Securities on the Computation of Basic Earnings Per Share"]

.1001 [Listed below are EITF Issues that provide interpretive guidance on specific material in this section.

Paragraph .103 (APB 14, ¶12)—EITF Issue No. 99-1
Paragraph .105 (APB 14, ¶16)—EITF Issue No. 88-9]

(The next page is 11657.)

DEBT: PRODUCT FINANCING ARRANGEMENTS SECTION D18

Source: FASB Statement 49

[**Note:** A list of Issues discussed by the Emerging Issues Task Force (EITF) that provide supplemental guidance for this section is presented in paragraph .1000.]

Summary

A product financing arrangement is a transaction in which an enterprise sells and agrees to repurchase inventory with the repurchase price equal to the original sale price plus carrying and financing costs, or other similar transactions. This section specifies criteria for determining when an arrangement involving the sale of inventory is in substance a financing arrangement. A product financing arrangement shall be accounted for as a borrowing rather than as a sale.

Applicability and Scope

.101 **Product financing arrangements** include agreements in which a sponsor (the enterprise seeking to finance product pending its future use or resale) either:

a. Sells the product to another enterprise (the enterprise through which the financing flows), and in a related transaction agrees to repurchase the product (or a substantially identical product)
b. Arranges for another enterprise to purchase the product on the sponsor's behalf and, in a related transaction, agrees to purchase the product from the other enterprise
c. Controls the disposition of the product that has been purchased by another enterprise in accordance with the arrangements described in either (a) or (b) above.

In all of the foregoing cases, the sponsor agrees to purchase the product, or processed goods of which the product is a component, from the other enterprise at specified prices over specified periods or, to the extent that it does not do so, guarantees resale prices to third parties (refer to paragraph .103(a)(1)). Paragraphs .108 through .114 illustrate each of the types of arrangements described in (a) and (b) above. [FAS49, ¶3]

.102 Other characteristics that commonly exist in product financing arrangements but that are not necessarily present in all such arrangements are:

a. The enterprise that purchases the product from the sponsor or purchases it directly from a third party on behalf of the sponsor was established expressly for that purpose or is an existing trust, nonbusiness organization, or credit grantor.

b. The product covered by the financing arrangement is to be used or sold by the sponsor, although a portion may be sold by the other enterprise directly to third parties.
c. The product covered by the financing arrangement is stored on the sponsor's premises.
d. The debt of the enterprise that purchases the product being financed is guaranteed by the sponsor.

[FAS49, ¶4]

.103 This section applies to product financing arrangements for products[1] that have been produced by or were originally purchased by the sponsor or purchased by another enterprise on behalf of the sponsor and have both of the following characteristics:

a. The financing arrangement requires the sponsor to purchase the product, a substantially identical product, or processed goods of which the product is a component at specified prices. The specified prices are not subject to change except for fluctuations due to finance and holding costs. This characteristic of predetermined prices also is present if any of the following circumstances exists:
   (1) The specified prices in the financing arrangement are in the form of resale price guarantees under which the sponsor agrees to make up any difference between the specified price and the resale price for products sold to third parties.
   (2) The sponsor is not required to purchase the product but has an option to purchase the product, the economic effect of which compels the sponsor to purchase the product; for example, an option arrangement that provides for a significant penalty if the sponsor does not exercise the option to purchase.
   (3) The sponsor is not required by the agreement to purchase the product but the other enterprise has an option whereby it can require the sponsor to purchase the product.
b. The payments that the other enterprise will receive on the transaction are established by the financing arrangement, and the amounts to be paid by the sponsor will be adjusted, as necessary, to cover substantially all fluctuations in costs incurred by the other enterprise in purchasing and holding the product (including interest).[2]

[FAS49, ¶5]

---

[1]Unmined or unharvested natural resources and financial instruments are not considered to be a product for purposes of this section. [FAS49, ¶5, fn2]

[2]The characteristic described in paragraph .103(b) ordinarily is not present in [FAS49, ¶5, fn3] (a) ordinary purchase commitments in which the risks and rewards of ownership are retained by the seller (for example, a manufacturer or other supplier) until the product is transferred to a purchaser or (b) typical contractor-subcontractor relationships in which the contractor is not in substance the owner of product held by the subcontractor and the obligation of the contractor is contingent on substantial performance on the part of the subcontractor. [FAS49, ¶18]

.104 This section does not modify any of the provisions of Section R75, "Revenue Recognition," paragraphs .105 through .109, and does not apply to transactions for which sales revenue is recognized currently in accordance with those provisions of that section. [FAS49, ¶6]

.105 The accounting for product financing arrangements specified by this section differs from the accounting for long-term unconditional purchase obligations (for example, take-or-pay contracts) specified by Section C32, "Commitments: Long-Term Obligations." [FAS49, ¶20] This section concludes that, [in a product financing arrangement that has the characteristics described in paragraph .103,] the sponsor is in substance the owner of the product and that the sponsor should, therefore, report the product as an asset and the related obligation as a liability. At the time a take-or-pay contract is entered into, by contrast, either the product does not yet exist (for example, electricity) or the product exists in a form unsuitable to the purchaser (for example, unmined coal); the purchaser has a right to receive future product but is not the substantive owner of existing product. [FAS49, ¶22]

Accounting for Product Financing Arrangements

.106 Product and obligations under product financing arrangements that have both of the characteristics described in paragraph .103 shall be accounted for by the sponsor as follows:

a. If a sponsor sells a product to another enterprise and, in a related transaction, agrees to repurchase the product (or a substantially identical product) or processed goods of which the product is a component, the sponsor shall record a liability at the time the proceeds are received from the other enterprise to the extent that the product is covered by the financing arrangement. The sponsor shall not record the transaction as a sale and shall not remove the covered product from its balance sheet.
b. If the sponsor is a party to an arrangement whereby another enterprise purchases a product on the sponsor's behalf and, in a related transaction, the sponsor agrees to purchase the product or processed goods of which the product is a component from the enterprise, the sponsor shall record the asset and the related liability when the product is purchased by the other enterprise.

[FAS49, ¶8]

.107 Costs of the product, excluding processing costs, in excess of the sponsor's original production or purchase costs or the other enterprise's purchase costs represent financing and holding costs. The sponsor shall account for such costs in accordance with the sponsor's accounting policies applicable to financing and holding costs as those costs are incurred by the other enterprise. For example, if insurance costs ordinarily are accounted for as period costs by the sponsor, similar costs associated with the product covered by financing arrangements shall be expensed by the sponsor as those costs are incurred by the other enterprise. Interest costs associated with the product covered by financing arrangements shall be identified separately and accounted for by the sponsor in accordance with Section I67, "Interest: Capitalization of Interest Costs," as those costs are incurred by the other enterprise. [FAS49, ¶9]

Illustrations of the Application of This Section to Common Product Financing Arrangements

.108 Paragraphs .109 through .114 illustrate how this section applies to two common product financing arrangements. The facts assumed in the examples are illustrative only and are not intended to modify or limit in any way the provisions of this section. The facts assumed in each case could vary in one or more respects without altering the application of the provisions of this section. [FAS49, ¶25]

Example 1

.109 An enterprise (sponsor) sells a portion of its inventory to another enterprise (the enterprise through which the financing flows), and in a related transaction agrees to repurchase the inventory (refer to paragraph .101(a)). [FAS49, ¶26]

Assumptions and Provisions of the Financing Arrangement

.110 The sponsor arranges for the other enterprise to acquire a portion of the sponsor's inventory. The other enterprise's sole asset is the transferred inventory that is, in turn, used as collateral for bank financing. The proceeds of the bank financing are then remitted to the sponsor. The debt of the other enterprise is guaranteed by the sponsor. The inventory is stored in a public warehouse during the holding period. The sponsor, in connection with the "sale" (legal title passes to the enterprise), enters into a financing arrangement under which:

a. The sponsor agrees to pay all costs of the other enterprise associated with the inventory, including holding and storage costs.
b. The sponsor agrees to pay the other enterprise interest on the purchase price of the inventory equivalent to the interest and fees incurred in connection with the bank financing.
c. The sponsor agrees to repurchase the inventory from the other enterprise at a specified future date for the same price originally paid by the enterprise to purchase the inventory irrespective of changes in market prices during the holding period.
d. The other enterprise agrees not to assign or otherwise encumber the inventory during its ownership period, except to the extent of providing collateral for the bank financing.

[FAS49, ¶27]

Application of the Provisions of This Section

.111 In the product financing arrangement outlined above, both of the characteristics in paragraph .103 are present; accordingly, the sponsor neither records the transaction as a sale of inventory nor removes the inventory from its balance sheet. The sponsor recognizes a liability when the proceeds are received from the other enterprise. Financing and holding costs are accrued by the sponsor as incurred by the other enterprise and accounted for in accordance with the sponsor's accounting policies for such costs. Interest costs are separately identified and accounted for in accordance with Section I67. [FAS49, ¶28]

Example 2

.112 A sponsor arranges for another enterprise to buy product on the sponsor's behalf with a related agreement to purchase the product from the other enterprise (refer to paragraph .101(b)). [FAS49, ¶29]

Assumptions and Provisions of the Financing Arrangement

.113 The sponsor arranges for the other enterprise to purchase on its behalf an existing supply of fuel. In a related agreement, the sponsor agrees to purchase the fuel from the other enterprise over a specified period and at specified prices. The prices established are adequate to cover all financing and holding costs of the other enterprise. The other enterprise finances the purchase of fuel using the fuel and the agreement as collateral. [FAS49, ¶30]

Application of the Provisions of This Section

.114 In the product financing arrangement described above, both of the characteristics in paragraph .103 are present; accordingly, the sponsor reports the asset (fuel) and the related liability on its balance sheet when the fuel is acquired by the other enterprise. Financing and holding costs are accrued by the sponsor as incurred by the other enterprise and accounted for in accordance with the sponsor's accounting policies for financing and holding costs. Interest costs are separately identified and accounted for in accordance with Section I67. [FAS49, ¶31]

[illegible]

Application of the Provisions of This Section

[illegible]

[illegible]

[illegible]

[illegible]

Application of the Provisions of This Section

[illegible]

[illegible]

Glossary

.401 **Product financing arrangements.** Includes agreements in which a sponsor (the enterprise seeking to finance product pending its future use or resale):

a. Sells the product to another enterprise (the enterprise through which the financing flows), and in a related transaction agrees to repurchase the product (or a substantially identical product)
b. Arranges for another enterprise to purchase the product on the sponsor's behalf and, in a related transaction, agrees to purchase the product from the other enterprise
c. Controls the disposition of the product that has been purchased by another enterprise in accordance with the arrangements described in either (a) or (b) above.

In all of the foregoing cases, the sponsor agrees to purchase the product, or processed goods of which the product is a component, from the other enterprise at specified prices over specified periods or, to the extent that it does not do so, guarantees resale to third parties [(refer to paragraphs .101 through .103)]. [FAS49, ¶3]

Supplemental Guidance: Emerging Issues Task Force (EITF) Issues

.1000 [Listed below is an EITF Issue that provides supplemental guidance for this section. This Issue is related by topic to the guidance in this section.

EITF Issue No. 98-12, "Application of Issue No. 00-19 to Forward Equity Sales Transactions"]

(The next page is 11825.)

DEBT: RESTRUCTURINGS SECTION D22

Sources: FASB Statement 15; FASB Statement 91; FASB Statement 114; FASB Statement 141; FASB Statement 144; FASB Technical Bulletin 80-2; FASB Technical Bulletin 81-6

[**Note:** A list of Issues discussed by the Emerging Issues Task Force (EITF) that provide supplemental guidance for this section is presented in paragraph .1000.]

Summary

This section presents standards of financial accounting and reporting by debtors and creditors for a troubled debt restructuring. A restructuring of debt constitutes a troubled debt restructuring if the creditor, for reasons related to the debtor's financial difficulties, grants a concession to the debtor that it would not otherwise consider. This section does not apply to routine changes in debt terms.

The accounting for a troubled debt restructuring is based on the type of the restructuring, and this section identifies two primary types of restructurings: (a) a transfer of assets (or equity interest) from a debtor to a creditor in full settlement of a debt and (b) a modification of terms.

If a debtor satisfies a debt in full by transferring assets, or by granting an equity interest, to a creditor and the fair market value of the assets transferred or equity interest granted is less than the carrying value of the debt (or, in the case of the creditor, is less than the recorded investment in the debt) the difference generally is an extraordinary gain to the debtor and ordinary loss to the creditor. Also, the debtor must recognize a gain or loss for any difference between the carrying value of the assets transferred and their fair value. Subsequent accounting for assets received in a troubled debt restructuring is the same as if the assets were acquired for cash.

If a creditor receives assets or an equity interest in the debtor in full satisfaction of a receivable, the creditor accounts for those assets at their fair value at the time of the restructuring and accounts for those assets received the same as if the assets had been acquired for cash.

For a creditor in a troubled debt restructuring in fiscal years beginning before December 16, 1994 involving only a modification of terms, the effects of the restructuring shall be accounted for prospectively from the time of restructuring, as long as the loan is not impaired based on the terms of the restructuring agreement. No gain or loss shall be recorded at the time of restructuring unless the carrying amount of the debt (or, in the case of the creditor, the recorded investment in the debt) exceeds the total future cash payments (or receipts) specified by the new terms. A creditor in a troubled debt restructuring in fiscal years beginning after December 15, 1994 involving a modification of terms or in a troubled debt restructuring in fiscal years beginning before December 16, 1994 that becomes impaired after that date based on the terms of the restructuring agreement shall account for the restructured loan in accordance with the provisions of Section I08, "Impairment."

Scope

.101 This section [presents] standards of financial accounting and reporting by the debtor and by the creditor for a troubled **debt** restructuring. [FAS15, ¶1]

.101A A creditor in a troubled debt restructuring involving a modification of terms shall account for the restructured loan in accordance with [paragraphs .139 through .146 and] the provisions of paragraphs .102 through .119 of Section I08, "Impairment," except that a troubled debt restructuring involving a modification of terms in fiscal years beginning before December 16, 1994[a] may continue to be accounted for and disclosed in accordance with this section [(paragraphs .126 through .138)] as long as the restructured loan [(a)] is not impaired based on the terms of the restructuring agreement [FAS114, ¶22(a)] [and (b) is not a *security* as defined in paragraph .406 of Section I80, "Investments: Debt and Equity Securities." Also refer to paragraphs .503 and .504 of Section I80 for further guidance on that section's applicability to loans restructured in a troubled debt restructuring.]

.102 For purposes of this section, **troubled debt restructurings** do not include changes in lease agreements (the accounting [for which] is prescribed by Section L10, "Leases") or employment-related agreements (for example, pension plans and deferred compensation contracts). Nor do troubled debt restructurings include debtors' failures to pay trade accounts according to their terms or creditors' delays in taking legal action to collect overdue amounts of interest and principal, unless they involve an agreement between debtor and creditor to restructure. [FAS15, ¶8]

[[a]Restructurings in those fiscal years are before the required effective date for the provisions of Section I08, paragraphs .102 through .119. If a creditor initially applies Section I08, paragraphs .102 through .119 earlier than the required effective date (fiscal years beginning after December 15, 1994), the provisions described in paragraph .123(b)(1) become effective at that time.]

.103 This section shall be applied to troubled debt restructurings consummated under reorganization, arrangement, or other provisions of the Federal Bankruptcy Act or other federal statutes related thereto.[1] [FAS15, ¶10]

Troubled Debt Restructuring

.104 A restructuring of debt constitutes a *troubled debt restructuring,* for purposes of this section, if the creditor for economic or legal reasons related to the debtor's financial difficulties grants a concession to the debtor that it would not otherwise consider. That concession either stems from an agreement between the creditor and the debtor or is imposed by law or a court. For example, a creditor may restructure the terms of a debt to alleviate the burden of the debtor's near-term cash requirements, and many troubled debt restructurings involve modifying terms to reduce or defer cash payments required of the debtor in the near future to help the debtor attempt to improve its financial condition and eventually be able to pay the creditor. Or, for example, the creditor may accept cash, other assets, or an equity interest in the debtor in satisfaction of the debt though the value received is less than the amount of the debt because the creditor concludes that step will maximize recovery of its investment.[2] [FAS15, ¶2]

.105 A troubled debt restructuring may include, but is not necessarily limited to, one or a combination of the following:

a. Transfer from the debtor to the creditor of receivables from third parties, real estate, or other assets to satisfy fully or partially a debt (including a transfer resulting from foreclosure or repossession)
b. Issuance or other granting of an equity interest to the creditor by the debtor to satisfy fully or partially a debt unless the equity interest is granted pursuant to existing terms for converting the debt into an equity interest
c. Modification of terms of a debt, such as one or a combination of:
   (1) Reduction (absolute or contingent) of the stated interest rate for the remaining original life of the debt
   (2) Extension of the maturity date or dates at a stated interest rate lower than the current market rate for new debt with similar risk

[1]The section does not apply, however, if under provisions of those federal statutes or in a quasi reorganization or corporate readjustment (refer to Section Q15, "Quasi Reorganizations") with which a troubled debt restructuring coincides, the debtor restates its liabilities generally. [FAS15, ¶10, fn4] [Refer to paragraphs .509 through .513 for guidance regarding a general restatement of a debtor's liabilities in bankruptcy situations.]

[2]Although troubled debt that is fully satisfied by foreclosure, repossession, or other transfer of assets or by grant of equity securities by the debtor is, in a technical sense, not restructured, that kind of event is included in the term *troubled debt restructuring* in this section. [FAS15, ¶2, fn1] [Refer to paragraph .1001 for an EITF Issue that provides interpretive guidance on this footnote.]

(3) Reduction (absolute or contingent) of the face amount or maturity amount of the debt as stated in the instrument or other agreement
(4) Reduction (absolute or contingent) of accrued interest.

[FAS15, ¶5]

.106 Whatever the form of concession granted by the creditor to the debtor in a troubled debt restructuring, the creditor's objective is to make the best of a difficult situation. That is, the creditor expects to obtain more cash or other value from the debtor, or to increase the probability of receipt, by granting the concession than by not granting it. [FAS15, ¶3]

.107 A debt restructuring is not necessarily a troubled debt restructuring, for purposes of this section, even if the debtor is experiencing some financial difficulties. For example, a troubled debt restructuring is not involved if (a) the fair value of cash, other assets, or an equity interest accepted by a creditor from a debtor in full satisfaction of its receivable at least equals the creditor's **recorded investment in the receivable;**[3] (b) the fair value of cash, other assets, or an equity interest transferred by a debtor to a creditor in full settlement of its payable at least equals the debtor's **carrying amount of the payable;** (c) the creditor reduces the effective interest rate on the debt primarily to reflect a decrease in market interest rates in general or a decrease in the risk so as to maintain a relationship with a debtor that can readily obtain funds from other sources at the current market interest rate; or (d) the debtor issues in exchange for its debt new marketable debt having an effective interest rate based on its market price that is at or near the current market interest rates of debt with similar maturity dates and stated interest rates issued by nontroubled debtors. In general, a debtor that can obtain funds from sources other than the existing creditor at market interest rates at or near those for nontroubled debt is not involved in a troubled debt restructuring. A debtor in a troubled debt restructuring can obtain funds from sources other than the existing creditor in the troubled debt restructuring, if at all, only at effective interest rates (based on market prices) so high that it cannot afford to pay them. [FAS15, ¶7]

Accounting by Debtors

.108 A debtor shall account for a troubled debt restructuring according to the type of the restructuring as prescribed in paragraphs .109 through .122. [FAS15, ¶12]

[3][Refer to paragraphs .506 through .508 for further guidance regarding when a debt restructuring can be a troubled debt restructuring for the debtor but not for the creditor.]

Transfer of Assets in Full Settlement

.109 A debtor that transfers its receivables from third parties, real estate, or other assets to a creditor to settle fully a payable shall recognize a gain on restructuring of payables. The gain shall be measured by the excess of (a) the carrying amount of the payable settled over (b) the fair value of the assets transferred to the creditor.[4] The fair value of the assets transferred is the amount that the debtor could reasonably expect to receive for them in a current sale between a willing buyer and a willing seller, that is, other than in a forced or liquidation sale. Fair value of assets shall be measured by their market value if an active market for them exists. If no active market exists for the assets transferred but exists for similar assets, the selling prices in that market may be helpful in estimating the fair value of the assets transferred. If no market price is available, a forecast of expected cash flows may aid in estimating the fair value of assets transferred, provided the expected cash flows are discounted at a rate commensurate with the risk involved.[5] [FAS15, ¶13]

.110 A difference between the fair value and the carrying amount of assets transferred to a creditor to settle a payable is a gain or loss on transfer of assets.[6] The debtor shall include that gain or loss in measuring net income for the period of transfer, reported as provided in Section I17, "Income Statement Presentation: Extraordinary Items," or Section I22, "Income Statement Presentation: Unusual or Infrequent Items." [FAS15, ¶14]

---

[4]Paragraphs .109, .111, and .115 indicate that the fair value of assets transferred or the fair value of an equity interest granted shall be used in accounting for a settlement of a payable in a troubled debt restructuring. That guidance is not intended to preclude using the fair value of the payable settled if more clearly evident than the fair value of the assets transferred or of the equity interest granted in a full settlement of a payable (refer to paragraphs .109 and .111). [FAS15, ¶13, fn5] (Refer to Section B51, "Business Combinations," paragraph .105.) [FAS141, ¶E6(a)] However, in a partial settlement of a payable (refer to paragraph .115), the fair value of the assets transferred or of the equity interest granted shall be used in all cases to avoid the need to allocate the fair value of the payable between the part settled and the part still outstanding. [FAS15, ¶13, fn5]

[5]Some factors that may be relevant in estimating the fair value of various kinds of assets are described in [FAS15, ¶13, fn6] Section B51, paragraphs .136 and .137, [FAS141, ¶E6(b)] Section I69, "Interest: Imputation of an Interest Cost," paragraphs .105 through .107, and Section N35, "Nonmonetary Transactions," paragraph .111. [FAS15, ¶13, fn6]

[6]The carrying amount of a receivable encompasses not only unamortized premium, discount, acquisition costs, and the like but also an allowance for uncollectible amounts and other *valuation* accounts, if any. A loss on transferring receivables to creditors may therefore have been wholly or partially recognized in measuring net income before the transfer and be wholly or partly a reduction of a valuation account rather than a gain or loss in measuring net income for the period of the transfer. [FAS15, ¶14, fn7]

Grant of Equity Interest in Full Settlement

.111 A debtor that issues or otherwise grants an equity interest to a creditor to settle fully a payable shall account for the equity interest at its fair value.[7] The difference between the fair value of the equity interest granted and the carrying amount of the payable settled shall be recognized as a gain on restructuring of payables. [FAS15, ¶15]

Modification of Terms

.112 A debtor in a troubled debt restructuring involving only modification of terms of a payable—that is, not involving a transfer of assets or grant of an equity interest—shall account for the effects of the restructuring prospectively from the **time of restructuring,** and shall not change the carrying amount of the payable at the time of the restructuring unless the carrying amount exceeds the total future cash payments specified by the new terms.[8] That is, the effects of changes in the amounts or timing (or both) of future cash payments designated as either interest or face amount shall be reflected in future periods.[9] Interest expense shall be computed in a way that a constant effective interest rate is applied to the carrying amount of the payable at the beginning of each period between restructuring and maturity (in substance the *interest* method prescribed by Section I69, "Interest: Imputation of an Interest Cost," paragraph .108). The new effective interest rate shall be the discount rate that equates the present value of the future cash payments specified by the new terms (excluding amounts contingently payable) with the carrying amount of the payable. [FAS15, ¶16] [Refer to paragraph .1001 for an EITF Issue that provides interpretive guidance on paragraphs .112 through .114.]

.113 If, however, the total future cash payments specified by the new terms of a payable, including both payments designated as interest and those designated as face amount, are less than the carrying amount of the payable, the debtor shall reduce the carrying amount to an amount equal to the total future cash payments specified by the new terms and shall recognize a gain on restructuring of payables equal to the amount of the reduc-

[7]Refer to footnote 4. [FAS15, ¶15, fn8]

[8]In this section, *total future cash payments* includes related accrued interest, if any, at the time of the restructuring that continues to be payable under the new terms. [FAS15, ¶16, fn9]

[9]All or a portion of the carrying amount of the payable at the time of the restructuring may need to be reclassified in the balance sheet because of changes in the terms, for example, a change in the amount of the payable due within one year after the date of the debtor's balance sheet. A troubled debt restructuring of a short-term obligation after the date of a debtor's balance sheet but before that balance sheet is issued may affect the classification of that obligation in accordance with Section B05, "Balance Sheet Classification: Current Assets and Current Liabilities." [FAS15, ¶16, fn10]

tion.[10] Thereafter, all cash payments under the terms of the payable shall be accounted for as reductions of the carrying amount of the payable, and no interest expense shall be recognized on the payable for any period between the restructuring and maturity of the payable.[11] [FAS15, ¶17]

.114 A debtor shall not recognize a gain on a restructured payable involving indeterminate future cash payments as long as the maximum total future cash payments may exceed the carrying amount of the payable. Amounts designated either as interest or as face amount by the new terms may be payable contingent on a specified event or circumstance (for example, the debtor may be required to pay specified amounts if its financial condition improves to a specified degree within a specified period). To determine whether the debtor shall recognize a gain according to the provisions of paragraphs .111 and .112, those contingent amounts shall be included in the *total future cash payments specified by the new terms* to the extent necessary to prevent recognizing a gain at the time of restructuring that may be offset by future interest expense. Thus, the debtor shall apply [the provisions of] Section C59, "Contingencies," paragraph .118, in which probability of occurrence of a gain contingency is not a factor, and shall assume that contingent future payments will have to be paid. The same principle applies to amounts of future cash payments that must sometimes be estimated to apply the provisions of paragraphs .112 and .113. For example, if the number of future interest payments is flexible because the face amount and accrued interest is payable on demand or becomes payable on demand, estimates of total future cash payments shall be based on the maximum number of periods possible under the restructured terms. [FAS15, ¶18]

Combination of Types

.115 A troubled debt restructuring may involve partial settlement of a payable by the debtor's transferring assets or granting an equity interest (or both) to the creditor and modification of terms of the remaining payable.[12] A debtor shall account for a troubled debt restructuring involving a partial settlement and a modification of terms as prescribed in paragraphs .112 through .114 except that, first, assets transferred or an equity

[10] If the carrying amount of the payable comprises several accounts (for example, face amount, accrued interest, and unamortized premium, discount, finance charges, and issue costs) that are to be continued after the restructuring, some possibly being combined, the reduction in carrying amount may need to be allocated among the remaining accounts in proportion to the previous balances. However, the debtor may choose to carry the amount designated as face amount by the new terms in a separate account and adjust another account accordingly. [FAS15, ¶17, fn11]

[11] The only exception is to recognize interest expense according to paragraph .118. [FAS15, ¶17, fn12]

[12] Even if the stated terms of the remaining payable, for example, the stated interest rate and the maturity date or dates, are not changed in connection with the transfer of assets or grant of an equity interest, the restructuring shall be accounted for as prescribed by paragraph .115. [FAS15, ¶19, fn13]

interest granted in that partial settlement shall be measured as prescribed in paragraphs .109 and .111, respectively, and the carrying amount of the payable shall be reduced by the total fair value of those assets or equity interest.[13] A difference between the fair value and the carrying amount of assets transferred to the creditor shall be recognized as a gain or loss on transfer of assets. No gain on restructuring of payables shall be recognized unless the remaining carrying amount of the payable exceeds the total future cash payments (including amounts contingently payable) specified by the terms of the debt remaining unsettled after the restructuring. Future interest expense, if any, shall be determined according to the provisions of paragraphs .112 through .114. [FAS15, ¶19]

Related Matters

.116 A troubled debt restructuring that is in substance a repossession or foreclosure by the creditor or other transfer of assets to the creditor shall be accounted for according to the provisions of paragraphs .109, .110, and .115. [FAS15, ¶20]

.117 [Deleted 4/02 because of FASB Statement 145, *Rescission of FASB Statements No. 4, 44, and 64, Amendment of FASB Statement No. 13, and Technical Corrections*.]

.118 If a troubled debt restructuring involves amounts contingently payable, those contingent amounts shall be recognized as a payable and as interest expense in future periods in accordance with Section C59. Thus, in general, interest expense for contingent payments shall be recognized in each period in which (a) it is probable that a liability has been incurred and (b) the amount of that liability can be reasonably estimated. Before recognizing a payable and interest expense for amounts contingently payable, however, accrual or payment of those amounts shall be deducted from the carrying amount of the restructured payable to the extent that contingent payments included in *total future cash payments specified by the new terms* prevented recognition of a gain at the time of restructuring (refer to paragraph .114). [FAS15, ¶22]

.119 If amounts of future cash payments must be estimated to apply the provisions of paragraphs .112 through .114 because future interest payments are expected to fluctuate—for example, the restructured terms may specify the stated interest rate to be the prime interest rate increased by a specified amount or proportion—estimates of maximum total future payments shall be based on the interest rate in effect at the time of the restructuring. Fluctuations in the effective interest rate after the restructuring from changes in the prime rate or other causes shall be accounted for as changes in estimates in the periods the changes occur. However, the accounting for those fluctuations shall not result in rec-

[13]If cash is paid in partial settlement of a payable in a troubled debt restructuring, the carrying amount of the payable shall be reduced by the amount of cash paid. [FAS15, ¶19, fn14]

ognizing a gain on restructuring that may be offset by future cash payments (refer to paragraphs .114 and .118). Rather, the carrying amount of the restructured payable shall remain unchanged, and future cash payments shall reduce the carrying amount until the time that any gain recognized cannot be offset by future cash payments. [FAS15, ¶23]

.120 Legal fees and other direct costs that a debtor incurs in granting an equity interest to a creditor in a troubled debt restructuring shall reduce the amount otherwise recorded for that equity interest according to paragraphs .111 and .115. All other direct costs that a debtor incurs to effect a troubled debt restructuring shall be deducted in measuring gain on restructuring of payables or shall be included in expense for the period if no gain on restructuring is recognized. [FAS15, ¶24]

Disclosure by Debtors

.121 A debtor shall disclose, either in the body of the financial statements or in the accompanying notes, the following information about troubled debt restructurings that have occurred during a period for which financial statements are presented:

a. For each restructuring:[14] a description of the principal changes in terms, the major features of settlement, or both
b. Aggregate gain on restructuring of payables
c. Aggregate net gain or loss on transfers of assets recognized during the period (refer to paragraphs .110 and .115)
d. Per share amount of the aggregate gain on restructuring of payables.

[FAS15, ¶25]

.122 A debtor shall disclose in financial statements for periods after a troubled debt restructuring the extent to which amounts contingently payable are included in the carrying amount of restructured payables pursuant to the provisions of paragraph .114. If required by Section C59, a debtor shall also disclose in those financial statements total amounts that are contingently payable on restructured payables and the conditions under which those amounts would become payable or would be forgiven. [Refer to Section F25, "Financial Instruments: Disclosure," for guidance on possible additional disclosure requirements.] [FAS15, ¶26]

[14]Separate restructurings within a fiscal period for the same category of payables (for example, accounts payable or subordinated debentures) may be grouped for disclosure purposes. [FAS15, ¶25, fn15]

Accounting by Creditors

.123 A creditor shall account for a troubled debt restructuring according to the type of the restructuring as prescribed in the following paragraphs: [FAS15, ¶27]

[a. A restructuring where there is a receipt of assets in full satisfaction of the loan is accounted for in accordance with paragraphs .124 and .125.

b. A restructuring where there is only a modification of terms or a restructuring where there is a combination of types (that is, both a receipt of assets and a modification of terms) is accounted for as follows:

(1) *Restructurings in fiscal years beginning before December 16, 1994*[14a]

(a) A troubled debt restructuring involving a modification of terms which *is not* impaired based on the terms of the restructuring agreement may be accounted for in accordance with paragraphs .126 through .138.

(b) A troubled debt restructuring involving a modification of terms which *is* impaired based on the terms of the restructuring agreement is accounted for in accordance with paragraphs .139 through .146 and Section I08, paragraphs .102 through .119.

(2) *Restructurings in fiscal years beginning after December 15, 1994*[14b]

A troubled debt restructuring involving a modification of terms is accounted for in accordance with the provisions of paragraphs .139 through .146 and Section I08, paragraphs .102 through .119.]

Paragraphs .124 through [.146] do not apply to a receivable that the creditor is accounting for at market value in accordance with specialized industry practice (for example, a marketable debt security accounted for at market value by a mutual fund). Estimated cash expected to be received less estimated costs expected to be incurred is not market value in accordance with specialized industry practice as that term is used in this paragraph. [FAS15, ¶27]

[[14a]Restructurings in those fiscal years are before the required effective date for the provisions of Section I08, paragraphs .102 through .119. If a creditor initially applies Section I08, paragraphs .102 through .119 earlier than the required effective date (fiscal years beginning after December 15, 1994), the provisions described in paragraph .123(b)(2) above should be applied to all loans restructured on or after that date of initial application.]

[[14b]Restructurings in those fiscal years are after the required effective date for the provisions of Section I08, paragraphs .102 through .119. If a creditor initially applies Section I08, paragraphs .102 through .119 earlier than the required effective date (fiscal years beginning after December 15, 1994), the provisions described in .123(b)(2) above become effective at that time.]

Receipt of Assets in Full Satisfaction

.124 A creditor that receives from a debtor in full satisfaction of a receivable either (a) receivables from third parties, real estate, or other assets or (b) shares of stock or other evidence of an equity interest in the debtor, or both, shall account for those assets (including an equity interest) at their fair value at the time of the restructuring (refer to paragraph .109 for how to measure fair value).[15] [FAS15, ¶28] A creditor that receives long-lived assets that will be sold from a debtor in full satisfaction of a receivable shall account for those assets at their fair value less cost to sell, as that term is used in paragraph .111 of Section D60, "Disposal of Long-Lived Assets." [FAS144, ¶C24(a)] The excess of (a) the recorded investment in the receivable satisfied over (b) the fair value of assets received (less cost to sell, if required above) is a loss to be recognized. For purposes of this paragraph, losses, to the extent they are not offset against allowances for uncollectible amounts or other valuation accounts, shall be included in measuring net income for the period. [FAS144, ¶C24(b)] [Refer to paragraph .1001 for EITF Issues that provide interpretive guidance on this paragraph.]

.125 After a troubled debt restructuring, a creditor shall account for assets received in satisfaction of a receivable the same as if the assets had been acquired for cash. [FAS15, ¶29]

Restructurings in Fiscal Years Beginning before December 16, 1994[15a]

Modification of Terms

.126 A creditor in a troubled debt restructuring involving only modification of terms of a receivable—that is, not involving receipt of assets (including an equity interest in the debtor)—shall account for the effects of the restructuring prospectively and shall not change the recorded investment in the receivable at the time of the restructuring unless that amount exceeds the *total future cash receipts specified by the new terms.*[16] That is, the effects of changes in the amounts or timing (or both) of future cash receipts designated either as

[15]Paragraphs .124 and .129 indicate that the fair value of assets received shall be used in accounting for satisfaction of a receivable in a troubled debt restructuring. That guidance is not intended to preclude using the fair value of the receivable satisfied if more clearly evident than the fair value of the assets received in full satisfaction of a receivable (refer to paragraph .124). [FAS15, ¶28, fn16] (Refer to Section B51, paragraph .105.) [FAS141, ¶E6(c)] However, in a partial satisfaction of a receivable (refer to paragraph .129), the fair value of the assets received shall be used in all cases to avoid the need to allocate the fair value of the receivable between the part satisfied and the part still outstanding. [FAS15, ¶28, fn16]

[[15a] Refer to footnote 14a.]

[16]In this section, *total future cash receipts* include related accrued interest, if any, at the time of the restructuring that continues to be receivable under the new terms. Uncertainty of collection of noncontingent amounts specified by the new terms (refer to paragraph .128 for inclusion of contingent amounts) is not a factor in applying paragraphs .126 through .128 but should, of course, be considered in accounting for allowances for uncollectible amounts. [FAS15, ¶30, fn18]

interest or as face amount shall be reflected in future periods.[17] Interest income shall be computed in a way that a constant effective interest rate is applied to the recorded investment in the receivable at the beginning of each period between restructuring and maturity (in substance the *interest* method prescribed by Section I69, paragraph .108). The new effective interest rate shall be the discount rate that equates the present value of the future cash receipts specified by the new terms (excluding amounts contingently receivable) with the recorded investment in the receivable. [FAS15, ¶30]

.127 If, however, the total future cash receipts specified by the new terms of the receivable, including both receipts designated as interest and those designated as face amount, are less than the recorded investment in the receivable before restructuring, the creditor shall reduce the recorded investment in the receivable to an amount equal to the total future cash receipts specified by the new terms. The amount of the reduction is a loss to be recognized according to paragraph .131. Thereafter, all cash receipts by the creditor under the terms of the restructured receivable, whether designated as interest or as face amount, shall be accounted for as recovery of the recorded investment in the receivable, and no interest income shall be recognized on the receivable for any period between the restructuring and maturity of the receivable.[19] [FAS15, ¶31]

.128 A creditor shall recognize a loss on a restructured receivable involving indeterminate future cash receipts unless the minimum future cash receipts specified by the new terms at least equal the recorded investment in the receivable. Amounts designated either as interest or as face amount that are receivable from the debtor may be contingent on a specified event or circumstance (for example, specified amounts may be receivable from the debtor if the debtor's financial condition improves to a specified degree within a specified period). To determine whether the creditor shall recognize a loss according to the provisions of paragraphs .126 and .127, those contingent amounts shall be included in the *total future cash receipts specified by the new terms* only if at the time of restructuring those amounts meet the conditions that would be applied under the provisions of Section C59, in accruing a loss. That is, a creditor shall recognize a loss unless contingent future cash receipts needed to make total future cash receipts specified by the new terms at least equal to the recorded investment in the receivable both are probable and can be reasonably estimated. The same principle applies to amounts of future cash receipts that must sometimes be estimated to apply the provisions of paragraphs .126 and .127. For example, if the number of interest receipts is flexible because the face amount and

---

[17]All or a portion of the recorded investment in the receivable at the time of restructuring may need to be reclassified in the balance sheet because of changes in the terms. [FAS15, ¶30, fn19]

[18][Deleted 11/92 because of FASB Statement 111, *Rescission of FASB Statement No. 32 and Technical Corrections.*]

[19]The only exception is to recognize interest income according to paragraph .132. [FAS15, ¶31, fn21]

accrued interest is collectible on demand or becomes collectible on demand after a specified period, estimates of total future cash receipts should be based on the minimum number of periods possible under the restructured terms. [FAS15, ¶32]

Combination of Types

.129 A troubled debt restructuring may involve receipt of assets (including an equity interest in the debtor) in partial satisfaction of a receivable and a modification of terms of the remaining receivable.[20] A creditor shall account for a troubled debt restructuring involving a partial satisfaction and modification of terms as prescribed in paragraphs .126 through .128 except that, first, the assets received shall be accounted for as prescribed in paragraph .124 and the recorded investment in the receivable shall be reduced by the fair value [FAS15, ¶33] less cost to sell [FAS144, ¶C24(c)] of the assets received.[21] No loss on the restructuring shall be recognized unless the remaining recorded investment in the receivable exceeds the total future cash receipts specified by the terms of the receivable remaining unsatisfied after the restructuring. Future interest income, if any, shall be determined according to the provisions of paragraphs .126 through .128. [FAS15, ¶33]

.129A Fees received in connection with a modification of terms of a troubled debt restructuring as defined in this section shall be applied as a reduction of the recorded investment in the loan. [FAS91, ¶14]

Related Matters

.130 A troubled debt restructuring that is in substance a repossession or foreclosure by the creditor, or in which the creditor otherwise obtains one or more of the debtor's assets in place of all or part of the receivable, shall be accounted for according to the provisions of paragraphs .124 and .129 and, if appropriate, .135. [FAS15, ¶34]

.131 Losses determined by applying the provisions of paragraphs .124 through .130 of this section shall, to the extent that they are not offset against allowances for uncollectible amounts or other valuation accounts, be included in measuring net income for the period of restructuring and reported according to Section I17. Although this section does not address questions concerning estimating uncollectible amounts or accounting for the related valuation allowance (refer to paragraph .101), it recognizes that creditors use al-

---

[20]Even if the stated terms of the remaining receivable, for example, the stated interest rate and the maturity date or dates, are not changed in connection with the receipt of assets (including an equity interest in the debtor), the restructuring shall be accounted for as prescribed by paragraph.129. [FAS15, ¶33, fn22]

[21]If cash is received in a partial satisfaction of a receivable, the recorded investment in the receivable shall be reduced by the amount of cash received. [FAS15, ¶33, fn23]

lowances for uncollectible amounts. Thus, a loss from reducing the recorded investment in a receivable may have been recognized before the restructuring by deducting an estimate of uncollectible amounts in measuring net income and increasing an appropriate valuation allowance. If so, a reduction in the recorded investment in the receivable in a troubled debt restructuring is a deduction from the valuation allowance rather than a loss in measuring net income for the period of restructuring. A valuation allowance can also be used to recognize a loss determined by applying paragraphs .124 through .130 that has not been previously recognized in measuring income. For example, a creditor with an allowance for uncollectible amounts pertaining to a group of receivables that includes the restructured receivable may deduct from the allowance the reduction of recorded investment in the restructured receivable and recognize the loss in measuring net income for the period of restructuring by estimating the appropriate allowance for remaining receivables, including the restructured receivable. [FAS15, ¶35]

.132 If a troubled debt restructuring involves amounts contingently receivable, those contingent amounts shall not be recognized as interest income in future periods before they become receivable—that is, they shall not be recognized as interest income before both the contingency has been removed and the interest has been earned.[22] Before recognizing those amounts as interest income, however, they shall be deducted from the recorded investment in the restructured receivable to the extent that contingent receipts included in *total future cash receipts specified by the new terms* avoided recognition of a loss at the time of restructuring (refer to paragraph .128). [FAS15, ¶36]

.133 If amounts of future cash receipts must be estimated to apply the provisions of paragraphs .126 through .128 because future interest receipts are expected to fluctuate—for example, the restructured terms may specify the stated interest rate to be the prime interest rate increased by a specified amount or proportion—estimates of the minimum total future receipts shall be based on the interest rate in effect at the time of restructuring. Fluctuations in the effective interest rate after the restructuring from changes in the prime rate or other causes shall be accounted for as changes in estimates in the periods the changes occur except that a creditor shall recognize a loss and reduce the recorded investment in a restructured receivable if the interest rate decreases to an extent that the minimum total future cash receipts determined using that interest rate fall below the recorded investment in the receivable at that time. [FAS15, ¶37]

---

[22]Section C59, paragraph .118, states, in part: "Contingencies that might result in gains usually are not reflected in the accounts since to do so might be to recognize revenue prior to its realization." [FAS15, ¶36, fn24]

.134 Legal fees and other direct costs [FAS15, ¶38] including direct loan origination costs [FAS91, ¶14] incurred by a creditor to effect a troubled debt restructuring shall be included in expense when incurred. [FAS15, ¶38]

.135 A receivable from the sale of assets previously obtained in a troubled debt restructuring shall be accounted for according to Section I69, regardless of whether the assets were obtained in satisfaction (full or partial) of a receivable to which that section was not intended to apply. A difference, if any, between the amount of the new receivable and the carrying amount of the assets sold is a gain or loss on sale of assets. [FAS15, ¶39]

Disclosures by Creditors

.136 A creditor shall disclose, either in the body of the financial statements or in the accompanying notes, the following information about troubled debt restructurings as of the date of each balance sheet presented:

a. For outstanding receivables whose terms have been modified in troubled debt restructurings, by major category:[23] (1) the aggregate recorded investment; (2) the gross interest income that would have been recorded in the period then ended if those receivables had been current in accordance with their original terms and had been outstanding throughout the period or since origination, if held for part of the period; and (3) the amount of interest income on those receivables that was included in net income for the period. A receivable whose terms have been modified need not be included in that disclosure if, subsequent to restructuring, its effective interest rate (refer to paragraph .126) had been equal to or greater than the rate that the creditor was willing to accept for a new receivable with comparable risk.
b. The amount of commitments, if any, to lend additional funds to debtors owing receivables whose terms have been modified in troubled debt restructurings. [Refer to Section F25 for guidance on possible additional disclosure requirements.]

[FAS15, ¶40]

.137 A financial institution, or other creditor, may appropriately disclose the information prescribed by paragraph .136, by major category, for the aggregate of outstanding reduced-earning and nonearning receivables rather than separately for outstanding receivables whose terms have been modified in troubled debt restructurings. [FAS15, ¶41]

[23]The appropriate major categories depend on various factors, including the industry or industries in which the creditor is involved. For example, for a commercial banking enterprise, at a minimum, the appropriate categories are investments in debt securities and loans. Information need not be disclosed, however, for noninterest-bearing trade receivables; loans to individuals for household, family, and other personal expenditures; and real estate loans secured by one-to-four family residential properties. [FAS15, ¶40, fn25]

Substitution or Addition of Debtors

.138 A troubled debt restructuring may involve substituting debt of another business enterprise, individual, or governmental unit[24] for that of the troubled debtor or adding another debtor (for example, as a joint debtor). That kind of restructuring should be accounted for according to its substance. For example, a restructuring in which, after the restructuring, the substitute or additional debtor controls, is controlled by, or is under common control[25] with the original debtor is an example of one that shall be accounted for by the creditor according to the provisions of paragraphs .126 through .128. Those paragraphs also shall apply to a restructuring in which the substitute or additional debtor and original debtor are related after the restructuring by an agency, trust, or other relationship that in substance earmarks certain of the original debtor's funds or funds flows for the creditor although payments to the creditor may be made by the substitute or additional debtor. In contrast, a restructuring in which the substitute or additional debtor and the original debtor do not have any of the relationships described above after the restructuring shall be accounted for by the creditor according to the provisions of paragraphs .124 and .129. [FAS15, ¶42]

Restructurings in Fiscal Years Beginning after December 15, 1994[26]

Modification of Terms

.139 A creditor in a troubled debt restructuring involving only a modification of terms of a receivable—that is, not involving receipt of assets (including an equity interest in the debtor)—shall account for the troubled debt restructuring in accordance with the provisions of Section I08, paragraphs .102 through .119. [FAS114, ¶22(b)]

Combination of Types

.140 A troubled debt restructuring may involve receipt of assets (including an equity interest in the debtor) in partial satisfaction of a receivable and a modification of terms

---

[24]Governmental units include, but are not limited to, states, counties, townships, municipalities, school districts, authorities, and commissions. [FAS15, ¶42, fn26]

[25]*Control* in this paragraph has the meaning described in Section I82, "Investments: Equity Method," paragraph .408: "The usual condition for control is ownership of a majority (over 50 percent) of the outstanding voting stock. The power to control may also exist with a lesser percentage of ownership, for example, by contract, lease, agreement with other stockholders, or by court decree." [FAS15, ¶42, fn27]

[[26]Refer to footnote 14b.]

of the remaining receivable.[27] A creditor shall account for a troubled debt restructuring involving a partial satisfaction and modification of terms as prescribed in [FAS15, ¶33] Section I08, paragraphs .102 through .119, [FAS114, ¶22(c)] except that, first, the assets received shall be accounted for as prescribed in paragraph .124 and the recorded investment in the receivable shall be reduced by the fair value [FAS15, ¶33] less cost to sell [FAS144, ¶C24(c)] of the assets received.[28] [FAS15, ¶33]

.141 Fees received in connection with a modification of terms of a troubled debt restructuring as defined in this section shall be applied as a reduction of the recorded investment in the loan. [FAS91, ¶14]

Related Matters

.142 A troubled debt restructuring that is in substance a repossession or foreclosure by the creditor, [FAS15, ¶34] that is, the creditor receives physical possession of the debtor's assets regardless of whether formal foreclosure proceedings take place, [FAS114, ¶22(d)] or in which the creditor otherwise obtains one or more of the debtor's assets in place of all or part of the receivable, shall be accounted for according to the provisions of paragraphs .124 and .140 and, if appropriate, .144. [FAS15, ¶34] [Refer to paragraph .1001 for EITF Issues that provide interpretive guidance on this paragraph.]

.143 Legal fees and other direct costs [FAS15, ¶38] including direct loan origination costs [FAS91, ¶14] incurred by a creditor to effect a troubled debt restructuring shall be included in expense when incurred. [FAS15, ¶38]

.144 A receivable from the sale of assets previously obtained in a troubled debt restructuring shall be accounted for according to Section I69, regardless of whether the assets were obtained in satisfaction (full or partial) of a receivable to which that section was not intended to apply. A difference, if any, between the amount of the new receivable and the carrying amount of the assets sold is a gain or loss on sale of assets. [FAS15, ¶39]

Disclosures by Creditors

.145 A creditor shall disclose, either in the body of the financial statements or in the accompanying notes, the amount of commitments, if any, to lend additional funds to debtors owing receivables whose terms have been modified in troubled debt restructurings,

[27]Even if the stated terms of the remaining receivable, for example, the stated interest rate and the maturity date or dates, are not changed in connection with the receipt of assets (including an equity interest in the debtor), the restructuring shall be accounted for as prescribed by paragraph .129. [FAS15, ¶33, fn22]

[28]If cash is received in a partial satisfaction of a receivable, the recorded investment in the receivable shall be reduced by the amount of cash received. [FAS15, ¶33, fn23]

as of the date of each balance sheet presented. [FAS15, ¶40] [Refer to Section F25 and Section I08 for guidance on additional disclosure requirements.]

Substitution or Addition of Debtors

.146 A troubled debt restructuring may involve substituting debt of another business enterprise, individual, or governmental unit[29] for that of the troubled debtor or adding another debtor (for example, as a joint debtor). That kind of restructuring should be accounted for according to its substance. For example, a restructuring in which, after the restructuring, the substitute or additional debtor controls, is controlled by, or is under common control[30] with the original debtor is an example of one that shall be accounted for by the creditor [FAS15, ¶42] as prescribed in Section I08, paragraphs .102 through .119. That section [FAS114, ¶22(e)] also shall apply to a restructuring in which the substitute or additional debtor and original debtor are related after the restructuring by an agency, trust, or other relationship that in substance earmarks certain of the original debtor's funds or funds flows for the creditor although payments to the creditor may be made by the substitute or additional debtor. In contrast, a restructuring in which the substitute or additional debtor and the original debtor do not have any of the relationships described above after the restructuring shall be accounted for by the creditor according to the provisions of paragraphs .124 and .140. [FAS15, ¶42]

---

[29] Governmental units include, but are not limited to, states, counties, townships, municipalities, school districts, authorities, and commissions. [FAS15, ¶42, fn26]

[30] *Control* in this paragraph has the meaning described in Section I82, "Investments: Equity Method," paragraph .408: "The usual condition for control is ownership of a majority (over 50 percent) of the outstanding voting stock. The power to control may also exist with a lesser percentage of ownership, for example, by contract, lease, agreement with other stockholders, or by court decree." [FAS15, ¶42, fn27]

Glossary

.401 **Carrying amount of the payable.** Face amount increased or decreased by applicable accrued interest and applicable unamortized premium, discount, finance charges, or issue costs. [FAS15, ¶13]

.402 **Debt.** A *receivable* or *payable* (collectively referred to as *debt*) represents a contractual right to receive money or a contractual obligation to pay money on demand or on fixed or determinable dates that is already included as an asset or liability in the creditor's or debtor's balance sheet at the time of the restructuring. Receivables or payables that may be involved in troubled debt restructurings commonly result from lending or borrowing of cash or selling or purchasing goods or services on credit. Examples are accounts receivable or payable, notes, debentures and bonds (whether those receivables or payables are secured or unsecured and whether they are convertible or nonconvertible), and related accrued interest, if any. Typically, each receivable or payable is negotiated separately, but sometimes two or more receivables or payables are negotiated together. For example, a debtor may negotiate with a group of creditors but sign separate debt instruments with each creditor. For purposes of this section, restructuring of each receivable or payable, including those negotiated and restructured jointly, shall be accounted for individually. The substance rather than the form of the receivable or payable shall govern. For example, to a debtor, a bond constitutes one payable even though there are many bondholders. [FAS15, ¶4]

.403 **Recorded investment in the receivable.** Face amount increased or decreased by applicable accrued interest and unamortized premium, discount, finance charges, or acquisition costs. The recorded investment in the receivable may reflect a previous direct write-down of the investment [but differs from the *carrying amount of receivable* in that] the latter is net of an allowance for estimated uncollectible amounts or other valuation account, if any. [FAS15, ¶28, fn17]

.404 **Time of restructuring.** Troubled debt restructurings may occur before, at, or after the stated maturity of debt, and time may elapse between the agreement, court order, etc., and the transfer of assets or equity interest, the effective date of new terms, or the occurrence of another event that constitutes consummation of the restructuring. The date of consummation is the time of the restructuring. [FAS15, ¶6]

.405 **Troubled debt restructuring.** The creditor for economic or legal reasons related to the debtor's financial difficulties grants a concession to the debtor that it would not otherwise consider. [Refer to paragraphs .104 through .107 for examples and clarification.] [FAS15, ¶2]

Supplemental Guidance

.501-.505 [Deleted 5/93 because of FASB Statement 114, *Accounting by Creditors for Impairment of a Loan.*]

Classification of Debt Restructurings by Debtors and Creditors

.506 *Question*—In applying this section can a debt restructuring be a troubled debt restructuring for a debtor but not for the creditor? [FTB80-2, ¶1]

.507 *Response*—Yes, a debtor may have a troubled debt restructuring even though the related creditor does not have a troubled debt restructuring. The debtor and creditor must individually apply this section to the specific facts and circumstances to determine whether a troubled debt restructuring has occurred. Example (a) in paragraph .107 identifies a type of debt restructuring that is *not* a troubled debt restructuring for the creditor; similarly, example (b) in paragraph .107 identifies a type of debt restructuring that is *not* a troubled debt restructuring for the debtor. This section establishes tests for applicability that are not symmetrical as between the debtor and the creditor when the debtor's carrying amount and the creditor's recorded investment differ. [FTB80-2, ¶3]

.508 *Illustration*—Creditor A makes a $10,000 interest-bearing loan to Debtor X and, when Debtor X later encounters financial difficulties, sells its receivable from Debtor X to Creditor B for $4,000 on a nonrecourse basis. Following the sale, the carrying amount of the loan payable by Debtor X would still be $10,000 and the recorded investment of the loan by Creditor B would be $4,000. If Debtor X subsequently transfers to Creditor B assets with a fair value of $5,500 in full settlement of the loan, that transaction would be a troubled debt restructuring for Debtor X because the fair value of the assets is less than the carrying amount of the loan, whereas Creditor B would not have a troubled debt restructuring because the fair value of the assets received exceeds its recorded investment in the loan. [FTB80-2, ¶4]

Applicability to Debtors in Bankruptcy Situations

.509 *Question*—Does this section apply to troubled debt restructurings of debtors involved in bankruptcy proceedings? [FTB81-6, ¶1]

.510 *Background*—Some confusion has arisen about the interaction of paragraph .104 and footnote 1. Paragraph .103 indicates that this section applies to troubled debt restructurings consummated under reorganization, arrangement, or other provisions of the Federal Bankruptcy Act or other federal statutes related thereto. However, footnote 1 to that paragraph states that this section does not apply ". . . if, under provisions of those federal statutes or in a quasi reorganization or corporate readjustment [(refer to Section Q15, "Quasi Reorganizations")] with which a troubled debt restructuring coincides, the debtor restates its liabilities generally." [FTB81-6, ¶2]

.511 *Response*—This section does not apply to debtors who, in connection with bankruptcy proceedings, enter into troubled debt restructurings that result in a general restatement of the debtor's liabilities, that is, when such restructurings or modifications accomplished under purview of the bankruptcy court encompass most of the amount of the debtor's liabilities. [FTB81-6, ¶3]

.512 For example, enterprises involved with Chapter XI bankruptcy proceedings frequently reduce all or most of their indebtedness with the approval of their creditors and the court in order to provide an opportunity for the enterprise to have a fresh start. Such reductions are usually by a stated percentage so that, for example, the debtor owes only 60 cents on the dollar. Because the debtor would be restating its liabilities generally, this section would not apply to the debtor's accounting for such reduction of liabilities. [FTB81-6, ¶4]

.513 On the other hand, this section would apply to an isolated troubled debt restructuring by a debtor involved in bankruptcy proceedings if such restructuring did not result in a general restatement of the debtor's liabilities. [FTB81-6, ¶5]

Supplemental Guidance: Emerging Issues Task Force (EITF) Issues

.1000 [Listed below are EITF Issues that provide supplemental guidance for this section. These Issues are grouped by subject matter and may be either interpretive of or related by topic to the guidance in this section.

Modification of Debt Terms

EITF Issue No. 84-19, "Mortgage Loan Payment Modifications"
EITF Issue No. 89-15, "Accounting for a Modification of Debt Terms When the Debtor Is Experiencing Financial Difficulties"

Troubled Debt Restructurings

EITF Issue No. 87-18, "Use of Zero Coupon Bonds in a Troubled Debt Restructuring"
EITF Issue No. 87-19, "Substituted Debtors in a Troubled Debt Restructuring"
EITF Issue No. 96-22, "Applicability of the Disclosures Required by FASB Statement No. 114 When a Loan Is Restructured in a Troubled Debt Restructuring into Two (or More) Loans"
EITF Issue No. 02-4, "Determining Whether a Debtor's Modification or Exchange of Debt Instruments Is within the Scope of FASB Statement No. 15"

Other

EITF Issue No. 85-44, "Differences between Loan Loss Allowances for GAAP and RAP"
EITF Issue No. 89-14, "Valuation of Repossessed Real Estate"
EITF Issue No. 91-2, "Debtor's Accounting for Forfeiture of Real Estate Subject to a Nonrecourse Mortgage"
EITF Issue No. 94-8, "Accounting for Conversion of a Loan into a Debt Security in a Debt Restructuring"
EITF Topic No. D-4, "Argentine Government Guarantee of U.S. Dollar-Denominated Loans to the Argentine Private Sector"]

.1001 [Listed below are those EITF Issues that provide interpretive guidance on specific material in this section.

Paragraph .104, footnote 2 (FAS 15, fn1)—EITF Issue No. 91-2
Paragraphs .112 through .114 (FAS 15, ¶16-18)—EITF Issue No. 89-15
Paragraph .124 (FAS 15, ¶28)—EITF Issues No. 87-18 and 87-19
Paragraph .142 (FAS 15, ¶34)—EITF Issues No. 87-18 and 87-19]

(The next page is 12607.)

DEPRECIATION — SECTION D40

Sources: ARB 43, Chapter 9C; APB Opinion 6; APB Opinion 12; FASB Statement 92; FASB Statement 93; FASB Statement 109; FASB Statement 135

Summary

Depreciation is the method of allocating the cost of a tangible capital asset, less salvage (if any), over the estimated useful life of the asset in a systematic and rational manner. Except when an enterprise is undergoing a reorganization, capital assets shall not be depreciated at appraisal, market, or current values that are above cost to the enterprise.

This section applies to both business enterprises and not-for-profit organizations.

Basic Principle

.101 The cost of an [asset] is one of the costs of the services it renders during its useful economic life. Generally accepted accounting principles require that this cost be spread over the expected useful life of the [asset] in such a way as to allocate it as equitably as possible to the periods during which services are obtained from the use of the [asset]. This procedure is known as **depreciation accounting,** a system of accounting that aims to distribute the cost or other basic value of tangible capital assets, less salvage (if any), over the estimated useful life of the unit (which may be a group of assets) in a systematic and rational manner. It is a process of allocation, not of valuation. [ARB43, ch9C, ¶5] Not-for-profit organizations[a] [also] shall recognize the cost of using up the future economic benefits or service potentials of their long-lived tangible assets [as] depreciation. [FAS93, ¶5]

[a]The term *not-for-profit organizations* in this section encompasses all entities described by FASB Concepts Statement 4, *Objectives of Financial Reporting by Nonbusiness Organizations,* as possessing characteristics that distinguish them from business enterprises. Concepts Statement 4, paragraph 6, lists as the distinguishing characteristics of not-for-profit organizations (a) contributions of significant amounts of resources from resource providers who do not expect commensurate or proportionate pecuniary return, (b) operating purposes other than to provide goods or services at a profit, and (c) absence of ownership interests like those of business enterprises. Not-for-profit organizations have those characteristics in varying degrees. The term not-for-profit organizations encompasses the kinds of organizations covered by the AICPA specialized industry pronouncements: [FAS93, ¶1, fn1] *Health Care Organizations* and *Not-for-Profit Organizations.* [FAS135, ¶5(a)]

.101A Consistent with the accepted practice for land used as a building site,[b] depreciation need not be recognized on individual works of art or historical treasures whose economic benefit or service potential is used up so slowly that their estimated useful lives are extraordinarily long. A work of art or historical treasure shall be deemed to have that characteristic only if verifiable[c] evidence exists demonstrating that (a) the asset individually has cultural, aesthetic, or historical value that is worth preserving perpetually and (b) the holder has the technological and financial ability to protect and preserve essentially undiminished the service potential of the asset and is doing that. [FAS93, ¶6] [A] recognized cultural, aesthetic, or historical value and, generally, [an] already long existence have established each [work of art and historical treasure] as a member of a group of rare works with that characteristic. Most of them are acquired by purchase, gift, or discovery with that characteristic already having been demonstrated, and the holder or acquirer usually takes steps to protect and preserve it, for example, by keeping a work of art in a protective environment and limiting its use solely to display. While that characteristic is not limited to assets with an already long existence, an asset that has come into existence relatively recently cannot be assumed to have it in the absence of the verifiable evidence described above. For example, to put a painting in a protective environment is not by itself evidence of cultural, aesthetic, or historical value that is worth preserving perpetually. [FAS93, ¶36]

.101B The future economic benefits or service potentials of individual items comprising "collections" and of buildings and other structures—including those designated as landmarks, monuments, cathedrals, or historical treasures—are used up not only by wear and tear in intended uses but also by the continuous destructive effects of pollutants, vibrations, and so forth. The cultural, aesthetic, or historical values of those assets can be preserved, if at all, only by periodic major efforts to protect, clean, and restore them, usually at significant cost. Thus, depreciation of those assets [shall] be recognized. [FAS93, ¶35]

.101C Depreciation should be recognized, of course, on any capitalized costs of major preservation or restoration devices or efforts, which provide future economic benefits or

[b]The process of using up the future economic benefit or service potential of land often takes place over a period so long that its occurrence is imperceptible—land used as a building site is perhaps the most common example. In contrast, however, that process also sometimes occurs much more rapidly—land used as a site for toxic waste, as a source of gravel or ore, or for farming under conditions in which fertility dissipates relatively quickly and cannot be restored economically are examples. [FAS93, ¶34]

[c]*Verifiability* means that several measurers or observers are likely to obtain essentially the same measure or conclude that a description of an item faithfully represents what it purports to represent. (Refer to FASB Concepts Statement 2, *Qualitative Characteristics of Accounting Information,* paragraphs 81 through 89.) [FAS93, ¶6, fn2]

service potentials until the next expected preservation or restoration, regardless of whether depreciation is recognized on the asset being protected or restored. [FAS93, ¶37]

.102 Property, plant, and equipment shall not be written up by an enterprise to reflect appraisal, market, or current values which are above cost to the enterprise. This section is not intended to change accounting practices followed in connection with quasi reorganizations[1] or reorganizations. This section may not apply to foreign operations under unusual conditions such as serious inflation or currency devaluation. However, when the accounts of an enterprise with foreign operations are translated into U.S. currency for consolidation, such write-ups normally are eliminated. Whenever appreciation has been recorded on the books, income shall be charged with depreciation computed on the written-up amounts. [APB6, ¶17]

Application

.103 [Deleted 2/92 because of FASB Statement 109, *Accounting for Income Taxes.*]

.104 The declining-balance method is one that meets the requirements of being systematic and rational.[3] If the expected productivity or revenue-earning power of the asset is relatively greater during the earlier years of its life, or where maintenance charges tend to increase during later years, the declining-balance method may provide the most satisfactory allocation of cost. That conclusion also applies to other methods, including the sum-of-the-years'-digits method, that produce substantially similar results. [FAS109, ¶288(a)] Annuity methods of depreciation are not acceptable under generally accepted accounting principles applicable to enterprises in general. [FAS92, ¶37]

Disclosure

.105 Because of the significant effects on financial position and results of operations of the depreciation method or methods used, the following disclosures shall be made in the financial statements or in notes thereto:

a. Depreciation expense for the period
b. Balances of major classes of depreciable assets, by nature or function, at the balance sheet date
c. Accumulated depreciation, either by major classes of depreciable assets or in total, at the balance sheet date

---

[1]Refer to Section Q15, "Quasi Reorganizations." [APB6, ¶17, fn6]

[[2]Deleted 12/87 because guidance is no longer applicable.]

[3]Accounting Terminology Bulletin No. 1, *Review and Résumé,* paragraph 56. [FAS109, ¶288(a)]

d. A general description of the method or methods used in computing depreciation with respect to major classes of depreciable assets.

[APB12, ¶5]

.106 [Deleted 12/82 because of FASB Statement 71, *Accounting for the Effects of Certain Types of Regulation.*]

.107 [Deleted 12/86 because of FASB Statement 89, *Financial Reporting and Changing Prices.*]

Glossary

.401 **Depreciation accounting.** A system of accounting that aims to distribute the cost or other basic value of tangible capital assets, less salvage (if any), over the estimated useful life of the unit (which may be a group of assets) in a systematic and rational manner. It is a process of allocation, not of valuation. [ARB43, ch9C, ¶5]

(The next page is 13001.)

DERIVATIVE INSTRUMENTS AND HEDGING ACTIVITIES — SECTION D50

Sources: FASB Statement 133; FASB Statement 138; FASB Statement 140; FASB Statement 141; FASB Statement 145

[**Note:** A list of Issues discussed by the Emerging Issues Task Force (EITF) that provide supplemental guidance for this section is presented in paragraph .1000.]

Summary

This section presents accounting and reporting standards for derivative instruments, including certain derivative instruments embedded in other contracts, (collectively referred to as derivatives) and for hedging activities. It requires that an entity recognize all derivatives as either assets or liabilities in the statement of financial position and measure those instruments at fair value. If certain conditions are met, a derivative may be specifically designated as (a) a hedge of the exposure to changes in the fair value of a recognized asset or liability or an unrecognized firm commitment, (b) a hedge of the exposure to variable cash flows of a forecasted transaction, or (c) a hedge of the foreign currency exposure of a net investment in a foreign operation, an unrecognized firm commitment, a recognized foreign-currency-denominated asset or liability (including an available-for-sale security), or a foreign-currency-denominated forecasted transaction.

The accounting for changes in the fair value of a derivative (that is, gains and losses) depends on the intended use of the derivative and the resulting designation.

- For a derivative designated as hedging the exposure to changes in the fair value of a recognized asset or liability or a firm commitment (referred to as a fair value hedge), the gain or loss is recognized in earnings in the period of change together with the offsetting loss or gain on the hedged item attributable to the risk being hedged. The effect of that accounting is to reflect in earnings the extent to which the hedge is not effective in achieving offsetting changes in fair value.
- For a derivative designated as hedging the exposure to variable cash flows of a forecasted transaction (referred to as a cash flow hedge), the effective portion of the derivative's gain or loss is initially reported as a component of other comprehensive income (outside earnings) and subsequently reclassified into earnings when

the forecasted transaction affects earnings. The ineffective portion of the gain or loss is reported in earnings immediately.

- For a derivative designated as hedging the foreign currency exposure of a net investment in a foreign operation, the gain or loss is reported in other comprehensive income (outside earnings) as part of the cumulative translation adjustment. The accounting for a fair value hedge described above applies to a derivative designated as a hedge of the foreign currency exposure of an unrecognized firm commitment or a recognized foreign-currency-denominated asset or liability. Similarly, the accounting for a cash flow hedge described above applies to a derivative designated as a hedge of the foreign currency exposure of a foreign-currency-denominated forecasted transaction or a recognized foreign-currency-denominated asset or liability.
- For a derivative not designated as a hedging instrument, the gain or loss is recognized in earnings in the period of change.

Under this section, an entity that elects to apply hedge accounting is required to establish at the inception of the hedge the method it will use for assessing the effectiveness of the hedging derivative and the measurement approach for determining the ineffective aspect of the hedge. Those methods must be consistent with the entity's approach to managing risk.

This section applies to all entities. A not-for-profit organization should recognize the change in fair value of all derivatives as a change in net assets in the period of change. In a fair value hedge, the changes in the fair value of the hedged item attributable to the risk being hedged also are recognized. However, because of the format of their statement of financial performance, not-for-profit organizations are not permitted special hedge accounting for derivatives used to hedge forecasted transactions. This section does not address how a not-for-profit organization should determine the components of an operating measure if one is presented.

This section precludes designating a nonderivative financial instrument as a hedge of an asset, liability, unrecognized firm commitment, or forecasted transaction except that a nonderivative instrument denominated in a foreign currency may be designated as a hedge of the foreign currency exposure of an unrecognized firm commitment denominated in a foreign currency or a net investment in a foreign operation.

Introduction

.101 This section standardizes the accounting for **derivative instruments,** including certain derivative instruments embedded in other contracts, by requiring that an entity recognize those items as assets or liabilities in the statement of financial position and measure them at **fair value.** If certain conditions are met, an entity may elect to designate a derivative instrument as follows:

a. A hedge of the exposure to changes in the fair value of a recognized asset or liability, or of an unrecognized **firm commitment,**[1] that are attributable to a particular risk (referred to as a fair value hedge)
b. A hedge of the exposure to variability in the cash flows of a recognized asset or liability, or of a **forecasted transaction,** that is attributable to a particular risk (referred to as a cash flow hedge)
c. A hedge of the foreign currency exposure of (1) an unrecognized firm commitment (a foreign currency fair value hedge), (2) an available-for-sale security (a foreign currency fair value hedge), (3) a forecasted transaction (a foreign currency cash flow hedge), or (4) a net investment in a foreign operation.

This section generally provides for matching the timing of gain or loss recognition on the hedging instrument with the recognition of (a) the changes in the fair value of the hedged asset or liability that are attributable to the hedged risk or (b) the earnings effect of the hedged forecasted transaction. Paragraphs .145 through .191 of this section provide guidance on identifying derivative instruments subject to the scope of this section and on assessing hedge effectiveness and is an integral part of the standards provided in this section. Paragraphs .192 through .288 contain examples that illustrate application of this section. Exhibit 289A provides a diagram for determining whether a contract is a freestanding derivative subject to the scope of this section. [FAS133, ¶4]

Scope and Definition

.102 This section applies to all entities. Some entities, such as not-for-profit organizations and defined benefit pension plans, do not report earnings as a separate caption in a statement of financial performance. The application of this section to those entities is set forth in paragraph .140. [FAS133, ¶5]

[1] An unrecognized firm commitment can be viewed as an executory contract that represents both a right and an obligation. When a previously unrecognized firm commitment that is designated as a hedged item is accounted for in accordance with this section, an asset or a liability is recognized and reported in the statement of financial position related to the recognition of the gain or loss on the firm commitment. Consequently, subsequent references to an asset or a liability in this section include a firm commitment. [FAS133, ¶4, fn2]

Derivative Instruments

.103 A derivative instrument is a **financial instrument** or other contract with all three of the following characteristics:

a. It has (1) one or more **underlyings** and (2) one or more **notional amounts**[2] or payment provisions or both. Those terms determine the amount of the settlement or settlements, and, in some cases, whether or not a settlement is required.[3]
b. It requires no initial net investment or an initial net investment that is smaller than would be required for other types of contracts that would be expected to have a similar response to changes in market factors.
c. Its terms require or permit net settlement, it can readily be settled net by a means outside the contract, or it provides for delivery of an asset that puts the recipient in a position not substantially different from net settlement.

[FAS133, ¶6]

.104 *Underlying, notional amount, and payment provision.* An underlying is a specified interest rate, security price, commodity price, foreign exchange rate, index of prices or rates, or other variable. An underlying may be a price or rate of an asset or liability but is not the asset or liability itself. A notional amount is a number of currency units, shares, bushels, pounds, or other units specified in the contract. The settlement of a derivative instrument with a notional amount is determined by interaction of that notional amount with the underlying. The interaction may be simple multiplication, or it may involve a formula with leverage factors or other constants. A payment provision specifies a fixed or determinable settlement to be made if the underlying behaves in a specified manner. [FAS133, ¶7] For example, a derivative might require a specified payment if a referenced interest rate increases by 300 basis points. Reference to either a notional amount or a payment provision is needed to compute the contract's periodic settlements and resulting changes in fair value. [FAS133, ¶251]

.105 *Initial net investment.* Many derivative instruments require no initial net investment. Some require an initial net investment as compensation for time value (for example, a premium on an option) or for terms that are more or less favorable than market conditions (for example, a premium on a forward purchase contract with a price less

---

[2]Sometimes other names are used. For example, the notional amount is called a face amount in some contracts. [FAS133, ¶6, fn3]

[3]The terms *underlying, notional amount, payment provision,* and *settlement* are intended to include the plural forms in the remainder of this section. Including both the singular and plural forms used in this paragraph is more accurate but much more awkward and impairs the readability. [FAS133, ¶6, fn4]

than the current forward price). Others require a mutual exchange of currencies or other assets at inception, in which case the net investment is the difference in the fair values of the assets exchanged. A derivative instrument does not require an initial net investment in the contract that is equal to the notional amount (or the notional amount plus a premium or minus a discount) or that is determined by applying the notional amount to the underlying. [FAS133, ¶8]

.106 *Net settlement.* A contract fits the description in paragraph .103(c) if its settlement provisions meet one of the following criteria:

a. Neither party is required to deliver an asset that is associated with the underlying or that has a principal amount, stated amount, face value, number of shares, or other denomination that is equal to the notional amount (or the notional amount plus a premium or minus a discount). For example, most interest rate swaps do not require that either party deliver interest-bearing assets with a principal amount equal to the notional amount of the contract.
b. One of the parties is required to deliver an asset of the type described in paragraph .106(a), but there is a market mechanism that facilitates net settlement, for example, an exchange that offers a ready opportunity to sell the contract or to enter into an offsetting contract.
c. One of the parties is required to deliver an asset of the type described in paragraph .106(a), but that asset is readily convertible to cash[4] or is itself a derivative instrument. An example of that type of contract is a forward contract that requires delivery of an exchange-traded equity security. Even though the number of shares to be delivered is the same as the notional amount of the contract and the price of the shares is the underlying, an exchange-traded security is readily convertible to cash. Another example is a swaption—an option to require delivery of a swap contract, which is a derivative.

Derivative instruments embedded in other contracts are addressed in paragraphs .109 through .113. [FAS133, ¶9]

---

[4]FASB Concepts Statement No. 5, *Recognition and Measurement in Financial Statements of Business Enterprises,* states that assets that are readily convertible to cash "have (i) interchangeable (fungible) units and (ii) quoted prices available in an active market that can rapidly absorb the quantity held by the entity without significantly affecting the price" (paragraph 83(a)). For contracts that involve multiple deliveries of the asset, the phrase *in an active market that can rapidly absorb the quantity held by the entity* should be applied separately to the expected quantity in each delivery. [FAS133, ¶9, fn5]

.107 Notwithstanding the conditions in paragraphs .103 through .106, the following contracts are not subject to the requirements of this section:

a. *"Regular-way" security trades.* Regular-way security trades are contracts with no net settlement provision and no market mechanism to facilitate net settlement (as described in paragraphs .106(a) and .106(b)). They provide for delivery of a security within the time generally established by regulations or conventions in the marketplace or exchange in which the transaction is being executed.[5] [FAS133, ¶10]
b. *Normal purchases and normal sales.* Normal purchases and normal sales are contracts that provide for the purchase or sale of something other than a financial instrument or derivative instrument that will be delivered in quantities expected to be used or sold by the reporting entity over a reasonable period in the normal course of business. However, contracts that have a price based on an underlying that is not clearly and closely related to the asset being sold or purchased (such as a price in a contract for the sale of a grain commodity based in part on changes in the S&P index) or that are denominated in a foreign currency that meets neither of the criteria in paragraphs .112(a) and .112(b) shall not be considered normal purchases and normal sales. Contracts that contain net settlement provisions as described in paragraphs .106(a) and .106(b) may qualify for the normal purchases and normal sales exception if it is probable at inception and throughout the term of the individual contract that the contract will not settle net and will result in physical delivery. Net settlement (as described in paragraphs .106(a) and .106(b)) of contracts in a group of contracts similarly designated as normal purchases and normal sales would call into question the classification of all such contracts as normal purchases or normal sales. Contracts that require cash settlements of gains or losses or are otherwise settled net on a periodic basis, including individual contracts that are part of a series of sequential contracts intended to accomplish ultimate acquisition or sale of a commodity, do not qualify for this exception.[5a] For contracts that qualify for the normal purchases and normal sales exception, the entity shall document the basis for concluding that it is probable

[5]The regular-way exemption [is extended] to purchases and sales of when-issued and to-be-announced securities. However, the exemption applies only if (a) there is no other way to purchase or sell the security and (b) the trade will settle within the shortest period permitted for the security. [FAS133, ¶276]

[5a]An entity may designate those contracts as a hedged item in an all-in-one hedge, pursuant to Statement 133 Implementation Issue No. G2, "Hedged Transactions That Arise from Gross Settlement of a Derivative ('All in One' Hedges)." [FAS138, ¶12]

that the contract will result in physical delivery. The documentation requirements can be applied either to groups of similarly designated contracts or to each individual contract.[6] [FAS138, ¶4(a)] [Refer to paragraph .1001 for an EITF Issue that provides interpretive guidance on this subparagraph.]

c. *Certain insurance contracts.* Generally, contracts of the type that are within the scope of Section In6, "Insurance Industry," are not subject to the requirements of this section whether or not they are written by insurance enterprises. That is, a contract is not subject to the requirements of this section if it entitles the holder to be compensated only if, as a result of an identifiable insurable event (other than a change in price), the holder incurs a liability or there is an adverse change in the value of a specific asset or liability for which the holder is at risk. The following types of contracts written by insurance enterprises or held by the insureds are not subject to the requirements of this section for the reasons given:

   (1) *Traditional life insurance contracts.* The payment of death benefits is the result of an identifiable insurable event (death of the insured) instead of changes in a variable.

   (2) *Traditional property and casualty contracts.* The payment of benefits is the result of an identifiable insurable event (for example, theft or fire) instead of changes in a variable.

   However, insurance enterprises enter into other types of contracts that may be subject to the provisions of this section. In addition, some contracts with insurance or other enterprises combine derivative instruments, as defined in this section, with other insurance products or nonderivative contracts, for example, indexed annuity contracts, variable life insurance contracts, and property and casualty contracts that combine traditional coverages with foreign currency options. Contracts that consist of both derivative portions and nonderivative portions are addressed in paragraph .109.

d. *Certain financial guarantee contracts.* Financial guarantee contracts are not subject to this section if they provide for payments to be made only to reimburse the guaranteed party for a loss incurred because the debtor fails to pay when payment is due, which is an identifiable insurable event. In contrast, financial guarantee contracts are subject to this section if they provide for payments to be made in response to changes in an underlying (for example, a decrease in a specified debtor's creditworthiness).

[6]The normal purchases and normal sales provision sometimes will result in different parties to a contract reaching different conclusions about whether the contract is required to be accounted for as a derivative instrument. For example, the contract may be for ordinary sales by one party (and therefore not [subject to this section]) but not for ordinary purchases by the counterparty (and therefore [subject to this section]). [FAS133, ¶272]

e. *Certain contracts that are not traded on an exchange.* Contracts that are not exchange-traded are not subject to the requirements of this section if the underlying on which the settlement is based is one of the following:
   (1) A climatic or geological variable or other physical variable
   (2) The price or value of (a) a nonfinancial asset of one of the parties to the contract provided that the asset is not readily convertible to cash or (b) a nonfinancial liability of one of the parties to the contract provided that the liability does not require delivery of an asset that is readily convertible to cash
   (3) Specified volumes of sales or service revenues of one of the parties to the contract.

   If a contract has more than one underlying and some, but not all, of them qualify for one of the exceptions in paragraphs .107(e)(1), .107(e)(2), and .107(e)(3), the application of this section to that contract depends on its predominant characteristics. That is, the contract is subject to the requirements of this section if all of its underlyings, considered in combination, behave in a manner that is highly correlated with the behavior of any of the component variables that do not qualify for an exception.
f. *Derivatives that serve as impediments to sales accounting.* A derivative instrument (whether freestanding or embedded in another contract) whose existence serves as an impediment to recognizing a related contract as a sale by one party or a purchase by the counterparty is not subject to this section. For example, the existence of a guarantee of the residual value of a leased asset by the lessor may be an impediment to treating a contract as a sales-type lease, in which case the contract would be treated by the lessor as an operating lease. Another example is the existence of a call option enabling a transferor to repurchase transferred assets that is an impediment to sales accounting under [FAS133, ¶10] Section F39, "Financial Instruments: Transfers." [FAS140, ¶353(a)]

.108 Notwithstanding the conditions of paragraphs .103 through .107, the reporting entity shall *not* consider the following contracts to be derivative instruments for purposes of this section:

a. Contracts issued or held by that reporting entity that are both (1) indexed to its own stock and (2) classified in stockholders' equity in its statement of financial position [Refer to paragraph .1001 for EITF Issues that provide interpretive guidance on this subparagraph.]
b. Contracts issued by the entity in connection with stock-based compensation arrangements addressed in Section C36, "Compensation: Stock-Based"
c. Contracts issued by the entity as contingent consideration from a business combination. [FAS133, ¶11] The purchaser's accounting for the instrument is explicitly excluded from the scope of this section, but the seller who receives the instrument must account for it according to the requirements of this section. [FAS133, ¶289] The ac-

counting for contingent consideration issued in a business combination is addressed in [FAS133, ¶11] Section B51, "Business Combinations." [FAS141, ¶E18(a)] In applying this paragraph, the issuer is considered to be the entity that is accounting for the combination using the purchase method.

In contrast, the above exceptions do not apply to the counterparty in those contracts. In addition, a contract that an entity either can or must settle by issuing its own equity instruments but that is indexed in part or in full to something other than its own stock can be a derivative instrument for the issuer under paragraphs .103 through .107, in which case it would be accounted for as a liability or an asset in accordance with the requirements of this section. [FAS133, ¶11]

Embedded Derivative Instruments

.109 Contracts that do not in their entirety meet the definition of a derivative instrument (refer to paragraphs .103 through .106), such as bonds, insurance policies, and leases, may contain "embedded" derivative instruments—implicit or explicit terms that affect some or all of the cash flows or the value of other exchanges required by the contract in a manner similar to a derivative instrument. The effect of embedding a derivative instrument in another type of contract ("the host contract") is that some or all of the cash flows or other exchanges that otherwise would be required by the [FAS133, ¶12] host [FAS138, ¶4(p)] contract, whether unconditional or contingent upon the occurrence of a specified event, will be modified based on one or more underlyings. An embedded derivative instrument shall be separated from the host contract[7] and accounted for as a derivative instrument pursuant to this section if and only if all of the following criteria are met:

a. The economic characteristics and risks of the embedded derivative instrument are not clearly and closely related to the economic characteristics and risks of the host contract. Additional guidance on applying this criterion to various contracts containing embedded derivative instruments is included in paragraphs .145 through .191 of this section.
b. The contract ("the hybrid instrument") that embodies both the embedded derivative instrument and the host contract is not remeasured at fair value under otherwise applicable generally accepted accounting principles with changes in fair value reported in earnings as they occur.

[7]The objective is to estimate the fair value of the derivative features separately from the fair value of the nonderivative portions of the contract. Estimates of fair value should reflect all relevant features of each component and their effect on a current exchange between willing parties. For example, an embedded purchased option that expires if the contract in which it is embedded is prepaid would have a different value than an option whose term is a specified period that is not subject to truncation. [FAS133, ¶303]

c. A separate instrument with the same terms as the embedded derivative instrument would, pursuant to paragraphs .103 through .108, be a derivative instrument subject to the requirements of this section. (The initial net investment for the hybrid instrument shall not be considered to be the initial net investment for the embedded derivative.) [FAS133, ¶12]

.110 For purposes of applying the provisions of paragraph .109, an embedded derivative instrument in which the underlying is an interest rate or interest rate index[8] that alters net interest payments that otherwise would be paid or received on an interest-bearing host contract is considered to be clearly and closely related to the host contract unless either of the following conditions exist:

a. The hybrid instrument can contractually be settled in a such a way that the investor (holder) would not recover *substantially all* of its initial recorded investment.
b. The embedded derivative could at least double the investor's initial rate of return on the host contract and could also result in a rate of return that is at least twice what otherwise would be the market return for a contract that has the same terms as the host contract and that involves a debtor with a similar credit quality.

Even though the above conditions focus on the investor's rate of return and the investor's recovery of its investment, the existence of either of those conditions would result in the embedded derivative instrument not being considered clearly and closely related to the host contract by both parties to the hybrid instrument. Because the existence of those conditions is assessed at the date that the hybrid instrument is acquired (or incurred) by the reporting entity, the acquirer of a hybrid instrument in the secondary market could potentially reach a different conclusion than could the issuer of the hybrid instrument due to applying the conditions in this paragraph at different points in time. [FAS133, ¶13]

.111 However, interest-only strips and principal-only strips are not subject to the requirements of this section provided they (a) initially resulted from separating the rights to receive contractual cash flows of a financial instrument that, in and of itself, did not contain an embedded derivative that otherwise would have been accounted for separately as

[8]Examples are an interest rate cap or an interest rate collar. An embedded derivative instrument that alters net interest payments based on changes in a stock price index (or another non-interest-rate index) is not addressed in paragraph .110. [FAS133, ¶13, fn6]

a derivative pursuant to the provisions of paragraphs .109 and .110 and (b) do not incorporate any terms not present in the original financial instrument described above. [FAS133, ¶14]

.112 An embedded foreign currency derivative instrument shall *not* be separated from the host contract and considered a derivative instrument under paragraph .109 if the host contract is not a financial instrument and it requires payment(s) denominated in (a) the currency of the primary economic environment in which any substantial party to that contract operates (that is, its functional currency) or (b) the currency in which the price of the related good or service that is acquired or delivered is routinely denominated in international commerce (for example, the U.S. dollar for crude oil transactions). Unsettled foreign currency transactions, including financial instruments, that are monetary items and have their principal payments, interest payments, or both denominated in a foreign currency are subject to the requirement in Section F60, "Foreign Currency Translation," to recognize any foreign currency transaction gain or loss in earnings and shall not be considered to contain embedded foreign currency derivative instruments under this section. The same proscription applies to available-for-sale or trading securities that have cash flows denominated in a foreign currency. [FAS133, ¶15]

.113 In subsequent provisions of this section, both (a) a derivative instrument included within the scope of this section by paragraphs .103 through .108 and (b) an embedded derivative instrument that has been separated from a host contract as required by paragraph .109 are collectively referred to as derivative instruments. If an embedded derivative instrument is separated from its host contract, the host contract shall be accounted for based on generally accepted accounting principles applicable to instruments of that type that do not contain embedded derivative instruments. If an entity cannot reliably identify and measure the embedded derivative instrument that paragraph .109 requires be separated from the host contract, the entire contract shall be measured at fair value with gain or loss recognized in earnings, but it may not be designated as a hedging instrument pursuant to this section. [FAS133, ¶16]

Recognition of Derivatives and Measurement of Derivatives and Hedged Items

.114 An entity shall recognize all of its derivative instruments in its statement of financial position as either assets or liabilities depending on the rights or obligations under the contracts. All derivative instruments shall be measured at fair value.[9] The guidance in Section F25, "Financial Instruments: Disclosure," shall apply in determining the fair value of a financial instrument (derivative or hedged item). If expected future cash flows are used to estimate fair value, those expected cash flows shall be the best estimate based on reasonable and supportable assumptions and projections. All available evidence shall be considered in developing estimates of expected future cash flows. The weight given to the evidence shall be commensurate with the extent to which the evidence can be verified objectively. If a range is estimated for either the amount or the timing of possible cash flows, the likelihood of possible outcomes shall be considered in determining the best estimate of future cash flows. [FAS133, ¶17]

.115 The accounting for changes in the fair value (that is, gains or losses) of a derivative depends on whether it has been designated and qualifies as part of a hedging relationship and, if so, on the reason for holding it. Either all or a proportion of a derivative may be designated as the hedging instrument. The proportion must be expressed as a percentage of the entire derivative so that the profile of risk exposures in the hedging portion of the derivative is the same as that in the entire derivative. (Thus, an entity is prohibited from separating a compound derivative into components representing different risks and designating any such component as the hedging instrument, except as permitted at the date of initial application of this section.) Subsequent references in this section to a derivative as a hedging instrument include the use of only a proportion of a derivative as a hedging instrument. Two or more derivatives, or proportions thereof, may also be viewed in combination and jointly designated as the hedging instrument. Gains and losses on derivative instruments are accounted for as follows:

a. *No hedging designation.* The gain or loss on a derivative instrument not designated as a hedging instrument shall be recognized currently in earnings.
b. *Fair value hedge.* The gain or loss on a derivative instrument designated and qualifying as a fair value hedging instrument as well as the offsetting loss or gain on the hedged item attributable to the hedged risk shall be recognized currently in earnings in the same accounting period, as provided in paragraphs .119 and .120.
c. *Cash flow hedge.* The effective portion of the gain or loss on a derivative instrument designated and qualifying as a cash flow hedging instrument shall be reported as a component of other **comprehensive income** (outside earnings) and reclassified into earnings in the same period or periods during which the hedged forecasted transac-

[9]Unlike Section F25, "Financial Instruments: Disclosure," this section provides no *practicability* exception that would permit an entity to avoid the required fair value measurements. [It is] believed that prudent risk management generally would require an entity to measure the fair value of any derivative that it holds as well as any item (or the portion of the item attributable to the identified risk) designated as being hedged in a fair value hedge. [FAS133, ¶318]

tion affects earnings, as provided in paragraphs .127 and .128. The remaining gain or loss on the derivative instrument, if any, shall be recognized currently in earnings, as provided in paragraph .127.

d. *Foreign currency hedge.* The gain or loss on a derivative instrument or nonderivative financial instrument designated and qualifying as a foreign currency hedging instrument shall be accounted for as follows:
   (1) The gain or loss on the hedging derivative or nonderivative instrument in a hedge of a foreign-currency-denominated firm commitment and the offsetting loss or gain on the hedged firm commitment shall be recognized currently in earnings in the same accounting period, as provided in paragraph .134.
   (2) The gain or loss on the hedging derivative instrument in a hedge of an available-for-sale security and the offsetting loss or gain on the hedged available-for-sale security shall be recognized currently in earnings in the same accounting period, as provided in paragraph .135.
   (3) The effective portion of the gain or loss on the hedging derivative instrument in a hedge of a forecasted foreign-currency-denominated transaction shall be reported as a component of other comprehensive income (outside earnings) and reclassified into earnings in the same period or periods during which the hedged forecasted transaction affects earnings, as provided in paragraph .138. The remaining gain or loss on the hedging instrument shall be recognized currently in earnings.
   (4) The gain or loss on the hedging derivative or nonderivative instrument in a hedge of a net investment in a foreign operation shall be reported in other comprehensive income (outside earnings) as part of the cumulative translation adjustment to the extent it is effective as a hedge, as provided in paragraph .139.

[FAS133, ¶18]

.116 In this section, the *change in the fair value* of an entire financial asset or liability for a period refers to the difference between its fair value at the beginning of the period (or acquisition date) and the end of the period adjusted to exclude (a) changes in fair value due to the passage of time and (b) changes in fair value related to any payments received or made, such as in partially recovering the asset or partially settling the liability. [FAS133, ¶19]

Fair Value Hedges

General

.117 An entity may designate a derivative instrument as hedging the exposure to changes in the fair value of an asset or a liability or an identified portion thereof ("hedged item") that is attributable to a particular risk. Designated hedging instruments and hedged items qualify for fair value hedge accounting if all of the following criteria and those in paragraph .118 are met:

a. At inception of the hedge, there is formal documentation of the hedging relationship and the entity's risk management objective and strategy for undertaking the hedge, including identification of the hedging instrument, the hedged item, the nature of the risk being hedged, and how the hedging instrument's effectiveness in offsetting the exposure to changes in the hedged item's fair value attributable to the hedged risk will be assessed. There must be a reasonable basis for how the entity plans to assess the hedging instrument's effectiveness.
   (1) For a fair value hedge of a firm commitment, the entity's formal documentation at the inception of the hedge must include a reasonable method for recognizing in earnings the asset or liability representing the gain or loss on the hedged firm commitment.
   (2) An entity's defined risk management strategy for a particular hedging relationship may exclude certain components of a specific hedging derivative's change in fair value, such as time value, from the assessment of hedge effectiveness, as discussed in paragraph .151.

   [Refer to paragraph .1001 for an EITF Issue that provides interpretive guidance on this subparagraph.]
b. Both at inception of the hedge and on an ongoing basis, the hedging relationship is expected to be highly effective[10] in achieving offsetting changes in fair value attributable to the hedged risk during the period that the hedge is designated. An assessment of effectiveness is required whenever financial statements or earnings are reported, and at least every three months. If the hedging instrument (such as an at-the-money option contract) provides only one-sided offset of the hedged risk, the increases (or decreases) in the fair value of the hedging instrument must be expected to be highly effective in offsetting the decreases (or increases) in the fair value of the hedged item. All assessments of effectiveness shall be consistent with the risk management strategy documented for that particular hedging relationship (in accordance with paragraph .117(a) above).[11]
c. If a written option is designated as hedging a recognized asset or liability, the combination of the hedged item and the written option provides at least as much potential for gains as a result of a favorable change in the fair value of the combined instru-

---

[10]"Highly effective" [is intended] to be essentially the same as the notion of "high correlation" in FASB Statement 80, *Accounting for Futures Contracts.* [FAS133, ¶389]

[11]The same method [should] be used for similar hedges unless different methods are explicitly justified. If an entity [subsequently] identifies an improved method for assessing effectiveness, it may discontinue the existing hedging relationship and then designate and document a new hedging relationship using the improved method prospectively. [FAS133, ¶386]

ments[12] as exposure to losses from an unfavorable change in their combined fair value. That test is met if all possible percentage favorable changes in the underlying (from zero percent to 100 percent) would provide at least as much gain as the loss that would be incurred from an unfavorable change in the underlying of the same percentage.

(1) A combination of options (for example, an interest rate collar) entered into contemporaneously shall be considered a written option if either at inception or over the life of the contracts a net premium is received in cash or as a favorable rate or other term. (Thus, a collar can be designated as a hedging instrument in a fair value hedge without regard to the test in paragraph .117(c) unless a net premium is received.) Furthermore, a derivative instrument that results from combining a written option and any other nonoption derivative shall be considered a written option.

A nonderivative instrument, such as a Treasury note, shall not be designated as a hedging instrument, except as provided in paragraphs .134 and .139 of this section. [FAS133, ¶20]

The Hedged Item

.118 An asset or a liability is eligible for designation as a hedged item in a fair value hedge if all of the following criteria are met:

a. The hedged item is specifically identified as either all or a specific portion of a recognized asset or liability or of an unrecognized firm commitment.[13] The hedged item is a single asset or liability (or a specific portion thereof) or is a portfolio of similar assets or a portfolio of similar liabilities (or a specific portion thereof).

   (1) If similar assets or similar liabilities are aggregated and hedged as a portfolio, the individual assets or individual liabilities must share the risk exposure for which they are designated as being hedged. The change in fair value attributable to the hedged risk for each individual item in a hedged portfolio must be expected to respond in a generally proportionate manner to the overall change in fair value of

[12]The reference to *combined instruments* refers to the written option and the hedged item, such as an embedded purchased option. [FAS133, ¶20, fn7]

[13]A firm commitment that represents an asset or liability that a specific accounting standard prohibits recognizing (such as a noncancelable operating lease or an unrecognized mortgage servicing right) may nevertheless be designated as the hedged item in a fair value hedge. A mortgage banker's unrecognized "interest rate lock commitment" (IRLC) does not qualify as a firm commitment (because as an option it does not obligate both parties) and thus is not eligible for fair value hedge accounting as the hedged item. (However, a mortgage banker's "forward sale commitments," which are derivatives that lock in the prices at which the mortgage loans will be sold to investors, may qualify as hedging instruments in cash flow hedges of the forecasted sales of mortgage loans.) [FAS133, ¶21, fn8]

the aggregate portfolio attributable to the hedged risk. That is, if the change in fair value of a hedged portfolio attributable to the hedged risk was 10 percent during a reporting period, the change in the fair values attributable to the hedged risk for each item constituting the portfolio should be expected to be within a fairly narrow range, such as 9 percent to 11 percent. In contrast, an expectation that the change in fair value attributable to the hedged risk for individual items in the portfolio would range from 7 percent to 13 percent would be inconsistent with this provision. In aggregating loans in a portfolio to be hedged, an entity may choose to consider some of the following characteristics, as appropriate: loan type, loan size, nature and location of collateral, interest rate type (fixed or variable) and the coupon interest rate (if fixed), scheduled maturity, prepayment history of the loans (if seasoned), and expected prepayment performance in varying interest rate scenarios.[14]

(2) If the hedged item is a specific portion of an asset or liability (or of a portfolio of similar assets or a portfolio of similar liabilities), the hedged item is one of the following:
   (a) A percentage of the entire asset or liability (or of the entire portfolio)
   (b) One or more selected contractual cash flows (such as the portion of the asset or liability representing the present value of the interest payments in the first two years of a four-year debt instrument)
   (c) A put option, a call option, an interest rate cap, or an interest rate floor embedded in an existing asset or liability that is not an embedded derivative accounted for separately pursuant to paragraph .109 of this section
   (d) The residual value in a lessor's net investment in a direct financing or sales-type lease.

   If the entire asset or liability is an instrument with variable cash flows, the hedged item cannot be deemed to be an implicit fixed-to-variable swap (or similar instrument) perceived to be embedded in a host contract with fixed cash flows.

b. The hedged item presents an exposure to changes in fair value attributable to the hedged risk that could affect reported earnings. The reference to affecting reported earnings does not apply to an entity that does not report earnings as a separate caption in a statement of financial performance, such as a not-for-profit organization, as discussed in paragraph .140.

[14]Mortgage bankers and other servicers of financial assets that designate a hedged portfolio by aggregating servicing rights within one or more risk strata used under paragraph .106(g) of Section F35, "Financial Instruments: Servicing," would not necessarily comply with the requirement in this paragraph for portfolios of similar assets. The risk stratum under paragraph .106(g) of Section F35 can be based on any predominant risk characteristic, including date of origination or geographic location. [FAS133, ¶21, fn9]

c. The hedged item is not (1) an asset or liability that is remeasured with the changes in fair value attributable to the hedged risk reported currently in earnings, (2) an investment accounted for by the equity method in accordance with the requirements of Section I82, "Investments: Equity Method," (3) a minority interest in one or more consolidated subsidiaries, (4) an equity investment in a consolidated subsidiary, (5) a firm commitment either to enter into a business combination or to acquire or dispose of a subsidiary, a minority interest, or an equity method investee, or (6) an equity instrument issued by the entity and classified in stockholders' equity in the statement of financial position. [FAS133, ¶21]

d. If the hedged item is all or a portion of a debt security (or a portfolio of similar debt securities) that is classified as held-to-maturity in accordance with Section I80, "Investments: Debt and Equity Securities," the designated risk being hedged is the risk of changes in its fair value attributable to credit risk, foreign exchange risk, or both. If the hedged item is an option component of a held-to-maturity security that permits its prepayment, the designated risk being hedged is the risk of changes in the entire fair value of that option component. [FAS138, ¶4(b)(1)] (The designated hedged risk for a held-to-maturity security may not be the risk of changes in its fair value attributable to [FAS133, ¶21] interest rate risk. [FAS138, ¶4(c)(2)] If the hedged item is other than an option component that permits its prepayment, the designated hedged risk also may not be the risk of changes in its overall fair value.)

e. If the hedged item is a nonfinancial asset or liability (other than a recognized loan servicing right or a nonfinancial firm commitment with financial components), the designated risk being hedged is the risk of changes in the fair value of the entire hedged asset or liability (reflecting its actual location if a physical asset). That is, the price risk of a similar asset in a different location or of a major ingredient may not be the hedged risk. Thus, in hedging the exposure to changes in the fair value of gasoline, an entity may not designate the risk of changes in the price of crude oil as the risk being hedged for purposes of determining effectiveness of the fair value hedge of gasoline.

f. If the hedged item is a financial asset or liability, a recognized loan servicing right, or a nonfinancial firm commitment with financial components, the designated risk being hedged is (1) the risk of changes in the overall fair value of the entire hedged item, (2) the risk of changes in its fair value attributable to changes in [FAS133, ¶21] the designated **benchmark interest rate** (referred to as interest rate risk), [FAS138, ¶4(b)(3)] (3) the risk of changes in its fair value attributable to changes in the related foreign currency exchange rates [FAS133, ¶21] (referred to as foreign exchange risk) (refer to paragraphs .134, .134A, and .135), [FAS138, ¶4(b)(4)] or (4) the risk of changes in its fair value attributable to [FAS133, ¶21] both [FAS138, ¶4(b)(5)] changes in [FAS133, ¶21] the obligor's creditworthiness and changes in the spread over the benchmark interest rate with respect to the hedged item's credit sector at inception of the hedge (referred to as credit risk). [FAS138, ¶4(b)(5)] If the risk designated as being hedged is not the risk in paragraph .118(f)(1) above, two or more of the other risks (market interest rate risk, foreign currency exchange risk, and credit risk) may simultaneously be designated as being hedged. [FAS133, ¶21] The benchmark interest rate being hedged in a hedge of interest rate risk must be specifically identified as part of the designation and documentation at the inception of the hedging relationship. Ordinarily, an entity should designate the same benchmark interest rate as the risk being hedged for similar hedges, consistent with paragraph .150; the use of different benchmark interest rates for similar hedges should be rare and must be justified. In calculating the change in the hedged item's fair value attributable to changes in the benchmark interest rate, the estimated cash flows used in calculating fair value must be based on all of the contractual cash flows of the entire hedged item. Excluding some of the hedged item's contractual cash flows (for example, the portion of the interest coupon in excess of the benchmark interest rate) from the calculation is not permitted.[14a, [14b]] [FAS138, ¶4(b)(7)] An entity may not simply designate prepayment risk as the risk being hedged for a financial asset. However, it can designate the option component of a prepayable instrument as the hedged item in a fair value hedge of the entity's exposure to changes in the [FAS133, ¶21] overall [FAS138, ¶4(b)(8)] fair value of that "prepayment" option, perhaps thereby achieving the objective of its desire to hedge prepayment risk. The effect of an embedded derivative of the same risk class must be considered in designating a hedge of an individual risk. For example, the effect of an embedded prepayment option must be considered in designating a hedge of market interest rate risk. [FAS133, ¶21]

.119 Gains and losses on a qualifying fair value hedge shall be accounted for as follows:

a. The gain or loss on the hedging instrument shall be recognized currently in earnings.
b. The gain or loss (that is, the change in fair value) on the hedged item attributable to the hedged risk shall adjust the carrying amount of the hedged item and be recognized currently in earnings.

If the fair value hedge is fully effective, the gain or loss on the hedging instrument, adjusted for the component, if any, of that gain or loss that is excluded from the assessment of effectiveness under the entity's defined risk management strategy for that particular hedging relationship (as discussed in paragraph .151), would exactly offset the loss or gain on the hedged item attributable to the hedged risk. Any difference that does arise

---

[14a]The first sentence of paragraph .118(a) that specifically permits the hedged item to be identified as either all or a specific portion of a recognized asset or liability or of an unrecognized firm commitment is not affected by the provisions in this subparagraph. [FAS138, ¶4(b)(7)]

[[14b]This section] does not mandate the use of any one method. [FAS138, ¶24]

would be the effect of hedge ineffectiveness, which consequently is recognized currently in earnings. The measurement of hedge ineffectiveness for a particular hedging relationship shall be consistent with the entity's risk management strategy and the method of assessing hedge effectiveness that was documented at the inception of the hedging relationship, as discussed in paragraph .117(a). Nevertheless, the amount of hedge ineffectiveness recognized in earnings is based on the extent to which exact offset is not achieved. Although a hedging relationship must comply with an entity's established policy range of what is considered "highly effective" pursuant to paragraph .117(b) in order for that relationship to qualify for hedge accounting, that compliance does not assure zero ineffectiveness. Paragraphs .150 through .191 illustrate assessing hedge effectiveness and measuring hedge ineffectiveness. Any hedge ineffectiveness directly affects earnings because there will be no offsetting adjustment of a hedged item's carrying amount for the ineffective aspect of the gain or loss on the related hedging instrument. [FAS133, ¶22]

.120 If a hedged item is otherwise measured at fair value with changes in fair value reported in other comprehensive income (such as an available-for-sale security), the adjustment of the hedged item's carrying amount discussed in paragraph .119 shall be recognized in earnings rather than in other comprehensive income in order to offset the gain or loss on the hedging instrument. [FAS133, ¶23]

.121 The adjustment of the carrying amount of a hedged asset or liability required by paragraph .119 shall be accounted for in the same manner as other components of the carrying amount of that asset or liability. For example, an adjustment of the carrying amount of a hedged asset held for sale (such as inventory) would remain part of the carrying amount of that asset until the asset is sold, at which point the entire carrying amount of the hedged asset would be recognized as the cost of the item sold in determining earnings. An adjustment of the carrying amount of a hedged interest-bearing financial instrument shall be amortized to earnings; amortization shall begin no later than when the hedged item ceases to be adjusted for changes in its fair value attributable to the risk being hedged. [FAS133, ¶24]

.122 An entity shall discontinue prospectively the accounting specified in paragraphs .119 and .120 for an existing hedge if any one of the following occurs:

a. Any criterion in paragraphs .117 and .118 is no longer met.
b. The derivative expires or is sold, terminated, or exercised.
c. The entity removes the designation of the fair value hedge.

In those circumstances, the entity may elect to designate prospectively a new hedging relationship with a different hedging instrument or, in the circumstances described in paragraphs .122(a) and .122(c) above, a different hedged item or a hedged transaction if the hedging relationship meets the criteria specified in paragraphs .117 and .118 for a fair value hedge or paragraphs .125 and .126 for a cash flow hedge. [FAS133, ¶25]

.123 In general, if a periodic assessment indicates noncompliance with the effectiveness criterion in paragraph .117(b), an entity shall not recognize the adjustment of the carrying amount of the hedged item described in paragraphs .119 and .120 after the last date on which compliance with the effectiveness criterion was established. However, if the event or change in circumstances that caused the hedging relationship to fail the effectiveness criterion can be identified, the entity shall recognize in earnings the changes in the hedged item's fair value attributable to the risk being hedged that occurred prior to that event or change in circumstances. If a fair value hedge of a firm commitment is discontinued because the hedged item no longer meets the definition of a firm commitment, the entity shall derecognize any asset or liability previously recognized pursuant to paragraph .119 (as a result of an adjustment to the carrying amount for the firm commitment) and recognize a corresponding loss or gain currently in earnings.[15] [FAS133, ¶26]

Impairment

.124 An asset or liability that has been designated as being hedged and accounted for pursuant to paragraphs .119 through .121 remains subject to the applicable requirements in generally accepted accounting principles for assessing impairment for that type of asset or for recognizing an increased obligation for that type of liability. Those impairment requirements shall be applied after hedge accounting has been applied for the period and the carrying amount of the hedged asset or liability has been adjusted pursuant to paragraph .119 of this section. Because the hedging instrument is recognized separately as an asset or liability, its fair value or expected cash flows shall not be considered in applying those impairment requirements to the hedged asset or liability. [FAS133, ¶27]

Cash Flow Hedges

General

.125 An entity may designate a derivative instrument as hedging the exposure to variability in expected future cash flows that is attributable to a particular risk. That exposure may be associated with an existing recognized asset or liability (such as all or certain future interest payments on variable-rate debt) or a forecasted transaction (such as a

[15] A pattern of discontinuing hedge accounting and derecognizing firm commitments would call into question the "firmness" of future hedged firm commitments and the entity's accounting for future hedges of firm commitments. [FAS133, ¶491]

forecasted purchase or sale).[16] Designated hedging instruments and hedged items or transactions qualify for cash flow hedge accounting if all of the following criteria and those in paragraph .126 are met:

a. At inception of the hedge, there is formal documentation of the hedging relationship and the entity's risk management objective and strategy for undertaking the hedge, including identification of the hedging instrument, the hedged transaction, the nature of the risk being hedged, and how the hedging instrument's effectiveness in hedging the exposure to the hedged transaction's variability in cash flows attributable to the hedged risk will be assessed. There must be a reasonable basis for how the entity plans to assess the hedging instrument's effectiveness.
   (1) An entity's defined risk management strategy for a particular hedging relationship may exclude certain components of a specific hedging derivative's change in fair value from the assessment of hedge effectiveness, as discussed in paragraph .151.
   (2) Documentation shall include all relevant details, including the date on or period within which the forecasted transaction is expected to occur, the specific nature of asset or liability involved (if any), and the expected currency amount or quantity of the forecasted transaction.
      (a) The phrase *expected currency amount* refers to hedges of foreign currency exchange risk and requires specification of the exact amount of foreign currency being hedged.
      (b) The phrase *expected . . . quantity* refers to hedges of other risks and requires specification of the physical quantity (that is, the number of items or units of measure) encompassed by the hedged forecasted transaction. If a forecasted sale or purchase is being hedged for price risk, the hedged transaction cannot be specified solely in terms of expected currency amounts, nor can it be specified as a percentage of sales or purchases during a period. The current price of a forecasted transaction also should be identified to satisfy the criterion in paragraph .125(b) for offsetting cash flows.

   The hedged forecasted transaction shall be described with sufficient specificity so that when a transaction occurs, it is clear whether that transaction is or is not the hedged transaction. Thus, the forecasted transaction could be identified as the sale of either the first 15,000 units of a specific product sold during a specified 3-month period or the first 5,000 units of a specific product sold in each of 3 specific months, but it could not be identified as the sale of the last 15,000 units of that product

[16]For purposes of paragraphs .125 through .132, the individual cash flows related to a recognized asset or liability and the cash flows related to a forecasted transaction are both referred to as a *forecasted transaction* or *hedged transaction.* [FAS133, ¶28, fn10]

sold during a 3-month period (because the last 15,000 units cannot be identified when they occur, but only when the period has ended).[17]

[Refer to paragraph .1001 for an EITF Issue that provides interpretive guidance on this subparagraph.]

b. Both at inception of the hedge and on an ongoing basis, the hedging relationship is expected to be highly effective[18] in achieving offsetting cash flows[19] attributable to the hedged risk during the term of the hedge, except as indicated in paragraph .125(d) below. An assessment of effectiveness is required whenever financial statements or earnings are reported, and at least every three months. If the hedging instrument, such as an at-the-money option contract, provides only one-sided offset against the hedged risk, the cash inflows (outflows) from the hedging instrument must be expected to be highly effective in offsetting the corresponding change in the cash outflows or inflows of the hedged transaction. All assessments of effectiveness shall be consistent with the originally documented risk management strategy for that particular hedging relationship.[20]

c. If a written option is designated as hedging the variability in cash flows for a recognized asset or liability, the combination of the hedged item and the written option provides at least as much potential for favorable cash flows as exposure to unfavor-

---

[17]The following example illustrates the requirement for specific identification of the hedged transaction. Company A determines with a high degree of probability that it will issue $5,000,000 of fixed-rate bonds with a 5-year maturity sometime during the next 6 months, but it cannot predict exactly when the debt issuance will occur. That situation might occur, for example, if the funds from the debt issuance are needed to finance a major project to which Company A is already committed but the precise timing of which has not yet been determined. To qualify for cash flow hedge accounting, Company A might identify the hedged forecasted transaction as, for example, the first issuance of five-year, fixed-rate bonds that occurs during the next six months. [FAS133, ¶460]

[18]"Highly effective" [is intended] to be essentially the same as the notion of "high correlation" in Statement 80. [FAS133, ¶389]

[19]The offset criterion precludes hedge accounting for certain risk management techniques, such as hedges of strategic risk. For example, a U.S. manufacturer, with no export business, that designates a forward contract to buy U.S. dollars for Japanese yen as a hedge of its U.S. dollar sales would fail the requirement that the cash flows of the derivative are expected to be highly effective in achieving offsetting cash flows on the hedged transaction. A weakened yen might allow a competitor to sell goods imported from Japan more cheaply, undercutting the domestic manufacturer's prices and reducing its sales volume and revenues. However, it would be difficult for the U.S. manufacturer to expect a high degree of offset between a decline in U.S. sales revenue due to increased competition and cash inflows on a foreign currency derivative. Any relationship between the exposure and the "hedging" derivative typically would be quite indirect, would depend on price elasticities, and would be only one of many factors influencing future results. In addition, the risk that a desired or expected number of transactions will not occur, that is, the potential absence of a transaction, is not a hedgeable risk under this section. [FAS133, ¶231]

[20]The same method [should] be used for similar hedges unless different methods are explicitly justified. If an entity [subsequently] identifies an improved method for assessing effectiveness, it may discontinue the existing hedging relationship and then designate and document a new hedging relationship using the improved method prospectively. [FAS133, ¶386]

able cash flows. That test is met if all possible percentage favorable changes in the underlying (from zero percent to 100 percent) would provide at least as much favorable cash flows as the unfavorable cash flows that would be incurred from an unfavorable change in the underlying of the same percentage. (Refer to paragraph .117(c)(1).)[21]

d. If a hedging instrument is used to modify the interest receipts or payments associated with a recognized financial asset or liability from one variable rate to another variable rate, the hedging instrument must be a link between an existing designated asset (or group of similar assets) with variable cash flows and an existing designated liability (or group of similar liabilities) with variable cash flows and be highly effective at achieving offsetting cash flows. A link exists if the basis (that is, the rate index on which the interest rate is based) of one leg of an interest rate swap is the same as the basis of the interest receipts for the designated asset and the basis of the other leg of the swap is the same as the basis of the interest payments for the designated liability. In this situation, the criterion in the first sentence in paragraph .126(a) is applied separately to the designated asset and the designated liability.

A nonderivative instrument, such as a Treasury note, shall not be designated as a hedging instrument for a cash flow hedge. [FAS133, ¶28]

The Hedged Forecasted Transaction

.126 A forecasted transaction is eligible for designation as a hedged transaction in a cash flow hedge if all of the following additional criteria are met:

a. The forecasted transaction is specifically identified as a single transaction or a group of individual transactions. If the hedged transaction is a group of individual transactions, those individual transactions must share the same risk exposure for which they

[21]This section does not permit hedge accounting for "covered call" strategies—strategies in which an entity writes an option on an asset that it owns (unless that asset is a call option that is embedded in another instrument). In that strategy, any loss on the written option will be covered by the gain on the owned asset. However, a covered call strategy will not qualify for hedge accounting because the risk profile of the combined position is asymmetrical (the exposure to losses is greater than the potential for gains). In contrast, the risk profile of the asset alone is "symmetrical or better" (the potential for gains is at least as great as the exposure to losses). [FAS133, ¶399] The symmetry requirement for hedges with written options is intended to preclude a written option that is used to sell a portion of the gain potential on an asset or liability from being eligible for hedge accounting. [FAS133, ¶400]

are designated as being hedged. Thus, a forecasted purchase and a forecasted sale cannot both be included in the same group of individual transactions that constitute the hedged transaction.[22]

b. The occurrence of the forecasted transaction is probable.[23]

---

[22]To illustrate, under the guidance in this section, a single derivative of appropriate size could be designated as hedging a given amount of aggregated forecasted transactions such as the following:

a. Forecasted sales of a particular product to numerous customers within a specified time period, such as a month, a quarter, or a year
b. Forecasted purchases of a particular product from the same or different vendors at different dates within a specified time period
c. Forecasted interest payments on several variable-rate debt instruments within a specified time period.

However, the transactions in each group must share the risk exposure for which they are being hedged. For example, the interest payments in group (c) above must vary with the same index to qualify for hedging with a single derivative. [FAS133, ¶462]

[23]An assessment of the likelihood that a forecasted transaction will take place should not be based solely on management's intent because intent is not verifiable. The transaction's probability should be supported by observable facts and the attendant circumstances. Consideration should be given to the following circumstances in assessing the likelihood that a transaction will occur.

a. The frequency of similar past transactions
b. The financial and operational ability of the entity to carry out the transaction
c. Substantial commitments of resources to a particular activity (for example, a manufacturing facility that can be used in the short run only to process a particular type of commodity)
d. The extent of loss or disruption of operations that could result if the transaction does not occur
e. The likelihood that transactions with substantially different characteristics might be used to achieve the same business purpose (for example, an entity that intends to raise cash may have several ways of doing so, ranging from a short-term bank loan to a common stock offering). [FAS133, ¶463]

Both the length of time until a forecasted transaction is projected to occur and the quantity of the forecasted transaction are considerations in determining probability. Other factors being equal, the more distant or the greater the physical quantity or future value of a forecasted transaction is, the less likely it is that the transaction would be considered probable and the stronger the evidence that would be needed to support an assertion that it is probable. [FAS133, ¶465]

c. The forecasted transaction is a transaction[24] with a party external to the reporting entity (except as permitted by paragraph .137) and presents an exposure to variations in cash flows for the hedged risk that could affect reported earnings.[25]
d. The forecasted transaction is not the acquisition of an asset or incurrence of a liability that will subsequently be remeasured with changes in fair value attributable to the hedged risk reported currently in earnings. If the forecasted transaction relates to a recognized asset or liability, the asset or liability is not remeasured with changes in fair value attributable to the hedged risk reported currently in earnings.
e. If the variable cash flows of the forecasted transaction relate to a debt security that is classified as held-to-maturity under Section I80, the risk being hedged is the risk of changes in its cash flows attributable to [FAS133, ¶29] credit risk, foreign exchange risk, or both. [FAS138, ¶4(c)(1)] For those variable cash flows, the risk being hedged cannot be the risk of changes in its cash flows attributable to [FAS133, ¶29] interest rate risk. [FAS138, ¶4(c)(2)]
f. The forecasted transaction does not involve a business combination subject to the provisions of [FAS133, ¶29] Section B51 [FAS141, ¶E18(b)] and is not a transaction (such as a forecasted purchase, sale, or dividend) involving (1) a parent company's interests in consolidated subsidiaries, (2) a minority interest in a consolidated subsidiary, (3) an equity-method investment, or (4) an entity's own equity instruments.
g. If the hedged transaction is the forecasted purchase or sale of a nonfinancial asset, the designated risk being hedged is (1) the risk of changes in the functional-currency-equivalent cash flows attributable to changes in the related foreign currency exchange rates or (2) the risk of changes in the cash flows relating to all changes in the

---

[24]FASB Concepts Statement 6, *Elements of Financial Statements,* defines a *transaction* as an external event involving transfer of something of value (future economic benefit) between two (or more) entities. That definition was intended to clearly distinguish a transaction from an internal cost allocation or an event that happens within an entity. [FAS133, ¶469]

[25]For example, the future sale of an asset or settlement of a liability that exposes an entity to the risk of a change in fair value may result in recognizing a gain or loss in earnings when the sale or settlement occurs. Changes in market price could change the amount for which the asset or liability could be sold or settled and, consequently, change the amount of gain or loss recognized. Forecasted transactions that expose an entity to cash flow risk have the potential to affect reported earnings because the amount of related revenue or expense may differ depending on the price eventually paid or received. Thus, an entity could designate the forecasted sale of a product at the market price at the date of sale as a hedged transaction because revenue will be recorded at that future sales price. [FAS133, ¶402] The earnings exposure criterion specifically precludes hedge accounting for derivatives used to hedge (a) transactions with stockholders as stockholders, such as projected purchases of treasury stock or payments of dividends, (b) intercompany transactions (except for foreign currency denominated forecasted intercompany transactions) between entities included in consolidated financial statements, and (c) the price of stock expected to be issued pursuant to a stock option plan for which recognized compensation expense is not based on changes in stock prices after the date of grant. However, intercompany transactions may present an earnings exposure for a subsidiary in its freestanding financial statements; a hedge of an intercompany transaction would be eligible for hedge accounting for purposes of those statements. [FAS133, ¶404]

purchase price or sales price of the asset [FAS133, ¶29] reflecting its actual location if a physical asset (regardless of whether that price and the related cash flows are stated in the entity's functional currency or a foreign currency), [FAS138, ¶4(h)] not the risk of changes in the cash flows relating to the purchase or sale of a similar asset in a different location or of a major ingredient. Thus, for example, in hedging the exposure to changes in the cash flows relating to the purchase of its bronze bar inventory, an entity may not designate the risk of changes in the cash flows relating to purchasing the copper component in bronze as the risk being hedged for purposes of assessing offset as required by paragraph .125(b).

h. If the hedged transaction is the forecasted purchase or sale of a financial asset or liability [FAS133, ¶29] (or the interest payments on that financial asset or liability) [FAS138, ¶4(c)(3)] or the variable cash inflow or outflow of an existing financial asset or liability, the designated risk being hedged is (1) [FAS133, ¶29] the risk of overall changes in the hedged cash flows related to the asset or liability [FAS138, ¶4(c)(4)] such as those relating to all changes in the purchase price or sales price (regardless of whether that price and the related cash flows are stated in the entity's functional currency or a foreign currency), (2) the risk of changes in its cash flows attributable to changes in [FAS133, ¶29] the designated benchmark interest rate (referred to as interest rate risk), [FAS138, ¶4(c)(5)] (3) the risk of changes in the functional-currency-equivalent cash flows attributable to changes in the related foreign currency exchange rates [FAS133, ¶29] (referred to as foreign exchange risk) (refer to paragraphs .137 through .137C), [FAS138, ¶4(c)(6)] or (4) the risk of changes in its cash flows attributable to [FAS133, ¶29] default, changes in the obligor's creditworthiness, and changes in the spread over the benchmark interest rate with respect to the hedged item's credit sector at inception of the hedge (referred to as credit risk). [FAS138, ¶4(c)(7)] Two or more of the above risks may be designated simultaneously as being hedged. [FAS133, ¶29] The benchmark interest rate being hedged in a hedge of interest rate risk must be specifically identified as part of the designation and documentation at the inception of the hedging relationship. Ordinarily, an entity should designate the same benchmark interest rate as the risk being hedged for similar hedges, consistent with paragraph .150; the use of different benchmark interest rates for similar hedges should be rare and must be justified. In a cash flow hedge of a variable-rate financial asset or liability, either existing or forecasted, the designated risk being hedged cannot be the risk of changes in its cash flows attributable to changes in the specifically identified benchmark interest rate if the cash flows of the hedged transaction are explicitly based on a different index, for example, based on a specific bank's prime rate, which cannot qualify as the benchmark rate.[25a] However, the risk designated as being hedged could potentially be the risk of overall changes in the hedged cash flows related to the asset or liability, provided that the other criteria for a cash flow hedge have been met. [FAS138, ¶4(c)(8)] An entity may not designate prepayment risk as the risk being hedged (refer to paragraph .118(f)). [FAS133, ¶29]

.127 The effective portion of the gain or loss on a derivative designated as a cash flow hedge is reported in other comprehensive income, and the ineffective portion is reported in earnings. More specifically, a qualifying cash flow hedge shall be accounted for as follows:

a. If an entity's defined risk management strategy for a particular hedging relationship excludes a specific component of the gain or loss, or related cash flows, on the hedging derivative from the assessment of hedge effectiveness (as discussed in paragraph .151), that excluded component of the gain or loss shall be recognized currently in earnings. For example, if the effectiveness of a hedge with an option contract is assessed based on changes in the option's intrinsic value, the changes in the option's time value would be recognized in earnings. Time value is equal to the fair value of the option less its intrinsic value.
b. Accumulated other comprehensive income associated with the hedged transaction shall be adjusted to a balance that reflects the *lesser* of the following (in absolute amounts):
   (1) The cumulative gain or loss on the derivative from inception of the hedge less (a) the excluded component discussed in paragraph .127(a) above and (b) the derivative's gains or losses previously reclassified from accumulated other comprehensive income into earnings pursuant to paragraph .128
   (2) The portion of the cumulative gain or loss on the derivative necessary to offset the cumulative change in expected future cash flows on the hedged transaction from inception of the hedge less the derivative's gains or losses previously reclassified from accumulated other comprehensive income into earnings pursuant to paragraph .128.

[25a]The effectiveness of a cash flow hedge of the variability in interest payments of a variable-rate financial asset or liability, either existing or forecasted, is affected by the interest rate index on which the variability is based and the extent to which the hedging instrument provides offset. Changes in credit sector spreads embodied within the interest rate index on which the variability is based do not affect the assessment and measurement of hedge effectiveness if both the cash flows on the hedging instrument and the hedged cash flows of the existing financial asset or liability or the variable rate financial asset or liability that is forecasted to be acquired or issued are based on the same index. However, if the cash flows on the hedging instrument and the hedged cash flows of the existing financial asset or liability or the variable-rate financial asset or liability that is forecasted to be acquired or issued are based on different indexes, the basis difference between those indexes would affect the assessment and measurement of hedge effectiveness. [FAS138, ¶21]

That adjustment of accumulated other comprehensive income shall incorporate recognition in other comprehensive income of part or all of the gain or loss on the hedging derivative, as necessary. [Refer to paragraph .1001 for an EITF Issue that provides interpretive guidance on this subparagraph.]

c. A gain or loss shall be recognized in earnings, as necessary, for any remaining gain or loss on the hedging derivative or to adjust other comprehensive income to the balance specified in paragraph .127(b) above. [FAS133, ¶30]
d. In a cash flow hedge of the variability of the functional-currency-equivalent cash flows for a recognized foreign-currency-denominated asset or liability that is remeasured at spot exchange rates under paragraph .122 of Section F60, an amount that will offset the related transaction gain or loss arising from the remeasurement and adjust earnings for the cost to the purchaser (income to the seller) of the hedging instrument shall be reclassified each period from other comprehensive income to earnings. [FAS138, ¶4(i)]

Paragraphs .150 through .191 illustrate assessing hedge effectiveness and measuring hedge ineffectiveness. Paragraphs .228 through .231 and .250 through .252 illustrate the application of this paragraph. [FAS133, ¶30]

.128 Amounts in accumulated other comprehensive income shall be reclassified into earnings in the same period or periods during which the hedged forecasted transaction affects earnings (for example, when a forecasted sale actually occurs). If the hedged transaction results in the acquisition of an asset or the incurrence of a liability, the gains and losses in accumulated other comprehensive income shall be reclassified into earnings in the same period or periods during which the asset acquired or liability incurred affects earnings (such as in the periods that depreciation expense, interest expense, or cost of sales is recognized). However, if an entity expects at any time that continued reporting of a loss in accumulated other comprehensive income would lead to recognizing a net loss on the combination of the hedging instrument and the hedged transaction (and related asset acquired or liability incurred) in one or more future periods, a loss shall be reclassified immediately into earnings for the amount that is not expected to be recovered. For example, a loss shall be reported in earnings for a derivative that is designated as hedging the forecasted purchase of inventory to the extent that the cost basis of the inventory plus the related amount reported in accumulated other comprehensive income exceeds the amount expected to be recovered through sales of that inventory. (Impairment guidance is provided in paragraphs .131 and .132.) [FAS133, ¶31]

.129 An entity shall discontinue prospectively the accounting specified in paragraphs .127 and .128 for an existing hedge if any one of the following occurs:

a. Any criterion in paragraphs .125 and .126 is no longer met.
b. The derivative expires or is sold, terminated, or exercised.
c. The entity removes the designation of the cash flow hedge.

In those circumstances, the net gain or loss shall remain in accumulated other comprehensive income and be reclassified into earnings as specified in paragraph .128. Furthermore, the entity may elect to designate prospectively a new hedging relationship with a different hedging instrument or, in the circumstances described in paragraphs .129(a) and .129(c), a different hedged transaction or a hedged item if the hedging relationship meets the criteria specified in paragraphs .125 and .126 for a cash flow hedge or paragraphs .117 and .118 for a fair value hedge. [FAS133, ¶32]

.130 The net derivative gain or loss related to a discontinued cash flow hedge shall continue to be reported in accumulated other comprehensive income unless it is probable that the forecasted transaction will *not* occur by the end of the originally specified time period (as documented at the inception of the hedging relationship) or within an additional two-month period of time thereafter, except as indicated in the following sentence. In rare cases, the existence of extenuating circumstances that are related to the nature of the forecasted transaction and are outside the control or influence of the reporting entity may cause the forecasted transaction to be probable of occurring on a date that is beyond the additional two-month period of time, in which case the net derivative gain or loss related to the discontinued cash flow hedge shall continue to be reported in accumulated other comprehensive income until it is reclassified into earnings pursuant to paragraph .128. If it is probable that the hedged forecasted transaction will not occur either by the end of the originally specified time period or within the additional two-month period of time and the hedged forecasted transaction also does not qualify for the exception described in the preceding sentence, that derivative gain or loss reported in accumulated other comprehensive income shall be reclassified into earnings immediately.[26] [FAS138, ¶4(q)]

.131 Existing requirements in generally accepted accounting principles for assessing asset impairment or recognizing an increased obligation apply to an asset or liability that gives rise to variable cash flows (such as a variable-rate financial instrument), for which the variable cash flows (the forecasted transactions) have been designated as being hedged and accounted for pursuant to paragraphs .127 and .128. Those impairment requirements shall be applied each period after hedge accounting has been applied for the period, pursuant to paragraphs .127 and .128 of this section. The fair value or expected

---

[26]A pattern of determining that hedged forecasted transactions probably will not occur would call into question both an entity's ability to accurately predict forecasted transactions and the propriety of using hedge accounting in the future for similar forecasted transactions. [FAS133, ¶494]

cash flows of a hedging instrument shall not be considered in applying those requirements. The gain or loss on the hedging instrument in accumulated other comprehensive income shall, however, be accounted for as discussed in paragraph .128. [FAS133, ¶34]

.132 If, under existing requirements in generally accepted accounting principles, an impairment loss is recognized on an asset or an additional obligation is recognized on a liability to which a hedged forecasted transaction relates, any offsetting net gain related to that transaction in accumulated other comprehensive income shall be reclassified immediately into earnings. Similarly, if a recovery is recognized on the asset or liability to which the forecasted transaction relates, any offsetting net loss that has been accumulated in other comprehensive income shall be reclassified immediately into earnings. [FAS133, ¶35]

Foreign Currency Hedges

.133 If the hedged item is denominated in a foreign currency, [FAS138, ¶4(j)(1)] an entity may designate the following types of hedges of foreign currency exposure, as specified in paragraphs .134 through .139:

a. A fair value hedge of an unrecognized firm commitment or [FAS133, ¶36] a recognized asset or liability (including an available-for-sale security) [FAS138, ¶4(j)(2)]
b. A cash flow hedge of a forecasted transaction, an unrecognized firm commitment, the forecasted functional-currency-equivalent cash flows associated with a recognized asset or liability, or a forecasted intercompany transaction [FAS138, ¶4(j)(3)]
c. A hedge of a net investment in a foreign operation. [FAS133, ¶36]

The recognition in earnings of the foreign currency transaction gain or loss on a foreign-currency-denominated asset or liability based on changes in the foreign currency spot rate is not considered to be the remeasurement of that asset or liability with changes in fair value attributable to foreign exchange risk recognized in earnings, which is discussed in the criteria in paragraphs .118(c)(1) and .126(d). Thus, those criteria are not impediments to either a foreign currency fair value or cash flow hedge of such a foreign-currency-denominated asset or liability or a foreign currency cash flow hedge of the forecasted acquisition or incurrence of a foreign-currency-denominated asset or liability whose carrying amount will be remeasured at spot exchange rates under paragraph .122 of Section F60. [FAS138, ¶4(j)(4)] A foreign currency derivative instrument that has been entered into with another member of a consolidated group can be a hedging instrument [FAS133, ¶36] in a fair value hedge or in a cash flow hedge of a recognized foreign-currency-denominated asset or liability or in a net investment hedge [FAS138, ¶4(n)] in the consolidated financial statements only if that other member has entered into an offsetting contract with an unrelated third party to hedge the exposure it acquired from issuing the derivative instrument to the affiliate that initiated the hedge. [FAS133, ¶36]

.133A The provisions in paragraph .133 that permit a recognized foreign-currency-denominated asset or liability to be the hedged item in a fair value or cash flow hedge of foreign currency exposure also pertain to a recognized foreign-currency-denominated receivable or payable that results from a hedged forecasted foreign-currency-denominated sale or purchase on credit. An entity may choose to designate a single cash flow hedge that encompasses the variability of functional currency cash flows attributable to foreign exchange risk related to the settlement of the foreign-currency-denominated receivable or payable resulting from a forecasted sale or purchase on credit. Alternatively, an entity may choose to designate a cash flow hedge of the variability of functional currency cash flows attributable to foreign exchange risk related to a forecasted foreign-currency-denominated sale or purchase on credit and then separately designate a foreign currency fair value hedge of the resulting recognized foreign-currency-denominated receivable or payable. In that case, the cash flow hedge would terminate (be dedesignated) when the hedged sale or purchase occurs and the foreign-currency-denominated receivable or payable is recognized. The use of the same foreign currency derivative instrument for both the cash flow hedge and the fair value hedge is not prohibited though some ineffectiveness may result. [FAS138, ¶4(k)]

Foreign Currency Fair Value Hedges

.134 *Unrecognized firm commitment.* A derivative instrument or a nonderivative financial instrument[27] that may give rise to a foreign currency transaction gain or loss under Section F60 can be designated as hedging changes in the fair value of an unrecognized firm commitment, or a specific portion thereof, attributable to foreign currency exchange rates. The designated hedging relationship qualifies for the accounting specified in paragraphs .119 through .124 if all the fair value hedge criteria in paragraphs .117 and .118 [FAS133, ¶37] and the conditions in paragraphs .137(a) and .137(b) [FAS138, ¶4(s)] are met. [FAS133, ¶37]

.134A *Recognized asset or liability.* A nonderivative financial instrument shall not be designated as the hedging instrument in a fair value hedge of the foreign currency exposure of a recognized asset or liability. A derivative instrument can be designated as hedging the changes in the fair value of a recognized asset or liability (or a specific portion

[27]The carrying basis for a nonderivative financial instrument that gives rise to a foreign currency transaction gain or loss under Section F60 is not addressed by this section. [FAS133, ¶37, fn11]

thereof) for which a foreign currency transaction gain or loss is recognized in earnings under the provisions of paragraph .122 of Section F60. All recognized foreign-currency-denominated assets or liabilities for which a foreign currency transaction gain or loss is recorded in earnings may qualify for the accounting specified in paragraphs .119 through .124 if all the fair value hedge criteria in paragraphs .117 and .118 and the conditions in paragraphs .137(a) and .137(b) are met. [FAS138, ¶4(l)]

.135 *Available-for-sale security.* A nonderivative financial instrument shall not be designated as the hedging instrument in a fair value hedge of the foreign currency exposure of an available-for-sale security. A derivative instrument can be designated as hedging the changes in the fair value of an available-for-sale *debt* security (or a specific portion thereof) attributable to changes in foreign currency exchange rates. The designated hedging relationship qualifies for the accounting specified in paragraphs .119 through .124 if all the fair value hedge criteria in paragraphs .117 and .118 [FAS133, ¶38] and the conditions in paragraphs .137(a) and .137(b) [FAS138, ¶4(t)] are met. An available-for-sale *equity* security can be hedged for changes in the fair value attributable to changes in foreign currency exchange rates and qualify for the accounting specified in paragraphs .119 through .124 only if the fair value hedge criteria in paragraphs .117 and .118 are met and the following two conditions are satisfied:

a. The security is not traded on an exchange (or other established marketplace) on which trades are denominated in the investor's functional currency.
b. Dividends or other cash flows to holders of the security are all denominated in the same foreign currency as the currency expected to be received upon sale of the security.

The change in fair value of the hedged available-for-sale equity security attributable to foreign exchange risk is reported in earnings pursuant to paragraph .120 and not in other comprehensive income. [FAS133, ¶38]

.136 Gains and losses on a qualifying foreign currency fair value hedge shall be accounted for as specified in paragraphs .119 through .124. The gain or loss on a nonderivative hedging instrument attributable to foreign currency risk is the foreign currency transaction gain or loss as determined under Section F60.[28] That foreign currency transaction gain or loss shall be recognized currently in earnings along with the change in the carrying amount of the hedged firm commitment. [FAS133, ¶39]

---

[28]The foreign currency transaction gain or loss on a hedging instrument is determined, consistent with paragraph .122 of Section F60, as the increase or decrease in functional currency cash flows attributable to the change in spot exchange rates between the functional currency and the currency in which the hedging instrument is denominated. [FAS133, ¶39, fn12]

Foreign Currency Cash Flow Hedges

.137 A nonderivative financial instrument shall not be designated as a hedging instrument in a foreign currency cash flow hedge. [FAS133, ¶40] A derivative instrument designated as hedging the foreign currency exposure to variability in the functional-currency-equivalent cash flows associated with a forecasted transaction (for example, a forecasted export sale to an unaffiliated entity with the price to be denominated in a foreign currency), a recognized asset or liability, an unrecognized firm commitment, or a forecasted intercompany transaction (for example, a forecasted sale to a foreign subsidiary or a forecasted royalty from a foreign subsidiary) qualifies for hedge accounting if all of the following criteria are met: [FAS138, ¶4(m)(1)]

a. For consolidated financial statements, either (1) the operating unit that has the foreign currency exposure is a party to the hedging instrument or (2) another member of the consolidated group that has the same functional currency as that operating unit (subject to the restrictions in this subparagraph and related footnote) is a party to the hedging instrument. To qualify for applying the guidance in (2) above, there may be no intervening subsidiary with a different functional currency.[28a] (Refer to paragraphs .133, .137A, and .137B for conditions for which an intercompany foreign currency derivative can be the hedging instrument in a cash flow hedge of foreign exchange risk.) [FAS138, ¶4(v)(1)]
b. The hedged transaction is denominated in a currency other than [FAS133, ¶40] the hedging [FAS138, ¶4(v)(2)] unit's functional currency.
c. All of the criteria in paragraphs .125 and .126 are met, except for the criterion in paragraph .126(c) that requires that the forecasted transaction be with a party external to the reporting entity.
d. If the hedged transaction is a group of individual forecasted foreign-currency-denominated transactions, a forecasted inflow of a foreign currency and a forecasted outflow of the foreign currency cannot both be included in the same group. [FAS133, ¶40]

[28a]For example, if a dollar-functional, second-tier subsidiary has a Euro exposure, the dollar-functional consolidated parent company could designate its U.S. dollar–Euro derivative as a hedge of the second-tier subsidiary's exposure provided that the functional currency of the intervening first-tier subsidiary (that is, the parent of the second-tier subsidiary) is also the U.S. dollar. In contrast, if the functional currency of the intervening first-tier subsidiary was the Japanese yen (thus requiring the financial statements of the second-tier subsidiary to be translated into yen before the yen-denominated financial statements of the first-tier subsidiary are translated into U.S. dollars for consolidation), the consolidated parent company could not designate its U.S. dollar–Euro derivative as a hedge of the second-tier subsidiary's exposure. [FAS138, ¶4(v)(1)]

[[29]Deleted 6/00 because of FASB Statement 138, *Accounting for Certain Derivatives and Certain Hedging Activities.*]

e. If the hedged item is a recognized foreign-currency-denominated asset or liability, all the variability in the hedged item's functional-currency-equivalent cash flows must be eliminated by the effect of the hedge. (For example, a cash flow hedge cannot be used with a variable-rate foreign-currency-denominated asset or liability and a derivative based solely on changes in exchange rates because the derivative does not eliminate all the variability in the functional currency cash flows.) [FAS138, ¶4(m)(2)]

.137A *Internal derivative.* A foreign currency derivative contract that has been entered into with another member of a consolidated group (such as a treasury center) can be a hedging instrument in a foreign currency cash flow hedge of a forecasted borrowing, purchase, or sale or an unrecognized firm commitment in the consolidated financial statements only if the following two conditions are satisfied. (That foreign currency derivative instrument is hereafter in this section referred to as an *internal derivative.*)

a. From the perspective of the member of the consolidated group using the derivative as a hedging instrument (hereafter in this section referred to as the *hedging affiliate*), the criteria for foreign currency cash flow hedge accounting in paragraph .137 must be satisfied.
b. The member of the consolidated group not using the derivative as a hedging instrument (hereafter in this section referred to as the *issuing affiliate*) must either (1) enter into a derivative contract with an unrelated third party to offset the exposure that results from that internal derivative or (2) if the conditions in paragraph .137B are met, enter into derivative contracts with unrelated third parties that would offset, on a net basis for each foreign currency, the foreign exchange risk arising from multiple internal derivative contracts.

[FAS138, ¶4(o)]

.137B *Offsetting net exposures.* If an issuing affiliate chooses to offset exposure arising from multiple internal derivative contracts on an aggregate or net basis, the derivatives issued to hedging affiliates may qualify as cash flow hedges in the consolidated financial statements only if all of the following conditions are satisfied:

a. The issuing affiliate enters into a derivative contract with an unrelated third party to offset, on a net basis for each foreign currency, the foreign exchange risk arising from multiple internal derivative contracts, and the derivative contract with the unrelated third party generates equal or closely approximating gains and losses when compared with the aggregate or net losses and gains generated by the derivative contracts issued to affiliates.
b. Internal derivatives that are not designated as hedging instruments are excluded from the determination of the foreign currency exposure on a net basis that is offset by the

third-party derivative. In addition, nonderivative contracts may not be used as hedging instruments to offset exposures arising from internal derivative contracts.

c. Foreign currency exposure that is offset by a single net third-party contract arises from internal derivative contracts that mature within the same 31-day period and that involve the same currency exposure as the net third-party derivative. The offsetting net third-party derivative related to that group of contracts must offset the aggregate or net exposure to that currency, must mature within the same 31-day period, and must be entered into within 3 business days after the designation of the internal derivatives as hedging instruments.
d. The issuing affiliate tracks the exposure that it acquires from each hedging affiliate and maintains documentation supporting linkage of each internal derivative contract and the offsetting aggregate or net derivative contract with an unrelated third party.
e. The issuing affiliate does not alter or terminate the offsetting derivative with an unrelated third party unless the hedging affiliate initiates that action. If the issuing affiliate does alter or terminate any offsetting third-party derivative (which should be rare), the hedging affiliate must prospectively cease hedge accounting for the internal derivatives that are offset by that third-party derivative.

[FAS138, ¶4(o)]

.137C A member of a consolidated group is not permitted to offset exposures arising from multiple internal derivative contracts on a net basis for foreign currency cash flow exposures related to recognized foreign-currency-denominated assets or liabilities. That prohibition includes situations in which a recognized foreign-currency-denominated asset or liability in a fair value hedge or cash flow hedge results from the occurrence of a specifically identified forecasted transaction initially designated as a cash flow hedge. [FAS138, ¶4(o)]

.138 A qualifying foreign currency cash flow hedge shall be accounted for as specified in paragraphs .127 through .132. [FAS133, ¶41]

Hedges of the Foreign Currency Exposure of a Net Investment in a Foreign Operation

.139 A derivative instrument or a nonderivative financial instrument that may give rise to a foreign currency transaction gain or loss under Section F60 can be designated as hedging the foreign currency exposure of a net investment in a foreign operation [FAS133, ¶42] provided that the conditions in paragraphs .137(a) and .137(b) are met. [FAS138, ¶4(u)] The gain or loss on a hedging derivative instrument (or the foreign currency transaction gain or loss on the nonderivative hedging instrument) that is designated as, and is effective as, an economic hedge of the net investment in a foreign operation shall be reported in the same manner as a translation adjustment to the extent it is effective as a hedge. The hedged net investment shall be accounted for consistent with Section F60; the provisions of this section for recognizing the gain or loss on assets designated as being hedged in a fair value hedge do not apply to the hedge of a net investment in a foreign operation. [FAS133, ¶42]

Accounting by Not-for-Profit Organizations and Other Entities That Do Not Report Earnings

.140 An entity that does not report earnings as a separate caption in a statement of financial performance (for example, a not-for-profit organization or a defined benefit pension plan) shall recognize the gain or loss on a hedging instrument and a nonhedging derivative instrument as a change in net assets in the period of change unless the hedging instrument is designated as a hedge of the foreign currency exposure of a net investment in a foreign operation. In that case, the provisions of paragraph .139 of this section shall be applied. Entities that do not report earnings shall recognize the changes in the carrying amount of the hedged item pursuant to paragraph .119 in a fair value hedge as a change in net assets in the period of change. Those entities are not permitted to use cash flow hedge accounting because they do not report earnings separately. Consistent with the provisions of Section No5, "Not-for-Profit Organizations," this section does not prescribe how a not-for-profit organization should determine the components of an operating measure, if one is presented. [FAS133, ¶43]

Disclosures

.141 An entity that holds or issues derivative instruments (or nonderivative instruments that are designated and qualify as hedging instruments pursuant to paragraphs .134 and .139) shall disclose its objectives for holding or issuing those instruments, the context needed to understand those objectives, and its strategies for achieving those objectives. The description shall distinguish between derivative instruments (and nonderivative instruments) designated as fair value hedging instruments, derivative instruments designated as cash flow hedging instruments, derivative instruments (and nonderivative instruments) designated as hedging instruments for hedges of the foreign currency exposure of a net investment in a foreign operation, and all other derivatives. The description also shall indicate the entity's risk management policy for each of those types of hedges, including a description of the items or transactions for which risks are hedged. For derivative instruments not designated as hedging instruments, the description shall indicate the purpose of the derivative activity. Qualitative disclosures about an entity's objectives and strategies for using derivative instruments may be more meaningful if such objectives and strategies are described in the context of an entity's overall risk management profile. If appropriate, an entity is encouraged, but not required, to provide such additional qualitative disclosures. [FAS133, ¶44]

.142 An entity's disclosures for every reporting period for which a complete set of financial statements is presented also shall include the following:

Fair value hedges

a. For derivative instruments, as well as nonderivative instruments that may give rise to foreign currency transaction gains or losses under Section F60, that have been designated and have qualified as fair value hedging instruments and for the related hedged items:
   (1) The net gain or loss recognized in earnings during the reporting period representing (a) the amount of the hedges' ineffectiveness and (b) the component of the derivative instruments' gain or loss, if any, excluded from the assessment of hedge effectiveness, and a description of where the net gain or loss is reported in the statement of income or other statement of financial performance
   (2) The amount of net gain or loss recognized in earnings when a hedged firm commitment no longer qualifies as a fair value hedge.

Cash flow hedges

b. For derivative instruments that have been designated and have qualified as cash flow hedging instruments and for the related hedged transactions:
   (1) The net gain or loss recognized in earnings during the reporting period representing (a) the amount of the hedges' ineffectiveness and (b) the component of the derivative instruments' gain or loss, if any, excluded from the assessment of hedge effectiveness, and a description of where the net gain or loss is reported in the statement of income or other statement of financial performance
   (2) A description of the transactions or other events that will result in the reclassification into earnings of gains and losses that are reported in accumulated other comprehensive income, and the estimated net amount of the existing gains or losses at the reporting date that is expected to be reclassified into earnings within the next 12 months
   (3) The maximum length of time over which the entity is hedging its exposure to the variability in future cash flows for forecasted transactions excluding those forecasted transactions related to the payment of variable interest on existing financial instruments
   (4) The amount of gains and losses reclassified into earnings as a result of the discontinuance of cash flow hedges because it is probable that the original forecasted transactions will not occur [FAS133, ¶45] by the end of the originally specified time period or within the additional period of time discussed in paragraph .130. [FAS138, ¶4(r)]

Hedges of the net investment in a foreign operation

c. For derivative instruments, as well as nonderivative instruments that may give rise to foreign currency transaction gains or losses under Section F60, that have been designated and have qualified as hedging instruments for hedges of the foreign currency exposure of a net investment in a foreign operation, the net amount of gains or losses included in the cumulative translation adjustment during the reporting period.

The quantitative disclosures about derivative instruments may be more useful, and less likely to be perceived to be out of context or otherwise misunderstood, if similar information is disclosed about other financial instruments or nonfinancial assets and liabilities to which the derivative instruments are related by activity. Accordingly, in those situations, an entity is encouraged, but not required, to present a more complete picture of its activities by disclosing that information. [FAS133, ¶45]

Reporting Changes in the Components of Comprehensive Income

.143 An entity shall display as a separate classification within other comprehensive income the net gain or loss on derivative instruments designated and qualifying as cash flow hedging instruments that are reported in comprehensive income pursuant to paragraphs .127 and .138. [FAS133, ¶46]

.144 As part of the disclosures of accumulated other comprehensive income, pursuant to paragraph .120 of Section C49, "Comprehensive Income: Financial Statement Presentation," an entity shall separately disclose the beginning and ending accumulated derivative gain or loss, the related net change associated with current period hedging transactions, and the net amount of any reclassification into earnings. [FAS133, ¶47]

Implementation Guidance

Scope and Definition: Application of Paragraphs .103 through .108

.145 The following discussion further explains the three characteristics of a derivative instrument discussed in paragraphs .103 through .106.

a. *Underlying*. An underlying is a variable that, along with either a notional amount or a payment provision, determines the settlement of a derivative. An underlying usually is one or a combination of the following:
   (1) A security price or security price index
   (2) A commodity price or commodity price index
   (3) An interest rate or interest rate index
   (4) A credit rating or credit index

(5) An exchange rate or exchange rate index
(6) An insurance index or catastrophe loss index
(7) A climatic or geological condition (such as temperature, earthquake severity, or rainfall), another physical variable, or a related index.

However, an underlying may be any variable whose changes are observable or otherwise objectively verifiable. Paragraph .107(e) specifically excludes a contract with settlement based on certain variables unless the contract is exchange-traded. A contract based on any variable that is not specifically excluded is subject to the requirements of this section if it has the other two characteristics identified in paragraph .103 (which also are discussed in paragraphs .145(b) and .145(c) below).

b. *Initial net investment.* A derivative requires no initial net investment or a smaller initial net investment than other types of contracts that have a similar response to changes in market factors. For example, entering into a commodity futures contract generally requires no net investment, while purchasing the same commodity requires an initial net investment equal to its market price. However, both contracts reflect changes in the price of the commodity in the same way (that is, similar gains or losses will be incurred). A swap or forward contract also generally does not require an initial net investment unless the terms favor one party over the other. An option generally requires that one party make an initial net investment (a premium) because that party has the rights under the contract and the other party has the obligations. The phrase *initial net investment* is stated from the perspective of only one party to the contract, but it determines the application of the section for both parties.[30]

c. *Net settlement.* A contract that meets any one of the following criteria has the characteristic described as net settlement:

(1) Its terms implicitly or explicitly require or permit net settlement. For example, a penalty for nonperformance in a purchase order is a net settlement provision if the amount of the penalty is based on changes in the price of the items that are the subject of the contract. Net settlement may be made in cash or by delivery of any other asset, whether or not it is readily convertible to cash. A fixed penalty for nonperformance is not a net settlement provision.

---

[30]Even though a contract may be a derivative as described in paragraphs .103 through .107 for both parties, the exceptions in paragraph .108 apply only to the issuer of the contract and will result in different reporting by the two parties. The exception in paragraph .107(b) also may apply to one of the parties but not the other. [FAS133, ¶57, fn15] The definition of a derivative instrument includes a contract that requires gross exchanges of currencies (for example, currency swaps that require an exchange of different currencies at both inception and maturity). The initial exchange of currencies of equal fair values in those arrangements does not constitute an initial net *investment* in the contract. Instead, it is the exchange of one kind of *cash* for another kind of *cash* of equal value. The balance of the agreement, a forward contract that obligates and entitles both parties to exchange specified currencies, on specified dates, at specified prices, is a derivative instrument. [FAS133, ¶257]

(2) There is an established market mechanism that facilitates net settlement outside the contract. The term *market mechanism* is to be interpreted broadly. Any institutional arrangement or other agreement that enables either party to be relieved of all rights and obligations under the contract and to liquidate its net position without incurring a significant transaction cost is considered net settlement.

(3) It requires delivery of an asset that is readily convertible to cash. The definition of *readily convertible to cash* in FASB Concepts Statement No. 5, *Recognition and Measurement in Financial Statements of Business Enterprises,* includes, for example, a security or commodity traded in an active market and a unit of foreign currency that is readily convertible into the functional currency of the reporting entity. A security that is publicly traded but for which the market is not very active is readily convertible to cash if the number of shares or other units of the security to be exchanged is small relative to the daily transaction volume. That same security would not be readily convertible if the number of shares to be exchanged is large relative to the daily transaction volume. The ability to use a security that is not publicly traded or an agricultural or mineral product without an active market as collateral in a borrowing does not, in and of itself, mean that the security or the commodity is readily convertible to cash.

[FAS133, ¶57]

.146 The following discussion further explains some of the exceptions discussed in paragraph .107.

a. *"Regular-way" security trades.* The exception in paragraph .107(a) applies only to a contract that requires delivery of securities that are readily convertible to cash.[31] To qualify, a contract must require delivery of such a security within the period of time after the trade date that is customary in the market in which the trade takes place. For example, a contract to purchase or sell a publicly traded equity security in the United States customarily requires settlement within three business days. If a contract for purchase of that type of security requires settlement in three business days, the regular-way exception applies, but if the contract requires settlement in five days, the regular-way exception does not apply. This section does not change whether an entity recognizes regular-way security trades on the trade date or the settlement date. However, trades that do not qualify for the regular-way exception are subject to the requirements of this section regardless of the method an entity uses to report its security trades.

[31]Contracts that require delivery of securities that are not readily convertible to cash are not subject to the requirements of this section unless there is a market mechanism outside the contract to facilitate net settlement. [FAS133, ¶58, fn16]

b. *Normal purchases and normal sales.* The exception in paragraph .107(b) applies only to a contract that [FAS133, ¶58] involves [FAS138, ¶4(x)(1)] future delivery of assets (other than financial instruments or derivative instruments). To qualify for the exception, a contract's terms also must be consistent with the terms of an entity's normal purchases or normal sales, that is, the quantity purchased or sold must be reasonable in relation to the entity's business needs. Determining whether or not the terms are consistent will require judgment. In making those judgments, an entity should consider all relevant factors, such as (1) the quantities provided under the contract and the entity's need for the related assets, (2) the locations to which delivery of the items will be made, (3) the period of time between entering into the contract and delivery, and (4) the entity's prior practices with regard to such contracts. Evidence such as past trends, expected future demand, other contracts for delivery of similar items, an entity's and industry's customs for acquiring and storing the related commodities, and an entity's operating locations should help in identifying contracts that qualify as normal purchases or normal sales. [FAS133, ¶58] Also, in order for a contract that meets the net settlement provisions of paragraphs .106(a) and .145(c)(1) and the market mechanism provisions of paragraphs .106(b) and .145(c)(2) to qualify for the exception, it must be probable at inception and throughout the term of the individual contract that the contract will not settle net and will result in physical delivery. [FAS138, ¶4(x)(2)]

c. *Certain contracts that are not traded on an exchange.* A contract that is not traded on an exchange is not subject to the requirements of this section if the underlying is:
   (1) A climatic or geological variable or other physical variable. Climatic, geological, and other physical variables include things like the number of inches of rainfall or snow in a particular area and the severity of an earthquake as measured by the Richter scale.
   (2) The price or value of (a) a nonfinancial asset of one of the parties to the contract unless that asset is readily convertible to cash or (b) a nonfinancial liability of one of the parties to the contract unless that liability requires delivery of an asset that is readily convertible to cash. [FAS133, ¶58] This exception applies only to nonfinancial assets that are unique and only if a nonfinancial asset related to the underlying is owned by the party that would *not* benefit *under the contract* from an increase in the price or value of the nonfinancial asset. If the contract is a call option contract, the exception applies only if that nonfinancial asset is owned by the party that would not benefit under the contract from an increase in the price or value of the nonfinancial asset above the option's strike price. [FAS138, ¶4(x)(3)]
   (3) Specified volumes of sales or service revenues by one of the parties. That exception is intended to apply to contracts with settlements based on the volume of items sold or services rendered, for example, royalty agreements. It is not in-

[32] [Deleted 6/00 because of Statement 138.]

tended to apply to contracts based on changes in sales or revenues due to changes in market prices.

If a contract's underlying is the combination of two or more variables, and one or more would not qualify for one of the exceptions above, the application of this section to that contract depends on the predominant characteristics of the combined variable. The contract is subject to the requirements of this section if the changes in its combined underlying are highly correlated with changes in one of the component variables that would not qualify for an exception. [FAS133, ¶58]

.147 The following discussion illustrates the application of paragraphs .103 through .108 in several situations.

a. *Forward purchases or sales of to-be-announced securities or securities when-issued, as-issued, or if-issued.* A contract for the purchase and sale of a security when, as, or if issued or to be announced is excluded from the requirements of this section as a regular-way security trade if (1) there is no other way to purchase or sell that security and (2) settlement will occur within the shortest period possible for that security.
b. *Credit-indexed contracts (often referred to as credit derivatives).* Many different types of contracts are indexed to the creditworthiness of a specified entity or group of entities, but not all of them are derivative instruments. Credit-indexed contracts that have certain characteristics described in paragraph .107(d) are guarantees and are not subject to the requirements of this section. Credit-indexed contracts that do not have the characteristics necessary to qualify for the exception in paragraph .107(d) are subject to the requirements of this section. One example of the latter is a credit-indexed contract that requires a payment due to changes in the creditworthiness of a specified entity even if neither party incurs a loss due to the change (other than a loss caused by the payment under the credit-indexed contract).
c. *Take-or-pay contracts.* Under a take-or-pay contract, an entity agrees to pay a specified price for a specified quantity of a product whether or not it takes delivery. Whether a take-or-pay contract is subject to this section depends on its terms. For example, if the product to be delivered is not readily convertible to cash and there is no net settlement option, the contract fails to meet the criterion in paragraph .103(c) and is not subject to the requirements of this section. However, a contract that meets all of the following conditions is subject to the requirements of this section: (1) the product to be delivered is readily convertible to cash, (2) the contract does not qualify for the normal purchases and normal sales exception in paragraph .107(b), and (3) little or no initial net investment in the contract is required.

d. *Short sales (sales of borrowed securities).*[33] Short sales typically involve the following activities:
   (1) Selling a security (by the short seller to the purchaser)
   (2) Borrowing a security (by the short seller from the lender)
   (3) Delivering the borrowed security (by the short seller to the purchaser)
   (4) Purchasing a security (by the short seller from the market)
   (5) Delivering the purchased security (by the short seller to the lender).

   Those five activities involve three separate contracts. A contract that distinguishes a short sale involves activities (2) and (5), borrowing a security and replacing it by delivering an identical security. Such a contract has two of the three characteristics of a derivative instrument. The settlement is based on an underlying (the price of the security) and a notional amount (the face amount of the security or the number of shares), and the settlement is made by delivery of a security that is readily convertible to cash. However, the other characteristic, little or no initial net investment, is not present. The borrowed security is the lender's initial net investment in the contract. Consequently, the contract relating to activities (2) and (5) is not a derivative instrument. The other two contracts (one for activities (1) and (3) and the other for activity (4)) are routine and do not generally involve derivative instruments. However, if a forward purchase or sale is involved, and the contract does not qualify for the exception in paragraph .107(a), it is subject to the requirements of this section.

e. *Repurchase agreements and "wash sales"* (accounted for as sales as described in [FAS133, ¶59] paragraphs .177 and .178 of Section F39). [FAS140, ¶353(d)] A transfer of financial assets accounted for as a sale under [FAS133, ¶59] Section F39 [FAS145, ¶9(j)] in which the transferor is both obligated and entitled to repurchase the transferred asset at a fixed or determinable price contains two separate features, one of which may be a derivative. The initial exchange of financial assets for cash is a sale-purchase transaction—generally not a transaction that involves a derivative instrument. However, the accompanying forward contract that gives the transferor the right and obligation to repurchase the transferred asset involves an underlying and a notional amount (the price of the security and its denomination), and it does not require an initial net investment in the contract. Consequently, if the forward contract requires delivery of a security that is readily convertible to cash or otherwise meets the net settlement criterion in paragraph .106, it is subject to the requirements of this section. [FAS133, ¶59]

[33]This discussion applies only to short sales with the characteristics described here. Some groups of transactions that are referred to as short sales may have different characteristics. If so, a different analysis would be appropriate, and other derivative instruments may be involved. [FAS133, ¶59, fn18]

Application of the Clearly-and-Closely-Related Criterion in Paragraphs .109 through .113

.148 In discussing whether a hybrid instrument contains an embedded derivative instrument (also simply referred to as an *embedded derivative*) that warrants separate accounting, paragraph .109 focuses on whether the economic characteristics and risks of the embedded derivative are clearly and closely related to the economic characteristics and risks of the host contract. If the host contract encompasses a residual interest in an entity, then its economic characteristics and risks should be considered that of an equity instrument and an embedded derivative would need to possess principally equity characteristics (related to the same entity) to be considered clearly and closely related to the host contract. However, most commonly, a financial instrument host contract will not embody a claim to the residual interest in an entity and, thus, the economic characteristics and risks of the host contract should be considered that of a debt instrument. For example, even though the overall hybrid instrument that provides for repayment of principal may include a return based on the market price (the underlying as defined in this section) of XYZ Corporation common stock, the host contract does not involve any existing or potential residual interest rights (that is, rights of ownership) and thus would not be an equity instrument. The host contract would instead be considered a debt instrument, and the embedded derivative that incorporates the equity-based return would not be clearly and closely related to the host contract. If the embedded derivative is considered *not* to be clearly and closely related to the host contract, the embedded derivative must be separated from the host contract and accounted for as a derivative instrument *by both parties* to the hybrid instrument, except as provided by paragraph .108(a). [FAS133, ¶60]

.149 The following guidance is relevant in deciding whether the economic characteristics and risks of the embedded derivative are clearly and closely related to the economic characteristics and risks of the host contract.

a. *Interest rate indexes.* An embedded derivative in which the underlying is an interest rate or interest rate index and a host contract that is considered a debt instrument are considered to be clearly and closely related unless, as discussed in paragraph .110, the embedded derivative contains a provision that (1) permits any possibility whatsoever that the investor's (or creditor's) undiscounted net cash inflows over the life of the instrument would not recover substantially all of its initial recorded investment in the hybrid instrument under its contractual terms or (2) could under any possibility whatsoever at least double the investor's initial rate of return on the host contract and also result in a rate of return that is at least twice what otherwise would be the market return for a contract that has the same terms as the host contract and that involves a debtor with a similar credit quality. The requirement to separate the embedded derivative from the host contract applies to *both parties* to the hybrid instrument even though the above tests focus on the investor's net cash inflows. Plain-vanilla servicing rights, which involve an obligation to perform servicing and the right to receive fees for performing that servicing, do not contain an embedded derivative that would be separated from those servicing rights and accounted for as a derivative.

b. *Inflation-indexed interest payments.* The interest rate and the rate of inflation in the economic environment for the currency in which a debt instrument is denominated are considered to be clearly and closely related. Thus, nonleveraged inflation-indexed contracts (debt instruments, capitalized lease obligations, pension obligations, and so forth) would *not* have the inflation-related embedded derivative separated from the host contract.

c. *Credit-sensitive payments.* The creditworthiness of the debtor and the interest rate on a debt instrument are considered to be clearly and closely related. Thus, for debt instruments that have the interest rate reset in the event of (1) default (such as violation of a credit-risk-related covenant), (2) a change in the debtor's published credit rating, or (3) a change in the debtor's creditworthiness indicated by a change in its spread over Treasury bonds, the related embedded derivative would *not* be separated from the host contract.

d. *Calls and puts on debt instruments.* Call options (or put options) that can accelerate the repayment of principal on a debt instrument are considered to be clearly and closely related to a debt instrument that requires principal repayments unless both (1) the debt involves a substantial premium or discount (which is common with zero-coupon bonds) and (2) the put or call option is only contingently exercisable. Thus, if a substantial premium or discount is not involved, embedded calls and puts (including contingent call or put options that are not exercisable unless an event of default occurs) would *not* be separated from the host contract. However, for contingently exercisable calls and puts to be considered clearly and closely related, they can be indexed only to interest rates or credit risk, not some extraneous event or factor. In contrast, call options (or put options) that do not accelerate the repayment of principal on a debt instrument but instead require a cash settlement that is equal to the price of the option at the date of exercise would *not* be considered to be clearly and closely related to the debt instrument in which it is embedded and would be separated from the host contract.

e. *Calls and puts on equity instruments.* A put option that enables the holder to require the issuer of an equity instrument to reacquire that equity instrument for cash or other assets is *not* clearly and closely related to that equity instrument. Thus, such a put option embedded in [FAS133, ¶61] a publicly traded equity instrument [FAS138, ¶4(y)(2)] to which it relates should be separated from the host contract by the holder of the equity instrument. That put option also should be separated from the host contract by the issuer of the equity instrument except in those cases in which the put option is not considered to be a derivative instrument pursuant to paragraph .108(a) because it is classified in stockholders' equity. A purchased call option that enables the issuer of an equity instrument (such as common stock) to reacquire that equity instrument would not be considered to be a derivative instrument by the issuer of the equity instrument pursuant to paragraph .108(a). Thus, if the call option were embedded in the related equity instrument, it would not be separated from the host contract by the issuer. However, for the holder of the related equity instrument, the embedded written call option would *not* be considered to be clearly and closely related to the equity instrument and should be separated from the host contract.

f. *Floors, caps, and collars.* Floors or caps (or collars, which are combinations of caps and floors) on interest rates and the interest rate on a debt instrument are considered to be clearly and closely related, provided the cap is at or above the current market price (or rate) and the floor is at or below the current market price (or rate) at issuance of the instrument. Thus, the derivative embedded in a variable-rate debt instrument that has a floor on the interest rate (that is, the floor option) would not be separated from the host contract and accounted for separately even though, in a falling interest rate environment, the debt instrument may have a return to the investor that is a significant amount above the market return of a debt instrument without the floor provision (refer to paragraph .110(b)).

g. *Term-extending options.* An embedded derivative provision that either (1) unilaterally enables one party to extend significantly the remaining term to maturity or (2) automatically extends significantly the remaining term triggered by specific events or conditions is *not* clearly and closely related to the interest rate on a debt instrument unless the interest rate is concurrently reset to the approximate current market rate for the extended term and the debt instrument initially involved no significant discount. Thus, if there is no reset of interest rates, the embedded derivative must be separated from the host contract and accounted for as a derivative instrument. That is, a term-extending option cannot be used to circumvent the restriction in paragraph .149(a) regarding the investor's not recovering substantially all of its initial recorded investment.

h. *Equity-indexed interest payments.* The changes in fair value of an equity interest and the interest yield on a debt instrument are *not* clearly and closely related. Thus, an equity-related derivative embedded in an equity-indexed debt instrument (whether based on the price of a specific common stock or on an index that is based on a basket of equity instruments) must be separated from the host contract and accounted for as a derivative instrument.

i. *Commodity-indexed interest or principal payments.* The changes in fair value of a commodity (or other asset) and the interest yield on a debt instrument are *not* clearly and closely related. Thus, a commodity-related derivative embedded in a commodity-indexed debt instrument must be separated from the noncommodity host contract and accounted for as a derivative instrument.

j. *Indexed rentals:*
   (1) *Inflation-indexed rentals.* Rentals for the use of leased assets and adjustments for inflation on similar property are considered to be clearly and closely related. Thus, unless a significant leverage factor is involved, the inflation-related derivative embedded in an inflation-indexed lease contract would *not* be separated from the host contract.
   (2) *Contingent rentals based on related sales.* Lease contracts that include contingent rentals based on certain sales of the lessee would *not* have the contingent-rental-related embedded derivative separated from the host contract because, under paragraph .107(e)(3), a non-exchange-traded contract whose underlying is specified volumes of sales by one of the parties to the contract would not be subject to the requirements of this section.
   (3) *Contingent rentals based on a variable interest rate.* The obligation to make future payments for the use of leased assets and the adjustment of those payments to reflect changes in a variable-interest-rate index are considered to be clearly and closely related. Thus, lease contracts that include contingent rentals based on changes in the prime rate would *not* have the contingent-rental-related embedded derivative separated from the host contract.

k. *Convertible debt.* The changes in fair value of an equity interest and the interest rates on a debt instrument are not clearly and closely related. Thus, for a debt security that is convertible into a specified number of shares of the debtor's common stock or another entity's common stock, the embedded derivative (that is, the conversion option) must be separated from the debt host contract and accounted for as a derivative instrument provided that the conversion option would, as a freestanding instrument, be a derivative instrument subject to the requirements of this section. (For example, if the common stock was not readily convertible to cash, a conversion option that requires purchase of the common stock would not be accounted for as a derivative.) That accounting applies only to the holder (investor) if the debt is convertible to the debtor's common stock because, under paragraph .108(a), a separate option with the same terms would not be considered to be a derivative for the issuer.

l. *Convertible preferred stock.* Because the changes in fair value of an equity interest and interest rates on a debt instrument are not clearly and closely related, the terms of the preferred stock (other than the conversion option) must be analyzed to determine whether the preferred stock (and thus the potential host contract) is more akin to an equity instrument or a debt instrument. A typical cumulative fixed-rate preferred stock that has a mandatory redemption feature is more akin to debt, whereas cumulative participating perpetual preferred stock is more akin to an equity instrument. [FAS133, ¶61]

Assessment of Hedge Effectiveness

Hedge Effectiveness Requirements of This Section

.150 This section requires that an entity define at the time it designates a hedging relationship the method it will use to assess the hedge's effectiveness in achieving offsetting changes in fair value or offsetting cash flows attributable to the risk being hedged. It also requires that an entity use that defined method consistently throughout the hedge period (a) to assess at inception of the hedge and on an ongoing basis whether it expects the hedging relationship to be highly effective in achieving offset and (b) to measure the ineffective part of the hedge. If the entity identifies an improved method and wants to apply that method prospectively, it must discontinue the existing hedging relationship and designate the relationship anew using the improved method. This section does not specify a single method for either assessing whether a hedge is expected to be highly effective or measuring hedge ineffectiveness. The appropriateness of a given method of assessing hedge effectiveness can depend on the nature of the risk being hedged and the type of hedging instrument used. Ordinarily, however, an entity should assess effectiveness for similar hedges in a similar manner; use of different methods for similar hedges should be justified. [FAS133, ¶62] [Refer to paragraph .1001 for an EITF Issue that provides interpretive guidance on this subparagraph.]

.151 In defining how hedge effectiveness will be assessed, an entity must specify whether it will include in that assessment all of the gain or loss on a hedging instrument. This section permits (but does not require) an entity to exclude all or a part of the hedging instrument's time value from the assessment of hedge effectiveness, as follows:

a. If the effectiveness of a hedge with an option contract is assessed based on changes in the option's intrinsic value, the change in the time value of the contract would be excluded from the assessment of hedge effectiveness.
b. If the effectiveness of a hedge with an option contract is assessed based on changes in the option's minimum value, that is, its intrinsic value plus the effect of discounting, the change in the volatility value of the contract would be excluded from the assessment of hedge effectiveness.
c. If the effectiveness of a hedge with a forward or futures contract is assessed based on changes in fair value attributable to changes in spot prices, the change in the fair value of the contract related to the changes in the difference between the spot price and the forward or futures price would be excluded from the assessment of hedge effectiveness.

In each circumstance above, changes in the excluded component would be included currently in earnings, together with any ineffectiveness that results under the defined method of assessing ineffectiveness. As noted in paragraph .150, the effectiveness of similar hedges generally should be assessed similarly; that includes whether a component of the gain or loss on a derivative is excluded in assessing effectiveness. No other components of a gain or loss on the designated hedging instrument may be excluded from the assessment of hedge effectiveness. [FAS133, ¶63]

.152 In assessing the effectiveness of a cash flow hedge, an entity generally will need to consider the time value of money if significant in the circumstances. Considering the effect of the time value of money is especially important if the hedging instrument involves periodic cash settlements. An example of a situation in which an entity likely would reflect the time value of money is a tailing strategy with futures contracts. When using a tailing strategy, an entity adjusts the size or contract amount of futures contracts used in a hedge so that earnings (or expense) from reinvestment (or funding) of daily settlement gains (or losses) on the futures do not distort the results of the hedge. To assess offset of expected cash flows when a tailing strategy has been used, an entity could reflect the time value of money, perhaps by comparing the present value of the hedged forecasted cash flow with the results of the hedging instrument. [FAS133, ¶64]

.153 Whether a hedging relationship qualifies as highly effective sometimes will be easy to assess, and there will be no ineffectiveness to recognize in earnings during the term of the hedge. If the critical terms of the hedging instrument and of the entire hedged asset or liability (as opposed to selected cash flows) or hedged forecasted transaction are the same, the entity could conclude that changes in fair value or cash flows attributable to the risk being hedged are expected to completely offset at inception and on an ongoing basis. For example, an entity may assume that a hedge of a forecasted purchase of a commodity with a forward contract will be highly effective and that there will be no ineffectiveness to be recognized in earnings if:

a. The forward contract is for purchase of the same quantity of the same commodity at the same time and location as the hedged forecasted purchase.
b. The fair value of the forward contract at inception is zero.
c. Either the change in the discount or premium on the forward contract is excluded from the assessment of effectiveness and included directly in earnings pursuant to paragraph .151 or the change in expected cash flows on the forecasted transaction is based on the forward price for the commodity.

[FAS133, ¶65]

.154 Assessing hedge effectiveness and measuring the ineffective part of the hedge, however, can be more complex. For example, hedge ineffectiveness would result from the following circumstances, among others:

a. A difference between the basis of the hedging instrument and the hedged item or hedged transaction (such as a Deutsche mark–based hedging instrument and Dutch guilder–based hedged item), to the extent that those bases do not move in tandem
b. Differences in critical terms of the hedging instrument and hedged item or hedged transaction, such as differences in notional amounts, maturities, quantity, location, or delivery dates.

Ineffectiveness also would result if part of the change in the fair value of a derivative is attributable to a change in the counterparty's creditworthiness. [FAS133, ¶66]

.155 A hedge that meets the effectiveness test specified in paragraphs .117(b) and .125(b) (that is, both at inception and on an ongoing basis, the entity expects the hedge to be highly effective at achieving offsetting changes in fair values or cash flows) also must meet the other hedge accounting criteria to qualify for hedge accounting. If the hedge initially qualifies for hedge accounting, the entity would continue to assess whether the hedge meets the effectiveness test and also would measure any ineffectiveness during the hedge period. If the hedge fails the effectiveness test at any time (that is, if the entity does not expect the hedge to be highly effective at achieving offsetting changes in fair values or cash flows), the hedge ceases to qualify for hedge accounting. The discussions of measuring hedge ineffectiveness in the examples in paragraphs .156 through .191 assume that the hedge satisfied all of the criteria for hedge accounting at inception. [FAS133, ¶67]

Assuming No Ineffectiveness in a Hedge with an Interest Rate Swap

.156 An assumption of no ineffectiveness is especially important in a hedging relationship involving an interest-bearing financial instrument and an interest rate swap because it significantly simplifies the computations necessary to make the accounting entries. An entity may assume no ineffectiveness in a hedging relationship of interest rate risk involving [FAS133, ¶68] a recognized interest-bearing asset or liability [FAS138, ¶4(z)(1)] and an interest rate swap if all of the applicable conditions in the following list are met:

Conditions applicable to both fair value hedges and cash flow hedges

a. The notional amount of the swap matches the principal amount of the interest-bearing asset or liability.
b. The fair value of the swap at [FAS133, ¶68] the inception of the hedging relationship [FAS138, ¶4(z)(2)] is zero.
c. The formula for computing net settlements under the interest rate swap is the same for each net settlement. (That is, the fixed rate is the same throughout the term, and the variable rate is based on the same index and includes the same constant adjustment or no adjustment.)

d. The interest-bearing asset or liability is not prepayable [FAS133, ¶68] (that is, able to be settled by either party prior to its scheduled maturity), except as indicated in the following sentences. This criterion does not apply to an interest-bearing asset or liability that is prepayable solely due to an embedded call option provided that the hedging interest rate swap contains an embedded mirror-image call option. The call option embedded in the swap is considered a mirror image of the call option embedded in the hedged item if (1) the terms of the two call options match (including matching maturities, strike price, related notional amounts, timing and frequency of payments, and dates on which the instruments may be called) and (2) the entity is the writer of one call option and the holder (or purchaser) of the other call option. Similarly, this criterion does not apply to an interest-bearing asset or liability that is prepayable solely due to an embedded put option provided that the hedging interest rate swap contains an embedded mirror-image put option. [FAS138, ¶4(z)(3)]

dd. The index on which the variable leg of the swap is based matches the benchmark interest rate designated as the interest rate risk being hedged for that hedging relationship.[33a] [FAS138, ¶4(z)(4)]

e. Any other terms in the interest-bearing financial instruments or interest rate swaps are typical of those instruments and do not invalidate the assumption of no ineffectiveness.

Conditions applicable to fair value hedges only

f. The expiration date of the swap matches the maturity date of the interest-bearing asset or liability.

g. There is no floor or ceiling on the variable interest rate of the swap.

h. The interval between repricings of the variable interest rate in the swap is frequent enough to justify an assumption that the variable payment or receipt is at a market rate (generally three to six months or less).

Conditions applicable to cash flow hedges only

i. All interest receipts or payments on the variable-rate asset or liability during the term of the swap are designated as hedged, and no interest payments beyond the term of the swap are designated as hedged.

j. There is no floor or cap on the variable interest rate of the swap unless the variable-rate asset or liability has a floor or cap. In that case, the swap must have a floor or cap on the variable interest rate that is comparable to the floor or cap on the variable-rate

[33a]For cash flow hedge situations in which the cash flows of the hedged item and the hedging instrument are based on the same index but that index is not the benchmark interest rate, the shortcut method is not permitted. However, the entity may obtain results similar to results obtained if the shortcut method was permitted. [FAS138, ¶4(z)(4)]

asset or liability. (For this purpose, comparable does not necessarily mean equal. For example, if a swap's variable rate is LIBOR and an asset's variable rate is LIBOR plus 2 percent, a 10 percent cap on the swap would be comparable to a 12 percent cap on the asset.)

k. The repricing dates match those of the variable-rate asset or liability. [FAS133, ¶68]

.157 The fixed rate on a hedged item need not exactly match the fixed rate on a swap designated as a fair value hedge. Nor does the variable rate on an interest-bearing asset or liability need to be the same as the variable rate on a swap designated as a cash flow hedge. A swap's fair value comes from its net settlements. The fixed and variable rates on a swap can be changed without affecting the net settlement if both are changed by the same amount. That is, a swap with a payment based on LIBOR and a receipt based on a fixed rate of 5 percent has the same net settlements and fair value as a swap with a payment based on LIBOR plus 1 percent and a receipt based on a fixed rate of 6 percent. [FAS133, ¶69]

.158 Comparable credit risk at inception is not a condition for assuming no ineffectiveness even though actually achieving perfect offset would require that the same discount rate be used to determine the fair value of the swap and of the hedged item or hedged transaction. To justify using the same discount rate, the credit risk related to both parties to the swap as well as to the debtor on the hedged interest-bearing asset (in a fair value hedge) or the variable-rate asset on which the interest payments are hedged (in a cash flow hedge) would have to be the same. However, because that complication is caused by the interaction of interest rate risk and credit risk, which are not easily separable, comparable creditworthiness is not considered a necessary condition to assume no ineffectiveness in a hedge of interest rate risk. [FAS133, ¶70]

After-Tax Hedging of Foreign Currency Risk

.159 Section F60 permitted hedging of foreign currency risk on an after-tax basis. The portion of the gain or loss on the hedging instrument that exceeded the loss or gain on the hedged item was required to be included as an offset to the related tax effects in the period in which those tax effects are recognized. This section continues those provisions. [FAS133, ¶71]

Illustrations of Assessing Effectiveness and Measuring Ineffectiveness

.160 The following examples illustrate some ways in which an entity may assess hedge effectiveness and measures hedge ineffectiveness for specific strategies. The examples are not intended to imply that other reasonable methods are precluded. However, not all possible methods are reasonable or consistent with this section. Paragraphs .150

through .191 also discuss some methods of assessing hedge effectiveness and determining hedge ineffecti veness that are not consistent with this section and thus may not be used. [FAS133, ¶72]

Example 1: Fair Value Hedge of Natural Gas Inventory with Futures Contracts

.161 Company A has 20,000 MMBTU's of natural gas stored at its location in West Texas. To hedge the fair value exposure of the natural gas, the company sells the equivalent of 20,000 MMBTU's of natural gas futures contracts on a national mercantile exchange. The futures prices are based on delivery of natural gas at the Henry Hub gàs collection point in Louisiana. [FAS133, ¶73]

Assessing the hedge's expected effectiveness

.162 The price of Company A's natural gas inventory in West Texas and the price of the natural gas that is the underlying for the futures it sold will differ as a result of regional factors (such as location, pipeline transmission costs, and supply and demand).[34] Company A therefore may not automatically assume that the hedge will be highly effective at achieving offsetting changes in fair value, and it cannot assess effectiveness by looking solely to the change in the price of natural gas delivered to the Henry Hub. [FAS133, ¶74]

.163 Both at inception of the hedge and on an ongoing basis, Company A might assess the hedge's expected effectiveness based on the extent of correlation in recent years for periods similar to the spot prices term of the futures contracts between the spot prices of natural gas in West Texas and at the Henry Hub.[35] If those prices have been and are expected to continue to be highly correlated, Company A might reasonably expect the changes in the fair value of the futures contracts attributable to changes in the spot price of natural gas at the Henry Hub to be highly effective in offsetting the changes in the fair value of its natural gas inventory. In assessing effectiveness during the term of the hedge, Company A must take into account actual changes in spot prices in West Texas and at the Henry Hub. [FAS133, ¶75]

---

[34]The use of a hedging instrument with a different underlying basis than the item or transaction being hedged is generally referred to as a *cross-hedge*. The principles for cross-hedges illustrated in this example also apply to hedges involving other risks. For example, the effectiveness of a hedge of market interest rate risk in which one interest rate is used as a surrogate for another interest rate would be evaluated in the same way as the natural gas cross-hedge in this example. [FAS133, ¶74, fn19]

[35]The period of time over which correlation of prices should be assessed would be based on management's judgment in the particular circumstance. [FAS133, ¶75, fn20]

.164 Company A may not assume that the change in the spot price of natural gas located at Henry Hub, Louisiana, is the same as the change in fair value of its West Texas inventory. The physical hedged item is natural gas in West Texas, not natural gas at the Henry Hub. In identifying the price risk that is being hedged, the company also may not assume that its natural gas in West Texas has a Louisiana natural gas "component." Use of a price for natural gas located somewhere other than West Texas to assess the effectiveness of a fair value hedge of natural gas in West Texas would be inconsistent with this section and could result in an assumption that a hedge was highly effective when it was not. If the price of natural gas in West Texas is not readily available, Company A might use a price for natural gas located elsewhere as a base for estimating the price of natural gas in West Texas. However, that base price must be adjusted to reflect the effects of factors, such as location, transmission costs, and supply and demand, that would cause the price of natural gas in West Texas to differ from the base price. [FAS133, ¶76]

Measuring hedge ineffectiveness

.165 Consistent with the company's method of assessing whether the hedge is expected to be highly effective, the hedge would be ineffective to the extent that (a) the actual change in the fair value of the futures contracts attributable to changes in the spot price of natural gas at the Henry Hub did not offset (b) the actual change in the spot price of natural gas in West Texas per MMBTU multiplied by 20,000. That method excludes the change in the fair value of the futures contracts attributable to changes in the difference between the spot price and the forward price of natural gas at the Henry Hub in determining ineffectiveness. The excluded amount would be reported directly in earnings. [FAS133, ¶77]

Example 2: Fair Value Hedge of Tire Inventory with a Forward Contract

.166 Company B manufactures tires. The production of those tires incorporates a variety of physical components, of which rubber and steel are the most significant, as well as labor and overhead. The company hedges its exposure to changes in the fair value of its inventory of 8,000 steel-belted radial tires by entering into a forward contract to sell rubber at a fixed price. [FAS133, ¶78]

Assessing the hedge's expected effectiveness

.167 Company B decides to base its assessment of hedge effectiveness on changes in the fair value of the forward contract attributable to changes in the spot price of rubber. To determine whether the forward contract is expected to be highly effective at offsetting the change in fair value of the tire inventory, Company B could estimate and compare such changes in the fair value of the forward contract and changes in the fair value of the tires (computed as the market price per tire multiplied by 8,000 tires) for different rubber and tire prices. Company B also should consider the extent to which past changes in the spot prices of rubber and tires have been correlated. Because tires are a nonfinancial asset and rubber is only an ingredient in manufacturing them, Company B may not assess hedge effectiveness by looking to the change in the fair value of only the rubber component of the steel-belted radial tires (paragraph .118(e)). Both at inception of the hedge and during its term, the company must base its assessment of hedge effectiveness on changes in the market price of steel-belted radial tires and changes in the fair value of the forward contract attributable to changes in the spot price of rubber. [FAS133, ¶79]

Measuring hedge ineffectiveness

.168 It is unlikely that this transaction would be highly effective in achieving offsetting changes in fair value. However, if Company B concludes that the hedge will be highly effective and the hedge otherwise qualifies for hedge accounting, the ineffective part of the hedge would be measured consistent with the company's method of assessing whether the hedge is expected to be highly effective. Based on that method, the hedge would be ineffective to the extent that the actual changes in (a) the fair value of the forward contract attributable to the change in the spot price of rubber and (b) the market price of steel-belted radials multiplied by the number of tires in inventory did not offset. Because Company B bases its assessment of effectiveness on changes in spot prices, the change in the fair value of the forward contract attributable to changes in the difference between the spot and forward price of rubber would be excluded from the measure of effectiveness and reported directly in earnings. [FAS133, ¶80]

Example 3: Fair Value Hedge of Growing Wheat with Futures Contracts

.169 Company C has a tract of land on which it is growing wheat. Historically, Company C has harvested at least 40,000 bushels of wheat from that tract of land. Two months before its expected harvest, the company sells 2-month futures contracts for 40,000 bushels of wheat, which it wants to designate as a fair value hedge of its growing wheat, rather than as a cash flow hedge of the projected sale of the wheat after harvest. [FAS133, ¶81]

Assessing the hedge's expected effectiveness and measuring ineffectiveness

.170 Even though the futures contracts are for the same type of wheat that Company C expects to harvest in two months, the futures contracts and hedged wheat have different bases because the futures contracts are based on fully grown, harvested wheat, while the hedged item is unharvested wheat with two months left in its growing cycle. The company therefore may not automatically assume that the hedge will be highly effective in achieving offsetting changes in fair value. [FAS133, ¶82]

.171 To determine whether the futures contracts are expected to be highly effective in providing offsetting changes in fair value for the growing wheat, Company C would need to estimate and compare the fair value of its growing wheat and of the futures contracts for different levels of wheat prices. Company C may not base its estimate of the value of its growing wheat solely on the current price of wheat because that price is for grown, harvested wheat. The company might, however, use the current price of harvested wheat together with other relevant factors, such as additional production and harvesting costs and the physical condition of the growing wheat, to estimate the current fair value of its growing wheat crop. [FAS133, ¶83]

.172 It is unlikely that wheat futures would be highly effective in offsetting the changes in value of growing wheat. However, if Company C concludes that the hedge qualifies as highly effective, it would use the same method for measuring actual hedge effectiveness that it uses initially and on an ongoing basis to assess whether the hedge is expected to be highly effective. The hedge would be ineffective to the extent that the actual changes in fair value of the futures contract and of the growing wheat crop did not offset. [FAS133, ¶84]

Example 4: Fair Value Hedge of Equity Securities with Option Contracts

.173 Company D holds 10,000 shares of XYZ stock. It purchases put option contracts on 20,000 shares of XYZ stock with a strike price equal to the current price of the stock to hedge its exposure to changes in the fair value of its investment position attributable to changes in the price of XYZ stock. Company D manages the position using a "delta-neutral" strategy. That is, it monitors the option's "delta"—the ratio of changes in the option's price to changes in the price of XYZ stock. As the delta ratio changes, Company D buys or sells put options so that the next change in the fair value of all of the options held can be expected to counterbalance the next change in the value of its investment in XYZ stock. For put options, the delta ratio moves closer to one as the share price of the stock falls and moves closer to zero as the share price rises. The delta ratio also changes as the exercise period decreases, as interest rates change, and as expected volatility changes. Company D designates the put options as a fair value hedge of its investment in XYZ stock. [FAS133, ¶85]

Assessing the hedge's expected effectiveness and measuring ineffectiveness

.174 Because Company D plans to change the number of options that it holds to the extent necessary to maintain a delta-neutral position, it may not automatically assume that the hedge will be highly effective at achieving offsetting changes in fair value. Also, because the "delta-neutral" hedging strategy is based on expected changes in the option's fair value, the company may not assess effectiveness based on changes in the option's intrinsic value. Instead, Company D would estimate (a) the gain or loss on the option position that would result from various decreases or increases in the market price of XYZ stock and (b) the loss or gain on its investment in XYZ stock for the same market price changes. To assess the effectiveness of the hedge both at inception and on an ongoing basis, the company could compare the respective gains and losses from different market price changes. The ongoing assessment of effectiveness also must consider the actual changes in the fair value of the put options held and of the investment in XYZ stock during the hedge period. [FAS133, ¶86]

.175 Consistent with the company's method of assessing effectiveness, the hedge would be ineffective to the extent that the actual realized and unrealized gains or losses from changes in the fair value of the options held is greater or less than the change in value of the investment in XYZ stock. The underlying for the put option contracts is the market price of XYZ stock. Therefore, if Company D continually monitors the delta ratio and adjusts the number of options held accordingly, the changes in the fair value of the options and of the hedged item may almost completely offset, resulting in only a small amount of ineffectiveness to be recognized in earnings. [FAS133, ¶87]

Example 5: Fair Value Hedge of a Treasury Bond with a Put Option Contract

.176 Company E owns a Treasury bond and wants to protect itself against the fair value exposure to declines in the price of the bond. The company purchases an at-the-money put option on a Treasury security with the same terms (remaining maturity, notional amount, and interest rate) as the Treasury bond held and designates the option as a hedge of the fair value exposure of the Treasury bond. Company E plans to hold the put option until it expires. [FAS133, ¶88]

Assessing the hedge's expected effectiveness and measuring ineffectiveness

.177 Because Company E plans to hold the put option (a static hedge) rather than manage the position with a delta-neutral strategy, it could assess whether it expects the hedge to be highly effective at achieving offsetting changes in fair value by calculating and comparing the changes in the intrinsic value of the option and changes in the price (fair value) of the Treasury bond for different possible market prices. In assessing the expectation of effectiveness on an ongoing basis, the company also must consider the actual changes in the fair value of the Treasury bond and in the intrinsic value of the option during the hedge period. [FAS133, ¶89]

.178 However, because the pertinent critical terms of the option and the bond are the same in this example, the company could expect the changes in value of the bond attributable to changes in interest rates and changes in the intrinsic value of the option to offset completely during the period that the option is in the money. That is, there will be no ineffectiveness because the company has chosen to exclude changes in the option's time value from the effectiveness test. Because of that choice, Company E must recognize changes in the time value of the option directly in earnings. [FAS133, ¶90]

Example 6: Fair Value Hedge of an Embedded Purchased Option with a Written Option

.179 Company F issues five-year, fixed-rate debt with an embedded (purchased) call option and, with a different counterparty, writes a call option to neutralize the call feature in the debt. The embedded call option and the written call option have the same effective notional amount, underlying fixed interest rate, and strike price. (The strike price of the option in the debt usually is referred to as the call price.) The embedded option also can be exercised at the same times as the written option. Company F designates the written option as a fair value hedge of the embedded prepayment option component of the fixed-rate debt. [FAS133, ¶91]

Assessing the hedge's expected effectiveness and measuring ineffectiveness

.180 To assess whether the hedge is expected to be highly effective in achieving offsetting changes in fair value, Company F could estimate and compare the changes in fair values of the two options for different market interest rates. Because this section does not permit derivatives, including embedded derivatives whether or not they are required to be accounted for separately, to be separated into components, Company F can only designate a hedge of the entire change in fair value of the embedded purchased call option. The resulting changes in fair value will be included currently in earnings. Changes in the fair value of the written option also will be included currently in earnings; any ineffectiveness thus will be automatically reflected in earnings. (The hedge is likely to have some ineffectiveness because the premium for the written call option is unlikely to be the same as the premium for the embedded purchased call option.) [FAS133, ¶92]

Example 7: Cash Flow Hedge of a Forecasted Purchase of Inventory with a Forward Contract

.181 Company G forecasts the purchase of 500,000 pounds of Brazilian coffee for U.S. dollars in 6 months. It wants to hedge the cash flow exposure associated with changes in the U.S. dollar price of Brazilian coffee. Rather than acquire a derivative based on Brazilian coffee, the company enters into a 6-month forward contract to purchase 500,000 pounds of Colombian coffee for U.S. dollars and designates the forward contract as a cash flow hedge of its forecasted purchase of Brazilian coffee. All other terms of the forward contract and the forecasted purchase, such as delivery locations, are the same. [FAS133, ¶93]

Assessing the hedge's expected effectiveness and measuring ineffectiveness

.182 Company G bases its assessment of hedge effectiveness and measure of ineffectiveness on changes in forward prices, with the resulting gain or loss discounted to reflect the time value of money. Because of the difference in the bases of the forecasted transaction (Brazilian coffee) and forward contract (Colombian coffee), Company G may not assume that the hedge will automatically be highly effective in achieving offsetting cash flows. Both at inception and on an ongoing basis, Company G could assess the effectiveness of the hedge by comparing changes in the expected cash flows from the Colombian coffee forward contract with the expected net change in cash outflows for purchasing the Brazilian coffee for different market prices. (A simpler method that should produce the same results would consider the expected future correlation of the prices of Brazilian and Colombian coffee, based on the correlation of those prices over past six-month periods.) [FAS133, ¶94]

.183 In assessing hedge effectiveness on an ongoing basis, Company G also must consider the extent of offset between the change in expected cash flows on its Colombian coffee contract and the change in expected cash flows for the forecasted purchase of Brazilian coffee. Both changes would be measured on a cumulative basis for actual changes in the forward price of the respective coffees during the hedge period. [FAS133, ¶95]

.184 Because the only difference between the forward contract and forecasted purchase relates to the type of coffee (Colombian versus Brazilian), Company G could consider the changes in the cash flows on a forward contract for Brazilian coffee to be a measure of perfectly offsetting changes in cash flows for its forecasted purchase of Brazilian coffee. For example, for given changes in the U.S. dollar prices of six-month and three-month Brazilian and Colombian contracts, Company G could compute the effect of a change in the price of coffee on the expected cash flows of its forward contract on Colombian coffee and of a forward contract for Brazilian coffee as [shown in Exhibit 184A]. [FAS133, ¶96]

Exhibit 184A

Effect of a Change in the Price of Coffee on Expected Cash Flows of a Forward Contract

	Estimate of Change in Cash Flows	
	Hedging Instrument: **Forward Contract on Colombian Coffee**	***Estimate of Forecasted Transaction:*** **Forward Contract on Brazilian Coffee**
Forward price of Colombian and Brazilian coffee:		
At hedge inception—6-month price	$ 2.54	$ 2.43
3 months later—3-month price	2.63	2.53
Cumulative change in price—gain	$ .09	$ .10
× 500,000 pounds of coffee	× 500,000	× 500,000
Estimate of change in cash flows	$ 45,000	$ 50,000

[FAS133, ¶96]

.185 Using the above amounts, Company G could evaluate effectiveness 3 months into the hedge by comparing the $45,000 change on its Colombian coffee contract with what would have been a perfectly offsetting change in cash flow for its forecasted purchase—the $50,000 change on an otherwise identical forward contract for Brazilian coffee. The hedge would be ineffective to the extent that there was a difference between the changes in the present value of the expected cash flows on (a) the company's Colombian coffee contract and (b) a comparable forward contract for Brazilian coffee (the equivalent of the present value of $5,000 in the numerical example). [FAS133, ¶97]

Example 8: Cash Flow Hedge with a Basis Swap

.186 Company H has a 5-year, $100,000 variable-rate asset and a 7-year, $150,000 variable-rate liability. The interest on the asset is payable by the counterparty at the end of each month based on the prime rate as of the first of the month. The interest on the liability is payable by Company H at the end of each month based on LIBOR as of the tenth day of the month (the liability's anniversary date). The company enters into a 5-year interest rate swap to pay interest at the prime rate and receive interest at LIBOR at the end of each month based on a notional amount of $100,000. Both rates are determined as of the first of the month. Company H designates the swap as a hedge of 5 years of interest receipts on the $100,000 variable-rate asset and the first 5 years of interest payments on $100,000 of the variable-rate liability. [FAS133, ¶98]

Assessing the hedge's expected effectiveness and measuring ineffectiveness

.187 Company H may not automatically assume that the hedge always will be highly effective at achieving offsetting changes in cash flows because the reset date on the receive leg of the swap differs from the reset date on the corresponding variable-rate liability. Both at hedge inception and on an ongoing basis, the company's assessment of expected effectiveness could be based on the extent to which changes in LIBOR have occurred during comparable 10-day periods in the past. Company H's ongoing assessment of expected effectiveness and measurement of actual ineffectiveness would be on a cumulative basis and would incorporate the actual interest rate changes to date. The hedge would be ineffective to the extent that the cumulative change in cash flows on the prime leg of the swap did not offset the cumulative change in expected cash flows on the asset, *and* the cumulative change in cash flows on the LIBOR leg of the swap did not offset the change in expected cash flows on the hedged portion of the liability. The terms of the swap, the asset, and the portion of the liability that is hedged are the same, with the exception of the reset dates on the liability and the receive leg of the swap. Thus, the hedge will only be ineffective to the extent that LIBOR has changed between the first of the month (the reset date for the swap) and the tenth of the month (the reset date for the liability). [FAS133, ¶99]

Example 9: Cash Flow Hedge of Forecasted Sale with a Forward Contract

.188 Company I, a U.S. dollar functional currency company, forecasts the sale of 10,000 units of its principal product in 6 months to French customers for FF500,000 (French francs). The company wants to hedge the cash flow exposure of the French franc sale related to changes in the US$-FF exchange rate. It enters into a 6-month forward contract to exchange the FF500,000 it expects to receive in the forecasted sale for the U.S. dollar equivalent specified in the forward contract and designates the forward contract as a cash flow hedge of the forecasted sale. [FAS133, ¶100]

Assessing the hedge's expected effectiveness and measuring ineffectiveness

.189 Company I chooses to assess hedge effectiveness at inception and during the term of the hedge based on (a) changes in the fair value of the forward contract attributable to changes in the US$-FF spot rate and (b) changes in the present value of the current U.S. dollar equivalent of the forecasted receipt of FF500,000. Because the critical terms of the forward contract and the forecasted transaction are the same, presumably there would be no ineffectiveness unless there is a reduction in the expected sales proceeds from the forecasted sales. Because Company I is assessing effectiveness based on spot rates, it would exclude the change in the fair value of the forward contract attributable to changes in the difference between the forward rate and spot rate from the measure of hedge ineffectiveness and report it directly in earnings. [FAS133, ¶101]

Example 10: Attempted Hedge of a Forecasted Sale with a Written Call Option

.190 Company J forecasts the sale in 9 months of 100 units of product with a current market price of $95 per unit. The company's objective is to sell the upside potential associated with the forecasted sale by writing a call option for a premium. The company plans to use the premium from the call option as an offset to decreases in future cash inflows from the forecasted sale that will occur if the market price of the product decreases below $95. Accordingly, Company J sells an at-the-money call option on 100 units of product with a strike price of $95 for a premium. The premium represents only the time value of the option. The option is exercisable at any time within nine months. [FAS133, ¶102]

.191 Company J's objective of using the premium from the written call option as an offset to any decrease in future cash inflows would not meet the notion of effectiveness in this section. Future changes in the market price of the company's product will not affect the premium that Company J received, which is all related to time value in this example and thus is the maximum amount by which Company J can benefit. That is, the company could not expect the cash flows on the option to increase so that, at different price levels, a decrease in cash flows from the forecasted sale would be offset by an increase in cash flows on the option. [FAS133, ¶103]

Examples Illustrating Application of This Section

Hedging Relationships

.192 Paragraphs .193 through .288 present examples that illustrate the application of this section. The examples do not address all possible uses of derivatives as hedging instruments. For simplicity, commissions and most other transaction costs, initial margin, and income taxes are ignored unless otherwise stated in an example. It is also assumed in each example that there are no changes in creditworthiness that would alter the effectiveness of any of the hedging relationships. [FAS133, ¶104]

Example 1: Fair Value Hedge of a Commodity Inventory

.193 This example illustrates the accounting for a fair value hedge of a commodity inventory. In the first scenario, the terms of the hedging derivative have been negotiated to produce no ineffectiveness in the hedging relationship. In the second scenario, there is ineffectiveness in the hedging relationship. To simplify the illustration and focus on basic concepts, the derivative in these two scenarios is assumed to have no time value. In practice, a derivative used for a fair value hedge of a commodity would have a time value that would change over the term of the hedging relationship. The changes in that time value would be recognized in earnings as they occur, either because they represent ineffectiveness or because they are excluded from the assessment of effectiveness (as discussed in paragraph .151). Other examples in paragraphs .194 through .263 illustrate accounting for the time value component of a derivative. [FAS133, ¶105]

Scenario 1—No ineffectiveness in the hedging relationship

.194 ABC Company decides to hedge the risk of changes during the period in the overall fair value of its entire inventory of Commodity A by entering into a derivative contract, Derivative Z. On the first day of period 1, ABC enters into Derivative Z and neither receives nor pays a premium (that is, the fair value at inception is zero). ABC designates the derivative as a hedge of the changes in fair value of the inventory due to changes in the price of Commodity A during period 1. The hedging relationship qualifies for fair value hedge accounting. ABC will assess effectiveness by comparing the entire change in fair value of Derivative Z with the change in the market price of the hedged commodity inventory. ABC expects no ineffectiveness because (a) the notional amount of Derivative Z matches the amount of the hedged inventory (that is, Derivative Z is based on the same number of bushels as the number of bushels of the commodity that ABC designated as hedged) and (b) the underlying of Derivative Z is the price of the same variety and grade of Commodity A as the inventory at the same location. [FAS133, ¶106]

.195 At inception of the hedge, Derivative Z has a fair value of zero and the hedged inventory has a carrying amount of $1,000,000 and a fair value of $1,100,000. On the last day of period 1, the fair value of Derivative Z has increased by $25,000, and the fair value of the inventory has decreased by $25,000. The inventory is sold, and Derivative Z is settled on the last day of period 1. Exhibit 195A illustrates the accounting for the situation described above. [FAS133, ¶107]

Exhibit 195A

Fair Value Hedge of a Commodity Inventory—No Effectiveness in the Hedging Relationship

	Debit (Credit)			
	Cash	**Derivative**	**Inventory**	**Earnings**
Period 1				
Recognize change in fair value of derivative		$ 25,000		$ (25,000)
Recognize change in fair value of inventory			$ (25,000)	25,000
Recognize revenue from sale	$1,075,000			(1,075,000)
Recognize cost of sale of inventory			(975,000)	975,000
Recognize settlement of derivative	25,000	(25,000)		
Total	$1,100,000	$ 0	$(1,000,000)	$ (100,000)

[FAS133, ¶107]

.196 If ABC had sold the hedged inventory at the inception of the hedge, its gross profit on that sale would have been $100,000. The above example illustrates that, by hedging the risk of changes in the overall fair value of its inventory, ABC recognized the same gross profit at the end of the hedge period even though the fair value of its inventory decreased by $25,000. [FAS133, ¶108]

Scenario 2—Ineffectiveness in the hedging relationship

.197 No ineffectiveness was recognized in earnings in the above situation because the gain on Derivative Z exactly offsets the loss on the inventory. However, if the terms of Derivative Z did not perfectly match the inventory and its fair value had increased by $22,500 as compared with the decline in fair value of the inventory of $25,000, then ineffectiveness of $2,500 would have been recognized in earnings. Exhibit 197A illustrates that situation (all other facts are assumed to be the same as in Scenario 1). [FAS133, ¶109]

Exhibit 197A

Fair Value Hedge of a Commodity Inventory—Ineffectiveness in the Hedging Relationship

	Debit (Credit)			
	Cash	**Derivative**	**Inventory**	**Earnings**
Period 1				
Recognize change in fair value of derivative		$ 22,500		$ (22,500)
Recognize change in fair value of inventory			$ (25,000)	25,000
Recognize revenue from sale	$1,075,000			(1,075,000)
Recognize cost of sale of inventory			(975,000)	975,000
Recognize settlement of derivative	22,500	(22,500)		
Total	$1,097,500	$ 0	$(1,000,000)	$ (97,500)

[FAS133, ¶109]

.198 The difference between the effect on earnings in this scenario and the effect on earnings in Scenario 1 is the $2,500 of hedge ineffectiveness. [FAS133, ¶110]

Example 2: Fair Value Hedge of Fixed-Rate Interest-Bearing Debt

Purpose of the example

.199 This example demonstrates the mechanics of reporting an interest rate swap used as a fair value hedge of an interest-bearing liability. It is not intended to demonstrate how to compute the fair value of an interest rate swap or an interest-bearing liability. This example has been simplified by assuming that the interest rate applicable to a payment due at any future date is the same as the rate for a payment due at any other date (that is, the yield curve is flat). Although that is an unrealistic assumption, it makes the amounts used in the example easier to understand without detracting from the purpose of the example. [FAS133, ¶111]

.200 The fair values of the swap in this example are determined using the "zero-coupon method." That method involves computing and summing the present value of each future net settlement that would be required by the contract terms if future spot interest rates match the forward rates implied by the current yield curve. The discount rates used are the spot interest rates implied by the current yield curve for hypothetical zero coupon bonds due on the date of each future net settlement on the swap. The zero-coupon method is not the only acceptable method. Explanations of other acceptable methods of determining the fair value of an interest rate swap can be obtained from various published sources. Fair values also may be available from dealers in interest rate swaps and other derivatives. [FAS133, ¶112]

.201 In this example, the term and notional amount of the interest rate swap match the term and principal amount of the interest-bearing liability being hedged. The fixed and variable interest rates used to determine the net settlements on the swap match the current yield curve, and the sum of the present values of the expected net settlements is zero at inception. Thus, paragraph .156 of this section permits the reporting entity to assume that there will be no ineffectiveness. Assessment of effectiveness at one of the swap's repricing dates would confirm the validity of that assumption. [FAS133, ¶113]

.202 A shortcut method can be used to produce the same reporting results as the method illustrated in this example. This shortcut is only appropriate for a fair value hedge of a fixed-rate asset or liability using an interest rate swap and only if the assumption of no ineffectiveness is appropriate.[36] The steps in the shortcut method are as follows:

a. Determine the difference between the fixed rate to be received on the swap and the fixed rate to be paid on the bonds.

[36]A slightly different shortcut method for interest rate swaps used as cash flow hedges is illustrated in Example 5. [FAS133, ¶114, fn21]

b. Combine that difference with the variable rate to be paid on the swap.
c. Compute and recognize interest expense using that combined rate and the fixed-rate liability's principal amount. (Amortization of any purchase premium or discount on the liability also must be considered, although that complication is not incorporated in this example.)
d. Determine the fair value of the interest rate swap.
e. Adjust the carrying amount of the swap to its fair value and adjust the carrying amount of the liability by an offsetting amount.

Amounts determined using the shortcut method and the facts in this example will match the amounts in Exhibit 205A even though the shortcut does not involve explicitly amortizing the hedge accounting adjustments on the debt. That is, the quarterly adjustments of the debt and explicit amortization of previous adjustments will have the same net effect on earnings as the shortcut method. [FAS133, ¶114]

Assumptions

.203 On July 1, 20X1, ABC Company borrows $1,000,000 to be repaid on June 30, 20X3. On that same date, ABC also enters into a two-year receive-fixed, pay-variable interest rate swap. ABC designates the interest rate swap as a hedge of the changes in the fair value of the fixed-rate debt attributable to changes in [FAS133, ¶115] the designated benchmark interest rate. ABC designates changes in **LIBOR swap rates** as the benchmark interest rate in hedging interest rate risk. [FAS138, ¶4(bb)] The terms of the interest rate swap and the debt are as follows:

	Interest Rate Swap	Fixed-Rate Debt
Trade date and borrowing date*	July 1, 20X1	July 1, 20X1
Termination date and maturity date	June 30, 20X3	June 30, 20X3
Notional amount and principal amount	$1,000,000	$1,000,000
Fixed interest rate*	6.41%	6.41%
Variable interest rate	3-month US$ LIBOR	Not applicable
Settlement dates and interest payment dates*	End of each calendar quarter	End of each calendar quarter
Reset dates	End of each calendar quarter through March 31, 20X3	Not applicable

*These terms need not match for the assumption of no ineffectiveness to be appropriate. (Refer to paragraphs .156 and .157.)

[FAS133, ¶115]

.204 The US$ LIBOR rates that are in effect at inception of the hedging relationship and at the end of each of the quarterly reset dates are assumed to be as follows:

Reset Date	3-Month LIBOR Rate
7/1/X1	6.41%
9/30/X1	6.48%
12/31/X1	6.41%
3/31/X2	6.32%
6/30/X2	7.60%
9/30/X2	7.71%
12/31/X2	7.82%
3/31/X3	7.42%

[FAS133, ¶116]

Amounts to be reported

.205 Exhibit 205A summarizes the fair values of the debt and the swap at each quarter end, the details of the changes in the fair values during each quarter (including accrual and payment of interest, the effect of changes in rates, and level-yield amortization of hedge accounting adjustments), the expense for each quarter, and the net cash payments for each quarter. The calculations of fair value of both the debt and the swap are made using LIBOR. (A discussion of the appropriate discount rate appears in paragraph .158.) [FAS133, ¶117]

Exhibit 205A

Fair Value Hedge of Fixed-Rate Interest-Bearing Debt

	Fixed-Rate Debt	Interest Rate Swap	Expense	Net Payment
July 1, 20X1	$(1,000,000)	$ 0		
Interest accrued	(16,025)	0	$(16,025)	
Payments (receipts)	16,025	0		$ 16,025
Effect of change in rates	1,149	(1,149)	0	
September 30, 20X1	(998,851)	(1,149)	$(16,025)	$ 16,025
Interest accrued	(16,025)	(19)	$(16,044)	
Payments (receipts)	16,025	175		$ 16,200
Amortization of basis adjustments	(156)	0	(156)	
Effect of change in rates	(993)	993	0	
December 31, 20X1	(1,000,000)	0	$(16,200)	$ 16,200
Interest accrued	(16,025)	0	$(16,025)	
Payments (receipts)	16,025	0		$ 16,025
Amortization of basis adjustments	0	0	0	
Effect of change in rates	(1,074)	1,074	0	
March 31, 20X2	(1,001,074)	1,074	$(16,025)	$ 16,025
Interest accrued	(16,025)	17	$(16,008)	
Payments (receipts)	16,025	(225)		$ 15,800
Amortization of basis adjustments	208	0	208	
Effect of change in rates	12,221	(12,221)	0	
June 30, 20X2	(988,645)	(11,355)	$(15,800)	$ 15,800
Interest accrued	(16,025)	(216)	$(16,241)	
Payments (receipts)	16,025	2,975		$ 19,000
Amortization of basis adjustments	(2,759)	0	(2,759)	
Effect of change in rates	789	(789)	0	
September 30, 20X2	(990,615)	(9,385)	$(19,000)	$ 19,000
Interest accrued	(16,025)	(181)	$(16,206)	
Payments (receipts)	16,025	3,250		$ 19,275
Amortization of basis adjustments	(3,069)	0	(3,069)	
Effect of change in rates	532	(532)	0	
December 31, 20X2	(993,152)	(6,848)	$(19,275)	$ 19,275
Interest accrued	(16,025)	(134)	$(16,159)	
Payments (receipts)	16,025	3,525		$ 19,550
Amortization of basis adjustments	(3,391)	0	(3,391)	
Effect of change in rates	(978)	978	0	
March 31, 20X3	(997,521)	(2,479)	$(19,550)	$ 19,550
Interest accrued	(16,025)	(46)	$(16,071)	
Payments (receipts)	1,016,025	2,525		$1,018,550
Amortization of basis adjustments	(2,479)	0	(2,479)	
June 30, 20X3	$ 0	$ 0	$(18,550)	$1,018,550

[FAS133, ¶117]

.206 Exhibit 205A demonstrates two important points that explain why the shortcut method described in paragraph .202 produces the same results as the computation in the above table when there is no ineffectiveness in the hedging relationship.

a. In every quarter, the effect of changes in rates on the swap completely offsets the effect of changes in rates on the debt. That is as expected because there is no ineffectiveness.
b. In every quarter except the last when the principal is repaid, the expense equals the cash payment.

[FAS133, ¶118]

.207 Exhibit 207A illustrates the computation of interest expense using the shortcut method described in paragraph .202. The results are the same as the results computed in Exhibit 205A. [FAS133, ¶119]

Exhibit 207A

Shortcut Method of Computing Interest Expense

Quarter Ended	(a) Difference between Fixed Rates	(b) Variable Rate on Swap	(c) Sum (a) + (b)	(d) Debt's Principal Amount	(e) Interest Expense ((c) × (d))/4
September 30, 20X1	0.00%	6.41%	6.41%	$1,000,000	$16,025
December 31, 20X1	0.00%	6.48%	6.48%	1,000,000	16,200
March 31, 20X2	0.00%	6.41%	6.41%	1,000,000	16,025
June 30, 20X2	0.00%	6.32%	6.32%	1,000,000	15,800
September 30, 20X2	0.00%	7.60%	7.60%	1,000,000	19,000
December 31, 20X2	0.00%	7.71%	7.71%	1,000,000	19,275
March 31, 20X3	0.00%	7.82%	7.82%	1,000,000	19,550
June 30, 20X3	0.00%	7.42%	7.42%	1,000,000	18,550

[FAS133, ¶119]

.208 As stated in the introduction to this example, a flat yield curve is assumed for simplicity. An upward-sloping yield curve would have made the computations more complex. Paragraph .204 would have shown different interest rates for each quarterly repricing date, and the present value of each future payment would have been computed using a different rate (as described in paragraph .200). However, the basic principles are the same. As long as there is no ineffectiveness in the hedging relationship, the shortcut method is appropriate. [FAS133, ¶120]

Example 2A: Fair Value Hedge of the LIBOR Swap Rate in a $100,000 BBB-Quality 5-Year Fixed-Rate Noncallable Note

.208A This example illustrates one method that could be used in determining the hedged item's change in fair value attributable to changes in the benchmark interest rate. Other methods could be used in determining the hedged item's change in fair value attributable to changes in the benchmark interest rate as long as those methods meet the criteria in paragraph .118(f). [FAS138, ¶4(cc)]

.208B On January 1, 20X0, GHI Company issues at par a $100,000 BBB-quality 5-year fixed-rate noncallable debt instrument with an annual 10 percent interest coupon. On that date, the issuer enters into a 5-year interest rate swap based on the LIBOR swap rate and designates it as the hedging instrument in a fair value hedge of the $100,000 liability. Under the terms of the swap, GHI will receive fixed interest at 7 percent and pay variable interest at LIBOR. The variable leg of the swap resets each year on December 31 for the payments due the following year. This example has been simplified by assuming that the interest rate applicable to a payment due at any future date is the same as the rate for a payment at any other date (that is, the yield curve is flat). During the hedge period, the gain or loss on the swap will be recorded in earnings. The example assumes that immediately before the interest rate on the variable leg resets on December 31, 20X0, the LIBOR swap rate increased by 50 basis points to 7.50 percent, and the change in fair value of the swap for the period from January 1 to December 31, 20X0 is a loss in value of $1,675. [FAS138, ¶4(cc)]

Changes in the fair value of the hedged item attributable to the changes in the benchmark interest rate for a specific period

.208C Under this method, the change in a hedged item's fair value attributable to changes in the benchmark interest rate for a specific period is determined as the difference between two present value calculations as of the end of the period that exclude or include, respectively, the effect of the changes in the benchmark interest rate during the period. The discount rates used for those present value calculations would be, respectively, (a) the discount rate equal to the market interest rate for that hedged item at the inception of the hedge adjusted (up or down) for changes in the benchmark rate (designated as the interest rate risk being hedged) from the inception of the hedge to the beginning date of the period for which the change in fair value is being calculated[36a] and (b) the discount rate equal to the market interest rate for that hedged item at the inception of the hedge adjusted (up or down) for changes in the designated benchmark rate from the inception of the hedge to the ending date of the period for which the change in fair value is being calculated. Both present value calculations are computed using the estimated future cash flows for the hedged item (which typically would be its remaining contractual cash flows). [FAS138, ¶4(cc)]

.208D In GHI's quarterly assessments of hedge effectiveness for each of the first three quarters of year 20X0 in this example, there was zero change in the hedged item's fair value attributable to changes in the benchmark interest rate because there was no change in the LIBOR swap rate. However, in the assessment for the fourth quarter 20X0, the discount rate for the beginning of the period is 10 percent (the hedged item's original market interest rate with an adjustment of zero), and the discount rate for the end of the period is 10.50 percent (the hedged item's original market interest rate adjusted for the change during the period in the LIBOR swap rate [+0.50 percent]).

December 31, 20X0

Calculate the present value using the beginning-of-period discount rate of 10 percent:

$10,000pmt, 10%i, 4n, PV =	$ 31,699	(interest payments)
$100,000fv, 10%i, 4n, PV =	68,301	(principal payment)
Total present value	$100,000	

Calculate the present value using the end-of-period discount rate of 10.50 percent (that is, the beginning-of-period discount rate adjusted for the change during the period in the LIBOR swap rate of 50 basis points):

$10,000pmt, 10.50%i, 4n, PV =	$31,359	(interest payments)
$100,000fv, 10.50%i, 4n, PV =	67,073	(principal payment)
Total present value	$98,432	

[36a]This section does not provide specific guidance on the discount rate that must be used in the calculation. However, the method chosen by GHI and described in this illustration requires that the discount rate be based on the market interest rate for the hedged item at the inception of the hedging relationship. [FAS138, ¶4(cc)]

The change in fair value of the hedged item attributable to the change in the benchmark interest rate is $100,000 – $98,432 = $1,568 (the fair value decrease in the liability is a gain on debt).

When the change in fair value of the hedged item ($1,568 gain) attributable to the risk being hedged is compared with the change in fair value of the hedging instrument ($1,675 loss), ineffectiveness of $107 results. That ineffectiveness will be reported in earnings, because both changes in fair value are recorded in earnings. [FAS138, ¶4(cc)]

Example 3: Fair Value Hedge—Using a Forward Contract to Purchase Foreign Currency to Hedge a Firm Commitment Denominated in a Different Foreign Currency

.209 This example illustrates a fair value hedge of a firm commitment to purchase an asset for a price denominated in a foreign currency. In this example, the hedging instrument and the firm commitment are denominated in different foreign currencies. Consequently, the hedge is not perfectly effective, and ineffectiveness is recognized immediately in earnings. (The entity in the example could have designed a hedge with no ineffectiveness by using a hedging instrument denominated in the same foreign currency as the firm commitment with terms that match the appropriate terms in the firm commitment.) [FAS133, ¶121]

.210 MNO Company's functional currency is the U.S. dollar. On February 3, 20X7, MNO enters into a firm commitment to purchase a machine for delivery on May 1, 20X7. The price of the machine will be 270,000 Dutch guilders (Dfl270,000). Also on February 3, 20X7, MNO enters into a forward contract to purchase 240,000 Deutsche marks (DM240,000) on May 1, 20X7. MNO will pay $0.6125 per DM1 (a total of $147,000), which is the current forward rate for an exchange on May 1, 20X7. MNO designates the forward contract as a hedge of its risk of changes in the fair value of the firm commitment resulting from changes in the U.S. dollar–Dutch guilder forward exchange rate. [FAS133, ¶122]

.211 MNO will assess effectiveness by comparing the overall changes in the fair value of the forward contract to the changes in fair value in U.S. dollars of the firm commitment due to changes in U.S. dollar–Dutch guilder forward exchange rates. MNO expects the forward contract to be highly effective as a hedge because:

a. DM240,000 is approximately equal to Dfl270,000 at the May 1, 20X1 forward exchange rate in effect on February 3, 20X7.
b. Settlement of the forward contract and the firm commitment will occur on the same date.

c. In recent years, changes in the value in U.S. dollars of Deutsche marks over three-month periods have been highly correlated with changes in the value in U.S. dollars of Dutch guilders over those same periods.

Ineffectiveness will result from the difference between changes in the U.S. dollar equivalent of DM240,000 (the notional amount of the forward contract) and changes in the U.S. dollar equivalent of Dfl270,000 (the amount to be paid for the machine). The difference between the spot rate and the forward exchange rate is not excluded from the hedging relationship because changes in the fair value of the firm commitment are being measured using forward exchange rates.[37] [FAS133, ¶123]

.212 The forward exchange rates in effect on certain key dates are assumed to be as follows:

Date	$-DM Forward Exchange Rate for Settlement on 5/1/X7	$-Dfl Forward Exchange Rate for Settlement on 5/1/X7
Inception of the hedge—2/3/X7	$0.6125 = DM1	$0.5454 = Dfl1
Quarter end—3/31/X7	$0.5983 = DM1	$0.5317 = Dfl1
Machine purchase—5/1/X7	$0.5777 = DM1	$0.5137 = Dfl1

[FAS133, ¶124]

.213 The U.S. dollar equivalent and changes in the U.S. dollar equivalent of the forward contract and the firm commitment, the changes in fair value of the forward contract and the firm commitment, and the ineffectiveness of the hedge on those same key dates are shown in Exhibit 213A. A 6 percent discount rate is used in this example. This section requires that MNO recognize immediately in earnings all changes in fair values of the forward contract. Because MNO is hedging the risk of changes in fair value of the firm commitment attributable to changes in the forward exchange rates, this section also requires recognizing those changes immediately in earnings. [FAS133, ¶125]

[37]If the hedged item were a foreign-currency-denominated available-for-sale security instead of a firm commitment, Section F60 would have required its carrying value to be measured using the spot exchange rate. Therefore, the spot-forward difference would have been recognized immediately in earnings either because it represented ineffectiveness or because it was excluded from the assessment of effectiveness. [FAS133, ¶123, fn22]

Exhibit 213A

Changes in Fair Values of Forward Contract and Firm Commitment Denominated in a Foreign Currency

	2/3/X7	3/31/X7	5/1/X7
Forward contract			
$-DM forward exchange rate for settlement on May 1, 20X7	$ 0.6125	$ 0.5983	$ 0.5777
Units of currency (DM)	× 240,000	× 240,000	× 240,000
Forward price of DM240,000 in dollars	147,000	143,592	138,648
Contract price in dollars	(147,000)	(147,000)	(147,000)
Difference	$ 0	$ (3,408)	$ (8,352)
Fair value (present value of the difference)	$ 0	$ (3,391)	$ (8,352)
Change in fair value during the period		$ (3,391)	$ (4,961)
Firm commitment			
$-Dfl forward exchange rate for settlement on May 1, 20X7	$ 0.5454	$ 0.5317	$ 0.5137
Units of currency (Dfl)	× 270,000	× 270,000	× 270,000
Forward price of Dfl270,000 in dollars	(147,258)	(143,559)	(138,699)
Initial forward price in dollars	147,258	147,258	147,258
Difference	$ 0	$ 3,699	$ 8,559
Fair value (present value of the difference)	$ 0	$ 3,681	$ 8,559
Change in fair value during the period		$ 3,681	$ 4,878
Hedge ineffectiveness (difference between changes in fair values of the forward contract denominated in Deutsche marks and the firm commitment denominated in Dutch guilders)		$ 290	$ (83)

[FAS133, ¶125]

.214 On May 1, 20X7, MNO fulfills the firm commitment to purchase the machine and settles the forward contract. The entries illustrating fair value hedge accounting for the hedging relationship and the purchase of the machine are summarized in Exhibit 214A.

The effect of the hedge is to recognize the machine at its price in Dutch guilders (Dfl270,000) translated at the forward rate in effect at the inception of the hedge ($0.5454 per Dfl1). [FAS133, ¶126]

Exhibit 214A

Entries for Fair Value Hedge and Purchase of Machine

	Debit (Credit)				
	Cash	**Firm Commitment**	**Forward Contract**	**Machine**	**Earnings**
March 31, 20X7					
Recognize change in fair value of firm commitment		$ 3,681			$(3,681)
Recognize change in fair value of forward contract			$(3,391)		3,391
					(290)
April 30, 20X7					
Recognize change in fair value of firm commitment		4,878			(4,878)
Recognize change in fair value of forward contract			(4,961)		4,961
					83
May 1, 20X7					
Recognize settlement of forward contract	$ (8,352)		8,352		
Recognize purchase of machine	(138,699)	(8,559)		$147,258	
Total	$(147,051)	$ 0	$ 0	$147,258	$ (207)

Note: To simplify this example and focus on the effects of the hedging relationship, other amounts that would be involved in the purchase of the machine by MNO (for example, shipping costs and installation costs) have been ignored.

[FAS133, ¶126]

Example 4: Cash Flow Hedge of the Forecasted Sale of a Commodity Inventory

.215 This example illustrates the accounting for a cash flow hedge of a forecasted sale of a commodity. The terms of the hedging derivative have been negotiated to match the terms of the forecasted transaction. Thus, there is no ineffectiveness. The assumptions in this example are similar to those in Example 1, including the assumption that there is no time value in the derivative. However, the entity has chosen to hedge the variability of the cash flows from the forecasted sale of the commodity instead of the changes in its fair value. [FAS133, ¶127]

.216 ABC Company decides to hedge the risk of changes in its cash flows relating to a forecasted sale of 100,000 bushels of Commodity A by entering into a derivative contract, Derivative Z. ABC expects to sell the 100,000 bushels of Commodity A on the last day of period 1. On the first day of period 1, ABC enters into Derivative Z and designates it as a cash flow hedge of the forecasted sale. ABC neither pays nor receives a premium on Derivative Z (that is, its fair value is zero). The hedging relationship qualifies for cash flow hedge accounting. ABC expects that there will be no ineffectiveness from the hedge because (a) the notional amount of Derivative Z is 100,000 bushels and the forecasted sale is for 100,000 bushels, (b) the underlying of Derivative Z is the price of the same variety and grade of Commodity A that ABC expects to sell (assuming delivery to ABC's selling point), and (c) the settlement date of Derivative Z is the last day of period 1 and the forecasted sale is expected to occur on the last day of period 1. [FAS133, ¶128]

.217 At inception of the hedge, the expected sales price of 100,000 bushels of Commodity A is $1,100,000. On the last day of period 1, the fair value of Derivative Z has increased by $25,000, and the expected sales price of 100,000 bushels of Commodity A has decreased by $25,000. Both the sale of 100,000 bushels of Commodity A and the settlement of Derivative Z occur on the last day of period 1. Exhibit 217A illustrates the accounting, including the net impact on earnings and other comprehensive income (OCI), for the situation described above. [FAS133, ¶129]

Exhibit 217A

Impact of Cash Flow Hedge on Forecasted Sale of a Commodity Inventory

	Debit (Credit)			
	Cash	**Derivative**	**OCI**	**Earnings**
Recognize change in fair value of derivative		$ 25,000	$(25,000)	
Recognize revenue from sale	$1,075,000			$(1,075,000)
Recognize settlement of derivative	25,000	(25,000)		
Reclassify change in fair value of derivative to earnings			25,000	(25,000)
Total	$1,100,000	$ 0	$ 0	$(1,100,000)

[FAS133, ¶129]

.218 At the inception of the hedge, ABC anticipated that it would receive $1,100,000 from the sale of 100,000 bushels of Commodity A. The above example illustrates that by hedging the risk of changes in its cash flows relating to the forecasted sale of 100,000 bushels of Commodity A, ABC still received a total of $1,100,000 in cash flows even though the sales price of Commodity A declined during the period. [FAS133, ¶130]

Example 5: Cash Flow Hedge of Variable-Rate Interest-Bearing Asset

Purpose of the example

.219 This example demonstrates the mechanics of accounting for an interest rate swap used as a cash flow hedge of variable interest receipts. It is not intended to demonstrate how to compute the fair value of an interest rate swap. As in Example 2, the zero-coupon method[38] is used to determine the fair values. (Unlike Example 2, the yield curve in this example is assumed to be upward sloping, that is, interest rates are higher for payments due further into the future). In this example, the term, notional amount, and repricing date of the interest rate swap match the term, repricing date, and principal amount of the interest-bearing asset on which the hedged interest receipts are due. The swap terms are "at the market" (as described in paragraphs .156 and .157), so it has a zero value at inception. Thus, the reporting entity is permitted to assume that there will be no ineffectiveness. [FAS133, ¶131]

.220 A shortcut method can be used to produce the same reporting results as the method illustrated in this example. This shortcut is only appropriate if the assumption of no ineffectiveness applies for an interest rate swap used as a cash flow hedge of interest receipts on a variable-rate asset (or interest payments on a variable-rate liability). The steps in the shortcut method are as follows:[39]

a. Determine the difference between the variable rate to be paid on the swap and the variable rate to be received on the bonds.
b. Combine that difference with the fixed rate to be received on the swap.
c. Compute and recognize interest income using that combined rate and the variable-rate asset's principal amount. (Amortization of any purchase premium or discount on the asset must also be considered, although that complication is not incorporated in this example.)
d. Determine the fair value of the interest rate swap.
e. Adjust the carrying amount of the swap to its fair value and adjust other comprehensive income by an offsetting amount.

[FAS133, ¶132]

---

[38] Paragraph .200 discusses the zero-coupon method. [FAS133, ¶131, fn23]

[39] A slightly different shortcut method for interest rate swaps used as fair value hedges is illustrated in Example 2. [FAS133, ¶132, fn24]

Background and assumptions

.221 On July 1, 20X1, XYZ Company invests $10,000,000 in variable-rate corporate bonds that pay interest quarterly at a rate equal to the 3-month US$ LIBOR rate plus 2.25 percent. The $10,000,000 principal will be repaid on June 30, 20X3. [FAS133, ¶133]

.222 Also on July 1, 20X1, XYZ enters into a two-year receive-fixed, pay-variable interest rate swap and designates it as a cash flow hedge of the variable-rate interest receipts on the corporate bonds. The risk designated as being hedged is the risk of changes in cash flows attributable to changes in [FAS133, ¶134] the designated benchmark interest rate. XYZ designates changes in LIBOR swap rates as the benchmark interest rate in hedging interest rate risk. [FAS138, ¶4(dd)] The terms of the interest rate swap and the corporate bonds are shown below.

	Interest Rate Swap	Corporate Bonds
Trade date and borrowing date*	July 1, 20X1	July 1, 20X1
Termination date	June 30, 20X3	June 30, 20X3
Notional amount	$10,000,000	$10,000,000
Fixed interest rate	6.65%	Not applicable
Variable interest rate†	3-month US$ LIBOR	3-month US$ LIBOR + 2.25%
Settlement dates and interest payment dates*	End of each calendar quarter	End of each calendar quarter
Reset dates	End of each calendar quarter through March 31, 20X3	End of each calendar quarter through March 31, 20X3

*These terms need not match for the assumption of no ineffectiveness to be appropriate. (Refer to paragraphs .156 and .157.)

†Only the interest rate basis (for example, LIBOR) must match. The spread over LIBOR does not invalidate the assumption of no ineffectiveness.

[FAS133, ¶134]

.223 Because the conditions described in paragraph .156 are met, XYZ is permitted to assume that there is no ineffectiveness in the hedging relationship and to recognize in other comprehensive income the entire change in the fair value of the swap. [FAS133, ¶135]

.224 The three-month US$ LIBOR rates in effect at the inception of the hedging relationship and at each of the quarterly reset dates are assumed to be as follows:

Reset Date	3-Month LIBOR Rate
7/1/X1	5.56%
9/30/X1	5.63%
12/31/X1	5.56%
3/31/X2	5.47%
6/30/X2	6.75%
9/30/X2	6.86%
12/31/X2	6.97%
3/31/X3	6.57%

[FAS133, ¶136]

Amounts to be reported

.225 XYZ must reclassify to earnings the amount in accumulated other comprehensive income as each interest receipt affects earnings. In determining the amounts to reclassify each quarter, it is important to recognize that the interest rate swap does not hedge the bonds. Instead, it hedges the eight variable interest payments to be received. That is, each of the eight quarterly settlements on the swap is associated with an interest payment to be received on the bonds. Under the zero-coupon method discussed in paragraph .219, the present value of each quarterly settlement is computed separately. Because each payment occurs at a different point on the yield curve, a different interest rate must be used to determine its present value. As each individual interest receipt on the bonds is recognized in earnings, the fair value of the related quarterly settlement on the swap is reclassified to earnings. The fair values and changes in fair values of the interest rate swap and the effects on earnings and other comprehensive income (OCI) for each quarter are [presented in Exhibit 225A]. [FAS133, ¶137]

Exhibit 225A

Cash Flow Hedge of Variable-Risk Interest-Bearing Asset

	Swap Debit (Credit)	OCI Debit (Credit)	Earnings Debit (Credit)	Cash Debit (Credit)
July 1, 20X1	$ 0			
Interest accrued	0			
Payment (receipt)	(27,250)			$27,250
Effect of change in rates	52,100	$ (52,100)		
Reclassification to earnings		27,250	$(27,250)	
September 30, 20X1	24,850	(24,850)	$(27,250)	$27,250
Interest accrued	330	(330)		
Payment (receipt)	(25,500)			$25,500
Effect of change in rates	74,120	(74,120)		
Reclassification to earnings		25,500	$(25,500)	
December 31, 20X1	73,800	(73,800)	$(25,500)	$25,500
Interest accrued	1,210	(1,210)		
Payment (receipt)	(27,250)			$27,250
Effect of change in rates	38,150	(38,150)		
Reclassification to earnings		27,250	$(27,250)	
March 31, 20X2	85,910	(85,910)	$(27,250)	$27,250
Interest accrued	1,380	(1,380)		
Payment (receipt)	(29,500)			$29,500
Effect of change in rates	(100,610)	100,610		
Reclassification to earnings		29,500	$(29,500)	
June 30, 20X2	(42,820)	42,820	$(29,500)	$29,500
Interest accrued	(870)	870		
Payment (receipt)	2,500			$ (2,500)
Effect of change in rates	8,030	(8,030)		
Reclassification to earnings		(2,500)	$ 2,500	
September 30, 20X2	(33,160)	33,160	$ 2,500	$ (2,500)
Interest accrued	(670)	670		
Payment (receipt)	5,250			$ (5,250)
Effect of change in rates	6,730	(6,730)		
Reclassification to earnings		(5,250)	$ 5,250	
December 31, 20X2	(21,850)	21,850	$ 5,250	$ (5,250)
Interest accrued	(440)	440		
Payment (receipt)	8,000			$ (8,000)
Effect of change in rates	16,250	(16,250)		
Reclassification to earnings		(8,000)	$ 8,000	
March 31, 20X3	1,960	(1,960)	$ 8,000	$ (8,000)
Interest accrued	40	(40)		
Payment (receipt)	(2,000)			$ 2,000
Reclassification to earnings		2,000	$ (2,000)	
June 30, 20X3	$ 0	$ 0	$ (2,000)	$ 2,000

[FAS133, ¶137]

.226 Exhibit 225A shows that, in each quarter, the net cash receipt or payment on the swap equals the income or expense to be recorded. The net effect on earnings of the interest on the bonds and the reclassification of gains or losses on the swap is in Exhibit 226A. [FAS133, ¶138]

Exhibit 226A

Effect on Earnings of the Interest on Bonds and the Reclassification of Gains or Losses on the Swap

	Earnings		
For the Quarter Ending	**Interest on Bonds**	**Gains (Losses) Reclassified from OCI**	**Net Effect**
9/30/X1	$ 195,250	$27,250	$ 222,500
12/31/X1	197,000	25,500	222,500
3/31/X2	195,250	27,250	222,500
6/30/X2	193,000	29,500	222,500
9/30/X2	225,000	(2,500)	222,500
12/31/X2	227,750	(5,250)	222,500
3/31/X3	230,500	(8,000)	222,500
6/30/X3	220,500	2,000	222,500
Totals	$1,684,250	$95,750	$1,780,000

[FAS133, ¶138]

.227 In this example, the shortcut method described in paragraph .220 works as follows. The difference between the variable rate on the swap and the variable rate on the asset is a net receipt of 2.25 percent. That rate combined with the 6.65 percent fixed rate received on the swap is 8.9 percent. The computed interest income is $890,000 per year or $222,500 per quarter, which is the same as the amount in the table in paragraph .226. [FAS133, ¶139]

Example 6: Accounting for a Derivative's Gain or Loss in a Cash Flow Hedge—Effectiveness Based on the Entire Change in the Derivative's Fair Value

.228 This example has been designed to illustrate application of the guidance for cash flow hedges described in paragraph .127 of this section. At the beginning of period 1, XYZ Company enters into a qualifying cash flow hedge of a transaction forecasted to occur early in period 6. XYZ's documented policy is to assess hedge effectiveness by comparing the changes in present value of the expected future cash flows on the forecasted transaction to all of the hedging derivative's gain or loss (that is, no time value component will be excluded as discussed in paragraph .151). In this hedging relationship, XYZ has designated changes in cash flows related to the forecasted transaction attributable to any cause as the hedged risk. [FAS133, ¶140]

.229 Exhibit 229A includes the assumptions for this example and details the steps necessary to account for a cash flow hedge that is not perfectly effective. [FAS133, ¶141]

Exhibit 229A

Steps to Account for a Cash Flow Hedge That Is Not Perfectly Effective

	Fair Value of Derivative Increase (Decrease)		Present Value of Expected Future Cash Flows on Hedged Transaction Increase (Decrease)			
	(A)	(B)	(C)	(D)	(E)	(F)
Period	Change during the Period	Cumulative Change	Change during the Period	Cumulative Change	Lesser of the Two Cumulative Changes	Adjustment to OCI
1	$ 100	$100	$ (96)	$ (96)	$ 96	$ 96
2	94	194	(101)	(197)	194	98
3	(162)	32	160	(37)	32	(162)
4	(101)	(69)	103	66	(66)	(98)
5	30	(39)	(32)	34	(34)	32

Step 1: Determine the change in fair value of the derivative and the change in present value of the cash flows on the hedged transaction (columns A and C).

Step 2: Determine the cumulative changes in fair value of the derivative and the cumulative changes in present value of the cash flows on the hedged transaction (columns B and D).

Step 3: Determine the lesser of the absolute values of the two amounts in Step 2 (column E).

Step 4: Determine the change during the period in the lesser of the absolute values (column F).

Step 5: Adjust the derivative to reflect its change in fair value and adjust other comprehensive income by the amount determined in Step 4. Balance the entry, if necessary, with an adjustment to earnings.

[FAS133, ¶141]

.230 The following are the entries required to account for the above cash flow hedge.

		Debit (Credit)		
Period	**Description**	**Derivative**	**Earnings**	**OCI**
1	Adjust derivative to fair value and OCI by the calculated amount	$ 100	$(4)	$ (96)
2	Adjust derivative to fair value and OCI by the calculated amount	94	4	(98)
3	Adjust derivative to fair value and OCI by the calculated amount	(162)	0	162
4	Adjust derivative to fair value and OCI by the calculated amount	(101)	3	98
5	Adjust derivative to fair value and OCI by the calculated amount	30	2	(32)

[FAS133, ¶142]

.231 The following table reconciles the beginning and ending balances in accumulated other comprehensive income.

	Accumulated Other Comprehensive Income—Debit (Credit)			
Period	**Beginning Balance**	**Change in Fair Value**	**Reclassification**	**Ending Balance**
1	$ 0	$ (96)	$ 0	$ (96)
2	(96)	(94)	(4)	(194)
3	(194)	162	0	(32)
4	(32)	98	0	66
5	66	(30)	(2)	34

The reclassification column relates to reclassifications between earnings and other comprehensive income. In period 2, the $(4) in that column relates to the prior period's derivative gain that was previously recognized in earnings. That amount is reclassified to other comprehensive income in period 2 because the cumulative gain on the derivative is less than the amount necessary to offset the cumulative change in the present value of expected future cash flows on the hedged transaction. In period 5, the $(2) in the reclassification column relates to the derivative loss that was recognized in other comprehensive income in a prior period. At the end of period 4, the derivative's cumulative loss of $69 was greater in absolute terms than the $66 increase in the present value of expected future cash flows on the hedged transaction. That $3 excess had been recognized in earnings during period 4. In period 5, the value of the derivative increased (and reduced the cumulative loss) by $30. The present value of the expected cash flows on the hedged transaction decreased (and reduced the cumulative increase) by $32. The gain on the derivative in period 5 was $2 smaller, in absolute terms, than the decrease in the present value of the expected cash flows on the hedged transaction. Consequently, the entire gain on the derivative is recognized in other comprehensive income. In addition, in absolute terms, the $3 cumulative excess of the loss on the derivative over the increase in the present value of the expected cash flows on the hedged transaction (which had previously been recognized in earnings) increased to $5. As a result, $2 is reclassified from other comprehensive income to earnings so that the $5 cumulative excess has been recognized in earnings. [FAS133, ¶143]

Example 7: Designation and Discontinuance of a Cash Flow Hedge of the Forecasted Purchase of Inventory

.232 This example illustrates the effect on earnings and other comprehensive income of discontinuing a cash flow hedge by dedesignating the hedging derivative before the variability of the cash flows from the hedged forecasted transaction has been eliminated. It also discusses the effect that the location of a physical asset has on the effectiveness of a hedging relationship. [FAS133, ¶144]

.233 On February 3, 20X1, JKL Company forecasts the purchase of 100,000 bushels of corn on May 20, 20X1. It expects to sell finished products produced from the corn on May 31, 20X1. On February 3, 20X1, JKL enters into 20 futures contracts, each for the purchase of 5,000 bushels of corn on May 20, 20X1 (100,000 in total) and immediately designates those contracts as a hedge of the forecasted purchase of corn. [FAS133, ¶145]

.234 JKL chooses to assess effectiveness by comparing the entire change in fair value of the futures contracts to changes in the cash flows on the forecasted transaction. JKL estimates its cash flows on the forecasted transaction based on the futures price of corn adjusted for the difference between the cost of corn delivered to Chicago and the cost of corn delivered to Minneapolis. JKL does not choose to use a tailing strategy (as described in paragraph .152). JKL expects changes in fair value of the futures contracts to be highly effective at offsetting changes in the expected cash outflows for the forecasted purchase of corn because (a) the futures contracts are for the same variety and grade of corn that JKL plans to purchase and (b) on May 20, 20X1, the futures price for delivery on May 20, 20X1 will be equal to the spot price (because futures prices and spot prices converge as the delivery date approaches). However, the hedge may not be perfectly effective. JKL will purchase corn for delivery to its production facilities in Minneapolis, but the price of the futures contracts is based on delivery of corn to Chicago. If the difference between the price of corn delivered to Chicago and the price of corn delivered to

Minneapolis changes during the period of the hedge, the effect of that change will be included currently in earnings according to the provisions of paragraph .127 of this section. [FAS133, ¶146]

.235 On February 3, 20X1, the futures price of corn for delivery to Chicago on May 20, 20X1 is $2.6875 per bushel resulting in a total price of $268,750 for 100,000 bushels. [FAS133, ¶147]

.236 On May 1, 20X1, JKL dedesignates the related futures contracts and closes them out by entering into offsetting contracts on the same exchange. As of that date, JKL had recognized in accumulated other comprehensive income gains on the futures contracts of $26,250. JKL still plans to purchase 100,000 bushels of corn on May 20, 20X1. Consequently, the gains that occurred prior to dedesignation will remain in other comprehensive income until the finished product is sold. If JKL had not closed out the futures contracts when it dedesignated them, any further gains or losses would have been recognized in earnings. [FAS133, ¶148]

.237 On May 20, 20X1, JKL purchases 100,000 bushels of corn, and on May 31, 20X1, JKL sells the finished product. [FAS133, ¶149]

.238 The futures prices of corn that are in effect on key dates are assumed to be as follows:

Date	Futures Price per Bushel for Delivery to Chicago on May 20, 20X1	Futures Price Adjusted for Delivery to Minneapolis on May 20, 20X1
Inception of hedging relationship—February 3, 20X1	$2.6875	$2.7375
End of quarter—March 31, 20X1	3.1000	3.1500
Discontinuc hcdgc—May 1, 20X1	2.9500	3.0000
Purchase of corn—May 20, 20X1	2.8500	2.9000

[FAS133, ¶150]

.239 The changes in fair value of the futures contracts between inception (February 3, 20X1) and discontinuation (May 1, 20X1) of the hedge are as follows:

	February 3– March 31, 20X1	April 1– May 1, 20X1
Futures price at beginning of period	$ 2.6875	$ 3.1000
Futures price at end of period	3.1000	2.9500
Change in price per bushel	0.4125	(0.1500)
Bushels under contract		
(20 contracts @ 5,000 bushels each)	× 100,000	× 100,000
Change in fair value—gain (loss)	$ 41,250	$ (15,000)

[FAS133, ¶151]

.240 Exhibit 240A displays the entries to recognize the effects of (a) entering into futures contracts as a hedge of the forecasted purchase of corn, (b) dedesignating and closing out the futures contracts, (c) completing the forecasted purchase of corn, and (d) selling the finished products produced from the corn. Because the difference in prices between corn delivered to Chicago and corn delivered to Minneapolis ($.05 per bushel, as illustrated in paragraph .238) did not change during the period of the hedge, no ineffectiveness is recognized in earnings. If that difference had changed, the resulting ineffectiveness would have been recognized immediately in earnings. The effect of the hedging strategy is that the cost of the corn recognized in earnings when the finished product was sold was $263,750. If the hedging relationship had not been discontinued early, the cost recognized in earnings would have been $273,750, which was the futures price of the corn, adjusted for delivery to Minneapolis, at the inception of the hedge. Without the strategy, JKL would have recognized $290,000, which was the price of corn delivered to Minneapolis at the time it was purchased. [FAS133, ¶152]

Exhibit 240A

Effect on Earnings and Other Comprehensive Income of Discontinuing a Cash Flow Hedge

	Debit (Credit)			
	Cash	**Inventory**	**OCI**	**Earnings**
March 31, 20X1 (end of quarter)				
Recognize change in fair value of futures contracts	$ 41,250		$(41,250)	
May 1, 20X1 (discontinue hedge)				
Recognize change in fair value of futures contracts	(15,000)		15,000	
May 20, 20X1				
Recognize purchase of corn	(290,000)	$ 290,000		
May 31, 20X1				
Recognize cost of sale of product		(290,000)		$290,000
Reclassify changes in fair value of futures contracts to earnings			26,250	(26,250)
Total	$(263,750)	$ 0	$ 0	$263,750

Note: To simplify this example and focus on the effects of the hedging relationship, the margin account with the clearinghouse and certain amounts that would be involved in a sale of JKL's inventory (for example, additional costs of production, selling costs, and sales revenue) have been ignored.

[FAS133, ¶152]

Example 8: Changes in a Cash Flow Hedge of Forecasted Interest Payments with an Interest Rate Swap

Background

.241 This example describes the effects on earnings and other comprehensive income of certain changes in a cash flow hedging relationship. It presents two different scenarios. In the first, the variability of the hedged interest payments is eliminated before the hedging derivative expires. In the second, the interest rate index that is the basis for the hedged interest payments is changed to a different index before the hedging derivative expires. [FAS133, ¶153]

.242 MNO Company enters into an interest rate swap (Swap 1) and designates it as a hedge of the variable interest payments on a series of $5 million notes with 90-day terms. MNO plans to continue issuing new 90-day notes over the next five years as each outstanding note matures. The interest on each note will be determined based on LIBOR at the time each note is issued. Swap 1 requires a settlement every 90 days, and the variable interest rate is reset immediately following each payment. MNO pays a fixed rate of interest (6.5 percent) and receives interest at LIBOR. MNO neither pays nor receives a premium at the inception of Swap 1. The notional amount of the contract is $5 million, and it expires in 5 years. [FAS133, ¶154]

.243 Because Swap 1 and the hedged forecasted interest payments are based on the same notional amount, have the same reset dates, and are based on the same benchmark interest rate designated under paragraph .126(h), MNO may conclude that there will be no ineffectiveness in the hedging relationship (absent a default by the swap counterparty). [FAS138, ¶4(ee)]

Scenario 1—Two undesignated interest rate swaps

.244 At the end of the second year of the 5-year hedging relationship, MNO discontinues its practice of issuing 90-day notes. Instead, MNO issues a 3-year, $5 million note with a fixed rate of interest (7.25 percent). Because the interest rate on the three-year note is fixed, the variability of the future interest payments has been eliminated. Thus, Swap 1 no longer qualifies for cash flow hedge accounting. However, the net gain or loss on Swap 1 in accumulated other comprehensive income is not reclassified to earnings immediately. Immediate reclassification is required (and permitted) only if it becomes probable that the hedged transactions (future interest payments) will not occur. The variability of the payments has been eliminated, but it still is probable that they will occur.

Thus, those gains or losses will continue to be reclassified from accumulated other comprehensive income to earnings as the interest payments affect earnings (as required by paragraph .128).[40] [FAS133, ¶156]

.245 Rather than liquidate the pay-fixed, receive-variable Swap 1, MNO enters into a pay-variable, receive-fixed interest rate swap (Swap 2) with a 3-year term and a notional amount of $5 million. MNO neither pays nor receives a premium. Like Swap 1, Swap 2 requires a settlement every 90 days and reprices immediately following each settlement. The relationship between 90-day interest rates and longer term rates has changed since MNO entered into Swap 1 (that is, the shape of the yield curve is different). As a result, Swap 2 has different terms and its settlements do not exactly offset the settlements on Swap 1. Under the terms of Swap 2, MNO will receive a fixed rate of 7.25 percent and pay interest at LIBOR. [FAS133, ¶157]

.246 The two swaps are not designated as hedging instruments and are reported at fair value. The changes in fair value are reported immediately in earnings and offset each other to a significant degree. [FAS133, ¶158]

Scenario 2—Two interest rate swaps designated as a hedge of future variable interest payments

.247 At the end of the second year of the 5-year hedging relationship, MNO discontinues its practice of issuing 90-day notes and issues a 3-year, $5 million note with a rate of interest that adjusts every 90 days to the prime rate quoted on that day. Swap 1 is no longer effective as a cash flow hedge because the receive-variable rate on the swap is LIBOR, and the prime rate and LIBOR are expected to change differently. Thus, the cash flows from the swap will not effectively offset changes in cash flows from the three-year note. [FAS133, ¶159]

.248 The net gain or loss on Swap 1 in accumulated other comprehensive income as of the date MNO issues the three-year note is not reclassified into earnings immediately. Immediate reclassification would be required only if it becomes probable that the hedged transactions (future interest payments) will not occur. The expected amounts of those payments have changed (because they will be based on prime instead of LIBOR, as originally expected), but it still is probable that the payments will occur. Thus, those gains or losses will continue to be reclassified to earnings as the interest payments affect earnings. [FAS133, ¶160]

---

[40] If the term of the fixed rate note had been longer than three years, the amounts in accumulated other comprehensive income still would have been reclassified into earnings over the next three years, which was the term of the designated hedging relationship. [FAS133, ¶156, fn25]

.249 Rather than liquidate Swap 1 and obtain a separate derivative to hedge the variability of the prime-rate-based interest payments, MNO enters into a pay-LIBOR, receive-prime basis swap. The basis swap has a $5 million notional amount and a 3-year term and requires a settlement every 90 days. MNO designates Swap 1 and the basis swap in combination as the hedging instrument in a cash flow hedge of the variable interest payments on the three-year note. On the three-year note, MNO pays interest at prime. On the basis swap, MNO receives interest at prime and pays interest at LIBOR. On Swap 1, MNO receives interest at LIBOR and pays interest at 6.5 percent. Together, the cash flows from the two derivatives are effective at offsetting changes in the interest payments on the three-year note. Changes in fair values of the two swaps are recognized in other comprehensive income and are reclassified to earnings when the hedged forecasted transactions (the variable interest payments) affect earnings (as required by paragraph .128). [FAS133, ¶161]

Example 9: Accounting for a Derivative's Gain or Loss in a Cash Flow Hedge—Effectiveness Based on Changes in Intrinsic Value

.250 Exhibit 250A illustrates application of the accounting guidance for cash flow hedges described in paragraph .127 of this section. At the beginning of period 1, XYZ Company purchases for $9.25 an at-the-money call option on 1 unit of Commodity X with a strike price of $125.00 to hedge a purchase of 1 unit of that commodity projected to occur early in period 5. XYZ's documented policy is to assess hedge effectiveness by comparing changes in cash flows on the hedged transaction (based on changes in the spot price) with changes in the option contract's intrinsic value. Because the hedging instrument is a purchased call option, its intrinsic value cannot be less than zero. If the price of the commodity is less than the option's strike price, the option is out-of-the-money. Its intrinsic value cannot decrease further regardless of how far the commodity price falls, and the intrinsic value will not increase until the commodity price increases to exceed the strike price. Thus, changes in cash flows from the option due to changes in its intrinsic value will offset changes in cash flows on the forecasted purchase only when the option is in-the-money or at-the-money. That phenomenon is demonstrated in period 3 in the following table when the commodity price declines by $1.25. Because the commodity price is $.75 below the option's strike price, the option's intrinsic value declines by only $.50 (to zero). The effect reverses in period 4 when the commodity price increases by $6.50 and the option's intrinsic value increases by $5.75. [FAS133, ¶162]

Exhibit 250A

Changes in a Cash Flow Hedge of Forecasted Interest Payments—Effectiveness Based on Changes in Intrinsic Value

	Period 1	Period 2	Period 3	Period 4
Assumptions				
Ending market price of Commodity X	$127.25	$125.50	$124.25	$130.75
Ending fair value of option:				
Time value	$ 7.50	$ 5.50	$ 3.00	$ 0.00
Intrinsic value	2.25	0.50	0.00	5.75
Total	$ 9.75	$ 6.00	$ 3.00	$ 5.75
Change in time value	$ (1.75)	$ (2.00)	$ (2.50)	$ (3.00)
Change in intrinsic value	2.25	(1.75)	(0.50)	5.75
Total current-period gain (loss) on derivative	$ 0.50	$ (3.75)	$ (3.00)	$ 2.75
Gain (loss) on derivative, adjusted to remove the component excluded from effectiveness test:				
For the current period	$ 2.25	$ (1.75)	$ (0.50)	$ 5.75
Cumulative	2.25	0.50	0.00	5.75
Change in expected future cash flows on hedged transaction:				
For the current period	(2.25)	1.75	1.25	(6.50)
Cumulative	(2.25)	(0.50)	0.75	(5.75)
Balance to be reflected in accumulated other comprehensive income (paragraph .127(b))				
Lesser (in absolute amounts) of derivative's cumulative gain (loss) or amount necessary to offset the cumulative change in expected future cash flows on hedged transaction	$ 2.25	$ 0.50	$ 0.00	$ 5.75

[FAS133, ¶162]

.251 The following are the entries required to account for the above cash flow hedge. The steps involved in determining the amounts are the same as in Example 6.

Period	Description	Debit (Credit) Derivative	Earnings	OCI
1	Adjust derivative to fair value and OCI by the calculated amount	$ 0.50	$1.75	$(2.25)
2	Adjust derivative to fair value and OCI by the calculated amount	(3.75)	2.00	1.75
3	Adjust derivative to fair value and OCI by the calculated amount	(3.00)	2.50	0.50
4	Adjust derivative to fair value and OCI by the calculated amount	2.75	3.00	(5.75)

[FAS133, ¶163]

.252 The following table reconciles the beginning and ending balances in accumulated other comprehensive income.

Period	Accumulated Other Comprehensive Income—Debit (Credit) Beginning Balance	Change in Intrinsic Value	Ending Balance
1	$ 0.00	$(2.25)	$(2.25)
2	(2.25)	1.75	(0.50)
3	(0.50)	0.50	0.00
4	0.00	(5.75)	(5.75)

The amount reflected in earnings relates to the component excluded from the effectiveness test, that is, the time value component. No reclassifications between other comprehensive income and earnings of the type illustrated in Example 6 are required because no hedge ineffectiveness is illustrated in this example. (The change in cash flows from the hedged transaction was not fully offset in period 3. However, that is not considered ineffectiveness. As described in paragraph .117(b), a purchased call option is considered effective if it provides one-sided offset.) [FAS133, ¶164]

Example 10: Cash Flow Hedge of the Foreign Currency Exposure in a Royalty Arrangement

.253 This example illustrates the accounting for a hedging relationship involving a single hedging derivative and three separate forecasted transactions. The three transactions occur on three separate dates, but the payment on receivables related to all three occurs on the same date. The settlement of the hedging derivative will occur on the date the receivable is paid. [FAS133, ¶165]

.254 DEF Company's functional currency is the U.S. dollar. ZYX's functional currency is the Deutsche mark (DM). Effective January 1, 20X1, DEF enters into a royalty agreement with ZYX Company that gives ZYX the right to use DEF's technology in manufacturing Product X. On April 30, 20X1, ZYX will pay DEF a royalty of DM1 million for each unit of Product X sold by that date. DEF expects ZYX to sell one unit of Product X on January 31, one on February 28, and one on March 31. The forecasted royalty is probable because ZYX has identified a demand for Product X and no other supplier has the capacity to fill that demand. [FAS133, ¶166]

.255 Also on January 1, 20X1, DEF enters into a forward contract to sell DM3 million on April 30, 20X1 for a price equal to the forward price of $0.6057 per Deutsche mark. DEF designates the forward contract as a hedge of the risk of changes in its functional-currency-equivalent cash flows attributable to changes in the Deutsche mark–U.S. dollar exchange rates related to the forecasted receipt of DM3 million from the royalty agreement. The spot price and forward price of Deutsche marks at January 1, 20X1 and the U.S. dollar equivalent of DM3 million at those prices are assumed to be as follows:

Prices at January 1, 20X1	$ per DM	$ Equivalent of DM3 Million
Spot price	$0.6019	$1,805,700
4-month forward price	0.6057	1,817,100

[FAS133, ¶167]

.256 DEF will exclude from its assessment of effectiveness the portion of the fair value of the forward contract attributable to the spot-forward difference (the difference between the spot exchange rate and the forward exchange rate). That is, DEF will recognize changes in that portion of the derivative's fair value in earnings but will not consider those changes to represent ineffectiveness. DEF will estimate the cash flows on the forecasted transactions based on the current spot exchange rate and will discount that amount. Thus, DEF will assess effectiveness by comparing (a) changes in the fair value of the forward contract attributable to changes in the dollar spot price of Deutsche marks and (b) changes in the present value of the forecasted cash flows based on the current spot exchange rate. Those two changes will exactly offset because the currency and the notional amount of the forward contract match the currency and the total of the expected foreign currency amounts of the forecasted transactions. Thus, if DEF dedesignates a proportion of the forward contract each time a royalty is earned (as described in the following paragraph), the hedging relationship will meet the "highly effective" criterion. [FAS133, ¶168]

.257 As each royalty is earned, DEF recognizes a receivable and royalty income. The forecasted transaction (the earning of royalty income) has occurred. The receivable is an asset, not a forecasted transaction, and [FAS133, ¶169] would separately be eligible to be designated as a fair value hedge of foreign exchange risk or continue to be eligible as a cash flow hedge of foreign exchange risk. [FAS138, ¶4(gg)(1)] Consequently, if the variability of the functional currency cash flows related to the royalty receivable is not being hedged, DEF will dedesignate a proportion of the hedging instrument in the original hedge relationship with respect to the proportion of the forward contract corresponding to the earned royalty. [FAS138, ¶4(gg)(3)] As the royalty is recognized in earnings and each proportion of the derivative is dedesignated, the related derivative gain or loss in accumulated other comprehensive income is reclassified into earnings. After that date, any gain or loss on the dedesignated proportion of the derivative and any transaction loss or gain on the royalty receivable[41] will be recognized in earnings and [FAS133, ¶169] may substantially offset [FAS138, ¶4(gg)(4)] each other. [FAS133, ¶169]

.258 The spot prices and forward prices for settlement on April 30, 20X1 in effect at inception of the hedge (January 1, 20X1) and at the end of each month between inception and April 30, 20X1 are assumed to be as follows:

	$ per DM	
	Spot Price	**Forward Price for Settlement on 4/30/X1**
January 1	$0.6019	$0.6057
January 31	0.5970	0.6000
February 28	0.5909	0.5926
March 31	0.5847	0.5855
April 30	0.5729	0.5729

[FAS133, ¶170]

[41] Section F60 requires immediate recognition in earnings of any foreign currency transaction gain or loss on a foreign-currency-denominated receivable that is not designated as a hedging instrument. Therefore, the effect of changes in spot prices on the royalty receivable must be recognized immediately in earnings. [FAS133, ¶169, fn26]

.259 The changes in fair value of the forward contract that are recognized each month in earnings and other comprehensive income are shown in Exhibit 259A. The fair value of the forward is the present value of the difference between the U.S. dollars to be received on the forward ($1,817,100) and the U.S. dollar equivalent of DM3 million based on the current forward rate. A 6 percent discount rate is used in this example. [FAS133, ¶171]

Exhibit 259A

Change in Fair Value of the Forward Contract in a Cash Flow Hedge of the Foreign Currency Exposure in a Royalty Agreement

	Debit (Credit)		
	Forward Contract	**Earnings**	**OCI**
Fair value on January 1	$ 0		
Period ended January 31:			
Change in spot-forward difference	2,364	$ (2,364)	
Change in fair value of dedesignated proportion	0	0	
Change in fair value of designated proportion	14,482		$(14,482)
Reclassification of gain	0	(4,827)	4,827
Fair value on January 31	16,846		
Period ended February 28:			
Change in spot-forward difference	3,873	(3,873)	
Change in fair value of dedesignated proportion	6,063	(6,063)	
Change in fair value of designated proportion	12,127		(12,127)
Reclassification of gain	0	(10,891)	10,891
Fair value on February 28	38,909		
Period ended March 31:			
Change in spot-forward difference	2,718	(2,718)	
Change in fair value of dedesignated proportion	12,458	(12,458)	
Change in fair value of designated proportion	6,213		(6,213)
Reclassification of gain	0	(17,104)	17,104
Fair value on March 31	60,298		
Period ended April 30:			
Change in spot-forward difference	2,445	(2,445)	
Change in fair value of dedesignated proportion	35,657	(35,657)	
Change in fair value of designated proportion	0		0
Fair value on April 30	$98,400		
Cumulative effect		$(98,400)	$ 0

[FAS133, ¶171]

.260 The effect on earnings of the royalty agreement and hedging relationship illustrated in this example is summarized by month in Exhibit 260A. [FAS133, ¶172]

Exhibit 260A

Effect on Earnings of the Royalty Agreement and Hedging Relationship

	Amounts Recognized in Earnings Related to					
	Receivable		Forward Contract			
Period Ended	$ Equivalent of DM1 Million Royalty	Foreign Currency Transaction Gain (Loss)	Amount Attributable to the Dedesignated Proportion	Reclassifications from OCI	Amount Attributable to the Difference between the Spot and Forward Rates	Total Amount Reported in Earnings
January 31	$ 597,000	$ 0	$ 0	$ 4,827	$ 2,364	$ 604,191
February 28	590,900	(6,100)	6,063	10,891	3,873	605,627
March 31	584,700	(12,400)	12,458	17,104	2,718	604,580
April 30	0	(35,400)	35,657	0	2,445	2,702
	$1,772,600	$(53,900)	$54,178	$32,822	$11,400	$1,817,100
				$98,400		

[FAS133, ¶172]

Example 11: Reporting Cash Flow Hedges in Comprehensive Income and Accumulated Other Comprehensive Income

.261 TUV Company's cash flow hedge transactions following adoption of this section through the end of 20X4 are as follows:

a. It continually purchases pork belly futures contracts to hedge its anticipated purchases of pork belly inventory.
b. In 20X2, it entered into a Deutsche mark forward exchange contract to hedge the foreign currency risk associated with the expected purchase of a pork belly processing machine with a five-year life that it bought from a vendor in Germany at the end of 20X2.
c. In 20X2, it entered into a 10-year interest rate swap concurrent with the issuance of 10-year variable rate debt (cash flow hedge of future variable interest payments).

d. In January 20X4, it entered into a two-year French franc forward exchange contract to hedge a forecasted export sale (denominated in French francs, expected to occur in December 20X5) of hot dogs to a large customer in France. In June 20X4, it closed the forward contract, but the forecasted transaction is still expected to occur.

[FAS133, ¶173]

.262 Exhibit 262A reconciles the beginning and ending accumulated other comprehensive income balances for 20X4. It supports the comprehensive income display and disclosures that are required under Section C49. It is assumed that there are no other amounts in accumulated other comprehensive income. The after-tax amounts assume a 30 percent effective tax rate. [FAS133, ¶174]

Exhibit 262A

Reconciliation of Accumulated Other Comprehensive Income Balance

	Other Comprehensive Income—Debit (Credit)			
	Accumulated Other Comprehensive Income as of 1/1/X4	**Changes in Fair Value Recognized in 20X4**	**Reclassification Adjustments**	**Accumulated Other Comprehensive Income as of 12/31/X4**
Derivatives designated as hedges of:				
Inventory purchases	$230	$ 85	$(270)	$ 45
Equipment purchase	120		(30)	90
Variable interest rate payments	(40)	10	5	(25)
Export sale	0	(50)	0	(50)
Before-tax totals	$310	$ 45	$(295)	$ 60
After-tax totals	$217	$ 32	$(207)	$ 42

[FAS133, ¶174]

.263 Exhibits 263A and 263B illustrate an acceptable method, under the provisions of Section C49, of reporting the transactions described in paragraphs .261 and .262 in earnings, comprehensive income, and shareholders' equity. [FAS133, ¶175]

Exhibit 263A

Effect of Selected Items on Earnings and Comprehensive Income
Year Ended December 31, 20X4

	Debit (Credit)	
Effect on earnings before taxes:		
Cost of goods sold	$ 270	
Depreciation	30	
Interest	(5)	
Total	295	
Income tax effect	(88)*	
Effect on earnings after taxes		$ 207
Other comprehensive income, net of tax:		
Cash flow hedges:		
Net derivative losses, net of tax effect of $13	32	
Reclassification adjustments, net of tax effect of $88	(207)	
Net change		(175)
Effect on total comprehensive income		$ 32

*This example assumes that it is appropriate under the circumstances, in accordance with Section I27, "Income Taxes," to recognize the related income tax benefit in the current year.

[FAS133, ¶175]

Exhibit 263B

Effect of Selected Items on Shareholders' Equity
Year Ended December 31, 20X4

	Debit (Credit)
Accumulated other comprehensive income:	
Balance on December 31, 20X3	$ 217
Net change during the year related to cash flow hedges	(175)
Balance on December 31, 20X4	$ 42

[FAS133, ¶175]

Examples Illustrating Application of the Clearly-and-Closely-Related Criterion to Derivative Instruments Embedded in Hybrid Instruments

.264 The following examples discuss instruments that contain a variety of embedded derivative instruments. They illustrate how the provisions of paragraphs .109 through .113 of this section would be applied to contracts with the described terms. If the terms of a contract are different from the described terms, the application of this section by either party to the contract may be affected. The illustrative instruments and related assumptions in Examples 12 through 27 are based on examples in Exhibit 96-12A of EITF Issue No. 96-12, "Recognition of Interest Income and Balance Sheet Classification of Structured Notes." [FAS133, ¶176]

.265 Specifically, each example (a) provides a brief discussion of the terms of an instrument that contains an embedded derivative and (b) analyzes the instrument (as of the date of inception) in relation to the provisions of paragraphs .109 through .113 that require an embedded derivative to be accounted for according to this section if it is not clearly and closely related to the host contract. Unless otherwise stated, the examples are based on the assumptions (1) that if the embedded derivative and host portions of the contract are not clearly and closely related, a separate instrument with the same terms as the embedded derivative would meet the scope requirements in paragraphs .103 through .108 and (2) that the contract is not remeasured at fair value under otherwise applicable generally accepted accounting principles with changes in fair value currently included in earnings. [FAS133, ¶177]

.266 **Example 12: Inverse Floater.** A bond with a coupon rate of interest that varies inversely with changes in specified general interest rate levels or indexes (for example, LIBOR).

> *Example:* Coupon = 5.25 percent for 3 months to July 19X4; thereafter at 8.75 percent – 6-month US$ LIBOR to January 19X5. "Stepping" option allows for spread and caps to step semiannually to maturity.
>
> *Scope Application:* An inverse floater contains an embedded derivative (a fixed-for-floating interest rate swap) that is referenced to an interest rate index (in this example, LIBOR) that alters net interest payments that otherwise would be paid by the debtor or received by the investor on an interest-bearing host contract. If the embedded derivative could potentially result in the investor's not recovering substantially all of its initial recorded investment in the bond (that is, if the inverse floater contains no floor to prevent any erosion of principal due to a negative interest rate), the embedded derivative is not considered to be clearly and closely related to the host contract (refer to paragraph .110(a)). In that case, the embedded

derivative should be separated from the host contract and accounted for by both parties pursuant to the provisions of this section. (In this example, there appears to be no possibility of the embedded derivative increasing the investor's rate of return on the host contract to an amount that is at least double the initial rate of return on the host contract [refer to paragraph .110(b)].) In contrast, if the embedded derivative could not potentially result in the investor's failing to recover substantially all of its initial recorded investment in the bond, the embedded derivative is considered to be clearly and closely related to the host contract and separate accounting for the derivative is neither required nor permitted.

[FAS133, ¶178]

.267 **Example 13: Levered Inverse Floater.** A bond with a coupon that varies indirectly with changes in general interest rate levels and applies a multiplier (greater than 1.00) to the specified index in its calculation of interest.

Example: Accrues at 6 percent to June 19X4; thereafter at 14.55 percent – (2.5 × 3-month US$ LIBOR).

Scope Application: A levered inverse floater can be viewed as an inverse floater in which the embedded interest rate swap is leveraged. Similar to Example 12, the embedded derivative would not be clearly and closely related to the host contract if it potentially could result in the investor's not recovering substantially all of its initial recorded investment in the bond (refer to paragraph .110(a)) because there is no floor to the interest rate. In that case, the embedded derivative (the leveraged interest rate swap) should be separated from the host contract and accounted for by both parties pursuant to the provisions of this section. In contrast, if an embedded derivative could not potentially result in the investor's failing to recover substantially all of its initial recorded investment in the bond and if there was no possibility of the embedded derivative increasing the investor's rate of return on the host contract to an amount that is at least double the initial rate of return on the host contract (refer to paragraph .110(b), the embedded derivative is considered to be clearly and closely related to the host contract and no separate accounting for the derivative is required or permitted.

[FAS133, ¶179]

.268 **Example 14: Delevered Floater.** A bond with a coupon rate of interest that lags overall movements in specified general interest rate levels or indices.

> *Example:* Coupon = (.5 × 10-year constant maturity treasuries (CMT)) + 1.25 percent.
>
> *Scope Application:* A delevered floater may be viewed as containing an embedded derivative (a deleveraged swap or a series of forward agreements) that is referenced to an interest rate index (for example, 50 percent of 10-year CMT) that alters net interest payments that otherwise would be paid or received on an interest-bearing host contract but could not potentially result in the investor's failing to recover substantially all of its initial recorded investment in the bond (refer to paragraph .110(a)). (In this example, there appears to be no possibility of the embedded derivative increasing the investor's rate of return on the host contract to an amount that is at least double the initial rate of return on the host contract [refer to paragraph .110(b)].) The embedded derivative is considered to be clearly and closely related to the host contract as described in paragraph .110 of this section. Therefore, the embedded derivative should *not* be separated from the host contract.

[FAS133, ¶180]

.269 **Example 15: Range Floater.** A bond with a coupon that depends on the *number of days* that a reference rate stays within a preestablished collar; otherwise, the bond pays either zero percent interest or a below-market rate.

> *Example:* Standard range floater—The investor receives 5.5 percent on *each day* that 3-month US$ LIBOR is between 3 percent and 4 percent, with the upper limit increasing annually after a specified date. The coupon will be equal to zero percent for each day that 3-month US$ LIBOR is *outside* that range.
>
> *Scope Application:* A range floater may be viewed as containing embedded derivatives (two written conditional exchange option contracts with notional amounts equal to the par value of the fixed-rate instrument) that are referenced to an interest rate index (in this example, LIBOR) that alter net interest payments that otherwise would be paid by the debtor or received by the investor on an interest-bearing host contract but could not potentially result in the investor's failing to recover substantially all of its initial recorded investment in the bond (refer to paragraph .110(a)). In this example, there appears to be no possibility of increasing the investor's rate of return on the host contract to an amount that is at least double the initial rate of return on the host contract (refer to paragraph .110(b)). The embedded derivatives are considered to be clearly and closely related to the host contract

as described in paragraph .110 of this section. Therefore, the embedded derivatives should *not* be separated from the host contract.

[FAS133, ¶181]

.270 **Example 16: Ratchet Floater.** A bond that pays a floating rate of interest and has an adjustable cap, adjustable floor, or both that move in sync with each new reset rate.

Example: Coupon = 3-month US$ LIBOR + 50 basis points. In addition to having a lifetime cap of 7.25 percent, the coupon will be collared each period between the previous coupon and the previous coupon plus 25 basis points.

Scope Application: A ratchet floater may be viewed as containing embedded derivatives (combinations of purchased and written options that create changing caps and floors) that are referenced to an interest rate index (in this example, LIBOR) that alter net interest payments that otherwise would be paid by the debtor or received by the investor on an interest-bearing host contract but could not potentially result in the investor's failing to recover substantially all of its initial recorded investment in the bond (refer to paragraph .110(a)). In this example, there appears to be no possibility of increasing the investor's rate of return on the host contract to an amount that is at least double the initial rate of return on the host contract (refer to paragraph .110(b)). The embedded derivatives are considered to be clearly and closely related to the host contract as described in paragraph .110 of this section. Therefore, the embedded derivatives should *not* be separated from the host contract.

[FAS133, ¶182]

.271 **Example 17: Fixed-to-Floating Note.** A bond that pays a varying coupon (first-year coupon is fixed; second- and third-year coupons are based on LIBOR, Treasury bills, or prime rate).

Scope Application: A fixed-to-floating note may be viewed as containing an embedded derivative (a forward-starting interest rate swap) that is referenced to an interest rate index (such as LIBOR) that alters net interest payments that otherwise would be paid by the debtor or received by the investor on an interest-bearing host instrument but could not potentially result in the investor's failing to recover substantially all of its initial recorded investment in the bond (refer to paragraph .110(a)). Likewise, there is no possibility of increasing the investor's rate of return on the host contract to an amount that is both at least double the initial rate of return on the host contract and at least twice what otherwise would be the market return for a contract that has the same terms as the host contract and that involves a debtor with a similar credit quality (refer to paragraph .110(b)). The embedded derivative is considered to be clearly and closely related to the host contract as described in paragraph .110 of this section. Therefore, the embedded derivative should *not* be separated from the host contract.

[FAS133, ¶183]

.272 **Example 18: Indexed Amortizing Note.** A bond that repays principal based on a predetermined amortization schedule or target value. The amortization is linked to changes in a specific mortgage-backed security index or interest rate index. The maturity of the bond changes as the related index changes. This instrument includes a varying maturity. (It is assumed for this example that the bond's terms could not potentially result in the investor's failing to recover substantially all of its initial recorded investment in the bond [refer to paragraph .110(a)] nor is there the possibility of increasing the investor's rate of return on the host contract to an amount that is both at least double the initial rate of return on the host contract and at least twice what otherwise would be the market return for a contract that has the same terms as the host contract and that involves a debtor with a similar credit quality [refer to paragraph .110(b)].)

Scope Application: An indexed amortizing note can be viewed as a fixed-rate amortizing note combined with a conditional exchange option contract that requires partial or total "early" payment of the note based on changes in a specific mortgage-backed security index or a specified change in an interest rate index. Because the requirement to prepay is ultimately tied to changing interest rates, the embedded derivative is considered to be clearly and closely related to a fixed-rate note. Therefore, the embedded derivative should *not* be separated from the host contract.

[FAS133, ¶184]

.273 **Example 19: Equity-Indexed Note.** A bond for which the return of interest, principal, or both is tied to a specified equity security or index (for example, the Standard and Poor's 500 [S&P 500] index). This instrument may contain a fixed or varying coupon rate and may place all or a portion of principal at risk.

Scope Application: An equity-indexed note essentially combines an interest-bearing instrument with a series of forward exchange contracts or option contracts. Often, a portion of the coupon interest rate is, in effect, used to purchase options that provide some form of floor on the potential loss of principal that would result from a decline in the referenced equity index. Because forward or option contracts for which the underlying is an equity index are not clearly and closely related to an investment in an interest-bearing note, those embedded derivatives should be separated from the host contract and accounted for by both parties pursuant to the provisions of this section.

[FAS133, ¶185]

.274 **Example 20: Variable Principal Redemption Bond.** A bond whose principal redemption value at maturity depends on the change in an underlying index over a predetermined observation period. A typical example would be a bond that guarantees a minimum par redemption value of 100 percent and provides the potential for a supplemental principal payment at maturity as compensation for the below-market rate of interest offered with the instrument.

> *Example:* A supplemental principal payment will be paid to the investor, at maturity, if the final S&P 500 closing value (determined at a specified date) is less than its initial value at date of issuance *and* the 10-year CMT is greater than 2 percent as of a specified date. In all cases, the minimum principal redemption will be 100 percent of par.
>
> *Scope Application:* A variable principal redemption bond essentially combines an interest-bearing investment with an option that is purchased with a portion of the bond's coupon interest payments. Because the embedded option entitling the investor to an additional return is partially contingent on the S&P 500 index closing above a specified amount, it is not clearly and closely related to an investment in a debt instrument. Therefore, the embedded option should be separated from the host contract and accounted for by both parties pursuant to the provisions of this section.

[FAS133, ¶186]

.275 **Example 21: Crude Oil Knock-in Note.** A bond that has a 1 percent coupon and guarantees repayment of principal with upside potential based on the strength of the oil market.

> *Scope Application:* A crude oil knock-in note essentially combines an interest-bearing instrument with a series of option contracts. A significant portion of the coupon interest rate is, in effect, used to purchase options that provide the investor with potential gains resulting from increases in specified crude oil prices. Because the option contracts are indexed to the price of crude oil, they are not clearly and closely related to an investment in an interest-bearing note. Therefore, the embedded option contract should be separated from the host contract and accounted for by both parties pursuant to the provisions of this section.

[FAS133, ¶187]

.276 **Example 22: Gold-Linked Bull Note.** A bond that has a fixed 3 percent coupon and guarantees repayment of principal with upside potential if the price of gold increases.

> *Scope Application:* A gold-linked bull note can be viewed as combining an interest-bearing instrument with a series of option contracts. A portion of the coupon interest rate is, in effect, used to purchase call options that provide the investor with potential gains resulting from increases in gold prices. Because the option contracts are indexed to the price of gold, they are not clearly and closely related to an investment in an interest-bearing note. Therefore, the embedded option contracts should be separated from the host contract and accounted for by both parties pursuant to the provisions of this section.

[FAS133, ¶188]

.277 **Example 23: Step-up Bond.** A bond that provides an introductory above-market yield and steps up to a new coupon, which will be below then-current market rates or, alternatively, the bond may be called in lieu of the step-up in the coupon rate.

> *Scope Application:* A step-up bond can be viewed as a fixed-rate bond with an embedded call option and a changing interest rate feature. The bond pays an initial above-market interest rate to compensate for the call option and the future below-market rate (that is, below the forward yield curve, as determined at issuance based on the existing upward-sloping yield curve). Because the call option is related to changes in interest rates, it is clearly and closely related to an investment in a fixed-rate bond. Therefore, the embedded derivatives should *not* be separated from the host contract.

[FAS133, ¶189]

.278 **Example 24: Credit-Sensitive Bond.** A bond that has a coupon rate of interest that resets based on changes in the issuer's credit rating.

> *Scope Application:* A credit-sensitive bond can be viewed as combining a fixed-rate bond with a conditional exchange contract (or an option) that entitles the investor to a higher rate of interest if the credit rating of the issuer declines. Because the creditworthiness of the debtor and the interest rate on a debt instrument are clearly and closely related, the embedded derivative should *not* be separated from the host contract.

[FAS133, ¶190]

.279 **Example 25: Inflation Bond.** A bond with a contractual principal amount that is indexed to the inflation rate but cannot decrease below par; the coupon rate is typically below that of traditional bonds of similar maturity.

> *Scope Application:* An inflation bond can be viewed as a fixed-rate bond for which a portion of the coupon interest rate has been exchanged for a conditional exchange contract (or option) indexed to the consumer price index, or other index of inflation in the economic environment for the currency in which the bond is denominated, that entitles the investor to payment of additional principal based on increases in the referenced index. Such rates of inflation and interest rates on the debt instrument are considered to be clearly and closely related. Therefore, the embedded derivative should *not* be separated from the host contract.

[FAS133, ¶191]

.280 **Example 26: Disaster Bond.** A bond that pays a coupon above that of an otherwise comparable traditional bond; however, all or a substantial portion of the principal amount is subject to loss if a specified disaster experience occurs.

> *Scope Application:* A disaster bond can be viewed as a fixed-rate bond combined with a conditional exchange contract (an option). The investor receives an additional coupon interest payment in return for giving the issuer an option indexed to industry loss experience on a specified disaster. Because the option contract is indexed to the specified disaster experience, it cannot be viewed as being clearly and closely related to an investment in a fixed-rate bond. Therefore, the embedded derivative should be separated from the host contract and accounted for by both parties pursuant to the provisions of this section.
>
> However, if the "embedded derivative" entitles the holder of the option (that is, the issuer of the disaster bond) to be compensated only for changes in the value of specified assets or liabilities for which the holder is at risk (including the liability for insurance claims payable due to the specified disaster) as a result of an identified insurable event (refer to paragraph .107(c)(2)), a separate instrument with the same terms as the "embedded derivative" would *not* meet the section's definition of a derivative in paragraphs .103 through .108. In that circumstance, because the criterion in paragraph .109(c) would not be met, there is no embedded derivative to be separated from the host contract, and the disaster bond would not be subject to the requirements of this section. The investor is essentially providing a form of insurance or reinsurance coverage to the issuer.

[FAS133, ¶192]

.281 **Example 27: Specific Equity-Linked Bond.** A bond that pays a coupon slightly below that of traditional bonds of similar maturity; however, the principal amount is linked to the stock market performance of an equity investee of the issuer. The issuer may settle the obligation by delivering the shares of the equity investee or may deliver the equivalent fair value in cash.

> *Scope Application:* A specific equity-linked bond can be viewed as combining an interest-bearing instrument with, depending on its terms, a series of forward exchange contracts or option contracts based on an equity instrument. Often, a portion of the coupon interest rate is used to purchase options that provide some form of floor on the loss of principal due to a decline in the price of the referenced equity instrument. The forward or option contracts do not qualify for the exception in paragraph .107(e)(2) because the shares in the equity investee owned by the issuer meet the definition of a *financial instrument.* Because forward or option contracts for which the underlying is the price of a specific equity instrument are not clearly and closely related to an investment in an interest-bearing note, the embedded derivative should be separated from the host contract and accounted for by both parties pursuant to the provisions of this section.

[FAS133, ¶193]

.282 **Example 28: Dual Currency Bond.** A bond providing for repayment of principal in U.S. dollars and periodic interest payments denominated in a foreign currency. In this example, a U.S. entity with the dollar as its functional currency is borrowing funds from an independent party with those repayment terms as described.

> *Scope Application:* Because the portion of this instrument relating to the periodic interest payments denominated in a foreign currency is subject to the requirement in Section F60 to recognize the foreign currency transaction gain or loss in earnings, the instrument should not be considered as containing an embedded foreign currency derivative instrument pursuant to paragraph .112 of this section. In this example, the U.S. entity has the dollar as the functional currency and is making interest payments in a foreign currency. Remeasurement of the liability is required using future equivalent dollar interest payments determined by the current spot exchange rate and discounted at the historical effective interest rate.

[FAS133, ¶194]

.283 **Example 29: Short-Term Loan with a Foreign Currency Option.** A U.S. lender issues a loan at an above-market interest rate. The loan is made in U.S. dollars, the borrower's functional currency, and the borrower has the option to repay the loan in U.S. dollars or in a fixed amount of a specified foreign currency.

Scope Application: This instrument can be viewed as combining a loan at prevailing market interest rates and a foreign currency option. The lender has written a foreign currency option exposing it to changes in foreign currency exchange rates during the outstanding period of the loan. The premium for the option has been paid as part of the interest rate. Because the borrower has the option to repay the loan in U.S. dollars or in a fixed amount of a specified foreign currency, the provisions of paragraph .112 are not relevant to this example. Paragraph .112 addresses foreign-currency-denominated interest or principal payments but does not apply to foreign currency options. Because a foreign currency option is not clearly and closely related to issuing a loan, the embedded option should be separated from the host contract and accounted for by both parties pursuant to the provisions of this section. In contrast, if both the principal payment and the interest payments on the loan had been payable only in a fixed amount of a specified foreign currency, there would be no embedded foreign currency derivative pursuant to this section.

[FAS133, ¶195]

.284 **Example 30: Lease Payment in Foreign Currency.** A U.S. company's operating lease with a Japanese lessor is payable in yen. The functional currency of the U.S. company is the U.S. dollar.

Scope Application: Paragraph .112(a) provides that contracts, other than financial instruments, that specify payments denominated in the currency of the primary economic environment in which any substantial party to that contract operates shall *not* be separated from the host contract and considered a derivative instrument for purposes of this section. Using available information about the lessor and its operations, the U.S. company may decide it is reasonable to conclude that the yen would be the currency of the primary economic environment in which the Japanese lessor operates, consistent with the functional currency notion in Section F60. (That decision can be based on available information and reasonable assumptions about the counterparty; representations from the counterparty are not required.) Thus, the lease should *not* be viewed as containing an embedded swap converting U.S. dollar lease payments to yen. Alternatively, if the lease payments are specified in a currency seemingly unrelated to each party's functional currency, such as drachmas (assuming the leased property is not in Greece), the embedded foreign currency swap should be separated from the host contract and accounted for as a derivative for purposes of this section because the provisions of paragraph .112 would not apply and a separate instrument with the same terms would meet the definition of a derivative instrument in paragraphs .103 through .108.

[FAS133, ¶196]

.285 **Example 31: Certain Purchases in a Foreign Currency.** A U.S. company enters into a contract to purchase corn from a local American supplier in six months for a fixed amount of Japanese yen; the yen is the functional currency of neither party to the transaction. The corn is expected to be delivered and used over a reasonable period in the normal course of business.

> *Scope Application:* Paragraph .107(b) excludes contracts that require future delivery of commodities that are readily convertible to cash from the accounting for derivatives if the commodities will be delivered in quantities expected to be used or sold by the reporting entity over a reasonable period in the normal course of business. However, that paragraph also states that contracts that are denominated in a foreign currency that meets neither of the criteria in paragraphs .112(a) and .112(b) shall not be considered normal purchases and normal sales. Because the Japanese yen is not the functional currency of either party to the contract and the purchase of corn is transacted internationally in many different currencies, the contract does not qualify for the normal purchases and normal sales exception. The contract is a compound derivative comprising a U.S. dollar-denominated forward contract for the purchase of corn and an embedded foreign currency swap from the purchaser's functional currency (the U.S. dollar) to yen. Consistent with [transition guidance that an entity may not separate a compound derivative into components representing different risks after the date of initial application of this section,] the compound derivative cannot be separated into its components (representing the foreign currency derivative and the forward commodity contract) and accounted for separately under this section.

[FAS138, ¶4(hh)]

.286 **Example 32: Participating Mortgage.** A mortgage in which the investor receives a below-market interest rate and is entitled to participate in the appreciation in the market value of the project that is financed by the mortgage upon sale of the project, at a deemed sale date, or at the maturity or refinancing of the loan. The mortgagor must continue to own the project over the term of the mortgage.

> *Scope Application:* This instrument has a provision that entitles the investor to participate in the appreciation of the referenced real estate (the "project"). However, a separate contract with the same terms would be excluded by the exception in paragraph .107(e)(2) because settlement is based on the value of a nonfinancial asset of one of the parties that is not readily convertible to cash. (This section does not modify the guidance in AICPA Statement of Position 97-1, *Accounting by Participating Mortgage Loan Borrowers.*)

[FAS133, ¶198]

.287 **Example 33: Convertible Debt.** An investor receives a below-market interest rate and receives the option to convert its debt instrument into the equity of the issuer at an established conversion rate. The terms of the conversion require that the issuer deliver shares of stock to the investor.

> *Scope Application:* This instrument essentially contains a call option on the issuer's stock. Under the provisions of this section, the accounting by the issuer and investor can differ. The issuer's accounting depends on whether a separate instrument with the same terms as the embedded written option would be a derivative instrument pursuant to paragraphs .103 through .108 of this section. Because the option is indexed to the issuer's own stock and a separate instrument with the same terms would be classified in stockholders' equity in the statement of financial position, the written option is not considered to be a derivative instrument for the issuer under paragraph .108(a) and should *not* be separated from the host contract.
>
> In contrast, if the terms of the conversion allow for a cash settlement rather than delivery of the issuer's shares at the investor's option, the exception in paragraph .108(a) for the issuer does not apply because the contract would not be classified in stockholders' equity in the issuer's statement of financial position. In that case, the issuer should separate the embedded derivative from the host contract and account for it pursuant to the provisions of this section because (a) an option based on the entity's stock price is not clearly and closely related to an interest-bearing debt instrument and (b) the option would not be considered an equity instrument of the issuer.
>
> Similarly, if the convertible debt is indexed to another entity's publicly traded common stock, the issuer should separate the embedded derivative from the host contract and account for it pursuant to the provisions of this section because (a) an option based on another entity's stock price is not clearly and closely related to an investment in an interest-bearing note and (b) the option would not be considered an equity instrument of the issuer.
>
> The exception in paragraph .108 does not apply to the investor's accounting. Therefore, in both cases described above, the investor should separate the embedded option contract from the host contract and account for the embedded option contract pursuant to the provisions of this section because the option contract is based on the price of another entity's equity instrument and thus is not clearly and closely related to an investment in an interest-bearing note. However, if the terms of conversion do not allow for a cash settlement and if the common stock delivered upon

conversion is privately held (that is, is not readily convertible to cash), the embedded derivative would not be separated from the host contract because it would not meet the criteria in paragraph .106.

[FAS133, ¶199]

.288 **Example 34: Variable Annuity Products.** These products are investment contracts as contemplated in Section In6, "Insurance Industry." Similar to variable life insurance products, policyholders direct their investment account asset mix among a variety of mutual funds composed of equities, bonds, or both, and assume the risks and rewards of investment performance. The funds are generally maintained in separate accounts by the insurance company. Contract terms provide that if the policyholder dies, the greater of the account market value or a minimum death benefit guarantee will be paid. The minimum death benefit guarantee is generally limited to a return of premium plus a minimum return (such as 3 or 4 percent); this life insurance feature represents the fundamental difference from the life insurance contracts that include significant (rather than minimal) levels of life insurance. The investment account may have various payment alternatives at the end of the accumulation period. One alternative is the right to purchase a life annuity at a fixed price determined at the initiation of the contract.

Scope Application: Variable annuity product structures as contemplated in Section In6 are generally not subject to the scope of this section (except for payment options at the end of the accumulation period), as follows:

- *Death benefit component.* Paragraph .107(c)(1) excludes a death benefit from the scope of this section because the payment of the death benefit is the result of an identifiable insurable event instead of changes in an underlying. The death benefit in this example is limited to the floor guarantee of the investment account, calculated as the premiums paid into the investment account plus a guaranteed rate of return, less the account market value. Section In6 remains the applicable guidance for the insurance-related liability accounting.
- *Investment component.* The policyholder directs certain premium investments in the investment account that includes equities, bonds, or both, which are held in separate accounts that are [FAS133, ¶200] distinct [FAS138, ¶4(ii)(1)] from the insurer's general account assets. This component is not [FAS133, ¶200] considered [FAS138, ¶4(ii)(1)] a derivative because [FAS133, ¶200] of the unique attributes of traditional variable annuity contracts issued by insurance companies. [FAS138, ¶4(ii)(1)] Furthermore, any embedded derivatives within those investments should not be separated from the host contract by the insurer because the separate account assets are already marked-to-market under Section In6. In contrast, if the product were an equity-index-based interest annuity

(rather than a [FAS133, ¶200] traditional [FAS138, ¶4(ii)(1)] variable annuity), the investment component would [FAS133, ¶200] contain an embedded derivative (the equity index-based derivative) that meets all the requirements of paragraph .109 of this section for separate accounting: (a) the economic characteristics and risks of the embedded derivative would not be clearly and closely related to the economic characteristics and risks of the host contract (that is, the host contract is a debt instrument and the embedded option is equity-indexed), (b) the hybrid instrument would not be remeasured at fair value with changes in fair value reported in earnings as they occur under GAAP, and (c) a separate instrument with the same terms as the embedded derivative instrument would be a derivative instrument pursuant to paragraphs .103 through .108 of this section. [FAS138, ¶4(ii)(1)]

- *Investment account surrender right at market value.* Because this right is exercised only at the fund market value (without the insurer's floor guarantee) and relates to [FAS133, ¶200] a traditional variable annuity contract issued by an insurance company, [FAS138, ¶4(ii)(2)] this right is not within the scope of this section.
- *Payment alternatives at the end of the accumulation period.* Payment alternatives are options subject to the requirements of this section if interest rates or other underlying variables affect the value. [FAS133, ¶200]

The guidance in the second and third bullets above is an exception for traditional variable annuity contracts issued by insurance companies. In determining the accounting for other seemingly similar structures, it would be inappropriate to analogize to the above guidance due to the unique attributes of traditional variable annuity contracts. [FAS138, ¶4(ii)(3)]

Diagram for Determining Whether a Contract Is a Freestanding Derivative Subject to the Scope of This Section

.289 The diagram in Exhibit 289A depicts the process for determining whether a freestanding contract is within the scope of this section. The diagram is a visual supplement to paragraphs .101 through .288. It should not be interpreted to alter any requirements of this section nor should it be considered a substitute for the requirements. The relevant paragraphs are identified in the parenthetical note after the question. [FAS133, ¶539]

Exhibit 289A

Diagram for Determining Whether a Freestanding Contract Is within the Scope of This Section

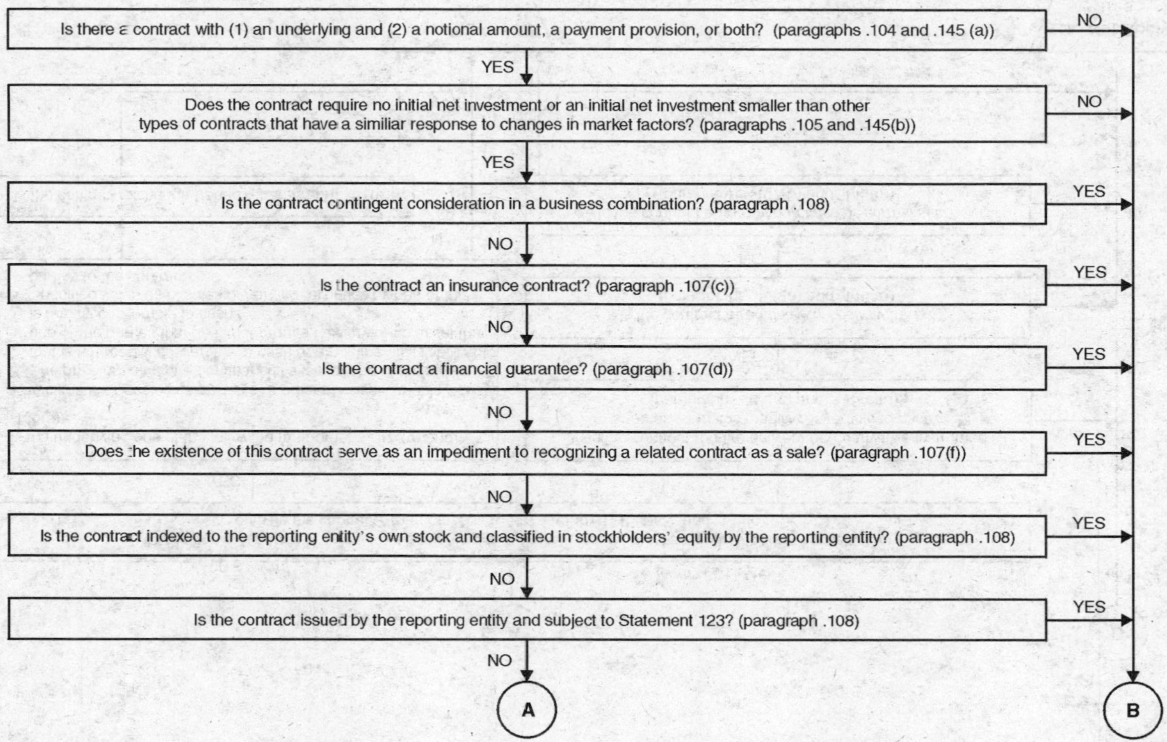

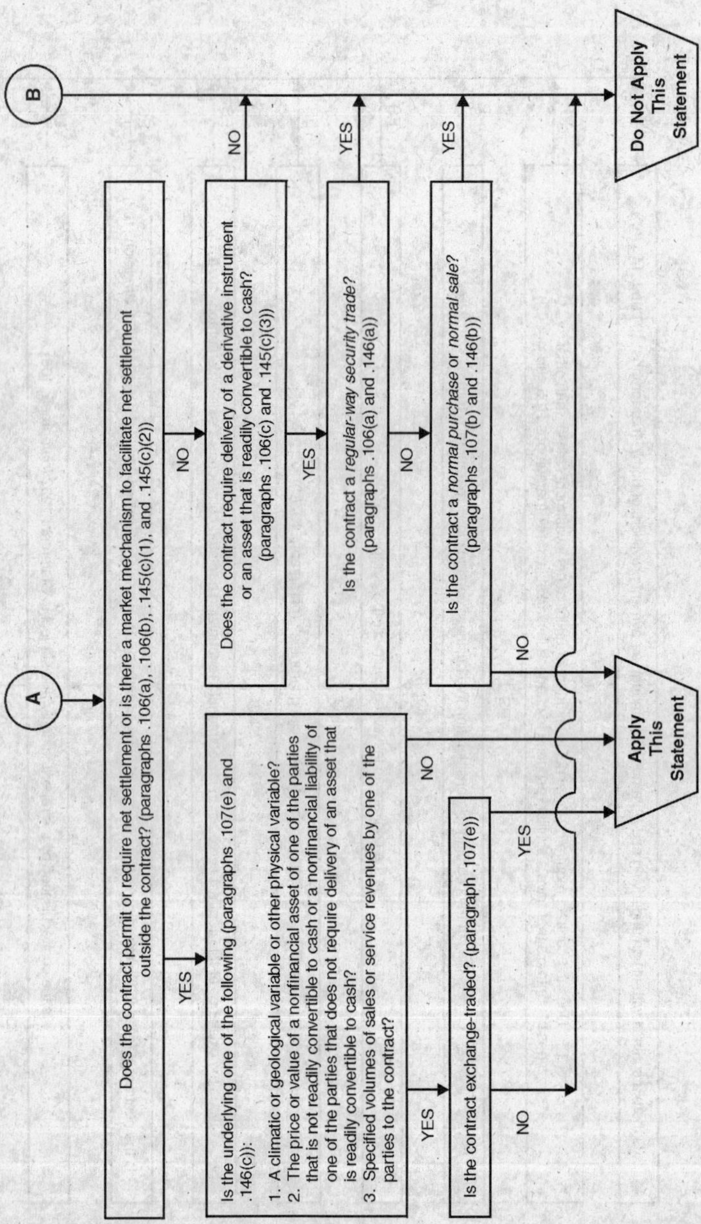
A
Does the contract permit or require net settlement or is there a market mechanism to facilitate net settlement outside the contract? (paragraphs .106(a), .106(b), .145(c)(1), and .145(c)(2))
NO
Does the contract require delivery of a derivative instrument or an asset that is readily convertible to cash? (paragraphs .106(c) and .145(c)(3))
YES
Is the contract a regular-way security trade? (paragraphs .106(a) and .146(a))
NO
Is the contract a normal purchase or normal sale? (paragraphs .107(b) and .146(b))
NO
YES
YES
NO
B
Do Not Apply This Statement
YES
Is the underlying one of the following (paragraphs .107(e) and .146(c)):
1. A climatic or geological variable or other physical variable?
2. The price or value of a nonfinancial asset of one of the parties that is not readily convertible to cash or a nonfinancial liability of one of the parties that does not require delivery of an asset that is readily convertible to cash?
3. Specified volumes of sales or service revenues by one of the parties to the contract?
NO
YES
Is the contract exchange-traded? (paragraph .107(e))
YES
NO
Apply This Statement

[FAS133, ¶539]

Glossary

.400 **Benchmark interest rate.** A widely recognized and quoted rate in an active financial market that is broadly indicative of the overall level of interest rates attributable to high-credit-quality obligors in that market. It is a rate that is widely used in a given financial market as an underlying basis for determining the interest rates of individual financial instruments and commonly referenced in interest-rate-related transactions.

In theory, the benchmark interest rate should be a risk-free rate (that is, has no risk of default). In some markets, government borrowing rates may serve as a benchmark. In other markets, the benchmark interest rate may be an interbank offered rate. In the United States, currently only the interest rates on direct Treasury obligations of the U.S. government and, for practical reasons, the LIBOR swap rate are considered to be benchmark interest rates. In each financial market, only the one or two most widely used and quoted rates that meet the above criteria may be considered benchmark interest rates. [FAS138, ¶4(jj)]

.401 **Comprehensive income.** The change in equity of a business enterprise during a period from transactions and other events and circumstances from nonowner sources. It includes all changes in equity during a period except those resulting from investments by owners and distributions to owners (FASB Concepts Statement No. 6, *Elements of Financial Statements,* paragraph 70). [FAS133, ¶540]

.402 **Derivative instrument.** Refer to paragraphs .103 through .106. [FAS133, ¶540]

.403 **Fair value.** The amount at which an asset (liability) could be bought (incurred) or sold (settled) in a current transaction between willing parties, that is, other than in a forced or liquidation sale. Quoted market prices in active markets are the best evidence of fair value and should be used as the basis for the measurement, if available. If a quoted market price is available, the fair value is the product of the number of trading units times that market price. If a quoted market price is not available, the estimate of fair value should be based on the best information available in the circumstances. The estimate of fair value should consider prices for similar assets or similar liabilities and the results of valuation techniques to the extent available in the circumstances. Examples of valuation techniques include the present value of estimated expected future cash flows using discount rates commensurate with the risks involved, option-pricing models, matrix pricing, option-adjusted spread models, and fundamental analysis. Valuation techniques for measuring assets and liabilities should be consistent with the objective of measuring fair value. Those techniques should incorporate assumptions that market participants would use in their estimates of values, future revenues, and future expenses, including assumptions about interest rates, default, prepayment, and volatility. In measuring forward contracts, such as foreign currency forward contracts, at fair value by discounting estimated future cash flows, an entity should base the estimate of future cash flows on the changes in the forward rate (rather than the spot rate). In measuring financial liabilities and nonfinancial derivatives that are liabilities at fair value by discounting estimated future cash flows (or equivalent outflows of other assets), an objective is to use discount rates at which those liabilities could be settled in an arm's-length transaction. [FAS133, ¶540]

.404 **Financial instrument.** Cash, evidence of an ownership interest in an entity, or a contract that both:

a. Imposes on one entity a contractual obligation* (1) to deliver cash or another financial instrument† to a second entity or (2) to exchange other financial instruments on potentially unfavorable terms with the second entity
b. Conveys to that second entity a contractual right‡ (1) to receive cash or another financial instrument from the first entity or (2) to exchange other financial instruments on potentially favorable terms with the first entity.

**Contractual obligations* encompass both those that are conditioned on the occurrence of a specified event and those that are not. All contractual obligations that are financial instruments meet the definition of *liability* set forth in Concepts Statement 6, although some may not be recognized as liabilities in financial statements—may be "off-balance-sheet"—because they fail to meet some other criterion for recognition. For some financial instruments, the obligation is owed to or by a group of entities rather than a single entity.

†The use of the term *financial instrument* in this definition is recursive (because the term *financial instrument* is included in it), though it is not circular. The definition requires a chain of contractual obligations that ends with the delivery of cash or an ownership interest in an entity. Any number of obligations to deliver financial instruments can be links in a chain that qualifies a particular contract as a financial instrument.

‡Contractual rights encompass both those that are conditioned on the occurrence of a specified event and those that are not. All contractual rights that are financial instruments meet the definition of *asset* set forth in Concepts Statement 6, although some may not be recognized as assets in financial statements—may be "off-balance-sheet"—because they fail to meet some other criterion for recognition. For some financial instruments, the right is held by or the obligation is due from a group of entities rather than a single entity.

[FAS133, ¶540]

.405 **Firm commitment.** An agreement with an unrelated party, binding on both parties and usually legally enforceable, with the following characteristics:

a. The agreement specifies all significant terms, including the quantity to be exchanged, the fixed price, and the timing of the transaction. The fixed price may be expressed as a specified amount of an entity's functional currency or of a foreign currency. It may also be expressed as a specified interest rate or specified effective yield. [FAS133, ¶540] A price that varies with the market price of the item that is the subject of the firm commitment cannot qualify as a "fixed" price. For example, a price that is specified in terms of ounces of gold would not be a fixed price if the market price of the item to be purchased or sold under the firm commitment varied with the price of gold. [FAS133, ¶442]

b. The agreement includes a disincentive for nonperformance that is sufficiently large to make performance probable.

[FAS133, ¶540]

.406 **Forecasted transaction.** A transaction that is expected to occur for which there is no firm commitment. Because no transaction or event has yet occurred and the transaction or event when it occurs will be at the prevailing market price, a forecasted transaction does not give an entity any present rights to future benefits or a present obligation for future sacrifices. [FAS133, ¶540]

.406A **LIBOR swap rate.** The fixed rate on a single-currency, constant-notional interest rate swap that has its floating-rate leg referenced to the London Interbank Offered Rate (LIBOR) with no additional spread over LIBOR on that floating-rate leg. That fixed rate is the derived rate that would result in the swap having a zero fair value at inception because the present value of fixed cash flows, based on that rate, equate to the present value of the floating cash flows. [FAS138, ¶4(jj)]

.407 **Notional amount.** A number of currency units, shares, bushels, pounds, or other units specified in a derivative instrument. [FAS133, ¶540]

.408 **Underlying.** A specified interest rate, security price, commodity price, foreign exchange rate, index of prices or rates, or other variable. An underlying may be a price or rate of an asset or liability but is not the asset or liability itself. [FAS133, ¶540]

Supplemental Guidance: Emerging Issues Task Force (EITF) Issues

.1000 [Listed below are EITF Issues that provide supplemental guidance for this section. These Issues are grouped by subject matter and may be either interpretive of or related by topic to the guidance in this section.

Business Combinations

EITF Issue No. 97-8, "Accounting for Contingent Consideration Issued in a Purchase Business Combination"

EITF Issue No. 97-15, "Accounting for Contingency Arrangements Based on Security Prices in a Purchase Business Combination"

Consolidated Subsidiaries

EITF Issue No. 99-1, "Accounting for Debt Convertible into the Stock of a Consolidated Subsidiary"

EITF Issue No. 00-4, "Majority Owner's Accounting for a Transaction in the Shares of a Consolidated Subsidiary and a Derivative Indexed to the Minority Interest in That Subsidiary"

EITF Issue No. 00-6, "Accounting for Freestanding Derivative Financial Instruments Indexed to, and Potentially Settled in, the Stock of a Consolidated Subsidiary"

Energy Contracts

EITF Issue No. 98-10, "Accounting for Contracts Involved in Energy Trading and Risk Management Activities"

EITF Issue No. 00-17, "Measuring the Fair Value of Energy-Related Contracts in Applying Issue No. 98-10"

EITF Topic No. D-105, "Accounting in Consolidation for Energy Trading Contracts between Affiliated Entities When the Activities of One but Not Both Affiliates Are within the Scope of Issue No. 98-10"

Other

EITF Issue No. 86-25, "Offsetting Foreign Currency Swaps"

EITF Issue No. 98-12, "Application of Issue No. 00-19 to Forward Equity Sales Transactions"

EITF Issue No. 99-2, "Accounting for Weather Derivatives"

EITF Issue No. 99-7, "Accounting for an Accelerated Share Repurchase Program"

EITF Issue No. 99-8, "Accounting for Transfers of Assets That Are Derivative Instruments but That Are Not Financial Assets"
EITF Issue No. 99-9, "Effect of Derivative Gains and Losses on the Capitalization of Interest"
EITF Issue No. 00-8, "Accounting by a Grantee for an Equity Instrument to Be Received in Conjunction with Providing Goods or Services"
EITF Issue No. 00-9, "Classification of a Gain or Loss from a Hedge of Debt That Is Extinguished"
EITF Issue No. 00-18, "Accounting Recognition for Certain Transactions involving Equity Instruments Granted to Other Than Employees"
EITF Issue No. 00-19, "Accounting for Derivative Financial Instruments Indexed to, and Potentially Settled in, a Company's Own Stock"
EITF Issue No. 01-6, "The Meaning of 'Indexed to a Company's Own Stock'"
EITF Issue No. 01-11, "Application of Issue No. 00-19 to a Contemporaneous Forward Purchase Contract and Written Put Option"
EITF Issue No. 01-12, "The Impact of the Requirements of FASB Statement No. 133 on Residual Value Guarantees in Connection with a Lease"
EITF Issue No. 02-2, "When Separate Contracts That Meet the Definition of Financial Instruments Should Be Combined for Accounting Purposes"
EITF Issue No. 02-8, "Accounting for Options Granted to Employees in Unrestricted, Publicly Traded Shares of an Unrelated Entity"
EITF Topic No. D-51, "The Applicability of FASB Statement No. 115 to Desecuritizations of Financial Assets"
EITF Topic No. D-71, "Accounting Issues Relating to the Introduction of the European Economic and Monetary Union (EMU)"
EITF Topic No. D-73, "Reclassification and Subsequent Sales of Securities in Connection with the Adoption of FASB Statement No. 133"
EITF Topic No. D-98, "Classification and Measurement of Redeemable Securities"
EITF Topic No. D-102, "Documentation of the Method Used to Measure Hedge Ineffectiveness under FASB Statement No. 133"]

.1001 [Listed below are EITF Issues that provide interpretive guidance on specific material in this section.

Paragraph .107(a) (FAS 138, ¶4(a))—EITF Topic No. D-105
Paragraph .108(a) (FAS 133, ¶11(a))—EITF Issues No. 99-1 and 01-6
Paragraph .117(a) (FAS 133, ¶20(a))—EITF Topic No. D-102
Paragraph .125(a) (FAS 133, ¶28(a))—EITF Topic No. D-102
Paragraph .127(b) (FAS 133, ¶30(b))—EITF Topic No. D-102
Paragraph .150 (FAS 133, ¶62)—EITF Topic No. D-102]

(The next page is 13501.)

DISPOSAL OF LONG-LIVED ASSETS SECTION D60

Sources: FASB Statement 144; FASB Statement 145

[**Note:** A list of Issues discussed by the Emerging Issues Task Force (EITF) that provide supplemental guidance for this section is presented in paragraph .1000.]

Summary

This section addresses financial accounting and reporting for long-lived assets to be disposed of.

A long-lived asset to be disposed of other than by sale shall continue to be classified as held and used until it is disposed of. If the asset is to be abandoned, the depreciable life of the asset shall be revised in accordance with Section A06, "Accounting Changes." If the asset is to be exchanged for a similar productive asset or distributed to owners in a spinoff, an impairment loss shall be recognized at the disposal date if the carrying amount of the asset exceeds its fair value.

A long-lived asset to be disposed of by sale shall be classified as held for sale and measured at the lower of its carrying amount or fair value less cost to sell when certain criteria are met. Depreciation shall cease.

Long-Lived Assets to Be Disposed Of

Scope

.101 Except as indicated in paragraphs .102 and .103, this section applies to recognized long-lived assets of an *entity*[1] to be disposed of, including (a) capital leases of lessees, (b) long-lived assets of lessors subject to operating leases, (c) proved oil and gas properties that are being accounted for using the successful efforts method of accounting,[2] and (d) long-term prepaid assets.[3] [FAS144, ¶3]

---

[1]This section applies to a business enterprise and a not-for-profit organization, each of which is referred to herein as an *entity.* [FAS144, ¶3, fn1]

[2]Accounting requirements for oil and gas properties that are accounted for using the full-cost method of accounting are prescribed by the Securities and Exchange Commission (Regulation S-X, Rule 4-10, "Financial Accounting and Reporting for Oil and Gas Producing Activities Pursuant to the Federal Securities Laws and the Energy Policy and Conservation Act of 1975"). [FAS144, ¶3, fn2]

[3]In this section, all references to a *long-lived asset* refer to a long-lived asset covered by this section. [FAS144, ¶3, fn3]

.102 If a long-lived asset (or assets) is part of a group that includes other assets and liabilities not covered by this section, this section applies to the group. In those situations, the unit of accounting for the long-lived asset is its group. For a long-lived asset or assets to be disposed of by sale or otherwise, that group (hereinafter referred to as a *disposal group*) represents assets to be disposed of together as a group in a single transaction and liabilities directly associated with those assets that will be transferred in the transaction.[4] This section does not change generally accepted accounting principles applicable to those other individual assets (such as accounts receivable and inventory) and liabilities (such as accounts payable, long-term debt, and asset retirement obligations) not covered by this section that are included in such groups. [FAS144, ¶4]

.103 This section does not apply to (a) goodwill, (b) long-term customer relationships of a financial institution, such as core deposit intangibles, credit cardholder intangibles, and servicing assets, (c) financial instruments, including investments in equity securities accounted for under the cost or equity method, (d) deferred policy acquisition costs, (e) deferred tax assets, and (f) unproved oil and gas properties that are being accounted for using the successful-efforts method of accounting. This section also does not apply to long-lived assets for which the accounting is prescribed by:

- Section Br5, "Broadcasting Industry"
- Section Co2, "Computer Software to Be Sold, Leased, or Otherwise Marketed"
- Section Re4, "Record and Music Industry"
- Section Re6, "Regulated Operations," (for accounting for abandonments and disallowances of plant costs, paragraphs .127A through .127E) [FAS144, ¶5]
- [AICPA Statement of Position 00-2, *Accounting by Producers or Distributors of Films.*]

Long-Lived Assets to Be Disposed Of Other Than by Sale

.104 A long-lived asset to be disposed of other than by sale (for example, by abandonment, in an exchange for a similar productive long-lived asset, or in a distribution to owners in a spinoff) shall continue to be classified as held and used until it is disposed of. Paragraphs .142 through .161 of Section I08, "Impairment," shall apply while the asset is classified as held and used. If a long-lived asset is to be abandoned or distributed to owners in a spinoff together with other assets (and liabilities) as a group and that dis-

[4]Examples of such liabilities include, but are not limited to, legal obligations that transfer with a long-lived asset, such as certain environmental obligations, and obligations that, for business reasons, a potential buyer would prefer to settle when assumed as part of a group, such as warranty obligations that relate to an acquired customer base. [FAS144, ¶4, fn4]

posal group is a *component of an entity,*[5] paragraphs .101 through .104 of Section I14, "Income Statement Presentation: Discontinued Operations," shall apply to the disposal group at the date it is disposed of. [FAS144, ¶27]

Long-Lived Asset to Be Abandoned

.105 For purposes of this section, a long-lived asset to be abandoned is disposed of when it ceases to be used. If an entity commits to a plan to abandon a long-lived asset before the end of its previously estimated useful life, depreciation estimates shall be revised in accordance with Section A06, "Accounting Changes," to reflect the use of the asset over its shortened useful life (refer to paragraph .144 of Section I08).[6] A long-lived asset that has been temporarily idled shall not be accounted for as if abandoned. [FAS144, ¶28]

Long-Lived Asset to Be Exchanged for a Similar Productive Long-Lived Asset or to Be Distributed to Owners in a Spinoff

.106 For purposes of this section, a long-lived asset to be exchanged for a similar productive long-lived asset or to be distributed to owners in a spinoff is disposed of when it is exchanged or distributed. If the asset (asset group) is tested for recoverability while it is classified as held and used, the estimates of future cash flows used in that test shall be based on the use of the asset for its remaining useful life, assuming that the disposal transaction will not occur. [FAS144, ¶29] An undiscounted cash flows recoverability test should apply prior to the disposal date. [FAS144, ¶B67] In addition to any impairment losses required to be recognized while the asset is classified as held and used, an impairment loss, if any, shall be recognized when the asset is disposed of if the carrying amount of the asset (disposal group) exceeds its fair value.[7] [FAS144, ¶29]

---

[5]A *component of an entity* is defined in paragraph .101 of Section I14 as comprising operations and cash flows that can be clearly distinguished, operationally and for financial reporting purposes, from the rest of the entity. [FAS144, ¶27, fn15]

[6]Because the continued use of a long-lived asset demonstrates the presence of service potential, only in unusual situations would the fair value of a long-lived asset to be abandoned be zero while it is being used. When a long-lived asset ceases to be used, the carrying amount of the asset should equal its salvage value, if any. The salvage value of the asset should not be reduced to an amount less than zero. [FAS144, ¶28, fn16]

[7]The provisions of this paragraph apply to those transactions described in paragraphs .108 and .110 of Section N35, "Nonmonetary Transactions," for which the accounting is based on the recorded amount (after reduction, if appropriate, for an indicated impairment of value) of a long-lived asset exchanged or distributed. [FAS144, ¶29, fn17]

Long-Lived Assets to Be Disposed Of by Sale

Recognition

.107 A long-lived asset (disposal group) to be sold shall be classified as held for sale in the period in which all of the following criteria are met:

a. Management, having the authority to approve the action, commits to a plan to sell the asset (disposal group).
b. The asset (disposal group) is available for immediate sale in its present condition subject only to terms that are usual and customary for sales of such assets (disposal groups). (Examples 1 through 3 (paragraphs .123 through .126) illustrate when that criterion would be met.)
c. An active program to locate a buyer and other actions required to complete the plan to sell the asset (disposal group) have been initiated.
d. The sale of the asset (disposal group) is probable,[8] and transfer of the asset (disposal group) is expected to qualify for recognition as a completed sale, within one year, except as permitted by paragraph .108. (Example 4 (paragraph .127) illustrates when that criterion would be met.)
e. The asset (disposal group) is being actively marketed for sale at a price that is reasonable in relation to its current fair value.
f. Actions required to complete the plan indicate that it is unlikely that significant changes to the plan will be made or that the plan will be withdrawn.

If at any time the criteria in this paragraph are no longer met (except as permitted by paragraph .108), a long-lived asset (disposal group) classified as held for sale shall be reclassified as held and used in accordance with paragraph .115.

[FAS144, ¶30]

.108 Events or circumstances beyond an entity's control may extend the period required to complete the sale of a long-lived asset (disposal group) beyond one year. An exception to the one-year requirement in paragraph .107(d) shall apply in the following situations in which such events or circumstances arise:

a. If at the date an entity commits to a plan to sell a long-lived asset (disposal group) the entity reasonably expects that others (not a buyer) will impose conditions on the transfer of the asset (group) that will extend the period required to complete the sale and

[8]The term *probable* is used consistent with the meaning associated with it in paragraph .104(a) of Section C59, "Contingencies," and refers to a future sale that is "likely to occur." [FAS144, ¶30, fn18]

(1) actions necessary to respond to those conditions cannot be initiated until after a *firm purchase commitment*[9] is obtained and (2) a firm purchase commitment is probable within one year. (Example 5 (paragraph .129) illustrates that situation.)

b. If an entity obtains a firm purchase commitment and, as a result, a buyer or others unexpectedly impose conditions on the transfer of a long-lived asset (disposal group) previously classified as held for sale that will extend the period required to complete the sale and (1) actions necessary to respond to the conditions have been or will be timely initiated and (2) a favorable resolution of the delaying factors is expected. (Example 6 (paragraph .130) illustrates that situation.)
c. If during the initial one-year period, circumstances arise that previously were considered unlikely and, as a result, a long-lived asset (disposal group) previously classified as held for sale is not sold by the end of that period and (1) during the initial one-year period the entity initiated actions necessary to respond to the change in circumstances, (2) the asset (group) is being actively marketed at a price that is reasonable given the change in circumstances, and (3) the criteria in paragraph .107 are met. (Example 7 of paragraph .131 illustrates that situation.)

[FAS144, ¶31]

.109 A long-lived asset (disposal group) that is newly acquired and that will be sold rather than held and used shall be classified as held for sale at the acquisition date only if the one-year requirement in paragraph .107(d) is met (except as permitted by paragraph .108) and any other criteria in paragraph .107 that are not met at that date are probable of being met within a short period following the acquisition (usually within three months). [FAS144, ¶32]

.110 If the criteria in paragraph .107 are met after the balance sheet date but before issuance of the financial statements, a long-lived asset shall continue to be classified as held and used in those financial statements when issued.[10] The information required by paragraph .120(a) shall be disclosed in the notes to the financial statements. If the asset (asset group) is tested for recoverability (on a held-and-used basis) as of the balance sheet date, the estimates of future cash flows used in that test shall consider the likelihood of possible outcomes that existed at the balance sheet date, including the assessment of the likelihood of the future sale of the asset. That assessment made as of the balance sheet

[9]A *firm purchase commitment* is an agreement with an unrelated party, binding on both parties and usually legally enforceable, that (a) specifies all significant terms, including the price and timing of the transaction, and (b) includes a disincentive for nonperformance that is sufficiently large to make performance probable. [FAS144, ¶31, fn19]

[10]Refer to AICPA Statement on Auditing Standards No. 1, *Codification of Auditing Standards and Procedures,* Section 560, "Subsequent Events." [FAS144, ¶33, fn20]

date shall not be revised for a decision to sell the asset after the balance sheet date.[11] An impairment loss, if any, to be recognized shall be measured as the amount by which the carrying amount of the asset (asset group) exceeds its fair value at the balance sheet date. [FAS144, ¶33]

Measurement

.111 A long-lived asset (disposal group) classified as held for sale shall be measured at the lower of its carrying amount or fair value less cost to sell. If the asset (disposal group) is newly acquired, the carrying amount of the asset (disposal group) shall be established based on its fair value less cost to sell at the acquisition date. A long-lived asset shall not be depreciated (amortized) while it is classified as held for sale. Interest and other expenses attributable to the liabilities of a disposal group classified as held for sale shall continue to be accrued. [FAS144, ¶34]

.112 Costs to sell are the incremental direct costs to transact a sale, that is, the costs that result directly from and are essential to a sale transaction and that would not have been incurred by the entity had the decision to sell not been made. Those costs include broker commissions, legal and title transfer fees, and closing costs that must be incurred before legal title can be transferred. Those costs exclude expected future losses associated with the operations of a long-lived asset (disposal group) while it is classified as held for sale.[12] If the sale is expected to occur beyond one year as permitted in limited situations by paragraph .108, the cost to sell shall be discounted. [FAS144, ¶35]

.113 The carrying amounts of any assets that are not covered by this section, including goodwill, that are included in a disposal group classified as held for sale shall be adjusted in accordance with other applicable generally accepted accounting principles prior to measuring the fair value less cost to sell of the disposal group.[13] [FAS144, ¶36]

---

[11]Because it is difficult to separate the benefit of hindsight when assessing conditions that existed at a prior date, it is important that judgments about those conditions, the need to test an asset for recoverability, and the application of a recoverability test be made and documented together with supporting evidence on a timely basis. [FAS144, ¶33, fn21]

[12]Expected future operating losses that marketplace participants would not similarly consider in their estimates of the fair value less cost to sell of a long-lived asset (disposal group) classified as held for sale shall not be indirectly recognized as part of an expected loss on the sale by reducing the carrying amount of the asset (disposal group) to an amount less than its current fair value less cost to sell. [FAS144, ¶35, fn22]

[13]Paragraph .138 of Section G40 provides guidance for allocating goodwill to a lower-level asset group to be disposed of that is part of a reporting unit and that constitutes a business. Goodwill is not included in a lower-level asset group to be disposed of that is part of a reporting unit if it does not constitute a business. [FAS144, ¶36, fn23]

.114 A loss shall be recognized for any initial or subsequent write-down to fair value less cost to sell. A gain shall be recognized for any subsequent increase in fair value less cost to sell, but not in excess of the cumulative loss previously recognized (for a write-down to fair value less cost to sell). The loss or gain shall adjust only the carrying amount of a long-lived asset, whether classified as held for sale individually or as part of a disposal group. A gain or loss not previously recognized that results from the sale of a long-lived asset (disposal group) shall be recognized at the date of sale. [FAS144, ¶37]

Changes to a Plan of Sale

.115 If circumstances arise that previously were considered unlikely and, as a result, an entity decides not to sell a long-lived asset (disposal group) previously classified as held for sale, the asset (disposal group) shall be reclassified as held and used. A long-lived asset that is reclassified shall be measured individually at the lower of its (a) carrying amount before the asset (disposal group) was classified as held for sale, adjusted for any depreciation (amortization) expense that would have been recognized had the asset (disposal group) been continuously classified as held and used, or (b) fair value at the date of the subsequent decision not to sell. [FAS144, ¶38]

.116 Any required adjustment to the carrying amount of a long-lived asset that is reclassified as held and used shall be included in income from continuing operations in the period of the subsequent decision not to sell. That adjustment shall be reported in the same income statement caption used to report a loss, if any, recognized in accordance with paragraph .118. If a component of an entity is reclassified as held and used, the results of operations of the component previously reported in discontinued operations in accordance with paragraph .103 of Section I14 shall be reclassified and included in income from continuing operations for all periods presented. [FAS144, ¶39]

.117 If an entity removes an individual asset or liability from a disposal group previously classified as held for sale, the remaining assets and liabilities of the disposal group to be sold shall continue to be measured as a group only if the criteria in paragraph .107 are met. Otherwise, the remaining long-lived assets of the group shall be measured individually at the lower of their carrying amounts or fair values less cost to sell at that date. Any long-lived assets that will not be sold shall be reclassified as held and used in accordance with paragraph .115. [FAS144, ¶40]

Reporting Gains or Losses on the Sale of a Long-Lived Asset or Disposal Group in Continuing Operations

.118 A gain or loss recognized [FAS144, ¶45] on the sale of a long-lived asset (disposal group) [FAS145, ¶9(n)] that is not a component of an entity shall be included in income from continuing operations before income taxes in the income statement of a business enterprise and in income from continuing operations in the statement of activities of a not-for-profit organization. If a subtotal such as "income from operations" is presented, it shall include the amounts of those gains or losses. [FAS144, ¶45]

Reporting a Long-Lived Asset or Disposal Group Classified as Held for Sale

.119 A long-lived asset classified as held for sale shall be presented separately in the statement of financial position. The assets and liabilities of a disposal group [including a component of an entity that is a discontinued operation] classified as held for sale shall be presented separately in the asset and liability sections, respectively, of the statement of financial position. Those assets and liabilities shall not be offset and presented as a single amount. The major classes of assets and liabilities classified as held for sale shall be separately disclosed either on the face of the statement of financial position or in the notes to financial statements (paragraph .120(a)). [FAS144, ¶46]

Disclosure

.120 The following information shall be disclosed in the notes to the financial statements that cover the period in which a long-lived asset (disposal group) either has been sold or is classified as held for sale:

a. A description of the facts and circumstances leading to the expected disposal, the expected manner and timing of that disposal, and, if not separately presented on the face of the statement, the carrying amount(s) of the major classes of assets and liabilities included as part of a disposal group
b. The gain or loss recognized in accordance with paragraph .114 and if not separately presented on the face of the income statement, the caption in the income statement or the statement of activities that includes that gain or loss
c. If applicable, amounts of revenue and pretax profit or loss reported in discontinued operations
d. If applicable, the segment in which the long-lived asset (disposal group) is reported under Section S30.

[FAS144, ¶47]

.121 If either paragraph .115 or paragraph .117 applies, a description of the facts and circumstances leading to the decision to change the plan to sell the long-lived asset (disposal group) and its effect on the results of operations for the period and any prior periods presented shall be disclosed in the notes to financial statements that include the period of that decision. [FAS144, ¶48]

Implementation Guidance

Introduction

.122 Paragraphs .123 through .131 illustrate application of some of the provisions of this section in certain specific situations. The relevant paragraphs of this section are identified in the parenthetical notes. The examples do not address all possible situations or applications of this section. Paragraphs .123 through .131 are an integral part of the standards provided in this section. [FAS144, ¶A1]

Examples 1 through 3—Plan-of-Sale Criterion .107(b)

.123 To qualify for classification as held for sale, a long-lived asset (disposal group) must be available for immediate sale in its present condition subject only to terms that are usual and customary for sales of such assets (disposal groups) (paragraph .107(b)). A long-lived asset (disposal group) is available for immediate sale if an entity currently has the intent and ability to transfer the asset (disposal group) to a buyer in its present condition. Examples 1 through 3 illustrate situations in which the criterion in paragraph .107(b) would or would not be met. [FAS144, ¶A15]

Example 1

.124 An entity commits to a plan to sell its headquarters building and has initiated actions to locate a buyer.

a. The entity intends to transfer the building to a buyer after it vacates the building. The time necessary to vacate the building is usual and customary for sales of such assets. The criterion in paragraph .107(b) would be met at the plan commitment date.
b. The entity will continue to use the building until construction of a new headquarters building is completed. The entity does not intend to transfer the existing building to a buyer until after construction of the new building is completed (and it vacates the existing building). The delay in the timing of the transfer of the existing building imposed by the entity (seller) demonstrates that the building is not available for immediate sale. The criterion in paragraph .107(b) would not be met until construction of the new building is completed, even if a firm purchase commitment for the future transfer of the existing building is obtained earlier.

[FAS144, ¶A16]

Example 2

.125 An entity commits to a plan to sell a manufacturing facility and has initiated actions to locate a buyer. At the plan commitment date, there is a backlog of uncompleted customer orders.

a. The entity intends to sell the manufacturing facility with its operations. Any uncompleted customer orders at the sale date would transfer to the buyer. The transfer of uncompleted customer orders at the sale date will not affect the timing of the transfer of the facility. The criterion in paragraph .107(b) would be met at the plan commitment date.
b. The entity intends to sell the manufacturing facility, but without its operations. The entity does not intend to transfer the facility to a buyer until after it ceases all operations of the facility and eliminates the backlog of uncompleted customer orders. The delay in the timing of the transfer of the facility imposed by the entity (seller) demonstrates that the facility is not available for immediate sale. The criterion in paragraph .107(b) would not be met until the operations of the facility cease, even if a firm purchase commitment for the future transfer of the facility is obtained earlier.

[FAS144, ¶A17]

Example 3

.126 An entity acquires through foreclosure a real estate property that it intends to sell.

a. The entity does not intend to transfer the property to a buyer until after it completes renovations to increase its sales value. The delay in the timing of the transfer of the property imposed by the entity (seller) demonstrates that the property is not available for immediate sale. The criterion in paragraph .107(b) would not be met until the renovations are completed.
b. After the renovations are completed and the property is classified as held for sale but before a firm purchase commitment is obtained, the entity becomes aware of environmental damage requiring remediation. The entity still intends to sell the property. However, the entity does not have the ability to transfer the property to a buyer until after the remediation is completed. The delay in the timing of the transfer of the property imposed by others before a firm purchase commitment is obtained demonstrates that the property is not available for immediate sale. The criterion in paragraph .107(b) would not continue to be met. The property would be reclassified as held and used in accordance with paragraph .116.

[FAS144, ¶A18]

Example 4—Plan-of-Sale Criterion .107(d)

.127 To qualify for classification as held for sale, the sale of a long-lived asset (disposal group) must be probable, and transfer of the asset (disposal group) must be expected to qualify for recognition as a completed sale, within one year (paragraph .107(d)). That criterion would not be met if, for example:

a. An entity that is a commercial leasing and finance company is holding for sale or lease equipment that has recently come off lease and the ultimate form of a future transaction (sale or lease) has not yet been determined.
b. An entity commits to a plan to "sell" a property that is in use, and the transfer of the property will be accounted for as a sale-leaseback through which the seller-lessee will retain more than a minor portion of the use of the property. The property would continue to be classified as held and used and paragraphs .142 through .161 of Section I08 would apply.[14]

[FAS144, ¶A19]

Examples 5 through 7—Exceptions to Plan-of-Sale Criterion .107(d)

.128 An exception to the one-year requirement in paragraph .107(d) applies in limited situations in which the period required to complete the sale of a long-lived asset (disposal group) will be (or has been) extended by events or circumstances beyond an entity's control and certain conditions are met (paragraph .108). Examples 5 through 7 illustrate those situations. [FAS144, ¶A20]

Example 5

.129 An entity in the utility industry commits to a plan to sell a disposal group that represents a significant portion of its regulated operations. The sale will require regulatory approval, which could extend the period required to complete the sale beyond one year. Actions necessary to obtain that approval cannot be initiated until after a buyer is known and a firm purchase commitment is obtained. However, a firm purchase commitment is probable within one year. In that situation, the conditions in paragraph .108(a) for an exception to the one-year requirement in paragraph .107(d) would be met. [FAS144, ¶A21]

[14]If at the date of the sale-leaseback the fair value of the property is less than its undepreciated cost, a loss would be recognized immediately up to the amount of the difference between undepreciated cost and fair value in accordance with paragraph .129(c) of Section L10, "Leases." [FAS144, ¶A19, fn30]

Example 6

.130 An entity commits to a plan to sell a manufacturing facility in its present condition and classifies the facility as held for sale at that date. After a firm purchase commitment is obtained, the buyer's inspection of the property identifies environmental damage not previously known to exist. The entity is required by the buyer to remediate the damage, which will extend the period required to complete the sale beyond one year. However, the entity has initiated actions to remediate the damage, and satisfactory remediation of the damage is probable. In that situation, the conditions in paragraph .108(b) for an exception to the one-year requirement in paragraph .107(d) would be met. [FAS144, ¶A22]

Example 7

.131 An entity commits to a plan to sell a long-lived asset and classifies the asset as held for sale at that date.

a. During the initial one-year period, the market conditions that existed at the date the asset was classified initially as held for sale deteriorate and, as a result, the asset is not sold by the end of that period. During that period, the entity actively solicited but did not receive any reasonable offers to purchase the asset and, in response, reduced the price. The asset continues to be actively marketed at a price that is reasonable given the change in market conditions, and the criteria in paragraph .107 are met. In that situation, the conditions in paragraph .108(c) for an exception to the one-year requirement in paragraph .107(d) would be met. At the end of the initial one-year period, the asset would continue to be classified as held for sale.
b. During the following one-year period, market conditions deteriorate further, and the asset is not sold by the end of that period. The entity believes that the market conditions will improve and has not further reduced the price of the asset. The asset continues to be held for sale, but at a price in excess of its current fair value. In that situation, the absence of a price reduction demonstrates that the asset is not available for immediate sale as required by the criterion in paragraph .107(b). In addition, the criterion in paragraph .107(e) requires that an asset be marketed at a price that is reasonable in relation to its current fair value. Therefore, the conditions in paragraph .108(c) for an exception to the one-year requirement in paragraph .107(d) would not be met. The asset would be reclassified as held and used in accordance with paragraph .115.

[FAS144, ¶A23]

Supplemental Guidance: Emerging Issues Task Force (EITF) Issues

.1000 [Listed below are EITF Issues that provide supplemental guidance for this section. These Issues are related by topic to the guidance in this section.

EITF Issue No. 94-3, "Liability Recognition for Certain Employee Termination Benefits and Other Costs to Exit an Activity (including Certain Costs Incurred in a Restructuring)"
EITF Issue No. 01-2, "Interpretations of APB Opinion No. 29"
EITF Topic No. D-104, "Clarification of Transition Guidance in Paragraph 51 of FASB Statement No. 144"]

(The next page is 14129.)

EARNINGS PER SHARE SECTION E11

Sources: FASB Statement 128; FASB Statement 135

[**Note:** A list of Issues discussed by the Emerging Issues Task Force (EITF) that provide supplemental guidance for this section is presented in paragraph .1000.]

Summary

This section presents standards for computing and presenting earnings per share (EPS) and applies to entities with publicly held common stock or potential common stock. This section simplifies previous standards for computing earnings per share and makes them comparable to international EPS standards. It replaces the presentation of primary EPS with a presentation of basic EPS. It also requires dual presentation of basic and diluted EPS on the face of the income statement for all entities with complex capital structures and requires a reconciliation of the numerator and denominator of the basic EPS computation to the numerator and denominator of the diluted EPS computation.

Basic EPS excludes dilution and is computed by dividing income available to common stockholders by the weighted-average number of common shares outstanding for the period. Diluted EPS reflects the potential dilution that could occur if securities or other contracts to issue common stock were exercised or converted into common stock or resulted in the issuance of common stock that then shared in the earnings of the entity. Diluted EPS is computed similarly to fully diluted EPS.

Introduction and Scope

.101 This section specifies the computation, presentation, and disclosure requirements for **earnings per share** (EPS) for entities with publicly held **common stock** or **potential common stock.** This section's objective is to simplify the computation of earnings per share and to make the U.S. standard for computing earnings per share more compatible with the EPS standards of other countries and with that of the International Accounting Standards Committee (IASC). [FAS128, ¶1]

.102 This section requires presentation of earnings per share by all entities that have issued common stock or potential common stock (that is, **securities** such as **options, warrants, convertible securities,** or **contingent stock agreements**) if those securities trade in a public market either on a stock exchange (domestic or foreign) or in the over-the-counter market, including securities quoted only locally or regionally. This section also requires presentation of earnings per share by an entity that has made a filing or is in the process of filing with a regulatory agency in preparation for the sale of those securities in a public market. This section does not require presentation of earnings per share for investment companies[1] or in statements of wholly owned subsidiaries. Any entity that is not required by this section to present earnings per share in its financial statements that chooses to present earnings per share in its financial statements shall do so in accordance with the provisions of this section. [FAS128, ¶6] All prior-period EPS data presented shall be restated (including interim financial statements, summaries of earnings, and selected financial data) to conform with the provisions of this section.[2] [FAS128, ¶43]

Basic Earnings per Share

.103 The objective of **basic EPS** is to measure the performance of an entity over the reporting period. Basic EPS shall be computed by dividing **income available to common stockholders** (the numerator) by the **weighted-average number of common shares outstanding** (the denominator) during the period. Shares issued during the period and shares reacquired during the period shall be weighted for the portion of the period that they were outstanding. [FAS128, ¶8] [Refer to paragraph .1001 for an EITF Issue that provides interpretive guidance on paragraphs .103 and .104.]

[1]That is, investment companies that comply with the requirements of the AICPA Audit and Accounting Guide, *Audits of Investment Companies,* to present selected per-share data. [FAS128, ¶6, fn2]

[[2]For example,] entities that present tables of 10-year selected data must restate and compute that data in accordance with the provisions of this section. [However,] this section does not require presentation of EPS data for 10 years. [FAS128, ¶145]

.104 Income available to common stockholders shall be computed by deducting both the dividends declared in the period on **preferred stock** (whether or not paid) and the dividends accumulated for the period on cumulative preferred stock (whether or not earned)[3] from income from continuing operations (if that amount appears in the income statement)[4] and also from net income. If there is a loss from continuing operations or a net loss, the amount of the loss shall be increased by those preferred dividends. [FAS128, ¶9]

.105 Shares issuable for little or no cash consideration upon the satisfaction of certain conditions **(contingently issuable shares)** shall be considered outstanding common shares and included in the computation of basic EPS as of the date that all necessary conditions have been satisfied (in essence, when issuance of the shares is no longer contingent).[5],[6] Outstanding common shares that are contingently returnable (that is, subject to recall) shall be treated in the same manner as contingently issuable shares.[7] [FAS128, ¶10]

Diluted Earnings per Share

.106 The objective of **diluted EPS** is consistent with that of basic EPS—to measure the performance of an entity over the reporting period—while giving effect to all **dilutive** potential common shares that were outstanding during the period. The computation of diluted EPS is similar to the computation of basic EPS except that the denominator is increased to include the number of additional common shares that would have been outstanding if the dilutive potential common shares had been issued. In addition, in computing the dilutive effect of convertible securities, the numerator is adjusted to add back (a) any convertible preferred dividends and (b) the after-tax amount of interest recognized in the period associated with any convertible debt. The numerator also is adjusted

[3]Preferred dividends that are cumulative only if earned shall be deducted only to the extent that they are earned. [FAS128, ¶9, fn3]

[4]An entity that does not report a discontinued operation but reports an extraordinary item or the cumulative effect of an accounting change in the period shall use that line item (for example, *income before extraordinary items* or *income before accounting change*) whenever the line item *income from continuing operations* is referred to in this section. [FAS128, ¶9, fn4]

[5]Those shares should be included in basic EPS on a weighted-average basis. In most cases, the shares would be included as of the last day of the period because whether the condition has been satisfied may not be certain until the end of the period. [FAS128, ¶121]

[6]"Vested" contingently issuable shares should be considered in the computation of basic EPS because consideration for those shares has been received. [FAS128, ¶92]

[7]Thus, contingently issuable shares include shares that (a) will be issued in the future upon the satisfaction of specified conditions, (b) have been placed in escrow and all or part must be returned if specified conditions are not met, or (c) have been issued but the holder must return all or part if specified conditions are not met. [FAS128, ¶10, fn5]

for any other changes in income or loss that would result from the assumed conversion of those potential common shares, such as profit-sharing expenses. Similar adjustments also may be necessary for certain contracts that provide the issuer or holder with a choice between settlement methods. [FAS128, ¶11]

.107 Diluted EPS shall be based on the most advantageous **conversion rate** or **exercise price** from the standpoint of the security holder. Previously reported diluted EPS data shall not be retroactively adjusted for subsequent conversions or subsequent changes in the market price of the common stock. [FAS128, ¶12]

No Antidilution

.108 The computation of diluted EPS shall not assume conversion, exercise, or **contingent issuance** of securities that would have an **antidilutive** effect on earnings per share. Shares issued on actual conversion, exercise, or satisfaction of certain conditions for which the underlying potential common shares were antidilutive shall be included in the computation as outstanding common shares from the date of conversion, exercise, or satisfaction of those conditions, respectively. In determining whether potential common shares are dilutive or antidilutive, each issue or series of issues of potential common shares shall be considered separately rather than in the aggregate. [FAS128, ¶13]

.109 Convertible securities may be dilutive on their own but antidilutive when included with other potential common shares in computing diluted EPS. To reflect maximum potential dilution, each issue or series of issues of potential common shares shall be considered in sequence from the most dilutive to the least dilutive. That is, dilutive potential common shares with the lowest "earnings per incremental share" shall be included in diluted EPS before those with a higher earnings per incremental share.[8] Paragraph .164 provides an example of that provision. [FAS128, ¶14]

.110 An entity that reports a discontinued operation, an extraordinary item, or the cumulative effect of an accounting change in a period shall use income from continuing operations[9] (adjusted for preferred dividends as described in paragraph .104) as the "control number" in determining whether those potential common shares are dilutive or antidilutive. That is, the same number of potential common shares used in computing the diluted per-share amount for income from continuing operations shall be used in com-

---

[8]Options and warrants generally will be included first because use of the treasury stock method does not impact the numerator of the computation. [FAS128, ¶14, fn6]

[9]Refer to footnote 4. [FAS128, ¶15, fn7]

puting all other reported diluted per-share amounts even if those amounts will be antidilutive to their respective basic per-share amounts.[10] [FAS128, ¶15]

.111 Including potential common shares in the denominator of a diluted per-share computation for continuing operations always will result in an antidilutive per-share amount when an entity has a *loss* from continuing operations or a *loss* from continuing operations available to common stockholders (that is, after any preferred dividend deductions). Although including those potential common shares in the other diluted per-share computations may be dilutive to their comparable basic per-share amounts, no potential common shares shall be included in the computation of any diluted per-share amount when a loss from continuing operations exists, even if the entity reports net income. [FAS128, ¶16]

Options and Warrants and Their Equivalents

.112 The dilutive effect of outstanding **call options** and warrants (and their equivalents) issued by the reporting entity shall be reflected in diluted EPS by application of the **treasury stock method** unless the provisions of paragraphs .119 and .143 through .146 require that another method be applied. Equivalents of options and warrants include nonvested stock granted to employees, stock purchase contracts, and partially paid stock subscriptions.[11] Under the treasury stock method:

a. Exercise of options and warrants shall be assumed at the beginning of the period (or at time of issuance, if later) and common shares shall be assumed to be issued.
b. The proceeds from exercise shall be assumed to be used to purchase common stock at the average market price during the period.[12]

[10]For example, assume that Corporation X has income from continuing operations of $2,400, a loss from discontinued operations of $(3,600), a net loss of $(1,200), and 1,000 common shares and 200 potential common shares outstanding. Corporation X's basic per-share amounts would be $2.40 for continuing operations, $(3.60) for the discontinued operation, and $(1.20) for the net loss. Corporation X would include the 200 potential common shares in the denominator of its diluted per-share computation for continuing operations because the resulting $2.00 per share is dilutive. (For illustrative purposes, assume no numerator impact of those 200 potential common shares.) Because income from continuing operations is the control number, Corporation X also must include those 200 potential common shares in the denominator for the other per-share amounts, even though the resulting per-share amounts—$(3.00) per share for the loss from discontinued operation and $(1.00) per share for the net loss—are antidilutive to their comparable basic per-share amounts; that is, the loss per-share amounts are less. [FAS128, ¶15, fn8]

[11]Refer to paragraph .157. [FAS128, ¶17, fn9]

[12]Refer to paragraphs .116, .140, and .141. [FAS128, ¶17, fn10]

c. The incremental shares (the difference between the number of shares assumed issued and the number of shares assumed purchased) shall be included in the denominator of the diluted EPS computation.[13]

[FAS128, ¶17]

.113 Options and warrants will have a dilutive effect under the treasury stock method only when the average market price of the common stock during the period exceeds the exercise price of the options or warrants (they are "in the money"). Previously reported EPS data shall not be retroactively adjusted as a result of changes in market prices of common stock. [FAS128, ¶18]

.114 Dilutive options or warrants that are issued during a period or that expire or are canceled during a period shall be included in the denominator of diluted EPS for the period that they were outstanding. Likewise, dilutive options or warrants exercised during the period shall be included in the denominator for the period prior to actual exercise. The common shares issued upon exercise of options or warrants shall be included in the denominator for the period after the exercise date. Consequently, incremental shares assumed issued shall be weighted for the period the options or warrants were outstanding, and common shares actually issued shall be weighted for the period the shares were outstanding. [FAS128, ¶19]

---

[13]Consider Corporation Y that has 10,000 warrants outstanding exercisable at $54 per share; the average market price of the common stock during the reporting period is $60. Exercise of the warrants and issuance of 10,000 shares of common stock would be assumed. The $540,000 that would be realized from exercise of the warrants ($54 × 10,000) would be an amount sufficient to acquire 9,000 shares ($540,000/$60). Thus, 1,000 incremental shares (10,000 – 9,000) would be added to the outstanding common shares in computing diluted EPS for the period.

A shortcut formula for that computation follows (note that this formula may not be appropriate for stock-based compensation awards (refer to paragraph .116)):

> Incremental shares = [(market price – exercise price)/market price] × shares assumed issued under option; thus, [($60 – $54)/$60] × 10,000 = 1,000 incremental shares.

[FAS128, ¶17, fn11]

Stock-Based Compensation Arrangements

.115 Fixed awards and nonvested stock[14] (as defined in Section C36, "Compensation: Stock-Based") to be issued to an employee[15] under a stock-based compensation arrangement are considered options for purposes of computing diluted EPS.[16] Such stock-based awards shall be considered to be outstanding as of the grant date for purposes of computing diluted EPS even though their exercise may be contingent upon vesting. Those stock-based awards are included in the diluted EPS computation even if the employee may not receive (or be able to sell) the stock until some future date. Accordingly, all shares to be issued shall be included in computing diluted EPS if the effect is dilutive. The dilutive effect of stock-based compensation arrangements shall be computed using the treasury stock method. If the stock-based awards were granted during the period, the shares issuable must be weighted to reflect the portion of the period during which the awards were outstanding. [FAS128, ¶20]

.116 In applying the treasury stock method described in paragraph .112, the assumed proceeds shall be the sum of (a) the amount, if any, the employee must pay upon exercise, (b) the amount of compensation cost attributed to future services and not yet recognized,[17] and (c) the amount of tax benefits (both deferred and current), if any, that would be credited to additional paid-in capital assuming exercise of the options. Assumed proceeds shall not include compensation ascribed to past services. The tax benefit is the amount resulting from a tax deduction for compensation in excess of compensation expense recognized for financial reporting purposes. That deduction arises from an increase in the market price of the stock under option between the measurement date and the date at which the compensation deduction for income tax purposes is determinable. The amount of the tax benefit shall be determined by a "with-and-without" computation. Paragraph .117 of Section C47, "Compensation to Employees: Stock Purchase and Option Plans," states that in some instances the tax deduction for compensation may be less than the compensation expense recognized for financial reporting purposes. If the result-

---

[14]Restricted stock [is also] included in the computation of diluted EPS based on the provisions for options and warrants in paragraphs .112 through .120. [FAS128, ¶109]

[15]The provisions in paragraphs .115 through .118 also apply to stock-based awards issued to other than employees in exchange for goods and services. [FAS128, ¶20, fn12]

[16]Stock appreciation rights and other variable plan awards are included in the computation of diluted earnings per share pursuant to the provisions of paragraphs .115 through .118. [FAS128, ¶168] Paragraphs .115 through .118 [also] provide guidance on when and how junior stock plans should be reflected in the diluted earnings per share computation. [FAS128, ¶169]

[17]This provision applies only to those stock-based awards for which compensation cost will be recognized in the financial statements in accordance with Section C47, "Compensation to Employees: Stock Purchase and Option Plans," or Section C36. [FAS128, ¶21, fn13]

ing difference in income tax will be deducted from capital in accordance with that paragraph, such taxes to be deducted from capital shall be treated as a reduction of assumed proceeds. [FAS128, ¶21]

.117 If stock-based compensation arrangements are payable in common stock or in cash at the election of either the entity or the employee, the determination of whether such stock-based awards are potential common shares shall be made based on the provisions in paragraph .124. If an entity has a tandem plan (as defined in Section C36) that allows the entity or the employee to make an election involving two or more types of equity instruments, diluted EPS for the period shall be computed based on the terms used in the computation of compensation expense for that period. [FAS128, ¶22]

.118 Performance awards (as defined in Section C36) shall be included in diluted EPS pursuant to the contingent share provisions in paragraphs .125 through .130 of this section. As discussed in paragraph .125 of Section C36, targeted stock price options are not considered to be a performance award. However, because options with a target stock price have a market price contingency, the contingent share provisions of this section shall be applied in determining whether those options are included in the computation of diluted EPS. [FAS128, ¶23]

Written Put Options

.119 Contracts that require that the reporting entity repurchase its own stock, such as written **put options** and forward purchase contracts, shall be reflected in the computation of diluted EPS if the effect is dilutive. If those contracts are "in the money" during the reporting period (the exercise price is above the average market price for that period), the potential dilutive effect on EPS shall be computed using the **reverse treasury stock method.** Under that method:

a. Issuance of sufficient common shares shall be assumed at the beginning of the period (at the average market price during the period) to raise enough proceeds to satisfy the contract.
b. The proceeds from issuance shall be assumed to be used to satisfy the contract (that is, to buy back shares).

c. The incremental shares (the difference between the number of shares assumed issued and the number of shares received from satisfying the contract) shall be included in the denominator of the diluted EPS computation.[18]

[FAS128, ¶24]

Purchased Options

.120 Contracts such as purchased put options and **purchased call options** (options held by the entity on its own stock) shall not be included in the computation of diluted EPS because including them would be antidilutive. That is, the put option would be exercised only when the exercise price is higher than the market price and the call option would be exercised only when the exercise price is lower than the market price; in both instances, the effect would be antidilutive under both the treasury stock method and the reverse treasury stock method, respectively. [FAS128, ¶25]

Convertible Securities

.121 The dilutive effect of convertible securities shall be reflected in diluted EPS by application of the **if-converted method.** Under that method:

a. If an entity has convertible preferred stock outstanding, the preferred dividends applicable to convertible preferred stock shall be added back to the numerator.[19]
b. If an entity has convertible debt outstanding, (1) interest charges applicable to the convertible debt shall be added back to the numerator, (2) to the extent nondiscretionary adjustments based on income[20] made during the period would have been computed differently had the interest on convertible debt never been recognized, the numerator shall be appropriately adjusted, and (3) the numerator shall be adjusted for the income tax effect of (1) and (2).

---

[18]For example, Corporation Z sells 100 put options with an exercise price of $25; the average market price for the period is $20. In computing diluted EPS at the end of the period, Corporation Z assumes it issues 125 shares at $20 per share to satisfy its put obligation of $2,500. The difference between the 125 shares issued and the 100 shares received from satisfying the put option (25 incremental shares) would be added to the denominator of diluted EPS. [FAS128, ¶24, fn14]

[19]The amount of preferred dividends added back will be the amount of preferred dividends for convertible preferred stock deducted from income from continuing operations (and from net income) in computing income available to common stockholders pursuant to paragraph .104. [FAS128, ¶26, fn15]

[20]Nondiscretionary adjustments include any expenses or charges that are determined based on the income (loss) for the period, such as profit-sharing and royalty agreements. [FAS128, ¶26, fn16]

c. The convertible preferred stock or convertible debt shall be assumed to have been converted at the beginning of the period (or at time of issuance, if later), and the resulting common shares shall be included in the denominator.

[FAS128, ¶26]

.122 In applying the if-converted method, conversion shall not be assumed for purposes of computing diluted EPS if the effect would be antidilutive. Convertible preferred stock is antidilutive whenever the amount of the dividend declared in or accumulated for the current period per common share obtainable on conversion exceeds basic EPS. Similarly, convertible debt is antidilutive whenever its interest (net of tax and nondiscretionary adjustments) per common share obtainable on conversion exceeds basic EPS. [FAS128, ¶27]

.123 Dilutive securities that are issued during a period and dilutive convertible securities for which conversion options lapse, for which preferred stock is redeemed, or for which related debt is extinguished during a period shall be included in the denominator of diluted EPS for the period that they were outstanding. [FAS135, ¶4(v)] Likewise, dilutive convertible securities converted during a period shall be included in the denominator for the period prior to actual conversion. The common shares issued upon actual conversion shall be included in the denominator for the period after the date of conversion. Consequently, shares assumed issued shall be weighted for the period the convertible securities were outstanding, and common shares actually issued shall be weighted for the period the shares were outstanding. [FAS128, ¶28]

Contracts That May Be Settled in Stock or Cash

.124 If an entity issues a contract that may be settled in common stock or in cash at the election of either the entity or the holder, the determination of whether that contract shall be reflected in the computation of diluted EPS shall be made based on the facts available each period.[21] It shall be presumed that the contract will be settled in common stock and the resulting potential common shares included in diluted EPS (in accordance with the relevant provisions of this section) if the effect is more dilutive. A contract that is reported as an asset or liability for accounting purposes may require an adjustment to the numerator for any changes in income or loss that would result if the contract had been reported as an equity instrument for accounting purposes during the period. That adjustment is similar to the adjustments required for convertible debt in paragraph .121(b). The presumption that the contract will be settled in common stock may be overcome if

[21] An example of such a contract is a written put option that gives the holder a choice of settling in common stock or in cash. Stock-based compensation arrangements that are payable in common stock or in cash at the election of either the entity or the employee shall be accounted for pursuant to this paragraph. [FAS128, ¶29, fn17]

past experience or a stated policy provides a reasonable basis to believe that the contract will be paid partially or wholly in cash. [FAS128, ¶29] [Refer to paragraph .1001 for an EITF Issue that provides interpretive guidance on this paragraph.]

Contingently Issuable Shares

.125 Shares whose issuance is contingent upon the satisfaction of certain conditions shall be considered outstanding and included in the computation of diluted EPS as follows:

a. If all necessary conditions have been satisfied by the end of the period (the events have occurred), those shares shall be included as of the beginning of the period in which the conditions were satisfied (or as of the date of the contingent stock agreement, if later).
b. If all necessary conditions have not been satisfied by the end of the period, the number of contingently issuable shares included in diluted EPS shall be based on the number of shares, if any, that would be issuable if the end of the reporting period were the end of the contingency period (for example, the number of shares that would be issuable based on current period earnings or period-end market price) and if the result would be dilutive. Those contingently issuable shares shall be included in the denominator of diluted EPS as of the beginning of the period (or as of the date of the contingent stock agreement, if later).[22]

Paragraphs .126 through .129 provide general guidelines that shall be applied in determining the EPS impact of different types of contingencies that may be included in contingent stock agreements. [FAS128, ¶30]

.126 If attainment or maintenance of a specified amount of earnings is the condition and if that amount has been attained, the additional shares shall be considered to be outstanding for the purpose of computing diluted EPS if the effect is dilutive. The diluted EPS computation shall include those shares that would be issued under the conditions of the contract based on the assumption that the current amount of earnings will remain unchanged until the end of the agreement, but only if the effect would be dilutive. Because the amount of earnings may change in a future period, basic EPS shall not include such contingently issuable shares because all necessary conditions have not been satisfied. Paragraph .163 provides an example of that provision. [FAS128, ¶31]

---

[22]For year-to-date computations, contingent shares shall be included on a weighted-average basis. That is, contingent shares shall be weighted for the interim periods in which they were included in the computation of diluted EPS. [FAS128, ¶30, fn18] That approach is similar to the method used for including incremental shares in year-to-date computations when applying the treasury stock method [as discussed in paragraph .139]. [FAS128, ¶121] [Refer to paragraph .1001 for an EITF Issue that provides interpretive guidance on this footnote.]

.127 The number of shares contingently issuable may depend on the market price of the stock at a future date. In that case, computations of diluted EPS shall reflect the number of shares that would be issued based on the current market price at the end of the period being reported on if the effect is dilutive. If the condition is based on an average of market prices over some period of time, the average for that period shall be used. Because the market price may change in a future period, basic EPS shall not include such contingently issuable shares because all necessary conditions have not been satisfied. [FAS128, ¶32]

.128 In some cases, the number of shares contingently issuable may depend on both future earnings and future prices of the shares. In that case, the determination of the number of shares included in diluted EPS shall be based on both conditions, that is, earnings to date and current market price—as they exist at the end of each reporting period. If *both* conditions are not met at the end of the reporting period, no contingently issuable shares shall be included in diluted EPS. [FAS128, ¶33]

.129 If the contingency is based on a condition other than earnings or market price (for example, opening a certain number of retail stores), the contingent shares shall be included in the computation of diluted EPS based on the assumption that the current status of the condition will remain unchanged until the end of the contingency period. Paragraph .163 provides an example of that provision. [FAS128, ¶34]

.130 Contingently issuable potential common shares (other than those covered by a contingent stock agreement, such as contingently issuable convertible securities) shall be included in diluted EPS as follows:

a. An entity shall determine whether the potential common shares may be assumed to be issuable based on the conditions specified for their issuance pursuant to the contingent share provisions in paragraphs .125 through .129.
b. If those potential common shares should be reflected in diluted EPS, an entity shall determine their impact on the computation of diluted EPS by following the provisions for options and warrants in paragraphs .112 through .120, the provisions for convertible securities in paragraphs .121 through .123, and the provisions for contracts that may be settled in stock or cash in paragraph .124, as appropriate.[23]

However, exercise or conversion shall not be assumed for purposes of computing diluted EPS unless exercise or conversion of similar outstanding potential common shares that are not contingently issuable is assumed. [FAS128, ¶35]

---

[23]Neither interest nor dividends shall be imputed for the additional contingently issuable convertible securities because any imputed amount would be reversed by the if-converted adjustments for assumed conversions. [FAS128, ¶35, fn19]

Presentation on Face of Income Statement

.131 Entities with simple capital structures, that is, those with only common stock outstanding, shall present basic per-share amounts for income from continuing operations[24] and for net income on the face of the income statement. All other entities shall present basic and diluted per-share amounts for income from continuing operations and for net income on the face of the income statement with equal prominence. [FAS128, ¶36]

.132 An entity that reports a discontinued operation, an extraordinary item, or the cumulative effect of an accounting change in a period shall present basic and diluted per-share amounts for those line items either on the face of the income statement or in the notes to the financial statements. Per-share amounts not required to be presented by this section that an entity chooses to disclose shall be computed in accordance with this section and disclosed only in the notes to the financial statements; it shall be noted whether the per-share amounts are pretax or net of tax.[25] [FAS128, ¶37]

Periods Presented

.133 Earnings per share data shall be presented for all periods for which an income statement or summary of earnings is presented. If diluted EPS data are reported for at least one period, they shall be reported for all periods presented, even if they are the same amounts as basic EPS. If basic and diluted EPS are the same amount, dual presentation can be accomplished in one line on the income statement. [FAS128, ¶38]

Terminology

.134 The terms *basic EPS* and *diluted EPS* are used in this section to identify EPS data to be presented and are not required to be captions used in the income statement. There are no explicit requirements for the terms to be used in the presentation of basic and diluted EPS; terms such as *earnings per common share* and *earnings per common share—assuming dilution,* respectively, are appropriate. [FAS128, ¶39]

---

[24]Refer to footnote 4. [FAS128, ¶36, fn20]

[25]Paragraph .135 of Section C25, "Cash Flows Statement," prohibits reporting an amount of cash flow per share. [FAS128, ¶37, fn21]

Disclosure Requirements

.135 For each period for which an income statement is presented, an entity shall disclose the following:

a. A reconciliation of the numerators and the denominators of the basic and diluted per-share computations for income from continuing operations.[26] The reconciliation shall include the individual income and share amount effects of all securities that affect earnings per share.[27] [FAS128, ¶40] Insignificant reconciling items need not be itemized as part of the reconciliation and [can] be combined (aggregated). [FAS128, ¶138] Paragraph .162 provides an example of that disclosure.
b. The effect that has been given to preferred dividends in arriving at income available to common stockholders in computing basic EPS.
c. Securities (including those issuable pursuant to contingent stock agreements) that could potentially dilute basic EPS in the future that were not included in the computation of diluted EPS because to do so would have been antidilutive for the period(s) presented. [FAS128, ¶40]

.136 For the latest period for which an income statement is presented, an entity shall provide a description of any transaction that occurs after the end of the most recent period but before issuance of the financial statements that would have changed materially the number of common shares or potential common shares outstanding at the end of the period if the transaction had occurred before the end of the period. Examples of those transactions include the issuance or acquisition of common shares; the issuance of warrants, options, or convertible securities; the resolution of a contingency pursuant to a contingent stock agreement; and the conversion or exercise of potential common shares outstanding at the end of the period into common shares. [FAS128, ¶41]

Computational Guidance

.137 The determination of EPS data as required by this section considers the complexities of the capital structures of some entities. The calculations also shall give effect to matters such as stock dividends or splits and business combinations. Guidelines for dealing with some common computational matters and some complex capital structures are set forth in paragraphs .138 through .157. [Those paragraphs are] an integral part of the requirements of this section. [FAS128, ¶42]

---

[26]Refer to footnote 4. [FAS128, ¶40, fn22]

[27]An entity is encouraged to refer to pertinent information about securities included in the EPS computations that is provided elsewhere in the financial statements as prescribed by Section C24, "Capital Structure: Disclosures," and other accounting pronouncements. [FAS128, ¶40, fn23]

Computing a Weighted Average

.138 The weighted-average number of shares discussed in this section is an arithmetical mean average of shares outstanding and assumed to be outstanding for EPS computations. The most precise average would be the sum of the shares determined on a daily basis divided by the number of days in the period. Less-precise averaging methods may be used, however, as long as they produce reasonable results. Methods that introduce artificial weighting, such as the "Rule of 78" method, are not acceptable for computing a weighted-average number of shares for EPS computations. [FAS128, ¶45]

Applying the Treasury Stock Method

Year-to-Date Computations

.139 The number of incremental shares included in quarterly diluted EPS shall be computed using the average market prices during the three months included in the reporting period. For year-to-date diluted EPS, the number of incremental shares to be included in the denominator shall be determined by computing a year-to-date weighted average of the number of incremental shares included in each quarterly diluted EPS computation. Exhibit 159E (footnote a) provides an example of that provision. [FAS128, ¶46] [Refer to paragraph .1001 for an EITF Issue that provides interpretive guidance on this paragraph.]

Average Market Price

.140 In applying the treasury stock method, the average market price of common stock shall represent a meaningful average. Theoretically, every market transaction for an entity's common stock could be included in determining the average market price. As a practical matter, however, a simple average of weekly or monthly prices usually will be adequate. [FAS128, ¶47]

.141 Generally, closing market prices are adequate for use in computing the average market price. When prices fluctuate widely, however, an average of the high and low prices for the period that the price represents usually would produce a more representative price. The method used to compute the average market price shall be used consistently unless it is no longer representative because of changed conditions. For example, an entity that uses closing market prices to compute the average market price for several years of relatively stable market prices might need to change to an average of high and low prices if prices start fluctuating greatly and the closing market prices no longer produce a representative average market price. [FAS128, ¶48]

Options and Warrants and Their Equivalents

.142 Options or warrants to purchase convertible securities shall be assumed to be exercised to purchase the convertible security whenever the average prices of both the convertible security and the common stock obtainable upon conversion are above the exercise price of the options or warrants. However, exercise shall not be assumed unless conversion of similar outstanding convertible securities, if any, also is assumed. The treasury stock method shall be applied to determine the incremental number of convertible securities that are assumed to be issued and immediately converted into common stock. Interest or dividends shall not be imputed for the incremental convertible securities because any imputed amount would be reversed by the if-converted adjustments for assumed conversions. [FAS128, ¶49]

.143 Paragraphs .144 through .146 provide guidance on how certain options, warrants, and convertible securities should be included in the computation of diluted EPS. Conversion or exercise of the potential common shares discussed in those paragraphs shall not be reflected in diluted EPS unless the effect is dilutive. Those potential common shares will have a dilutive effect if (a) the average market price of the related common stock for the period exceeds the exercise price or (b) the security to be tendered is selling at a price below that at which it may be tendered under the option or warrant agreement and the resulting discount is sufficient to establish an effective exercise price below the market price of the common stock obtainable upon exercise. When several conversion alternatives exist, the computation shall give effect to the alternative that is most advantageous to the holder of the convertible security. Similar treatment shall be given to preferred stock that has similar provisions or to other securities that have conversion options that permit the investor to pay cash for a more favorable conversion rate. [FAS128, ¶50]

.144 Options or warrants may permit or require the tendering of debt or other securities of the issuer (or its parent or its subsidiary) in payment of all or a portion of the exercise price. In computing diluted EPS, those options or warrants shall be assumed to be exercised and the debt or other securities shall be assumed to be tendered. If tendering cash would be more advantageous to the option holder or warrant holder and the contract permits tendering cash, the treasury stock method shall be applied. Interest (net of tax) on any debt assumed to be tendered shall be added back as an adjustment to the numerator. The numerator also shall be adjusted for any nondiscretionary adjustments based on income (net of tax). The treasury stock method shall be applied for proceeds assumed to be received in cash. [FAS128, ¶51]

.145 The underlying terms of certain options or warrants may require that the proceeds received from the exercise of those securities be applied to retire debt or other securities of the issuer (or its parent or its subsidiary). In computing diluted EPS, those options or warrants shall be assumed to be exercised and the proceeds applied to purchase the debt at its average market price rather than to purchase common stock under the treasury stock method. The treasury stock method shall be applied, however, for excess proceeds received from the assumed exercise. Interest, net of tax, on any debt assumed to be purchased shall be added back as an adjustment to the numerator. The numerator also shall be adjusted for any nondiscretionary adjustments based on income (net of tax). [FAS128, ¶52]

.146 Convertible securities that permit or require the payment of cash by the holder of the security at conversion are considered the equivalent of warrants. In computing diluted EPS, the proceeds assumed to be received shall be assumed to be applied to purchase common stock under the treasury stock method and the convertible security shall be assumed to be converted under the if-converted method. [FAS128, ¶53]

Restatement of EPS Data

Stock Dividends or Stock Splits

.147 If the number of common shares outstanding increases as a result of a stock dividend or stock split[28] or decreases as a result of a reverse stock split, the computations of basic and diluted EPS shall be adjusted retroactively for all periods presented to reflect that change in capital structure. If changes in common stock resulting from stock dividends, stock splits, or reverse stock splits occur after the close of the period but before issuance of the financial statements, the per-share computations for those and any prior-period financial statements presented shall be based on the new number of shares. If per-share computations reflect such changes in the number of shares, that fact shall be disclosed. [FAS128, ¶54]

Rights Issues

.148 A **rights issue** whose exercise price at issuance is less than the fair value of the stock contains a bonus element that is somewhat similar to a stock dividend. If a rights issue contains a bonus element and the rights issue is offered to all existing stockholders, basic and diluted EPS shall be adjusted retroactively for the bonus element for all periods presented. If the ability to exercise the rights issue is contingent on some event other than the passage of time, the provisions of this paragraph shall not be applicable until that contingency is resolved. [FAS128, ¶55]

---

[28]Refer to Section C20, "Capital Stock: Stock Dividends and Stock Splits." [FAS128, ¶54, fn24]

.149 The number of common shares used in computing basic and diluted EPS for all periods prior to the rights issue shall be the number of common shares outstanding immediately prior to the issue multiplied by the following factor: (fair value per share immediately prior to the exercise of the rights)/(theoretical ex-rights fair value per share). Theoretical ex-rights fair value per share shall be computed by adding the aggregate fair value of the shares immediately prior to the exercise of the rights to the proceeds expected from the exercise of the rights and dividing by the number of shares outstanding after the exercise of the rights. Paragraph .165 provides an example of that provision. If the rights themselves are to be publicly traded separately from the shares prior to the exercise date, fair value for the purposes of this computation shall be established at the close of the last day on which the shares are traded together with the rights. [FAS128, ¶56]

Prior-Period Adjustments

.150 Certain sections require that a restatement of the results of operations of a prior period be included in the income statement or summary of earnings. In those instances, EPS data given for the prior period or periods shall be restated. The effect of the restatement, expressed in per-share terms, shall be disclosed in the period of restatement. [FAS128, ¶57]

.151 Restated EPS data shall be computed as if the restated income or loss had been reported originally in the prior period or periods. Thus, it is possible that common stock assumed to be issued upon exercise, conversion, or issuance of potential common shares in accordance with the provisions of this section may not be included in the computation of restated EPS amounts. That is, retroactive restatement of income from continuing operations could cause potential common shares originally determined to be dilutive to become antidilutive pursuant to the control number provision in paragraph .110. The reverse also is true. Retroactive restatement also may cause the numerator of the EPS computation to change by an amount that differs from the amount of the retroactive adjustment. [FAS128, ¶58]

Business Combinations and Reorganizations

.152 When common shares are issued to acquire a business in a business combination, the computations of earnings per share shall recognize the existence of the new shares only from the acquisition date. In reorganizations, EPS computations shall be based on analysis of the particular transaction and the provisions of this section. [FAS128, ¶59]

Participating Securities and Two-Class Common Stock

.153 The capital structures of some entities include:

a. Securities that may participate in dividends with common stocks according to a predetermined formula (for example, two for one) with, at times, an upper limit on the extent of participation (for example, up to, but not beyond, a specified amount per share)
b. A class of common stock with different dividend rates from those of another class of common stock but without prior or senior rights.

[FAS128, ¶60]

.154 The if-converted method shall be used for those securities that are convertible into common stock if the effect is dilutive. For those securities that are not convertible into a class of common stock, the "two class" method of computing earnings per share shall be used. The two-class method is an earnings allocation formula that determines earnings per share for each class of common stock and participating security according to dividends declared (or accumulated) and participation rights in undistributed earnings. Under that method:

a. Income from continuing operations (or net income) shall be reduced by the amount of dividends declared in the current period for each class of stock and by the contractual amount of dividends (or interest on participating income bonds) that must be paid for the current period (for example, unpaid cumulative dividends).[29]
b. The remaining earnings shall be allocated to common stock and participating securities to the extent that each security may share in earnings as if all of the earnings for the period had been distributed. The total earnings allocated to each security shall be determined by adding together the amount allocated for dividends and the amount allocated for a participation feature.
c. The total earnings allocated to each security shall be divided by the number of outstanding shares of the security to which the earnings are allocated to determine the earnings per share for the security.
d. Basic and diluted EPS data shall be presented for each class of common stock.

[29]Dividends declared in the current period do not include dividends declared in respect of prior-year unpaid cumulative dividends. Preferred dividends that are cumulative only if earned are deducted only to the extent that they are earned. [FAS128, ¶61, fn25]

For the diluted EPS computation, outstanding common shares shall include all potential common shares assumed issued. Paragraph .166 provides an example of that provision. [FAS128, ¶61]

Securities of Subsidiaries

.155 The effect on consolidated EPS of options, warrants, and convertible securities issued by a subsidiary depends on whether the securities issued by the subsidiary enable their holders to obtain common stock of the subsidiary company or common stock of the parent company. The following general guidelines shall be used for computing consolidated diluted EPS by entities with subsidiaries that have issued common stock or potential common shares to parties other than the parent company:[30]

a. Securities issued by a subsidiary that enable their holders to obtain the subsidiary's common stock shall be included in computing the subsidiary's EPS data. Those per-share earnings of the subsidiary shall then be included in the consolidated EPS computations based on the consolidated group's holding of the subsidiary's securities. Paragraph .167 provides an example of that provision.
b. Securities of a subsidiary that are convertible into its parent company's common stock shall be considered among the potential common shares of the parent company for the purpose of computing consolidated diluted EPS. Likewise, a subsidiary's options or warrants to purchase common stock of the parent company shall be considered among the potential common shares of the parent company in computing consolidated diluted EPS. Paragraph .167 provides an example of that provision.

As noted in paragraph .105 of Section I82, "Investments: Equity Method," the above provisions are applicable to investments in common stock of corporate joint ventures and investee companies accounted for under the equity method. [FAS128, ¶62]

.156 The if-converted method shall be used in determining the EPS impact of securities issued by a parent company that are convertible into common stock of a subsidiary company or an investee company accounted for under the equity method. That is, the securities shall be assumed to be converted and the numerator (income available to common stockholders) adjusted as necessary in accordance with the provisions in paragraph .121(a)

---

[30]This section is based on the current practice of deducting income attributable to the noncontrolling interest (minority interest) to arrive at consolidated net income in the consolidated financial statements. The October 1995 FASB Exposure Draft, *Consolidated Financial Statements: Policy and Procedures,* would change that practice to require that net income attributable to the noncontrolling interest be deducted from consolidated net income to arrive at an amount called *net income attributable to the controlling interest.* [However,] the EPS computation would continue to be based only on net income attributable to the controlling interest. [FAS128, ¶140]

and (b). In addition to those adjustments, the numerator shall be adjusted appropriately for any change in the income recorded by the parent (such as dividend income or equity method income) due to the increase in the number of common shares of the subsidiary or equity method investee outstanding as a result of the assumed conversion. The denominator of the diluted EPS computation would not be affected because the number of shares of parent company common stock outstanding would not change upon assumed conversion. [FAS128, ¶63]

Partially Paid Shares and Partially Paid Stock Subscriptions

.157 If an entity has common shares issued in a partially paid form[31] and those shares are entitled to dividends in proportion to the amount paid, the common-share equivalent of those partially paid shares shall be included in the computation of basic EPS to the extent that they were entitled to participate in dividends. Partially paid stock subscriptions that do not share in dividends until fully paid are considered the equivalent of warrants and shall be included in diluted EPS by use of the treasury stock method. That is, the unpaid balance shall be assumed to be proceeds used to purchase stock under the treasury stock method. The number of shares included in diluted EPS shall be the difference between the number of shares subscribed and the number of shares assumed to be purchased. [FAS128, ¶64]

Illustrations

.158 Paragraphs .159 through .170 illustrate this section's application to entities with complex capital structures. Certain assumptions have been made to simplify the computations and focus on the issue at hand in each illustration. [FAS128, ¶147]

Illustration 1—Computation of Basic and Diluted Earnings per Share and Income Statement Presentation

.159 Exhibits 159A through 159E illustrate the quarterly and annual computations of basic and diluted EPS in the year 20X1 for Corporation A, which has a complex capital structure. The control number used in this illustration (and in Illustration 2) is income before extraordinary item and accounting change because Corporation A has no discontinued operations. Paragraph .160 illustrates the presentation of basic and diluted EPS on the face of the income statement. The facts assumed are as follows:

[31] Issuing common shares that are not fully paid is permitted in some countries. [FAS128, ¶64, fn27]

Average market price of common stock. The average market prices of common stock for the calendar-year 20X1 were as follows:

First quarter	$59
Second quarter	$70
Third quarter	$72
Fourth quarter	$72

The average market price of common stock from July 1 to September 1, 20X1 was $71.

Common stock. The number of shares of common stock outstanding at the beginning of 20X1 was 3,300,000. On March 1, 20X1, 100,000 shares of common stock were issued for cash.

Convertible debentures. In the last quarter of 20X0, 4 percent convertible debentures with a principal amount of $10,000,000 due in 20 years were sold for cash at $1,000 (par). Interest is payable semiannually on November 1 and May 1. Each $1,000 debenture is convertible into 20 shares of common stock. No debentures were converted in 20X0. The entire issue was converted on April 1, 20X1, because the issue was called by the Corporation.

Convertible preferred stock. In the second quarter of 20X0, 600,000 shares of convertible preferred stock were issued for assets in a purchase transaction. The quarterly dividend on each share of that convertible preferred stock is $0.05, payable at the end of the quarter. Each share is convertible into one share of common stock. Holders of 500,000 shares of that convertible preferred stock converted their preferred stock into common stock on June 1, 20X1.

Warrants. Warrants to buy 500,000 shares of common stock at $60 per share for a period of 5 years were issued on January 1, 20X1. All outstanding warrants were exercised on September 1, 20X1.

Options. Options to buy 1,000,000 shares of common stock at $85 per share for a period of 10 years were issued on July 1, 20X1. No options were exercised during 20X1 because the exercise price of the options exceeded the market price of the common stock.

Tax rate. The tax rate was 40 percent for 20X1.

Year 20X1	Income (Loss) before Extraordinary Item and Accounting Change[a]	Net Income (Loss)
First quarter	$3,000,000	$ 3,000,000
Second quarter	4,500,000	4,500,000
Third quarter	500,000	(1,500,000)[b]
Fourth quarter	(500,000)	3,750,000[c]
Full year	$7,500,000	$ 9,750,000

[a]This is the control number (before adjusting for preferred dividends). Refer to paragraph .110.

[b]Corporation A had a $2 million extraordinary loss (net of tax) in the third quarter.

[c]Corporation A had a $4.25 million cumulative effect of an accounting change (net of tax) in the fourth quarter.

[FAS128, ¶148]

Exhibit 159A

Computation of Basic and Diluted EPS for First Quarter 20X1

Basic EPS Computation

Net income	$3,000,000
Less: Preferred stock dividends	(30,000)[a]
Income available to common stockholders	$2,970,000

[a]600,000 shares × $0.05

Dates Outstanding	Shares Outstanding	Fraction of Period	Weighted-Average Shares
January 1–February 28	3,300,000	2/3	2,200,000
Issuance of common stock on March 1	100,000		
March 1–March 31	3,400,000	1/3	1,133,333
Weighted-average shares			3,333,333

Basic EPS $0.89

The equation for computing basic EPS is:

$$\frac{\text{Income available to common stockholders}}{\text{Weighted-average shares}}$$

Diluted EPS Computation

Income available to common stockholders		$2,970,000
Plus: Income impact of assumed conversions		
Preferred stock dividends	$ 30,000[a]	
Interest on 4% convertible debentures	60,000[b]	
Effect of assumed conversions		90,000
Income available to common stockholders + assumed conversions		$3,060,000
Weighted-average shares		3,333,333
Plus: Incremental shares from assumed conversions		
Warrants	0[c]	
Convertible preferred stock	600,000	
4% convertible debentures	200,000	
Dilutive potential common shares		800,000
Adjusted weighted-average shares		4,133,333

Diluted EPS $0.74

The equation for computing diluted EPS is:

$$\frac{\text{Income available to common stockholders + Effect of assumed conversions}}{\text{Weighted-average shares + Dilutive potential common shares}}$$

[a]600,000 shares × $0.05

[b]($10,000,000 × 4%) ÷ 4; less taxes at 40%

[c]The warrants were not assumed exercised because they were antidilutive in the period ($60 exercise price > $59 average price).

[FAS128, ¶148]

Exhibit 159B

Computation of Basic and Diluted EPS for Second Quarter 20X1

Basic EPS Computation

Net income	$4,500,000
Less: Preferred stock dividends	(5,000)[a]
Income available to common stockholders	$4,495,000

[a]600,000 shares × $0.05

Dates Outstanding	Shares Outstanding	Fraction of Period	Weighted-Average Shares
April 1	3,400,000		
Conversion of 4% debentures on April 1	200,000		
April 1–May 31	3,600,000	2/3	2,400,000
Conversion of preferred stock on June 1	500,000		
June 1–June 30	4,100,000	1/3	1,366,667
Weighted-average shares			3,766,667

Basic EPS $1.19

The equation for computing basic EPS is:

$$\frac{\text{Income available to common stockholders}}{\text{Weighted-average shares}}$$

Diluted EPS Computation

Income available to common stockholders		$4,495,000
Plus: Income impact of assumed conversions		
Preferred stock dividends	$ 5,000[a]	
Effect of assumed conversions		5,000
Income available to common stockholders + assumed conversions		$4,500,000
Weighted-average shares		3,766,667
Plus: Incremental shares from assumed conversions		
Warrants	71,429[b]	
Convertible preferred stock	433,333[c]	
Dilutive potential common shares		504,762
Adjusted weighted-average shares		4,271,429

Diluted EPS $1.05

The equation for computing diluted EPS is:

$$\frac{\text{Income available to common stockholders + Effect of assumed conversions}}{\text{Weighted-average shares + Dilutive potential common shares}}$$

[a]100,000 shares × $0.05

[b]$60 × 500,000 = $30,000,000; $30,000,000 ÷ $70 = 428,571; 500,000 – 428,571 = 71,429 shares **OR** [($70 – $60) ÷ $70] × 500,000 shares = 71,429 shares

[c](600,000 shares × 2/3) + (100,000 shares × 1/3)

[FAS128, ¶148]

Exhibit 159C

Computation of Basic and Diluted EPS for Third Quarter 20X1

Basic EPS Computation

Income before extraordinary item	$ 500,000
Less: Preferred stock dividends	(5,000)
Income available to common stockholders	495,000
Extraordinary item	(2,000,000)
Net loss available to common stockholders	$(1,505,000)

Dates Outstanding	Shares Outstanding	Fraction of Period	Weighted-Average Shares
July 1–August 31	4,100,000	2/3	2,733,333
Exercise of warrants on September 1	500,000		
September 1–September 30	4,600,000	1/3	1,533,333
Weighted-average shares			4,266,666

Basic EPS

Income before extraordinary item	**$ 0.12**
Extraordinary item	**$(0.47)**
Net loss	**$(0.35)**

The equation for computing basic EPS is:

$$\frac{\text{Income available to common stockholders}}{\text{Weighted-average shares}}$$

Diluted EPS Computation

Income available to common stockholders		$ 495,000
Plus: Income impact of assumed conversions		
Preferred stock dividends	$ 5,000	
Effect of assumed conversions		5,000
Income available to common stockholders + assumed conversions		500,000
Extraordinary item		(2,000,000)
Net loss available to common stockholders + assumed conversions		$(1,500,000)
Weighted-average shares		4,266,666
Plus: Incremental shares from assumed conversions		
Warrants	51,643[a]	
Convertible preferred stock	100,000	
Dilutive potential common shares		151,643
Adjusted weighted-average shares		4,418,309

Diluted EPS

Income before extraordinary item	**$ 0.11**
Extraordinary item	**$(0.45)**
Net loss	**$(0.34)**

The equation for computing diluted EPS is:

$$\frac{\text{Income available to common stockholders + Effect of assumed conversions}}{\text{Weighted-average shares + Dilutive potential common shares}}$$

Note: The incremental shares from assumed conversions are included in computing the diluted per-share amounts for the extraordinary item and net loss even though they are antidilutive. This is because the control number (income before extraordinary item, adjusted for preferred dividends) was income, not a loss. (Refer to paragraphs .110 and .111.)

[a] [($71 – $60) ÷ $71] × 500,000 = 77,465 shares; 77,465 × 2/3 = 51,643 shares

[FAS128, ¶148]

Exhibit 159D

Computation of Basic and Diluted EPS for Fourth Quarter 20X1

Basic and Diluted EPS Computation

Loss before accounting change	$ (500,000)
Plus: Preferred stock dividends	(5,000)
Loss available to common stockholders	(505,000)
Accounting change	4,250,000
Net income available to common stockholders	$3,745,000

Dates Outstanding	Shares Outstanding	Fraction of Period	Weighted-Average Shares
October 1–December 31	4,600,000	3/3	4,600,000
Weighted-average shares			4,600,000

Basic and Diluted EPS

Loss before accounting change	**$(0.11)**
Accounting change	**$ 0.92**
Net income	**$ 0.81**

The equation for computing basic (and diluted) EPS is:

$$\frac{\text{Income available to common stockholders}}{\text{Weighted-average shares}}$$

Note: The incremental shares from assumed conversions are not included in computing the diluted per-share amounts for the accounting change and net income because the control number (loss before accounting change, adjusted for preferred dividends) was a loss, not income. (Refer to paragraphs .110 and .111.)

[FAS128, ¶148]

(This page intentionally left blank.)

Exhibit 159E

Computation of Basic and Diluted EPS for Full Year 20X1

Basic EPS Computation

Income before extraordinary item and accounting change	$ 7,500,000
Less: Preferred stock dividends	(45,000)
Income available to common stockholders	7,455,000
Extraordinary item	(2,000,000)
Accounting change	4,250,000
Net income available to common stockholders	$ 9,705,000

Dates Outstanding	Shares Outstanding	Fraction of Period	Weighted-Average Shares
January 1–February 28	3,300,000	2/12	550,000
Issuance of common stock on March 1	100,000		
March 1–March 31	3,400,000	1/12	283,333
Conversion of 4% debenture on April 1	200,000		
April 1–May 31	3,600,000	2/12	600,000
Conversion of preferred stock on June 1	500,000		
June 1–August 31	4,100,000	3/12	1,025,000
Exercise of warrants on September 1	500,000		
September 1–December 31	4,600,000	4/12	1,533,333
Weighted-average shares			3,991,666

Basic EPS

Income before extraordinary item and accounting change	**$ 1.87**
Extraordinary item	**$(0.50)**
Accounting change	**$ 1.06**
Net income	**$ 2.43**

The equation for computing basic EPS is:

$$\frac{\text{Income available to common stockholders}}{\text{Weighted-average shares}}$$

Diluted EPS Computation

Income available to common stockholders		$ 7,455,000
Plus: Income impact of assumed conversions		
Preferred stock dividends	$ 45,000	
Interest on 4% convertible debentures	60,000	
Effect of assumed conversions		105,000
Income available to common stockholders + assumed conversions		7,560,000
Extraordinary item		(2,000,000)
Accounting change		4,250,000
Net income available to common stockholders + assumed conversions		$ 9,810,000
Weighted-average shares		3,991,666
Plus: Incremental shares from assumed conversions		
Warrants	30,768[a]	
Convertible preferred stock	308,333[b]	
4% convertible debentures	50,000[c]	
Dilutive potential common shares		389,101
Adjusted weighted-average shares		4,380,767

Diluted EPS

Income before extraordinary item and accounting change	**$ 1.73**
Extraordinary item	**$(0.46)**
Accounting change	**$ 0.97**
Net income	**$ 2.24**

The equation for computing diluted EPS is:

$$\frac{\text{Income available to common stockholders + Effect of assumed conversions}}{\text{Weighted-average shares + Dilutive potential common shares}}$$

[a](71,429 shares × 3/12) + (51,643 shares × 3/12)

[b](600,000 shares × 5/12) + (100,000 shares × 7/12)

[c]200,000 shares × 3/12

[FAS128, ¶148]

.160 Exhibit 160A illustrates how Corporation A might present its EPS data on its income statement. Note that the per-share amounts for the extraordinary item and the accounting change are not required to be shown on the face of the income statement. [FAS128, ¶149]

Exhibit 160A

Corporation A
EPS Presentation on Income Statement

	For the Year Ended 20X1
Earnings per common share	
Income before extraordinary item and accounting change	$ 1.87
Extraordinary item	(0.50)
Cumulative effect of a change in accounting principle	1.06
Net income	$ 2.43
Earnings per common share—assuming dilution	
Income before extraordinary item and accounting change	$ 1.73
Extraordinary item	(0.46)
Cumulative effect of a change in accounting principle	0.97
Net income	$ 2.24

[FAS128, ¶149]

.161 Exhibit 161A includes the quarterly and annual EPS data for Corporation A. The purpose of this exhibit is to illustrate that the sum of the four quarters' EPS data will not necessarily equal the annual EPS data. This section does not require disclosure of this information. [FAS128, ¶150]

Exhibit 161A

Optional Quarterly and Annual EPS Presentation

	First Quarter	Second Quarter	Third Quarter	Fourth Quarter	Full Year
Basic EPS					
Income (loss) before extraordinary item and accounting change	$0.89	$1.19	$ 0.12	$(0.11)	$ 1.87
Extraordinary item	—	—	(0.47)	—	(0.50)
Accounting change	—	—	—	0.92	1.06
Net income (loss)	$0.89	$1.19	$(0.35)	$ 0.81	$ 2.43
Diluted EPS					
Income (loss) before extraordinary item and accounting change	$0.74	$1.05	$ 0.11	$(0.11)	$ 1.73
Extraordinary item	—	—	(0.45)	—	(0.46)
Accounting change	—	—	—	0.92	0.97
Net income (loss)	$0.74	$1.05	$(0.34)	$ 0.81	$ 2.24

[FAS128, ¶150]

Illustration 2—Earnings per Share Disclosures

.162 Exhibit 162A is an illustration of the reconciliation of the numerators and denominators of the basic and diluted EPS computations for "income before extraordinary item and accounting change" and other related disclosures required by paragraph .135 for Corporation A in Illustration 1. **Note:** Section C36, paragraphs .144 through .147, has specific disclosure requirements related to stock-based compensation arrangements. [FAS128, ¶151]

Exhibit 162A

Corporation A
Earnings per Share Disclosure

	For the Year Ended 20X1		
	Income (Numerator)	**Shares (Denominator)**	**Per-Share Amount**
Income before extraordinary item and accounting change	$7,500,000		
Less: Preferred stock dividends	(45,000)		
Basic EPS			
Income available to common stockholders	7,455,000	3,991,666	$1.87
Effect of Dilutive Securities			
Warrants		30,768	
Convertible preferred stock	45,000	308,333	
4% convertible debentures	60,000	50,000	
Diluted EPS			
Income available to common stockholders + assumed conversions	$7,560,000	4,380,767	$1.73

Options to purchase 1,000,000 shares of common stock at $85 per share were outstanding during the second half of 20X1 but were not included in the computation of diluted EPS because the options' exercise price was greater than the average market price of the common shares. The options, which expire on June 30, 20Y1, were still outstanding at the end of year 20X1. [FAS128, ¶151]

Illustration 3—Contingently Issuable Shares

.163 Exhibit 163A illustrates the contingent share provisions described in paragraphs .105 and .125 through .130. The facts assumed are as follows:

- Corporation B had 100,000 shares of common stock outstanding during the entire year ended December 31, 20X1. It had no options, warrants, or convertible securities outstanding during the period.
- Terms of a contingent stock agreement related to a recent business combination provided the following to certain shareholders of the Corporation:
  - 1,000 additional common shares for each new retail site opened during 20X1
  - 5 additional common shares for each $100 of consolidated, after-tax net income in excess of $500,000 for the year ended December 31, 20X1.
- The Corporation opened two new retail sites during the year:
  - One on May 1, 20X1
  - One on September 1, 20X1.
- Corporation B's consolidated, year-to-date after-tax net income was:
  - $400,000 as of March 31, 20X1
  - $600,000 as of June 30, 20X1
  - $450,000 as of September 30, 20X1
  - $700,000 as of December 31, 20X1.

Note: In computing diluted EPS for an interim period, contingent shares are included as of the beginning of the period. For year-to-date computations, footnote 22 of this section requires that contingent shares be included on a weighted-average basis. [FAS128, ¶152]

Exhibit 163A

EPS Computation with Contingently Issuable Shares

	First Quarter	Second Quarter	Third Quarter	Fourth Quarter	Full Year
Basic EPS Computation					
Numerator	$400,000	$200,000	$(150,000)	$250,000	$700,000
Denominator:					
Common shares outstanding	100,000	100,000	100,000	100,000	100,000
Retail site contingency	0	667[a]	1,333[b]	2,000	1,000[c]
Earnings contingency[d]	0	0	0	0	0
Total shares	100,000	100,667	101,333	102,000	101,000
Basic EPS	$ 4.00	$ 1.99	$ (1.48)	$ 2.45	$ 6.93

	First Quarter	Second Quarter	Third Quarter	Fourth Quarter	Full Year
Diluted EPS Computation					
Numerator	$400,000	$200,000	$(150,000)	$250,000	$700,000
Denominator:					
Common shares outstanding	100,000	100,000	100,000	100,000	100,000
Retail site contingency	0	1,000	2,000	2,000	1,250[e]
Earnings contingency	0[f]	5,000[g]	0[h]	10,000[i]	3,750[j]
Total shares	100,000	106,000	102,000	112,000	105,000
Diluted EPS	$ 4.00	$ 1.89	$ (1.47)[k]	$ 2.23	$ 6.67

[a] 1,000 shares × 2/3

[b] 1,000 shares + (1,000 shares × 1/3)

[c] (1,000 shares × 8/12) + (1,000 shares × 4/12)

[d] The earnings contingency has no effect on basic EPS because it is not certain that the condition is satisfied until the end of the contingency period (paragraphs .105 and .126). The effect is negligible for the fourth-quarter and full-year computations because it is not certain that the condition is met until the last day of the period.

[e] (0 + 1,000 + 2,000 + 2,000) ÷ 4

[f] Corporation B did not have $500,000 year-to-date, after-tax net income at March 31, 20X1. Projecting future earnings levels and including the related contingent shares are not permitted by this section.

[g] [($600,000 – $500,000) ÷ $100] × 5 shares

[h] Year-to-date, after-tax net income was less than $500,000.

[i] [($700,000 – $500,000) ÷ $100] × 5 shares

[j] (0 + 5,000 + 0 + 10,000) ÷ 4

[k] Loss during the third quarter is due to a change in accounting principle; therefore, antidilution rules (paragraph .110) do not apply.

[FAS128, ¶152]

Illustration 4—Antidilution Sequencing

.164 Exhibit 164A illustrates the antidilution sequencing provisions described in paragraph .109 for Corporation C for the year ended December 31, 20X0. The facts assumed are as follows:

- Corporation C had income available to common stockholders of $10,000,000 for the year 20X0.
- 2,000,000 shares of common stock were outstanding for the entire year 20X0.
- The average market price of the common stock was $75.
- Corporation C had the following potential common shares outstanding during the year:
  - Options (not compensation related) to buy 100,000 shares of common stock at $60 per share.
  - 800,000 shares of convertible preferred stock entitled to a cumulative dividend of $8 per share. Each preferred share is convertible into 2 shares of common stock.
  - 5 percent convertible debentures with a principal amount of $100,000,000 (issued at par). Each $1,000 debenture is convertible into 20 shares of common stock.
- The tax rate was 40 percent for 20X0.

[FAS128, ¶153]

Exhibit 164A

Illustration of Antidilution Sequencing Provisions

Determination of Earnings per Incremental Share

	Increase in Income	Increase in Number of Common Shares	Earnings per Incremental Share
Options	0	20,000[a]	—
Convertible preferred stock	$6,400,000[b]	1,600,000[c]	$4.00
5% convertible debentures	3,000,000[d]	2,000,000[e]	1.50

[a][($75 – $60) ÷ $75] × 100,000

[b]800,000 shares × $8

[c]800,000 shares × 2

[d]($100,000,000 × 5%) less taxes at 40%

[e]100,000 debentures × 20

Computation of Diluted Earnings per Share

	Income Available	Common Shares	Per Share	
As reported	$10,000,000	2,000,000	$5.00	
Options	0	20,000		
	10,000,000	2,020,000	4.95	Dilutive
5% convertible debentures	3,000,000	2,000,000		
	13,000,000	4,020,000	3.23	Dilutive
Convertible preferred stock	6,400,000	1,600,000		
	$19,400,000	5,620,000	3.45	Antidilutive

Note: Because diluted EPS *increases* from $3.23 to $3.45 when convertible preferred shares are included in the computation, those convertible preferred shares are antidilutive and are ignored in the computation of diluted EPS. Therefore, diluted EPS is reported as $3.23. [FAS128, ¶153]

Illustration 5—Rights Issues

.165 The following example illustrates the provisions for stock rights issues that contain a bonus element as described in paragraphs .148 and .149. The facts assumed are as follows:

- Net income was $1,100 for the year ended December 31, 20X0.
- 500 common shares were outstanding for the entire year ended December 31, 20X0.
- A rights issue was offered to all existing shareholders in January 20X1. The last date to exercise the rights was March 1, 20X1. The offer provided 1 common share for each 5 outstanding common shares (100 new shares).
- The exercise price for the rights issue was $5 per share acquired.
- The fair value of 1 common share was $11 at March 1, 20X1.
- Basic EPS for the year 20X0 (prior to the rights issuance) was $2.20.

As a result of the bonus element in the January 20X1 rights issue, basic and diluted EPS for 20X0 will have to be adjusted retroactively. The number of common shares used in computing basic and diluted EPS is the number of shares outstanding immediately prior to the rights issue (500) multiplied by an *adjustment factor.* Prior to computing the adjustment factor, the *theoretical ex-rights fair value per share* must be computed. Those computations follow:

Theoretical ex-rights fair value per share[a]	\$10	=	$\frac{(500 \times \$11) + (100 \times \$5)}{(500 + 100)}$
Adjustment factor[b]	1.1	=	\$11 ÷ \$10
Denominator for restating basic EPS	550	=	500 × 1.1
Restated basic EPS for 20X0	\$2.00	=	\$1,100 ÷ 550

Diluted EPS would be adjusted retroactively by adding 50 shares to the denominator that was used in computing diluted EPS prior to the restatement.

---

[a]The equation for computing the theoretical ex-rights fair value per share is:

$$\frac{\text{Aggregate fair value of shares prior to exercise of rights} + \text{Proceeds from exercise of rights}}{\text{Total shares outstanding after exercise of rights}}$$

[b]The equation for computing the adjustment factor is:

$$\frac{\text{Fair value per share immediately prior to exercise of rights}}{\text{Theoretical ex-rights fair value per share}}$$

[FAS128, ¶154]

Illustration 6—Two-Class Method

.166 The two-class method of computing basic EPS for an entity that has more than one class of nonconvertible securities is illustrated in the following example. This method is described in paragraph .154; as noted in that paragraph, diluted EPS would be computed in a similar manner. The facts assumed for the year 20X0 are as follows:

- Net income was \$65,000.
- 10,000 shares of \$50 par value common stock were outstanding.
- 5,000 shares of \$100 par value nonconvertible preferred stock were outstanding.
- The preferred stock was entitled to a noncumulative annual dividend of \$5 per share before any dividend is paid on common stock.
- After common stock has been paid a dividend of \$2 per share, the preferred stock then participates in any additional dividends on a 40:60 *per-share* ratio with common stock. (That is, after preferred and common stock have been paid dividends of \$5 and

$2 per share, respectively, preferred stock participates in any additional dividends at a rate of two-thirds of the additional amount paid to common stock on a per-share basis.)

- Preferred stockholders have been paid $27,000 ($5.40 per share).
- Common stockholders have been paid $26,000 ($2.60 per share).

Basic EPS for 20X0 would be computed as follows:

Net income		$65,000
Less dividends paid:		
Preferred	$27,000	
Common	26,000	53,000
Undistributed 20X0 earnings		$12,000

Allocation of undistributed earnings:

To preferred:

0.4(5,000) ÷ [0.4(5,000) + 0.6(10,000)] × $12,000 = $3,000
$3,000 ÷ 5,000 shares = $0.60 per share

To common:

0.6(10,000) ÷ [0.4(5,000) + 0.6(10,000)] × $12,000 = $9,000
$9,000 ÷ 10,000 shares = $0.90 per share

Basic per-share amounts:

	Preferred Stock	Common Stock
Distributed earnings	$5.40	$2.60
Undistributed earnings	0.60	0.90
Totals	$6.00	$3.50

[FAS128, ¶155]

Illustration 7—Securities of a Subsidiary: Computation of Basic and Diluted Earnings per Share

.167 Exhibit 167A illustrates the EPS computations for a subsidiary's securities that enable their holders to obtain the subsidiary's common stock based on the provisions in paragraph .155.[32] The facts assumed are as follows:

Parent corporation:

- Net income was $10,000 (excluding any earnings of or dividends paid by the subsidiary).
- 10,000 shares of common stock were outstanding; the parent corporation had not issued any other securities.
- The parent corporation owned 900 common shares of a domestic subsidiary corporation.
- The parent corporation owned 40 warrants issued by the subsidiary.
- The parent corporation owned 100 shares of convertible preferred stock issued by the subsidiary.

Subsidiary corporation:

- Net income was $3,600.
- 1,000 shares of common stock were outstanding.
- Warrants exercisable to purchase 200 shares of its common stock at $10 per share (assume $20 average market price for common stock) were outstanding.
- 200 shares of convertible preferred stock were outstanding. Each share is convertible into two shares of common stock.
- The convertible preferred stock paid a dividend of $1.50 per share.
- No intercompany eliminations or adjustments were necessary except for dividends.
- Income taxes have been ignored for simplicity.

[FAS128, ¶156]

[32]This example is based on current practice. Based on the provisions of the consolidations Exposure Draft, the presentation of earnings per share would differ from that illustrated in this example for an entity that includes subsidiaries that are not wholly owned. [Refer to footnote 30.] [FAS128, ¶156]

Exhibit 167A

EPS Computation for Securities of a Subsidiary

Subsidiary's Earnings per Share

Basic EPS	\$3.30	Computed:	(\$3,600[a] – \$300[b]) ÷ 1,000[c]
Diluted EPS	\$2.40	Computed:	\$3,600[d] ÷ (1,000 + 100[e] + 400[f])

Consolidated Earnings per Share

Basic EPS	\$1.31	Computed:	(\$10,000[g] + \$3,120[h]) ÷ 10,000[i]
Diluted EPS	\$1.27	Computed:	(\$10,000 + \$2,160[j] + \$48[k] + \$480[l]) ÷ 10,000

[a]Subsidiary's net income

[b]Dividends paid by subsidiary on convertible preferred stock

[c]Shares of subsidiary's common stock outstanding

[d]Subsidiary's income available to common stockholders (\$3,300) increased by \$300 preferred dividends from applying the if-converted method for convertible preferred stock

[e]Incremental shares from warrants from applying the treasury stock method, computed: [(\$20 – \$10) ÷ \$20] × 200

[f]Shares of subsidiary's common stock assumed outstanding from conversion of convertible preferred stock, computed: 200 convertible preferred shares × conversion factor of 2

[g]Parent's net income

[h]Portion of subsidiary's income to be included in consolidated basic EPS, computed: (900 × \$3.30) + (100 × \$1.50)

[i]Shares of parent's common stock outstanding

[j]Parent's proportionate interest in subsidiary's earnings attributable to common stock, computed: (900 ÷ 1,000) × (1,000 shares × \$2.40 per share)

[k]Parent's proportionate interest in subsidiary's earnings attributable to warrants, computed: (40 ÷ 200) × (100 incremental shares × \$2.40 per share)

[l]Parent's proportionate interest in subsidiary's earnings attributable to convertible preferred stock, computed: (100 ÷ 200) × (400 shares from conversion × \$2.40 per share)

[FAS128, ¶156]

Illustration 8—Application of the Treasury Stock Method for Stock Appreciation Rights and Other Variable Stock Option Award Plans

.168 The following examples illustrate the provisions in paragraphs .115 through .117 for computing the effect on diluted EPS of stock appreciation rights and other variable stock option or award plans when the service period is presumed to be the vesting period. The examples do not comprehend all possible combinations of circumstances. Amounts and quantities have been rounded for simplicity. The terminology and compensation cost is based on the guidance in Section C47.

The provisions of the agreements are as follows:

Date of grant	January 1, 19X9
Expiration date	December 31, 20Y8
Vesting	100% at the end of 20Y2
Number of shares under option	1,000
Option exercise price	$10 per share
Quoted market price at date of grant	$10 per share

- Stock appreciation rights are granted in tandem with stock options for market value appreciation in excess of the option price.
- Exercise of the rights cancels the options for an equal number of shares and vice versa.
- Share appreciation is payable in stock, cash, or a combination of stock and cash at the entity's election.

The facts assumed are as follows:

- There are no circumstances in these two examples that would overcome the presumption that the rights are payable in stock (refer to paragraph .124).
- The tax deduction for compensation will equal the compensation recognized for financial reporting purposes.
- The quoted market prices of common stock on December 31 of the years 19X9 20X4 were as follows:

19X9	$11
20Y0	$12
20Y1	$15
20Y2	$14
20Y3	$15
20Y4	$18

[FAS128, ¶157]

Example 1

.169 Exhibit 169A illustrates the annual computation of incremental shares for the above-described stock appreciation right plan. A single annual computation is shown for simplicity in this and in the following example. Normally, a computation would be done monthly or quarterly. [FAS128, ¶158]

Exhibit 169A

Annual Computation of Incremental Shares for Use in EPS Calculations

		Compensation							Additional Shares for Diluted EPS		
Date	Market Price	Per Share[a]	Aggregate[b]	Percentage Accrued[c]	Compensation Accrued to Date	Measurable Compensation Attributed to Future Periods[d]	Amount to Be Paid by Employee	Assumed Proceeds	Shares Issuable[e]	Treasury Shares Assumed Repurchased[f]	Incremental Shares
12/31/X9	$11	$1	$1,000	25%	$ 250	$ 750	—	$ 750	47	35	12
12/31/Y0	12	2	2,000	50	1,000	1,000	—	1,000	130	76	54
12/31/Y1	15	5	5,000	75	3,750	1,250	—	1,250	259	83	176
12/31/Y2	14	4	4,000	100	4,000	0	—	0	310[g]	43[g]	267[g]
12/31/Y3	15	5	5,000	100	5,000	0	—	0	310	0	310
12/31/Y4	18	8	8,000	100	8,000	0	—	0	394	0	394

[a]Market price less exercise price ($10).

[b]Aggregate compensation for unexercised shares to be allocated to periods in which service is performed (shares under option × compensation per share).

[c]The percentage accrued is based on the four-year vesting period.

[d]Unaccrued compensation in this example.

[e]Average aggregate compensation ÷ average market price.

[f]Average assumed proceeds ÷ average market price.

[g]Illustration of computation of additional shares for one year (20Y2) follows:

Date	Market Price	Aggregate Compensation	Assumed Proceeds
12/31/Y1	$15.00	$5,000	$1,250
12/31/Y2	14.00	4,000	0
Average	14.50	4,500	625

Additional shares for diluted EPS:

Shares issuable	310	(4,500 ÷ $14.50)
Treasury shares	(43)	(625 ÷ $14.50)
Incremental shares	267	

[FAS128, ¶153]

Example 2

.170 If the stock appreciation rights vested 25 percent per year commencing in 19X9, the annual computation of incremental shares for diluted EPS in Example 1 would change as illustrated in Exhibit 170A. The computation of compensation expense is explained in Section C47, paragraphs .142 through .144.

The additional facts assumed are as follows:

- On December 31, 20Y1, the employee exercises the right to receive share appreciation on 300 shares.
- On March 15, 20Y2, the employee exercises the right to receive share appreciation on 100 shares; quoted market price $15 per share.
- On June 15, 20Y3, the employee exercises the right to receive share appreciation on 100 shares; quoted market price $16 per share.
- On December 31, 20Y3, the employee exercises the right to receive share appreciation on 300 shares.
- On December 31, 20Y4, the employee exercises the right to receive share appreciation on 200 shares.

[FAS128, ¶159]

Exhibit 170A

Annual Computation of Incremental Shares for Use in EPS Calculations

				Compensation							Additional Shares for Diluted EPS				
Date	Transaction	Number of Shares under Option	Market Price	Per Share[a]	Aggregate[b]	Percentage Accrued[c]	Compensation Accrued to Date	Measurable Compensation Attributed to Future Periods[d]	Amount to Be Paid by Employee	Assumed Proceeds	Shares Issuable[e]	Treasury Shares Assumed Repurchased[f]	Incremental Shares	Weighted-Average Shares Outstanding[g]	Total Shares
12/31/X9			$11	$1	$1,000	52%	$ 520	$480	—	$480	47	22	25	—	25
12/31/Y0			12	2	2,000	79	1,580	420	—	420	130	39	91	—	91
12/31/Y1			15	5	5,000	94	4,700	300	—	300	259	26	233	—	233
12/31/Y1	SAR	300	15	5											
3/15/Y2	SAR	100	15	5											
12/31/Y2			14	4	2,400	100	2,400	0	—	0	193	10	183	126	309
6/15/Y3	SAR	100	16	6											
12/31/Y3			15	5	2,500	100	2,500	0	—	0	170[h]	0	170	153[i]	323
12/31/Y3	SAR	300	15	5											
12/31/Y4			18	8	1,600	100	1,600	0	—	0	78	0	78	270	348
12/31/Y4	SAR	200	18	8											

Transaction code:
SAR—Exercise of a stock appreciation right.

---

[a]Market price for the year less exercise price ($10).

[b]Aggregate compensation for unexercised shares to be allocated to periods in which the service is performed (shares under option × compensation per share).

[c]Refer to the schedule in Section C47, paragraph .143.

[d]Unaccrued compensation in this example.

[e]Average aggregate compensation ÷ average market price, weighted for portion of period during which rights were unexercised.

[f]Average assumed proceeds ÷ average market price

[g]Shares issued upon exercise of stock appreciation rights. These would be included in the enterprise's total weighted-average shares outstanding.

[h]Illustration of computation of shares issuable for one year (20Y3) follows:

	Number of Shares under Option	Average Compensation per Share	Average Aggregate Compensation	Average Market Price	Aggregate Shares Issuable	Weighing Factor	Shares Issuable
Rights outstanding:							
Entire year 20Y3	500	$4.50	$2,250	$14.50	155	12/12	155
1/1–6/15	100	5.00	500	15.00	33	5.5/12	15
							170

[i]Illustration of computation of weighted-average shares outstanding for one year (20Y3) follows:

	Number of Shares under Option	Compensation per Share	Aggregate Compensation	Market Price	Aggregate Shares Outstanding	Weighing Factor	Weighted-Average Shares Outstanding
Shares issued:							
12/31/Y1	300	$5	$1,500	$15	100	12/12	100
3/15/Y2	100	5	500	15	33	12/12	33
6/15/Y3	100	6	600	16	38	6.5/12	20
							153

[FAS128, ¶159]

Other Authoritative Guidance on Earnings per Share

.171 This paragraph [presents a list] of SEC guidance on earnings per share. [Refer to paragraph .1000 for Emerging Issues Task Force (EITF) Issues that are related by topic to this section.]

Staff Accounting Bulletin No. 64, *Accounting for Redeemable Preferred Stock* (Topic 3C)—Section E11 does not address numerator issues relating to the EPS computation. The SEC guidance for redeemable preferred stock continues to apply.

Accounting Series Release (ASR) No. 280, *General Revision of Regulation S-X* (Topic 6B)—Section E11 does not require income available to common shareholders to be presented on the face of the income statement. The SEC disclosure guidance continues to apply.

Staff Accounting Bulletin No. 68, *Increasing Rate Preferred Stock* (Topic 5Q)—Section E11 does not address numerator issues relating to the EPS computation. The SEC guidance for increasing rate preferred stock continues to apply. [FAS128, ¶172]

[Staff Accounting Bulletin No. 98, *Earnings per Share Computations in an Initial Public Offering* (Topic 4D)—For periods covered by income statements included in the registration statement and in subsequent filings with the SEC, SAB 98 requires nominal issuances of potential common shares (that is, those issued for nominal consideration) to be reflected in basic and diluted EPS in a manner similar to a stock dividend or a stock split. Section E11 would permit those potentially dilutive common shares to be included only in the computation of *diluted* EPS and only from the date of issuance. The SEC guidance applies to SEC registrants involved in an IPO that have issued such potentially dilutive common shares.]

Glossary

.401 **Antidilution (antidilutive).** An increase in earnings per share amounts or a decrease in loss per share amounts. [FAS128, ¶171]

.402 **Basic earnings per share (basic EPS).** The amount of earnings for the period available to each share of common stock outstanding during the reporting period. [FAS128, ¶171]

.403 **Call option.** A contract that allows the holder to buy a specified quantity of stock from the writer of the contract at a fixed price for a given period. Refer to **option** and **purchased call option.** [FAS128, ¶171]

.404 **Common stock (common shares).** A stock that is subordinate to all other stock of the issuer. [FAS128, ¶171]

.405 **Contingent issuance.** A possible issuance of shares of common stock that is dependent on the satisfaction of certain conditions. [FAS128, ¶171]

.406 **Contingent stock agreement.** An agreement to issue common stock (usually in connection with a business combination) that is dependent on the satisfaction of certain conditions. Refer to **contingently issuable shares.** [FAS128, ¶171]

.407 **Contingently issuable shares (contingently issuable stock).** Shares issuable for little or no cash consideration upon the satisfaction of certain conditions pursuant to a contingent stock agreement. Refer to **contingent stock agreement.** [FAS128, ¶171]

.408 **Conversion rate (conversion ratio).** The ratio of the number of common shares issuable upon conversion to a unit of a convertible security. For example, $100 face value of debt convertible into 5 shares of common stock would have a conversion ratio of 5 to 1. [FAS128, ¶171]

.409 **Convertible security.** A security that is convertible into another security based on a conversion rate; for example, convertible preferred stock that is convertible into common stock on a two-for-one basis (two shares of common for each share of preferred). [FAS128, ¶171]

.410 **Diluted earnings per share (diluted EPS).** The amount of earnings for the period available to each share of common stock outstanding during the reporting period and to each share that would have been outstanding assuming the issuance of common shares for all dilutive potential common shares outstanding during the reporting period. [FAS128, ¶171]

.411 **Dilution (dilutive).** A reduction in earnings per share resulting from the assumption that convertible securities were converted, that options or warrants were exercised, or that other shares were issued upon the satisfaction of certain conditions. [FAS128, ¶171]

.412 **Earnings per share (EPS).** The amount of earnings attributable to each share of common stock. For convenience, the term is used in this section to refer to either earnings or loss per share. [FAS128, ¶171]

.413 **Exercise price.** The amount that must be paid for a share of common stock upon exercise of an option or warrant. [FAS128, ¶171]

.414 **If-converted method.** A method of computing EPS data that assumes conversion of convertible securities at the beginning of the reporting period (or at time of issuance, if later). [FAS128, ¶171]

.415 **Income available to common stockholders.** Income (or loss) from continuing operations or net income (or net loss) adjusted for preferred stock dividends. [FAS128, ¶171]

.416 **Option.** Unless otherwise stated in this section, a call option that gives the holder the right to purchase shares of common stock from the reporting entity in accordance with an agreement upon payment of a specified amount. As used in this section, options include, but are not limited to, options granted to employees and stock purchase agreements entered into with employees. Options are considered "securities" in this section. Refer to **call option.** [FAS128, ¶171]

.417 **Potential common stock.** A security or other contract that may entitle its holder to obtain common stock during the reporting period or after the end of the reporting period. [FAS128, ¶171]

.418 **Preferred stock.** A security that has rights that are preferential to common stock. [FAS128, ¶171]

.419 **Purchased call option.** A contract that allows the reporting entity to buy a specified quantity of its own stock from the writer of the contract at a fixed price for a given period. Refer to **call option.** [FAS128, ¶171]

.420 **Put option.** A contract that allows the holder to sell a specified quantity of stock to the writer of the contract at a fixed price during a given period. [FAS128, ¶171]

.421 **Reverse treasury stock method.** A method of recognizing the dilutive effect on earnings per share of satisfying a put obligation. It assumes that the proceeds used to buy back common stock (pursuant to the terms of a put option) will be raised from issuing shares at the average market price during the period. Refer to **put option.** [FAS128, ¶171]

.422 **Rights issue.** An offer to existing shareholders to purchase additional shares of common stock in accordance with an agreement for a specified amount (which is generally substantially less than the fair value of the shares) for a given period. [FAS128, ¶171]

.423 **Security.** The evidence of debt or ownership or a related right. For purposes of this section, it includes options and warrants as well as debt and stock. [FAS128, ¶171]

.424 **Treasury stock method.** A method of recognizing the use of proceeds that could be obtained upon exercise of options and warrants in computing diluted EPS. It assumes that any proceeds would be used to purchase common stock at the average market price during the period. [FAS128, ¶171]

.425 **Warrant.** A security that gives the holder the right to purchase shares of common stock in accordance with the terms of the instrument, usually upon payment of a specified amount. [FAS128, ¶171]

.426 **Weighted-average number of common shares outstanding.** The number of shares determined by relating (a) the portion of time within a reporting period that common shares have been outstanding to (b) the total time in that period. In computing diluted EPS, equivalent common shares are considered for all dilutive potential common shares. [FAS128, ¶171]

Supplemental Guidance: Emerging Issues Task Force (EITF) Issues

.1000 [Listed below are EITF Issues that provide supplemental guidance for this section. These Issues are grouped by subject matter and may be either interpretive of or related by topic to the guidance in this section.

Debt Securities

EITF Issue No. 85-18, "Earnings-per-Share Effect of Equity Commitment Notes"
EITF Issue No. 90-19, "Convertible Bonds with Issuer Option to Settle for Cash upon Conversion"

Employee Stock Ownership Plans (ESOPs)

EITF Issue No. 90-4, "Earnings-per-Share Treatment of Tax Benefits for Dividends on Stock Held by an Employee Stock Ownership Plan"
EITF Issue No. 92-3, "Earnings-per-Share Treatment of Tax Benefits for Dividends on Unallocated Stock Held by an Employee Stock Ownership Plan"

Preferred Stock

EITF Topic No. D-42, "The Effect on the Calculation of Earnings per Share for the Redemption or Induced Conversion of Preferred Stock"
EITF Topic No. D-53, "Computation of Earnings per Share for a Period That Includes a Redemption or an Induced Conversion of a Portion of a Class of Preferred Stock"
EITF Topic No. D-82, "Effect of Preferred Stock Dividends Payable in Common Shares on Computation of Income Available to Common Stockholders"

Other

EITF Issue No. 84-22, "Prior Years' Earnings per Share following a Savings and Loan Association Conversion and Pooling"
EITF Issue No. 88-9, "Put Warrants"
EITF Issue No. 98-12, "Application of Issue No. 00-19 to Forward Equity Sales Transactions"
EITF Issue No. 99-7, "Accounting for an Accelerated Share Repurchase Program"
EITF Issue No. 00-19, "Accounting for Derivative Financial Instruments Indexed to, and Potentially Settled in, a Company's Own Stock"
EITF Topic No. D-62, "Computing Year-to-Date Earnings per Share under FASB Statement No. 128"

EITF Topic No. D-72, "Effect of Contracts That May Be Settled in Stock or Cash on the Computation of Diluted Earnings per Share"
EITF Topic No. D-93, "Accounting for the Rescission of the Exercise of Employee Stock Options"
EITF Topic No. D-95, "Effect of Participating Convertible Securities on the Computation of Basic Earnings per Share"]

.1001 [Listed below are those EITF Issues that provide interpretive guidance on specific material in this section.

Paragraphs .103 and .104 (FAS 128, ¶8–9)—EITF Topic No. D-82
Paragraph .124 (FAS 128, ¶29)—EITF Topic No. D-72
Paragraph .125, footnote 22 (FAS 128, fn18)—EITF Topic No. D-62
Paragraph .139 (FAS 128, ¶46)—EITF Topic No. D-62
Paragraph .154 (FAS 128, ¶61)—EITF Topic No. D-95]

(The next page is 14261.)

EMPLOYEE STOCK OWNERSHIP PLANS (ESOPs) SECTION E55

Source: EITF Issues

Supplemental Guidance: Emerging Issues Task Force (EITF) Issues

.1000 [Listed below are EITF Issues that provide supplemental guidance for the authoritative literature governing an employer's financial reporting of ESOP transactions. The authoritative guidance on accounting for ESOPs is provided in the AICPA's Statements of Position 76-3, *Accounting Practices for Certain Employee Stock Ownership Plans,* and 93-6, *Employers' Accounting for Employee Stock Ownership Plans.* The AICPA issued SOP 93-6 in December 1993 which supersedes SOP 76-3. Under the transition provisions in SOP 93-6, employers may continue their current accounting for shares acquired before January 1, 1993.

Business Combinations

EITF Issue No. 85-11, "Use of an Employee Stock Ownership Plan in a Leveraged Buyout"

EITF Issue No. 88-27, "Effect of Unallocated Shares in an Employee Stock Ownership Plan on Accounting for Business Combinations"

EITF Issue No. 93-2, "Effect of Acquisition of Employer Shares for/by an Employee Benefit Trust on Accounting for Business Combinations"

EITF Topic No. D-19, "Impact on Pooling-of-Interests Accounting of Treasury Shares Acquired to Satisfy Conversions in a Leveraged Preferred Stock ESOP"

Earnings per Share Computational Guidelines

EITF Issue No. 89-12, "Earnings-per-Share Issues Related to Convertible Preferred Stock Held by an Employee Stock Ownership Plan"

EITF Issue No. 90-4, "Earnings per Share Treatment of Tax Benefits for Dividends on Stock Held by an Employee Stock Ownership Plan"

EITF Issue No. 92-3, "Earnings-per-Share Treatment of Tax Benefits for Dividends on Unallocated Stock Held by an Employee Stock Ownership Plan"

Other

EITF Issue No. 86-27, "Measurement of Excess Contributions to a Defined Contribution Plan or Employee Stock Ownership Plan"
EITF Issue No. 87-23, "Book Value Stock Purchase Plans"
EITF Issue No. 89-8, "Expense Recognition for Employee Stock Ownership Plans"
EITF Issue No. 89-10, "Sponsor's Recognition of Employee Stock Ownership Plan Debt"
EITF Issue No. 89-11, "Sponsor's Balance Sheet Classification of Capital Stock with a Put Option Held by an Employee Stock Ownership Plan"]

(The next page is 16501.)

FINANCIAL INSTRUMENTS: DISCLOSURE SECTION F25

Sources: FASB Statement 107; FASB Statement 112; FASB Statement 123; FASB Statement 126; FASB Statement 133; FASB Statement 140

[**Note:** A list of Issues discussed by the Emerging Issues Task Force (EITF) that provide supplemental guidance for this section is presented in paragraph .1000.]

Summary

This section presents requirements for all entities to disclose certain information about their financial instruments. However, certain disclosures are optional for nonpublic entities that meet specific criteria and certain specified financial instruments are exempt from the disclosure requirements of this section.

Disclosure of information about significant concentrations of credit risk from an individual counterparty or groups of counterparties for all financial instruments is required.

In addition, all entities except certain nonpublic entities are required to disclose the fair value of financial instruments, both assets and liabilities recognized and not recognized in the statement of financial position, for which it is practicable to estimate fair value. If estimating fair value is not practicable, this section requires disclosure of descriptive information pertinent to estimating the value of a financial instrument.

This section also encourages, but does not require, quantitative information about market risks of derivative instruments, and also of other assets and liabilities, that is consistent with the way the entity manages or adjusts those risks.

Applicability and Scope

.101–.105 [Deleted 6/98 because of FASB Statement 133, *Accounting for Derivative Instruments and Hedging Activities.*]

.105A–.105C [Deleted 10/94 and renumbered as .105G through .105I.]

.105D–.105F [Deleted 6/98 because of Statement 133.]

.105G [Paragraph .116A of this section requires disclosure about financial instruments (refer to paragraph .106 for the definition of financial instrument) with concentrations of credit risk except as specifically modified in paragraph .116B.] This section [also] requires disclosures about fair value [(refer to paragraph .115A for the definition of fair value)] for all financial instruments, whether recognized or not recognized in the statement of financial position, except for those specifically listed in paragraph .105H. [Disclosures about fair value] apply to all entities [FAS107, ¶7] but are optional for those entities covered by paragraphs .105J through .105L of this section. [FAS126, ¶5] [This section] does not change any requirements for recognition, measurement, or classification of financial instruments in financial statements. [FAS107, ¶7]

.105H The disclosures about fair value prescribed in paragraphs .115C through .115F, .115I, and .115J are not required for the following:

a. Employers' and plans' obligations for pension benefits, other postretirement benefits including health care and life insurance benefits, [FAS107, ¶8] postemployment benefits, [FAS112, ¶11] employee stock option and stock purchase plans, and other forms of deferred compensation arrangements, as defined in Sections Pe5, "Pension Funds: Accounting and Reporting by Defined Benefit Pension Plans," P16, "Pension Costs," P40, "Postretirement Benefits Other Than Pensions," [FAS107, ¶8] P32, "Postemployment Benefits," [FAS112, ¶11] C36, "Compensation: Stock-Based," [FAS123, ¶389(a)] C38, "Compensation to Employees: Deferred Compensation Agreements," and C44, "Compensation to Employees: Paid Absences" [FAS107, ¶8]
b. Substantively extinguished debt subject to the disclosure requirements of paragraphs .109(a) and .109(b) of Section L35, "Liabilities: Extinguishments" [FAS140, ¶361(a)]
c. Insurance contracts, other than financial guarantees and investment contracts, as discussed in Section In6, "Insurance Industry"

[1–5][Deleted 6/98 because of FASB Statement 133, *Accounting for Derivative Instruments and Hedging Activities.*]

d. Lease contracts as defined in Section L10, "Leases," (a contingent obligation arising out of a cancelled lease and a guarantee of a third-party lease obligation are not lease contracts and are included in the scope of this section)
e. Warranty obligations and rights
f. Unconditional purchase obligations as defined in paragraph .101 of Section C32, "Commitments: Long-Term Obligations"
g. Investments accounted for under the equity method in accordance with the requirements of Section I82, "Investments: Equity Method"
h. Minority interests in consolidated subsidiaries
i. Equity investments in consolidated subsidiaries
j. Equity instruments issued by the entity and classified in stockholders' equity in the statement of financial position. [FAS107, ¶8]

.105I Generally accepted accounting principles already require disclosure of or subsequent measurement at fair value for many classes of financial instruments. Although the definitions or the methods of estimation of fair value vary to some extent, and various terms such as *market value, current value, or mark-to-market* are used, the amounts computed under those requirements satisfy the requirements of this section and those requirements are not superseded or modified by this section. [FAS107, ¶9] [In addition, generally accepted accounting principles and regulatory accounting requirements have been and will be developed for certain specified financial instruments. Specific disclosure and accounting requirements for those instruments are found in other sections. For example, Section C32, paragraph .105, presents disclosure requirements for all long-term debt, Section D50, "Derivative Instruments and Hedging Activities," paragraphs .141 and .142, presents disclosure requirements for derivative instruments, and Section F39, "Financial Instruments: Transfers," paragraph .109, presents disclosure requirements for collateral, securitization transactions, and retained interests in securitizations.]

Exemption for Certain Nonpublic Entities

.105J Disclosures about the fair value of financial instruments prescribed in paragraphs .115C through .115F and .115I though .115K of this section, shall be optional for an entity that meets each of the following criteria:

a. The entity is a nonpublic entity [(refer to paragraph .105K for the definition of nonpublic entity)].
b. The entity's total assets are less than $100 million on the date of the financial statements. [FAS126, ¶2]
c. The entity has no instrument that, in whole or in part, is accounted for as a derivative instrument under Section D50 during the reporting period. [FAS133, ¶537]

The criteria shall be applied to the most recent year presented in comparative financial statements to determine applicability of this paragraph. If disclosures are not required in the current period, the disclosures for previous years may be omitted if financial statements for those years are presented for comparative purposes. If disclosures are required in the current period, disclosures about the fair value of financial instruments prescribed in paragraphs .115C through .115F and .115I through .115K of this section that have not been reported previously need not be included in financial statements that are presented for comparative purposes. [FAS126, ¶2] The following table presents the requirements for disclosures when prior periods are presented in comparative financial statements.

If Disclosures for the Current Period Are:	And Disclosures for Prior Periods Were:	Then Disclosures for Prior Periods Presented in Comparative Statements Are:
Optional	Optional	Optional
Optional	Required	Optional
Required	Optional	Optional
Required	Required	Required

[FAS126, ¶25]

.105K For purposes of paragraph .105J, a nonpublic entity is any entity other than one (a) whose debt or equity securities trade in a public market either on a stock exchange (domestic or foreign) or in the over-the-counter market, including securities quoted only locally or regionally, (b) that makes a filing with a regulatory agency in preparation for the sale of any class of debt or equity securities in a public market, or (c) that is controlled by an entity covered by (a) or (b). [FAS126, ¶3]

.105L [The guidance in] paragraphs .105J and .105K does not change the requirements of Sections I80, "Investments: Debt and Equity Securities," and No5, "Not-for-Profit Organizations," paragraphs .148 through .175 (including disclosures about financial instruments other than equity and debt securities that are measured at fair value in the statement of financial position), or any requirements, other than those specified in paragraph .105J, for recognition, measurement, classification, or disclosure of financial instruments in financial statements. [FAS126, ¶4]

Definition of a Financial Instrument

.106 A financial instrument is defined as cash, evidence of an ownership interest in an entity, or a contract that both:

a. Imposes on one entity a contractual obligation[6] (1) to deliver cash or another financial instrument[7] to a second entity or (2) to exchange other financial instruments on potentially unfavorable terms with the second entity
b. Conveys to that second entity a contractual right[8] (1) to receive cash or another financial instrument from the first entity or (2) to exchange other financial instruments on potentially favorable terms with the first entity.

[FAS107, ¶3]

.106A–.115 [Deleted 6/98 because of Statement 133.]

Fair Value of Financial Instruments

.115A For purposes of this section, the fair value of a financial instrument is the amount at which the instrument could be exchanged in a current transaction between willing parties, other than in a forced or liquidation sale. If a quoted market price is available for an instrument, the fair value to be disclosed for that instrument is the product of the number of trading units of the instrument times that market price. [FAS107, ¶5]

.115B Under the definition of fair value in paragraph .115A, the quoted price for a single trading unit in the most active market is the basis for determining market price and reporting fair value. This is the case even if placing orders to sell all of an entity's holdings

---

[6]*Contractual obligations* encompass both those that are conditioned on the occurrence of a specified event and those that are not. All contractual obligations that are financial instruments meet the definition of *liability* set forth in FASB Concepts Statement 6, *Elements of Financial Statements,* although some may not be recognized as liabilities in financial statements—may be "off-balance-sheet"—because they fail to meet some other criterion for recognition. For some financial instruments, the obligation is owed to or by a group of entities rather than a single entity. [FAS107, ¶3, fn1]

[7]The use of the term *financial instrument* in this definition is recursive (because the term *financial instrument* is included in it), though it is not circular. The definition requires a chain of contractual obligations that ends with the delivery of cash or an ownership interest in an entity. Any number of obligations to deliver financial instruments can be links in a chain that qualifies a particular contract as a financial instrument. [FAS107, ¶3, fn2]

[8]*Contractual rights* encompass both those that are conditioned on the occurrence of a specified event and those that are not. All contractual rights that are financial instruments meet the definition of *asset* set forth in Concepts Statement 6, although some may not be recognized as assets in financial statements—may be "off-balance-sheet"—because they fail to meet some other criterion for recognition. For some financial instruments, the right is held by or the obligation is due from a group of entities rather than a single entity. [FAS107, ¶3, fn3]

[9–16][Deleted 6/98 because of Statement 133.]

of an asset or to buy back all of a liability might affect the price, or if a market's normal volume for one day might not be sufficient to absorb the quantity held or owed by an entity. [FAS107, ¶6]

Disclosures about Fair Value of Financial Instruments

.115C An entity shall disclose, either in the body of the financial statements or in the accompanying notes,[16a] the fair value of financial instruments for which it is practicable to estimate that value. [FAS107, ¶10] Fair value disclosed in the notes shall be presented together with the related carrying amount in a form that makes it clear whether the fair value and carrying amount represent assets or liabilities and how the carrying amounts relate to what is reported in the statement of financial position. [FAS133, ¶532(b)] An entity also shall disclose the method(s) and significant assumptions used to estimate the fair value of financial instruments. [FAS107, ¶10] [Refer to paragraph .1001 for an EITF Issue that provides interpretive guidance on this paragraph.]

.115D Quoted market prices, if available, are the best evidence of the fair value of financial instruments. If quoted market prices are not available, management's best estimate of fair value may be based on the quoted market price of a financial instrument with similar characteristics or on valuation techniques (for example, the present value of estimated future cash flows using a discount rate commensurate with the risks involved, option pricing models, or matrix pricing models). Paragraphs .141 through .152 contain examples of procedures for estimating fair value. [FAS107, ¶11]

.115E In estimating the fair value of deposit liabilities, a financial entity shall not take into account the value of its long-term relationships with depositors, commonly known as core deposit intangibles, which are separate intangible assets, not financial instruments. For deposit liabilities with no defined maturities, the fair value to be disclosed under this section is the amount payable on demand at the reporting date. This section does not prohibit an entity from disclosing separately the estimated fair value of any of its nonfinancial intangible and tangible assets and nonfinancial liabilities. [FAS107, ¶12]

.115F For trade receivables and payables, no disclosure is required under paragraph .115C if the carrying amount approximates fair value. [FAS107, ¶13]

[16a]If disclosed in more than a single note, one of the notes shall include a summary table. The summary table shall contain the fair value and related carrying amounts and cross-references to the location(s) of the remaining disclosures required by this section. [FAS133, ¶532(a)]

.115G–.115H [Deleted 10/94 and renumbered as paragraphs .115J and .115K.]

.115I In disclosing the fair value of a financial instrument, an entity shall not net that fair value with the fair value of other financial instruments—even if those financial instruments are of the same class or are otherwise considered to be related, for example, by a risk management strategy—except to the extent that the offsetting of carrying amounts in the statement of financial position is permitted under the general principle in paragraphs .101A and .101B of Section B10, "Balance Sheet Display: Offsetting," or the exceptions for master netting arrangements in paragraph .106 of Section B10 and for amounts related to certain repurchase and reverse repurchase agreements in paragraphs .106A and .106B of Section B10. [FAS133, ¶531(c)]

.115J If it is not practicable for an entity to estimate the fair value of a financial instrument or a class of financial instruments, the following shall be disclosed:

a. Information pertinent to estimating the fair value of that financial instrument or class of financial instruments, such as the carrying amount, effective interest rate, and maturity
b. The reasons why it is not practicable to estimate fair value.

[FAS107, ¶14]

.115K In the context of paragraphs .115C through .115F and .115J, *practicable* means that an estimate of fair value can be made without incurring excessive costs. It is a dynamic concept: what is practicable for one entity might not be for another; what is not practicable in one year might be in another. For example, it might not be practicable for an entity to estimate the fair value of a class of financial instruments for which a quoted market price is not available because it has not yet obtained or developed the valuation model necessary to make the estimate, and the cost of obtaining an independent valuation appears excessive considering the materiality of the instruments to the entity. Practicability, that is, cost considerations, also may affect the required precision of the estimate; for example, while in many cases it might seem impracticable to estimate fair value on an individual instrument basis, it may be practicable for a class of financial instruments in a portfolio or on a portfolio basis. In those cases, the fair value of that class or of the portfolio shall be disclosed. Finally, it might be practicable for an entity to estimate the fair value only of a subset of a class of financial instruments; the fair value of that subset shall be disclosed. [FAS107, ¶15]

.115L–.116 [Deleted 6/98 because of Statement 133.]

[16b–16m] [Deleted 6/98 because of Statement 133.]

Disclosures about Concentrations of Credit Risk of All Financial Instruments

.116A Except as indicated in paragraph .116B, an entity shall disclose all significant concentrations of credit risk arising from *all* financial instruments, whether from an individual counterparty or groups of counterparties. *Group concentrations* of credit risk exist if a number of counterparties are engaged in similar activities and have similar economic characteristics that would cause their ability to meet contractual obligations to be similarly affected by changes in economic or other conditions. The following shall be disclosed about each significant concentration:

a. Information about the (shared) activity, region, or economic characteristic that identifies the concentration
b. The maximum amount of loss due to credit risk that, based on the gross fair value of the financial instrument, the entity would incur if parties to the financial instruments that make up the concentration failed completely to perform according to the terms of the contracts and the collateral or other security, if any, for the amount due proved to be of no value to the entity
c. The entity's policy of requiring collateral or other security to support financial instruments subject to credit risk, information about the entity's access to that collateral or other security, and the nature and a brief description of the collateral or other security supporting those financial instruments
d. The entity's policy of entering into master netting arrangements to mitigate the credit risk of financial instruments, information about the arrangements for which the entity is a party, and a brief description of the terms of those arrangements, including the extent to which they would reduce the entity's maximum amount of loss due to credit risk.

[FAS133, ¶531(d)]

.116B The requirements of the preceding paragraph do not apply to the following financial instruments, whether written or held:

a. Financial instruments of a pension plan, including plan assets, when subject to the accounting and reporting requirements of Section P16[16n]
b. The financial instruments described in paragraphs .105H(a), .105H(c), .105H(e), and .105H(f) of this section, except for reinsurance receivables and prepaid reinsurance premiums.

[FAS133, ¶531(d)]

[16n]Financial instruments of a pension plan, other than the obligations for pension benefits, when subject to the accounting and reporting requirements of Section Pe5, are subject to the requirements of paragraph .116A. [FAS133, ¶531(d)]

Encouraged Disclosure about Market Risk of All Financial Instruments

.116C An entity is encouraged, but not required, to disclose quantitative information about the market risks of financial instruments that is consistent with the way it manages or adjusts those risks. [FAS133, ¶531(d)]

.116D Appropriate ways of reporting the quantitative information encouraged in paragraph .116C will differ for different entities and will likely evolve over time as management approaches and measurement techniques evolve. Possibilities include disclosing (a) more details about current positions and perhaps activity during the period, (b) the hypothetical effects on comprehensive income (or net assets), or annual income, of several possible changes in market prices, (c) a gap analysis of interest rate repricing or maturity dates, (d) the duration of the financial instruments, or (e) the entity's value at risk from derivatives and from other positions at the end of the reporting period and the average value at risk during the year. This list is not exhaustive, and an entity is encouraged to develop other ways of reporting quantitative information. [FAS133, ¶531(d)]

.117–.140 [Deleted 6/98 because of Statement 133.]

Examples of Procedures for Estimating Fair Value

.141 Paragraphs .142 through .152 provide examples of procedures for estimating the fair value of financial instruments. The examples are illustrative and are not meant to portray all possible ways of estimating the fair value of a financial instrument in order to comply with the provisions of paragraphs .115C through .115F and .115I through .115K. [FAS107, ¶18]

.142 Fair value information is frequently based on information obtained from market sources. In broad terms, there are four kinds of markets in which financial instruments can be bought, sold, or originated; available information about prices differs by kind of market:

a. *Exchange market.* An exchange or "auction" market provides high visibility and order to the trading of financial instruments. Typically, closing prices and volume levels are readily available in an exchange market.
b. *Dealer market.* In a dealer market, dealers stand ready to trade—either buy or sell—for their own account, thereby providing liquidity to the market. Typically, current bid and asked prices are more readily available than information about closing prices and volume levels. "Over-the-counter" markets are dealer markets.

[17–20][Deleted 6/98 because of Statement 133.]

c. *Brokered market.* In a brokered market, brokers attempt to match buyers with sellers but do not stand ready to trade for their own account. The broker knows the prices bid and asked by the respective parties, but each party is typically unaware of another party's price requirements; prices of completed transactions are sometimes available.
d. *Principal-to-principal market.* Principal-to-principal transactions, both originations and resales, are negotiated independently, with no intermediary, and little, if any, information is typically released publicly.

[FAS107, ¶19]

Financial Instruments with Quoted Prices

.143 As indicated in paragraph .115D, quoted market prices, if available, are the best evidence of fair value of financial instruments. Prices for financial instruments may be quoted in several markets; generally, the price in the most active market will be the best indicator of fair value. [FAS107, ¶20]

.144 In some cases, an entity's management may decide to provide further information about the fair value of a financial instrument. For example, an entity may want to explain that although the fair value of its long-term debt is less than the carrying amount, settlement at the reported fair value may not be possible or may not be a prudent management decision for other reasons; or the entity may want to state that potential taxes and other expenses that would be incurred in an actual sale or settlement are not taken into consideration. [FAS107, ¶21]

Financial Instruments with No Quoted Prices

.145 For financial instruments that do not trade regularly, or that trade only in principal-to-principal markets, an entity shall provide its best estimate of fair value. Judgments about the methods and assumptions to be used in various circumstances must be made by those who prepare and attest to an entity's financial statements. The following discussion provides some examples of how fair value might be estimated. [FAS107, ¶22]

.146 For some short-term financial instruments, the carrying amount in the financial statements may approximate fair value because of the relatively short period of time between the origination of the instruments and their expected realization. Likewise, for loans that reprice frequently at market rates, the carrying amount may normally be close enough to fair value to satisfy these disclosure requirements, provided there is no significant change in the credit risk of those loans. [FAS107, ¶23]

.147 Some financial instruments (for example, interest rate swaps and foreign currency contracts) may be "custom-tailored" and, thus, may not have a quoted market price. In those cases, an estimate of fair value might be based on the quoted market price of a similar financial instrument, adjusted as appropriate for the effects of the tailoring. Alternatively, the estimate might be based on the estimated current replacement cost of that instrument. [FAS107, ¶24]

.148 Other financial instruments that are commonly "custom-tailored" include various types of options (for example, put and call options on stock, foreign currency, or interest rate contracts). A variety of option pricing models that have been developed in recent years (such as the Black-Scholes model and binomial models) are regularly used to value options. The use of those pricing models to estimate fair value is appropriate under the requirements of this section. [FAS107, ¶25]

.149 For some predominantly financial entities, loans receivable may be the most significant category of financial instruments. Market prices may be more readily available for some categories of loans (such as residential mortgage loans) than for others. If no quoted market price exists for a category of loans, an estimate of fair value may be based on (a) the market prices of similar traded loans with similar credit ratings, interest rates, and maturity dates, (b) current prices (interest rates) offered for similar loans in the entity's own lending activities, or (c) valuations obtained from loan pricing services offered by various specialist firms or from other sources. [FAS107, ¶26]

.150 An estimate of the fair value of a loan or group of loans may be based on the discounted value of the future cash flows expected to be received from the loan or group of loans. The selection of an appropriate current discount rate reflecting the relative risks involved requires judgment, and several alternative rates and approaches are available to an entity. A single discount rate could be used to estimate the fair value of a homogeneous category of loans; for example, an entity might apply a single rate to each aggregated category of loans reported for regulatory purposes. An entity could use a discount rate commensurate with the credit, interest rate, and prepayment risks involved, which could be the rate at which the same loans would be made under current conditions. An entity also could select a discount rate that reflects the effects of interest rate changes and then make adjustments to reflect the effects of changes in credit risk. Those adjustments could include (a) revising cash flow estimates for cash flows not expected to be collected, (b) revising the discount rate to reflect any additional credit risk associated with that group of loans, or some combination of (a) and (b). [FAS107, ¶27]

.151 A fair value for financial liabilities for which quoted market prices are not available can generally be estimated using the same techniques used for estimating the value of financial assets. For example, a loan payable to a bank could be valued at the discounted amount of future cash flows using an entity's current incremental rate of borrowing for a similar liability; alternatively, the discount rate could be the rate that an entity would have to pay to a creditworthy third party to assume its obligation, with the creditor's legal consent (sometimes referred to as the "settlement rate"). [FAS107, ¶28]

.152 For deposit liabilities with defined maturities, such as certificates of deposit, an estimate of fair value might also be based on the discounted value of the future cash flows expected to be paid on the deposits. The discount rate could be the current rate offered for similar deposits with the same remaining maturities. For deposit liabilities with no defined maturities, paragraph .115E requires that the fair value to be disclosed be the amount payable on demand at the reporting date. [FAS107, ¶29]

Illustrations Applying the Disclosure Requirements about Fair Value of Financial Instruments

.153 The examples that follow are guides to implementation of the disclosure requirements of paragraphs .115C through .115F and .115I through .115K. Entities are not required to display the information contained herein in the specific manner illustrated. Alternative ways of disclosing the information are permissible as long as they satisfy the disclosure requirements of paragraphs .115C through .115F and .115I through .115K. Paragraphs .115E and .144 describe possible additional voluntary disclosures that may be appropriate in certain circumstances. [FAS107, ¶30]

Example 1—Financial Entity

.154 Bank A might disclose the following:

Note V: Disclosures about Fair Value of Financial Instruments

The following methods and assumptions were used to estimate the fair value of each class of financial instruments for which it is practicable to estimate that value:

Cash and short-term investments
For those short-term instruments, the carrying amount is a reasonable estimate of fair value.

Investment securities and trading account assets
For securities and derivative instruments held for trading purposes (which include bonds, interest rate futures, options, interest rate swaps, securities sold not owned, caps and floors, foreign currency contracts, and forward contracts) and marketable equity securities held for investment purposes, fair values are based on quoted market prices or dealer quotes.

For other securities held as investments, fair value equals quoted market price, if available. If a quoted market price is not available, fair value is estimated using quoted market prices for similar securities.

Loan receivables
For certain homogeneous categories of loans, such as some residential mortgages, credit card receivables, and other consumer loans, fair value is estimated using the quoted market prices for securities backed by similar loans, adjusted for differences in loan characteristics. The fair value of other types of loans is estimated by discounting the future cash flows using the current rates at which similar loans would be made to borrowers with similar credit ratings and for the same remaining maturities.

Deposit liabilities
The fair value of demand deposits, savings accounts, and certain money market deposits is the amount payable on demand at the reporting date. The fair value of fixed-maturity certificates of deposit is estimated using the rates currently offered for deposits of similar remaining maturities.

Long-term debt
Rates currently available to the Bank for debt with similar terms and remaining maturities are used to estimate fair value of existing debt.

Commitments to extend credit, standby letters of credit, and financial guarantees written
The fair value of commitments is estimated using the fees currently charged to enter into similar agreements, taking into account the remaining terms of the agreements and the present creditworthiness of the counterparties. For fixed-rate loan commitments, fair value also considers the difference between current levels of interest rates and the committed rates. The fair value of guarantees and letters of credit is based on fees currently charged for similar agreements or on the estimated cost to terminate them or otherwise settle the obligations with the counterparties at the reporting date.

The estimated fair values of the Bank's financial instruments are as follows:

	19X9		19X8	
	Carrying Amount	**Fair Value**	**Carrying Amount**	**Fair Value**
Financial assets:				
Cash and short-term investments	$ XXX	$ XXX	$ XXX	$ XXX
Trading account assets	XXX	XXX	XXX	XXX
Investment securities	XXX	XXX	XXX	XXX
Loans	XXX		XXX	
Less: allowance for loan losses	(XXX)		(XXX)	
Loans, net of allowance	XXX	XXX	XXX	XXX
Financial liabilities:				
Deposits	XXX	XXX	XXX	XXX
Securities sold not owned	XXX	XXX	XXX	XXX
Long-term debt	XXX	XXX	XXX	XXX
Unrecognized financial instruments:*				
Commitments to extend credit	(XXX)	(XXX)	(XXX)	(XXX)
Standby letters of credit	(XXX)	(XXX)	(XXX)	(XXX)
Financial guarantees written	(XXX)	(XXX)	(XXX)	(XXX)

*The amounts shown under "carrying amount" represent accruals or deferred income (fees) arising from those unrecognized financial instruments. Other derivative instruments entered into as trading activities are included in "trading account assets" or "securities sold not owned." [FAS107, ¶31]

Example 2—Nonfinancial Entity

[In this example, it is assumed that the carrying amounts of the short-term trade receivables and payables approximate their fair values.]

.155 Corporation B might disclose the following:

Note X: Disclosures about Fair Value of Financial Instruments

The following methods and assumptions were used to estimate the fair value of each class of financial instruments for which it is practicable to estimate that value:

Cash and short-term investments
The carrying amount approximates fair value because of the short maturity of those instruments.

Long-term investments
The fair values of some investments are estimated based on quoted market prices for those or similar investments. For other investments for which there are no quoted market prices, a reasonable estimate of fair value could not be made without incurring excessive costs. Additional information pertinent to the value of an unquoted investment is provided below.

Long-term debt
The fair value of the Corporation's long-term debt is estimated based on the quoted market prices for the same or similar issues or on the current rates offered to the Corporation for debt of the same remaining maturities.

Foreign currency contracts
The fair value of foreign currency contracts (used for hedging purposes) is estimated by obtaining quotes from brokers.

The estimated fair values of the Corporation's financial instruments are as follows:

	19X9		**19X8**	
	Carrying Amount	**Fair Value**	**Carrying Amount**	**Fair Value**
Cash and short-term investments	$ XXX	$ XXX	$ XXX	$ XXX
Long-term investments for which it is:				
Practicable to estimate fair value	XXX	XXX	XXX	XXX
Not practicable	XXX	—	XXX	—
Long-term debt	(XXX)	(XXX)	(XXX)	(XXX)
Foreign currency contracts	XXX	XXX	(XXX)	(XXX)

It was not practicable to estimate the fair value of an investment representing 12 percent of the issued common stock of an untraded company; that investment is carried at its original cost of $XXX (19X8, $XXX) in the statement of financial position. At year-end, the total assets reported by the untraded company were $XXX (19X8, $XXX) and the common stockholders' equity was $XXX (19X8, $XXX), revenues were $XXX (19X8, $XXX), and net income was $XXX (19X8, $XXX). [FAS107, ¶32]

Example 3—Small Nonfinancial Entity

.156 Corporation C, whose only financial instruments are cash, short-term trade receivables and payables for which their carrying amounts approximate fair values, and long-term debt, might disclose the following:

Note Z: Long-Term Debt

Based on the borrowing rates currently available to the Corporation for bank loans with similar terms and average maturities, the fair value of long-term debt is $XXX (19X8, $XXX). [FAS107, ¶33]

Glossary

.401–.404 [Deleted 6/98 because of Statement 133 and editorial deletions.]

Supplemental Guidance: Emerging Issues Task Force (EITF) Issues

.1000 [Listed below are EITF Issues that provide supplemental guidance for this section. These Issues may be either interpretive of or related by topic to the guidance in this section.

EITF Issue No. 84-23, "Leveraged Buyout Holding Company Debt"
EITF Issue No. 98-10, "Accounting for Contracts Involved in Energy Trading and Risk Management Activities"
EITF Topic No. D-69, "Gain Recognition on Transfers of Financial Assets under FASB Statement No. 125"]

.1001 [Listed below is an EITF Issue that provides interpretive guidance on specific material in this section.

Paragraph .115C (FAS107, ¶10)—EITF Topic No. D-69]

(The next page is 17503.)

FINANCIAL INSTRUMENTS: SERVICING SECTION F35

Source: FASB Statement 140

[**Note:** A list of Issues discussed by the Emerging Issues Task Force (EITF) that provide supplemental guidance for this section is presented in paragraph .1000.]

Summary

This section presents accounting and reporting standards for servicing of financial assets. Servicing assets purchased or servicing liabilities assumed should be initially measured at fair value. The initial measurement of servicing assets or liabilities retained in a sale or securitization is specified in Section F39, "Financial Instruments: Transfers."

This section also requires that servicing assets and liabilities be subsequently measured by (a) amortization in proportion to and over the period of estimated net servicing income or loss and (b) assessment for asset impairment or increased obligation based on their fair values.

Scope

.101 This section [presents] accounting [and reporting standards] for servicing of **financial assets.** [FAS140, ¶1] [This section addresses the recognition and initial measurement of] **servicing assets** and **[servicing] liabilities** purchased or assumed [or] undertaken in a sale or securitization of the financial assets being serviced. [FAS140, ¶13] This section [also addresses the] subsequent measurement of servicing assets and servicing liabilities. This section does not address [sales or other] transfers of servicing assets. [FAS140, ¶4] [Section F39, "Financial Instruments: Transfers," presents accounting guidance for the initial measurement of servicing assets or liabilities undertaken in a sale or **securitization.**]

Recognition and Measurement of Servicing Assets and Liabilities

.102 Each time an entity undertakes an obligation to service financial assets it shall recognize either a servicing asset or a servicing liability for that servicing contract, unless it transfers the assets to a qualifying SPE in a **guaranteed mortgage securitization,** retains all of the resulting securities, and classifies them as debt securities held-to-maturity in accordance with Section I80, "Investments: Debt and Equity Securities."* If the servicing asset or liability was purchased or assumed rather than undertaken in a sale or securitization of the financial assets being serviced, it shall be measured initially at its fair value, presumptively the price paid. A servicing asset or liability shall be amortized in proportion to and over the period of estimated net servicing income (if servicing revenues exceed servicing costs) or net servicing loss (if servicing costs exceed servicing revenues). A servicing asset or liability shall be assessed for impairment or increased obligation based on its fair value (paragraphs .104 through .107). [FAS140, ¶13] [Refer to Section F39, paragraphs .149 through .151, for the definition of and guidance about fair value.]

Disclosures

.102A An entity shall disclose the following for all servicing assets and servicing liabilities:

a. The amounts of servicing assets or liabilities recognized and amortized during the period
b. The fair value of recognized servicing assets and liabilities for which it is practicable to estimate that value [as determined according to paragraphs .149 through .151 of Section F39] and the method and significant assumptions used to estimate the fair value
c. The risk characteristics of the underlying financial assets used to stratify recognized servicing assets for purposes of measuring impairment in accordance with paragraph .106 of this section
d. The activity in any valuation allowance for impairment of recognized servicing assets—including beginning and ending balances, aggregate additions charged and reductions credited to operations, and aggregate direct write-downs charged against the allowances—for each period for which results of operations are presented.

[FAS140, ¶17(e)] [Refer to paragraph .1001 for an EITF Issue that provides interpretive guidance on this paragraph.]

Implementation Guidance

.103 Paragraphs .104 through .107 describe certain provisions of this section in more detail and describe how they apply to certain types of transactions. Facts and circum-

[*The exception in paragraph .102 applies after March 31, 2001. On or before March 31, 2001, a slightly different exception applies, under which servicing contracts are subject to the remaining guidance in paragraph .102, unless the entity securitizes the assets, retains all the resulting securities, and classifies them as debt securities held to maturity.]

stances and specific contracts need to be considered carefully in applying this section. Paragraphs .104 through .107 are an integral part of the standards provided in this section. [FAS140, ¶26]

Servicing Assets and Liabilities

.104 Servicing of mortgage loans, credit card receivables, or other financial assets commonly includes, but is not limited to, collecting principal, interest, and escrow payments from borrowers; paying taxes and insurance from escrowed funds; monitoring delinquencies; executing foreclosure if necessary; temporarily investing funds pending distribution; remitting fees to guarantors, trustees, and others providing services; and accounting for and remitting principal and interest payments to the holders of beneficial interests in the financial assets. Servicing is inherent in all financial assets; it becomes a distinct asset or liability only when contractually separated from the underlying assets by sale or securitization of the assets with servicing retained or separate purchase or assumption of the servicing. [FAS140, ¶61] [Refer to paragraph .1001 for an EITF Issue that provides interpretive guidance on this paragraph.]

.105 An entity that undertakes a contract to service financial assets shall recognize either a servicing asset or a servicing liability, with only one exception. (That exception is if the **transferor** transfers the assets in a guaranteed mortgage securitization, retains all of the resulting securities, and classifies them as debt securities held-to-maturity in accordance with Section I80, in which case the servicing asset or liability may be reported together with the asset being serviced.) Each sale or securitization with servicing retained or separate purchase or assumption of servicing results in a servicing contract.[1] A servicer of financial assets commonly receives the **benefits of servicing**—revenues from **contractually specified servicing fees,** late charges, and other ancillary sources, including “float,” all of which it is entitled to receive only if it performs the servicing—and incurs the costs of servicing the assets. Each servicing contract results in a servicing asset or servicing liability. Typically, the benefits of servicing are expected to be more than **adequate compensation** to the servicer for performing the servicing, and the contract results in a servicing asset. However, if the benefits of servicing are not expected to adequately compensate the servicer for performing the servicing, the contract results in a servicing liability. (A servicing asset may become a servicing liability, or vice versa, if circumstances change, and the initial measure for servicing may be zero if the benefits of servicing are just adequate to compensate the servicer for its servicing responsibilities.) [FAS140, ¶62]

---

[1]Recognition of servicing assets or liabilities for revolving-period receivables is similarly limited to the servicing for the receivables that exist and have been transferred. As new receivables are sold, rights to service them become assets or liabilities and are recognized. [FAS140, ¶78]

.106 A servicer that recognizes a servicing asset or servicing liability shall account for the contract to service financial assets separately from those assets, as follows:

a. Report servicing assets separately from servicing liabilities in the statement of financial position (paragraph .102).
b. Initially measure servicing assets retained in a sale or securitization of the assets being serviced at their allocated previous carrying amount based on relative fair values, if practicable, at the date of the sale or securitization. (Refer to Section F39, paragraphs .105, .143 through .145, and .149 through .153 [for guidance on and illustrations of initial measurement of servicing assets retained in a sale or securitization].)
c. Initially measure servicing assets purchased or servicing liabilities assumed at fair value (paragraph .102).
d. Initially measure servicing liabilities undertaken in a sale or securitization at fair value, if practicable. (Refer to Section F39, paragraphs .106(b), .106(c), and .149 through .153 [for guidance and illustrations of initial measurement of servicing liabilities in a sale or securitization].)
e. Account separately for rights to future interest income from the serviced assets that exceeds contractually specified servicing fees. Those rights are not servicing assets; they are financial assets, effectively [they are] **interest-only strips** to be accounted for in accordance with Section F39, paragraph .108.
f. Subsequently measure servicing assets by amortizing the amount recognized in proportion to and over the period of estimated net servicing income—the excess of servicing revenues over servicing costs (paragraph .102).
g. Subsequently evaluate and measure impairment of servicing assets as follows:
   (1) Stratify servicing assets based on one or more of the predominant risk characteristics of the underlying financial assets. Those characteristics may include financial asset type,[2] size, interest rate, date of origination, term, and geographic location.
   (2) Recognize impairment through a valuation allowance for an individual stratum. The amount of impairment recognized shall be the amount by which the carrying amount of servicing assets for a stratum exceeds their fair value. The fair value of servicing assets that have not been recognized shall not be used in the evaluation of impairment.
   (3) Adjust the valuation allowance to reflect changes in the measurement of impairment subsequent to the initial measurement of impairment. Fair value in excess of the carrying amount of servicing assets for that stratum, however, shall not be recognized. This section does not address when an entity should record a direct write-down of recognized servicing assets (paragraph .102).

[2]For example, for mortgage loans, financial asset type refers to the various conventional or government guaranteed or insured mortgage loans and adjustable-rate or fixed-rate mortgage loans. [FAS140, ¶63, fn19]

h. Subsequently measure servicing liabilities by amortizing the amount recognized in proportion to and over the period of estimated net servicing loss—the excess of servicing costs over servicing revenues. However, if subsequent events have increased the fair value of the liability above the carrying amount, for example, because of significant changes in the amount or timing of actual or expected future cash flows from the cash flows previously projected, the servicer shall revise its earlier estimates and recognize the increased obligation as a loss in earnings (paragraph .102).

[FAS140, ¶63]

.107 As indicated above, transferors sometimes agree to take on servicing responsibilities when the future benefits of servicing are not expected to adequately compensate them for performing that servicing. In that circumstance, the result is a servicing liability rather than a servicing asset. For example, if in the transaction illustrated in Section F39, paragraph .142, the transferor had agreed to service the loans without explicit compensation and it estimated the fair value of that servicing obligation at $50, net proceeds would be reduced to $1,050, gain on sale would be reduced to $50, and the transferor would report a servicing liability of $50. [FAS140, ¶64]

.108 [Deleted 12/00 and renumbered as paragraph .102A.]

[**Note:** Additional guidance with respect to implementing Section F35 is presented in *A Guide to Implementation of Statement 140 on Accounting for Transfers and Servicing of Financial Assets and Extinguishments of Liabilities: Questions and Answers*. This publication addresses 123 questions and was written by FASB staff members Halsey G. Bullen, Victoria A. Lusniak, and Stephen J. Young. This publication is available from the Order Department, Financial Accounting Standards Board, 401 Merritt 7, P.O. Box 5116, Norwalk, CT 06856-5116, telephone (203) 847-0700.]

Glossary

.401 **Adequate compensation.** The amount of benefits of servicing that would fairly compensate a substitute servicer should one be required, which includes the profit that would be demanded in the marketplace. [FAS140, ¶364]

.402 **Benefits of servicing.** Revenues from contractually specified servicing fees, late charges, and other ancillary sources, including "float." [FAS140, ¶364]

.403 **Contractually specified servicing fees.** All amounts that, per contract, are due to the servicer in exchange for servicing the financial asset and would no longer be received by a servicer if the beneficial owners of the serviced assets (or their trustees or agents) were to exercise their actual or potential authority under the contract to shift the servicing to another servicer. Depending on the servicing contract, those fees may include some or all of the difference between the interest rate collectible on the asset being serviced and the rate to be paid to the beneficial owners of those assets. [FAS140, ¶364]

.404 **Financial asset.** Cash, evidence of an ownership interest in an entity, or a contract that conveys to a second entity a contractual right (a) to receive cash or another financial instrument from a first entity or (b) to exchange other financial instruments on potentially favorable terms with the first entity. (This definition is essentially the same as that used in Section F25, "Financial Instruments: Disclosure," paragraph .106(b).) [FAS140, ¶364]

.404A **Guaranteed mortgage securitization.** A securitization of mortgage loans that is within the scope of Section Mo4, "Mortgage Banking Activities," and includes a substantive guarantee by a third party. [FAS140, ¶364]

.405 **Interest-only strip.** A contractual right to receive some or all of the interest due on a bond, mortgage loan, collateralized mortgage obligation, or other interest-bearing financial asset. [FAS140, ¶364]

.406 **Securitization.** The process by which financial assets are transformed into securities. [FAS140, ¶364]

.407 **Servicing asset.** A contract to service financial assets under which the estimated future revenues from contractually specified servicing fees, late charges, and other ancillary revenues are expected to more than adequately compensate the servicer for performing the servicing. A servicing contract is either (a) undertaken in conjunction with selling or securitizing the financial assets being serviced or (b) purchased or assumed separately. [FAS140, ¶364]

.408 **Servicing liability.** A contract to service financial assets under which the estimated future revenues from [contractually specified] servicing fees, late charges, and other ancillary revenues are not expected to adequately compensate the servicer for performing the servicing. [FAS140, ¶364]

.408A **Transfer.** The conveyance of a noncash financial asset by and to someone other than the issuer of that financial asset. Thus, a transfer includes selling a receivable, putting it into a securitization trust, or posting it as collateral but excludes the origination of that receivable, the settlement of that receivable, or the restructuring of that receivable into a security in a troubled debt restructuring. [FAS140, ¶364]

.409 **Transferor.** An entity that transfers a financial asset, a portion of a financial asset, or a group of financial assets that it controls to another entity. [FAS140, ¶364]

Supplemental Guidance: Emerging Issues Task Force (EITF) Issues

.1000 [Listed below are EITF Issues that provide supplemental guidance for this section. These Issues are grouped by subject matter and may be either interpretive of or related by topic to the guidance in this section.

Sale of Mortgage Servicing Rights

EITF Issue No. 85-13, "Sale of Mortgage Service Rights on Mortgages Owned by Others"
EITF Issue No. 87-34, "Sale of Mortgage Servicing Rights with a Subservicing Agreement"
EITF Issue No. 90-21, "Balance Sheet Treatment of a Sale of Mortgage Servicing Rights with a Subservicing Agreement"
EITF Issue No. 95-5, "Determination of What Risks and Rewards, If Any, Can Be Retained and Whether Any Unresolved Contingencies May Exist in a Sale of Mortgage Loan Servicing Rights"

Other

EITF Issue No. 88-11, "Allocation of Recorded Investment When a Loan or Part of a Loan Is Sold"
EITF Issue No. 88-22, "Securitization of Credit Card and Other Portfolios"
EITF Topic No. D-69, "Gain Recognition on Transfers of Financial Assets under FASB Statement No. 125"
EITF Topic No. D-99, "Questions and Answers Related to Servicing Activities in a Qualifying Special-Purpose Entity under FASB Statement No. 140"]

.1001 [Listed below is an EITF Issue that provides interpretive guidance on specific material in this section.

Paragraph .102A (FAS 140, ¶17(e))—EITF Topic No. D-69
Paragraph .104 (FAS 140, ¶61)—EITF Topic No. D-99]

(The next page is 17811.)

[illegible] Internet Engineering Task Force (IETF) Issues

[illegible]

[illegible]

[illegible]

FINANCIAL INSTRUMENTS: TRANSFERS (FAS 125) SECTION F38

The material in this section has been superseded by FASB Statement 140, *Accounting for Transfers and Servicing of Financial Assets and Extinguishments of Liabilities.* Due to the delayed effective date of Statement 140 and the prohibition of early or retroactive application, this section has been moved to Appendix E, "*Current Text* Sections That Are Superseded by Pronouncements with Delayed Effective Dates," for continued reference by users until the effective date. For transfers of financial assets occurring on or before March 31, 2001, Section F38 must be applied. (Refer to Appendix C, "Effective Dates of Pronouncements," for details of the effective date and transition provisions of Statement 140.)

FINANCIAL INSTRUMENTS: TRANSFERS (FAS140) SECTION F39

Sources: FASB Statement 140; FASB Technical Bulletin 01-1

[**Note:** A list of Issues discussed by the Emerging Issues Task Force (EITF) that provide supplemental guidance for this section is presented in paragraph .1000.]

Summary

This section presents accounting and reporting standards for transfers of financial assets. Those standards are based on consistent application of a *financial-components approach* that focuses on control. Under that approach, after a transfer of financial assets, an entity recognizes the financial and servicing assets it controls and the liabilities it has incurred, derecognizes financial assets when control has been surrendered, and derecognizes liabilities when extinguished. This section provides consistent standards for distinguishing transfers of financial assets that are sales from transfers that are secured borrowings.

A transfer of financial assets in which the transferor surrenders control over those assets is accounted for as a sale to the extent that consideration other than beneficial interests in the transferred assets is received in exchange. The transferor has surrendered control over transferred assets if and only if all of the following conditions are met:

a. The transferred assets have been isolated from the transferor—put presumptively beyond the reach of the transferor and its creditors, even in bankruptcy or other receivership.
b. Each transferee (or, if the transferee is a qualifying special-purpose entity (SPE), each holder of its beneficial interests) has the right to pledge or exchange the assets (or beneficial interests) it received, and no condition both constrains the transferee (or holder) from taking advantage of its right to pledge or exchange and provides more than a trivial benefit to the transferor.
c. The transferor does not maintain effective control over the transferred assets through either (1) an agreement that both entitles and obligates the transferor to repurchase or redeem them before their maturity or (2) the ability to unilaterally cause the holder to return specific assets, other than through a cleanup call.

This section requires that liabilities and derivatives incurred or obtained by transferors as part of a transfer of financial assets be initially measured at fair value, if practicable. It also requires that servicing assets and other retained interests in the transferred assets be measured by allocating the previous carrying amount between the assets sold, if any, and retained interests, if any, based on their relative fair values at the date of the transfer. Guidance on the initial measurement of servicing assets and liabilities purchased or assumed and the subsequent accounting for servicing assets is presented in Section F35, "Financial Instruments: Servicing."

This section provides implementation guidance for assessing isolation of transferred assets, conditions that constrain a transferee, conditions for an entity to be a qualifying SPE, accounting for transfers of partial interests, measurement of retained interests, securitizations, transfers of sales-type and direct financing lease receivables, securities lending transactions, repurchase agreements including "dollar rolls," "wash sales," loan syndications and participations, risk participations in banker's acceptances, factoring arrangements, and transfers of receivables with recourse. This section also provides guidance about whether a transferor has retained effective control over assets transferred to qualifying SPEs through removal-of-accounts provisions, liquidation provisions, or other arrangements.

This section requires a debtor to (a) reclassify financial assets pledged as collateral and report those assets in its statement of financial position separately from other assets not so encumbered if the secured party has the right by contract or custom to sell or repledge the collateral and (b) disclose assets pledged as collateral that have not been reclassified and separately reported in the statement of financial position. This section also requires a secured party to disclose information about collateral that it has accepted and is permitted by contract or custom to sell or repledge. The required disclosure includes the fair value at the end of the period of that collateral, and of the portion of that collateral that it has sold or repledged, and information about the sources and uses of that collateral.

This section requires an entity that has securitized financial assets to disclose information about accounting policies, volume, cash flows, key assumptions made in determining fair values of retained interests, and sensitivity of those fair values to changes in key assumptions. It also requires that entities that securitize assets disclose for the securitized assets and any other financial assets it manages together with them (a) the total principal amount outstanding, the portion that has been derecognized, and the portion that continues to be recognized in each category reported in the statement of financial position, at the end of the period; (b) delinquencies at the end of the period; and (c) credit losses during the period.

Scope

.101 **Transfers** of **financial assets** take many forms. [Many] transfers [occur] in which the **transferor** has no continuing involvement with the transferred assets or with the **transferee.** However, transfers of financial assets often occur in which the transferor has some continuing involvement either with the assets transferred or with the transferee. Examples of continuing involvement are **recourse,** servicing, agreements to reacquire, options written or held, and pledges of **collateral**. Transfers of financial assets with continuing involvement raise issues about the circumstances under which the transfers should be considered as sales of all or part of the assets or as secured borrowings and about how transferors and transferees should account for sales and secured borrowings. This section establishes standards for resolving those issues. [FAS140, ¶2] This section [is based on] a *financial-components approach* for [dealing with transfers of financial assets] that focuses on control and recognizes that financial assets and liabilities can be divided into a variety of components. [FAS140, ¶7]

.102 [One] objective in accounting for transfers of financial assets is for each entity that is a party to the transaction to recognize only assets it controls and liabilities it has incurred, [and] to **derecognize** assets only when control has been surrendered. [FAS140, ¶5] Another objective is that recognition of financial assets and liabilities should not be affected by the sequence of transactions that result in their acquisition or incurrence unless the effect of those transactions is to maintain effective control over a transferred financial asset. For example, if a transferor sells financial assets it owns and at the same time writes an "at-the-money" put option (such as a guarantee or recourse obligation) on those assets, it should recognize the put obligation in the same manner as would another unrelated entity that writes an identical put option on assets it never owned. [FAS140, ¶6]

.103 This section does not address transfers of custody of financial assets for safekeeping, contributions,[1] transfers of ownership interests that are in substance sales of real estate, exchanges of equity method investments for similar productive assets, or investments by owners or distributions to owners of a business enterprise. This section does not address

---

[1]Contributions—unconditional nonreciprocal transfers of assets—are addressed in Section C67, "Contributions." [FAS140, ¶4, fn2]

subsequent measurement of assets and liabilities, except for **interest-only strips,** securities, retained interests in securitizations, loans, other receivables, or other financial assets that can contractually be prepaid or otherwise settled in such a way that the holder would not recover substantially all of its recorded investment and that are not within the scope of Section D50, "Derivative Instruments and Hedging Activities." This section does not change the accounting for employee benefits subject to the provisions of Sections P16, "Pension Costs," or P40, "Postretirement Benefits Other Than Pensions." This section does not change the provisions relating to leveraged leases in Section L10, "Leases," or money-over-money and wrap lease transactions involving nonrecourse debt subject to the provisions of paragraphs .542 through .545 of Section L10. This section does not address transfers of nonfinancial assets, for example, **servicing assets,** or transfers of unrecognized financial assets, for example, minimum lease payments to be received under operating leases. [FAS140, ¶4]

Accounting for Transfers

.104 A transfer of financial assets (or all or a portion of a financial asset) in which the transferor surrenders control over those financial assets shall be accounted for as a sale to the extent that consideration other than **beneficial interests** in the transferred assets is received in exchange. The transferor has surrendered control over transferred assets if and only if *all of the following conditions* are met:

a. The transferred assets have been isolated from the transferor—put presumptively beyond the reach of the transferor and its creditors, even in bankruptcy or other receivership (paragraphs .112 and .113).[1a]
b. Each transferee (or, if the transferee is a qualifying SPE (paragraph .120), each holder of its beneficial interests) has the right to pledge or exchange the assets (or beneficial interests) it received, and no condition both constrains the transferee (or holder) from

[1a]For banks and other financial institutions subject to possible receivership under the FDIC (and for other affected entities that have previously considered their transfers of financial assets in "single-step" securitizations to have isolated those assets in circumstances similar to those of entities subject to possible FDIC receivership), paragraphs .104(a), .112, .113, and .161 through .165 shall be effective for transfers of financial assets occurring after December 31, 2001. [FTB01-1, ¶5] [An] additional transition period applies to voluntary transfers that under prior contractual arrangements with qualifying SPE BIHs other than the transferor, its affiliates, or its agents, are constrained to be made in such a way that the transfer cannot meet all the requirements for sale accounting in paragraphs .104(a), .112, .113, and .161 through .165 of this section. That additional transition period is available only for such transfers by banks and other financial institutions subject to possible receivership under the FDIC (and for other affected entities that have previously considered their transfers of financial assets in "single-step" securitizations to have isolated those assets in circumstances similar to those of entities subject to possible FDIC receivership). The additional transition period is available only if all beneficial interests issued by the qualifying SPE after [July 23, 2001] permit the necessary changes in structure. The additional transition period ends three months after the earliest date at which sufficient approvals to permit the necessary changes can be obtained from BIHs and any other persons whose approvals are required by the terms of the prior contractual arrangement, but in no event later than June 30, 2006. [FTB01-1, ¶8, fn*]

taking advantage of its right to pledge or exchange and provides more than a trivial benefit to the transferor (paragraphs .114 through .119).

c. The transferor does not maintain effective control over the transferred assets through either (1) an agreement that both entitles and obligates the transferor to repurchase or redeem them before their maturity (paragraphs .132 through .134) or (2) the ability to unilaterally cause the holder to return specific assets, other than through a **cleanup call** (paragraphs .135 through .139).

[FAS140, ¶9] [Refer to paragraph .1001 for EITF Issues that provide interpretive guidance on this paragraph.]

.105 Upon completion of any transfer of financial assets, the transferor shall:

a. Continue to carry in its statement of financial position any retained interest in the transferred assets, including, if applicable, servicing assets (paragraphs .146 through .148 of this section and .104 through .107 of Section F35), beneficial interests in assets transferred to a qualifying SPE in a **securitization** (paragraphs .154 through .165), and retained **undivided interests** (paragraphs .143 and .144)
b. Allocate the previous carrying amount between the assets sold, if any, and the retained interests, if any, based on their relative **fair values** at the date of transfer (paragraphs .141 through .145).

[FAS140, ¶10] [Refer to paragraph .1001 for an EITF Issue that provides interpretive guidance on this paragraph.]

.106 Upon completion[2] of a transfer of assets that satisfies the conditions to be accounted for as a sale (paragraph .105), the transferor (**seller**) shall:

a. Derecognize all assets sold
b. Recognize all assets obtained and liabilities incurred in consideration as **proceeds** of the sale, including cash, put or call options held or written (for example, guarantee or recourse obligations), forward commitments (for example, commitments to deliver additional receivables during the revolving periods of some securitizations), swaps (for example, provisions that convert interest rates from fixed to variable), and servicing liabilities, if applicable (paragraphs .141, .142, and .146 through .148 of this section and paragraphs .104 through .107 of Section F35)

[2] Although a transfer of securities may not be considered to have reached completion until the settlement date, this section does not modify other generally accepted accounting principles, including Section Pe5, "Pension Funds: Accounting and Reporting by Defined Benefit Pension Plans," and AICPA Statements of Position and audit and accounting Guides for certain industries, that require accounting at the trade date for certain contracts to purchase or sell securities. [FAS140, ¶11, fn3]

c. Initially measure at fair value assets obtained and liabilities incurred in a sale (paragraphs .149 through .151) or, if it is not practicable to estimate the fair value of an asset or a liability, apply alternative measures (paragraphs .152 and .153)
d. Recognize in earnings any gain or loss on the sale.

The transferee shall recognize all assets obtained and any liabilities incurred and initially measure them at fair value (in aggregate, presumptively the price paid). [FAS140, ¶11] [Refer to paragraph .1001 for an EITF Issue that provides interpretive guidance on this paragraph.]

.107 If a transfer of financial assets in exchange for cash or other consideration (other than beneficial interests in the transferred assets) does not meet the criteria for a sale in paragraph .104, the transferor and transferee shall account for the transfer as a secured borrowing with pledge of collateral (paragraph .109). [FAS140, ¶12]

Financial Assets Subject to Prepayment

.108 Interest-only strips, retained interests in securitizations, loans, other receivables, or other financial assets that can contractually be prepaid or otherwise settled in such a way that the holder would not recover substantially all of its recorded investment, except for instruments that are within the scope of Section D50, shall be subsequently measured like investments in debt securities classified as available-for-sale or trading under Section I80, "Investments: Debt and Equity Securities," paragraphs .104 and .109.[3] [FAS 140, ¶14]

Secured Borrowings and Collateral

.109 A debtor may grant a **security interest** in certain assets to a lender (the secured party) to serve as collateral for its obligation under a borrowing, with or without recourse to other assets of the debtor. An obligor under other kinds of current or potential obligations, for example, interest rate swaps, also may grant a security interest in certain assets to a secured party. If collateral is transferred to the secured party, the custodial arrangement is commonly referred to as a pledge. Secured parties sometimes are permitted to sell or repledge (or otherwise transfer) collateral held under a pledge. The same relationships occur, under different names, in transfers documented as sales that are

[3]The provisions of paragraph .108 do not apply to situations in which events that are not the result of contractual provisions, for example, borrower default or changes in the value of an instrument's denominated currency relative to the entity's functional currency, cause the holder not to recover substantially all of its recorded investment. [FAS140, ¶295]

accounted for as secured borrowings (paragraph .107). The accounting for noncash[4] collateral by the debtor (or obligor) and the secured party depends on whether the secured party has the right to sell or repledge the collateral and on whether the debtor has defaulted.

a. If the secured party (transferee) has the right by contract or custom to sell or repledge the collateral, then the debtor (transferor) shall reclassify that asset and report that asset in its statement of financial position separately (for example, as security pledged to creditors) from other assets not so encumbered.
b. If the secured party (transferee) sells collateral pledged to it, it shall recognize the proceeds from the sale and its obligation to return the collateral.[5] The sale of the collateral is a transfer subject to the provisions of this section.
c. If the debtor (transferor) defaults under the terms of the secured contract and is no longer entitled to redeem the pledged asset, it shall derecognize the pledged asset, and the secured party (transferee) shall recognize the collateral as its asset initially measured at fair value or, if it has already sold the collateral, derecognize its obligation to return the collateral.
d. Except as provided in paragraph .109(c), the debtor (transferor) shall continue to carry the collateral as its asset, and the secured party (transferee) shall not recognize the pledged asset.

[FAS140, ¶15]

Disclosures

.110 An entity shall disclose the following:

a. For collateral:
   (1) If the entity has entered into repurchase agreements or securities lending transactions, its policy for requiring collateral or other security
   (2) If the entity has pledged any of its assets as collateral that are not reclassified and separately reported in the statement of financial position pursuant to paragraph .109(a), the carrying amount and classification of those assets as of the date of the latest statement of financial position presented

---

[4]Cash "collateral," sometimes used, for example, in securities lending transactions (paragraphs .172 through .176), shall be derecognized by the payer and recognized by the recipient, not as collateral but rather as proceeds of either a sale or a borrowing. [FAS140, ¶15, fn4] All cash collateral should be recorded as an asset by the party receiving it, together with a liability for the obligation to return it to the payer, whose asset is a receivable. [FAS140, ¶241]

[5]Obligations to return to the transferor assets borrowed and then sold have sometimes been effectively recognized as part of a liability for securities sold but not yet purchased, and [this section does] not require any change in that practice. [FAS140, ¶244]

(3) If the entity has accepted collateral that it is permitted by contract or custom to sell or repledge, the fair value as of the date of each statement of financial position presented of that collateral and of the portion of that collateral that it has sold or repledged, and information about the sources and uses of that collateral [FAS140, ¶17(a)]

b. If it is not practicable to estimate the fair value of certain assets obtained or liabilities incurred in transfers of financial assets during the period, a description of those items and the reasons why it is not practicable to estimate their fair value [FAS140, ¶17(d)]

c. If the entity has securitized financial assets during any period presented and accounts for that transfer as a sale, for each major asset type (for example, mortgage loans, credit card receivables, and automobile loans):

(1) Its accounting policies for initially measuring the retained interests, if any, including the methodology (whether quoted market price, prices based on sales of similar assets and liabilities, or prices based on valuation techniques) used in determining their fair value (paragraphs .149 through .151)

(2) The characteristics of securitizations (a description of the transferor's continuing involvement with the transferred assets, including, but not limited to, servicing, recourse, and restrictions on retained interests) and the gain or loss from sale of financial assets in securitizations

(3) The key assumptions[6] used in measuring the fair value of retained interests at the time of securitization (including, at a minimum, quantitative information about discount rates, expected prepayments including the expected weighted-average life of prepayable financial assets,[7] and anticipated credit losses, if applicable)

(4) Cash flows between the securitization SPE and the transferor, unless reported separately elsewhere in the financial statements or notes (including proceeds from new securitizations, proceeds from collections reinvested in revolving-period securitizations, purchases of delinquent or foreclosed loans, servicing fees, and cash flows received on interests retained) [FAS140, ¶17(f)]

d. If the entity has retained interests in securitized financial assets at the date of the latest statement of financial position presented, for each major asset type (for example, mortgage loans, credit card receivables, and automobile loans):

(1) Its accounting policies for subsequently measuring those retained interests, including the methodology (whether quoted market price, prices based on sales of similar assets and liabilities, or prices based on valuation techniques) used in determining their fair value (paragraphs .149 through .151)

---

[6]If an entity has made multiple securitizations of the same major asset type during a period, it may disclose the range of assumptions. [FAS140, ¶17, fn7]

[7]The weighted-average life of prepayable assets in periods (for example, months or years) can be calculated by multiplying the principal collections expected in each future period by the number of periods until that future period, summing those products, and dividing the sum by the initial principal balance. [FAS140, ¶17, fn8]

(2) The key assumptions used in subsequently measuring the fair value of those interests (including, at a minimum, quantitative information about discount rates, expected prepayments including the expected weighted-average life of prepayable financial assets, and anticipated credit losses, including expected static pool losses,[8] if applicable)
(3) A sensitivity analysis or stress test showing the hypothetical effect on the fair value of those interests of two or more unfavorable variations from the expected levels for each key assumption that is reported under (2) above independently from any change in another key assumption, and a description of the objectives, methodology, and limitations of the sensitivity analysis or stress test
(4) For the securitized assets and any other financial assets that it manages together with them:[9]
   (a) The total principal amount outstanding, the portion that has been derecognized, and the portion that continues to be recognized in each category reported in the statement of financial position, at the end of the period
   (b) Delinquencies at the end of the period
   (c) Credit losses, net of recoveries, during the period

   Disclosure of average balances during the period is encouraged, but not required. [FAS140, ¶17(g)]

[Refer to paragraph .1001 for an EITF Issue that provides interpretive guidance on this paragraph.]

Implementation Guidance

.111 Paragraphs .112 through .194 describe certain provisions of this section in more detail and describe how they apply to certain types of transactions. These paragraphs discuss generalized situations. Facts and circumstances and specific contracts need to be considered carefully in applying this section. Paragraphs .112 through .194 are an integral part of the standards provided in this section. [FAS140, ¶26]

Isolation beyond the Reach of the Transferor and Its Creditors

.112 The nature and extent of supporting evidence required for an assertion in financial statements that transferred financial assets have been isolated—put presumptively beyond the reach of the transferor and its creditors, either by a single transaction or a series

[8]Expected static pool losses can be calculated by summing the actual and projected future credit losses and dividing the sum by the original balance of the pool of assets. [FAS140, ¶17, fn9]

[9]Excluding securitized assets that an entity continues to service but with which it has no other continuing involvement. [FAS140, ¶17, fn10]

of transactions taken as a whole—depend on the facts and circumstances. All available evidence that either supports or questions an assertion shall be considered. That consideration includes making judgments about whether the contract or circumstances permit the transferor to revoke the transfer. It also may include making judgments about the kind of bankruptcy or other receivership into which a transferor or SPE might be placed, whether a transfer of financial assets would likely be deemed a true sale at law, whether the transferor is affiliated with the transferee, and other factors pertinent under applicable law. Derecognition of transferred assets is appropriate only if the available evidence provides reasonable assurance that the transferred assets would be beyond the reach of the powers of a bankruptcy trustee or other receiver for the transferor or any **consolidated affiliate of the transferor** that is not a special-purpose corporation or other entity designed to make remote the possibility that it would enter bankruptcy or other receivership (paragraph .164(c)).[9a] [FAS140, ¶27]

.113 Whether securitizations isolate transferred assets may depend on such factors as whether the securitization is accomplished in one step or two steps (paragraphs .161 through .165). Many common financial transactions, for example, typical repurchase agreements and securities lending transactions, isolate transferred assets from the transferor, although they may not meet the other criteria for surrender of control.[9b] [FAS140, ¶28]

Conditions That Constrain a Transferee

.114 Sale accounting is allowed under paragraph .104(b) only if each transferee has the right to pledge, or the right to exchange, the transferred assets or beneficial interests it received, but constraints on that right also matter. Many transferor-imposed or other conditions on a transferee's right to pledge or exchange a transferred asset both constrain a transferee from pledging or exchanging the transferred assets and, through that constraint, provide more than a trivial benefit to the transferor. For example, a provision in the transfer contract that prohibits selling or pledging a transferred loan receivable not only constrains the transferee but also provides the transferor with the more-than-trivial benefits of knowing who has the asset, a prerequisite to repurchasing the asset, and of being able to block the asset from finding its way into the hands of a competitor for the loan customer's business or someone that the loan customer might consider an undesirable creditor. Transferor-imposed contractual constraints that narrowly limit timing or terms, for example, allowing a transferee to pledge only on the day assets are obtained or only on terms agreed with the transferor, also constrain the transferee and presumptively provide the transferor with more-than-trivial benefits. [FAS140, ¶29]

[[9a]Refer to footnote 1a.]

[[9b]Refer to footnote 1a.]

.115 However, some conditions do not constrain a transferee from pledging or exchanging the asset and therefore do not preclude a transfer subject to such a condition from being accounted for as a sale. For example, a transferor's right of first refusal on the occurrence of a bona fide offer to the transferee from a third party presumptively would not constrain a transferee, because that right in itself does not enable the transferor to compel the transferee to sell the assets and the transferee would be in a position to receive the sum offered by exchanging the asset, albeit possibly from the transferor rather than the third party. Further examples of conditions that presumptively would not constrain a transferee include (a) a requirement to obtain the transferor's permission to sell or pledge that is not to be unreasonably withheld, (b) a prohibition on sale to the transferor's competitor if other potential willing buyers exist, (c) a regulatory limitation such as on the number or nature of eligible transferees (as in the case of securities issued under Securities Act Rule 144A or debt placed privately), and (d) illiquidity, for example, the absence of an active market. Judgment is required to assess the significance of some conditions. For example, a prohibition on sale to the transferor's competitor would be a significant constraint if that competitor were the only potential willing buyer other than the transferor. [FAS140, ¶30]

.116 A condition imposed by a transferor that constrains the transferee presumptively provides more than a trivial benefit to the transferor. A condition *not* imposed by the transferor that constrains the transferee may or may not provide more than a trivial benefit to the transferor. For example, if the transferor refrains from imposing its usual contractual constraint on a specific transfer because it knows an equivalent constraint is already imposed on the transferee by a third party, it presumptively benefits more than trivially from that constraint. However, the transferor cannot benefit from a constraint if it is unaware at the time of the transfer that the transferee is constrained. [FAS140, ¶31]

Transferor's Rights or Obligations to Reacquire Transferred Assets

.117 Some rights or obligations to reacquire transferred assets both constrain the transferee and provide more than a trivial benefit to the transferor, thus precluding sale accounting under paragraph .104(b). For example, a **freestanding call** option written by a transferee to the transferor benefits the transferor and, if the transferred assets are not readily obtainable in the marketplace, is likely to constrain a transferee because it might have to default if the call was exercised and it had exchanged or pledged the assets. A freestanding forward purchase-sale contract between the transferor and the transferee on transferred assets not readily obtainable in the marketplace would benefit the transferor and is likely to constrain a transferee in much the same manner. Judgment is necessary to assess constraint and benefit. For example, put options written to the transferee generally do not constrain it, but a put option on a not-readily-obtainable asset may benefit the transferor and effectively constrain the transferee if the option is sufficiently deep-in-the-money when it is written that it is probable that the transferee will exercise it and the transferor will reacquire the transferred asset. In contrast, a sufficiently out-of-the-money call option held by the transferor may not constrain a transferee if it is probable when the option is written that it will not be exercised. Freestanding rights to reacquire transferred assets that are readily obtainable presumptively do not constrain the transferee from exchanging or pledging them and thus do not preclude sale accounting under paragraph .104(b). [FAS140, ¶32]

.118 Other rights or obligations to reacquire transferred assets, regardless of whether they constrain the transferee, may result in the transferor's maintaining effective control over the transferred assets, as discussed in paragraphs .135 through .139, thus precluding sale accounting under paragraph .104(c)(2).[10] [FAS140, ¶33]

Conditions That Constrain a Holder of Beneficial Interests in a Qualifying SPE

.119 The considerations in paragraphs .114 through .117, about conditions that may or may not constrain a transferee that is not a qualifying SPE from pledging or exchanging the transferred assets, also extend to conditions that may or may not constrain a BIH from pledging or exchanging its beneficial interests in assets transferred to a qualifying SPE. For example, if BIHs agree to sell their beneficial interests in a qualifying SPE back to the transferor upon request at the price paid plus a stated return, that arrangement clearly conveys more than a trivial benefit to the transferor; sale accounting for the transfer to the qualifying SPE would be precluded if that agreement constrained a BIH from exchanging or pledging its beneficial interest. [FAS140, ¶34]

Qualifying SPE

.120 A qualifying SPE[11] is a trust or other legal vehicle that meets *all* of the following conditions:

a. It is demonstrably distinct from the transferor (paragraph .121).
b. Its permitted activities (1) are significantly limited, (2) were entirely specified in the legal documents that established the SPE or created the beneficial interests in the transferred assets that it holds, and (3) may be significantly changed only with the ap-

---

[10]And it is necessary to consider the overall effect of related rights and obligations in assessing such matters as whether a transferee is constrained or a transferor has maintained effective control. For example, if the transferor or its affiliate or agent is the servicer for the transferred asset and is empowered to decide to put the asset up for sale, and has the right of first refusal, that combination would place the transferor in position to unilaterally cause the return of a specific transferred asset and thus maintain the transferor's effective control of the transferred asset as discussed in paragraphs .104(c)(2) and .135. [FAS140, ¶33, fn15]

[11]The description of a qualifying SPE is restrictive. The accounting for qualifying SPEs and transfers of financial assets to them should not be extended to any entity that does not currently satisfy all of the conditions articulated in this paragraph. [FAS140, ¶35, fn16]

proval of the holders of at least a majority of the beneficial interests held by entities other than any transferor, its affiliates[12], and its **agents** (paragraphs .122 and .123).

c. It may hold only:
   (1) Financial assets transferred to it that are passive in nature (paragraph .124)
   (2) Passive **derivative financial instruments** that pertain to beneficial interests (other than another derivative financial instrument) issued or sold to parties other than the transferor, its affiliates, or its agents (paragraphs .124 and .125)
   (3) Financial assets (for example, guarantees or rights to collateral) that would reimburse it if others were to fail to adequately service financial assets transferred to it or to timely pay obligations due to it and that it entered into when it was established, when assets were transferred to it, or when beneficial interests (other than derivative financial instruments) were issued by the SPE
   (4) Servicing rights related to financial assets that it holds
   (5) Temporarily, nonfinancial assets obtained in connection with the collection of financial assets that it holds (paragraph .126)
   (6) Cash collected from assets that it holds and investments purchased with that cash pending distribution to holders of beneficial interests that are appropriate for that purpose (that is, money-market or other relatively risk-free instruments without options and with maturities no later than the expected distribution date).

d. If it can sell or otherwise dispose of noncash financial assets, it can do so only in automatic response to one of the following conditions:
   (1) Occurrence of an event or circumstance that (a) is specified in the legal documents that established the SPE or created the beneficial interests in the transferred assets that it holds; (b) is outside the control of the transferor, its affiliates, or its agents; and (c) causes, or is expected at the date of transfer to cause, the fair value of those financial assets to decline by a specified degree below the fair value of those assets when the SPE obtained them (paragraphs .127 through .128)
   (2) Exercise by a BIH (other than the transferor, its affiliates, or its agents) of a right to put that holder's beneficial interest back to the SPE (paragraph .129)
   (3) Exercise by the transferor of a call or ROAP specified in the legal documents that established the SPE, transferred assets to the SPE, or created the beneficial interests in the transferred assets that it holds (paragraphs .136 through .139 and .166 through .169)
   (4) Termination of the SPE or maturity of the beneficial interests in those financial assets on a fixed or determinable date that is specified at inception (paragraph .130).

[FAS140, ¶35] [Refer to paragraph .1001 for an EITF Issue that provides interpretive guidance on this paragraph.]

---

[12]In this section, the term *affiliate* is used in the same sense as it is used in Section R36, "Related Parties." [FAS140, ¶24, fn12]

Need to Be Demonstrably Distinct from the Transferor

.121 A qualifying SPE is demonstrably distinct from the transferor only if it cannot be unilaterally dissolved by any transferor, its affiliates, or its agents and either (a) at least 10 percent of the fair value of its beneficial interests is held by parties other than any transferor, its affiliates, or its agents or (b) the transfer is a **guaranteed mortgage securitization.**[13] An ability to unilaterally dissolve an SPE can take many forms, including but not limited to holding sufficient beneficial interests to demand that the trustee dissolve the SPE, the right to call all the assets transferred to the SPE, and a right to call or a prepayment privilege on the beneficial interests held by other parties. [FAS140, ¶36]

Limits on Permitted Activities

.122 The powers of the SPE must be limited to those activities allowed by paragraph .120 for it to be a qualifying SPE. Many kinds of entities are not so limited. For example, any bank, insurance company, pension plan, or investment company has powers that cannot be sufficiently limited for it to be a qualifying SPE. [FAS140, ¶37] [Refer to paragraph .1001 for an EITF Issue that provides interpretive guidance on this paragraph.]

.123 The BIHs other than any transferor, its affiliates, or its agents may have the ability to change the powers of a qualifying SPE. If the powers of a previously qualifying SPE are changed so that the SPE is no longer qualifying, unless the conditions in paragraph .104(b) are then met by the SPE itself and the conditions in paragraphs .104(a) and .104(c) continue to be met, that change would bring the transferred assets held in the SPE back under the control of the transferor (paragraph .140). [FAS140, ¶38]

Limits on What a Qualifying SPE May Hold

.124 A financial asset or derivative financial instrument is passive only if holding the asset or instrument does not involve its holder in making decisions other than the decisions inherent in servicing (paragraph .104 of Section F35). An equity instrument is not passive if the qualifying SPE can exercise the voting rights and is permitted to choose how to vote. Investments are not passive if through them, either in themselves or in combination with other investments or rights, the SPE or any related entity, such as the transferor, its affiliates, or its agents, is able to exercise control or significant influence (as defined in generally accepted accounting principles for consolidation policy and for the equity method, respectively) over the investee. A derivative financial instrument is not passive if, for example,

---

[13]An effect of that provision, in conjunction with paragraph .131, is that mortgage-backed securities retained in a guaranteed mortgage securitization in which the SPE meets all conditions for being a qualifying SPE are classified in the financial statements of the transferor as securities that are subsequently measured under Section I80. [FAS140, ¶36, fn17]

it includes an option allowing the SPE to choose to call or put other financial instruments; but other derivative financial instruments can be passive, for example, interest rate caps and swaps and forward contracts. Derivative financial instruments that result in liabilities, like other liabilities of a qualifying SPE, are a kind of beneficial interest in the qualifying SPE's assets. [FAS140, ¶39]

.125 A derivative financial instrument pertains to beneficial interests (other than another derivative financial instrument) issued only if it:

a. Is entered into (1) when the beneficial interests are issued by the qualifying SPE to parties other than the transferor, its affiliates, or its agents or sold to such other parties after being issued by the qualifying SPE to the transferor, its affiliates, or its agents or (2) when a passive derivative financial instrument needs to be replaced upon occurrence of an event or circumstance (specified in the legal documents that established the SPE or created the beneficial interests in the transferred assets that it holds) outside the control of the transferor, its affiliates, or its agents, for example, when the counterparty to the derivative defaults or is downgraded below a specified threshold
b. Has a notional amount that does not initially exceed the amount of those beneficial interests and is not expected to exceed them subsequently
c. Has characteristics that relate to, and partly or fully but not excessively counteract, some risk associated with those beneficial interests or the related transferred assets.

[FAS140, ¶40]

.126 A qualifying SPE may hold nonfinancial assets other than servicing rights only temporarily and only if those nonfinancial assets result from collecting the transferred financial assets. For example, a qualifying SPE could be permitted to temporarily hold foreclosed nonfinancial collateral. In contrast, an entity cannot be a qualifying SPE if, for example, it receives from a transferor significant secured financial assets likely to default with the expectation that it will foreclose on and profitably manage the securing nonfinancial assets. A qualifying SPE also may hold the residual value of a sales-type or a direct financing lease only to the extent that it is guaranteed at the inception of the lease either by the lessee or by a third party financially capable of discharging the obligations that may arise from the guarantee (paragraph .170). [FAS140, ¶41] [Refer to paragraph .1001 for an EITF Issue that provides interpretive guidance on paragraphs .126 through .129.]

Limits on Sales or Other Dispositions of Assets

.127 Examples of requirements to sell, exchange, put, or distribute (hereinafter referred to collectively as dispose of) noncash financial assets that *are* permitted activities of a qualifying SPE—because they respond automatically to the occurrence of an event or circumstance that (a) is specified in the legal documents that established the SPE or created the beneficial interests in the transferred assets that it holds; (b) is outside the control of the transferor, its affiliates, or its agents; and (c) causes, or is expected to cause, the fair value of those assets to decline by a specified degree below the fair value of those assets when the qualifying SPE obtained them—include requirements to dispose of transferred assets in response to:

a. A failure to properly service transferred assets that could result in the loss of a substantial third-party credit guarantee
b. A default by the obligor
c. A downgrade by a major rating agency of the transferred assets or of the underlying obligor to a rating below a specified minimum rating
d. The involuntary insolvency of the transferor
e. A decline in the fair value of the transferred assets to a specified value less than their fair value at the time they were transferred to the SPE.

[FAS140, ¶42]

.128 The following are examples of powers or requirements to dispose of noncash financial assets that *are not* permitted activities of a qualifying SPE, because they do not respond automatically to the occurrence of a specified event or circumstance outside the control of the transferor, its affiliates, or its agents that causes, or is expected to cause, the fair value of those transferred assets to decline by a specified degree below the fair value of those assets when the SPE obtained them:

a. A power that allows an SPE to choose to either dispose of transferred assets or hold them in response to a default, a downgrade, a decline in fair value, or a servicing failure
b. A requirement to dispose of marketable equity securities upon a specified decline from their "highest fair value" if that power could result in disposing of the asset in exchange for an amount that is more than the fair value of those assets at the time they were transferred to the SPE
c. A requirement to dispose of transferred assets in response to the violation of a nonsubstantive contractual provision (that is, a provision for which there is not a sufficiently large disincentive to ensure performance).

[FAS140, ¶43]

.129 A qualifying SPE may dispose of transferred assets automatically to the extent necessary to comply with the exercise by a BIH (other than the transferor, its affiliates, or its agents) of its right to put beneficial interests back to the SPE in exchange for:

a. A full or partial distribution of those assets
b. Cash (which may require that the SPE dispose of those assets or issue beneficial interests to generate cash to fund settlement of the put)
c. New beneficial interests in those assets.

[FAS140, ¶44]

.130 A qualifying SPE may have the power to dispose of assets to a party other than the transferor, its affiliate, or its agent on termination of the SPE or maturity of the beneficial interests, but only automatically on fixed or determinable dates that are specified at inception. For example, if an SPE is required to dispose of long-term mortgage loans and terminate itself at the earlier of (a) the specified maturity of beneficial interests in those mortgage loans or (b) the date of prepayment of a specified amount of the transferred mortgage loans, the termination date is a fixed or determinable date that was specified at inception. In contrast, if that SPE has the power to dispose of transferred assets on two specified dates and the SPE can decide which transferred assets to sell on each date, the termination date is *not* a fixed or determinable date that was specified at inception. [FAS140, ¶45]

Qualifying SPEs and Consolidated Financial Statements

.131 A qualifying SPE shall not be consolidated in the financial statements of a transferor or its affiliates.[14] [FAS140, ¶46]

Maintaining Effective Control over Transferred Assets

Agreement to Repurchase or Redeem Transferred Assets

.132 An agreement that both entitles and obligates the transferor to repurchase or redeem transferred assets from the transferee maintains the transferor's effective control over those assets under paragraph .104(c)(1), and the transfer is therefore to be accounted for as a secured borrowing, if and only if all of the following conditions are met:

a. The assets to be repurchased or redeemed are the same or substantially the same as those transferred (paragraph .133).
b. The transferor is able to repurchase or redeem them on substantially the agreed terms, even in the event of default by the transferee (paragraph .134).
c. The agreement is to repurchase or redeem them before maturity, at a fixed or determinable price.
d. The agreement is entered into concurrently with the transfer.

[FAS140, ¶47] [Refer to paragraph .1001 for an EITF Issue that provides interpretive guidance on this paragraph.]

[14]Any entity that is not a transferor of assets to a qualifying SPE, or an affiliate of the transferor, needs to consider other existing or future generally accepted accounting principles on consolidation policy to determine whether it is required to consolidate a qualifying SPE in the financial statements being presented. [FAS140, ¶199]

.133 To be substantially the same,[15] the asset that was transferred and the asset that is to be repurchased or redeemed need to have all of the following characteristics:

a. The same primary obligor (except for debt guaranteed by a sovereign government, central bank, government-sponsored enterprise or agency thereof, in which case the guarantor and the terms of the guarantee must be the same)
b. Identical form and type so as to provide the same risks and rights
c. The same maturity (or in the case of mortgage-backed pass-through and pay-through securities, similar remaining weighted-average maturities that result in approximately the same market yield)
d. Identical contractual interest rates
e. Similar assets as collateral
f. The same aggregate unpaid principal amount or principal amounts within accepted "good delivery" standards for the type of security involved.

[FAS140, ¶48]

.134 To be able to repurchase or redeem assets on substantially the agreed terms, even in the event of default by the transferee, a transferor must at all times during the contract term have obtained cash or other collateral sufficient to fund substantially all of the cost of purchasing replacement assets from others.[16] [FAS140, ¶49] [Refer to paragraph .1001 for an EITF Issue that provides interpretive guidance on this paragraph.]

Ability to Unilaterally Cause the Return of Specific Transferred Assets

.135 Some rights to reacquire transferred assets (or to acquire beneficial interests in transferred assets held by a qualifying SPE), regardless of whether they constrain the transferee, may result in the transferor's maintaining effective control over the transferred assets through the **unilateral ability** to cause the return of specific transferred assets. Such rights preclude sale accounting under paragraph .104(c)(2). For example, an **attached call** in itself would not constrain a transferee who is able, by exchanging or

---

[15]In this section, the term *substantially the same* is used consistently with the usage of that term in the AICPA Statement of Position 90-3, *Definition of the Term Substantially the Same for Holders of Debt Instruments, as Used in Certain Audit Guides and a Statement of Position*. [FAS140, ¶48, fn18]

[16]Judgment is needed to interpret the term *substantially all* and other aspects of the criterion that the terms of a repurchase agreement do not maintain effective control over the transferred asset. However, arrangements to repurchase or lend readily obtainable securities, typically with as much as 98 percent collateralization (for entities agreeing to repurchase) or as little as 102 percent overcollateralization (for securities lenders), valued daily and adjusted up or down frequently for changes in the market price of the security transferred and with clear powers to use that collateral quickly in the event of default, typically fall clearly within that guideline. Other collateral arrangements [are believed to] typically fall well outside that guideline. [FAS140, ¶218]

pledging the asset subject to that call, to obtain substantially all of its economic benefits. An attached call could result, however, in the transferor's maintaining effective control over the transferred asset(s) because the attached call gives the transferor the ability to unilaterally cause whoever holds that specific asset to return it. In contrast, transfers of financial assets subject to calls embedded by the issuers of the financial instruments, for example, callable bonds or prepayable mortgage loans, do not preclude sale accounting. Such an **embedded call** does not result in the transferor's maintaining effective control, because it is the issuer rather than the transferor who holds the call. [FAS140, ¶50]

.136 If the transferee is a qualifying SPE, it has met the conditions in paragraph .120(d) and therefore must be constrained from choosing to exchange or pledge the transferred assets. In that circumstance, any call held by the transferor is effectively attached to the assets and could—depending on the price and other terms of the call—maintain the transferor's effective control over transferred assets through the ability to unilaterally cause the transferee to return specific assets. For example, a transferor's unilateral ability to cause a qualifying SPE to return to the transferor or otherwise dispose of specific transferred assets at will or, for example, in response to its decision to exit a market or a particular activity, could provide the transferor with effective control over the transferred assets. [FAS140, ¶51]

.137 A call that is attached to transferred assets maintains the transferor's effective control over those assets if, under its price and other terms, the call conveys more than a trivial benefit to the transferor. Similarly, any unilateral right to reclaim specific assets transferred to a qualifying SPE maintains the transferor's effective control over those assets if the right conveys more than a trivial benefit to the transferor. A call or other right conveys more than a trivial benefit if the price to be paid is fixed, determinable, or otherwise potentially advantageous, unless because that price is so far out of the money or for other reasons it is probable when the option is written that the transferor will not exercise it. Thus, for example, a call on specific assets transferred to a qualifying SPE at a price fixed at their principal amount maintains the transferor's effective control over the assets subject to that call. Effective control over transferred assets can be present even if the right to reclaim is indirect. For example, if an embedded call allows a transferor to buy back the beneficial interests of a qualifying SPE at a fixed price, then the transferor remains in effective control of the assets underlying those beneficial interests. A cleanup call, however, is permitted as an exception to that general principle. [FAS140, ¶52]

.138 A right to reclaim specific transferred assets by paying their fair value when reclaimed generally does not maintain effective control, because it does not convey a more than trivial benefit to the transferor. However, a transferor has maintained effective control if it has such a right and also holds the residual interest in the transferred assets. For example, if a transferor can reclaim such assets at termination of the qualifying SPE by purchasing them in an auction, and thus at what might appear to be fair value, then sale accounting for the assets it can reclaim would be precluded. Such circumstances provide the transferor with a more than trivial benefit and effective control over the assets, because it can pay any price it chooses in the auction and recover any excess paid over fair value through its residual interest. [FAS140, ¶53]

.139 A transferor that has a right to reacquire transferred assets from a qualifying SPE does not maintain effective control if the reclaimed assets would be randomly selected and the amount of the assets reacquired is sufficiently limited (paragraph .168(a)), because that would not be a right to reacquire *specific* assets. Nor does a transferor maintain effective control through an obligation to reacquire transferred assets from a qualifying SPE if the transfer could occur only after a specified failure of the servicer to properly service the transferred assets that could result in the loss of a third-party guarantee (paragraph .127(a)) or only after a BIH other than the transferor, its affiliate, or its agent requires a qualifying SPE to repurchase that beneficial interest (paragraph .129(b)), because the transferor could not cause that reacquisition *unilaterally*. [FAS140, ¶54]

Changes That Result in the Transferor's Regaining Control of Assets Sold

.140 A change in law, status of the transferee as a qualifying SPE, or other circumstance may result in the transferor's regaining control of assets previously accounted for appropriately as having been sold, because one or more of the conditions in paragraph .104 are no longer met. Such a change, unless it arises solely from either the initial application of this section or a change in market prices (for example, an increase in price that moves into-the-money a freestanding call that was originally sufficiently out-of-the-money that it was judged not to constrain the transferee), is accounted for in the same manner as a purchase of the assets from the former transferee(s) in exchange for liabilities assumed (paragraph .106). After that change, the transferor recognizes in its financial statements those assets together with liabilities to the former transferee(s) or BIHs in those assets (paragraph .123). The transferor initially measures those assets and liabilities at fair value on the date of the change, as if the transferor purchased the assets and assumed the liabilities on that date. The former transferee would derecognize the assets on that date, as if it had sold the assets in exchange for a receivable from the transferor. [FAS140, ¶55]

Measurement of Interests Held after a Transfer of Financial Assets

Assets Obtained and Liabilities Incurred as Proceeds

.141 The proceeds from a sale of financial assets consist of the cash and any other assets obtained in the transfer less any liabilities incurred. Any asset obtained that is not an interest in the transferred asset is part of the proceeds from the sale. Any liability incurred, even if it is related to the transferred assets, is a reduction of the proceeds. Any derivative financial instrument entered into concurrently with a transfer of financial assets is either an asset obtained or a liability incurred and part of the proceeds received in the transfer. All proceeds and reductions of proceeds from a sale shall be initially measured at fair value, if practicable. [FAS140, ¶56]

Illustration—Recording Transfers with Proceeds of Cash, Derivatives, and Other Liabilities

.142 Company A sells loans with a fair value of $1,100 and a carrying amount of $1,000. Company A retains no servicing responsibilities but obtains an option to purchase from the transferee loans similar to the loans sold (which are readily obtainable in the marketplace) and assumes a limited recourse obligation to repurchase delinquent loans. Company A agrees to provide the transferee a return at a floating rate of interest even though the contractual terms of the loan are fixed rate in nature (that provision is effectively an interest rate swap).

Fair Values	
Cash proceeds	$1,050
Interest rate swap	40
Call option	70
Recourse obligation	60

Net Proceeds	
Cash received	$1,050
Plus: Call option	70
Interest rate swap	40
Less: Recourse obligation	(60)
Net proceeds	$1,100

Gain on Sale	
Net proceeds	$1,100
Carrying amount of loans sold	1,000
Gain on sale	$ 100

Journal Entry		
Cash	1,050	
Interest rate swap	40	
Call option	70	
Loans		1,000
Recourse obligation		60
Gain on sale		100
To record transfer		

[FAS140, ¶57]

Retained Interests

.143 Other interests in transferred assets—those that are not part of the proceeds of the transfer—are retained interests over which the transferor has not relinquished control. They shall be measured at the date of the transfer by allocating the previous carrying amount between the assets sold, if any, and the retained interests, based on their relative fair values. Allocation procedures shall be applied to all transfers in which interests are retained, even those that do not qualify as sales. Examples of retained interests include securities backed by the transferred assets, undivided interests, servicing assets, and cash reserve accounts and residual interests in securitization trusts. If a transferor cannot determine whether an asset is a retained interest or proceeds from the sale, the asset shall be treated as proceeds from the sale and accounted for in accordance with paragraph .141.[17] [FAS140, ¶58]

.144 If the retained interests are subordinated to more senior interests held by others, that subordination may concentrate into the retained interests most of the risks inherent in the transferred assets and shall be taken into consideration in estimating the fair value of the retained interests. For example, if the amount of the gain recognized, after allocation, on a securitization with a subordinated retained interest is greater than the gain would have been had the entire asset been sold, the transferor needs to be able to identify why that can occur. Otherwise, it is likely that the impact of the retained interest being subordinate to a senior interest has not been adequately considered in the determination of the fair value of the subordinated retained interest. [FAS140, ¶59]

Illustration—Recording Transfers of Partial Interests

.145 Company B sells a pro rata nine-tenths interest in loans with a fair value of $1,100 and a carrying amount of $1,000. There is no servicing asset or liability, because Company B estimates that the **benefits of servicing** are just adequate to compensate it for its servicing responsibilities.

Fair Values	
Cash proceeds for nine-tenths interest sold	$990
One-tenth interest retained [($990 $\div \frac{9}{10}$) $\times \frac{1}{10}$]	110

[17][That treatment is required because] at the margin, it may be difficult to distinguish between a retained interest in the asset transferred and a newly created asset. It is impractical to provide detailed guidance that would cover all possibilities. A careful examination of cash flows, risks, and other provisions should provide a basis for resolving most questions. [FAS140, ¶272]

Carrying Amount Based on Relative Fair Values

	Fair Value	Percentage of Total Fair Value	Allocated Carrying Amount
Nine-tenths interest sold	$ 990	90	$ 900
One-tenth interest retained	110	10	100
Total	$1,100	100	$1,000

Gain on Sale	
Net proceeds	$990
Carrying amount of loans sold	900
Gain on sale	$ 90

Journal Entry

Cash	990	
Loans		900
Gain on sale		90
To record transfer		

[FAS140, ¶60]

Illustration—Sale of Receivables with Servicing Retained

.146 Company C originates $1,000 of loans that yield 10 percent interest income for their estimated lives of 9 years. Company C sells the $1,000 principal plus the right to receive interest income of 8 percent to another entity for $1,000. Company C will continue to service the loans, and the contract stipulates that its compensation for performing the servicing is the right to receive half of the interest income not sold. The remaining half of the interest income not sold is considered an interest-only strip receivable. At the date of the transfer, the fair value of the loans, including servicing, is $1,100. The fair value of the servicing asset is $40.

Fair Values	
Cash proceeds	$1,000
Servicing asset	40
Interest-only strip receivable	60

Carrying Amount Based on Relative Fair Values

	Fair Value	Percentage of Total Fair Value	Allocated Carrying Amount
Loans sold	$1,000	91.0	$ 910
Servicing asset	40	3.6	36
Interest-only strip receivable	60	5.4	54
Total	$1,100	100.0	$1,000

Gain on Sale

Net proceeds	$1,000
Carrying amount of loans sold	910
Gain on sale	$ 90

Journal Entries

	Debit	Credit
Cash	1,000	
Loans		910
Gain on sale		90
To record transfer		
Servicing asset	36	
Interest-only strip receivable	54	
Loans		90
To record servicing asset and interest-only strip receivable		
Interest-only strip receivable	6	
Equity		6
To begin to subsequently measure interest-only strip receivable like an available-for-sale security (paragraph .108 of Section F39)		

[FAS140, ¶65]

.147 The previous illustration demonstrates how a transferor would account for a simple sale or securitization in which servicing is retained. Company C might instead transfer the financial assets to a corporation or a trust that is a qualifying SPE. The qualifying SPE then securitizes the loans by selling beneficial interests to the public. The qualifying SPE pays the cash proceeds to the original transferor, which accounts for the transfer as a sale and derecognizes the financial assets assuming that the criteria in paragraph .104 of this section are met. Securitizations often combine the elements shown in paragraphs .142, .145, and .146 of this section as illustrated below. [FAS140, ¶66]

Illustration—Recording Transfers of Partial Interests with Proceeds of Cash, Derivatives, Other Liabilities, and Servicing

.148 Company D originates $1,000 of prepayable loans that yield 10 percent interest income for their 9-year expected lives. Company D sells nine-tenths of the principal plus interest of 8 percent to another entity. Company D will continue to service the loans, and the contract stipulates that its compensation for performing the servicing is the 2 percent of the interest income not sold. Company D obtains an option to purchase from the transferee loans similar to the loans sold (which are readily obtainable in the marketplace) and incurs a limited recourse obligation to repurchase delinquent loans.

Fair Values	
Cash proceeds	$900
Call option	70
Recourse obligation	60
Servicing asset	90
One-tenth interest retained	100

Net Proceeds	
Cash received	$900
Plus: Call option	70
Less: Recourse obligation	(60)
Net proceeds	$910

Carrying Amount Based on Relative Fair Values

	Fair Value	Percentage of Total Fair Value	Allocated Carrying Amount
Interest sold	$ 910	83	$ 830
Servicing asset	90	8	80
One-tenth interest retained	100	9	90
Total	$1,100	100	$1,000

Gain on Sale

Net proceeds	$910
Carrying amount of loans sold	830
Gain on sale	$ 80

Journal Entries

Cash	900	
Call option	70	
Loans		830
Recourse obligation		60
Gain on sale		80
To record transfer		
Servicing asset	80	
Loans		80
To record servicing asset		

At the time of the transfer, Company D reports its one-tenth retained interest in the loans at its allocated carrying amount of $90. [FAS140, ¶67]

Fair Value

.149 The fair value of an asset (or liability) is the amount at which that asset (or liability) could be bought (or incurred) or sold (or settled) in a current transaction between willing parties, that is, other than in a forced or liquidation sale. Quoted market prices in active markets are the best evidence of fair value and shall be used as the basis for the measurement, if available. If a quoted market price is available, the fair value is the product of the number of trading units times that market price. [FAS140, ¶68]

.150 If quoted market prices are not available, the estimate of fair value shall be based on the best information available in the circumstances. The estimate of fair value shall consider prices for similar assets and liabilities and the results of valuation techniques to the extent available in the circumstances. Examples of valuation techniques include the present value of estimated future cash flows,[18] option-pricing models, matrix pricing, option-adjusted spread models, and fundamental analysis. Valuation techniques for measuring financial assets and liabilities and servicing assets and liabilities shall be consistent with the objective of measuring fair value. Those techniques shall incorporate assumptions that market participants would use in their estimates of values, future revenues, and future expenses, including assumptions about interest rates, default, prepayment, and volatility.[19] In measuring **financial liabilities** and servicing liabilities at fair value, the objective is to estimate the value of the assets required currently to (a) settle the liability with the holder or (b) transfer a liability to an entity of comparable credit standing. [FAS140, ¶69] [Refer to paragraph .1001 for an EITF Issue that provides interpretive guidance on this paragraph.]

.151 Estimates of expected future cash flows, if used to estimate fair value, shall be based on reasonable and supportable assumptions and projections. All available evidence shall be considered in developing estimates of expected future cash flows. The weight given to the evidence shall be commensurate with the extent to which the evidence can be verified objectively. If a range is estimated for either the amount or timing of possible cash flows, the likelihood of possible outcomes shall be considered either directly, if applying an expected cash flow approach, or indirectly through the risk-adjusted discount rate, if determining the best estimate of future cash flows. [FAS140, ¶70]

If It Is Not Practicable to Estimate Fair Values

.152 If it is not practicable to estimate the fair values of assets, the transferor shall record those assets at zero. If it is not practicable to estimate the fair values of liabilities, the transferor shall recognize no gain on the transaction and shall record those liabilities at the greater of:

a. The excess, if any, of (1) the fair values of assets obtained less the fair values of other liabilities incurred, over (2) the sum of the carrying values of the assets transferred
b. The amount that would be recognized in accordance with Section C59, "Contingencies."

[FAS140, ¶71]

---

[18]FASB Concepts Statement No. 7, *Using Cash Flow Information and Present Value in Accounting Measurements,* discusses the use of present value techniques in measuring the fair value of an asset (or liability) in paragraphs 42 through 54 and 75 through 88. [It is noted] that an expected present value technique is superior to traditional "best estimate" techniques, especially in situations in which the timing or amount of estimated cash flows is uncertain, as is often the case for retained interests in transferred financial assets. Concepts Statement 7 also discusses in paragraph 44 the steps needed to complete a proper search for the "rate commensurate with the risk" in applying the traditional technique. [FAS140, ¶69, fn20]

[19]The timing and amount of future cash flows for retained interests in securitizations are commonly uncertain, especially if those interests are subordinate to more senior beneficial interests. Applying the present value approach depends heavily on assumptions about default and prepayment of all the assets securitized, because of the implicit credit or prepayment risk enhancement arising from the subordination. [FAS140, ¶69, fn21]

Illustration—Recording Transfers If It Is Not Practicable to Estimate a Fair Value

.153 Company E sells loans with a carrying amount of $1,000 to another entity for cash plus a call option to purchase loans similar to the loans sold (which are readily obtainable in the marketplace) and incurs a limited recourse obligation to repurchase any delinquent loans. Company E undertakes to service the transferred assets for the other entity. In Case 1, Company E finds it impracticable to estimate the fair value of the servicing contract, although it is confident that servicing revenues will be more than **adequate compensation** for performing the servicing. In Case 2, Company E finds it impracticable to estimate the fair value of the recourse obligation.

Fair Values	Case 1	Case 2
Cash proceeds	$1,050	$1,050
Servicing asset	XX*	40
Call option	70	70
Recourse obligation	60	XX*
Fair value of loans transferred	1,100	1,100

*Not practicable to estimate fair value.

Net Proceeds	Case 1	Case 2
Cash received	$1,050	$1,050
Plus: Call option	70	70
Less: Recourse obligation	(60)	XX
Net proceeds	$1,060	$1,120

Carrying Amount Based on Relative Fair Values (Case 1)

	Fair Value	Percentage of Total Fair Value	Allocated Carrying Amount
Loans sold	$1,060	100	$1,000
Servicing asset	0	0	0
Total	$1,060	100	$1,000

Carrying Amount Based on Relative Fair Values (Case 2)

	Fair Value	Percentage of Total Fair Value	Allocated Carrying Amount
Loans sold	$1,120	97	$ 970
Servicing asset	40	3	30
Total	$1,160	100	$1,000

Journal Entries	Case 1		Case 2	
Cash	1,050		1,050	
Servicing asset	0*		30	
Call option	70		70	
Loans		1,000		1,000
Recourse obligation		60		150†
Gain on sale		60		0
To record transfer				

*Assets shall be recorded at zero if an estimate of the fair value of the assets is not practicable.

†The amount recorded as a liability in this example equals the sum of the known assets less the fair value of the known liabilities, that is, the amount that results in no gain or loss.

[FAS140, ¶72]

Securitizations

.154 Financial assets such as mortgage loans, automobile loans, trade receivables, credit card receivables, and other revolving charge accounts are assets commonly transferred in securitizations. Securitizations of mortgage loans may include pools of single-family residential mortgages or other types of real estate mortgage loans, for example, multi-family residential mortgages and commercial property mortgages. Securitizations of loans secured by chattel mortgages on automotive vehicles as well as other equipment (including direct financing or sales-type leases) also are common. Both financial and nonfinancial assets can be securitized; life insurance policy loans, patent and copyright royalties, and even taxi medallions also have been securitized. But securitizations of nonfinancial assets are outside the scope of this section. [FAS140, ¶73]

.155 An originator of a typical securitization (the transferor) transfers a portfolio of financial assets to an SPE, commonly a trust. In "pass-through" and "pay-through" securitizations, receivables are transferred to the SPE at the inception of the securitization, and no further transfers are made; all cash collections are paid to the holders of beneficial interests in the SPE. In "revolving-period" securitizations, receivables are transferred at the inception and also periodically (daily or monthly) thereafter for a defined period (commonly three to eight years), referred to as the revolving period. During the revolving period, the SPE uses most of the cash collections to purchase additional receivables from the transferor on prearranged terms. [FAS140, ¶74]

.156 Beneficial interests in the SPE are sold to investors and the proceeds are used to pay the transferor for the assets transferred. Those beneficial interests may comprise either a single class having equity characteristics or multiple classes of interests, some having debt characteristics and others having equity characteristics. The cash collected from the portfolio is distributed to the investors and others as specified by the legal documents that established the SPE. [FAS140, ¶75]

.157 Pass-through, pay-through, and revolving-period securitizations that meet the criteria in paragraph .104 qualify for sale accounting under this section. All financial assets obtained or retained and liabilities incurred by the originator of a securitization that qualifies as a sale shall be recognized and measured as provided in paragraph .106; that includes the implicit forward contract to sell new receivables during a revolving period, which may become valuable or onerous to the transferor as interest rates and other market conditions change. [FAS140, ¶76]

Revolving-Period Securitizations

.158 The value of the forward contract implicit in a revolving-period securitization arises from the difference between the agreed-upon rate of return to investors on their beneficial interests in the trust and current market rates of return on similar investments. For example, if the agreed-upon annual rate of return to investors in a trust is 6 percent, and later market rates of return for those investments increased to 7 percent, the forward contract's value to the transferor (and burden to the investors) would approximate the present value of 1 percent of the amount of the investment for each year remaining in the revolving structure after the receivables already transferred have been collected. If a forward contract to sell receivables is entered into at the market rate, its value at inception may be zero. Changes in the fair value of the forward contract are likely to be greater if the investors receive a fixed rate than if the investors receive a rate that varies based on changes in market rates. [FAS140, ¶77]

.159 Gain or loss recognition for revolving-period receivables sold to a securitization trust is limited to receivables that exist and have been sold. Recognition of servicing assets or liabilities for revolving-period receivables is similarly limited to the servicing for the receivables that exist and have been transferred. As new receivables are sold, rights to service them become assets or liabilities and are recognized. [FAS140, ¶78]

.160 Revolving-period securitizations may use either a discrete trust, used for a single securitization, or a master trust, used for many securitizations. To achieve another securitization using an existing master trust, a transferor first transfers additional receivables to the trust and then sells additional ownership interests in the trust to investors. Adding receivables to a master trust, in itself, is neither a sale nor a secured borrowing under paragraph .104, because that transfer only increases the transferor's beneficial interest in the trust's assets. A sale or secured borrowing does not occur until the transferor receives consideration other than beneficial interests in the transferred assets. Transfers that result in an exchange of cash, that is, either transfers that in essence replace previously transferred receivables that have been collected or sales of beneficial interests to outside investors, are transfers in exchange for consideration other than beneficial interests in the transferred assets and thus are accounted for as sales (if they satisfy all the criteria in paragraph .104) or as secured borrowings. [FAS140, ¶79]

Isolation of Transferred Assets in Securitizations

.161 A securitization carried out in one transfer or a series of transfers may or may not isolate the transferred assets beyond the reach of the transferor and its creditors. Whether it does depends on the structure of the securitization transaction taken as a whole, considering such factors as the type and extent of further involvement in arrangements to protect investors from credit and interest rate risks, the availability of other assets, and the powers of bankruptcy courts or other receivers.[19a] [FAS140, ¶80]

.162 In certain securitizations, a corporation that, if it failed, would be subject to the U.S. Bankruptcy Code transfers financial assets to a special-purpose trust in exchange for cash. The trust raises that cash by issuing to investors beneficial interests that pass

[19a]For banks and other financial institutions subject to possible receivership under the FDIC (and for other affected entities that have previously considered their transfers of financial assets in "single-step" securitizations to have isolated those assets in circumstances similar to those of entities subject to possible FDIC receivership), paragraphs .104(a), .112, .113, and .161 through .165 shall be effective for transfers of financial assets occurring after December 31, 2001. [FTB01-1, ¶5] [An] additional transition period applies to voluntary transfers that under prior contractual arrangements with qualifying SPE BIHs other than the transferor, its affiliates, or its agents, are constrained to be made in such a way that the transfer cannot meet all the requirements for sale accounting in paragraphs .104(a), .112, .113, and .161 through .165 of this section. That additional transition period is available only for such transfers by banks and other financial institutions subject to possible receivership under the FDIC (and for other affected entities that have previously considered their transfers of financial assets in "single-step" securitizations to have isolated those assets in circumstances similar to those of entities subject to possible FDIC receivership). The additional transition period is available only if all beneficial interests issued by the qualifying SPE after [July 23, 2001] permit the necessary changes in structure. The additional transition period ends three months after the earliest date at which sufficient approvals to permit the necessary changes can be obtained from BIHs and any other persons whose approvals are required by the terms of the prior contractual arrangement, but in no event later than June 30, 2006. [FTB01-1, ¶8, fn*]

through all cash received from the financial assets, and the transferor has no further involvement with the trust or the transferred assets. The Board understands that those securitizations generally would be judged as having isolated the assets, because in the absence of any continuing involvement there would be reasonable assurance that the transfer would be found to be a true sale at law that places the assets beyond the reach of the transferor and its creditors, even in bankruptcy or other receivership.[19b] [FAS140, ¶81]

.163 In other securitizations, a similar corporation transfers financial assets to an SPE in exchange for cash and beneficial interests in the transferred assets. That entity raises the cash by issuing to investors commercial paper that gives them a senior interest in cash received from the financial assets. The beneficial interests retained by the transferring corporation represent a junior interest to be reduced by any credit losses on the financial assets in trust. The commercial paper interests are highly rated by credit rating agencies only if both (a) the credit enhancement from the junior interest is sufficient and (b) the transferor is highly rated. Depending on facts and circumstances, the Board understands that those "single-step" securitizations often would be judged in the United States as not having isolated the assets, because the nature of the continuing involvement may make it difficult to obtain reasonable assurance that the transfer would be found to be a true sale at law that places the assets beyond the reach of the transferor and its creditors in U.S. bankruptcy (paragraph .194). If the transferor fell into bankruptcy and the transfer was found not to be a true sale at law, investors in the transferred assets might be subjected to an automatic stay that would delay payments due them, and they might have to share in bankruptcy expenses and suffer further losses if the transfer was recharacterized as a secured loan.[19c] [FAS140, ¶82]

.164 Still other securitizations use two transfers intended to isolate transferred assets beyond the reach of the transferor and its creditors, even in bankruptcy. In those "two-step" structures:

a. First, the corporation transfers financial assets to a special-purpose corporation that, although wholly owned, is so designed that the possibility that the transferor or its creditors could reclaim the assets is remote. This first transfer is designed to be judged to be a true sale at law, in part because the transferor does not provide "excessive" credit or yield protection to the special-purpose corporation, and the Board understands that transferred assets are likely to be judged beyond the reach of the transferor or the transferor's creditors even in bankruptcy.
b. Second, the special-purpose corporation transfers the assets to a trust or other legal vehicle with a sufficient increase in the credit or yield protection on the second transfer (provided by a junior retained beneficial interest or other means) to merit the high

[19b]Refer to footnote 19a.]

[19c]Refer to footnote 19a.]

credit rating sought by third-party investors who buy senior beneficial interests in the trust. Because of that aspect of its design, that second transfer might not be judged to be a true sale at law and, thus, the transferred assets could at least in theory be reached by a bankruptcy trustee for the special-purpose corporation.

c. However, the special-purpose corporation is designed to make remote the possibility that it would enter bankruptcy, either by itself or by substantive consolidation into a bankruptcy of its parent should that occur. For example, its charter forbids it from undertaking any other business or incurring any liabilities, so that there can be no creditors to petition to place it in bankruptcy. Furthermore, its dedication to a single purpose is intended to make it extremely unlikely, even if it somehow entered bankruptcy, that a receiver under the U.S. Bankruptcy Code could reclaim the transferred assets because it has no other assets to substitute for the transferred assets.

[It is understood] that the "two-step" securitizations described above, taken as a whole, generally would be judged under present U.S. law as having isolated the assets beyond the reach of the transferor and its creditors, even in bankruptcy or other receivership.[19d] [FAS140, ¶83]

.165 The powers of receivers for entities not subject to the U.S. Bankruptcy Code (for example, banks subject to receivership by the FDIC) vary considerably, and therefore some receivers may be able to reach financial assets transferred under a particular arrangement and others may not. A securitization may isolate transferred assets from a transferor subject to such a receiver and its creditors even though it is accomplished by only one transfer directly to an SPE that issues beneficial interests to investors and the transferor provides credit or yield protection. For entities that are subject to other possible bankruptcy, conservatorship, or other receivership procedures in the United States or other jurisdictions, judgments about whether transferred assets have been isolated need to be made in relation to the powers of bankruptcy courts or trustees, conservators, or receivers in those jurisdictions.[19e] [FAS140, ¶84]

Removal-of-Accounts Provisions

.166 Many transfers of financial assets in securitizations empower the transferor to reclaim assets subject to certain restrictions. Such a power is sometimes called a removal-of-accounts provision (ROAP). Whether a ROAP precludes sale accounting depends on whether the ROAP results in the transferor's maintaining effective control over specific transferred assets (paragraphs .104(c)(2) and .136 through .139). [FAS140, ¶85]

[[19d]Refer to footnote 19a.]

[[19e]Refer to footnote 19a.]

.167 The following are examples of ROAPs that preclude transfers from being accounted for as sales:

a. An unconditional ROAP or repurchase agreement that allows the transferor to specify the assets that may be removed, because such a provision allows the transferor unilaterally to remove specific assets
b. A ROAP conditioned on a transferor's decision to exit some portion of its business, because whether it can be triggered by canceling an affinity relationship, spinning off a business segment, or accepting a third party's bid to purchase a specified (for example, geographic) portion of the transferor's business, such a provision allows the transferor unilaterally to remove specific assets.

[FAS140, ¶86]

.168 The following are examples of ROAPs that *do not* preclude transfers from being accounted for as sales:

a. A ROAP for random removal of excess assets, if the ROAP is sufficiently limited so that the transferor cannot remove specific transferred assets, for example, by limiting removals to the amount of the transferor's retained interest and to one removal per month
b. A ROAP for defaulted receivables, because the removal would be allowed only after a third party's action (default) and could not be caused unilaterally by the transferor
c. A ROAP conditioned on a third-party cancellation, or expiration without renewal, of an affinity or private-label arrangement, because the removal would be allowed only after a third party's action (cancellation) or decision not to act (expiration) and could not be caused unilaterally by the transferor.

[FAS140, ¶87]

.169 A ROAP that can be exercised only in response to a third party's action that has not yet occurred does not maintain the transferor's effective control over assets potentially subject to that ROAP. However, when a third party's action (such as default or cancellation) or decision not to act (expiration) occurs that allows removal of assets to be initiated solely by the transferor, the transferor must recognize any assets subject to the ROAP, whether the ROAP is exercised or not. If the ROAP is exercised, the assets are recognized because the transferor has reclaimed the assets. If the ROAP is not exercised, the assets are recognized because the transferor now can unilaterally cause the qualifying SPE to return those specific assets and, therefore, the transferor once again has effective control over those transferred assets (paragraph .140). [FAS140, ¶88]

Sales-Type and Direct Financing Lease Receivables

.170 Sales-type and direct financing receivables secured by leased equipment, referred to as gross investment in lease receivables, are made up of two components: minimum lease payments and residual values. Minimum lease payments are requirements for lessees to pay cash to lessors and meet the definition of a financial asset. Thus, transfers of minimum lease payments are subject to the requirements of this section. Residual values represent the lessor's estimate of the "salvage" value of the leased equipment at the end of the lease term and may be either guaranteed or unguaranteed; residual values meet the definition of financial assets *to the extent that they are guaranteed at the inception of the lease.* Thus, transfers of residual values guaranteed at inception also are subject to the requirements of this section. Unguaranteed residual values do not meet the definition of financial assets, nor do residual values guaranteed after inception, and transfers of them are not subject to the requirements of this section. Transfers of residual values not guaranteed at inception continue to be subject to Section L10. Because residual values guaranteed at inception are financial assets, increases to their estimated value over the life of the related lease are recognized. Entities selling or securitizing lease financing receivables shall allocate the gross investment in receivables between minimum lease payments, residual values guaranteed at inception, and residual values not guaranteed at inception using the individual carrying amounts of those components at the date of transfer. Those entities also shall record a servicing asset or liability in accordance with paragraph .105 of this section and .102 of Section F35, if appropriate. [FAS140, ¶89]

Illustration—Recording Transfers of Lease Financing Receivables with Residual Values

.171 At the beginning of the second year in a 10-year sales-type lease, Company F sells for $505 a nine-tenths interest in the minimum lease payments and retains a one-tenth interest in the minimum lease payments and a 100 percent interest in the unguaranteed residual value of leased equipment. Company F receives no explicit compensation for servicing, but it estimates that the other benefits of servicing are just adequate to compensate it for its servicing responsibilities and hence initially records no servicing asset or liability. The carrying amounts and related gain computation are as follows:

Carrying Amounts

Minimum lease payments		$ 540
Unearned income related to minimum lease payments		370
Gross investment in minimum lease payments		910
Unguaranteed residual value	$ 30	
Unearned income related to residual value	60	
Gross investment in residual value		90
Total gross investment in financing lease receivable		$1,000

Gain on Sale

Cash received		$ 505
Nine-tenths of carrying amount of gross investment in minimum lease payments	$819	
Nine-tenths of carrying amount of unearned income related to minimum lease payments	333	
Net carrying amount of minimum lease payments sold		486
Gain on sale		$ 19

Journal Entry

Cash	505	
Unearned income	333	
Lease receivable		819
Gain on sale		19

To record sale of nine-tenths of the minimum lease payments at the beginning of year 2

[FAS140, ¶90]

Securities Lending Transactions

.172 Securities lending transactions are initiated by broker-dealers and other financial institutions that need specific securities to cover a short sale or a customer's failure to deliver securities sold. Transferees ("borrowers") of securities generally are required to provide "collateral" to the transferor ("lender") of securities, commonly cash but sometimes other securities or standby letters of credit, with a value slightly higher than that of the securities "borrowed." If the "collateral" is cash, the transferor typically earns a return by investing that cash at rates higher than the rate paid or "rebated" to the transferee. If the "collateral" is other than cash, the transferor typically receives a fee. Securities custodians or other agents commonly carry out securities lending activities on behalf of clients. Because of the protection of "collateral" (typically valued daily and adjusted frequently for changes in the market price of the securities transferred) and the short terms of the transactions, most securities lending transactions in themselves do not impose significant credit risks on either party. Other risks arise from what the parties to the transaction do with the assets they receive. For example, investments made with cash "collateral" impose market and credit risks on the transferor. [FAS140, ¶91]

.173 In some securities lending transactions, the criteria in paragraph .104 are met, including the effective control criterion in paragraph .104(c), and consideration other than beneficial interests in the transferred assets is received. Those transactions shall be accounted for (a) by the transferor as a sale of the "loaned" securities for proceeds consisting of the cash "collateral"[20] and a forward repurchase commitment and (b) by the transferee as a purchase of the "borrowed" securities in exchange for the "collateral" and a forward resale commitment. During the term of that agreement, the transferor has surrendered control over the securities transferred and the transferee has obtained control over those securities with the ability to sell or transfer them at will. In that case, creditors of the transferor have a claim only to the "collateral" and the forward repurchase commitment. [FAS140, ¶92]

.174 However, many securities lending transactions are accompanied by an agreement that entitles and obligates the transferor to repurchase or redeem the transferred assets before their maturity under which the transferor maintains effective control over those assets (paragraphs .132 through .134). Those transactions shall be accounted for as secured borrowings, in which cash (or securities that the holder is permitted by contract or custom to sell or repledge) received as "collateral" is considered the amount borrowed, the securities "loaned" are considered pledged as collateral against the cash borrowed and reclassified as set forth in paragraph .109(a), and any "rebate" paid to the transferee of securities is interest on the cash the transferor is considered to have borrowed. [FAS140, ¶93]

.175 The transferor of securities being "loaned" accounts for cash received in the same way whether the transfer is accounted for as a sale or a secured borrowing. The cash received shall be recognized as the transferor's asset—as shall investments made with that cash, even if made by agents or in pools with other securities lenders—along with the obligation to return the cash. If securities that may be sold or repledged are received, the transferor of the securities being "loaned" accounts for those securities in the same way as it would account for cash received. [FAS140, ¶94]

---

[20]If the "collateral" in a transaction that meets the criteria in paragraph .104 is a financial asset that the holder is permitted by contract or custom to sell or repledge, that financial asset is proceeds of the sale of the "loaned" securities. To the extent that the "collateral" consists of letters of credit or other financial instruments that the holder is not permitted by contract or custom to sell or repledge, a securities lending transaction does not satisfy the sale criteria and is accounted for as a loan of securities by the transferor to the transferee. [FAS140, ¶92, fn22]

Illustration—Securities Lending Transaction Treated as a Secured Borrowing

.176 The following example illustrates the accounting for a securities lending transaction treated as a secured borrowing, in which the securities borrower sells the securities upon receipt and later buys similar securities to return to the securities lender:

Facts

Transferor's carrying amount and fair value of security loaned	$1,000
Cash "collateral"	1,020
Transferor's return from investing cash collateral at a 5 percent annual rate	5
Transferor's rebate to the securities borrower at a 4 percent annual rate	4

For simplicity, the fair value of the security is assumed not to change during the 35-day term of the transaction.

Journal Entries for the Transferor

At inception:

Cash	1,020	
Payable under securities loan agreements		1,020
To record the receipt of cash collateral		
Securities pledged to creditors	1,000	
Securities		1,000
To reclassify loaned securities that the secured party has the right to sell or repledge		
Money market instrument	1,020	
Cash		1,020
To record investment of cash collateral		

At conclusion:

Cash	1,025	
Interest		5
Money market instrument		1,020
To record results of investment		
Securities	1,000	
Securities pledged to creditors		1,000
To record return of security		
Payable under securities loan agreements	1,020	
Interest ("rebate")	4	
Cash		1,024
To record repayment of cash collateral plus interest		

Journal Entries for the Transferee

At inception:

Receivable under securities loan agreements	1,020	
Cash		1,020
To record transfer of cash collateral		
Cash	1,000	
Obligation to return borrowed securities		1,000
To record sale of borrowed securities to a third party and the resulting obligation to return securities that it no longer holds		

At conclusion:

Obligation to return borrowed securities	1,000	
Cash		1,000
To record the repurchase of securities borrowed		
Cash	1,024	
Receivable under securities loan agreements		1,020
Interest revenue ("rebate")		4
To record the receipt of cash collateral and rebate interest		

[FAS140, ¶95]

Repurchase Agreements and "Wash Sales"

.177 Government securities dealers, banks, other financial institutions, and corporate investors commonly use repurchase agreements to obtain or use short-term funds. Under those agreements, the transferor ("repo party") transfers a security to a transferee ("repo counterparty" or "reverse party") in exchange for cash[21] and concurrently agrees to reacquire that security at a future date for an amount equal to the cash exchanged plus a stipulated "interest" factor. [FAS140, ¶96]

.178 Repurchase agreements can be effected in a variety of ways. Some repurchase agreements are similar to securities lending transactions in that the transferee has the right to sell or repledge the securities to a third party during the term of the repurchase agree-

[21]Instead of cash, other securities or letters of credit sometimes are exchanged. Those transactions are accounted for in the same manner as securities lending transactions (paragraphs .173 through .175). [FAS140, ¶96, fn23]

ment. In other repurchase agreements, the transferee does not have the right to sell or repledge the securities during the term of the repurchase agreement. For example, in a tri-party repurchase agreement, the transferor transfers securities to an independent third-party custodian that holds the securities during the term of the repurchase agreement. Also, many repurchase agreements are for short terms, often overnight, or have indefinite terms that allow either party to terminate the arrangement on short notice. However, other repurchase agreements are for longer terms, sometimes until the maturity of the transferred asset. Some repurchase agreements call for repurchase of securities that need not be identical to the securities transferred. [FAS140, ¶97]

.179 If the criteria in paragraph .104 are met, including the criterion in paragraph .104(c)(1), the transferor shall account for the repurchase agreement as a sale of financial assets and a forward repurchase commitment, and the transferee shall account for the agreement as a purchase of financial assets and a forward resale commitment. Other transfers that are accompanied by an agreement to repurchase the transferred assets that shall be accounted for as sales include transfers with agreements to repurchase at maturity and transfers with repurchase agreements in which the transferee has not obtained collateral sufficient to fund substantially all of the cost of purchasing replacement assets. [FAS140, ¶98]

.180 Furthermore, "wash sales" that previously were not recognized if the same financial asset was purchased soon before or after the sale shall be accounted for as sales under this section. Unless there is a concurrent contract to repurchase or redeem the transferred financial assets from the transferee, the transferor does not maintain effective control over the transferred assets. [FAS140, ¶99]

.181 As with securities lending transactions, under many agreements to repurchase transferred assets before their maturity the transferor maintains effective control over those assets. Repurchase agreements that do not meet all the criteria in paragraph .104 shall be treated as secured borrowings. Fixed-coupon and dollar-roll repurchase agreements, and other contracts under which the securities to be repurchased need not be the same as the securities sold, qualify as borrowings if the return of substantially the same (paragraph .133) securities as those concurrently transferred is assured. Therefore, those transactions shall be accounted for as secured borrowings by both parties to the transfer. [FAS140, ¶100]

.182 If a transferor has transferred securities to an independent third-party custodian, or to a transferee, under conditions that preclude the transferee from selling or repledging the assets during the term of the repurchase agreement (as in most tri-party repurchase agreements), the transferor has not surrendered control over those assets. [FAS140, ¶101]

Loan Syndications

.183 Borrowers often borrow amounts greater than any one lender is willing to lend. Therefore, it is common for groups of lenders to jointly fund those loans. That may be accomplished by a syndication under which several lenders share in lending to a single borrower, but each lender loans a specific amount to the borrower and has the right to repayment from the borrower. [FAS140, ¶102]

.184 A loan syndication is not a transfer of financial assets. Each lender in the syndication shall account for the amounts it is owed by the borrower. Repayments by the borrower may be made to a lead lender that then distributes the collections to the other lenders of the syndicate. In those circumstances, the lead lender is simply functioning as a servicer and, therefore, shall not recognize the aggregate loan as an asset. [FAS140, ¶103]

Loan Participations

.185 Groups of banks or other entities also may jointly fund large borrowings through loan participations in which a single lender makes a large loan to a borrower and subsequently transfers undivided interests in the loan to other entities. [FAS140, ¶104]

.186 Transfers by the originating lender may take the legal form of either assignments or participations. The transfers are usually on a nonrecourse basis, and the transferor ("originating lender") continues to service the loan. The transferee ("participating entity") may or may not have the right to sell or transfer its participation during the term of the loan, depending upon the terms of the participation agreement. [FAS140, ¶105]

.187 If the loan participation agreement gives the transferee the right to pledge or exchange those participations and the other criteria in paragraph .104 are met, the transfers to the transferee shall be accounted for by the transferor as sales of financial assets. A transferor's right of first refusal on a bona fide offer from a third party, a requirement to obtain the transferor's permission that shall not be unreasonably withheld, or a prohibition on sale to the transferor's competitor if other potential willing buyers exist is a limitation on the transferee's rights but presumptively does not constrain a transferee from exercising its right to pledge or exchange. However, if the loan participation agreement constrains the transferees from pledging or exchanging their participations, the transferor presumptively receives a more than trivial benefit, has not relinquished control over the loan, and shall account for the transfers as secured borrowings. [FAS140, ¶106]

Banker's Acceptances and Risk Participations in Them

.188 Banker's acceptances provide a way for a bank to finance a customer's purchase of goods from a vendor for periods usually not exceeding six months. Under an agreement between the bank, the customer, and the vendor, the bank agrees to pay the customer's liability to the vendor upon presentation of specified documents that provide evidence of delivery and acceptance of the purchased goods. The principal document is a draft or bill of exchange drawn by the customer that the bank stamps to signify its "acceptance" of the liability to make payment on the draft on its due date. [FAS140, ¶107]

.189 Once the bank accepts a draft, the customer is liable to repay the bank at the time the draft matures. The bank recognizes a receivable from the customer and a liability for the acceptance it has issued to the vendor. The accepted draft becomes a negotiable financial instrument. The vendor typically sells the accepted draft at a discount either to the accepting bank or in the marketplace. [FAS140, ¶108]

.190 A risk participation is a contract between the accepting bank and a participating bank in which the participating bank agrees, in exchange for a fee, to reimburse the accepting bank in the event that the accepting bank's customer fails to honor its liability to the accepting bank in connection with the banker's acceptance. The participating bank becomes a guarantor of the credit of the accepting bank's customer. [FAS140, ¶109]

.191 An accepting bank that obtains a risk participation shall not derecognize the liability for the banker's acceptance, because the accepting bank is still primarily liable to the holder of the banker's acceptance even though it benefits from a guarantee of reimbursement by a participating bank. The accepting bank shall not derecognize the receivable from the customer because it has not transferred the receivable: it controls the benefits inherent in that receivable and it is still entitled to receive payment from the customer. The accepting bank shall, however, record the guarantee purchased, and the participating bank shall record a liability for the guarantee issued. [FAS140, ¶110]

Illustration—Banker's Acceptance with a Risk Participation

.192 An accepting bank assumes a liability to pay a customer's vendor and obtains a risk participation from another bank. The details of the banker's acceptance are provided below:

Facts

Face value of the draft provided to vendor	$1,000
Term of the draft provided to vendor	90 days
Commission with an annual rate of 10 percent	25
Fee paid for risk participation	10

Journal Entries for Accepting Bank

At issuance of acceptance:

Receivable from customer	1,000	
Cash	25	
Time draft payable to vendor		1,000
Deferred acceptance commission revenue		25

At purchase of risk participation from a participating bank:

Guarantee purchased	10	
Cash		10

Upon presentation of the accepted time draft:

Time draft payable to vendor	1,000	
Deferred acceptance commission revenue	25	
Cash		1,000
Acceptance commission revenue		25

Upon collection from the customer (or the participating bank, if the customer defaults):

Cash	1,000	
Guarantee expense	10	
Receivable from customer		1,000
Guarantee purchased		10

Journal Entries for Participating Bank

Upon issuing the risk participation:

Cash	10	
Guarantee liability		10

Upon payment by the customer to the accepting bank:

Guarantee liability	10	
Guarantee revenue		10

OR:

In the event of total default by the customer:

Guarantee loss	990	
Guarantee liability	10	
Cash (paid to accepting bank)		1,000

[FAS140, ¶111]

Factoring Arrangements

.193 Factoring arrangements are a means of discounting accounts receivable on a nonrecourse, notification basis. Accounts receivable are sold outright, usually to a transferee (the factor) that assumes the full risk of collection, without recourse to the transferor in the event of a loss. Debtors are directed to send payments to the transferee. Factoring arrangements that meet the criteria in paragraph .104 shall be accounted for as sales of financial assets because the transferor surrenders control over the receivables to the factor. [FAS140, ¶112]

Transfers of Receivables with Recourse

.194 In a transfer of receivables with recourse, the transferor provides the transferee with full or limited recourse. The transferor is obligated under the terms of the recourse provision to make payments to the transferee or to repurchase receivables sold under certain circumstances, typically for defaults up to a specified percentage. The effect of a recourse provision on the application of paragraph .104 may vary by jurisdiction. In some jurisdictions, transfers with full recourse may not place transferred assets beyond the reach of the transferor and its creditors, but transfers with limited recourse may. A transfer of receivables with recourse shall be accounted for as a sale, with the proceeds of the sale reduced by the fair value of the recourse obligation, if the criteria in paragraph .104 are met. Otherwise, a transfer of receivables with recourse shall be accounted for as a secured borrowing. [FAS140, ¶113]

Illustrative Guidance

.195 Paragraphs .196 through .202 provide specific examples that illustrate the disclosures that are required by this section. The formats in the illustrations are not required by this section. Entities [are] encouraged to use a format that displays the information in the most understandable manner in the specific circumstances. References to paragraphs of this section in which the relevant requirements appear are given in parentheses. [FAS140, ¶342]

.196 Exhibit 196A illustrates the disclosure of accounting policies for retained interests. In particular, it describes the accounting policies for (a) initial measurement (paragraph .110(c)(1)) and (b) subsequent measurement (paragraph .110(d)(1)), including determination of fair value. [FAS140, ¶343]

Exhibit 196A

Illustrative Disclosure of Accounting Policies for Retained Interests

NOTE X—SUMMARY OF SIGNIFICANT ACCOUNTING POLICIES

Receivable Sales

When the Company sells receivables in securitizations of automobile loans, credit card loans, and residential mortgage loans, it retains interest-only strips, one or more subordinated tranches, servicing rights, and in some cases a cash reserve account, all of which are retained interests in the securitized receivables. Gain or loss on sale of the receivables depends in part on the previous carrying amount of the financial assets involved in the transfer, allocated between the assets sold and the retained interests based on their relative fair value at the date of transfer. To obtain fair values, quoted market prices are used if available. However, quotes are generally not available for retained interests, so the Company generally estimates fair value based on the present value of future expected cash flows estimated using management's best estimates of the key assumptions—credit losses, prepayment speeds, forward yield curves, and discount rates commensurate with the risks involved.

[FAS140, ¶343]

.197 In addition to the disclosure of assumptions used in determining the values of retained interests at the time of securitization that are presented in paragraph .196, this section also requires similar disclosures at the end of the latest period being presented. Exhibit 197A illustrates disclosures about the characteristics of securitizations and gain or loss from securitizations and other sales by major type of asset (paragraph .110(c)(2)). [FAS140, ¶344]

Exhibit 197A

Illustrative Disclosures about Characterization and Gains from Securitizations

NOTE Y—SALES OF RECEIVABLES

During 20X2 and 20X1, the Company sold automobile loans, residential mortgage loans, and credit card loans in securitization transactions. In all those securitizations, the Company retained servicing responsibilities and subordinated interests. The Company receives annual servicing fees approximating 0.5 percent (for mortgage loans), 2 percent (for credit card loans), and 1.5 percent (for automobile loans) of the outstanding balance and rights to future cash flows arising after the investors in the securitization trust have received the return for which they contracted. The investors and the securitization trusts have no recourse to the Company's other assets for failure of debtors to pay when due. The Company's retained interests are subordinate to investor's interests. Their value is subject to credit, prepayment, and interest rate risks on the transferred financial assets.

In 20X2, the Company recognized pretax gains of $22.3 million on the securitization of the automobile loans, $30.2 million on the securitization of credit card loans, and $25.6 million on the securitization of residential mortgage loans.

In 20X1, the Company recognized pretax gains of $16.9, $21.4, and $15.0 million on the securitization of the automobile loans, credit card loans, and residential mortgage loans, respectively.

[FAS140, ¶344]

.198 Exhibit 198A is an illustration of the quantitative information about key assumptions used in measuring retained interests at the date of sale or securitization for each financial period presented (paragraph .110(c)(3)). [FAS140, ¶345]

Exhibit 198A

Illustrative Disclosures about Key Assumptions in Measuring Retained Interests

Key economic assumptions used in measuring the retained interests at the date of securitization resulting from securitizations completed during the year were as follows (rates* per annum):

	20X2				20X1			
			Residential Mortgage Loans				Residential Mortgage Loans	
	Automobile Loans	Credit Card Loans	Fixed-Rate	Adjustable†	Automobile Loans	Credit Card Loans	Fixed-Rate	Adjustable†
Prepayment speed	1.00%	15.0%	10.00%	8.0%	1.00%	12.85%	8.00%	6.00%
Weighted-average life (in years)[22]	1.8	0.4	7.2	6.5	1.8	0.4	8.5	7.2
Expected credit losses	3.10–3.40%	6.10%	1.25%	1.30%	3.50–3.80%	5.30%	1.25%	2.10%
Residual cash flows discounted at	12.0–13.0%	12.00%	10.00%	8.50%	13.00–13.50%	13.00%	11.75%	11.00%
Variable returns to transferees	Forward Eurodollar yield curve plus contractual spread over LIBOR ranging from 30 to 80 basis points		Not applicable		Forward Eurodollar yield curve plus contractual spread over LIBOR ranging from 28 to 70 basis points		Not applicable	

Notes:

*Weighted-average rates for securitizations entered into during the period for securitizations of loans with similar characteristics.

†Rates for these loans are adjusted based on an index (for most loans, the 1-year Treasury note rate plus 2.75 percent). Contract terms vary, but for most loans, the rate is adjusted every 12 months by no more than 2 percent.

[FAS140, ¶345]

---

[22]The weighted-average life in periods (for example, months or years) of prepayable assets is calculated by summing the product of (a) the sum of the principal collections expected in each future period times (b) the number of periods until collection, and then dividing that total by (c) the initial principal balance. [FAS140, ¶345, fn33]

.199 Exhibit 199A is an illustration that combines disclosure of the key assumptions used in valuing retained interests at the end of the latest period (paragraph .110(d)(2)) and the hypothetical effect on current fair value of two or more pessimistic variations from the expected levels for each of the key assumptions (paragraph .110(d)(3)). [FAS140, ¶346]

Exhibit 199A

Illustrative Disclosures about Key Assumptions in Valuing Retained Interests and Sensitivity to Change in Assumptions

At December 31, 20X2, key economic assumptions and the sensitivity of the current fair value of residual cash flows to immediate 10 percent and 20 percent adverse changes in those assumptions are as follows ($ in millions):

			Residential Mortgage Loans	
	Automobile Loans	**Credit Card Loans**	**Fixed-Rate**	**Adjustable**
Carrying amount/fair value of retained interests	$15.6	$21.25	$12.0	$13.3
Weighted-average life (in years)[23]	1.7	0.4	6.5	6.1
Prepayment speed assumption (annual rate)	**1.3%**	**15.0%**	**11.5%**	**9.3%**
Impact on fair value of 10% adverse change	*$0.3*	*$1.6*	*$3.3*	*$2.6*
Impact on fair value of 20% adverse change	*$0.7*	*$3.0*	*$7.8*	*$6.0*
Expected credit losses (annual rate)	**3.0%**	**6.1%**	**0.9%**	**1.8%**
Impact on fair value of 10% adverse change	*$4.2*	*$3.2*	*$1.1*	*$1.2*
Impact on fair value of 20% adverse change	*$8.4*	*$6.5*	*$2.2*	*$3.0*
Residual cash flows discount rate (annual)	**14.0%**	**14.0%**	**12.0%**	**9.0%**
Impact on fair value of 10% adverse change	*$1.0*	*$0.1*	*$0.6*	*$0.5*
Impact on fair value of 20% adverse change	*$1.8*	*$0.1*	*$0.9*	*$0.9*
Interest rates on variable and adjustable contracts	**Forward Eurodollar yield curve plus contracted spread**			
Impact on fair value of 10% adverse change	*$1.5*	*$4.0*	*$0.4*	*$1.5*
Impact on fair value of 20% adverse change	*$2.5*	*$8.1*	*$0.7*	*$3.8*

These sensitivities are hypothetical and should be used with caution. As the figures indicate, changes in fair value based on a 10 percent variation in assumptions generally cannot be extrapolated because the relationship of the change in assumption to the change in fair value may not be linear. Also, in this table, the effect of a variation in a particular assumption on the fair value of the retained interest is calculated without changing any other assumption; in reality, changes in one fac-

[23]Footnote 5, paragraph .110(c)(3), describes how weighted-average life can be calculated. [FAS140, ¶346, fn34]

tor may result in changes in another (for example, increases in market interest rates may result in lower prepayments and increased credit losses), which might magnify or counteract the sensitivities.

[FAS140, ¶346]

.200 Exhibit 200A is an illustration of disclosure of expected static pool credit losses (paragraph .110(d)(2)). [FAS140, ¶347]

Exhibit 200A

Illustrative Disclosure of Expected Credit Losses for Static Pools

	Automobile Loans Securitized in		
Actual and Projected Credit Losses (%) as of:	**20X0**	**20X1**	**20X2**
December 31, 20X2	5.0	5.9	5.1
December 31, 20X1	5.1	5.0	
December 31, 20X0	4.5		

Note: Static pool losses are calculated by summing the actual and projected future credit losses and dividing them by the original balance of each pool of assets. The amount shown here for each year is a weighted average for all securitizations during the period.

[FAS140, ¶347]

.201 Exhibit 201A is an illustration of the disclosure of cash flows between the securitization SPE and the transferor (paragraph .110(c)(4)). [FAS140, ¶348]

Exhibit 201A

Illustrative Disclosure of Cash Flows between Securitization SPEs and the Transferor

The table below summarizes certain cash flows received from and paid to securitization trusts ($ in millions):

	Year Ended December 31	
	20X2	**20X1**
Proceeds from new securitizations	$1,413	$ 971
Proceeds from collections reinvested in previous credit card securitizations	3,150	2,565
Servicing fees received	23	19
Other cash flows received on retained interests*	81	52
Purchases of delinquent or foreclosed assets	(45)	(25)
Servicing advances	(102)	(73)
Repayments of servicing advances	90	63

Note:

*This amount represents total cash flows received from retained interests by the transferor other than servicing fees. Other cash flows include, for example, all cash flows from interest-only strips and cash above the minimum required level in cash collateral accounts.

[FAS140, ¶348]

.202 Exhibit 202A presents quantitative information about delinquencies, net credit losses, and components of securitized financial assets and other assets managed together with them ($ in millions). [FAS140, ¶349]

Exhibit 202A

Illustrative Disclosure about Delinquencies, and Net Credit Losses, on Securitized Financial Assets and Other Assets Managed Together with Them

	Total Principal Amount of Loans		Principal Amount of Loans 60 Days or More Past Due*		Average Balances[24]		Net Credit Losses†	
	At December 31				During the Year			
Type of Loan	**20X2**	**20X1**	**20X2**	**20X1**	**20X2**	**20X1**	**20X2**	**20X1**
Automobile loans	$830	$488	$42.3	$26.8	$720	$370	$21.6	$12.6
Residential mortgage loans (fixed-rate)	482	302	5.8	3.6	470	270	5.6	3.2
Residential mortgage loans (adjustable)	544	341	7.1	6.8	520	300	6.2	6.0
Credit card loans	300	250	15	12.5	350	300	16	15
Total loans managed or securitized ‡	2,156	1,381	$70.2	$49.7	2,060	1,240	$49.4	$36.8
Less:								
Loans securitized§	1,485	905			1,368	752		
Loans held for sale or securitization	19	11			17	9		
Loans held in portfolio[25]	$652	$465			$675	$479		

Notes:

*Loans 60 days or more past due are based on end of period total loans.

†Net credit losses are charge-offs and are based on total loans outstanding.

‡Owned and securitized loans are customer loans, credit card loans, mortgage loans, auto loans, and other loans, as applicable, in which the transferor retains a subordinate interest or retains any risk of loss (for example, 10 percent recourse).

§Represents the principal amount of the loan. Interest-only strips and servicing rights (or other retained interests) held for securitized assets are excluded from this table because they are recognized separately.

[FAS140, ¶349]

---

[24] This disclosure is optional. [FAS140, ¶349, fn35]

[25] Loans held in portfolio are reported separately from loans held for securitization because they are measured differently. [FAS141, ¶349, fn36]

[**Note:** Additional guidance with respect to implementing Section F39 is presented in *A Guide to Implementation of Statement 140 on Accounting for Transfers and Servicing of Financial Assets and Extinguishments of Liabilities: Questions and Answers.* The publication, which addresses 123 questions, was written by FASB staff members Halsey G. Bullen, Victoria A. Lusniak, and Stephen J. Young. This publication is available from the Order Department, Financial Accounting Standards Board, 401 Merritt 7, P.O. Box 5116, Norwalk, CT 06856-5116, telephone (203) 847-0700.]

Glossary

.401 **Adequate compensation.** The amount of benefits of servicing that would fairly compensate a substitute servicer should one be required, which includes the profit that would be demanded in the marketplace. [FAS140, ¶364]

.402 **Agent.** A party that acts for and on behalf of another party. For example, a third-party intermediary is an agent of the transferor if it acts on behalf of the transferor. [FAS140, ¶364]

.403 **Attached call.** A call option held by the transferor of a financial asset that becomes part of and is traded with the underlying instrument. Rather than being an obligation of the transferee, an attached call is traded with and diminishes the value of the underlying instrument transferred subject to that call. [FAS140, ¶364]

.404 **Beneficial interests.** Rights to receive all or portions of specified cash inflows to a trust or other entity, including senior and subordinated shares of interest, principal, or other cash inflows to be "passed-through" or "paid-through," premiums due to guarantors, commercial paper obligations, and residual interests, whether in the form of debt or equity. [FAS140, ¶364]

.405 **Benefits of servicing.** Revenues from contractually specified servicing fees, late charges, and other ancillary sources, including "float." [FAS140, ¶364]

.406 **Cleanup call.** An option held by the servicer or its affiliate, which may be the transferor, to purchase the remaining transferred financial assets, or the remaining beneficial interests not held by the transferor, its affiliates, or its agents in a qualifying SPE (or in a series of beneficial interests in transferred assets within a qualifying SPE), if the amount of outstanding assets or beneficial interests falls to a level at which the cost of servicing those assets or beneficial interests becomes burdensome in relation to the benefits of servicing. [FAS140, ¶364]

.407 **Collateral.** Personal or real property in which a security interest has been given. [FAS140, ¶364]

.408 **Consolidated affiliate of the transferor.** An entity whose assets and liabilities are included with those of the transferor in the consolidated, combined, or other financial statements being presented. [FAS140, ¶364]

.409 **Derecognize.** Remove previously recognized assets or liabilities from the statement of financial position. [FAS140, ¶364]

.410 **Derivative financial instrument.** A derivative instrument (as defined in Section D50, paragraphs .103 through .106) that is a financial instrument (refer to Section F25, "Financial Instruments: Disclosure," paragraph .106). [FAS140, ¶364]

.411 **Embedded call.** A call option held by the issuer of a financial instrument that is part of and trades with the underlying instrument. For example, a bond may allow the issuer to call it by posting a public notice well before its stated maturity that asks the current holder to submit it for early redemption and provides that interest ceases to accrue on the bond after the early redemption date. Rather than being an obligation of the initial purchaser of the bond, an embedded call trades with and diminishes the value of the underlying bond. [FAS140, ¶364]

.412 **Fair value.** Refer to paragraphs .149 through .151. [FAS140, ¶364]

.413 **Financial asset.** Cash, evidence of an ownership interest in an entity, or a contract that conveys to a second entity a contractual right (a) to receive cash or another financial instrument from a first entity or (b) to exchange other financial instruments on potentially favorable terms with the first entity (Section F25, paragraph .106(b)). [FAS140, ¶364]

.414 **Financial liability.** A contract that imposes on one entity a contractual obligation (a) to deliver cash or another financial instrument to a second entity or (b) to exchange other financial instruments on potentially unfavorable terms with the second entity (Section F25, paragraph .106(a)). [FAS140, ¶364]

.415 **Freestanding call.** A call that is neither embedded in nor attached to an asset subject to that call. [FAS140, ¶364]

.416 **Guaranteed mortgage securitization.** A securitization of mortgage loans that is within the scope of Section Mo4, "Mortgage Banking Activities" and includes a substantive guarantee by a third party. [FAS140, ¶364]

.417 **Interest-only strip.** A contractual right to receive some or all of the interest due on a bond, mortgage loan, collateralized mortgage obligation, or other interest-bearing financial asset. [FAS140, ¶364]

.418 **Proceeds.** Cash, derivatives, or other assets that are obtained in a transfer of financial assets, less any liabilities incurred. [FAS140, ¶364]

.419 **Recourse.** The right of a transferee of receivables to receive payment from the transferor of those receivables for (a) failure of debtors to pay when due, (b) the effects of prepayments, or (c) adjustments resulting from defects in the eligibility of the transferred receivables. [FAS140, ¶364]

.420 **Securitization.** The process by which financial assets are transformed into securities. [FAS140, ¶364]

.421 **Security interest.** A form of interest in property that provides that upon default of the obligation for which the security interest is given, the property may be sold in order to satisfy that obligation. [FAS140, ¶364]

.422 **Seller.** A transferor that relinquishes control over financial assets by transferring them to a transferee in exchange for consideration. [FAS140, ¶364]

.423 **Servicing asset.** A contract to service financial assets under which the estimated future revenues from contractually specified servicing fees, late charges, and other ancillary revenues are expected to more than adequately compensate the servicer for performing the servicing. A servicing contract is either (a) undertaken in conjunction with selling or securitizing the financial assets being serviced or (b) purchased or assumed separately. [FAS140, ¶364]

.424 **Servicing liability.** A contract to service financial assets under which the estimated future revenues from contractually specified servicing fees, late charges, and other ancillary revenues are not expected to adequately compensate the servicer for performing the servicing. [FAS140, ¶364]

.425 **Transfer.** The conveyance of a noncash financial asset by and to someone other than the issuer of that financial asset. Thus, a transfer includes selling a receivable, putting it into a securitization trust, or posting it as collateral but excludes the origination of that receivable, the settlement of that receivable, or the restructuring of that receivable into a security in a troubled debt restructuring. [FAS140, ¶364]

.426 **Transferee.** An entity that receives a financial asset, a portion of a financial asset, or a group of financial assets from a transferor. [FAS140, ¶364]

.427 **Transferor.** An entity that transfers a financial asset, a portion of a financial asset, or a group of financial assets that it controls to another entity. [FAS140, ¶364]

.428 **Undivided interest.** Partial legal or beneficial ownership of an asset as a tenant in common with others. The proportion owned may be pro rata, for example, the right to receive 50 percent of all cash flows from a security, or non–pro rata, for example, the right to receive the interest from a security while another has the right to the principal. [FAS140, ¶364]

.429 **Unilateral ability.** A capacity for action not dependent on the actions (or failure to act) of any other party. [FAS140, ¶364]

Supplemental Guidance: Emerging Issues Task Force (EITF) Issues

.1000 [Listed below are EITF Issues that provide supplemental guidance for this section. These Issues are grouped by subject matter and may be either interpretive of or related by topic to the guidance in this section.

Credit Card Securitizations

EITF Issue No. 88-20, "Difference between Initial Investment and Principal Amount of Loans in a Purchased Credit Card Portfolio"

EITF Issue No. 88-22, "Securitization of Credit Card and Other Receivable Portfolios"

EITF Issue No. 90-18, "Effect of a 'Removal of Accounts' Provision on the Accounting for a Credit Card Securitization"

Transfer of Financial Assets

EITF Issue No. 84-5, "Sale of Marketable Securities with a Put Option"

EITF Issue No. 84-30, "Sales of Loans to Special-Purpose Entities"

EITF Issue No. 85-25, "Sale of Preferred Stocks with a Put Option"

EITF Issue No. 85-40, "Comprehensive Review of Sales of Marketable Securities with Put Arrangements"

EITF Issue No. 87-30, "Sale of a Short-Term Loan Made under a Long-Term Credit Commitment"

EITF Issue No. 88-11, "Allocation of Recorded Investment When a Loan or Part of a Loan is Sold"

EITF Issue No. 89-2, "Maximum Maturity Guarantees on Transfers of Receivables with Recourse"

EITF Issue No. 92-2, "Measuring Loss Accruals by Transferors for Transfers of Receivables with Recourse"

EITF Issue No. 98-15, "Structured Notes Acquired for a Specified Investment Strategy"

EITF Topic No. D-14, "Transactions involving Special-Purpose Entities"

EITF Topic No. D-63, "Call Options 'Embedded' in Beneficial Interests Issued by a Qualifying Special-Purpose Entity"

EITF Topic No. D-65, "Maintaining Collateral in Repurchase Agreements and Similar Transactions under FASB Statement No. 125"

EITF Topic No. D-66, "Effect of a Special-Purpose Entity's Powers to Sell, Exchange, Repledge, or Distribute Transferred Financial Assets under FASB Statement No. 125"

EITF Topic No. D-69, "Gain Recognition on Transfers of Financial Assets under FASB Statement No. 125"

EITF Topic No. D-94, "Questions and Answers Related to the Implementation of FASB Statement No. 140"

EITF Topic No. D-99, "Questions and Answers Related to Servicing Activities in a Qualifying Special-Purpose Entity under FASB Statement No. 140"

Other

EITF Issue No. 84-15, "Grantor Trusts Consolidation"

EITF Issue No. 86-8, "Sale of Bad-Debt Recovery Rights"

EITF Issue No. 87-18, "Use of Zero Coupon Bonds in a Troubled Debt Restructuring"

EITF Issue No. 88-18, "Sales of Future Revenues"

EITF Issue No. 96-10, "Impact of Certain Transactions on the Held-to-Maturity Classification under FASB Statement No. 115"

EITF Issue No. 97-3, "Accounting for Fees and Costs Associated with Loan Syndications and Loan Participations after the Issuance of FASB Statement No. 125"

EITF Issue No. 97-14, "Accounting for Deferred Compensation Arrangements Where Amounts Earned Are Held in a Rabbi Trust and Invested"

EITF Issue No. 98-8, "Accounting for Transfers of Investments That Are in Substance Real Estate"

EITF Issue No. 98-12, "Application of Issue No. 00-19 to Forward Equity Sales Transactions"

EITF Issue No. 99-8, "Accounting for Transfers of Assets That Are Derivative Instruments but That Are Not Financial Assets"

EITF Issue No. 00-17, "Measuring the Fair Value of Energy-Related Contracts in Applying Issue No. 98-10"

EITF Issue No. 01-2, "Interpretations of APB Opinion No. 29"

EITF Issue No. 02-2, "When Separate Contracts That Meet the Definition of Financial Instruments Should Be Combined for Accounting Purposes"

EITF Topic No. D-51, "The Applicability of FASB Statement No. 115 to Desecuritizations of Financial Assets"]

.1001 [Listed below are those EITF Issues that provide interpretive guidance on specific material in this section.

Paragraph .104 (FAS 140, ¶9)—EITF Topics No. D-51, D-65, and D-99
Paragraph .104(a) (FAS 140, ¶9(a))—EITF Topic No. D-94
Paragraph .105 (FAS 140, ¶10)—EITF Issue No. 98-15
Paragraph .106 (FAS 140, ¶11)—EITF Topic No. D-69
Paragraph .110 (FAS 140, ¶17)—EITF Topic No. D-65
Paragraphs .112 and .113 (FAS 140, ¶27–28)—EITF Topic No. D-94
Paragraph .120 (FAS 140, ¶35)—EITF Topic No. D-99
Paragraph .122 (FAS 140, ¶37)—EITF Topic No. D-99
Paragraphs .126 through .129 (FAS 140, ¶41–44)—EITF Topic No. D-99
Paragraph .132 (FAS 140, ¶47)—EITF Topic No. D-65
Paragraph .134 (FAS 140, ¶49)—EITF Topic No. D-65
Paragraph .150 (FAS 140, ¶69)—EITF Topic No. D-69
Paragraphs .161 through .165 (FAS 140, ¶80–84)—EITF Topic No. D-94]

(The next page is 18351.)

FINANCIAL STATEMENTS: COMPARATIVE FINANCIAL STATEMENTS — SECTION F43

Source: ARB 43, Chapter 2A

[**Note:** A list of Issues discussed by the Emerging Issues Task Force (EITF) that provide supplemental guidance for this section is presented in paragraph .1000.]

Summary

The presentation of comparative financial statements enhances the usefulness of annual and other reports. Ordinarily, it is desirable that financial statements of two or more periods be presented.

.101 The presentation of comparative financial statements in annual and other reports enhances the usefulness of such reports and brings out more clearly the nature and trends of current changes affecting the enterprise. Such presentation emphasizes the fact that statements for a series of periods are far more significant than those for a single period and that the accounts for one period are but an installment of what is essentially a continuous history. [ARB43, ch2A, ¶1]

.102 In any one year it is ordinarily desirable that the balance sheet, the income statement, [the statement of cash flows,] and the statement of [retained earnings] be given for one or more preceding years as well as for the current year.[1] Footnotes [and] explanations that appeared on the statements for the preceding years should be repeated, or at least referred to, in the comparative statements to the extent that they continue to be of significance. [ARB43, ch2A, ¶2]

.103 It is necessary that prior-year figures shown for comparative purposes be in fact comparable with those shown for the most recent period, or that any exceptions to comparability be clearly brought out. [ARB43, ch2A, ¶3]

---

[1]Refer to Section A06, "Accounting Changes," concerning disclosure of changes made in the manner of or basis for presenting corresponding items for two or more periods. [ARB43, ch2A, ¶2]

Supplemental Guidance: Emerging Issues Task Force (EITF)

.1000 [Listed below is an EITF Issue that provides supplemental guidance for this section. This Issue is related by topic to the guidance in this section.

EITF Topic No. D-85, "Application of Certain Transition Provisions in SEC Staff Accounting Bulletin No. 101"]

(The next page is 19251.)

FOREIGN CURRENCY TRANSLATION SECTION F60

Sources: FASB Statement 52; FASB Statement 95; FASB Statement 104; FASB Statement 109; FASB Statement 130; FASB Statement 133; FASB Statement 135; FASB Interpretation 37

[**Note:** A list of Issues discussed by the Emerging Issues Task Force (EITF) that provide supplemental guidance for this section is presented in paragraph .1000.]

Summary

The requirements in this section reflect these general conclusions:

a. The economic effects of an exchange rate change on an operation that is relatively self-contained and integrated within a foreign country relate to the net investment in that operation. Translation adjustments that arise from consolidating that foreign operation do not impact cash flows and are not included in net income.
b. The economic effects of an exchange rate change on a foreign operation that is an extension of the parent's domestic operations relate to individual assets and liabilities and impact the parent's cash flows directly. Accordingly, the exchange gains and losses in such an operation are included in net income.
c. Contracts, transactions, or balances that are, in fact, effective hedges of foreign exchange risk will be accounted for as hedges without regard to their form.

More specifically, this section presents standards for foreign currency translation that are designed to (a) provide information that is generally compatible with the expected economic effects of a rate change on an enterprise's cash flows and equity and (b) reflect in consolidated statements the financial results and relationships as measured in the primary currency in which each entity conducts its business (referred to as its *functional currency*).

An entity's functional currency is the currency of the primary economic environment in which that entity operates. The functional currency can be the dollar or a foreign currency depending on the facts. Normally, it will be the currency of the economic environment in which cash is generated and expended by the entity. An entity can be any form of operation, including a subsidiary, division, branch, or joint venture. This section provides guidance for this key determination in which management's judgment is essential in assessing the facts.

A currency in a highly inflationary environment (3-year inflation rate of approximately 100 percent or more) is not considered stable enough to serve as a functional currency and the more stable currency of the reporting parent is to be used instead.

The functional currency translation approach adopted in this section encompasses:

a. Identifying the functional currency of the entity's economic environment
b. Measuring all elements of the financial statements in the functional currency
c. Using the current exchange rate for translation from the functional currency to the reporting currency, if they are different
d. Distinguishing the economic impact of changes in exchange rates on a net investment from the impact of such changes on individual assets and liabilities that are receivable or payable in currencies other than the functional currency

Translation adjustments are an inherent result of the process of translating a foreign entity's financial statements from the functional currency to U.S. dollars. Translation adjustments are *not* included in determining net income for the period but are included in other comprehensive income and accumulated in equity until a sale in whole or in part or a complete or substantially complete liquidation of the net investment in the foreign entity takes place.

Transaction gains and losses are a result of the effect of exchange rate changes on transactions denominated in currencies other than the functional currency (for example, a U.S. enterprise may borrow Swiss francs or a French subsidiary may have a receivable denominated in kroner from a Danish customer). Gains and losses on those foreign currency transactions are generally included in determining net income for the period in which exchange rates change unless the transaction hedges a foreign currency commitment or a net investment in a foreign entity. Intercompany transactions of a long-term investment nature are considered part of a parent's net investment and hence do not give rise to gains or losses.

Introduction and Scope

.101 This section [contains] standards of financial accounting and reporting for **foreign currency transactions** in financial statements of a **reporting enterprise** (hereinafter, **enterprise**). It also [contains] the standards for translating foreign currency financial statements (hereinafter, **foreign currency statements**) that are incorporated in the financial statements of an enterprise by consolidation, combination, or the equity method of accounting. **Translation** of financial statements from one currency to another for purposes other than consolidation, combination, or the equity method is beyond the scope of this section. For example, this section does not cover translation of the financial statements of an enterprise from its **reporting currency** into another currency for the convenience of readers accustomed to that other currency. [FAS52, ¶2]

.102 The **functional currency** approach [described herein] applies equally to translation of financial statements of foreign investees whether accounted for by the equity method or consolidated. It also applies to translation after a business combination. Therefore, the foreign statements and the foreign currency transactions of an investee that are accounted for by the equity method should be translated in conformity with the requirements of this section in applying the equity method. Likewise, after a business combination, the amount allocated at the date of acquisition to the assets acquired and the liabilities assumed (including *goodwill* or *excess over cost,* as those terms are used in [Section B51, "Business Combinations"]) should be translated in conformity with the requirements of this section. Accumulated **translation adjustments** attributable to minority interests should beallocated to and reported as part of the minority interest in the consolidated enterprise. [FAS52, ¶101]

Objectives of Translation

.103 Financial statements are intended to present information in financial terms about the performance, financial position, and cash flows of an enterprise. For this purpose, the financial statements of separate **entities** within an enterprise, which may exist and operate in different economic and currency environments, are consolidated and presented as though they were the financial statements of a single enterprise. Because it is not possible to combine, add, or subtract measurements expressed in different currencies, it is necessary to translate into a single reporting currency[1] those assets, liabilities, revenues,

[1]For convenience, this section assumes that the enterprise uses the U.S. dollar (dollar) as its reporting currency. However, a currency other than the dollar may be the reporting currency in financial statements that are prepared in conformity with U.S. generally accepted accounting principles. For example, a foreign enterprise may report in its **local currency** in conformity with U.S. generally accepted accounting principles. If so, the requirements of this section apply. [FAS52,¶4, fn2]

expenses, gains, and losses that are measured or denominated in a **foreign currency.**[2] However, the unity presented by such translation does not alter the underlying significance of the results and relationships of the constituent parts of the enterprise. It is only through the effective operation of its constituent parts that the enterprise as a whole is able to achieve its purpose. Accordingly, the translation of the financial statements of each component entity of an enterprise should accomplish the following objectives:

a. Provide information that is generally compatible with the expected economic effects of a rate change on an enterprise's cash flows and equity
b. Reflect in consolidated statements the financial results and relationships of the individual consolidated entities as measured in their functional currencies in conformity with U.S. generally accepted accounting principles

[FAS52, ¶4]

The Functional Currency

.104 The assets, liabilities, and operations of a **foreign entity** shall be measured using the functional currency of that entity. An entity's functional currency is the currency of the primary economic environment in which the entity operates; normally, that is the currency of the environment in which an entity primarily generates and expends cash. Paragraphs .106 through .112 provide guidance for determination of the functional currency. [FAS52, ¶5]

.105 It is neither possible nor desirable to provide unequivocal criteria to identify the functional currency of foreign entities under all possible facts and circumstances and still fulfill the objectives of **foreign currency translation.** Arbitrary rules that might dictate the identification of the functional currency in each case would accomplish a degree of superficial uniformity but, in the process, might diminish the relevance and reliability of the resulting information. [FAS52, ¶40]

---

[2]To measure in foreign currency is to quantify an **attribute** of an item in a unit of currency other than the reporting currency. Assets and liabilities are denominated in a foreign currency if their amounts are fixed in terms of that foreign currency regardless of exchange rate changes. An asset or liability may be both measured and denominated in one currency, or it may be measured in one currency and denominated in another. To illustrate: Two foreign branches of a U.S. enterprise, one Swiss and one German, purchase identical assets on credit from a Swiss vendor at identical prices stated in Swiss francs. The German branch measures the cost (an attribute) of that asset in German marks. Although the corresponding liability is also measured in marks, it remains denominated in Swiss francs since the liability must be settled in a specified number of Swiss francs. The Swiss branch measures the asset and liability in Swiss francs. Its liability is both measured and denominated in Swiss francs. Although assets and liabilities can be measured in various currencies, rights to receive or obligations to pay fixed amounts of a currency are, by definition, denominated in that currency. [FAS52, ¶4, fn3]

.106 Multinational enterprises may consist of entities operating in a number of economic environments and dealing in a number of foreign currencies. All foreign operations are not alike. In order to fulfill the objective in paragraph .102, it is necessary to recognize at least two broad classes of foreign operations. [FAS52, ¶79]

.107 In the first class are foreign operations that are relatively self-contained and integrated within a particular country or economic environment. The day-to-day operations are not dependent upon the economic environment of the parent's functional currency; the foreign operation primarily generates and expends foreign currency. The foreign currency net cash flows that it generates may be reinvested or converted and distributed to the parent. For this class, the foreign currency is the functional currency. [FAS52, ¶80]

.108 In the second class are foreign operations that are primarily a direct and integral component or extension of the parent company's operations. Significant assets may be acquired from the parent company or otherwise by expending dollars and, similarly, the sale of assets may generate dollars that are available to the parent. Financing is primarily by the parent or otherwise from dollar sources. In other words, the day-to-day operations are dependent on the economic environment of the parent's currency, and the changes in the foreign entity's individual assets and liabilities impact directly on the cash flows of the parent company in the parent's currency. For this case, the dollar is the functional currency. [FAS52, ¶81]

.109 The functional currency of an entity is, in principle, a matter of fact. In some cases, the facts will clearly identify the functional currency; in other cases they will not. [FAS52, ¶39] For example, if a foreign entity conducts significant amounts of business in two or more currencies, the functional currency might not be clearly identified. [FAS52, ¶8] In those instances in which the indicators are mixed and the functional currency is not obvious, management's judgment will be required in order to determine the functional currency that most faithfully portrays the economic results of the entity's operations and thereby best achieves the objectives of foreign currency translation set forth in paragraph .102. Management is in the best position to obtain the pertinent facts and weigh their relative importance in determining the functional currency for each operation. It is important to recognize that management's judgment is essential and paramount in this determination, provided only that it is not contradicted by the facts. [FAS52, ¶41]

.110 The salient economic factors set forth below, and possibly others, should be considered both individually and collectively when determining the functional currency.

a. Cash flow indicators
   (1) Foreign Currency—Cash flows related to the foreign entity's individual assets and liabilities are primarily in the foreign currency and do not directly impact the parent company's cash flows.

(2) Parent's Currency—Cash flows related to the foreign entity's individual assets and liabilities directly impact the parent's cash flows on a current basis and are readily available for remittance to the parent company.

b. Sales price indicators

(1) Foreign Currency—Sales prices for the foreign entity's products are not primarily responsive on a short-term basis to changes in exchange rates but are determined more by local competition or local government regulation.

(2) Parent's Currency—Sales prices for the foreign entity's products are primarily responsive on a short-term basis to changes in exchange rates; for example, sales prices are determined more by worldwide competition or by international prices.

c. Sales market indicators

(1) Foreign Currency—There is an active local sales market for the foreign entity's products, although there also might be significant amounts of exports.

(2) Parent's Currency—The sales market is mostly in the parent's country or sales contracts are denominated in the parent's currency.

d. Expense indicators

(1) Foreign Currency—Labor, materials, and other costs for the foreign entity's products or services are primarily local costs, even though there also might be imports from other countries.

(2) Parent's Currency—Labor, materials, and other costs for the foreign entity's products or services, on a continuing basis, are primarily costs for components obtained from the country in which the parent company is located.

e. Financing indicators

(1) Foreign Currency—Financing is primarily denominated in foreign currency, and funds generated by the foreign entity's operations are sufficient to service existing and normally expected debt obligations.

(2) Parent's Currency—Financing is primarily from the parent or other dollar-denominated obligations, or funds generated by the foreign entity's operations are not sufficient to service existing and normally expected debt obligations without the infusion of additional funds from the parent company. Infusion of additional funds from the parent company for expansion is not a factor, provided funds generated by the foreign entity's expanded operations are expected to be sufficient to service that additional financing.

f. Intercompany transactions and arrangements indicators

(1) Foreign Currency—There is a low volume of intercompany transactions and there is not an extensive interrelationship between the operations of the foreign entity and the parent company. However, the foreign entity's operations may rely on the parent's or affiliates' competitive advantages, such as patents and trademarks.

(2) Parent's Currency—There is a high volume of intercompany transactions and there is an extensive interrelationship between the operations of the foreign entity and the parent company. Additionally, the parent's currency generally would be the

functional currency if the foreign entity is a device or shell corporation for holding investments, obligations, intangible assets, etc., that could readily be carried on the parent's or an affiliate's books.

[FAS52, ¶42]

.111 An entity might have more than one distinct and separable operation, such as a division or branch, in which case each operation may be considered a separate entity. If those operations are conducted in different economic environments, they might have different functional currencies. [FAS52, ¶7] Similarly, a single subsidiary of a financial institution might have relatively self-contained and integrated operations in each of several different countries. In circumstances such as those described above, each operation may be considered to be an entity as that term is used in this section; and, based on the facts and circumstances, each operation might have a different functional currency. [FAS52, ¶43]

.112 Foreign investments that are consolidated or accounted for by the equity method are controlled by or subject to significant influence by the parent company. Likewise, the parent's currency is often used for measurements, assessments, evaluations, projections, etc., pertaining to foreign investments as part of the management decision-making process. Such management control, decisions, and resultant actions may reflect, indicate, or create economic facts and circumstances. However, the exercise of significant management control and the use of the parent's currency for decision-making purposes do not determine, per se, that the parent's currency is the functional currency for foreign operations. [FAS52, ¶44]

.113 Once the functional currency for a foreign entity is determined, that determination shall be used consistently unless significant changes in economic facts and circumstances indicate clearly that the functional currency has changed. Previously issued financial statements shall not be restated for any change in the functional currency. [FAS52, ¶9] (Section A06, "Accounting Changes," paragraph .106, states that "adoption or modification of an accounting principle necessitated by transactions or events that are clearly different in substance from those previously occurring" is not a change in accounting principles.) [FAS52, ¶45]

.114 If the functional currency changes from a foreign currency to the reporting currency, translation adjustments for prior periods should not be removed from equity and the translated amounts for nonmonetary assets at the end of the prior period become the accounting basis for those assets in the period of the change and subsequent periods. If the functional currency changes from the reporting currency to a foreign currency, the adjustment attributable to current-rate translation of nonmonetary assets as of the date of the change should be reported in [FAS52, ¶46] other comprehensive income. [FAS135, ¶4(l)] [Refer to paragraph .1001 for EITF Issues that provide interpretive guidance on this paragraph.]

.115 If an entity's books of record are not maintained in its functional currency, remeasurement into the functional currency is required. That remeasurement is required before translation into the reporting currency. If a foreign entity's functional currency is the reporting currency, remeasurement into the reporting currency obviates translation. The remeasurement process is intended to produce the same result as if the entity's books of record had been maintained in the functional currency. The remeasurement of and subsequent accounting for transactions denominated in a currency other than the functional currency shall be in accordance with the requirements of this section (refer to paragraphs .122 and .123). Paragraphs .146 through .152 provide guidance for remeasurement into the functional currency. [FAS52, ¶10]

Translation of Operations in Highly Inflationary Economies

.116 The financial statements of a foreign entity in a highly inflationary economy shall be remeasured as if the functional currency were the reporting currency. Accordingly, the financial statements of those entities shall be remeasured into the reporting currency according to the requirements of paragraph .115. For the purposes of this requirement, a highly inflationary economy is one that has cumulative inflation of approximately 100 percent or more over a 3-year period. [FAS52, ¶11] [Refer to paragraph .1001 for an EITF Issue that provides interpretive guidance on this paragraph.]

.117 The definition of a highly inflationary economy as one that has cumulative inflation of *approximately* 100 percent or more over a 3-year period is necessarily an arbitrary decision. In some instances, the trend of inflation might be as important as the absolute rate. The definition of a highly inflationary economy [shall] be applied with judgment. [FAS52, ¶109]

Translation of Foreign Currency Statements

.118 All elements of financial statements shall be translated by using a **current exchange rate.** For assets and liabilities, the exchange rate at the balance sheet date shall be used. For revenues, expenses, gains, and losses, the exchange rate at the dates on which those elements are recognized shall be used. Because translation at the exchange rates at the dates the numerous revenues, expenses, gains, and losses are recognized is generally impractical, an appropriately weighted average exchange rate for the period may be used to translate those elements. [FAS52, ¶12] This also applies to accounting allocations (for example, depreciation, cost of sales, and amortization of deferred revenues and expenses) and requires translation at the current exchange rates applicable to the dates those allocations are included in revenues and expenses (that is, not the rates on the dates the related items originated). [FAS52, ¶99]

.118A A statement of cash flows of an enterprise with foreign currency transactions or foreign operations shall report the reporting currency equivalent of foreign currency cash flows using the exchange rates in effect at the time of the cash flows. An appropriately weighted average exchange rate for the period may be used for translation if the result is substantially the same as if the rates at the dates of the cash flows were used.[2aa] The statement shall report the effect of exchange rate changes on cash balances held in foreign currencies as a separate part of the reconciliation of the change in cash and cash equivalents during the period. [FAS95, ¶25] [Paragraphs .142 through .152 of Section C25, "Cash Flows Statement," present an example of a consolidating statement of cash flows for a U.S. parent company with two foreign subsidiaries.]

.119 If an entity's functional currency is a foreign currency, translation adjustments result from the process of translating that entity's financial statements into the reporting currency. Translation adjustments shall not be included in determining net income but shall be reported [FAS52, ¶13] in other comprehensive income [as required in Section C49, "Comprehensive Income: Financial Statement Presentation"]. [FAS130, ¶29] [Refer to paragraph .1001 for an EITF Issue that provides interpretive guidance on this paragraph.]

.120 Upon sale or upon complete or substantially complete liquidation of an investment in a foreign entity, the amount attributable to that entity and accumulated in the translation adjustment component of equity shall be removed from the separate component of equity and shall be reported as part of the gain or loss on sale or liquidation of the investment for the period during which the sale or liquidation occurs.[[2a]] [FAS52, ¶14] If an enterprise sells part of its ownership interest in a foreign entity, a pro rata portion of the accumulated translation adjustment component of equity attributable to that investment shall be recognized in measuring the gain or loss on the sale.[2b] [FIN37, ¶2]

.121 [Deleted 11/87 because of FASB Statement 95, *Statement of Cash Flows*.]

[2aa]Paragraph .118 recognizes the general impracticality of translating revenues, expenses, gains, and losses at the exchange rates on dates they are recognized and permits an appropriately weighted average exchange rate for the period to be used to translate those elements. Section C25, "Cash Flows Statement," applies that provision to cash receipts and cash payments. [FAS95, ¶25, fn9]

[[2a]][Some consider] a partial liquidation by a subsidiary may be considered to be similar to a sale of part of an ownership interest if the liquidation proceeds are distributed to the parent. However, extending pro rata recognition to such partial liquidations would require that their substance be distinguished from ordinary dividends. [It is felt] that such a distinction is [neither] possible nor desirable. This paragraph is restricted to clarifying that a sale includes an investor's partial, as well as complete, disposal of its ownership interest. [FIN37, ¶8]

[2b]Under Section I13, "Income Statement Presentation: Discontinued Operations," a gain or loss on disposal of part or all of a net investment may be recognized in a period other than that in which actual sale or liquidation occurs. This paragraph does not alter the period in which a gain or loss on sale or liquidation is recognized under existing generally accepted accounting principles. [FIN37, ¶2, fn1]

Foreign Currency Transactions

.121A Section D50, "Derivative Instruments and Hedging Activities," addresses the accounting for freestanding foreign currency derivatives and certain foreign currency derivatives embedded in other instruments. This section does not address the accounting for derivative instruments. [FAS133, ¶527(a)]

.122 Foreign currency transactions are transactions denominated in a currency other than the entity's functional currency. Foreign currency transactions may produce receivables or payables that are fixed in terms of the amount of foreign currency that will be received or paid. [FAS52, ¶15] Examples [of foreign currency transactions] include a sale denominated in Swiss francs, a Swiss franc loan, and the holding of Swiss francs by an entity whose functional currency is the dollar. Likewise, a Swiss franc denominated transaction by a German entity or other entity whose functional currency is not the Swiss franc is a foreign currency transaction. For any entity whose functional currency is *not* the dollar, a dollar-denominated transaction is also a foreign currency transaction. [FAS52, ¶120] A change in exchange rates between the functional currency and the currency in which a transaction is denominated increases or decreases the expected amount of functional currency cash flows upon settlement of the transaction. [FAS52, ¶15] That is equally the case for transactions of the foreign entity denominated in the reporting currency. [FAS52, ¶96] That increase or decrease in expected functional currency cash flows is a foreign currency **transaction gain or loss** that generally shall be included in determining net income for the period in which the exchange rate changes. Likewise, a transaction gain or loss (measured from the **transaction date** or the most recent intervening balance sheet date, whichever is later) realized upon settlement of a foreign currency transaction generally shall be included in determining net income for the period in which the transaction is settled. The exceptions to this requirement for inclusion in net income of transaction gains and losses are set forth in [FAS52, ¶15] paragraph .127 [FAS133, ¶527(b)] and pertain to certain intercompany transactions and to transactions that are designated as, and effective as, economic hedges of net investments. [FAS52, ¶15] [Refer to paragraph .1001 for an EITF Issue that provides interpretive guidance on this paragraph.]

.123 For other than [FAS52, ¶16] **derivative instruments** (refer to Section D50), [FAS133, ¶527(c)] the following shall apply to all foreign currency transactions of an enterprise and its investees:

a. At the date the transaction is recognized, each asset, liability, revenue, expense, gain, or loss arising from the transaction shall be measured and recorded in the functional currency of the recording entity by use of the exchange rate in effect at that date (refer to paragraphs .136 through .138).

b. At each balance sheet date, recorded balances that are denominated in a currency other than the functional currency of the recording entity shall be adjusted to reflect the current exchange rate.

[FAS52, ¶16]

.124–.126 [Deleted 6/98 because of FASB Statement 133, *Accounting for Derivative Instruments and Hedging Activities.*]

.126A [Editorial deletion, 6/98.]

Transaction Gains and Losses to Be Excluded from Determination of Net Income

.127 Gains and losses on the following foreign currency transactions shall not be included in determining net income but shall be reported in the same manner as translation adjustments (refer to paragraph .119):

a. Foreign currency transactions that are designated as, and are effective as, economic hedges of a net investment in a foreign entity, commencing as of the designation date
b. Intercompany foreign currency transactions that are of a long-term investment nature (that is, settlement is not planned or anticipated in the foreseeable future), when the entities to the transaction are consolidated, combined, or accounted for by the equity method in the reporting enterprise's financial statements. [FAS52, ¶20] [Intercompany] transactions and balances for which settlement is not planned or anticipated in the foreseeable future are considered to be part of the net investment. This might include balances that take the form of an advance or a demand note payable provided that payment is not planned or anticipated in the foreseeable future. [FAS52, ¶131]

.128–.129 [Editorial deletion, 5/02.]

Hedges of Firm Commitments

.130 The accounting for a gain or loss on a foreign currency transaction that is intended to hedge an identifiable foreign currency commitment (for example, an agreement to purchase or sell equipment) is addressed by paragraph .134 of Section D50. [FAS133, ¶527(e)]

.131 [Editorial deletion, 6/98.]

Income Tax Consequences of Rate Changes

.132 Interperiod tax allocation is required in accordance with [FAS52, ¶22] Section I27, "Income Taxes," [FAS109, ¶287] if taxable exchange gains or tax-deductible exchange losses resulting from an entity's foreign currency transactions are included in net income in a different period for financial statement purposes from that for tax purposes. [FAS52, ¶22]

.133 Translation adjustments are accumulated and reported in a separate component of equity. Reported as such, translation adjustments do not affect pretax accounting income and most such adjustments also do not affect taxable income. Adjustments that do not affect either accounting income or taxable income do not create [temporary differences] as defined by [Section I27]. However, reporting those adjustments as a component of equity does have the effect of increasing or decreasing equity, that is, increasing or decreasing an enterprise's net assets. Potential future tax effects related to those adjustments would partially offset the increase or decrease in net assets. Therefore, [temporary differences] relating to translation adjustments shall be accounted for in the same way as [temporary differences] relating to accounting income. The need for and the amount of deferred taxes shall be determined according to the requirements of [Section I27]. [FAS52, ¶135] [Section I27] provides that deferred taxes shall not be provided for unremitted earnings of a subsidiary in certain instances; in those instances, deferred taxes shall not be provided on translation adjustments. [FAS52, ¶23] [Similarly, Section I27] provides guidance as to how to compute the amount of deferred taxes; deferred taxes on translation adjustments should be computed in the same manner. [FAS52, ¶135]

.134 Section I27 [FAS109, ¶287] requires income tax expense to be allocated among income before extraordinary items, extraordinary items, adjustments of prior periods (or of the opening balance of retained earnings), and direct entries to other equity accounts. Some transaction gains and losses and all translation adjustments are reported in [FAS52, ¶24] other comprehensive income. [FAS135, ¶4(l)] Any income taxes related to those transaction gains and losses and translation adjustments shall be allocated to [FAS52, ¶24] other comprehensive income. [FAS135, ¶4(l)]

Elimination of Intercompany Profits

.135 The elimination of intercompany profits that are attributable to sales or other transfers between entities that are consolidated, combined, or accounted for by the equity method in the enterprise's financial statements shall be based on the exchange rates at the dates of the sales or transfers. The use of reasonable approximations or averages is permitted. [FAS52, ¶25]

Exchange Rates

.136 The exchange rate is the ratio between a unit of one currency and the amount of another currency for which that unit can be exchanged at a particular time. If exchangeability between two currencies is temporarily lacking at the transaction date or balance sheet date, the first subsequent rate at which exchanges could be made shall be used for purposes of this section. If the lack of exchangeability is other than temporary, the propriety of consolidating, combining, or accounting for the foreign operation by the equity method in the financial statements of the enterprise shall be carefully considered. [FAS52, ¶26] [Refer to paragraph .1001 for an EITF Issue that provides interpretive guidance on this paragraph.]

.137 The exchange rates to be used for translation of foreign currency transactions and foreign currency statements are as follows:

a. *Foreign Currency Transactions*—The applicable rate at which a particular transaction could be settled at the transaction date shall be used to translate and record the transaction. At a subsequent balance sheet date, the current rate is that rate at which the related receivable or payable could be settled at that date.
b. *Foreign Currency Statements*—In the absence of unusual circumstances, the rate applicable to **conversion** of a currency for purposes of dividend remittances shall be used to translate foreign currency statements.[3]

[FAS52, ¶27]

.138 If a foreign entity whose balance sheet date differs from that of the enterprise is consolidated or combined with or accounted for by the equity method in the financial

[3]If unsettled intercompany transactions are subject to and translated using preference or penalty rates, translation of foreign currency statements at the rate applicable to dividend remittances may cause a difference between intercompany receivables and payables. Until that difference is eliminated by settlement of the intercompany transaction, the difference shall be treated as a receivable or payable in the enterprise's financial statements. [FAS52, ¶27, fn4]

statements of the enterprise, the current rate is the rate in effect at the foreign entity's balance sheet date for purposes of applying the requirements of this section to that foreign entity. [FAS52, ¶28]

Use of Averages or Other Methods of Approximation

.139 Literal application of the standards in this section might require a degree of detail in record keeping and computations that could be burdensome as well as unnecessary to produce reasonable approximations of the results. Accordingly, it is acceptable to use averages or other methods of approximation. For example, the propriety of using average rates to translate revenue and expense amounts is noted in paragraph .118. Likewise, the use of other time- and effort-saving methods to approximate the results of detailed calculations is permitted. [FAS52, ¶29] Average rates used should be appropriately weighted by the volume of functional currency transactions occurring during the accounting period. For example, to translate revenue and expense accounts for an annual period, individual revenue and expense accounts for each quarter or month may be translated at that quarter's or that month's average rate. The translated amounts for each quarter or month should then be combined for the annual totals. [FAS52, ¶140]

Disclosure

.140 The aggregate transaction gain or loss included in determining net income for the period shall be disclosed in the financial statements or notes thereto. For that disclosure, gains and losses on [FAS52, ¶30] derivative instruments shall comply with paragraph .142 of Section D50. [FAS133, ¶527(f)] Certain enterprises, primarily banks, are dealers in foreign exchange. Although certain gains or losses from dealer transactions may fit the definition of transaction gains or losses in this section, they may be disclosed as dealer gains or losses rather than as transaction gains or losses. [Refer to Section F25, "Financial Instruments: Disclosure," for guidance on possible additional disclosure requirements.] [FAS52, ¶30]

.141 An analysis of the changes during the period in the [FAS52, ¶31] accumulated amount of [FAS135, ¶4(l)] translation adjustments [FAS52, ¶31] reported in equity [FAS135, ¶4(l)] shall be provided in a separate financial statement, in notes to the financial statements, or as part of a statement of changes in equity. [FAS52, ¶31] This [accumulated amount in] equity might be titled "Equity Adjustment from Foreign Currency Translation" or given a similar title. [FAS52, ¶142] At a minimum, the analysis shall disclose:

a. Beginning and ending amount of cumulative translation adjustments
b. The aggregate adjustment for the period resulting from translation adjustments (refer to paragraph .119) and gains and losses from certain hedges and intercompany bal-

ances (refer to paragraph .127) [FAS52, ¶31] (Paragraph .142(c) of Section D50 specifies additional disclosures for instruments designated as hedges of the foreign currency exposure of a net investment in a foreign operation.) [FAS133, ¶527(g)]

c. The amount of income taxes for the period allocated to translation adjustments (refer to paragraph .134)

d. The amounts transferred from cumulative translation adjustments and included in determining net income for the period as a result of the sale or complete or substantially complete liquidation of an investment in a foreign entity (refer to paragraph .120). [FAS52, ¶31]

.142 An enterprise's financial statements shall not be adjusted for a rate change that occurs after the date of the enterprise's financial statements or after the date of the foreign currency statements of a foreign entity if they are consolidated, combined, or accounted for by the equity method in the financial statements of the enterprise. However, disclosure of the rate change and its effects on unsettled balances pertaining to foreign currency transactions, if significant, may be necessary. [FAS52, ¶32] If disclosed, the disclosure should include consideration of changes in unsettled transactions from the date of the financial statements to the date the rate changed. In some cases it may not be practicable to determine these changes; if so, that fact should be stated. [FAS52, ¶143]

.143 Management [is encouraged] to supplement the disclosures required by this section with an analysis and discussion of the effects of rate changes on the reported results of operations. This type of disclosure might include the mathematical effects of translating revenue and expenses at rates that are different from those used in a preceding period as well as the economic effects of rate changes, such as the effects on selling prices, sales volume, and cost structures. The purpose is to assist financial report users in understanding the broader economic implications of rate changes and to compare recent results with those of prior periods. [FAS52, ¶144]

.144 [Editorial deletion; this paragraph is contained in Section F65, "Foreign Operations," paragraph .102.]

.145 [Editorial deletion; this paragraph is contained in Section F65, "Foreign Operations," paragraph .103.]

Remeasurement of the Books of Record into the Functional Currency[4]

.146 If an entity's books of record are not maintained in its functional currency, this section (refer to paragraph .115) requires remeasurement into the functional currency prior to the translation process. If a foreign entity's functional currency is the reporting currency, remeasurement into the reporting currency obviates translation. The remeasurement process should produce the same result as if the entity's books of record had been initially recorded in the functional currency. To accomplish that result, it is necessary to use historical exchange rates between the functional currency and another currency in the remeasurement process for certain accounts (the current rate will be used for all others), and paragraph .147 identifies those accounts. To accomplish that result, it is also necessary to recognize currently in income all exchange gains and losses from remeasurement of monetary assets and liabilities that are not denominated in the functional currency (for example, assets and liabilities that are not denominated in dollars if the dollar is the functional currency). [FAS52, ¶47]

.147 The table below lists common nonmonetary balance sheet items and related revenue, expense, gain, and loss accounts that should be remeasured using historical rates in order to produce the same result in terms of the functional currency that would have occurred if those items had been initially recorded in the functional currency.

Accounts to Be Remeasured Using Historical Exchange Rates

Marketable securities carried at cost
- Equity securities
- Debt securities not intended to be held until maturity

Inventories carried at cost

Prepaid expenses such as insurance, advertising, and rent

Property, plant, and equipment

Accumulated depreciation on property, plant, and equipment

Patents, trademarks, licenses, and formulas

Goodwill

[4]The guidance in paragraphs .146 through .153 applies only to those instances in which the books of record are not maintained in the functional currency. [FAS52, ¶47, fn*]

Other intangible assets

Deferred charges and credits, except policy acquisition costs for life insurance enterprises

Deferred income

Common stock

Preferred stock carried at issuance price

Examples of revenues and expenses related to nonmonetary items:
- Cost of goods sold
- Depreciation of property, plant, and equipment
- Amortization of intangible items such as patents, licenses, etc.
- Amortization of deferred charges or credits except policy acquisition costs for life insurance enterprises

[FAS52, ¶48]

Inventories—Applying the Rule of Cost or Market, Whichever Is Lower, to Remeasure Inventory Not Recorded in the Functional Currency

.148 The rule of cost or market, whichever is lower (described in Section I78, "Inventory," [as *lower of cost or market*]), requires special application when the books of record are not kept in the functional currency. Inventories carried at cost in the books of record in another currency should be first remeasured to cost in the functional currency using historical exchange rates. Then, historical cost in the functional currency is compared with market as stated in the functional currency. Application of the rule in functional currency may require write-downs to market in the functional currency statements even though no write-down has been made in the books of record maintained in another currency. Likewise, a write-down in the books of record may need to be reversed if market exceeds historical cost as stated in the functional currency. If inventory[5] has been written down to market in the functional currency statements, that functional currency amount shall continue to be the carrying amount in the functional currency financial statements until the inventory is sold or a further write-down is necessary. [FAS52, ¶49]

[5]An asset other than inventory may sometimes be written down from historical cost. Although that write-down is not under the rule of cost or market, whichever is lower, the approach described in this paragraph might be appropriate. That is, a write-down may be required in the functional currency statements even though not required in the books of record, and a write-down in the books of record may need to be reversed before remeasurement to prevent the remeasured amount from exceeding functional currency historical cost. [FAS52, ¶49, fn5]

.149 Literal application of the rule of cost or market, whichever is lower, may require an inventory write-down[6] in functional currency financial statements for locally acquired inventory[7] if the value of the currency in which the books of record are maintained has declined in relation to the functional currency between the date the inventory was acquired and the date of the balance sheet. Such a write-down may not be necessary, however, if the replacement costs or selling prices expressed in the currency in which the books of record are maintained have increased sufficiently so that market exceeds historical cost as measured in functional currency. Paragraphs .150 through .152 illustrate this situation. [FAS52, ¶50]

.150 Assume the following:

a. When the rate is BR1 = FC2.40, a foreign subsidiary of a U.S. enterprise purchases a unit of inventory at a cost of BR500 (measured in functional currency, FC1,200).[8]
b. At the foreign subsidiary's balance sheet date, the current rate is BR1 = FC2.00 and the current replacement cost of the unit of inventory is BR560 (measured in functional currency, FC1,120).
c. Net realizable value is BR630 (measured in functional currency, FC1,260).
d. Net realizable value reduced by an allowance for an approximately normal profit margin is BR550 (measured in functional currency, FC1,100).

Because current replacement cost as measured in the functional currency (FC1,120) is less than historical cost as measured in the functional currency (FC1,200), an inventory write-down of FC80 is required in the functional currency financial statements. [FAS52, ¶51]

---

[6]This paragraph is not intended to preclude recognition of gains in a later interim period to the extent of inventory losses recognized from market declines in earlier interim periods if losses on the same inventory are recovered in the same year, as provided by Section I73, "Interim Financial Reporting," paragraph .107(c), which states: "Inventory losses from market declines should not be deferred beyond the interim period in which the decline occurs. Recoveries of such losses on the same inventory in later interim periods of the same fiscal year through market price recoveries should be recognized as gains in the later interim period. Such gains should not exceed previously recognized losses. Some market declines at interim dates, however, can reasonably be expected to be restored in the fiscal year. Such *temporary* market declines need not be recognized at the interim date since no loss is expected to be incurred in the fiscal year." [FAS52, ¶50, fn6]

[7]An inventory write-down also may be required for imported inventory. [FAS52, ¶50, fn7]

[8][The following abbreviations are used:]

BR = currency in which the books of record are maintained
FC = functional currency

[FAS52, ¶51, fn*]

.151 Continue to assume the same information in the preceding example but substitute a current replacement cost at the foreign subsidiary's balance sheet date of BR620. Because market as measured in the functional currency (BR620 × FC2.00 = FC1,240) exceeds historical cost as measured in the functional currency (BR500 × FC2.40 = FC1,200), an inventory write-down is not required in the financial statements. [FAS52, ¶52]

.152 As another example, assume the information in paragraph .150, except that selling prices in terms of the currency in which the books of record are maintained have increased so that net realizable value is BR720 and net realizable value reduced by an allowance for an approximately normal profit margin is BR640. In that case, because replacement cost measured in functional currency (BR560 × FC2.00 = FC1,120) is less than net realizable value reduced by an allowance for an approximately normal profit margin measured in functional currency (BR640 × FC2.00 = FC1,280), market is FC1,280. Because market as measured in the functional currency (FC1,280) exceeds historical cost as measured in the functional currency (BR500 × FC2.40 = FC1,200), an inventory write-down is not required in the functional currency financial statements. [FAS52, ¶53]

.153 [Deleted 12/82 because of FASB Statement 70, *Financial Reporting and Changing Prices: Foreign Currency Translation.*]

Glossary

.401 **Attribute.** The quantifiable characteristic of an item that is measured for accounting purposes. For example, historical cost and current cost are attributes of an asset. [FAS52, ¶162]

.402 **Conversion.** The exchange of one currency for another. [FAS52, ¶162]

.403 [Deleted 6/98 because of Statement 133.]

.404 **Current exchange rate.** The current exchange rate is the rate at which one unit of a currency can be exchanged for (converted into) another currency. For purposes of translation of financial statements referred to in this section, the current exchange rate is the rate as of the end of the period covered by the financial statements or as of the dates of recognition in those statements in the case of revenues, expenses, gains, and losses. The requirements for applying the current exchange rate for translating financial statements are set forth in paragraph .113. Further information regarding exchange rates is provided in paragraphs .127 through .129. [FAS52, ¶162]

.405 [Deleted 6/98 because of Statement 133.]

.406 **Enterprise.** Refer to **reporting enterprise.** [FAS52, ¶162]

.407 **Entity.** Refer to **foreign entity.** [FAS52, ¶162]

.408 **Foreign currency.** A currency other than the functional currency of the entity being referred to (for example, the dollar could be a foreign currency for a foreign entity). Composites of currencies, such as the Special Drawing Rights on the International Monetary Fund (SDRs), used to set prices or denominate amounts of loans, etc., have the characteristics of foreign currency for purposes of applying this section. [FAS52, ¶162]

.409 **Foreign currency statements.** Financial statements that employ as the unit of measure a functional currency that is not the reporting currency of the enterprise. [FAS52, ¶162]

.410 **Foreign currency transactions.** Transactions whose terms are denominated in a currency other than the entity's functional currency. Foreign currency transactions arise when an enterprise (a) buys or sells on credit goods or services whose prices are denominated in foreign currency, (b) borrows or lends funds and the amounts payable or receivable are denominated in foreign currency, (c) is a party to an unperformed forward exchange contract, or (d) for other reasons, acquires or disposes of assets, or incurs or settles liabilities denominated in foreign currency. [FAS52, ¶162]

.411 **Foreign currency translation.** The process of expressing in the reporting currency of the enterprise those amounts that are denominated or measured in a different currency. [FAS52, ¶162]

.412 **Foreign entity.** An operation (for example, subsidiary, division, branch, joint venture, etc.) whose financial statements (a) are prepared in a currency other than the reporting currency of the reporting enterprise and (b) are combined or consolidated with or accounted for on the equity basis in the financial statements of the reporting enterprise. [FAS52, ¶162]

.413 [Deleted 6/98 because of Statement 133.]

.414 [Deleted 6/98 because of Statement 133.]

.415 **Functional currency.** An entity's functional currency is the currency of the primary economic environment in which the entity operates; normally, that is the currency of the environment in which an entity primarily generates and expends cash (refer to paragraphs .104 through .115). [FAS52, ¶162]

.416 **Local currency.** The currency of a particular country being referred to. [FAS52, ¶162]

.417 **Reporting currency.** The currency in which an enterprise prepares its financial statements. [FAS52, ¶162]

.418 **Reporting enterprise.** An entity or group whose financial statements are being referred to. In this section, those financial statements reflect (a) the financial statements of one or more foreign operations by combination, consolidation, or equity accounting; (b) foreign currency transactions; or (c) both of the foregoing. [FAS52, ¶162]

.419 [Editorial deletion, 6/98.]

.420 **Transaction date.** The date at which a transaction (for example, a sale or purchase of merchandise or services) is recorded in accounting records in conformity with generally accepted accounting principles. A long-term commitment may have more than one transaction date (for example, the due date of each progress payment under a construction contract is an anticipated transaction date). [FAS52, ¶162]

.421 **Transaction gain or loss.** Transaction gains or losses result from a change in exchange rates between the functional currency and the currency in which a foreign currency transaction is denominated. They represent an increase or decrease in (a) the actual functional currency cash flows realized upon settlement of foreign currency transactions and (b) the expected functional currency cash flows on unsettled foreign currency transactions. [FAS52, ¶162]

.422 **Translation.** Refer to **foreign currency translation.** [FAS52, ¶162]

.423 **Translation adjustments.** Translation adjustments result from the process of translating financial statements from the entity's functional currency into the reporting currency. [FAS52, ¶162]

Supplemental Guidance: Emerging Issues Task Force (EITF) Issues

.1000 [Listed below are EITF Issues that provide supplemental guidance for this section. These Issues are grouped by subject matter and may be either interpretive of or related by topic to the guidance in this section.

Hedges

EITF Issue No. 96-15, "Accounting for the Effects of Changes in Foreign Currency Exchange Rates on Foreign-Currency-Denominated Available-for-Sale Debt Securities"
EITF Issue No. 97-7, "Accounting for Hedges of the Foreign Currency Risk Inherent in an Available-for-Sale Marketable Equity Security"

Highly Inflationary Economies

EITF Issue No. 92-4, "Accounting for a Change in Functional Currency When an Economy Ceases to Be Considered Highly Inflationary"
EITF Issue No. 92-8, "Accounting for the Income Tax Effects under FASB Statement No. 109 of a Change in Functional Currency When an Economy Ceases to Be Considered Highly Inflationary"
EITF Topic No. D-55, "Determining a Highly Inflationary Economy under FASB Statement No. 52"
EITF Topic No. D-56, "Accounting for a Change in Functional Currency and Deferred Taxes When an Economy Becomes Highly Inflationary"

Other

EITF Issue No. 87-12, "Foreign Debt-for-Equity Swaps"
EITF Issue No. 88-18, "Sales of Future Revenues"
EITF Issue No. 96-11, "Accounting for Forward Contracts and Purchased Options to Acquire Securities Covered by FASB Statement No. 115"
EITF Issue No. 01-5, "Application of FASB Statement No. 52 to an Investment Being Evaluated for Impairment That Will Be Disposed Of"
EITF Topic No. D-4, "Argentine Government Guarantee of U.S. Dollar-Denominated Loans to the Argentine Private Sector"
EITF Topic No. D-12, "Foreign Currency Translation—Selection of Exchange Rate When Trading Is Temporarily Suspended"
EITF Topic No. D-71, "Accounting Issues Relating to the Introduction of the European Economic and Monetary Union (EMU)"]

.1001 [Listed below are those EITF Issues that provide interpretive guidance on specific material in this section.

Paragraph .114 (FAS 52, ¶46)—EITF Issues No. 92-4 and 92-8 and Topic No. D-56
Paragraph .116 (FAS 52, ¶11)—EITF Topic No. D-55
Paragraph .119 (FAS 52, ¶13)—EITF Issue No. 01-5
Paragraph .122 (FAS 52, ¶15)—EITF Issue No. 96-15
Paragraph .136 (FAS 52, ¶26)—EITF Topic No. D-12]

(The next page is 19501.)

Sources: ARB 43, Chapter 12; FASB Statement 131

Summary

Any foreign earnings reported beyond the amounts received in the United States shall be carefully considered in the light of all the facts.

.100A The recommendations made in this section apply to U.S. enterprises which have branches or subsidiaries operating in foreign countries. [ARB43, ch12, ¶1]

.100B Since World War I foreign operations have been influenced to a marked degree by wars, departures from the gold standard, devaluations of currencies, currency restrictions, government regulations, etc. [ARB43, ch12, ¶2]

.100C Although comparatively few countries in recent years have had unrestricted currencies and exchanges, it is nevertheless true that many companies have been doing business in foreign countries having varying degrees of restrictions; in some cases they have been carrying on all operations regarded as normal, including the transmission of funds. In view of the difficulties mentioned above, however, the accounting treatment of assets, liabilities, losses, and gains involved in the conduct of foreign business and to be included or reflected in the financial statements of the U.S. companies requires careful consideration. [ARB43, ch12, ¶3]

.101 A sound procedure for U.S. enterprises to follow is to show earnings from foreign operations in their own accounts only to the extent that funds have been received in the United States or unrestricted funds are available for transmission thereto. Appropriate provision shall be made for known losses. [ARB43, ch12, ¶4]

.102 Any foreign earnings reported beyond the amounts received in the United States shall be carefully considered in the light of all the facts. The amounts shall be disclosed if they are significant. [ARB43, ch12, ¶5] Section S30, "Segment Disclosures and Related Information," discusses the requirements for reporting revenues from foreign operations. [FAS131, ¶129(a)]

.103 Section S30 discusses the requirements for reporting assets located outside the United States. [FAS131, ¶129(b)]

(The next page is 22001.)

GOODWILL AND OTHER INTANGIBLE ASSETS SECTION G40

Sources: FASB Statement 72; FASB Statement 141; FASB Statement 142; FASB Statement 144; FASB Statement 145; FASB Interpretation 9; FASB Technical Bulletin 85-6

[**Note:** A list of Issues discussed by the Emerging Issues Task Force (EITF) that provide supplemental guidance for this section is presented in paragraph .1000.]

Summary

This section addresses financial accounting and reporting for acquired goodwill and other intangible assets. It addresses how intangible assets that are acquired individually or with a group of other assets (but not those acquired in a business combination) should be accounted for in financial statements upon their acquisition. This section also addresses how goodwill and other intangible assets should be accounted for after they have been initially recognized in the financial statements. This section presents the following significant aspects of the subsequent accounting for goodwill and other intangible assets:

- This section adopts an aggregate view of goodwill and bases the accounting for goodwill on the units of the combined entity into which an acquired entity is integrated (those units are referred to as reporting units).
- This section does not presume that goodwill and all other intangible assets are wasting assets. Instead, goodwill and intangible assets that have indefinite useful lives will not be amortized but rather will be tested at least annually for impairment. Intangible assets that have finite useful lives will continue to be amortized over their useful lives, but without the constraint of an arbitrary ceiling.
- This section provides specific guidance for testing goodwill for impairment. Goodwill will be tested for impairment at least annually using a two-step process that begins with an estimation of the fair value of a reporting unit. The first step is a screen for potential impairment, and the second step measures the amount of impairment, if any.
- In addition, this section provides specific guidance on testing intangible assets that will not be amortized for impairment and thus removes those intangible assets from the scope of other impairment guidance. Intangible assets that are not amortized will be tested

for impairment at least annually by comparing the fair values of those assets with their recorded amounts.

- This section requires disclosure of information about goodwill and other intangible assets in the years subsequent to their acquisition. Required disclosures include information about the changes in the carrying amount of goodwill from period to period (in the aggregate and by reportable segment), the carrying amount of intangible assets by major intangible asset class for those assets subject to amortization and for those not subject to amortization, and the estimated intangible asset amortization expense for the next five years.

This section does not change the requirement to expense the cost of certain acquired research and development assets at the date of acquisition as required by Section R50, "Research and Development" and Section B51, "Business Combinations."

This section utilizes the guidance in FASB Concepts Statement 7, *Using Cash Flow Information and Present Value in Accounting Measurements,* for estimating the fair values used in testing both goodwill and other intangible assets that are not being amortized for impairment. The provisions of this section are not applicable to goodwill and other intangible assets arising from combinations between mutual enterprises or to not-for-profit organizations.

Introduction

.101 This section addresses financial accounting and reporting for **intangible assets** acquired individually or with a group of other assets (but not those acquired in a business combination) at acquisition. This section also addresses financial accounting and reporting for goodwill and other intangible assets subsequent to their acquisition. Section B51, "Business Combinations," addresses financial accounting and reporting for goodwill and other intangible assets acquired in a business combination at acquisition. [FAS142, ¶1]

.102 Paragraphs .161 through .169 of this section provide implementation guidance on how intangible assets should be accounted for in accordance with this section [and are] an integral part of the standards provided in this section. Paragraph .148 provides [an] illustration of some of the financial statement disclosures that this section requires. [FAS142, ¶3]

Scope

.103 The initial recognition and measurement provisions of this section apply to intangible assets acquired individually or with a group of other assets (but not those acquired in a business combination).[1] The remaining provisions of this section apply to **goodwill** that an entity[2] recognizes in accordance with Section B51 and to other intangible assets that an entity acquires, whether individually, with a group of other assets, or in a business combination. While goodwill is an intangible asset, the term *intangible asset* is used in this section to refer to an intangible asset other than goodwill. [FAS142, ¶4]

.104 This section applies to costs of internally developing goodwill and other unidentifiable intangible assets with indeterminate lives. Some entities capitalize costs incurred to develop identifiable intangible assets, while others expense those costs as incurred. This section also applies to costs of internally developing identifiable intangible assets that an entity recognizes as assets. [FAS142, ¶5]

.105 This section applies to goodwill and other intangible assets recognized on the acquisition of some or all of the noncontrolling interests in a subsidiary—whether acquired by the parent, the subsidiary itself, or another affiliate.[3] This section, including its transition provisions, applies to amounts recognized as goodwill in applying the equity method of accounting and to the excess reorganization value recognized by entities that adopt fresh-start reporting in accordance with AICPA Statement of Position 90-7, *Financial Reporting by Entities in Reorganization Under the Bankruptcy Code.* That excess reorganization value shall be reported as goodwill and accounted for in the same manner as goodwill. [FAS142, ¶6]

.106 This section does not change the accounting prescribed in the following sections:

a. Section B51, "Business Combinations," paragraphs .144 and .145
b. Section Br5, "Broadcasting Industry"
c. Section Bt7, "Banking and Thrift Industries," paragraphs .106 through .110
d. Section Co2, "Computer Software to be Sold, Leased, or Otherwise Marketed"
e. Section F35, "Financial Instruments: Servicing" (a servicing asset or liability)

---

[1]Section B51 addresses the initial recognition and measurement of intangible assets acquired in a business combination. [FAS142, ¶4, fn3]

[2]This section applies to a business enterprise, a **mutual enterprise,** and a **not-for-profit organization,** each of which is referred to herein as an *entity*. [FAS142, ¶4, fn4]

[3]Section B51 requires that the acquisition of some or all of the noncontrolling interests in a subsidiary be accounted for using the purchase method. [FAS142, ¶6, fn5]

f. Section I27, "Income Taxes" (a deferred tax asset)
g. Section Oi5, "Oil and Gas Producing Activities"
h. Section R50, "Research and Development"
i. Section Re4, "Record and Music Industry"
j. Section Re6, "Regulated Operations," paragraphs .134 and .135
k. Section Ti7, "Title Plant."

[FAS142, ¶8]

Initial Recognition and Measurement of Intangible Assets

.107 An intangible asset that is acquired either individually or with a group of other assets (but not those acquired in a business combination) shall be initially recognized and measured based on its **fair value.**[4] General concepts related to the initial measurement of assets acquired in exchange transactions, including intangible assets, are provided in paragraphs .104 through .106 of Section B51.[5] The cost of a group of assets acquired in a transaction other than a business combination shall be allocated to the individual assets acquired based on their relative fair values and shall not give rise to goodwill.[6] Intangible assets acquired in a business combination are initially recognized and measured in accordance with Section B51.[7] [FAS142, ¶9]

---

[4]Intangible assets that are acquired individually or with a group of assets in a transaction other than a business combination may meet the asset recognition criteria in FASB Concepts Statement 5, *Recognition and Measurement in Financial Statements of Business Enterprises,* even though they do not meet either the contractual-legal criterion or the separability criterion (for example, specially-trained employees or a unique manufacturing process related to an acquired manufacturing plant). Thus, those assets should be recognized as intangible assets. [FAS142, ¶B37]

[5]Although those paragraphs refer to determining the cost of the assets acquired, both paragraph .105 of Section B51 and paragraph .105 of Section N35, "Nonmonetary Transactions," note that, in general, cost should be measured based on the fair value of the consideration given or the fair value of the net assets acquired, whichever is more reliably measurable. [FAS142, ¶9, fn6]

[6]Section B51 requires intangible assets acquired in a business combination that do not meet certain criteria to be included in the amount initially recognized as goodwill. Those recognition criteria do not apply to intangible assets acquired in transactions other than business combinations. [FAS142, ¶9, fn7]

[7]Section R50 requires amounts assigned to acquired intangible assets that are to be used in a particular research and development project and that *have no alternative future use* to be charged to expense at the acquisition date. Section B51 does not change that requirement, nor does this section. [FAS142, ¶9, fn8]

Internally Developed Intangible Assets

.108 Costs of internally developing, maintaining, or restoring intangible assets (including goodwill) that are not specifically identifiable, that have indeterminate lives, or that are inherent in a continuing business and related to an entity as a whole, shall be recognized as an expense when incurred. [FAS142, ¶10] [Refer to paragraph .1001 for an EITF Issue that provides interpretive guidance on this paragraph.]

Accounting for Intangible Assets

Determining the Useful Life of an Intangible Asset

.109 The accounting for a recognized intangible asset is based on its **useful life** to the reporting entity. An intangible asset with a finite useful life is amortized; an intangible asset with an indefinite useful life is not amortized. The useful life of an intangible asset to an entity is the period over which the asset is expected to contribute directly or indirectly to the future cash flows of that entity.[8] The estimate of the useful life of an intangible asset to an entity shall be based on an analysis of all pertinent factors, in particular:

a. The expected use of the asset by the entity
b. The expected useful life of another asset or a group of assets to which the useful life of the intangible asset may relate (such as mineral rights to depleting assets)
c. Any legal, regulatory, or contractual provisions that may limit the useful life [9]
d. Any legal, regulatory, or contractual provisions that enable renewal or extension of the asset's legal or contractual life without substantial cost (provided there is evidence to support renewal or extension and renewal or extension can be accomplished without material modifications of the existing terms and conditions)[10]
e. The effects of obsolescence, demand, competition, and other economic factors (such as the stability of the industry, known technological advances, legislative action that results in an uncertain or changing regulatory environment, and expected changes in distribution channels)

---

[8]The useful life of an intangible asset shall reflect the period over which it will contribute to the cash flows of the reporting entity, not the period of time that it would take that entity to internally develop an intangible asset that would provide similar benefits. [FAS142, ¶11, fn9]

[9]The useful lives of intangible assets cannot extend beyond the length of their legal rights and may be shorter. [FAS142, ¶B46]

[10]Whether the cost of renewal is substantial should be determined based on the relationship of the renewal cost to the fair value of the intangible asset at the time it is acquired. [FAS142, ¶B60]

f. The level of maintenance expenditures required to obtain the expected future cash flows from the asset (for example, a material level of required maintenance in relation to the carrying amount of the asset may suggest a very limited useful life).[11]

If no legal, regulatory, contractual, competitive, economic, or other factors limit the useful life of an intangible asset to the reporting entity, the useful life of the asset shall be considered to be indefinite.[12] The term *indefinite* does not mean infinite [FAS142, ¶11] or indeterminate. [FAS142, ¶B59] Paragraphs .161 through .169 include illustrative examples of different intangible assets and how they should be accounted for in accordance with this section, including determining whether the useful life of an intangible asset is indefinite. [FAS142, ¶11]

Intangible Assets Subject to Amortization

.110 A recognized intangible asset shall be amortized over its useful life to the reporting entity unless that life is determined to be indefinite. If an intangible asset has a finite useful life, but the precise length of that life is not known, that intangible asset shall be amortized over the best estimate of its useful life. The method of amortization shall reflect the pattern in which the economic benefits of the intangible asset are consumed or otherwise used up. If that pattern cannot be reliably determined, a straight-line amortization method shall be used. An intangible asset shall not be written down or off in the period of acquisition unless it becomes impaired during that period.[13] [FAS142, ¶12]

.111 The amount of an intangible asset to be amortized shall be the amount initially assigned to that asset less any **residual value.** The residual value of an intangible asset shall be assumed to be zero unless at the end of its useful life to the entity the asset is expected to continue to have a useful life to another entity and (a) the reporting entity has a commitment from a third party to purchase the asset at the end of its useful life or

[11] As in determining the useful life of depreciable tangible assets, regular maintenance may be assumed but enhancements may not. [FAS142, ¶11, fn10]

[12] The useful life of an intangible asset is indefinite if that life extends beyond the foreseeable horizon—that is, there is no foreseeable limit on the period of time over which it is expected to contribute to the cash flows of the reporting entity. [FAS142, ¶B45] Examples of intangible assets [with indefinite lives] might be airport route authorities, certain trademarks, and taxicab medallions. [FAS142, ¶B56]

[13] However, both Section B51 and Section R50 require amounts assigned to acquired intangible assets that are to be used in a particular research and development project and that have no alternative future use to be charged to expense at the acquisition date. [FAS142, ¶12, fn11]

(b) the residual value can be determined by reference to an exchange transaction in an existing market for that asset and that market is expected to exist at the end of the asset's useful life. [FAS142, ¶13]

.112 An entity shall evaluate the remaining useful life of an intangible asset that is being amortized each reporting period to determine whether events and circumstances warrant a revision to the remaining period of amortization. If the estimate of an intangible asset's remaining useful life is changed, the remaining carrying amount of the intangible asset shall be amortized prospectively over that revised remaining useful life. If an intangible asset that is being amortized is subsequently determined to have an indefinite useful life, the asset shall be tested for impairment in accordance with paragraph .115 [FAS142, ¶14] (for example, due to a change in legal requirements).[14] [FAS142, ¶B61] That intangible asset shall no longer be amortized and shall be accounted for in the same manner as other intangible assets that are not subject to amortization. [FAS142, ¶14]

Recognition and Measurement of an Impairment Loss

.113 An intangible asset that is subject to amortization shall be reviewed for impairment in accordance with Section I08, "Impairment," by applying the recognition and measurement provisions in [FAS142, ¶15] paragraphs .142 through .159 [of that section]. [FAS144, ¶C17(b)] In accordance with Section I08, an impairment loss shall be recognized if the carrying amount of an intangible asset is not recoverable and its carrying amount exceeds its fair value. After an impairment loss is recognized, the adjusted carrying amount of the intangible asset shall be its new accounting basis. Subsequent reversal of a previously recognized impairment loss is prohibited. [FAS142, ¶15]

Intangible Assets Not Subject to Amortization

.114 If an intangible asset is determined to have an indefinite useful life, it shall not be amortized until its useful life is determined to be no longer indefinite. An entity shall evaluate the remaining useful life of an intangible asset that is not being amortized each reporting period to determine whether events and circumstances continue to support an indefinite useful life. If an intangible asset that is not being amortized is subsequently determined to have a finite useful life, [FAS142, ¶16] such as when unanticipated com-

[14]Any resulting impairment loss would be due to a change in accounting estimate and thus, consistent with Section A06, "Accounting Changes," should be recognized as a change in estimate, not as a change in accounting principle. Therefore, that loss would be presented in the income statement in the same manner as other impairment losses. [FAS142, ¶B66]

petition enters the market,[15] [FAS142, ¶B61] the asset shall be tested for impairment in accordance with paragraph .115. That intangible asset shall then be amortized prospectively over its estimated remaining useful life and accounted for in the same manner as other intangible assets that are subject to amortization. [FAS142, ¶16]

Recognition and Measurement of an Impairment Loss

.115 An intangible asset that is not subject to amortization shall be tested for impairment annually, or more frequently if events or changes in circumstances indicate that the asset might be impaired. [FAS142, ¶17] (Paragraph .143 of Section I08 includes examples of impairment indicators.) [FAS144, ¶C17(c)] The impairment test shall consist of a comparison of the fair value of an intangible asset with its carrying amount.[16] If the carrying amount of an intangible asset exceeds its fair value, an impairment loss shall be recognized in an amount equal to that excess. After an impairment loss is recognized, the adjusted carrying amount of the intangible asset shall be its new accounting basis. Subsequent reversal of a previously recognized impairment loss is prohibited. [FAS142, ¶17] [Refer to paragraph .1001 for an EITF Issue that provides interpretive guidance on this paragraph.]

Accounting for Goodwill

.116 Goodwill shall not be amortized. Goodwill shall be tested for impairment at a level of reporting referred to as a reporting unit. (Paragraphs .128 through .135 provide guidance on determining reporting units.) Impairment is the condition that exists when the carrying amount of goodwill exceeds its implied fair value.[17] The two-step impairment test discussed in paragraphs .117 through .120 shall be used to identify potential goodwill impairment and measure the amount of a goodwill impairment loss to be recognized (if any). [FAS142, ¶18]

---

[15]Any resulting impairment loss would be due to a change in accounting estimate and thus, consistent with Section A06, should be recognized as a change in estimate, not as a change in accounting principle. Therefore, that loss would be presented in the income statement in the same manner as other impairment losses. [FAS142, ¶B66]

[16]The fair value of an intangible asset shall be estimated using the guidance in paragraphs .121 through .123 (except the guidance specific to estimating the fair value of a **reporting unit**). [FAS142, ¶17, fn12]

[17]The fair value of goodwill can be measured only as a residual and cannot be measured directly. Therefore, this section includes a methodology to determine an amount that achieves a reasonable estimate of the value of goodwill for purposes of measuring an impairment loss. That estimate is referred to herein as the *implied fair value of goodwill*. [FAS142, ¶18, fn13]

Recognition and Measurement of an Impairment Loss

.117 The first step of the goodwill impairment test, used to identify potential impairment, compares the fair value of a reporting unit with its carrying amount, including goodwill. The guidance in paragraphs .121 through .123 shall be used to determine the fair value of a reporting unit. If the fair value of a reporting unit exceeds its carrying amount, goodwill of the reporting unit is considered not impaired, thus the second step of the impairment test is unnecessary. If the carrying amount of a reporting unit exceeds its fair value, the second step of the goodwill impairment test shall be performed to measure the amount of impairment loss, if any. [FAS142, ¶19]

.118 The second step of the goodwill impairment test, used to measure the amount of impairment loss, compares the implied fair value of reporting unit goodwill with the carrying amount of that goodwill. The guidance in paragraph .119 shall be used to estimate the implied fair value of goodwill. If the carrying amount of reporting unit goodwill exceeds the implied fair value of that goodwill, an impairment loss shall be recognized in an amount equal to that excess. The loss recognized cannot exceed the carrying amount of goodwill. After a goodwill impairment loss is recognized, the adjusted carrying amount of goodwill shall be its new accounting basis. Subsequent reversal of a previously recognized goodwill impairment loss is prohibited once the measurement of that loss is completed. [FAS142, ¶20] [Refer to paragraph .1001 for an EITF Issue that provides interpretive guidance on this paragraph.]

.119 The implied fair value of goodwill shall be determined in the same manner as the amount of goodwill recognized in a business combination is determined. That is, an entity shall allocate the fair value of a reporting unit to all of the assets and liabilities of that unit (including any unrecognized intangible assets) as if the reporting unit had been acquired in a business combination and the fair value of the reporting unit was the price paid to acquire the reporting unit.[18] The excess of the fair value of a reporting unit over the amounts assigned to its assets and liabilities is the implied fair value of goodwill. That allocation process shall be performed only for purposes of testing goodwill for impairment; an entity shall not write up or write down a recognized asset or liability, nor should it recognize a previously unrecognized intangible asset as a result of that allocation process. [FAS142, ¶21]

.120 If the second step of the goodwill impairment test is not complete before the financial statements are issued and a goodwill impairment loss is probable and can be

[18]The relevant guidance in paragraphs .134 through .137 of Section B51 shall be used in determining how to allocate the fair value of a reporting unit to the assets and liabilities of that unit. Included in that allocation would be research and development assets that meet the criteria in paragraph .130 of this section, even if Section B51 or Section R50 would require those assets to be written off to earnings when acquired. [FAS142, ¶21, fn14]

reasonably estimated, the best estimate of that loss shall be recognized in those financial statements.[19] Paragraph .146(c) requires disclosure of the fact that the measurement of the impairment loss is an estimate. Any adjustment to that estimated loss based on the completion of the measurement of the impairment loss shall be recognized in the subsequent reporting period. [FAS142, ¶22]

Fair Value Measurements

.121 The fair value of an asset (or liability) is the amount at which that asset (or liability) could be bought (or incurred) or sold (or settled) in a current transaction between willing parties, that is, other than in a forced or liquidation sale. Thus, the fair value of a reporting unit refers to the amount at which the unit as a whole could be bought or sold in a current transaction between willing parties. Quoted market prices in active markets are the best evidence of fair value and shall be used as the basis for the measurement, if available. However, the market price of an individual equity security (and thus the market capitalization of a reporting unit with publicly traded equity securities) may not be representative of the fair value of the reporting unit as a whole.[20] The quoted market price of an individual equity security, therefore, need not be the sole measurement basis of the fair value of a reporting unit. [FAS142, ¶23]

.122 If quoted market prices are not available, the estimate of fair value shall be based on the best information available, including prices for similar assets and liabilities and the results of using other valuation techniques.[[21]] A present value technique is often the best available technique with which to estimate the fair value of a group of net assets (such as a reporting unit). If a present value technique is used to measure fair value, estimates of future cash flows used in that technique shall be consistent with the objective of measuring fair value. Those cash flow estimates shall incorporate assumptions

---

[19]Refer to Section C59, "Contingencies." [FAS142, ¶22, fn15]

[20]Substantial value may arise from the ability to take advantage of synergies and other benefits that flow from control over another entity. Consequently, measuring the fair value of a collection of assets and liabilities that operate together in a controlled entity is different from measuring the fair value of that entity's individual equity securities. An acquiring entity often is willing to pay more for equity securities that give it a controlling interest than an investor would pay for a number of equity securities representing less than a controlling interest. That control premium may cause the fair value of a reporting unit to exceed its market capitalization. [FAS142, ¶23, fn16]

[[21]]If an acquired entity is a significant portion of a reporting unit (or a reporting unit itself) and the technique used to value the acquisition (determine the purchase price) is consistent with the objective of measuring fair value, the assumptions underlying that valuation should be used in measuring the fair value of the reporting unit. A valuation technique similar to that used to value the acquisition would most likely be used by the entity to determine the fair value of the reporting unit. For example, if the purchase price were based on an expected cash flow model, that cash flow model and related assumptions would be used to measure the fair value of the reporting unit. [FAS142, ¶B155]

that marketplace participants would use in their estimates of fair value. If that information is not available without undue cost and effort, an entity may use its own assumptions. Those cash flow estimates shall be based on reasonable and supportable assumptions and shall consider all available evidence.[22] The weight given to the evidence shall be commensurate with the extent to which the evidence can be verified objectively. If a range is estimated for the amounts or timing of possible cash flows, the likelihood of possible outcomes shall be considered. Concepts Statement 7 discusses the essential elements of a present value measurement (paragraph 23), provides examples of circumstances in which an entity's cash flows might differ from the market cash flows (paragraph 32), and discusses the use of present value techniques in measuring the fair value of an asset or a liability (paragraphs 39 through 54 and 75 through 88). Refer to Appendix H, "Excerpts from Concepts Statement 7," in the *Current Text,* for those paragraphs of Concepts Statement 7. [FAS142, ¶24]

.123 In estimating the fair value of a reporting unit, a valuation technique based on multiples of earnings or revenue or a similar performance measure may be used if that technique is consistent with the objective of measuring fair value. Use of multiples of earnings or revenue in determining the fair value of a reporting unit may be appropriate, for example, when the fair value of an entity that has comparable operations and economic characteristics is observable and the relevant multiples of the comparable entity are known. Conversely, use of multiples would not be appropriate in situations in which the operations or activities of an entity for which the multiples are known are not of a comparable nature, scope, or size as the reporting unit for which fair value is being estimated. [FAS142, ¶25]

When to Test Goodwill for Impairment

.124 Goodwill of a reporting unit shall be tested for impairment on an annual basis and between annual tests in certain circumstances (refer to paragraph .126). The annual goodwill impairment test may be performed any time during the fiscal year provided the test is performed at the same time every year. Different reporting units may be tested for impairment at different times. [FAS142, ¶26]

.125 A detailed determination of the fair value of a reporting unit may be carried forward from one year to the next if all of the following criteria have been met:

a. The assets and liabilities that make up the reporting unit have not changed significantly since the most recent fair value determination. (A recent significant acquisi-

[22]When cash flows are used to estimate fair value, those cash flows should be consistent with the most recent budgets and plans used by management. In estimating cash flows for purposes of determining the fair value of a reporting unit, some consideration should be given to industry trends. [FAS142, ¶B152]

tion or a reorganization of an entity's segment reporting structure is an example of an event that might significantly change the composition of a reporting unit.)

b. The most recent fair value determination resulted in an amount that exceeded the carrying amount of the reporting unit by a substantial margin.

c. Based on an analysis of events that have occurred and circumstances that have changed since the most recent fair value determination, the likelihood that a current fair value determination would be less than the current carrying amount of the reporting unit is remote.

[FAS142, ¶27]

.126 Goodwill of a reporting unit shall be tested for impairment between annual tests if an event occurs or circumstances change that would more likely than not reduce the fair value of a reporting unit below its carrying amount. Examples of such events or circumstances include:

a. A significant adverse change in legal factors or in the business climate
b. An adverse action or assessment by a regulator
c. Unanticipated competition
d. A loss of key personnel
e. A more-likely-than-not expectation that a reporting unit or a significant portion of a reporting unit will be sold or otherwise disposed of
f. The testing for recoverability under Section I08 of a significant asset group within a reporting unit
g. Recognition of a goodwill impairment loss in the financial statements of a subsidiary that is a component of a reporting unit.

In addition, paragraph .138 requires that goodwill be tested for impairment after a portion of goodwill has been allocated to a business to be disposed of. [FAS142, ¶28]

.127 If goodwill and another asset (or asset group) of a reporting unit are tested for impairment at the same time, the other asset (or asset group) shall be tested for impairment before goodwill.[23] For example, if a significant asset group is to be tested for impairment under Section I08 (thus potentially requiring a goodwill impairment test), the impairment test for the significant asset group would be performed before the goodwill impairment test. If the asset group was impaired, the impairment loss would be recognized prior to goodwill being tested for impairment. [FAS142, ¶29]

[23]That requirement applies to all assets that are tested for impairment, not just those included in the scope of Section I08. [FAS142, ¶B167]

Reporting Unit

.128 A reporting unit is an operating segment or one level below an operating segment (referred to as a component).[24] A component of an operating segment is a reporting unit if the component constitutes a business[25] for which discrete financial information is available and segment management[26] regularly reviews the operating results of that component. However, two or more components of an operating segment shall be aggregated and deemed a single reporting unit if the components have similar economic characteristics.[27] An operating segment shall be deemed to be a reporting unit if all of its components are similar, if none of its components is a reporting unit, or if it comprises only a single component. [FAS142, ¶30] A reporting unit could be the same as an operating segment, which could be the same as a reportable segment, which could be the same as the entity as a whole (entity level). Reporting units will vary depending on the level at which performance of the segment is reviewed, how many businesses the operating segment includes, and the similarity of those businesses. [FAS142, ¶B112] The relevant provisions of Section S30 and related interpretive literature shall be used to determine the reporting units of an entity. [FAS142, ¶30] [Refer to paragraph .1001 for an EITF Issue that provides interpretive guidance on this paragraph.]

.129 An entity that is not required to report segment information in accordance with Section S30 is nonetheless required to test goodwill for impairment at the reporting unit level. That entity shall use the guidance in paragraphs .109 through .114 of Section S30 to determine its operating segments for purposes of determining its reporting units. [FAS142, ¶31] As with public entities, the reporting unit level for many nonpublic entities may be the same as the entity level. Thus, nonpublic entities would not be precluded from testing for impairment at the entity level—if in fact that level meets the definition of a reporting unit. [FAS142, ¶B113]

---

[24]For purposes of determining reporting units, an operating segment is as defined in paragraph .109 of Section S30, "Segment Disclosures and Related Information." [FAS142, ¶30, fn17]

[25]EITF Issue No. 98-3, "Determining Whether a Nonmonetary Transaction Involves Receipt of Productive Assets or of a Business," includes guidance on determining whether an asset group constitutes a business. [FAS142, ¶30, fn18]

[26]Segment management consists of one or more segment managers, as that term is defined in paragraph .113 of Section S30. [FAS142, ¶30, fn19]

[27]Paragraph .116 of Section S30 shall be considered in determining if the components of an operating segment have similar economic characteristics. [FAS142, ¶30, fn20]

Assigning acquired assets and assumed liabilities to reporting units

.130 For the purpose of testing goodwill for impairment, acquired assets and assumed liabilities shall be assigned to a reporting unit as of the acquisition date if both of the following criteria are met:

a. The asset will be employed in or the liability relates to the operations of a reporting unit.
b. The asset or liability will be considered in determining the fair value of the reporting unit.

Assets or liabilities that an entity considers part of its corporate assets or liabilities shall also be assigned to a reporting unit if both of the above criteria are met. Examples of corporate items that may meet those criteria and therefore would be assigned to a reporting unit are environmental liabilities that relate to an existing operating facility of the reporting unit and a pension obligation that would be included in the determination of the fair value of the reporting unit. This provision applies to assets acquired and liabilities assumed in a business combination and to those acquired or assumed individually or with a group of other assets. [FAS142, ¶32]

.131 Some assets or liabilities may be employed in or relate to the operations of multiple reporting units. The methodology used to determine the amount of those assets or liabilities to assign to a reporting unit shall be reasonable and supportable and shall be applied in a consistent manner.[28] For example, assets and liabilities not directly related to a specific reporting unit, but from which the reporting unit benefits, could be allocated according to the benefit received by the different reporting units (or based on the relative fair values of the different reporting units). In the case of pension items, for example, a pro rata allocation based on payroll expense might be used. [FAS142, ¶33]

Assigning goodwill to reporting units

.132 For the purpose of testing goodwill for impairment, *all* goodwill acquired in a business combination shall be assigned to one or more reporting units as of the acquisition date. Goodwill shall be assigned to reporting units of the acquiring entity that are expected to benefit from the synergies of the combination even though other assets or liabilities of the acquired entity may not be assigned to that reporting unit. The total amount of acquired goodwill may be divided among a number of reporting units. The methodology used to determine the amount of goodwill to assign to a reporting unit shall be reasonable and supportable and shall be applied in a consistent manner. In addition, that

[28]It is possible for a reasonable allocation method to be very general. [FAS142, ¶B118]

methodology shall be consistent with the objectives of the process of assigning goodwill to reporting units described in paragraph .133. [FAS142, ¶34]

.133 In concept, the amount of goodwill assigned to a reporting unit would be determined in a manner similar to how the amount of goodwill recognized in a business combination is determined. [FAS142, ¶35] An entity would determine the fair value of the acquired business (or portion thereof) to be included in a reporting unit—in essence a "purchase price" for that business. The entity would then allocate that purchase price to the individual assets acquired and liabilities assumed related to that acquired business (or portion thereof).[29] Any excess purchase price is the amount of goodwill assigned to that reporting unit. [FAS145, ¶9(m)] However, if goodwill is to be assigned to a reporting unit that has not been assigned any of the assets acquired or liabilities assumed in that acquisition, the amount of goodwill to be assigned to that unit might be determined by applying a "with and without" computation. That is, the difference between the fair value of that reporting unit before the acquisition and its fair value after the acquisition represents the amount of goodwill to be assigned to that reporting unit. [FAS142, ¶35]

.134 This section does not require that goodwill and all other related assets and liabilities assigned to reporting units for purposes of testing goodwill for impairment be reflected in the entity's reported segments. However, even though an asset may not be included in reported segment assets, the asset (or liability) should be allocated to a reporting unit for purposes of testing for [goodwill] impairment if it meets the criteria in paragraph .130 of this section. [FAS142, ¶B121]

Reorganization of reporting structure

.135 When an entity reorganizes its reporting structure in a manner that changes the composition of one or more of its reporting units, the guidance in paragraphs .130 and .131 shall be used to reassign assets and liabilities to the reporting units affected. However, goodwill shall be reassigned to the reporting units affected using a relative fair value allocation approach similar to that used when a portion of a reporting unit is to be disposed of (refer to paragraph .138). For example, if existing reporting unit A is to be integrated with reporting units B, C, and D, goodwill in reporting unit A would be assigned to units B, C, and D based on the relative fair values of the three portions of reporting unit A prior to those portions being integrated with reporting units B, C, and D. [FAS142, ¶36]

---

[29] Paragraphs .134 through .137 of Section B51 provide guidance on allocating the purchase price to the assets acquired and liabilities assumed in a business combination. [FAS142, ¶35, fn21]

Goodwill Impairment Testing by a Subsidiary

.136 All goodwill recognized by a public or nonpublic subsidiary (subsidiary goodwill) in its separate financial statements that are prepared in accordance with generally accepted accounting principles shall be accounted for in accordance with this section.[30] Subsidiary goodwill shall be tested for impairment at the subsidiary level using the subsidiary's reporting units. If a goodwill impairment loss is recognized at the subsidiary level, goodwill of the reporting unit or units (at the higher consolidated level) in which the subsidiary's reporting unit with impaired goodwill resides must be tested for impairment if the event that gave rise to the loss at the subsidiary level would more likely than not reduce the fair value of the reporting unit (at the higher consolidated level) below its carrying amount (refer to paragraph .126(g)). Only if goodwill of that higher-level reporting unit is impaired would a goodwill impairment loss be recognized at the consolidated level.[31][FAS142, ¶37]

Goodwill Impairment Testing When a Noncontrolling Interest Exists

.137 Goodwill arising from a business combination with a continuing noncontrolling interest shall be tested for impairment using an approach consistent with the approach used to measure the noncontrolling interest at the acquisition date. (A noncontrolling interest is sometimes referred to as a minority interest.) For example, if goodwill is initially recognized based only on the controlling interest of the parent, the fair value of the reporting unit used in the impairment test should be based on that controlling interest and should not reflect the portion of fair value attributable to the noncontrolling interest. Similarly, the implied fair value of goodwill that is determined in the second step of the impairment test and used to measure the impairment loss should reflect only the parent company's interest in that goodwill. [FAS142, ¶38]

Disposal of All or a Portion of a Reporting Unit

.138 When a reporting unit is to be disposed of in its entirety, goodwill of that reporting unit shall be included in the carrying amount of the reporting unit in determin-

---

[30]Subsidiary goodwill might arise from (a) acquisitions that a subsidiary made prior to its being acquired by the parent, (b) acquisitions that a subsidiary made subsequent to its being acquired by the parent, and (c) goodwill arising from the business combination in which a subsidiary was acquired that the parent company pushed down to the subsidiary's financial statements. [FAS142, ¶B157]

[31]If testing at the consolidated level leads to an impairment loss, that loss should be recognized at that level separately from the subsidiary's loss. [FAS142, ¶B159]

ing the gain or loss on disposal. When a portion of a reporting unit that constitutes a business[33] is to be disposed of, goodwill associated with that business shall be included in the carrying amount of the business in determining the gain or loss on disposal. The amount of goodwill to be included in that carrying amount shall be based on the relative fair values of the business to be disposed of and the portion of the reporting unit that will be retained. For example, if a business is being sold for $100 and the fair value of the reporting unit excluding the business being sold is $300, 25 percent of the goodwill residing in the reporting unit would be included in the carrying amount of the business to be sold. However, if the business to be disposed of was never integrated into the reporting unit after its acquisition and thus the benefits of the acquired goodwill were never realized by the rest of the reporting unit, the current carrying amount of that acquired goodwill shall be included in the carrying amount of the business to be disposed of. That situation might occur when the acquired business is operated as a stand-alone entity or when the business is to be disposed of shortly after it is acquired.[34] When only a portion of goodwill is allocated to a business to be disposed of, the goodwill remaining in the portion of the reporting unit to be retained shall be tested for impairment in accordance with paragraphs .117 through .120 (using its adjusted carrying amount). [FAS142, ¶39]

Equity Method Investments

.139 The portion of the difference between the cost of an investment and the amount of underlying equity in net assets of an equity method investee that is recognized as goodwill in accordance with paragraph .109(b) of Section I82, "Investments: Equity Method," (equity method goodwill) shall not be amortized. However, equity method goodwill shall not be reviewed for impairment in accordance with this section. [Since] equity method goodwill is not separable from the related investment, that goodwill should not be tested for impairment in accordance with this section. [FAS142, ¶B170] Equity method investments shall continue to be reviewed for impairment in accordance with paragraph .109(h) of Section I82. [FAS142, ¶40]

---

[32] [Deleted 8/01 because of FASB Statement 144, *Accounting for the Impairment or Disposal of Long-Lived Assets.*]

[33] Refer to footnote 25. [FAS142, ¶39, fn23]

[34] Those situations would be infrequent because some amount of integration generally occurs after an acquisition. [FAS142, ¶B166]

Deferred Income Taxes

.140 Paragraph .129 of Section I27 states that deferred income taxes are not recognized for any portion of goodwill for which amortization is not deductible for income tax purposes. Paragraphs .188 and .189 of Section I27 provide additional guidance for recognition of deferred income taxes related to goodwill when amortization of goodwill is deductible for tax purposes. This section does not change the requirements in Section I27 for recognition of deferred income taxes related to goodwill and intangible assets. [FAS142, ¶41]

Financial Statement Presentation

Intangible Assets

.141 At a minimum, all intangible assets shall be aggregated and presented as a separate line item in the statement of financial position. However, that requirement does not preclude presentation of individual intangible assets or classes of intangible assets as separate line items. The amortization expense and impairment losses for intangible assets shall be presented in income statement line items within continuing operations as deemed appropriate for each entity. Paragraphs .112 and .114 require that an intangible asset be tested for impairment when it is determined that the asset should no longer be amortized or should begin to be amortized due to a reassessment of its remaining useful life. An impairment loss resulting from that impairment test shall *not* be recognized as a change in accounting principle. [FAS142, ¶42]

Goodwill

.142 The aggregate amount of goodwill shall be presented as a separate line item in the statement of financial position. The aggregate amount of goodwill impairment losses shall be presented as a separate line item in the income statement before the subtotal *income from continuing operations* (or similar caption) unless a goodwill impairment loss is associated with a discontinued operation. A goodwill impairment loss associated with a discontinued operation shall be included (on a net-of-tax basis) within the results of discontinued operations. [FAS142, ¶43]

Disclosures

.143 For intangible assets acquired either individually or with a group of assets, the following information shall be disclosed in the notes to the financial statements in the period of acquisition:

a. For intangible assets subject to amortization:
   (1) The total amount assigned and the amount assigned to any major **intangible asset class**
   (2) The amount of any significant residual value, in total and by major intangible asset class
   (3) The weighted-average amortization period, in total and by major intangible asset class
b. For intangible assets *not* subject to amortization, the total amount assigned and the amount assigned to any major intangible asset class
c. The amount of research and development assets acquired and written off in the period and the line item in the income statement in which the amounts written off are aggregated.

[FAS142, ¶44]

.144 The following information shall be disclosed in the financial statements or the notes to the financial statements for each period for which a statement of financial position is presented:

a. For intangible assets subject to amortization:
   (1) The gross carrying amount and accumulated amortization, in total and by major intangible asset class
   (2) The aggregate amortization expense for the period
   (3) The estimated aggregate amortization expense for each of the five succeeding fiscal years
b. For intangible assets *not* subject to amortization, the total carrying amount and the carrying amount for each major intangible asset class
c. The changes in the carrying amount of goodwill during the period including:
   (1) The aggregate amount of goodwill acquired
   (2) The aggregate amount of impairment losses recognized
   (3) The amount of goodwill included in the gain or loss on disposal of all or a portion of a reporting unit.

   Entities that report segment information in accordance with Section S30 shall provide the above information about goodwill in total and for each reportable segment and shall disclose any significant changes in the allocation of goodwill by reportable segment. If any portion of goodwill has not yet been allocated to a reporting unit at the date the financial statements are issued, that unallocated amount and the reasons for not allocating that amount shall be disclosed.

The illustration in Exhibit 148A provides an example of those disclosure requirements. [FAS142, ¶45]

.145 For each impairment loss recognized related to an intangible asset, the following information shall be disclosed in the notes to the financial statements that include the period in which the impairment loss is recognized:

a. A description of the impaired intangible asset and the facts and circumstances leading to the impairment
b. The amount of the impairment loss and the method for determining fair value
c. The caption in the income statement or the statement of activities in which the impairment loss is aggregated
d. If applicable, the segment in which the impaired intangible asset is reported under Section S30.

[FAS142, ¶46]

.146 For each goodwill impairment loss recognized, the following information shall be disclosed in the notes to the financial statements that include the period in which the impairment loss is recognized:

a. A description of the facts and circumstances leading to the impairment
b. The amount of the impairment loss and the method of determining the fair value of the associated reporting unit (whether based on quoted market prices, prices of comparable businesses, a present value or other valuation technique, or a combination thereof)
c. If a recognized impairment loss is an estimate that has not yet been finalized (refer to paragraph .120), that fact and the reasons therefor and, in subsequent periods, the nature and amount of any significant adjustments made to the initial estimate of the impairment loss.

The illustration in Exhibit 148A provides an example of those disclosure requirements. [FAS142, ¶47]

Illustration of Disclosure Requirements in Periods Subsequent to a Business Combination

.147 Exhibit 148A provides [an] illustration of the financial statement disclosure requirements of this section. The information presented in the following example has been included for illustrative purposes only and, therefore, may not be representative of

[an] actual transaction. For simplicity, the illustrative disclosures do not provide all of the background information that would be necessary to arrive at the disclosed information. [FAS142, ¶C1]

.148 In accordance with paragraphs .144 and .146, the following disclosures would be made by Theta Company in its December 31, 20X3 financial statements relating to acquired intangible assets and goodwill. Theta Company has two reporting units with goodwill—Technology and Communications—which also are reportable segments. [FAS142, ¶C2]

Exhibit 148A

Illustrative Disclosures Relating to Acquired Assets and Goodwill

Note B: Acquired Intangible Assets

	As of December 31, 20X3	
($000s)	**Gross Carrying Amount**	**Accumulated Amortization**
Amortized intangible assets		
Trademark	$1,078	$ (66)
Unpatented technology	475	(380)
Other	90	(30)
Total	$1,643	$(476)
Unamortized intangible assets		
Broadcast licenses	$1,400	
Trademark	600	
Total	$2,000	

Aggregate Amortization Expense:

For year ended 12/31/X3	$319

Estimated Amortization Expense:

For year ended 12/31/X4	$199
For year ended 12/31/X5	$ 74
For year ended 12/31/X6	$ 74
For year ended 12/31/X7	$ 64
For year ended 12/31/X8	$ 54

Note C: Goodwill

The changes in the carrying amount of goodwill for the year ended December 31, 20X3, are as follows:

($000s)	Technology Segment	Communications Segment	Total
Balance as of January 1, 20X3	$1,413	$904	$2,317
Goodwill acquired during year	189	115	304
Impairment losses	—	(46)	(46)
Goodwill written off related to sale of business unit	(484)	—	(484)
Balance as of December 31, 20X3	$1,118	$973	$2,091

The Communications segment is tested for impairment in the third quarter, after the annual forecasting process. Due to an increase in competition in the Texas and Louisiana cable industry, operating profits and cash flows were lower than expected in the fourth quarter of 20X2 and the first and second quarters of 20X3. Based on that trend, the earnings forecast for the next five years was revised. In September 20X3, a goodwill impairment loss of $46 was recognized in the Communications reporting unit. The fair value of that reporting unit was estimated using the expected present value of future cash flows. [FAS142, ¶C2]

.149–.154 [Deleted 4/02 because of FASB Statement 145, *Rescission of FASB Statements No. 4, 44, and 64, Amendment of FASB Statement No. 13, and Technical Corrections*.]

[35–38][Deleted 4/02 because of Statement 145.]

Acquisition of a Banking or Thrift Institution

.155 Paragraphs .156 through .159 [apply] to the acquisition of a commercial bank, a savings and loan association, a mutual savings bank, a credit union, other depository institutions having assets and liabilities of the same types as those institutions, and branches of such enterprises. Paragraphs .157 and .159 apply to only those acquisitions in which the fair value of liabilities assumed by the acquiring enterprise exceeds the fair value of tangible and identifiable intangible assets acquired, and those provisions specify an amortization method for the portion of any unidentifiable intangible asset up to the amount of that excess. [FAS72, ¶2] Paragraphs .109 through .112 [FAS142, ¶D9(a)] also provide guidance as to the amortization of any additional unidentifiable intangible asset recognized in the acquisition. The provisions of paragraphs .156 and .159 apply to all acquisitions of banking and thrift institutions. [FAS72, ¶2]

Recognized Intangible Assets

.156 In a business combination involving the acquisition of a banking or thrift institution, intangible assets acquired that meet the criteria in paragraph .138 of Section B51 shall be recognized as assets apart from goodwill. [FAS141, ¶E11(a)] [For example,] the purchase price paid for a [banking or thrift institution] may include an amount for one or more factors, such as the following:

a. Capacity of existing savings accounts and loan accounts to generate future income
b. Capacity of existing savings accounts and loan accounts to generate additional business or new business
c. Nature of territory served. [FIN9, ¶8]

If any of those factors meet the criteria in paragraph .138 of Section B51, the fair value of that factor shall be recognized as an asset apart from goodwill. [FAS141, ¶E20(e)] An acquired intangible asset that does not meet the criteria in paragraph .138 of Section B51 shall be included in the amount recorded as goodwill. [FAS141, ¶E20(e)] The fair values of [FAS72, ¶4] separately recognized intangible assets [FAS141, ¶E20(e)] that relate to depositor or borrower relationships ([such as] (a) and (b) [above]) shall be based on the estimated benefits attributable to the relationships that *exist* at the date of acquisition without regard to new depositors or borrowers that may replace them. Those [FAS72, ¶4] separately recognized intangible assets [FAS141, ¶E20(e)] shall be amortized over the estimated lives of those existing relationships. [FAS72, ¶4] An enterprise shall evaluate the periods of amortization [for those intangible assets] continually to determine whether later events and circumstances warrant revised estimates of useful lives. If estimates are changed, the unamortized cost shall be allocated to the increased or reduced number of remaining periods in the revised useful life but not to exceed 40 years after acquisition. Estimation of value and future benefits of an intangible asset may indicate that the unamortized cost should be reduced significantly. However, a single loss year or even a few loss years together do not necessarily justify an unusual charge to income for all or a large part of the unamortized cost of intangible assets. The reason for an unusual deduction shall be disclosed. [FAS142, ¶D9(b)] The [FIN9, ¶8] fair value for [other] separately recognized intangible asset[s] [FAS141, ¶E20(e)] shall be recorded as the cost of the intangible [asset] and [FIN9, ¶8] accounted for in accordance with the provisions of [paragraphs .109 through .115 of] this section. [FAS142, ¶D11(a)]

Unidentifiable Intangible Asset

.157 If, in a combination [involving a banking or thrift institution], the fair value of liabilities assumed exceeds the fair value of tangible and identified intangible assets acquired, that excess constitutes an unidentifiable intangible asset. That asset shall be amortized to expense over a period no greater than the estimated remaining life of the long-term interest-bearing assets[39] acquired. Amortization shall be at a constant rate when applied to the carrying amount[40] of those interest-bearing assets that, based on their terms, are expected to be outstanding at the beginning of each subsequent period. The prepayment assumptions, if any, used to determine the fair value of the long-term interest-bearing assets acquired also shall be used in determining the amount of those assets expected to be outstanding. However, if the assets acquired in such a combination do not include a significant amount of long-term interest-bearing assets, the unidentifiable intangible asset shall be amortized over a period not exceeding the estimated average remaining life of the existing customer (deposit) base acquired. The periodic amounts of amortization shall be determined as of the acquisition date and shall not be subsequently adjusted except as provided by paragraphs .158 and .159. Notwithstanding the other provisions of this paragraph, the period of amortization shall not exceed 40 years. [FAS72, ¶5] [Refer to paragraph .1001 for EITF Issues that provide interpretive guidance on this paragraph.]

.158 Paragraph .112 specifies that an entity should evaluate the remaining useful life of an intangible asset that is being amortized each reporting period to determine whether events and circumstances warrant a revision to the remaining period of amortization. [FAS142, ¶D9(c)] In no event, however, shall the useful life of the unidentifiable intangible asset described in paragraph .157 be revised upward. [FAS72, ¶6]

---

[39]For purposes of paragraph .156, long-term interest-bearing assets are interest-bearing assets with a remaining term to maturity of more than one year. [FAS72, ¶5, fn3]

[40]*Carrying amount* is the face amount of the interest-bearing asset plus (or minus) the unamortized premium (or discount). [FAS72, ¶5, fn4]

.159 If a large segment or separable group of the operating assets of an acquired banking or thrift institution, such as branches, is sold or liquidated, the portion of the unidentifiable intangible asset attributable to that segment or separable group shall be included in the cost of the assets sold. If a large segment or separable group of the interest-bearing assets of an acquired institution is sold or liquidated and if the benefits attributable to the unidentifiable intangible asset have been significantly reduced, that reduction shall be recognized as a charge to income. [FAS72, ¶7]

Implementation Guidance on Intangible Assets

.160 Paragraphs .161 through .169 provide guidance on how intangible assets should be accounted for in accordance with paragraphs .109 through .115 of this section and are an integral part of this section. Each of the following examples describes an acquired intangible asset and the facts and circumstances surrounding the determination of its useful life and the subsequent accounting based on that determination. The facts and circumstances unique to each acquired intangible asset need to be considered in making similar determinations. [FAS142, ¶A1]

Example 1

.161 ***An acquired customer list.*** A direct-mail marketing company acquired the customer list and expects that it will be able to derive benefit from the information on the acquired customer list for at least one year but for no more than three years.

The customer list would be amortized over 18 months, management's best estimate of its useful life, following the pattern in which the expected benefits will be consumed or otherwise used up. Although the acquiring entity may intend to add customer names and other information to the list in the future, the expected benefits of the acquired customer list relate only to the customers on that list at the date of acquisition (a closed-group notion). The customer list would be reviewed for impairment under Section I08. [FAS142, ¶A1]

Example 2

.162 ***An acquired patent that expires in 15 years.*** The product protected by the patented technology is expected to be a source of cash flows for at least 15 years. The reporting entity has a commitment from a third party to purchase that patent in 5 years for 60 percent of the fair value of the patent at the date it was acquired, and the entity intends to sell the patent in 5 years.

The patent would be amortized over its five-year useful life to the reporting entity following the pattern in which the expected benefits will be consumed or otherwise used up. The amount to be amortized is 40 percent of the patent's fair value at the acquisition date (residual value is 60 percent). The patent would be reviewed for impairment under Section I08. [FAS142, ¶A1]

Example 3

.163 ***An acquired copyright that has a remaining legal life of 50 years.*** An analysis of consumer habits and market trends provides evidence that the copyrighted material will generate cash flows for approximately 30 more years.

The copyright would be amortized over its 30-year estimated useful life following the pattern in which the expected benefits will be consumed or otherwise used up and reviewed for impairment under Section I08. [FAS142, ¶A1]

Example 4

.164 ***An acquired broadcast license that expires in five years.*** The broadcast license is renewable every 10 years if the company provides at least an average level of service to its customers and complies with the applicable Federal Communications Commission (FCC) rules and policies and the FCC Communications Act of 1934. The license may be renewed indefinitely at little cost and was renewed twice prior to its recent acquisition. The acquiring entity intends to renew the license indefinitely, and evidence supports its ability to do so. Historically, there has been no compelling challenge to the license renewal. The technology used in broadcasting is not expected to be replaced by another technology any time in the foreseeable future. Therefore, the cash flows from that license are expected to continue indefinitely.

The broadcast license would be deemed to have an indefinite useful life because cash flows are expected to continue indefinitely. Therefore, the license would not be amortized until its useful life is deemed to be no longer indefinite. The license would be tested for impairment in accordance with paragraph .115 of this section. [FAS142, ¶A1]

Example 5

.165 ***The broadcast license in Example 4.*** The FCC subsequently decides that it will no longer renew broadcast licenses, but rather will auction those licenses. At the time the FCC decision is made, the broadcast license has three years until it expires. The cash flows from that license are expected to continue until the license expires.

Because the broadcast license can no longer be renewed, its useful life is no longer indefinite. Thus, the acquired license would be tested for impairment in accordance with paragraph .115 of this section. The license would then be amortized over its remaining three-year useful life following the pattern in which the expected benefits will be consumed or otherwise used up. Because the license will be subject to amortization, in the future it would be reviewed for impairment under Section I08. [FAS142, ¶A1]

Example 6

.166 ***An acquired airline route authority from the United States to the United Kingdom that expires in three years.*** The route authority may be renewed every five years, and the acquiring entity intends to comply with the applicable rules and regulations surrounding renewal. Route authority renewals are routinely granted at a minimal cost and have historically been renewed when the airline has complied with the applicable rules and regulations. The acquiring entity expects to provide service to the United Kingdom from its hub airports indefinitely and expects that the related supporting infrastructure (airport gates, slots, and terminal facility leases) will remain in place at those airports for as long as it has the route authority. An analysis of demand and cash flows supports those assumptions.

Because the facts and circumstances support the acquiring entity's ability to continue providing air service to the United Kingdom from its U.S. hub airports indefinitely, the intangible asset related to the route authority is considered to have an indefinite useful life. Therefore, the route authority would not be amortized until its useful life is deemed to be no longer indefinite and would be tested for impairment in accordance with paragraph .115 of this section. [FAS142, ¶A1]

Example 7

.167 ***An acquired trademark that is used to identify and distinguish a leading consumer product that has been a market-share leader for the past eight years.*** The trademark has a remaining legal life of 5 years but is renewable every 10 years at little cost. The acquiring entity intends to continuously renew the trademark, and evidence supports its ability to do so. An analysis of product life cycle studies; market, competitive, and environmental trends; and brand extension opportunities provides evidence that the trademarked product will generate cash flows for the acquiring entity for an indefinite period of time.

The trademark would be deemed to have an indefinite useful life because it is expected to contribute to cash flows indefinitely. Therefore, the trademark would not be amortized until its useful life is no longer indefinite. The trademark would be tested for impairment in accordance with paragraph .115 of this section. [FAS142, ¶A1]

Example 8

.168 ***A trademark that distinguished a leading consumer product that was acquired 10 years ago.*** When it was acquired, the trademark was considered to have an indefinite useful life because the product was expected to generate cash flows indefinitely. During the annual impairment test of the intangible asset, the entity determines that unexpected competition has entered the market that will reduce future sales of the product. Management estimates that cash flows generated by that consumer product will be 20 percent less for the foreseeable future; however, management expects that the product will continue to generate cash flows indefinitely at those reduced amounts.

As a result of the projected decrease in future cash flows, the entity determines that the estimated fair value of the trademark is less than its carrying amount, and an impairment loss is recognized. Because it is still deemed to have an indefinite useful life, the trademark would continue to not be amortized and would continue to be tested for impairment in accordance with paragraph .115 of this section. [FAS142, ¶A1]

Example 9

.169 ***A trademark for a line of automobiles that was acquired several years ago in an acquisition of an automobile company.*** The line of automobiles had been produced by the acquired entity for 35 years with numerous new models developed under the trademark. At the acquisition date, the acquiring entity expected to continue to produce that line of automobiles, and an analysis of various economic factors indicated there was no limit to the period of time the trademark would contribute to cash flows. Because cash flows were expected to continue indefinitely, the trademark was not amortized. Management recently decided to phase out production of that automobile line over the next four years.

Because the useful life of that acquired trademark is no longer deemed to be indefinite, the trademark would be tested for impairment in accordance with paragraph .115 of this section. The carrying amount of the trademark after adjustment, if any, would then be amortized over its remaining four-year useful life following the pattern in which the expected benefits will be consumed or otherwise used up. Because the trademark will be subject to amortization, in the future it would be reviewed for impairment under Section I08. [FAS142, ¶A1]

Glossary

.401 **Fair value.** The amount at which an asset (or liability) could be bought (or incurred) or sold (or settled) in a current transaction between willing parties, that is, other than in a forced or liquidation sale. [FAS142, ¶F1]

.402 **Goodwill.** The excess of the cost of an acquired entity over the net of the amounts assigned to assets acquired and liabilities assumed. The amount recognized as goodwill includes acquired intangible assets that do not meet the criteria in Section B51 for recognition as an asset apart from goodwill. [FAS142, ¶F1]

.403 **Intangible assets.** Assets (not including financial assets) that lack physical substance. (The term *intangible assets* is used in this section to refer to intangible assets other than goodwill.) [FAS142, ¶F1]

.404 **Intangible asset class.** A group of intangible assets that are similar, either by their nature or by their use in the operations of an entity. [FAS142, ¶F1]

.405 **Mutual enterprise.** An entity other than an investor-owned entity that provides dividends, lower costs, or other economic benefits directly and proportionately to its owners, members, or participants. Mutual insurance companies, credit unions, and farm and rural electric cooperatives are examples of mutual enterprises (FASB Concepts Statement 4, *Objectives of Financial Reporting by Nonbusiness Organizations,* paragraph 7). [FAS142, ¶F1]

.406 **Not-for-profit organization.** An entity that possesses the following characteristics that distinguish it from a business enterprise: (a) contributions of significant amounts of resources from resource providers who do not expect commensurate or proportionate pecuniary return, (b) operating purposes other than to provide goods or services at a profit, and (c) absence of ownership interests like those of business enterprises. Not-for-profit organizations have those characteristics in varying degrees (Concepts Statement 4, paragraph 6). Entities that clearly fall outside this definition include all investor-owned entities and mutual enterprises. [FAS142, ¶F1]

.407 **Reporting unit.** The level of reporting at which goodwill is tested for impairment. A reporting unit is an operating segment or one level below an operating segment (as that term is defined in paragraph .109 of Section S30). [FAS142, ¶F1]

.408 **Residual value.** The estimated fair value of an intangible asset at the end of its useful life to an entity, less any disposal costs. [FAS142, ¶F1]

.409 **Useful life.** The period over which an asset is expected to contribute directly or indirectly to future cash flows. [FAS142, ¶F1]

Supplemental Guidance

Amounts Paid by an Enterprise to a Shareholder or Former Shareholder Attributed to an Agreement Precluding the Shareholder or Former Shareholder from Purchasing Additional Shares

.501 *Question*—Should amounts paid by an enterprise to a shareholder or former shareholder attributed to an agreement precluding the shareholder or former shareholder from purchasing additional shares be capitalized as assets and amortized over the period of the agreement? [FTB85-6, ¶4]

.502 *Response*—No. Payments by an enterprise to a shareholder or former shareholder attributed, for example, to a "standstill" agreement, or any agreement in which a shareholder or former shareholder agrees not to purchase additional shares, should be expensed as incurred. Such payments do not give rise to assets of the enterprise as defined in Concepts Statement 6. [FTB85-6, ¶5]

Supplemental Guidance: Emerging Issues Task Force (EITF) Issues

.1000 [Listed below are EITF Issues that provide supplemental guidance for this section. These Issues are grouped by subject matter and may be either interpretive of or related by topic to the guidance in this section.

Banking and Thrift Institutions

EITF Issue No. 85-8, "Amortization of Thrift Intangibles"
EITF Issue No. 85-41, "Accounting for Savings and Loan Associations under FSLIC Management Consignment Program"
EITF Issue No. 85-42, "Amortization of Goodwill Resulting from Recording Time Savings Deposits at Fair Values"
EITF Issue No. 88-19, "FSLIC-Assisted Acquisitions of Thrifts"

Credit Cards

EITF Issue No. 88-20, "Difference between Initial Investment and Principal Amount of Loans in a Purchased Credit Card Portfolio"
EITF Issue No. 93-1, "Accounting for Individual Credit Card Acquisitions"

Other

EITF Issue No. 89-19, "Accounting for a Change in Goodwill Amortization for Business Combinations Initiated Prior to the Effective Date of FASB Statement No. 72"
EITF Issue No. 90-6, "Accounting for Certain Events Not Addressed in Issue No. 87-11 Relating to an Acquired Operating Unit to Be Sold"
EITF Issue No. 92-9, "Accounting for the Present Value of Future Profits Resulting from the Acquisition of a Life Insurance Company"
EITF Issue No. 97-13, "Accounting for Costs Incurred in Connection with a Consulting Contract or an Internal Project That Combines Business Process Reengineering and Information Technology Transformation"
EITF Issue No. 02-7, "Unit of Accounting for Testing Impairment of Indefinite-Lived Intangible Assets"
EITF Topic No. D-100, "Clarification of Paragraph 61(b) of FASB Statement No. 141 and Paragraph 49(b) of FASB Statement No. 142"
EITF Topic No. D-101, "Clarification of Reporting Unit Guidance in Paragraph 30 of FASB Statement No. 142"]

.1001 [Listed below are those EITF Issues that provide interpretive guidance on specific material in this section.

Paragraph .108 (FAS 142, ¶10)—EITF Issue No. 97-13
Paragraph .115 (FAS 142, ¶17)—EITF Issue No. 02-7
Paragraph .118 (FAS 142, ¶20)—EITF Issue No. 02-7
Paragraph .128 (FAS 142, ¶30)—EITF Topic No. D-101
Paragraph .157 (FAS 72, ¶5)—EITF Issues No. 85-8, 85-42, and 88-19]

(The next page is 23701.)

(Refer to Volume II for the rest of the General Standards sections.)

IMPAIRMENT SECTION I08

Sources: FASB Statement 114; FASB Statement 115; FASB Statement 118; FASB Statement 130; FASB Statement 133; FASB Statement 135; FASB Statement 139; FASB Statement 144; FASB Statement 145

[**Note:** A list of Issues discussed by the Emerging Issues Task Force (EITF) that provide supplemental guidance for this section is presented in paragraph .1000.]

Summary

This section presents standards for accounting for the impairment of (1) certain loans, (2) certain investments in debt and equity securities, and (3) long-lived assets that will be held and used. It also includes references to other sections in which impairment considerations are discussed.

For impaired loans this section is applicable to all creditors and, with limited exceptions, to all loans, uncollateralized as well as collateralized, that have been identified for impairment evaluation. It also applies to all loans that are restructured in a troubled debt restructuring involving a modification of terms.

Impaired loans that are within the scope of this section shall be measured based on the present value of expected future cash flows discounted at the loan's effective interest rate or, as a practical expedient, at the loan's observable market price or the fair value of the collateral if the loan is collateral dependent. Changes in these values are reflected in income and as adjustments to the allowance for credit losses.

This section presents standards for recognizing other-than-temporary impairment of certain investments in debt and equity securities.

This section also addresses financial accounting and reporting for the impairment of long-lived assets. A long-lived asset within the scope of this section shall be tested for impairment whenever events or changes in circumstances indicate that the carrying amount of the asset may not be recoverable from its undiscounted cash flows (without interest charges). An impairment loss shall be recognized only if the carrying amount of the asset is not recoverable. The loss shall be measured as the difference between the carrying amount and fair value of the asset.

.101 [This section addresses the impairment of (a) loans in paragraphs .102 through .119A, (b) certain investments in debt and equity securities in paragraph .120, and (c) long-lived assets to be held and used in paragraphs .139 through .175. The accounting for impairment as it relates to other specific topics is included in other sections, such as the following:

Asset or Topic	Section/Paragraph
Capitalized costs of the broadcasting industry	Br5.108
Capitalized computer software costs	Co2.109
Deferred policy acquisition costs of the insurance industry	In6.137D, .138-.143
Deferred tax assets	I27.119-.125
Disallowed costs of recently completed plants of regulated enterprises	Re6.127E
Equity method of investments in common stock	I82.109(h)
Estimated residual value for sales-type, direct financing, and leveraged leases of lessors	L10.113
Goodwill	G40.116-.137
Identifiable intangibles specifically excluded in paragraph .141 of Section I08	G40.115
Long-term investments in mortgage loans by mortgage bankers	Mo4.108
Recognized intangible assets in certain acquisitions of banking or thrift institutions	G40.156
Record masters of the record and music industry	Re4.106
Unproved properties of oil and gas producing companies	Oi5.104, .118-.120, .122(b), .124, .131, .138(g), and .138(h)

This section does not change the provisions of those sections.]

Impairment of a Loan

Scope

.102 For purposes of this section, a loan is a contractual right to receive money on demand or on fixed or determinable dates that is recognized as an asset in the creditor's statement of financial position. Examples include but are not limited to accounts receivable (with terms exceeding one year) and notes receivable. [FAS114, ¶4]

.103 This section applies to all creditors. It addresses the accounting by creditors for impairment of a loan by specifying how allowances for credit losses related to certain loans should be determined. This section also addresses the accounting by creditors for all loans that are restructured in a troubled debt restructuring involving a modification of terms of a receivable (except restructurings of loans excluded from the scope of this section in paragraph .104(b) through (d)) including [restructurings] involving a receipt of assets in partial satisfaction of a receivable. The term *troubled debt restructuring* is used in this section consistent with its use in Section D22, "Debt: Restructurings." [FAS114, ¶5] [A creditor in a troubled debt restructuring involving a modification of terms before the initial application of this section where the restructured loan is impaired based on the terms of the restructuring agreement shall apply this section and the relevant paragraphs of Section D22. A creditor in a troubled debt restructuring involving a modification of terms before the initial application of this section where the restructured loan is *not* impaired based on the terms of the restructuring agreement, may apply the relevant paragraphs of Section D22 unless the restructured loan meets the definition of a *security* in paragraph .406 of Section I80, "Investments: Debt and Equity Securities," in which case the provisions of Section I80 would apply.]

.104 This section applies to all loans that are identified for evaluation, uncollateralized as well as collateralized, except:

a. Large groups of smaller-balance homogeneous loans that are collectively evaluated for impairment. Those loans may include but are not limited to credit card, residential mortgage, and consumer installment loans.
b. Loans that are measured at fair value or at the lower of cost or fair value, for example, in accordance with Section Mo4, "Mortgage Banking Activities," or other specialized industry practice.
c. Leases as defined in Section L10, "Leases."
d. Debt securities as defined in Section I80.

[FAS114, ¶6]

.105 This section does not specify how a creditor should identify loans that are to be evaluated for collectibility.[1] A creditor should apply its normal loan review procedures in making that judgment. This section does not address when a creditor should record a direct write-down of an impaired loan, nor does it address how a creditor should assess the overall adequacy of the allowance for credit losses. In addition to the allowance calculated in accordance with this section, a creditor should continue to recognize an allowance for credit losses necessary to comply with Section C59, "Contingencies." [FAS114, ¶7]

Recognition of Impairment

.106 A loan is impaired when, based on current information and events, it is probable that a creditor will be unable to collect all amounts due according to the contractual terms of the loan agreement. As used in this section and in Section C59, *all amounts due according to the contractual terms* means that both the contractual interest payments and the contractual principal payments of a loan will be collected as scheduled in the loan agreement. [FAS114, ¶8] For a loan that has been restructured in a troubled debt restructuring, *the contractual terms of the loan agreement* refers to the contractual terms specified by the original loan agreement, not the contractual terms specified by the restructuring agreement. [FAS118, ¶6(a)] This section does not specify how a creditor should determine that it is probable that it will be unable to collect all amounts due according to the contractual terms of a loan. A creditor should apply its normal loan review procedures in making that judgment. An insignificant delay or insignificant shortfall in amount of payments does not require application of this section. A loan is not impaired during a period of delay in payment if the creditor expects to collect all amounts due including interest accrued at the contractual interest rate for the period of delay. Thus, a demand loan or other loan with no stated maturity is not impaired if the creditor expects to collect all amounts due including interest accrued at the contractual interest rate during the period the loan is outstanding. [FAS114, ¶8]

[1] Sources of information useful in identifying loans for evaluation that are listed in the AICPA's Auditing Procedure Study, *Auditing the Allowance for Credit Losses of Banks,* include a specific materiality criterion; regulatory reports of examination; internally generated listings such as "watch lists," past due reports, overdraft listings, and listings of loans to insiders; management reports of total loan amounts by borrower; historical loss experience by type of loan; loan files lacking current financial data related to borrowers and guarantors; borrowers experiencing problems such as operating losses, marginal working capital, inadequate cash flow, or business interruptions; loans secured by collateral that is not readily marketable or that is susceptible to deterioration in realizable value; loans to borrowers in industries or countries experiencing economic instability; and loan documentation and compliance exception reports. [FAS114, ¶7, fn1]

.107 Usually, a loan whose terms are modified in a troubled debt restructuring already will have been identified as impaired because the condition specified in paragraph .106 will have existed before a formal restructuring. However, if a loan is excluded from the scope of this section under paragraph .104(a), a creditor may not have accounted for that loan in accordance with this section before the loan was restructured. The creditor shall apply the provisions of this section to that loan when it is restructured. [FAS114, ¶9]

.108 The term *probable* is used in this section consistent with its use in paragraph .104 of Section C59. The conditions for accrual in paragraph .105 of Section C59 are not inconsistent with the accounting concept of conservatism. *Those conditions are not intended to be so rigid that they require virtual certainty before a loss is accrued.* They require only that it be *probable* that an asset has been impaired or a liability has been incurred and that the amount of loss be *reasonably* estimable. [FAS114, ¶10]

Measurement of Impairment

.109 Measuring [FAS114, ¶11] impairment of a loan [FAS118, ¶6(b)] requires judgment and estimates, and the eventual outcomes may differ from those estimates. Creditors should have latitude to develop measurement methods that are practical in their circumstances. Paragraphs .110 through .114 address those measurement methods. [FAS114, ¶11]

.110 Some impaired loans have risk characteristics that are unique to an individual borrower, and the creditor will apply the measurement methods described in paragraphs .111 through .114 on a loan-by-loan basis. However, some impaired loans may have risk characteristics in common with other impaired loans. A creditor may aggregate those loans and may use historical statistics, such as average recovery period and average amount recovered, along with a composite effective interest rate as a means of measuring [FAS114, ¶12] impairment of those loans. [FAS118, ¶6(c)]

.111 When a loan is impaired as defined in paragraph .106, a creditor shall measure impairment based on the present value of expected future cash flows discounted at the loan's effective interest rate, except that as a practical expedient, a creditor may measure impairment based on a loan's observable market price, or the fair value of the collateral if the loan is collateral dependent. Regardless of the measurement method, a creditor shall measure impairment based on the fair value of the collateral when the creditor determines that foreclosure is probable.[2] A loan is collateral dependent if the repayment of the loan is expected to be provided solely by the underlying collateral. The creditor may choose a measurement method on a loan-by-loan basis.[3] A creditor shall consider estimated costs to sell, on a discounted basis, in the measure of impairment if those costs are expected to reduce the cash flows available to repay or otherwise satisfy the loan.[4] If the [FAS114, ¶13] present value of expected future cash flows (or, alternatively, the observable market price of the loan or the fair value of the collateral) [FAS118, ¶6(d)] is less than the recorded investment in the loan[5] (including accrued interest, net deferred loan fees or costs, and unamortized premium or discount), a creditor shall recognize an impairment by creating a valuation allowance with a corresponding charge to bad-debt expense or by adjusting an existing valuation allowance for the impaired loan with a corresponding charge or credit to bad-debt expense. [FAS114, ¶13] [Refer to paragraph .1001 for an EITF Issue that provides interpretive guidance on this paragraph.]

.112 If a creditor [FAS114, ¶14] bases its measure of loan impairment on [FAS118, ¶6(e)] a present value amount, the creditor shall calculate that present value amount based on an estimate of the expected future cash flows of the impaired loan, discounted at the loan's effective interest rate. The effective interest rate of a loan is the rate of return implicit in the loan (that is, the contractual interest rate adjusted for any net deferred loan

---

[2]When a creditor determines that foreclosure is probable, a creditor should remeasure the loan at the fair value of the collateral so that loss recognition is not delayed until actual foreclosure. The requirement in this section to discount expected future cash flows may not preclude the need to recognize additional loss when foreclosure is probable because estimates of expected future cash flows are not remeasured using a market rate and because estimates of expected future cash flows may change when a creditor determines that foreclosure is probable. [FAS114, ¶69] [Because of] the practical problems of accounting for the operations of an asset [(the collateral) that] the creditor does not possess, a loan for which foreclosure is probable should continue to be accounted for as a loan. [FAS114, ¶71]

[3]The measurement method for an individual impaired loan shall be applied consistently to that loan and a change in method shall be justified by a change in circumstance. [FAS114, ¶53]

[4]For example, if repayment of a loan is dependent on the sale of the collateral, a creditor that uses a discounted cash flow method to measure impairment shall reduce its estimate of expected future cash flows by its estimates of costs to sell. Likewise, if a creditor uses the fair value of the collateral to measure impairment of a collateral-dependent loan and repayment or satisfaction of a loan is dependent on the sale of the collateral, the fair value of the collateral shall be adjusted to consider estimated costs to sell. However, if repayment or satisfaction of the loan is dependent only on the operation, rather than the sale, of the collateral, the measure of impairment would not incorporate estimated costs to sell the collateral. [FAS114, ¶46]

[5]The term *recorded investment in the loan* is distinguished from *net carrying amount of the loan* because the latter term is net of a valuation allowance, while the former term is not. The recorded investment in the loan does, however, reflect any direct write-down of the investment. [FAS114, ¶13, fn2]

fees or costs, premium, or discount existing at the origination or acquisition of the loan).[6] The effective interest rate for a loan restructured in a troubled debt restructuring is based on the original contractual rate, not the rate specified in the restructuring agreement. If the loan's contractual interest rate varies based on subsequent changes in an independent factor, such as an index or rate (for example, the prime rate, the London interbank offered rate, or the U.S. Treasury bill weekly average), that loan's effective interest rate may be calculated based on the factor as it changes over the life of the loan or may be fixed at the rate in effect at the date the loan meets the impairment criterion in paragraph .106. The creditor's choice shall be applied consistently for all loans whose contractual interest rate varies based on subsequent changes in an independent factor. Projections of changes in the factor should not be made for purposes of determining the effective interest rate or estimating expected future cash flows. [FAS114, ¶14] [Refer to paragraph .1001 for an EITF Issue that provides interpretive guidance on this paragraph.]

.113 If a creditor [FAS114, ¶15] bases its measure of loan impairment on [FAS118, ¶6(f)] a present value calculation, the estimates of expected future cash flows shall be the creditor's best estimate based on reasonable and supportable assumptions and projections. All available evidence, including estimated costs to sell if those costs are expected to reduce the cash flows available to repay or otherwise satisfy the loan, should be considered in developing the estimate of expected future cash flows. The weight given to the evidence should be commensurate with the extent to which the evidence can be verified objectively. If a creditor estimates a range for either the amount or timing of possible cash flows, the likelihood of the possible outcomes shall be considered in determining the best estimate of expected future cash flows. [FAS114, ¶15]

.114 Subsequent to the initial measurement of impairment, if there is a significant change (increase or decrease) in the amount or timing of an impaired loan's expected future cash flows, or if actual cash flows are significantly different from the cash flows previously projected, a creditor shall recalculate the impairment by applying the procedures specified in paragraphs .110 through .113 and by adjusting the valuation allowance. Similarly, a creditor that measures impairment based on the observable market price of an impaired loan or the fair value of the collateral of an impaired collateral-dependent loan shall adjust the valuation allowance if there is a significant change (increase or decrease) in either of those bases. However, the net carrying amount of the loan shall at no time exceed the recorded investment in the loan. [FAS114, ¶16]

[6] A loan may be acquired at a discount because of a change in credit quality or rate or both. When a loan is acquired at a discount that relates, at least in part, to the loan's credit quality, the effective interest rate is the discount rate that equates the present value of the investor's estimate of the loan's future cash flows with the purchase price of the loan. [FAS114, ¶14, fn3]

Income Recognition

.115 This section does not address how a creditor should recognize, measure, or display interest income on an impaired loan.[6a] Some accounting methods for recognizing income may result in a recorded investment in an impaired loan that is less than the present value of expected future cash flows (or, alternatively, the observable market price of the loan or the fair value of the collateral). In that case, while the loan would meet the definition of an impaired loan in paragraph .106, no additional impairment would be recognized. Those accounting methods include recognition of interest income using a cost-recovery method, a cash-basis method, or some combination of those methods. The recorded investment in an impaired loan also may be less than the present value of expected future cash flows (or, alternatively, the observable market price of the loan or the fair value of the collateral) because the creditor has charged off part of the loan. [FAS118, ¶6(g)] [Refer to paragraph .1001 for an EITF Issue that provides interpretive guidance on this paragraph.]

.116–.117 [Deleted 10/94 because of FASB Statement 118, *Accounting by Creditors for Impairment of a Loan—Income Recognition and Disclosures.*]

Disclosures

.118 A creditor shall disclose, either in the body of the financial statements or in the accompanying notes,[7] the following information about loans that meet the definition of an impaired loan in paragraph .106 of this section:

a. As of the date of each statement of financial position presented, the total recorded investment in the impaired loans at the end of each period and (1) the amount of that recorded investment for which there is a related allowance for credit losses determined in accordance with this section and the amount of that allowance and (2) the amount of that recorded investment for which there is no related allowance for credit losses determined in accordance with this section [Refer to Exhibit 119A for a summary of these disclosure requirements.]
b. The creditor's policy for recognizing interest income on impaired loans, including how cash receipts are recorded

[6a]This section does not preclude a creditor [from accruing] interest on the net carrying amount of the impaired loan and [reporting] other changes in the net carrying amount of the loan as an adjustment to bad-debt expense. This section [also] does not preclude a creditor [from recognizing] all changes in the net carrying amount of the loan as an adjustment to bad-debt expense. [FAS118, ¶4]

[7]This section does not preclude a creditor from disclosing in the notes to the financial statements the effect of initially applying this section if the creditor believes it is practical to do so. [FAS114, ¶74]

c. For each period for which results of operations are presented, the average recorded investment[7a] in the impaired loans during each period, the related amount of interest income recognized during the time within that period that the loans were impaired, and, unless not practicable, the amount of interest income recognized using a cash-basis method of accounting during the time within that period that the loans were impaired.

Information about an impaired loan that has been restructured in a troubled debt restructuring involving a modification of terms need not be included in the disclosures required by (a) and (c) [above] in years after the restructuring if (i) the restructuring agreement specifies an interest rate equal to or greater than the rate that the creditor was willing to accept at the time of the restructuring for a new loan with comparable risk and (ii) the loan is not impaired based on the terms specified by the restructuring agreement. That exception shall be applied consistently for (a) and (c) [above] to all loans restructured in a troubled debt restructuring that meet the criteria in (i) and (ii) [above]. [FAS118, ¶6(i)] [Refer to paragraph .1001 for an EITF Issue that provides interpretive guidance on paragraphs .118 and .118A.]

.118A For each period for which results of operations are presented, a creditor also shall disclose the activity in the total allowance for credit losses related to loans, including the balance in the allowance at the beginning and end of each period, additions charged to operations, direct write-downs charged against the allowance, and recoveries of amounts previously charged off. The total allowance for credit losses related to loans includes those amounts that have been determined in accordance with Section C59 and with this section. [FAS118, ¶6(i)]

.119 [Deleted 10/94 because of FASB Statement 118.]

Illustration of Disclosure Requirements for Impaired Loans

.119A [Exhibit 119A presents a summary of the disclosure requirements in paragraph .118(a) for loans that are impaired under the definition in paragraph .106.]

[7a]This section does not specify how a creditor should calculate the average recorded investment in the impaired loans during the reporting period. A creditor should develop an appropriate method and averages based on month-end balances may be considered an appropriate method [by some creditors]. [FAS118, ¶17]

Exhibit 119A

Summary of Disclosure Requirements in Paragraph .118(a)

Description of Loans	Required Disclosures about the Recorded Investment in Loans That Meet the Definition of an Impaired Loan in Paragraph .106		
	(A) The Total Recorded Investment in the Impaired Loans	(B) The Amount of the Recorded Investment in (A) for Which There Is a Related Allowance for Credit Losses	(C) The Amount of the Recorded Investment in (A) for Which There Is No Related Allowance for Credit Losses
1. Loans that meet the definition of an impaired loan in paragraph .106 and that have *not* been charged off fully	Included. The amount disclosed in (A) must equal the sum of (B) and (C).	Included if there is a related allowance for credit losses.	Included if there is no related allowance for credit losses.
2. Loans that meet the definition of an impaired loan in paragraph .106 and that have been charged off fully	Excluded. The recorded investment and allowance for credit losses are equal to zero.		
3. Loans restructured in a troubled debt restructuring [before the date of adoption of the provisions in paragraphs .102-.119 and Section D22 (paragraphs .139-.146)] that are not impaired based on the terms specified by the restructuring agreement	Excluded. Disclosures should be provided in accordance with paragraphs .136 and .137 of Section D22.		

4. Loans restructured in a troubled debt restructuring [before the date of adoption of the provisions in paragraphs .102-.119 and Section D22 (paragraphs .139-.146)] that are impaired based on the terms specified by the restructuring agreement	Refer to items 1 and 2 above.
5. Loans restructured in a troubled debt restructuring [after the date of adoption of the provisions in paragraphs .102-.119 and Section D22 (paragraphs .139-.146)]	May be excluded in years after the restructuring if (a) the restructuring agreement specifies an interest rate equal to or greater than the rate that the creditor was willing to accept at the time of the restructuring for a new receivable with comparable risk and (b) the loan is not impaired based on the terms specified by the restructuring agreement. Otherwise, refer to items 1 and 2 above.
6. Large groups of smaller-balance homogeneous loans that are collectively evaluated for impairment and other loans that are excluded from the scope of this section as defined in paragraph .104	Excluded unless restructured in a troubled debt restructuring (refer to items 3-5 above and paragraph .107 for requirements for a restructured loan).

[FAS118, ¶24]

Impairment of Investments in Debt and Equity Securities

.120 For individual securities [as addressed in Section I80] classified as either available-for-sale or held-to-maturity, an enterprise shall determine whether a decline in fair value below the amortized cost basis is other than temporary. [FAS115, ¶16] (If a security has been the hedged item in a fair value hedge, the security's "amortized cost basis" shall reflect the effect of the adjustments of its carrying amount made pursuant to paragraph .119(b) of Section D50, "Derivative Instruments and Hedging Activities.") [FAS133, ¶534(d)] For example, if it is probable that the investor will be unable to collect all amounts due according to the contractual terms of a debt security not impaired at acquisition, an other-than-temporary impairment shall be considered to have occurred.[8] If the decline in fair value is judged to be other than temporary, the cost basis of the individual security shall be written down to fair value as a new cost basis and the amount of the write-down shall be included in earnings (that is, accounted for as a realized loss). The new cost basis shall not be changed for subsequent recoveries in fair value. Subsequent increases in the fair value of available-for-sale securities shall be included in [FAS115, ¶16] other comprehensive income [as required in Section C49, "Comprehensive Income: Financial Statement Presentation,"] [FAS130, ¶33(d)] pursuant to paragraph .110 of Section I80; subsequent decreases in fair value, if not an other-than-temporary impairment, also shall be included in [FAS115, ¶16] other comprehensive income. [FAS130, ¶33(d)] [Refer to paragraph .1001 for an EITF Issue that provides interpretive guidance on this paragraph.]

.121 [Deleted 8/01 and renumbered as .119A.]

The material in paragraphs .122 through .138 has been superseded by FASB Statement 144, *Accounting for the Impairment or Disposal of Long-Lived Assets.* Those paragraphs have been moved to Appendix E, "*Current Text* Sections That Are Superseded by Pronouncements with Delayed Effective Dates," for continued reference by users until the date Statement 144 is initially applied. The provisions of paragraphs .139 through .175 shall be effective for financial statements issued for fiscal years beginning after December 15, 2001 and interim periods within those fiscal years. (Refer to Appendix C, "Effective Dates of Pronouncements," for details of the effective date and transition provisions of Statement 144.)

.122–.130 [Deleted 8/01 because of FASB Statement 144, *Accounting for the Impairment or Disposal of Long-Lived Assets.*]

---

[8]A decline in the value of a security that is other than temporary is also discussed in [FAS115, ¶16, fn4] AICPA Statement on Auditing Standards No. 92, *Auditing Derivative Instruments, Hedging Activities, and Investments in Securities,* [FAS145, ¶9(h)] and in SEC Staff Accounting Bulletin No. 59, *Accounting for Noncurrent Marketable Equity Securities.* [FAS115, ¶16, fn4]

[9–15][Deleted 8/01 because of Statement 144.]

.131 [Deleted 6/01 because of FASB Statement 142, *Goodwill and Other Intangible Assets.*]

.132–.138 [Deleted 8/01 because of Statement 144.]

Impairment of Long-Lived Assets to Be Held and Used

Scope

.139 This section applies to recognized long-lived assets of an *entity*[16] to be held and used, including (a) capital leases of lessees, (b) long-lived assets of lessors subject to operating leases, (c) proved oil and gas properties that are being accounted for using the successful-efforts method of accounting,[17] and (d) long-term prepaid assets.[18] [FAS144, ¶3]

.140 If a long-lived asset (or assets) is part of a group that includes other assets and liabilities not covered by this section, this section applies to the group. In those situations, the unit of accounting for the long-lived asset is its group. For a long-lived asset or assets to be held and used, that group (hereinafter referred to as an *asset group*) represents the lowest level for which identifiable cash flows are largely independent of the cash flows of other groups of assets and liabilities. This section does not change generally accepted accounting principles applicable to those other individual assets (such as accounts receivable and inventory) and liabilities (such as accounts payable, long-term debt, and asset retirement obligations) not covered by this section that are included in such groups. [FAS144, ¶4]

.141 This section does not apply to (a) goodwill, (b) intangible assets not being amortized [FAS144, ¶5] that are to be held and used, [FAS145, ¶9(n)] (c) long-term customer relationships of a financial institution, such as core deposit intangibles, credit cardholder intangibles, and servicing assets, (d) financial instruments, including investments in equity securities accounted for under the cost or equity method, (e) deferred policy acquisition costs, (f) deferred tax assets, and (g) unproved oil and gas properties that are being

[16]This section applies to a business enterprise and a not-for-profit organization, each of which is referred to herein as an *entity*. [FAS144, ¶3, fn1]

[17]Accounting requirements for oil and gas properties that are accounted for using the full-cost method of accounting are prescribed by the Securities and Exchange Commission (Regulation S-X, Rule 4-10, "Financial Accounting and Reporting for Oil and Gas Producing Activities Pursuant to the Federal Securities Laws and the Energy Policy and Conservation Act of 1975"). [FAS144, ¶3, fn2]

[18]In this section, all references to a *long-lived asset* refer to a long-lived asset covered by this section. [FAS144, ¶3, fn3]

accounted for using the successful-efforts method of accounting. This section also does not apply to long-lived assets for which the accounting is prescribed by:

- Section Br5, "Broadcasting Industry"
- Section Co2, "Computer Software to Be Sold, Leased, or Otherwise Marketed"
- Section Re4, "Record and Music Industry"
- Section Re6, "Regulated Operations" (for accounting for abandonments and disallowances of plant costs, paragraphs .127A through .127E) [FAS144, ¶5]
- [AICPA Statement of Position 00-2, *Accounting by Producers or Distributors of Films*.]

Recognition and Measurement of an Impairment Loss

.142 For purposes of this section, *impairment* is the condition that exists when the carrying amount of a long-lived asset (asset group) exceeds its fair value. An impairment loss shall be recognized only if the carrying amount of a long-lived asset (asset group) is not recoverable and exceeds its fair value. The carrying amount of a long-lived asset (asset group) is not recoverable if it exceeds the sum of the undiscounted cash flows expected to result from the use and eventual disposition of the asset (asset group). That assessment shall be based on the carrying amount of the asset (asset group) at the date it is tested for recoverability, whether in use (paragraph .154) or under development (paragraph .155). An impairment loss shall be measured as the amount by which the carrying amount of a long-lived asset (asset group) exceeds its fair value. [FAS144, ¶7]

When to Test a Long-Lived Asset for Recoverability

.143 A long-lived asset (asset group) shall be tested for recoverability whenever events or changes in circumstances indicate that its carrying amount may not be recoverable. The following are examples of such events or changes in circumstances:

a. A significant decrease in the market price of a long-lived asset (asset group)
b. A significant adverse change in the extent or manner in which a long-lived asset (asset group) is being used or in its physical condition
c. A significant adverse change in legal factors or in the business climate that could affect the value of a long-lived asset (asset group), including an adverse action or assessment by a regulator
d. An accumulation of costs significantly in excess of the amount originally expected for the acquisition or construction of a long-lived asset (asset group)
e. A current-period operating or cash flow loss combined with a history of operating or cash flow losses or a projection or forecast that demonstrates continuing losses associated with the use of a long-lived asset (asset group)

f. A current expectation that, *more likely than not,*[19] a long-lived asset (asset group) will be sold or otherwise disposed of significantly before the end of its previously estimated useful life.

[FAS144, ¶8]

.144 When a long-lived asset (asset group) is tested for recoverability, it also may be necessary to review depreciation estimates and method as required by Section A06, "Accounting Changes," or the amortization period as required by Section G40.[20] Any revision to the remaining useful life of a long-lived asset resulting from that review also shall be considered in developing estimates of future cash flows used to test the asset (asset group) for recoverability (paragraph .153). However, any change in the accounting method for the asset resulting from that review shall be made only after applying this section. [FAS144, ¶9]

Grouping Long-Lived Assets to Be Held and Used

.145 For purposes of recognition and measurement of an impairment loss, a long-lived asset or assets shall be grouped with other assets and liabilities at the lowest level for which identifiable cash flows are largely independent of the cash flows of other assets and liabilities.[[21]] However, an impairment loss, if any, that results from applying this section shall reduce only the carrying amount of a long-lived asset or assets of the group in accordance with paragraph .149. [FAS144, ¶10]

.146 In limited circumstances, a long-lived asset (for example, a corporate headquarters facility) may not have identifiable cash flows that are largely independent of the cash

---

[19]The term *more likely than not* refers to a level of likelihood that is more than 50 percent. [FAS144, ¶8, fn6]

[20]Paragraphs .109 and .130 through .132 of Section A06 address the accounting for changes in estimates; paragraphs .119 and .120 of Section A06 address the accounting for changes in the method of depreciation. Paragraph .109 of Section G40 addresses the determination of the useful life of an intangible asset. [FAS144, ¶9, fn7]

[[21]]Grouping long-lived assets [for impairment consideration] requires significant judgment. Varying facts and circumstances inevitably [justify] different groupings. [Consider the case where] an entity operated a bus company that provided service under contract with a municipality that required minimum service on each of five separate routes. Assets devoted to serving each route and the cash flows from each route were discrete. One of the routes operated at a significant deficit that resulted in the inability to recover the carrying amounts of the dedicated assets. The five bus routes would be an appropriate level at which to group assets to test for and measure impairment because the entity did not have the option to curtail any one bus route. [FAS144, ¶B45]

flows of other assets and liabilities and of other asset groups. In those circumstances, the asset group for that long-lived asset shall include all assets and liabilities of the entity.[22] [FAS144, ¶11]

.147 Goodwill shall be included in an asset group to be tested for impairment under this section only if the asset group is or includes a *reporting unit*.[23] Goodwill shall not be included in a lower-level asset group that includes only part of a reporting unit. Estimates of future cash flows used to test that lower-level asset group for recoverability shall not be adjusted for the effect of excluding goodwill from the group. [FAS144, ¶12]

.148 Other than goodwill, the carrying amounts of any assets (such as accounts receivable and inventory) and liabilities (such as accounts payable, long-term debt, and asset retirement obligations) not covered by this section that are included in an asset group shall be adjusted in accordance with other applicable generally accepted accounting principles prior to testing the asset group for recoverability.[24] [FAS144, ¶13]

.149 An impairment loss for an asset group shall reduce only the carrying amounts of a long-lived asset or assets of the group. The loss shall be allocated to the long-lived assets of the group on a pro rata basis using the relative carrying amounts of those assets, except that the loss allocated to an individual long-lived asset of the group shall not reduce the carrying amount of that asset below its fair value whenever that fair value is determinable without undue cost and effort. (Example 1 (paragraphs .163 through .165) illustrates the allocation of an impairment loss for an asset group.) [FAS144, ¶14]

---

[22]Not-for-profit organizations that rely in part on contributions to maintain their assets may need to consider those contributions in determining the appropriate cash flows to compare with the carrying amount of an asset. If future unrestricted contributions to the organization as a whole are not considered, the sum of the expected future cash flows may be negative, or positive but less than the carrying amount of the asset. For example, the costs of administering a museum may exceed the admission fees charged, but the organization may fund the cash flow deficit with unrestricted contributions. Similar [situations might] be experienced by business enterprises. For example, the cost of operating assets such as corporate headquarters or centralized research facilities may be funded by revenue-producing activities at lower levels of the enterprise. Accordingly, in limited circumstances, the lowest level of identifiable cash flows that are largely independent of other asset groups may be the entity level. [FAS144, ¶B46]

[23]The term *reporting unit* is defined in Section G40 as the same level as or one level below an operating segment (as that term is defined in paragraph .109 of Section S30, "Segment Disclosures and Related Information"). Section G40 requires that goodwill be tested for impairment at the reporting unit level. [FAS144, ¶12, fn8]

[24]Paragraph .127 of Section G40 requires that goodwill be tested for impairment only after the carrying amounts of the other assets of the reporting unit, including the long-lived assets covered by this section, have been tested for impairment under other applicable accounting pronouncements. [FAS144, ¶13, fn9]

New Cost Basis

.150 If an impairment loss is recognized, the adjusted carrying amount of a long-lived asset shall be its new cost basis. For a depreciable long-lived asset, the new cost basis shall be depreciated (amortized) over the remaining useful life of that asset. Restoration of a previously recognized impairment loss is prohibited. [FAS144, ¶15]

Estimates of Future Cash Flows Used to Test a Long-Lived Asset for Recoverability

.151 Estimates of future cash flows used to test the recoverability of a long-lived asset (asset group) shall include only the future cash flows (cash inflows less associated cash outflows) that are directly associated with and that are expected to arise as a direct result of the use and eventual disposition of the asset (asset group). Those estimates shall exclude interest charges that will be recognized as an expense when incurred. [FAS144, ¶16]

.152 Estimates of future cash flows used to test the recoverability of a long-lived asset (asset group) shall incorporate the entity's own assumptions about its use of the asset (asset group) and shall consider all available evidence. The assumptions used in developing those estimates shall be reasonable in relation to the assumptions used in developing other information used by the entity for comparable periods, such as internal budgets and projections, accruals related to incentive compensation plans, or information communicated to others. However, if alternative courses of action to recover the carrying amount of a long-lived asset (asset group) are under consideration or if a range is estimated for the amount of possible future cash flows associated with the likely course of action, the likelihood of those possible outcomes shall be considered. A probability-weighted approach may be useful in considering the likelihood of those possible outcomes. (Example 2 (paragraphs .166 through .169) illustrates the use of that approach when alternative courses of action are under consideration.) [FAS144, ¶17]

.153 Estimates of future cash flows used to test the recoverability of a long-lived asset (asset group) shall be made for the remaining useful life of the asset (asset group) to the entity. The remaining useful life of an asset group shall be based on the remaining useful life of the primary asset of the group. For purposes of this section, the *primary asset* is the principal long-lived tangible asset being depreciated or intangible asset being amortized that is the most significant component asset from which the asset group derives its cash-flow-generating capacity.[25] Factors that an entity generally should consider in de-

[25]The primary asset of an asset group therefore cannot be land or an intangible asset not being amortized. [FAS144, ¶18, fn10]

termining whether a long-lived asset is the primary asset of an asset group include the following: (a) whether other assets of the group would have been acquired by the entity without the asset, (b) the level of investment that would be required to replace the asset, and (c) the remaining useful life of the asset relative to other assets of the group. If the primary asset is not the asset of the group with the longest remaining useful life, estimates of future cash flows for the group should assume the sale of the group at the end of the remaining useful life of the primary asset. [FAS144, ¶18]

.154 Estimates of future cash flows used to test the recoverability of a long-lived asset (asset group) that is in use, including a long-lived asset (asset group) for which development is substantially complete, shall be based on the existing service potential of the asset (asset group) at the date it is tested. The service potential of a long-lived asset (asset group) encompasses its remaining useful life, cash-flow-generating capacity, and for tangible assets, physical output capacity. Those estimates shall include cash flows associated with future expenditures necessary to maintain the existing service potential of a long-lived asset (asset group), including those that replace the service potential of component parts of a long-lived asset (for example, the roof of a building) and component assets other than the primary asset of an asset group. Those estimates shall exclude cash flows associated with future capital expenditures that would increase the service potential of a long-lived asset (asset group). [FAS144, ¶19]

.155 Estimates of future cash flows used to test the recoverability of a long-lived asset (asset group) that is under development shall be based on the expected service potential of the asset (asset group) when development is substantially complete. Those estimates shall include cash flows associated with all future expenditures necessary to develop a long-lived asset (asset group), including interest payments that will be capitalized as part of the cost of the asset (asset group).[26] [FAS144, ¶20]

.156 If a long-lived asset that is under development is part of an asset group that is in use, estimates of future cash flows used to test the recoverability of that group shall include the cash flows associated with future expenditures necessary to maintain the existing service potential of the group (paragraph .154) as well as the cash flows associated with all future expenditures necessary to substantially complete the asset that is under development (paragraph .155). (Example 3 (paragraphs .170 and .171) illustrates that situation.) [FAS144, ¶21]

[26]Section I67, "Interest: Capitalization of Interest Costs," states, "The capitalization period shall end when the asset is substantially complete and ready for its intended use" (paragraph .115). [FAS144, ¶20, fn11]

Fair Value

.157 The fair value of an asset (liability) is the amount at which that asset (liability) could be bought (incurred) or sold (settled) in a current transaction between willing parties, that is, other than in a forced or liquidation sale.[27] Quoted market prices in active markets are the best evidence of fair value and shall be used as the basis for the measurement, if available. However, in many instances, quoted market prices in active markets will not be available for the long-lived assets (asset groups) covered by this section. In those instances, the estimate of fair value shall be based on the best information available, including prices for similar assets (groups) and the results of using other valuation techniques. [FAS144, ¶22]

.158 A present value technique is often the best available valuation technique with which to estimate the fair value of a long-lived asset (asset group). Paragraphs 39 through 54 of FASB Concepts Statement No. 7, *Using Cash Flow Information and Present Value in Accounting Measurements,* discuss the use of two present value techniques to measure the fair value of an asset (liability).[28] The first is expected present value, in which multiple cash flow scenarios that reflect the range of possible outcomes and a risk-free rate are used to estimate fair value. The second is traditional present value, in which a single set of estimated cash flows and a single interest rate (a rate commensurate with the risk) are used to estimate fair value. Either present value technique can be used for a fair value measurement. However, for long-lived assets (asset groups) that have uncertainties both in timing and amount, an expected present value technique will often be the appropriate technique. (Example 4 (paragraphs .172 through .175) illustrates the use of that technique.) [FAS144, ¶23]

.159 If a present value technique is used, estimates of future cash flows shall be consistent with the objective of measuring fair value. Assumptions that marketplace partici-

[27] The fair value of an asset or a disposal group refers to the amount at which the group as a whole could be bought or sold in a current single transaction. Therefore, the fair value of the group would not necessarily equate to the sum of the fair values of the individual assets and liabilities of the group. [FAS144, ¶22, fn12] [It was] decided not to provide an exception for assets subject to nonrecourse debt. The recognition of an impairment loss and the recognition of a gain on the extinguishment of debt are separate events, and each event should be recognized in the period in which it occurs. The recognition of an impairment loss should be based on the measurement of the asset at its fair value and that the existence of nonrecourse debt should not influence that measurement. [FAS144, ¶B34]

[28] Appendix H, "Excerpts from FASB Concepts Statement 7," incorporates those paragraphs of Concepts Statement 7. [FAS144, ¶23, fn13]

pants would use in their estimates of fair value shall be incorporated whenever that information is available without undue cost and effort.[29] Otherwise, the entity may use its own assumptions. [FAS144, ¶24]

Reporting and Disclosure

.160 An impairment loss recognized for a long-lived asset (asset group) to be held and used shall be included in income from continuing operations before income taxes in the income statement of a business enterprise and in income from continuing operations in the statement of activities of a not-for-profit organization. If a subtotal such as "income from operations" is presented, it shall include the amount of that loss. [FAS144, ¶25]

.161 The following information shall be disclosed in the notes to the financial statements that include the period in which an impairment loss is recognized:

a. A description of the impaired long-lived asset (asset group) and the facts and circumstances leading to the impairment
b. If not separately presented on the face of the statement, the amount of the impairment loss and the caption in the income statement or the statement of activities that includes that loss
c. The method or methods for determining fair value (whether based on a quoted market price, prices for similar assets, or another valuation technique)
d. If applicable, the segment in which the impaired long-lived asset (asset group) is reported under Section S30.

[FAS144, ¶26]

Implementation Guidance

Introduction

.162 Paragraphs .163 through .175 illustrate application of some of the provisions of this section in certain specific situations. The relevant paragraphs of this section are identified in the parenthetical notes. The examples do not address all possible situations or applications of this section. Paragraphs .163 through .175 are an integral part of the standards provided in this section. [FAS144, ¶A1]

---

[29]Concepts Statement 7 discusses the essential elements of a present value measurement (paragraph 23) and provides reasons why an entity's estimates of cash flows might differ from those used by marketplace participants (paragraph 32). Appendix H incorporates those paragraphs. [FAS144, ¶24, fn14]

Example 1—Allocating an Impairment Loss

.163 This example illustrates the allocation of an impairment loss to the long-lived assets of an asset group (paragraph .149). [FAS144, ¶A2]

.164 An entity owns a manufacturing facility that together with other assets is tested for recoverability as a group. In addition to long-lived assets (Assets A–D), the asset group includes inventory, which is reported at the lower of cost or market in accordance with Section I78, "Inventory," and other current assets and liabilities that are not covered by this section. The $2.75 million aggregate carrying amount of the asset group is not recoverable and exceeds its fair value by $600,000. In accordance with paragraph .149, the impairment loss of $600,000 would be allocated as shown below to the long-lived assets of the group.

Asset Group	Carrying Amount	Pro Rata Allocation Factor	Allocation of Impairment (Loss)	Adjusted Carrying Amount
		(in $ 000s)		
Current assets	$ 400	—	—	$ 400
Liabilities	(150)	—	—	(150)
Long-lived assets:				
Asset A	590	24%	$(144)	446
Asset B	780	31	(186)	594
Asset C	950	38	(228)	722
Asset D	180	7	(42)	138
Subtotal—long-lived assets	2,500	100	(600)	1,900
Total	$2,750	100%	$(600)	$2,150

[FAS144, ¶A3]

.165 If the fair value of an individual long-lived asset of an asset group is determinable without undue cost and effort and exceeds the adjusted carrying amount of that asset after an impairment loss is allocated initially, the excess impairment loss initially allocated to that asset would be reallocated to the other long-lived assets of the group. For example, if the fair value of Asset C is $822,000, the excess impairment loss of $100,000 initially allocated to that asset (based on its adjusted carrying amount of $722,000) would be reallocated as shown below to the other long-lived assets of the group on a pro rata basis using the relative adjusted carrying amounts of those assets.

Long-Lived Assets of Asset Group	Adjusted Carrying Amount	Pro Rata Reallocation Factor	Reallocation of Excess Impairment (Loss)	Adjusted Carrying Amount after Reallocation
		(in $ 000s)		
Asset A	$ 446	38%	$ (38)	$ 408
Asset B	594	50	(50)	544
Asset D	138	12	(12)	126
Subtotal	1,178	100%	(100)	1,078
Asset C	722		100	822
Total—long-lived assets	$1,900		$ 0	$1,900

[FAS144, ¶A4]

Example 2—Probability-Weighted Cash Flows

.166 This example illustrates the use of a probability-weighted approach for developing estimates of future cash flows used to test a long-lived asset for recoverability when alternative courses of action are under consideration (paragraph .152). [FAS144, ¶A5]

.167 At December 31, 20X2, a manufacturing facility with a carrying amount of $48 million is tested for recoverability. At that date, 2 courses of action to recover the carrying amount of the facility are under consideration—sell in 2 years or sell at the end of its remaining useful life of 10 years. The facility has identifiable cash flows that are largely independent of the cash flows of other assets. [FAS144, ¶A6]

.168 The following table shows the range and probability of possible estimated cash flows expected to result from the use and eventual disposition of the facility assuming that (a) it is sold at the end of 2 years or (b) it is sold at the end of 10 years. Among other things, the range of possible estimated cash flows considers future sales levels (volume and price) and associated manufacturing costs in varying scenarios that consider (a) the likelihood that existing customer relationships will continue and (b) future economic (market) conditions. The probability assessments consider all information available without undue cost and effort. Such assessments are by their nature subjective and, in many situations, may be limited to management's best judgment about the probabilities of the best, worst, and most-likely scenarios.

Course of Action	Cash Flow Estimate (Use)	Cash Flow Estimate (Disposition)	Cash Flow Estimate	Probability Assessment	Probability-Weighted Cash Flows
		(in $ millions)			
Sell in 2 years	$ 8	$30	$38	20%	$ 7.6
	11	30	41	50	20.5
	13	30	43	30	12.9
					$41.0
Sell in 10 years	36	1	37	20%	$ 7.4
	48	1	49	50	24.5
	55	1	56	30	16.8
					$48.7

[FAS144, ¶A7]

.169 In computing the future cash flows used to test the facility for recoverability, the entity concludes that there is (a) a 60 percent probability that the facility will be sold at the end of 2 years and (b) a 40 percent probability that the facility will continue to be used for its remaining estimated useful life of 10 years. The following table shows the computation of future cash flows based on the probability of those alternative courses of action.[30] As shown, those future cash flows are $44.1 million (undiscounted). Therefore, the carrying amount of the facility of $48 million would not be recoverable.

[30]The alternatives of whether to sell or use an asset are not necessarily independent of each other. In many situations, after estimating the possible future cash flows relating to those potential courses of action, an entity might select the course of action that results in a significantly higher estimate of possible future cash flows. In that situation, the entity generally would use the estimates of possible future cash flows relating only to that course of action in computing future cash flows. [FAS144, ¶A8, fn27]

Course of Action	Probability-Weighted Cash Flows	Probability Assessment (Course of Action)	Expected Cash Flows
	(in $ millions)		
Sell in 2 years	$41.0	60%	$24.6
Sell in 10 years	48.7	40	19.5
			$44.1

[FAS144, ¶A8]

Example 3—Estimates of Future Cash Flows Used to Test an Asset Group for Recoverability

.170 A long-lived asset that is under development may be part of an asset group that is in use. In that situation, estimates of future cash flows used to test the recoverability of that group shall include the cash flows associated with future expenditures necessary to maintain the existing service potential of the group as well as the cash flows associated with future expenditures necessary to substantially complete the asset that is under development (paragraph .156). [FAS144, ¶A9]

.171 An entity engaged in mining and selling phosphate estimates future cash flows from its commercially minable phosphate deposits in order to test the recoverability of the asset group that includes the mine and related long-lived assets (plant and equipment). Deposits from the mined rock must be processed in order to extract the phosphate. As the active mining area expands along the geological structure of the mine, a new processing plant is constructed near the production area. Depending on the size of the mine, extracting the minable deposits may require building numerous processing plants over the life of the mine. In testing the recoverability of the mine and related long-lived assets, the estimates of future cash flows from its commercially minable phosphate deposits would include cash flows associated with future expenditures necessary to build all of the required processing plants. [FAS144, ¶A10]

Example 4—Expected Present Value Technique

.172 This example illustrates the application of an expected present value technique to estimate the fair value of a long-lived asset in the absence of an observable market price (paragraph .158).[31] It is based on the facts provided for the manufacturing facility in Example 2. [FAS144, ¶A11]

.173 Consistent with an objective of measuring fair value, the entity's estimates of future cash flows used to test the manufacturing facility for recoverability in Example 2 are adjusted to incorporate assumptions that, based on available information, marketplace participants would use in their estimates of the fair value of the asset. The net effect of those adjustments is to increase the entity's estimates of future cash flows (on an undiscounted basis) by approximately 15 percent.[32] [FAS144, ¶A12]

.174 The following table shows by year the range and probability of possible cash flows expected to result from the use and eventual disposition of the facility over its remaining useful life of ten years (Example 2), adjusted for market assumptions. It also shows by year the computation of expected cash flows.

---

[31]Present value is the current measure of an estimated future cash inflow, discounted at an interest rate for the number of periods between today and the date of the estimated cash flow. The present value of *$X* in *n* periods in the future and discounted at interest of *i* per period is computed using the formula $X / (1 + i)^n$. Because all of the risks are considered in the estimates of cash flows, the entity discounts the expected cash flows for each year using the risk-free rate of interest. The risk-free rate of interest is the interest rate on monetary assets that are essentially risk free and that have maturity dates that coincide with the expected timing of the cash flow. In the United States, the risk-free rate is the rate for zero-coupon U.S. Treasury instruments. A yield curve for U.S. Treasury instruments may be used to determine the appropriate risk-free rates of interest. [FAS144, ¶A11, fn28]

[32]In this example, a reliable estimate of the market risk premium is not available. Paragraph 62 of Concepts Statement 7 explains:

> An estimate of fair value should include the price that marketplace participants are able to receive for bearing the uncertainties in cash flows—the adjustment for risk—if the amount is identifiable, measurable, and significant. An arbitrary adjustment for risk, or one that cannot be evaluated by comparison to marketplace information, introduces an unjustified bias into the measurement. On the other hand, excluding a risk adjustment (if it is apparent that marketplace participants include one) would not produce a measurement that faithfully represents fair value. There are many techniques for estimating a risk adjustment, including matrix pricing, option-adjusted spread models, and fundamental analysis. However, in many cases a reliable estimate of the market risk premium may not be obtainable or the amount may be small relative to potential measurement error in the estimated cash flows. In such situations, the present value of expected cash flows, discounted at a risk-free rate of interest, may be the best available estimate of fair value in the circumstances.

[FAS144, ¶A12, fn29]

Year	Total Cash Flow Estimate (Market)	Probability Assessment	Expected Cash Flows
	(in $ millions)		
1	$4.6	20%	$ .9
	6.3	50	3.2
	7.5	30	2.3
			$6.4
2	$4.6	20%	$ .9
	6.3	50	3.2
	7.5	30	2.3
			$6.4
3	$4.3	20%	$ .9
	5.8	50	2.9
	6.7	30	2.0
			$5.8
4	$4.3	20%	$ .9
	5.8	50	2.9
	6.7	30	2.0
			$5.8
5	$4.0	20%	$ .8
	5.4	50	2.7
	6.4	30	1.9
			$5.4
6	$4.0	20%	$ .8
	5.4	50	2.7
	6.4	30	1.9
			$5.4
7	$3.9	20%	$ .8
	5.1	50	2.6
	5.6	30	1.7
			$5.1
8	$3.9	20%	$ .8
	5.1	50	2.6
	5.6	30	1.7
			$5.1

Year	Total Cash Flow Estimate (Market)	Probability Assessment	Expected Cash Flows
	(in $ millions)		
9	$3.9	20%	$ .8
	5.0	50	2.5
	5.5	30	1.7
			$5.0
10	$4.9	20%	$1.0
	6.0	50	3.0
	6.5	30	2.0
			$6.0

[FAS144, ¶A13]

.175 The following table shows the computation of the present value of the expected cash flows; that is, the sum of the present values of the expected cash flows by year, which are calculated by discounting those cash flows at a risk-free rate. As shown, the expected present value is $42.3 million. In accordance with paragraph .142, the entity would recognize an impairment loss of $5.7 million ($48 million less $42.3 million).

Year	Expected Cash Flows	Risk-Free Rate of Interest	Present Value	Expected Present Value
		(in $ millions)		
1	$6.4	5.0%	$6.1	
2	6.4	5.1	5.8	
3	5.8	5.2	5.0	
4	5.8	5.4	4.7	
5	5.4	5.6	4.1	
6	5.4	5.8	3.9	
7	5.1	6.0	3.4	
8	5.1	6.2	3.2	
9	5.0	6.4	2.9	
10	6.0	6.6	3.2	
				$42.3

[FAS144, ¶A14]

[**Note:** Additional guidance with respect to implementing Section I08 is presented in FASB *Viewpoints,* "Application of FASB Statements 5 and 114 to a Loan Portfolio," April 12, 1999. This article addresses 31 questions and was written by FASB staff members Sean Leonard, Tim Lucas, and Leslie Seidman. This article is available from the Order Department, Financial Accounting Standards Board, 401 Merritt 7, P.O. Box 5116, Norwalk, CT 06856-5116, telephone 800-748-0659.]

Supplemental Guidance: Emerging Issues Task Force (EITF) Issues

.1000 [Listed below are EITF Issues that provide supplemental guidance for this section. These Issues are grouped by subject matter and may be either interpretive of or related by topic to the guidance in this section.

Executory Contracts

EITF Issue No. 99-14, "Recognition by a Purchaser of Losses on Firmly Committed Executory Contracts"
EITF Issue No. 00-26, "Recognition by a Seller of Losses on Firmly Committed Executory Contracts"

Impairment of Assets

EITF Issue No. 93-4, "Accounting for Regulatory Assets"
EITF Issue No. 94-3, "Liability Recognition for Certain Employee Termination Benefits and Other Costs to Exit an Activity (including Certain Costs Incurred in a Restructuring)"
EITF Issue No. 97-4, "Deregulation of the Pricing of Electricity—Issues Related to the Application of FASB Statements No. 71 and 101"
EITF Issue No. 99-5, "Accounting for Pre-Production Costs Related to Long-Term Supply Arrangements"
EITF Issue No. 01-5, "Application of FASB Statement No. 52 to an Investment Being Evaluated for Impairment That Will Be Disposed Of"

Impairment of Investments in Debt and Equity Securities

EITF Issue No. 99-20, "Recognition of Interest Income and Impairment on Purchased and Retained Beneficial Interests in Securitized Financial Assets"
EITF Topic No. D-44, "Recognition of Other-Than-Temporary Impairment upon the Planned Sale of a Security Whose Cost Exceeds Fair Value"

Impairment of Loans

EITF Issue No. 84-4, "Acquisition, Development, and Construction Loans"
EITF Issue No. 84-19, "Mortgage Loan Payment Modifications"
EITF Issue No. 85-44, "Differences between Loan Loss Allowances for GAAP and RAP"
EITF Issue No. 87-18, "Use of Zero Coupon Bonds in a Troubled Debt Restructuring"
EITF Issue No. 87-19, "Substituted Debtors in a Troubled Debt Restructuring"
EITF Issue No. 94-8, "Accounting for Conversion of a Loan into a Debt Security in a Debt Restructuring"

EITF Issue No. 96-22, "Applicability of the Disclosures Required by FASB Statement No. 114 When a Loan Is Restructured in a Troubled Debt Restructuring into Two (or More) Loans"
EITF Topic No. D-80, "Application of FASB Statements No. 5 and No. 114 to a Loan Portfolio"

Other

EITF Issue No. 89-13, "Accounting for the Cost of Asbestos Removal"
EITF Issue No. 93-11, "Accounting for Barter Transactions Involving Barter Credits"
EITF Issue No. 98-13, "Accounting by an Equity Method Investor for Investee Losses When the Investor Has Loans to and Investments in Other Securities of the Investee"
EITF Topic No. D-104, "Clarification of Transition Guidance in Paragraph 51 of FASB Statement No. 144"]

.1001 [Listed below are those EITF Issues that provide interpretive guidance on specific material in this section.

Paragraph .111 (FAS 114, ¶13)—EITF Issue No. 98-13
Paragraph .115 (FAS 118, ¶6(g))—EITF Issue No. 98-13
Paragraphs .118 and .118A (FAS 118, ¶6(i))—EITF Issue No. 96-22
Paragraph .120 (FAS 115, ¶16)—EITF Topic No. D-44]

(The next page is 24275.)

INCOME STATEMENT PRESENTATION: DISCONTINUED OPERATIONS

SECTION I13

The material in this section has been superseded by FASB Statement 144, *Accounting for the Impairment or Disposal of Long-Lived Assets.* Due to the delayed effective date of Statement 144, this section has been moved to Appendix E, "*Current Text* Sections That Are Superseded by Pronouncements with Delayed Effective Dates," for continued reference by users until the date Statement 144 is initially applied. For financial statements issued for fiscal years beginning before December 15, 2001, Section I13 may be applied. (Refer to Appendix C, "Effective Dates of Pronouncements," for details of the effective date and transition provisions of Statement 144.)

INCOME STATEMENT PRESENTATION: DISCONTINUED OPERATIONS (FAS 144) — SECTION I14

Source: FASB Statement 144

[**Note:** A list of Issues discussed by the Emerging Issues Task Force (EITF) that provide supplemental guidance for this section is presented in paragraph .1000.]

Summary

This section specifies that the results of discontinued operations and the gain or loss on disposal shall be reported in the income statement separately from continuing operations but not as an extraordinary item.

Reporting Discontinued Operations

.101 For purposes of this section, a *component of an entity* comprises operations and cash flows that can be clearly distinguished, operationally and for financial reporting purposes, from the rest of the entity. A component of an entity may be a reportable segment or an operating segment (as those terms are defined in paragraph .109 of Section S30, "Segment Disclosures and Related Information"), a reporting unit (as that term is defined in paragraph .407 of Section G40, "Goodwill and Other Intangible Assets"), a subsidiary, or an asset group (as that term is defined in paragraph .140 of Section I08, "Impairment"). [FAS144, ¶41]

.102 The results of operations of a component of an entity that either has been disposed of or is classified as held for sale shall be reported in discontinued operations in accordance with paragraph .103 if both of the following conditions are met: (a) the operations and cash flows of the component have been (or will be) eliminated from the ongoing operations of the entity as a result of the disposal transaction and (b) the entity will not have any significant continuing involvement in the operations of the component after the disposal transaction. (Examples 1 through 4 (paragraphs .109 through .115) illustrate disposal activities that do or do not qualify for reporting as discontinued operations.) [FAS144, ¶42]

.103 In a period in which a component of an entity either has been disposed of or is classified as held for sale, the income statement of a business enterprise (or statement of activities of a not-for-profit organization) for current and prior periods shall report the results of operations of the component, including any gain or loss recognized in accordance with paragraph .114 of Section D60, "Disposal of Long-Lived Assets," in discontinued operations. The results of operations of a component classified as held for sale shall be reported in discontinued operations in the period(s) in which they occur. The results of discontinued operations, less applicable income taxes (benefit), shall be reported as a separate component of income before extraordinary items and the cumulative effect of accounting changes (if applicable). For example, the results of discontinued operations may be reported in the income statement of a business enterprise as follows:

Income from continuing operations before income taxes	$XXXX	
Income taxes	XXX	
Income from continuing operations[1]		$XXXX
Discontinued operations (Note X)		
Loss from operations of discontinued Component X (including loss on disposal of $XXX)	XXXX	
Income tax benefit	XXXX	
Loss on discontinued operations		XXXX
Net income		$XXXX

A gain or loss recognized on the disposal shall be disclosed either on the face of the income statement or in the notes to the financial statements (paragraph .106(b)). [FAS144, ¶43]

.104 Adjustments to amounts previously reported in discontinued operations that are directly related to the disposal of a component of an entity in a prior period shall be classified separately in the current period in discontinued operations. The nature and amount of such adjustments shall be disclosed. Examples of circumstances in which those types of adjustments may arise include the following:

a. The resolution of contingencies that arise pursuant to the terms of the disposal transaction, such as the resolution of purchase price adjustments and indemnification issues with the purchaser
b. The resolution of contingencies that arise from and that are directly related to the operations of the component prior to its disposal, such as environmental and product warranty obligations retained by the seller

[1]This caption shall be modified appropriately when an entity reports an extraordinary item or the cumulative effect of a change in accounting principle or both in accordance with Section A06, "Accounting Changes." If applicable, the presentation of per-share data will need similar modification. [FAS144, ¶43, fn24]

c. The settlement of employee benefit plan obligations (pension, postemployment benefits other than pensions, and other postemployment benefits), provided that the settlement is directly related to the disposal transaction.[2]

[FAS144, ¶44]

Disclosure

.105 The following information shall be disclosed in the notes to the financial statements that cover the period in which a long-lived asset (disposal group) either has been sold or is classified as held for sale:

a. A description of the facts and circumstances leading to the expected disposal, the expected manner and timing of that disposal, and, if not separately presented on the face of the statement, the carrying amount(s) of the major classes of assets and liabilities included as part of a disposal group
b. The gain or loss recognized in accordance with paragraph .114 of Section D60 and if not separately presented on the face of the income statement, the caption in the income statement or the statement of activities that includes that gain or loss
c. If applicable, amounts of revenue and pretax profit or loss reported in discontinued operations
d. If applicable, the segment in which the long-lived asset (disposal group) is reported under Section S30.

[FAS144, ¶47]

.106 If either paragraph .115 or paragraph .117 of Section D60 applies, a description of the facts and circumstances leading to the decision to change the plan to sell the long-lived asset (disposal group) and its effect on the results of operations for the period and any prior periods presented shall be disclosed in the notes to financial statements that include the period of that decision. [FAS144, ¶48]

[2]Paragraph .457 of Section P16, "Pension Costs," defines *settlement* as "a transaction that (a) is an irrevocable action, (b) relieves the employer (or the plan) of primary responsibility for a pension benefit obligation, and (c) eliminates significant risks related to the obligation and the assets used to effect the settlement." A settlement is directly related to the disposal transaction if there is a demonstrated direct cause-and-effect relationship and the settlement occurs no later than one year following the disposal transaction, unless it is delayed by events or circumstances beyond an entity's control (refer to paragraph .108 of Section D60). [FAS144, ¶44, fn25]

Implementation Guidance on Reporting Discontinued Operations

Introduction

.107 Paragraphs .108 through .115 illustrate application of some of the provisions of this section in certain specific situations. The relevant paragraphs of this section are identified in the parenthetical notes. The examples do not address all possible situations or applications of this section. Paragraphs .108 through .115 are an integral part of the standards provided in this section. [FAS144, ¶A1]

.108 The results of operations of a component of an entity that either has been disposed of or is classified as held for sale shall be reported in discontinued operations if (a) the operations and cash flows of the component have been (or will be) eliminated from the ongoing operations of the entity as a result of the disposal transaction and (b) the entity will not have any significant continuing involvement in the operations of the component after the disposal transaction (paragraph .102). Examples 1 through 4 (paragraphs .109 through .115) illustrate disposal activities that do or do not qualify for reporting as discontinued operations. [FAS144, ¶A24]

Example 1

.109 An entity that manufactures and sells consumer products has several product groups, each with different product lines and brands. For that entity, a product group is the lowest level at which the operations and cash flows can be clearly distinguished, operationally and for financial reporting purposes, from the rest of the entity. Therefore, each product group is a component of the entity. [FAS144, ¶A25]

.110 The entity has experienced losses associated with certain brands in its beauty care products group.

a. The entity decides to exit the beauty care business and commits to a plan to sell the product group with its operations. The product group is classified as held for sale at that date. The operations and cash flows of the product group will be eliminated from the ongoing operations of the entity as a result of the sale transaction, and the entity will not have any continuing involvement in the operations of the product group after it is sold. In that situation, the conditions in paragraph .102 for reporting in discontinued operations the operations of the product group while it is classified as held for sale would be met.
b. The entity decides to remain in the beauty care business but will discontinue the brands with which the losses are associated. Because the brands are part of a larger cash-flow-generating product group and, in the aggregate, do not represent a group that on

its own is a component of the entity, the conditions in paragraph .102 for reporting in discontinued operations the losses associated with the brands that are discontinued would not be met.

[FAS144, ¶A26]

Example 2

.111 An entity that is a franchisor in the quick-service restaurant business also operates company-owned restaurants. For that entity, an individual company-owned restaurant is the lowest level at which the operations and cash flows can be clearly distinguished, operationally and for financial reporting purposes, from the rest of the entity. Therefore, each company-owned restaurant is a component of the entity.

a. The entity has experienced losses on its company-owned restaurants in one region. The entity decides to exit the quick-service restaurant business in that region and commits to a plan to sell the restaurants in that region. The restaurants are classified as held for sale at that date. The operations and cash flows of the restaurants in that region will be eliminated from the ongoing operations of the entity as a result of the sale transaction, and the entity will not have any continuing involvement in the operations of the restaurants after they are sold. In that situation, the conditions in paragraph .102 for reporting in discontinued operations the operations of the restaurants while they are classified as held for sale would be met.
b. Based on its evaluation of the ownership mix of its system-wide restaurants in certain markets, the entity commits to a plan to sell its company-owned restaurants in one region to an existing franchisee. The restaurants are classified as held for sale at that date. Although each company-owned restaurant, on its own, is a component of the entity, through the franchise agreement, the entity will (1) receive franchise fees determined, in part, based on the future revenues of the restaurants and (2) have significant continuing involvement in the operations of the restaurants after they are sold. In that situation, the conditions in paragraph .102 for reporting in discontinued operations the operations of the restaurants would not be met.

[FAS144, ¶A27]

Example 3

.112 An entity that manufactures sporting goods has a bicycle division that designs, manufactures, markets, and distributes bicycles. For that entity, the bicycle division is the lowest level at which the operations and cash flows can be clearly distinguished, operationally and for financial reporting purposes, from the rest of the entity. Therefore, the bicycle division is a component of the entity. [FAS144, ¶A28]

.113 The entity has experienced losses in its bicycle division resulting from an increase in manufacturing costs (principally labor costs).

a. The entity decides to exit the bicycle business and commits to a plan to sell the division with its operations. The bicycle division is classified as held for sale at that date. The operations and cash flows of the division will be eliminated from the ongoing operations of the entity as a result of the sale transaction, and the entity will not have any continuing involvement in the operations of the division after it is sold. In that situation, the conditions in paragraph .102 for reporting in discontinued operations the operations of the division while it is classified as held for sale would be met.
b. The entity decides to remain in the bicycle business but will outsource the manufacturing operations and commits to a plan to sell the related manufacturing facility. The facility is classified as held for sale at that date. Because the manufacturing facility is part of a larger cash-flow-generating group (the bicycle division), and on its own is not a component of the entity, the conditions in paragraph .102 for reporting in discontinued operations the operations (losses) of the manufacturing facility would not be met. (Those conditions also would not be met if the manufacturing facility on its own was a component of the entity because the decision to outsource the manufacturing operations of the division will not eliminate the operations and cash flows of the division [and its bicycle business] from the ongoing operations of the entity.)

[FAS144, ¶A29]

Example 4

.114 An entity owns and operates retail stores that sell household goods. For that entity, each store is the lowest level at which the operations and cash flows can be clearly distinguished, operationally and for financial reporting purposes, from the rest of the entity. Therefore, each store is a component of the entity. [FAS144, ¶A30]

.115 To expand its retail store operations in one region, the entity decides to close two of its retail stores and open a new "superstore" in that region. The new superstore will continue to sell the household goods previously sold through the two retail stores as well as other related products not previously sold. Although each retail store on its own is a component of the entity, the operations and cash flows from the sale of household goods previously sold through the two retail stores in that region will not be eliminated from the ongoing operations of the entity. In that situation, the conditions in paragraph .102 for reporting in discontinued operations the operations of the stores would not be met. [FAS144, ¶A31]

Supplemental Guidance: Emerging Issues Task Force (EITF) Issues

.1000 [Listed below are EITF Issues that provide supplemental guidance for this section. These Issues are grouped by subject matter and are related by topic to the guidance in this section.

Restructuring of Business Operations

EITF Issue No. 86-22, "Display of Business Restructuring Provisions in the Income Statement"
EITF Issue No. 87-4, "Restructuring of Operations: Implications of SEC Staff Accounting Bulletin No. 67"
EITF Issue No. 94-3, "Liability Recognition for Certain Employee Termination Benefits and Other Costs to Exit an Activity (including Certain Costs Incurred in a Restructuring)"

Other

EITF Issue No. 87-24, "Allocation of Interest to Discontinued Operations"
EITF Issue No. 93-17, "Recognition of Deferred Tax Assets for a Parent Company's Excess Tax Basis in the Stock of a Subsidiary That Is Accounted for as a Discontinued Operation"
EITF Topic No. D-104, "Clarification of Transition Guidance in Paragraph 51 of FASB Statement No. 144"]

(The next page is 24467.)

INCOME STATEMENT PRESENTATION: EXTRAORDINARY ITEMS — SECTION I17

Sources: APB Opinion 9; APB Opinion 16; APB Opinion 30;
AICPA Interpretations of APB Opinion 9;
AICPA Interpretation of APB Opinion 30;
FASB Statement 101; FASB Statement 128; FASB Statement 141;
FASB Statement 144; FASB Technical Bulletin 85-6

[**Note:** A list of Issues discussed by the Emerging Issues Task Force (EITF) that provide supplemental guidance for this section is presented in paragraph .1000.]

Summary

This section specifies that an enterprise shall show extraordinary items separately as an item of net income for the period on the face of its income statement. Extraordinary items are events or transactions that are unusual and unrelated to the enterprise's ordinary activities and would occur infrequently.

Applicability

.101 This section applies to general purpose financial statements that purport to present results of operations in conformity with generally accepted accounting principles. Investment enterprises, insurance enterprises, and certain nonprofit enterprises have developed income statements with formats different from those of the typical commercial enterprise, designed to highlight the peculiar nature and sources of their income or operating results. The requirement of this section that net income be presented as one amount does not apply to such enterprises. [APB9, ¶6]

Income Statement Presentation and Disclosure

.102 In the absence of discontinued operations[a] (refer to Section I14, "Income Statement Presentation: Discontinued Operations") and changes in accounting principles

[a]Paragraphs .101 through .104 of Section I14, "Income Statement Presentation: Discontinued Operations," address the reporting of discontinued operations. [FAS144, ¶C5(c)]

(refer to Section A06, "Accounting Changes"), the following main captions shall appear in an income statement if **extraordinary items** are reported:

Income before extraordinary items[1]	$XXX
Extraordinary items (less applicable income taxes of $XXX) (Note A)	XXX
Net income	$XXX

The caption "extraordinary items" shall be used to identify separately the effects of events and transactions, other than the disposal of a [APB30, ¶11] component of an entity, [FAS144, ¶C5(c)] that meet the criteria for classification as extraordinary as discussed in paragraphs .106 through .111. Descriptive captions and the amounts for *individual* extraordinary events or transactions shall be presented, preferably on the face of the income statement, if practicable; otherwise, disclosure in related notes is acceptable. The nature of an extraordinary event or transaction and the principal items entering into the determination of an extraordinary gain or loss shall be described. The income taxes applicable to extraordinary items shall be disclosed on the face of the income statement; alternatively, disclosure in the related notes is acceptable. The caption *net income* shall replace the three captions shown above if the income statement includes no extraordinary items. [APB30, ¶11]

.103 Earnings per share data for extraordinary items shall be presented either on the face of the income statement or in the related notes, as prescribed by Section E11, "Earnings per Share." [FAS128, ¶165(b)]

.104 [Deleted 4/02 because of FASB Statement 145, *Rescission of FASB Statements No. 4, 44, and 64, Amendment of FASB Statement No. 13, and Technical Corrections*.]

[1]This caption shall be modified appropriately when an enterprise reports the cumulative effect of an accounting change (refer to Section A06). [APB30, ¶11, fn4]

.105 It has become customary for business enterprises to present historical, statistical-type summaries of financial data for a number of periods—commonly 5 or 10 years. The format for reporting extraordinary items described in paragraph .102 [is recommended] in such summaries. [APB9, ¶27]

Criteria for Extraordinary Items

.106 Judgment is required to segregate in the income statement the effects of events or transactions that are extraordinary items (as required by paragraph .102). An event or transaction shall be presumed to be an ordinary and usual activity of the reporting entity, the effects of which shall be included in income from operations, unless the evidence clearly supports its classification as an extraordinary item as defined in this section. [APB30, ¶19]

.107 Extraordinary items are events and transactions that are distinguished by their unusual nature *and* by the infrequency of their occurrence. Thus, *both* of the following criteria shall be met to classify an event or transaction as an extraordinary item:

a. *Unusual nature*—the underlying event or transaction possesses a high degree of abnormality and is of a type clearly unrelated to, or only incidentally related to, the ordinary and typical activities of the enterprise, taking into account the environment in which the enterprise operates (refer to paragraph .108).
b. *Infrequency of occurrence*—the underlying event or transaction is of a type that would not reasonably be expected to recur in the foreseeable future, taking into account the environment in which the enterprise operates (refer to paragraph .109). [APB30, ¶20]

However, the following items shall be recognized as extraordinary items regardless of whether those criteria are met:

(1) [Deleted 4/02 because of Statement 145.]
(2) The net effect of discontinuing the application of paragraphs .119 through .122 of Section Re6, "Regulated Operations," pursuant to paragraph .117A of this section
(3) The remaining excess of fair value of acquired net assets over cost pursuant to paragraphs .158 and .159 of Section B51, *Business Combinations.* [FAS141, ¶E5(b)]

[Refer to paragraph .1001 for EITF Issues that provide interpretive guidance on this paragraph.]

Unusual Nature

.108 The specific characteristics of the enterprise, such as type and scope of operations, lines of business, and operating policies, shall be considered in determining the enterprise's ordinary and typical activities. The environment in which an enterprise operates is a primary consideration in determining whether an underlying event or transaction is abnormal and significantly different from the ordinary and typical activities of the enterprise. The environment of an enterprise includes such factors as the characteristics of the industry or industries in which it operates, the geographical location of its operations, and the nature and extent of governmental regulation. Thus, an event or transaction may be unusual in nature for one enterprise but not for another because of differences in their respective environments. Unusual nature is not established by the fact that an event or transaction is beyond the control of management. [APB30, ¶21] [Refer to paragraph .1001 for an EITF Issue that provides interpretive guidance on paragraphs .108 and .109.]

Infrequency of Occurrence

.109 For purposes of this section, an event or transaction of a type not reasonably expected to recur in the foreseeable future is considered to occur infrequently. Determining the probability of recurrence of a particular event or transaction in the foreseeable future shall take into account the environment in which an enterprise operates. Accordingly, a specific transaction of one enterprise might meet that criterion and a similar transaction of another enterprise might not because of different probabilities of recurrence. The past occurrence of an event or transaction for a particular enterprise provides evidence to assess the probability of recurrence of that type of event or transaction in the foreseeable future. By definition, extraordinary items occur infrequently. However, mere infrequency of occurrence of a particular event or transaction does not alone imply that its effects should be classified as extraordinary. An event or transaction of a type that occurs frequently in the environment in which the enterprise operates cannot, by definition, be considered as extraordinary, regardless of its financial effect. [APB30, ¶22]

.110 Certain gains and losses shall not be reported as extraordinary items because they are usual in nature or may be expected to recur as a consequence of customary and continuing business activities. Examples include:

a. Write-down or write-off of receivables,[2] inventories, equipment leased to others, or intangible assets

---

[[2]Refer to paragraphs .501 and .502 as to accounting for railroads' losses arising from charging off receivables from bankrupt railroads.]

b. Gains or losses from exchange or translation of foreign currencies, including those relating to major devaluations and revaluations (refer to Section F60, "Foreign Currency Translation")
c. Gains or losses on disposal of a [APB30, ¶23] component of an entity [FAS144, ¶C5(f)] (refer to Section I14)
d. Other gains or losses from sale or abandonment of property, plant, or equipment used in the business
e. Effects of a strike, including those against competitors and major suppliers
f. Adjustment of accruals on long-term contracts.

[APB30, ¶23] [Refer to paragraph .1001 for EITF Issues that provide interpretive guidance on this paragraph.]

.110A [Refer to paragraphs .503 through .510 for a discussion of additional examples that should or should not be reported as extraordinary items.]

.111 In rare situations, an event or transaction may occur that clearly meets both criteria specified in paragraph .107 and thus gives rise to an extraordinary gain or loss that includes one or more of the gains or losses enumerated above. In these circumstances, gains or losses such as those described in subparagraphs .110(a) and .110(d) shall be included in the extraordinary item if they are a direct result of a major casualty (such as an earthquake), an expropriation, or a prohibition under a newly enacted law or regulation that clearly meets both criteria specified in paragraph .107. However, any portion of such losses that would have resulted from a valuation of assets on a going concern basis shall not be included in the extraordinary items. [APB30, ¶23] Disposals of a component of an entity shall be accounted for and presented in the income statement in accordance with Section I14 even though the circumstances of the disposal meet the criteria specified in paragraph .107 of this section.[3] [FAS144, ¶C5(f)] [Refer to paragraph .1001 for an EITF Issue that provides interpretive guidance on this paragraph.]

Exceptions to the Criteria for Extraordinary Items

.112 [Paragraphs .113 through .117A identify specific items that shall be reported as extraordinary items even though they do not meet the criteria set forth in paragraph .107.]

[[3]Refer to paragraphs .501 through .508 for further guidance in applying the criteria in paragraph .107.]

.113–.115 [Deleted 4/02 because of Statement 145.]

.116 [Deleted 2/92 because of FASB Statement 109, *Accounting for Income Taxes.*]

.117 [Deleted 6/01 because of FASB Statement 141, *Business Combinations.*]

Discontinuation of Accounting for the Effects of Certain Types of Regulation

.117A When an enterprise discontinues application of [the specialized accounting for the effects of certain types of regulation as described in] Section Re6, "Regulated Operations," to all or part of its operations, that enterprise shall eliminate from its statement of financial position prepared for general-purpose external financial reporting the effects of any actions of regulators that had been recognized as assets and liabilities pursuant to Section Re6 but would not have been recognized as assets and liabilities by enterprises in general. However, the carrying amounts of plant, equipment, and inventory measured and reported pursuant to Section Re6 shall not be adjusted unless those assets are impaired, in which case the carrying amounts of those assets shall be reduced to reflect that impairment. Whether those assets have been impaired shall be judged in the same manner as for enterprises in general [FAS101, ¶6] and paragraphs .139 through .161 of Section I08, "Impairment," shall apply, except for the provisions for income statement reporting in paragraphs .160 and .161 of that section. [FAS144, ¶C33] The net effect of the adjustments required by this paragraph shall be included in income of the period in which the discontinuation occurs and shall be classified as an extraordinary item. [FAS101, ¶6] [For further guidance, refer to Section Re6, paragraphs .204 through .216.]

Materiality

.118 The effect of an extraordinary event or transaction shall be classified separately in the income statement in the manner described in paragraph .102 if it is material in relation to income before extraordinary items or to the trend of annual earnings before extraordinary items, or is material by other appropriate criteria. Items shall be considered individually and not in the aggregate in determining whether an extraordinary event or transaction is material. However, the effects of a series of related transactions arising from a single specific and identifiable event or plan of action that otherwise meets the two criteria in paragraph .107 shall be aggregated to determine materiality. [APB30, ¶24] [Refer to paragraph .1001 for an EITF Issue that provides interpretive guidance on this paragraph.]

[4–5][Deleted 4/02 because of Statement 145.]

Adjustment of Amounts Reported in Prior Periods

.119 Circumstances attendant to extraordinary items frequently require estimates, for example, of associated costs and occasionally of associated revenue, based on judgment and evaluation of the facts known at the time of first accounting for the event. [APB30, ¶25] Each adjustment in the current period of an element of an extraordinary item that was reported in a prior period shall be separately disclosed as to year of origin, nature, and amount and classified separately in the current period [as an extraordinary item]. [FAS16, ¶16(c)] If the adjustment is the correction of an error, the provisions of Section A35, "Adjustments of Financial Statements for Prior Periods," paragraphs .103(a) and .105, shall be applied. [APB30, ¶25]

Glossary

.401 **Extraordinary items.** Events and transactions that are distinguished by their unusual nature *and* by the infrequency of their occurrence. Thus, *both* of the following criteria shall be met to classify an event or transaction as an extraordinary item:

a. *Unusual nature*—the underlying event or transaction possesses a high degree of abnormality and is of a type clearly unrelated to, or only incidentally related to, the ordinary and typical activities of the enterprise, taking into account the environment in which the enterprise operates.
b. *Infrequency of occurrence*—the underlying event or transaction is of a type that would not reasonably be expected to recur in the foreseeable future, taking into account the environment in which the enterprise operates. [APB30, ¶20]

However, the following items shall be recognized as extraordinary items regardless of whether those criteria are met:

(1) Classifications of gains or losses from extinguishment of debt pursuant to paragraph .113 of this section
(2) The net effect of discontinuing the application of paragraphs .119 through .122 of Section Re6, pursuant to paragraph .117A of this section
(3) The remaining excess of fair value of acquired net assets over cost pursuant to paragraphs .158 and .159 of Section B51. [FAS141, ¶E5(b)]

[Refer to paragraph .1001 for an EITF Issue that provides interpretive guidance on this paragraph.]

Supplemental Guidance

Losses Caused by Bankruptcies

.501 *Question*—Recent [1970] railroad bankruptcies raise the question of whether enterprises holding receivables from those railroads should account for losses arising from charging off such assets as ordinary losses or as extraordinary losses in determining net income. The Interstate Commerce Commission has ruled that railroads must write off certain past due payments from other railroads (for example, interline receivables) as extraordinary losses. Is this accounting treatment appropriate in the annual reports to railroads' shareholders and in the annual reports to shareholders of other (nonrailroad) enterprises? [AIN-APB9, #1]

.502 *Interpretation*—No, paragraph .110(a) specifies that, regardless of size, losses from receivables do *not* constitute extraordinary losses. The fact that the loss arises from a receivable from an enterprise in bankruptcy proceedings does not alter this answer in any way. Regulatory authorities often rule on the accounting treatment to be applied by enterprises under their jurisdiction. The above question is covered by [Section Re6, paragraph .114.] [AIN-APB9, #1]

Criteria for Extraordinary Items

.503 *Question*—As stated in paragraph .106, judgment is required to segregate in the income statement the effects of events or transactions that are extraordinary items. What factors must be considered in determining whether the effects of a particular event or transaction are extraordinary items or should otherwise be set forth in the income statement, and how are these factors applied in practice? [AIN-APB30, #1]

.504 *Interpretation*—The criteria for extraordinary items classification should be considered. That is: Does the event or transaction meet both criteria of *unusual nature* and *infrequency of occurrence?* [FAS144, ¶C6(a)]

.505 Events or transactions that would meet both criteria in the circumstances described are:

a. A large portion of a tobacco manufacturer's crops are destroyed by a hail storm. Severe damage from hail storms in the locality where the manufacturer grows tobacco is rare.
b. A steel fabricating enterprise sells the only land it owns. The land was acquired 10 years ago for future expansion, but shortly thereafter the enterprise abandoned all plans for expansion and held the land for appreciation.

c. [Deleted 2/99 because of FASB Statement 135, *Rescission of FASB Statement No. 75 and Technical Corrections.*]
d. An earthquake destroys one of the oil refineries owned by a large multinational oil enterprise.

[AIN-APB30, #1]

.506 The following illustrate events or transactions that do not meet both criteria in the circumstances described and thus should not be reported as extraordinary items:

a. A citrus grower's Florida crop is damaged by frost. Frost damage is normally experienced every three or four years. The criterion of infrequency of occurrence taking into account the environment in which the enterprise operates would not be met since the history of losses caused by frost damage provides evidence that such damage may reasonably be expected to recur in the foreseeable future.
b. An enterprise that operates a chain of warehouses sells the excess land surrounding one of its warehouses. When the enterprise buys property to establish a new warehouse, it usually buys more land than it expects to use for the warehouse with the expectation that the land will appreciate in value. In the past five years, there have been two instances in which the enterprise sold such excess land. The criterion of infrequency of occurrence has not been met since past experience indicates that such sales may reasonably be expected to recur in the foreseeable future.
c. A large diversified enterprise sells a block of shares from its portfolio of securities that it has acquired for investment purposes. This is the first sale from its portfolio of securities. Since the enterprise owns several securities for investment purposes, it should be concluded that sales of such securities are related to its ordinary and typical activities in the environment in which it operates and thus the criterion of unusual nature would not be met.
d. A textile manufacturer with only one plant moves to another location. It has not relocated a plant in 20 years and has no plans to do so in the foreseeable future. Notwithstanding the infrequency of occurrence of the event as it relates to this particular enterprise, moving from one location to another is an occurrence that is a consequence of customary and continuing business activities, some of which are finding more favorable labor markets, more modern facilities, and proximity to customers or suppliers. Therefore, the criterion of unusual nature has not been met and the moving expenses (and related gains and losses) should not be reported as an extraordinary item. Another example of an event that is a consequence of customary and typical business activities (namely financing) is an unsuccessful public registration, the cost of which should not be reported as an extraordinary item. (For additional examples refer to paragraph .110.)

[AIN-APB30, #1]

.507 [Deleted 8/01 because of FASB Statement 144, *Accounting for the Impairment or Disposal of Long-Lived Assets.*]

.508 [The foregoing examples are illustrative. It should be recognized that all attendant circumstances, which can vary from those above, need to be considered in making the judgments required by this section.]

Costs Incurred in Defending against a Takeover Attempt

.509 *Question*—Should the costs incurred by an enterprise to defend itself from a takeover attempt or the cost attributed to a "standstill" agreement be classified as extraordinary items? [FTB85-6, ¶6]

.510 *Response*—No. Neither the costs incurred by an enterprise to defend itself from a takeover attempt nor the costs incurred as part of a "standstill" agreement meet the criteria for extraordinary classification as discussed in paragraph .107. The *event* that gave rise to those costs—a takeover attempt—cannot be considered to be both *unusual* and *infrequent* as those terms are used in this section. [FTB85-6, ¶7]

Supplemental Guidance: Emerging Issues Task Force (EITF) Issues

.1000 [Listed below are EITF Issues that provide supplemental guidance for this section. These Issues are grouped by subject matter and may be either interpretive of or related by topic to the guidance in this section.

Extinguishment of Debt

EITF Issue No. 90-19, "Convertible Bonds with Issuer Option to Settle for Cash upon Conversion"
EITF Issue No. 96-19, "Debtor's Accounting for a Modification or Exchange of Debt Instruments"
EITF Issue No. 00-9, "Classification of a Gain or Loss from a Hedge of Debt That Is Extinguished"

Restructuring of Business Operations

EITF Issue No. 86-22, "Display of Business Restructuring Provisions in the Income Statement"
EITF Issue No. 94-3, "Liability Recognition for Certain Employee Termination Benefits and Other Costs to Exit an Activity (including Certain Costs Incurred in a Restructuring)"

Other

EITF Issue No. 85-2, "Classification of Costs Incurred in a Takeover Defense"
EITF Issue No. 86-15, "Increasing-Rate Debt"
EITF Issue No. 89-13, "Accounting for the Cost of Asbestos Removal"
EITF Issue No. 01-10, "Accounting for the Impact of the Terrorist Attacks of September 11, 2001"
EITF Issue No. 01-13, "Income Statement Display of Business Interruption Insurance Recoveries"
EITF Topic No. D-5, "Extraordinary Treatment Related to Abandoned Nuclear Power Plants"]

.1001 [Listed below are EITF Issues that provide interpretive guidance on specific material in this section.

Paragraph .107 (APB 30, ¶20)—EITF Issues No. 89-13 and 01-10
Paragraphs .108 and .109 (APB 30, ¶21–22)—EITF Issue No. 01-10
Paragraph .110 (APB 30, ¶23)—EITF Issues No. 89-13 and 01-10
Paragraph .111 (APB 30, ¶23)—EITF Issue No. 01-10
Paragraph .118 (APB 30, ¶24)—EITF Issue No. 01-10
Paragraph .401 (APB 30, ¶20)—EITF Issue No. 01-10]

(The next page is 24667.)

INCOME STATEMENT PRESENTATION: UNUSUAL OR INFREQUENT ITEMS — SECTION I22

Source: APB Opinion 30

[**Note:** A list of Issues discussed by the Emerging Issues Task Force (EITF) that provide supplemental guidance for this section is presented in paragraph .1000.]

Summary

An event or transaction that is either unusual in nature or occurs infrequently, but not both, shall be classified and reported as a separate component of income from continuing operations.

.101 A material event or transaction that is unusual in nature or occurs infrequently, but not both, and therefore does not meet both criteria for classification as an extraordinary item (refer to Section I17, "Income Statement Presentation: Extraordinary Items") shall be reported as a separate component of income from continuing operations. The nature and financial effects of each event or transaction shall be disclosed on the face of the income statement or, alternatively, in notes to the financial statements. Gains or losses of a similar nature that are not individually material shall be aggregated. Such items shall not be reported on the face of the income statement net of income taxes or in any other manner that may imply that they are extraordinary items. Similarly, the earnings per share effects of those items shall not be disclosed on the face of the income statement.[1] [APB30, ¶26]

---

[1][Deleted as of 12/87 because of FASB Statement 97, *Accounting and Reporting by Insurance Enterprises for Certain Long-Duration Contracts and for Realized Gains and Losses from the Sale of Investments.*]

Supplemental Guidance

.501-.502 [Deleted 8/01 because of FASB Statement 144, *Accounting for the Impairment or Disposal of Long-Lived Assets.*]

Supplemental Guidance: Emerging Issues Task Force (EITF) Issues

.1000 [Listed below are EITF Issues that provide supplemental guidance for this section. These Issues are related by topic to the guidance in this section.

EITF Issue No. 96-9, "Classification of Inventory Markdowns and Other Costs Associated with a Restructuring"

EITF Issue No. 99-4, "Accounting for Stock Received from the Demutualization of a Mutual Insurance Company"

EITF Issue No. 01-10, "Accounting for the Impact of the Terrorist Attacks of September 11, 2001"

EITF Issue No. 01-13, "Income Statement Display of Business Interruption Insurance Recoveries"]

(The next page is 25331.)

Supplemental Guidance: Emerging Issues Task Force (EITF) Issues

[illegible] EITF Issues that provide supplemental guidance [illegible] Issues [illegible]

- EITF Issue No. [illegible]
- EITF Issue No. [illegible]
- EITF Issue No. [illegible]
- EITF Issue No. [illegible] Business Interruption Insurance [illegible]

INCOME TAXES SECTION I27

Sources: APB Opinion 2; APB Opinion 4; APB Opinion 10; APB Opinion 23; AICPA Interpretations of APB Opinion 4; FASB Statement 37; FASB Statement 60; FASB Statement 95; FASB Statement 109; FASB Statement 115; FASB Statement 123; FASB Statement 130; FASB Statement 135; FASB Statement 141; FASB Technical Bulletin 82-1

[**Note:** A list of Issues discussed by the Emerging Issues Task Force (EITF) that provide supplemental guidance for this section is presented in paragraph .1000.]

Summary

This section presents financial accounting and reporting standards for the effects of income taxes that result from an enterprise's activities during the current and preceding years. An asset and liability approach is used in accounting for income taxes.

The objectives of accounting for income taxes are to recognize (a) the amount of taxes payable or refundable for the current year and (b) deferred tax liabilities and assets for the future tax consequences of events that have been recognized in an enterprise's financial statements or tax returns.

The following basic principles are applied in accounting for income taxes at the date of the financial statements:

a. A current tax liability or asset is recognized for the estimated taxes payable or refundable on tax returns for the current year.
b. A deferred tax liability or asset is recognized for the estimated future tax effects attributable to temporary differences and carryforwards.
c. The measurement of current and deferred tax liabilities and assets is based on provisions of the enacted tax law; the effects of future changes in tax laws or rates are not anticipated.
d. The measurement of deferred tax assets is reduced, if necessary, by the amount of any tax benefits that, based on available evidence, are not expected to be realized.

The tax consequences of most events recognized in the financial statements for a year are included in determining income taxes currently payable. However, tax laws often differ from the recognition and measurement requirements of financial accounting standards, and differences can arise between (a) the amount of taxable income and pretax financial income for a year and (b) the tax bases of assets or liabilities and their reported amounts in financial statements. All such differences collectively are referred to as *temporary differences* in this section.

Temporary differences ordinarily become taxable or deductible when the related asset is recovered or the related liability is settled. A deferred tax liability or asset represents the increase or decrease in taxes payable or refundable in future years as a result of temporary differences and carryforwards at the end of the current year.

A deferred tax liability is recognized for temporary differences that will result in taxable amounts in future years. For example, a temporary difference is created between the reported amount and the tax basis of an installment sale receivable if, for tax purposes, some or all of the gain on the installment sale will be included in the determination of taxable income in future years. Because amounts received upon recovery of that receivable will be taxable, a deferred tax liability is recognized in the current year for the related taxes payable in future years.

A deferred tax asset is recognized for temporary differences that will result in deductible amounts in future years and for carryforwards. For example, a temporary difference is created between the reported amount and the tax basis of a liability for estimated expenses if, for tax purposes, those estimated expenses are not deductible until a future year. Settlement of that liability will result in tax deductions in future years, and a deferred tax asset is recognized in the current year for the reduction in taxes payable in future years. A valuation allowance is recognized if, based on the weight of available evidence, it is *more likely than not* that some portion or all of the deferred tax asset will not be realized.

This section presents procedures to (a) measure deferred tax liabilities and assets using a tax rate convention and (b) assess whether a valuation allowance should be established for deferred tax assets. Enacted tax laws and rates are considered in determining the applicable tax rate and in assessing the need for a valuation allowance.

All available evidence, both positive and negative, is considered to determine whether, based on the weight of that evidence, a valuation allowance is needed for some portion or all of a deferred tax asset. Judgment must be used in considering the relative impact of negative and positive evidence. The weight given to the potential effect of negative and positive evidence should be commensurate with the extent to which it can be objectively verified. The more negative evidence that exists (a) the more positive evidence is necessary and (b) the more difficult it is to support a conclusion that a valuation allowance is not needed.

Deferred tax liabilities and assets are adjusted in the period of enactment for the effect of an enacted change in tax laws or rates. The effect is included in income from continuing operations.

This section also addresses the appropriate tax accounting treatment for the following areas:

a. Undistributed earnings of subsidiaries
b. Investments in corporate joint ventures
c. Bad-debt reserves of savings and loan associations
d. Policyholders' surplus of stock life insurance enterprises
e. Investment tax credits
f. Offsetting securities against taxes payable.

[**Note:** The reader should be aware that any references to income tax rules and regulations in this section are as they appear in the original pronouncement. No effect has been given to subsequent legislation, if any.]

Introduction

.101 This section addresses financial accounting and reporting for the effects of **income taxes** that result from an enterprise's activities during the current and preceding years. [FAS109, ¶1]

Scope

.102 This section [presents] standards of financial accounting and reporting for income taxes that are currently payable and for the tax consequences of:

a. Revenues, expenses, gains, or losses that are included in **taxable income** of an earlier or later year than the year in which they are recognized in financial income
b. Other **events** that create differences between the tax bases of assets and liabilities and their amounts for financial reporting
c. Operating loss or tax credit **carrybacks** for refunds of taxes paid in prior years and **carryforwards** to reduce taxes payable in future years.

[FAS109, ¶3]

.103 The principles and requirements of this section are applicable to:

a. Domestic federal (national) income taxes (U.S. federal income taxes for U.S. enterprises) and foreign, state, and local (including franchise) taxes based on income
b. An enterprise's[1] domestic and foreign operations that are consolidated, combined, or accounted for by the equity method
c. Foreign enterprises in preparing financial statements in accordance with U.S. generally accepted accounting principles.

[FAS109, ¶4]

.104 This section does not address accounting for income taxes in interim periods (other than the criteria for recognition of tax benefits and the effect of enacted changes in tax laws or rates and changes in valuation allowances). (Section I73, "Interim Financial Reporting," addresses that subject.) [FAS109, ¶5]

Objectives and Basic Principles

.105 One objective of accounting for income taxes is to recognize the amount of taxes payable or refundable for the current year. A second objective is to recognize **deferred tax liabilities and assets** for the future **tax consequences** of events[2] that have been recognized in an enterprise's financial statements or tax returns. [FAS109, ¶6]

.106 Ideally, the second objective might be stated more specifically to recognize the *expected* future tax consequences of events that have been recognized in the financial statements or tax returns. However, that objective is realistically constrained because (a) the tax payment or refund that results from a particular tax return is a joint result of all the items included in that return, (b) taxes that will be paid or refunded in future years are the joint result of events of the current or prior years and events of future years, and (c) information available about the future is limited. As a result, attribution of taxes to individual items and events is arbitrary and, except in the simplest situations, requires estimates and approximations. [FAS109, ¶7]

---

[1]The term *enterprise* is used throughout this section because accounting for income taxes is primarily an issue for business enterprises. However, the requirements of this section apply to the activities of a not-for-profit organization that are subject to income taxes. [FAS109, ¶4, fn2]

[2]Some events do not have tax consequences. Certain revenues are exempt from taxation and certain expenses are not deductible. In the United States, for example, interest earned on certain municipal obligations is not taxable and fines are not deductible. [FAS109, ¶6, fn3]

.107 To implement the objectives in light of those constraints, the following basic principles (the only exceptions are identified in paragraph .108) are applied in accounting for income taxes at the date of the financial statements:

a. A current tax liability or asset is recognized for the estimated taxes payable or refundable on tax returns for the current year.
b. A deferred tax liability or asset is recognized for the estimated future tax effects attributable to **temporary differences** and carryforwards.
c. The measurement of current and deferred tax liabilities and assets is based on provisions of the enacted tax law; the effects of future changes in tax laws or rates are not anticipated.
d. The measurement of deferred tax assets is reduced, if necessary, by the amount of any tax benefits that, based on available evidence, are not expected to be realized.

[FAS109, ¶8]

.108 The only exceptions in applying those basic principles are:

a. The requirements for recognition of deferred taxes for the areas addressed in paragraphs .212 through .224
b. Special transitional procedures for temporary differences related to deposits in statutory reserve funds by U.S. steamship enterprises (refer to paragraph .131)
c. [The] accounting for leveraged leases, [including leveraged leases acquired in a purchase business combination], as required by Section L10, "Leases," (refer to paragraphs .183 through .185)
d. [The prohibition from recognizing] a deferred tax liability or asset related to goodwill (or the portion thereof) for which amortization is not deductible for tax purposes (refer to paragraph .129)
e. [The accounting] for income taxes paid on intercompany profits on assets remaining within the group, [as required by Section C51, "Consolidation,"] and [the prohibition from recognizing] a deferred tax asset for the difference between the tax basis of the assets in the buyer's tax jurisdiction and their cost as reported in the consolidated financial statements
f. [The prohibition from recognizing] a deferred tax liability or asset for differences related to assets and liabilities that, under [the provisions of] Section F60, "Foreign Currency Translation," are remeasured from the local currency into the functional currency using historical exchange rates and that result from (1) changes in exchange rates or (2) indexing for tax purposes.

[FAS109, ¶9] [Refer to paragraph .1001 for EITF Issues that provide interpretive guidance on this paragraph and on subparagraph (f).]

Temporary Differences

.109 **Income taxes currently payable**[3] for a particular year usually include the tax consequences of most events that are recognized in the financial statements for that year. However, because tax laws and financial accounting standards differ in their recognition and measurement of assets, liabilities, equity, revenues, expenses, gains, and losses, differences arise between:

a. The amount of taxable income and pretax financial income for a year
b. The tax bases of assets or liabilities and their reported amounts in financial statements.

[FAS109, ¶10]

.110 An assumption inherent in an enterprise's statement of financial position prepared in accordance with generally accepted accounting principles is that the reported amounts of assets and liabilities will be recovered and settled, respectively. Based on that assumption, a difference between the tax basis of an asset or a liability and its reported amount in the statement of financial position will result in taxable or deductible amounts in some future year(s) when the reported amounts of assets are recovered and the reported amounts of liabilities are settled. Examples follow:

a. *Revenues or gains that are taxable after they are recognized in financial income.* An asset (for example, a receivable from an installment sale) may be recognized for revenues or gains that will result in future taxable amounts when the asset is recovered.
b. *Expenses or losses that are deductible after they are recognized in financial income.* A liability (for example, a product warranty liability) may be recognized for expenses or losses that will result in future tax deductible amounts when the liability is settled.
c. *Revenues or gains that are taxable before they are recognized in financial income.* A liability (for example, subscriptions received in advance) may be recognized for an advance payment for goods or services to be provided in future years. For tax purposes, the advance payment is included in taxable income upon the receipt of cash. Future sacrifices to provide goods or services (or future refunds to those who cancel their orders) will result in future tax deductible amounts when the liability is settled.
d. *Expenses or losses that are deductible before they are recognized in financial income.* The cost of an asset (for example, depreciable personal property) may have been deducted for tax purposes faster than it was depreciated for financial reporting.

[3]References in this section to income taxes currently payable and (total) **income tax expense** are intended to include also **income taxes currently refundable** and (total) **income tax benefit,** respectively. [FAS109, ¶10, fn4]

Amounts received upon future recovery of the amount of the asset for financial reporting will exceed the remaining tax basis of the asset, and the excess will be taxable when the asset is recovered.

e. *A reduction in the tax basis of depreciable assets because of tax credits.*[4] Amounts received upon future recovery of the amount of the asset for financial reporting will exceed the remaining tax basis of the asset, and the excess will be taxable when the asset is recovered.
f. *Investment tax credit (ITC) accounted for by the deferral method.* In paragraph .228, ITC is viewed and accounted for as a reduction of the cost of the related asset (even though, for financial statement presentation, deferred ITC may be reported as deferred income). Amounts received upon future recovery of the reduced cost of the asset for financial reporting will be less than the tax basis of the asset, and the difference will be tax deductible when the asset is recovered.
g. *An increase in the tax basis of assets because of indexing whenever the local currency is the functional currency.* The tax law for a particular tax jurisdiction might require adjustment of the tax basis of a depreciable (or other) asset for the effects of inflation. The inflation-adjusted tax basis of the asset would be used to compute future tax deductions for depreciation or to compute gain or loss on sale of the asset. Amounts received upon future recovery of the local currency historical cost of the asset will be less than the remaining tax basis of the asset, and the difference will be tax deductible when the asset is recovered.
h. *Business combinations.* There may be differences between the assigned values and the tax bases of the assets and liabilities recognized in a business combination. Those differences will result in taxable or deductible amounts when the reported amounts of the assets and liabilities are recovered and settled, respectively.

[FAS109, ¶11] [Refer to paragraph .1001 for an EITF Issue that provides interpretive guidance on this paragraph.]

.111 Examples (a) through (d) in paragraph .110 illustrate revenues, expenses, gains, or losses that are included in taxable income of an earlier or later year than the year in which they are recognized in pretax financial income. Those differences between taxable income and pretax financial income also create differences (sometimes accumulating over more than one year) between the tax basis of an asset or liability and its reported amount in the financial statements. Examples (e) through (h) in paragraph .110 illustrate other events that create differences between the tax basis of an asset or liability and its re-

[4]The Tax Equity and Fiscal Responsibility Act of 1982 provided taxpayers with the choice of either (a) taking the full amount of Accelerated Cost Recovery System (ACRS) deductions and a reduced tax credit (that is, investment tax credit and certain other tax credits) or (b) taking the full tax credit and a reduced amount of ACRS deductions. [FAS109, ¶11, fn5]

ported amount in the financial statements. For all eight examples, the differences result in taxable or deductible amounts when the reported amount of an asset or liability in the financial statements is recovered or settled, respectively. [FAS109, ¶12]

.112 This section refers collectively to the types of differences illustrated by those eight examples and to the ones described in paragraph .114 as *temporary differences.* Temporary differences that will result in taxable amounts in future years when the related asset or liability is recovered or settled are often referred to in this section as **taxable temporary differences** (examples (a), (d), and (e) in paragraph .110 are taxable temporary differences). Likewise, temporary differences that will result in deductible amounts in future years are often referred to as **deductible temporary differences** (examples (b), (c), (f), and (g) in paragraph .110 are deductible temporary differences). Business combinations (example (h)) may give rise to both taxable and deductible temporary differences. [FAS109, ¶13]

.113 Certain basis differences may not result in taxable or deductible amounts in future years when the related asset or liability for financial reporting is recovered or settled and, therefore, may not be temporary differences for which a deferred tax liability or asset is recognized. One example under current U.S. tax law is the excess of cash surrender value of life insurance over premiums paid. That excess is a temporary difference if the cash surrender value is expected to be recovered by surrendering the policy, but is not a temporary difference if the asset is expected to be recovered without tax consequence upon the death of the insured (there will be no taxable amount if the insurance policy is held until the death of the insured). [FAS109, ¶14]

.114 Some temporary differences are deferred taxable income or tax deductions and have balances only on the income tax balance sheet and therefore cannot be identified with a particular asset or liability for financial reporting. That occurs, for example, if a long-term contract is accounted for by the percentage-of-completion method for financial reporting and by the completed-contract method for tax purposes. The temporary difference (income on the contract) is deferred income for tax purposes that becomes taxable when the contract is completed. Another example is organizational costs that are recognized as expenses when incurred for financial reporting and are deferred and deducted in a later year for tax purposes. In both instances, there is no related, identifiable asset or liability for financial reporting, but there is a temporary difference that results from an event that has been recognized in the financial statements and, based on provisions in the tax law, the temporary difference will result in taxable or deductible amounts in future years. [FAS109, ¶15] [Refer to paragraph .1001 for an EITF Issue that provides interpretive guidance on this paragraph.]

Recognition and Measurement

.115 An enterprise shall recognize a deferred tax liability or asset for all temporary differences[5] and operating loss and tax credit carryforwards in accordance with the provisions of paragraph .116. [FAS109, ¶16] [The deferred tax liability or asset] shall not be accounted for on a discounted basis. [APB10, ¶6] **Deferred tax expense or benefit** is the change during the year in an enterprise's deferred tax liabilities and assets.[6] For deferred tax liabilities and assets acquired in a purchase business combination during the year, it is the change since the combination date. Total income tax expense or benefit for the year is the sum of deferred tax expense or benefit and income taxes currently payable or refundable. [FAS109, ¶16]

Annual Computation of Deferred Tax Liabilities and Assets

.116 Deferred taxes shall be determined separately for each tax-paying component (an individual entity or group of entities that is consolidated for tax purposes) in each tax jurisdiction. That determination includes the following procedures:

a. Identify (1) the types and amounts of existing temporary differences and (2) the nature and amount of each type of operating loss and tax credit carryforward and the remaining length of the carryforward period
b. Measure the total deferred tax liability for taxable temporary differences using the applicable tax rate (refer to paragraph .117)
c. Measure the total deferred tax asset for deductible temporary differences and operating loss carryforwards using the applicable tax rate
d. Measure deferred tax assets for each type of tax credit carryforward
e. Reduce deferred tax assets by a **valuation allowance** if, based on the weight of available evidence, it is *more likely than not* (a likelihood of more than 50 percent) that some portion or all of the deferred tax assets will not be realized. The valuation allowance shall be sufficient to reduce the deferred tax asset to the amount that is more likely than not to be realized.

[FAS109, ¶17] [Refer to paragraph .1001 for EITF Issues that provide interpretive guidance on this paragraph.]

---

[5]Refer to paragraph .108. A deferred tax liability shall be recognized for the temporary differences addressed by paragraphs .212 through .224 in accordance with the requirements of paragraphs .130 through .133. [FAS109, ¶16, fn6]

[6]Paragraph .156 addresses the manner of reporting the transaction gain or loss that is included in the net change in a deferred foreign tax liability or asset if the reporting currency is the functional currency. [FAS109, ¶16, fn7]

.117 The objective is to measure a deferred tax liability or asset using the enacted tax rate(s) expected to apply to taxable income in the periods in which the deferred tax liability or asset is expected to be settled or realized. Under current U.S. federal tax law, if taxable income exceeds a specified amount, all taxable income is taxed, in substance, at a single flat tax rate. That tax rate shall be used for measurement of a deferred tax liability or asset by enterprises for which graduated tax rates are not a significant factor. Enterprises for which graduated tax rates are a significant factor shall measure a deferred tax liability or asset using the average graduated tax rate applicable to the amount of estimated annual taxable income in the periods in which the deferred tax liability or asset is estimated to be settled or realized (refer to paragraph .163). Other provisions of enacted tax laws should be considered when determining the tax rate to apply to certain types of temporary differences and carryforwards (for example, the tax law may provide for different tax rates on ordinary income and capital gains). If there is a phased-in change in tax rates, determination of the applicable tax rate requires knowledge about when deferred tax liabilities and assets will be settled and realized. [FAS109, ¶18] [Refer to paragraph .1001 for an EITF Issue that provides interpretive guidance on this paragraph.]

.118 In the U.S. federal tax jurisdiction, the applicable tax rate is the regular tax rate, and a deferred tax asset is recognized for alternative minimum tax credit carryforwards in accordance with the provisions of paragraph .116(d) and (e) of this section. If alternative tax systems exist in jurisdictions other than the U.S. federal jurisdiction, the applicable tax rate is determined in a manner consistent with the tax law after giving consideration to any interaction (that is, a mechanism similar to the U.S. alternative minimum tax credit) between the two systems. [FAS109, ¶19] [Refer to paragraph .1001 for an EITF Issue that provides interpretive guidance on this paragraph.]

.119 All available evidence, both positive and negative, shall be considered to determine whether, based on the weight of that evidence, a valuation allowance is needed. Information about an enterprise's current financial position and its results of operations for the current and preceding years ordinarily is readily available. That historical information is supplemented by all currently available information about future years. Sometimes, however, historical information may not be available (for example, start-up operations) or it may not be as relevant (for example, if there has been a significant, recent change in circumstances) and special attention is required. [FAS109, ¶20]

.120 Future realization of the tax benefit of an existing deductible temporary difference or carryforward ultimately depends on the existence of sufficient taxable income of the appropriate character (for example, ordinary income or capital gain) within the carryback, carryforward period available under the tax law. The following four possible sources of taxable income may be available under the tax law to realize a tax benefit for deductible temporary differences and carryforwards:

a. Future reversals of existing taxable temporary differences
b. Future taxable income exclusive of reversing temporary differences and carryforwards
c. Taxable income in prior carryback year(s) if carryback is permitted under the tax law
d. **Tax-planning strategies** (refer to paragraph .121) that would, if necessary, be implemented to, for example:
   (1) Accelerate taxable amounts to utilize expiring carryforwards
   (2) Change the character of taxable or deductible amounts from ordinary income or loss to capital gain or loss
   (3) Switch from tax-exempt to taxable investments.

Evidence available about each of those possible sources of taxable income will vary for different tax jurisdictions and, possibly, from year to year. To the extent evidence about one or more sources of taxable income is sufficient to support a conclusion that a valuation allowance is not necessary, other sources need not be considered. Consideration of each source is required, however, to determine the amount of the valuation allowance that is recognized for deferred tax assets. [FAS109, ¶21]

.121 In some circumstances, there are actions (including elections for tax purposes) that (a) are prudent and feasible, (b) an enterprise ordinarily might not take, but would take to prevent an operating loss or tax credit carryforward from expiring unused, and (c) would result in realization of deferred tax assets. This section refers to those actions as *tax-planning strategies.*[7] An enterprise shall consider tax-planning strategies[8] in determining the amount of valuation allowance required. Significant expenses to implement a tax-planning strategy or any significant losses that would be recognized if that strategy were implemented (net of any recognizable tax benefits associated with those expenses or losses) shall be included in the valuation allowance. Refer to paragraphs .173 through .178 for additional guidance. [FAS109, ¶22]

.122 Forming a conclusion that a valuation allowance is not needed is difficult if there is negative evidence such as cumulative losses in recent years. Other examples of negative evidence include (but are not limited to) the following:

a. A history of operating loss or tax credit carryforwards expiring unused
b. Losses expected in early future years (by a presently profitable entity)

---

[7]Implementation of the tax-planning strategies must be primarily within the control of management but need not be within the unilateral control of management. [FAS109, ¶107]

[8]Under this section, the requirements for consideration of tax-planning strategies pertain only to the determination of a valuation allowance for a deferred tax asset. A deferred tax liability ordinarily is recognized for all taxable temporary differences. [FAS109, ¶251]

c. Unsettled circumstances that, if unfavorably resolved, would adversely affect future operations and profit levels on a continuing basis in future years
d. A carryback, carryforward period that is so brief that it would limit realization of tax benefits if (1) a significant deductible temporary difference is expected to reverse in a single year or (2) the enterprise operates in a traditionally cyclical business.

[FAS109, ¶23]

.123 Examples (not prerequisites) of positive evidence that might support a conclusion that a valuation allowance is not needed if there is negative evidence include (but are not limited to) the following:

a. Existing contracts or firm sales backlog that will produce more than enough taxable income to realize the deferred tax asset based on existing sales prices and cost structures
b. An excess of appreciated asset value over the tax basis of the entity's net assets in an amount sufficient to realize the deferred tax asset
c. A strong earnings history exclusive of the loss that created the future deductible amount (tax loss carryforward or deductible temporary difference) coupled with evidence indicating that the loss (for example, an unusual, infrequent, or extraordinary item) is an aberration rather than a continuing condition.

[FAS109, ¶24]

.124 An enterprise must use judgment in considering the relative impact of negative and positive evidence. The weight given to the potential effect of negative and positive evidence shall be commensurate with the extent to which it can be objectively verified. The more negative evidence that exists (a) the more positive evidence is necessary and (b) the more difficult it is to support a conclusion that a valuation allowance is not needed for some portion or all of the deferred tax asset.[9] [FAS109, ¶25]

A Change in the Valuation Allowance

.125 The effect of a change in the beginning-of-the-year balance of a valuation allowance that results from a change in circumstances that causes a change in judgment about the realizability of the related deferred tax asset in future years ordinarily shall be included in income from continuing operations. The only exceptions are the initial recog-

[9]Future realization of a tax benefit sometimes will be expected for a portion but not all of a deferred tax asset, and the dividing line between the two portions may be unclear. In those circumstances, application of judgment based on a careful assessment of all available evidence is required to determine the portion of a deferred tax asset for which it is more likely than not a tax benefit will not be realized. [FAS109, ¶98]

nition (that is, by elimination of the valuation allowance) of certain tax benefits that are allocated as required by paragraph .129 and paragraph .135 (items (c) and (e) through (g)). The effect of other changes in the balance of a valuation allowance are allocated among continuing operations and items other than continuing operations as required by paragraph .134. [FAS109, ¶26] [Refer to paragraph .1001 for an EITF Issue that provides interpretive guidance on this paragraph.]

An Enacted Change in Tax Laws or Rates

.126 Deferred tax liabilities and assets shall be adjusted for the effect of a change in tax laws or rates. The effect shall be included in income from continuing operations for the period that includes the enactment date. [FAS109, ¶27] [Refer to paragraph .1001 for EITF Issues that provide interpretive guidance on this paragraph.]

A Change in the Tax Status of an Enterprise

.127 An enterprise's tax status may change from nontaxable to taxable or from taxable to nontaxable. An example is a change from a partnership to a corporation and vice versa. A deferred tax liability or asset[10] shall be recognized for temporary differences in accordance with the requirements of this section at the date that a nontaxable enterprise becomes a taxable enterprise. A deferred tax liability or asset shall be eliminated at the date an enterprise ceases to be a taxable enterprise. In either case, the effect of (a) an election for a voluntary change in tax status is recognized on the approval date or on the filing date if approval is not necessary and (b) a change in tax status that results from a change in tax law is recognized on the enactment date. The effect of recognizing or eliminating the deferred tax liability or asset shall be included in income from continuing operations. [FAS109, ¶28]

Regulated Enterprises

.128 Regulated enterprises that meet the criteria for application of Section Re6, "Regulated Operations," are not exempt from the requirements of this section. Specifically, this section:

a. Prohibits net-of-tax accounting and reporting
b. Requires recognition of a deferred tax liability (1) for tax benefits that are flowed through to customers when temporary differences originate and (2) for the equity component of the allowance for funds used during construction
c. Requires adjustment of a deferred tax liability or asset for an enacted change in tax laws or rates.

[[10]There are] tax jurisdictions that have [various types of] tax holidays. [FAS109, ¶183] Recognition of a deferred tax asset for *any* tax holiday [is prohibited.] [FAS109, ¶184]

If, as a result of an action by a regulator, it is probable that the future increase or decrease in taxes payable for items (b) and (c) above will be recovered from or returned to customers through future rates, an asset or liability is recognized for that probable future revenue or reduction in future revenue pursuant to paragraphs .119 through .121 of Section Re6. That asset or liability also is a temporary difference for which a deferred tax liability or asset shall be recognized. [FAS109, ¶29]

Business Combinations

.129 A deferred tax liability or asset shall be recognized[11] in accordance with the requirements of this section for differences between the assigned values and the tax bases of the assets and liabilities (except the portion of goodwill for which amortization is not deductible for tax purposes, unallocated [FAS109, ¶30] excess over cost (also referred to as negative goodwill), [FAS141, ¶E15(d)] leveraged leases, and acquired differences under paragraphs .212 through .224[12]) recognized in a purchase business combination (refer to paragraphs .186 through .199 for additional guidance). If a valuation allowance is recognized for the deferred tax asset for an acquired entity's deductible temporary differences or operating loss or tax credit carryforwards at the acquisition date, the tax benefits for those items that are first recognized (that is, by elimination of that valuation allowance) in financial statements after the acquisition date shall be applied (a) first to reduce to zero any goodwill related to the acquisition, (b) second to reduce to zero other noncurrent intangible assets related to the acquisition, and (c) third to reduce income tax expense. [FAS109, ¶30] [Refer to paragraph .1001 for EITF Issues that provide interpretive guidance on this paragraph.]

Temporary Differences under Paragraphs .212 through .224 and U.S. Steamship Enterprise Temporary Differences

.130 A deferred tax liability is not recognized for the following types of temporary differences unless it becomes apparent that those temporary differences will reverse in the foreseeable future:

a. An excess of the amount for financial reporting over the tax basis of an investment in a foreign subsidiary or a foreign corporate joint venture as defined in Section I82, "Investments: Equity Method," that is essentially permanent in duration

[11]Discounting deferred tax assets or liabilities shall be prohibited for temporary differences (except for leveraged leases) related to business combinations as it is for other temporary differences. [FAS109, ¶130] An acquired enterprise's deductible temporary differences and carryforwards are not included in measuring a purchase transaction if the criteria for recognition of tax benefits are not met. Retroactive restatement of the purchase transaction and results of operations for intervening years [is not permitted] if the criteria for recognition of tax benefits are met in subsequent periods. [FAS109, ¶136]

[12]Acquired differences under paragraphs .212 through .224 are accounted for in accordance with the requirements of paragraphs .130 through .133. [FAS109, ¶30, fn8]

b. Undistributed earnings of a domestic subsidiary or a domestic corporate joint venture that is essentially permanent in duration that arose in fiscal years beginning on or before December 15, 1992[13]
c. "Bad debt reserves" for tax purposes of U.S. savings and loan associations (and other "qualified" thrift lenders) that arose in tax years beginning before December 31, 1987 (that is, the base-year amount)
d. "Policyholders' surplus" of stock life insurance companies that arose in fiscal years beginning on or before December 15, 1992.

The indefinite reversal criterion in paragraph .215 shall not be applied to analogous types of temporary differences. [FAS109, ¶31] [Refer to paragraph .1001 for an EITF Issue that provides interpretive guidance on this paragraph.]

.131 A deferred tax liability shall be recognized for the following types of taxable temporary differences:

a. An excess of the amount for financial reporting over the tax basis of an investment in a domestic subsidiary that arises in fiscal years beginning after December 15, 1992
b. An excess of the amount for financial reporting over the tax basis of an investment in a 50-percent-or-less-owned investee except as provided in paragraph .130(a) and (b) for a corporate joint venture that is essentially permanent in duration
c. "Bad debt reserves" for tax purposes of U.S. savings and loan associations (and other "qualified" thrift lenders) that arise in tax years beginning after December 31, 1987 (that is, amounts in excess of the base-year amount).

The tax effects of temporary differences related to deposits in statutory reserve funds by U.S. steamship enterprises that arose in fiscal years beginning on or before December 15, 1992 and that were not previously recognized shall be recognized when those temporary differences reverse or in their entirety at the beginning of the fiscal year for which this section is first applied. [FAS109, ¶32]

.132 Whether an excess of the amount for financial reporting over the tax basis of an investment in a more-than-50-percent-owned domestic subsidiary is a taxable temporary difference must be assessed. It is not a taxable temporary difference if the tax law provides a means by which the reported amount of that investment can be recovered tax-free and the enterprise expects that it will ultimately use that means. For example, under current U.S. federal tax law:

a. An enterprise may elect to determine taxable gain or loss on the liquidation of an 80-percent-or-more-owned subsidiary by reference to the tax basis of the subsid-

[13]A last-in, first-out (LIFO) pattern determines whether reversals pertain to differences that arose in fiscal years beginning on or before December 15, 1992. [FAS109, ¶31, fn9]

iary's net assets rather than by reference to the parent company's tax basis for the stock of that subsidiary.

b. An enterprise may execute a statutory merger whereby a subsidiary is merged into the parent company, the minority shareholders receive stock of the parent, the subsidiary's stock is cancelled, and no taxable gain or loss results if the continuity of ownership, continuity of business enterprise, and certain other requirements of the tax law are met.

Some elections for tax purposes are available only if the parent company owns a specified percentage of the subsidiary's stock. The parent company sometimes may own less than that specified percentage, and the price per share to acquire a minority interest may significantly exceed the per share equivalent of the amount reported as minority interest in the consolidated financial statements. In those circumstances, the excess of the amount for financial reporting over the tax basis of the parent's investment in the subsidiary is not a taxable temporary difference if settlement of the minority interest is expected to occur at the point in time when settlement would not result in a significant cost. That could occur, for example, toward the end of the life of the subsidiary, after it has recovered and settled most of its assets and liabilities, respectively. The fair value of the minority interest ordinarily will approximately equal its percentage of the subsidiary's net assets if those net assets consist primarily of cash. [FAS109, ¶33]

.133 A deferred tax asset shall be recognized for an excess of the tax basis over the amount for financial reporting of an investment in a subsidiary or corporate joint venture that is essentially permanent in duration only if it is apparent that the temporary difference will reverse in the foreseeable future. The need for a valuation allowance for that deferred tax asset and other deferred tax assets related to temporary differences under paragraphs .212 through .224 (for example, a deferred tax asset for foreign tax credit carryforwards or for a savings and loan association's bad-debt reserve for financial reporting) shall be assessed. Paragraph .120 identifies four sources of taxable income to be considered in determining the need for and amount of a valuation allowance for those and other deferred tax assets. One source is future reversals of temporary differences. Future reversals of taxable differences for which a deferred tax liability has not been recognized based on the exceptions cited in paragraph .130, however, shall not be considered. Another source is future taxable income exclusive of reversing temporary differences and carryforwards. Future distributions of future earnings of a subsidiary or corporate joint venture, however, shall not be considered except to the extent that a deferred tax liability has been recognized for existing undistributed earnings or earnings have been remitted in the past. [FAS109, ¶34] [Refer to paragraph .1001 for an EITF Issue that provides interpretive guidance on this paragraph.]

Intraperiod Tax Allocation

.134 Income tax expense or benefit for the year shall be allocated among continuing operations, discontinued operations, extraordinary items, [FAS109, ¶35] other comprehensive income, [FAS130, ¶32(a)] and items charged or credited directly to shareholders' equity (refer to paragraph .135). The amount allocated to continuing operations is the tax effect of the pretax income or loss from continuing operations that occurred during the year, plus or minus income tax effects of (a) changes in circumstances that cause a change in judgment about the realization of deferred tax assets in future years (refer to paragraph .125), (b) changes in tax laws or rates (refer to paragraph .126), (c) changes in tax status (refer to paragraph .127), and (d) tax-deductible dividends paid to shareholders (except as set forth in paragraph .135 for dividends paid on unallocated shares held by an employee stock ownership plan [ESOP] or any other stock compensation arrangement). The remainder is allocated to items other than continuing operations in accordance with the provisions of paragraph .137. [FAS109, ¶35] [Refer to paragraph .1001 for EITF Issues that provide interpretive guidance on this paragraph.]

.135 The tax effects of the following items occurring during the year are charged or credited directly [FAS109, ¶36] to other comprehensive income [as required by Section C49, "Comprehensive Income: Financial Statement Presentation,"] or [FAS130, ¶32(b)] to related components of shareholders' equity:

a. Adjustments of the opening balance of retained earnings for certain changes in accounting principles or a correction of an error
b. **Gains and losses included in comprehensive income but excluded from net income** (for example, translation adjustments under Section F60 and [FAS109, ¶36] changes in the unrealized holding gains and losses of securities classified as available-for-sale under Section I80, "Investments: Debt and Equity Securities") [FAS115, ¶133]
c. An increase or decrease in contributed capital (for example, deductible expenditures reported as a reduction of the proceeds from issuing capital stock)
d. An increase in the tax basis of assets acquired in a taxable business combination accounted for as a pooling of interests[13a] and for which a tax benefit is recognized at the date of the business combination
e. Expenses for employee stock options recognized differently for financial reporting and tax purposes (refer to [FAS109, ¶36] paragraphs .140 through .143 of Section C36, "Compensation: Stock-Based," and [FAS123, ¶390] paragraph .117 of Section C47, "Compensation to Employees: Stock Purchase and Option Plans")
f. Dividends that are paid on unallocated shares held by an ESOP and that are charged to retained earnings

---

[13a]Section B51, "Business Combinations," prohibits the use of the pooling-of-interests method for all business combinations initiated after June 30, 2001. [FAS141, ¶E15(e)]

g. Deductible temporary differences and carryforwards that existed at the date of a quasi reorganization (except as set forth in paragraph .138).

[FAS109, ¶36] [Refer to paragraph .1001 for EITF Issues that provide interpretive guidance on this paragraph and subparagraph (f).]

.136 The tax benefit of an operating loss carryforward or carryback (other than those carryforwards referred to at the end of this paragraph) shall be reported in the same manner as the source of the income or loss in the current year and not in the same manner as (a) the source of the operating loss carryforward or taxes paid in a prior year or (b) the source of expected future income that will result in realization of a deferred tax asset for an operating loss carryforward from the current year. The only exceptions are as follows:

a. Tax effects of deductible temporary differences and carryforwards that existed at the date of a purchase business combination and for which a tax benefit is initially recognized in subsequent years in accordance with the provisions of paragraph .129
b. Tax effects of deductible temporary differences and carryforwards that are allocated to shareholders' equity in accordance with the provisions of paragraph .135 (items (c) and (e) through (g)).

[FAS109, ¶37] [Refer to paragraph .1001 for an EITF Issue that provides interpretive guidance on paragraphs .136 and .137.]

.137 If there is only one item other than continuing operations, the portion of income tax expense or benefit for the year that remains after the allocation to continuing operations is allocated to that item. If there are two or more items other than continuing operations, the amount that remains after the allocation to continuing operations shall be allocated among those other items in proportion to their individual effects on income tax expense or benefit for the year. If there are two or more items other than continuing operations, the sum of the separately calculated, individual effects of each item sometimes may not equal the amount of income tax expense or benefit for the year that remains after the allocation to continuing operations. In those circumstances, the procedures to allocate the remaining amount to items other than continuing operations are as follows:

a. Determine the effect on income tax expense or benefit for the year of the total net loss for all net loss items
b. Apportion the tax benefit determined in (a) ratably to each net loss item
c. Determine the amount that remains, that is, the difference between (1) the amount to be allocated to all items other than continuing operations and (2) the amount allocated to all net loss items
d. Apportion the tax expense determined in (c) ratably to each net gain item.

Refer to paragraphs .200 through .203 for additional guidance. [FAS109, ¶38]

Certain Quasi Reorganizations

.138 The tax benefits of deductible temporary differences and carryforwards as of the date of a quasi reorganization as defined and contemplated in Section Q15, "Quasi Reorganizations," ordinarily are reported as a direct addition to contributed capital if the tax benefits are recognized in subsequent years. The only exception is for enterprises that have previously both adopted [the provisions of] FASB Statement 96, *Accounting for Income Taxes,* and effected a quasi reorganization that involves only the elimination of a deficit in retained earnings by a concurrent reduction in contributed capital prior to adopting [the provisions of] this section. For those enterprises, subsequent recognition of the tax benefit of prior deductible temporary differences and carryforwards is included in income and reported as required by paragraph .136 (without regard to the referenced exceptions) and then reclassified from retained earnings to contributed capital. Those enterprises shall disclose (a) the date of the quasi reorganization, (b) the manner of reporting the tax benefits and that it differs from present accounting requirements for other enterprises, and (c) the effect of those tax benefits on income from continuing operations, income before extraordinary items, and on net income (and on related per share amounts). [FAS109, ¶39]

Separate Financial Statements of a Subsidiary

.139 The consolidated amount of current and deferred tax expense for a group that files a consolidated tax return shall be allocated among the members of the group if those members issue separate financial statements. This section does not require a single allocation method. The method adopted, however, shall be systematic, rational, and consistent with the broad principles established by this section. A method that allocates current and deferred taxes to members of the group by applying this section to each member as if it were a separate taxpayer[14] meets those criteria. Examples of methods that are not consistent with the broad principles established by this section include:

a. A method that allocates only current taxes payable to a member of the group that has taxable temporary differences
b. A method that allocates deferred taxes to a member of the group using a method fundamentally different from the asset and liability method described in this section
c. A method that allocates no current or deferred tax expense to a member of the group that has taxable income because the consolidated group has no current or deferred tax expense.

Certain disclosures are also required (refer to paragraph .147). [FAS109, ¶40]

---

[14] In that situation, the sum of the amounts allocated to individual members of the group may not equal the consolidated amount. That may also be the result if there are intercompany transactions between members of the group. The criteria are satisfied, nevertheless, after giving effect to the type of adjustments (including eliminations) normally present in preparing consolidated financial statements. [FAS109, ¶40, fn10]

Financial Statement Presentation

.140 In a classified statement of financial position, an enterprise shall separate deferred tax liabilities and assets into a current amount and a noncurrent amount. Deferred tax liabilities and assets shall be classified as current or noncurrent based on the classification of the related[15] asset or liability for financial reporting. A deferred tax liability or asset that is not related to an asset or liability for financial reporting (refer to paragraph .114), including deferred tax assets related to carryforwards, shall be classified according to the expected reversal date of the [FAS109, ¶41] specific temporary difference. Such classification disregards any additional temporary differences that may arise and is based on the criteria used for classifying other assets and liabilities. [FAS109, ¶288(p)] [Refer to paragraphs .204 through .211 for illustrations of balance sheet classification.] The valuation allowance for a particular tax jurisdiction shall be allocated between current and noncurrent deferred tax assets for that tax jurisdiction on a pro rata basis. [FAS109, ¶41]

.141 For a particular tax-paying component of an enterprise and within a particular tax jurisdiction, (a) all current deferred tax liabilities and assets shall be offset and presented as a single amount and (b) all noncurrent deferred tax liabilities and assets shall be offset and presented as a single amount. However, an enterprise shall not offset deferred tax liabilities and assets attributable to different tax-paying components of the enterprise or to different tax jurisdictions. [FAS109, ¶42]

Financial Statement Disclosure

.142 The components of the net deferred tax liability or asset recognized in an enterprise's statement of financial position shall be disclosed as follows:

a. The total of all deferred tax liabilities measured in procedure (b) of paragraph .116
b. The total of all deferred tax assets measured in procedures (c) and (d) of paragraph .116
c. The total valuation allowance recognized for deferred tax assets determined in procedure (e) of paragraph .116.

The net change during the year in the total valuation allowance also shall be disclosed. A **public enterprise** shall disclose the approximate tax effect of each type of temporary difference and carryforward that gives rise to a significant portion of deferred tax liabilities and deferred tax assets (before allocation of valuation allowances). A **nonpublic**

[15]A temporary difference is related to an asset or liability if reduction of the asset or liability causes the temporary difference to reverse. As used here, the term *reduction* includes amortization, sale, or other realization of an asset and amortization, payment, or other satisfaction of a liability. [FAS109, ¶288(p)]

enterprise shall disclose the types of significant temporary differences and carryforwards but may omit disclosure of the tax effects of each type. A public enterprise that is not subject to income taxes because its income is taxed directly to its owners shall disclose that fact and the net difference between the tax bases and the reported amounts of the enterprise's assets and liabilities. [FAS109, ¶43]

.143 The following information shall be disclosed whenever a deferred tax liability is not recognized because of the exceptions to comprehensive recognition of deferred taxes for any of the areas addressed by paragraphs .212 through .224 or for deposits in statutory reserve funds by U.S. steamship enterprises:

a. A description of the types of temporary differences for which a deferred tax liability has not been recognized and the types of events that would cause those temporary differences to become taxable
b. The cumulative amount of each type of temporary difference
c. The amount of the unrecognized deferred tax liability for temporary differences related to investments in foreign subsidiaries and foreign corporate joint ventures that are essentially permanent in duration if determination of that liability is practicable or a statement that determination is not practicable
d. The amount of the deferred tax liability for temporary differences other than those in (c) above (that is, undistributed domestic earnings, the bad-debt reserve for tax purposes of a U.S. savings and loan association or other qualified thrift lender, the policyholders' surplus of a life insurance enterprise, and the statutory reserve funds of a U.S. steamship enterprise) that is not recognized in accordance with the provisions of paragraphs .130 and .131.

[FAS109, ¶44]

.144 The significant components of income tax expense attributable to continuing operations for each year presented shall be disclosed in the financial statements or notes thereto. Those components would include, for example:

a. **Current tax expense or benefit**
b. Deferred tax expense or benefit (exclusive of the effects of other components listed below)
c. Investment tax credits
d. Government grants (to the extent recognized as a reduction of income tax expense)
e. The benefits of operating loss carryforwards
f. Tax expense that results from allocating certain tax benefits either directly to contributed capital or to reduce goodwill or other noncurrent intangible assets of an acquired entity

g. Adjustments of a deferred tax liability or asset for enacted changes in tax laws or rates or a change in the tax status of the enterprise
h. Adjustments of the beginning-of-the-year balance of a valuation allowance because of a change in circumstances that causes a change in judgment about the realizability of the related deferred tax asset in future years.

[FAS109, ¶45]

.145 The amount of income tax expense or benefit allocated to continuing operations and the amounts separately allocated to other items (in accordance with the provisions of paragraphs .134 through .138) shall be disclosed for each year for which those items are presented. [FAS109, ¶46]

.146 A public enterprise shall disclose a reconciliation using percentages or dollar amounts of (a) the reported amount of income tax expense attributable to continuing operations for the year to (b) the amount of income tax expense that would result from applying domestic federal statutory tax rates to pretax income from continuing operations. The "statutory" tax rates shall be the regular tax rates if there are alternative tax systems. The estimated amount and the nature of each significant reconciling item shall be disclosed. A nonpublic enterprise shall disclose the nature of significant reconciling items but may omit a numerical reconciliation. If not otherwise evident from the disclosures required by this paragraph and paragraphs .142 through .145, all enterprises shall disclose the nature and effect of any other significant matters affecting comparability of information for all periods presented. [FAS109, ¶47]

.147 An enterprise shall disclose (a) the amounts and expiration dates of operating loss and tax credit carryforwards for tax purposes and (b) any portion of the valuation allowance for deferred tax assets for which subsequently recognized tax benefits will be allocated to reduce goodwill or other noncurrent intangible assets of an acquired entity or directly to contributed capital (refer to paragraphs .129 and .135). [FAS109, ¶48]

.148 An entity that is a member of a group that files a consolidated tax return shall disclose in its separately issued financial statements:

a. The aggregate amount of current and deferred tax expense for each statement of earnings presented and the amount of any tax-related balances due to or from affiliates as of the date of each statement of financial position presented
b. The principal provisions of the method by which the consolidated amount of current and deferred tax expense is allocated to members of the group and the nature and effect of any changes in that method (and in determining related balances to or from affiliates) during the years for which the disclosures in (a) above are presented.

[FAS109, ¶49]

Application of the Standards in Paragraphs .101 Through .148 to Specific Aspects of Accounting for Income Taxes

.149 Paragraphs .150 through .211 provide additional discussion and examples[16] that illustrate application of the standards [in paragraphs .101 through .148] to specific aspects of accounting for income taxes. [FAS109, ¶223]

CONTENTS

[16]The discussion and examples in paragraphs .150 through .203 assume that the tax law requires offsetting net deductions in a particular year against net taxable amounts in the 3 preceding years and then in the 15 succeeding years. [These] assumptions about the tax law are for illustrative purposes only. The enacted tax law for a particular tax jurisdiction shall be used for recognition and measurement of deferred tax liabilities and assets. [FAS109, ¶223, fn14]

Recognition of Deferred Tax Assets and Deferred Tax Liabilities

.150 A deferred tax liability is recognized for all taxable temporary differences,[17] and a deferred tax asset is recognized for all deductible temporary differences and operating loss and tax credit carryforwards. A valuation allowance is recognized if it is more likely than not that some portion or all of the deferred tax asset will not be realized. [FAS109, ¶224]

.151 Exhibit 151A illustrates recognition of deferred tax assets and liabilities.

Exhibit 151A

Recognition of Deferred Tax Assets and Liabilities

At the end of year 3 (the current year), an enterprise has $2,400 of deductible temporary differences and $1,500 of taxable temporary differences.

A deferred tax liability is recognized at the end of year 3 for the $1,500 of taxable temporary differences, and a deferred tax asset is recognized for the $2,400 of deductible temporary differences. All available evidence, both positive and negative, is considered to determine whether, based on the weight of that evidence, a valuation allowance is needed for some portion or all of the deferred tax asset. If evidence about one or more sources of taxable income (refer to paragraph .120) is sufficient to support a conclusion that a valuation allowance is not needed, other sources of taxable income need not be considered. For example, if the weight of available evidence indicates that taxable income will exceed $2,400 in each future year, a conclusion that no valuation allowance is needed can be reached without considering the pattern and timing of the reversal of the temporary differences, the existence of qualifying tax-planning strategies, and so forth.

Similarly, if the deductible temporary differences will reverse within the next 3 years and taxable income in the current year exceeds $2,400, nothing needs to be known about future taxable income exclusive of reversing temporary differences because the deferred tax asset could be realized by carryback to the current year. A valuation allowance is needed, however, if the weight of available evidence indicates that some portion or all of the $2,400 of tax deductions from future reversals of the deductible temporary differences will not be realized by offsetting:

a. The $1,500 of taxable temporary differences and $900 of future taxable income exclusive of reversing temporary differences

[17] Refer to paragraph .108. [FAS109, ¶224, fn15]

Exhibit 151A (continued)

b. $2,400 of future taxable income exclusive of reversing temporary differences
c. $2,400 of taxable income in the current or prior years by loss carryback to those years
d. $2,400 of taxable income in one or more of the circumstances described above and as a result of a qualifying tax-planning strategy (refer to paragraphs .173 through .178).

To the extent that evidence about one or more sources of taxable income is sufficient to eliminate any need for a valuation allowance, other sources need not be considered. Detailed forecasts, projections, or other types of analyses[18] are unnecessary if expected future taxable income is more than sufficient to realize a tax benefit. Detailed analyses are not necessary, for example, if the enterprise earned $500 of taxable income in each of years 1 through 3 and there is no evidence to suggest it will not continue to earn that level of taxable income in future years. That level of future taxable income is more than sufficient to realize the tax benefit of $2,400 of tax deductions over a period of at least 19 years (the year(s) of the deductions, 3 carryback years, and 15 carryforward years) in the U.S. federal tax jurisdiction. [FAS109, ¶225]

.152 Exhibit 152A illustrates recognition of a valuation allowance for a portion of a deferred tax asset in one year and a subsequent change in circumstances that requires adjustment of the valuation allowance at the end of the following year.

Exhibit 152A

Change in a Valuation Allowance

The assumptions are as follows:

a. At the end of the current year (year 3), an enterprise's only temporary differences are deductible temporary differences in the amount of $900.
b. Pretax financial income, taxable income, and taxes paid for each of years 1 through 3 are all positive, but relatively negligible, amounts.
c. The enacted tax rate is 40 percent for all years.

---

[18]The terms *forecast* and *projection* refer to any process by which available evidence is accumulated and evaluated for purposes of estimating whether future taxable income will be sufficient to realize a deferred tax asset. Judgment is necessary to determine how detailed or formalized that evaluation process should be. Furthermore, information about expected future taxable income is necessary only to the extent positive evidence available from other sources (refer to paragraph .120) is not sufficient to support a conclusion that a valuation allowance is not needed. This section does not require either a *financial forecast* or a *financial projection* within the meaning of those terms in the Statements on Standards for Accountants' Services on Prospective Financial Information issued by the Auditing Standards Board of the American Institute of Certified Public Accountants. [FAS109, ¶225, fn16]

Exhibit 152A (continued)

A deferred tax asset in the amount of $360 ($900 at 40 percent) is recognized at the end of year 3. If management concludes, based on an assessment of all available evidence (refer to guidance in paragraphs .119 through .124), that it is more likely than not that future taxable income will not be sufficient to realize a tax benefit for $400 of the $900 of deductible temporary differences at the end of the current year, a $160 valuation allowance ($400 at 40 percent) is recognized at the end of year 3.

Assume that pretax financial income and taxable income for year 4 turn out to be as follows:

Pretax financial loss	$ (50)
Reversing deductible temporary differences	(300)
Loss carryforward for tax purposes	$(350)

The $50 pretax loss in year 4 is additional negative evidence that must be weighed against available positive evidence to determine the amount of valuation allowance necessary at the end of year 4. Deductible temporary differences and carryforwards at the end of year 4 are as follows:

Loss carryforward from year 4 for tax purposes (refer to the above)	$350
Unreversed deductible temporary differences ($900 – $300)	600
	$950

The $360 deferred tax asset recognized at the end of year 3 is increased to $380 ($950 at 40 percent) at the end of year 4. Based on an assessment of all evidence available at the end of year 4, management concludes that it is more likely than not that $240 of the deferred tax asset will not be realized and, therefore, that a $240 valuation allowance is necessary. The $160 valuation allowance recognized at the end of year 3 is increased to $240 at the end of year 4. The $60 net effect of those 2 adjustments (the $80 increase in the valuation allowance less the $20 increase in the deferred tax asset) results in $60 of deferred tax expense that is recognized in year 4. [FAS109, ¶226]

Offset of Taxable and Deductible Amounts

.153 The tax law determines whether future reversals of temporary differences will result in taxable and deductible amounts that offset each other in future years. The tax law also determines the extent to which deductible temporary differences and carryforwards will offset the tax consequences of income that is expected to be earned in future years.

For example, the tax law may provide that capital losses are deductible only to the extent of capital gains. In that case, a tax benefit is not recognized for temporary differences that will result in future deductions in the form of capital losses unless those deductions will offset either (a) other existing temporary differences that will result in future capital gains, (b) capital gains that are expected to occur in future years, or (c) capital gains of the current year or prior years if carryback (of those capital loss deductions from the future reversal years) is expected. [FAS109, ¶227]

Pattern of Taxable or Deductible Amounts

.154 The particular years in which temporary differences result in taxable or deductible amounts generally are determined by the timing of the recovery of the related asset or settlement of the related liability. However, there are exceptions to that general rule. For example, a temporary difference between the tax basis and the reported amount of inventory for which cost is determined on a LIFO basis does not reverse when present inventory is sold in future years if it is replaced by purchases or production of inventory in those same future years. A LIFO inventory temporary difference becomes taxable or deductible in the future year that inventory is liquidated and not replaced. [FAS109, ¶228]

.155 For some assets or liabilities, temporary differences may accumulate over several years and then reverse over several years. That pattern is common for depreciable assets. Future originating differences for existing depreciable assets and their subsequent reversals are a factor to be considered when assessing the likelihood of future taxable income (refer to paragraph .120(b)) for realization of a tax benefit for existing deductible temporary differences and carryforwards. [FAS109, ¶229]

Change in Deferred Foreign Tax Assets and Liabilities

.156 When the reporting currency (not the foreign currency) is the functional currency, remeasurement of an enterprise's deferred foreign tax liability or asset after a change in the exchange rate will result in a transaction gain or loss that is recognized currently in determining net income. Section F60 requires disclosure of the aggregate transaction gain or loss included in determining net income but does not specify how to display that transaction gain or loss or its components for financial reporting. Accordingly, a transaction gain or loss that results from remeasuring a deferred foreign tax liability or asset may be included in the reported amount of deferred tax benefit or expense if that presentation is considered to be more useful. If reported in that manner, that transaction gain or loss is still included in the aggregate transaction gain or loss for the period to be disclosed as required by Section F60. [FAS109, ¶230]

Special Deductions

.157 The tax benefit of statutory depletion [, as described in paragraph .141 of Section Oi5, "Oil and Gas Producing Activities,"] and other types of special deductions such as those for Blue Cross-Blue Shield and small life insurance companies in future years shall not be anticipated for purposes of offsetting a deferred tax liability for taxable temporary differences at the end of the current year. [FAS109, ¶231]

.158 As required above, the tax benefit of special deductions ordinarily is recognized no earlier than the year in which those special deductions are deductible on the tax return. However, some portion of the future tax effects of special deductions are implicitly recognized in determining (a) the average graduated tax rate to be used for measuring deferred taxes when graduated tax rates are a significant factor and (b) the need for a valuation allowance for deferred tax assets. In those circumstances, implicit recognition is unavoidable because (1) those special deductions are one of the determinants of future taxable income and (2) future taxable income determines the average graduated tax rate and sometimes determines the need for a valuation allowance. [FAS109, ¶232]

The Incremental Effect of Future Losses

.159 The tax consequences of tax losses expected in future years [shall not] be anticipated for purposes of:

a. Nonrecognition of a deferred tax liability for taxable temporary differences if there will be no future sacrifice because of future tax losses that otherwise would expire unused
b. Recognition of a deferred tax asset for the carryback refund of taxes paid for the current or a prior year because of future tax losses that otherwise would expire unused.

[FAS109, ¶185]

Measurement of Deferred Tax Liabilities and Assets

.160 The tax rate that is used to measure deferred tax liabilities and deferred tax assets is the enacted tax rate(s) expected to apply to taxable income in the years that the liability is expected to be settled or the asset recovered. Measurements are based on elections (for example, an election for loss carryforward instead of carryback) that are expected to be made for tax purposes in future years. Presently enacted changes in tax laws and rates that become effective for a particular future year or years must be considered when determining the tax rate to apply to temporary differences reversing in that year or years. Tax laws and rates for the current year are used if no changes have been enacted for future years. An asset for deductible temporary differences that are expected to be realized in future years through carryback of a future loss to the current or a prior year (or a liability for taxable temporary differences that are expected to reduce the refund claimed for the carryback of a future loss to the current or a prior year) is measured using tax laws and rates for the current or a prior year, that is, the year for which a refund is expected to be realized based on loss carryback provisions of the tax law. [FAS109, ¶233]

.161 Exhibit 161A illustrates determination of the tax rate for measurement of a deferred tax liability for taxable temporary differences when there is a phased-in change in tax rates.

Exhibit 161A

Determination of the Tax Rate for Measurement of a Deferred Tax Liability with a Phased-in Change in Tax Rates

At the end of year 3 (the current year), an enterprise has $2,400 of taxable temporary differences, which are expected to result in taxable amounts of approximately $800 on the future tax returns for each of years 4 through 6. Enacted tax rates are 35 percent for years 1 through 3, 40 percent for years 4 through 6, and 45 percent for year 7 and thereafter.

The tax rate that is used to measure the deferred tax liability for the $2,400 of taxable temporary differences differs depending on whether the tax effect of future reversals of those temporary differences is on taxes payable for years 1 through 3, years 4 through 6, or year 7 and thereafter. The tax rate for measurement of the deferred tax liability is 40 percent whenever taxable income is expected in years 4 through 6. If tax losses are expected in years 4 through 6, however, the tax rate is:

a. 35 percent if realization of a tax benefit for those tax losses in years 4 through 6 will be by loss carryback to years 1 through 3
b. 45 percent if realization of a tax benefit for those tax losses in years 4 through 6 will be by loss carryforward to year 7 and thereafter.

[FAS109, ¶234]

.162 Exhibit 162A illustrates determination of the tax rate for measurement of a deferred tax asset for deductible temporary differences when there is a change in tax rates.

Exhibit 162A

Determination of the Tax Rate for Measurement of a Deferred Tax Asset When There Is a Change in Tax Rates

The assumptions are as follows:

a. Enacted tax rates are 30 percent for years 1 through 3 and 40 percent for year 4 and thereafter.
b. At the end of year 3 (the current year), an enterprise has $900 of deductible temporary differences, which are expected to result in tax deductions of approximately $300 on the future tax returns for each of years 4 through 6.

The tax rate is 40 percent if the enterprise expects to realize a tax benefit for the deductible temporary differences by offsetting taxable income earned in future years. Alternatively, the tax rate is 30 percent if the enterprise expects to realize a tax benefit for the deductible temporary differences by loss carryback refund.

Assume that (a) the enterprise recognizes a $360 ($900 at 40 percent) deferred tax asset to be realized by offsetting taxable income in future years and (b) taxable income and taxes payable in each of years 1 through 3 were $300 and $90, respectively. Realization of a tax benefit of at least $270 ($900 at 30 percent) is assured because carryback refunds totalling $270 may be realized even if no taxable income is earned in future years. Recognition of a valuation allowance for the other $90 ($360 - $270) of the deferred tax asset depends on management's assessment of whether, based on the weight of available evidence, a portion or all of the tax benefit of the $900 of deductible temporary differences will not be realized at 40 percent tax rates in future years.

Alternatively, if enacted tax rates are 40 percent for years 1 through 3 and 30 percent for year 4 and thereafter, measurement of the deferred tax asset at a 40 percent tax rate could only occur if tax losses are expected in future years 4 through 6. [FAS109, ¶235]

.163 Exhibit 163A illustrates determination of the average graduated tax rate for measurement of deferred tax liabilities and assets by an enterprise for which graduated tax rates ordinarily are a significant factor.

Exhibit 163A

Determination of the Average Graduated Tax Rate for Measurement of Deferred Tax Liabilities and Assets

At the end of year 3 (the current year), an enterprise has $1,500 of taxable temporary differences and $900 of deductible temporary differences, which are expected to result in net taxable amounts of approximately $200 on the future tax returns for each of years 4 through 6. Enacted tax rates are 15 percent for the first $500 of taxable income, 25 percent for the next $500, and 40 percent for taxable income over $1,000. This example assumes that there is no income (for example, capital gains) subject to special tax rates.

The deferred tax liability and asset for those reversing taxable and deductible temporary differences in years 4 through 6 are measured using the average graduated tax rate for the estimated amount of annual taxable income in future years. Thus, the average graduated tax rate will differ depending on the expected level of annual taxable income (including reversing temporary differences) in years 4 through 6. The average tax rate will be:

a. 15 percent if the estimated annual level of taxable income in years 4 through 6 is $500 or less
b. 20 percent if the estimated annual level of taxable income in years 4 through 6 is $1,000
c. 30 percent if the estimated annual level of taxable income in years 4 through 6 is $2,000.

Temporary differences usually do not reverse in equal annual amounts as in the example above, and a different average graduated tax rate might apply to reversals in different future years. However, a detailed analysis to determine the net reversals of temporary differences in each future year usually is not warranted. It is not warranted because the other variable (that is, taxable income or losses exclusive of reversing temporary differences in each of those future years) for determination of the average graduated tax rate in each future year is no more than an estimate. For that reason, an aggregate calculation using a single estimated average graduated tax rate based on estimated average annual taxable income in future years is sufficient. Judgment is permitted, however, to deal with unusual situations, for example, an abnormally large temporary difference that will re-

Exhibit 163A (continued)

verse in a single future year, or an abnormal level of taxable income that is expected for a single future year. The lowest graduated tax rate shall be used whenever the estimated average graduated tax rate otherwise would be zero. [FAS109, ¶236]

.164 Deferred tax liabilities and assets are measured using enacted tax rates applicable to capital gains, ordinary income, and so forth, based on the expected type of taxable or deductible amounts in future years. For example, evidence based on all facts and circumstances should determine whether an investor's liability for the tax consequences of temporary differences related to its equity in the earnings of an investee should be measured using enacted tax rates applicable to a capital gain or a dividend. Computation of a deferred tax liability for undistributed earnings based on dividends shall also reflect any related dividends received deductions or foreign tax credits, and taxes that would be withheld from the dividend. [FAS109, ¶237]

Alternative Minimum Tax

.165 Temporary differences such as depreciation differences are one reason why [tentative minimum tax] (TMT) may exceed regular tax. Temporary differences, however, ultimately reverse and, absent a significant amount of preference items, total taxes paid over the entire life of the enterprise will be based on the regular tax system. Preference items are another reason why TMT may exceed regular tax. If preference items are large enough, an enterprise could be subject, over its lifetime, to the AMT system; and the cumulative amount of AMT credit carryforwards would expire unused. No one can know beforehand which scenario will prevail because that determination can only be made after the fact. In the meantime, this section requires procedures that provide a practical solution to that problem. [FAS109, ¶238]

.166 Under the requirements of this section, an enterprise shall:

a. Measure the total deferred tax liability and asset for regular tax temporary differences and carryforwards using the regular tax rate
b. Measure the total deferred tax asset for all AMT credit carryforward
c. Reduce the deferred tax asset for AMT credit carryforward by a valuation allowance if, based on the weight of available evidence, it is more likely than not that some portion or all of that deferred tax asset will not be realized.

Paragraph .120 identifies four sources of taxable income that shall be considered in determining the need for and amount of a valuation allowance. No valuation allowance is necessary if the deferred tax asset for AMT credit carryforward can be realized:

1. Under paragraph .120(a), by reducing a deferred tax liability from the amount of regular tax on regular tax temporary differences to not less than the amount of TMT on AMT temporary differences
2. Under paragraph .120(b), by reducing taxes on future income from the amount of regular tax on regular taxable income to not less than the amount of TMT on AMT income
3. Under paragraph .120(c), by loss carryback
4. Under paragraph .120(d), by a tax-planning strategy such as switching from tax-exempt to taxable interest income.

[FAS109, ¶239]

Operating Loss and Tax Credit Carryforwards and Carrybacks

Recognition of a Tax Benefit for Carrybacks

.167 An operating loss, certain deductible items that are subject to limitations, and some tax credits arising but not utilized in the current year may be carried back for refund of taxes paid in prior years or carried forward to reduce taxes payable in future years. A receivable is recognized for the amount of taxes paid in prior years that is refundable by carryback of an operating loss or unused tax credits of the current year. [FAS109, ¶240]

Recognition of a Tax Benefit for Carryforwards

.168 A deferred tax asset is recognized for an operating loss or tax credit carryforward.[19] In assessing the need for a valuation allowance, provisions in the tax law that limit utilization of an operating loss or tax credit carryforward are applied in determining whether it is more likely than not that some portion or all of the deferred tax asset will not be realized by reduction of taxes payable on taxable income during the carryforward period. [FAS109, ¶241]

.169 Exhibit 169A illustrates recognition of the tax benefit of an operating loss in the loss year and in subsequent carryforward years when a valuation allowance is necessary in the loss year.

---

[19]This requirement pertains to all ITC carryforwards regardless of whether the flow-through or deferral method is used to account for ITC. [FAS109, ¶241, fn17]

Exhibit 169A

Recognition of the Tax Benefit of an Operating Loss When a Valuation Allowance Is Necessary in the Loss Year

The assumptions are as follows:

a. The enacted tax rate is 40 percent for all years.
b. An operating loss occurs in year 5.
c. The only difference between financial and taxable income results from use of accelerated depreciation for tax purposes. Differences that arise between the reported amount and the tax basis of depreciable assets in years 1 through 7 will result in taxable amounts before the end of the loss carryforward period from year 5.
d. Financial income, taxable income, and taxes currently payable or refundable are as follows:

	Year 1	Years 2-4	Year 5	Year 6	Year 7
Pretax financial income (loss)	$2,000	$ 5,000	$(8,000)	$ 2,200	$ 7,000
Depreciation differences	(800)	(2,200)	(800)	(700)	(600)
Loss carryback	—	—	2,800	—	—
Loss carryforward	—	—	—	(6,000)	(4,500)
Taxable income (loss)	$1,200	$ 2,800	$(6,000)	$(4,500)	$ 1,900
Taxes payable (refundable)	$ 480	$ 1,120	$(1,120)	$ —	$ 760

e. At the end of year 5, profits are not expected in years 6 and 7 and later years, and it is concluded that a valuation allowance is necessary to the extent realization of the deferred tax asset for the operating loss carryforward depends on taxable income (exclusive of reversing temporary differences) in future years.

The deferred tax liability for the taxable temporary differences is calculated at the end of each year as follows:

	Year 1	Years 2-4	Year 5	Year 6	Year 7
Unreversed differences:					
Beginning amount	$ —	$ 800	$3,000	$3,800	$4,500
Additional amount	800	2,200	800	700	600
Total	$800	$3,000	$3,800	$4,500	$5,100
Deferred tax liability (40 percent)	$320	$1,200	$1,520	$1,800	$2,040

Exhibit 169A (continued)

The deferred tax asset and related valuation allowance for the loss carryforward are calculated at the end of each year as follows:

	Year 1	Years 2-4	Year 5	Year 6	Year 7
Loss carryforward for tax purposes	$—	$—	$6,000	$4,500	$—
Deferred tax assset (40 percent)	$—	$—	$2,400	$1,800	$—
Valuation allowance equal to the amount by which the deferred tax asset exceeds the deferred tax liability	—	—	(880)	—	—
Net deferred tax asset	$—	$—	$1,520	$1,800	$—

Total tax expense for each period is as follows:

	Year 1	Years 2-4	Year 5	Year 6	Year 7
Deferred tax expense (benefit)					
Increase in deferred tax liability	$320	$ 880	$ 320	$ 280	$ 240
(Increase) decrease in net deferred tax asset	—	—	(1,520)	(280)	1,800
	320	880	(1,200)	—	2,040
Currently payable (refundable)	480	1,120	(1,120)	—	760
Total tax expense (benefit)	$800	$2,000	$(2,320)	$ —	$2,800

In year 5, $2,800 of the loss is carried back to reduce taxable income in years 2 through 4, and $1,120 of taxes paid for those years is refunded. In addition, a $1,520 deferred tax liability is recognized for $3,800 of taxable temporary differences, and a $2,400 deferred tax asset is recognized for the $6,000 loss carryforward. However, based on the conclusion described in assumption (e), a valuation allowance is recognized for the amount by which that deferred tax asset exceeds the deferred tax liability.

In year 6, a portion of the deferred tax asset for the loss carryforward is realized because taxable income is earned in that year. The remaining balance of the deferred tax asset for the loss carryforward at the end of year 6 equals the deferred tax liability for the taxable temporary differences. A valuation allowance is not needed.

In year 7, the remaining balance of the loss carryforward is realized, and $760 of taxes are payable on net taxable income of $1,900. A $2,040 deferred tax liability is recognized for the $5,100 of taxable temporary differences. [FAS109, ¶242]

.170 An operating loss or tax credit carryforward from a prior year (for which the deferred tax asset was offset by a valuation allowance) may sometimes reduce taxable income and taxes payable that are attributable to certain revenues or gains that the tax law requires be included in taxable income for the year that cash is received. For financial reporting, however, there may have been no revenue or gain and a liability is recognized for the cash received. Future sacrifices to settle the liability will result in deductible amounts in future years. Under those circumstances, the reduction in taxable income and taxes payable from utilization of the operating loss or tax credit carryforward gives no cause for recognition of a tax benefit because, in effect, the operating loss or tax credit carryforward has been replaced by temporary differences that will result in deductible amounts when a nontax liability is settled in future years. The requirements for recognition of a tax benefit for deductible temporary differences and for operating loss carryforwards are the same, and the manner of reporting the eventual tax benefit recognized (that is, in income or as required by paragraph .136) is not affected by the intervening transaction reported for tax purposes. [FAS109, ¶243]

.171 Exhibit 171A illustrates the interaction of loss carryforwards and temporary differences that will result in net deductible amounts in future years.

Exhibit 171A

Interaction of Loss Carryforwards and Temporary Differences That Will Result in Net Deductible Amounts in Future Years

The assumptions are as follows:

a. The financial loss and the loss reported on the tax return for an enterprise's first year of operations are the same.
b. In year 2, a gain of $2,500 from a transaction that is a sale for tax purposes but a sale and leaseback for financial reporting is the only difference between pretax financial income and taxable income.

		Financial Income	Taxable Income
Year 1:	Income (loss) from operations	$(4,000)	$(4,000)
Year 2:	Income (loss) from operations	$ —	$ —
	Taxable gain on sale		2,500
	Taxable income before loss carryforward		2,500
	Loss carryforward from year 1		(4,000)
	Taxable income		$ —

Exhibit 171A (continued)

The $4,000 operating loss carryforward at the end of year 1 is reduced to $1,500 at the end of year 2 because $2,500 of it is used to reduce taxable income. The $2,500 reduction in the loss carryforward becomes $2,500 of deductible temporary differences that will reverse and result in future tax deductions when lease payments are made. The enterprise has no deferred tax liability to be offset by those future tax deductions, the future tax deductions cannot be realized by loss carryback because no taxes have been paid, and the enterprise has had pretax losses for financial reporting since inception. Unless positive evidence exists that is sufficient to overcome the negative evidence associated with those losses, a valuation allowance is recognized at the end of year 2 for the full amount of the deferred tax asset related to the $2,500 of deductible temporary differences and the remaining $1,500 of operating loss carryforward. [FAS109, ¶244]

Reporting the Tax Benefit of Operating Loss Carryforwards or Carrybacks

.172 Except as noted in paragraph .136, the manner of reporting the tax benefit of an operating loss carryforward or carryback is determined by the source of the income or loss in the current year and not by (a) the source of the operating loss carryforward or taxes paid in a prior year or (b) the source of expected future income that will result in realization of a deferred tax asset for an operating loss carryforward from the current year. Deferred tax expense or benefit that results because a change in circumstances causes a change in judgment about the future realization of the tax benefit of an operating loss carryforward is allocated to continuing operations (refer to paragraph .125). Thus, for example:

a. The tax benefit of an operating loss carryforward that resulted from an extraordinary loss in a prior year and that is first recognized in the financial statements for the current year:
   (1) Is allocated to continuing operations if it offsets the current or deferred tax consequences of income from continuing operations
   (2) Is allocated to an extraordinary gain if it offsets the current or deferred tax consequences of that extraordinary gain
   (3) Is allocated to continuing operations if it results from a change in circumstances that causes a change in judgment about future realization of a tax benefit
b. The current or deferred tax benefit of a loss from continuing operations in the current year is allocated to continuing operations regardless of whether that loss offsets the current or deferred tax consequences of an extraordinary gain that:
   (1) Occurred in the current year

(2) Occurred in a prior year (that is, if realization of the tax benefit will be by carryback refund)
(3) Is expected to occur in a future year.

[FAS109, ¶245]

Tax-Planning Strategies

.173 Expectations about future taxable income incorporate numerous assumptions about actions, elections, and strategies to minimize income taxes in future years. For example, an enterprise may have a practice of deferring taxable income whenever possible by structuring sales to qualify as installment sales for tax purposes. Actions such as that are not *tax-planning strategies,* as that term is used in this section, because they are actions that management takes in the normal course of business. For purposes of applying the requirements of this section, a *tax-planning strategy* is an action that management ordinarily might not take but would take, if necessary, to realize a tax benefit for a carryforward before it expires. For example, a strategy to sell property and lease it back for the expressed purpose of generating taxable income to utilize a carryforward before it expires is not an action that management takes in the normal course of business. A qualifying tax-planning strategy is an action that:

a. *Is prudent and feasible.* Management must have the ability to implement the strategy and expect to do so unless the need is eliminated in future years. For example, management would not have to apply the strategy if income earned in a later year uses the entire amount of carryforward from the current year.
b. *An enterprise ordinarily might not take, but would take to prevent an operating loss or tax credit carryforward from expiring unused.* All of the various strategies that are expected to be employed for business or tax purposes other than utilization of carryforwards that would otherwise expire unused are, for purposes of this section, implicit in management's estimate of future taxable income and, therefore, are not tax-planning strategies as that term is used in this section.
c. *Would result in realization of deferred tax assets.* The effect of qualifying tax-planning strategies must be recognized in the determination of the amount of a valuation allowance. Tax-planning strategies need not be considered, however, if positive evidence available from other sources (refer to paragraph .120) is sufficient to support a conclusion that a valuation allowance is *not* necessary.

[FAS109, ¶246]

.174 Tax-planning strategies may shift estimated future taxable income between future years. For example, assume that an enterprise has a $1,500 operating loss carryforward that expires at the end of next year and that its estimate of taxable income exclusive of the future reversal of existing temporary differences and carryforwards is approximately $1,000 per year for each of the next several years. That estimate is based, in part, on the enterprise's present practice of making sales on the installment basis and on provisions in the tax law that result in temporary deferral of gains on installment sales. A tax-planning strategy to increase taxable income next year and realize the full tax benefit of that operating loss carryforward might be to structure next year's sales in a manner that does not meet the tax rules to qualify as installment sales. Another strategy might be to change next year's depreciation procedures for tax purposes. [FAS109, ¶247]

.175 Tax-planning strategies also may shift the estimated pattern and timing of future reversals of temporary differences. For example, if an operating loss carryforward otherwise would expire unused at the end of next year, a tax-planning strategy to sell the enterprise's installment sale receivables next year would accelerate the future reversal of *taxable* temporary differences for the gains on those installment sales. In other circumstances, a tax-planning strategy to accelerate the future reversal of *deductible* temporary differences in time to offset taxable income that is expected in an early future year might be the only means to realize a tax benefit for those deductible temporary differences if they otherwise would reverse and provide no tax benefit in some later future year(s). Examples of actions that would accelerate the future reversal of deductible temporary differences include:

a. An annual payment that is larger than an enterprise's usual annual payment to reduce a long-term pension obligation (recognized as a liability in the financial statements) might accelerate a tax deduction for pension expense to an earlier year than would otherwise have occurred.
b. Disposal of obsolete inventory that is reported at net realizable value in the financial statements would accelerate a tax deduction for the amount by which the tax basis exceeds the net realizable value of the inventory.
c. Sale of loans at their reported amount (that is, net of an allowance for bad debts) would accelerate a tax deduction for the allowance for bad debts.

[FAS109, ¶248]

.176 A significant expense might need to be incurred to implement a particular tax-planning strategy, or a significant loss might need to be recognized as a result of implementing a particular tax-planning strategy. In either case, that expense or loss (net of any future tax benefit that would result from that expense or loss) reduces the amount of tax benefit that is recognized for the expected effect of a qualifying tax-planning strategy. For that purpose, the future effect of a differential in interest rates (for example, between the rate that would be earned on installment sale receivables and the rate that could be earned on an alternative investment if the tax-planning strategy is to sell those receivables to accelerate the future reversal of related taxable temporary differences) is not considered. [FAS109, ¶249]

.177 Exhibit 177A illustrates recognition of a deferred tax asset based on the expected effect of a qualifying tax-planning strategy when a significant expense would be incurred to implement the strategy.

Exhibit 177A

Qualifying Tax-Planning Strategy with Significant Expense to Implement the Strategy

The assumptions are as follows:

a. A $900 operating loss carryforward expires at the end of next year.
b. Based on historical results and the weight of other available evidence, the estimated level of taxable income exclusive of the future reversal of existing temporary differences and the operating loss carryforward next year is $100.
c. Taxable temporary differences in the amount of $1,200 ordinarily would result in taxable amounts of approximately $400 in each of the next 3 years.
d. There is a qualifying tax-planning strategy to accelerate the future reversal of all $1,200 of taxable temporary differences to next year.
e. Estimated legal and other expenses to implement that tax-planning strategy are $150.
f. The enacted tax rate is 40 percent for all years.

Without the tax-planning strategy, only $500 of the $900 operating loss carryforward could be realized next year by offsetting (a) $100 of taxable income exclusive of reversing temporary differences and (b) $400 of reversing taxable temporary differences. The other $400 of operating loss carryforward would expire unused at the end of next year. Therefore, the $360 deferred tax asset ($900 at 40 percent) would be offset by a $160 valuation allowance ($400 at 40 percent), and a $200 net deferred tax asset would be recognized for the operating loss carryforward.

With the tax-planning strategy, the $900 operating loss carryforward could be applied against $1,300 of taxable income next year ($100 of taxable income exclusive of reversing temporary differences and $1,200 of reversing taxable temporary differences). The $360 deferred tax asset is reduced by a $90 valuation allowance recognized for the net-

Exhibit 177A (continued)

of-tax expenses necessary to implement the tax-planning strategy. The amount of that valuation allowance is determined as follows:

Legal and other expenses to implement the tax-planning strategy	$150
Future tax benefit of those legal and other expenses—$150 at 40 percent	60
	$ 90

In summary, a $480 deferred tax liability is recognized for the $1,200 of taxable temporary differences, a $360 deferred tax asset is recognized for the $900 operating loss carryforward, and a $90 valuation allowance is recognized for the net-of-tax expenses of implementing the tax-planning strategy. [FAS109, ¶250]

.178 Under this section, the requirements for consideration of tax-planning strategies pertain only to the determination of a valuation allowance for a deferred tax asset. A deferred tax liability ordinarily is recognized for all taxable temporary differences. The only exceptions are identified in paragraph .108. Certain seemingly taxable temporary differences, however, may or may not result in taxable amounts when those differences reverse in future years. One example is an excess of cash surrender value of life insurance over premiums paid (paragraph .113). Another example is an excess of the book over the tax basis of an investment in a domestic subsidiary (paragraph .132). The determination of whether those differences are taxable temporary differences does not involve a tax-planning strategy as that term is used in this section. [FAS109, ¶251]

Regulated Enterprises

.179 [The provisions of] paragraph .119 of Section Re6 require a regulated enterprise that applies Section Re6 to capitalize an incurred cost that would otherwise be charged to expense if the following criteria are met:

a. It is probable that future revenue in an amount at least equal to the capitalized cost will result from inclusion of that cost in allowable costs for rate-making purposes.
b. Based on available evidence, the future revenue will be provided to permit recovery of the previously incurred cost rather than to provide for expected levels of similar future costs.

If the income taxes that result from recording a deferred tax liability in accordance with this section meet those criteria, an asset is recognized for those income taxes when the deferred tax liability is recognized. That asset and the deferred tax liability are not offset for general-purpose financial reporting; rather, each is displayed separately. [FAS109, ¶252]

.180 Exhibit 180A illustrates recognition of an asset for the probable future revenue to recover future income taxes related to the deferred tax liability for the equity component of the allowance for funds used during construction (AFUDC).

Exhibit 180A

Regulated Enterprises—Equity Component of AFUDC

The assumptions are as follows:

a. During year 1, the first year of operations, total construction costs for financial reporting and tax purposes are $400,000 (exclusive of AFUDC).
b. The enacted tax rate is 34 percent for all future years.
c. AFUDC (consisting entirely of the equity component) is $26,000. The asset for probable future revenue to recover the related income taxes is calculated as follows:

   34 percent of ($26,000 + A) = A (where A equals the asset for probable future revenue)

   A = $13,394

At the end of year 1, the related accounts[20] are as follows:

Construction in progress	$426,000
Probable future revenue	$ 13,394
Deferred tax liability [34 percent of ($26,000 + $13,394)]	$ 13,394

[FAS109, ¶253]

[20]In this example, if AFUDC had consisted entirely of a net-of-tax debt component in the amount of $26,000, the related accounts and their balances at the end of year 1 would be construction in progress in the amount of $439,394 and a deferred tax liability in the amount of $13,394. [FAS109, ¶253, fn18]

.181 Exhibit 181A illustrates adjustment of a deferred tax liability for an enacted change in tax rates.

Exhibit 181A

Regulated Enterprises—Enacted Change in Tax Rates

The assumptions are the same as for the example in Exhibit 180A except that a change in the tax rate from 34 percent to 30 percent is enacted on the first day of year 2. As of the first day of year 2, the related accounts are adjusted so that the balances are as follows:

Construction in progress	$426,000
Probable future revenue	$ 11,143
Deferred tax liability [30 percent of ($26,000 + $11,143)]	$ 11,143

[FAS109, ¶254]

.182 Exhibit 182A illustrates adjustment of a deferred tax liability for an enacted change in tax rates when that deferred tax liability represents amounts already collected from customers for the future payment of income taxes. In that case, there would be no asset for "probable future revenue."

Exhibit 182A

Regulated Enterprises—Enacted Change in Tax Rates with Refund to Customers of Previously Collected Income Taxes

The assumptions are as follows:

a. Amounts at the end of year 1, the current year, are as follows:

Construction in progress for financial reporting	$400,000
Tax basis of construction in progress	$300,000
Deferred tax liability (34 percent of $100,000)	$ 34,000

b. A change in the tax rate from 34 percent to 30 percent is enacted on the first day of year 2. As a result of the reduction in tax rates, it is probable that $4,000 of the $34,000 (previously collected from customers for the future payment of income taxes) will be refunded to customers, together with the tax benefit of that refund, through a future

Exhibit 182A (continued)

rate reduction. The liability for the future rate reduction to refund a portion of the deferred taxes previously collected from customers is calculated as follows:

$4,000 + (30 percent of R) = R (where R equals the probable future reduction in revenue)

R = $5,714

As of the first day of year 2, the related accounts are adjusted so that the balances are as follows:

Construction in progress	$400,000
Probable reduction in future revenue	$ 5,714
Deferred tax liability [30 percent of ($100,000 - $5,714)]	$ 28,286

[FAS109, ¶255]

Leveraged Leases

.183 This section does not change (a) the pattern of recognition of after-tax income for leveraged leases as required by paragraph .141 in Section L10 or (b) the allocation of the purchase price in a purchase business combination to acquired leveraged leases as required by that section. Integration[21] of the results of income tax accounting for leveraged leases with the other results of accounting for income taxes under this section is required when deferred tax credits related to leveraged leases are the only source (refer to paragraph .120) for recognition of a tax benefit for deductible temporary differences and carryforwards not related to leveraged leases. A valuation allowance is not necessary if deductible temporary differences and carryforwards will offset taxable amounts

---

[21]Integration is an issue when all of the following exist:

(1) The accounting for a leveraged lease requires recognition of deferred tax credits.
(2) The requirements of this section limit the recognition of a tax benefit for deductible temporary differences and carryforwards not related to the leveraged lease.
(3) Unrecognized tax benefits could offset taxable amounts that result from future recovery of the net investment in the leveraged lease.

In those circumstances, integration should be required. However, integration should not override any results that are unique to income tax accounting for leveraged leases, for example, the manner of recognizing the tax effect of an enacted change in tax rates. [FAS109, ¶126]

from future recovery of the net investment in the leveraged lease. However, to the extent that the amount of deferred tax credits for a leveraged lease as determined under Section L10 differs from the amount of the deferred tax liability related to the leveraged lease that would otherwise result from applying the requirements of this section, that difference is preserved and is not a source of taxable income for recognition of the tax benefit of deductible temporary differences and operating loss or tax credit carryforwards. [FAS109, ¶256]

.184 Paragraph .141 of Section L10 requires that the tax effect of any difference between the assigned value and the tax basis of a leveraged lease at the date of a business combination not be accounted for as a deferred tax credit. This section does not change that requirement. Any tax effects included in unearned and deferred income as required by Section L10 are not offset by the deferred tax consequences of other temporary differences or by the tax benefit of operating loss or tax credit carryforwards. However, deferred tax credits that arise after the date of a business combination are accounted for in the same manner as described above for leveraged leases that were not acquired in a purchase business combination. [FAS109, ¶257]

.185 Exhibit 185A illustrates integration of the results of income tax accounting for leveraged leases with the other results of accounting for income taxes as required by this section.

Exhibit 185A

Integration of the Results of Income Tax Accounting for Leveraged Leases with Other Results of Accounting for Income Taxes

a. At the end of year 1, the current year, an enterprise has two temporary differences. One temporary difference is for a leveraged lease that was entered into in a prior year. During year 1, the enacted tax rate for year 2 and thereafter changed from 40 percent to 35 percent. After adjusting for the change in estimated total net income from the lease as a result of the change in tax rates as required by Section L10, the components of the investment in the leveraged lease at the end of year 1 are as follows:

Net rentals receivable plus residual value less unearned pretax income		$150,000
Reduced by:		
Deferred ITC	$ 9,000	
Deferred tax credits	39,000	48,000
Net investment in leveraged lease for financial reporting		$102,000

Exhibit 185A (continued)

b. The other temporary difference is for a $120,000 estimated liability for warranty expense that will result in a tax deduction in year 5 when the liability is expected to be paid. Absent consideration of the deferred tax credits attributable to the leveraged lease, the weight of available evidence indicates that a valuation allowance is needed for the entire amount of the deferred tax asset related to that $120,000 deductible temporary difference.

c. The tax basis of the investment in the leveraged lease at the end of year 1 is $41,000. The amount of the deferred tax liability for that leveraged lease that would otherwise result from the requirements of this section is determined as follows:

Net rentals receivable plus residual value less unearned pretax income	$150,000
Temporary difference for deferred ITC	9,000
	141,000
Tax basis of leveraged lease	41,000
Temporary difference	$100,000
Deferred tax liability (35 percent)	$ 35,000

d. Loss carryback (to year 2) and loss carryforward (to year 20) of the $120,000 tax deduction for warranty expense in year 5 would offset the $100,000 of taxable amounts resulting from future recovery of the net investment in the leveraged lease over the remainder of the lease term.

e. At the end of year 1, the enterprise recognizes a $42,000 ($120,000 at 35 percent) deferred tax asset and a related $7,000 valuation allowance. The effect is to recognize a $35,000 net deferred tax benefit for the reduction in deferred tax credits attributable to the leveraged lease. Deferred tax credits attributable to the leveraged lease determined under the requirements of Section L10 are $39,000. However, the deferred tax liability determined under the requirements of this section is only $35,000. The $4,000 difference is not available for offsetting.

[FAS109, ¶258]

Business Combinations

.186 This section requires recognition of deferred tax liabilities and deferred tax assets (and related valuation allowances, if necessary) for the deferred tax consequences of differences between the assigned values and the tax bases of the assets and liabilities recognized in a business combination. A deferred tax liability or asset is not recognized for a difference between the reported amount and the tax basis of goodwill or the portion thereof for which amortization is not deductible for tax purposes (refer to paragraphs .189 and .190), unallocated "negative" goodwill, and leveraged leases (refer to paragraphs .183 through .185). Acquired differences under paragraphs .212 through .224 are accounted for in accordance with the requirements of paragraphs .130 through .133. [FAS109, ¶259]

Nontaxable Business Combinations

.187 Exhibit 187A illustrates recognition and measurement of a deferred tax liability and asset in a nontaxable business combination.

Exhibit 187A

Deferred Tax Liability and Asset in a Nontaxable Business Combination

The assumptions are as follows:

a. The enacted tax rate is 40 percent for all future years, and amortization of goodwill is not deductible for tax purposes.
b. An enterprise is acquired for $20,000, and the enterprise has no leveraged leases.
c. The tax basis of the net assets acquired is $5,000, and the assigned value (other than goodwill) is $12,000. Future recovery of the assets and settlement of the liabilities at their assigned values will result in $20,000 of taxable amounts and $13,000 of deductible amounts that can be offset against each other. Therefore, no valuation allowance is necessary.

The amounts recorded to account for the purchase transaction are as follows:

Assigned value of the net assets (other than goodwill) acquired	$12,000
Deferred tax liability for $20,000 of taxable temporary differences	(8,000)
Deferred tax asset for $13,000 of deductible temporary differences	5,200
Goodwill	10,800
Purchase price of the acquired enterprise	$20,000

[FAS109, ¶260]

Taxable Business Combinations

.188 In a taxable business combination, the purchase price is assigned to the assets and liabilities recognized for tax purposes as well as for financial reporting. However, the amounts assigned to particular assets and liabilities may differ for financial reporting and tax purposes. A deferred tax liability and asset are recognized for the deferred tax consequences of those temporary differences in accordance with the recognition and measurement requirements of this section. For example, a portion of the amount of goodwill for financial reporting may be allocated to some other asset for tax purposes, and amortization of that other asset may be deductible for tax purposes. If a valuation allowance is recognized for that deferred tax asset at the acquisition date, recognized benefits for those tax deductions after the acquisition date shall be applied (a) first to reduce to zero any goodwill related to that acquisition, (b) second to reduce to zero other noncurrent intangible assets related to that acquisition, and (c) third to reduce income tax expense. [FAS109, ¶261]

.189 Amortization of goodwill is deductible for tax purposes in some tax jurisdictions. In those tax jurisdictions, the reported amount of goodwill and the tax basis of goodwill are each separated into two components as of the combination date for purposes of deferred tax calculations. The first component of each equals the lesser of (a) goodwill for financial reporting or (b) tax-deductible goodwill. The second component of each equals the remainder of each, that is, (1) the remainder, if any, of goodwill for financial reporting or (2) the remainder, if any, of tax-deductible goodwill. Any difference that arises between the book and tax basis of that first component of goodwill in future years is a temporary difference for which a deferred tax liability or asset is recognized based on the requirements of this section. No deferred taxes are recognized for the second component of goodwill. If that second component is an excess of tax-deductible goodwill over the reported amount of goodwill, the tax benefit for that excess is recognized when realized on the tax return, and that tax benefit is applied first to reduce to zero the goodwill related to that acquisition, second to reduce to zero other noncurrent intangible assets related to that acquisition, and third to reduce income tax expense. [FAS109, ¶262]

.190 Exhibit 190A illustrates accounting for the tax consequences of goodwill when amortization of goodwill is deductible for tax purposes.

Exhibit 190A

Accounting for Tax Consequences of Tax-Deductible Goodwill

The assumptions are as follows:

a. At the combination date, the reported amount and tax basis of goodwill are $600 and $800, respectively.
b. For tax purposes, amortization of goodwill will result in tax deductions of $400 in each of years 1 and 2. Those deductions result in a current tax benefit in years 1 and 2.
c. For financial reporting, amortization of goodwill is straight-line over years 1 through 4.
d. For purposes of simplification, the consequences of other temporary differences are ignored for years 1 through 4.
e. Income before amortization of goodwill and income taxes in each of years 1 through 4 is $1,000.
f. The tax rate is 40 percent for all years.

Income taxes payable for years 1 through 4 are:

	Year			
	1	**2**	**3**	**4**
Income before amortization of goodwill	$1,000	$1,000	$1,000	$1,000
Amortization of goodwill	400	400	—	—
Taxable income	$ 600	$ 600	$1,000	$1,000
Income taxes payable (40 percent)	$ 240	$ 240	$ 400	$ 400

At the combination date, goodwill is separated into two components as follows:

	Reported Amount	**Tax Basis**
First component	$600	$600
Second component	—	200
Total goodwill	$600	$800

A deferred tax liability is recognized at the end of years 1 through 3 for the excess of the reported amount over the tax basis of the first component of goodwill. A deferred tax asset is not recognized for the second component of goodwill; the tax benefit is allocated to reduce goodwill when realized on the tax returns for years 1 and 2.

Exhibit 190A (continued)

The second component of goodwill is deductible $100 per year in years 1 and 2. Those tax deductions provide $40 ($100 at 40 percent) of tax benefits that are realized in years 1 and 2. Allocation of those realized tax benefits to reduce the first component of goodwill produces a deferred tax benefit by reducing the taxable temporary difference related to that component of goodwill. Thus, the total tax benefit allocated to reduce the first component of goodwill in each of years 1 and 2 is the sum of (a) the $40 realized tax benefit allocated to reduce goodwill and (b) the deferred tax benefit from reducing the deferred tax liability related to goodwill. That total tax benefit (TTB) is determined as follows:

TTB = realized tax benefit plus (tax rate times TTB)
TTB = $40 + (.40 × TTB)
TTB = $67

Goodwill for financial reporting for years 1 through 4 is:

	Year			
	1	2	3	4
Balance at beginning of year	$600	$383	$188	$94
Amortization:				
$600 ÷ 4 years	150			
$383 ÷ 3 years		128		
$188 ÷ 2 years			94	94
Total tax benefit allocated to reduce goodwill	67	67	—	—
Balance at end of year	$383	$188	$ 94	$—

The deferred tax liability for the first component of goodwill and the related amount of deferred tax expense (benefit) for years 1 through 4 are:

	Year			
	1	2	3	4
Reported amount of goodwill at end of year	$383	$188	$ 94	$ —
Tax basis of goodwill (first component)	300	—	—	—
Taxable temporary difference	$ 83	$188	$ 94	$ —
Deferred tax liability:				
At end of year (40 percent)	$ 33	$ 75	$ 38	$ —
At beginning of year	—	33	75	38
Deferred tax expense (benefit) for the year	$ 33	$ 42	$(37)	$(38)

Exhibit 190A (continued)

Income for financial reporting for years 1 through 4 is:

	Year			
	1	**2**	**3**	**4**
Income before amortization of goodwill and income taxes	$1,000	$1,000	$1,000	$1,000
Amortization of goodwill	150	128	94	94
Pretax income	850	872	906	906
Income tax expense (benefit):				
Current	240	240	400	400
Deferred	33	42	(37)	(38)
Benefit applied to reduce goodwill	67	67	—	—
Income tax expense	340	349	363	362
Net income	$ 510	$ 523	$ 543	$ 544

[FAS109, ¶263]

Carryforwards—Purchase Method

.191 Accounting for a business combination shall reflect any provisions in the tax law that restrict the future use of either of the combining enterprises' deductible temporary differences or carryforwards to reduce taxable income or taxes payable attributable to the other enterprise subsequent to the business combination. For example, the tax law may limit the use of the acquired enterprise's deductible temporary differences and carryforwards to subsequent taxable income of the acquired enterprise in a consolidated tax return for the combined enterprise. In that circumstance, or if the acquired enterprise will file a separate tax return, the need for a valuation allowance for some portion or all of the acquired enterprise's deferred tax assets for deductible temporary differences and carryforwards is assessed based on the acquired enterprise's *separate* past and expected future results of operations. [FAS109, ¶264]

.192 Exhibit 192A illustrates (a) recognition of a deferred tax asset and the related valuation allowance for acquired deductible temporary differences at the date of a nontaxable business combination and in subsequent periods when (b) the tax law limits the use of an acquired enterprise's deductible temporary differences and carryforwards to subsequent taxable income of the acquired enterprise in a consolidated tax return.

Exhibit 192A

Recognition of a Deferred Tax Asset and the Related Valuation Allowance in a Nontaxable Business Combination When the Tax Law Limits the Use of Acquired Tax Benefits

The assumptions are as follows:

a. The enacted tax rate is 40 percent for all future years.
b. The purchase price is $20,000, and the assigned value of the net assets acquired is also $20,000.
c. The tax basis of the net assets acquired is $60,000. The $40,000 ($60,000 – $20,000) of deductible temporary differences at the combination date is primarily attributable to an allowance for loan losses. Provisions in the tax law limit the use of those future tax deductions to subsequent taxable income of the acquired enterprise.
d. The acquired enterprise's actual pretax results for the two preceding years and the expected results for the year of the business combination are as follows:

Year 1	$(15,000)
Year 2	(10,000)
Year 3 to the combination date	(5,000)
Expected results for the remainder of year 3	(5,000)

e. Based on assessments of all evidence available at the date of the business combination in year 3 and at the end of year 3, management concludes that a valuation allowance is needed at both dates for the entire amount of the deferred tax asset related to the acquired deductible temporary differences.

The acquired enterprise's pretax financial income and taxable income for year 3 (after the business combination) and year 4 are as follows:

	Year 3	Year 4
Pretax financial income	$ 15,000	$ 10,000
Reversals of acquired deductible temporary differences	(15,000)	(10,000)
Taxable income	$ —	$ —

At the end of year 4, the remaining balance of acquired deductible temporary differences is $15,000 ($40,000 – $25,000). The deferred tax asset is $6,000 ($15,000 at 40 percent). Based on an assessment of all available evidence at the end of year 4, management concludes that no valuation allowance is needed for that $6,000 deferred tax asset. Elimination of the $6,000 valuation allowance results in a $6,000 deferred tax benefit that is reported as a reduction of deferred income tax expense because there is no goodwill or

Exhibit 192A (continued)

other noncurrent intangible assets related to the acquisition. For the same reason, tax benefits realized in years 3 and 4 attributable to reversals of acquired deductible temporary differences are reported as a zero current income tax expense. The consolidated statement of earnings would include the following amounts attributable to the acquired enterprise for year 3 (after the business combination) and year 4:

	Year 3	Year 4
Pretax financial income	$15,000	$10,000
Income tax expense (benefit):		
Current	—	—
Deferred	—	(6,000)
Net income	$15,000	$16,000

[FAS109, ¶265]

.193 The tax law in some tax jurisdictions may permit the future use of either of the combining enterprises' deductible temporary differences or carryforwards to reduce taxable income or taxes payable attributable to the other enterprise subsequent to the business combination. If the combined enterprise expects to file a consolidated tax return, a deferred tax asset (net of a valuation allowance, if necessary) is recognized for deductible temporary differences or carryforwards of either combining enterprise based on an assessment of the *combined* enterprise's past and expected future results of operations as of the acquisition date. This either reduces goodwill or noncurrent assets (except long-term investments in marketable securities) of the acquired enterprise or creates or increases negative goodwill. [FAS109, ¶266]

.194 Exhibit 194A illustrates (a) elimination of the need for a valuation allowance for the deferred tax asset for an acquired loss carryforward based on offset against taxable temporary differences of the acquiring enterprise in a nontaxable business combination when (b) the tax law permits use of an acquired enterprise's deductible temporary differences and carryforwards to reduce taxable income or taxes payable attributable to the acquiring enterprise in a consolidated tax return.

Exhibit 194A

Recognition of an Acquired Loss Carryforward When the Tax Law Permits Acquired Tax Benefits to Be Utilized by the Acquiring Corporation

The assumptions are as follows:

a. The enacted tax rate is 40 percent for all future years.
b. The purchase price is $20,000. The tax basis of the identified net assets acquired is $5,000, and the assigned value is $12,000, that is, there are $7,000 of taxable temporary differences. The acquired enterprise also has a $16,000 operating loss carryforward, which, under the tax law, may be used by the acquiring enterprise in the consolidated tax return.
c. The acquiring enterprise has temporary differences that will result in $30,000 of net taxable amounts in future years.
d. All temporary differences of the acquired and acquiring enterprises will result in taxable amounts before the end of the acquired enterprise's loss carryforward period.

In assessing the need for a valuation allowance, future taxable income exclusive of reversing temporary differences and carryforwards (paragraph .120(b)) need not be considered because the $16,000 operating loss carryforward will offset (a) the *acquired* enterprise's $7,000 of taxable temporary differences and (b) another $9,000 of the *acquiring* enterprise's taxable temporary differences. The amounts recorded to account for the purchase transaction are as follows:

Assigned value of the identified net assets acquired	$12,000
Deferred tax liability recognized for the acquired company's taxable temporary differences ($7,000 at 40 percent)	(2,800)
Deferred tax asset recognized for the acquired loss carryforward based on offset against the acquired company's taxable temporary differences ($7,000 at 40 percent)	2,800
Deferred tax asset recognized for the acquired loss carryforward based on offset against the acquiring company's taxable temporary differences ($9,000 at 40 percent)	3,600
Goodwill	4,400
Purchase price of the acquired enterprise	$20,000

[FAS109, ¶267]

Subsequent Recognition of Carryforward Benefits—Purchase Method

.195 If a valuation allowance is recognized for some portion or all of an acquired enterprise's deferred tax asset for deductible temporary differences and operating loss or tax credit carryforwards at the acquisition date, tax benefits for those items recognized in financial statements for a subsequent year(s) are:

a. First applied to reduce to zero any goodwill related to the acquisition
b. Second applied to reduce to zero other noncurrent intangible assets related to the acquisition
c. Third applied to reduce income tax expense.

Additional amounts of deductible temporary differences and operating loss or tax credit carryforwards may arise after the acquisition date and before recognition of the tax benefit of amounts existing at the acquisition date. Tax benefits are recognized in later years as follows:

a. The tax benefit of amounts existing at the acquisition date is first applied to reduce goodwill and other noncurrent intangible assets to zero. Any additional tax benefit reduces income tax expense.
b. The tax benefit of amounts arising after the acquisition date is recognized as a reduction of income tax expense.

Whether a tax benefit recognized in later years is attributable to an amount (for example, an operating loss carryforward) existing at or arising after the acquisition date is determined for financial reporting by provisions in the tax law that identify the sequence in which those amounts are utilized for tax purposes. If not determinable by provisions in the tax law, a tax benefit recognized for financial reporting is prorated between a reduction of (a) goodwill and other noncurrent intangible assets and (b) income tax expense. [FAS109, ¶268] [Refer to paragraph .1001 for an EITF Issue that provides interpretive guidance on this paragraph.]

.196 Exhibit 196A illustrates recognition of tax benefits subsequent to a business combination.

Exhibit 196A

Recognition of Tax Benefits Subsequent to a Business Combination

The assumptions are as follows:

a. A nontaxable business combination occurs on the first day of year 1. Before considering any acquired deferred tax assets, the purchase transaction is summarized as follows:

	Assigned Value	Tax Basis
Net assets acquired	$5,000	$6,000
Excess of purchase price over the fair value of the net assets acquired*	1,500	
Purchase price	$6,500	

*There are no other noncurrent intangible assets.

b. The only difference between pretax financial income and taxable income (amortization of goodwill is disregarded for this example) for years 1 through 3 is a $1,000 loss for tax purposes in year 1 from disposal of the acquired identified net assets at amounts equal to their $5,000 assigned value on the acquisition date.

	Year 1	Year 2	Year 3
Pretax financial income (loss)	$(3,000)	$ 2,500	$ 1,500
Disposal of acquired identified net assets	(1,000)	—	—
Taxable income (loss) before loss carryforward	(4,000)	2,500	1,500
Loss carryforward (loss carryback not permitted)	4,000	(2,500)	(1,500)
Taxable income after loss carryforward	$ —	$ —	$ —

c. The tax rate is 40 percent for all years.

d. Based on an assessment of all available evidence, management reaches the following conclusions at the acquisition date and at the end of years 1 and 2:

(1) At the acquisition date, the portion of the $1,000 of deductible temporary differences ($6,000 – $5,000) for which it is more likely than not that a tax benefit will not be realized is $500.

Exhibit 196A (continued)

(2) At the end of year 1, the portion of the $4,000 loss carryforward for which it is more likely than not that a tax benefit will not be realized is $1,750.

(3) At the end of year 2, it is more likely than not that a tax benefit will be realized for all of the remaining $1,500 of loss carryforward.

At the acquisition date, a $400 ($1,000 at 40 percent) deferred tax asset and a $200 ($500 at 40 percent) valuation allowance are recognized. The $200 net tax benefit reduces the excess of purchase price over the fair value of the net assets acquired from $1,500 to $1,300. Thus, the amount of goodwill recognized at the acquisition date is $1,300.

During year 1, the $1,000 of net deductible temporary differences at the acquisition date reverse and are part of the $4,000 loss carryforward for tax purposes at the end of year 1. An analysis of the components of that $4,000 loss carryforward follows:

	Acquired Deductions	Loss in Year 1	Total
Tax loss carryforward	$1,000	$3,000	$4,000
Portion for which a tax benefit was recognized at the acquisition date	500	—	500
Remainder available for recognition of a tax benefit at the end of year 1	$ 500	$3,000	$3,500

Provisions in the tax law do not distinguish between those two components of the $3,500, and the component that is used first for tax purposes is indeterminable. However, the $500 of acquired deductions for which a tax benefit has not been recognized is one-seventh of the $3,500 total, and the $3,000 loss in year 1 is six-sevenths of the $3,500 total. The tax benefit of that $3,500 is prorated one-seventh to reduce goodwill and six-sevenths to reduce income tax expense when recognized in years 1 and 2.

At the end of year 1, a $1,600 ($4,000 at 40 percent) deferred tax asset and a $700 ($1,750 at 40 percent) valuation allowance are recognized. The tax benefit for the $700 increase in the net deferred tax asset (from $200 at the acquisition date to $900 at the end of year 1) is prorated as follows:

a. One-seventh or $100 to reduce goodwill
b. Six-sevenths or $600 to reduce tax expense.

During year 2, $1,000 ($2,500 at 40 percent) of the deferred tax asset recognized at the end of year 1 is realized. In addition, a tax benefit is recognized for the remaining $1,750 of future tax deductions by eliminating the $700 valuation allowance. That tax benefit is

Exhibit 196A (continued)

prorated $100 to reduce goodwill and $600 to reduce tax expense. The combined effect of the changes in the deferred tax asset and the related valuation allowance during year 2 is illustrated below:

	Deferred Tax Asset		Tax Expense
	Year 1	Year 2	or (Benefit)
Deferred tax asset	$1,600	$600	$1,000
Valuation allowance	(700)	—	(700)
	$ 900	$600	300
Portion of $700 tax benefit allocated to reduce goodwill			100
Deferred tax expense for year 2			$ 400

The $600 deferred tax asset at the end of year 2 is realized in year 3, resulting in $600 of deferred tax expense for year 3. The consolidated statement of earnings would include the following amounts attributable to the acquired enterprise:

	Year 1	Year 2	Year 3
Pretax financial income (loss)	$(3,000)	$2,500	$1,500
Net deferred tax expense (benefit)	(600)	400	600
Net income (loss)	$(2,400)	$2,100	$ 900

[FAS109, ¶269]

Carryforwards—Pooling-of-Interests Method

.197 The separate financial statements of combining enterprises for prior periods are restated on a combined basis when a business combination is accounted for by the pooling-of-interests method.[21a] For restatement of periods prior to the combination date, a combining enterprise's operating loss carryforward does not offset the other enterprise's taxable income because consolidated tax returns cannot be filed for those periods. However, provisions in the tax law may permit an operating loss carryforward of either of the combining enterprises to offset combined taxable income subsequent to the combination date. [FAS109, ¶270]

.198 If the combined enterprise expects to file consolidated tax returns, a deferred tax asset is recognized for either combining enterprise's operating loss carryforward in a

[21a]Section B51 prohibits the use of the pooling-of-interests method for all business combinations initiated after June 30, 2001. [FAS141, ¶E15(g)]

prior period. A valuation allowance is necessary to the extent it is more likely than not that a tax benefit will not be realized for that loss carryforward through offset of either (a) the other enterprise's deferred tax liability for taxable temporary differences that will reverse subsequent to the combination date or (b) combined taxable income subsequent to the combination date. Determined in that manner, the valuation allowance may be less than the sum of the valuation allowances in the separate financial statements of the combining enterprises prior to the combination date. That tax benefit is recognized as part of the adjustment to restate financial statements on a combined basis for prior periods. The same requirements apply to deductible temporary differences and tax credit carryforwards. [FAS109, ¶271]

.199 A taxable business combination may sometimes be accounted for by the pooling-of-interests method. The increase in the tax basis of the net assets acquired results in temporary differences. The deferred tax consequences of those temporary differences are recognized and measured the same as for other temporary differences. As of the combination date, recognizable tax benefits attributable to the increase in tax basis are allocated to contributed capital. Tax benefits attributable to the increase in tax basis that become recognizable after the combination date (that is, by elimination of a valuation allowance) are reported as a reduction of income tax expense. [FAS109, ¶272]

Intraperiod Tax Allocation

.200 If there is only one item other than continuing operations, the portion of income tax expense or benefit for the year that remains after the allocation to continuing operations is allocated to that item. If there are two or more items other than continuing operations, the amount that remains after the allocation to continuing operations is allocated among those other items in proportion to their individual effects on income tax expense or benefit for the year. [FAS109, ¶273]

.201 Exhibit 201A illustrates allocation of income tax expense if there is only one item other than income from continuing operations.

Exhibit 201A

Allocation of Income Tax Expense—One Item Other Than Income from Continuing Operations

The assumptions are as follows:

a. The enterprise's pretax financial income and taxable income are the same.
b. The enterprise's ordinary loss from continuing operations is $500.

Exhibit 201A (continued)

c. The enterprise also has an extraordinary gain of $900 that is a capital gain for tax purposes.
d. The tax rate is 40 percent on ordinary income and 30 percent on capital gains. Income taxes currently payable are $120 ($400 at 30 percent).

Income tax expense is allocated between the pretax loss from operations and the extraordinary gain as follows:

Total income tax expense	$ 120
Tax benefit allocated to the loss from operations	(150)
Incremental tax expense allocated to the extraordinary gain	$ 270

The effect of the $500 loss from continuing operations was to offset an equal amount of capital gains that otherwise would be taxed at a 30 percent tax rate. Thus, $150 ($500 at 30 percent) of tax benefit is allocated to continuing operations. The $270 incremental effect of the extraordinary gain is the difference between $120 of total tax expense and the $150 tax benefit from continuing operations. [FAS109, ¶274]

.202 Exhibit 202A illustrates allocation of the tax benefit of a tax credit carryforward that is recognized as a deferred tax asset in the current year.

Exhibit 202A

Allocation of the Tax Benefit of an Originating Tax Credit Carryforward

The assumptions are as follows:

a. The enterprise's pretax financial income and taxable income are the same.
b. Pretax financial income for the year comprises $300 from continuing operations and $400 from an extraordinary gain.
c. The tax rate is 40 percent. Taxes payable for the year are zero because $330 of tax credits that arose in the current year more than offset the $280 of tax otherwise payable on $700 of taxable income.
d. A $50 deferred tax asset is recognized for the $50 ($330 – $280) tax credit carryforward. Based on the weight of available evidence, management concludes that no valuation allowance is necessary.

Exhibit 202A (continued)

Income tax expense or benefit is allocated between pretax income from continuing operations and the extraordinary gain as follows:

Total income tax benefit		$ (50)
Tax expense (benefit) allocated to income from continuing operations:		
Tax (before tax credits) on $300 of taxable income at 40 percent	$ 120	
Tax credits	(330)	(210)
Tax expense allocated to the extraordinary gain		$ 160

Absent the extraordinary gain and assuming it was not the deciding factor in reaching a conclusion that a valuation allowance is not needed, the entire tax benefit of the $330 of tax credits would be allocated to continuing operations. The presence of the extraordinary gain does not change that allocation. [FAS109, ¶275]

.203 Income taxes are sometimes allocated directly to shareholders' equity [FAS109, ¶276] or to other comprehensive income. [FAS135, ¶4(s)] Exhibit 203A illustrates the allocation of income taxes for translation adjustments under Section F60 [FAS109, ¶276] to other comprehensive income. [FAS135, ¶4(s)]

Exhibit 203A

Allocation of Income Taxes to Other Comprehensive Income

a. A foreign subsidiary has earnings of FC600 for year 2. Its net assets (and unremitted earnings) are FC1,000 and FC1,600 at the end of years 1 and 2, respectively.
b. The foreign currency is the functional currency. For year 2, translated amounts are as follows:

	Foreign Currency	Exchange Rate	Dollars
Unremitted earnings, beginning of year	1,000	FC1=$1.20	1,200
Earnings for the year	600	FC1=$1.10	660
Unremitted earnings, end of year	1,600	FC1=$1.00	1,600

c. A $260 translation adjustment ($1,200 + $660 – $1,600) is [FAS109, ¶276] reported in other comprehensive income and accumulated [FAS135, ¶4(s)] in shareholders' equity for year 2.

Exhibit 203A (continued)

d. The U.S. parent expects that all of the foreign subsidiary's unremitted earnings will be remitted in the foreseeable future, and under paragraph .209, a deferred U.S. tax liability is recognized for those unremitted earnings.
e. The U.S. parent accrues the deferred tax liability at a 20 percent tax rate (that is, net of foreign tax credits, foreign tax credit carryforwards, and so forth). An analysis of the net investment in the foreign subsidiary and the related deferred tax liability for year 2 is as follows:

	Net Investment	Deferred Tax Liability
Balances, beginning of year	$1,200	$240
Earnings and related taxes	660	132
Translation adjustment and related taxes	(260)	(52)
Balances, end of year	$1,600	$320

f. For year 2, $132 of deferred taxes are charged against earnings, and $52 of deferred taxes are [FAS109, ¶276] reported in other comprehensive income and accumulated [FAS135, ¶4(s)] in shareholders' equity.

[FAS109, ¶276]

Balance Sheet Classification of Deferred Income Taxes

.204 Paragraphs .205 through .211 illustrate the balance sheet classification of certain types of deferred income taxes but do not encompass all possible circumstances. Accordingly, each situation should be resolved based on an evaluation of the facts, using these examples as guides to the extent that they are applicable. [FAS37, ¶16]

Accounting Change for Tax Purposes

.205 The deferred tax liability or asset [FAS109, ¶288(p)] associated with an accounting change for tax purposes would be classified like the associated asset or liability if reduction of that associated asset or liability will cause the [FAS37, ¶19] temporary difference [FAS109, ¶287] to reverse. If there is no associated asset or liability or if the [FAS37, ¶19] temporary difference [FAS109, ¶287] will reverse only over a period of time, the [FAS37, ¶19] deferred tax liability or asset [FAS109, ¶288(p)] would be classified based on the expected reversal date of the specific [FAS37, ¶19] temporary difference. [FAS109, ¶287]

.206 An enterprise changes its method of handling bad debts for tax purposes from the cash method to the reserve method. Ten percent of the effect of the change at the beginning of calendar year 19X1 will be included as a deduction from taxable income each year for 10 years. The enterprise uses a one-year time period as the basis for classifying current assets and current liabilities on its balance sheet. At December 31, 19X1, the amount of the effect of the change that is yet to be included as a deduction from taxable income and the balance of the related deferred income taxes are as follows:

Amount of the effect of the change that is yet to be included as a deduction from taxable income (9/10 of total effect of the change)	$5,125,000

[FAS37, ¶20]

Deferred Tax Asset (40 percent is the enacted tax rate—no valuation allowance deemed necessary)	$2,050,000

[FAS109, ¶288(p)]

.207 The deferred tax asset does [FAS109, ¶288(p)] not relate to trade receivables or provisions for doubtful accounts because collection or write-off of the receivables will not cause the [FAS37, ¶21] temporary differences [FAS109, ¶287] to reverse; the [FAS37, ¶21] temporary differences [FAS109, ¶287] will reverse over time. Accordingly, the enterprise would classify the [FAS37, ¶21] deferred tax asset [FAS109, ¶288(p)] based on the scheduled reversal of the related [FAS37, ¶21] temporary differences. [FAS109, ¶287] One-ninth of the remaining [FAS37, ¶21] temporary differences [FAS109, ¶287] are scheduled to reverse in 19X2, so one-ninth of the related [FAS37, ¶21] deferred tax asset [FAS109, ¶288(p)] would be classified as current at December 31, 19X1 [FAS37, ¶21] ($227,778). [FAS109, ¶288(p)]

Method of Reporting Construction Contracts

.208 An enterprise reports profits on construction contracts on the completed contract method for tax purposes and the percentage-of-completion method for financial reporting purposes. The [FAS37, ¶22] temporary differences [FAS109, ¶288(p)] do not relate to an asset or liability that appears on the enterprise's balance sheet; the [FAS37, ¶22] temporary differences [FAS109, ¶287] will only reverse when the contracts are completed. Receivables that result from progress billings can be collected with no effect on the [FAS37, ¶22] temporary differences; [FAS109, ¶287] likewise, contract retentions can be collected with no effect on [FAS37, ¶22] temporary differences, [FAS109, ¶287] and the [FAS37, ¶22] temporary differences [FAS109, ¶287] will reverse when the contracts are deemed to be complete even if there is a waiting period before retentions will be received. Accordingly, the enterprise would classify the [FAS37, ¶22] deferred tax liability [FAS109, ¶288(p)] based on the estimated reversal of the related [FAS37, ¶22] temporary differences. [FAS109, ¶287] Deferred tax liabilities [FAS109, ¶288(p)] related to [FAS37, ¶22] temporary differences [FAS109, ¶287] that will reverse within the same time period used in classifying other contract-related assets and liabilities as current (for example, an operating cycle) would be classified as current. [FAS37, ¶22]

Unremitted Foreign Earnings of Subsidiaries

.209 An enterprise provides U.S. income taxes on the portion of its unremitted foreign earnings that are not considered to be permanently reinvested in its consolidated foreign subsidiary. The foreign earnings are included in U.S. taxable income in the year in which dividends are paid. The enterprise uses a one-year time period as the basis for classifying current assets and current liabilities on its balance sheet. At December 31, 19X1, the accumulated amount of unremitted earnings on which taxes have been provided and the balance of the related deferred income taxes are as follows:

Accumulated unremitted earnings on which taxes have been provided:	
Expected to be remitted within one year	$ 9,800,000
Not expected to be remitted within one year	2,700,000
Total	$12,500,000
Accumulated [FAS37, ¶23] Deferred Tax Liability [FAS109, ¶288(p)] Related to Unremitted Earnings	$ 1,250,000

[FAS37, ¶23]

.210 The [FAS37, ¶24] deferred tax liability does [FAS109, ¶288(p)] not relate to an asset or liability on the consolidated balance sheet; the [FAS37, ¶24] temporary difference [FAS109, ¶287] will only reverse when the unremitted earnings are received from the foreign subsidiary by the parent. A payment between consolidated affiliates does not change the consolidated balance sheet, so no item on the consolidated balance sheet would be liquidated. Unremitted earnings expected to be remitted within the next year represent 78 percent of the total unremitted earnings for which tax has been provided ($9,800,000 ÷ $12,500,000). Therefore, 78 percent of the related [FAS37, ¶24] deferred tax liability [FAS109, ¶288(p)] would be classified as current on the consolidated balance sheet ($975,000). [FAS37, ¶24]

.211 If the subsidiary were accounted for on the equity method rather than consolidated (for example, a subsidiary reported on the equity method in separate parent company financial statements), the deferred income taxes would relate to the recorded investment in the subsidiary. The payment of dividends that causes the reversal of the [FAS37, ¶25] temporary difference [FAS109, ¶287] would be accompanied by a reduction of the recorded investment in the subsidiary. Therefore, the [FAS37, ¶25] deferred tax liability [FAS109, ¶288(p)] would be classified the same as the related investment in the subsidiary. [FAS37, ¶25]

Undistributed Earnings of Subsidiaries

.212 The inclusion of undistributed earnings of a subsidiary[22] in the pretax accounting income of a parent company, either through consolidation or accounting for the investment by the equity method [APB23, ¶9] results in a temporary difference. [FAS109, ¶288(f)]

Temporary Difference

.213 It should be presumed that all undistributed earnings of a subsidiary will be transferred to the parent company. Accordingly, the undistributed earnings of a subsidiary included in consolidated income shall be accounted for as a temporary difference unless the tax law provides a means by which the investment in a domestic subsidiary can be recovered tax free. However, a deferred tax liability is not recognized for (a) an excess of the amount for financial reporting over the tax basis of an investment in a foreign subsidiary that meets the criteria in paragraph .215 and (b) undistributed earnings of a domestic subsidiary that arose in fiscal years beginning on or before December 15, 1992 and that meet the criteria in paragraph .215. The criteria in paragraph .215 do not apply to undistributed earnings of domestic subsidiaries that arise in fiscal years beginning after December 15, 1992, and a deferred tax liability shall be recognized if the undistributed earnings are a taxable temporary difference. [FAS109, ¶288(f)]

.214 A deferred tax asset shall be recognized for an excess of the tax basis over the amount for financial reporting of an investment in a subsidiary in accordance with the requirements of paragraph .133. [FAS109, ¶288(f)]

Indefinite Reversal Criterion

.215 The presumption that all undistributed earnings will be transferred to the parent company may be overcome, and no income taxes shall be accrued by the parent company, if sufficient evidence shows that the subsidiary has invested or will invest the undistributed earnings indefinitely or that the earnings will be remitted in a tax-free liquidation. A parent company shall have evidence of specific plans for reinvestment of undistributed earnings of a subsidiary that demonstrate that remittance of the earnings will be post-

[22]The conclusions of this section on undistributed earnings of a subsidiary also apply to the portion of the earnings of a Domestic International Sales Corporation (DISC) that is eligible for tax deferral. [APB23, ¶9, fn2]

poned indefinitely. Experience of the enterprises and definite future programs of operations and remittances are examples of the types of evidence required to substantiate the parent company's representation of indefinite postponement of remittances from a subsidiary. If circumstances change and it becomes apparent that some or all of the undistributed earnings of a subsidiary will be remitted in the foreseeable future but income taxes have not been recognized by the parent company, it shall accrue as an expense of the current period income taxes attributable to that remittance; income tax expense for such undistributed earnings shall not be accounted for as an extraordinary item. If it becomes apparent that some or all of the undistributed earnings of a subsidiary on which income taxes have been accrued will not be remitted in the foreseeable future, the parent company shall adjust income tax expense of the current period; such adjustment of income tax expense shall not be accounted for as an extraordinary item. [APB23, ¶12] [Refer to paragraph .1001 for an EITF Issue that provides interpretive guidance on this paragraph.]

Change in Investment

.216 An investment in common stock of a subsidiary may change so that it is no longer a subsidiary because the parent company sells a portion of the investment, the subsidiary sells additional stock, or other transactions affect the investment. If the remaining investment in common stock should be accounted for by the equity method, the investor shall recognize income taxes on its share of current earnings of the investee enterprise in accordance with [APB23, ¶13] this section. [FAS109, ¶287] If a parent company did not recognize income taxes on its equity in undistributed earnings of a subsidiary for the reasons cited in paragraph .215 (and the enterprise in which the investment is held ceases to be a subsidiary), it shall accrue as a current period expense income taxes on undistributed earnings in the period that it becomes apparent[23] that any of those undistributed earnings (prior to the change in status) will be remitted; the accrual of those income taxes shall not be accounted for as an extraordinary item. [APB23, ¶13] If a parent company recognizes a deferred tax liability for the temporary difference arising from its equity in undistributed earnings of a subsidiary and subsequently reduces its investment in the subsidiary through a taxable sale or other transaction, the amount of the temporary difference and the related deferred tax liability will change. An investment in common stock of an investee (other than a subsidiary or corporate joint venture) may change so that the investee becomes a subsidiary because the investor acquires additional common stock, the investee acquires or retires common stock, or other transactions affect the investment. A temporary difference for the investor's share of the undistributed earnings of the investee prior to the date it becomes a subsidiary shall continue to be treated as a temporary difference for which a deferred tax liability shall continue to be recognized to the

[23]The change in the status of an investment would not by itself mean that remittance of these undistributed earnings should be considered apparent. [APB23, ¶13, fn5]

extent that dividends from the subsidiary do not exceed the parent company's share of the subsidiary's earnings subsequent to the date it became a subsidiary. [FAS109, ¶288(f)]

Disclosure

.217 Paragraphs .142 through .148 specify the requirements for financial statement disclosures [about income taxes]. [FAS109, ¶288(f)]

Investments in Corporate Joint Ventures

.218 The principles applicable to undistributed earnings of subsidiaries (refer to paragraphs .212 through .216) also apply to tax effects of differences between taxable income and pretax accounting income attributable to earnings of corporate joint ventures that are essentially permanent in duration and are accounted for by the equity method.[24] [APB23, ¶17]

Disclosure

.219 The disclosure requirements set forth in paragraphs .142 through .148 also apply to earnings of corporate joint ventures. [APB23, ¶18]

Bad-Debt Reserves of Savings and Loan Associations

.220 Regulatory authorities require both stock and mutual savings and loan associations to appropriate a portion of earnings to general reserves[25] and to retain the reserves as a protection for depositors. Provisions of the U.S. Internal Revenue Code permit a savings and loan association to deduct an annual addition to a reserve for bad debts[26] in determining taxable income, subject to certain limitations. This annual addition permitted by the Code generally differs significantly from the bad-debt experience upon which determination of pretax accounting income is based. Thus, taxable income and pretax accounting income of an association usually differ. [APB23, ¶19]

---

[24]Certain corporate joint ventures have a life limited by the nature of the venture, project, or other business activity. Therefore, a reasonable assumption is that a part or all of the undistributed earnings of the venture will be transferred to the investor in a taxable distribution. Deferred taxes shall be recorded, in accordance with [APB23, ¶17, fn7] this section [FAS109, ¶287], at the time the earnings (or losses) are included in the investor's income. [APB23, ¶17, fn7]

[25]The term *general reserves* is used in the context of the special meaning this term has in regulatory pronouncements and in the U.S. Internal Revenue Code. [APB23, ¶19, fn8]

[26]The term *reserve for bad debts* is used in the context of the special meaning this term has in regulatory pronouncements and in the U.S. Internal Revenue Code. [APB23, ¶19, fn8]

.221 Although a general reserve determined according to requirements of the regulatory authorities is not directly related to a reserve for bad debts computed according to provisions of the U.S. Internal Revenue Code, the purposes and restrictions of each reserve are similar. Amounts of bad-debt deductions for income tax purposes are includable in taxable income of later years only if the bad-debt reserves are used subsequently for purposes other than to absorb bad-debt losses. [APB23, ¶20]

.222 The term *pretax accounting income,* as used in paragraphs .220 through .222, represents income or loss for a period, exclusive of related income tax expense, determined in conformity with generally accepted accounting principles. The term *taxable income,* as used in paragraphs .220 through .222, represents pretax accounting income (a) adjusted for reversal of provisions for estimated losses on loans and property acquired in settlement of loans, gains or losses on the sales of such property, and adjusted for [APB23, ¶21] events that do not have tax consequences [FAS109, ¶288(f)] and (b) after giving effect to the bad-debt deduction allowable by the U.S. Internal Revenue Code assuming the applicable tax return were to be prepared based on such adjusted pretax accounting income. [APB23, ¶21]

.223 As described in paragraph .130, a savings and loan association[27] shall not provide deferred taxes on taxable temporary differences related to bad-debt reserves for tax purposes that arose in tax years beginning before December 31, 1987 (the base-year amount). [FAS109, ¶288(f)] However, if circumstances indicate that the association is likely to pay income taxes, either currently or in later years, because of known or expected reductions in the bad-debt reserve, income taxes attributable to that reduction shall be accrued as tax expense of the current period; the accrual of those income taxes shall not be accounted for as an extraordinary item. [APB23, ¶23]

Disclosure

.224 Paragraphs .142 through .148 specify the requirements for financial statement disclosures. [FAS109, ¶288(f)] [Those] disclosure requirements also apply to a parent company of a savings and loan association accounting for that investment either through consolidation or by the equity method. [APB23, ¶25]

---

[27]The conclusions in this section apply to stock and mutual savings and loan associations and mutual savings banks. [APB23, ¶23, fn9]

Income Taxes of Stock Life Insurance Enterprises

Deferred Income Taxes

.225 Except as noted in paragraph .226, a deferred tax liability or asset shall be recognized for the deferred tax consequences of temporary differences in accordance with this section. [FAS109, ¶288(t)]

Policyholders' Surplus

.226 As described in paragraph .130, a life insurance enterprise shall not provide deferred taxes on taxable temporary differences related to policyholders' surplus that arose in fiscal years beginning on or before December 15, 1992. [FAS109, ¶288(t)] However, if circumstances indicate that the insurance enterprise is likely to pay income taxes, either currently or in later years, because of a known or expected reduction in policyholders' surplus, income taxes attributable to that reduction shall be accrued as a tax expense of the current period; the accrual of those income taxes shall not be accounted for as an extraordinary item. [FAS60, ¶59] Paragraphs .142 through .148 specify the requirements for financial statement disclosures about income taxes. [FAS109, ¶288(t)]

Accounting for Investment Tax Credits

.227 [Tax law and regulations may] provide for an *investment [tax] credit* that, in general, is equal to a specified percentage of the cost of certain depreciable assets acquired and placed in service [during specified periods]. [APB2, ¶1]

.228 [It] shall be considered preferable [APB4, ¶10] [for] the allowable investment credit [to] be reflected in net income over the productive life of acquired property [(the deferral method)]. [APB2, ¶13] [However,] treating the credit as a reduction of federal income taxes of the year in which the credit arises [(the flow-through method)] is also acceptable. [APB4, ¶10]

.229 Disclosure [shall] be made of the method followed and amounts involved, when material. [APB4, ¶11]

.230 An investment credit shall be reflected in the financial statements to the extent it has been used as an offset against income taxes otherwise currently payable or to the extent its benefit is recognizable under the provisions of this section. Refer to paragraph .147 for required disclosures related to (a) tax credit carryforwards for tax purposes and (b) tax credit carryforwards for which a tax benefit has not been recognized for financial reporting. [FAS109, ¶288(b)]

Deferral Method

.231 While reflection of the allowable credit [on the balance sheet] as a reduction in the net amount at which the acquired property is stated (either directly or by inclusion in an offsetting account) may be preferable in many cases, [it is] recognized as equally appropriate [to display] the credit as deferred income, provided it is amortized over the productive life of the acquired property. [APB2, ¶14] [(Refer to paragraph .509 for supplemental guidance on applying the deferral method.)]

.232 It [is] preferable that the statement of income in the year in which the allowable investment credit arises shall be affected only by the results that flow from the accounting for the credit [under the deferral method] set forth in paragraph .228. Nevertheless, reflection of income tax provisions, in the income statement, in the amount payable (that is, after deduction of the allowable investment credit) is appropriate provided that a corresponding charge is made to an appropriate cost or expense (for example, to the provision for depreciation). [APB2, ¶15]

Offsetting Securities against Taxes Payable

.233 It is a general principle of accounting that the offsetting of assets and liabilities in the balance sheet is improper except when a right of setoff exists. [Refer to Section B10, "Balance Sheet Display: Offsetting," paragraphs .101A, .101B, and .107, for guidance on determining whether a right of setoff exists.] Accordingly, the offset of cash or other assets against the tax liability or other amounts owing to governmental bodies is not acceptable except in the circumstances described in paragraph .235. [APB10, ¶7(1)]

.234 Most securities now issued by governments are not by their terms designed specifically for the payment of taxes and, accordingly, shall not be deducted from taxes payable on the balance sheet. [APB10, ¶7(2)]

.235 The only exception to the general principle [in paragraph .233] occurs when it is clear that a purchase of securities (acceptable for the payment of taxes) is in substance an advance payment of taxes that will be payable in the relatively near future, so that in the special circumstances the purchase is tantamount to the prepayment of taxes. This occurs at times, for example, as an accommodation to a local government and in some instances when governments issue securities that are specifically designated as being acceptable for the payment of taxes of those governments. [APB10, ¶7(3)]

[**Note:** Additional guidance with respect to implementing Section I27 is presented in *A Guide to Implementation of Statement 109 on Accounting for Income Taxes: Questions and Answers.* The publication addresses 28 questions and was written by FASB staff members, Raymond E. Perry and E. Raymond Simpson. This publication is available from the Order Department, Financial Accounting Standards Board, 401 Merritt 7, P.O. Box 5116, Norwalk, CT 06856-5116, telephone (203) 847-0700.]

Glossary

.401 **Carrybacks.** Deductions or credits that cannot be utilized on the tax return during a year that may be carried back to reduce taxable income or taxes payable in a prior year. An operating loss carryback is an excess of tax deductions over gross income in a year; a tax credit carryback is the amount by which tax credits available for utilization exceed statutory limitations. Different tax jurisdictions have different rules about whether excess deductions or credits may be carried back and the length of the carryback period. [FAS109, ¶289]

.402 **Carryforwards.** Deductions or credits that cannot be utilized on the tax return during a year that may be carried forward to reduce taxable income or taxes payable in a future year. An operating loss carryforward is an excess of tax deductions over gross income in a year; a tax credit carryforward is the amount by which tax credits available for utilization exceed statutory limitations. Different tax jurisdictions have different rules about whether excess deductions or credits may be carried forward and the length of the carryforward period. The terms *carryforward, operating loss carryforward,* and *tax credit carryforward* refer to the amounts of those items, if any, reported in the tax return for the current year. [FAS109, ¶289]

.403 **Current tax expense or benefit.** The amount of income taxes paid or payable (or refundable) for a year as determined by applying the provisions of the enacted tax law to the taxable income or excess of deductions over revenues for that year. [FAS109, ¶289]

.404 **Deductible temporary difference.** Temporary differences that result in deductible amounts in future years when the related asset or liability is recovered or settled, respectively. Also refer to **Temporary difference.** [FAS109, ¶289]

.405 **Deferred tax asset.** The deferred tax consequences attributable to deductible temporary differences and carryforwards. A deferred tax asset is measured using the applicable enacted tax rate and provisions of the enacted tax law. A deferred tax asset is reduced by a valuation allowance if, based on the weight of evidence available, it is more likely than not that some portion or all of a deferred tax asset will not be realized. [FAS109, ¶289]

.406 **Deferred tax expense or benefit.** The change during the year in an enterprise's deferred tax liabilities and assets. For deferred tax liabilities and assets acquired in a purchase business combination during the year, it is the change since the combination date. Income tax expense or benefit for the year is allocated among continuing operations, discontinued operations, extraordinary items, and items charged or credited directly to shareholders' equity. [FAS109, ¶289]

.407 **Deferred tax liability.** The deferred tax consequences attributable to taxable temporary differences. A deferred tax liability is measured using the applicable enacted tax rate and provisions of the enacted tax law. [FAS109, ¶289]

.408 **Event.** A happening of consequence to an enterprise. The term encompasses both transactions and other events affecting an enterprise. [FAS109, ¶289]

.409 **Gains and losses included in comprehensive income but excluded from net income.** Under present practice, gains and losses included in comprehensive income but excluded from net income include certain changes in market values of investments in marketable equity securities classified as noncurrent assets, certain changes in market values of investments in industries having specialized accounting practices for marketable securities, adjustments from recognizing certain additional pension liabilities, and foreign currency translation adjustments. Future changes to generally accepted accounting principles may change what is included in this category. [FAS109, ¶289]

.410 **Income taxes.** Domestic and foreign federal (national), state, and local (including franchise) taxes based on income. [FAS109, ¶289]

.411 **Income taxes currently payable (refundable).** Refer to **Current tax expense or benefit**. [FAS109, ¶289]

.412 **Income tax expense (benefit).** The sum of current tax expense (benefit) and deferred tax expense (benefit). [FAS109, ¶289]

.413 **Nonpublic enterprise.** An enterprise other than one (a) whose debt or equity securities are traded in a public market, including those traded on a stock exchange or in the over-the-counter market (including securities quoted only locally or regionally), or (b) whose financial statements are filed with a regulatory agency in preparation for the sale of any class of securities. [FAS109, ¶289]

.414 **Public enterprise.** An enterprise (a) whose debt or equity securities are traded in a public market, including those traded on a stock exchange or in the over-the-counter market (including securities quoted only locally or regionally), or (b) whose financial statements are filed with a regulatory agency in preparation for the sale of any class of securities. [FAS109, ¶289]

.415 **Taxable income.** The excess of taxable revenues over tax deductible expenses and exemptions for the year as defined by the governmental taxing authority. [FAS109, ¶289]

.416 **Taxable temporary difference.** Temporary differences that result in taxable amounts in future years when the related asset or liability is recovered or settled, respectively. Also refer to **Temporary difference.** [FAS109, ¶289]

.417 **Tax consequences.** The effects on income taxes—current or deferred—of an event. [FAS109, ¶289]

.418 **Tax-planning strategy.** An action (including elections for tax purposes) that meets certain criteria (paragraph .121) and that would be implemented to realize a tax benefit for an operating loss or tax credit carryforward before it expires. Tax-planning strategies are considered when assessing the need for and amount of a valuation allowance for deferred tax assets. [FAS109, ¶289]

.419 **Temporary difference.** A difference between the tax basis of an asset or liability and its reported amount in the financial statements that will result in taxable or deductible amounts in future years when the reported amount of the asset or liability is recovered or settled, respectively. Paragraph .110 cites 8 examples of temporary differences. Some temporary differences cannot be identified with a particular asset or liability for financial reporting (refer to paragraph .114), but those temporary differences (a) result from events that have been recognized in the financial statements and (b) will result in taxable or deductible amounts in future years based on provisions of the tax law. Some events recognized in financial statements do not have tax consequences. Certain revenues are exempt from taxation and certain expenses are not deductible. Events that do not have tax consequences do not give rise to temporary differences. [FAS109, ¶289]

.420 **Valuation allowance.** The portion of a deferred tax asset for which it is more likely than not that a tax benefit will not be realized. [FAS109, ¶289]

Supplemental Guidance

Disclosure of the Sale or Purchase of Tax Benefits through Tax Leases

.501 *Question*—What disclosures are required for the sale or purchase of tax benefits through tax leases? [FTB82-1, ¶1] (This section does not address the accounting for the sale or purchase of tax benefits through tax leases.) [FTB82-1, ¶8]

.502 *Background*—The term *tax leases,* as used in this section, refers to leases that are entered into to transfer certain tax benefits as allowed by the leasing provisions of the Economic Recovery Tax Act of 1981. The tax benefits that can be transferred are deductions under the Accelerated Cost Recovery System and credits such as the investment tax credit and energy credit. Temporary Treasury regulations were issued on October 20, 1981, November 10, 1981, and December 28, 1981 that prescribe the conditions that must be met for a transaction to be characterized as a "safe harbor" lease for federal income tax purposes, thus enabling the parties to the transaction to transfer certain tax benefits between them. [FTB82-1, ¶2]

.503 *Response*—Section A10, "Accounting Policies," requires disclosure of all significant accounting policies for which alternative accounting principles or practices exist, including the methods of applying those accounting principles that materially affect the determination of financial position, [FTB82-1, ¶4] cash flows, [FAS95, ¶152(h)] and results of operations. Because alternative accounting practices exist, the accounting policies or practices followed for those transactions should be disclosed in accordance with Section A10. The disclosure should include the method of recognizing revenue and allocating the income tax benefits and asset costs to current and future periods. [FTB82-1, ¶4]

.504 Paragraph .145 requires that (a) the reported amount of income tax expense attributable to continuing operations for the year be reconciled to the amount of income tax expense that would result from applying domestic federal statutory tax rates to pretax income from continuing operations and (b) the estimated amount and the nature of each significant reconciling item be disclosed. Transactions involving the sale or purchase of tax benefits through tax leases may give rise to a significant reconciling item that should be disclosed pursuant to the requirements of this section. [FAS109, ¶288(cc)]

.505 Section I22, "Income Statement Presentation: Unusual or Infrequent Items," paragraph .101, requires disclosure of material events or transactions that are unusual in nature or occur infrequently as a separate component of income from continuing operations. If material and unusual or infrequent to the enterprise, the nature and financial effects of transactions involving the sale or purchase of tax benefits through tax leases should be disclosed on the face of the income statement or, alternatively, in notes to the financial statements. [FTB82-1, ¶6]

.506 Disclosures in addition to those required by Sections A10, I22, and [FTB82-1, ¶7] this section [FAS109, ¶287] as discussed above may also be appropriate depending on the circumstances involved. For example, if significant contingencies exist with respect to the sale or purchase of tax benefits, disclosures in accordance with Section C59, "Contingencies," may be warranted. Also, as referred to in Section F43, "Financial Statements: Comparative Financial Statements," paragraph .102, if comparative financial statements are presented, disclosure should be made of any change in practice that significantly affects comparability. [FTB82-1, ¶7]

Investment Credit from Leased Property

.507 A financing institution may include the investment credit as part of the proceeds from leased property accounted for by the financing method and include it in determining the yield from the "loan," which is reflected in income over the term of the lease. However, the financing institution may account for the investment credit on property purchased for its own use by either the flow-through or the deferral method. [AIN-APB4, #3]

.508 The investment credit may be passed through to a lessee for leased property. The lessee should account for the credit by whichever method is used for purchased property. If the deferral method is used and the leased property is not capitalized, the term of the lease, generally including renewal options that are reasonably expected to be exercised, is the period over which the credit should be amortized. [AIN-APB4, #3]

Applying the Deferral Method of Accounting for Investment Credit

.509 Under the deferral method, the credit is reflected as a reduction of tax expense ratably over the period during which the asset is depreciated and follows the depreciation method used for financial reporting purposes. The amortization period may be the specific life of each asset or the composite life of all depreciable assets. However, amortization over the period [that] the asset must be held to avoid recapture of the credit rather than [over] the life of the asset is not acceptable because it is not based on depreciable life. [AIN-APB4, #3]

Supplemental Guidance: Emerging Issues Task Force (EITF) Issues

.1000 [Listed below are EITF Issues that provide supplemental guidance for this section. These Issues are grouped by subject matter and may be either interpretive of or related by topic to the guidance in this section.

Banking and Thrift Industries

EITF Issue No. 85-31, "Comptroller of the Currency's Rule on Deferred Tax Debits"
EITF Issue No. 85-41, "Accounting for Savings and Loan Associations under FSLIC Management Consignment Program"
EITF Issue No. 88-19, "FSLIC-Assisted Acquisitions of Thrifts"

Business Combinations

EITF Issue No. 86-9, "IRC Section 338 and Push-Down Accounting"
EITF Issue No. 86-31, "Reporting the Tax Implications of a Pooling of a Bank and a Savings and Loan Association"
EITF Issue No. 93-7, "Uncertainties Related to Income Taxes in a Purchase Business Combination"

Change in Tax Laws/Rates

EITF Issue No. 93-12, "Recognition and Measurement of the Tax Benefit of Excess Tax-Deductible Goodwill Resulting from a Retroactive Change in Tax Law"
EITF Issue No. 93-13, "Effect of a Retroactive Change in Enacted Tax Rates That Is Included in Income from Continuing Operations"
EITF Issue No. 99-15, "Accounting for Decreases in Deferred Tax Asset Valuation Allowances Established in a Purchase Business Combination As a Result of a Change in Tax Regulations"
EITF Topic No. D-30, "Adjustment Due to Effect of a Change in Tax Laws or Rates"

Deferred Taxes

EITF Issue No. 93-17, "Recognition of Deferred Tax Assets for a Parent Company's Excess Tax Basis in the Stock of a Subsidiary That Is Accounted for as a Discontinued Operation"
EITF Issue No. 96-7, "Accounting for Deferred Taxes on In-Process Research and Development Activities Acquired in a Purchase Business Combination"

Foreign Dividend Payments

EITF Issue No. 95-9, "Accounting for Tax Effects of Dividends in France in Accordance with FASB Statement No. 109"
EITF Issue No. 95-10, "Accounting for Tax Credits Related to Dividend Payments in Accordance with FASB Statement No. 109"
EITF Issue No. 95-20, "Measurement in the Consolidated Financial Statements of a Parent of the Tax Effects Related to the Operations of a Foreign Subsidiary That Receives Tax Credits Related to Dividend Payments"

Highly Inflationary Economies

EITF Issue No. 92-8, "Accounting for the Income Tax Effects under FASB Statement No. 109 of a Change in Functional Currency When an Economy Ceases to Be Considered Highly Inflationary"
EITF Topic No. D-56, "Accounting for a Change in Functional Currency and Deferred Taxes When an Economy Becomes Highly Inflationary"

Other

EITF Issue No. 87-8, "Tax Reform Act of 1986: Issues Related to the Alternative Minimum Tax"
EITF Issue No. 88-4, "Classification of Payment Made to IRS to Retain Fiscal Year"
EITF Issue No. 88-5, "Recognition of Insurance Death Benefits"
EITF Issue No. 91-8, "Application of FASB Statement No. 96 to a State Tax Based on the Greater of a Franchise Tax or an Income Tax"
EITF Issue No. 92-3, "Earnings-per-Share Treatment of Tax Benefits for Dividends on Unallocated Stock Held by an Employee Stock Ownership Plan"
EITF Issue No. 93-9, "Application of FASB Statement No. 109 in Foreign Financial Statements Restated for General Price-Level Changes"
EITF Issue No. 93-16, "Application of FASB Statement No. 109 to Basis Differences within Foreign Subsidiaries That Meet the Indefinite Reversal Criterion of APB Opinion No. 23"
EITF Issue No. 94-1, "Accounting for Tax Benefits Resulting from Investments in Affordable Housing Projects"
EITF Issue No. 94-10, "Accounting by a Company for the Income Tax Effects of Transactions among or with Its Shareholders under FASB Statement No. 109"
EITF Issue No. 98-11, "Accounting for Acquired Temporary Differences in Certain Purchase Transactions That Are Not Accounted for as Business Combinations"

EITF Issue No. 00-15, "Classification in the Statement of Cash Flows of the Income Tax Benefit Received by a Company upon Exercise of a Nonqualified Employee Stock Option"

EITF Topic No. D-31, "Temporary Differences Related to LIFO Inventory and Tax-to-Tax Differences"

EITF Topic No. D-32, "Intraperiod Tax Allocation of the Tax Effect of Pretax Income from Continuing Operations"

EITF Topic No. D-33, "Timing of Recognition of Tax Benefits for Pre-reorganization Temporary Differences and Carryforwards"]

.1001 [Listed below are those EITF Issues that provide interpretive guidance on specific material in this section.

Paragraph .108 (FAS 109, ¶9)—EITF Topic No. D-31
Paragraph .108(f) (FAS 109, ¶9(f))—EITF Issues No. 92-8 and 93-9 and Topic No. D-56
Paragraph .110 (FAS 109, ¶11)—EITF Issue No. 93-9
Paragraph .114 (FAS 109, ¶15)—EITF Issue No. 93-16
Paragraph .116 (FAS 109, ¶17)—EITF Issue No. 94-1 and Topic No. D-31
Paragraph .117 (FAS 109, ¶18)—EITF Issue No. 95-10
Paragraph .118 (FAS 109, ¶19)—EITF Issue No. 95-20
Paragraph .125 (FAS 109, ¶26)—EITF Issue No. 94-10
Paragraph .126 (FAS 109, ¶27)—EITF Issues No. 93-12, 93-13, and 99-15 and Topic No. D-30
Paragraph .129 (FAS 109, ¶30)—EITF Issues No. 93-7 and 99-15
Paragraph .130 (FAS 109, ¶31)—EITF Issue No. 93-16
Paragraph .133 (FAS 109, ¶34)—EITF Issue No. 93-17
Paragraph .134 (FAS 109, ¶35)—EITF Issue No. 95-9 and Topic No. D-32
Paragraph .135 (FAS 109, ¶36)—EITF Issue No. 94-10 and Topic No. D-32
Paragraph .135(f) (FAS 109, ¶36(f))—EITF Issue No. 92-3
Paragraphs .136 and .137 (FAS 109, ¶37-38)—EITF Topic No. D-32
Paragraph .195 (FAS 109, ¶268)—EITF Topic No. D-33
Paragraph .215 (APB 23, ¶12)—EITF Issue No. 93-16]

(The next page is 26155.)

Sources: FASB Statement 5; FASB Statement 113; FASB Technical Bulletin 85-4

[**Note:** A list of Issues discussed by the Emerging Issues Task Force (EITF) that provide supplemental guidance for this section is presented in paragraph .1000.]

Summary

Payments to insurance enterprises that do not involve transfer of risk shall be accounted for as a deposit by the insured or by the ceding enterprise in the case of reinsurance.

The amount that could be realized under a life insurance contract as of the date of the statement of financial position should be reported as an asset. The change in cash surrender or contract value during the period is an adjustment of premiums paid in determining the expense or income to be recognized under the contract for the period.

Payments to Insurance Enterprises That May Not Involve Transfer of Risk

.101 To the extent that an insurance contract or reinsurance contract does not, despite its form, provide for indemnification of the insured or the ceding enterprise by the insurer or reinsurer against loss or liability, the premium paid less the amount of the premium to be retained by the insurer or reinsurer shall be accounted for as a deposit by the insured or the ceding enterprise. Those contracts may be structured in various ways, but if, regardless of form, their substance is that all or part of the premium paid by the insured or the ceding enterprise is a deposit, it shall be accounted for as such.[1] [FAS5, ¶44]

.102 Operations in certain industries may be subject to such high risks that insurance is unavailable or is available only at what is considered to be a prohibitively high cost. Some enterprises in those industries have "pooled" their risks by forming a mutual insurance enterprise in which they retain an equity interest and to which they pay insurance premiums. For example, some electric utility enterprises have formed such a mutual insurance enterprise to insure risks related to nuclear power plants, and some oil enterprises have formed an enterprise to insure against risks associated with petroleum exploration and production. Whether the premium paid represents a payment for the transfer of risk or whether it represents merely a deposit will depend on the circumstances

[1]Paragraphs .171 through .177 of Section In6, "Insurance Industry," identify conditions that are required for a reinsurance contract to indemnify the ceding enterprise against loss or liability and to be accounted for as reinsurance. Any transaction between enterprises to which Section In6 applies must meet those conditions to be accounted for as reinsurance. [FAS113, ¶30]

surrounding each enterprise's interest in and insurance arrangement with the mutual insurance enterprise. An analysis of the contract is required to determine whether risk has been transferred and to what extent. [FAS5, ¶45] [Refer to paragraph .1001 for an EITF Issue that provides interpretive guidance on this paragraph.]

Supplemental Guidance

.501-.503 [Deleted 11/85 because of FASB Technical Bulletin No. 85-4, *Accounting for Purchases of Life Insurance.*]

Accounting for Purchases of Life Insurance

.504 *Question*—How should an enterprise[501] account for an investment in life insurance? [FTB85-4, ¶1]

.505 *Background*—A premium paid by a purchaser of life insurance serves a variety of purposes. A portion of the premium pays the insurer for assumption of mortality risk and provides for recovery of the insurer's contract acquisition, initiation, and maintenance costs. Another portion of the premium contributes to the accumulation of contract values. The relative amounts of premium payment credited to various contract attributes change over time as the age of the insured party increases and as earnings are credited to previously established contract values. [FTB85-4, ¶5]

.506 An insurance contract is significantly different from most investment agreements. The various attributes of the policy could be obtained separately through term insurance and purchase of investments. The combination of benefits and contract values could not, however, typically be acquired absent the insurance contract. Continued protection from mortality risk and realization of scheduled increases in contract accumulation usually requires payment of future premiums. [FTB85-4, ¶6]

.507 The payment of insurance premiums may take a number of different forms. The insurance contract may be purchased through payment of a single premium, as opposed to the typical series of future premiums. Alternatively, the premium payments may be made through loans from the insurance company that are secured by policy cash surrender values. The pattern of premium payments is a decision that does not alter the underlying nature of the insurance contract. [FTB85-4, ¶7]

.508 *Response*—The amount that could be realized under the insurance contract as of the date of the statement of financial position should be reported as an asset. The change

[501]The provisions of paragraphs .504 through .509 apply to all enterprises that purchase life insurance in which the enterprise is either the owner or beneficiary of the contract, without regard to the funding objective of the purchase. Such purchases would typically include those intended to meet loan covenants or to fund deferred compensation agreements, buy-sell agreements, or postemployment death benefits. Purchases of life insurance by retirement plans that are subject to Section Pe5, "Pension Funds: Accounting and Reporting," are not covered by paragraphs .504 through .509. [FTB85-4, ¶1, fn1]

in cash surrender or contract value during the period is an adjustment of premiums paid in determining the expense or income to be recognized under the contract for the period. [FTB85-4, ¶2]

.509 [A] business exchange rider allows an enterprise to use values in an existing policy to insure a different employee when the originally insured employee leaves the enterprise. [FTB85-4, ¶14] The business exchange rider is a significant development in the design of business insurance products and reduces additional policy costs if a covered employee leaves the enterprise. Such a provision does not affect the realization of future benefits under the insurance contract, nor does it change the traditional underwriting decisions involved in insuring a new life. Instead, the provision only reduces the cost of obtaining those benefits by allowing a new employee to be insured without the costs that are typically associated with obtaining a new policy. [FTB85-4, ¶15]

Supplemental Guidance: Emerging Issues Task Force (EITF) Issues

.1000 [Listed below are EITF Issues that provide supplemental guidance for this section. These Issues may be either interpretive of or related by topic to the guidance in this section.

EITF Issue No. 88-5, "Recognition of Insurance Death Benefits"
EITF Issue No. 93-14, "Accounting for Multiple-Year Retrospectively Rated Insurance Contracts by Insurance Enterprises and Other Enterprises"]

.1001 [Listed below is an EITF Issue that provides interpretive guidance on specific material in this section.

Paragraph .102 (FAS 5, ¶45)—EITF Issue No. 93-14]

(The next page is 26635.)

INTANGIBLE ASSETS (APB 17) SECTION I60

Most of the material in this section has been superseded by FASB Statement 142, *Goodwill and Other Intangible Assets*. Due to the delayed effective date of Statement 142, this section has been moved to Appendix E for continued reference by users. For goodwill and intangible assets acquired on or before June 30, 2001, this section may be applied. Section I60 must be applied for goodwill and other intangible assets arising from combinations between mutual enterprises or not-for-profit organizations. (Refer to Appendix C, "Effective Dates of Pronouncements," for details of the effective date and transition provisions of Statement 142.)

The guidance in this section provided by FASB Statements 4, 72, and 109, FASB Interpretation 9, and FASB Technical Bulletin 85-6 is still current and has been carried forward to Section G40, "Goodwill and Other Intangible Assets."

(The next page is 26971.)

INTEREST: CAPITALIZATION OF INTEREST COSTS

SECTION I67

Sources: FASB Statement 34; FASB Statement 42; FASB Statement 58; FASB Statement 62; FASB Statement 87; FASB Statement 144; FASB Interpretation 33

[**Note:** A list of Issues discussed by the Emerging Issues Task Force (EITF) that provide supplemental guidance for this section is presented in paragraph .1000.]

Summary

Interest cost shall be capitalized as part of the historical cost of acquiring certain assets. To qualify for interest capitalization, assets must require a period of time to get them ready for their intended use. Examples are assets that an enterprise constructs for its own use (such as facilities) and assets intended for sale or lease that are constructed as discrete projects (such as ships or real estate projects). Interest capitalization is required for those assets if its effect, compared with the effect of expensing interest, is material. If the net effect is not material, interest capitalization is not required. However, interest cannot be capitalized for inventories that are routinely manufactured or otherwise produced in large quantities on a repetitive basis, or on qualifying assets acquired using gifts or grants that are restricted by the donor or grantor to acquisition of those assets to the extent that funds are available from such gifts or grants.

In situations involving qualifying assets financed with the proceeds of restricted tax-exempt borrowings, the amount of interest cost to be capitalized shall be all interest cost of those borrowings less any interest earned on temporary investment of the proceeds of those borrowings from the date of borrowing until the specified qualifying assets acquired with those borrowings are ready for their intended use.

In all other situations, the interest cost eligible for capitalization shall be the interest cost recognized on borrowings and other obligations. The amount capitalized is to be an allocation of the interest cost incurred during the period required to complete the asset. The interest rate for capitalization purposes is to be based on the rates of the enterprise's outstanding borrowings. If the enterprise associates a specific new borrowing with the asset, it may apply the rate on that borrowing to the appropriate portion of the expenditures for the asset. A weighted average of the rates on other borrowings is to be applied to expenditures not covered by specific new borrowings. Judgment is required in identifying the borrowings on which the average rate is based.

.101 This section [presents] standards of financial accounting and reporting for capitalizing interest cost as a part of the historical cost of acquiring certain assets. For the purposes of this section, *interest cost* includes interest recognized on obligations having explicit interest rates,[1] interest imputed on certain types of payables in accordance with Section I69, "Interest: Imputation of an Interest Cost," and interest related to a capital lease determined in accordance with Section L10, "Leases." [FAS34, ¶1] The interest cost component of net periodic pension cost [(Section P16, "Pension Costs")] shall not be considered to be interest for purposes of this section. [FAS87, ¶16, fn4]

.102 The historical cost of acquiring an asset includes the costs necessarily incurred to bring it to the condition and location necessary for its intended use.[2] If an asset requires a period of time in which to carry out the activities[3] necessary to bring it to that condition and location, the interest cost incurred during that period as a result of expenditures for the asset is a part of the historical cost of acquiring the asset. [FAS34, ¶6]

.103 The objectives of capitalizing interest are (a) to obtain a measure of acquisition cost that more closely reflects the enterprise's total investment in the asset and (b) to charge a cost that relates to the acquisition of a resource that will benefit future periods against the revenues of the periods benefited. [FAS34, ¶7]

.104 In concept, interest cost is capitalizable for all assets that require a period of time to get them ready for their intended use (an *acquisition period*). However, in many cases, the benefit in terms of information about enterprise resources and earnings may not justify the additional accounting and administrative cost involved in providing the information. [FAS34, ¶8] Accordingly, interest shall not be capitalized in the situations described in paragraph .106. [FAS42, ¶4]

Assets Qualifying for Interest Capitalization

.105 Interest shall be capitalized for the following types of assets ([referred to as] *qualifying assets*): [FAS42, ¶4]

a. Assets that are constructed or otherwise produced for an enterprise's own use (including assets constructed or produced for the enterprise by others for which deposits or progress payments have been made)

[1]Interest cost on these obligations includes amounts resulting from periodic amortization of discount or premium and issue costs on debt. [FAS34, ¶1, fn1]

[2]The term *intended use* embraces both readiness for use and readiness for sale, depending on the purpose of acquisition. [FAS34, ¶6, fn3]

[3]Refer to paragraph .114 for a definition of those activities for purposes of this section. [FAS34, ¶6, fn4]

b. Assets intended for sale or lease that are constructed or otherwise produced as discrete projects (for example, ships or real estate developments) [FAS34, ¶9]
c. Investments (equity, loans, and advances) accounted for by the equity method while the investee has activities in progress necessary to commence its planned principal operations provided that the investee's activities include the use of funds to acquire qualifying assets for its operations. [FAS58, ¶5]

.106 However, interest cost shall not be capitalized for inventories that are routinely manufactured or otherwise produced in large quantities on a repetitive basis because the informational benefit does not justify the cost of so doing. In addition, interest shall not be capitalized for the following types of assets:

a. Assets that are in use or ready for their intended use in the earning activities of the enterprise
b. Assets that are not being used in the earning activities of the enterprise and that are not undergoing the activities necessary to get them ready for use [FAS34, ¶10]
c. Assets that are not included in the consolidated balance sheet of the parent company and consolidated subsidiaries
d. Investments accounted for by the equity method after the planned principal operations of the investee begin
e. Investments in regulated investees that are capitalizing both the cost of debt and equity capital [FAS58, ¶6]
f. Assets acquired with gifts and grants that are restricted by the donor or grantor to acquisition of those assets to the extent that funds are available from such gifts and grants. Interest earned from temporary investment of those funds that is similarly restricted shall be considered an addition to the gift or grant for this purpose. [FAS62, ¶5]

.107 Land that is not undergoing activities necessary to get it ready for its intended use is not a qualifying asset. If activities are undertaken for the purpose of developing land for a particular use, the expenditures to acquire the land qualify for interest capitalization while those activities are in progress. The interest cost capitalized on those expenditures is a cost of acquiring the asset that results from those activities. If the resulting asset is a structure, such as a plant or a shopping center, interest capitalized on the land expenditures is part of the acquisition cost of the structure. If the resulting asset is developed land, such as land that is to be sold as developed lots, interest capitalized on the land expenditures is part of the acquisition cost of the developed land. [FAS34, ¶11]

.108 For oil and gas producing operations accounted for by the full cost method, assets whose costs are being currently depreciated, depleted, or amortized are assets in use in the earning activities of the enterprise and are not assets qualifying for capitalization of interest cost. Unusually significant investments in unproved properties and major development projects[4] that are not being currently depreciated, depleted, or amortized and on which exploration or development activities are in progress are assets qualifying for capitalization of interest cost. Similarly, in a cost center with no production, significant properties and projects on which exploration or development activities are in progress are assets qualifying for capitalization of interest cost. [FIN33, ¶2]

The Amount of Interest Cost to Be Capitalized

.109 The amount of interest cost to be capitalized for qualifying assets is intended to be that portion of the interest cost incurred during the assets' acquisition periods that theoretically could have been avoided (for example, by avoiding additional borrowings or by using the funds expended for the assets to repay existing borrowings) if expenditures for the assets had not been made. [FAS34, ¶12] [Refer to paragraph .1001 for an EITF Issue that provides interpretive guidance on paragraphs .109 through .111.]

.110 The amount capitalized in an accounting period shall be determined by applying an interest rate(s) ([referred to as] the *capitalization rate*) to the average amount of accumulated expenditures for the asset during the period.[5] The capitalization rates used in an accounting period shall be based on the rates applicable to borrowings outstanding during the period. If an enterprise's financing plans associate a specific new borrowing with a qualifying asset, the enterprise may use the rate on that borrowing as the capitalization rate to be applied to that portion of the average accumulated expenditures for the asset that does not exceed that amount of that borrowing. If average accumulated expenditures for the asset exceed the amounts of specific new borrowings associated with the asset, the capitalization rate to be applied to such excess shall be a weighted average of the rates applicable to other borrowings of the enterprise. [FAS34, ¶13]

.111 In identifying the borrowings to be included in the weighted average rate, the objective is a reasonable measure of the cost of financing acquisition of the asset in terms of the interest cost incurred that otherwise could have been avoided. Accordingly, judgment will be required to make a selection of borrowings that best accomplishes that objective in the circumstances. For example, in some circumstances, it will be appropriate to include all borrowings of the parent company and its consolidated subsidiaries; for some multinational enterprises, it may be appropriate for each foreign subsidiary to use

---

[4]Judgments as to what constitute *unusually significant* investments and *major* projects should be determined by an enterprise and its auditors based upon the enterprise's facts and circumstances. [FIN33, ¶12]

[5]If qualifying assets are financed with the proceeds of tax-exempt borrowings and those funds are externally restricted to the acquisition of specified qualifying assets or to service the related debt, the amount of interest cost capitalized shall be determined in accordance with paragraphs .116A and .116B of this section. [FAS62, ¶6]

an average of the rates applicable to its own borrowings. However, the use of judgment in determining capitalization rates shall not circumvent the requirement that a capitalization rate be applied to all capitalized expenditures for a qualifying asset to the extent that interest cost has been incurred during an accounting period. [FAS34, ¶14]

.112 The total amount of interest cost capitalized in an accounting period shall not exceed the total amount of interest cost incurred by the enterprise in that period. In consolidated financial statements, that limitation shall be applied by reference to the total amount of interest cost incurred by the parent company and consolidated subsidiaries on a consolidated basis. In any separately issued financial statements of a parent company or a consolidated subsidiary and in the financial statements (whether separately issued or not) of unconsolidated subsidiaries and other investees accounted for by the equity method, the limitation shall be applied by reference to the total amount of interest cost (including interest on intercompany borrowings) incurred by the separate entity. [FAS34, ¶15]

.113 For purposes of this section, *expenditures* to which capitalization rates are to be applied are capitalized expenditures (net of progress payment collections) for the qualifying asset that have required the payment of cash, the transfer of other assets, or the incurring of a liability on which interest is recognized (in contrast to liabilities, such as trade payables, accruals, and retainages on which interest is not recognized). However, reasonable approximations of net capitalized expenditures may be used. For example, capitalized costs for an asset may be used as a reasonable approximation of capitalized expenditures unless the difference is material. [FAS34, ¶16]

The Capitalization Period

.114 In situations involving qualifying assets financed with the proceeds of tax-exempt borrowings that are externally restricted as specified in paragraph .116A, the capitalization period begins at the date of the borrowing. [FAS62, ¶7] [In other situations,] the capitalization period shall begin when [the following] three conditions are present:

a. Expenditures (as defined in paragraph .113) for the asset have been made.
b. Activities that are necessary to get the asset ready for its intended use are in progress.
c. Interest cost is being incurred.

Interest capitalization shall continue as long as those three conditions are present. The term *activities* is to be construed broadly. It encompasses more than physical construction; it includes all the steps required to prepare the asset for its intended use. For example, it includes administrative and technical activities during the preconstruction stage, such as the development of plans or the process of obtaining permits from governmental authorities; it includes activities undertaken after construction has begun in order to overcome unforeseen obstacles, such as technical problems, labor disputes, or litigation. If the enterprise suspends substantially all activities related to acquisition of the asset, interest capitalization shall cease until activities are resumed. However, brief interruptions in activities, interruptions that are externally imposed, and delays that are inherent in the asset acquisition process shall not require cessation of interest capitalization. [FAS34, ¶17]

.115 The capitalization period shall end when the asset is substantially complete[6] and ready for its intended use. Some assets are completed in parts, and each part is capable of being used independently while work is continuing on other parts. An example is a condominium. For such assets, interest capitalization shall stop on each part when it is substantially complete and ready for use. Some assets must be completed in their entirety before any part of the asset can be used. An example is a facility designed to manufacture products by sequential processes. For such assets, interest capitalization shall continue until the entire asset is substantially complete and ready for use. Some assets cannot be used effectively until a separate facility has been completed. Examples are the oil wells drilled in Alaska before completion of the pipeline. For such assets, interest capitalization shall continue until the separate facility is substantially complete and ready for use. [FAS34, ¶18]

.116 Interest capitalization shall not cease when present accounting principles require recognition of a lower value for the asset than acquisition cost; the provision required to reduce acquisition cost to such lower value shall be increased appropriately. [FAS34, ¶19] The provisions of paragraphs .139 through .161 of Section I08, "Impairment," apply in recognizing impairment of long-lived assets held for use. [FAS144, ¶C26]

Capitalization of Interest Cost in Situations Involving Certain Tax-Exempt Borrowings and Certain Gifts and Grants

.116A Interest earned shall not be offset against interest cost in determining either capitalization rates or limitations on the amount of interest cost to be capitalized except in situations involving acquisition of qualifying assets financed with the proceeds of tax-exempt borrowings if those funds are externally restricted to finance acquisition of specified qualifying assets or to service the related debt. [FAS62, ¶3]

[6]The term *substantially complete* is used to prohibit continuation of interest capitalization in situations in which completion of the asset is intentionally delayed. For example, it is customary for a condominium developer to defer installation of certain fixtures and fittings until units are sold, so that buyers may choose the types and colors they want. An intentional delay of that kind is related more to marketing of the asset than to the exigencies of the asset acquisition process. Similarly, interest is not to be capitalized during periods when the enterprise intentionally defers or suspends activities related to the asset. Interest cost incurred during such periods is a holding cost, not an acquisition cost. [FAS34, ¶58]

.116B The amount of interest cost capitalized on qualifying assets acquired with proceeds of tax-exempt borrowings that are externally restricted as specified in paragraph .116A shall be all interest cost of the borrowing less any interest earned on related interest-bearing investments acquired with proceeds of the related tax-exempt borrowings[7] from the date of the borrowing until the assets are ready for their intended use. Interest cost of a tax-exempt borrowing shall be eligible for capitalization on other qualifying assets of the entity when the specified qualifying assets are no longer eligible for interest capitalization. [FAS62, ¶4]

Example

.116C The following example illustrates the application of [paragraphs .116A and .116B] in the situation described below:

a. The entity is committed to construct Project A at a cost of $10 million. Project A is to be financed from three sources:
   (1) $4 million government grant restricted to use for the specified construction project, payable $1 million per year
   (2) $4 million tax-exempt borrowing at an interest rate of 8 percent ($320,000 per year)
   (3) $2 million from operations
b. The entity has $10 million in other borrowings that are outstanding throughout the construction of Project A. The interest rate on those borrowings is 6 percent. Other qualifying assets of the entity never exceed $5 million during the construction of Project A.
c. The proceeds from the borrowing and the initial phase of the grant are received 1 year in advance of starting construction on Project A and are temporarily invested in interest-bearing investments yielding 12 percent. Interest income earned from temporary investments is not reinvested.
d. Project A will take 4 years after start of construction to complete.
e. The table on the following page sets forth the amount of interest to be capitalized as part of the entity's investment in Project A.
f. Over the course of construction the net cost of financing is $678,000, the sum of the interest capitalized for the 5 years. Accordingly, the entity's total net investment in Project A will be $10,678,000.

[7]The interest cost and interest earned on any portion of the proceeds of the tax-exempt borrowings that are not designated for the acquisition of specified qualifying assets and servicing the related debt are excluded. The entire interest cost on that portion of the proceeds that is available for other uses (such as refunding of an existing debt issue other than a construction loan related to those assets) is eligible for capitalization on other qualifying assets. [FAS62, ¶4, fn1]

	Year				
	19X1	**19X2**	**19X3**	**19X4**	**19X5**
	(amounts in thousands)				
(1) Assumed average qualifying assets	$ 0	$2,000	$5,000	$8,000	$9,000
(2) Average funding received					
borrowing	4,000	4,000	4,000	4,000	4,000
grant	1,000	2,000	3,000	4,000	4,000
(3) Average temporary investments ((2) – (1), not less than zero)*					
borrowing	4,000	3,000	1,000	0	0
grant	1,000	1,000	1,000	0	0
(4) Interest earned ((3) × 12 percent)					
(a) borrowing	480	360	120	0	0
(b) grant	120	120	120	0	0
(5) Average qualifying assets in excess of borrowing, grant, and interest earned on grant†	0	0	0	0	640
(6) Interest cost capitalized—other borrowings ((5) × 6 percent)	0	0	0	0	38
(7) Interest cost—tax-exempt borrowings	320	320	320	320	320
(8) Interest capitalized ((6) + (7) – (4)(a))‡	(160)	(40)	200	320	358

*Balances of unexpended borrowings and unexpended grants can vary depending on the source from which the entity elects to disburse funds.

†That is, (1) average qualifying assets minus the sum of ((2) average funding received plus (4)(b) cumulative interest earned on grant), not less than zero.

‡Note that amounts in parentheses are reductions in the cost of the asset.

[FAS62, ¶10]

Disposition of the Amount Capitalized

.117 Because interest cost is an integral part of the total cost of acquiring a qualifying asset, its disposition shall be the same as that of other components of asset cost. [FAS34, ¶20] Interest capitalized on an investment accounted for by the equity method shall be accounted for in accordance with Section I82, "Investments: Equity Method," paragraph .109(b), which states: "A difference between the cost of an investment and the amount of underlying equity in net assets of an investee should be accounted for as if the investee were a consolidated subsidiary." [FAS58, ¶7]

Disclosures

.118 The following information with respect to interest cost shall be disclosed in the financial statements or related notes:

a. For an accounting period in which no interest cost is capitalized, the amount of interest cost incurred and charged to expense during the period
b. For an accounting period in which some interest cost is capitalized, the total amount of interest cost incurred during the period and the amount thereof that has been capitalized. [FAS34, ¶21]

Supplemental Guidance

.501–.503 [Deleted 6/82 because of FASB Statement 62, *Capitalization of Interest Cost in Situations Involving Certain Tax-Exempt Borrowings and Certain Gifts and Grants.*]

Supplemental Guidance: Emerging Issues Task Force (EITF) Issues

.1000 [Listed below is an EITF Issue that provides supplemental guidance for this section. This Issue is interpretive of the guidance in this section.

EITF Issue No. 99-9, "Effect of Derivative Gains and Losses on the Capitalization of Interest"]

.1001 [Listed below is an EITF Issue that provides interpretive guidance on specific material in this section.

Paragraphs .109 through .111 (FAS 34, ¶12–14)—EITF Issue No. 99-9]

(The next page is 27087.)

INTEREST: IMPUTATION OF AN INTEREST COST SECTION I69

Sources: APB Opinion 12; APB Opinion 21; AICPA Interpretation of APB Opinion 21; FASB Statement 34; FASB Statement 109

[**Note:** A list of Issues discussed by the Emerging Issues Task Force (EITF) that provide supplemental guidance for this section is presented in paragraph .1000.]

Summary

Receivables and payables (notes) that are contractual rights to receive or pay money at a fixed or determinable date are recorded at the present value of the consideration given or received in the exchange.

This section does not apply to:

a. Receivables and payables from the normal course of business maturing in less than one year
b. Amounts that will be applied to the purchase price of property, goods, or services
c. Security deposits and retainages
d. Financial institutions' customary lending activities
e. Transactions when interest rates are affected by tax attributes or legal restrictions prescribed by a governmental agency
f. Parent-subsidiary transactions.

When a note is exchanged for cash only, the present value of the note is measured by the cash proceeds given or received. If rights or privileges are exchanged in addition to cash, the difference between the present value of the note and the cash exchanged is considered applicable to those rights and privileges.

When a note is exchanged for property, goods, or services in an arm's-length transaction, there is a general presumption that the note's stipulated rate of interest is fair and adequate unless (a) no interest rate is stated, (b) the stated rate is unreasonable, or (c) the face amount of the note differs materially from the current cash sales price of the property, goods, or services exchanged for the note or the market value of the note. In these circumstances, the exchange is valued at the fair value of the property, goods, or services or at an amount that reasonably approximates the market value of the note, whichever is more clearly determinable. In the absence of established exchange prices for the property, goods, or services or evidence of the market price of the note, the present value of the note is determined by discounting all future payments using an imputed rate of interest. The imputed interest rate used is one that approximates the rate that an independent borrower and lender would have negotiated in a similar transaction.

Any difference between the face amount of the note and its present value is accounted for as a discount or premium and amortized over the life of the note by the interest method or any other method that produces approximately the same results.

Applicability

.101 This section is applicable to receivables and payables that represent contractual rights to receive money or contractual obligations to pay money on fixed or determinable dates, whether or not there is any stated provision for interest, except as stated in paragraphs .102 and .103. Such receivables and payables are collectively referred to in this section as *notes*. Examples are secured and unsecured notes, debentures, bonds, mortgage notes, equipment obligations, and some accounts receivable and payable. [APB21, ¶2]

.102 Except that paragraph .109 covering statement presentation of discount and premium is applicable in all circumstances, this section is not intended to apply to:

a. Receivables and payables arising from transactions with customers or suppliers in the normal course of business that are due in customary trade terms not exceeding approximately one year
b. Amounts that do not require repayment in the future, but rather will be applied to the purchase price of the property, goods, or services involved (for example, deposits or progress payments on construction contracts, advance payments for acquisition of resources and raw materials, advances to encourage exploration in the extractive industries)
c. Amounts intended to provide security for one party to an agreement (for example, security deposits, retainages on contracts)
d. The customary cash lending activities and demand or savings deposit activities of financial institutions whose primary business is lending money
e. Transactions when interest rates are affected by the tax attributes or legal restrictions prescribed by a governmental agency (for example, industrial revenue bonds, tax-exempt obligations, government-guaranteed obligations, income tax settlements)
f. Transactions between parent company and subsidiaries and between subsidiaries of a common parent.

[APB21, ¶3]

.103 This section is also not intended to apply to the application of the *present value*[1] measurement (valuation) technique to estimates of contractual or other obligations assumed in connection with sales of property, goods, or services—for example, a warranty for product performance. [APB21, ¶4]

Notes Exchanged for Cash or for Cash and Rights or Privileges

.104 When a note[2] is received or issued solely for cash and no other right or privilege is exchanged, it is presumed to have a present value at issuance measured by the cash proceeds exchanged. If cash and some other rights or privileges are exchanged for a note, the value of the rights or privileges shall be given accounting recognition [APB21, ¶11] by establishing a note discount or premium account. In such instances, the effective interest rate differs from the stated rate. For example, an enterprise may lend a supplier cash which is to be repaid five years hence with no stated interest. Such a noninterest-bearing loan may be partial consideration under a purchase contract for supplier products at lower than the prevailing market prices. In this circumstance, the difference between the present value of the receivable and the cash loaned to the supplier is appropriately regarded as an addition to the cost of products purchased during the contract term. The note discount is amortized as interest income over the five-year life of the note. [APB21, ¶7]

Notes Exchanged for Property, Goods, or Services

.105 When a note is exchanged for property, goods, or services in a bargained transaction entered into at arm's length, there shall be a general presumption that the rate of interest stipulated by the parties to the transaction represents fair and adequate compensation to the supplier for the use of the related funds. That presumption, however, must not permit the form of the transaction to prevail over its economic substance and thus would not apply if (a) interest is not stated or (b) the stated interest rate is unreasonable (refer to paragraphs .106 and .107) or (c) the stated face amount of the note is materially different from the current cash sales price for the same or similar items or from the market value of the note at the date of the transaction. In these circumstances, the note, the sales price, and the cost of the property, goods, or services exchanged for the note shall be recorded at the fair value of the property, goods, or services or at an amount that reasonably approximates the market value of the note, whichever is the more clearly determinable. That amount may or may not be the same as its face amount, and any resulting discount or premium shall be accounted for as an element of interest over the life of the note (refer to paragraph .108). In the absence of established exchange prices for the

[1]*Present value* is the sum of the future payments discounted to the present date at an appropriate rate of interest (refer to paragraphs .111 and .112 for examples). [APB21, ¶1, fn1]

[2]Paragraphs .101 through .103 describe the applicability of this section. [APB21, ¶11, fn6]

related property, goods, or services or evidence of the market value of the note, the present value of a note that stipulates either no interest or a rate of interest that is clearly unreasonable shall be determined by discounting all future payments on the notes using an imputed rate of interest as described in paragraphs .106 and .107. This determination shall be made at the time the note is issued, assumed, or acquired; any subsequent changes in prevailing interest rates shall be ignored. [APB21, ¶12]

Determining an Appropriate Interest Rate

.106 The variety of transactions encountered precludes any specific interest rate from being applicable in all circumstances. However, some general guides may be stated. The choice of a rate may be affected by the credit standing of the issuer, restrictive covenants, the collateral payment and other terms pertaining to the debt, and, if appropriate, the tax consequences to the buyer and seller. The prevailing rates for similar instruments of issuers with similar credit ratings will normally help determine the appropriate interest rate for determining the present value of a specific note at its date of issuance. In any event, the rate used for valuation purposes will normally be at least equal to the rate at which the debtor can obtain financing of a similar nature from other sources at the date of the transaction. The objective is to approximate the rate that would have resulted if an independent borrower and an independent lender had negotiated a similar transaction under comparable terms and conditions with the option to pay the cash price upon purchase or to give a note for the amount of the purchase which bears the prevailing rate of interest to maturity. [APB21, ¶13]

.107 The selection of a rate may be affected by many considerations. For instance, where applicable, the choice of a rate may be influenced by (a) an approximation of the prevailing market rates for the source of credit that would provide a market for sale or assignment of the note; (b) the prime or higher rate for notes that are discounted with banks, giving due weight to the credit standing of the maker; (c) published market rates for similar quality bonds; (d) current rates for debentures with substantially identical terms and risks that are traded in open markets; and (e) the current rate charged by investors for first or second mortgage loans on similar property. [APB21, ¶14]

Amortization of Discount and Premium

.108 With respect to a note that by the provisions of this section requires the imputation of interest, the difference between the present value and the face amount shall be treated as discount or premium[3] and amortized as interest expense or income over the life of the note in such a way as to result in a constant rate of interest when applied to the amount outstanding at the beginning of any given period. This is the *interest* method.[4] Other methods of amortization may be used if the results obtained are not materially different from those that would result from the *interest* method. [APB21, ¶15]

Statement Presentation of Discount and Premium

.109 The discount or premium resulting from the determination of present value in cash or noncash transactions is not an asset or liability separable from the note that gives rise to it. Therefore, the discount or premium shall be reported in the balance sheet as a direct deduction from or addition to the face amount of the note. It shall not be classified as a deferred charge or deferred credit. The description of the note shall include the effective interest rate; the face amount shall also be disclosed in the financial statements or in the notes to the statements.[5] Amortization of discount or premium shall be reported as interest expense. Issue costs shall be reported in the balance sheet as deferred charges. [APB21, ¶16]

Eligibility for Interest Capitalization

.110 Paragraphs .108 and .109 provide that the discount or premium that results from imputing interest for certain types of payables shall be amortized as interest expense over the life of the payable and reported as such in the statement of income. The amount chargeable to interest expense under the provisions of those paragraphs is eligible for inclusion in the amount of interest cost [that is] capitalizable [as a part of the historical cost of acquiring certain assets] in accordance with Section I67, "Interest: Capitalization of Interest Costs." [FAS34, ¶2]

---

[3]Differences between the recognition for financial accounting purposes and income tax purposes of discount or premium resulting from determination of the present value of a note should be treated as [APB21, ¶15, fn8] temporary differences [in accordance with] Section I27, "Income Taxes." [FAS109, ¶287]

[4]The *interest* method of amortization is an acceptable method [APB12, ¶17] [for determining] the periodic amortization of discount and expense or premium on debt (that is, the difference between the net proceeds, after expense, received upon issuance of debt and the amount repayable at its maturity) over its term. The objective of the interest method is to arrive at a periodic interest cost (including amortization) which will represent a level effective rate on the sum of the face amount of the debt and (plus or minus) the unamortized premium or discount and expense at the beginning of each period. The difference between the periodic interest cost so calculated and the nominal interest on the outstanding amount of the debt is the amount of periodic amortization. [APB12, ¶16]

[5]Refer to paragraph .113 for illustrations of balance sheet presentation. [APB21, ¶16, fn9]

Examples of Determining Present Value

Example 1

.111 Consider the issuance of a $1,000, 20-year bond which bears interest at 10 percent annually. If we assume that 10 percent is an appropriate market rate of interest for such a bond, the proceeds at issuance will be $1,000. The bond payable would be recorded at $1,000 which represents the amount repayable at maturity and also the present value at issuance which is equal to the proceeds. However, under similar circumstances, if the prevailing market rate were more (less) than 10 percent, a 20-year, 10-percent bond with a face amount of $1,000 would usually have a value at issuance and provide cash proceeds of less (more) than $1,000. The significant point is that, upon issuance, a bond is valued at (a) the present value of the future coupon interest payments plus (b) the present value of the future principal payments (face amount). These two sets of future cash payments are discounted at the prevailing market rate of interest (for an equivalent security) at the date of issuance of the debt. As the 8-percent and 12-percent columns show, premium or discount arises when the prevailing market rate of interest differs from the coupon rate:

	Assume prevailing market rate of		
	10%	**8%**	**12%**
1. Present value of annual interest payments of $100 (the coupon rate of 10% of $1,000) for 20 years	$ 851	$ 982	$747
2. Present value of payment of the face amount of $1,000 at the end of year 20	149	215	104
Present value and proceeds at date of issuance	$1,000	$1,197	$851

[APB21, ¶18]

Example 2

.112 In the case of a $1,000, non-interest-bearing 20-year note, when the prevailing market rate for comparable credit risks is 10 percent, the following valuation shall be made:

1. Present value of no annual interest payments	$ 0
2. Present value of payment of the face amount of $1,000 at the end of year 20	149
Present value and proceeds at date of issuance	$149

Comparison of the results of the illustrations in paragraph .111 with the illustration above shows the significant impact of interest. [APB21, ¶19]

Illustrations of Balance Sheet Presentation of Notes That Are Discounted

Example 1

.113 [Balance sheet presentation of] discount presented in the caption [is as follows:]

	December 31,	
	19Y0	19X9
Note Receivable from Sale of Property:		
$1,000,000 face amount, noninterest bearing, due December 31, 19Y5 (less unamortized discount based on imputed interest rate of 8%—19Y0, $320,000; 19X9, $370,000)	$680,000	$630,000

[APB21, ¶20]

Example 2

.114 [Balance sheet presentation of] discount presented separately [is as follows:]

	December 31,	
	19Y0	19X9
Note Receivable from Sale of Property:		
Non-interest-bearing note due December 31, 19Y5	$1,000,000	$1,000,000
Less unamortized discount based on imputed interest rate of 8%	320,000	370,000
Note receivable less unamortized discount	$ 680,000	$ 630,000

[APB21, ¶20]

Example 3

.115 [Balance sheet presentation of] several notes involved [is as follows:]

	December 31, 19Y0	December 31, 19X9
Long-Term Debt (Note A):		
Principal amount	$24,000,000	$24,000,000
Less unamortized discount	2,070,000	2,192,000
Long-term debt less unamortized discount	$21,930,000	$21,808,000

Note A—Long-Term Debt: Long-term debt at December 31, 19Y0 consisted of the following:

	Principal	Unamortized Discount
6% subordinated debentures, due 19Z4 (discount is based on imputed interest rate of 7%)	$20,000,000	$1,750,000
6½% of bank loan, due 19Y3	3,000,000	
Non-interest-bearing note issued in connection with acquisition of property, due 19Y5 (discount is based on imputed interest rate of 8%)	1,000,000	320,000
Total	$24,000,000	$2,070,000

[APB21, ¶20]

Supplemental Guidance

Advance Not Requiring Imputation

.501 *Question*—This section requires interest to be imputed for some rights to receive or obligations to pay money on fixed or determinable dates. In certain transactions, pipeline enterprises make advances to encourage exploration. These advances are satisfied by delivery of future production, but there is also a definite obligation to repay if the future production is insufficient to discharge the obligation by a definite date. Does this section apply to such advances? [AIN-APB21]

.502 *Interpretation*—No, paragraph .102 states that this section is not intended to apply to "amounts that do not require repayment in the future, but rather will be applied to the purchase price of the property, goods, or services involved (for example, deposits or progress payments on construction contracts, advance payments for acquisition of resources and raw materials, advances to encourage exploration in the extractive industries)." The advance described in the paragraph above is covered by the exclusion in paragraph .102 even though there may be an obligation to repay should the future production prove insufficient to discharge the obligation. [AIN-APB21]

Supplemental Guidance: Emerging Issues Task Force (EITF) Issues

.1000 [Listed below are EITF Issues that provide supplemental guidance for this section. These Issues are related by topic to the guidance in this section.

EITF Issue No. 86-15, "Increasing-Rate Debt"

EITF Issue No. 86-28, "Accounting Implications of Indexed Debt Instruments"

EITF Issue No. 86-45, "Imputation of Dividends on Preferred Stock Redeemable at the Issuer's Option with Initial Below-Market Dividend Rate"

EITF Issue No. 96-12, "Recognition of Interest Income and Balance Sheet Classification of Structured Notes"

EITF Issue No. 98-14, "Debtor's Accounting for Changes in Line-of-Credit or Revolving-Debt Arrangements"]

(The next page is 27279.)

INTERIM FINANCIAL REPORTING SECTION I73

Sources: APB Opinion 28; FASB Statement 3; FASB Statement 16; FASB Statement 69; FASB Statement 95; FASB Statement 109; FASB Statement 128; FASB Statement 130; FASB Statement 131; FASB Statement 135; FASB Statement 141; FASB Statement 144; FASB Interpretation 18; FASB Technical Bulletin 79-9

[**Note:** A list of Issues discussed by the Emerging Issues Task Force (EITF) that provide supplemental guidance for this section is presented in paragraph .1000.]

Summary

Each interim period shall be viewed primarily as an integral part of an annual period. The results for each interim period shall be based on the accounting principles and practices used by an enterprise in the preparation of its latest annual financial statements unless a change in an accounting practice or policy has been adopted in the current year. However, certain accounting principles and practices followed for annual reporting purposes may require modification at interim reporting dates so that the reported results for the interim period may better relate to the results of operations for the annual period.

This section provides guidance concerning modifications that are necessary or desirable at interim dates in accounting principles or practices followed for annual periods. It also requires that an enterprise make at the end of each interim period its best estimate of the effective tax rate expected to be applicable for the full fiscal year. The rate so determined shall be used in providing for income taxes on a current year-to-date basis.

Introduction

.101 This section indicates the applicability of generally accepted accounting principles [APB28, ¶3] to interim reporting and sets forth minimum disclosure requirements for interim financial reports of publicly traded enterprises.[1] This section does not deal with unresolved matters of accounting related to annual reporting. [APB28, ¶6]

[1] A publicly traded enterprise for purposes of this section includes any enterprise whose securities trade in a public market on either (a) a stock exchange (domestic or foreign) or (b) in the over-the-counter market (including securities quoted only locally or regionally). When an enterprise makes a filing with a regulatory agency in preparation for sale of its securities in a public market, it is considered a publicly traded enterprise for this purpose. [APB28, ¶6, fn1]

.102 [Generally accepted] accounting principles and reporting practices shall apply to interim financial information in the manner set forth in this section. The guides expressed in this section are applicable whenever an enterprise issues interim financial information. [APB28, ¶7]

Determining Interim Financial Information

.103 Each interim period shall be viewed primarily as an integral part of an annual period. [APB28, ¶9] The results for each interim period shall be based on the accounting principles and practices used by an enterprise in the preparation of its latest annual financial statements unless a change in an accounting practice or policy has been adopted in the current year (refer to paragraphs .131 through .145). However, certain accounting principles and practices followed for annual reporting purposes shall require modification at interim reporting dates so that the reported results for the interim period may better relate to the results of operations for the annual period. Paragraphs .105 through .123 set forth the modifications that are necessary or desirable at interim dates in accounting principles or practices followed for annual periods. [APB28, ¶10]

Revenue

.104 Revenue from products sold or services rendered shall be recognized as earned during an interim period on the same basis as followed for the full year.[2] [APB28, ¶11]

Costs and Expenses

.105 Costs and expenses for interim reporting purposes shall be classified as:

a. Costs associated with revenue—those costs that are associated directly with or allocated to the products sold or to the services rendered and are charged against income in those interim periods in which the related revenue is recognized.
b. All other costs and expenses—those costs and expenses that are not allocated to the products sold or to the services rendered and are charged against income in interim fiscal periods as incurred, or are allocated among interim periods based on an estimate of time expired, benefit received, or other activity associated with the periods.

[APB28, ¶12]

[2]For example, revenues from long-term construction-type contracts accounted for under the percentage-of-completion method shall be recognized in interim periods on the same basis followed for the full year. Losses projected on such contracts shall be recognized in full during the interim period in which the existence of such losses becomes evident. [APB28, ¶11]

Costs Associated with Revenue

.106 Those costs and expenses that are associated directly with or allocated to the products sold or to the services rendered for annual reporting purposes (including, for example, material costs, wages and salaries and related fringe benefits, manufacturing overhead, and warranties) shall be similarly treated for interim reporting purposes. [APB28, ¶13]

.107 [An enterprise shall] generally use the same inventory pricing methods and make provisions for write-downs to market at interim dates on the same basis as used at annual inventory dates with the following exceptions, as appropriate, at interim reporting dates:

a. Some enterprises use estimated gross profit rates to determine the costs of goods sold during interim periods or use other methods different from those used at annual inventory dates. Those enterprises shall disclose the method used at the interim date and any significant adjustments that result from reconciliations with the annual physical inventory.
b. An enterprise that uses the LIFO method may encounter a liquidation of base period inventories at an interim date that is expected to be replaced by the end of the annual period. In such a case the inventory at the interim reporting date shall not give effect to the LIFO liquidation, and costs of sales for the interim reporting period shall include the expected cost of replacement of the liquidated LIFO base.
c. Inventory losses from market declines shall not be deferred beyond the interim period in which the decline occurs. Recoveries of such losses on the same inventory in later interim periods of the same fiscal year through market price recoveries shall be recognized as gains in the later interim period. Such gains shall not exceed previously recognized losses. Some market declines at interim dates, however, can reasonably be expected to be restored in the fiscal year. Such *temporary* market declines need not be recognized at the interim date since no loss is expected to be incurred in the fiscal year.
d. An enterprise that uses standard cost accounting systems for determining inventory and product costs shall generally follow the same procedures in reporting purchase price, wage rate, usage or efficiency variances from standard cost at the end of an interim period as followed at the end of a fiscal year. Purchase price variances or volume or capacity cost variances that are planned and expected to be absorbed by the end of the annual period shall be deferred at interim reporting dates. The effect of unplanned or unanticipated purchase price or volume variances, however, shall be reported at the end of an interim period following the same procedures used at the end of a fiscal year.

[APB28, ¶14] [Refer to paragraph .1001 for an EITF Issue that provides interpretive guidance on this paragraph.]

All Other Costs and Expenses

.108 The following standards shall apply in accounting for costs and expenses other than product costs in interim periods:

a. Costs and expenses other than product costs shall be charged to income in interim periods as incurred, or be allocated among interim periods based on an estimate of time expired, benefit received or activity associated with the periods. Procedures adopted for assigning specific cost and expense items to an interim period shall be consistent with the bases followed by the enterprise in reporting results of operations at annual reporting dates. However, if a specific cost or expense item charged to expense for annual reporting purposes benefits more than one interim period, the cost or expense item shall be allocated to those interim periods (refer to paragraph .150).
b. Costs and expenses incurred in an interim period that cannot be readily identified with the activities or benefits of other interim periods shall be charged to the interim period in which incurred. Disclosure shall be made as to the nature and amount of such costs unless items of a comparable nature are included in both the current interim period and in the corresponding interim period of the preceding year.
c. Arbitrary assignment of the amount of such costs to an interim period shall not be made.
d. Gains and losses that arise in any interim period similar to those that would not be deferred at year-end shall not be deferred to later interim periods within the same fiscal year.

[APB28, ¶15] [Refer to paragraph .150 for examples of accounting for costs and expenses other than product costs.]

.109 The amounts of certain costs and expenses are frequently subjected to year-end adjustments even though they can reasonably be approximated at interim dates. To the extent possible, such adjustments shall be estimated and the estimated costs and expenses assigned to interim periods so that the interim periods bear a reasonable portion of the anticipated annual amount. Examples of such items include inventory shrinkage, allowances for uncollectible accounts, allowances for quantity discounts, and discretionary year-end bonuses. [APB28, ¶17]

Seasonal Revenue, Costs, or Expenses

.110 Revenues of certain enterprises are subject to material seasonal variations. To avoid the possibility that interim results with material seasonal variations may be taken as fairly indicative of the estimated results for a full fiscal year, such businesses shall disclose the seasonal nature of their activities, and consider supplementing their interim reports with information for 12-month periods ended at the interim date for the current and preceding years. [APB28, ¶18]

Income Tax Provisions

Estimated Annual Effective Tax Rate[3]

.111 At the end of each interim period the enterprise shall make its best estimate of the effective tax rate expected to be applicable for the full fiscal year. The rate so determined shall be used in providing for income taxes on a current year-to-date basis. The effective tax rate shall reflect anticipated investment tax credits, foreign tax rates, percentage depletion, capital gains rates, and other available tax planning alternatives.[4] [APB28, ¶19] It also includes the effect of any valuation allowance expected to be necessary at the end of the year for deferred tax assets related to originating deductible temporary differences and carryforwards during the year. [FAS109, ¶288(y)] However, in arriving at this effective tax rate no effect shall be included for the tax related to significant, unusual, or extraordinary items that will be separately reported or reported net of their related tax effect in reports for the interim period or for the fiscal year. [APB28, ¶19]

.112 The rate is revised, if necessary, as of the end of each successive interim period during the fiscal year to the enterprise's best *current* estimate of its annual effective tax rate. In some cases, the rate will be the statutory rate modified as may be appropriate in particular circumstances. In other cases, the rate will be the enterprise's estimate of the **tax (or benefit)** that will be provided for the fiscal year, stated as a percentage of its

---

[3]Refer also to paragraph .113 when the enterprise has operations taxable in multiple jurisdictions. [FIN18, ¶8, fn3]

[4]Certain investment tax credits may be excluded from the estimated annual effective tax rate. If an enterprise includes allowable investment tax credits as part of its provision for income taxes over the productive life of acquired property and not entirely in the year the property is placed in service, amortization of deferred investment tax credits need not be taken into account in estimating the annual effective tax rate; however, if the investment tax credits are taken into account in the estimated annual effective tax rate, the amount taken into account shall be the amount of amortization that is anticipated to be included in income in the current year (refer to Section I27, "Income Taxes," paragraphs .228 and .232). Further, Section L10, "Leases," paragraphs .145 and .146, specifies that the investment tax credits related to leases that are accounted for as leveraged leases shall be deferred and accounted for as return on the net investment in the leveraged leases in the years in which the net investment is positive. Section L10, footnote 39, explains that the use of the term *years* is not intended to preclude application of the accounting described to shorter periods. If an enterprise accounts for investment tax credits related to leveraged leases in accordance with Section L10, paragraphs .145 and .146, for interim periods, those investment tax credits shall not be taken into account in estimating the annual effective tax rate. [FIN18, ¶8, fn6]

estimated **ordinary income (or loss)** for the fiscal year (refer to paragraphs .121 through .123 if an ordinary loss is anticipated for the fiscal year).[5] [FIN18, ¶8] The tax (or benefit) related to ordinary income (or loss) shall be computed at an estimated annual effective tax rate[6] and the tax (or benefit) related to all other items shall be individually computed and recognized when the items occur. [FIN18, ¶6] Disclosure shall be made of the reasons for significant variations in the customary relationship between income tax expense and pretax accounting income, if they are not otherwise apparent from the financial statements or from the nature of the enterprise's business [APB28, ¶19, fn2] (refer to Section I27, paragraph .147). [FAS109, ¶288(h)]

Operations Taxable in Multiple Jurisdictions

.113 If an enterprise that is subject to tax in multiple jurisdictions pays taxes based on identified income in one or more individual jurisdictions, interim period tax (or benefit) related to consolidated ordinary income (or loss) for the year to date shall be computed in accordance with paragraphs .116 through .123 using one overall estimated annual effective tax rate except that:

a. If in a separate jurisdiction an enterprise anticipates an ordinary loss for the fiscal year or has an ordinary loss for the year to date for which, in accordance with paragraphs .121 through .123, no tax benefit can be recognized, the enterprise shall exclude ordinary income (or loss) in that jurisdiction and the related tax (or benefit) from the overall computations of the estimated annual effective tax rate and interim period tax (or benefit). A separate estimated annual effective tax rate shall be computed for that jurisdiction and applied to ordinary income (or loss) in that jurisdiction in accordance with paragraphs .116 through .123.
b. If an enterprise is unable to estimate an annual effective tax rate in a foreign jurisdiction in dollars or is otherwise unable to make a reliable estimate of its ordinary income (or loss) or of the related tax (or benefit) for the fiscal year in a jurisdiction, the enterprise shall exclude ordinary income (or loss) in that jurisdiction and the related tax (or benefit) from the overall computations of the estimated annual effective tax rate and interim period tax (or benefit). The tax (or benefit) related to ordinary in-

[5]Estimates of the annual effective tax rate at the end of interim periods are, of necessity, based on evaluations of possible future events and transactions and may be subject to subsequent refinement or revision. If a reliable estimate cannot be made, the actual effective tax rate for the year to date may be the best estimate of the annual effective tax rate. If an enterprise is unable to estimate a part of its ordinary income (or loss) or the related tax (or benefit) but is otherwise able to make a reliable estimate, the tax (or benefit) applicable to the item that cannot be estimated shall be reported in the interim period in which the item is reported. [FIN18, ¶8, fn7]

[[6]Deleted 11/92 because of FASB Statement 111, *Rescission of FASB Statement No. 32 and Technical Corrections.*]

come (or loss) in that jurisdiction[7] shall be recognized in the interim period in which the ordinary income (or loss) is reported. [FIN18, ¶22]

(1) The effect of translating foreign currency financial statements may make it difficult to estimate an annual effective foreign currency tax rate in dollars. For example, depreciation is translated at historical exchange rates, whereas many transactions included in income are translated at current period average exchange rates. If depreciation is large in relation to earnings, a change in the estimated ordinary income that does not change the effective foreign currency tax rate can change the effective tax rate in the dollar financial statements. This result can occur with no change in exchange rates during the current year if there have been exchange rate changes in past years. If the enterprise is unable to estimate its annual effective tax rate in dollars or is otherwise unable to make a reliable estimate of its ordinary income (or loss) or of the related tax (or benefit) for the fiscal year in a jurisdiction, the tax (or benefit) applicable to ordinary income (or loss) in that jurisdiction shall be recognized in the interim period in which the ordinary income (or loss) is reported. [FIN18, ¶85]

Effect of New Tax Legislation

.114 Paragraph .122 sets forth the requirements for recognition of the tax effects of a change in tax law or rates. That paragraph refers to effective dates prescribed in the statutes. Paragraph .115 describes the determination of when new legislation becomes effective. [FAS109, ¶288(y)]

Effective Date

.115 Legislation generally becomes effective on the date prescribed in the statutes. However, tax legislation may prescribe changes that become effective during an enterprise's fiscal year that are administratively implemented by applying a portion of the change to the full fiscal year. For example, if the statutory tax rate applicable to calendar-year corporations were increased from 48 percent to 52 percent, effective January 1, the increased statutory rate might be administratively applied to a corporation with a fiscal year ending at June 30 in the year of the change by applying a 50 percent rate to its taxable income for the fiscal year, rather than 48 percent for the first 6 months and 52 percent for the last 6 months. In that case the legislation becomes effective for that

[7]The tax (or benefit) related to ordinary income (or loss) in a jurisdiction may not be limited to tax (or benefit) in that jurisdiction. It might also include tax (or benefit) in another jurisdiction that results from providing taxes on unremitted earnings, foreign tax credits, etc. [FIN18, ¶22, fn24]

[[7a]Deleted 2/92 because of FASB Statement 109, *Accounting for Income Taxes*.]

enterprise at the beginning of the enterprise's fiscal year. [FIN18, ¶24] (Refer to paragraphs .501 through .503 for supplemental guidance.)

Computation of Interim Period Tax (or Benefit)

.116 The estimated annual effective tax rate, described in paragraph .111 above, shall be applied to the year-to-date ordinary income (or loss) at the end of each interim period to compute the year-to-date tax (or benefit) related to ordinary income (or loss).[8] The interim period tax (or benefit) related to ordinary income (or loss) shall be the difference between the amount so computed and the amounts reported for previous interim periods of the fiscal year. [FIN18, ¶9]

Ordinary Income Anticipated for Fiscal Year

Year-to-Date Ordinary Income

.117 If an enterprise has ordinary income for the year to date at the end of an interim period and anticipates ordinary income for the fiscal year, the interim period tax shall be computed as described in paragraph .116. [FIN18, ¶10]

Year-to-Date Ordinary Loss

.118 If an enterprise has an ordinary loss for the year to date at the end of an interim period and anticipates ordinary income for the fiscal year, the interim period tax benefit shall be computed as described in paragraph .116 except that the year-to-date tax benefit recognized shall be limited to the amount determined in accordance with paragraphs .121 and .123. [FIN18, ¶11]

Ordinary Loss Anticipated for Fiscal Year

Year-to-Date Ordinary Income

.119 If an enterprise has ordinary income for the year to date at the end of an interim period and anticipates an ordinary loss for the fiscal year, the interim period tax shall be computed as described in paragraph .116. The estimated tax benefit for the fiscal year,

---

[8]One result of the year-to-date computation is that, if the tax benefit of an ordinary loss that occurs in the early portions of the fiscal year is not recognized because [FIN18, ¶9, fn8] it is more likely than not that the tax benefit will not be realized, [FAS135, ¶4(z)] tax is not provided for subsequent ordinary income until the unrecognized tax benefit of the earlier ordinary loss is offset (refer to paragraph .122). [FIN18, ¶9, fn8]

used to determine the estimated annual effective tax rate described in paragraph .112, shall not exceed the tax benefit determined in accordance with paragraphs .121 through .123. [FIN18, ¶12]

Year-to-Date Ordinary Loss

.120 If an enterprise has an ordinary loss for the year to date at the end of an interim period and anticipates an ordinary loss for the fiscal year, the interim period tax benefit shall be computed as described in paragraph .116. The estimated tax benefit for the fiscal year, used to determine the estimated annual effective tax rate described in paragraph .112, shall not exceed the tax benefit determined in accordance with paragraphs .121 through .123. In addition to that limitation in the effective rate computation, if the year-to-date ordinary loss exceeds the anticipated ordinary loss for the fiscal year, the tax benefit recognized for the year to date shall not exceed the tax benefit determined, based on the year-to-date ordinary loss, in accordance with paragraphs .121 through .123. [FIN18, ¶13]

Limitations Applicable to Losses

Recognition of the Tax Benefit of a Loss

.121 Paragraph .122 provides that a tax benefit is recognized for a loss that arises early in a fiscal year if the tax benefits are expected to be (a) realized during the year or (b) recognizable as a deferred tax asset at the end of the year in accordance with the provisions of Section I27. Paragraph .116(e) of Section I27 requires that a valuation allowance be recognized if it is more likely than not that the tax benefit of some portion or all of a deferred tax asset will not be realized. Those limitations shall be applied in determining the estimated tax benefit of an ordinary loss for the fiscal year, used to determine the estimated annual effective tax rate described in paragraph .112, and the year-to-date tax benefit of a loss. [FAS109, ¶288(y)]

.122 The tax effects of losses that arise in the early portion of a fiscal year shall be recognized only when [APB28, ¶20] the tax benefits are expected to be (a) realized during the year or (b) recognizable as a deferred tax asset at the end of the year in accordance with the provisions of Section I27. [FAS109, ¶288(h)] An established seasonal pattern of loss in early interim periods offset by income in later interim periods shall constitute evidence that realization is [APB28, ¶20] more likely than not [FAS109, ¶288(h)], unless other evidence indicates the established seasonal pattern will not prevail. The tax effects of losses incurred in early interim periods shall be recognized in a later interim period of a fiscal year if their realization, although initially uncertain, later becomes [APB28, ¶20] more likely than not. [FAS109, ¶288(h)] If the tax effects of losses that

[[8a]Deleted 2/92 because of FASB Statement 109.]

arise in the early portions of a fiscal year are not recognized in that interim period, no tax provision shall be made for income that arises in later interim periods until the tax effects of the previous interim losses are utilized.[9] [APB28, ¶20] The tax effect of a valuation allowance expected to be necessary for a deferred tax asset at the end of the year for originating deductible temporary differences and carryforwards during the year should be included in the effective tax rate. The effect of a change in the beginning-of-the-year balance of a valuation allowance as a result of a change in judgment about the realizability of the related deferred tax asset in future years shall not be apportioned among interim periods through an adjustment of the effective tax rate but shall be recognized in the interim period in which the change occurs. The effects of new tax legislation shall not be recognized prior to enactment. The tax effect of a change in tax laws or rates on taxes currently payable or refundable for the current year shall be reflected after the effective dates prescribed in the statutes in the computation of the annual effective tax rate beginning no earlier than the first interim period that includes the enactment date of the new legislation. The effect of a change in tax laws or rates on a deferred tax liability or asset shall not be apportioned among interim periods through an adjustment of the annual effective tax rate. The tax effect of a change in tax laws or rates on taxes payable or refundable for a prior year shall be recognized as of the enactment date of the change as tax expense (benefit) for the current year. [FAS109, ¶288(h)]

Reversal of Taxable Temporary Differences

.123 A deferred tax liability related to existing taxable temporary differences is a source of evidence for recognition of a tax benefit when (a) an enterprise anticipates an ordinary loss for the fiscal year or has a year-to-date ordinary loss in excess of the anticipated ordinary loss for the fiscal year, (b) the tax benefit of that loss is not expected to be realized during the year, and (c) recognition of a deferred tax asset for that loss at the end of the fiscal year is expected to depend on taxable income from the reversal of existing taxable temporary differences (that is, a higher valuation allowance (refer to paragraph .116(e) of Section I27) would be necessary absent the existing taxable temporary differences). If the tax benefit relates to an estimated ordinary loss for the fiscal year, it shall be considered in determining the estimated annual effective tax rate described in paragraph .112. If the tax benefit relates to a year-to-date ordinary loss, it shall be considered in computing the maximum tax benefit that shall be recognized for the year-to-date. [FAS109, ¶288(y)]

---

[9]The tax benefits of interim losses accounted for in this manner would not be reported as extraordinary items in the results of operations of the interim period. [APB28, ¶20, fn3]

[10][Deleted 2/92 because of FASB Statement 109.]

[11][Deleted 2/92 because of FASB Statement 109.]

Disposal of a Component of an Entity and Extraordinary, Unusual, Infrequently Occurring, and Contingent Items

.124 Extraordinary items shall be disclosed separately and included in the determination of net income for the interim period in which they occur. In determining materiality, extraordinary items shall be related to the estimated income for the full fiscal year. Effects of disposals of a [APB28, ¶21] component of an entity [FAS144, ¶C3] and unusual and infrequently occurring transactions and events that are material with respect to the operating results of the interim period but that are not designated as extraordinary items in the interim statements shall be reported separately. In addition, matters such as unusual seasonal results [APB28, ¶21] and business combinations [FAS141, ¶E3(a)] shall be disclosed to provide information needed for a proper understanding of interim financial reports.[11a] Extraordinary items, gains or losses from disposal of a [APB28, ¶21] component of an entity, [FAS144, ¶C3] and unusual or infrequently occurring items shall not be prorated over the balance of the fiscal year. [APB28, ¶21]

Contingent Items

.125 Contingencies and other uncertainties that affect the fairness of presentation of financial data at an interim date shall be disclosed in interim reports in the same manner required for annual reports.[12] Such disclosures shall be repeated in interim and annual reports until the contingencies have been removed, resolved, or have become immaterial. [APB28, ¶22]

Tax (or Benefit) Applicable to Significant Unusual or Infrequently Occurring Items, Discontinued Operations, or Extraordinary Items

Basis of Tax Provision

.126 Paragraph .111 excludes taxes related to "significant unusual or extraordinary items that will be separately reported or reported net of their related tax effect"[13] from the estimated annual effective tax rate calculation. [FIN18, ¶16] Paragraph .122 excludes

[11a]Disclosures required in interim financial information related to a business combination are set forth in paragraph .171 of Section B51, "Business Combinations." [FAS141, ¶E3(b)]

[12]The significance of a contingency or uncertainty shall be judged in relation to annual financial statements. Disclosures of such items shall include, but not be limited to, those matters that form the basis of a qualification of an independent auditor's report. [APB28, ¶22, fn4]

[13]In the context of paragraph .124, which is consistent with Sections I17, "Income Statement Presentation: Extraordinary Items," and I22, "Income Statement Presentation: Unusual or Infrequent Items," this description includes unusual items, infrequently occurring items, discontinued operations, and extraordinary items. [FIN18, ¶16, fn16]

the effects of changes in judgment about beginning-of-year valuation allowances and effects of changes in tax laws or rates from the estimated effective tax rate calculation. [FAS109, ¶288(y)] Paragraph .124 requires that those items be recognized in the interim period in which they occur. [FIN18, ¶16] Section I27, paragraphs .134 through .137, [FAS109, ¶288(y)] describes the method of applying tax allocation within a period. This computation shall be made using the estimated fiscal-year ordinary income and the items described in footnote 13 for the year to date. [FIN18, ¶16]

Financial Statement Presentation

.127 Extraordinary items and discontinued operations that will be presented net of related tax effects in the financial statements for the fiscal year shall be presented net of related tax effects in interim financial statements. Unusual or infrequently occurring items that will be separately disclosed in the financial statements for the fiscal year shall be separately disclosed as a component of pretax income from continuing operations, and the tax (or benefit) related to such items shall be included in the tax (or benefit) related to continuing operations. Paragraphs .128 and .129 describe the application of the above to specific situations. [FIN18, ¶17]

Recognition of the Tax Benefit of a Loss

.128 If an enterprise has a significant unusual, infrequently occurring, or extraordinary loss or a loss from discontinued operations, the tax benefit of that loss [FIN18, ¶18] shall be recognized when the tax benefit of the loss is expected to be (a) realized during the year or (b) recognizable as a deferred tax asset at the end of the year in accordance with the provisions of Section I27. Realization would appear to be more likely than not if future taxable income from (ordinary) income during the current year is expected based on an established seasonal pattern of loss in early interim periods offset by income in later interim periods.[14] If recognition of a deferred tax asset at the end of the fiscal year for all or a portion of the tax benefit of the loss depends on taxable income from the reversal of existing taxable temporary differences, refer to paragraph .123 above. [FAS109, ¶288(y)] If all or a part of the tax benefit is not realized and future realization is not [FIN18, ¶18] more likely than not [FAS109, ¶288(y)] in the interim period of occurrence but becomes [FIN18, ¶18] more likely than not [FAS109, ¶288(y)] in a subsequent interim period of the same fiscal year, the previously unrecognized tax benefit shall be reported in that subsequent interim period in the same manner that it would have been reported if realization had been [FIN18, ¶18] more likely than not [FAS109, ¶288(y)] in the interim period of occurrence, that is, as a tax benefit relating to continuing operations, discontinued operations, or an extraordinary item. [FIN18, ¶18]

---

[14]Refer to paragraph .122. [FIN18, ¶18, fn19]

Discontinued Operations

.129 The computations described in paragraphs .126 through .128 shall be the basis for the tax (or benefit) related to the income (or loss) from operations of the [FIN18, ¶19] discontinued component [FAS144, ¶C19(b)][15] prior to the [FIN18, ¶19] date on which the criteria in paragraph .107 of Section D60, "Disposal of Long-Lived Assets," are met. [FAS144, ¶C19(b)] Income (or loss) from operations of the [FIN18, ¶19] discontinued component [FAS144, ¶C19(b)] prior to the interim period in which the [FIN18, ¶19] criteria in paragraph .107 of Section D60 are met [FAS144, ¶C19(b)] will have been included in ordinary income (or loss) of prior periods and thus will have been included in the estimated annual effective tax rate and tax (or benefit) calculations. The *total* tax (or benefit) provided in the prior interim periods shall not be recomputed but shall be divided into two components, applicable to the remaining ordinary income (or loss) and to the income (or loss) from operations of the [FIN18, ¶19] discontinued component [FAS144, ¶C19(b)] as follows. A revised estimated annual effective tax rate and resulting tax (or benefit) shall be computed, in accordance with paragraphs .111 through .123, for the remaining ordinary income (or loss), based on the estimates applicable to such operations used in the original calculations for each prior interim period. The tax (or benefit) related to the operations of the [FIN18, ¶19] discontinued component [FAS144, ¶C19(b)] shall be the total of (a) the difference between the tax (or benefit) originally computed for ordinary income (or loss) and the recomputed amount for the remaining ordinary income (or loss) and (b) the tax computed in accordance with paragraphs .126 through .128 for any unusual or infrequently occurring items of the [FIN18, ¶19] discontinued component. [FAS144, ¶C19(b)]

Using a Prior-Year Operating Loss Carryforward

.130 Paragraph .136 of Section I27 requires that the manner of reporting the tax benefit of an operating loss carryforward recognized in a subsequent year generally is determined by the source of the income in that year, and not by (a) the source of the operating loss carryforward or (b) the source of expected future income that will result in realization of a deferred tax asset for the operating loss carryforward. The tax benefit is allocated first to reduce tax expense from continuing operations to zero with any excess allocated to the other source(s) of income that provides the means of realization, for example, extraordinary items, discontinued operations, and so forth. That requirement also pertains to reporting the tax benefit of an operating loss carryforward in interim periods. The tax benefit of an operating loss carryforward from prior years shall be included in the effective tax rate computation if the tax benefit is expected to be realized as a result

[15]The term *discontinued component* refers to the disposal of a component of an entity as described in paragraph .101 of Section I14, "Income Statement Presentation: Discontinued Operations." [FAS144, ¶C19(b)]

of ordinary income in the current year. Otherwise, the tax benefit shall be recognized in the manner described above in each interim period to the extent that income in the period and for the year to date is available to offset the operating loss carryforward or, in the case of a change in judgment about realizability of the related deferred tax asset in future years, the effect shall be recognized in the interim period in which the change occurs. [FAS109, ¶288(y)]

Accounting Changes in Interim Periods

.131 Each report of interim financial information shall indicate any change in accounting principles or practices from those applied in (a) the comparable interim period of the prior annual period, (b) the preceding interim periods in the current annual period, and (c) the prior annual report. [APB28, ¶23]

.132 Changes in an interim or annual accounting practice or policy made in an interim period shall be reported in the period in which the change is made in accordance with the provisions of Section A06, "Accounting Changes." [APB28, ¶24]

.133 The effect of a change in an accounting estimate, including a change in the estimated effective annual tax rate, shall be accounted for in the period in which the change in estimate is made. No restatement of previously reported interim information shall be made for changes in estimates, but the effect on earnings of a change in estimate made in a current interim period shall be reported in the current and subsequent interim periods, if material in relation to any period presented and shall continue to be reported in the interim financial information of the subsequent year for as many periods as necessary to avoid misleading comparisons. Such disclosure shall conform with Section A06, paragraph .132. [APB28, ¶26]

.134 If possible, [it is recommended that] enterprises adopt any accounting changes during the first interim period of a fiscal year. Changes in accounting principles and practices adopted after the first interim period in a fiscal year tend to obscure operating results and complicate disclosure of interim financial information. [APB28, ¶28]

Cumulative Effect-Type Accounting Changes Other Than Changes to LIFO

.135 If a cumulative effect-type accounting change is made during the *first* interim period of an enterprise's fiscal year, the cumulative effect of the change on retained earnings at the *beginning of that fiscal year* shall be included in net income of the first interim period (and in last-12-months-to-date financial reports that include that first interim period). [FAS3, ¶9]

.136 If a cumulative effect-type accounting change is made in *other than the first* interim period of an enterprise's fiscal year, *no* cumulative effect of the change shall be included in net income of the period of change. Instead, financial information for the prechange interim periods of the fiscal year in which the change is made shall be restated by applying the newly adopted accounting principle to those prechange interim periods. The cumulative effect of the change on retained earnings at the *beginning of that fiscal year* shall be included in restated net income of the first interim period of the fiscal year in which the change is made (and in any year-to-date or last-12-months-to-date financial reports that include the first interim period). If financial information that includes those prechange interim periods is presented, it shall be presented on the restated basis. [FAS3, ¶10]

.137 The following disclosures about a cumulative effect-type accounting change shall be made in interim financial reports:

a. In financial reports for the interim period in which the new accounting principle is adopted, disclosure shall be made of the nature of and justification for the change.
b. In financial reports for the interim period in which the new accounting principle is adopted, disclosure shall be made of the effect of the change on income from continuing operations, net income, and related per share amounts for the interim period in which the change is made. In addition, if the change is made in other than the first interim period of a fiscal year, financial reports for the period of change shall also disclose (1) the effect of the change on income from continuing operations, net income, and related per share amounts for each prechange interim period of that fiscal year and (2) income from continuing operations, net income, and related per share amounts for each prechange interim period restated in accordance with paragraph .136.
c. In financial reports for the interim period in which the new accounting principle is adopted, disclosure shall be made of income from continuing operations, net income, and related per share amounts computed on a pro forma basis for (1) the interim period in which the change is made and (2) any interim periods of prior fiscal years for which financial information is being presented. If no financial information for interim periods of prior fiscal years is being presented, disclosure shall be made, in the period of change, of the actual and pro forma amounts of income from continuing operations, net income, and related per share amounts for the interim period of the immediately preceding fiscal year that corresponds to the interim period in which the changes are made. In all cases, the pro forma amounts shall be computed and presented in conformity with Section A06, paragraphs .115, .117, .118, and .121.
d. In year-to-date and last-12-months-to-date financial reports that include the interim period in which the new accounting principle is adopted, the disclosures specified in the first sentence of subparagraph (b) above and in subparagraph (c) above shall be made.
e. In financial reports for a subsequent (postchange) interim period of the fiscal year in which the new accounting principle is adopted, disclosure shall be made of the effect

of the change on income from continuing operations, net income, and related per share amounts for that postchange interim period.

[FAS3, ¶11]

.138 In determining materiality for the purpose of reporting the cumulative effect of an accounting change or correction of an error, amounts shall be related to the estimated income for the full fiscal year and also to the effect on the trend of earnings. Changes that are material with respect to an interim period but not material with respect to the estimated income for the full fiscal year or to the trend of earnings shall be separately disclosed in the interim period. [APB28, ¶29]

.139 Section A06 specifies that the related income tax effect of a cumulative effect-type accounting change shall be computed as though the new accounting principle had been applied retroactively for all prior periods that would have been affected. [FIN18, ¶21]

Changes to the LIFO Method of Inventory Pricing and Similar Situations

.140 Section A06, paragraph .122, indicates that in rare situations—principally a change to the LIFO method of inventory pricing[16]—neither the cumulative effect of the change on retained earnings at the beginning of the fiscal year in which the change is made nor the pro forma amounts can be computed. In those situations, the paragraph requires an explanation of the reasons for omitting (a) accounting for a cumulative effect and (b) disclosure of pro forma amounts for prior years. If a change of that type is made in the *first* interim period of an enterprise's fiscal year, the disclosures specified in paragraph .137 shall be made (except the pro forma amounts for interim periods of prior fiscal years called for by paragraph .137(c) will not be disclosed). [FAS3, ¶12]

.141 If the change is made in *other than the first* interim period of an enterprise's fiscal year, the disclosure specified in paragraph .137 shall be made (except the pro forma amounts for interim periods of prior fiscal years called for by paragraph .137(c) will not be disclosed) and in addition, financial information for the prechange interim periods of that fiscal year shall be restated by applying the newly adopted accounting principle to those prechange interim periods. If financial information that includes those prechange interim periods is presented, it shall be presented on the restated basis. [FAS3, ¶13]

.142 Certain changes in accounting principle, such as those described in Section A06, paragraphs .103 and .123, require retroactive restatement of previously issued financial

[16]In making disclosures about changes to the LIFO method, enterprises should be aware of the limitations the Internal Revenue Service has placed on such disclosures. [FAS3, ¶12, fn1]

statements. Section A35, "Adjustments of Financial Statements for Prior Periods," paragraph .107, requires similar treatment for prior period adjustments. Previously issued financial statements also must be restated for a change in the reporting entity (refer to Section A35, paragraphs .112 and .113) and for correction of an error (refer to Section A35, paragraphs .103 and .105). Previously issued interim financial information shall be similarly restated. Sections A06 and A35 specify the required disclosures. [APB28, ¶25]

Adjustments Related to Prior Interim Periods of the Current Fiscal Year

.143 For purposes of this section, an "adjustment related to prior *interim* periods of the current fiscal year" is an adjustment or settlement of litigation or similar claims, of income taxes [FAS16, ¶13] (except for the effects of retroactive tax legislation) [FAS109, ¶288(n)], of renegotiation proceedings, or of utility revenue under rate-making processes provided that the adjustment or settlement meets each of the following criteria:

a. The effect of the adjustment or settlement is material in relation to income from continuing operations of the current fiscal year or in relation to the trend of income from continuing operations or is material by other appropriate criteria.
b. All or part of the adjustment or settlement can be specifically identified with and is directly related to business activities of specific prior interim periods of the current fiscal year.
c. The amount of the adjustment or settlement could not be reasonably estimated prior to the current interim period but becomes reasonably estimable in the current interim period.

Criterion (b) is not met solely because of incidental effects such as interest on a settlement. Criterion (c) would be met by the occurrence of an event with currently measurable effects such as a final decision on a rate order. Treatment as adjustments related to prior interim periods of the current fiscal year shall not be applied to the normal recurring corrections and adjustments that are the result of the use of estimates inherent in the accounting process. Changes in provisions for doubtful accounts shall not be considered to be adjustments related to prior interim periods of the current fiscal year even though the changes result from litigation or similar claims. [FAS16, ¶13]

.144 If an item of profit or loss occurs in *other than the first* interim period of the enterprise's fiscal year and all or a part of the item of profit or loss is an adjustment related to prior interim periods of the current fiscal year, as defined in paragraph .143, the item shall be reported as follows:

[[16a]Deleted 2/92 because of FASB Statement 109.]

a. The portion of the item that is directly related to business activities of the enterprise during the current interim period, if any, shall be included in the determination of net income for that period.
b. Prior interim periods of the current fiscal year shall be restated to include the portion of the item that is directly related to business activities of the enterprise during each prior interim period in the determination of net income for that period.
c. The portion of the item that is directly related to business activities of the enterprise during prior fiscal years, if any, shall be included in the determination of net income of the first interim period of the current fiscal year.

[FAS16, ¶14]

.145 The following disclosures shall be made in interim financial reports about an adjustment related to prior interim periods of the current fiscal year. In financial reports for the interim period in which the adjustment occurs, disclosure shall be made of (a) the effect on income from continuing operations, net income, and related per share amounts for each prior interim period of the current fiscal year and (b) income from continuing operations, net income, and related per share amounts for each prior interim period restated in accordance with paragraph .144. [FAS16, ¶15]

Disclosure of Summarized Interim Financial Data by Publicly Traded Companies

.146 If publicly traded companies[17] report summarized financial information at interim dates (including reports on fourth quarters), the following data shall be reported, as a minimum:[18]

a. Sales or gross revenues, provision for income taxes, extraordinary items (including related income tax effects), cumulative effect of a change in accounting principles or practices, [APB28, ¶30] net income, and comprehensive income [as required in Section C49, "Comprehensive Income: Financial Statement Presentation"] [FAS130, ¶28(b)]
b. Basic and diluted earnings per share data for each period presented, determined in accordance with the provisions of Section E11, "Earnings per Share" [FAS128, ¶164]
c. Seasonal revenue, costs, or expenses (refer to paragraph .110)

[17] Refer to footnote 1. [APB28, ¶30, fn6]

[18] The minimum disclosures of summarized interim financial data required of publicly traded companies by this section do not constitute a fair presentation of financial position and results of operations in conformity with generally accepted accounting principles. [APB28, ¶30, fn7]

d. Significant changes in estimates or provisions for income taxes (refer to paragraphs .111 and .112)
e. Disposal of a [APB28, ¶30] component of an entity [FAS144, ¶C3] and extraordinary, unusual or infrequently occurring items (refer to paragraph .124)
f. Contingent items (refer to paragraph .125)
g. Changes in accounting principles or estimates (refer to paragraphs .131 through .145)
h. Significant changes in financial position (refer to paragraph .149) [APB28, ¶30]
i. The following information about reportable operating segments determined according to the provisions of Section S30, "Segment Disclosures and Related Information," including provisions related to restatement of segment information in previously issued financial statements:
   (1) Revenues from external customers
   (2) Intersegment revenues
   (3) A measure of segment profit or loss
   (4) Total assets for which there has been a material change from the amount disclosed in the last annual report
   (5) A description of differences from the last annual report in the basis of segmentation or in the measurement of segment profit or loss
   (6) A reconciliation of the total of the reportable segments' measures of profit or loss to the enterprise's consolidated income before income taxes, extraordinary items, discontinued operations, and the cumulative effect of changes in accounting principles. However, if, for example, an enterprise allocates items such as income taxes and extraordinary items to segments, the enterprise may choose to reconcile the total of the segments' measures of profit or loss to consolidated income after those items. Significant reconciling items shall be separately identified and described in that reconciliation. [FAS131, ¶131]

If summarized financial data are regularly reported on a quarterly basis, the foregoing information with respect to the current quarter and the current year to date or the last 12 months to date shall be furnished together with comparable data for the preceding year. [APB28, ¶30]

.147 If interim financial data and disclosures are not separately reported for the fourth quarter, [APB28, ¶31] users of the interim financial information [FAS135, ¶4(e)] often make inferences about that quarter by subtracting data based on the third quarter interim report from the annual results. In the absence of a separate fourth quarter report or disclosure of the results (as outlined in paragraph .146) for that quarter in the annual report, [accounting changes made during the fourth quarter,] disposals of [APB28, ¶31] components of an entity, [FAS144, ¶C3] and extraordinary, unusual, or infrequently occurring items recognized in the fourth quarter, as well as the aggregate effect of year-end adjustments that are material to the results of that quarter (refer to paragraph .109), shall be disclosed in the annual report in a note to the annual financial statements. [APB28, ¶31] Disclosures about the effect of an accounting change on interim periods that are required by paragraphs .131 through .137 and .140 and .141 shall be included, as appropriate. [FAS3, ¶14]

.148 Disclosure of the impact on the financial results for interim periods of the matters discussed in paragraphs .124 through .141 is desirable for as many subsequent periods as necessary to keep the reader fully informed. There is a presumption that users of summarized interim financial data will have read the latest published annual report, including the financial disclosures required by generally accepted accounting principles and management's commentary concerning the annual financial results, and that the summarized interim data will be viewed in that context. In this connection, the management is encouraged to provide commentary relating to the effects of significant events upon the interim financial results. [APB28, ¶32]

.149 Publicly traded enterprises are encouraged to publish balance sheet and [APB28, ¶33] cash flow data [FAS95, ¶151(a)] at interim dates since these data often assist [APB28, ¶33] users of the interim financial information [FAS135, ¶4(e)] in their understanding and interpretation of the income data reported. If condensed interim balance sheet information or [APB28, ¶33] cash flow data [FAS95, ¶151(a)] are not presented at interim reporting dates, significant changes since the last reporting period with respect to liquid assets, net working capital, long-term liabilities, or stockholders' equity shall be disclosed. [APB28, ¶33]

Disclosures Required by Publicly Traded[19] Enterprises with Oil and Gas Producing Activities

.149A The disclosures set forth in Section Oi5, "Oil and Gas Producing Activities," paragraphs .156 through .186, are not required in interim financial reports. However, interim financial reports [of publicly traded enterprises with significant oil and gas producing activities] shall include information about a major discovery or other favorable or adverse event that causes a significant change from the information presented in the most recent annual financial report concerning oil and gas reserve quantities [refer to Section Oi5, paragraphs .160 through .167]. [FAS69, ¶9]

[[19]Refer to Section Oi5, "Oil and Gas Producing Activities," paragraph .157.]

Examples of Accounting for Costs and Expenses Other Than Product Costs

.150 A complete listing of examples of application of the standards set forth in paragraph .108 is not practical; however, the following examples of applications may be helpful:

a. If a cost that is expensed for annual reporting purposes clearly benefits two or more interim periods (for example, annual major repairs), each interim period shall be charged for an appropriate portion of the annual cost by the use of accruals or deferrals.
b. If quantity discounts are allowed customers based upon annual sales volume, the amount of such discounts charged to each interim period shall be based on the sales to customers during the interim period in relation to estimated annual sales.
c. Property taxes (and similar costs such as interest and rent) may be accrued or deferred at the annual reporting date, to achieve a full year's charge of taxes to costs and expenses. Similar procedures shall be adopted at each interim reporting date to provide an appropriate cost in each period.
d. Advertising costs may be deferred within a fiscal year if the benefits of an expenditure made clearly extend beyond the interim period in which the expenditure is made. Advertising costs may be accrued and assigned to interim periods in relation to sales prior to the time the service is received if the advertising program is clearly implicit in the sales arrangement.

[APB28, ¶16]

Examples of Reporting a Cumulative Effect-Type Accounting Change (Other Than a Change to LIFO)

.151 The following are examples of application of this section, and the requirements of Section A06 as they are incorporated by reference in this section. The examples do not encompass all possible circumstances and are not intended to indicate a preference for a particular format. [FAS3, Appendix A]

Assumptions

.152 In the year 19X5, ABC Company decides to adopt the straight-line method of depreciation for plant equipment. The straight-line method will be used for new acquisitions as well as for previously acquired plant equipment for which depreciation had been provided on an accelerated method. [FAS3, Appendix A]

.153 These examples assume that the effects of the change are limited to the effect on depreciation, incentive compensation, and related income tax provisions and that the effect on inventories is not material. The pro forma amounts have been adjusted for an assumed 10 percent pretax effect of the change on the provisions for incentive compensation and an assumed 50 percent income tax rate. The per share amounts are computed assuming that throughout the 2 years 19X4 and 19X5, 1,000,000 shares of common stock were issued and outstanding with no potential dilution. Other data assumed for these examples are:

Period	Net Income on the Basis of Old Accounting Principle (Accelerated Depreciation)	Gross Effect of Change to Straight-Line Depreciation	Gross Effect Less Income Taxes	Net Effect after Incentive Compensation and Related Income Taxes
Prior to first quarter 19X4		$ 20,000	$ 10,000	$ 9,000
First quarter 19X4	$1,000,000	30,000	15,000	13,500
Second quarter 19X4	1,200,000	70,000	35,000	31,500
Third quarter 19X4	1,100,000	50,000	25,000	22,500
Fourth quarter 19X4	1,100,000	80,000	40,000	36,000
Total at beginning of 19X5	$4,400,000	$250,000	$125,000	$112,500
First quarter 19X5	$1,059,500	$ 90,000	$ 45,000	$ 40,500
Second quarter 19X5	1,255,000	100,000	50,000	45,000
Third quarter 19X5	1,150,500	110,000	55,000	49,500
Fourth quarter 19X5	1,146,000	120,000	60,000	54,000
[Total at end of 19X5]	$4,611,000	$420,000	$210,000	$189,000

[FAS3, Appendix A]

Example 1

.154 The change in depreciation method is made in the first quarter of 19X5. The manner of reporting the change in the first quarter of 19X5, with comparative information for the first quarter of 19X4, is as follows:

	3 Months Ended March 31,	
	19X5	**19X4**
Income before cumulative effect of a change in accounting principle	$1,100,000	$1,000,000
Cumulative effect on prior years (to December 31, 19X4) of changing to a different depreciation method (Note A)	125,000	
Net income	$1,225,000	$1,000,000
Amounts per common share:		
Income before cumulative effect of a change in accounting principle	$1.10	$1.00
Cumulative effect on prior years (to December 31, 19X4) of changing to a different depreciation method (Note A)	.13	
Net income	$1.23	$1.00
Pro forma amounts assuming the new depreciation method is applied retroactively (Note A):		
Net income	$1,100,000	$1,013,500
Net income per common share	$1.10	$1.01

Note A—Change in Depreciation Method for Plant Equipment

In the first quarter of 19X5, the method of computing depreciation of plant equipment was changed from the . . . (state previous method) . . . used in prior years, to the straight-line method . . . (state justification for the change in method) . . . and the new method has been applied to equipment acquisitions of prior years. The $125,000 cumulative effect of the change on prior years (after reduction for income taxes of $125,000) is included in income of the first quarter of 19X5. The effect of the change on the first quarter of 19X5 was to increase income before cumulative effect of a change in accounting principle $40,500 ($.04 per share) and net income $165,500 ($.17 per share). The pro forma amounts reflect the effect of retroactive application on depreciation, the change in provisions for incentive compensation that would have been made in 19X4 had the new method been in effect, and related income taxes. [FAS3, Appendix A]

Example 2

.155 Assume the same facts as in Example 1, except that the change is made in the third quarter of 19X5. [FAS3, Appendix A]

.156 The manner of reporting the change in the third quarter of 19X5, with year-to-date information and comparative information for similar periods of 19X4, is as follows:

	3 Months Ended September 30,		9 Months Ended September 30,	
	19X5	**19X4**	**19X5**	**19X4**
Income before cumulative effect of a change in accounting principle	$1,200,000	$1,100,000	$3,600,000	$3,300,000
Cumulative effect on prior years (to December 31, 19X4) of changing to a different depreciation method (Note A)			125,000	
Net income	$1,200,000	$1,100,000	$3,725,000	$3,300,000
Amounts per common share:				
Income before cumulative effect of a change in accounting principle	$1.20	$1.10	$3.60	$3.30
Cumulative effect on prior years (to December 31, 19X4) of changing to a different depreciation method (Note A)			.13	
Net income	$1.20	$1.10	$3.73	$3.30
Pro forma amounts assuming the new depreciation method is applied retroactively (Note A):				
Net income	$1,200,000	$1,122,500	$3,600,000	$3,367,500
Net income per common share	$1.20	$1.12	$3.60	$3.37

Note A—Change in Depreciation Method for Plant Equipment

In the third quarter of 19X5, the method of computing depreciation of plant equipment was changed from the . . . (state previous method) . . . used in prior years, to the straight-line method . . . (state justification for the change in method) . . . and the new method has been applied to equipment acquisitions of prior years. The $125,000 cumulative effect of the change on prior years (after reduction for income taxes of $125,000) is included in income of the 9 months ended September 30, 19X5. The effect of the change on the 3 months ended September 30, 19X5 was to increase net income $49,500 ($.05 per share); the effect of the change on the 9 months ended September 30, 19X5 was to increase income before cumulative effect of a change in accounting principle $135,000 ($.14 per share) and net income $260,000 ($.26 per share). The pro forma amounts reflect the effect of retroactive application on depreciation, the change in provisions for incentive compensation that would have been made in 19X4 had the new method been in effect, and related income taxes. The effect of the change on the first quarter of 19X5 was to increase income before cumulative effect of a change in accounting principle $40,500 ($.04 per share) to $1,100,000 ($1.10 per share) and net income $165,500 ($.17 per share) to $1,225,000 ($1.23 per share); the effect of the change on the second quarter was to increase net income $45,000 ($.04 per share) to $1,300,000 ($1.30 per share). [FAS3, Appendix A]

.157 Alternatively, the last sentence of Note A could be replaced with the following tabular disclosure:

The effect of the change on the first and second quarters of 19X5 is as follows:

	3 Months Ended	
	March 31, 19X5	**June 30, 19X5**
Net income as originally reported*	$1,059,500	$1,255,000
Effect of change in depreciation method	40,500	45,000
Income before cumulative effect of a change in accounting principle	1,100,000	1,300,000
Cumulative effect on prior years (to December 31, 19X4) of changing to a different depreciation method	125,000	
Net income as restated	$1,225,000	$1,300,000
Per share amounts:		
Net income as originally reported*	$ 1.06	$ 1.26
Effect of change in depreciation method	.04	.04
Income before cumulative effect of a change in accounting principle	1.10	1.30
Cumulative effect on prior years (to December 31, 19X4) of changing to a different depreciation method	.13	
Net income as restated	$ 1.23	$ 1.30

*Disclosure of net income as originally reported is not required.

[FAS3, Appendix A]

Reporting a Change to the LIFO Method of Inventory Pricing

.158 The following are examples of application of this section, and the requirements of Section A06 as they are incorporated by reference in this section. The examples do not encompass all possible circumstances and are not intended to indicate a preference for a particular format. [FAS3, Appendix B]

Assumptions

.159 In the year 19X5, XYZ Company decides to change to the LIFO method of inventory pricing. These examples assume that the effects of the change are limited to the effect on inventory, incentive compensation, and related income tax provisions. A 10 percent pretax effect of the change on incentive compensation and a 50 percent income tax rate are assumed. The per share amounts are computed assuming that throughout 19X4 and 19X5, 1,000,000 shares of common stock were issued and outstanding with no potential dilution. Other data assumed for these examples are:

Period	Net Income on the Basis of Old Accounting Principle	Gross Effect of Change to LIFO	Net Effect after Incentive Compensation and Income Taxes
First quarter 19X5	$1,095,500	$ (90,000)	$ (40,500)
Second quarter 19X5	1,295,000	(100,000)	(45,000)
Third quarter 19X5	1,194,500	(110,000)	(49,500)
Fourth quarter 19X5	1,194,000	(120,000)	(54,000)
[Total]	$4,779,000	$(420,000)	$(189,000)

[FAS3, Appendix B]

Example 3

.160 The change to LIFO is made in the first quarter of 19X5. The manner of reporting the change in the first quarter of 19X5, with comparative information for the first quarter of 19X4, is as follows:

	3 Months Ended March 31,	
	19X5	19X4
Net income (Note A)	$1,055,000	$1,000,000
Net income per common share (Note A)	$1.06	$1.00

Note A—Change to LIFO Method of Inventory Pricing

In the first quarter of 19X5, the enterprise changed its method of inventory pricing from . . . (state previous method) . . . used previously to the LIFO method because . . . (state justification for change and reasons for not disclosing a cumulative effect on, and pro forma amounts for, prior periods). The effect of the change on the first quarter of 19X5 was to decrease net income $40,500 ($.04 per share). [FAS3, Appendix B]

Example 4

.161 Assume the same facts as in Example 3, except that the change is made in the third quarter of 19X5. [FAS3, Appendix B]

.162 The manner of reporting the change in the third quarter of 19X5, with year-to-date information and comparative information for similar periods of 19X4, is as follows:

	3 Months Ended September 30,		9 Months Ended September 30,	
	19X5	**19X4**	**19X5**	**19X4**
Net income (Note A)	$1,145,000	$1,200,000	$3,450,000	$3,400,000
Net income per common share (Note A)	$1.15	$1.20	$3.45	$3.40

Note A—Change to LIFO Method of Inventory Pricing

In the third quarter of 19X5, the enterprise changed its method of inventory pricing from . . . (state previous method) . . . used previously to the LIFO method because . . . (state justification for change and reasons for not disclosing a cumulative effect on, and pro forma amounts for, prior periods). The effect of the change on the 3 months and 9 months ended September 30, 19X5 was to decrease net income $49,500 ($.05 per share) and $135,000 ($.14 per share), respectively. The effect of the change on the first and second quarters of 19X5 was to decrease net income $40,500 ($.04 per share) to $1,055,000 ($1.06 per share) and $45,000 ($.05 per share) to $1,250,000 ($1.25 per share), respectively. [FAS3, Appendix B]

.163 Alternatively, the last sentence of Note A could be replaced with the following tabular disclosure:

The effect of the change on the first and second quarters of 19X5 is as follows:

	3 Months Ended	
	March 31, 19X5	**June 30, 19X5**
Net income as originally reported*	$1,095,500	$1,295,000
Effect of change to LIFO method of inventory pricing	(40,500)	(45,000)
Net income as restated	$1,055,000	$1,250,000
Per share amounts:		
Net income as originally reported*	$1.10	$1.30
Effect of change to LIFO method of inventory pricing	(.04)	(.05)
Net income as restated	$1.06	$1.25

*Disclosure of net income as originally reported is not required.

[FAS3, Appendix B]

.164 This paragraph provides a cross-reference from the paragraphs of this section to other paragraphs that illustrate the application of those paragraphs.

Text Paragraph Numbers		**Example at Paragraph Numbers**
.112	Estimated annual effective tax rate	.167, .174, .178, .179
	Changes in estimates	.172, .173
.113	Operations taxable in multiple jurisdictions	.198
.113(a)	Ordinary loss, realization not assured	.200
.113(b)	Unable to estimate in a jurisdiction	.201
	Effect of new tax legislation:	
.114	Effective in future interim period	.204, .205
.116	Computation of interim period tax (or benefit) applicable to ordinary income (or loss):	
	Ordinary income anticipated for fiscal year:	
.117	Year-to-date ordinary income	.168, .169
.118	Year-to-date ordinary loss	.170, .171

Text Paragraph Numbers		Example at Paragraph Numbers
	Ordinary loss anticipated for fiscal year:	
.119	Year-to-date ordinary income	.176, .179
.120	Year-to-date ordinary loss	.175, .177, .178
.121	Recognition of the tax benefit of a loss	.175, .177, .178, .179
	Year-to-date loss—special computation	.170, .171, .176
.123	Reversal of net deferred tax credits	.180, .181
.126	Tax (or benefit) applicable to significant unusual, infrequently occurring, or extraordinary items	.183, .184
.127	Financial statement presentation	.208
.128	Recognition of the tax benefit of a loss	.183, .184
.129	Tax (or benefit) applicable to discontinued operations	.188, .189, .190, .191, .192, .193, .194, .195
.139	Cumulative effects of changes in accounting principles	.196, .197

[FIN18, ¶40]

Examples of Computations of Interim Period Income Taxes

.165 Paragraphs .167 through .208 provide examples of application of this section for some specific situations. In general, the examples illustrate matters unique to accounting for income taxes at interim dates. The examples do not include consideration of the nature of tax credits and [FIN18, ¶41] events that do not have tax consequences [FAS109, ¶288(y)] or illustrate all possible combinations of circumstances. [FIN18, ¶41]

.166 Specific situations illustrated are:

	Paragraph Numbers
Accounting for income taxes applicable to ordinary income (or loss) at an interim date if ordinary income is anticipated for the fiscal year:	
Facts, paragraphs .168 through .171	.167
Ordinary income on all interim periods	.168
Ordinary income and losses in interim periods:	
Year-to-date ordinary income	.169
Year-to-date ordinary losses, realization assured	.170
Year-to-date ordinary losses, realization not assured	.171
Changes in estimates	.172, .173

	Paragraph Numbers
Accounting for income taxes applicable to ordinary income (or loss) at an interim date if an ordinary loss is anticipated for the fiscal year:	
Facts, paragraphs .175 through .179	.174
Realization of the tax benefit of the loss is assured:	
Ordinary losses in all interim periods	.175
Ordinary income and losses in interim periods	.176
Realization of the tax benefit of the loss is not assured	.177
Partial realization of the tax benefit of the loss is assured:	
Ordinary losses in all interim periods	.178
Ordinary income and losses in interim periods	.179
[Reduction of deferred tax liability]	.180, .181
Accounting for income taxes applicable to unusual, infrequently occurring, or extraordinary items:	
Ordinary income expected for the fiscal year:	
Explanation of paragraphs .183 and .184	.182
Unusual, infrequently occurring, or extraordinary loss with:	
Realization of the tax benefit assured at date of occurrence	.183
Realization of the tax benefit not assured at date of occurrence	.184
Accounting for income taxes applicable to income (or loss) from discounted operations at an interim date	.188-.195
Accounting for income taxes applicable to the cumulative effect of a change in accounting principle:	
Cumulative effect of the change on retained earnings at the beginning of the fiscal year	.196
Effect of the change on prechange interim periods of the current fiscal year	.197
Accounting for income taxes applicable to ordinary income if an enterprise is subject to tax in multiple jurisdictions:	
Ordinary income in all jurisdictions	.198, .199
Ordinary loss in a jurisdiction; realization of the tax benefit not assured	.200
Ordinary income tax cannot be estimated in one jurisdiction	.201, .202
Effect of new tax legislation:	
Facts, paragraphs .204 through [.205]	.203
Legislation effective in a future interim period	.204, .205

[FIN18, ¶42]

Accounting for Income Taxes Applicable to Ordinary Income (or Loss) at an Interim Date If Ordinary Income Is Anticipated for the Fiscal Year

.167 The following assumed facts are applicable to the examples of application of this section in paragraphs .168 through .171:

> For the full fiscal year, an enterprise anticipates ordinary income of $100,000. All income is taxable in 1 jurisdiction at a 50-percent rate. Anticipated tax credits for the fiscal year total $10,000. No [FIN18, ¶43] events that do not have tax consequences [FAS109, ¶288(y)] are anticipated. No changes in estimated ordinary income, tax rates, or tax credits occur during the year.
>
> Computation of the estimated annual effective tax rate applicable to ordinary income is as follows:

Tax at statutory rate ($100,000 at 50%)	$ 50,000
Less anticipated tax credits	(10,000)
Net tax to be provided	$ 40,000
Estimated annual effective tax rate ($40,000 ÷ $100,000)	40%

Tax credits are generally subject to limitations, usually based on the amount of tax payable before the credits. In computing the estimated annual effective tax rate, anticipated tax credits are limited to the amounts that are expected to be realized or are expected to be [FIN18, ¶43] recognizable at the end of the current year in accordance with the provisions of Section I27. [FAS109, ¶288(y)] If an enterprise is unable to estimate the amount of its tax credits for the year, refer to paragraph .112, footnote 5. [FIN18, ¶43]

.168 Assume the facts stated in paragraph .167. The enterprise has ordinary income in all interim periods. Quarterly tax computations are:

	Ordinary Income		Estimated	Tax		
			Annual		Less	
	Reporting	Year-to-	Effective	Year-to-	Previously	Reporting
Reporting Period	**Period**	**Date**	**Tax Rate**	**Date**	**Provided**	**Period**
First quarter	$ 20,000	$ 20,000	40%	$ 8,000	—	$ 8,000
Second quarter	20,000	40,000	40%	16,000	$ 8,000	8,000
Third quarter	20,000	60,000	40%	24,000	16,000	8,000
Fourth quarter	40,000	100,000	40%	40,000	24,000	16,000
Fiscal year	$100,000					$40,000

[FIN18, ¶44]

.169 Assume the facts stated in paragraph .167. The enterprise has ordinary income and losses in interim periods; there is not an ordinary loss for the fiscal year to date at the end of any interim period. Quarterly tax computations are:

Reporting Period	Ordinary Income (Loss) Reporting Period	Ordinary Income (Loss) Year-to-Date	Estimated Annual Effective Tax Rate	Tax (or Benefit) Year-to-Date	Tax (or Benefit) Less Previously Provided	Tax (or Benefit) Reporting Period
First quarter	$ 40,000	$ 40,000	40%	$16,000	—	$16,000
Second quarter	40,000	80,000	40%	32,000	$16,000	16,000
Third quarter	(20,000)	60,000	40%	24,000	32,000	(8,000)
Fourth quarter	40,000	100,000	40%	40,000	24,000	16,000
Fiscal year	$100,000					$40,000

[FIN18, ¶45]

.170 Assume the facts stated in paragraph .167. The enterprise has ordinary income and losses in interim periods, and there is an ordinary loss for the year to date at the end of an interim period. [FIN18, ¶46] Established seasonal patterns provide evidence that realization in the current year of the tax benefit of the year-to-date loss and of anticipated tax credits is more likely than not. [FAS109, ¶288(y)] Quarterly tax computations are:

Reporting Period	Ordinary Income (Loss) Reporting Period	Ordinary Income (Loss) Year-to-Date	Estimated Annual Effective Tax Rate	Tax (or Benefit) Year-to-Date	Tax (or Benefit) Less Previously Provided	Tax (or Benefit) Reporting Period
First quarter	$ (20,000)	$ (20,000)	40%	$ (8,000)	—	$ (8,000)
Second quarter	10,000	(10,000)	40%	(4,000)	$(8,000)	4,000
Third quarter	15,000	5,000	40%	2,000	(4,000)	6,000
Fourth quarter	95,000	100,000	40%	40,000	2,000	38,000
Fiscal year	$100,000					$40,000

[FIN18, ¶46]

.171 Assume the facts stated in paragraph .167. The enterprise has ordinary income and losses in interim periods, and there is a year-to-date ordinary loss during the year. [FIN18, ¶47] There is no established seasonal pattern and it is more likely than not that the tax benefit of the year-to-date loss and the anticipated tax credits will not be realized in the current or future years. [FAS109, ¶288(y)] Quarterly tax computations are:

	Ordinary Income (Loss)		Estimated	Tax		
			Annual		Less	
	Reporting	Year-to-	Effective	Year-to-	Previously	Reporting
Reporting Period	**Period**	**Date**	**Tax Rate**	**Date**	**Provided**	**Period**
First quarter	$ (20,000)	$ (20,000)	—*	—	—	—
Second quarter	10,000	(10,000)	—*	—	—	—
Third quarter	15,000	5,000	40%	$ 2,000	—	$ 2,000
Fourth quarter	95,000	100,000	40%	40,000	$2,000	38,000
Fiscal year	$100,000					$40,000

*No benefit recognized because the tax benefit of the year-to-date loss is not [FIN18, ¶47] expected to be (a) realized during the current year or (b) recognizable as a deferred tax asset at the end of the current year in accordance with the provisions of Section I27. [FAS109, ¶288(y)].

.172 During the fiscal year, all of an enterprise's operations are taxable in one jurisdiction at a 50 percent rate. No [FIN18, ¶48] events that do not have tax consequences [FAS109, ¶288(y)] are anticipated. Estimates of ordinary income for the year and of anticipated credits at the end of each interim period are as shown below. Changes in the estimated annual effective tax rate result from changes in the ratio of anticipated tax credits to tax computed at the statutory rate. Changes consist of an unanticipated strike that reduced income in the second quarter, an increase in the capital budget resulting in an increase in anticipated investment tax credit in the third quarter, and better than anticipated sales and income in all interim periods. Computations of the estimated annual effective tax rate based on the estimate made at the end of each quarter are:

	Estimated, End of			
	First Quarter	**Second Quarter**	**Third Quarter**	**Actual Fiscal Year**
Estimated ordinary income for the fiscal year	$100,000	$80,000	$ 80,000	$100,000
Tax at 50% statutory rate	$ 50,000	$40,000	$ 40,000	$ 50,000
Less anticipated credits	(5,000)	(5,000)	(10,000)	(10,000)
Net tax to be provided	$ 45,000	$35,000	$ 30,000	$ 40,000
Estimated annual effective tax rate	45%	43.75%	37.5%	40%

[FIN18, ¶48]

.173 Quarterly tax computations are:

	Ordinary Income		Estimated Annual	Tax		
					Less	
Reporting Period	Reporting Period	Year-to-Date	Effective Tax Rate	Year-to-Date	Previously Provided	Reporting Period
First quarter	$ 25,000	$ 25,000	45%	$11,250	—	$11,250
Second quarter	5,000	30,000	43.75%	13,125	$11,250	1,875
Third quarter	25,000	55,000	37.5%	20,625	13,125	7,500
Fourth quarter	45,000	100,000	40%	40,000	20,625	19,375
Fiscal year	$100,000					$40,000

[FIN18, ¶48]

Accounting for Income Taxes Applicable to Ordinary Income (or Loss) at an Interim Date If an Ordinary Loss Is Anticipated for the Fiscal Year

.174 The following assumed facts are applicable to the examples of application of this section in paragraphs .175 through .179:

> For the full fiscal year, an enterprise anticipates an ordinary loss of $100,000. The enterprise operates entirely in one jurisdiction where the tax rate is 50 percent. Anticipated tax credits for the fiscal year total $10,000. No [FIN18, ¶49] events that do not have tax consequences [FAS109, ¶288(y)] are anticipated. [FIN18, ¶49]
>
> If there is a recognizable tax benefit for [both] the loss and the tax credits pursuant to the requirements of Section I27 [FAS109, ¶288(y)], computation of the estimated annual effective tax rate applicable to the ordinary loss would be as follows:

Tax benefit at statutory rate ($100,000 at 50%)	$(50,000)
Tax credits	(10,000)
Net tax benefit	$(60,000)
Estimated annual effective tax rate ($60,000 ÷ $100,000)	60%

The examples in paragraphs .175 through .179 state varying assumptions with respect to assurance of realization of the components of the net tax benefit. When realization of a component of the benefit is not [FIN18, ¶49] expected to be (a) realized during the current year or (b) recognizable as a deferred tax asset at the end of the current year in accordance with the provisions of Section I27, [FAS109, ¶288(y)] that component is not included in the computation of the estimated annual effective tax rate. [FIN18, ¶49]

.175 Assume the facts stated in paragraph .174. The enterprise has ordinary losses in all interim periods. [FIN18, ¶50] The full tax benefit of the anticipated ordinary loss and the anticipated tax credits will be realized by carryback. [FAS109, ¶288(y)] Quarterly tax computations are:

Reporting Period	Ordinary Loss: Reporting Period	Ordinary Loss: Year-to-Date	Estimated Annual Effective Tax Rate	Tax Benefit: Year-to-Date	Tax Benefit: Less Previously Provided	Tax Benefit: Reporting Period
First quarter	$ (20,000)	$ (20,000)	60%	$(12,000)	—	$(12,000)
Second quarter	(20,000)	(40,000)	60%	(24,000)	$(12,000)	(12,000)
Third quarter	(20,000)	(60,000)	60%	(36,000)	(24,000)	(12,000)
Fourth quarter	(40,000)	(100,000)	60%	(60,000)	(36,000)	(24,000)
Fiscal year	$100,000					$(60,000)

[FIN18, ¶50]

.176 Assume the facts stated in paragraph .174. The enterprise has ordinary income and losses in interim periods and for the year to date. [FIN18, ¶51] The full tax benefit of the anticipated ordinary loss and the anticipated tax credits will be realized by carryback. The full tax benefit of the maximum year-to-date ordinary loss can also be realized by carryback. [FAS109, ¶288(y)] Quarterly tax computations are:

Reporting Period	Ordinary Income (Loss): Reporting Period	Ordinary Income (Loss): Year-to-Date	Estimated Annual Effective Tax Rate	Tax (or Benefit): Year-to-Date Computed	Tax (or Benefit): Year-to-Date Limited To	Tax (or Benefit): Less Previously Provided	Tax (or Benefit): Reporting Period
First quarter	$ 20,000	$ 20,000	60%	$ 12,000		—	$ 12,000
Second quarter	(80,000)	(60,000)	60%	(36,000)		$ 12,000	(48,000)
Third quarter	(80,000)	(140,000)	60%	(84,000)	$(80,000)*	(36,000)	(44,000)
Fourth quarter	40,000	(100,000)	60%	(60,000)		(80,000)	20,000
Fiscal year	$(100,000)						$(60,000)

*Because the year-to-date ordinary loss exceeds the anticipated ordinary loss for the fiscal year, the tax benefit recognized for the year to date is limited to the amount that would be recognized if the year-to-date ordinary loss were the anticipated ordinary loss for the fiscal year. The limitation is computed as follows:

Year-to-date ordinary loss times the statutory rate ($140,000 at 50%)	$(70,000)
Estimated tax credits for the year	(10,000)
Year-to-date benefit limited to	$(80,000)

[FIN18, ¶51]

.177 In the examples in paragraphs .175 and .176, if neither the tax benefit of the anticipated loss for the fiscal year [FIN18, ¶52] nor [FAS109, ¶288(y)] anticipated tax credits were [FIN18, ¶52] recognizable pursuant to Section I27 [FAS109, ¶288(y)], the estimated annual effective tax rate for the year would be zero and no tax (or benefit) would be recognized in any quarter. That conclusion is not affected by changes in the mix of income and loss in interim periods during a fiscal year. However, refer to paragraph .112, footnote 5. [FIN18, ¶52]

Partial Realization of the Tax Benefit of the Loss Is Assured

.178 Assume the facts stated in paragraph .174. The enterprise has an ordinary loss in all interim periods. [FIN18, ¶53] It is more likely than not that [FAS109, ¶288(y)] the tax benefit of the loss [FIN18, ¶53] in excess [FAS109, ¶288(y)] of $40,000 of prior income available to be offset by carryback ($20,000 of tax at the 50 percent statutory rate) [FIN18, ¶53] will not be realized. [FAS109, ¶288(y)] Therefore, the estimated annual effective tax rate is 20 percent ($20,000 benefit assured divided by $100,000 estimated fiscal-year ordinary loss). Quarterly tax computations are:

	Ordinary Loss		Estimated	Tax Benefit		
Reporting Period	Reporting Period	Year-to-Date	Annual Effective Tax Rate	Year-to-Date	Less Previously Provided	Reporting Period
First quarter	$(20,000)	$ (20,000)	20%	$ (4,000)	—	$ (4,000)
Second quarter	(20,000)	(40,000)	20%	(8,000)	$ (4,000)	(4,000)
Third quarter	(20,000)	(60,000)	20%	(12,000)	(8,000)	(4,000)
Fourth quarter	(40,000)	(100,000)	20%	(20,000)	(12,000)	(8,000)
Fiscal year	$100,000					$(20,000)

[FIN18, ¶53]

.179 Assume the facts stated in paragraph .174. The enterprise has ordinary income and losses in interim periods and for the year to date. [FIN18, ¶54] It is more likely than not that [FAS109, ¶288(y)] the tax benefit of the anticipated ordinary loss [FIN18, ¶54] in excess [FAS109, ¶288(y)] of $40,000 of prior income available to be offset by carryback ($20,000 of tax at the 50 percent statutory rate) [FIN18, ¶54] will not be realized. [FAS109, ¶288(y)] Therefore, the estimated annual effective tax rate is 20 percent ($20,000 benefit assured divided by $100,000 estimated fiscal-year ordinary loss), and the benefit that can be recognized for the year to date is limited to $20,000 (the benefit that is assured of realization). Quarterly tax computations are:

	Ordinary Income (Loss)		Estimated Annual	Tax (or Benefit)			
				Year-to-Date		Less	
Reporting Period	**Reporting Period**	**Year-to-Date**	**Effective Tax Rate**	**Computed**	**Limited To**	**Previously Provided**	**Reporting Period**
First quarter	$ 20,000	$ 20,000	20%	$ 4,000		—	$ 4,000
Second quarter	(80,000)	(60,000)	20%	(12,000)		$ 4,000	(16,000)
Third quarter	(80,000)	(140,000)	20%	(28,000)	$(20,000)	(12,000)	(8,000)
Fourth quarter	40,000	(100,000)	20%	(20,000)		(20,000)	—
Fiscal year	$(100,000)						$(20,000)

[FIN18, ¶54]

.180 The enterprise anticipates a fiscal year ordinary loss. The loss cannot be carried back, and future profits [FIN18, ¶55] exclusive of reversing temporary differences are unlikely. [FAS109, ¶288(y)] Net deferred tax [FIN18, ¶55] liabilities [FAS109, ¶288(y)] arising from [FIN18, ¶55] existing net taxable temporary differences [FAS109, ¶288(y)] are present. A portion of the [FIN18, ¶55] existing net taxable temporary differences [FAS109, ¶288(y)] relating to those [FIN18, ¶55] liabilities [FAS109, ¶288(y)] will reverse within the loss carryforward period. Computation of the estimated annual tax rate to be used [FIN18, ¶55] (refer to paragraph .123) [FAS109, ¶288(y)] is as follows:

Estimated fiscal year ordinary loss		$(100,000)
The tax benefit to be recognized is the lesser of:		
Tax effect of the loss carryforward ($100,000 at 50% statutory rate)	$50,000	
Amount of the net deferred tax [FIN18, ¶55] liabilities [FAS109, ¶288(y)] that would otherwise have been [FIN18, ¶55] settled [FAS109, ¶288(y)] during the carryforward period	$24,000	
Estimated annual effective tax rate ($24,000 ÷ $100,000)		24%

[FIN18, ¶55]

.181 Quarterly tax computations are:

Reporting Period	Ordinary Loss Reporting Period	Ordinary Loss Year-to-Date	Estimated Annual Effective Tax Rate	Tax Benefit Year-to-Date	Tax Benefit Less Previously Provided	Tax Benefit Reporting Period
First quarter	$ (20,000)	$ (20,000)	24%	$ (4,800)	—	$ (4,800)
Second quarter	(20,000)	(40,000)	24%	(9,600)	$ (4,800)	(4,800)
Third quarter	(20,000)	(60,000)	24%	(14,400)	(9,600)	(4,800)
Fourth quarter	(40,000)	(100,000)	24%	(24,000)	(14,400)	(9,600)
Fiscal year	$100,000					$(24,000)

Note: Changes in the timing of the loss by quarter would not change the above computation. [FIN18, ¶55]

Accounting for Income Taxes Applicable to Unusual, Infrequently Occurring, or Extraordinary Items

.182 The examples of computations in paragraphs .183 and .184 illustrate the computation of the tax (or benefit) applicable to unusual, infrequently occurring, or extraordinary items when ordinary income is anticipated for the fiscal year. These examples are based on the facts and computations given in paragraphs .167 through .171 plus additional information supplied in paragraphs .183 and .184. The computation of the tax (or benefit) applicable to the ordinary income is not affected by the occurrence of an unusual, infrequently occurring, or extraordinary item; therefore, each example refers to one or more of the examples of that computation in paragraphs .168 through .171 and does not reproduce the computation and the facts assumed. The income statement display for tax (or benefit applicable to unusual, infrequently occurring, or extraordinary items) is illustrated in paragraph .208. [FIN18, ¶56]

.183 As explained in paragraph .182, this example is based on the computations of tax applicable to ordinary income that are illustrated in paragraph .168. In addition, the enterprise experiences a tax-deductible unusual, infrequently occurring, or extraordinary loss of $50,000 (tax benefit $25,000) in the second quarter. Because the loss can be carried back, the benefit of the loss is assured beyond any reasonable doubt at the time of occurrence. Quarterly tax provisions are:

			Tax (or Benefit) Applicable to	
Reporting Period	**Ordinary Income**	**Unusual, Infrequently Occurring, or Extraordinary Loss**	**Ordinary Income**	**Unusual, Infrequently Occurring, or Extraordinary Loss**
First quarter	$ 20,000		$ 8,000	
Second quarter	20,000	$(50,000)	8,000	$(25,000)
Third quarter	20,000		8,000	
Fourth quarter	40,000		16,000	
Fiscal year	$100,000	$(50,000)	$40,000	$(25,000)

Note: Changes in assumptions would not change the timing of the recognition of the tax benefit applicable to the unusual, infrequently occurring, or extraordinary item as long as realization is assured beyond any reasonable doubt. [FIN18, ¶57]

.184 As explained in paragraph .182, this example is based on the computations of tax applicable to ordinary income that are illustrated in paragraphs .168 and .169. In addition, the enterprise experiences a tax-deductible unusual, infrequently occurring, or extraordinary loss of $50,000 (potential benefit $25,000) in the second quarter. [FIN18, ¶58] The loss cannot be carried back, and available evidence indicates that a valuation allowance is needed for all of the deferred tax asset. [FAS109, ¶288(y)] As a result, the tax benefit of the unusual, infrequently occurring, or extraordinary loss is [FIN18, ¶58] recognized only [FAS109, ¶288(y)] to the extent of offsetting ordinary income for the year to date. Quarterly tax provisions under two different assumptions for the occurrence of ordinary income are:

Assumptions and Reporting Period	Ordinary Income (Loss)	Unusual, Infrequently Occurring, or Extraordinary Loss	Tax (or Benefit) Applicable to Ordinary Income (Loss): Reporting Period	Ordinary Income (Loss): Year-to-Date	Unusual, Infrequently Occurring, or Extraordinary Loss: Year-to-Date	Less Previously Provided	Reporting Period
Income in all quarters:							
First quarter	$ 20,000		$ 8,000	$ 8,000			
Second quarter	20,000	$(50,000)	8,000	16,000	$(16,000)	—	$(16,000)
Third quarter	20,000		8,000	24,000	(24,000)	$(16,000)	(8,000)
Fourth quarter	40,000		16,000	40,000	(25,000)	(24,000)	(1,000)
Fiscal year	$100,000	$(50,000)	$40,000				$(25,000)
Income and loss quarters:							
First quarter	$ 40,000		$16,000	$16,000			
Second quarter	40,000	$(50,000)	16,000	32,000	$(25,000)	—	$(25,000)
Third quarter	(20,000)		(8,000)	24,000	(24,000)	$(25,000)	1,000
Fourth quarter	40,000		16,000	40,000	(25,000)	(24,000)	(1,000)
Fiscal year	$100,000	$(50,000)	$40,000				$(25,000)

[FIN18, ¶58]

.185-.187 [Deleted 2/92 because of FASB Statement 109.]

Accounting for Income Taxes Applicable to Income (or Loss) from Discontinued Operations at an Interim Date

.188 An enterprise anticipates ordinary income for the year of $100,000 and tax credits of $10,000. The enterprise has ordinary income in all interim periods. The estimated annual effective tax rate is 40 percent, computed as follows:

Estimated pretax income	$100,000
Tax at 50% statutory rate	$ 50,000
Less anticipated credits	(10,000)
Net tax to be provided	$ 40,000
Estimated annual effective tax rate	40%

[FIN18, ¶62]

.189 Quarterly tax computations for the first two quarters are:

	Ordinary Income		Estimated Annual	Tax Benefit		
Reporting Period	**Reporting Period**	**Year-to-Date**	**Effective Tax Rate**	**Year-to-Date**	**Less Previously Provided**	**Reporting Period**
First quarter	$(20,000)	$20,000	40%	$ 8,000	$ —	$ 8,000
Second quarter	25,000	45,000	40%	18,000	8,000	10,000

[FIN18, ¶62]

.190 In the third quarter a decision is made to discontinue the operations of Division X, a segment of the business that has recently operated at a loss (before income taxes). The pretax income (and losses) of the continuing operations of the enterprise and of Division X through the third quarter and the estimated fourth quarter results are as follows:

		Division X	
Reporting Period	**Revised Ordinary Income from Continuing Operations**	**Loss from Operations**	**Provision for Loss on Disposal**
First quarter	$ 25,000	$ (5,000)	
Second quarter	35,000	(10,000)	
Third quarter	50,000	(10,000)	$(55,000)
Fourth quarter	50,000*	—	—
Fiscal year	$160,000	$(25,000)	$(55,000)

*Estimated.

[FIN18, ¶62]

.191 No changes have occurred in continuing operations that would affect the estimated annual effective tax rate. Anticipated annual tax credits of $10,000 included $2,000 of credits related to the operations of Division X. The revised estimated annual effective tax rate applicable to ordinary income from continuing operations is 45 percent, computed as follows:

Estimated ordinary income from continuing operations	$160,000
Tax at 50% statutory rate	$ 80,000
Less anticipated tax credits applicable to continuing operations	(8,000)
Net tax to be provided	$ 72,000
Estimated annual effective tax rate	45%

[FIN18, ¶62]

.192 Quarterly computations of tax applicable to ordinary income from continuing operations are as follows:

Reporting Period	Ordinary Income: Reporting Period	Ordinary Income: Year-to-Date	Estimated Annual Effective Tax Rate	Tax: Year-to-Date	Tax: Less Previously Provided	Tax: Reporting Period
First quarter	$ 25,000	$ 25,000	45%	$11,250	—	$11,250
Second quarter	35,000	60,000	45%	27,000	$11,250	15,750
Third quarter	50,000	110,000	45%	49,500	27,000	22,500
Fourth quarter	50,000	160,000	45%	72,000	49,500	22,500
Fiscal year	$160,000					$72,000

[FIN18, ¶62]

.193 Tax benefit applicable to Division X for the first two quarters is computed as follows:

Reporting Period	Tax Applicable to Ordinary Income: Previously Reported (A)	Tax Applicable to Ordinary Income: Recomputed (above) (B)	Tax Benefit Applicable to Division X (A – B)
First quarter	$ 8,000	$11,250	$(3,250)
Second quarter	10,000	15,750	(5,750)
			$(9,000)

[FIN18, ¶62]

.194 The third quarter tax benefits applicable to both the loss from operations and the provision for loss on disposal of Division X are computed based on estimated annual income with and without the effects of the Division X losses. Current year tax credits related to the operations of Division X have not been recognized. It is assumed that the tax benefit of those credits will not be realized because of the discontinuance of Division X operations. Any reduction in tax benefits resulting from recapture of previously recognized tax credits resulting from discontinuance or current year tax credits applicable to the discontinued operations would be reflected in the tax benefit recognized for the loss on disposal or loss from operations as appropriate. If, because of capital gains and losses, etc., the individually computed tax effects of the items do not equal the aggregate tax effects of the items, the aggregate tax effects are allocated to the individual items in the same manner that they will be allocated in the annual financial statements. The computations are as follows:

	Loss from Operations of Division X	Provision for Loss on Disposal
Estimated annual income from continuing operations	$160,000	$160,000
Loss from Division X operations	(25,000)	
Provision for loss on disposal of Division X		(55,000)
Total	$135,000	$105,000
Tax at 50% statutory rate	$ 67,500	$ 52,500
Anticipated credits from continuing operations	(8,000)	(8,000)
Tax credits of Division X and recapture of previously recognized tax credits resulting from discontinuance	—	—
Taxes on income after effect of Division X losses	59,500	44,500
Taxes on income before effect of Division X losses—refer to computation above	72,000	72,000
Tax benefit applicable to the losses of Division X	(12,500)	(27,500)
Amounts previously recognized—refer to computation above	(9,000)	—
Tax benefit recognized in third quarter	$ (3,500)	$ (27,500)

[FIN18, ¶62]

.195 The resulting revised quarterly tax provisions are summarized as follows:

	Pretax Income (Loss)			Tax (or Benefit) Applicable to		
Reporting Period	Continuing Operations	Operations of Division X	Provision for Loss on Disposal	Continuing Operations	Operations of Division X	Provision for Loss on Disposal
First quarter	$ 25,000	$ (5,000)		$11,250	$ (3,250)	
Second quarter	35,000	(10,000)		15,750	(5,750)	
Third quarter	50,000	(10,000)	$(55,000)	22,500	(3,500)	$(27,500)
Fourth quarter	50,000			22,500		
Fiscal year	$160,000	$(25,000)	$(55,000)	$72,000	$(12,500)	$(27,500)

[FIN18, ¶62]

Accounting for Income Taxes Applicable to the Cumulative Effect of a Change in Accounting Principle

.196 The tax (or benefit) applicable to the cumulative effect of the change on retained earnings at the beginning of the fiscal year shall be computed the same as for the annual financial statements. [FIN18, ¶63]

.197 When an enterprise makes a cumulative effect-type accounting change in other than the first interim period of the enterprise's fiscal year, paragraph .136 requires that financial information for the prechange interim periods of the fiscal year shall be restated by applying the newly adopted accounting principle to those prechange interim periods. The tax (or benefit) applicable to those prechange interim periods shall be recomputed. The restated tax (or benefit) shall reflect the year-to-date amounts and annual estimates originally used for the prechange interim periods, modified only for the effect of the change in accounting principle on those year-to-date and estimated annual amounts. [FIN18, ¶64]

Accounting for Income Taxes Applicable to Ordinary Income If an Enterprise Is Subject to Tax in Multiple Jurisdictions

.198 An enterprise operates through separate corporate entities in two countries. Applicable tax rates are 50 percent in the United States and 20 percent in Country A. The enterprise has no unusual or extraordinary items during the fiscal year and anticipates no tax credits or [FIN18, ¶65] events that do not have tax consequences. [FAS109, ¶288(y)] (The effect of foreign tax credits and the necessity of providing tax on undistributed earnings are ignored because of the wide range of tax-planning alternatives available.) For the full fiscal year the enterprise anticipates ordinary income of $60,000 in the United States and $40,000 in Country A. The enterprise is able to make a reliable estimate of its Country A ordinary income and tax for the fiscal year in dollars. Computation of the overall estimated annual effective tax rate is as follows:

Anticipated ordinary income for the fiscal year:	
In the United States	$ 60,000
In Country A	40,000
Total	$100,000
Anticipated tax for the fiscal year:	
In the United States ($60,000 at 50% statutory rate)	$ 30,000
In Country A ($40,000 at 20% statutory rate)	8,000
Total	$ 38,000
Overall estimated annual effective tax rate ($38,000 ÷ $100,000)	38%

[FIN18, ¶65]

.199 Quarterly tax computations are as follows:

Reporting Period	Ordinary Income U.S.	Country A	Total	Year-to-Date	Overall Estimated Annual Effective Tax Rate	Tax Year-to-Date	Less Previously Reported	Reporting Period
First quarter	$ 5,000	$15,000	$ 20,000	$ 20,000	38%	$ 7,600	$ —	$ 7,600
Second quarter	10,000	10,000	20,000	40,000	38%	15,200	7,600	7,600
Third quarter	10,000	10,000	20,000	60,000	38%	22,800	15,200	7,600
Fourth quarter	35,000	5,000	40,000	100,000	38%	38,000	22,800	15,200
Fiscal year	$60,000	$40,000	$100,000					$38,000

[FIN18, ¶65]

.200 Assume the facts stated in paragraphs .198 and .199. In addition, the enterprise operates through a separate corporate entity in Country B. Applicable tax rates in Country B are 40 percent. Operations in Country B have resulted in losses in recent years and an ordinary loss is anticipated for the current fiscal year in Country B. [FIN18, ¶66] It is expected that [FAS109, ¶288(y)] the tax benefit of those losses [FIN18, ¶66] will not be recognizable as a deferred tax asset at the end of the current year pursuant to Section I27 [FAS109, ¶288(y)]; accordingly, no tax benefit is recognized for losses in Country B, and interim period tax (or benefit) is separately computed for the ordinary loss in Country B and for the overall ordinary income in the United States and Country A. The tax applicable to the overall ordinary income in the United States and Country A is computed as in paragraphs .198 and .199. Quarterly tax provisions are as follows:

Reporting Period	Ordinary Income (or Loss) U.S.	Country A	Combined Excluding Country B	Country B	Total	Tax (or Benefit) Overall Excluding Country B	Country B	Total
First quarter	$ 5,000	$15,000	$ 20,000	$ (5,000)	$15,000	$ 7,600	$—	$ 7,600
Second quarter	10,000	10,000	20,000	(25,000)	(5,000)	7,600	—	7,600
Third quarter	10,000	10,000	20,000	(5,000)	15,000	7,600	—	7,600
Fourth quarter	35,000	5,000	40,000	(5,000)	35,000	15,200	—	15,200
Fiscal year	$60,000	$40,000	$100,000	$(40,000)	$60,000	$38,000	$—	$38,000

[FIN18, ¶66]

.201 Assume the facts stated in paragraphs .198 and .199. In addition, the enterprise operates through a separate corporate entity in Country C. Applicable tax rates in Country C are 40 percent in foreign currency. Depreciation in that country is large and exchange rates have changed in prior years. The enterprise is unable to make a reasonable estimate of its ordinary income for the year in Country C and thus is unable to reasonably estimate its annual effective tax rate in Country C in dollars. Accordingly, tax (or benefit) in Country C is separately computed as ordinary income (or loss) occurs in Country C. The tax applicable to the overall ordinary income in the United States and Country A is computed as in paragraphs .198 and .199. Quarterly computations of tax applicable to Country C are as follows:

	Foreign Currency Amounts		Translated Amounts in Dollars	
Reporting Period	Ordinary Income in Reporting Period	Tax (at 40% Rate)	Ordinary Income in Reporting Period	Tax
First quarter	FC10,000	FC 4,000	$12,500	$ 3,000
Second quarter	5,000	2,000	8,750	1,500
Third quarter	30,000	12,000	27,500	9,000
Fourth quarter	15,000	6,000	16,250	4,500
Fiscal year	FC60,000	FC24,000	$65,000	$18,000

[FIN18, ¶67]

.202 Quarterly tax provisions are as follows:

	Ordinary Income					Tax		
Reporting Period	U.S.	Country A	Combined Excluding Country C	Country C	Total	Overall Excluding Country C	Country C	Total
First quarter	$ 5,000	$15,000	$ 20,000	$12,500	$ 32,500	$ 7,600	$ 3,000	$10,600
Second quarter	10,000	10,000	20,000	8,750	28,750	7,600	1,500	9,100
Third quarter	10,000	10,000	20,000	27,500	47,500	7,600	9,000	16,600
Fourth quarter	35,000	5,000	40,000	16,250	56,250	15,200	4,500	19,700
Fiscal year	$60,000	$40,000	$100,000	$65,000	$165,000	$38,000	$18,000	$56,000

[FIN18, ¶67]

Effect of New Tax Legislation

.203 The following assumed facts are applicable to the examples of application in paragraphs .204 and .205:

> For the full fiscal year, an enterprise anticipates ordinary income of $100,000. All income is taxable in 1 jurisdiction at a 50 percent rate. Anticipated tax credits for the fiscal year total $10,000. No [FIN18, ¶68] events that do not have tax consequences [FAS109, ¶288(y)] are anticipated.

Computation of the estimated annual effective tax rate applicable to ordinary income is as follows:

Tax at statutory rate ($100,000 at 50%)	$ 50,000
Less anticipated tax credits	(10,000)
Net tax to be provided	$ 40,000
Estimated annual effective tax rate ($40,000 ÷ $100,000)	40%

[FIN18, ¶68]

.204 Assume the facts stated in paragraph .203. In addition, assume that new legislation creating additional tax credits is enacted during the second quarter of the enterprise's fiscal year. The new legislation is effective on the first day of the third quarter. As a result of the estimated effect of the new legislation, the enterprise revises its estimate of its annual effective tax rate to the following:

Tax at statutory rate ($100,000 at 50%)	$ 50,000
Less anticipated tax credits	(12,000)
Net tax to be provided	$ 38,000
Estimated annual effective tax rate ($38,000 ÷ $100,000)	38%

[FIN18, ¶69]

.205 The effect of the new legislation shall not be reflected until it is effective or administratively effective. Accordingly, quarterly tax computations are:

	Ordinary Income		Estimated Annual Effective	Tax	Tax Less	
Reporting Period	**Reporting Period**	**Year-to-Date**	**Tax Rate**	**Year-to-Date**	**Previously Provided**	**Reporting Period**
First quarter	$ 20,000	$ 20,000	40%	$ 8,000	—	$ 8,000
Second quarter	20,000	40,000	40%	16,000	$ 8,000	8,000
Third quarter	20,000	60,000	38%	22,800	16,000	6,800
Fourth quarter	40,000	100,000	38%	38,000	22,800	15,200
Fiscal year	$100,000					$38,000

[FIN18, ¶69]

.206-.207 [Deleted 2/92 because of FASB Statement 109.]

[[19a]Deleted 2/92 because of FASB Statement 109.]

Illustration of Income Taxes in Income Statement Display

.208 Exhibit 208A illustrates the location in an income statement display of the various tax amounts computed under this section. [FIN18, ¶71]

Exhibit 208A

Illustrative Income Statement

*Net sales		$XXXX
*Other income		XXX
		XXXX
Costs and expenses:		
*Cost of sales	$XXXX	
*Selling, general, and administrative expenses	XXXX	
*Interest expense	XXX	
*Other deductions	XX	
Unusual items	XXX	
Infrequently occurring items	XXX	XXXX
Income (loss) from continuing operations before income taxes and other items listed below		XXXX
†Provision for income taxes (benefit)		XXXX
Income (loss) from continuing operations before other items listed below		XXXX
Discontinued operations:		
Income (loss) from operations of discontinued [FIN18, ¶71] Component [FAS144, ¶C19(d)] X (less applicable income taxes of $XXXX)		XXXX
Income (loss) before extraordinary items and cumulative effect of a change in accounting principle		XXXX
Extraordinary items (less applicable income taxes of $XXXX)		XXXX
‡Cumulative effect on prior years of a change in accounting principle (less applicable income taxes of $XXXX)		XXXX
Net income (loss)		$XXXX

*Components of ordinary income (loss)

†Consists of the total income taxes (or benefits) applicable to (a) ordinary income, (b) unusual items, and (c) infrequently occurring items.

‡This amount is net of applicable income taxes. The amount of the applicable income taxes is usually separately disclosed but that is not required.

[FIN18, ¶71]

Glossary

.401 **Annual effective tax rate.** Best estimate of [an enterprise's] effective tax rate expected to be applicable for the full fiscal year [(refer to paragraph .111)]. [APB28, ¶19]

.402 **Ordinary income or loss.** "Income (or loss) from continuing operations before income taxes (or benefits)" excluding significant "unusual or infrequently occurring items." Extraordinary items, discontinued operations, and cumulative effects of changes in accounting principles are also excluded from this term.[401] The term is *not* used in the income tax context of ordinary income versus capital gain. [FIN18, ¶5]

.403 **Tax (or benefit).** The total income tax expense (or benefit) including the provision (or benefit) for income taxes both currently payable and deferred. [FIN18, ¶5]

[401]The terms used in this definition are described in Sections A06, I14, I17, and I22. See Section I17, [paragraphs .107 and .401,] for *extraordinary items* and paragraph .101 of Section I22 for *unusual items* and *infrequently occurring items.* See paragraph .116 of Section A06 for *cumulative effects of changes in accounting principles.* See paragraphs .101 through .104 of Section I14 for *discontinued operations.* [FAS144, ¶C19(a)]

[illegible]

Discussion

101. [illegible] effective [illegible] estimate of the [illegible]

102. [illegible]

103. [illegible]

[illegible]

Supplemental Guidance

Reduction in Tax Rate Effective for Part of Fiscal Year

.501 *Question*—How should an enterprise with a fiscal year other than a calendar year account during interim periods for the reduction in the corporate tax rate resulting from the Revenue Act of 1978? [FTB79-9, ¶1]

.502 *Background*—The Revenue Act of 1978, among other things, reduced the corporate income tax rate from 48 percent to 46 percent. [FTB79-9, ¶2]

.503 *Response*—Paragraph .115 requires that the effect of a change in tax rates be reflected in a revised annual effective tax rate calculation in the same way that the change will be applied to the enterprise's taxable income for the year. The revised annual effective tax rate would then be applied to pretax income for the year to date at the end of the current interim period. [FTB79-9, ¶3]

.504-.507 [Deleted 2/92 because of FASB Statement 109.]

Supplemental Guidance: Emerging Issues Task Force (EITF) Issues

.1000 [Listed below are EITF Issues that provide supplemental guidance for this section. These Issues may be either interpretive of or related by topic to the guidance in this section.

EITF Issue No. 86-13, "Recognition of Inventory Market Declines at Interim Reporting Dates"
EITF Issue No. 95-7, "Implementation Issues Related to the Treatment of Minority Interests in Certain Real Estate Investment Trusts"
EITF Issue No. 98-9, "Accounting for Contingent Rent"
EITF Topic No. D-96, "Accounting for Management Fees Based on a Formula"]

.1001 [Listed below is an EITF Issue that provides interpretive guidance on specific material in this section.

Paragraph .107 (APB 28, ¶14)—EITF Issue No. 86-13]

(The next page is 27519.)

Supplemental Guidance: Emerging Issues Task Force (EITF) Issues

.1001 Listed below are EITF Issues that provide supplemental guidance on this section. These issues may be cited as [illegible] guidance in this section.

EITF Issue No. 86-13, Recognition of Inventory Market Declines at Interim Reporting Dates

EITF Issue No. [illegible], Implementation Issues Related to the Treatment of Minority Interests in Certain Real Estate Investment Trusts

EITF Issue No. [illegible], Accounting for Contingent Rent

EITF Issue No. [illegible], Accounting for Management Fees Based on a Formula

.1002 Listed below is an EITF Issue that provides [illegible] guidance [illegible] this section.

[illegible]

INVENTORY SECTION I78

Sources: FASB Statement 133; ARB 43, Chapter 3A; ARB 43, Chapter 4

[**Note:** A list of Issues discussed by the Emerging Issues Task Force (EITF) that provide supplemental guidance for this section is presented in paragraph .1000.]

Summary

Inventory shall be stated at the lower of cost or market except in certain exceptional cases when it may be stated above cost. *Cost* is defined as the sum of the applicable expenditures and charges directly or indirectly incurred in bringing inventories to their existing condition and location. Cost for inventory purposes may be determined under any one of several assumptions as to the flow of cost factors (such as first-in, first-out; average; and last-in, first-out).

Introduction

.101 Whenever the operation of a business includes the ownership of a stock of goods, it is necessary for adequate financial accounting purposes that **inventories** be properly compiled periodically and recorded in the accounts.[1] [ARB43, ch4, ¶1] This section sets forth the general principles applicable to the pricing of inventories of mercantile and manufacturing enterprises. Its conclusions are not directed to or necessarily applicable to noncommercial businesses or to regulated utilities. [ARB43, ch4, ¶2]

Definition of Inventory

.102 [In this section,] the term *inventory* is used to designate the aggregate of those items of tangible personal property that (a) are held for sale in the ordinary course of business [(finished goods)], (b) are in process of production for such sale [(work in process)], or (c) are to be currently consumed either directly or indirectly in the production of goods or services to be available for sale [(raw materials and supplies)]. [ARB43, ch4, ¶3]

.103 This definition of inventories excludes long-term assets subject to depreciation accounting or goods that, when put into use, will be so classified. [In addition,] a depreciable asset [that] is retired from regular use and held for sale [shall] not be classified as part of the inventory. Raw materials and supplies purchased for production may be used or consumed for the construction of long-term assets or other purposes not related to

---

[1]Prudent reliance upon perpetual inventory records is not precluded. [ARB43, ch4, ¶1, fn1]

production, but the fact that inventory items representing a small portion of the total [inventory] may not be absorbed ultimately in the production process shall not require separate classification. By trade practice, operating materials and supplies of certain types of enterprises, such as oil producers, are usually treated as inventory. [ARB43, ch4, ¶3]

Accounting Objective

.104 [Revenues from the sale of inventory, or from the sale of the goods or services in whose production it is used, normally arise] in a continuous repetitive process or cycle of operations by which goods are acquired and sold, and further goods are acquired for additional sales. The major objective [in accounting for the goods in the inventory] is the matching of appropriate **costs** against revenues in order that there may be a proper determination of the realized income. Thus, the inventory at any given date is the balance of costs applicable to goods on hand remaining after the matching of absorbed costs with concurrent revenues. This balance [shall be] carried to future periods provided it does not exceed an amount properly chargeable against the revenues expected to be obtained from ultimate disposition of the goods carried forward.[2] In practice, this balance is determined by the process of pricing the articles in the inventory.[3] [ARB43, ch4, ¶4]

Accounting for Inventories

Cost Basis

.105 In keeping with the principle that accounting is primarily based on cost, there is a presumption that inventories shall be stated at cost.[3] [ARB43, ch4, ¶5]

.106 Although principles for the determination of inventory costs may be easily stated, their application, particularly to such inventory items as work in process and finished goods, is difficult because of the variety of problems encountered in the allocation of costs and charges. For example, under some circumstances, items such as idle facility expense, excessive spoilage, double freight, and rehandling costs may be so abnormal as to require treatment as current period charges rather than as a portion of the inventory cost. Also, general and administrative expenses shall be included as period charges, except for the portion of such expenses that [are] clearly related to production and thus constitute a part of inventory costs (product charges). Selling expenses [are not] part of inventory costs. Exclusion of all overheads from inventory costs does not constitute an accepted accounting procedure. [ARB43, ch4, ¶5]

[2Refer to paragraph .109 for guidance if the utility of inventory is not as great as its cost.]

[3Refer to paragraphs .109 and .119 for exceptions to this rule.]

.107 Cost for inventory purposes shall be determined under any one of several assumptions as to the flow of cost factors (such as first-in, first-out; average; and last-in, first-out); the major objective in selecting a method shall be to choose the one that most clearly reflects periodic income. [ARB43, ch4, ¶6] [Refer to Section I73, "Interim Financial Reporting," paragraph .107, for a discussion of the application of those methods at an interim reporting date.]

.108 The cost to be matched against revenue from a sale may not be the identified cost of the specific item that is sold, especially in cases in which similar goods are purchased at different times and at different prices. While in some lines of business specific lots are clearly identified from the time of purchase through the time of sale and are costed on this basis, ordinarily the identity of goods is lost between the time of acquisition and the time of sale. If the materials purchased in various lots are identical and interchangeable, the use of identified cost of the various lots may not produce the most useful financial statements. This fact has resulted in the development of general acceptance of several assumptions with respect to the flow of cost factors (such as first-in, first-out; average; and last-in, first-out) to provide practical bases for the measurement of periodic income.[4] In some situations, a reversed mark-up procedure of inventory pricing, such as the retail inventory method, may be both practical and appropriate. The business operations in some cases may be such as to make it desirable to apply one of the acceptable methods of determining cost to one portion of the inventory or components thereof and another of the acceptable methods to other portions of the inventory. [ARB43, ch4, ¶6]

Lower of Cost or Market Basis

.109 A departure from the cost basis of pricing the inventory is required when the utility of the goods is no longer as great as its cost. If the utility of goods is impaired by damage, deterioration, obsolescence, changes in price levels, or other causes, a loss [shall] be reflected as a charge against the revenues of the period in which it occurs. The measurement of such losses shall be accomplished by applying the rule of pricing inventories at **cost or market, whichever is lower.** [ARB43, ch4, ¶8] (If inventory has been the hedged item in a fair value hedge, the inventory's "cost" basis used in the cost-or-market-whichever-is-lower accounting shall reflect the effect of the adjustments of its carrying amount made pursuant to paragraph .119(b) of Section D50, "Derivative Instruments and Hedging Activities.") [FAS133, ¶526] This provides a practical means of measuring utility and thereby determining the amount of the loss to be recognized and accounted for in the current period. [ARB43, ch4, ¶8]

---

[4]Standard costs are acceptable if adjusted at reasonable intervals to reflect current conditions so that at the balance sheet date standard costs reasonably approximate costs computed under one of the recognized bases. In such cases, descriptive language shall be used that will express this relationship, as, for instance, "approximate costs determined on the first-in, first-out basis," or, if it is desired to mention standard costs, "at standard costs, approximating average costs." [ARB43, ch4, ¶6, fn3]

.110 As used in the phrase *lower of cost or market* the term **market** means current replacement cost (by purchase or by reproduction, as the case may be) except that:

a. Market shall not exceed the net realizable value (i.e., estimated selling price in the ordinary course of business less reasonably predictable costs of completion and disposal); and
b. Market shall not be less than net realizable value reduced by an allowance for an approximately normal profit margin. [ARB43, ch4, ¶9]

.111 The rule of *cost or market, whichever is lower* [shall] provide a means of measuring the residual usefulness of an inventory expenditure. The term *market* shall therefore be interpreted as indicating utility on the inventory date and should be thought of in terms of the equivalent expenditure that would have to be made in the ordinary course [of business] at that date to procure corresponding utility. As a general guide, utility is indicated primarily by the current cost of replacement of the goods as they would be obtained by purchase or reproduction. In applying the rule, however, judgment should always be exercised and no loss shall be recognized unless the evidence indicates clearly that a loss has been sustained. There are exceptions to such a standard. Replacement or reproduction prices [are] not appropriate as a measure of utility [if] the estimated sales value, reduced by the costs of completion and disposal, is lower, in which case the realizable value so determined more appropriately measures utility. Furthermore, [if] the evidence indicates that cost will be recovered with an approximately normal profit upon sale in the ordinary course of business, no loss shall be recognized even though replacement or reproduction costs are lower. This might be true, for example, in the case of production under firm sales contracts at fixed prices, or [if] a reasonable volume of future orders is assured at stable selling prices. [ARB43, ch4, ¶9]

.112 Because of the many variations of circumstances encountered in inventory pricing, paragraphs .110 and .111 are intended as a guide rather than a literal rule. They should be applied realistically in the light of the objectives expressed in this section and with due regard to the form, content, and composition of the inventory. For example, the retail inventory method, if adequate markdowns are currently taken, accomplishes the objectives described herein. If a business is expected to lose money for a sustained period, the inventory shall not be written down to offset a loss inherent in the subsequent operations. [ARB43, ch4, ¶10]

.113 Depending on the character and composition of the inventory, the rule of *cost or market, whichever is lower* may be properly applied either directly to each item or to the total of the inventory (or, in some cases, to the total of the components of each major category). The method shall be that which most clearly reflects periodic income. [ARB43, ch4, ¶11]

.114 The purpose of reducing inventory to *market* is to reflect fairly the income of the period. The most common practice is to apply the *lower of cost or market* rule separately to each item of the inventory. However, if there is only one end-product category the cost utility of the total stock—the inventory in its entirety—may have the greatest significance for accounting purposes. Accordingly, the reduction of individual items to *market* may not always lead to the most useful result if the utility of the total inventory to the business is not below its cost. This might be the case if selling prices are not affected by temporary or small fluctuations in current costs of purchase or manufacture. Similarly, [if] more than one major product or operational category exists, the application of the *cost or market, whichever is lower* rule to the total of the items included in such major categories may result in the most useful determination of income. [ARB43, ch4, ¶11]

.115 [If] no loss of income is expected to take place as a result of a reduction of cost prices of certain goods because others forming components of the same general categories of finished products have a market equally in excess of cost, such components need not be adjusted to market to the extent that they are in balanced quantities. Thus, in such cases, the rule of *cost or market, whichever is lower* shall be applied directly to the totals of the entire inventory, rather than to the individual inventory items, if they enter into the same category of finished product and if they are in balanced quantities, provided the procedure is applied consistently from year to year. [ARB43, ch4, ¶12]

.116 To the extent, however, that the stocks of particular materials or components are excessive in relation to others, the more widely recognized procedure of applying the *lower of cost or market* to the individual items constituting the excess shall be followed. This would also apply in cases in which the items enter into the production of unrelated products or products having a material variation in the rate of turnover. Unless an effective method of classifying categories is practicable, the rule shall be applied to each item in the inventory. [ARB43, ch4, ¶13]

.117 [If] substantial and unusual losses result from the application of this rule, the amount of the loss [shall be disclosed] in the income statement as a charge separately identified from the consumed inventory costs described as *cost of goods sold.* [ARB43, ch4, ¶14]

.118 [The application of the lower of cost or market rule to inventories in translated financial statements is discussed in Section F60, "Foreign Currency Translation," paragraphs .148 through .152.]

Stating Inventories above Cost

.119 Only in exceptional cases may inventories be stated above cost. For example, precious metals having a fixed monetary value with no substantial cost of marketing may be stated at such monetary value; any other exceptions must be justifiable by inability to determine appropriate approximate costs, immediate marketability at quoted market price, and the characteristic of unit interchangeability. [Stating inventories above cost] is not uncommon for inventories representing agricultural, mineral, and other products, units of which are interchangeable and have an immediate marketability at quoted prices and for which appropriate costs may be difficult to obtain. [If] such inventories are stated at sales prices, they [shall be] reduced by expenditures to be incurred in disposal. [If goods are stated above cost, this fact] shall be fully disclosed. [ARB43, ch4, ¶16]

Disclosure

.120 The amounts at which [inventories] are stated [shall] be supplemented by information which reveals for the various classifications of inventory items, the basis upon which their amounts are stated and, where practicable, [an] indication of the method of determining the cost—e.g., *average cost, first-in first-out, last-in first-out,* etc. [ARB43, ch3A, ¶9] The basis of stating inventories shall be consistently applied and shall be disclosed in the financial statements;[5] whenever a significant change is made therein, there shall be disclosure of the nature of the change and, if material, the effect on income, [as discussed in Section A06, "Accounting Changes," paragraphs .107 and .108 and .113 through .124]. [ARB43, ch4, ¶15]

Net Losses on Firm Purchase Commitments

.121 Accrued net losses on firm purchase commitments for goods for inventory, measured in the same way as are inventory losses, shall, if material, be recognized in the accounts and the amounts thereof separately disclosed in the income statement. [ARB43, ch4, ¶17]

.122 The recognition in a current period of losses arising from the decline in the utility of cost expenditures is equally applicable to similar losses that are expected to arise from firm, uncancelable, and unhedged commitments for the future purchase of inventory items. The net loss on such commitments shall be measured in the same way as are inventory losses and, if material, shall be recognized in the [financial statements] and separately disclosed in the income statement. The utility of such commitments is not impaired, and hence there is no loss, [if] the amounts to be realized from the disposition of the future inventory items are adequately protected by firm sales contracts or if there are other circumstances that reasonably assure continuing sales without price decline. [ARB43, ch4, ¶17]

[[5]Refer to Section A10, "Accounting Policies," for guidance regarding disclosure.]

Glossary

.401 **Cost.**[401] The price paid or consideration given to acquire an asset; [it includes] the applicable expenditures and charges directly or indirectly incurred in bringing [the asset] to its existing condition and location. [ARB43, ch4, ¶5]

.402 **Inventory.** The aggregate of those items of tangible personal property that (a) are held for sale in the ordinary course of business (finished goods), (b) are in process of production for such sale (work in process), or (c) are to be currently consumed either directly or indirectly in the production of goods or services to be available for sale (raw materials and supplies). [ARB43, ch4, ¶3]

.403 **Lower of Cost or Market [Rule].** The rule of **cost or market, whichever is lower** [shall] provide a means of measuring the residual usefulness of an inventory expenditure. In applying the rule, however, judgment should always be exercised and no loss shall be recognized unless the evidence indicates clearly that a loss has been sustained. There are exceptions to such a standard. Replacement or reproduction prices [are] not appropriate as a measure of utility [if] the estimated sales value, reduced by the costs of completion and disposal, is lower, in which case the realizable value so determined more appropriately measures utility. Furthermore, [if] the evidence indicates that cost will be recovered with an approximately normal profit upon sale in the ordinary course of business, no loss shall be recognized even though replacement or reproduction costs are lower. This might be true, for example, in the case of production under firm sales contracts at fixed prices, or [if] a reasonable volume of future orders is assured at stable selling prices. [ARB43, ch4, ¶9]

.404 **Market.** The term **market** means current replacement cost (by purchase or by reproduction, as the case may be) except that:

a. Market shall not exceed the net realizable value (i.e., estimated selling price in the ordinary course of business less reasonably predictable costs of completion and disposal); and
b. Market shall not be less than net realizable value reduced by an allowance for an approximately normal profit margin.

The term *market* shall be interpreted as indicating utility on the inventory date and should be thought of in terms of the equivalent expenditure that would have to be made in the ordinary course [of business] at that date to procure corresponding utility. As a general guide, utility is indicated primarily by the current cost of replacement of the goods as they would be obtained by purchase or reproduction. [ARB43, ch4, ¶9]

---

[401] In the case of goods that have been written down below cost at the close of a fiscal period (refer to paragraph .109), such reduced amounts shall be considered the cost for subsequent accounting purposes. [ARB43, ch4, ¶5, fn2]

Glossary

[illegible]

[illegible]

[illegible]

[illegible]

[illegible]

[illegible]

[illegible]

[illegible]

[illegible]

Supplemental Guidance: Emerging Issues Task Force (EITF) Issues

.1000 [Listed below are EITF Issues that provide supplemental guidance for this section. These Issues are grouped by subject matter and are related by topic to the guidance in this section.

Last-In, First-Out (LIFO)

EITF Issue No. 84-10, "LIFO Conformity of Companies Relying on *Insilco* Tax Court Decision"

EITF Issue No. 84-24, "LIFO Accounting Issues"

Other

EITF Issue No. 86-46, "Uniform Capitalization Rules for Inventory under the Tax Reform Act of 1986"

EITF Issue No. 96-9, "Classification of Inventory Markdowns and Other Costs Associated with a Restructuring"

EITF Issue No. 98-10, "Accounting for Contracts Involved in Energy Trading and Risk Management Activities"

EITF Issue No. 01-9, "Accounting for Consideration Given by a Vendor to a Customer (Including a Reseller of the Vendor's Products)"]

(The next page is 27631.)

INVESTMENTS: DEBT AND EQUITY SECURITIES SECTION I80

Sources: ARB 43; FASB Statement 91; FASB Statement 115; FASB Statement 124; FASB Statement 130; FASB Statement 133; FASB Statement 135; FASB Statement 140; FASB Statement 144; FASB Statement 145; FASB Technical Bulletin 79-19; FASB Technical Bulletin 94-1

[**Note:** A list of Issues discussed by the Emerging Issues Task Force (EITF) that provide supplemental guidance for this section is presented in paragraph .1000.]

Summary

This section addresses the accounting and reporting for investments in equity securities that have readily determinable fair values and for all investments in debt securities. Those investments are to be classified in three categories and accounted for as follows:

- Debt securities that the enterprise has the positive intent and ability to hold to maturity are classified as *held-to-maturity securities* and reported at amortized cost.
- Debt and equity securities that are bought and held principally for the purpose of selling them in the near term are classified as *trading securities* and reported at fair value, with unrealized gains and losses included in earnings.
- Debt and equity securities not classified as either held-to-maturity securities or trading securities are classified as *available-for-sale securities* and reported at fair value, with unrealized gains and losses excluded from earnings and reported in other comprehensive income.

This section does not apply to unsecuritized loans. However, after mortgage loans are converted to mortgage-backed securities, they are subject to its provisions.

Scope

.101 This section addresses the accounting and reporting for certain investments in **debt securities** and **equity securities.** [FAS115, ¶1] Except as indicated in paragraph .102, this section establishes standards of financial accounting and reporting for investments in equity securities that have readily determinable **fair values** and for all investments in debt securities.

a. The fair value of an equity security is readily determinable if sales prices or bid-and-asked quotations are currently available on a **securities** exchange registered with the Securities and Exchange Commission (SEC) or in the over-the-counter market, provided that those prices or quotations for the over-the-counter market are publicly reported by the National Association of Securities Dealers Automated Quotations systems or by the National Quotation Bureau. Restricted stock[1] does not meet that definition.
b. The fair value of an equity security traded only in a foreign market is readily determinable if that foreign market is of a breadth and scope comparable to one of the U.S. markets referred to above.
c. The fair value of an investment in a mutual fund is readily determinable if the fair value per share (unit) is determined and published and is the basis for current transactions.

[FAS115, ¶3] [Refer to paragraph .1001 for an EITF Issue that provides interpretive guidance on this paragraph.]

.102 This section does not apply to investments in equity securities accounted for under the equity method nor to investments in consolidated subsidiaries. [Refer to Section I82, "Investments: Equity Method."] This section does not apply to enterprises whose specialized accounting practices include accounting for substantially all investments in debt and equity securities at market value or fair value, with changes in value recognized in earnings (income) or in the change in net assets. Examples of those enterprises are brokers and dealers in securities, defined benefit pension plans, and investment companies. [FAS115, ¶4] This section applies to cooperatives and mutual enterprises, including credit unions and mutual insurance companies, but does not apply to not-for-profit organizations.[2] Section No5, "Not-for-Profit Organizations," paragraphs .148 through .175, establishes standards for not-for-profit organizations. [FAS124, ¶110] This section does not apply to investments in derivative instruments that are subject to the requirements of Section D50, "Derivative Instruments and Hedging Activities." If an investment would otherwise be in the scope of this section and it has within it an embedded derivative that

[1]*Restricted stock,* for the purpose of this section, means equity securities for which sale is restricted by governmental or contractual requirement (other than in connection with being pledged as collateral) except if that requirement terminates within one year or if the holder has the power by contract or otherwise to cause the requirement to be met within one year. Any portion of the security that can be reasonably expected to qualify for sale within one year, such as may be the case under Rule 144 or similar rules of the SEC, is not considered restricted. [FAS115, ¶3, fn2]

[[2]Editorial deletion, 10/95.]

is subject to Section D50, the host instrument (as described in Section D50) remains within the scope of this section. A transaction gain or loss on a held-to-maturity foreign-currency-denominated debt security shall be accounted for pursuant to Section F60, "Foreign Currency Translation." [FAS133, ¶534(a)] The accounting for discounts, premiums, and commitment fees associated with the purchase of loans and other debt securities such as corporate bonds, Treasury notes and bonds, groups of loans, and loan-backed securities (such as pass-through certificates, collateralized mortgage obligations, and other so-called "securitized" loans) is addressed in Section L20, "Lending Activities." [FAS91, ¶3] [Refer to paragraphs .503 and .504 for further guidance on the applicability of this section to loans restructured in a troubled debt restructuring.]

Accounting for Certain Investments in Debt and Equity Securities

.103 At acquisition, an enterprise shall classify debt and equity securities into one of three categories: held-to-maturity, available-for-sale, or trading. At each reporting date, the appropriateness of the classification shall be reassessed. [FAS115, ¶6]

Held-to-Maturity Securities

.104 Investments in debt securities shall be classified as *held-to-maturity* and measured at amortized cost in the statement of financial position only if the reporting enterprise has the positive intent[3] and ability to hold those securities to maturity. [FAS115, ¶7] A security may not be classified as held-to-maturity if that security can contractually be prepaid or otherwise settled in such a way that the holder of the security would not recover substantially all of its recorded investment.[3a, 3b, 3c] [FAS140, ¶362] A debt security with those characteristics should be evaluated in accordance with paragraphs .109 through .113 of Section D50 to determine whether it contains an embedded derivative that must be accounted for separately. [FAS135, ¶4(t)] Interest-only strips, retained interests in securitizations, loans, other receivables, or other financial assets that can contractually be prepaid or otherwise settled in such a way that the holder would not recover substantially all of its recorded investment, except for instruments that are within the

[3]In establishing intent, an enterprise shall consider pertinent historical experience, such as sales and transfers of debt securities classified as held-to-maturity. A pattern of sales or transfers of those securities is inconsistent with an expressed current intent to hold similar debt securities to maturity. [FAS115, ¶59]

[[3a]Deleted 12/00 because of FASB Statement No. 140, *Accounting for Transfers and Servicing of Financial Assets and Extinguishments of Liabilities*.]

[3b]The provisions of the second sentence of paragraph .104 do not apply to situations in which events that are not the result of contractual provisions, for example, borrower default or changes in the value of an instrument's denominated currency relative to the entity's functional currency, cause the holder not to recover substantially all of its recorded investment. [FAS140, ¶295]

[[3c]Deleted 12/00 because of Statement 140.]

scope of Section D50, shall be subsequently measured like investments in debt securities classified as available-for-sale or trading under the guidance in paragraphs .104 and .109. [FAS140, ¶14] [Refer to paragraph .1001 for EITF Issues that provide interpretive guidance on this paragraph.]

.105 The following changes in circumstances, however, may cause the enterprise to change its intent to hold a certain security to maturity without calling into question its intent to hold other debt securities to maturity in the future. Thus, the sale or transfer of a held-to-maturity security due to one of the following changes in circumstances shall not be considered to be inconsistent with its original classification:

a. Evidence of a significant deterioration[4] in the issuer's creditworthiness
b. A change in tax law that eliminates or reduces the tax-exempt status of interest on the debt security (but not a change in tax law that revises the marginal tax rates applicable to interest income[5])
c. A major business combination or major disposition (such as sale of a [FAS115, ¶8] component of an entity [FAS144, ¶C13]) that necessitates the sale or transfer of held-to-maturity securities to maintain the enterprise's existing interest rate risk position or credit risk policy[6]

[4]The sale of a held-to-maturity security must be in response to an actual deterioration, not mere speculation. That deterioration shall be supported by evidence about the issuer's creditworthiness; however, the enterprise need not await an actual downgrading in the issuer's published credit rating or inclusion on a "credit watch" list. [FAS115, ¶72]

[5Similarly, selling] held-to-maturity securities to generate taxable gains to offset existing taxable losses, or vice versa, [or selling] those securities in response to changes in the enterprise's anticipated future profitability [is not permitted]. Securities that may need to be sold to implement tax-planning strategies should be classified as available-for-sale, not held-to-maturity. [FAS115, ¶71]

[6]Those necessary transfers or sales should occur concurrent with or shortly after the business combination or disposition. [FAS115, ¶74]

d. A change in statutory or regulatory requirements significantly modifying either what constitutes a permissible investment or the maximum level of investments in certain kinds of securities, thereby causing an enterprise to dispose of a held-to-maturity security
e. A significant increase by the regulator in the industry's capital requirements that causes the enterprise to downsize by selling held-to-maturity securities[7]
f. A significant increase in the risk weights of debt securities used for regulatory risk-based capital purposes.

In addition to the foregoing changes in circumstances, other events that are isolated, nonrecurring, and unusual for the reporting enterprise that could not have been reasonably anticipated may cause the enterprise to sell or transfer a held-to-maturity security without necessarily calling into question its intent to hold other debt securities to maturity. All sales and transfers of held-to-maturity securities shall be disclosed pursuant to paragraph .121. [FAS115, ¶8]

.106 An enterprise shall not classify a debt security as held-to-maturity if the enterprise has the intent to hold the security for only an indefinite period. Consequently, a debt security should not, for example, be classified as held-to-maturity if the enterprise anticipates that the security would be available to be sold in response to:

a. Changes in market interest rates and related changes in the security's prepayment risk
b. Needs for liquidity (for example, due to the withdrawal of deposits, increased demand for loans, surrender of insurance policies, or payment of insurance claims)
c. Changes in the availability of and the yield on alternative investments
d. Changes in funding sources and terms
e. Changes in foreign currency risk.

[FAS115, ¶9] [Refer to paragraph .1001 for an EITF Issue that provides interpretive guidance on this paragraph.]

.107 Although its asset-liability management may encompass consideration of the maturity and repricing characteristics of all investments in debt securities, an enterprise may decide that it can accomplish the necessary adjustments under its asset-liability management without having all of its debt securities available for disposition. In that case, the enterprise may choose to designate certain debt securities as unavailable to be sold to accomplish those ongoing adjustments deemed necessary under its asset-liability man-

[7However,] an enterprise's ability and intent to hold securities to maturity would be called into question by the sale of held-to-maturity securities to realize gains to replenish regulatory capital that had been reduced by a provision for loan losses. [FAS115, ¶76]

agement, thereby enabling those debt securities to be accounted for at amortized cost on the basis of a positive intent and ability to hold them to maturity. [FAS115, ¶10]

.108 Sales of debt securities that meet either of the following two conditions may be considered as maturities for purposes of the classification of securities under paragraphs .104 and .109 and the disclosure requirements under paragraph .121:

a. The sale of a security occurs near enough to its maturity date (or call date if exercise of the call is probable) that interest rate risk is substantially eliminated as a pricing factor. That is, the date of sale is so near the maturity or call date (for example, within three months) that changes in market interest rates would not have a significant effect on the security's fair value.
b. The sale of a security occurs after the enterprise has already collected a substantial portion (at least 85 percent) of the principal outstanding at acquisition [FAS115, ¶11] (not the principal outstanding at issuance for securities purchased in the secondary market) [FAS115, ¶66] due either to prepayments on the debt security or to scheduled payments on a debt security payable in equal installments (both principal and interest) over its term. For variable-rate securities, the scheduled payments need not be equal.

[FAS115, ¶11]

Trading Securities and Available-for-Sale Securities

.109 Investments in debt securities that are not classified as held-to-maturity and equity securities that have readily determinable fair values shall be classified in one of the following categories and measured at fair value in the statement of financial position:

a. *Trading securities.* Securities that are bought and held principally for the purpose of selling them in the near term (thus held for only a short period of time) shall be classified as *trading securities.* Trading generally reflects active and frequent buying and selling, and trading securities are generally used with the objective of generating profits on short-term differences in price.
b. *Available-for-sale securities.* Investments not classified as trading securities (nor as held-to-maturity securities) shall be classified as *available-for-sale securities.*

[FAS115, ¶12] [Refer to paragraph .1001 for an EITF Issue that provides interpretive guidance on this paragraph.]

Reporting Changes in Fair Value

.110 Unrealized **holding gains and losses** for trading securities shall be included in earnings. Unrealized holding gains and losses for available-for-sale securities (including those classified as current assets) shall be excluded from earnings and reported [FAS115, ¶13] in other comprehensive income [as required in Section C49, "Comprehensive Income: Financial Statement Presentation,"] [FAS130, ¶33(a)] until realized except as indicated in the following sentence. All or a portion of the unrealized holding gain and loss of an available-for-sale security that is designated as being hedged in a fair value hedge shall be recognized in earnings during the period of the hedge, pursuant to paragraph .119 of Section D50. [FAS133, ¶534(b)] Paragraph .135 of Section I27, "Income Taxes," provides guidance on reporting the tax effects of unrealized holding gains and losses reported in [FAS115, ¶13] other comprehensive income. [FAS130, ¶33(a)] [Refer to paragraph .1001 for an EITF Issue that provides interpretive guidance on this paragraph.]

.111 Dividend and interest income, including amortization of the premium and discount arising at acquisition, for all three categories of investments in securities shall continue to be included in earnings. This section does not affect the methods used for recognizing and measuring the amount of dividend and interest income. Realized gains and losses for securities classified as either available-for-sale or held-to-maturity also shall continue to be reported in earnings. [FAS115, ¶14]

Determining Fair Value

.112 Quoted market prices, if available, provide the most reliable measure of fair value. [FAS115, ¶110] Although quoted market prices are not available for all debt securities, a reasonable estimate of fair value can be made or obtained for the remaining debt securities required to be valued at fair value by this section. For debt securities that do not trade regularly or that trade only in principal-to-principal markets, a reasonable estimate of fair value can be made using a variety of pricing techniques, including, but not limited to, discounted cash flow analysis, matrix pricing, option-adjusted spread models, and fundamental analysis. [FAS115, ¶111]

.113 [Deleted 6/98 because of FASB Statement 133, *Accounting for Derivative Instruments and Hedging Activities.*]

Transfers between Categories of Investments

.114 The transfer of a security between categories of investments shall be accounted for at fair value.[8] At the date of the transfer, the security's unrealized holding gain or loss shall be accounted for as follows:

a. For a security transferred from the trading category, the unrealized holding gain or loss at the date of the transfer will have already been recognized in earnings and shall not be reversed.
b. For a security transferred into the trading category, the [FAS115, ¶15] portion of the [FAS133, ¶534(c)] unrealized holding gain or loss at the date of the transfer [FAS115, ¶15] that has not been previously recognized in earnings [FAS133, ¶534(c)] shall be recognized in earnings immediately.
c. For a debt security transferred into the available-for-sale category from the held-to-maturity category, the unrealized holding gain or loss at the date of the transfer shall be [FAS115, ¶15] reported in other comprehensive income. [FAS130, ¶33(b)]
d. For a debt security transferred into the held-to-maturity category from the available-for-sale category, the unrealized holding gain or loss at the date of the transfer shall continue to be reported in a separate component of shareholders' equity [FAS115, ¶15] such as accumulated other comprehensive income, [FAS130, ¶33(c)] but shall be amortized over the remaining life of the security as an adjustment of yield in a manner consistent with the amortization of any premium or discount. The amortization of an unrealized holding gain or loss reported in equity will offset or mitigate the effect on interest income of the amortization of the premium or discount (discussed in footnote 8) for that held-to-maturity security.

Consistent with paragraphs .104 through .106, transfers from the held-to-maturity category should be rare, except for transfers due to the changes in circumstances identified in subparagraphs .105(a) through .105(f). Given the nature of a trading security, transfers into or from the trading category also should be rare. [FAS115, ¶15]

Impairment of Securities

.115 For individual securities classified as either available-for-sale or held-to-maturity, an enterprise shall determine whether a decline in fair value below the amortized cost basis is other than temporary. [FAS115, ¶16] (If a security has been the hedged item in a fair value hedge, the security's "amortized cost basis" shall reflect the effect of the adjustments of its

[8]For a debt security transferred into the held-to-maturity category, the use of fair value may create a premium or discount that, under amortized cost accounting, shall be amortized thereafter as an adjustment of yield pursuant to Section L20. [FAS115, ¶15, fn3]

carrying amount made pursuant to paragraph .119(b) of Section D50.) [FAS133, ¶534(d)] For example, if it is probable that the investor will be unable to collect all amounts due according to the contractual terms of a debt security not impaired at acquisition, an other-than-temporary impairment shall be considered to have occurred.[9] If the decline in fair value is judged to be other than temporary, the cost basis of the individual security shall be written down to fair value as a new cost basis and the amount of the write-down shall be included in earnings (that is, accounted for as a realized loss).[10] The new cost basis shall not be changed for subsequent recoveries in fair value. Subsequent increases in the fair value of available-for-sale securities shall be included in [FAS115, ¶16] other comprehensive income [FAS130, ¶33(d)] pursuant to paragraph .110; subsequent decreases in fair value, if not an other-than-temporary impairment, also shall be included in [FAS115, ¶16] other comprehensive income. [FAS130, ¶33(d)] [Refer to paragraph .1001 for an EITF Issue that provides interpretive guidance on this paragraph.]

Financial Statement Presentation

.116 An enterprise that presents a classified statement of financial position shall report individual held-to-maturity securities, individual available-for-sale securities, and individual trading securities as either current or noncurrent, as appropriate, under the provisions of Section B05, "Balance Sheet Classification: Current Assets and Current Liabilities."[11] [FAS135, ¶4(t)] Presentation of individual amounts for the three categories of investments on the face of the statement of financial position [is not required], provided the information is presented in the notes. [FAS115, ¶117]

.117 Cash flows from purchases, sales, and maturities of available-for-sale securities and held-to-maturity securities shall be classified as cash flows from investing activities and reported gross for each security classification in the statement of cash flows. Cash

---

[9] A decline in the value of a security that is other than temporary is also discussed in [FAS115, ¶16, fn4] AICPA Statement on Auditing Standards No. 92, *Auditing Derivative Instruments, Hedging Activities, and Investments in Securities,* [FAS145, ¶9(h)] and in SEC Staff Accounting Bulletin No. 59, *Accounting for Noncurrent Marketable Equity Securities.* [FAS115, ¶16, fn4]

[10] The impairment provisions of this section differ from those in Section I08, "Impairment," [paragraphs .102 through .119, in that] this section requires that the measure of impairment be based on the fair value of the security, whereas Section I08 permits measurement of an unsecuritized loan's impairment based on either fair value (of the loan or the collateral) or the present value of the expected cash flows discounted at the loan's effective interest rate. [FAS115, ¶113]

[11] Section B05, paragraph .105, indicates that "the term *current assets* is used to designate cash and other assets or resources commonly identified as those which are reasonably expected to be realized in cash or sold or consumed during the normal operating cycle of the business." That paragraph further indicates that the term also comprehends "marketable securities representing the investment of cash available for current operations." Paragraph .106 indicates that "a one-year time period is to be used as a basis for the segregation of current assets in cases where there are several operating cycles occurring within a year." [FAS115, ¶17, fn5]

flows from purchases, sales, and maturities of trading securities shall be classified as cash flows from operating activities. [FAS115, ¶18]

Disclosures

.118 For securities classified as available-for-sale, all reporting enterprises shall disclose the aggregate fair value, the total gains for securities with net gains in accumulated other comprehensive income, and the total losses for securities with net losses in accumulated other comprehensive income, by major security type as of each date for which a statement of financial position is presented. For securities classified as held-to-maturity, all reporting enterprises shall disclose the aggregate fair value, gross unrecognized holding gains, gross unrecognized holding losses, the net carrying amount, and the gross gains and losses in accumulated other comprehensive income for any derivatives that hedged the forecasted acquisition of the held-to-maturity securities, by major security type as of each date for which a statement of financial position is presented. [FAS133, ¶534(e)] In complying with this requirement, financial institutions[12] shall include in their disclosure the following major security types, though additional types also may be included as appropriate:

a. Equity securities
b. Debt securities issued by the U.S. Treasury and other U.S. government corporations and agencies
c. Debt securities issued by states of the United States and political subdivisions of the states
d. Debt securities issued by foreign governments
e. Corporate debt securities
f. Mortgage-backed securities
g. Other debt securities.

[FAS115, ¶19]

.119 For investments in debt securities classified as available-for-sale and separately for securities classified as held-to-maturity, all reporting enterprises shall disclose information about the contractual maturities of those securities as of the date of the most recent statement of financial position presented. Maturity information may be combined in appropriate groupings. In complying with this requirement, financial institutions shall disclose the fair value and the [FAS115, ¶20] net carrying amount (if different from fair

[12]For purposes of the disclosure requirements of paragraphs .118 and .119, the term *financial institutions* includes banks, savings and loan associations, savings banks, credit unions, finance companies, and insurance companies, consistent with the usage of that term in AICPA Statement of Position 90-11, *Disclosure of Certain Information by Financial Institutions About Debt Securities Held as Assets.* [FAS115, ¶19, fn6]

value) [FAS133, ¶534(f)] of debt securities based on at least 4 maturity groupings: (a) within 1 year, (b) after 1 year through 5 years, (c) after 5 years through 10 years, and (d) after 10 years. Securities not due at a single maturity date, such as mortgage-backed securities, may be disclosed separately rather than allocated over several maturity groupings; if allocated, the basis for allocation also shall be disclosed. [FAS115, ¶20]

.120 For each period for which the results of operations are presented, an enterprise shall disclose:

a. The proceeds from sales of available-for-sale securities and the gross realized gains and gross realized losses [FAS115, ¶21] that have been included in earnings as a result of those sales [FAS133, ¶534(g)]
b. The basis on which [FAS115, ¶21] the cost of a security sold or the amount reclassified out of accumulated other comprehensive income into earnings was determined [FAS133, ¶534(g)] (that is, specific identification, average cost, or other method used)
c. The gross gains and gross losses included in earnings from transfers of securities from the available-for-sale category into the trading category [FAS115, ¶21]
d. The amount of the net unrealized holding gain or loss on available-for-sale securities for the period that has been included in accumulated other comprehensive income and the amount of gains and losses reclassified out of accumulated other comprehensive income for the period
e. The portion of trading gains and losses for the period that relates to trading securities still held at the reporting date. [FAS133, ¶534(g)]

.121 For any sales of or transfers from securities classified as held-to-maturity, the [FAS115, ¶22] net carrying [FAS133, ¶534(h)] amount of the sold or transferred security, [FAS115, ¶22] the net gain or loss in accumulated other comprehensive income for any derivative that hedged the forecasted acquisition of the held-to-maturity security, [FAS133,¶534(h)] the related realized or unrealized gain or loss, and the circumstances leading to the decision to sell or transfer the security shall be disclosed in the notes to the financial statements for each period for which the results of operations are presented. Such sales or transfers should be rare except for sales and transfers due to the changes in circumstances identified in subparagraphs .105(a) through .105(f). [FAS115, ¶22]

[**Note:** Additional guidance with respect to implementing Section I80 is presented in *A Guide to Implementation of Statement 115 on Accounting for Certain Investments in Debt and Equity Securities: Questions and Answers.* The publication addresses 61 questions and was written by FASB staff members, Leslie French Seidman and Robert C. Wilkins. This publication is available from the Order Department, Financial Accounting Standards Board, 401 Merritt 7, P.O. Box 5116, Norwalk, CT 06856-5116, telephone (203) 847-0700.]

[illegible]

[illegible]

[illegible]

[illegible]

[illegible]

[illegible]

[illegible]

Glossary

.401 **Debt security.** Any security representing a creditor relationship with an enterprise. It also includes (a) preferred stock that by its terms either must be redeemed by the issuing enterprise or is redeemable at the option of the investor and (b) a collateralized mortgage obligation (CMO) (or other instrument) that is issued in equity form but is required to be accounted for as a nonequity instrument regardless of how that instrument is classified (that is, whether equity or debt) in the issuer's statement of financial position. However, it excludes option contracts, financial futures contracts, forward contracts, and lease contracts.

- Thus, the term *debt security* includes, among other items, U.S. Treasury securities, U.S. government agency securities, municipal securities, corporate bonds, convertible debt, commercial paper, all securitized debt instruments, such as CMOs and real estate mortgage investment conduits (REMICs), and interest-only and principal-only strips.
- Trade accounts receivable arising from sales on credit by industrial or commercial enterprises and loans receivable arising from consumer, commercial, and real estate lending activities of financial institutions are examples of receivables that do not meet the definition of *security;* thus, those receivables are not debt securities (unless they have been securitized, in which case they would meet the definition).

[FAS115, ¶137]

.402 **Equity security.** Any security representing an ownership interest in an enterprise (for example, common, preferred, or other capital stock) or the right to acquire (for example, warrants, rights, and call options) or dispose of (for example, put options) an ownership interest in an enterprise at fixed or determinable prices. However, the term does not include convertible debt or preferred stock that by its terms either must be redeemed by the issuing enterprise or is redeemable at the option of the investor. [FAS115, ¶137]

.403 **Fair value.** The amount at which an asset could be bought or sold in a current transaction between willing parties, that is, other than in a forced or liquidation sale. Quoted market prices in active markets are the best evidence of fair value and should be used as the basis for the measurement, if available. If a quoted market price is available, the fair value is the product of the number of trading units times that market price. If a quoted market price is not available, the estimate of fair value should be based on the best information available in the circumstances. The estimate of fair value should consider prices for similar assets and the results of valuation techniques to the extent available in the circumstances. Examples of valuation techniques include the present value of estimated expected future cash flows using a discount rate commensurate with the risks involved, option-pricing models, matrix pricing, option-adjusted spread models, and fundamental analysis. Valuation techniques for measuring assets should be consistent with the objective of measuring fair value. Those techniques should incorporate assumptions that market participants would use in their estimates of values, including assumptions about interest rates, default, prepayment, and volatility. [FAS133, ¶534(j)]

.404 **Holding gain or loss.** The net change in fair value of a security exclusive of dividend or interest income recognized but not yet received and exclusive of any write-downs for other-than-temporary impairment. [FAS115, ¶137]

.405 **Restricted stock.** Equity securities for which sale is restricted by governmental or contractual requirement (other than in connection with being pledged as collateral) except if that requirement terminates within one year or if the holder has the power by contract or otherwise to cause the requirement to be met within one year. Any portion of the security that can be reasonably expected to qualify for sale within one year, such as may be the case under Rule 144 or similar rules of the SEC, is not considered restricted. [FAS115, ¶3, fn2]

.406 **Security.** A share, participation, or other interest in property or in an enterprise of the issuer or an obligation of the issuer that (a) either is represented by an instrument issued in bearer or registered form or, if not represented by an instrument, is registered in books maintained to record transfers by or on behalf of the issuer, (b) is of a type commonly dealt in on securities exchanges or markets or, when represented by an instrument, is commonly recognized in any area in which it is issued or dealt in as a medium for investment, and (c) either is one of a class or series or by its terms is divisible into a class or series of shares, participations, interests, or obligations. [FAS115, ¶137]

Supplemental Guidance

Unrealized Losses on Marketable Securities Owned by an Equity Method Investee

.501 *Question*—How should a parent or investor account for its share of the [FTB79-19, ¶1] unrealized holding gains or losses on investments in debt and equity securities [FAS115, ¶135(a)] included in stockholders' equity of an investee accounted for under the equity method? [FTB79-19, ¶1]

.502 *Response*—If an investee that is accounted for by the equity method is required to include unrealized holding gains and losses on investments in debt and equity securities in other comprehensive income pursuant to the provisions of this section, the investor shall adjust its investment in that investee by its proportionate share of the unrealized gains and losses and a like amount shall be included in its other comprehensive income. [FAS133, ¶538]

Application of This Section to Debt Securities Restructured in a Troubled Debt Restructuring

.503 *Question*—For a loan that was restructured in a troubled debt restructuring involving a modification of terms, does this section apply to the accounting by the creditor (that is, investor) [as described in paragraph .101A of Section D22, "Debt: Restructurings,"] if the restructured loan meets the definition of a *security* in paragraph .406? [FTB94-1, ¶1]

.504 *Response*—This section applies to all loans that meet the definition of a *security* in paragraph .406. Thus, any loan that was restructured in a troubled debt restructuring involving a modification of terms, [as described in paragraph .126 of Section D22] including those restructured [in fiscal years beginning before December 16, 1994] would be subject to the provisions of this section if the debt instrument meets the definition of a *security*. [FTB94-1, ¶3]

Supplemental Guidance: Emerging Issues Task Force (EITF) Issues

.1000 [Listed below are EITF Issues that provide supplemental guidance for this section. These Issues are grouped by subject matter and may be either interpretive of or related by topic to the guidance in this section.

Convertible Instruments

EITF Issue No. 98-5, "Accounting for Convertible Securities with Beneficial Conversion Features or Contingently Adjustable Conversion Ratios"
EITF Issue No. 00-27, "Application of Issue No. 98-5 to Certain Convertible Instruments"
EITF Issue No. 01-1, "Accounting for a Convertible Instrument Granted or Issued to a Nonemployee for Goods or Services or a Combination of Goods or Services and Cash"

Foreign Currency Issues

EITF Issue No. 96-15, "Accounting for the Effects of Changes in Foreign Currency Exchange Rates on Foreign-Currency-Denominated Available-for-Sale Debt Securities"
EITF Issue No. 97-7, "Accounting for Hedges of the Foreign Currency Risk Inherent in an Available-for-Sale Marketable Equity Security"

Implementation of FASB Statement 115

EITF Topic No. D-39, "Questions Related to the Implementation of FASB Statement No. 115"
EITF Topic No. D-41, "Adjustments in Assets and Liabilities for Holding Gains and Losses as Related to the Implementation of FASB Statement No. 115"

Structured Notes

EITF Issue No. 96-12, "Recognition of Interest Income and Balance Sheet Classification of Structured Notes"
EITF Issue No. 98-15, "Structured Notes Acquired for a Specified Investment Strategy"

Other

EITF Issue No. 84-20, "GNMA Dollar Rolls"
EITF Issue No. 85-23, "Effect of a Redemption Agreement on Carrying Value of a Security"
EITF Issue No. 85-25, "Sale of Preferred Stocks with a Put Option"
EITF Issue No. 85-39, "Implications of SEC Staff Accounting Bulletin No. 59 on Noncurrent Marketable Equity Securities"

EITF Issue No. 86-40, "Investments in Open-End Mutual Funds That Invest in U.S. Government Securities"
EITF Issue No. 89-18, "Divestitures of Certain Investment Securities to an Unregulated Commonly Controlled Entity under FIRREA"
EITF Issue No. 91-5, "Nonmonetary Exchange of Cost-Method Investments"
EITF Issue No. 94-8, "Accounting for Conversion of a Loan into a Debt Security in a Debt Restructuring"
EITF Issue No. 96-10, "Impact of Certain Transactions on the Held-to-Maturity Classification under FASB Statement No. 115"
EITF Issue No. 96-11, "Accounting for Forward Contracts and Purchased Options to Acquire Securities Covered by FASB Statement No. 115"
EITF Issue No. 97-14, "Accounting for Deferred Compensation Arrangements Where Amounts Earned Are Held in a Rabbi Trust and Invested"
EITF Issue No. 98-2, "Accounting by a Subsidiary or Joint Venture for an Investment in the Stock of Its Parent Company or Joint Venture Partner"
EITF Issue No. 98-13, "Accounting by an Equity Method Investor for Investee Losses When the Investor Has Loans to and Investments in Other Securities of the Investee"
EITF Issue No. 99-4, "Accounting for Stock Received from the Demutualization of a Mutual Insurance Company"
EITF Issue No. 99-20, "Recognition of Interest Income and Impairment on Purchased and Retained Beneficial Interests in Securitized Financial Assets"
EITF Issue No. 00-8, "Accounting by a Grantee for an Equity Instrument to Be Received in Conjunction with Providing Goods or Services"
EITF Issue No. 00-18, "Accounting Recognition for Certain Transactions involving Equity Instruments Granted to Other Than Employees"
EITF Issue No. 02-2, "When Separate Contracts That Meet the Definition of Financial Instruments Should Be Combined for Accounting Purposes"
EITF Topic No. D-11, "Impact of Stock Market Decline"
EITF Topic No. D-40, "Planned Sale of Securities following a Business Combination Expected to Be Accounted for as a Pooling of Interests"
EITF Topic No. D-44, "Recognition of Other-Than-Temporary Impairment upon the Planned Sale of a Security Whose Cost Exceeds Fair Value"
EITF Topic No. D-51, "The Applicability of FASB Statement No. 115 to Desecuritizations of Financial Assets"
EITF Topic No. D-73, "Reclassification and Subsequent Sales of Securities in Connection with the Adoption of FASB Statement No. 133"
EITF Topic No. D-74, "Issues Concerning the Scope of the AICPA Guide on Investment Companies"]

.1001 [Listed below are those EITF Issues that provide interpretive guidance on specific material in this section.

Paragraph .101 (FAS 115, ¶3)—EITF Topic No. D-39
Paragraph .104 (FAS 115, ¶7)—EITF Issue No. 96-10 and Topic No. D-39
Paragraph .106 (FAS 115, ¶9)—EITF Topic No. D-51
Paragraph .109 (FAS 115, ¶12)—EITF Issue No. 98-13
Paragraph .110 (FAS 115, ¶13)—EITF Topic No. D-41
Paragraph .115 (FAS 115, ¶16)—EITF Topic No. D-44]

(The next page is 27715.)

INVESTMENTS: EQUITY METHOD SECTION I82

Sources: APB Opinion 18; AICPA Interpretations of APB Opinion 18;
FASB Statement 58; FASB Statement 94; FASB Statement 109;
FASB Statement 115; FASB Statement 128; FASB Statement 133;
FASB Statement 142; FASB Interpretation 35; FASB Technical Bulletin 79-19

[**Note:** A list of Issues discussed by the Emerging Issues Task Force (EITF) that provide supplemental guidance for this section is presented in paragraph .1000.]

Summary

The equity method is a method of accounting for investments. An investor using the equity method initially records an investment at cost. Subsequently, the carrying amount of the investment is increased to reflect the investor's share of income of the investee and is reduced to reflect the investor's share of losses of the investee or dividends received from the investee. The investor's share of the income or losses of the investee is included in the investor's net income as the investee reports them. Adjustments similar to those made in preparing consolidated financial statements, such as elimination of intercompany gains and losses and amortization of the difference between cost and underlying equity in net assets, also are applicable to the equity method. Under the equity method, an investment in common stock is generally shown in the balance sheet of an investor as a single amount. Likewise, an investor's share of earnings or losses from its investment is ordinarily shown in its income statement as a single amount.

This section requires that an investor use the equity method to account for investments in corporate joint ventures. This section also requires use of the equity method to account for other investments in common stock if the investor has the ability to exercise significant influence over operating and financial policies of the investee enterprise. That ability is presumed to exist for investments of 20 percent or more and is presumed not to exist for investments of less than 20 percent; both presumptions may be overcome by predominant evidence to the contrary.

Scope

.101 This section does not apply to investments in common stock held by (a) investment enterprises registered under the Investment Company Act of 1940 or investment enterprises that would be included under the Act (including small business investment enterprises) except that the number of stockholders is limited and the securities are not offered publicly or (b) nonbusiness entities, such as estates, trusts, and individuals. The section also does not apply to investments in common stock other than those described in this section. [APB18, ¶2] This section [does not address] parent-company financial statements prepared for purposes other than issuance as the general-purpose financial statements of the primary reporting entity. [FAS94, ¶15, fn3]

Criteria for Applying the Equity Method

.102 Section C51, "Consolidation," paragraphs .102 and .103, requires consolidation of all majority-owned **subsidiaries** except the few that meet conditions described in paragraph .102 of that section. The **equity method** is not a valid substitute for consolidation. Moreover, since Section C51 requires the general-purpose financial statements of companies having one or more majority-owned subsidiaries to be consolidated statements, parent-company statements are not a valid substitute for consolidated financial statements.[1] [FAS94, ¶15(c)]

.103 Investors shall account for investments in common stock of **corporate joint ventures** by the equity method in consolidated financial statements.[2] [FAS94, ¶15(e)]

.104 The equity method of accounting for an investment in common stock also shall be followed by an **investor** whose investment in voting stock gives it the ability to exercise significant influence over operating and financial policies of an **investee** even though the investor holds 50 percent or less of the voting stock. Ability to exercise that influence may be indicated in several ways, such as representation on the board of directors, participation in policymaking processes, material intercompany transactions, interchange of managerial personnel, or technological dependency. Another important consideration is the extent of ownership by an investor in relation to the concentration of other shareholdings, but substantial or majority ownership of the voting stock of an investee by another investor does not necessarily preclude the ability to exercise significant influence by the investor. Determining the ability of an investor to exercise such influence is not always clear and applying judgment is necessary to assess the status of each investment. In order to achieve a reasonable degree of uniformity in application, an investment (direct or indirect) of 20 percent or more of the voting stock of an investee shall lead to a presumption that in the absence of evidence to the contrary an investor has the

[1]Paragraphs .102 and .103 of Section C51 describe the conditions under which a majority-owned subsidiary shall not be consolidated. The limitations in paragraphs .102 and .103 of Section C51 shall also be applied as limitations to the use of the equity method. [FAS94, ¶15(d)]

[2]The equity method shall not be applied to the investments described in this paragraph insofar as the limitations on the use of the equity method outlined in footnote 1 would be applicable to investments other than those in subsidiaries. [APB18, ¶16, fn6] [Supplemental guidance regarding applicability to investments in partnerships and unincorporated joint ventures is provided in paragraphs .508 through .512.]

ability to exercise significant influence over an investee. Conversely, an investment of less than 20 percent of the voting stock of an investee shall lead to a presumption that an investor does not have the ability to exercise significant influence unless such ability can be demonstrated.[3] [APB18, ¶17] [Refer to paragraph .1001 for an EITF Issue that provides interpretive guidance on this paragraph.]

.105 An investor's *voting stock interest* in an investee shall be based on those currently outstanding securities whose holders have present voting privileges. Potential voting privileges that may become available to holders of securities of an investee shall be disregarded. [APB18, ¶18] An investor's *share of the earnings or losses* of an investee should be based on the shares of *common stock* held by an investor.[4] [FAS128, ¶162]

.106 Paragraph .104 requires that the equity method of accounting be followed by an investor whose investment in voting stock gives it the ability to exercise significant influence over operating and financial policies of an investee. The presumptions in paragraph .104 are intended to provide a reasonable degree of uniformity in applying the equity method. The presumptions can be overcome by predominant evidence to the contrary. [FIN35, ¶2]

---

[3]The equity method shall not be applied to the investments described in this paragraph insofar as the limitations on the use of the equity method outlined in footnote 1 would be applicable to investments other than those in subsidiaries. [APB18, ¶17, fn7]

[4]Paragraph .155 of Section E11, "Earnings per Share," discusses the treatment of common shares or potential common shares for purposes of computing consolidated EPS. The provisions of that paragraph also apply to investments in common stock of corporate joint ventures and investee companies accounted for under the equity method. [FAS128, ¶162]

.107 Evidence that an investor owning 20 percent or more of the voting stock of an investee may be unable to exercise significant influence over the investee's operating and financial policies requires an evaluation of all the facts and circumstances relating to the investment. The presumption that the investor has the ability to exercise significant influence over the investee's operating and financial policies stands until overcome by predominant evidence to the contrary.[5] [FIN35, ¶3]

.108 Examples of indications that an investor may be unable to exercise significant influence over the operating and financial policies of an investee include:

a. Opposition by the investee, such as litigation or complaints to governmental regulatory authorities, challenges the investor's ability to exercise significant influence.
b. The investor and investee sign an agreement under which the investor surrenders significant rights as a shareholder.[6]
c. Majority ownership of the investee is concentrated among a small group of shareholders who operate the investee without regard to the views of the investor.
d. The investor needs or wants more financial information to apply the equity method than is available to the investee's other shareholders (for example, the investor wants quarterly financial information from an investee that publicly reports only annually), tries to obtain that information, and fails.[7]
e. The investor tries and fails to obtain representation on the investee's board of directors.

This list is illustrative and is not all-inclusive. None of the individual circumstances is necessarily conclusive that the investor is unable to exercise significant influence over the investee's operating and financial policies. However, if any of these or similar circumstances exists, an investor with ownership of 20 percent or more shall evaluate all facts and circumstances relating to the investment to reach a judgment about whether the presumption that the investor has the ability to exercise significant influence over the investee's operating and financial policies is overcome. It may be necessary to evaluate the facts and circumstances for a period of time before reaching a judgment. [FIN35, ¶4]

---

[5] Subject to the limitations on the use of the equity method identified in footnote 1. [FIN35, ¶3, fn1]

[6] [Sometimes,] an investor and an investee have signed an agreement under which the investor agrees to limit its shareholding in the investee. (Because the investor usually agrees not to increase its current holdings, such agreements often are called *stand-still agreements.*) Those agreements commonly are used to compromise disputes when an investee is fighting against a takeover attempt or an increase in an investor's percentage ownership. Depending on their provisions, the agreements may modify an investor's rights or may increase certain rights and restrict others compared with the situation of an investor without such an agreement. If the investor surrenders significant rights as a shareholder under the provisions of such an agreement, the investor shall assess all the facts and circumstances of the investment to determine whether they are sufficient to overcome the presumption. [FIN35, ¶9]

[7] The subject of inability to obtain financial information also is addressed in the American Institute of Certified Public Accountants' *Codification of Statements on Auditing Standards,* AU Section 332, "Evidential Matter for Long-Term Investments," paragraph 9. [FIN35, ¶4, fn3]

Applying the Equity Method

.109 The procedures set forth below shall be followed by an investor in applying the equity method of accounting to investments in common stock of corporate joint ventures and other investees that qualify for the equity method:

a. Intercompany profits and losses shall be eliminated until realized by the investor or investee as if a corporate joint venture or investee enterprise were consolidated.[8]
b. A difference between the cost of an investment and the amount of underlying equity in net assets of an investee shall be accounted for as if the investee were a consolidated subsidiary.[9]
c. The investment(s) in common stock shall be shown in the balance sheet of an investor as a single amount, and the investor's share of earnings or losses of an investee(s) shall ordinarily be shown in the income statement as a single amount except for the extraordinary items as specified in (d) below.
d. The investor's share of extraordinary items and its share of prior period adjustments reported in the financial statements of the investee in accordance with Section I17, "Income Statement Presentation: Extraordinary Items," and Section A06, "Accounting Changes," shall be classified in a similar manner unless they are immaterial in the income statement of the investor.
e. A transaction of an investee of a capital nature that affects the investor's share of stockholders' equity of the investee shall be accounted for as if the investee were a consolidated subsidiary. [For purchases by an investee of its own stock, refer to Section B51, "Business Combinations," paragraph .1B.]
f. Sales of stock of an investee by an investor shall be accounted for as gains or losses equal to the difference at the time of sale between selling price and carrying amount of the stock sold.
g. If financial statements of an investee are not sufficiently timely for an investor to apply the equity method currently, the investor ordinarily shall record its share of the earnings or losses of an investee from the most recent available financial statements. A lag in reporting shall be consistent from period to period.
h. A loss in value of an investment that is other than a temporary decline shall be recognized. Evidence of a loss in value might include, but would not necessarily be limited to, absence of an ability to recover the carrying amount of the investment or inability of the investee to sustain an earnings capacity that would justify the carrying amount of the investment. A current fair value of an investment that is less than its carrying

---

[[8]Supplemental guidance on eliminating intercompany profits is provided in paragraphs .501 through .507.]

[9]Investors shall not amortize goodwill associated with equity method investments after the date [that an] entity [is required to be in full compliance with the provisions of] Section G40, "Goodwill and Other Intangible Assets." [FAS142, ¶D2(a)]

amount may indicate a loss in value of the investment. However, a decline in the quoted market price below the carrying amount or the existence of operating losses is not necessarily indicative of a loss in value that is other than temporary. All are factors to be evaluated.[10]

i. An investor's share of losses of an investee may equal or exceed the carrying amount of an investment accounted for by the equity method plus advances made by the investor. The investor ordinarily shall discontinue applying the equity method when the investment (and net advances) is reduced to zero and shall not provide for additional losses unless the investor has guaranteed obligations of the investee or is otherwise committed to provide further financial support for the investee.[11] If the investee subsequently reports net income, the investor shall resume applying the equity method only after its share of that net income equals the share of net losses not recognized during the period the equity method was suspended. [Refer to paragraph .1001 for EITF Issues that provide interpretive guidance on this subparagraph.]
j. [Accounting for income taxes on undistributed earnings of investees accounted for by the equity method is discussed in Section I27, "Income Taxes," paragraphs .212 through .217.]
k. If an investee has outstanding cumulative preferred stock, an investor shall compute its share of earnings (losses) after deducting the investee's preferred **dividends,** whether or not such dividends are declared.
l. An investment in voting stock of an investee enterprise may fall below the level of ownership described in paragraph .104 from sale of a portion of an investment by the investor, sale of additional stock by an investee, or other transactions and the investor may thereby lose the ability to influence policy, as described in that paragraph. An investor shall discontinue accruing its share of the earnings or losses of the investee for an investment that no longer qualifies for the equity method. The earnings or losses that relate to the stock retained by the investor and that were previously accrued shall remain as a part of the carrying amount of the investment. The investment account shall not be adjusted retroactively under the conditions described in this subparagraph. However, dividends received by the investor in subsequent periods that exceed [the investor's] share of earnings for such periods shall be applied in reduction of the carrying amount of the investment (refer to paragraph .402). [APB18, ¶19] Section I80, "Investments: Debt and Equity Securities," addresses the accounting for investments in equity securities with readily determinable fair values that are not consolidated or accounted for under the equity method. [FAS115, ¶126]

[[10]Supplemental guidance on reporting unrealized losses on marketable securities owned by an equity method investee is provided in paragraphs .513 and .514.]

[11]An investor shall, however, provide for additional losses when the imminent return to profitable operations by an investee appears to be assured. For example, a material, nonrecurring loss of an isolated nature may reduce an investment below zero even though the underlying profitable operating pattern of an investee is unimpaired. [APB18, ¶19, fn10]

m. An investment in common stock of an investee that was previously accounted for on other than the equity method [(that is, by the **cost method**)] may become qualified for use of the equity method by an increase in the level of ownership described in paragraph .104 (that is, acquisition of additional voting stock by the investor, acquisition or retirement of voting stock by the investee, or other transactions). When an investment qualifies for use of the equity method, the investor shall adopt the equity method of accounting. The investment, results of operations (current and prior periods presented), and retained earnings of the investor shall be adjusted retroactively in a manner consistent with the accounting for a step-by-step acquisition of a subsidiary.[12] [APB18, ¶19] If that retroactive adjustment is made on or after the date [that an entity is required to be in full compliance with the provisions of] Section G40, the goodwill related to that investment (including goodwill related to step purchases made prior to the initial application of [the provisions of] Section G40) shall not be amortized in determining the amount of the adjustment. [FAS142, ¶D2(b)] [(Refer to Section C51, paragraph .111, for a description of the step-by-step acquisition method.)]

n. The carrying amount of an investment in common stock of an investee that qualifies for the equity method of accounting as described in subparagraph (m) may differ from the underlying equity in net assets of the investee. The difference shall affect the determination of the amount of the investor's share of earnings or losses of an investee as if the investee were a consolidated subsidiary. [APB18, ¶19] However, if the investor is unable to relate the difference to specific accounts of the investee, the difference shall be recognized as goodwill and not be amortized in accordance with Section G40. [FAS142, ¶D2(c)]

Disclosures

.110 The significance of an investment to the investor's financial position and results of operations shall be considered in evaluating the extent of disclosures of the financial position and results of operations of an investee. If the investor has more than one investment in common stock, disclosures wholly or partly on a combined basis may be appropriate. The following disclosures are generally applicable to the equity method of accounting for investments in common stock:

a. Financial statements of an investor shall disclose parenthetically, in notes to financial statements, or in separate statements or schedules (1) the name of each investee and

---

[12]The amount of interest cost capitalized through application of Section I67, "Interest: Capitalization of Interest Cost," shall not be changed when restating financial statements of prior periods [to reflect the use of the equity method for an investee that was previously accounted for on other than the equity method]. [FAS58, ¶8]

[13][Deleted 6/01 because of FASB Statement 142, *Goodwill and Other Intangible Assets*.]

percentage of ownership of common stock, (2) the accounting policies of the investor with respect to investments in common stock,[14] and (3) the difference, if any, between the amount at which an investment is carried and the amount of underlying equity in net assets and the accounting treatment of the difference.

b. For those investments in common stock for which a quoted market price is available, the aggregate value of each identified investment based on the quoted market price usually shall be disclosed. This disclosure is not required for investments in common stock of subsidiaries.
c. [Deleted 11/87 because of FASB Statement 94, *Consolidation of All Majority-Owned Subsidiaries.*]
d. If investments in common stock of corporate joint ventures or other investments accounted for under the equity method are, in the aggregate, material in relation to the financial position or results of operations of an investor, it may be necessary for summarized information as to assets, liabilities, and results of operations of the investees to be presented in the notes or in separate statements, either individually or in groups, as appropriate.
e. Conversion of outstanding convertible securities, exercise of outstanding options and warrants, and other contingent issuances of an investee may have a significant effect on an investor's share of reported earnings or losses. Accordingly, material effects of possible conversions, exercises, or contingent issuances shall be disclosed in notes to the financial statements of an investor.[15]

[APB18, ¶20]

---

[14]Disclosure shall include the names of any significant investee corporations in which the investor holds 20 percent or more of the voting stock, but the common stock is not accounted for on the equity method, together with the reasons why the equity method is not considered appropriate, and the names of any significant investee corporations in which the investor holds less than 20 percent of the voting stock and the common stock is accounted for on the equity method, together with the reasons why the equity method is considered appropriate. [APB18, ¶19, fn13]

[15]Refer to footnote 4. [APB18, ¶19, fn14]

Glossary

.401 **Corporate joint venture.** An enterprise owned and operated by a small group of businesses (the *joint venturers*) as a separate and specific business or project for the mutual benefit of the members of the group. A government also may be a member of the group. The purpose of a corporate joint venture frequently is to share risks and rewards in developing a new market, product, or technology; to combine complementary technological knowledge; or to pool resources in developing production or other facilities. A corporate joint venture also usually provides an arrangement under which each joint venturer may participate, directly or indirectly, in the overall management of the joint venture. Joint venturers thus have an interest or relationship other than as passive investors. An enterprise that is a subsidiary of one of the joint venturers is not a corporate joint venture. The ownership of a corporate joint venture seldom changes, and its stock is usually not traded publicly. A minority public ownership, however, does not preclude an enterprise from being a corporate joint venture. [APB18, ¶3]

.402 **Cost method.** [A method of accounting for an investment under which] an investor records an investment in the stock of an investee at cost, and recognizes as income dividends received that are distributed from net accumulated earnings of the investee since the date of acquisition by the investor. The net accumulated earnings of an investee subsequent to the date of investment are recognized by the investor only to the extent distributed by the investee as dividends. Dividends received in excess of earnings subsequent to the date of investment are considered a return of investment and are recorded as reductions of cost of the investment. [APB18, ¶6(a)]

.403 **Dividends.** Dividends paid or payable in cash, other assets, or another class of stock and does not include, for purposes of this section, stock dividends or stock splits. [APB18, ¶3] [Section C20, "Capital Stock: Stock Dividends and Stock Splits," discusses accounting for stock dividends and stock splits.]

.404 **Earnings or losses of an investee** and **financial position of an investee.** Net income (or net loss) and financial position of an investee determined in accordance with accounting principles generally accepted in the United States. [APB18, ¶3]

.405 **Equity method.** [A method of accounting for an investment under which] an investor initially records an investment in the stock of an investee at cost, and adjusts the carrying amount of the investment to recognize the investor's share of the earnings or losses of the investee after the date of acquisition. The amount of the adjustment is included in the determination of net income by the investor and such amount reflects adjustments similar to those made in preparing consolidated statements including adjustments to eliminate intercompany gains and losses, and to amortize, if appropriate, any difference between investor cost and underlying equity in net assets of the investee at the date of investment. The investment of an investor also is adjusted to reflect the investor's share of changes in the investee's capital. Dividends received from an investee reduce the carrying amount of the investment. [APB18, ¶6(b)] Under the equity method, an investment in common stock is generally shown in the balance sheet of an investor as a single amount. Likewise, an investor's share of earnings or losses from its investment is ordinarily shown in its income statement as a single amount. [APB18, ¶11]

.406 **Investee.** An enterprise that issued voting stock held by an investor. [APB18, ¶3]

.407 **Investor.** A business enterprise that holds an investment in voting stock of another enterprise. [APB18, ¶3]

.408 **Subsidiary.** An enterprise that is controlled, directly or indirectly, by another enterprise. The usual condition for control is ownership of a majority (over 50 percent) of the outstanding voting stock. The power to control also may exist with a lesser percentage of ownership, for example, by contract, lease, agreement with other stockholders, or by court decree. [APB18, ¶3]

Supplemental Guidance

Intercompany Profit Elimination

.501 *Question*—In applying the equity method of accounting, intercompany profits or losses on assets still remaining with an investor or investee should be eliminated, giving effect to any income taxes on the intercompany transactions (refer to paragraph .109(a) and Section C51, paragraphs .109 and .110). Should all of the intercompany profit or loss be eliminated or only that portion related to the investor's common stock interest in the investee? [AIN-APB18, #1]

.502 *Interpretation*—Paragraph .109 normally requires an investor's net income and stockholders' equity to be the same from application of the equity method as would result from consolidation. Because the equity method is a *one-line* consolidation, however, the details reported in the investor's financial statements under the equity method will not be the same as would be reported in consolidated financial statements (refer to paragraph .109(c)). All intercompany transactions are eliminated in consolidation, but under the equity method intercompany profits or losses are normally eliminated only on assets still remaining on the books of an investor or an investee. [AIN-APB18, #1]

.503 Section C51, paragraph .115, provides for complete elimination of intercompany profits or losses in consolidation. It also states that the elimination of intercompany profit or loss may be allocated proportionately between the majority and minority interests. Whether all or a proportionate part of the intercompany profit or loss shall be eliminated under the equity method depends largely upon the relationship between the investor and the investee. [AIN-APB18, #1]

.504 If an investor controls an investee through majority voting interest and enters into a transaction with an investee which is not on an *arm's-length* basis, none of the intercompany profit or loss from the transaction shall be recognized in income by the investor until it has been realized through transactions with third parties. The same treatment also applies for an investee established with the cooperation of an investor (including an investee established for the financing and operation or leasing of property sold to the investee by the investor) if control is exercised through guarantees of indebtedness, extension of credit and other special arrangements by the investor for the benefit of the investee, or because of ownership by the investor of warrants, convertible securities, etc., issued by the investee. [AIN-APB18, #1]

.505 In other cases, it would be appropriate for the investor to eliminate intercompany profit in relation to the investor's common stock interest in the investee. In these cases, the percentage of intercompany profit to be eliminated would be the same regardless of whether the transaction is *downstream* (that is, a sale by the investor to the investee) or *upstream* (that is, sale by the investee to the investor). The following examples illustrate how these eliminations might be made. The examples assume an investor owns 30 percent of the common stock of an investee, the investment is accounted for under the equity method, and the income tax rate to both the investor and the investee is 40 percent. [AIN-APB18, #1]

.506 Assume an investor sells inventory items to the investee (*downstream* [transaction]). At the investee's balance sheet date, the investee holds inventory for which the investor has recorded a gross profit of $100,000. The investor's net income would be reduced $18,000 to reflect a $30,000 reduction in gross profit and a $12,000 reduction in income tax expense. The elimination of intercompany profit might be reflected in the investor's balance sheet in various ways. The income statement and balance sheet presentations will depend upon what is the most meaningful in the circumstances. [AIN-APB18, #1]

.507 Assume an investee sells inventory items to the investor (*upstream* [transaction]). At the investor's balance sheet date, the investor holds inventory for which the investee has recorded a gross profit of $100,000. In computing the investor's equity "pickup," $60,000 ($100,000 less 40 percent of income tax) would be deducted from the investee's net income and $18,000 (the investor's share of the intercompany gross profit after income tax) would thereby be eliminated from the investor's equity income. Usually, the investor's investment account would also reflect the $18,000 intercompany profit elimination, but the elimination also might be reflected in various other ways; for example, the investor's inventory might be reduced $18,000. [AIN-APB18, #1]

Investments in Partnerships and Unincorporated Ventures

.508 *Question*—Do the provisions of this section apply to investments in partnerships and unincorporated joint ventures? [AIN-APB18, #2]

.509 *Interpretation*—This section applies only to investments in common stock of enterprises and does not cover investments in partnerships and unincorporated joint ventures (also called undivided interests in ventures). Many of the provisions of the section would be appropriate in accounting for investments in these unincorporated entities, however, as discussed below. [AIN-APB18, #2]

.510 Partnership profits and losses accrued by investor-partners are generally reflected in their financial statements as described in paragraphs .109(c) and .109(d). Likewise, most of the other provisions of paragraph .109 would be appropriate in accounting for a partnership interest, such as the elimination of intercompany profits and losses (refer to paragraph .109(a)). [AIN-APB18, #2]

.511 However, income taxes shall be provided on the profits accrued by investor-partners regardless of the tax basis employed in the partnership return. The tax liabilities applicable to partnership interests relate directly to the partners, and the accounting for income taxes generally contemplated by [AIN-APB18, #2] Section I27 [FAS109, ¶287] is appropriate. [AIN-APB18, #2]

.512 Generally, the above discussion of partnerships also would apply to unincorporated joint ventures, particularly the elimination of intercompany profits and the accounting for income taxes. However, because the investor-venturer owns an undivided interest in each asset and is proportionately liable for its share of each liability, the provisions of paragraph .109(c) may not apply in some industries. For example, if it is the established industry practice (such as in some oil and gas venture accounting), the investor-venturer may account in its financial statements for its pro rata share of the assets, liabilities, revenues, and expenses of the venture. [AIN-APB18, #2]

Unrealized Losses on Marketable Securities Owned by an Equity Method Investee

.513 *Question*—How should a parent or investor account for its share of the [FTB79-19, ¶1] unrealized holding gains or losses on investments in debt and equity securities [FAS115, ¶135(a)] included in stockholders' equity of an investee accounted for under the equity method? [FTB79-19, ¶1]

.514 *Response*—If an investee that is accounted for by the equity method is required to include unrealized holding gains and losses on investments in debt and equity securities in other comprehensive income pursuant to the provisions of Section I80, the investor shall adjust its investment in that investee by its proportionate share of the unrealized gains and losses and a like amount shall be included in its other comprehensive income. [FAS133, ¶538]

Supplemental Guidance: Emerging Issues Task Force (EITF) Issues

.1000 [Listed below are EITF Issues that provide supplemental guidance for this section. These Issues are grouped by subject matter and may be either interpretive of or related by topic to the guidance in this section.

Investee Losses

EITF Issue No. 98-13, "Accounting by an Equity Method Investor for Investee Losses When the Investor Has Loans to and Investments in Other Securities of the Investee"
EITF Issue No. 99-10, " Percentage Used to Determine the Amount of Equity Method Losses"
EITF Topic No. D-68, "Accounting by an Equity Method Investor for Investee Losses When the Investor Has Loans to and Investments in Other Securities of an Investee"

Limited Partnerships

EITF Issue No. 98-6, "Investor's Accounting for an Investment in a Limited Partnership When the Investor Is the Sole General Partner and the Limited Partners Have Certain Approval or Veto Rights"
EITF Topic No. D-46, "Accounting for Limited Partnership Investments"

Tax Issues

EITF Issue No. 84-33, "Acquisition of a Tax Loss Carryforward—Temporary Parent-Subsidiary Relationship"
EITF Issue No. 94-1, "Accounting for Tax Benefits Resulting from Investments in Affordable Housing Projects"

Other

EITF Issue No. 95-6, "Accounting by a Real Estate Investment Trust for an Investment in a Service Corporation"
EITF Issue No. 98-2, "Accounting by a Subsidiary or Joint Venture for an Investment in the Stock of Its Parent Company or Joint Venture Partner"
EITF Issue No. 00-1, "Investor Balance Sheet and Income Statement Display under the Equity Method for Investments in Certain Partnerships and Other Ventures"
EITF Issue No. 00-6, "Accounting for Freestanding Derivative Financial Instruments Indexed to, and Potentially Settled in, the Stock of a Consolidated Subsidiary"
EITF Issue No. 00-8, "Accounting by a Grantee for an Equity Instrument to Be Received in Conjunction with Providing Goods or Services"

EITF Issue No. 00-12, "Accounting by an Investor for Stock-Based Compensation Granted to Employees of an Equity Method Investee"
EITF Issue No. 00-18, "Accounting Recognition for Certain Transactions involving Equity Instruments Granted to Other Than Employees"
EITF Topic No. D-84, "Accounting for Subsequent Investments in an Investee After Suspension of Equity Method Loss Recognition When an Investor Increases Its Ownership Interest from Significant Influence to Control through a Market Purchase of Voting Securities"]

.1001 [Listed below are those EITF Issues that provide interpretive guidance on specific material in this section.

Paragraph .104 (APB 18, ¶17)—EITF Issue No. 95-6
Paragraph .109(i) (APB 18, ¶19(i))—EITF Issue No. 98-13 and Topics No. D-68 and D-84]

(The next page is 29141.)

LEASES SECTION L10

Sources: FASB Statement 13; FASB Statement 22; FASB Statement 23; FASB Statement 27; FASB Statement 28; FASB Statement 29; FASB Statement 91; FASB Statement 94; FASB Statement 98; FASB Statement 109; FASB Statement 140; FASB Statement 141; FASB Statement 145; FASB Interpretation 19; FASB Interpretation 21; FASB Interpretation 23; FASB Interpretation 24; FASB Interpretation 26; FASB Interpretation 27; FASB Technical Bulletin 79-10; F ASB Technical Bulletin 79-12; FASB Technical Bulletin 79-13; FASB Technical Bulletin 79-14; FASB Technical Bulletin 79-15; FASB Technical Bulletin 79-16(R); FASB Technical Bulletin 85-3; FASB Technical Bulletin 86-2; FASB Technical Bulletin 88-1

[**Note:** A list of Issues discussed by the Emerging Issues Task Force (EITF) that provide supplemental guidance for this section is presented in paragraph .1000.]

Summary

The accounting for leases, as provided in this section, is derived from the view that a lease that transfers substantially all of the benefits and risks of ownership should be accounted for as the acquisition of an asset and the incurrence of an obligation by the lessee (a capital lease) and as a sale or financing by the lessor (a sales-type, direct financing, or leveraged lease). Other leases should be accounted for as operating leases, that is, the rental of property.

A lessee classifies a lease as either a capital lease or an operating lease. If a particular lease meets any one of the following classification criteria, it is a capital lease:

a. The lease transfers ownership of the property to the lessee by the end of the lease term.
b. The lease contains an option to purchase the leased property at a bargain price.
c. The lease term is equal to or greater than 75 percent of the estimated economic life of the leased property.
d. The present value of rental and other minimum lease payments equals or exceeds 90 percent of the fair value of the leased property less any investment tax credit retained by the lessor.

The last 2 criteria are not applicable when the beginning of the lease term falls within the last 25 percent of the total estimated economic life of the leased property.

The amount to be recorded by the lessee as an asset and an obligation under a capital lease is the lesser of the present value of the rental and other minimum lease payments or the fair value of the leased property. Leased property under a capital lease is amortized in a manner consistent with the lessee's normal depreciation policy for owned assets; the amortization period is restricted to the lease term, rather than the life of the asset, unless the lease provides for transfer of title or includes a bargain purchase option. The periodic rental payments are treated as payments of the lease obligation and interest is recorded on the remaining balance of the obligation.

If none of the criteria is met, the lease is classified as an operating lease by a lessee. Neither an asset nor an obligation is recorded for operating leases. Rental payments are recorded as rental expense in the income statement in a systematic manner, which is usually straight-line.

From the lessor's perspective, a lease is classified as a sales-type, direct financing, leveraged, or operating lease. For a lease involving real estate whose fair value is different from its carrying amount, the lease is classified as a sales-type lease if the lease transfers ownership of the property to the lessee by the end of the lease term; otherwise, such lease is classified as an operating lease. For a lease involving real estate whose fair value is the same as its carrying amount and for all leases not involving real estate, to be classified as a sales-type, direct financing, or leveraged lease, a lease must meet one of the four classification criteria specified above and *both* of the following two further criteria:

a. Collectibility of the minimum lease payments is reasonably predictable.
b. No important uncertainties surround the amount of unreimbursable costs yet to be incurred by the lessor under the lease.

A lease not involving real estate that meets those criteria is classified as a sales-type lease if the fair value of the leased property is different from its carrying amount. Otherwise, unless the lease meets certain additional criteria for leveraged leases, a lease not involving real estate that meets one of the first four criteria and both of the last two is classified as a direct financing lease. Similarly, a lease involving real estate whose fair value is the same as its carrying amount is classified as a direct financing lease if it meets one of the first four criteria and both of the last two, unless the lease meets certain additional criteria for leveraged leases. Leases that fail to meet the foregoing criteria are classified as operating leases.

For sales-type leases of real estate, the method of profit recognition is determined under Section R10, "Real Estate." For other sales-type leases, the present value of the minimum lease payments receivable from the lessee is reported as sales and the carrying amount of the leased property plus any initial direct costs, less the present value of any unguaranteed residual value, is charged as cost of sales. The lessor reports as an asset on the balance sheet the net investment in a sales-type lease calculated by recording the gross investment (the sum of the minimum lease payments and the unguaranteed residual value) at its present value, using the interest rate implicit in the lease as the discount factor. The difference between the gross investment and the net investment is unearned income, which is amortized over the lease term so as to produce a constant periodic rate of return on the net investment.

For a lease classified as a direct financing lease, the lessor reports as an asset on the balance sheet the net investment in a lease consisting of gross investment less unearned income and the unamortized initial direct costs. The gross investment is calculated by adding the minimum lease payments and the unguaranteed residual value. Unearned income is determined by subtracting the sum of the cost or carrying amount of the leased property from the gross investment. Unearned income and the initial direct costs are amortized over the lease term so as to produce a constant periodic rate of return on the net investment. The practice of recognizing a portion of the unearned income at inception of the lease to offset initial direct costs or other costs of direct financing leases is not acceptable.

A leveraged lease is a direct financing lease that additionally has all of the following characteristics:

a. It involves at least three parties: a lessee, a long-term creditor, and a lessor.
b. The financing provided by the long-term creditor is substantial to the transaction and is nonrecourse to the lessor.
c. The lessor's net investment declines during the early years and increases during the later years of the lease term.
d. Any investment tax credit retained by the lessor is accounted for as one of the cash flow components of the lease.

The lessor records the investment in a leveraged lease net of the nonrecourse debt. Income is recognized only in periods in which the net investment net of related deferred taxes is positive. The total net income over the lease term is calculated by deducting the original investment from total cash receipts. By using projected cash receipts and disbursements, the rate of return on the net investment in the years in which the investment is positive is determined and applied to the net investment to determine the periodic income to be recognized. The assumption that underlies this accounting is that the lessor will earn other income during the years in which the investment is negative (net funds are provided by the lease) and will not expect the lease to provide income during those years.

A lessor accounts for leases not meeting the criteria for classification as sales-type, direct financing, or leveraged leases as operating leases. Leased property under operating leases is recorded in the same way as other property, plant, and equipment; rent is reported as income over the lease term in a systematic manner, which is usually straight-line; and the leased property is depreciated like other productive assets.

Leases involving real estate are also addressed. Briefly, if the leased property is land only, the lease is classified as an operating lease unless it provides for transfer of title or includes a bargain purchase option. If the leased property is land and buildings, this section specifies whether and how the elements are to be separated and which criteria are to be applied. Leases that cover only part of a building are addressed and guidance is provided in determining whether the fair value of that part of a building can be determined objectively.

A sale-leaseback transaction involving real estate, including real estate with equipment, is accounted for as a sale only if the transaction qualifies as a sale under the provisions of Section R10 and the seller-lessee will actively use the property during the lease term. If the transaction does not qualify as a sale, it should be accounted for by the deposit method or as a financing.

Required disclosures of lessees and lessors are specified and special guidance is provided for various matters, including leveraged leases, leases involving real estate, leases involving related parties, subleases, the effect of business combinations on the classification of leases, and sale-leaseback transactions.

Scope

.101 This section [presents] standards of financial accounting and reporting for leases by lessees and lessors.[1] A **lease** is defined as an agreement conveying the right to use property, plant, or equipment (land or depreciable assets or both) usually for a stated period of time. It includes agreements that, although not nominally identified as leases, meet the above definition, such as a *heat supply contract* for nuclear fuel.[2] This definition does not include agreements that are contracts for services that do not transfer the right to use property, plant, or equipment from one contracting party to the other. On the other hand, agreements that do transfer the right to use property, plant, or equipment meet the definition of a lease even though substantial services by the contractor (lessor) may be called for in connection with the operation or maintenance of such assets. This section does not apply to lease agreements concerning the rights to explore for or to exploit natural resources such as oil, gas, minerals, and timber. Nor does it apply to licensing agreements for items such as motion picture films, plays, manuscripts, patents, and copyrights. [FAS13, ¶1] [Refer to paragraph .1001 for an EITF Issue that provides interpretive guidance on this paragraph.]

Classification of Leases

.102 For purposes of applying the accounting and reporting standards [herein], leases are classified as follows:

a. Classifications from the standpoint of the lessee:
   (1) ***Capital leases.*** Leases that meet one or more of the criteria in paragraph .103.
   (2) ***Operating leases.*** All other leases.
b. Classifications from the standpoint of the lessor: [FAS13, ¶6]
   (1) ***Sales-type leases.*** Leases that give rise to manufacturer's or dealer's profit (or loss) to the lessor (that is, the **fair value of the leased property** at the **inception of the lease** is greater or less than its cost or carrying amount, if different) and that meet one or more of the criteria in paragraph .103 and both of the criteria in paragraph .104, except as indicated in the following sentence. A lease involving real estate shall be classified as a sales-type lease only if it meets the criterion in paragraph .103(a),) in which case the criteria in paragraph .104 do not apply. [FAS98, ¶22(c)] Normally, sales-type leases will arise when manufacturers or dealers use leasing as a means of marketing their products. Leases involving les-

[[1]Paragraphs .512 and .513 discuss the applicability of this section to current value financial statements.]

[2]Under present generally accepted accounting principles, a nuclear fuel installation constitutes a depreciable asset. Thus, a nuclear fuel lease conveys the right to use a depreciable asset, whereas contracts to supply coal or oil do not. [FAS13, ¶64] Heat supply (also called *burn-up*) contracts usually provide for payments by the user-lessee based upon nuclear fuel utilization in the period plus a charge for the unrecovered cost base. The residual value usually accrues to the lessee, and the lessor furnishes no service other than the financing. [FAS13, ¶1, fn1]

sors that are primarily engaged in financing operations normally will not be sales-type leases if they qualify under paragraphs .103 and .104, but will most often be **direct financing leases,** described in paragraph .102(b)(2) below. However, a lessor need not be a dealer to realize dealer's profit (or loss) on a transaction, for example, if a lessor, not a dealer, leases an asset that at the inception of the lease has a fair value that is greater or less than its cost or carrying amount, if different, such a transaction is a sales-type lease, assuming the criteria referred to are met. [FAS13, ¶6] Leases of a manufacturing company's equipment sold to a leasing subsidiary that are accounted for as direct financing leases on the subsidiary's financial statements normally would be sales-type capital leases in the consolidated financial statements. [FAS94, ¶52] A **renewal or extension** of an existing sales-type or direct financing lease that otherwise qualifies as a sales-type lease shall be classified as a direct financing lease unless the renewal or extension occurs at or near the end of the original term[3] specified in the existing lease, in which case it shall be classified as a sales-type lease (refer to paragraph .113(f)). [FAS27, ¶6]

(2) ***Direct financing leases.*** Leases other than **leveraged leases** that do not give rise to manufacturer's or dealer's profit (or loss) to the lessor but that meet one or more of the criteria in paragraph .103 and both of the criteria in paragraph .104. In such leases, the cost or carrying amount, if different, and fair value of the leased property are the same at the inception of the lease. [FAS13, ¶6] An exception arises when an existing sales-type or direct financing lease is renewed or extended[4] during the term of the existing lease. [FAS27, ¶7] In such cases, the fact that the carrying amount of the property at the end of the original lease term is different from its fair value at that date shall not preclude the classification of the renewal or extension as a direct financing lease (refer to paragraph .113(f)).

(3) ***Leveraged leases.*** Leases that meet the criteria of paragraph .144. [FAS13, ¶6]

(4) ***Operating leases.*** All other leases, including leases that involve real estate and give rise to manufacturer's or dealer's profit (or loss) to the lessor but do not meet the criterion in paragraph .103(a). [FAS98, ¶22(d)]

Criteria for Classifying Leases (Other Than Leveraged Leases)

.103 The criteria for classifying leases set forth in this paragraph and in paragraph .104 derive from the concept [FAS13, ¶7] that a lease that transfers substantially all of the benefits and risks incident to the ownership of property should be accounted for as the acquisition of an asset and the incurrence of an obligation by the lessee and as a sale or financing by the lessor. All other leases should be accounted for as operating leases. In a

[3]A renewal or extension that occurs in the last few months of an existing lease is considered to have occurred at or near the end of the existing **lease term.** [FAS27, ¶6]

[4]Refer to paragraph .419. [FAS13, ¶6, fn10]

lease that transfers substantially all of the benefits and risks of ownership, the economic effect on the parties is similar, in many respects, to that of an installment purchase. [FAS13, ¶60] If at its inception a lease meets one or more of the following four criteria, the lease shall be classified as a capital lease by the lessee. Otherwise, it shall be classified as an operating lease. (Refer to paragraph .150 and Exhibit 150C for an illustration of the application of these criteria.)

a. The lease transfers ownership of the property to the lessee by the end of the lease term.[4a]
b. The lease contains a **bargain purchase option.**
c. The lease term is equal to 75 percent or more of the estimated economic life of the leased property. However, if the beginning of the lease term falls within the last 25 percent of the total **estimated economic life of the leased property,** including earlier years of use, this criterion shall not be used for purposes of classifying the lease.
d. The present value[5] at the beginning of the lease term of the **minimum lease payments,** excluding that portion of the payments representing **executory costs,** to be paid by the lessor, including any profit thereon, equals or exceeds 90 percent of the excess of the fair value of the leased property to the lessor at the inception of the lease over any related investment tax credit retained by the lessor and expected to be realized by [the lessor].[6] However, if the beginning of the lease term falls within the last 25 percent of the total estimated economic life of the leased property, including earlier years of use, this criterion shall not be used for purposes of classifying the lease. A lessor shall compute the present value of the minimum lease payments using the interest rate implicit in the lease. A lessee shall compute the present value of the minimum lease payments using its incremental borrowing rate, unless (1) it is practicable for [the lessee] to learn the implicit rate computed by the lessor and (2) the implicit rate computed by the lessor is less than the lessee's incremental borrowing rate. If both of those conditions are met, the lessee shall use the implicit rate. [Refer to paragraph .1001 for an EITF Issue that provides interpretive guidance on this subparagraph.]

[FAS13, ¶7] [Refer to paragraph .1001 for an EITF Issue that provides interpretive guidance on this paragraph.]

[4a]This criterion is met in situations in which the lease agreement provides for the transfer of title at or shortly after the end of the lease term in exchange for the payment of a nominal fee, for example, the minimum required by statutory regulation to transfer title. [FAS98, ¶22(e)]

[[5]Refer to paragraphs .509 through .511 for supplemental guidance on the interest rate to be used in calculating the present value of minimum lease payments.]

[6]The 90 percent test is stated as a lower limit rather than as a guideline. [FIN19, ¶4]

.104 From the standpoint of the lessor, a lease involving real estate shall be classified as a sales-type lease only if it meets the criterion in paragraph .103(a) as appropriate under paragraph .102(b)(1). Otherwise, if the lease at inception meets any one of the four criteria in paragraph .103 and in addition meets both of the following criteria, it shall be classified as a sales-type lease, a direct financing lease, a leveraged lease, or an operating lease as appropriate under paragraph .102(b). If the lease does not meet any of the criteria of paragraph .103 or both of the following criteria, the lease shall be classified as an operating lease.

a. Collectibility of the minimum lease payments is reasonably predictable. A lessor shall not be precluded from classifying a lease as a sales-type lease, a direct financing lease, or a leveraged lease simply because the receivable is subject to an estimate of uncollectibility based on experience with groups of similar receivables. [FAS98, ¶22(f)]
b. No important uncertainties surround the amount of unreimbursable costs yet to be incurred by the lessor under the lease.[7] Important uncertainties might include commitments by the lessor to guarantee performance of the leased property in a manner more extensive than the typical product warranty or to effectively protect the lessee from obsolescence of the leased property. However, the necessity of estimating executory costs to be paid by the lessor (refer to paragraphs .113(a) and .114(a)) shall not by itself constitute an important uncertainty as referred to herein. [FAS13, ¶8]

.105 If at any time the lessee and lessor agree to change the provisions of the lease, other than by renewing the lease or extending its term, in a manner that would have resulted in a different classification of the lease under the criteria in paragraphs .103 and .104 had the changed terms been in effect at the inception of the lease, the revised agreement shall be considered as a new agreement over its term, and the criteria in paragraphs .103 and .104 shall be applied for purposes of classifying the new lease. Likewise, except when a guarantee or **penalty** is rendered inoperative as described in paragraphs .108 and .113(e), any action that extends the lease beyond the expiration of the existing lease term, such as the exercise of a lease renewal option other than those already included in the lease term, shall be considered as a new agreement, which shall be classified according to the provisions of paragraphs .102 through .104. Changes in estimates (for example, changes in estimates of the economic life or of the residual value of the leased property) or changes in circumstances (for example, default by the lessee), however, shall not give rise to a new classification of a lease for accounting purposes. [FAS13, ¶9]

---

[7]If the property covered by the lease is yet to be constructed or has not been acquired by the lessor at the inception of the lease, the classification criterion of paragraph .104(b) shall be applied at the date that construction of the property is completed or the property is acquired by the lessor. [FAS23, ¶7]

Accounting and Reporting by Lessees

Capital Leases

.106 The lessee shall record a capital lease as an asset and an obligation at an amount equal to the present value at the beginning of the lease term of minimum lease payments during the lease term, excluding that portion of the payments representing executory costs to be paid by the lessor, together with any profit thereon. However, if the amount so determined exceeds the fair value of the leased property at the inception of the lease, the amount recorded as the asset and obligation shall be the fair value.[8] If the portion of the minimum lease payments representing executory costs, including profit thereon, is not determinable from the provisions of the lease, an estimate of the amount shall be made. The discount rate to be used in determining present value of the minimum lease payments shall be that prescribed for the lessee in paragraph .103(d). (Refer to paragraph .150 and Exhibit 150C for an illustration.) [FAS13, ¶10]

.107 Except as provided in paragraphs .121 and .122 with respect to leases involving land, the asset recorded under a capital lease shall be amortized as follows:

a. If the lease meets the criterion of either paragraph .103(a) or .103(b), the asset shall be amortized in a manner consistent with the lessee's normal depreciation policy for owned assets.
b. If the lease does not meet either criterion .103(a) or .103(b), the asset shall be amortized in a manner consistent with the lessee's normal depreciation policy except that the period of amortization shall be the lease term. The asset shall be amortized to its expected value, if any, to the lessee at the end of the lease term. As an example, if the lessee guarantees a residual value at the end of the lease term and has no interest in any excess which might be realized, the expected value of the leased property to [the lessee] is the amount that can be realized from it up to the amount of the guarantee.

[FAS13, ¶11]

.108 During the lease term, each minimum lease payment shall be allocated between a reduction of the obligation and interest expense so as to produce a constant periodic rate

[8]If the lease agreement or commitment, if earlier, includes a provision to escalate minimum lease payments for increases in construction or acquisition cost of the leased property or for increases in some other measure of cost or value, such as general price levels, during the construction or preacquisition period, the effect of any increases that have occurred shall be considered in the determination of "fair value of the leased property at the inception of the lease" for purposes of this paragraph. [FAS23, ¶8]

of interest on the remaining balance of the obligation.[9] (Refer to paragraph .150 for illustrations.) In leases containing a residual guarantee by the lessee or a penalty for failure to renew the lease at the end of the lease term,[10] following the above method of amortization will result in a balance of the obligation at the end of the lease term that will equal the amount of the guarantee or penalty at that date. In the event that a renewal or extension of the lease term renders the guarantee or penalty inoperative, the asset and the obligation under the lease shall be adjusted by an amount equal to the difference between the present value of the future minimum lease payments under the revised agreement and the present balance of the obligation. The present value of the future minimum lease payments under the revised agreement shall be computed using the rate of interest used to record the lease initially. In accordance with paragraph .105, other renewals and extensions of the lease term shall be considered new agreements, which shall be accounted for in accordance with the provisions of paragraph .109. [FAS13, ¶12] **Contingent rentals** shall be included in the determination of income as accruable. [FAS29, ¶13] [(Refer to paragraph .165 for an illustration involving contingent rentals.)]

.109 Except for a change in the provisions of a lease that results from a refunding by the lessor of tax-exempt debt, including an advance refunding in which the perceived economic advantages of the refunding are passed through to the lessee by a change in the provisions of the lease agreement and the revised agreement is classified as a capital lease (refer to paragraph .110), a change in the provisions of a lease, a renewal or extension of an existing lease, and a termination of a lease prior to the expiration of the lease term shall be accounted for as follows: [FAS22, ¶14]

a. If the provisions of the lease are changed in a way that changes the amount of the remaining minimum lease payments and the change either (1) does not give rise to a new agreement under the provisions of paragraph .105 or (2) does give rise to a new agreement but such agreement is also classified as a capital lease, the present balances of the asset and the obligation shall be adjusted by an amount equal to the difference between the present value of the future minimum lease payments under the revised or new agreement and the present balance of the obligation. The present value of the future minimum lease payments under the revised or new agreement shall be computed using the rate of interest used to record the lease initially. [FAS13, ¶14] If the change in the lease provisions gives rise to a new agreement classified as an operating lease, the transaction shall be accounted for under the sale-leaseback

[9]This is the *interest* method described in Section I69, "Interest: Imputation of an Interest Cost," paragraph .108 and footnote 4. [FAS13, ¶12, fn11]

[10]Residual guarantees and termination penalties that serve to extend the lease term are excluded from minimum lease payments and are thus distinguished from those guarantees and penalties referred to in this paragraph. [FAS13, ¶12, fn12]

requirements in paragraphs .130C through .130J, .130K through .130M, or .128 and .129 of this section, as applicable. [FAS145, ¶8]

b. Except when a guarantee or penalty is rendered inoperative as described in paragraph .108, a renewal or an extension of an existing lease shall be accounted for as follows:
   (1) If the renewal or extension is classified as a capital lease, it shall be accounted for as described in subparagraph (a) above.
   (2) If the renewal or extension is classified as an operating lease, the existing lease shall continue to be accounted for as a capital lease to the end of its original term, and the renewal or extension shall be accounted for as any other operating lease.
c. A termination of a capital lease shall be accounted for by removing the asset and obligation, with gain or loss recognized for the difference.[11] [FAS13, ¶14]

.110 If prior to the expiration of the lease term a change in the provisions of the lease results from a refunding by the lessor of tax-exempt debt, including an advance refunding,[12] in which the perceived economic advantages of the refunding are passed through to the lessee and the revised agreement is classified as a capital lease by the lessee, the change shall be accounted for [by the lessee] as follows:

a. If a change in the provisions of a lease results from a refunding by the lessor of tax-exempt debt, including an advance refunding that is accounted for as an early extinguishment of debt, the lessee shall adjust the lease obligation to the present value of the future minimum lease payments under the revised lease using the effective interest rate applicable to the revised agreement and shall recognize any resulting gain or loss currently as a gain or loss on early extinguishment of debt. [Paragraphs .162 and .163 illustrate the accounting prescribed by this subparagraph.]

[11]The termination of the capital lease that results from the purchase of a leased asset by the lessee is not the type of transaction contemplated by this paragraph but rather is an integral part of the purchase of the leased asset. The purchase by the lessee of property under a capital lease shall be accounted for like a renewal or extension of a capital lease that, in turn, is classified as a capital lease, that is, any difference between the purchase price and the carrying amount of the lease obligation shall be recorded as an adjustment of the carrying amount of the asset. [FIN26, ¶5]

[12]An advance refunding involves the issuance of new debt to replace existing debt with the proceeds from the new debt placed in trust or otherwise restricted to retire the existing debt at a determinable future date or dates. [FAS22, ¶1, fn1]

b. If the provisions of a lease are changed in connection with an advance refunding by the lessor of tax-exempt debt that is not accounted for as an early extinguishment of debt at the date of the advance refunding and the lessee is obligated to reimburse the lessor for any costs related to the debt to be refunded that have been or will be incurred, such as unamortized discount or issue costs or a call premium, the lessee shall accrue those costs by the *interest* method[13] over the period from the date of the advance refunding to the call date of the debt to be refunded.

[FAS22, ¶12]

Operating Leases

.111 Normally, rental on an operating lease shall be charged to expense over the lease term as it becomes payable. If rental payments are not made on a straight-line basis,[13a] rental expense nevertheless shall be recognized on a straight-line basis unless another systematic and rational basis is more representative of the time pattern in which use benefit is derived from the leased property, in which case that basis shall be used. [FAS13, ¶15] [Refer to paragraph .1001 for an EITF Issue that provides interpretive guidance on this paragraph.]

Disclosures

.112 The following information with respect to leases shall be disclosed in the lessee's financial statements or the footnotes thereto. (Refer to paragraphs .151 and .152 for illustrations.)

a. For capital leases:
   (1) The gross amount of assets recorded under capital leases as of the date of each balance sheet presented by major classes according to nature or function. This information may be combined with the comparable information for owned assets.
   (2) Future *minimum lease payments* as of the date of the latest balance sheet presented, in the aggregate and for each of the five succeeding fiscal years, with separate deductions from the total for the amount representing *executory costs,* including any profit thereon, included in the *minimum lease payments* and for the amount of the imputed interest necessary to reduce the net *minimum lease payments* to present value.

---

[13]Refer to paragraph .108 and footnote 9 thereto. [FAS22, ¶12, fn3]

[[13a]Refer to paragraphs .525 through .527F for supplemental guidance on accounting for operating leases with scheduled rent increases and lease incentives.]

(3) The total of minimum sublease rentals to be received in the future under noncancelable subleases as of the date of the latest balance sheet presented.
(4) Total *contingent rentals* actually incurred for each period for which an income statement is presented. [FAS13, ¶16]
(5) Assets recorded under capital leases and the accumulated amortization thereon shall be separately identified in the lessee's balance sheet or in footnotes thereto. Likewise, the related obligations shall be separately identified in the balance sheet as obligations under capital leases and shall be subject to the same considerations as other obligations in classifying them with current and noncurrent liabilities in classified balance sheets. Unless the charge to income resulting from amortization of assets recorded under capital leases is included with depreciation expense and the fact that it is so included is disclosed, the amortization charge shall be separately disclosed in the financial statements or footnotes thereto. [FAS13, ¶13]

b. For operating leases having initial or remaining noncancelable *lease terms* in excess of one year:
(1) Future minimum rental payments required as of the date of the latest balance sheet presented, in the aggregate and for each of the five succeeding fiscal years.
(2) The total of minimum rentals to be received in the future under noncancelable subleases as of the date of the latest balance sheet presented.

c. For all operating leases, rental expense for each period for which an income statement is presented, with separate amounts for minimum rentals, contingent rentals, and sublease rentals. Rental payments under leases with *terms* of a month or less that were not renewed need not be included.

d. A general description of the lessee's leasing arrangements including, but not limited to, the following:
(1) The basis on which contingent rental payments are determined.
(2) The existence and terms of renewal or purchase options and escalation clauses.
(3) Restrictions imposed by lease agreements, such as those concerning dividends, additional debt, and further leasing. [FAS13, ¶16]

Accounting and Reporting by Lessors

Sales-Type Leases

.113 Sales-type leases shall be accounted for by the lessor as follows:

a. The minimum lease payments (net of amounts, if any, included therein with respect to executory costs to be paid by the lessor, together with any profit thereon) plus the **unguaranteed residual value** accruing to the benefit of the lessor shall be recorded as the gross investment in the lease.[13b] [FAS13, ¶17] The estimated residual value used to compute the unguaranteed residual value accruing to the benefit of the lessor shall not exceed the amount estimated at the inception of the lease.[14] [FAS23, ¶9] However, if the sales-type lease involves real estate, the lessor shall account for the transaction under the provisions of Section R10, "Real Estate," in the same manner as a *seller* of the same property. [FAS98, ¶22(g)]

b. The difference between the gross investment in the lease in (a) above and the sum of the present values of the two components of the gross investment shall be recorded as unearned income. The discount rate to be used in determining the present values shall be the interest rate implicit in the lease. The net investment in the lease shall consist of the gross investment less the unearned income. The unearned income shall be amortized to income over the lease term so as to produce a constant periodic rate of return on the net investment in the lease.[15] However, other methods of income recognition may be used if the results obtained are not materially different from those which would result from the prescribed method. The net investment in the lease shall be subject to the same considerations as other assets in classification as current or noncurrent assets in a classified balance sheet. [FAS13, ¶17] Contingent rentals shall be included in the determination of income as accruable. [FAS29, ¶13] [(Refer to paragraph .165 for an illustration involving contingent rentals.)]
c. The present value of the minimum lease payments (net of executory costs, including any profit thereon), computed at the interest rate implicit in the lease, shall be recorded as the sales price. The cost or carrying amount, if different, of the leased property, plus any **initial direct costs,** less the present value of the unguaranteed residual value accruing to the benefit of the lessor, computed at the interest rate implicit in the lease, shall be charged against income in the same period.
d. The estimated residual value shall be reviewed at least annually.[16] If the review results in a lower estimate than had been previously established, a determination must be made as to whether the decline in estimated residual value is other than temporary. If the decline in estimated residual value is judged to be other than temporary, the accounting for the transaction shall be revised using the changed estimate. The resulting reduction in the net investment shall be recognized as a loss in the period in which

[[13b] Paragraphs .536 and .537 further discuss residual value retained by a lessor that sells rental payments.]

[14]If the lease agreement or commitment, if earlier, includes a provision to escalate minimum lease payments for increases in construction or acquisition cost of the leased property or for increases in some other measure of cost or value, such as general price levels, during the construction or preacquisition period, the effect of any increases that have occurred shall be considered in the determination of "the **estimated residual value of the leased property** at the inception of the lease" for purposes of this paragraph. [FAS23, ¶9]

[15]This is the interest method described in Section I69, paragraph .108 and footnote 4. [FAS13, ¶12, fn11]

[[16]Paragraphs .514 through .517 discuss upward adjustment of guaranteed residual values.]

the estimate is changed. An upward adjustment of the estimated residual value shall not be made.

e. In leases containing a residual guarantee or a penalty for failure to renew the lease at the end of the lease term,[17] following the method of amortization described in (b) above will result in a balance of minimum lease payments receivable at the end of the lease term that will equal the amount of the guarantee or penalty at that date. In the event that a renewal or other extension of the lease term renders the guarantee or penalty inoperative, the existing balances of the minimum lease payments receivable and the estimated residual value shall be adjusted for the changes resulting from the revised agreement (subject to the limitation on the residual value imposed by subparagraph (d) above) and the net adjustment shall be charged or credited to unearned income. [FAS13, ¶17]

f. Except for a change in the provisions of a lease that results from a refunding by the lessor of tax-exempt debt, including an advance refunding, in which the perceived economic advantages of the refunding are passed through to the lessee by a change in the provisions of the lease agreement and the revised agreement is classified as a direct financing lease (refer to paragraph .110), a change in the provisions of a lease, a renewal or extension of an existing lease, and a termination of a lease prior to the expiration of the lease term shall be accounted for as follows: [FAS22, ¶15]

  (1) If the provisions of a lease are changed in a way that changes the amount of the remaining minimum lease payments and the change either (a) does not give rise to a new agreement under the provisions of paragraph .105 or (b) does give rise to a new agreement but such agreement is classified as a direct financing lease, the balance of the minimum lease payments receivable and the estimated residual value, if affected, shall be adjusted to reflect the change (subject to the limitation on the residual value imposed by subparagraph (d) above), and the net adjustment shall be charged or credited to unearned income. If the change in the lease provisions gives rise to a new agreement classified as an operating lease, the remaining net investment shall be removed from the accounts, the leased asset shall be recorded as an asset at the lower of its original cost, present fair value, or present carrying amount, and the net adjustment shall be charged to income of the period. The new lease shall thereafter be accounted for as any other operating lease.

  (2) Except when a guarantee or penalty is rendered inoperative as described in subparagraph (e) above, a renewal or an extension of an existing lease shall be accounted for as follows:

    (a) If the renewal or extension is classified as a direct financing lease, it shall be accounted for as described in subparagraph (f)(1) above.

[17] Residual guarantees and termination penalties that serve to extend the lease term are excluded from minimum lease payments and are thus distinguished from those guarantees and penalties referred to in this paragraph. [FAS13, ¶17, fn17]

(b) If the renewal or extension is classified as an operating lease, the existing lease shall continue to be accounted for as a sales-type lease to the end of its original term, and the renewal or extension shall be accounted for as any other operating lease. [FAS13, ¶17]

(c) If a renewal or extension that occurs at or near the end of the term[18] of the existing lease is classified as a sales-type lease, the renewal or extension shall be accounted for as a sales-type lease. [FAS27, ¶8]

(3) A termination of the lease shall be accounted for by removing the net investment from the accounts, recording the leased asset at the lower of its original cost, present fair value, or present carrying amount, and the net adjustment shall be charged to income of the period. [FAS13, ¶17]

g. If prior to the expiration of the lease term a change in the provisions of a lease results from a refunding by the lessor of tax-exempt debt, including an advance refunding,[19] in which the perceived economic advantages of the refunding are passed through to the lessee and the revised agreement is classified as a direct financing lease by the lessor, the change shall be accounted for as follows:[20]

(1) If a change in the provisions of a lease results from a refunding of tax-exempt debt, including an advance refunding that is accounted for as an early extinguishment of debt, the lessor shall adjust the balance of the minimum lease payments receivable and the estimated residual value, if affected (that is, the gross investment in the lease), in accordance with the requirements of paragraphs .114(c) and .113(f)(1). The adjustment of unearned income shall be the amount required to adjust the net investment in the lease to the sum of the present values of the two components of the gross investment based on the interest rate applicable to the revised lease agreement. The combined adjustment resulting from applying the two preceding sentences shall be recognized as a gain or loss in the current period. [Paragraphs .162 and .163 illustrate the accounting prescribed by this paragraph.]

(2) If a change in the provisions of the lease results from an advance refunding that is not accounted for as an early extinguishment of debt at the date of the advance refunding, the lessor shall systematically recognize, as revenue, any reimbursements to be received from the lessee for costs related to the debt to be refunded,

---

[18]A renewal or extension that occurs in the last few months of an existing lease is considered to have occurred at or near the end of the existing lease term. [FAS27, ¶8]

[19]An advance refunding involves the issuance of new debt to replace existing debt with the proceeds from the new debt placed in trust or otherwise restricted to retire the existing debt at a determinable future date or dates. [FAS22, ¶1, fn1]

[20]This paragraph prescribes the accounting for a direct financing lease by governmental units that classify and account for leases of that kind. [FAS22, ¶12, fn4]

such as unamortized discount or issue costs or a call premium, over the period from the date of the advance refunding to the call date of debt to be refunded. [FAS22, ¶12]

Direct Financing Leases

.114 Direct financing leases shall be accounted for by the lessor as follows (refer to paragraph .150 for illustrations): [FAS13, ¶18]

a. The sum of (1) the minimum lease payments (net of amounts, if any, included therein with respect to executory costs, such as maintenance, taxes, and insurance, to be paid by the lessor, together with any profit thereon) and (2) the unguaranteed residual value accruing to the benefit of the lessor shall be recorded as the gross investment in the lease.[20a] The estimated residual value used to compute the unguaranteed residual value accruing to the benefit of the lessor shall not exceed the amount estimated at the inception of the lease.[21] [FAS98, ¶22(h)]
b. The difference between the gross investment in the lease in (a) above and the cost or carrying amount, if different, of the leased property shall be recorded as unearned income. The net investment in the lease shall consist of the gross investment plus any unamortized initial direct costs less the unearned income. The unearned income and initial direct costs shall be amortized to income over the lease term[21a] so as to produce a constant periodic rate of return on the net investment in the lease.[22] However, other methods of income recognition may be used if the results obtained are not materially different from those that would result from the prescribed method in the preceding sentence. The net investment in the lease shall be subject to the same considerations as other assets in classification as current or noncurrent assets in a classified balance sheet. Contingent rentals shall be included in the determination of income as accruable. [FAS98, ¶22(i)]

[[20a]Paragraphs .536 and .537 further discuss residual value retained by a lessor that sells rental payments.]

[21]If the lease agreement or commitment, if earlier, includes a provision to escalate minimum lease payments for increases in construction or acquisition cost of the leased property or for increases in some other measure of cost or value, such as general price levels, during the construction or preacquisition period, the effect of any increases that have occurred shall be considered in the determination of "the estimated residual value of the leased property at the inception of the lease" for purposes of this paragraph. [FAS23, ¶9]

[[21a]]The practice of accelerating the recognition of lease finance revenues to offset initial direct costs or other costs of direct financing leases [is not] acceptable. [FAS91, ¶44]

[22]This is the interest method described in Section I69, paragraph .108 and footnote 4, [FAS13, ¶12, fn11] [and in Section L20, "Lending Activities," paragraph .117].

c. In leases containing a residual guarantee or penalty for failure to renew the lease at the end of the lease term,[23] the lessor shall follow the accounting procedure described in paragraph .113(e). The accounting provisions of paragraphs .113(f) and .113(g) with respect to renewals and extensions not dealt with in paragraph .113(e), terminations, and other changes in lease provisions shall also be followed with respect to direct financing leases.
d. The estimated residual value shall be reviewed at least annually[24] and, if necessary, adjusted in the manner prescribed in paragraph .113(d). [FAS13, ¶18]

Operating Leases

.115 Operating leases shall be accounted for by the lessor as follows:

a. The leased property shall be included with or near property, plant, and equipment in the balance sheet. The property shall be depreciated following the lessor's normal depreciation policy, and in the balance sheet the accumulated depreciation shall be deducted from the investment in the leased property.
b. Rent shall be reported as income over the lease term as it becomes receivable according to the provisions of the lease. However, if the rentals vary from a straight-line basis,[24a] the income shall be recognized on a straight-line basis unless another systematic and rational basis is more representative of the time pattern in which use benefit from the leased property is diminished, in which case that basis shall be used.
c. Initial direct costs shall be deferred and allocated over the lease term in proportion to the recognition of rental income. However, initial direct costs may be charged to expense as incurred if the effect is not materially different from that which would have resulted from the use of the method prescribed in the preceding sentence. [FAS13, ¶19]
d. If, at the inception of the lease, the fair value of the property in an operating lease involving real estate that would have been classified as a sales-type lease except that it did not meet the criterion in paragraph .103(a) is less than its cost or carrying amount, if different, then a loss equal to that difference shall be recognized at the inception of the lease. [FAS98, ¶22(j)]

---

[23]Residual guarantees and termination penalties that serve to extend the lease term are excluded from minimum lease payments and are thus distinguished from those guarantees and penalties referred to in this paragraph. [FAS13, ¶12, fn12]

[[24]Paragraphs .514 through .517 discuss upward adjustment of guaranteed residual values.]

[[24a]Refer to paragraphs .525 through .527F for supplemental guidance on accounting for operating leases with scheduled rent increases and lease incentives.]

Participation by Third Parties

.116 The sale or assignment of a lease or of property subject to a lease that was accounted for as a sales-type lease or direct financing lease shall not negate the original accounting treatment accorded the lease. Any transfer of minimum lease payments under, or residual values that are guaranteed at the inception of, a sales-type lease or direct financing lease shall be accounted for in accordance with Section F39, "Financial Instruments: Transfers." However, transfers of unguaranteed residual values and residual values that are guaranteed after the inception of the lease are not subject to the provisions of Section F39. [FAS140, ¶352] [Refer to Section F39, paragraphs .168 and .169 for guidance on accounting for transfers of sales-type and direct financing lease receivables.]

.117 The sale of property subject to an operating lease, or of property that is leased by or intended to be leased by the third-party purchaser to another party, shall not be treated as a sale if the seller or any party related to the seller retains substantial risks of ownership in the leased property. A seller may by various arrangements assure recovery of the investment by the third-party purchaser in some operating lease transactions and thus retain substantial risks in connection with the property. For example, in the case of default by the lessee or termination of the lease, the arrangements may involve a formal or informal commitment by the seller to (a) acquire the lease or the property, (b) substitute an existing lease, or (c) secure a replacement lessee or a buyer for the property under a remarketing agreement. However, a remarketing agreement by itself shall not disqualify accounting for the transaction as a sale if the seller (1) will receive a reasonable fee commensurate with the effort involved at the time of securing a replacement lessee or buyer for the property and (2) is not required to give priority to the re-leasing or disposition of the property owned by the third-party purchaser over similar property owned or produced by the seller. (For example, a first-in, first-out remarketing arrangement is considered to be a priority.) [FAS13, ¶21] [Refer to paragraph .1001 for an EITF Issue that provides interpretive guidance on paragraphs .117 and .118.]

.118 If a sale to a third party of property subject to an operating lease or of property that is leased by or intended to be leased by the third-party purchaser to another party is not to be recorded as a sale because of the provisions of paragraph .117, the transaction shall be accounted for as a borrowing. (Transactions of these types are in effect collateralized borrowings.) The proceeds from the *sale* shall be recorded as an obligation on the books of the *seller.* Until that obligation has been amortized under the procedure described herein, rental payments made by the lessee(s) under the operating lease or leases shall be recorded as revenue by the *seller,* even if such rentals are paid directly to the third-party purchaser. A portion of each rental shall be recorded by the *seller* as interest expense, with the remainder to be recorded as a reduction of the obligation. The interest expense shall be calculated by application of a rate determined in accordance with the provisions of Section I69, paragraphs .106 and .107. The leased property shall be accounted for as prescribed in paragraph .115(a) for an operating lease, except that the term over which the asset is depreciated shall be limited to the estimated amortization period of the obligation. The sale or assignment by the lessor of lease payments due under an operating lease shall be accounted for as a borrowing as described above. [FAS13, ¶22]

Disclosures

.119 When leasing, exclusive of leveraged leasing, is a significant part of the lessor's business activities in terms of revenue, net income, or assets, the following information with respect to leases shall be disclosed in the financial statements or footnotes thereto (refer to paragraphs .151 and .153 for illustrations):

a. For sales-type and direct financing leases: [FAS13, ¶23]
   (1) The components of the net investment in sales-type and direct financing leases as of the date of each balance sheet presented:
      (a) Future minimum lease payments to be received, with separate deductions for (i) amounts representing executory costs, including any profit thereon, included in the minimum lease payments and (ii) the accumulated allowance for uncollectible minimum lease payments receivable.
      (b) The unguaranteed residual values accruing to the benefit of the lessor.
      (c) For direct financing leases only, initial direct costs (see paragraph .411).
      (d) Unearned income (refer to paragraphs .113(b) and .114(b)). [FAS91, ¶25(d)]
   (2) Future minimum lease payments to be received for each of the five succeeding fiscal years as of the date of the latest balance sheet presented.
   (3) [Deleted 12/86 because of the issuance of FASB Statement 91, *Accounting for Nonrefundable Fees and Costs Associated with Originating or Acquiring Loans and Initial Direct Costs of Leases.*]
   (4) Total contingent rentals included in income for each period for which an income statement is presented.
b. For operating leases:
   (1) The cost and carrying amount, if different, of property on lease or held for leasing by major classes of property according to nature or function, and the amount of accumulated depreciation in total as of the date of the latest balance sheet presented.
   (2) Minimum future rentals on noncancelable leases as of the date of the latest balance sheet presented, in the aggregate and for each of the five succeeding fiscal years.
   (3) Total contingent rentals included in income for each period for which an income statement is presented.
c. A general description of the lessor's leasing arrangements. [FAS13, ¶23]

Leases Involving Real Estate

.120 For purposes of this section, leases involving real estate can be divided into four categories: (a) leases involving land only, (b) leases involving land and building(s), (c) leases involving equipment as well as real estate, and (d) leases involving only part of a building. [FAS13, ¶24]

Leases Involving Land Only

.121 If land is the sole item of property leased and the criterion in either paragraph .103(a) or .103(b) is met, the lessee shall account for the lease as a capital lease otherwise, as an operating lease. If the lease gives rise to manufacturer's or dealer's profit (or loss) and the criterion of paragraph .103(a) is met, the lessor shall classify the lease as a sales-type lease as appropriate under paragraph .102(b)(1) and account for the transaction under the provisions of Section R10 in the same manner as a *seller* of the same property. If the lease does not give rise to manufacturer's or dealer's profit (or loss) and the criterion of paragraph .103(a) and both criteria of paragraph .104 are met, the lessor shall account for the lease as a direct financing lease or a leveraged lease as appropriate under paragraph .102(b). If the criterion of paragraph .103(b) and both criteria of paragraph .104 are met, the lessor shall account for the lease as a direct financing lease, a leveraged lease, or an operating lease as appropriate under paragraph .102(b). If the lease does not meet the criteria of paragraph .104, the lessor shall account for the lease as an operating lease. [FAS98, ¶22(k)] Criteria .103(c) and .103(d) are not applicable to land leases. Because ownership of the land is expected to pass to the lessee if either criterion .103(a) or .103(b) is met, the asset recorded under the capital lease would not normally be amortized. [FAS13, ¶25]

Leases Involving Land and Buildings

.122 Leases involving both land and building(s) shall be accounted for as follows:

a. Lease meets either criterion .103(a) or .103(b):
   (1) Lessee's accounting: If either criterion (a) or (b) of paragraph .103 is met, the land and building shall be separately capitalized by the lessee. For this purpose, the present value of the minimum lease payments after deducting executory costs, including any profit thereon, shall be allocated between the two elements in proportion to their fair values at the inception of the lease.[25] The building shall be

[25]If the lease agreement or commitment, if earlier, includes a provision to escalate *minimum lease payments* for increases in construction or acquisition cost of the leased property or for increases in some other measure of cost or value, such as general price levels, during the construction or preacquisition period, the effect of any increases that have occurred shall be considered in the determination of "fair value of the leased property at the inception of the lease" for purposes of this paragraph. [FAS23, ¶8]

amortized in accordance with the provisions of paragraph .107(a). As stated in paragraph .121, land capitalized under a lease that meets criterion (a) or (b) of paragraph .103 would not normally be amortized. [FAS13, ¶26]

(2) Lessor's accounting if the lease meets criterion .103(a): If the lease gives rise to manufacturer's or dealer's profit (or loss), the lessor shall classify the lease as a sales-type lease as appropriate under paragraph .102(b)(1) and account for the lease as a single unit under the provisions of Section R10 in the same manner as a *seller* of the same property. If the lease does not give rise to manufacturer's or dealer's profit (or loss) and meets both criteria of paragraph .104, the lessor shall account for the lease as a direct financing lease or a leveraged lease as appropriate under paragraph .102(b)(2) or .102(b)(3). If the lease does not give rise to manufacturer's or dealer's profit (or loss) and does not meet both criteria of paragraph .104, the lessor shall account for the lease as an operating lease.

(3) Lessor's accounting if the lease meets criterion .103(b): If the lease gives rise to manufacturer's or dealer's profit (or loss), the lessor shall classify the lease as an operating lease as appropriate under paragraph .102(b)(4). If the lease does not give rise to manufacturer's or dealer's profit (or loss) and meets both criteria of paragraph .104, the lessor shall account for the lease as a direct financing lease or a leveraged lease as appropriate under paragraph .102(b)(2) or .102(b)(3). If the lease does not give rise to manufacturer's or dealer's profit (or loss) and does not meet both criteria of paragraph .104, the lessor shall account for the lease as an operating lease. [FAS98, ¶22(l)]

b. Lease meets neither criterion .103(a) nor .103(b):

(1) If the fair value of the land is less than 25 percent of the total fair value of the leased property at the inception of the lease: Both the lessee and the lessor shall consider the land and the building as a single unit for purposes of applying the criteria of paragraphs .103(c) and .103(d). For purposes of applying the criterion of paragraph .103(c), the estimated economic life of the building shall be considered as the estimated economic life of the unit.

(a) Lessee's accounting: If either criterion (c) or (d) of paragraph .103 is met, the lessee shall capitalize the land and building as a single unit and amortize it in accordance with the provisions of paragraph .107(b); otherwise, the lease shall be accounted for as an operating lease. [FAS13, ¶26]

(b) Lessor's accounting: If either criterion (c) or (d) of paragraph .103 and both criteria of paragraph .104 are met, the lessor shall account for the lease as a single unit as a direct financing lease, a leveraged lease, or an operating lease as appropriate under paragraph .102(b). If the lease meets neither criterion (c) nor (d) of paragraph .103 or does not meet both criteria of paragraph .104, the lease shall be accounted for as an operating lease. [FAS98, ¶22(m)]

(2) If the fair value of the land is 25 percent or more of the total fair value of the leased property at the inception of the lease: Both the lessee and lessor shall consider the

land and the building separately for purposes of applying the criteria of paragraphs .103(c) and .103(d). The minimum lease payments after deducting executory costs, including any profit thereon, applicable to the land and the building shall be separated both by the lessee and the lessor by determining the fair value of the land and applying the lessee's incremental borrowing rate to it to determine the annual minimum lease payments applicable to the land element; the remaining minimum lease payments shall be attributed to the building element.

(a) Lessee's accounting: If the building element of the lease meets criterion (c) or (d) of paragraph .103, the building element shall be accounted for as a capital lease and amortized in accordance with the provisions of paragraph .107(b). The land element of the lease shall be accounted for separately as an operating lease. If the building element of the lease meets neither criterion (c) nor (d) of paragraph .103, both the building element and the land element shall be accounted for as a single operating lease. [FAS13, ¶26]

(b) Lessor's accounting: If the building element of the lease meets either criterion (c) or (d) of paragraph .103 and both criteria of paragraph .104, the building element shall be accounted for as a direct financing lease, a leveraged lease, or an operating lease as appropriate under paragraph .102(b). [FAS98, ¶22(n)] The land element of the lease shall be accounted for separately as an operating lease. If the building element of the lease meets neither criterion (c) nor (d) of paragraph .103 or does not meet the criteria of paragraph .104, both the building element and the land element shall be accounted for as a single operating lease. [FAS13, ¶26] [Refer to paragraph .1001 for an EITF Issue that provides interpretive guidance on subparagraph (b)(2).]

Leases Involving Equipment as Well as Real Estate

.123 If a lease involving real estate also includes equipment, the portion of the minimum lease payments applicable to the equipment element of the lease shall be estimated by whatever means are appropriate in the circumstances. The equipment shall be considered separately for purposes of applying the criteria in paragraphs .103 and .104 and shall be accounted for separately according to its classification by both lessees and lessors. [FAS13, ¶27]

Leases Involving Only Part of a Building

.124 When the leased property is part of a larger whole, its cost (or carrying amount) and fair value[26] may not be objectively determinable, as for example, when an office or floor of a building is leased. If the cost and fair value of the leased property are objectively determinable, both the lessee and the lessor shall classify and account for the lease according to the provisions of paragraph .122. Unless both the cost and the fair value are objectively determinable, the lease shall be classified and accounted for as follows:

a. Lessee:
   (1) If the fair value of the leased property is objectively determinable, the lessee shall classify and account for the lease according to the provisions of paragraph .122.
   (2) If the fair value of the leased property is not objectively determinable, the lessee shall classify the lease according to the criterion of paragraph .103(c) only, using the estimated economic life of the building in which the leased premises are located. If that criterion is met, the leased property shall be capitalized as a unit and amortized in accordance with the provisions of paragraph .107(b).
b. Lessor:
   If either the cost or the fair value of the property is not objectively determinable, the lessor shall account for the lease as an operating lease.

Because of special provisions normally present in leases involving terminal space and other airport facilities owned by a governmental unit or authority, the economic life of such facilities for purposes of classifying the lease is essentially indeterminate. Likewise, the concept of fair value is not applicable to such leases. Since such leases also do not provide for a transfer of ownership or a bargain purchase option, they shall be clas-

[26]If there are no sales of property similar to the leased property, other evidence may provide a basis for an objective determination of fair value. For example, reasonable estimates of the leased property's fair value might be objectively determined by referring to an independent appraisal of the leased property or to estimated replacement cost information. [FIN24, ¶6] [However,] this section does not intend to impose a requirement to obtain an appraisal or similar valuation as a general matter but does [indicate] that kind of information be obtained whenever possible if (a) classification as a capital lease seems likely and (b) the effects of capital lease classification would be significant to the financial statements of a lessee. [Although] the applicability of this paragraph [is not] limited to lessees of a significant portion of a facility, [it is] recognized that a lessee's ability to make a reasonable estimate of the leased property's fair value will vary depending on the size of the leased property in relation to the entire facility. For example, obtaining a meaningful appraisal of an office or a floor of a multi-story building may not be possible, whereas similar information may be readily obtainable if the leased property is a major part of that facility. [FIN24, ¶4]

sified as operating leases.[27] Leases of other facilities owned by a governmental unit or authority wherein the rights of the parties are essentially the same as in a lease of airport facilities described above shall also be classified as operating leases. Examples of such leases may be those involving facilities at ports and bus terminals. [FAS13, ¶28]

Leases between Related Parties

.125 Except as noted below, leases between **related parties** shall be classified in accordance with the criteria in paragraphs .103 and .104. Insofar as the separate financial statements of the related parties are concerned, the classification and accounting shall be the same as for similar leases between **unrelated parties,** except in cases in which it is clear that the terms of the transaction have been significantly affected by the fact that the lessee and lessor are related. In such cases, the classification or accounting or both shall be modified as necessary to recognize economic substance rather than legal form. The nature and extent of leasing transactions with related parties shall be disclosed. [FAS13, ¶29]

.126 In consolidated financial statements or in financial statements for which an interest in an investee is accounted for on the equity basis, any profit or loss on a leasing transaction with the related party shall be accounted for in accordance with the principles set forth in Section C51, "Consolidation," or Section I82, "Investments: Equity Method," whichever is applicable. [FAS13, ¶30]

---

[27][This automatic classification as an operating lease applies] only if all of the following conditions are met:

a. The leased property is owned by a governmental unit or authority.
b. The leased property is part of a larger facility, such as an airport, operated by or on behalf of the lessor.
c. The leased property is a permanent structure or a part of a permanent structure, such as a building, that normally could not be moved to a new location.
d. The lessor, or in some cases a higher governmental authority, has the explicit right under the lease agreement or existing statutes or regulations applicable to the leased property to terminate the lease at any time during the lease term, such as by closing the facility containing the leased property or by taking possession of the facility. [FIN23, ¶8] ([However, it is not intended] that leases of government-owned property would be classified as operating leases merely because sovereign rights, such as the right of eminent domain, exist.) [FIN23, ¶6]
e. The lease neither transfers ownership of the leased property to the lessee nor allows the lessee to purchase or otherwise acquire ownership of the leased property.
f. The leased property or equivalent property in the same service area [FIN23, ¶8] (property that would allow continuation of essentially the same service or activity as afforded by the leased property without any appreciable difference in economic results to the lessee) [FIN23, ¶8, fn1] cannot be purchased nor can such property be leased from a nongovernmental unit or authority. [FIN23, ¶8]

Leases of property not meeting all of these conditions are subject to the same criteria for classifying leases that are applicable to leases not involving government-owned property. [FIN23, ¶9]

.127 The accounts of subsidiaries (regardless of when organized or acquired) whose principal business activity is leasing property or facilities to the parent or other affiliated enterprises shall be consolidated. The equity method is not adequate for fair presentation of those subsidiaries because their assets and liabilities are significant to the consolidated financial position of the enterprise. [FAS13, ¶31]

Sale-Leaseback Transactions

.128 Sale-leaseback transactions involve the sale of property by the owner and a lease of the property back to the seller. A sale of property that is accompanied by a leaseback of all or any part of the property for all or part of its remaining economic life shall be accounted for by the seller-lessee in accordance with the provisions of paragraph .129 [except that a sale-leaseback involving real estate, property improvements, or integral equipment[27a] shall be accounted for in accordance with the provisions of paragraphs .130A through .130M]. A sale of property that is accompanied by a leaseback of all or any part of the property for all or part of its remaining economic life shall be accounted for by the [buyer-lessor] in accordance with the provisions of paragraph .130. [FAS28, ¶2] [See paragraphs .544 through .545 for supplemental guidance in accounting for sale-leaseback transactions when nonrecourse debt is obtained using the lease rentals or lease rentals and the leased asset as collateral and the nonrecourse debt is sold with the asset to a third-party investor (a wrap lease transaction).] [Refer to paragraph .1001 for EITF Issues that provide interpretive guidance on this paragraph.]

.129 If the lease meets one of the criteria for treatment as a capital lease (refer to paragraph .103), the seller-lessee shall account for the lease as a capital lease; otherwise, as an operating lease. Any profit or loss on the sale[28] shall be deferred and amortized in proportion to the amortization of the leased asset,[29] if a capital lease, or in proportion to

[[27a]The terms *property improvements* and *integral equipment* are discussed in paragraph .130A and footnote 32a.]

[28]*Profit or loss on the sale* is used in this paragraph to refer to the profit or loss that would be recognized on the sale if there were no leaseback. For example, on a sale of real estate subject to Section R10, the profit on the sale to be deferred and amortized in proportion to the leaseback would be the profit that could otherwise be recognized in accordance with that section. [FAS28, ¶3]

[29]If the leased asset is land only, the amortization shall be on a straight-line basis over the lease term. [FAS13, ¶33, fn23]

the related gross rental charged to expense over the lease term, if an operating lease, unless:

a. The seller-lessee relinquishes the right to substantially all of the remaining use of the property sold (retaining only a minor portion of such use),[30] in which case the sale and the leaseback shall be accounted for as separate transactions based on their respective terms. However, if the amount of rentals called for by the lease is unreasonable under market conditions at the inception of the lease, an appropriate amount shall be deferred or accrued, by adjusting the profit or loss on the sale, and amortized as specified in the introduction of this paragraph to adjust those rentals to a reasonable amount.
b. The seller-lessee retains more than a minor part but less than substantially all[31] of the use of the property through the leaseback and realizes a profit on the sale[32] in excess of (1) the present value of the minimum lease payments over the lease term, if the leaseback is classified as an operating lease, or (2) the recorded amount of the leased asset, if the leaseback is classified as a capital lease. In that case, the profit on the sale in excess of either the present value of the minimum lease payments or the recorded amount of the leased asset, whichever is appropriate, shall be recognized at the date of the sale. For purposes of applying this provision, the present value of the minimum lease payments for an operating lease shall be computed using the interest rate that would be used to apply the 90 percent recovery criterion of paragraph .103(d).
c. The fair value of the property at the time of the transaction is less than its undepreciated cost, in which case a loss shall be recognized immediately up to the amount of the difference between undepreciated cost and fair value.

[FAS28, ¶3] [Refer to paragraph .1001 for EITF Issues that provide interpretive guidance on this paragraph.]

---

[30] *Substantially all* and *minor* are used here in the context of the concepts underlying the classification criteria of this section. In that context, a test based on the 90 percent recovery criterion of paragraph .103(d) could be used as a guideline; that is, if the present value of a reasonable amount of rental for the leaseback represents 10 percent or less of the *fair value* of the asset sold, the seller-lessee could be presumed to have transferred to the [buyer-lessor] the right to substantially all of the remaining use of the property sold, and the seller-lessee could be presumed to have retained only a minor portion of such use. [FAS28, ¶3(a)]

[31] *Substantially all* is used here in the context of the concepts underlying the classification criteria of this section. In that context, if a leaseback of *the entire property sold* meets the criteria of this section for classification as a capital lease, the seller-lessee would be presumed to have retained substantially all of the remaining use of the property sold. [FAS28, ¶3(b)]

[32] *Profit or loss on the sale* is used in this paragraph to refer to the profit or loss that would be recognized on the sale if there were no leaseback. For example, on a sale of real estate subject to Section R10, the profit on the sale to be deferred and amortized in proportion to the leaseback would be the profit that could otherwise be recognized in accordance with that section. [FAS28, ¶3]

.130 If the lease meets the criteria in paragraphs .103 and .104, the [buyer-lessor] shall record the transaction as a purchase and a direct financing lease; otherwise, the [buyer-lessor] shall record the transaction as a purchase and an operating lease. [FAS13, ¶34] [Refer to paragraph .1001 for an EITF Issue that provides interpretive guidance on this paragraph.]

Sale-Leaseback Transactions Involving Real Estate

.130A Paragraphs .130A through .130M [present] standards of financial accounting and reporting by a seller-lessee for sale-leaseback transactions involving real estate, including real estate with equipment, such as manufacturing facilities, power plants, and office buildings with furniture and fixtures. A sale-leaseback transaction involving real estate with equipment includes any sale-leaseback transaction in which the equipment and the real estate are sold and leased back as a package, irrespective of the relative value of the equipment and the real estate. Those paragraphs also address sale-leaseback transactions in which the seller-lessee sells property improvements or integral equipment[32a] to a buyer-lessor and leases them back while retaining the underlying land.[32b] [FAS98, ¶6]

Sale-Leaseback Accounting

.130B **Sale-leaseback accounting** is a method of accounting for a sale-leaseback transaction in which the seller-lessee records the sale, removes all property and related liabilities from its balance sheet, recognizes gain or loss from the sale in accordance with [paragraphs .129 and .130A through .130M] and Section R10, and classifies the leaseback in accordance with this section. [FAS98, ¶70]

Criteria for Sale-Leaseback Accounting

.130C Sale-leaseback accounting shall be used by a seller-lessee only if a sale-leaseback transaction includes all of the following:

[32a]The terms *property improvements* or *integral equipment* as used in paragraphs .130A through .130M of this section refer to any physical structure or equipment attached to the real estate, or other parts thereof, that cannot be removed and used separately without incurring significant cost. Examples include an office building, a manufacturing facility, a power plant, and a refinery. [FAS98, ¶6, fn2]

[32b]Paragraphs .141 and .142 of Section R10 address transactions in which the seller sells property improvements to a buyer and leases the underlying land to the buyer of the improvements. Under certain circumstances, paragraph .141 of Section R10 precludes **sales recognition** for such transactions and requires that they be accounted for as leases of both the land and improvements. Paragraphs .130A through .130M of this section are not intended to modify paragraph .141 of Section R10; thus, they do not address a sale-leaseback transaction that does not qualify for sales recognition under the provisions of paragraph .141 of Section R10. However, those paragraphs do address a sale-leaseback transaction that qualifies for sales recognition under the provisions of paragraph .142 of Section R10. [FAS98, ¶6, fn3]

a. A normal leaseback as described in paragraph .130D
b. Payment terms and provisions that adequately demonstrate the buyer-lessor's initial and continuing investment in the property (refer to paragraphs .111 through .119 of Section R10)
c. Payment terms and provisions that transfer *all* of the other risks and rewards of ownership as demonstrated by the absence of *any* other continuing involvement by the seller-lessee described in paragraphs .130G through .130I of this section and paragraphs .128 through .142 and .144 through .146 of Section R10.

[FAS98, ¶7]

.130D A *normal leaseback* is a lessee-lessor relationship that involves the active use of the property by the seller-lessee in consideration for payment of rent, including contingent rentals that are based on the future operations of the seller-lessee,[32c] and excludes other continuing involvement provisions or conditions described in paragraphs .130G through .130I of this section. The phrase *active use of the property by the seller-lessee* refers to the use of the property during the lease term in the seller-lessee's trade or business, provided that subleasing of the leased back property is minor.[32d] If the present value of a reasonable amount of rental for that portion of the leaseback that is subleased is not more than 10 percent of the fair value of the asset sold, the leased back property under sublease is considered minor. Active use of the property may involve the providing of services where the occupancy of the property is generally transient or short-term and is integral to the ancillary services being provided. Those ancillary services include, but are not limited to, housekeeping, inventory control, entertainment, bookkeeping, and food services. Thus, the use of property by a seller-lessee engaged in the hotel or bonded warehouse business or the operation of a golf course or a parking lot, for example, is considered active use. [FAS98, ¶8]

Terms of the Sale-Leaseback Transaction

.130E Terms of the sale-leaseback transaction that are substantially different from terms that an independent third-party lessor or lessee would accept represent an exchange of some stated or unstated rights or privileges. Those rights or privileges shall be considered in evaluating the continuing involvement provisions in paragraphs .130G through .130I of this section. Those terms or conditions include, but are not limited to, the sales

[32c]Paragraphs .130A through .130M distinguish between contingent rentals that are based on the future operations of the seller-lessee and those that are based on some predetermined or determinable level of future operations of the buyer-lessor. The latter type of contingent rental is addressed in paragraph .130H(e) of this section. [FAS98, ¶8, fn4]

[32d][The term] *minor* is used here in the context of the definition in footnote 30 to paragraph .129. [FAS98, ¶8, fn6]

price, the interest rate, and other terms of any loan from the seller-lessee to the buyer-lessor. The fair value of the property used in making that evaluation shall be based on objective evidence, for example, an independent third-party appraisal or recent sales of comparable property. [FAS98, ¶9]

Continuing Involvement

.130F A sale-leaseback transaction that does not qualify for sale-leaseback accounting because of any form of continuing involvement by the seller-lessee other than a normal leaseback shall be accounted for by the deposit method or as a financing, whichever is appropriate under Section R10. The provisions or conditions described in paragraphs .130G through .130I of this section are examples of continuing involvement for the purpose of applying paragraphs .130A through .130M. [FAS98, ¶10] [Refer to paragraph .1001 for EITF Issues that provide interpretive guidance on this paragraph.]

.130G Paragraphs .128 through .142 and .144 through .146 of Section R10 describe forms of continuing involvement by the seller-lessee with the leased property that result in the seller-lessee not transferring the risks or rewards of ownership to the buyer-lessor. Two examples of continuing involvement specified in those paragraphs that are frequently found in sale-leaseback transactions are provisions or conditions in which:

a. The seller-lessee has an obligation or an option[32e] to repurchase the property or the buyer-lessor can compel the seller-lessee to repurchase the property.
b. The seller-lessee guarantees the buyer-lessor's investment or a return on that investment for a limited or extended period of time.

[FAS98, ¶11] [Refer to paragraph .1001 for EITF Issues that provide interpretive guidance on this paragraph.]

.130H Other provisions or conditions that are guarantees and that do not transfer all of the risks of ownership shall constitute continuing involvement for the purpose of applying paragraphs .130A through .130M to sale-leaseback transactions and include, but are not limited to, the following:

a. The seller-lessee is required to pay the buyer-lessor at the end of the lease term for a decline in the fair value of the property below the estimated residual value on some basis other than excess wear and tear of the property levied on inspection of the property at the termination of the lease.

[32e]A right of first refusal based on a bona fide offer by a third party ordinarily is not an obligation or an option to repurchase. An agreement that allows the seller-lessee to repurchase the asset in the event no third-party offer is made is an option to repurchase. [FAS98, ¶11, fn7]

b. The seller-lessee provides **nonrecourse financing** to the buyer-lessor for any portion of the sales proceeds or provides recourse financing in which the only recourse is to the leased asset.
c. The seller-lessee is not relieved of the obligation under any existing debt related to the property.
d. The seller-lessee provides collateral on behalf of the buyer-lessor other than the property directly involved in the sale-leaseback transaction, the seller-lessee or a related party to the seller-lessee guarantees the buyer-lessor's debt, or a related party to the seller-lessee guarantees a return of or on the buyer-lessor's investment.
e. The seller-lessee's rental payment is contingent on some predetermined or determinable level of future operations of the buyer-lessor.[32f]

[FAS98, ¶12] [Refer to paragraph .1001 for EITF Issues that provide interpretive guidance on paragraphs .130H and .130I.]

.130I The following provisions or conditions also shall be considered examples of continuing involvement for the purpose of applying paragraphs .130A through .130M to sale-leaseback transactions:

a. The seller-lessee enters into a sale-leaseback transaction involving property improvements or integral equipment[32g] without leasing the underlying land to the buyer-lessor.[32h]
b. The buyer-lessor is obligated to share with the seller-lessee any portion of the appreciation of the property.
c. Any other provision or circumstance that allows the seller-lessee to participate in any future profits of the buyer-lessor or the appreciation of the leased property, for

---

[32f]Paragraphs .130A through .130M distinguish between contingent rentals that are based on the future operations of the seller-lessee and those that are based on some predetermined or determinable level of future operations of the buyer-lessor. [FAS98, ¶8, fn4]

[32g]The terms *property improvements* or *integral equipment* as used in paragraphs .130A through .130M refer to any physical structure or equipment attached to the real estate, or other parts thereof, that cannot be removed and used separately without incurring significant cost. Examples include an office building, a manufacturing facility, a power plant, and a refinery. [FAS98, ¶6, fn2]

[32h]Paragraphs .141 and .142 of Section R10 address transactions in which the seller sells property improvements to a buyer and leases the underlying land to the buyer of the improvements. Under certain circumstances, paragraph .141 of Section R10 precludes sales recognition for such transactions and requires that they be accounted for as leases of both the land and improvements. Paragraph .130A through .130M of this section are not intended to modify paragraph .141 of Section R10; thus, they do not address a sale-leaseback transaction that does not qualify for sales recognition under the provisions of paragraph .141 of Section R10. However, those paragraphs do address a sale-leaseback transaction that qualifies for sales recognition under the provisions of paragraph .142 of Section R10. [FAS98, ¶6, fn3]

example, a situation in which the seller-lessee owns or has an option to acquire any interest in the buyer-lessor.

[FAS98, ¶13]

Sale-Leaseback Transactions by Regulated Enterprises

.130J The provisions of paragraphs .130A through .130M apply to sale-leaseback transactions of a regulated enterprise subject to Section Re6, "Regulated Operations." That accounting may result in a difference between the timing of income and expense recognition required by those paragraphs and the timing of income and expense recognition for rate-making purposes. That difference shall be accounted for as follows:

a. If the difference in timing of income and expense recognition constitutes all or a part of a phase-in plan, as defined in paragraph .125A of Section Re6, it shall be accounted for in accordance with paragraphs .125A through .125F of Section Re6.
b. Otherwise, the timing of income and expense recognition related to the sale-leaseback transaction shall be modified as necessary to conform to Section Re6. That modification required for a transaction that is accounted for by the deposit method or as a financing is further described in paragraphs .125I and .125J of Section Re6.

[FAS98, ¶14]

Financial Statement Presentation and Disclosure

.130K In addition to the [other] disclosure requirements of this section and Section R10, the financial statements of a seller-lessee shall include a description of the terms of the sale-leaseback transaction, including future commitments, obligations, provisions, or circumstances that require or result in the seller-lessee's continuing involvement. [FAS98, ¶17]

.130L The financial statements of a seller-lessee that has accounted for a sale-leaseback transaction by the deposit method or as a financing according to the provisions of this section and Section R10 also shall disclose:

a. The obligation for future minimum lease payments as of the date of the latest balance sheet presented in the aggregate and for each of the five succeeding fiscal years
b. The total of minimum sublease rentals, if any, to be received in the future under noncancelable subleases in the aggregate and for each of the five succeeding fiscal years.

[FAS98, ¶18]

Other

.130M Paragraphs .160A through .160M provide additional discussion and illustrations of how the provisions of paragraphs .130A through .130M shall be applied to specific aspects of accounting for sale-leaseback transactions [involving real estate, property improvements, and equipment integral to real estate]. Paragraphs .160A through .160M constitute an integral part of the requirements of paragraphs .130A through .130M. [FAS98, ¶19]

Accounting and Reporting for Subleases and Similar Transactions

.131 Paragraphs .132 through .136 deal with the following types of leasing transactions:

a. The leased property is re-leased by the original lessee[33] to a third party, and the lease agreement between the two original parties remains in effect (a sublease).
b. A new lessee is substituted under the original lease agreement. The new lessee becomes the primary obligor under the agreement, and the original lessee may or may not be secondarily liable.
c. A new lessee is substituted through a new agreement, with cancellation of the original lease agreement.

[FAS13, ¶35]

Accounting by the Original Lessor

.132 If the original lessee enters into a sublease or the original lease agreement is sold or transferred by the original lessee to a third party, the original lessor shall continue to account for the lease as before. [FAS13, ¶36]

.133 If the original lease agreement is replaced by a new agreement with a new lessee, the lessor shall account for the termination of the original lease as provided in paragraph .113(f) and shall classify and account for the new lease as a separate transaction. [FAS13, ¶37]

Accounting by the Original Lessee

.134 If the nature of the transaction is such that the original lessee is relieved of the primary obligation under the original lease, as would be the case in transactions of the

[33] An *original lessee* includes any lessee who acts as sublessor on a sublease. [FIN27, ¶1, fn1]

type described in paragraphs .131(b) and .131(c), the termination of the original lease agreement shall be accounted for as follows:

a. If the original lease was a capital lease of property other than real estate (including integral equipment), the asset and obligation representing the original lease shall be removed from the accounts, a gain or loss shall be recognized for the difference, and, if the original lessee is secondarily liable, the guarantee obligation shall be recognized in accordance with paragraph .104 of Section L35, "Liabilities: Extinguishments." Any consideration paid or received upon termination shall be included in the determination of gain or loss to be recognized.
b. If the original lease was a capital lease of real estate (including integral equipment), the determination as to whether the asset held under the capital lease and the related obligation may be removed from the balance sheet shall be made in accordance with the requirements of Section R10, "Real Estate." If the criteria for recognition of a sale in Section R10 are met, the asset and obligation representing the original lease shall be removed from the accounts and any consideration paid or received upon termination and any guarantee obligation shall be recognized in accordance with the requirements above for property other than real estate. If the transaction results in a gain, that gain may be recognized if the criteria in Section R10 for recognition of profit by the full accrual method are met. Otherwise, the gain shall be recognized in accordance with one of the other profit recognition methods discussed in Section R10. Any loss on the transaction shall be recognized immediately.
c. If the original lease was an operating lease and the original lessee is secondarily liable, the guarantee obligation shall be recognized in accordance with paragraph .104 of Section L35.

[FAS145, ¶9(c)]

.135 If the nature of the transaction[34] is such that the original lessee is not relieved of the primary obligation under the original lease, as would be the case in transactions of the type described in paragraph .131(a), the original lessee, as sublessor, shall account for the transaction as follows:

a. If the original lease met either criterion (a) or (b) of paragraph .103, the original lessee shall classify the new lease in accordance with the criteria of paragraphs .103 and .104. If the new lease meets one of the criteria of paragraph .103 and both of the criteria of paragraph .104, it shall be accounted for as a sales-type or direct financing lease, as appropriate, and the unamortized balance of the asset under the original lease

[34]Paragraphs .518 through .520 discuss the accounting for loss on a sublease not involving the disposal of a segment.]

shall be treated as the cost of the leased property. If the new lease does not qualify as a sales-type or direct financing lease, it shall be accounted for as an operating lease. In either case, the original lessee shall continue to account for the obligation related to the original lease as before.

b. If the original lease met either criterion (c) or (d) but not criterion (a) or (b) of paragraph .103, the original lessee shall, with one exception, classify the new lease in accordance with the criteria of paragraphs .103(c) and .104 only. If it meets those criteria, it shall be accounted for as a direct financing lease, with the unamortized balance of the asset under the original lease treated as the cost of the leased property; otherwise, as an operating lease. In either case, the original lessee shall continue to account for the obligation related to the original lease as before. The one exception arises when the timing and other circumstances surrounding the sublease are such as to suggest that the sublease was intended as an integral part of an overall transaction in which the original lessee serves only as an intermediary. In that case, the sublease shall be classified according to the criteria of paragraphs .103(c) and .103(d), as well as the criteria of paragraph .104. In applying the criterion of paragraph .103(d), the fair value of the leased property shall be the fair value to the original lessor at the inception of the original lease.

c. If the original lease is an operating lease, the original lessee shall account for both it and the new lease as operating leases. [FAS13, ¶39]

This paragraph does not prohibit the recognition of a loss by an original lessee who disposes of leased property or mitigates the cost of an existing lease commitment by subleasing the property.[34a] [FIN27, ¶2]

Accounting by the New Lessee

.136 The new lessee shall classify the lease in accordance with the criteria of paragraph .103 and account for it accordingly. [FAS13, ¶40]

[34a See paragraphs .527C through .527F for guidance on the lessee's recognition of a loss on a lease that is assumed by a new lessor as an incentive to enter into a new lease with that lessor.]

35 [Deleted 2/99 because of FASB Statement 135, Rescission of FASB Statement No. 75 and Technical Corrections.]

Accounting for Leases in a Business Combination

Summary

.137 The classification of a lease in accordance with the criteria of this section shall not be changed as a result of a business combination unless the provisions of the lease are modified (refer to paragraph .138). [FIN21, ¶12]

Changes in the Provisions of the Lease

.138 If in connection with a business combination, the provisions of a lease are modified in a way that would require the revised agreement to be considered a new agreement under paragraph .105, the new lease shall be classified by the combined enterprise according to the criteria set forth in this section, based on conditions as of the date of the modification of the lease. [FIN21, ¶13]

.139 [Deleted 6/01 because of FASB Statement 141, *Business Combinations.*]

Business Combination

.140 In a business combination, the acquiring enterprise shall retain the previous classification in accordance with this section for the leases of an acquired enterprise unless the provisions of the lease are modified as indicated in paragraph .138. The amounts assigned to individual assets acquired and liabilities assumed at the date of the combination shall be determined in accordance with the general guides for that type of asset or liability in [FIN21, ¶15] Section B51, "Business Combinations," paragraphs .135 through .138. [FAS141, ¶E21(c)] Subsequent to the recording of the amounts called for by that section, the leases shall thereafter be accounted for in accordance with this section.[36] Paragraphs .141 and .142 explain application of this paragraph to a leveraged lease by an enterprise that acquires a lessor. [FIN21, ¶15]

.141 In a business combination, the acquiring enterprise shall apply the following procedures to the acquired enterprise's investment as a lessor in a leveraged lease. The acquiring enterprise shall retain the classification of a leveraged lease at the date of the combination. The acquiring enterprise shall assign an amount to the acquired net investment in the leveraged lease in accordance with the general guides in [FIN21, ¶16] Section B51, paragraphs .136 and .137, [FAS141, ¶E21(d)] based on the remaining future cash flows and giving appropriate recognition to the estimated future tax effects of

---

[36]The subsequent accounting for amounts recorded for favorable or unfavorable operating leases [is not addressed here]. Accordingly, present practice is not changed with respect to the amortization of those amounts. [FIN21, ¶15, fn3]

those cash flows. Once determined, that net investment shall be broken down into its components, namely, net rentals receivable, estimated residual value, and unearned income including discount to adjust other components to present value. The acquiring enterprise thereafter shall account for that investment in a leveraged lease in accordance with the provisions of this section. [FIN21, ¶16]

.142 Paragraph .161 illustrates the application of paragraph .141. [FIN21, ¶16]

Accounting and Reporting for Leveraged Leases

.143 From the standpoint of the lessee, leveraged leases shall be classified and accounted for in the same manner as nonleveraged leases. The balance of this section deals with leveraged leases from the standpoint of the lessor. [FAS13, ¶41]

.144 For the purposes of this section, a leveraged lease is defined as one having all of the following characteristics:

a. Except for the exclusion of leveraged leases from the definition of a direct financing lease as set forth in paragraph .102(b)(2), it otherwise meets that definition. Leases that meet the definition of sales-type leases set forth in paragraph .102(b)(1) shall not be accounted for as leveraged leases but shall be accounted for as prescribed in paragraph .113.
b. It involves at least three parties: a lessee, a long-term creditor, and a lessor (commonly called the equity participant).
c. The financing provided by the long-term creditor is nonrecourse as to the general credit of the lessor (although the creditor may have recourse to the specific property leased and the unremitted rentals relating to it). The amount of the financing is sufficient to provide the lessor with substantial *leverage* in the transaction. [Refer to paragraph .1001 for an EITF Issue that provides interpretive guidance on this subparagraph.]
d. The lessor's net investment, as defined in paragraph .145, declines during the early years once the investment has been completed and rises during the later years of the lease before its final elimination. Such decreases and increases in the net investment balance may occur more than once.

A lease meeting the preceding definition shall be accounted for by the lessor using the method described in paragraphs .145 through .149.[36a] An exception arises if the invest-

[[36a]Paragraphs .536 and .537 further discuss residual value retained by a lessor that sells rental payments.]

ment tax credit is accounted for other than as stated in paragraphs .145 and .146,[37] in which case the lease shall be classified as a direct financing lease and accounted for in accordance with paragraph .114. A lease not meeting the definition of a leveraged lease shall be accounted for in accordance with its classification under paragraph .102(b). [FAS13, ¶42]

.145 The lessor shall record its investment in a leveraged lease net of the nonrecourse debt.[37a] The net of the balances of the following accounts shall represent the initial and continuing investment in leveraged leases:

a. Rentals receivable, net of that portion of the rental applicable to principal and interest on the nonrecourse debt.
b. A receivable for the amount of the investment tax credit to be realized on the transaction.
c. The estimated residual value of the leased asset. [FAS13, ¶43] The estimated residual value shall not exceed the amount estimated at the inception of the lease except as provided in footnote 38.[38] [FAS23, ¶10]
d. Unearned and deferred income consisting of (1) the estimated pretax lease income (or loss), after deducting initial direct costs, remaining to be allocated to income over the lease term and (2) the investment tax credit remaining to be allocated to income over the lease term.

The investment in leveraged leases less deferred taxes arising from differences between pretax accounting income and taxable income shall represent the lessor's net investment in leveraged leases for purposes of computing periodic net income from the lease, as described in paragraph .146. [FAS13, ¶43]

.146 Given the original investment and using the projected cash receipts and disbursements over the term of the lease, the rate of return on the net investment in the years[39] in which it is positive shall be computed. The rate is that rate which when applied to the net investment in the years in which the net investment is positive will distribute the net

[37]It is recognized that the investment tax credit may be accounted for other than as prescribed here, as provided by Congress in the Revenue Act of 1971. [FAS13, ¶42, fn24]

[[37a]Footnote 502 further discusses nonrecourse debt collateralized by a lease receivable.]

[38]If the lease agreement or commitment, if earlier, includes a provision to escalate minimum lease payments for increases in construction or acquisition cost of the leased property or for increases in some other measure of cost or value, such as general price levels, during the construction or preacquisition period, the effect of any increases that have occurred shall be considered in the determination of "the estimated residual value of the leased property at the inception of the lease" for purposes of this paragraph. [FAS23, ¶10]

[39]The use of the term *years* is not intended to preclude application of the accounting prescribed in this paragraph to shorter accounting periods. [FAS13, ¶44, fn25]

income to those years (refer to Exhibit 154C) and is distinct from the *interest rate implicit in the lease.* In each year whether positive or not, the difference between the net cash flow and the amount of income recognized, if any, shall serve to increase or reduce the net investment balance. The net income recognized shall be composed of three elements: two, pretax lease income (or loss) and investment tax credit, shall be allocated in proportionate amounts from the unearned and deferred income included in net investment, as described in paragraph .145; the third element is the tax effect of the pretax lease income (or loss) recognized, which shall be reflected in tax expense for the year. The tax effect of the difference between pretax accounting income (or loss) and taxable income (or loss) for the year shall be charged or credited to deferred taxes. The accounting prescribed in paragraph .145 and in this paragraph is illustrated in paragraph .154. [FAS13, ¶44]

.147 If the projected net cash receipts[40] over the term of the lease are less than the lessor's initial investment, the deficiency shall be recognized as a loss at the inception of the lease. Likewise, if at any time during the lease term the application of the method prescribed in paragraphs .145 and .146 would result in a loss being allocated to future years, that loss shall be recognized immediately. This situation might arise in cases in which one of the important assumptions affecting net income is revised (refer to paragraph .148). [FAS13, ¶45]

.148 Any estimated residual value and all other important assumptions affecting estimated total net income from the lease shall be reviewed at least annually.[41] If during the lease term the estimate of the residual value is determined to be excessive and the decline in the residual value is judged to be other than temporary or if the revision of another important assumption changes the estimated total net income from the lease, the rate of return and the allocation of income to positive investment years shall be recalculated from the inception of the lease following the method described in paragraph .146 and using the revised assumption. The accounts constituting the net investment balance shall be adjusted to conform to the recalculated balances, and the change in the net investment shall be recognized as a gain or loss in the year in which the assumption is changed. An upward adjustment of the estimated residual value shall not be made.[41a] The accounting prescribed in this paragraph is illustrated in paragraph .154. [FAS13, ¶46] [Refer to paragraph .1001 for an EITF Issue that provides interpretive guidance on this paragraph.]

---

[40]For purposes of this paragraph, net cash receipts shall be gross cash receipts less gross cash disbursements exclusive of the lessor's initial investment. [FAS13, ¶45, fn26]

[[41]Refer to paragraphs .521 through .524 for supplemental guidance on the effect of a change in income tax rate on the accounting for leveraged leases.]

[[41a]Paragraphs .536 and .537 further discuss residual value retained by a lessor that sells rental payments.]

Accounting for Income Taxes

.148A Section I27, "Income Taxes," does not change (a) the pattern of recognition of after-tax income for leveraged leases as required by this section or (b) the allocation of the purchase price in a purchase business combination to acquired leveraged leases as required by paragraphs .140 through .142. Integration[41b] of the results of income tax accounting for leveraged leases with the other results of accounting for income taxes under Section I27 is required when deferred tax credits related to leveraged leases are the only source (refer to paragraph .120 of Section I27) for recognition of a tax benefit for deductible temporary differences and carryforwards not related to leveraged leases. A valuation allowance is not necessary if deductible temporary differences and carryforwards will offset taxable amounts from future recovery of the net investment in the leveraged lease. However, to the extent that the amount of deferred tax credits for a leveraged lease as determined under this section differs from the amount of the deferred tax liability related to the leveraged lease that would otherwise result from applying the requirements of Section I27, that difference is preserved and is not a source of taxable income for recognition of the tax benefit of deductible temporary differences and operating loss or tax credit carryforwards. [FAS109, ¶256]

.148B Paragraph .141 requires that the tax effect of any difference between the assigned value and the tax basis of a leveraged lease at the date of a business combination not be accounted for as a deferred tax credit. Section I27 does not change that requirement. Any tax effects included in unearned and deferred income as required by this section are not offset by the deferred tax consequences of other temporary differences or by the tax benefit of operating loss or tax credit carryforwards. However, deferred tax credits that arise after the date of a business combination are accounted for in the same manner as described above for leveraged leases that were not acquired in a purchase business combination. [FAS109, ¶257] [Exhibit 185A in Section I27 presents an example that integrates the] accounting for leveraged leases [as required by this section] and the accounting for income taxes required by Section I27. [FAS109, ¶258]

[41b]Integration is an issue when all of the following exist:

a. The accounting for a leveraged lease requires recognition of deferred tax credits.
b. The requirements of Section I27 limit the recognition of a tax benefit for deductible temporary differences and carryforwards not related to the leveraged lease.
c. Unrecognized tax benefits could offset taxable amounts that result from future recovery of the net investment in the leveraged lease.

In those circumstances, integration shall be required. However, integration should not override any results that are unique to income tax accounting for leveraged leases, for example, the manner of recognizing the tax effect of an enacted change in tax rates. [FAS109, ¶126]

Disclosures

.149 For purposes of presenting the investment in a leveraged lease in the lessor's balance sheet, the amount of related deferred taxes shall be presented separately (from the remainder of the net investment). In the income statement or the notes thereto, separate presentation (from each other) shall be made of pretax income from the leveraged lease, the tax effect of pretax income, and the amount of investment tax credit recognized as income during the period. When leveraged leasing is a significant part of the lessor's business activities in terms of revenue, net income, or assets, the components of the net investment balance in leveraged leases as set forth in paragraph .145 shall be disclosed in the footnotes to the financial statements. Paragraph .154 contains an illustration of the balance sheet, income statement, and footnote presentation for a leveraged lease. [FAS13, ¶47]

Illustrations of Accounting by Lessees and Lessors

.150 This paragraph contains the following exhibits illustrating the accounting requirements of this section as applied to a particular example (an automobile lease):

a. Lease example—terms and assumptions, Exhibit 150A
b. Computation of minimum lease payments (lessee and lessor) and lessor's computation of rate of interest implicit in the lease, Exhibit 150B
c. Classification of the lease, Exhibit 150C
d. Journal entries for the first month of the lease, as well as for the disposition of the leased property at the end of the lease term, Exhibit 150D.

[FAS13, ¶121]

Exhibit 150A

Lease Example
Terms and Assumptions

Lessor's cost of the leased property (automobile)	$5,000
Fair value of the leased property at inception of the lease (1/1/X7)	$5,000
Estimated economic life of the leased property	5 years

Lease terms and assumptions: The lease has a fixed noncancelable term of 30 months, with a rental of $135 payable at the beginning of each month. The lessee guarantees the residual value at the end of the 30-month lease term in the amount of $2,000. The lessee is to receive any excess of sales price of property over the guaranteed amount at the end of the lease term. The lessee pays executory costs. The lease is renewable periodically based on a schedule of rentals and guarantees of the residual values decreasing over time. The rentals specified are deemed to be fair rentals (as distinct from bargain rentals), and the guarantees of the residual are expected to approximate realizable values. No investment tax credit is available.

The residual value at the end of the lease term is estimated to be $2,000. The lessee depreciates its owned automobiles on a straight-line basis. The **lessee's incremental borrowing rate** is 10½ percent per year. There were no initial direct costs of negotiating and closing the transaction. At the end of the lease term the asset is sold for $2,100. [FAS13, ¶121]

Exhibit 150B

Computation of Minimum Lease Payments for Lessee and Lessor

In accordance with paragraph .416, minimum lease payments for both the lessee and lessor are computed as follows:

Minimum rental payments over the lease term ($135 × 30 months)	$4,050
Lessee guarantee of the residual value at the end of the lease term	2,000
Total minimum lease payments	$6,050

Lessor's Computation of Rate of Interest Implicit in the Lease

In accordance with paragraph .412, the **interest rate implicit in the lease** is that rate implicit in the recovery of the fair value of the property at the inception of the lease ($5,000) through the minimum lease payments (30 monthly payments of $135 and the lessee's guarantee of the residual value in the amount of $2,000 at the end of the lease term). That rate is 12.036 percent (1.003 percent per month). [FAS13, ¶121]

Exhibit 150C

Classification of the Lease

Criteria Set Forth in Paragraph	
.103(a)	*Not met.* The lease does not transfer ownership of the property to the lessee by the end of the lease term.
.103(b)	*Not met.* The lease does not contain a bargain purchase option.
.103(c)	*Not met.* The lease term is not equal to 75 percent or more of the estimated economic life of the property. (In this case, it represents only 50 percent of the estimated economic life of the property.)
.103(d)	*Met.* In the lessee's case, the present value ($5,120) of the minimum lease payments using the incremental borrowing rate (10½ percent) exceeds 90 percent of the fair value of the property at the inception of the lease. (Refer to [the following] computation.) Even if the lessee knows the implicit rate, the lessee uses its incremental rate because it is lower. The lessee classifies the lease as a capital lease. In the lessor's case, the present value ($5,000) of the minimum lease payments using the implicit rate also exceeds 90 percent of the fair value of the property. (Refer to [the following] computation.) Having met this criterion and assuming that the criteria of paragraph .104 are also met, the lessor will classify the lease as a direct financing lease (as opposed to a sales-type lease) because the cost and fair value of the asset are the same at the inception of the lease (refer to paragraph .102(b)(2)).

	Present Values	
	Lessee's Computation Using the Incremental Borrowing Rate of 10½% (.875% per Month)*	**Lessor's Computation Using the Implicit Interest Rate of 12.036% (1.003% per Month)**
Minimum lease payments:		
Rental payments	$3,580	$3,517
Residual guarantee by lessee	1,540	1,483
Total	$5,120	$5,000
Fair value of the property at inception of the leases	$5,000	$5,000
Minimum lease payments as a percentage of fair value	102%	100%

*In this case, the lessee's incremental borrowing rate is used because it is lower than the implicit rate (refer to paragraph .103(d)).

[FAS13, ¶121]

Exhibit 150D

Journal Entries for the First Month of the Lease as Well as for the Disposition of the Leased Property at the End of the Lease Term

First Month of the Lease

		Debit	Credit
LESSEE			
1/1/X7	Leased property under capital leases	5,000	
	Obligations under capital leases		5,000
	To record capital lease at the fair value of the property. (Since the present value of the minimum lease payments using the lessee's incremental borrowing rate as the discount rate [refer to paragraph .103(d) for selection of rate to be used] is greater than the fair value of the property, the lessee capitalizes only the fair value of the property [refer to paragraph .106].)		
1/1/X7	Obligations under capital leases	135	
	Cash		135
	To record first month's rental payment.		
1/31/X7	Interest expense	49	
	Accrued interest on obligations under capital leases		49*
	To recognize interest expense for the first month of the lease. Obligation balance outstanding during month $4,865 ($5,000 – $135) × 1.003% (rate implicit in the liquidation of the $5,000 obligation through (a) 30 monthly payments of $135 made at the beginning of each month and (b) a $2,000 guarantee of the residual value at the end of 30 months) = $49 (refer to paragraph .108).		

---

*In accordance with paragraph .108, the February 1, 19X7 rental payment of $135 will be allocated as follows: $86 (principal reduction) against obligations under capital leases and $49 against accrued interest on obligations under capital leases.

Exhibit 150D (continued)

Date	Account	Debit	Credit
LESSEE (continued)			
1/31/X7	Depreciation expense	100	
	Leased property under capital leases		100
	To record first month's depreciation on a straight-line basis over 30 months to a salvage value of $2,000, which is the estimated residual value to the lessee (refer to paragraph .107(b)).		
LESSOR			
1/1/X7	Minimum lease payments receivable	6,050	
	Automobile		5,000
	Unearned income		1,050
	To record lessor's investment in the direct financing lease (refer to paragraphs .114(a) and .114(b)).		
1/1/X7	Cash	135	
	Minimum lease payments receivable		135
	To record receipt of first month's rental payment under the lease.		
1/31/X7	Unearned income	49	
	Earned income		49
	To recognize the portion of unearned income that is earned during the first month of the lease. Net investment outstanding for month $4,865 (gross investment $5,915 [$6,050 – $135] less unearned income $1,050) × 1.003% (monthly implicit rate in the lease) = $49 (refer to paragraph .114(b)).		

Exhibit 150D (continued)

Disposition of Asset for $2,100
(refer to following Note)

		Debit	Credit
LESSEE			
7/1/X9	Cash	100	
	Obligations under capital leases	1,980	
	Accrued interest on obligations under capital leases	20	
	Leased property under capital leases		2,000
	Gain on disposition of leased property		100
	To record the liquidation of the obligations under capital leases and receipt of cash in excess of the residual guarantee through the sale of the leased property.		
LESSOR			
7/1/X9	Cash	2,000	
	Minimum lease payments receivable		2,000
	To record the receipt of the amount of the lessee's guarantee.		

Note to Disposition of Asset

Had the lessee elected at July 1, 19X9 to renew the lease, it would render inoperative the guarantee as of that date. For that reason, the renewal would not be treated as a new agreement, as would otherwise be the case under paragraph .105, but would instead be accounted for as provided in paragraph .108. The lessee would accordingly adjust the remaining balances of the asset and obligation from the original lease, which at June 30, 19X9 were equal, by an amount equal to the difference between the present value of the future minimum lease payments under the revised agreement and the remaining balance of the obligation. The present value of the future minimum lease payments would be computed using the rate of interest used to record the lease initially.

From the lessor's standpoint, the revised agreement would be accounted for in accordance with paragraph .113(e). Accordingly, the remaining balance of minimum lease payments receivable would be adjusted to the amount of the payments called for by the revised agreement, and the adjustment would be credited to unearned income. [FAS13, ¶121]

Illustrations of Disclosure by Lessees and Lessors

.151 Paragraphs .152 and .153 illustrate one way of meeting the disclosure requirements of this section, except for those relating to leveraged leases which are illustrated in paragraph .154. The illustrations do not encompass all types of leasing arrangements for which disclosures are required. For convenience, the illustrations have been constructed as if the section had been in effect in prior years. [FAS13, ¶122]

.152 Lessee's disclosure [is illustrated in Exhibits 152A and 152B]. [FAS13, ¶122]

Exhibit 152A

[Lessee] Company X
Balance Sheet

	Assets December 31, 19X6	Assets December 31, 19X5		Liabilities December 31, 19X6	Liabilities December 31, 19X5
Leased property under capital leases, less accumulated amortization (Note 2)	XXX	XXX	Current:		
			Obligations under capital leases (Note 2)	XXX	XXX
			Noncurrent:		
			Obligations under capital leases (Note 2)	XXX	XXX

Footnotes appear in Exhibit 152B. [FAS13, ¶122]

Exhibit 152B

Footnotes for Exhibit 152A

Note 1—Description of Leasing Arrangements

The Company conducts a major part of its operations from leased facilities which include a manufacturing plant, 4 warehouses, and 26 stores. The plant lease, which is for 40 years expiring in 19Z9, is classified as a capital lease. The warehouses are under operating leases that expire over the next seven years. Most of the leases of store facilities are classified as capital leases. All of the leases of store facilities expire over the next 15 years.

Most of the operating leases for warehouses and store facilities contain one of the following options: (a) the Company can, after the initial lease term, purchase the property at the then fair value of the property or (b) the Company can, at the end of the initial lease term, renew its lease at the then fair rental value for periods of 5 to 10 years. These options enable the Company to retain use of facilities in desirable operating areas. The rental payments under a store facility lease are based on a minimum rental plus a percentage of the store's sales in excess of stipulated amounts. Portions of store space and warehouse space are sublet under leases expiring during the next three years.

In addition, the Company leases transportation equipment (principally trucks) and data processing equipment under operating leases expiring during the next three years.

In most cases, management expects that in the normal course of business, leases will be renewed or replaced by other leases.

The plant lease prohibits the Company from entering into future lease agreements if, as a result of new lease agreements, aggregate annual rentals under all leases will exceed $XXX.

Note 2—Capital Leases

The following is an analysis of the leased property under capital leases by major classes:

	Asset Balances at December 31,	
Classes of Property	**19X6**	**19X5**
Manufacturing plant	$ XXX	$ XXX
Store facilities	XXX	XXX
Other	XXX	XXX
Less: Accumulated amortization	(XXX)	(XXX)
	$ XXX	$ XXX

Exhibit 152B (continued)

The following is a schedule by years of future minimum lease payments under capital leases together with the present value of the net minimum lease payments as of December 31, 19X6:

Year ending December 31:	
19X7	$ XXX
19X8	XXX
19X9	XXX
19Y0	XXX
19Y1	XXX
Later years	XXX
Total minimum lease payments*	XXX
Less: Amount representing estimated executory costs (such as taxes, maintenance, and insurance), including profit thereon, included in total minimum lease payments	(XXX)
Net minimum lease payments	XXX
Less: Amount representing interest†	(XXX)
Present value of net minimum lease payments‡	$ XXX

*Minimum payments have not been reduced by minimum sublease rentals of $XXX due in the future under noncancelable subleases. They also do not include contingent rentals which may be paid under certain store leases on the basis of a percentage of sales in excess of stipulated amounts. Contingent rentals amounted to $XXX in 19X6 and $XXX in 19X5.

†Amount necessary to reduce net minimum lease payments to present value calculated at the Company's incremental borrowing rate at the inception of the leases.

‡Reflected in the balance sheet as current and noncurrent obligations under capital leases of $XXX and $XXX, respectively.

Exhibit 152B (continued)

Note 3—Operating Leases

The following is a schedule by years of future minimum rental payments required under operating leases that have initial or remaining noncancelable lease terms in excess of one year as of December 31, 19X6:

Year ending December 31:	
19X7	$XXX
19X8	XXX
19X9	XXX
19Y0	XXX
19Y1	XXX
Later years	XXX
Total minimum payments required*	$XXX

*Minimum payments have not been reduced by minimum sublease rentals of $XXX due in the future under noncancelable subleases.

The following schedule shows the composition of total rental expense for all operating leases except those with terms of a month or less that were not renewed:

	Year Ending December 31,	
	19X6	**19X5**
Minimum rentals	$ XXX	$ XXX
Contingent rentals	XXX	XXX
Less: Sublease rentals	(XXX)	(XXX)
	$ XXX	$ XXX

[FAS13, ¶122]

.153 Lessor's disclosure (other than for leveraged leases) [is illustrated in Exhibits 153A and 153B]. [FAS13, ¶122]

Exhibit 153A

[Lessor] Company X
Balance Sheet

	December 31,	
Assets	**19X6**	**19X5**
Current assets:		
Net investment in direct financing and sales-type leases (Note 2)	XXX	XXX
Noncurrent assets:		
Net investment in direct financing and sales-type leases (Note 2)	XXX	XXX
Property on operating leases and property held for leases (net of accumulated depreciation of $XXX and $XXX for 19X6 and 19X5, respectively) (Note 3)	XXX	XXX

Footnotes appear in Exhibit 153B. [FAS13, ¶122]

Exhibit 153B

Footnotes to Exhibit 153A

Note 1—Description of Leasing Arrangements

The Company's leasing operations consist principally of the leasing of various types of heavy construction and mining equipment, data processing equipment, and transportation equipment. With the exception of the leases of transportation equipment, the bulk of the Company's leases are classified as direct financing leases. The construction equipment and mining equipment leases expire over the next 10 years and the data processing equipment leases expire over the next 8 years. Transportation equipment (principally trucks) is leased under operating leases that expire during the next three years.

Exhibit 153B (continued)

Note 2—Net Investment in Direct Financing and Sales-Type Leases

The following lists the components of the net investment in direct financing and sales-type leases as of December 31:

	19X6	19X5
Total minimum lease payments to be received*	$ XXX	$ XXX
Less: Amounts representing estimated executory costs (such as taxes, maintenance, and insurance), including profit thereon, included in total minimum lease payments	(XXX)	(XXX)
Minimum lease payments receivable	XXX	XXX
Less: Allowance for uncollectibles	(XXX)	(XXX)
Net minimum lease payments receivable	XXX	XXX
Estimated residual values of leased property (unguaranteed)	XXX	XXX
Less: Unearned income	(XXX)	(XXX)
Net investment in direct financing and sales-type leases	$ XXX	$ XXX

* Minimum lease payments do not include contingent rentals which may be received under certain leases of data processing equipment on the basis of hours of use in excess of stipulated minimums. Contingent rentals amounted to $XXX in 19X6 and $XXX in 19X5. At December 31, 19X6, minimum lease payments for each of the five succeeding fiscal years are as follows: $XXX in 19X7, $XXX in 19X8, $XXX in 19X9, $XXX in 19Y0, and $XXX in 19Y1.

Note 3—Property on Operating Leases and Property Held for Lease

The following schedule provides an analysis of the Company's investment in property on operating leases and property held for lease by major classes as of December 31, 19X6:

Construction equipment	$ XXX
Mining equipment	XXX
Data processing equipment	XXX
Transportation equipment	XXX
Other	XXX
	XXX
Less: Accumulated depreciation	(XXX)
	$ XXX

Exhibit 153B (continued)

Note 4—Rentals under Operating Leases

The following is a schedule by years of minimum future rentals on noncancelable operating leases as of December 31, 19X6:

Year ending December 31:	
19X7	$XXX
19X8	XXX
19X9	XXX
19Y0	XXX
19Y1	XXX
Later years	XXX
Total minimum future rentals*	$XXX

*This amount does not include contingent rentals which may be received under certain leases of data processing equipment on the basis of hours of use in excess of stipulated minimums. Contingent rentals amounted to $XXX in 19X6 and $XXX in 19X5.

[FAS13, ¶122]

Illustrations of Accounting and Financial Statement Presentation for Leveraged Leases

.154 This paragraph illustrates the accounting requirements of this section and one way of meeting its disclosure requirements as applied to a leveraged lease. The illustrations do not encompass all circumstances that may arise in connection with leveraged leases; rather, the illustrations are based on a single example of a leveraged lease, the terms and assumptions of which are stated in Exhibit 154A. The elements of accounting and reporting illustrated for this example of a leveraged lease are as follows:

a. Leveraged lease example—terms and assumptions, Exhibit 154A
b. Cash flow analysis by years, Exhibit 154B
c. Allocation of annual cash flow to investment and income, Exhibit 154C
d. Journal entries for lessor's initial investment and first year of operation, Exhibit 154D
e. Financial statements including footnotes at end of second year, Exhibit 154E
f. Accounting for a revision in the estimated residual value of the leased asset assumed to occur in the eleventh year of the lease (from $200,000 to $120,000):
    (1) Revised allocation of annual cash flow to investment and income, Exhibit 154F
    (2) Balances in investment accounts at beginning of the eleventh year before revised estimate, Exhibit 154G

(3) Journal entries, Exhibit 154H
(4) Adjustment of investment accounts, Exhibit 154I

[FAS13, ¶123]

Exhibit 154A

Leveraged Lease Example Terms and Assumptions

Cost of leased asset (equipment)	$1,000,000.
Lease term	15 years, dating from January 1, 19X5.
Lease rental payments	$90,000 per year (payable last day of each year).
Residual value	$200,000 estimated to be realized one year after lease termination. In the eleventh year of the lease the estimate is reduced to $120,000.
Financing:	
Equity investment by lessor	$400,000.
Long-term nonrecourse debt	$600,000, bearing interest at 9% and repayable in annu installments (on last day of each year) of $74,435.30.
Depreciation allowable to lessor for income tax purposes	7-year ADR life using double-declining-balance metho for the first 2 years (with the half-year convention ele tion applied in the first year) and sum-of-years'-digits method for remaining life, depreciated to $100,000 sa vage value.
Lessor's income tax rate (federal and state)	50.4% (assumed to continue in existence throughout th term of the lease).
Investment tax credit	10% of equipment cost or $100,000 (realized by the le sor on last day of first year of lease).
Initial direct costs	For simplicity, initial direct costs have not been includ in the illustration.

[FAS13, ¶123]

Exhibit 154B

Cash Flow Analysis by Years

Year	1 Gross Lease Rentals and Residual Value	2 Depreciation (for Income Tax Purposes)	3 Loan Interest Payments	4 Taxable Income (Loss) (Col. 1 – 2 – 3)	5 Income Tax Credits (Charges) (Col. 4 × 50.4%)	6 Loan Principal Payments	7 Investment Tax Credit Realized	8 Annual Cash Flow (Col. 1 – 3 + 5 – 6 + 7)	9 Cumulative Cash Flow
Initial investment	—	—	—	—	—	—	—	$(400,000)	$(400,000)
1	$ 90,000	$ 142,857	$ 54,000	$(106,857)	$ 53,856	$ 20,435	$100,000	169,421	(230,579)
2	90,000	244,898	52,161	(207,059)	104,358	22,274	—	119,923	(110,656)
3	90,000	187,075	50,156	(147,231)	74,204	24,279	—	89,769	(20,887)
4	90,000	153,061	47,971	(111,032)	55,960	26,464	—	71,525	50,638
5	90,000	119,048	45,589	(74,637)	37,617	28,846	—	53,182	103,820
6	90,000	53,061	42,993	(6,054)	3,051	31,442	—	18,616	122,436
7	90,000	—	40,163	49,837	(25,118)	34,272	—	(9,553)	112,883
8	90,000	—	37,079	52,921	(26,672)	37,357	—	(11,108)	101,775
9	90,000	—	33,717	56,283	(28,367)	40,719	—	(12,803)	88,972
10	90,000	—	30,052	59,948	(30,214)	44,383	—	(14,649)	74,323
11	90,000	—	26,058	63,942	(32,227)	48,378	—	(16,663)	57,660
12	90,000	—	21,704	68,296	(34,421)	52,732	—	(18,857)	38,803
13	90,000	—	16,957	73,043	(36,813)	57,478	—	(21,248)	17,555
14	90,000	—	11,785	78,215	(39,420)	62,651	—	(23,856)	(6,301)
15	90,000	—	6,145	83,855	(42,263)	68,290	—	(26,698)	(32,999)
16	200,000	100,000	—	100,000	(50,400)	—	—	149,600	116,601
Totals	$1,550,000	$1,000,000	$516,530	$ 33,470	$ (16,869)	$600,000	$100,000	$ 116,601	

[FAS13, ¶123]

Exhibit 154C

Allocation of Annual Cash Flow to Investment and Income

	1	2	3	4	5	6	7
		Annual Cash Flow			Components of Income†		
Year	Lessor's Net Investment at Beginning of Year	Total (from Exhibit 154B, Col. 8)	Allocated to Investment	Allocated to Income*	Pretax Income	Tax Effect of Pretax Income	Investment Tax Credit
1	$400,000	$169,421	$134,833	$ 34,588	$ 9,929	$ (5,004)	$ 29,663
2	265,167	119,923	96,994	22,929	6,582	(3,317)	19,664
3	168,173	89,769	75,227	14,542	4,174	(2,104)	12,472
4	92,946	71,525	63,488	8,037	2,307	(1,163)	6,893
5	29,458	53,182	50,635	2,547	731	(368)	2,184
6	(21,177)	18,616	18,616	—	—	—	—
7	(39,793)	(9,553)	(9,553)	—	—	—	—
8	(30,240)	(11,108)	(11,108)	—	—	—	—
9	(19,132)	(12,803)	(12,803)	—	—	—	—
10	(6,329)	(14,649)	(14,649)	—	—	—	—
11	8,320	(16,663)	(17,382)	719	206	(104)	617
12	25,702	(18,857)	(21,079)	2,222	637	(321)	1,906
13	46,781	(21,248)	(25,293)	4,045	1,161	(585)	3,469
14	72,074	(23,856)	(30,088)	6,232	1,789	(902)	5,345
15	102,162	(26,698)	(35,532)	8,834	2,536	(1,278)	7,576
16	137,694	149,600	137,694	11,906	3,418	(1,723)	10,211
Totals		$516,601	$400,000	$116,601	$33,470	$(16,869)	$100,000

*Lease income is recognized as 8.647 percent of the unrecovered investment at the beginning of each year in which the net investment is positive. The rate is that rate which when applied to the net investment in the years in which the net investment is positive will distribute the net income (net cash flow) to those years. The rate for allocation used in this exhibit is calculated by a trial and error process. The allocation is calculated based upon an initial estimate of the rate as a starting point. If the total thus allocated to income (column 4) differs under the estimated rate from the net cash flow (Exhibit 154B, column 8) the estimated rate is increased or decreased, as appropriate, to derive a revised allocation. This process is repeated until a rate is selected which develops a total amount allocated to income that is precisely equal to the net cash flow. As a practical matter, a computer program is used to calculate Exhibit 154C under successive interations until the correct rate is determined.

†Each component is allocated among the years of positive net investment in proportion to the allocation of net income in column 4.

[FAS13, ¶123]

Exhibit 154D

Illustrative Journal Entries for Year Ending December 31, 19X5

	Debit	Credit
Lessor's Initial Investment		
Rentals receivable (Exhibit 154B, total of column 1 less residual value, less totals of columns 3 and 6)	233,470	
Investment tax credit receivable (Exhibit 154B, column 7)	100,000	
Estimated residual value (Exhibit 154A)	200,000	
Unearned and deferred income (Exhibit 154C, totals of columns 5 and 7)		133,470
Cash		400,000
To record lessor's initial investment.		
First Year of Operation		
Journal Entry 1		
Cash	15,565	
Rentals receivable (Exhibit 154B, column 1 less columns 3 and 6)		15,565
Collection of first year's net rental		
Journal Entry 2		
Cash*	100,000	
Investment tax credit receivable (Exhibit 154B, column 7)		100,000
Receipt of investment tax credit		
Journal Entry 3		
Unearned and deferred income	9,929	
Income from leveraged leases (Exhibit 154C, column 5)		9,929
Recognition of first year's portion of pretax income allocated in the same proportion as the allocation of total income, [computed as follows:]		

$$\frac{34{,}588}{116{,}601} \times 33{,}470 = 9{,}929$$

*Receipts of the investment tax credit and other tax benefits are shown as cash receipts for simplicity only. Those receipts probably would not be in the form of immediate cash inflow. Instead, they likely would be in the form of reduced payments of taxes on other income of the lessor or on the combined income of the lessor and other entities whose operations are joined with the lessor's operations in a consolidated tax return.

Exhibit 154D (continued)

	Debit	Credit
Journal Entry 4		
Unearned and deferred income	29,663	
Investment tax credit recognized (Exhibit 154C, column 7)		29,663

Recognition of first year's portion of investment tax credit allocated in the same proportion as the allocation of total income, [computed as follows:]

$$\frac{34{,}588}{116{,}601} \times 100{,}000 = 29{,}663$$

	Debit	Credit
Journal Entry 5		
Cash (Exhibit 154B, column 5)	53,856	
Income tax expense (Exhibit 154C, column 6)	5,004	
Deferred taxes		58,860

To record receipt of first year's tax credit from lease operation, to charge income tax expense for tax effect of pretax accounting income, and to recognize as deferred taxes the tax effect of the difference between pretax accounting income and the tax loss for the year, calculated as follows:

Tax loss (Exhibit 154B, column 4)	$(106,857)
Pretax accounting income	9,929
Difference	$(116,786)
Deferred taxes ($116,786 × 50.4%)	$ 58,860

[FAS13, ¶123]

Exhibit 154E

Illustrative Partial Financial Statements Including Footnotes

Balance Sheet

Assets	December 31, 19X6	December 31, 19X5	Liabilities	December 31, 19X6	December 31, 19X5
Investment in leveraged leases	$334,708	$324,027	Deferred taxes arising from leveraged leases	$166,535	$58,860

Income Statement

(Ignoring all income and expense items other than those relating to leveraged leasing)

	19X6	19X5
Income from leveraged leases	$ 6,582	$ 9,929
Income before taxes and investment tax credit	6,582	9,929
Less: Income tax expense*	(3,317)	(5,004)
	3,265	4,925
Investment tax credit recognized*	19,664	29,663
Net income	$22,929	$34,588

Footnotes appear on the following page.

*These two items may be netted for purposes of presentation in the income statement, provided that the separate amounts are disclosed in a note to the financial statements.

Exhibit 154E (continued)

Footnotes

Investment in Leveraged Leases

The Company is the lessor in a leveraged lease agreement entered into in 19X5 under which mining equipment having an estimated economic life of 18 years was leased for a term of 15 years. The Company's equity investment represented 40 percent of the purchase price; the remaining 60 percent was furnished by third-party financing in the form of long-term debt that provides for no recourse against the Company and is secured by a first lien on the property. At the end of the lease term, the equipment is turned back to the Company. The residual value at that time is estimated to be 20 percent of cost. For federal income tax purposes, the Company receives the investment tax credit and has the benefit of tax deductions for depreciation on the entire leased asset and for interest on the long-term debt. Since during the early years of the lease those deductions exceed the lease rental income, substantial excess deductions are available to be applied against the Company's other income. In the later years of the lease, rental income will exceed the deductions and taxes will be payable. Deferred taxes are provided to reflect this reversal.

The Company's net investment in leveraged leases is composed of the following elements:

	December 31,	
	19X6	**19X5**
Rentals receivable (net of principal and interest on the nonrecourse debt)	$ 202,340	$217,905
Estimated residual value of leased assets	200,000	200,000
Less: Unearned and deferred income	(67,632)	(93,878)
Investment in leveraged leases	334,708	324,027
Less: Deferred taxes arising from leveraged leases	(166,535)	(58,860)
Net investment in leveraged leases	$ 168,173	$265,167

[FAS13, ¶123]

Exhibit 154F

Allocation of Annual Cash Flow to Investment and Income Revised to Include New Residual Value Estimate

	1	2	3	4	5	6	7
		Annual Cash Flow			Components of Income		
Year	Lessor's Net Investment at Beginning of Year	Total	Allocated to Investment	Allocated to Income*	Pretax Loss	Tax Effect of Pretax Loss	Investment Tax Credit
1	$400,000	$169,421	$142,458	$26,963	$(16,309)	$ 8,220	$ 35,052
2	257,542	119,923	102,563	17,360	(10,501)	5,293	22,568
3	154,979	89,769	79,323	10,446	(6,319)	3,184	13,581
4	75,656	71,525	66,425	5,100	(3,085)	1,555	6,630
5	9,231	53,182	52,560	622	(377)	190	809
6	(43,329)	18,616	18,616	—	—	—	—
7	(61,945)	(9,553)	(9,553)	—	—	—	—
8	(52,392)	(11,108)	(11,108)	—	—	—	—
9	(41,284)	(12,803)	(12,803)	—	—	—	—
10	(28,481)	(14,649)	(14,649)	—	—	—	—
11	(13,832)	(16,663)	(16,663)	—	—	—	—
12	2,831	(18,857)	(19,048)	191	(115)	58	248
13	21,879	(21,248)	(22,723)	1,475	(892)	450	1,917
14	44,602	(23,856)	(26,862)	3,006	(1,819)	916	3,909
15	71,464	(26,698)	(31,515)	4,817	(2,914)	1,469	6,262
16	102,979	109,920	102,979	6,941	(4,199)	2,116	9,024
Totals		$476,921	$400,000	$76,921	$(46,530)	$23,451	$100,000

*The revised allocation rate is 6.741%.

[FAS13, ¶123]

Exhibit 154G

Balances in Investment Accounts before Revised Estimate of Residual Value

	1	2	3	4	5	6	7
				Unearned and Deferred Income			
	Rentals Receivable*	Estimated Residual Value	Investment Tax Credit Receivable	Pretax Income (Loss)†	Investment Tax Credit‡	Deferred Taxes§	Net Investment (Col. 1 + 2 + 3) Less (Col. 4 + 5 + 6)
Initial investment	$233,470	$200,000	$ 100,000	$33,470	$100,000	$ —	$ 400,000
Changes in year of operation							
1	(15,565)	—	(100,000)	(9,929)	(29,663)	58,860	(134,833)
2	(15,565)	—	—	(6,582)	(19,664)	107,675	(96,994)
3	(15,565)	—	—	(4,174)	(12,472)	76,308	(75,227)
4	(15,565)	—	—	(2,307)	(6,893)	57,123	(63,488)
5	(15,565)	—	—	(731)	(2,184)	37,985	(50,635)
6	(15,565)	—	—	—	—	3,051	(18,616)
7	(15,565)	—	—	—	—	(25,118)	9,553
8	(15,564)	—	—	—	—	(26,672)	11,108
9	(15,564)	—	—	—	—	(28,367)	12,803
10	(15,565)	—	—	—	—	(30,214)	14,649
Balances, beginning of eleventh year	$ 77,822	$200,000	$ —	$ 9,747	$ 29,124	$230,631	$ 8,320

*Exhibit 154B, column 1, excluding residual value, less columns 3 and 6.

†Exhibit 154C, column 5.

‡Exhibit 154C, column 7.

§50.4% of difference between taxable income (loss), Exhibit 154B, column 4, and pretax accounting income (loss), Exhibit 154C, column 5.

[FAS13, ¶123]

Exhibit 154H

Illustrative Journal Entries
Reduction in Residual Value in Eleventh Year

		Debit	Credit
Journal Entry 1			
Pretax income (or loss)		$60,314	
Unearned and deferred income		27,450	
Pretax income (loss):			
Balance at end of 10th year	$ 9,747[a]		
Revised balance	(9,939)[b]		
Adjustment	(19,686)		
Deferred investment tax credit:			
Balance at end of 10th year	29,124[c]		
Revised balance	21,360[d]		
Adjustment	(7,764)		
Investment tax credit recognized			$ 7,764
Estimated residual value			80,000

To record:

a. The cumulative effect on pretax income and the effect on future income resulting from the decrease in estimated residual value:

Reduction in estimated residual value	$ 80,000
Less portion attributable to future years (unearned and deferred income)	(19,686)
Cumulative effect (charged against current income)	$ 60,314

b. The cumulative and future effect of the change in allocation of the investment tax credit resulting from the reduction in estimated residual value

[a]Exhibit 154G, column 4.

[b]Exhibit 154F, total of column 5 less amounts applicable to the first 10 years.

[c]Exhibit 154G, column 5.

[d]Exhibit 154F, total of column 7 less amounts applicable to the first 10 years.

Exhibit 154H (continued)

		Debit	Credit
Journal Entry 2			
Deferred taxes		30,398	
Income tax expense			30,398
To recognize deferred taxes for the difference between pretax accounting income (or loss) and taxable income (or loss) for the effect of the reduction in estimated residual value:			
Pretax accounting loss per journal entry 1	$(60,314)		
Tax income (or loss)	—		
Difference	$(60,314)		
Deferred taxes ($60,314 × 50.4%)	$(30,398)		

[FAS13, ¶123]

Exhibit 154I

Adjustment of Investment Accounts for Revised Estimate of Residual Value in Eleventh Year

	1	2	3	4	5	6
			Unearned and Deferred Income			
	Rentals Receivable	Estimated Residual Value	Pretax Income (Loss)	Investment Tax Credit	Deferred Taxes	Net Investment (Col. 1 + 2) Less (Col. 3 + 4 + 5)
Balances, beginning of eleventh year (Exhibit 154G)	$77,822	$200,000	$ 9,747	$29,124	$230,631	$ 8,320
Adjustment of estimated residual value and unearned and deferred income (Exhibit 154H—journal entry 1)	—	(80,000)	(19,686)	(7,764)	—	(52,550)
Adjustment of deferred taxes for the cumulative effect on pretax accounting income (Exhibit 154H—journal entry 2)	—	—	—	—	(30,398)	30,398
Adjusted balances, beginning of eleventh year	$77,822	$120,000	$ (9,939)	$21,360	$200,233	$(13,832)*

*Exhibit 154F, column 1.

[FAS13, ¶123]

Illustrations of Accounting for Sale-Leaseback Transactions

.155 Paragraphs .156 through .160M illustrate the accounting for certain sales with leasebacks but do not encompass all possible circumstances. Accordingly, each situation should be resolved based on an evaluation of the facts, using the examples in these paragraphs as guidance to the extent that they are applicable to the facts of the individual sale and leaseback. [FAS28, ¶22] Examples [in paragraphs .160A through .160M] assume that the initial transaction occurs on the first day of the year and that subsequent transactions and payments are made on the last day of each year. [FAS98, ¶26]

Sales Qualifying for Full and Immediate Profit Recognition

Minor Leaseback

.156 An enterprise constructs a regional shopping center and sells it to a real estate management firm. The sale meets [the criteria of paragraph .130C for sale-leaseback accounting and] the criteria of Section R10 for full and immediate profit recognition. At the same time, the seller leases back for 40 years a part of the facility, estimated to be approximately 8 percent of the total rental value of the center. Pertinent data are:

Sales price	$11,200,000
Cost of shopping center	$10,000,000

The rental called for by the lease appears to be reasonable in view of current market conditions. The seller-lessee would record the sale and recognize $1,200,000 profit. The seller-lessee would account for the leaseback as though it were unrelated to the sale because the leaseback is minor as indicated in paragraph .129(a). [FAS28, ¶23]

.157 An enterprise sells real estate, consisting of land and a factory. The factory has an estimated remaining life of approximately 40 years. The sale meets [the criteria of paragraph .130C for sale-leaseback accounting and] the criteria of Section R10 for full and immediate profit recognition. The seller negotiates a leaseback of the factory for one year because its new facilities are under construction and approximately one year will be required to complete the new facilities and relocate. Pertinent data are:

Sales price	$20,000,000
Carrying value of real estate	$6,000,000
Annual rental under leaseback	$ 900,000
Estimated annual market rental	$1,800,000

The leaseback is minor as indicated in paragraph .129(a) because the present value of the leaseback ($1,800,000) is less than 10 percent of the fair value of the asset sold (approximately $20,900,000, based on the sales price and the prepaid rental that apparently has reduced the sales price). Accordingly, the seller-lessee would record the sale and would recognize profit. An amount of $900,000 would be deferred and amortized as additional rent expense over the term of the leaseback to adjust the leaseback rentals to a reasonable amount.[42] Accordingly, the seller-lessee would recognize $14,900,000 as profit on the sale ($14,000,000 of profit based on the terms of the sale increased by $900,000 to adjust the leaseback rentals to a reasonable amount). [FAS28, ¶24]

Leasebacks That Are Not Minor but Do Not Cover Substantially All of the Use of the Property Sold

.158 An enterprise sells an existing shopping center to a real estate management firm. The sale meets [the criteria of paragraph .130C for sale-leaseback accounting and] the criteria of Section R10 for full and immediate profit recognition. At the same time, the seller leases back the anchor store (with corresponding use of the related land), estimated to be approximately 30 percent of the total rental value of the shopping center, for 20 years, which is substantially all of the remaining economic life of the building. Pertinent data are:

Sales price of shopping center	$3,500,000
Estimated to consist of:	
Land	$1,000,000
Buildings and improvements	2,500,000
	$3,500,000
Carrying value of shopping center	$1,000,000
Monthly rentals called for by leaseback	$12,600
Seller-lessee's incremental borrowing rate*	10%

*Believed to be approximately the same as the implicit rate calculated by the lessor.

The seller-lessee estimates the ratio of land to building for the leaseback to be the same as for the property as a whole. The seller-lessee would apply paragraph .122(b)(2)(a) because the land value exceeds 25 percent of the total fair value of the leased property and would account for the leaseback of the land as a separate operating lease. The seller-lessee would account for $2,500 as monthly land rental (10 percent annual rate applied to the $300,000 value of the land leased back—30 percent of the land value of the shop-

[42]If the term of a prepayment of rent were significant, the amount deferred would be the amount required to adjust the rental to the market rental for an equivalent property if that rental were also prepaid. [FAS28, ¶24, fn††]

ping center). The balance of the monthly rental (10,000) would be allocated to the building and improvements and would be accounted for as a capital lease pursuant to the 75 percent of economic life criterion. The leased building and improvements would be recorded at the present value of the $10,100 monthly rentals for 20 years at the seller-lessee's 10 percent incremental borrowing rate, or $1,046,608. The seller-lessee would compute the profit to be recognized on the sale as follows:

Profit on the sale		$2,500,000
Recorded amount of leased asset (capital lease)	$1,046,608	
Present value of operating lease rentals at 10% rate	259,061	
Profit to be deferred and amortized		1,305,669
Profit to be recognized		$1,194,331

The deferred profit would be amortized in relation to the separate segments of the lease. The amount attributable to the capital lease ($1,046,608) would be amortized in proportion to the amortization of the leased asset over the term of the lease. The amount attributable to the operating lease ($259,061) would be amortized on a straight-line basis over the term of the lease. [FAS28, ¶25]

.159 An enterprise sells an airplane with an estimated remaining economic life of 10 years. At the same time, the seller leases back the airplane for three years. Pertinent data are:

Sales price	$600,000
Carrying value of airplane	$100,000
Monthly rental under leaseback	$6,330
Interest rate implicit in the lease as computed by the lessor*	12%

*Used because it is lower than the lessee's incremental borrowing rate.

The leaseback does not meet any of the criteria for classification as a capital lease; hence, it would be classified as an operating lease. The seller-lessee would compute the profit to be recognized on the sale as follows:

Profit on the sale	$500,000
Present value of operating lease rentals ($6,330 for 36 months at 12%)	190,581
Profit to be recognized	$309,419

The $190,581 deferred profit would be amortized in equal monthly amounts over the lease term because the leaseback is classified as an operating lease. [FAS28, ¶26]

Leaseback That Covers Substantially All of the Use of the Property Sold

.160 An enterprise sells equipment with an estimated remaining economic life of 15 years. At the same time, the seller leases back the equipment for 12 years. All profit on the sale would be deferred and amortized in relation to the amortization of the leased asset because the leaseback of *all* of the property sold covers a period in excess of 75 percent of the remaining economic life of the property and, thus, meets one of the criteria for classification as a capital lease. [FAS28, ¶27]

Sales Not Qualifying for Full and Immediate Profit Recognition

Sales Recognition

.160A A sale-leaseback transaction [that involves real estate, property improvements, or equipment integral to real estate and] that qualifies for sales recognition under the provisions of paragraphs .130A through .130M of this section is accounted for using sale-leaseback accounting by the seller-lessee whether the leaseback is classified as a capital lease or an operating lease in accordance with paragraph .102(a). The proper approach is first to determine the gain that would be recognized under Section R10 as if the transaction were a sale without a leaseback and then to allocate that gain as provided by this section over the remaining lease term. Under the provisions of footnote 28 to paragraph .129 of this section, the gain to be deferred and amortized in proportion to the leaseback is the gain that would otherwise be recognized in that year under the provisions of Section R10, except for the amount that can be recognized currently under paragraph .129 of this section. The total gain is recognized immediately if the leaseback is considered minor under the context of paragraph .129(a). The gain to be recognized currently under paragraph .129(b) is the amount of gain in excess of (a) the present value of the minimum lease payments if the leaseback is classified as an operating lease or (b) the recorded amount of the leased asset if the leaseback is classified as a capital lease. [FAS98, ¶27]

Example 1—Sale-Leaseback Transaction Accounted for as a Sale with Gain Recognized under the Installment Method and the Leaseback Classified as an Operating Lease

.160B Company A (a seller-lessee) sells the building at its principal manufacturing facility with an estimated remaining life of 15 years and a cost less accumulated depreciation of $800,000 to a buyer-lessor for $950,000 (the fair value of the property as determined by an independent third-party appraisal) and enters into an agreement to lease back the building. In exchange for the building, the seller-lessee receives $50,000 and a 10-year $900,000 recourse note with a 10 percent annual interest rate with annual payments of $146,471. Under the terms of the agreement, the seller-lessee is required to lease the building back for $100,000 a year for an initial period of 5 years. In addition, the seller-lessee has the option to renew the lease for an additional 5 years at $110,000 (estimated to be the then fair-market rental). [FAS98, ¶28]

.160C The sale-leaseback transaction does not include any form of continuing involvement that would preclude the seller-lessee from using sale-leaseback accounting. The initial down payment is inadequate for the seller-lessee to account for the transaction under the full accrual method described in Section R10. Under the provisions of Section R10, the seller-lessee elects to use the installment method to recognize the gain on the transaction. The property and any related debt would be removed from the seller-lessee's balance sheet and the note receivable net of unamortized deferred profit would be reported on the balance sheet. The renewal of the lease is included in the lease term for purposes of classifying the lease and amortizing income because the loss of the property at the end of the initial lease term is considered to be a penalty. The leaseback is classified as an operating lease because none of the criteria of paragraph .103 of this section is met. [FAS98, ¶29] [Exhibit 160A presents the calculation of the total gain and the portion to be recognized in each period.]

Exhibit 160A

Recognition of the Gain on the Transaction in Example 1

Calculation of the Gain

Sales price	$950,000
Cost less accumulated depreciation	800,000
Total gain to be recognized	$150,000

Gain Recognition under Section R10
(Installment Method Absent the Leaseback)

Day 1	$ 7,895
End of Year 1	8,916
Year 2	9,808
Year 3	123,381
Total	$150,000

Exhibit 160A (continued)

Gain Recognition for the Sale-Leaseback under This Section

Period Recognized	Day 1 Gain	End of Year 1 Gain	Year 2 Gain	Year 3 Gain	Total Gain Recognized
		Allocation of Annual Gain under the Installment Method with the Leaseback			
Year 1	$ 789				$ 789
Year 2	789	$ 990			1,779
Year 3	789	990	$1,226		3,005
Year 4	789	990	1,226	$ 17,625	20,630
Year 5	789	991	1,226	17,626	20,632
Year 6	790	991	1,226	17,626	20,633
Year 7	790	991	1,226	17,626	20,633
Year 8	790	991	1,226	17,626	20,633
Year 9	790	991	1,226	17,626	20,633
Year 10	790	991	1,226	17,626	20,633
Total	$7,895	$8,916	$9,808	$123,381	$150,000

Note: The installment method as described in paragraph .150 of Section R10 requires profit to be allocated to the down payment and subsequent collections on the buyer-lessor's note (principal portion only) by the percentage of profit inherent in the transaction (in this example, 15.79 percent). In addition, paragraph .155 of Section R10 allows a seller to switch from the installment method to the full accrual method of recognizing profit when the transaction meets the requirements for the full accrual method on a cumulative basis. In this example, it is assumed that for the seller-lessee to recognize profit in year 3 under the full accrual method, the buyer-lessor must have an investment in the property of 20 percent of the sales price to meet the minimum investment requirement and that the seller-lessee elects to switch to the full accrual method in the first full year after the minimum initial and continuing investment criteria are met.

[FAS98, ¶29, Illustration 1]

Deposit Method

.160D Paragraphs .123 through .125, .131, and .135 of Section R10 describe certain circumstances in which it is appropriate to account for a transaction using the deposit method (as described in paragraphs .159 through .161 of Section R10). If a sale-leaseback transaction is accounted for by the deposit method, lease payments decrease and collections on the buyer-lessor's note, if any, increase the seller-lessee's deposit account. The property and any related debt continue to be included in the seller-lessee's balance sheet, and the seller-lessee continues to depreciate the property. Under the provisions of paragraph .124 of Section R10, a seller-lessee that is accounting for any transaction by the deposit method according to the provisions of this section shall recognize a loss if at any time the net carrying amount of the property exceeds the sum of the balance in the deposit account, the fair value of the unrecorded note receivable, and any debt assumed by the buyer. [FAS98, ¶30]

.160E If a sale-leaseback transaction accounted for by the deposit method subsequently qualifies for sales recognition under this section and Section R10, the transaction is accounted for using sale-leaseback accounting, and the gain or loss is recognized in accordance with the provisions of paragraph .160A of this section. In addition, the leaseback is classified and accounted for in accordance with this section as if the sale had been recognized at the inception of the lease. If the leaseback meets one of the criteria for classification as a capital lease, the asset and liability accounts related to the leaseback, including accumulated amortization, are recorded as of the date that the sale is recognized to reflect amortization that would have been charged to expense had the lease been recorded as a capital lease at its inception. The change in the related lease accounts that would have been recorded from the inception of the lease had the transaction initially qualified for sale-leaseback accounting is included in computing the gain or loss recognized in accordance with paragraph .160A of this section. [FAS98, ¶31]

Example 2—Sale-Leaseback Transaction Accounted for by the Deposit Method with Subsequent Sales Recognition and the Leaseback Classified as a Capital Lease

.160F Company B (a seller-lessee) sells the building at one of its manufacturing facilities to a buyer-lessor for $950,000 (the fair value of the property as determined by an independent third-party appraisal) and enters into an agreement to lease the building back for 10 years at $150,000 per year. The property has a historical cost of $1,300,000 and accumulated depreciation at the date of the transaction of $400,000. Depreciation expense is $80,000 per year. In exchange for the building, the seller-lessee receives $50,000 and a 10-year $900,000 recourse note with a 10 percent annual interest rate with annual payments of $146,471. [FAS98, ¶32]

.160G The sale-leaseback transaction does not include any continuing involvement provisions, but the buyer-lessor has a questionable credit rating. Based on the poor credit standing of the buyer-lessor and the inadequate initial investment, the seller-lessee elects to account for the transaction by the deposit method. The initial and continuing investment must equal 20 percent of the sales price before it is appropriate to recognize profit by the full accrual method. Based on the amortization schedule of the buyer-lessor's note and assuming an improved credit rating of the buyer-lessor, income recognition under the full accrual method will be appropriate for the transaction at the end of year 3. The leaseback meets the criteria for classification as a capital lease in accordance with the provisions of paragraphs .103(c) and .103(d) of this section. [FAS98, ¶33] [Exhibit 160B presents the calculation of the total gain and the portion to be recognized in each period. Exhibit 160C presents the related journal entries. Exhibit 160D presents balance sheet information.]

Exhibit 160B

Recognition of the Gain on the Transaction in Example 2

Calculation of the Gain

Sales price (at inception)	$ 950,000
Cost less accumulated depreciation (end of year 3)	660,000
	290,000
Adjustments required by the deposit method or provisions of this section:	
Amortization of capital asset not recognized	(285,000)
Interest income credited to the deposit account in years 1-3 (credited to the deposit account as part of note payments received)	252,495
Interest expense charged to the deposit account in years 1-3 (charged to the deposit account as part of lease payments)	(247,363)
Total gain to be recognized	$ 10,132

Under the provisions of Section R10 and absent the leaseback, a gain of $10,132 would be recognized at the end of year 3 under the full accrual method.

Allocation of Gain Recognition under This Section

Period Recognized	Year 3 Gain
Year 4	$ 1,447
Year 5	1,447
Year 6	1,447
Year 7	1,447
Year 8	1,448
Year 9	1,448
Year 10	1,448
Total	$10,132

[FAS98, ¶33, Illustration 2]

Exhibit 160C

Journal Entries for Example 2

	Debit	Credit
At inception:		
Cash	50,000	
Deposit		50,000
To record the receipt of the down payment on the property		
Recurring journal entries in years 1-3:		
Cash	146,471	
Deposit		146,471
To record the receipt of collections on the buyer-lessor's note (the annual payment required for a 10-year $900,000 note)		
Deposit	150,000	
Cash		150,000
To record the lease payments		
Depreciation expense	80,000	
Accumulated depreciation		80,000
To record the depreciation expense		
When the sale is recognized at end of year 3:		
Deposit	39,413	
Capital asset	950,000	
Note receivable	713,082	
Accumulated depreciation	640,000	
Property, plant, and equipment		1,300,000
Capital lease obligation		747,363
Accumulated amortization of the capital asset		285,000
Deferred gain		10,132
To recognize the sale and to record the capitalization of the leased asset		

[FAS98, ¶33, Illustration 3]

Exhibit 160D

Annual Balances in the Related Balance Sheet Accounts for Example 2

(1)	(2)	(3)	(4)	(5)	(6)	(7)	(8)	(9)	(10)	(11)	(12)	(13)
					Memo Entries Only in Years 1-3							
Period	Deposit Account	Property, Plant, and Equipment	Accum. Depr.	Deferred Gain	Deferred Interest Income	Gross Note Receiv.	Net Note Receiv.	Deferred Interest Expense	Gross Lease Oblig.	Net Lease Oblig.	Capital Lease Asset	Capital Lease Accum. Amort.
At inception	$50,000	$1,300,000	$400,000	$ 0	$564,710	$1,464,710	$900,000	$550,000	$1,500,000	$950,000	$950,000	$ 0
Year 1	46,471	1,300,000	480,000	0	474,710	1,318,239	843,529	461,635	1,350,000	888,365	950,000	95,000
Year 2	42,942	1,300,000	560,000	0	390,357	1,171,768	781,411	379,003	1,200,000	820,997	950,000	190,000
Year 3	39,413	1,300,000	640,000	0	312,215	1,025,297	713,082	302,637	1,050,000	747,363	950,000	285,000
After sale is recognized	0	0	0	10,132	312,215	1,025,297	713,082	302,637	1,050,000	747,363	950,000	285,000
Year 4	0	0	0	8,685	240,907	878,826	637,919	233,120	900,000	666,880	950,000	380,000
Year 5	0	0	0	7,238	177,115	732,355	555,240	171,090	750,000	578,910	950,000	475,000
Year 6	0	0	0	5,791	121,591	585,884	464,293	117,242	600,000	482,758	950,000	570,000
Year 7	0	0	0	4,344	75,162	439,413	364,251	72,337	450,000	377,663	950,000	665,000
Year 8	0	0	0	2,896	38,736	292,942	254,206	37,209	300,000	262,791	950,000	760,000
Year 9	0	0	0	1,448	13,316	146,471	133,155	12,765	150,000	137,235	950,000	855,000
Year 10	0	0	0	0	0	0	0	0	0	0	950,000	950,000

Computations:

Column (2)	Original deposit plus collections on the buyer-lessor's note net of payments on the lease.
Column (3)	Plant balance at inception of lease.
Column (4)	Accumulated depreciation at inception of lease plus annual depreciation expense.
Column (5)	Deferred gain account less amount recognized annually per Exhibit 160B.
Column (6)	Column 7 less column 8.
Column (7)	Balance of remaining payments on the buyer-lessor's note.
Column (8)	The present value of the remaining note payments discounted at 10 percent.
Column (9)	Column 10 less column 11.
Column (10)	Accumulated balance of the remaining payments on the seller-lessee's lease obligation.
Column (11)	The present value of the remaining lease payments discounted at 9.301595 percent (assumed to be the seller-lessee's incremental borrowing rate).
Column (12)	Balance of the capital lease asset.
Column (13)	Accumulated balance of annual amortization of $95,000.

[FAS98, ¶33, Illustration 4]

Financing Method

.160H This section and paragraphs .128 through .142 and .144 through .146 of Section R10 describe some common forms of continuing involvement with the property by the seller that preclude a sale-leaseback transaction from sale-leaseback accounting. Depending on the nature and duration of the continuing involvement with the property, those provisions may require a sale-leaseback transaction to be accounted for as a financing. If a sale-leaseback transaction is reported as a financing, lease payments, exclusive of an interest portion, decrease and collections on the buyer-lessor's note increase the seller-lessee's liability account with a portion of the lease payments being recognized under the interest method. The seller-lessee reports the sales proceeds as a liability, continues to report the real estate or the real estate and equipment as an asset, and continues to depreciate the property. [FAS98, ¶34]

.160I If a sale-leaseback transaction accounted for as a financing subsequently qualifies for sales recognition under this section and Section R10, the transaction is then recorded using sale-leaseback accounting, and the cumulative change in the related balance sheet accounts is included in the computation of the gain recognized in accordance with the provisions of paragraph .160A of this section. In addition, the leaseback is classified and accounted for in accordance with paragraph .103 of this section as if the sale had been recognized at the inception of the lease. If the leaseback meets one of the criteria for classification as a capital lease, the related lease accounts, including accumulated amortization, are established as of the date the sale is recognized to reflect accumulated amortization and interest that would have been charged to expense had the lease been recorded at its inception. The change in the related lease accounts from the inception of the lease to the date the sale is recognized is included in the gain recognized in accordance with paragraph .160A of this section. [FAS98, ¶35]

Example 3—Sale-Leaseback Transaction (with Seller-Lessee Providing Financing) Accounted for as a Financing with Subsequent Sales Recognition and the Leaseback Classified as an Operating Lease

.160J Company C (a seller-lessee) sells one of its older special-purpose buildings at its principal manufacturing facility to a buyer-lessor for $950,000 (the fair value of the property as determined by an independent third-party appraisal) and enters into an agreement to lease the building back for 5 years at $100,000 per year. In addition, the agreement includes an option that allows the seller-lessee to renew the lease for an additional 5 years at $100,000 per year (estimated to be the then fair-market rental). The lease agreement also includes a fair value repurchase option during the initial lease term, and the seller-lessee guarantees that the residual value of the property will be no less than $920,000 at the end of the initial lease period. The special-purpose building has a historical cost of $3,510,000 and accumulated depreciation at the date of the transaction of $2,660,000.

Depreciation expense is $70,000 per year. In exchange for the building, the seller-lessee receives $50,000 and a 10-year $900,000 recourse note with a 10 percent annual interest rate. [FAS98, ¶36]

.160K The seller-lessee accounts for this transaction as a financing because of the continuing involvement associated with the guarantee and the repurchase option. At the end of year 5, the seller-lessee exercises the renewal option, and the continuing involvement with the property is no longer at issue because the repurchase option and the guarantee no longer exist. The seller-lessee recognizes the transaction as a sale and classifies the leaseback as an operating lease because none of the criteria of paragraph .103 of this section is met. [FAS98, ¶37] [Exhibit 160E presents the calculation of the total gain and the portion to be recognized in each period. Exhibit 160F presents the related journal entries. Exhibit 160G presents balance sheet information.]

Exhibit 160E

Recognition of the Gain on the Transaction in Example 3

Calculation of the Gain

Sales price (at inception)	$ 950,000
Cost less accumulated depreciation (end of year 5)	500,000
	450,000
Adjustments required by the provisions of this section:	
Rent charged to the finance obligation account in years 1-5	(500,000)
Interest expense charged to income during years 1-5	82,405
Interest income credited to the finance obligation account in years 1-5	387,595
Total gain to be recognized	$ 420,000

Under the provisions of Section R10 and absent the leaseback, a gain of $420,000 would be recognized at the end of year 5 under the full accrual method.

Exhibit 160E (continued)

Allocation of Gain Recognition under This Section

Period Recognized	Year 5 Gain
Year 5	$ 34,060*
Year 6	77,188
Year 7	77,188
Year 8	77,188
Year 9	77,188
Year 10	77,188
Total	$420,000

*Represents the amount by which the total gain to be recognized exceeds the present value of the future minimum lease payments discounted at the seller-lessee's incremental borrowing rate, assumed to be 9.301595 percent ($420,000 – $385,940 = $34,060).

[FAS98, ¶37, Illustration 5]

Exhibit 160F

Journal Entries for Example 3

	Debit	Credit
At inception:		
Cash	50,000	
Finance obligation		50,000
To record the receipt of the down payment on the property		
Recurring journal entries in years 1-5:		
Cash	146,471	
Finance obligation		146,471
To record the receipt of collections on the buyer-lessor's note (the annual payment required for a 10-year $900,000 note)		
Depreciation expense	70,000	
Accumulated depreciation		70,000
To record the depreciation expense		

Exhibit 160F (continued)

	Debit	Credit
Nonrecurring journal entries:		
Year 1		
Finance obligation	94,972	
Interest expense	5,028	
Cash		100,000
To record the lease payments (Interest expense is calculated under the interest method using an effective yield of 10.0562 percent and the guaranteed residual value as the last payment.)		
Year 2		
Finance obligation	89,793	
Interest expense	10,207	
Cash		100,000
To record the lease payments		
Year 3		
Finance obligation	84,093	
Interest expense	15,907	
Cash		100,000
To record the lease payments		
Year 4		
Finance obligation	77,820	
Interest expense	22,180	
Cash		100,000
To record the lease payments		
Year 5		
Finance obligation	70,917	
Interest expense	29,083	
Cash		100,000
To record the lease payments		
When the sale is recognized:		
Finance obligation	364,760	
Note receivable	555,240	
Accumulated depreciation	3,010,000	
Property, plant, and equipment		3,510,000
Deferred gain		385,940
Gain on sale		34,060
To record the transaction as a sale		

[FAS98, ¶37, Illustration 6]

Exhibit 160G

Annual Balances in the Related Balance Sheet Accounts for Example 3

(1)	(2)	(3)	(4)	(5)	(6)	(7)	(8)
					Memo Entries Only in Years 1-5		
Period	Finance Obligation	Property, Plant, and Equipment	Accumulated Depreciation	Deferred Gain	Deferred Interest Income	Gross Note Receivable	Net Note Receivable
At inception	$ 50,000	$3,510,000	$2,660,000	$ 0	$564,710	$1,464,710	$900,000
Year 1	101,499	3,510,000	2,730,000	0	474,710	1,318,239	843,529
Year 2	158,177	3,510,000	2,800,000	0	390,357	1,171,768	781,411
Year 3	220,555	3,510,000	2,870,000	0	312,215	1,025,297	713,082
Year 4	289,206	3,510,000	2,940,000	0	240,907	878,826	637,919
Year 5	364,760	3,510,000	3,010,000	0	177,115	732,355	555,240
After sale is recognized	0	0	0	385,940	177,115	732,355	555,240
Year 6	0	0	0	308,752	121,591	585,884	464,293
Year 7	0	0	0	231,564	75,162	439,413	364,251
Year 8	0	0	0	154,376	38,736	292,942	254,206
Year 9	0	0	0	77,188	13,316	146,471	133,155
Year 10	0	0	0	0	0	0	0

Computations:

Column (2)	Collections on the buyer-lessor's note net of payments on the lease applied to the finance obligation account.
Column (3)	Plant balance at inception of lease.
Column (4)	Accumulated depreciation at inception of lease plus annual depreciation expense.
Column (5)	Deferred gain less amounts recognized annually per Exhibit 160E.
Column (6)	Column 7 less column 8.
Column (7)	Balance of remaining payments on the buyer-lessor's note.
Column (8)	The present value of the remaining note payments discounted at 10 percent.

[FAS98, ¶37, Illustration 7]

Example 4—Sale-Leaseback Transaction (All Cash) Accounted for as a Financing with Subsequent Sales Recognition

.160L Company D (a seller-lessee) sells the building at one of its manufacturing facilities to a buyer-lessor for $950,000 (the fair value of the property as determined by an independent third-party appraisal) and enters into an agreement to lease the building back for 5 years at $100,000 per year. In addition, the seller-lessee has an option to renew the lease for an additional 5 years at $110,000 (estimated to be the then fair-market rental). The lease agreement also includes a fair value repurchase option, and the seller-lessee guarantees that the residual value of the property will be no less than $950,000 at the end of the initial lease period. The property has a historical cost of $1,200,000 and accumulated depreciation at the date of the transaction of $400,000. Depreciation expense is $80,000 per year. [FAS98, ¶38]

.160M Because of the continuing involvement associated with the guarantee and the repurchase option, the seller-lessee accounts for this transaction as a financing in accordance with the provisions of this section. At the inception of the lease, it is known that the seller-lessee is developing a new manufacturing process that will require a different manufacturing facility. The new technology becomes available at the end of the initial lease term, and the seller-lessee vacates the property. The fair value of the property (as determined by an independent third-party appraisal) at that time is $915,000. The seller-lessee honors the $950,000 guarantee of the property by paying the buyer-lessor $35,000 and recognizes the sale of the property. [FAS98, ¶39] [Exhibits 160H, 160I, and 160J present the calculation of the gain before the effect of the guarantee, the related journal entries, and balance sheet information, respectively.]

Exhibit 160H

Recognition of the Gain on the Transaction in Example 4

Calculation of the Gain before the Effect of the Guarantee

Sales price (at inception)	$950,000
Cost less accumulated depreciation (end of year 5)	400,000
Total gain to be recognized	$550,000

[FAS98, ¶39, Illustration 8]

Exhibit 160I

Journal Entries for Example 4

	Debit	Credit
At inception:		
Cash	950,000	
Finance obligation		950,000
To record the receipt of the proceeds from the sale of the property		
Recurring journal entries in years 1-5:		
Depreciation expense	80,000	
Accumulated depreciation		80,000
To record the depreciation expense		
Interest expense	100,000	
Cash		100,000
To record the lease payments (Interest expense is calculated under the interest method using an effective yield of 10.5263 percent and the guaranteed residual as the last payment.)		
When the sale is recognized:		
Accumulated depreciation	800,000	
Finance lease obligation	950,000	
Property, plant, and equipment		1,200,000
Cash		35,000
Gain on sale of property		515,000
To record the transaction as a sale		

Under the provisions of this section, gain deferral is not required because the seller-lessee no longer occupies or otherwise benefits from the property and no longer has any guarantee or other continuing involvement.

[FAS98, ¶39, Illustration 9]

Exhibit 160J

Annual Balances in the Related Balance Sheet Accounts for Example 4

(1) Period	(2) Finance Obligation	(3) Property, Plant, and Equipment	(4) Accumulated Depreciation
At inception	$950,000	$1,200,000	$400,000
Year 1	950,000	1,200,000	480,000
Year 2	950,000	1,200,000	560,000
Year 3	950,000	1,200,000	640,000
Year 4	950,000	1,200,000	720,000
Year 5	950,000	1,200,000	800,000
When property is vacated	0	0	0

[FAS98, ¶39, Illustration 10]

Illustration of the Accounting for a Leveraged Lease in a Business Combination

.161 This paragraph illustrates one way that a lessor's investment in a leveraged lease might be valued by the acquiring enterprise in a business combination and the subsequent accounting for the investment. The elements of accounting and reporting illustrated for this example are as follows:

a. Leveraged lease example—terms and assumptions, Exhibit 161A
b. Acquiring enterprise's cash flow analysis by years, Exhibit 161B
c. Acquiring enterprise's valuation of investment in the leveraged lease, Exhibit 161C
d. Acquiring enterprise's allocation of annual cash flow to investment and income, Exhibit 161D
e. Journal entry for recording allocation of purchase price to net investment in the leveraged lease, Exhibit 161E
f. Journal entries for the year ending December 31, 19Y4 (year 10 of the lease), Exhibit 161F.

[FIN21, ¶19]

Exhibit 161A

Leveraged Lease Example
Term and Assumptions

Cost of leased asset (equipment)	$1,000,000.
Lease term	15 years, dating from January 1, 19X5.
Lease rental payments	$90,000 per year (payable last day of each year).
Residual value	$200,000 estimated to be realized 1 year after lease termination.
Financing:	
Equity investment by lessor	$400,000.
Long-term nonrecourse debt	$600,000 bearing interest at 9% and repayable in annual installments (on last day of each year) of $74,435.30.
Depreciation allowable to lessor for income tax purposes	7-year ADR life using double-declining-balance method for the first 2 years (with the half-year convention election applied in the first year) and sum-of-years-digits' method for remaining life, depreciated to $100,000 salvage value.
Lessor's income tax rate (federal and state)	50.4% (assumed to continue in existence throughout the term of the lease).
Investment tax credit	10% of equipment cost or $100,000 (realized by the lessor on last day of first year of lease).
Initial direct costs	For simplicity, initial direct costs have not been included in the illustration.
Date of business combination	January 1, 19X2.
Tax status of business combination	Nontaxable transaction.
Appropriate interest rate for valuing net-of-tax return on investment	4½%

[FIN21, ¶19]

Exhibit 161B

Acquiring Enterprise's Cash Flow Analysis by Years

	1	2	3	4	5	6	7
Year	Gross Lease Rentals and Residual Value	Depreciation (for Income Tax Purposes)	Loan Interest Payments	Taxable Income (Col. 1–2–3)	Income Tax (Charges) (Col. 4×50.4%)	Loan Principal Payments	Annual Cash Flow (Col. 1–3+5–6)
8	$ 90,000	—	$ 37,079	$ 52,921	$ (26,672)	$ 37,357	$ (11,108)
9	90,000	—	33,717	56,283	(28,367)	40,719	(12,803)
10	90,000	—	30,052	59,948	(30,214)	44,383	(14,649)
11	90,000	—	26,058	63,942	(32,227)	48,378	(16,663)
12	90,000	—	21,704	68,296	(34,421)	52,732	(18,857)
13	90,000	—	16,957	73,043	(36,813)	57,478	(21,248)
14	90,000	—	11,785	78,215	(39,420)	62,651	(23,856)
15	90,000	—	6,145	83,855	(42,263)	68,290	(26,698)
16	200,000	$100,000	—	100,000	(50,400)	—	149,600
Totals	$920,000	$100,000	$183,497	$636,503	$(320,797)	$411,988	$ 3,718

[FIN21, ¶19]

Exhibit 161C

Acquiring Enterprise's Valuation of Investment in the Leveraged Lease

Cash Flow	Present Value at 4½% Net-of-Tax Rate
1. Rentals receivable (net of principal and interest on the nonrecourse debt) ($15,564.70 at the end of each year for 8 years)	$ 102,663
2. Estimated residual value ($200,000 realizable at the end of 9 years)	134,581
3. Future tax payments (various amounts payable over 9 years—refer to Exhibit 161B)	(253,489)
Net present value	$ (16,245)

[FIN21, ¶19]

Exhibit 161D

Acquiring Enterprise's Allocation of Annual Cash Flow to Investment and Income

	1	2	3	4	5	6
		Annual Cash Flow			Components of Income[b]	
Year	Net Investment at Beginning of Year	Total from Exhibit 161B Col. 7	Allocated to Investment	Allocated to Income[a]	Pretax Income	Tax Effect of Pretax Income
8	$ (16,245)	$ (11,108)	$ (11,108)	—	—	—
9	(5,137)	(12,803)	(12,803)	—	—	—
10	7,666	(14,649)	(14,973)	$ 324	$ 5,530	$ (5,206)
11	22,639	(16,663)	(17,621)	958	16,353	(15,395)
12	40,260	(18,857)	(20,561)	1,704	29,087	(27,383)
13	60,821	(21,248)	(23,822)	2,574	43,937	(41,363)
14	84,643	(23,856)	(27,439)	3,583	61,160	(57,577)
15	112,082	(26,698)	(31,443)	4,745	80,995	(76,250)
16	143,525	149,600	143,525	6,075	103,698	(97,623)
Totals		$ 3,718	$ (16,245)	$19,963	$340,760	$(320,797)

[a]Lease income is recognized as 4.233 percent of the unrecovered investment at the beginning of each year in which the net investment is positive. The rate is that rate which when applied to the net investment in the years in which the net investment is positive will distribute the net income (net cash flow) to those years. The rate for allocation used in this exhibit is calculated by a trial and error process. The allocation is calculated based upon an initial estimate of the rate as a starting point. If the total thus allocated to income (column 4) differs under the estimated rate from the net cash flow (column 2 less column 3), the estimated rate is increased or decreased, as appropriate, to derive a revised allocation. This process is repeated until a rate is selected which develops a total amount allocated to income that is precisely equal to the net cash flow. As a practical matter, a computer program is used to calculate Exhibit 161D under successive iterations until the correct rate is determined.

[b]Each component is allocated among the years of positive net investment in proportion to the allocation of net income in column 4. Journal entry 2 in Exhibit 161F of this paragraph includes an example of this computation.

[FIN21, ¶19]

Exhibit 161E

Illustrative Journal Entry for Recording Allocation of Purchase Price to Net Investment in the Leveraged Lease

	Debit	Credit
Rentals receivable (Exhibit 161B, total of column 1 less residual value, less totals of columns 3 and 6)	$124,515	
Estimated residual value (Exhibit 161A)	200,000	
Purchase price allocation clearing account (Exhibit 161C, present value)	16,245	
Unearned and deferred income (Exhibit 161C, present value, less total of rentals receivable and estimated residual value)		$340,760

[FIN21, ¶19]

Exhibit 161F

Illustrative Journal Entries for the Year Ending December 31, 19Y4

Third Year of Operation after the Business Combination
(Year 10 of the Lease)

	Debit	Credit
Journal Entry 1		
Cash	$15,565	
Rentals receivable (Exhibit 161B, column 1, less columns 3 and 6)		$15,565
Collection of year's net rental		
Journal Entry 2		
Unearned and deferred income	$ 5,530	
Income from leveraged leases (Exhibit 161D, column 5)		$ 5,530
Recognition of pretax income for the year allocated in the same proportion as the allocation of total income, [computed as follows:]		

$$\frac{\$324}{\$19,963} \times \$340,760 = \$5,530$$

	Debit	Credit
Journal Entry 3		
Deferred taxes (Exhibit 161B, column 5, less Exhibit 161D, column 6)	$25,008	
Income tax expense (Exhibit 161D, column 6)	$ 5,206	
Cash (Exhibit 161B, column 5)		$30,214
To record payment of tax for the year.		

[FIN21, ¶19]

Illustration of Lessor and Lessee Accounting Required by Paragraphs .110 and .113(g) regarding Refunding of Tax-Exempt Debt

.162 Exhibits 163B and 163C illustrate the application of the requirements of paragraphs .110(a) and .113(g)(1) when a refunding of tax-exempt debt results in a change in the provisions of a lease agreement and the revised lease is classified as a direct financing lease by the lessor and as a capital lease by the lessee. [FAS22, ¶17]

Computation Information

.163 Exhibit 163A summarizes the total debt service requirements of the serial obligation to be refunded and of the refunding obligation. It is presumed that the perceived economic advantages of the refunding results from the lower interest rate applicable to the refunding obligation. The resulting reduction in total debt service requirements will be passed through to the lessee by changing the terms of the lease to conform with the debt service requirements of the refunding obligation. All costs that have been or that will be incurred by the lessor in connection with the refunding transaction will be passed through to the lessee. [FAS22, ¶17]

Exhibit 163A

Fifteen-Year Serial Debt Service Requirements ($000 omitted)

Obligation to Be Refunded			Refunding Obligation*			
Face Amount	Interest 7%	Total	Face Amount	Interest 5%	Total	Difference
$50,000	$32,300	$82,300	$52,000	$23,150	$75,150	$7,150

*The face amount of the refunding obligation ($52,000,000) is equal to the face amount of the obligation to be refunded ($50,000,000) plus the redemption premium applicable to the obligation to be refunded ($1,500,000) and the costs of issuance ($500,000).

[FAS22, ¶17]

Exhibit 163B

Lessor Accounting

Computation of Required Adjustments to Reflect Changes in the Terms of a Lease Resulting from a Refunding of Tax-Exempt Debt

Adjustment to Balance of Minimum Lease Payments Receivable:	
Present balance of minimum lease payments receivable (equal to debt service requirements of obligation to be refunded)	$82,300,000
Minimum lease payments receivable under revised agreement (equal to debt service requirements of refunding obligation)	75,150,000
Adjustment to reflect reduction in minimum lease payments receivable	$ 7,150,000
Adjustment to Unearned Income:	
Change in the sum of the present value of the two components of the gross investment using the interest rate applicable to each agreement	$ 2,000,000
Change in sum of the present value of the two components of the gross investment using the interest rate applicable to each agreement	7,150,000
Adjustment to reflect reduction in balance of unearned income	$ 9,150,000

Summary of Adjustments ($000 omitted):

	Minimum Lease Payments Receivable	Unearned Income	Net Investment
Balance before refunding	$82,300	$32,300	$50,000
Adjustment	(7,150)	(9,150)	2,000
Balance after refunding	$75,150	$23,150	$52,000

Exhibit 163B (continued)

Journal Entries to Record the Refunding and Changes in the Terms of the Lease Resulting from Refunding of Tax-Exempt Debt

	Debit	Credit
Recoverable deferred issue costs	500,000	
Loss resulting from refunding of tax-exempt debt	1,500,000	
7% outstanding obligation	50,000,000	
5% refunding obligation		52,000,000
To record loss from refunding $50,000,000—7% obligation with $52,000,000—5% refunding obligation in accordance with the provisions of Section D18.		
Unearned income	9,150,000	
Minimum lease payments receivable		7,150,000
Gain resulting from adjustment of lease terms		1,500,000
Recoverable deferred issue costs		500,000
To adjust unearned income by the amount required to adjust the net investment in the lease to the sum of the present values of the two components of the gross investment based on the interest rate applicable to the revised lease agreement in accordance with this section.		

[FAS22, ¶17]

Exhibit 163C

Lessee Accounting

Computation of Required Adjustment to Lease Obligation to Reflect Changes in the Terms of the Lease Resulting from Refunding of Tax-Exempt Debt

Adjustment to Balance of Lease Obligation:	
Present balance of lease obligation under original agreement	$50,000,000
Present value of future minimum lease payments under revised agreement	51,500,000
Adjustment to Lease Obligation	$ 1,500,000

Journal Entry to Record Adjustment to Lease Obligation Resulting from Refunding of Tax-Exempt Debt

	Debit	Credit
Loss resulting from revision to lease agreement	1,500,000	
Obligation under capital lease		1,500,000
To record the loss resulting from changes in the lease terms resulting from a refunding of tax-exempt debt. For purposes of calculating the present value of the future minimum lease payments, deferred issue costs were considered as additional interest in determining the effective interest rate applicable to the revised agreement.		

[FAS22, ¶17]

Illustrations of Determining Contingent Rentals

.164 Paragraphs .165 and .166 illustrate the application of the provisions of this section in determining contingent rentals. The examples do not comprehend all possible combinations of circumstances. [FAS29, ¶15]

.165 Paragraph .404 indicates that lease payments that depend on an existing index or rate, such as the prime interest rate, shall be included in the minimum lease payments based on the index or rate existing at the inception of the lease. As an example, an equipment lease could stipulate a monthly base rental of $2,000 and a monthly supplemental rental of $15 for each percentage point in the prime interest rate in effect at the beginning of each month. If the prime interest rate at the inception of the lease is 10 percent, minimum lease payments would be based on a monthly rental of $2,150 [$2,000 + ($15 × 10) = $2,150]. If the lease term is 48 months and no executory costs are included in the rentals, minimum lease payments would be $103,200 [$2,150 × 48]. If the lease is classified as a capital lease and the prime interest rate subsequently increases to 11 percent, the $15 increase in the monthly rentals would be a contingent rental included in the determination of income as it accrues. If the prime interest rate subsequently decreases to 9 percent, the $15 reduction in the monthly rentals would affect income as accruable. In the case of either the increase or decrease, minimum lease payments would continue to be $103,200. [FAS29, ¶16]

.166 Paragraph .404 also indicates that lease payments that depend on a factor directly related to the future use of the leased property, such as machine hours of use or sales volume during the lease term, are contingent rentals and accordingly, are excluded from minimum lease payments in their entirety. For example, a lease agreement for retail store space could stipulate a monthly base rental of $200 and a monthly supplemental rental of ¼ of one percent of monthly sales volume during the lease term. Even if the lease agreement is a renewal for store space that had averaged monthly sales of $25,000 for the past 2 years, minimum lease payments would include only the $200 monthly base rental; the supplemental rental is a contingent rental that is excluded from minimum lease payments. The future sales for the lease term do not exist at the inception of the lease, and future rentals would be limited to $200 per month if the store were subsequently closed and no sales were made thereafter. [FAS29, ¶17]

Glossary

.401 **Bargain purchase option.** A provision allowing the lessee, at [the lessee's] option, to purchase the leased property for a price that is sufficiently lower than the expected fair value of the property at the date the option becomes exercisable that exercise of the option appears, at the inception of the lease, to be reasonably assured. [FAS13, ¶5(d)]

.402 **Bargain renewal option.** A provision allowing the lessee, at [the lessee's] option, to renew the lease for a rental sufficiently lower than the fair rental[401] of the property at the date the option becomes exercisable that exercise of the option appears, at the inception of the lease, to be reasonably assured. [FAS13, ¶5(e)]

.403 **Capital lease.** [Refer to paragraph .102(a)(1).]

.404 **Contingent rentals.** The increases or decreases in lease payments that result from changes occurring subsequent to the inception of the lease in the factors (other than the passage of time) on which lease payments are based, except as provided in the following sentence. Any escalation of minimum lease payments relating to increases in construction or acquisition cost of the leased property or for increases in some measure of cost or value during the construction or preconstruction period, as discussed in footnote 13, shall be excluded from contingent rentals. Lease payments that depend on a factor directly related to the future use of the leased property, such as machine hours of use or sales volume during the lease term, are contingent rentals and, accordingly, are excluded from minimum lease payments in their entirety. However, lease payments that depend on an existing index or rate, such as the consumer price index or the prime interest rate, shall be included in minimum lease payments based on the index or rate existing at the inception of the lease; any increases or decreases in lease payments that result from subsequent changes in the index or rate are contingent rentals and thus affect the determination of income as accruable. [FAS29, ¶11] [Refer to paragraph .1001 for an EITF Issue that provides interpretive guidance on this paragraph.]

.405 **Direct financing leases.** [Refer to paragraph .102(b)(2).]

.406 **Estimated economic life of leased property.** The estimated remaining period during which the property is expected to be economically usable by one or more users, with normal repairs and maintenance, for the purpose for which it was intended at the inception of the lease, without limitation by the lease term. [FAS13, ¶5(g)]

---

[401] *Fair rental* in this context shall mean the expected rental for equivalent property under similar terms and conditions. [FAS13, ¶5, fn2]

.407 **Estimated residual value of leased property.** The estimated fair value of the leased property at the end of the lease term. [FAS13, ¶5(h)]

.408 **Executory costs.** [Those costs] such as insurance, maintenance, and taxes [incurred for leased property, whether paid by the lessor or lessee. Amounts paid by a lessee in consideration for a guarantee from an unrelated third party of the residual value are also executory costs. If executory costs are paid by a lessor, any lessor's profit on those costs is considered the same as executory costs.] [FAS13, ¶7 and ¶10]

.409 **Fair value of the leased property.** The price for which the property could be sold in an arm's-length transaction between unrelated parties. The following are examples of the determination of fair value:

a. When the lessor is a manufacturer or dealer, the fair value of the property at the inception of the lease will ordinarily be its normal selling price, reflecting any volume or trade discounts that may be applicable. However, the determination of fair value shall be made in light of market conditions prevailing at the time, which may indicate that the fair value of the property is less than the normal selling price and, in some instances, less than the cost of the property.
b. When the lessor is not a manufacturer or dealer, the fair value of the property at the inception of the lease will ordinarily be its cost, reflecting any volume or trade discounts that may be applicable. However, when there has been a significant lapse of time between the acquisition of the property by the lessor and the inception of the lease, the determinaton of fair value shall be made in light of market conditions prevailing at the inception of the lease, which may indicate that the fair value of the property is greater or less than its cost or carrying amount, if different (refer to paragraph .102).

[FAS13, ¶5(c)]

.410 **Inception of the lease.** The date of the lease agreement or commitment, if earlier.[402] For purposes of this definition, a commitment shall be in writing, signed by the parties in interest to the transaction, and shall specifically set forth the principal pro-

[402]If a master lease agreement specifies that the lessee must take a minimum number of units or dollar value of equipment and if all other principal provisions are stated, the inception of the lease is the date of the master lease agreement with respect to the specified minimum. The inception of the lease for equipment *take-downs* in excess of the specified minimum is the date that the lessee orders the equipment because the lessee does not agree to lease the equipment until that date. To the extent that lease payments for required take-downs are based on value at the date of the take-down, the lease, in effect, has a preacquisition period escalator provision based on value. Footnotes 18, 24, 31, and 35 address that situation. If a master lease agreement does not require the lessee to take down any minimum quantity or dollar value of equipment, the agreement is merely an offer by the lessor to rent equipment at an agreed price and the inception of the lease is the date that the lessee orders the equipment. [FAS23, ¶14]

visions of the transaction. If any of the principal provisions [is] yet to be negotiated, such a preliminary agreement or commitment does not qualify for purposes of this definition. [FAS23, ¶6]

.411 **Initial direct costs.**[402a] Only those costs incurred by the lessor that are (a) costs to originate a lease incurred in transactions with independent third parties that (i) result directly from and are essential to acquire that lease and (ii) would not have been incurred had that leasing transaction not occurred and (b) certain costs directly related to specified activities performed by the lessor for that lease. Those activities are: evaluating the prospective lessee's financial condition; evaluating and recording guarantees, collateral, and other security arrangements; negotiating lease terms; preparing and processing lease documents; and closing the transaction. The costs directly related to those activities shall include only that portion of the employees' total compensation and payroll-related fringe benefits directly related to time spent performing those activities for that lease and other costs related to those activities that would not have been incurred but for that lease. Initial direct costs shall not include costs related to activities performed by the lessor for advertising, soliciting potential lessees, servicing existing leases, and other ancillary activities related to establishing and monitoring credit policies, supervision, and administration. Initial direct costs shall not include administrative costs, rent, depreciation, any other occupancy and equipment costs and employees' compensation and fringe benefits related to activities described in the previous sentence, unsuccessful origination efforts, and idle time. [FAS91, ¶24]

.412 **Interest rate implicit in the lease.** The discount rate that, when applied to (a) the minimum lease payments, excluding that portion of the payments representing executory costs to be paid by the lessor, together with any profit thereon, and (b) the unguaranteed residual value accruing to the benefit of the lessor[403] causes the aggregate present value at the beginning of the lease term to be equal to the fair value of the leased property to the lessor at the inception of the lease, minus any investment tax credit retained by the lessor and expected to be realized by him. (This definition does not necessarily purport to include all factors that a lessor might recognize in determining his rate of return, for example, refer to paragraph .146.) [FAS13, ¶5(k)]

.413 **Lease.** An agreement conveying the right to use property, plant, or equipment (land or depreciable assets or both) usually for a stated period of time. [FAS13, ¶1]

[402a]Initial direct cost shall be offset by nonrefundable fees that are yield adjustments as prescribed in Section L20. [FAS91, ¶24, fn*] The provisions of paragraphs .104 through .108 of Section L20 apply to lessors in determining the net amount of *initial direct costs*. [FAS91, ¶23] [Refer to paragraph .1001 for an EITF Issue that provides interpretive guidance on this footnote.]

[403]If the lessor is not entitled to any excess of the amount realized on disposition of the property over a guaranteed amount, no unguaranteed residual value would accrue to the lessor's benefit. [FAS13, ¶5(k), fn8]

.414 **Lease term.** The fixed noncancelable term of the lease plus (a) all periods, if any, covered by bargain renewal options (as defined in paragraph .402), (b) all periods, if any, for which failure to renew the lease imposes a penalty (as defined in paragraph .418A) on the lessee in such amount that a renewal appears, at the inception of the lease, to be reasonably assured, (c) all periods, if any, covered by ordinary renewal options[405] during which a guarantee by the lessee of the lessor's debt directly or indirectly related to the leased property[405a] is expected to be in effect or a loan from the lessee to the lessor directly or indirectly related to the leased property is expected to be outstanding, (d) all periods, if any, covered by ordinary renewal options preceding the date as of which a bargain purchase option (as defined in paragraph .401) is exercisable, and (e) all periods, if any, representing renewals or extensions of the lease at the lessor's option; however, in no case shall the lease term be assumed to extend beyond the date a bargain purchase option becomes exercisable. A lease that is cancelable (1) only upon the occurrence of some remote contingency, (2) only with the permission of the lessor, (3) only if the lessee enters into a new lease with the same lessor, or (4) only if the lessee incurs a penalty in such amount that continuation of the lease appears, at inception, reasonably assured shall be considered "noncancelable" for purposes of this definition. [FAS98, ¶22(a)]

.415 **Lessee's incremental borrowing rate.** The rate that, at the inception of the lease, the lessee would have incurred to borrow over a similar term the funds necessary to purchase the leased asset.[406] [FAS13, ¶5(l)]

.416 **Leveraged lease.** [Refer to paragraphs .102(b)(3) and .144.]

.417 **Minimum lease payments.**

a. *From the standpoint of the lessee:* The payments that the lessee is obligated to make or can be required to make in connection with the leased property. [FAS13, ¶5(j)] (Contingent rentals, as defined in paragraph .404, shall be excluded from minimum

---

[[404]Deleted 5/88 because of FASB Statement 98, *Accounting for Leases: Sale-Leaseback Transactions Involving Real Estate, Sales-Type Leases of Real Estate, Definition of the Lease Term, and Initial Direct Costs of Direct Financing Leases.*]

[[405]Paragraphs .501 through .505 address fiscal funding clauses in lease agreements.]

[405a]The phrase *indirectly related to the leased property* is used in this paragraph to describe provisions or conditions that in substance are guarantees of the lessor's debt or loans to the lessor by the lessee that are related to the leased property but are structured in such a manner that they do not represent a direct guarantee or loan. Examples include a party related to the lessee guaranteeing the lessor's debt on behalf of the lessee, or the lessee financing the lessor's purchase of the leased asset using collateral other than the leased property. [FAS98, ¶22(a)]

[[406]Paragraphs .509 through .511 further discuss the interest rate used in calculating the present value of the minimum lease payments.]

lease payments.) [FAS29, ¶10] However, a guarantee by the lessee of the lessor's debt and the lessee's obligation to pay (apart from the rental payments) executory costs in connection with the leased property shall be excluded. If the lease contains a bargain purchase option, only the minimum rental payments over the lease term (as defined in paragraph .413) and the payment called for by the bargain purchase option shall be included in the minimum lease payments. Otherwise, minimum lease payments include the following:

(1) The minimum rental payments called for by the lease over the lease term.

(2) Any guarantee by the lessee or any party related to the lessee of the residual value at the expiration of the lease term, whether or not payment of the guarantee constitutes a purchase of the leased property.[407] When the lessor has the right to require the lessee to purchase the property at termination of the lease for a certain or determinable amount, that amount shall be considered a lessee guarantee. When the lessee agrees to make up any deficiency[408] below a stated amount in the lessor's realization of the residual value, the guarantee to be included in the minimum lease payments shall be the stated amount,[409] rather than an estimate of the deficiency to be made up.

(3) Any payment that the lessee must make or can be required to make upon failure to renew or extend the lease at the expiration of the lease term, whether or not the payment would constitute a purchase of the lease property. In this connection, it should be noted that the definition of lease term (refer to paragraph .413) includes "all periods, if any, for which failure to renew the lease imposes a penalty

[407]A guarantee of the residual value obtained by the lessee from an unrelated third party for the benefit of the lessor shall not be used to reduce the amount of the lessee's minimum lease payments except to the extent that the lessor explicitly releases the lessee from obligation, including secondary obligation if the guarantor defaults, to make up a residual value deficiency. Amounts paid in consideration for a guarantee by an unrelated third party are executory costs and are not included in the lessee's minimum lease payments. [FIN19, ¶5]

[408]A lease provision requiring the lessee to make up a residual value deficiency that is attributable to damage, extraordinary wear and tear, or excessive usage is similar to contingent rentals in that the amount is not determinable at the inception of the lease. Such a provision does not constitute a lessee guarantee of the residual value. [FIN19, ¶3]

[409]If a lease limits the amount of the lessee's obligation to make up a residual value deficiency to an amount less than the stipulated residual value of the leased property at the end of the lease term, the amount of the lessee's guarantee to be included in minimum lease payments shall be limited to the specified maximum deficiency the lessee can be required to make up. The *stated amount* is the specified maximum deficiency that the lessee is obligated to make up. If that maximum deficiency clearly exceeds any reasonable estimate of a deficiency that might be expected to arise in normal circumstances, the lessor's risk associated with the portion of the residual in excess of the maximum may appear to be negligible. However, the fact remains that the lessor must look to the resale market or elsewhere rather than to the lessee to recover the unguaranteed portion of the stipulated residual value of the leased property. The lessee has not guaranteed full recovery of the residual value, and the parties should not base their accounting on the assumption that the lessee has guaranteed it. [FIN19, ¶4]

on the lessee in an amount such that renewal appears, at the inception of the lease, to be reasonably assured." If the lease term has been extended because of that provision, the related penalty shall not be included in minimum lease payments. [Refer to paragraph .1001 for an EITF Issue that provides interpretive guidance on subparagraph .417(a).]

b. *From the standpoint of the lessor:* The payments described above plus any guarantee of the residual value or of rental payments beyond the lease term by a third party unrelated to either the lessee or the lessor,[410] provided the third party is financially capable of discharging the obligations that may arise from the guarantee. [FAS13, ¶5(j)]

[Refer to paragraph .1001 for an EITF Issue that provides interpretive guidance on this paragraph.]

.417A [Deleted 1/89 and renumbered .417C.]

.417B **Money-over-money lease transaction.** [Refer to paragraph .542.]

.417C **Nonrecourse financing.** Lending or borrowing activities in which the creditor does not have general recourse to the debtor but rather has recourse only to the property used for collateral in the transaction or other specific property. [FAS98, ¶70]

.418 **Operating lease.** [Refer to paragraphs .102(a)(2) and 102(b)(4).]

.418A **Penalty.** Any requirement that is imposed or can be imposed on the lessee by the lease agreement or by factors outside the lease agreement to disburse cash, incur or assume a liability, perform services, surrender or transfer an asset or rights to an asset or otherwise forego an economic benefit, or suffer an economic detriment. Factors to consider when determining if an economic detriment may be incurred include, but are not limited to, the uniqueness of purpose or location of the property, the availability of a comparable replacement property, the relative importance or significance of the property to the continuation of the lessee's line of business or service to its customers, the existence of leasehold improvements or other assets whose value would be impaired by the lessee vacating or discontinuing use of the leased property, adverse tax consequences, and the ability or willingness of the lessee to bear the cost associated with relocation or replacement of the leased property at market rental rates or to tolerate other parties using the leased property. [FAS98, ¶22(b)]

.419 **Related parties.** A parent company and its subsidiaries, an owner enterprise and its joint ventures (corporate or otherwise) and partnerships, and an investor (including a

[410]If the guarantor is related to the lessor, the residual value shall be considered as unguaranteed. [FAS13, ¶5(j), fn8]

natural person) and its investees, provided that the parent company, owner enterprise, or investor has the ability to exercise significant influence over operating and financial policies of the related party, as significant influence is defined in Section I82, paragraph .104. In addition to the examples of significant influence set forth in that paragraph, significant influence may be exercised through guarantees of indebtedness, extensions of credit, or through ownership of warrants, debt obligations, or other securities. If two or more enterprises are subject to the significant influence of a parent company, owner enterprise, investor (including a natural person), or common officers or directors, those enterprises shall be considered related parties with respect to each other. [FAS13, ¶5(a)]

.420 **Renewal or extension of a lease.** [The continuation of a lease agreement beyond the original lease term including] a new lease under which the lessee continues to use the same property. [FAS13, ¶6, fn9]

.420A **Sale-leaseback accounting.** For purposes of this section, a method of accounting for a sale-leaseback transaction in which the seller-lessee records the sale, removes all property and related liabilities from its balance sheet, recognizes gain or loss from the sale, and classifies the leaseback in accordance with this section. [FAS98, ¶70]

.420B **Sales recognition.** Any method that is described in Section R10 as a method to record a transaction involving real estate, other than the deposit method, or the methods to record transactions accounted for as financing, leasing, or profit-sharing arrangements. Profit recognition methods described in Section R10 commonly used to record transactions involving real estate include, but are not limited to, the full accrual method, the installment method, the cost recovery method, and the reduced profit method. [FAS98, ¶70]

.421 **Sales-type lease.** [Refer to paragraph .102(b)(1).]

.422 **Unguaranteed residual value.** The estimated residual value of the leased property exclusive of any portion guaranteed by the lessee or by any party related to the lessee or by a third party unrelated to the lessor.[411] [FAS13, ¶5(i)]

.423 **Unrelated parties.** [All parties that are not related parties as defined above.]

.424 **Wrap lease transaction.** [Refer to paragraph .544.]

[411]If the guarantor is related to the lessor, the residual value shall be considered as unguaranteed. [FAS13, ¶5(i), fn4]

[illegible]

[illegible] Removal of exterior [illegible]

[illegible] accounting [illegible]

[illegible]

[illegible]

[illegible]

[illegible]

[illegible]

[illegible]

Supplemental Guidance

Fiscal Funding Clauses in Lease Agreements

.501 *Question*—What effect, if any, should the existence of a fiscal funding clause in a lease agreement have on the classification of the lease under this section? [FTB79-10, ¶1]

.502 *Background*—A fiscal funding clause is commonly found in a lease agreement in which the lessee is a governmental unit. A fiscal funding clause generally provides that the lease is cancelable if the legislature or other funding authority does not appropriate the funds necessary for the governmental unit to fulfill its obligations under the lease agreement. [FTB79-10, ¶2]

.503 *Response*—[Under] paragraph .413, a cancelable lease, such as a lease containing a fiscal funding clause, [must] be evaluated to determine whether the uncertainty of possible lease cancellation is a remote contingency. That paragraph states that "a lease which is cancelable (1) only upon occurrence of some *remote* contingency . . . shall be considered for purposes of this definition" of lease term. (Emphasis added.) [FTB79-10, ¶3]

.504 In discussing the likelihood of the occurrence of a future event or events to confirm a loss contingency, Section C59, paragraph .104, defines *remote* as relating to conditions when "the chance of the future event or events occurring is slight." The evaluation of the uncertainty of possible lease cancellation should be consistent with that definition. [FTB79-10, ¶4]

.505 The existence of a fiscal funding clause in a lease agreement would necessitate an assessment of the likelihood of lease cancellation through exercise of the fiscal funding clause. If the likelihood of exercise of the fiscal funding clause is assessed as being remote, a lease agreement containing such a clause would be considered a noncancelable lease; otherwise, the lease would be considered cancelable and thus classified as an operating lease. [FTB79-10, ¶5]

.506-.508 [Deleted 5/88 because of FASB Statement 98, *Accounting for Leases: Sale-Leaseback Transactions Involving Real Estate, Sales-Type Leases of Real Estate, Definition of the Lease Term, and Initial Direct Costs of Direct Financing Leases.*]

Interest Rate Used in Calculating the Present Value of Minimum Lease Payments

.509 *Question*—May a lessee use its secured borrowing rate in calculating the present value of minimum lease payments in applying the provisions of this section? [FTB79-12, ¶1]

.510 *Background*—Paragraph .103(d) requires the lessee to use its incremental borrowing rate (or the lessor's implicit interest rate in certain circumstances) to calculate the present value of minimum lease payments. The incremental borrowing rate is defined in paragraph .414 as "the rate that . . . the lessee would have incurred to borrow over a similar term the funds necessary to purchase the leased asset." [FTB79-12, ¶2]

.511 *Response*—Paragraph .414 does not proscribe the lessee's use of a secured borrowing rate as its incremental borrowing rate if that rate is determinable, reasonable, and consistent with the financing that would have been used in the particular circumstances. [FTB79-12, ¶3]

Applicability of This Section to Current Value Financial Statements

.512 *Question*—Are financial statements prepared on a current value basis exempt from the provisions of this section? [FTB79-13, ¶1]

.513 *Response*—This section would not be inapplicable merely because financial statements are prepared on a current value basis. For example, if at its inception a lease involving property meets one or more of the four criteria of paragraph .103 and both of the criteria of paragraph .104, the lessor would classify the lease as a sales-type or direct financing lease, whichever is appropriate. Subsequently, the carrying amount of the recorded investment in the lease payments receivable would be adjusted in accordance with the valuation techniques employed in preparing the financial statements on a current value basis. [FTB79-13, ¶2]

Upward Adjustment of Guaranteed Residual Values

.514 *Question*—Does the prohibition against upward adjustments of estimated residual values in this section also apply to upward adjustments that result from renegotiations of the guaranteed portions of residual values? [FTB79-14, ¶1]

.515 *Background*—Paragraphs .113(d), .114(d), and .148 require the lessor to review annually the estimated residual value of sales-type leases, direct financing leases, and leveraged leases, respectively. Those paragraphs also contain a provision that prohibits any upward adjustment of the estimated residual value. [FTB79-14, ¶2]

.516 *Response*—The prohibitions of paragraphs .113(d), .114(d), and .148 against upward adjustments to the leased property's estimated residual value are equally applicable to the guaranteed portion. If a lease initially transferred substantially all of the benefits and risks incident to the ownership of the leased property, it would not seem appropriate that the lessor could subsequently increase the benefits that were accounted for as having been retained initially. [FTB79-14, ¶3]

.517 Recording upward adjustments to the leased property's residual value would, in essence, result in recognizing a sale of the residual value interest. In this respect, the prohibition of an upward adjustment in the leased property's residual value is similar to the prohibition in Section C59, paragraph .118, of recognizing gain contingencies because to do so might be recognizing revenue before realization. Realization of the residual value interest might also be contingent on factors, such as the physical condition of the leased property or the requirements and related costs, if any, relating to remarketing agreements at the end of the lease term. [FTB79-14, ¶4]

Accounting for Loss on a Sublease Not Involving the Disposal of a Segment

.518 *Question*—Should a loss on a sublease not involving the disposal of a segment be recognized and how is it determined? [FTB79-15, ¶1]

.519 *Response*—The general principle of recognizing losses on transactions and the applicability of that general principle to contracts that are expected to result in a loss are well established. Accordingly, if costs expected to be incurred under an operating sublease (that is, executory costs and either amortization of the leased asset or rental payments on an operating lease, whichever is applicable) exceed anticipated revenue on the operating sublease, a loss should be recognized by the sublessor. Similarly, a loss should be recognized on a direct financing sublease if the carrying amount of the investment in the sublease exceeds the total of rentals expected to be received and estimated residual values unless the sublessor's tax benefits from the transaction are sufficient to justify that result. [FTB79-15, ¶2]

.520 The absence of explicit reference to accounting for these transactions in this section does not affect the necessity to follow general principles of loss recognition. [FTB79-15, ¶3]

Effect of a Change in Income Tax Rate on the Accounting for Leveraged Leases

.521 *Question*—What effect, if any, does a change in the income tax rate have on the accounting for leveraged leases under this section? [FTB79-16(R), ¶1]

.522 *Background*—Paragraph .148 provides that, when an important assumption changes, the rate of return and the allocation of income shall be recalculated from the inception of the lease, and the change in the recalculated balances of net investment shall be recognized as a gain or loss in the year in which the assumption is changed. [FTB79-16(R), ¶2]

.523 *Response*—The lessor's income tax rate is an important assumption in accounting for a leveraged lease. Accordingly, the income effect of a change in the income tax rate should be recognized in the first accounting period ending on or after the date on which the legislation effecting a rate change becomes law. [FTB79-16(R), ¶3] [Refer to paragraph .1001 for an EITF Issue that provides interpretive guidance on paragraphs .523 and .524.]

.524 If accounting for the effect on leveraged leases of the change in tax rates results in a significant variation from the customary relationship between income tax expense and pretax accounting income and the reason for that variation is not otherwise apparent, [FTB79-16(R), ¶4] Section I27, paragraph .146, [FAS109, ¶288(bb)] requires that the reason for that variation should be disclosed. [FTB79-16(R), ¶4]

Accounting for Operating Leases

Accounting for Operating Leases with Scheduled Rent Increases

.525 *Question*—Certain operating lease agreements specify scheduled rent increases over the lease term. Such scheduled rent increases may, for example, be designed to provide an inducement or "rent holiday" for the lessee, to reflect the anticipated effects of inflation, to ease the lessee's near-term cash flow requirements, or to acknowledge the time value of money. For operating leases that include scheduled rent increases, is it ever appropriate for lessees or lessors to recognize rent expense or rental income on a basis other than the straight-line basis required by this section? [FTB85-3, ¶1] [Refer to paragraph .1001 for an EITF Issue that provides interpretive guidance on paragraphs .525 and .526.]

.526 *Response*—The effects of those scheduled rent increases, which are included in minimum lease payments [refer to paragraph .417], should be recognized by lessors and lessees on a straight-line basis over the lease term unless another systematic and rational allocation basis is more representative of the time pattern in which the leased property is physically employed. [See paragraph .527B.] Using factors such as the time value of money, anticipated inflation, or expected future revenues to allocate scheduled rent increases is inappropriate because these factors do not relate to the *time pattern* of the physical usage of the leased property. However, such factors may affect the periodic reported rental income or expense if the lease agreement involves contingent rentals [refer to paragraph .404], which are excluded from minimum lease payments and accounted for separately [refer to paragraphs .108, .113, and .114]. [FTB85-3, ¶2]

.527 There is an important substantive difference between lease rentals that are contingent upon some specified future event and scheduled rent increases that are unaffected by future events. [FTB85-3, ¶13] This section differentiates between (a) scheduled rent increases that are not dependent on future events and (b) increases or decreases in rentals that are dependent on future events such as future sales volume, future inflation, future property taxes, and so forth. The former are minimum lease payments to be accounted for under paragraphs .111 and .115(b). The latter are contingent rentals that affect the measure of expense or income as accruable, as specified in paragraphs .108, .113, and .114. [FTB85-3, ¶12] If the lessor and lessee eliminate the risk of variable payments inherent in contingent rentals by agreeing to scheduled rent increases, the accounting should reflect those different circumstances. [FTB85-3, ¶13]

Time Pattern of the Physical Use of the Property in an Operating Lease

.527A *Question*—A lease agreement may include scheduled rent increases designed to accommodate the lessee's projected physical use of the property. For example, rents may escalate in contemplation of the lessee's physical use of the property even though the lessee takes possession of or controls the physical use of the property at the inception of the lease, or rents may escalate under a master lease agreement as the lessee adds additional equipment to the leased property or requires additional space or capacity (hereinafter referred to as additional leased property). For operating leases that include those provisions, how should the rental payment obligation be recognized by the lessee and lessor in accordance with paragraphs .111, [.115,] and .525 through .527? [FTB88-1, ¶1]

.527B *Response*—Both the lessee and the lessor should recognize the lease payments under paragraphs .111, [.115,] and .525 through .527 as follows:

a. If rents escalate in contemplation of the lessee's physical use of the leased property, including equipment, but the lessee takes possession of or controls the physical use[501a] of the property at the beginning of the lease term, all rental payments, including the escalated rents, should be recognized as rental expense or rental revenue on a straight-line basis in accordance with paragraphs .111, [.115,] and .525 through .527 starting with the beginning of the lease term.
b. If rents escalate under a master lease agreement because the lessee gains access to and control over additional leased property at the time of the escalation, the escalated rents should be considered rental expense or rental revenue attributable to the leased property and recognized in proportion to the additional leased property in the years that the lessee has control over the use of the additional leased property. The amount of rental expense or rental revenue attributed to the additional leased property should

[[501]Deleted 1/89 and renumbered as footnote 501b.]

[501a]The right to control the use of the leased property [is considered] the equivalent of physical use. When the lessee controls the use of the leased property, recognition of rental expense or rental revenue should not be affected by the extent to which the lessee utilizes that property. [FTB88-1, ¶4]

be proportionate to the relative fair value of the additional property, as determined at the inception of the lease, in the applicable time periods during which the lessee controls its use.

[FTB88-1, ¶2]

Lease Incentives in an Operating Lease

.527C *Question*—An operating lease agreement with a new lessor may include incentives for the lessee to sign the lease, such as an up-front cash payment to the lessee, payment of costs for the lessee (such as moving expenses), or the assumption by the lessor of the lessee's preexisting lease with a third party. For operating leases that include such incentives, should lessees or lessors ever recognize those incentives as rental expense or rental revenue other than on a straight-line basis in accordance with paragraphs .111, [.115,] and .525 through .527? [FTB88-1, ¶6]

.527D *Response*—Payments made to or on behalf of the lessee represent incentives that should be considered reductions of rental expense by the lessee and reductions of rental revenue by the lessor over the term of the new lease. Similarly, losses incurred by the lessor as a result of assuming a lessee's preexisting lease with a third party should be considered an incentive by both the lessor and the lessee. Incentives should be recognized on a straight-line basis over the term of the new lease in accordance with paragraphs .111, [.115,] and .525 through .527B. [FTB88-1, ¶7]

.527E The lessee's immediate recognition of expenses or losses, such as moving expenses, losses on subleases, or the write-off of abandoned leasehold improvements, is not changed by paragraph .527D. Rather, paragraph .527D addresses the question of when to recognize the incentive related to the new lessor's assumption of that expense or loss. The new lessor and the lessee should independently estimate any loss attributable to the assumption of a preexisting lease with a third party. For example, the lessee's estimate of the incentive could be based on a comparison of the new lease with the market rental rate available for similar lease property or the market rental rate from the same lessor without the lease assumption, and the lessor should estimate any loss based on the total remaining costs reduced by the expected benefits from the sublease or use of the assumed leased property. [FTB88-1, ¶8]

.527F For example, in conjunction with an operating lease of property for eight years, the lessor assumes the lessee's preexisting lease with a third party that has four years remaining. Assume that the old lease payment is $800 per year and the new lease payment is $1,200 per year. Also assume that the lessor estimates the loss on the assumed lease of $1,000 over its remaining term based on the ability to sublease the property for $550 per year. The lessee estimates the incentive as $960 based on a comparison of the preexisting lease rate to current rates for similar property. Exhibit 527A [presents the journal entries for] accounting for that incentive. [FTB88-1, ¶9]

Exhibit 527A

Journal Entries for Lease Incentives

	Debit	Credit
Lessor Accounting		
At inception:		
Incentive to lessee	1,000	
Liability on sublease assumed		1,000
To record deferred cost and liability related to loss on assumption of remaining lease		
Recurring journal entries in years 1 through 4:		
Liability on sublease assumed (1,000/4 years)	250	
Sublease expense	550	
Cash		800
To record cash payment on sublease assumed and amortization of the liability on the sublease assumed		
Cash	550	
Sublease revenue		550
To record cash received from sublease of the property		
Recurring journal entries in years 1 through 8:		
Cash	1,200	
Rental revenue		1,075
Incentive to lessee (1,000/8 years)		125
To record cash received on new lease and amortization of incentive over new lease term		
Lessee Accounting		
At inception:		
Loss on sublease assumed by lessor	960	
Incentive from lessor		960
To record loss on sublease assumed in conjunction with new lease agreement		
Recurring journal entries in years 1 through 8:		
Lease expense	1,080	
Incentive from lessor (960/8 years)	120	
Cash		1,200
To record cash payment on new lease and amortization of incentive over the new lease term		

[FTB88-1, ¶9]

Accounting for the Acquisition of an Interest in Residual Value

.528 *Question*—How should an enterprise account for the acquisition from a lessor of the unconditional right to own and possess, at the end of the lease term, an asset subject to a lease? Also, how should an enterprise account for the acquisition of the right to receive all, or a portion, of the proceeds from the sale of a leased asset at the end of the lease term? [FTB86-2, ¶1]

.529 *Response*—At the date the rights are acquired, both transactions involve a right to receive, at the end of the lease term, all, or a portion, of any future benefit to be derived from the leased asset and should be accounted for as the acquisition of an asset. (Hereinafter, both transactions are referred to as the acquisition of an interest in the residual value of a leased asset.) [FTB86-2, ¶2]

Measuring Cost of Acquired Residual Value

.530 *Question*—How should an enterprise acquiring an interest in the residual value of a leased asset measure the cost of the acquisition? [FTB86-2, ¶3]

.531 *Response*—An interest in the residual value of a leased asset should be recorded as an asset at the amount of cash disbursed, the fair value of other consideration given, and the present value of liabilities assumed at the date the right is acquired. The fair value of the interest in the residual value of the leased asset at the date of the agreement should be used to measure its cost if that fair value is more clearly evident than the fair value of assets surrendered, services rendered, or liabilities assumed. [FTB86-2, ¶4]

Accounting for an Interest in the Residual Value of a Leased Asset during Lease Term

.532 *Question*—A lessor recognizes increases in the residual value of a leased asset accounted for as a sales-type or direct financing lease to its estimated value at the end of the lease term. How should an enterprise acquiring an interest in the residual value of a leased asset account for that asset during the lease term? [FTB86-2, ¶5]

.533 *Response*—An enterprise acquiring an interest in the residual value of any leased asset, irrespective of the classification of the related lease by the lessor, should not recognize increases to the asset's estimated value over the remaining term of the related lease, and the asset should be reported at no more than its acquisition cost until sale or disposition. If it is subsequently determined that the fair value of the residual value of a leased asset has declined below the carrying amount of the acquired interest and that decline is other than temporary, the asset should be written down to fair value, and the amount of the write-down should be recognized as a loss. That fair value becomes the asset's new carrying amount, and the asset should not be increased for any subsequent increase in its fair value prior to its sale or disposition. [FTB86-2, ¶6]

Applicability to Lease Brokers

.534 *Question*—Do paragraphs .529, .531, and .533 apply to lease brokers? [FTB86-2, ¶7]

.535 *Response*—Yes. An interest in the residual value of a leased asset acquired by a lease broker for cash, liabilities assumed, and the fair value of other consideration given, including services rendered, should be accounted for under those paragraphs.[501b] [FTB86-2, ¶8]

Residual Value Retained by Lessor That Sells Rental Payments

.536 *Question*—If a lessor sells substantially all of the minimum rental payments associated with a sales-type, direct financing, or leveraged lease and retains an interest in the residual value of the leased asset, how should the lessor account for that asset over the remaining lease term? [FTB86-2, ¶9]

.537 *Response*—A lessor retaining an interest in the residual value of the leased asset should not recognize increases in the value of the lease residual to its estimated value over the remaining lease term. The lessor should report any remaining interest thereafter at its carrying amount at the date of the sale of the lease payments.[502] If it is subsequently determined that the fair value of the residual value of the leased asset has declined below the carrying amount of the interest retained and that decline is other than temporary, the asset should be written down to fair value, and the amount of the write-down should be recognized as a loss. That fair value becomes the asset's new carrying

---

[501b]This section prohibits a lease broker from recognizing increases in the asset's estimated value over the remaining term of the lease. In that respect, it differs from the AICPA Issues Paper, "Accounting by Lease Brokers." It does not address other areas of fee recognition by lease brokers, or any other provisions of that Issues Paper. [FTB86-2, ¶16]

[[502]This] paragraph only addresses those transactions structured as a sale of the related lease receivable and is not intended to consider any circumstance in which nonrecourse debt is collateralized by a lease receivable. In that circumstance, recognizing increases in the carrying amount of an interest in the residual value of a leased asset is appropriate under this section. However, Section I27, paragraph .233 states:

> It is a general principle of accounting that the offsetting of assets and liabilities in the balance sheet is improper except where a right of setoff exists.

Therefore, offsetting the lease receivable with nonrecourse debt is appropriate only in those circumstances in which a legal right of offset exists or when, at the inception of the lease, the lease meets all of the characteristics of paragraph .144 and is appropriately classified as a leveraged lease. Otherwise, the guidance provided in paragraph .233 of Section I27 should be applied. [FTB86-2, ¶21]

amount, and the asset should not be increased for any subsequent increase in its fair value prior to its sale or disposition. [FTB86-2, ¶10]

Guaranteed Residual Value of a Leased Asset

.538 *Question*—If an interest in the residual value of a leased asset is guaranteed, does the guarantee change the nature of the asset or the accounting [described in paragraphs .529, .531, .533, .535, and .537]? [FTB86-2, ¶11]

.539 [*Response*]—Yes. A residual value of a leased asset is a financial asset to the extent guaranteed at the inception of the lease. Accordingly, increases to its estimated value over the remaining lease term should be recognized. [FAS140, ¶356]

Applicability of Leveraged Lease Accounting to Existing Assets of the Lessor

.540 *Question*—Paragraph .102(b)(2) requires that the cost or carrying amount, if different, and the fair value of the asset be the same at the inception of the lease for it to be classified as a direct financing lease. Paragraph .144(a) requires that a lease qualify as a direct financing lease for the lessor to classify that lease as a leveraged lease. How does a lessor apply those requirements to leasing an asset the lessor has owned and had previously placed in service? [FTB88-1, ¶11]

.541 *Response*—Paragraphs .102(b)(2) and .144(a) should be applied literally. Although the carrying amount (cost less accumulated depreciation) of an asset previously placed in service may not be significantly different from its fair value, the two amounts will not likely be the same. Therefore, leveraged lease accounting will not be appropriate, generally, other than when an asset to be leased is acquired by the lessor. If the carrying amount of an existing asset of the lessor before any related write-down is equal to fair value as established in transactions by unrelated third parties, that asset could qualify for leveraged lease accounting. However, any write-down to the existing asset's fair value in contemplation of leasing the asset precludes the transaction from leveraged lease accounting. [FTB88-1, ¶12]

Money-over-Money Lease Transactions

.542 *Question*—An enterprise manufactures or purchases an asset, leases the asset to a lessee, and obtains nonrecourse financing in excess of the asset's cost using the leased asset and the future lease rentals as collateral (commonly referred to as a **money-over-money lease transaction**). Should the enterprise ever recognize any of the amount by which the cash received plus the present value of any estimated residual retained exceeds the carrying amount of the leased asset as profit on that transaction at the beginning of the lease term? If not, how should the enterprise account for the transaction? [FTB88-1, ¶16]

.543 *Response*—Other than the recognition of manufacturer's or dealer's profit in a sales-type lease, an enterprise should never recognize as income the proceeds from the borrowing in a money-over-money lease transaction at the beginning of the lease term. The enterprise should account for that transaction as (a) the manufacture or purchase of an asset, (b) the leasing of the asset under an operating, direct financing, or sales-type lease as required by paragraphs .102 through .104, and (c) the borrowing of funds. The asset (if an operating lease) or the lease receivable (if a direct financing or sales-type lease) and the liability for the nonrecourse financing should not be offset in the statement of financial position unless a right of setoff exists. [FTB88-1, ¶17] [See Section B10, "Balance Sheet Display: Offsetting," paragraphs .101A, .101B, and .107, for guidance on determining whether a right of setoff exists.]

Wrap Lease Transactions

.544 *Question*—An enterprise purchases an asset, leases the asset to a lessee, obtains nonrecourse financing using the lease rentals or the lease rentals and the asset as collateral, sells the asset subject to the lease and the nonrecourse debt to a third-party investor, and leases the asset back while remaining the substantive principal lessor under the original lease (commonly referred to as a **wrap lease transaction**). Other than as required by this section, should an enterprise ever recognize any profit on the wrap lease transaction at its inception? If not, how should the enterprise account for the transaction? [FTB88-1, ¶21]

.545 *Response*—If the property involved is real estate, paragraphs .130A through .130M and .160A through .160M of this section and paragraphs .125H through .125J of Section Re6 apply to the sale-leaseback transaction. If the property involved is not real estate, the enterprise should account for the transaction as a sale-leaseback transaction in accordance with paragraphs .128 through .130 and the lease to the end user should be accounted for as a sublease in accordance with paragraph .132. Under this section the asset should be removed from the books of the original enterprise, the leaseback should be classified in accordance with paragraph .102, and any gain on the transaction should be recognized or deferred and amortized in accordance with paragraph .129. The enterprise would also reflect the retained residual interest, gross sublease receivable, nonrecourse third-party debt, the leaseback obligation, and the note receivable from the investor in the statement of financial position. As in accounting for a money-over-money lease transaction (refer to paragraph .543), the sublease asset and the related nonrecourse debt should not be offset in the statement of financial position unless a right of setoff exists. [FTB88-1, ¶22] [See Section B10, paragraphs .101A, .101B, and .107, for guidance on determining whether a right of setoff exists.] [Refer to paragraph .1001 for an EITF Issue that provides interpretive guidance on this paragraph.]

Supplemental Guidance: Emerging Issues Task Force (EITF) Issues

.1000 [Listed below are EITF Issues that provide supplemental guidance for this section. These Issues are grouped by subject matter and may be either interpretive of or related by topic to the guidance in this section.

Lease Modifications

EITF Issue No. 88-10, "Costs Associated with Lease Modification or Termination"
EITF Issue No. 94-3, "Liability Recognition for Certain Employee Termination Benefits and Other Costs to Exit an Activity (including Certain Costs Incurred in a Restructuring)"
EITF Issue No. 95-17, "Accounting for Modifications to an Operating Lease That Do Not Change the Lease Classification"

Leases with Tax Issues

EITF Issue No. 86-33, "Tax Indemnifications in Lease Agreements"
EITF Issue No. 86-44, "Effect of a Change in Tax Law on Investments in Safe Harbor Leases"
EITF Issue No. 89-20, "Accounting for Cross Border Tax Benefit Leases"

Leveraged Leases

EITF Issue No. 85-16, "Leveraged Leases: Real Estate Leases and Sale-Leaseback Transactions and Delayed Equity Contributions by Lessors"
EITF Issue No. 86-43, "Effect of a Change in Tax Law or Rates on Leveraged Leases"
EITF Issue No. 87-8, "Tax Reform Act of 1986: Issues Related to the Alternative Minimum Tax"

Revenue Recognition

EITF Issue No. 95-1, "Revenue Recognition on Sales with a Guaranteed Minimum Resale Value"
EITF Issue No. 95-4, "Revenue Recognition on Equipment Sold and Subsequently Repurchased Subject to an Operating Lease"
EITF Issue No. 01-4, "Accounting for Sales of Fractional Interests in Equipment"

Sale-Leaseback

EITF Issue No. 84-37, "Sale-Leaseback Transaction with Repurchase Option"
EITF Issue No. 85-27, "Recognition of Receipts from Made-Up Rental Shortfalls"

EITF Issue No. 86-17, "Deferred Profit on Sale-Leaseback Transaction with Lessee Guarantee of Residual Value"

EITF Issue No. 88-21, "Accounting for the Sale of Property Subject to the Seller's Preexisting Lease"

EITF Issue No. 89-16, "Consideration of Executory Costs in Sale-Leaseback Transactions"

EITF Issue No. 90-14, "Unsecured Guarantee by Parent of Subsidiary's Lease Payments in a Sale-Leaseback Transaction"

EITF Issue No. 90-20, "Impact of an Uncollateralized Irrevocable Letter of Credit on a Real Estate Sale-Leaseback Transaction"

EITF Issue No. 93-8, "Accounting for the Sale and Leaseback of an Asset That Is Leased to Another Party"

EITF Issue No. 97-10, "The Effect of Lessee Involvement in Asset Construction"

EITF Issue No. 99-13, "Application of Issue No. 97-10 and FASB Interpretation No. 23 to Entities That Enter into Leases with Governmental Entities"

EITF Issue No. 00-11, "Lessors' Evaluation of Whether Leases of Certain Integral Equipment Meet the Ownership Transfer Requirements of FASB Statement No. 13"

EITF Issue No. 00-13, "Determining Whether Equipment Is 'Integral Equipment' Subject to FASB Statements No. 66 and No. 98"

EITF Topic No. D-24, "Sale-Leaseback Transactions with Continuing Involvement"

Special-Purpose Entities

EITF Issue No. 90-15, "Impact of Nonsubstantive Lessors, Residual Value Guarantees, and Other Provisions in Leasing Transactions"

EITF Issue No. 96-21, "Implementation Issues in Accounting for Leasing Transactions involving Special-Purpose Entities"

EITF Issue No. 97-1, "Implementation Issues in Accounting for Lease Transactions, including Those involving Special-Purpose Entities"

EITF Topic No. D-14, "Transactions involving Special-Purpose Entities"

Other

EITF Issue No. 87-7, "Sale of an Asset Subject to a Lease and Nonrecourse Financing: 'Wrap Lease Transactions'"

EITF Issue No. 92-1, "Allocation of Residual Value or First-Loss Guarantee to Minimum Lease Payments in Leases involving Land and Building(s)"

EITF Issue No. 95-6, "Accounting by a Real Estate Investment Trust for an Investment in a Service Corporation"

EITF Issue No. 98-9, "Accounting for Contingent Rent"

EITF Issue No. 01-8, "Determining Whether an Arrangement Is a Lease"

EITF Issue No. 01-10, "Accounting for the Impact of the Terrorist Attacks of September 11, 2001"

EITF Issue No. 01-12, "The Impact of the Requirements of FASB Statement No. 133 on Residual Value Guarantees in Connection with a Lease"

EITF Topic No. D-8, "Accruing Bad-Debt Expense at Inception of a Lease"]

.1001 [Listed below are those EITF Issues that provide interpretive guidance on specific material in this section.

Paragraph .101 (FAS 13, ¶1)—EITF Issue No. 95-1
Paragraph .103 (FAS 13, ¶7)—EITF Issues No. 97-1 and 00-11
Paragraph .103(d) (FAS 13, ¶7(d))—EITF Issue No. 96-21
Paragraph .111 (FAS 13, ¶15)—EITF Issue No. 98-9
Paragraphs .117 and .118 (FAS 13, ¶21-22)—EITF Issue No. 95-4
Paragraph .122(b)(2) (FAS 13, ¶26(b)(ii))—EITF Issue No. 92-1
Paragraph .128 (FAS 28, ¶2)—EITF Issues No. 88-21 and 93-8
Paragraph .129 (FAS 28, ¶3)—EITF Issues No. 86-17, 88-21, 89-16, and 93-8
Paragraph .130 (FAS 13, ¶34)—EITF Issue No. 88-21
Paragraph .130F (FAS 98, ¶10)—EITF Issues No. 90-14 and 90-20 and Topic No. D-24
Paragraph .130G (FAS 98, ¶11)—EITF Issues No. 90-14, 90-20, and 97-1 and Topic No. D-24
Paragraphs .130H and .130I (FAS 98, ¶12-13)—EITF Issues No. 90-14 and 90-20 and Topic No. D-24
Paragraph .144(c) (FAS 13, ¶42(c))—EITF Issue No. 85-16
Paragraph .148 (FAS 13, ¶46)—EITF Issue No. 86-43
Paragraph .404 (FAS 29, ¶11)—EITF Issue No. 86-33
Paragraph .411, fn402a (FAS 91, ¶23)—EITF Topic No. D-8
Paragraph .417 (FAS 13, ¶5(j))—EITF Issue No. 95-1
Paragraph .417(a) (FAS 13, ¶5(j)(i) and FAS 29, ¶10)—EITF Issue No. 86-33
Paragraphs .523 and .524 (FTB 79-16(R), ¶3-4)—EITF Issue No. 86-43
Paragraphs .525 and .526 (FTB 85-3, ¶1-2)—EITF Issue No. 86-33
Paragraph .545 (FTB 88-1, ¶22)—EITF Issue No. 89-16]

(The next page is 30101.)

LENDING ACTIVITIES SECTION L20

Sources: FASB Statement 91; FASB Statement 115; FASB Statement 124; FASB Statement 133; FASB Statement 140

[**Note:** A list of Issues discussed by the Emerging Issues Task Force (EITF) that provide supplemental guidance for this section is presented in paragraph .1000.]

Summary

This section presents the accounting for nonrefundable fees and costs associated with lending, committing to lend, or purchasing a loan or group of loans.

This section applies to all types of loans (including debt securities) as well as to all types of lenders (including banks, thrift institutions, insurance companies, mortgage bankers, and other financial and nonfinancial institutions).

The section specifies that:

- Loan origination fees shall be recognized over the life of the related loan as an adjustment of yield.
- Certain direct loan origination costs shall be recognized over the life of the related loan as a reduction of the loan's yield.
- All loan commitment fees shall be deferred except for certain retrospectively determined fees; commitment fees meeting specified criteria shall be recognized over the loan commitment period; all other commitment fees shall be recognized as an adjustment of yield over the related loan's life or, if the commitment expires unexercised, recognized in income upon expiration of the commitment.
- Loan fees, certain direct loan origination costs, and purchase premiums and discounts on loans shall be recognized as an adjustment of yield generally by the interest method based on the contractual terms of the loan. However, prepayments may be anticipated in certain specified circumstances.

Scope

.101 This section [presents] standards of financial accounting and reporting for nonrefundable fees and costs associated with lending activities and loan purchases. Lending, committing to lend, refinancing or restructuring loans, arranging standby letters of credit, syndicating loans, and leasing activities are "lending activities" for purposes of this section. The lender's activities that precede the disbursement of funds can generally be distinguished between (a) efforts to identify and attract potential borrowers and (b) efforts necessary to originate a loan or loan commitment after a potential borrower requests a loan or loan commitment. Nonrefundable fees have many different names in practice, such as **origination fees,** points, placement fees, **commitment fees,** application fees, management fees, restructuring fees, and syndication fees, but, for purposes of this section, they are referred to as loan origination fees, commitment fees, or syndication fees. [FAS91, ¶2]

.102 This section addresses the recognition and the balance sheet classification of nonrefundable fees and costs associated with lending activities. The accounting for discounts, premiums, and commitment fees associated with the purchase of loans and other debt securities such as corporate bonds, Treasury notes and bonds, groups of loans, and loan-backed securities (such as pass-through certificates, collateralized mortgage obligations, and other so-called "securitized" loans) is also addressed by this section. This section does not [address] loan origination or commitment fees that are refundable; however, the provisions of this section do apply when such fees subsequently become nonrefundable. It also does not [address] costs that are incurred by the lender in transactions with independent third parties if the lender bills those costs directly to the borrower. The provisions of this section do not apply to nonrefundable fees and costs associated with originating or acquiring loans that are carried at market value [FAS91, ¶3] if the changes in market value are included in earnings [FAS115, ¶130(a)] of a business enterprise or change in net assets of a not-for-profit organization. [FAS124, ¶109]

General

.103 An enterprise may acquire a loan by lending (originating the loan) or by purchasing (acquiring a loan from a party other than the borrower). This section applies to both a lender and a purchaser. This section shall be applied to individual loan contracts. Aggregation of similar loans for purposes of recognizing net fees or costs and purchase premiums or discounts is permitted if the provisions of paragraph .118 are met or if the resulting recognition does not differ materially from the amount that would have been recognized on an individual loan-by-loan basis. [FAS91, ¶4]

Loan Origination Fees and Costs

.104 Loan origination fees[1] shall be deferred and recognized over the life of the loan as an adjustment of yield[2] (interest income). Likewise, direct loan origination costs defined in paragraph .105 shall be deferred and recognized as a reduction in the yield of the loan except as set forth in paragraph .113 (for a troubled debt restructuring). Loan origination fees and related direct loan origination costs for a given loan shall be offset and only the net amount shall be deferred and amortized. The practice of recognizing a portion of loan origination fees as revenue in a period to offset all or part of the costs of origination shall no longer be acceptable. [FAS91, ¶5] [Refer to paragraph .1001 for an EITF Issue that provides interpretive guidance on this paragraph.]

.105 Direct loan origination costs of a completed loan shall include only (a) **incremental direct costs** of loan origination incurred in transactions with independent third parties for that loan and (b) certain costs directly related to specified activities performed by the lender for that loan. Those activities are: evaluating the prospective borrower's financial condition; evaluating and recording guarantees, collateral, and other security arrangements; negotiating loan terms; preparing and processing loan documents; and closing the transaction. The costs directly related to those activities shall include only that portion of the employees' total compensation and payroll-related fringe benefits directly related to time spent performing those activities for that loan and other costs related to those activities that would not have been incurred but for that loan. [FAS91, ¶6] [Refer to paragraph .1001 for EITF Issues that provide interpretive guidance on this paragraph.]

.106 All other lending-related costs, including costs related to activities performed by the lender for advertising, soliciting potential borrowers, servicing existing loans, and other ancillary activities related to establishing and monitoring credit policies, supervi-

---

[1]Origination fees consist of:

a. Fees that are being charged to the borrower as "prepaid" interest or to reduce the loan's nominal interest rate, such as interest "buy-downs" (explicit yield adjustments)
b. Fees to reimburse the lender for origination activities
c. Other fees charged to the borrower that relate directly to making the loan (for example, fees that are paid to the lender as compensation for granting a complex loan or agreeing to lend quickly)
d. Fees that are not conditional on a loan being granted by the lender that receives the fee but are, in substance, implicit yield adjustments because a loan is granted at rates or terms that would not have otherwise been considered absent the fee (for example, certain syndication fees addressed in paragraph .110).

Designation of a fee or cost as an origination fee or cost for a loan that is purchased is inappropriate because a purchased loan has already been originated by another party. [FAS91, ¶36]

[2]Methods for recognition of deferred fees and direct loan origination costs over the life of the loan as an adjustment of yield are set forth in paragraphs .117 through .119. [FAS91, ¶5, fn2]

sion, and administration, shall be charged to expense as incurred. Employees' compensation and fringe benefits related to those activities, unsuccessful loan origination efforts, and idle time shall be charged to expense as incurred. Administrative costs, rent, depreciation, and all other occupancy and equipment costs are considered indirect costs and shall be charged to expense as incurred. [FAS91, ¶7] [Refer to paragraph .1001 for an EITF Issue that provides interpretive guidance on this paragraph.]

Commitment Fees and Costs

.107 Except as set forth in subparagraphs (a) and (b) below, fees received for a commitment to originate or purchase a loan or group of loans shall be deferred and, if the commitment is exercised, recognized over the life of the loan as an adjustment of yield or, if the commitment expires unexercised, recognized in income upon expiration of the commitment.

a. If the enterprise's experience with similar arrangements indicates that the likelihood that the commitment will be exercised is remote,[3] the commitment fee shall be recognized over the commitment period on a straight-line basis as service fee income. If the commitment is subsequently exercised during the commitment period, the remaining unamortized commitment fee at the time of exercise shall be recognized over the life of the loan as an adjustment of yield.
b. If the amount of the commitment fee is determined retrospectively as a percentage of the line of credit available but unused in a previous period, if that percentage is nominal in relation to the stated interest rate on any related borrowing, and if that borrowing will bear a market interest rate at the date the loan is made, the commitment fee shall be recognized as service fee income as of the determination date.

[FAS91, ¶8] [Refer to paragraph .1001 for EITF Issues that provide interpretive guidance on this paragraph.]

.108 Direct loan origination costs (described in paragraph .105) incurred to make a commitment to originate a loan shall be offset against any related commitment fee and the net amount recognized as set forth in paragraph .107. [FAS91, ¶9]

.109 Available lines of credit under credit card and similar charge card arrangements are loan commitments, and fees collected in connection with such cards **(credit card fees)** are viewed in part as being loan commitment fees. However, those fees generally cover many services to cardholders. Accordingly, fees that are periodically charged to

[3] The term *remote* is used here, consistent with its use in Section C59, "Contingencies," to mean that the likelihood is slight that a loan commitment will be exercised prior to its expiration. [FAS91, ¶8, fn3]

cardholders shall be deferred and recognized on a straight-line basis over the period the fee entitles the cardholder to use the card. This accounting shall also apply to other similar card arrangements that involve an extension of credit by the card issuer. [FAS91, ¶10] [Refer to paragraph .1001 for an EITF Issue that provides interpretive guidance on this paragraph.]

Syndication Fees

.110 The enterprise managing a loan syndication (the syndicator) shall recognize loan syndication fees when the syndication is complete unless a portion of the syndication loan is retained. If the yield on the portion of the loan retained by the syndicator is less than the average yield to the other syndication participants after considering the fees passed through by the syndicator, the syndicator shall defer a portion of the syndication fee to produce a yield on the portion of the loan retained that is not less than the average yield on the loans held by the other syndication participants. [FAS91, ¶11]

Fees and Costs in Refinancings or Restructurings

.111 If the terms of the new loan resulting from a loan refinancing or restructuring other than a troubled debt restructuring are at least as favorable to the lender as the terms for comparable loans to other customers with similar collection risks who are not refinancing or restructuring a loan with the lender, the refinanced loan shall be accounted for as a new loan. This condition would be met if the new loan's effective yield is at least equal to the effective yield for such loans.[4] Any unamortized net fees or costs and any prepayment penalties from the original loan shall be recognized in interest income when the new loan is granted. [FAS91, ¶12]

.112 If the refinancing or restructuring does not meet the condition set forth in paragraph .111 or if only minor modifications are made to the original loan contract, the unamortized net fees or costs from the original loan and any prepayment penalties shall be carried forward as a part of the net investment in the new loan. In this case, the investment in the new loan shall consist of the remaining net investment in the original loan,[5] any additional amounts loaned, any fees received, and direct loan origination costs set forth in paragraph .105 associated with the refinancing or restructuring. [FAS91, ¶13]

[4]The effective yield comparison considers the level of nominal interest rate, commitment and origination fees, and direct loan origination costs and would also consider comparison of other factors where appropriate, such as compensating balance arrangements. [FAS91, ¶12, fn4]

[5]The net investment in the original loan includes the unpaid loan principal, any remaining unamortized net fees or costs, any remaining unamortized purchase premium or discount, and any accrued interest receivable. [FAS91, ¶13, fn5]

.113 Fees received in connection with a modification of terms of a troubled debt restructuring as defined in Section D22, "Debt: Restructurings," shall be applied as a reduction of the recorded investment in the loan. All related costs, including direct loan origination costs, shall be charged to expense as incurred. [FAS91, ¶14]

Purchase of a Loan or Group of Loans

.114 The initial investment in a purchased loan or group of loans shall include the amount paid to the seller plus any fees paid or less any fees received. The initial investment frequently differs from the related loan's principal amount at the date of purchase. This difference shall be recognized as an adjustment of yield over the life of the loan. All other costs incurred in connection with acquiring purchased loans or committing to purchase loans shall be charged to expense as incurred. [FAS91, ¶15]

.115 In applying the provisions of this section to loans purchased as a group, the purchaser may allocate the initial investment to the individual loans or may account for the initial investment in the aggregate. The cash flows provided by the underlying loan contracts shall be used to apply the interest method, except as set forth in paragraph .118. If prepayments are not anticipated pursuant to paragraph .118 and prepayments occur or a portion of the purchased loans is sold, a proportionate amount of the related deferred fees and purchase premium or discount shall be recognized in income so that the effective interest rate on the remaining portion of loans continues unchanged. [FAS91, ¶16] [Refer to paragraph .1001 for an EITF Issue that provides interpretive guidance on this paragraph.]

Other

.116 Deferred net fees or costs shall not be amortized during periods in which interest income on a loan is not being recognized because of concerns about the realization of loan principal or interest. [FAS91, ¶17]

Application of the Interest Method and Other Amortization Matters

.117 Net fees or costs that are required to be recognized as yield adjustments over the life of the related loan(s) shall be recognized by the interest method except as set forth in paragraph .119. The objective of the interest method is to arrive at periodic interest income (including recognition of fees and costs) at a constant effective yield on the net investment in the receivable (that is, the principal amount of the receivable adjusted by unamortized fees or costs and purchase premium or discount). The difference between the periodic interest income so determined and the stated interest on the outstanding principal amount of the receivable is the amount of periodic amortization.[6] Under the provisions of this section, the interest method shall be applied as follows when the stated interest rate is not constant throughout the term of the loan:

a. If the loan's stated interest rate increases during the term of the loan (so that interest accrued under the interest method in early periods would exceed interest at the stated rate), interest income shall not be recognized to the extent that the net investment in the loan would increase to an amount greater than the amount at which the borrower could settle the obligation.[7] Prepayment penalties shall be considered in determining the amount at which the borrower could settle the obligation only to the extent that such penalties are imposed throughout the loan term. (Refer to paragraphs .133 through .135.)
b. If the loan's stated interest rate decreases during the term of the loan, the stated periodic interest received early in the term of the loan would exceed the periodic interest income that is calculated under the interest method. In that circumstance, the excess shall be deferred and recognized in those future periods when the constant effective yield under the interest method exceeds the stated interest rate. (Refer to paragraph .136.)
c. If the loan's stated interest rate varies based on future changes in an independent factor, such as an index or rate (for example, the prime rate, the London Interbank Offered Rate (LIBOR), or the U.S. Treasury bill weekly average rate), the calculation of the constant effective yield necessary to recognize fees and costs shall be based either on the factor (the index or rate) that is in effect at the inception of the loan or on the factor as it changes over the life of the loan.[8] (Refer to paragraphs .137 and .138.)

[FAS91, ¶18] [Refer to paragraph .1001 for EITF Issues that provide interpretive guidance on this paragraph.]

.118 Except as stated in the following sentence, the calculation of the constant effective yield necessary to apply the interest method shall use the payment terms required by the loan contract, and prepayments of principal shall not be anticipated to shorten the loan

[6]The "interest" method is also described in footnote 4 of Section I69, "Interest: Imputation of an Interest Cost" and in the first sentence of paragraph .108 of that section. [FAS91, ¶18, fn6]

[7]This paragraph imposes a limit on the amount of periodic amortization that can be recognized. However, that limitation does not apply to the capitalization of costs incurred (such as direct loan origination costs and purchase premiums) that cause the investment in the loan to be in excess of the amount at which the borrower could settle the obligation. [It was] concluded that the capitalization of costs incurred is different from increasing the net investment in a loan through accrual of interest income that is only contingently receivable. [FAS91, ¶54]

[8]A variable rate loan whose initial rate differs from the rate its base factor would produce is also subject to the provisions of paragraphs .117(a) and (b). [FAS91, ¶18, fn7]

term. If the enterprise holds a large number of similar loans[9] for which prepayments are probable and the timing and amount of prepayments can be reasonably estimated, the enterprise may consider estimates of future principal prepayments in the calculation of the constant effective yield necessary to apply the interest method. If the enterprise anticipates prepayments in applying the interest method and a difference arises between the prepayments anticipated and actual prepayments received, the enterprise shall recalculate the effective yield to reflect actual payments to date and anticipated future payments. The net investment in the loans shall be adjusted to the amount that would have existed had the new effective yield been applied since the acquisition of the loans. The investment in the loans shall be adjusted to the new balance with a corresponding charge or credit to interest income. Enterprises that anticipate prepayments shall disclose that policy and the significant assumptions underlying the prepayment estimates. The practice of recognizing net fees over the estimated average life of a group of loans shall no longer be acceptable. (Refer to paragraphs .128 through .132.) [FAS91, ¶19] [Refer to paragraph .1001 for EITF Issues that provide interpretive guidance on paragraphs .118 and .119.]

.119 Certain loan agreements provide no scheduled payment terms (demand loans); others provide the borrower with the option to make multiple borrowings up to a specified maximum amount, to repay portions of previous borrowings, and then reborrow under the same contract (revolving lines of credit).

a. For a loan that is payable at the lender's demand, any net fees or costs may be recognized as an adjustment of yield on a straight-line basis over a period that is consistent with (1) the understanding between the borrower and lender or (2) if no understanding exists, the lender's estimate of the period of time over which the loan will remain outstanding; any unamortized amount shall be recognized when the loan is paid in full.
b. For revolving lines of credit (or similar loan arrangements), the net fees or costs shall be recognized in income on a straight-line basis over the period the revolving line of credit is active, assuming that borrowings are outstanding for the maximum term provided in the loan contract. If the borrower pays all borrowings and cannot reborrow under the contract, any unamortized net fees or costs shall be recognized in income upon payment. The interest method shall be applied to recognize net unamortized

[9]The loans [that are] grouped together should have sufficiently similar characteristics that prepayment experience of the loans can be expected to be similar in a variety of interest rate environments [and] should have sufficiently similar levels of net fees or costs so that, in the event that an individual loan is sold, recalculation of that loan's carrying amount will be practicable. [FAS91, ¶58]

fees or costs when the loan agreement provides a schedule for payment and no additional borrowings are provided for under the agreement.[10]

[FAS91, ¶20]

Measurement of Loans Subject to Prepayment

.119A Interest-only strips, retained interests in securitizations, loans, other receivables, or other financial assets that can contractually be prepaid or otherwise settled in such a way that the holder would not recover substantially all of its recorded investment, except for instruments that are within the scope of Section D50, "Derivative Instruments and Hedging Activities," shall be subsequently measured like investments in debt securities classified as available-for-sale or trading under Section I80, "Investments: Debt and Equity Securities," paragraphs .104 and .109. [FAS140, ¶14]

Balance Sheet Classification

.120 The unamortized balance of loan origination, commitment, and other fees and costs and purchase premiums and discounts that is being recognized as an adjustment of yield pursuant to this section shall be reported on the enterprise's balance sheet as part of the loan balance to which it relates. [FAS91, ¶21]

Income Statement Classification

.121 Amounts of loan origination, commitment, and other fees and costs recognized as an adjustment of yield shall be reported as part of interest income. Amortization of other fees, such as commitment fees that are being amortized on a straight-line basis over the commitment period or included in income when the commitment expires, shall be reported as service fee income. [FAS91, ¶22]

---

[10]For example, if the loan agreement provides the borrower with the option to convert a one-year revolving line of credit to a five-year term loan, during the term of the revolving line of credit the lender would recognize the net fees or costs as income on a straight-line basis using the combined life of the revolving line of credit and term loan. If the borrower elects to convert the line of credit to a term loan, the lender would recognize the unamortized net fees or costs as an adjustment of yield using the interest method. If the revolving line of credit expires and borrowings are extinguished, the unamortized net fees or costs would be recognized in income upon payment. [FAS91, ¶20, fn8]

Application to Leasing Activities

.122 [As discussed in Section L10, "Leases,"] the provisions of paragraphs .104 through .108 of this section apply to lessors in determining the net amount of *initial direct costs* as that term is used in Section L10. Lessors shall account for initial direct costs as part of the investment in a direct financing lease. The practice of recognizing a portion of the unearned income at inception of the lease to offset initial direct costs [is not] acceptable. [FAS91, ¶23] [Refer to paragraph .1001 for an EITF Issue that provides interpretive guidance on this paragraph.]

Examples of Application of This Section

.123 The examples and estimates used are illustrative only and are not intended to modify or limit in any way the provisions of this section. All examples assume that principal and interest payments are made on the last day of the year. [FAS91, ¶64]

Case 1—Amortization Based on Contractual Payment Terms

.124 On January 1, 19X7, Company A originates a 10-year $100,000 loan with a 10 percent stated interest rate. The contract specifies equal annual payments of $16,275 through December 31, 19Y6. The contract also specifies that no penalty will be charged for prepayments of the loan. Company A charges a 3 percent ($3,000) nonrefundable fee to the borrower and incurs $1,000 in direct loan origination costs (attorney fees, appraisal, title insurance, wages and payroll-related fringe benefits of employees performing origination activities, outside broker's fee). The carrying amount of the loan is computed as follows:

Loan principal	$100,000
Origination fees	(3,000)
Direct loan origination costs	1,000
Carrying amount of loan	$ 98,000

[FAS91, ¶65]

.125 Company A accounts for this loan using contractual payments to apply the interest method of amortization. In calculating the effective rate to apply the interest method, the discount rate necessary to equate 10 annual payments of $16,275 to the initial carrying amount of $98,000 is approximately 10.4736 percent. The amortization if no prepayment occurs is shown in Exhibit 125A. [FAS91, ¶66]

Exhibit 125A

Amortization Based on Contractual Payment Terms

Year	(1) Cash (Out) Inflow	(2) Stated Interest	(3) Amortization	(4) Interest Income	(5) Remaining Principal	(6) Unamortized Net Fees	(7) Carrying Amount
	$(98,000)				$100,000		$98,000
1	16,275	$10,000	$ 264	$10,264	93,725	$1,736	91,989
2	16,275	9,373	262	9,635	86,823	1,474	85,349
3	16,275	8,682	257	8,939	79,230	1,217	78,013
4	16,275	7,923	248	8,171	70,878	969	69,909
5	16,275	7,088	234	7,322	61,691	735	60,956
6	16,275	6,169	215	6,384	51,585	520	51,065
7	16,275	5,159	189	5,348	40,469	331	40,138
8	16,275	4,047	157	4,204	28,241	174	28,067
9	16,275	2,824	116	2,940	14,790	58	14,732
10	16,275	1,485[a]	58	1,543	0	0	0
Total amortization			$2,000				

Computations:
Column (1)—Contractual payments
Column (2)—Column (5) for prior year × the loan's stated interest rate (10%)
Column (3)—Column (4) – Column (2)
Column (4)—Column (7) for prior year × the effective interest rate (10.4736%)[b]
Column (5)—Column (5) for prior year – (Column (1) – Column (2))
Column (6)—Initial net fees – amortization to date
Column (7)—Column (5) – Column (6)

[a] $6 rounding adjustment.

[b] The effective interest rate is the discount rate that equates the present value of the future cash inflows to the initial net cash outflow of $98,000.

[FAS91, ¶66]

Case 2—Amortization Based on Contractual Payment Terms with Full Prepayment in Year 3

.126 On January 1, 19X7, Company B originates a 10-year $100,000 loan with a 10 percent stated interest rate. The contract specifies equal annual payments of $16,275 through December 31, 19Y6. The contract also specifies that no penalty will be charged for prepayments of the loan. Company B charges a 3 percent ($3,000) nonrefundable fee to the borrower and incurs $1,000 in direct loan origination costs. [FAS91, ¶67]

.127 Company B accounts for this loan using contractual payments to apply the interest method of amortization. The amortization if the borrower prepays the remaining principal at the end of year 3 is shown in Exhibit 127A. [FAS91, ¶68]

Exhibit 127A

Amortization Based on Contractual Payment Terms with Full Prepayment in Year 3

Year	(1) Cash (Out) Inflow	(2) Stated Interest	(3) Amortization	(4) Interest Income	(5) Remaining Principal	(6) Unamortized Net Fees	(7) Carrying Amount
	$(98,000)				$100,000		$98,000
1	16,275	$10,000	$ 264	$10,264	93,725	$1,736	91,989
2	16,275	9,373	262	9,635	86,823	1,474	85,349
3	95,505	8,682	1,474	10,156	0	0	0
Total amortization			$2,000				

Computations:
Column (1)—Contractual payments + prepayments
Column (2)—Column (5) for prior year × the loan's stated interest rate (10%)
Column (3)—Column (4) – Column (2)
Column (4)—Column (7) for prior year × the effective interest rate (10.4736%) plus in year 3 an adjustment of $1,217 representing the unamortized net fees recognized when the loan is paid in full
Column (5)—Column (5) for prior year – (Column (1) – Column (2))
Column (6)—Initial net fees – amortization to date
Column (7)—Column (5) – Column (6)

[FAS91, ¶68]

Case 3—Amortization Based on Estimated Prepayment Patterns

.128 On January 1, 19X7, Company C originates 1,000 10-year $10,000 loans with 10 percent stated interest rates. Each contract specifies equal annual payments through December 31, 19Y6. The contracts also specify that no penalty will be charged for prepayments. Company C charges each borrower a 3 percent ($300) fee and incurs $100 in direct origination costs for each loan. The carrying amount of the loans is computed as follows:

Loan principal amounts	$10,000,000
Origination fees	(300,000)
Direct loan origination costs	100,000
Carrying amount of loans	$ 9,800,000

[FAS91, ¶69]

.129 Company C chooses to account for this large number of loans using anticipated prepayment patterns to apply the interest method of amortization. Company C estimates a constant prepayment rate of 6 percent per year, which is consistent with Company C's prior experience with similar loans and Company C's expectation of ongoing experience. The amortization when prepayments occur as anticipated is shown in Exhibit 129A. [FAS91, ¶70]

Exhibit 129A

Amortization Based on Estimated Prepayment Patterns

Year	(1) Cash (Out) Inflow	(2) Stated Interest	(3) Amortization	(4) Interest Income	(5) Remaining Principal	(6) Unamortized Net Fees	(7) Carrying Amount
	$(9,800,000)				$10,000,000		$9,800,000
1	2,227,454	$1,000,000	$ 35,141	$1,035,141	8,772,546	$164,859	8,607,687
2	2,049,623	877,255	31,946	909,201	7,600,178	132,913	7,467,265
3	1,880,619	760,018	28,724	788,742	6,479,577	104,189	6,375,388
4	1,719,716	647,958	25,453	673,411	5,407,819	78,736	5,329,083
5	1,566,144	540,782	22,111	562,893	4,382,457	56,625	4,325,832
6	1,419,028	438,246	18,677	456,923	3,401,675	37,948	3,363,727
7	1,277,230	340,168	15,131	355,299	2,464,613	22,817	2,441,796
8	1,138,934	246,461	11,458	257,919	1,572,140	11,359	1,560,781
9	1,000,180	157,214	7,646	164,860	729,174	3,713	725,461
10	802,091	72,917	3,713	76,630	0	0	0
Total amortization			$200,000				

Computations:
Column (1)—Contractual payments + 6% of Column (5) for the prior year (except in year 10)
Column (2)—Column (5) for prior year × the loan's stated interest rate (10%)
Column (3)—Column (4) – Column (2)
Column (4)—Column (7) for the prior year × the effective interest rate (10.5627%)
Column (5)—Column (5) for prior year – (Column (1) – Column (2))
Column (6)—Initial net fees – amortization to date
Column (7)—Column (5) – Column (6)

[FAS91, ¶70]

Case 4—Amortization Based on Estimated Prepayment Patterns Adjusted for Change in Estimate

.130 On January 1, 19X7, Company D originates 1,000 10-year $10,000 loans with 10 percent stated interest rates. Each contract specifies equal annual payments through December 31, 19Y6. The contracts also specify that no penalty will be charged for prepayments. Company D charges each borrower a 3 percent ($300) fee and incurs $100 in direct origination costs for each loan. [FAS91, ¶71]

.131 Company D chooses to account for this portfolio of loans using anticipated prepayment patterns to apply the interest method of amortization. Company D estimates a constant prepayment rate of 6 percent per year, which is consistent with Company D's prior experience with similar loans and Company D's expectation of ongoing experience. [FAS91, ¶72]

.132 Exhibit 132A illustrates the adjustment required by paragraph .118 of this section when an enterprise's actual prepayment experience differs from the amounts anticipated. The loans have actually prepaid at a rate of 6 percent in years 1 and 2 and 20 percent in year 3, and based on the new information at the end of year 3, Company D revises its estimate of prepayment experience to anticipate that 10 percent of the loans will prepay in year 4 and 6 percent of the loans will prepay in remaining years. The carrying amount of the loans at the end of year 3 is adjusted to the amount that would have existed had the new effective yield been applied since January 1, 19X7. Included in amortization in year 3 is an adjustment for the difference in the prior effective yield and the new effective yield applied to amounts outstanding in years 1 and 2. Amortization in years 4-10 assumes the new estimates of prepayment experience occur as anticipated. [FAS91, ¶73]

Exhibit 132A

Amortization Based on Estimated Prepayment Patterns Adjusted for a Change in Estimate

Year	(1) Cash (Out) Inflow	(2) Stated Interest	(3) Amortization	(4) Interest Income	(5) Remaining Principal	(6) Unamortized Net Fees	(7) Carrying Amount
	$(9,800,000)				$10,000,000		$9,800,000
1	2,227,454	$1,000,000	$ 35,141	$1,035,141	8,772,546	$164,859	8,607,687
2	2,049,623	877,255	31,946	909,201	7,600,178	132,913	7,467,265
3	2,944,644	760,018	41,951	801,969	5,415,552	90,962	5,324,590
4	1,653,939	541,555	23,294	564,849	4,303,168	67,668	4,235,500
5	1,246,229	430,317	18,998	449,315	3,487,256	48,670	3,438,586
6	1,129,164	348,726	16,050	364,776	2,706,818	32,620	2,674,198
7	1,016,331	270,682	13,005	283,687	1,961,169	19,615	1,941,554
8	906,285	196,117	9,849	205,966	1,251,001	9,766	1,241,235
9	795,875	125,100	6,574	131,674	580,226	3,192	577,034
10	638,249	58,023	3,192	61,215	0	0	0
Total amortization			$200,000				

Computations:

Column (1)—Contractual payments + prepayments

Column (2)—Column (5) for prior year × the loan's stated interest rate (10%)

Column (3)—Column (4) – Column (2)

Column (4)—Column (7) for the prior year × the effective rate (10.5627% for years 1 and 2, and 10.6083% for years 3-10, + an adjustment of $8,876 in year 3 representing the cumulative effect[c] applicable to years 1 and 2 of changing the estimated effective rate)

Column (5)—Column (5) for prior year – (Column (1) – Column (2))

Column (6)—Initial net fees – amortization to date

Column (7)—Column (5) – Column (6)

[c]An adjustment would also be required if the level of prepayments realized was less than anticipated.

[FAS91, ¶73]

Case 5—Application of Paragraph .117(a)—When the Loan's Prepayment Penalty Is Effective throughout the Entire Term

.133 Company E grants a 10-year $100,000 loan with an 8 percent stated interest rate in year 1 and 10 percent in years 2-10. Company E receives net fees of $1,000 related to this loan. The contract specifies that the borrower must pay a penalty equal to 1 percent of any principal prepaid. Application of the effective yield to recognize an amount in excess of net fees is appropriate for a loan with an increasing stated interest rate only to the extent that the loan agreement provides for a prepayment penalty that is effective throughout the loan term. [Exhibit 133A illustrates the application of paragraph .117(a) when the prepayment penalty is effective throughout the entire term of the loan.] [FAS91, ¶74]

Exhibit 133A

Application of Paragraph .117(a)—When the Loan's Prepayment Penalty Is Effective throughout the Entire Term

Year	(1) Cash (Out) Inflow	(2) Stated Interest	(3) Amortization	(4) Interest Income	(5) Remaining Principal	(6) Unamortized Net Fees[d]	(7) Carrying Amount	(8) Settlement Amount
	$(99,000)				$100,000		$99,000	
1	14,903	$8,000	$1,710	$9,710	93,097	$(710)	93,807	$94,028
2	16,165	9,310	(108)	9,202	86,242	(602)	86,844	87,104
3	16,165	8,624	(106)	8,518	78,701	(496)	79,197	79,488
4	16,165	7,870	(102)	7,768	70,406	(394)	70,800	71,110
5	16,165	7,041	(97)	6,944	61,282	(297)	61,579	61,895
6	16,165	6,128	(88)	6,040	51,245	(209)	51,454	51,757
7	16,165	5,124	(78)	5,046	40,204	(131)	40,335	40,606
8	16,165	4,021	(65)	3,956	28,060	(66)	28,126	28,340
9	16,165	2,806	(47)	2,759	14,701	(19)	14,720	14,848
10	16,165	1,464[e]	(19)	1,445	0	0	0	0
Total amortization			$1,000					

Computations:
Column (1)—Contractual payments
Column (2)—Column (5) for prior year × the loan's stated interest rate (8% in year 1, 10% in years 2-10)
Column (3)—Column (4) – Column (2)
Column (4)—Column (7) for the prior year × the effective interest rate (9.8085%)
Column (5)—Column (5) for prior year – (Column (1) – Column (2))
Column (6)—Initial net fees – amortization to date
Column (7)—Column (5) – Column (6)
Column (8)—Column (5) × 1.01 (to calculate the settlement amount including prepayment penalty)

---

[d] Unamortized net fee and accrued interest.

[e] $6 rounding adjustment.

[FAS91, ¶74]

Case 6—Application of Paragraph .117(a)—With No Prepayment Penalty

.134 Company F grants a 10-year $100,000 loan. The contract provides for 8 percent interest in year 1 and 10 percent interest in years 2-10. Company F receives net fees of $1,000 related to this loan. The contract specifies that no penalty will be charged for prepayment of principal. [FAS91, ¶75]

.135 The discount factor that equates the present value of the cash inflows in Column 1 with the initial cash outflow of $99,000 is 9.8085 percent. In year 1, recognition of interest income on the investment of $99,000 at a rate of 9.8085 percent would cause the investment to be $93,807, or $710 greater than the amount at which the borrower could settle the obligation. Because the condition set forth in paragraph .117(a) is not met, recognition of an amount greater than the net fee is not permitted, [as illustrated in Exhibit 135A.] [FAS91, ¶76]

Exhibit 135A

Application of Paragraph .117(a)—With No Prepayment Penalty

Year	(1) Cash (Out) Inflow	(2) Stated Interest	(3) Amortization	(4) Interest Income	(5) Remaining Principal	(6) Unamortized Net Fees	(7) Carrying Amount
	$(99,000)				$100,000		$99,000
1	14,903	$8,000	$1,000	$9,000	93,097	$0	93,097
2	16,165	9,310	0	9,310	86,242	0	86,242
3	16,165	8,624	0	8,624	78,701	0	78,701
4	16,165	7,870	0	7,870	70,406	0	70,406
5	16,165	7,041	0	7,041	61,282	0	61,282
6	16,165	6,128	0	6,128	51,245	0	51,245
7	16,165	5,124	0	5,124	40,204	0	40,204
8	16,165	4,021	0	4,021	28,060	0	28,060
9	16,165	2,806	0	2,806	14,701	0	14,701
10	16,165	1,464[f]	0	1,464	0	0	0
Total amortization			$1,000				

Computations:
Column (1)—Contractual payments
Column (2)—Column (5) for prior year × the loan's stated interest rate (8% in year 1, 10% in year 2-10)
Column (3)—Column (4) – Column (2)
Column (4)—Column (7) for the prior year × the effective interest rate (9.8085%) as limited by paragraph .117(a) of this section
Column (5)—Column (5) for prior year – (Column (1) – Column (2))
Column (6)—Initial net fees – amortization to date
Column (7)—Column (5) – Column (6)

[f] $6 rounding adjustment.

[FAS91, ¶76]

Case 7—Application of Paragraph .117(b)

.136 Company G grants a 10-year $100,000 mortgage. Company G receives net fees of $1,000 related to this loan. The contract provides for an interest rate of 12 percent in year 1, 11 percent in year 2, and 10 percent thereafter. [Exhibit 136A illustrates the application of paragraph .117(b).] [FAS91, ¶77]

Exhibit 136A

Application of Paragraph .117(b)

Year	(1) Cash (Out) Inflow	(2) Stated Interest	(3) Amortization	(4) Interest Income	(5) Remaining Principal	(6) Unamortized Net Fees[g]	(7) Carrying Amount
	$(99,000)				$100,000		$99,000
1	17,698	$12,000	$(1,259)	$10,741	94,302	$2,259	92,043
2	17,031	10,373	(388)	9,985	87,644	2,647	84,997
3	16,428	8,764	458	9,222	79,980	2,189	77,791
4	16,428	7,998	441	8,439	71,550	1,748	69,802
5	16,428	7,155	418	7,573	62,277	1,330	60,947
6	16,428	6,228	385	6,613	52,077	945	51,132
7	16,428	5,208	339	5,547	40,857	606	40,251
8	16,428	4,086	281	4,367	28,515	325	28,190
9	16,428	2,852	206	3,058	14,939	119	14,820
10	16,428	1,489[h]	119	1,608	0	0	0
Total amortization			$ 1,000				

Computations:
Column (1)—Contractual payments
Column (2)—Column (5) for prior year × the loan's stated interest rate (12% in year 1, 11% for year 2, and 10% in years 3-10)
Column (3)—Column (4) – Column (2)
Column (4)—Column (7) for the prior year × the effective interest rate (10.8491%)
Column (5)—Column (5) for prior year – (Column (1) – Column (2))
Column (6)—Initial net fees – amortization to date
Column (7)—Column (5) – Column (6)

[g] Unamortized net fee and deferred interest.

[h] $5 rounding adjustment.

[FAS91, ¶77]

Case 8—Application of Paragraph .117(c)—Amortization Based on Factor at Inception

.137 Company H grants a 10-year variable rate mortgage. The loan's interest rate and payment are adjusted annually based on the weekly Treasury bill index plus 1 percent. At the date the loan is granted, this index is 7 percent and does not change until the end of year 3. The first year loan interest rate is 8 percent (equal to the Treasury bill index plus 1 percent). Company H receives net fees of $3,000. At the end of year 3 the index changes to 9 percent and does not change again. Therefore, the loan's stated interest rate is 8 percent for years 1-3 and 10 percent for years 4-10. Company H chooses to determine the amortization based on the index at the date the loan is granted and to ignore subsequent changes in the factor, [as illustrated in Exhibit 137A.] [FAS91, ¶78]

Exhibit 137A

Application of Paragraph .117(c)—Amortization Based on Factor at Inception

Year	(1) Cash (Out) Inflow	(2) Stated Interest	(3) Amortization	(4) Interest Income	(5) Remaining Principal	(6) Unamortized Net Fees	(7) Carrying Amount
	$(97,000)				$100,000		$97,000
1	14,903	$8,000	$ 420	$8,420	93,097	$2,580	90,517
2	14,903	7,448	410	7,858	85,642	2,170	83,472
3	14,903	6,851	395	7,246	77,590	1,775	75,815
4	15,937	7,759	375	8,134	69,412	1,400	68,012
5	15,937	6,941	347	7,288	60,416	1,053	59,363
6	15,937	6,042	314	6,356	50,521	739	49,782
7	15,937	5,052	272	5,324	39,636	467	39,169
8	15,937	3,964	221	4,185	27,663	246	27,417
9	15,937	2,766	160	2,926	14,492	86	14,406
10	15,937	1,445[i]	86	1,531	0	0	0
Total amortization			$3,000				

Computations:
Column (1)—Contractual payments
Column (2)—Column (5) for prior year × the loan's stated interest rate (8% in years 1-3, and 10% in years 4-10)
Column (3)—Calculated as if the index did not change—that is, the amount that would have been recognized for an 8%, 10-year $100,000 mortgage with no prepayments and a $3,000 net fee
Column (4)—Column (2) + Column (3)
Column (5)—Column (5) for prior year – (Column (1) – Column (2))
Column (6)—Initial net fees – amortization to date
Column (7)—Column (5) – Column (6)

[i] $4 rounding adjustment.

[FAS91, ¶78]

Case 9—Application of Paragraph .117(c)—Amortization Recalculated for Subsequent Changes in Factor

.138 Company I grants a 10-year variable rate mortgage. The loan's interest rate and payment are adjusted annually based on the weekly Treasury bill index plus 1 percent. At the date the loan is granted, this index is 7 percent and does not change until the end of year 3. The first year loan interest rate is 8 percent (equal to the Treasury bill index plus 1 percent). Company I receives net fees of $3,000. At the end of year 3 the index changes to 9 percent and does not change again. Therefore, the loan's stated interest rate is 8 percent for years 1-3 and 10 percent for years 4-10. Company I chooses to recalculate a new amortization schedule each time the loan's index changes, [as illustrated in Exhibit 138A.] [FAS91, ¶79]

Exhibit 138A

Application of Paragraph .117(c)—Amortization Recalculated for Subsequent Changes in Factor

Year	(1) Cash (Out) Inflow	(2) Stated Interest	(3) Amortization	(4) Interest Income	(5) Remaining Principal	(6) Unamortized Net Fees	(7) Carrying Amount
	$(97,000)				$100,000		$97,000
1	14,903	$8,000	$ 420	$8,420	93,097	$2,580	90,517
2	14,903	7,448	410	7,858	85,642	2,170	83,472
3	14,903	6,851	395	7,246	77,590	1,775	75,815
4	15,937	7,759	358	8,117	69,412	1,417	67,995
5	15,937	6,941	340	7,281	60,416	1,077	59,339
6	15,937	6,042	311	6,353	50,521	766	49,755
7	15,937	5,052	275	5,327	39,636	491	39,145
8	15,937	3,964	227	4,191	27,663	264	27,399
9	15,937	2,766	168	2,934	14,492	96	14,396
10	15,937	1,445[j]	96	1,541	0	0	0
Total amortization			$3,000				

Computations:
Column (1)—Contractual payments
Column (2)—Column (5) for prior year × the loan's stated interest rate (8% in years 1-3, and 10% in years 4-10)
Column (3)—Column (4) – Column (2)
Column (4)—Column (7) for the prior year × the effective interest rate (8.6809%) for years 1-3 and Column (7) for the prior year × the effective interest rate (10.7068%) for years 4-10
Column (5)—Column (5) for prior year – (Column (1) – Column (2))
Column (6)—Initial net fees – amortization to date
Column (7)—Column (5) – Column (6)

[j] $4 rounding adjustment.

[FAS91, ¶79]

[**Note:** Additional guidance with respect to implementing Section L20 is presented in *A Guide to Implementation of Statement 91 on Accounting for Nonrefundable Fees and Costs Associated with Originating or Acquiring Loans and Initial Direct Costs of Leases: Questions and Answers.* The publication, which addresses 65 questions and was edited by Christopher S. Lynch, FASB staff, is available from the Order Department, Financial Accounting Standards Board, 401 Merritt 7, P.O. Box 5116, Norwalk, CT 06856-5116, telephone (203) 847-0700.]

Glossary

.401 **Commitment fees.** Fees charged for entering into an agreement that obligates the enterprise to make or acquire a loan or to satisfy an obligation of the other party under a specified condition. For purposes of this section, the term *commitment fees* includes fees for letters of credit and obligations to purchase a loan or group of loans and pass-through certificates. [FAS91, ¶80]

.402 **Credit card fees.** The periodic uniform fees that entitle cardholders to use credit cards. The amount of such fees generally is not dependent upon the level of credit available or frequency of usage. Typically the use of credit cards facilitates the cardholder's payment for the purchase of goods and services on a periodic, as-billed basis (usually monthly), involves the extension of credit, and, if payment is not made when billed, involves imposition of interest or finance charges. For purposes of this section, the term *credit card fees* includes fees received in similar arrangements, such as charge card and cash card fees. [FAS91, ¶80]

.403 **Incremental direct costs.** Costs to originate a loan that (a) result directly from and are essential to the lending transaction and (b) would not have been incurred by the lender had that lending transaction not occurred. [FAS91, ¶80]

.404 **Origination fees.** Fees charged to the borrower in connection with the process of originating, refinancing, or restructuring a loan. This term includes, but is not limited to, points, management, arrangement, placement, application, underwriting, and other fees pursuant to a lending or leasing transaction and also includes syndication and participation fees to the extent they are associated with the portion of the loan retained by the lender. [FAS91, ¶80]

Supplemental Guidance: Emerging Issues Task Force (EITF) Issues

.1000 [Listed below are EITF Issues that provide supplemental guidance for this section. These Issues are grouped by subject matter and may be either interpretive of or related by topic to the guidance in this section.

ADC Loans

EITF Issue No. 84-4, "Acquisition, Development, and Construction Loans"
EITF Issue No. 86-21, "Application of the AICPA Notice to Practitioners regarding Acquisition, Development, and Construction Arrangements to Acquisition of an Operating Property"

Credit Cards

EITF Issue No. 88-20, "Difference between Initial Investment and Principal Amount of Loans in a Purchased Credit Card Portfolio"
EITF Issue No. 92-5, "Amortization Period for Net Deferred Credit Card Origination Costs"
EITF Issue No. 93-1, "Accounting for Individual Credit Card Acquisitions"

Interest Income Recognition

EITF Issue No. 96-12, "Recognition of Interest Income and Balance Sheet Classification of Structured Notes"
EITF Topic No. D-10, "Required Use of Interest Method in Recognizing Interest Income"

Lease Arrangements

EITF Issue No. 95-6, "Accounting by a Real Estate Investment Trust for an Investment in a Service Corporation"
EITF Topic No. D-8, "Accruing Bad-Debt Expense at Inception of a Lease"

Loan Guarantees

EITF Issue No. 85-20, "Recognition of Fees for Guaranteeing a Loan"
EITF Topic No. D-4, "Argentine Government Guarantee of U.S. Dollar-Denominated Loans to the Argentine Private Sector"

Other

EITF Issue No. 87-30, "Sale of a Short-Term Loan Made under a Long-Term Credit Commitment"
EITF Issue No. 97-3, "Accounting for Fees and Costs Associated with Loan Syndications and Loan Participations after the Issuance of FASB Statement No. 125"
EITF Issue No. 01-7, "Creditor's Accounting for a Modification or Exchange of Debt Instruments"]

.1001 [Listed below are those EITF Issues that provide interpretive guidance on specific material in this section.

Paragraph .104 (FAS 91, ¶5)—EITF Issue No. 93-1
Paragraph .105 (FAS 91, ¶6)—EITF Issues No. 92-5 and 93-1
Paragraph .106 (FAS 91, ¶7)—EITF Issue No. 93-1
Paragraph .107 (FAS 91, ¶8)—EITF Issues No. 85-20 and 87-30
Paragraph .109 (FAS 91, ¶10)—EITF Issue No. 92-5
Paragraph .115 (FAS 91, ¶16)—EITF Issue No. 88-20
Paragraph .117 (FAS 91, ¶18)—EITF Issues No. 88-20, 92-5, and 93-1 and Topic No. D-10
Paragraphs .118 and .119 (FAS 91, ¶19-20)—EITF Issues No. 88-20, 92-5, and 93-1
Paragraph .122 (FAS 91, ¶23)—EITF Topic No. D-8]

(The next page is 30733.)

Sources: APB Opinion 26; AICPA Interpretation of APB Opinion 26; FASB Statement 84; FASB Statement 111; FASB Statement 140; FASB Statement 145; FASB Technical Bulletin 80-1

[**Note:** A list of Issues discussed by the Emerging Issues Task Force (EITF) that provide supplemental guidance for this section is presented in paragraph .1000.]

Summary

This section presents accounting and reporting standards for extinguishments of liabilities. This section requires that a liability be derecognized if and only if either (a) the debtor pays the creditor and is relieved of its obligation for the liability or (b) the debtor is legally released from being the primary obligor under the liability either judicially or by the creditor. Therefore, a liability is not considered extinguished by an in-substance defeasance.

This section applies to all extinguishments of debt, whether early or not, other than debt conversions and troubled debt restructurings.

The difference between the amount paid to extinguish the debt and the net carrying amount of the debt shall be recognized currently in income.

Scope

.101 This section [applies to all] extinguishments of liabilities [by using] a *financial-components approach* that focuses on control. [FAS140, ¶7] [**Derecognition** of liabilities occurs] only when they have been extinguished. [FAS140, ¶5] Under the financial-components approach, an in-substance defeasance transaction does not meet the derecognition criteria for either the liability or the asset. [FAS140, ¶311]

.102 Paragraphs .105 through .108 apply to all extinguishments of debt, whether early or not, except debt that is extinguished through a troubled debt restructuring [refer to Section D22, "Debt: Restructurings"]; debt that is converted to equity securities of the debtor pursuant to conversion privileges provided in terms of the debt at issuance; [APB26, ¶2, as amended by FAS76, ¶7] [and] conversions of convertible debt when conversion privileges included in terms at issuance are changed, or additional consideration is paid, to induce conversion of the debt to equity securities [as described in Section D10, "Debt: Convertible Debt, Conversion of Convertible Debt, and Debt with Stock Purchase Warrants"]. [FAS84, ¶5] All extinguishments of debt are fundamentally alike. The accounting for such transactions shall be the same regardless of the means used to achieve the extinguishment. [APB26, ¶19]

Extinguishments of Liabilities

.103 A debtor shall derecognize a liability if and only if it has been extinguished. A liability has been extinguished if either of the following conditions is met:

a. The debtor pays the creditor and is relieved of its obligation for the liability. *Paying the creditor* includes delivery of cash, other financial assets, goods, or services or reacquisition by the debtor of its outstanding debt securities whether the securities are canceled or held as so-called treasury bonds.
b. The debtor is legally released[1] from being the primary obligor under the liability, either judicially or by the creditor.

[FAS140, ¶16] [Refer to paragraph .1001 for an EITF Issue that provides interpretive guidance on this paragraph.]

.104 If a creditor releases a debtor from primary obligation on the condition that a third party assumes the obligation and that the original debtor becomes secondarily liable, that release extinguishes the original debtor's liability. However, in those circumstances, whether or not explicit consideration was paid for that guarantee, the original debtor becomes a guarantor. As a guarantor, it shall recognize a guarantee obligation in the same manner as would a guarantor that had never been primarily liable to that creditor, with due regard for the likelihood that the third party will carry out its obligations. The guarantee obligation shall be initially measured at fair value, and that amount reduces the gain or increases the loss recognized on extinguishment. [FAS140, ¶114]

[1] If nonrecourse debt (such as certain mortgage loans) is assumed by a third party in conjunction with the sale of an asset that serves as sole collateral for that debt, the sale and related assumption effectively accomplish a legal release of the seller-debtor for purposes of applying this section. [FAS140, ¶16, fn5]

Accounting for Extinguishment of Debt

.105 The difference between the **reacquisition price** and the **net carrying amount** of the extinguished debt shall be recognized currently in income of the period of extinguishment as [a] loss or gain and identified as a separate item [refer to paragraph .106 below].[2] Gains and losses shall not be amortized to future periods. [APB26, ¶20]

.106 The extinguishment of convertible debt does not change the character of the security as between debt and equity at that time. Therefore, a difference between the cash acquisition price of the debt and its net carrying amount shall be recognized currently in income in the period of extinguishment as a loss or gain. [APB26, ¶21]

.107–.108 [Deleted 4/02 because of FASB Statement 145, *Rescission of FASB Statements No. 4, 44, and 64, Amendment of FASB Statement No. 13, and Technical Corrections*.]

---

[2]If upon extinguishment of debt, the parties also exchange unstated (or stated) rights or privileges, the portion of the consideration exchanged allocable to such unstated (or stated) rights or privileges should be given appropriate accounting recognition. Moreover, extinguishment transactions between related enterprises may be in essence capital transactions. [APB26, ¶20, fn1]

[3–4][Deleted 4/02 because of Statement 145.]

Disclosure

.109 An entity shall disclose the following:

a. If debt was considered to be extinguished by in-substance defeasance under the provisions of Section D14, "Debt: Extinguishments," prior to the effective date of this section [January 1, 1997], a general description of the transaction and the amount of debt that is considered extinguished at the end of the period so long as that debt remains outstanding [FAS140, ¶17(b)]
b. If assets are set aside after the effective date of this section solely for satisfying scheduled payments of a specific obligation, a description of the nature of restrictions placed on those assets [FAS140, ¶17(c)]
c. [Deleted 4/02 because of Statement 145.]

[**Note:** Additional guidance with respect to implementing Section L35 is presented in *A Guide to Implementation of Statement 140 on Accounting for Transfers and Servicing of Financial Assets and Extinguishments of Liabilities: Questions and Answers.* This publication addresses 123 questions and was written by FASB staff members Halsey G. Bullen, Victoria A. Lusniak, and Stephen J. Young. This publication is available from the Order Department, Financial Accounting Standards Board, 401 Merritt 7, P.O. Box 5116, Norwalk, CT 06856-5116, telephone (203) 847-0700.]

Glossary

.401 **Derecognize.** Remove previously recognized assets or liabilities from the statement of financial position. [FAS140, ¶364]

.402 **Net carrying amount [of debt].** The amount due at maturity, adjusted for unamortized premium, discount, and cost of issuance. [APB26, ¶3]

.403 **Reacquisition price [of debt].** The amount paid on extinguishment, including a call premium and miscellaneous costs of reacquisition. If extinguishment is achieved by a direct exchange of new securities, the reacquisition price is the total present value of the new securities. [APB26, ¶3]

Supplemental Guidance

Extinguishment of Debt through Exchange for Common or Preferred Stock

.501 *Question*—Does this section apply to extinguishments of debt effected by issuance of common or preferred stock, including redeemable and fixed-maturity preferred stock? [FTB80-1, ¶1]

.502 *Background*—The conversion of debt to common or preferred stock is not an extinguishment if the conversion represents the exercise of a conversion right contained in the terms of the debt issue. Other exchanges of common or preferred stock for debt would constitute extinguishment. [FTB80-1, ¶2]

.503 *Response*—All extinguishments of debt must be accounted for in accordance with either [FTB80-1, ¶3] Section D10, [FAS111, ¶8(bb)] Section D22, Section I17, "Income Statement Presentation: Extraordinary Items," or this section. [FAS145, ¶9(p)] [Section D10 applies to conversion of convertible debt,] Section D22 applies to extinguishments effected in a troubled debt restructuring, [Section I17 addresses the criteria for extraordinary item classification, and] this section applies to all other extinguishments of debt. [FTB80-1, ¶3]

.504 This section applies to all extinguishments of debt effected by issuance of common or preferred stock, including redeemable and fixed maturity preferred stock, unless the extinguishment is a troubled debt restructuring or [FTB80-1, ¶4] a conversion of debt to equity securities of the debtor (a) pursuant to conversion privileges provided in the terms of the debt at issuance or (b) when conversion privileges provided in the terms of the debt at issuance are changed (including changes that involve payment of consideration) to induce conversion of the debt to security equities in accordance with paragraph .103A of Section D10. [FAS111, ¶8(bb)] The reacquisition price of the extinguished debt is to be determined by the value of the common or preferred stock issued or the value of the debt—whichever is more clearly evident. [FTB80-1, ¶4]

Debt Tendered to Exercise Warrants

.505 *Question*—This section stipulates that gain or loss should be recognized currently in income when any form of debt security is reacquired by the issuer except through conversion by the holder. Does this section apply to debt tendered to exercise warrants that were originally issued with that debt but which were detachable? [AIN-APB26, #1]

.506 *Response*—This section does not apply to debt tendered to exercise detachable warrants that were originally issued with that debt if the debt is permitted to be tendered towards the exercise price of the warrants under the terms of the securities at issuance. The tendering of the debt in such a case would be a conversion [pursuant to conversion privileges provided in the terms of the debt at issuance]. [AIN-APB26, #1]

Supplemental Guidance: Emerging Issues Task Force (EITF) Issues

.1000 [Listed below are EITF Issues that provide supplemental guidance for this section. These Issues may be either interpretive of or related by topic to the guidance in this section.

EITF Issue No. 86-36, "Invasion of a Defeasance Trust"
EITF Issue No. 90-19, "Convertible Bonds with Issuer Option to Settle for Cash upon Conversion"
EITF Issue No. 96-19, "Debtor's Accounting for a Modification or Exchange of Debt Instruments
EITF Issue No. 98-14, "Debtor's Accounting for Changes in Line-of-Credit or Revolving-Debt Arrangements"
EITF Issue No. 00-9, "Classification of a Gain or Loss from a Hedge of Debt That Is Extinguished"]

.1001 [Listed below is an EITF Issue that provides interpretive guidance on specific material in this section.

Paragraph .103 (FAS 140, ¶16)—EITF Issue No. 96-19]

(The next page is 31981.)

Supplemental Guidance: Emerging Issues Task Force (EITF) Issues

[illegible]

NONMONETARY TRANSACTIONS SECTION N35

Sources: APB Opinion 29; FASB Statement 109; FASB Statement 123; FASB Statement 141; FASB Statement 144; FASB Interpretation 30

[**Note:** A list of Issues discussed by the Emerging Issues Task Force (EITF) that provide supplemental guidance for this section is presented in paragraph .1000.]

Summary

In general, accounting for nonmonetary transactions shall be based on the fair values of the assets (or services) involved. This is the same basis as that used for monetary transactions. If a nonmonetary asset is involuntarily converted to a monetary asset (such as cash), a gain or loss shall be recognized even though an enterprise reinvests or is obligated to reinvest the monetary assets in replacement nonmonetary assets.

Applicability

.101 This section does not apply to the following transactions:

a. A business combination accounted for by an enterprise according to the provisions of [APB29, ¶4] Section B51, "Business Combinations"[b] [FAS141, ¶E4]
b. A transfer of **nonmonetary assets** solely between enterprises or persons under common control, such as between a parent company and its subsidiaries or between two subsidiary enterprises of the same parent, or between a corporate joint venture and its owners
c. Acquisition of nonmonetary assets or services on issuance of the capital stock of an enterprise[c]
d. Stock issued or received in stock dividends and stock splits which are accounted for in accordance with Section C20, "Capital Stock: Stock Dividends and Stock Splits."

[[a]Deleted 6/01 and renumbered as footnote [c].]

[b]Paragraph .109 of Section B51, "Business Combinations," states that an exchange of a business for a business is a business combination. [FAS141, ¶E4]

[c]Section C36, "Compensation: Stock-Based," applies to all transactions in which an entity acquires goods or services by issuing equity instruments or by incurring liabilities to the supplier in amounts based on the price of the entity's common stock or other equity instruments [including transactions with suppliers other than employees]. [FAS123, ¶383]

Some exchanges of nonmonetary assets involve a small monetary consideration, referred to as *boot,* even though the exchange is essentially nonmonetary. This section also applies to those transactions. For purposes of applying this section, events and transactions in which nonmonetary assets are involuntarily converted[1] (for example, as a result of total or partial destruction, theft, seizure, or condemnation) to **monetary assets** that are then reinvested in other nonmonetary assets are monetary transactions. [APB29, ¶4]

Examples of Nonmonetary Transactions

Nonreciprocal Transfers with Owners

.102 Some **nonmonetary transactions** are **nonreciprocal transfers** between an enterprise and its owners. Examples include (a) distribution of nonmonetary assets, such as marketable equity securities, to stockholders as dividends [(refer to Section C11, "Capital Stock: Dividends-in-Kind")]; (b) distribution of nonmonetary assets, such as marketable equity securities, to stockholders to redeem or acquire outstanding capital stock of the enterprise; (c) distribution of nonmonetary assets, such as capital stock of subsidiaries, to stockholders in corporate liquidations or plans of reorganization that involve disposing of all or a significant segment of the business (the plans are variously referred to as spin-offs, split-ups, and split-offs); and (d) distribution of nonmonetary assets to groups of stockholders, pursuant to plans of rescission or other settlements relating to a prior business combination, to redeem or acquire shares of capital stock previously issued in a business combination. [APB29, ¶5]

Nonreciprocal Transfers with Other Than Owners

.103 Other nonmonetary transactions are nonreciprocal transfers between an enterprise and entities other than its owners. Examples are the contribution of nonmonetary assets by an enterprise to a charitable organization and the contribution of land by a governmental unit for construction of productive facilities by an enterprise. [APB29, ¶6]

Exchanges

.104 Many nonmonetary transactions are **exchanges** of nonmonetary assets or services with another entity. Examples include (a) exchange of product held for sale in the ordinary course of business (inventory) for dissimilar property as a means of selling the product to a customer; (b) exchange of product held for sale in the ordinary course of business (inventory) for similar product as an accommodation—that is, at least one party to

[[1]Paragraphs .114 through .119 discuss the appropriate accounting for *involuntary* conversions of nonmonetary assets to monetary assets.]

the exchange reduces transportation costs, meets immediate inventory needs, or otherwise reduces costs or facilitates ultimate sale of the product—and not as a means of selling the product to a customer; and (c) exchange of **productive assets**—assets employed in production rather than held for sale in the ordinary course of business—for similar productive assets or for an equivalent interest in **similar productive assets.** Examples of exchanges in category (c) include the trade of player contracts by professional sports organizations, exchange of leases on mineral properties, exchange of one form of interest in an oil-producing property for another form of interest, [and] exchange of real estate for real estate. [APB29, ¶7]

Basic Principle

.105 Accounting for nonmonetary transactions shall be based on the fair values[2] of the assets (or services) involved, which is the same basis as that used in monetary transactions. Thus, the cost of a nonmonetary asset acquired in exchange for another nonmonetary asset is the fair value of the asset surrendered to obtain it, and a gain or loss shall be recognized on the exchange. The fair value of the asset received shall be used to measure the cost if it is more clearly evident than the fair value of the asset surrendered. Similarly, a nonmonetary asset received in a nonreciprocal transfer shall be recorded at the fair value of the asset received. A transfer of a nonmonetary asset to a stockholder or to another entity in a nonreciprocal transfer shall be recorded at the fair value of the asset transferred, and a gain or loss should be recognized on the disposition of the asset. The fair value of an enterprise's own stock reacquired may be a more clearly evident measure of the fair value of the asset distributed in a nonreciprocal transfer if the transaction involves distribution of a nonmonetary asset to eliminate a disproportionate part of owners' interests (that is, to acquire stock for the treasury or for retirement). [APB29, ¶18] [Refer to paragraph .1001 for an EITF Issue that provides interpretive guidance on this paragraph.]

.106 Certain modifications of the basic principle are required to accommodate problems of measurement and questions about the conditions for recognizing revenue. These modifications are specified in paragraphs .107 through .110. [APB29, ¶19]

Modifications of the Basic Principle

Fair Value Not Determinable

.107 Accounting for a nonmonetary transaction shall not be based on the fair values of the assets transferred unless those fair values are determinable within reasonable limits (refer to paragraph .111). [APB29, ¶20] [Refer to paragraph .1001 for an EITF Issue that provides interpretive guidance on paragraphs .107 through .110.]

[2]Refer to paragraph .111 for determination of fair value. [APB29, ¶18, fn5]

Exchanges

.108 If the exchange is not essentially the culmination of an earning process, accounting for an exchange of a nonmonetary asset between an enterprise and another entity shall be based on the recorded amount (after reduction, if appropriate, for an indicated impairment of value) of the nonmonetary asset relinquished.[2a] The following two types of nonmonetary exchange transactions do not culminate an earning process:

a. An exchange of a product or property held for sale in the ordinary course of business for a product or property to be sold in the same line of business to facilitate sales to customers other than the parties to the exchange
b. An exchange of a productive asset not held for sale in the ordinary course of business for a similiar productive asset or an equivalent interest in the same or similar productive asset (examples are given in paragraph .104).[3]

[APB29, ¶21]

.109 The exchanges of nonmonetary assets that would otherwise be based on recorded amounts (refer to paragraph .108) may include an amount of monetary consideration. The recipient of the monetary consideration has realized gain on the exchange to the extent that the amount of the monetary receipt exceeds a proportionate share of the recorded amount of the asset surrendered. The portion of the cost applicable to the realized amount shall be based on the ratio of the monetary consideration to the total consideration received (monetary consideration plus the estimated fair value of the nonmonetary asset received) or, if more clearly evident, the fair value of the nonmonetary asset transferred. The enterprise paying the monetary consideration shall not recognize any gain on a transaction covered in paragraph .108 but shall record the asset received at the amount of the monetary consideration paid plus the recorded amount of the nonmonetary asset surrendered. If a loss is indicated by the terms of a transaction described in this paragraph or in paragraph .108, the entire indicated loss on the exchange shall be recognized. [APB29, ¶22]

Nonreciprocal Transfers to Owners

.110 Accounting for the distribution of nonmonetary assets to owners of an enterprise in a spin-off or other form of reorganization or liquidation or in a plan that is in substance the rescission of a prior business combination shall be based on the recorded amount (after reduction, if appropriate, for an indicated impairment of value)[3a] of the non-

[2a]An indicated impairment of value of a long-lived asset covered by Section D60, "Disposal of Long-Lived Assets," shall be determined in accordance with paragraph .106 of that section. [FAS144, ¶C4]

[3]The fact that an exchange of productive assets is not a taxable transaction for tax purposes may be evidence that the assets exchanged are similar for purposes of applying this section. [APB29, ¶21, fn6]

[3a][See footnote 2a.]

monetary assets distributed. A pro rata distribution to owners of an enterprise of shares of a subsidiary or other enterprise that has been or is being consolidated or that has been or is being accounted for under the equity method is to be considered to be equivalent to a spin-off. Other nonreciprocal transfers of nonmonetary assets to owners shall be accounted for at fair value if the fair value of the nonmonetary asset distributed is objectively measurable and would be clearly realizable to the distributing entity in an outright sale at or near the time of the distribution. [APB29, ¶23]

Applying the Basic Principle

.111 Fair value of a nonmonetary asset transferred to or from an enterprise in a nonmonetary transaction shall be determined by referring to estimated realizable values in cash transactions of the same or similar assets, quoted market prices, independent appraisals, estimated fair values of assets or services received in exchange, and other available evidence. If one of the parties in a nonmonetary transaction could have elected to receive cash instead of the nonmonetary asset, the amount of cash that could have been received may be evidence of the fair value of the nonmonetary assets exchanged. [APB29, ¶25]

.112 Fair value shall be regarded as not determinable within reasonable limits if major uncertainties exist about the realizability of the value that would be assigned to an asset received in a nonmonetary transaction accounted for at fair value. An exchange involving parties with essentially opposing interests is not considered a prerequisite to determining a fair value of a nonmonetary asset transferred; nor does an exchange insure that a fair value for accounting purposes can be ascertained within reasonable limits. If neither the fair value of a nonmonetary asset transferred nor the fair value of a nonmonetary asset received in exchange is determinable within reasonable limits, the recorded amount of the nonmonetary asset transferred from the enterprise may be the only available measure of the transaction. [APB29, ¶26]

.113 A difference between the amount of gain or loss recognized for tax purposes and that recognized for accounting purposes may constitute a [APB29, ¶27] temporary difference [FAS109, ¶287] to be accounted for according to [APB29, ¶27] Section I27, "Income Taxes." [FAS109, ¶287]

Accounting for Involuntary Conversions of Nonmonetary Assets to Monetary Assets

.114 Involuntary conversions of nonmonetary assets to monetary assets are monetary transactions for which gain or loss shall be recognized even though an enterprise reinvests or is obligated to reinvest the monetary assets in replacement nonmonetary assets. [FIN30, ¶2] The gain or loss on the involuntary conversion is the difference between the cost[4] of the nonmonetary asset and the amount of monetary assets received. [FIN30, ¶1]

.115 The requirement to recognize gain in paragraph .114 does not apply to certain involuntary conversions of LIFO inventories[5] [FIN30, ¶2] for which replacement is intended but not made by year-end and the taxpayer does not recognize gain for income tax reporting purposes. [FIN30, ¶11]

.116 An involuntary conversion of a nonmonetary asset to monetary assets and the subsequent reinvestment of the monetary assets is [not] equivalent to an exchange transaction between an enterprise and another entity. The conversion of a nonmonetary asset to monetary assets is a monetary transaction, whether the conversion is voluntary or involuntary, and such a conversion differs from exchange transactions that involve only nonmonetary assets. To the extent the cost of a nonmonetary asset differs from the amount of monetary assets received, the transaction results in the realization of a gain or loss that shall be recognized. The cost of subsequently acquired nonmonetary assets shall be measured by the consideration paid and not be affected by a previous transaction. [FIN30, ¶10]

.117 In some cases, a nonmonetary asset may be destroyed or damaged in one accounting period, and the amount of monetary assets to be received is not determinable until a subsequent accounting period. In those cases, gain or loss shall be recognized in accordance with Section C59, "Contingencies." [FIN30, ¶3]

.118 Gain or loss resulting from an involuntary conversion of a nonmonetary asset to monetary assets shall be classified in accordance with the provisions of Section I17, "Income Statement Presentation: Extraordinary Items," and Section I22, "Income Statement Presentation: Unusual or Infrequent Items." [FIN30, ¶4]

.119 Gain or loss resulting from an involuntary conversion of a nonmonetary asset to monetary assets that is not recognized for income tax reporting purposes in the same period in which the gain or loss is recognized for financial reporting purposes is a [FIN30, ¶5] temporary difference [FAS109, ¶287] for which comprehensive [recognition of deferred taxes], as described in [FIN30, ¶5] Section I27, [FAS109, ¶287] is required. [FIN30, ¶5]

---

[4]As used in this section, the term *cost* refers to the cost of a nonmonetary asset or to its carrying amount, if different. [FIN30, ¶1, fn2]

[5]Section I73, "Interim Financial Reporting," paragraph .107(b), provides an exception for the liquidation of a LIFO inventory at an interim date if replacement is expected by year-end. Accordingly, that exception applies to an involuntary conversion of a LIFO inventory if replacement is expected by year-end. [FIN30, ¶2, fn3]

Disclosure

.120 An enterprise that engages in one or more nonmonetary transactions during a period shall disclose in financial statements for the period the nature of the transactions, the basis of accounting for the assets transferred, and gains or losses recognized on transfers.[6] [APB29, ¶28]

[6]Section C51, "Consolidation," paragraph .113, includes additional disclosures that are preferred if a parent company disposes of a subsidiary during the year. [APB29, ¶28, fn7]

Glossary

.401 **Exchange (or exchange transaction).** A reciprocal transfer between an enterprise and another entity that results in the enterprise's acquiring assets or services or satisfying liabilities by surrendering other assets or services or incurring other obligations.[401] [APB29, ¶3] [Refer to paragraph .1001 for an EITF Issue that provides interpretive guidance on this paragraph.]

.402 **Monetary assets (and liabilities).** Assets and liabilities whose amounts are fixed in terms of units of currency by contract or otherwise. Examples are cash, short- or long-term accounts and notes receivable in cash, and short- or long-term accounts and notes payable in cash.[402] [APB29, ¶3]

.403 **Nonmonetary assets and (liabilities).** Assets and liabilities other than monetary ones. Examples are inventories; investments in common stocks; property, plant, and equipment; and liabilities for rent collected in advance.[403] [APB29, ¶3]

.404 **Nonmonetary transactions.** Exchanges and nonreciprocal transfers that involve little or no monetary assets or liabilities. [APB29, ¶1] [Some nonmonetary transactions are described in paragraphs .102 through .104.]

.405 **Nonreciprocal transfer.**[404] A transfer of assets or services in one direction, either from an enterprise to its owners (whether or not in exchange for their ownership interests) or another entity or from owners or another entity to the enterprise. An enterprise's reacquisition of its outstanding stock is an example of a nonreciprocal transfer. [APB29, ¶3]

.406 **Productive assets.** Assets held for or used in the production of goods or services by the enterprise. Productive assets include an investment in another entity if the investment is accounted for by the equity method but exclude an investment not accounted for by that method. [APB29, ¶3]

---

[401] APB Statement No. 4, *Basic Concepts and Accounting Principles Underlying Financial Statements of Business Enterprises,* paragraphs 180 through 183, contains a more complete explanation of exchanges and nonreciprocal transfers. [APB29, ¶3, fn3]

[402] Refer to APB Statement No. 3, *Financial Statements Restated for General Price Level Changes,* paragraphs 17 through 19 and Appendix B, [and Section C28, "Changing Prices: Reporting Their Effects in Financial Reports," for a] more complete explanation of monetary and nonmonetary items. [APB29, ¶3, fn2]

[403] [Refer to footnote 402.] [APB29, ¶3, fn2]

[404] [Refer to footnote 401.] [APB29, ¶3, fn3]

.407 **Similar productive assets.** Productive assets that are of the same general type, that perform the same function or that are employed in the same line of business. [APB29, ¶3]

Supplemental Guidance: Emerging Issues Task Force (EITF) Issues

.1000 [Listed below are EITF Issues that provide supplemental guidance for this section. These Issues are grouped by subject matter and may be either interpretive of or related by topic to the guidance in this section.

Advertising Barter Transactions

EITF Issue No. 93-11, "Accounting for Barter Transactions involving Barter Credits"
EITF Issue No. 99-17, "Accounting for Advertising Barter Transactions"

Other

EITF Issue No. 84-39, "Transfers of Monetary and Nonmonetary Assets among Individuals and Entities under Common Control"
EITF Issue No. 87-21, "Change of Accounting Basis in Master Limited Partnership Transactions"
EITF Issue No. 91-5, "Nonmonetary Exchange of Cost-Method Investments"
EITF Issue No. 98-3, "Determining Whether a Nonmonetary Transaction Involves Receipt of Productive Assets or of a Business"
EITF Issue No. 99-4, "Accounting for Stock Received from the Demutualization of a Mutual Insurance Company"
EITF Issue No. 01-2, "Interpretations of APB Opinion No. 29"]

.1001 [Listed below are those EITF Issues that provide interpretive guidance on specific material in this section.

Paragraph .105 (APB 29, ¶18)—EITF Issue No. 93-11
Paragraphs .107 through .110 (APB 29, ¶20–23)—EITF Issue No. 01-2
Paragraph .401 (APB 29, ¶3)—EITF Issue No. 01-2]

(The next page is 34201.)

PENSION COSTS SECTION P16

Sources: FASB Statement 87; FASB Statement 88; FASB Statement 106; FASB Statement 109; FASB Statement 130; FASB Statement 132; FASB Statement 135; FASB Statement 144

[**Note:** A list of Issues discussed by the Emerging Issues Task Force (EITF) that provide supplemental guidance for this section is presented in paragraph .1000.]

Summary

The conclusions in this section derive from the basic idea that a defined benefit pension is an exchange between the employer and the employee. In exchange for services provided by the employee, the employer promises to provide, in addition to current wages and other benefits, an amount of retirement income. It follows from that basic view that pension benefits are not gratuities but instead are part of an employee's compensation, and since payment is deferred, the pension is a type of deferred compensation. It also follows that the employer's obligation for that compensation is incurred when the services are rendered.

This section addresses three fundamental aspects of pension accounting: *delaying recognition* of certain events, reporting *net cost,* and *offsetting* liabilities and assets.

The *delayed recognition* feature means that changes in the pension obligation (including those resulting from plan amendments) and changes in the value of assets set aside to meet those obligations are not recognized as they occur but are recognized systematically and gradually over subsequent periods.

The *net cost* feature means that the recognized consequences of events and transactions affecting a pension plan are reported as a single net amount in the employer's financial statements. That approach aggregates at least three items that might be reported separately for any other part of an employer's operations: the compensation cost of benefits promised, interest cost resulting from deferred payment of those benefits, and the results of investing what are often significant amounts of assets.

The *offsetting* feature means that recognized values of assets contributed to a plan and liabilities for pensions recognized as net pension cost of past periods are shown net in the employer's statement of financial position, even though the liability has not been settled, the assets may still be largely controlled, and substantial risks and rewards associated with both of those amounts are clearly borne by the employer.

Within those three features that are retained from prior standards, more useful financial reporting is achieved through the following changes:

1. A standardized method is required for measuring net periodic pension cost that is intended to improve comparability and understandability by recognizing the compensation cost of an employee's pension (including prior service cost) over the employee's approximate service period and by relating cost more directly to the terms of the plan
2. Immediate recognition of a liability (the minimum liability) is required in certain circumstances when the accumulated benefit obligation exceeds the fair value of plan assets, although recognition of the offsetting amount as an increase in net periodic pension cost continues to be delayed
3. Expanded disclosures are required that are intended to provide more complete and more current information than that incorporated in the financial statements. However, reduced disclosures are permitted for nonpublic entities. The disclosures required by this section may be reported separately or may be presented in a combined format with the disclosures required by Section P40, "Postretirement Benefits Other Than Pensions," in a single note to the financial statements.

This section defines the limits of delayed recognition of certain previously unrecognized amounts. It also identifies certain events or transactions that trigger the immediate recognition of gains or losses and unrecognized prior service costs. Those events or transactions include settlements of pension obligations and curtailment of defined benefits. This section also addresses the accounting for termination benefits.

Prior to issuance of this section, an employer that entered into an asset reversion transaction involving the termination of one plan and the establishment of a successor defined benefit plan was precluded from immediately recognizing any resulting gain in earnings. This section specifies how that employer should determine the gain to be recognized in earnings at the time of initial application of this section.

.101 This section [presents] standards of financial accounting and reporting for an employer that offers **pension benefits** to its employees. Ordinarily, such benefits are periodic pension payments to retired employees or their survivors, but they may also include benefits payable as a single lump sum and, except as noted in the following paragraph, other types of **benefits** such as death benefits [(also referred to as life insurance)] provided through a pension plan. An employer's arrangement to provide pension benefits may take a variety of forms and may be financed in different ways. This section applies to any arrangement that is similar in substance to a pension plan regardless of the form or means of financing. This section applies to a written plan and to a plan whose existence may be implied from a well-defined, although perhaps unwritten, practice of paying postretirement benefits. [FAS87, ¶7] This section [also] applies to an employer that sponsors a **defined benefit pension plan** if all or part of the plan's pension benefit obligation is settled or the plan is curtailed. [In addition,] it applies to an employer that offers benefits to employees in connection with their termination of employment. [FAS88, ¶2]

.102 This section does not apply to life insurance benefits provided outside a pension plan or to other postretirement health and welfare benefits. The accounting for those benefits is set forth in Section P40, "Postretirement Benefits Other Than Pensions." [FAS106, ¶14] This section does not change or supersede any of the requirements set forth in Section Pe5, "Pension Funds: Accounting and Reporting by Defined Benefit Pension Plans," for the financial statements of a pension plan. [FAS87, ¶8]

.103 This section is intended to specify accounting objectives and results rather than specific computational means of obtaining those results. If estimates, averages, or computational shortcuts can reduce the cost of applying this section, their use is appropriate, provided the results are reasonably expected not to be materially different from the results of a detailed application. [FAS87, ¶10]

Single-Employer Defined Benefit Pension Plans

.104 For purposes of this section, a defined benefit pension plan is one that defines an amount of pension benefit to be provided, usually as a function of one or more factors such as age, years of **service,** or compensation. [FAS87, ¶11]

.105 A pension benefit is part of the compensation paid to an employee for services. In a defined benefit pension plan, the employer promises to provide, in addition to current wages, retirement income payments in future years after the employee retires or termi-

[1][Deleted 12/90 because of FASB Statement 106, *Employers' Accounting for Postretirement Benefits Other Than Pensions.*]

nates service. Generally, the amount of benefit to be paid depends on a number of future events that are incorporated in the **plan's benefit formula,** often including how long the employee and any survivors live, how many years of service the employee renders, and the employee's compensation in the years immediately before retirement or termination. In most cases, services are rendered over a number of years before an employee retires and begins collecting the pension. Even though the services rendered by an employee are complete and the employee has retired, the total amount of benefit that the employer has promised and the cost to the employer of the services rendered are not precisely determinable but can only be estimated using the **benefit formula** and estimates of the relevant future events, many of which the employer cannot control. [FAS87, ¶12]

Basic Elements of Pension Accounting

.106 Conceptually, compensation cost should be recognized in the period in which the employee renders services. Although the complexity and uncertainty of the pension arrangement may preclude complete achievement of that goal, a fundamental objective of this section is to approximate more closely the recognition of the compensation cost of an employee's pension benefits over that employee's service period. [FAS87, ¶95]

.107 Any method of pension accounting that recognizes cost before the payment of benefits to retirees must deal with two problems stemming from the nature of the defined benefit pension contract. First, estimates or **assumptions** must be made concerning the future events that will determine the amount and timing of the benefit payments. Second, some approach to attributing the cost of pension benefits to individual years of service must be selected. [FAS87, ¶13]

.108 This section requires use of assumptions, each of which individually represents the best estimate of a particular future event. [FAS87, ¶14] That method of selecting assumptions is referred to as an **explicit approach.** [FAS87, ¶191]

.109 The assumptions and the **attribution** of cost to periods of employee service are fundamental to the measurements of **net periodic pension cost** and pension obligations required by this section. The basic elements of pension accounting are described in paragraphs .110 through .113; they are the foundation of the accounting and reporting requirements set forth in this section. [FAS87, ¶15]

.110 Net periodic pension cost is made up of several *components* that reflect different aspects of the employer's financial arrangements as well as the cost of benefits earned by employees. The cost of a benefit can be determined without regard to how the employer decides to finance the plan. The **service cost component** of net periodic pension cost is the **actuarial present value** of benefits attributed by the plan's benefit formula to services rendered by employees during the period. The service cost component is conceptually the same for an unfunded plan, a plan with minimal funding, and a well-funded plan. The other components of net periodic pension cost are interest cost[2] (interest on the **projected benefit obligation,** which is a discounted amount), **actual return on plan assets, amortization** of **unrecognized prior service cost,** and **gain or loss.** Both the **return on plan assets** and interest cost components are in substance financial items rather than employee compensation costs. [FAS87, ¶16]

.111 The projected benefit obligation as of a date is the actuarial present value of all benefits attributed by the plan's benefit formula to employee service rendered prior to that date. The projected benefit obligation is measured using an assumption as to future compensation levels if the **pension benefit formula** is based on those future compensation levels. Plans for which the pension benefit formula is based on future compensation are sometimes called pay-related, **final-pay,** final-average-pay, or **career-average-pay plans.** Plans for which the pension benefit formula is not based on future compensation levels are called non-pay-related or **flat-benefit plans.** The projected benefit obligation is a measure of benefits attributed to service to date assuming that the plan continues in effect and that estimated future events (including compensation increases, **turnover,** and **mortality**) occur. [FAS87, ¶17]

.112 The **accumulated benefit obligation** as of a date is the actuarial present value of benefits attributed by the pension benefit formula to employee service rendered prior to that date and based on current and past compensation levels. The accumulated benefit obligation differs from the projected benefit obligation in that it includes no assumption about future compensation levels. For plans with flat-benefit or non-pay-related pension benefit formulas, the accumulated benefit obligation and the projected benefit obligation are the same. The accumulated benefit obligation and the **vested benefit obligation** provide information about the obligation the employer would have if the plan were discontinued. [FAS87, ¶18]

.113 **Plan assets** are assets—usually stocks, bonds, and other investments—that have been segregated and restricted (usually in a trust) to provide for pension benefits. The amount of plan assets includes amounts contributed by the employer (and by employees for a **contributory plan**) and amounts earned from investing the contributions, less benefits paid. Plan assets ordinarily cannot be withdrawn by the employer except under certain circumstances when a plan has assets in excess of obligations and the employer has taken certain steps to satisfy existing obligations. Assets not segregated in a trust or otherwise effectively restricted so that they cannot be used by the employer for other purposes are not plan

[2]The **interest cost component** of net periodic pension cost shall not be considered to be interest for purposes of applying Section I67, "Interest: Capitalization of Interest Costs." [FAS87, ¶16, fn4]

assets for purposes of this section even though it may be intended that such assets be used to provide pensions. Amounts accrued by the employer but not yet paid to the plan are not plan assets for purposes of this section. Securities of the employer held by the plan are includable in plan assets provided they are transferable. [FAS87, ¶19]

Recognition of Net Periodic Pension Cost

.114 The following components shall be included in the net pension cost recognized for a period by an employer sponsoring a defined benefit pension plan:

a. Service cost
b. Interest cost
c. Actual return on plan assets, if any
d. Amortization of unrecognized prior service cost, if any
e. Gain or loss (including the effects of changes in assumptions) to the extent recognized [(paragraphs .123 through .128)]
f. Amortization of the unrecognized net obligation (and loss or cost) or unrecognized net asset (and gain) existing at the date of initial application of this section.[3]

[FAS87, ¶20]

Service Cost

.115 The service cost component recognized in a period shall be determined as the actuarial present value of benefits attributed by the pension benefit formula to employee service during that period. The measurement of the service cost component requires use of an attribution method and assumptions. That measurement is discussed in paragraphs .133 through .138 and paragraphs .141 through .144 of this section. [FAS87, ¶21]

---

[3]For a defined benefit plan, an employer shall determine as of the **measurement date** (paragraph .148) for the beginning of the fiscal year in which this section is first applied, the amounts of (a) the projected benefit obligation and (b) the **fair value** of plan assets plus previously recognized **unfunded accrued pension cost** or less previously recognized **prepaid pension cost.** The difference between those two amounts, whether it represents an unrecognized net obligation (and loss or cost) or an unrecognized net asset (and gain), shall be amortized on a straight-line basis over the average remaining service period of employees expected to receive benefits under the plan, except that, (a) if the average remaining service period is less than 15 years, the employer may elect to use a 15-year period, and (b) if all or almost all of a plan's **participants** are inactive, the employer shall use the inactive participants' average remaining life expectancy period. That same amortization shall also be used to recognize any unrecognized net obligation related to a **defined contribution plan.** [FAS87, ¶77]

Interest Cost

.116 The interest cost component recognized in a period shall be determined as the increase in the projected benefit obligation due to the passage of time. Measuring the projected benefit obligation as a present value requires accrual of an interest cost at rates equal to the assumed **discount rates.** [FAS87, ¶22]

Actual Return on Plan Assets

.117 For a funded plan, the actual return on plan assets shall be determined based on the fair value of plan assets at the beginning and the end of the period, adjusted for contributions and benefit payments. [FAS87, ¶23]

Prior Service Cost

.118 **Plan amendments** (including initiation of a plan) often include provisions that grant increased benefits based on services rendered in prior periods. Because plan amendments are granted with the expectation that the employer will realize economic benefits in future periods, this section does not require the cost of providing such **retroactive benefits** (that is, **prior service cost**) to be included in net periodic pension cost entirely in the year of the amendment but provides for recognition during the future service periods of those employees active at the date of the amendment who are expected to receive benefits under the plan. [FAS87, ¶24] [Refer to paragraph .1001 for an EITF Issue that provides interpretive guidance on paragraphs .118 through .122.]

.119 The cost of retroactive benefits (including benefits that are granted to retirees) is the increase in the projected benefit obligation at the date of the amendment. Except as specified in paragraphs .120 and .121, that prior service cost shall be amortized by assigning an equal amount to each future period of service of each employee active at the date of the amendment who is expected to receive benefits under the plan. If all or almost all of a plan's participants are inactive, the cost of retroactive plan amendments affecting benefits of inactive participants shall be amortized based on the remaining life expectancy of those participants instead of based on the remaining service period. [FAS87, ¶25]

.120 To reduce the complexity and detail of the computations required, consistent use of an alternative amortization approach that more rapidly reduces the unrecognized cost of retroactive amendments is acceptable. For example, a straight-line amortization of the cost over the average remaining service period of employees expected to receive benefits under the plan is acceptable. The alternative method used shall be disclosed.

[FAS87, ¶26] Use of [a] more precise method [that] recognize[s] the cost of each individual's added benefits over that individual's remaining service period is, of course, appropriate. [FAS87, ¶163]

.121 In some situations a history of regular plan amendments and other evidence may indicate that the period during which the employer expects to realize economic benefits from an amendment granting retroactive benefits is shorter than the entire remaining service period of the active employees. Identification of such situations requires an assessment of the individual circumstances and the substance of the particular plan situation. In those circumstances [FAS87, ¶27] [and when] the benefits of a plan amendment have been impaired, [FAS87, ¶167] the amortization of prior service cost shall be accelerated to reflect the more rapid expiration of the employer's economic benefits and to recognize the cost in the periods benefited. [FAS87, ¶27]

.122 A plan amendment can reduce, rather than increase, the projected benefit obligation. Such a reduction shall be used to reduce any existing unrecognized prior service cost, and the excess, if any, shall be amortized on the same basis as the cost of benefit increases. [FAS87, ¶28]

Gains and Losses

.123 **Gains and losses** are changes in the amount of either the projected benefit obligation or plan assets resulting from experience different from that assumed and from changes in assumptions. This section does not distinguish between those sources of gains and losses. Gains and losses include amounts that have been realized, for example by sale of a security, as well as amounts that are unrealized. Because gains and losses may reflect refinements in estimates as well as real changes in economic values and because some gains in one period may be offset by losses in another or vice versa, this section does not require recognition of gains and losses as components of net pension cost of the period in which they arise.[4] [FAS87, ¶29]

.124 The **expected return on plan assets** shall be determined based on the **expected long-term rate of return on plan assets** and the **market-related value of plan assets.** The market-related value of plan assets shall be either fair value or a calculated value that recognizes changes in fair value in a systematic and rational manner over not more than five years. Different ways of calculating market-related value may be used for different classes of assets (for example, an employer might use fair value for bonds and a

[4] Accounting for **plan terminations** and **curtailments** and other circumstances in which recognition of gains and losses might not be delayed is addressed in paragraphs .171 through .188. [FAS87, ¶29, fn5]

five-year-moving-average value for equities), but the manner of determining market-related value shall be applied consistently from year to year for each asset class. [FAS87, ¶30]

.125 Asset gains and losses are differences between the actual return on assets during a period and the expected return on assets for that period. Asset gains and losses include both (a) changes reflected in the market-related value of assets and (b) changes not yet reflected in the market-related value (that is, the difference between the fair value of assets and the market-related value). Asset gains and losses not yet reflected in market-related value are not required to be amortized under paragraphs .126 and .127. [FAS87, ¶31]

.126 As a minimum, amortization of an **unrecognized net gain or loss** (excluding asset gains and losses not yet reflected in market-related value) shall be included as a component of net pension cost for a year if, as of the beginning of the year, that unrecognized net gain or loss exceeds 10 percent of the greater of the projected benefit obligation or the market-related value of plan assets. If amortization is required, the minimum amortization[5] shall be that excess divided by the average remaining service period of active employees expected to receive benefits under the plan. If all or almost all of a plan's participants are inactive, the average remaining life expectancy of the inactive participants shall be used instead of average remaining service. [FAS87, ¶32]

.127 Any systematic method of amortization of unrecognized gains or losses may be used in lieu of the minimum specified in the previous paragraph provided that (a) the minimum is used in any period in which the minimum amortization is greater (reduces the net balance by more), (b) the method is applied consistently, (c) the method is applied similarly to both gains and losses, and (d) the method used is disclosed. [FAS87, ¶33]

.128 The gain or loss component of net periodic pension cost shall consist of (a) the difference between the actual return on plan assets and the expected return on plan assets and (b) amortization of the unrecognized net gain or loss from previous periods. [FAS87, ¶34]

Recognition of Liabilities and Assets

.129 A liability (unfunded accrued pension cost) is recognized if net periodic pension cost recognized pursuant to this section exceeds amounts the employer has contributed

---

[5]The amortization must always reduce the beginning-of-the-year balance. Amortization of a net unrecognized gain results in a decrease in net periodic pension cost; amortization of a net unrecognized loss results in an increase in net periodic pension cost. [FAS87, ¶32, fn6]

to the plan. An asset (prepaid pension cost) is recognized if net periodic pension cost is less than amounts the employer has contributed to the plan. [FAS87, ¶35]

.130 If the accumulated benefit obligation exceeds the fair value of plan assets, the employer shall recognize in the statement of financial position a liability (including unfunded accrued pension cost) that is at least equal to the **unfunded accumulated benefit obligation.** Recognition of an additional minimum liability is required if an unfunded accumulated benefit obligation exists and (a) an asset has been recognized as prepaid pension cost, (b) the liability already recognized as unfunded accrued pension cost is less than the unfunded accumulated benefit obligation, or (c) no accrued or prepaid pension cost has been recognized. [FAS87, ¶36]

.131 If an additional minimum liability is recognized pursuant to paragraph .130, an equal amount shall be recognized as an intangible asset, provided that the asset recognized shall not exceed the amount of unrecognized prior service cost.[6] If an additional liability required to be recognized exceeds unrecognized prior service cost, the excess (which would represent a net loss not yet recognized as net periodic pension cost) shall be reported [FAS87, ¶37] in other comprehensive income [as required in Section C49, "Comprehensive Income: Financial Statement Presentation,"] [FAS130, ¶31(a)] net of any tax benefits that result from considering such losses as [FAS87, ¶37] temporary differences [FAS109, ¶287] for purposes of applying the provisions of [FAS87, ¶37] Section I27, "Income Taxes." [FAS109, ¶287]

.132 When a new determination of the amount of additional liability is made to prepare a statement of financial position, the related intangible asset and [FAS87, ¶38] the balance accumulated in a [FAS130, ¶31(b)] separate component of equity shall be eliminated or adjusted as necessary. [FAS87, ¶38] Eliminations of or adjustments to that balance shall be reported in other comprehensive income. [FAS130, ¶31(b)]

Measurement of Cost and Obligations

.133 The service component of net periodic pension cost, the projected benefit obligation, and the accumulated benefit obligation are based on an attribution of pension benefits to periods of employee service and on the use of actuarial assumptions to calculate the actuarial present value of those benefits. Actuarial assumptions reflect the time value of money (discount rate) and the probability of payment (assumptions as to mortality, turnover, early retirement, and so forth). [FAS87, ¶39]

---

[6]For purposes of this paragraph, an unrecognized net obligation existing at the date of initial application of this section [(see footnote 3)] shall be treated as unrecognized prior service cost. [FAS87, ¶37, fn7]

Attribution

.134 For purposes of this section, pension benefits ordinarily shall be attributed to periods of employee service based on the plan's benefit formula to the extent that the formula states or implies an attribution. For example, if a plan's formula provides for a pension benefit of $10 per month for life for each year of service, the benefit attributed to each year of an employee's service is $10 times the number of months of life expectancy after retirement, and the cost attributable to each year is the actuarial present value of that benefit. For plan benefit formulas that define benefits similarly for all years of service, that attribution is a **"benefit/years-of-service" approach** because it attributes the same amount of the pension benefit to each year of service.[7] For final-pay and career-average-pay plans, that attribution is also the same as the "projected unit credit" or "unit credit with service prorate" actuarial cost method. For a flat-benefit plan, it is the same as the "unit credit" actuarial cost method. [FAS87, ¶40] [The] use of a standardized [attribution approach will] improve comparability, even though some differences that are not necessarily reflective of real differences will remain because of the exercise of judgment in the selection of assumptions. [FAS87, ¶127]

.135 In some situations a history of regular increases in non-pay-related benefits or benefits under a career-average-pay plan and other evidence may indicate that an employer has a present commitment to make future amendments and that the substance of the plan is to provide benefits attributable to prior service that are greater than the benefits defined by the written terms of the plan. In those situations, the substantive commitment shall be the basis for the accounting, and the existence and nature of the commitment to make future amendments shall be disclosed. [FAS87, ¶41] [In the absence of such a commitment,] plan amendments should [not] be anticipated or estimated before they are made. [A] present obligation ordinarily [does not exist] for benefits to be promised in future amendments. [FAS87, ¶168]

.136 Some plans may have benefit formulas that attribute all or a disproportionate share of the total benefits provided to later years of service, thereby achieving in substance a delayed vesting of benefits. For example, a plan that provides no benefits for the first 19 years of service and a vested benefit of $10,000 for the 20th year is substantively the same as a plan that provides $500 per year for each of 20 years and requires 20 years of service before benefits vest. For such plans the total projected benefit shall be considered

[7]Some plans define different benefits for different years of service. For example, a step-rate plan might provide a benefit of 1 percent of final pay for each year of service up to 20 years and 1½ percent of final pay for years of service in excess of 20. Another plan might provide 1 percent of final pay for each year of service but limit the total benefit to no more than 20 percent of final pay. For such plans the attribution called for by this section will not assign the same amount of pension benefit to each year of service. [FAS87, ¶40, fn8]

to accumulate in proportion to the ratio of the number of completed years of service to the number that will have been completed when the benefit is first fully vested. If a plan's benefit formula does not specify how a particular benefit relates to services rendered, the benefit shall be considered to accumulate as follows:

a. For benefits of a type includable in **vested benefits,**[8] in proportion to the ratio of the number of completed years of service to the number that will have been completed when the benefit is first fully vested
b. For benefits of a type not includable in vested benefits,[9] in proportion to the ratio of completed years of service to total projected years of service.

[FAS87, ¶42]

Assumptions

.137 Each significant assumption used shall reflect the best estimate solely with respect to that individual assumption. All assumptions shall presume that the plan will continue in effect in the absence of evidence that it will not continue. [FAS87, ¶43]

.138 Assumed discount rates shall reflect the rates at which the pension benefits could be effectively settled.[9a] It is appropriate in estimating those rates to look to available information about rates implicit in current prices of **annuity contracts** that could be used to effect settlement of the obligation (including information about [FAS87, ¶44] [certain] [FAS87, ¶196] available annuity rates currently published by the Pension Benefit Guaranty Corporation). In making those estimates, employers may also look to rates of return on high-quality fixed-income investments currently available and expected to be

[8]For example, a supplemental early retirement benefit that is a vested benefit after a stated number of years. [FAS87, ¶42, fn9]

[9]For example, a death or disability benefit that is payable only if death or disability occurs during active service. [FAS87, ¶42, fn10]

[9a]As opposed to "settling" the obligation, which incorporates the insurer's risk factor, "effectively settling" the obligation focuses only on the time value of money and ignores the insurer's cost for assuming the risk of experience losses. [FAS106, ¶188]

available during the period to maturity of the pension benefits.[9b] Assumed discount rates are used in measurements of the projected, accumulated, and vested benefit obligations and the service and interest cost components of net periodic pension cost. [FAS87, ¶44] Material changes in long-term rates should [not] be ignored solely to avoid adjusting assumed interest discount rates. [FAS87, ¶201]

.139 **Interest rates** vary depending on the duration of investments; for example, U.S. Treasury bills, 7-year bonds, and 30-year bonds have different interest rates. Thus, the weighted-average discount rate (interest rate) inherent in the prices of annuities (or a dedicated bond portfolio) will vary depending on the length of time remaining until individual benefit payment dates. A plan covering only retired employees would be expected to have significantly different discount rates from one covering a work force of 30-year-olds. The disclosures required by this section regarding components of the pension benefit obligation will be more representationally faithful if individual discount rates applicable to various benefit deferral periods are selected. A properly weighted average rate can be used for aggregate computations such as the interest cost component of net pension cost for the period. [FAS87, ¶199]

.140 An insurance company deciding on the price of an annuity contract will consider the rates of return available to it for investing the premium received and the rates of return expected to be available to it for reinvestment of future cash flows from the initial investment during the period until benefits are payable. That consideration is indicative of a relationship between rates inherent in the prices of annuity contracts and rates available in investment markets. [It is] appropriate for employers to consider that relationship and information about investment rates in estimating the discount rates required for application of this section. [FAS87, ¶200] A current settlement rate best meets that objective and also is consistent with measurement of plan assets at fair value for purposes of disclosing the plan's funded status. [FAS87, ¶198] The volatility of the unfunded or over-

[9b]The objective of selecting assumed discount rates is to measure the single amount that, if invested at the measurement date in a portfolio of high-quality debt instruments, would provide the necessary future cash flows to pay the benefit [obligation] when due. Notionally, that single amount, the [projected,] accumulated [, or vested] benefit obligation, would equal the current market value of a portfolio of high-quality zero coupon bonds whose maturity dates and amounts would be the same as the timing and amount of the [respective] future benefit payments. Because cash inflows would equal cash outflows in timing and amount, there would be no reinvestment risk in the yields to maturity of the portfolio. However, in other than a zero coupon portfolio, such as a portfolio of long-term debt instruments that pay semiannual interest payments or whose maturities do not extend far enough into the future to meet expected benefit payments, the assumed discount rates (the yield to maturity) need to incorporate expected reinvestment rates available in the future. Those rates should be extrapolated from the existing yield curve at the measurement date. Assumed discount rates should be reevaluated at each measurement date. If the general level of interest rates rises or declines, the assumed discount rates should change in a similar manner. [FAS106, ¶186] [Refer to paragraph .1001 for an EITF Issue that provides interpretive guidance on this footnote.]

funded obligation may be less than some expect if the explicit assumptions used in the valuation of the obligation are changed to reflect fully the changes in interest rate structures that affect the fair values of plan assets, because changes in the assets may tend to offset changes in the obligation. [FAS87, ¶174] [Refer to paragraph .1001 for an EITF Issue that provides interpretive guidance on this paragraph.]

.141 The expected long-term rate of return on plan assets shall reflect the average rate of earnings expected on the funds invested or to be invested to provide for the benefits included in the projected benefit obligation. In estimating that rate, appropriate consideration should be given to the returns being earned by the plan assets in the **fund** and the rates of return expected to be available for reinvestment.[10] The expected long-term rate of return on plan assets is used (with the market-related value of assets) to compute the expected return on assets. [FAS87, ¶45]

.142 The service cost component of net periodic pension cost and the projected benefit obligation shall reflect future compensation levels to the extent that the pension benefit formula defines pension benefits wholly or partially as a function of future compensation levels (that is, for a final-pay plan or a career-average-pay plan). Future increases for which a present commitment exists as described in paragraph .135 shall be similarly considered. Assumed compensation levels shall reflect an estimate of the actual future compensation levels of the individual employees involved, including future changes attributed to general price levels, productivity, seniority, promotion, and other factors. All assumptions shall be consistent to the extent that each reflects expectations of the same future economic conditions, such as future rates of inflation. Measuring service cost and the projected benefit obligation based on estimated future compensation levels entails considering indirect effects, such as changes under existing law in social security benefits or benefit limitations[11] that would affect benefits provided by the plan. [FAS87, ¶46]

.143 The accumulated benefit obligation shall be measured based on employees' *history* of service and *compensation* without an estimate of future compensation levels. Excluding estimated future compensation levels also means excluding indirect effects of future changes such as increases in the social security wage base. In measuring the accumulated benefit obligation, projected years of service shall be a factor only in determining employees' expected eligibility for particular benefits, such as:

a. Increased benefits that are granted provided a specified number of years of service are rendered (for example, a pension benefit that is increased from $9 per month to $10 per month for each year of service if 20 or more years of service are rendered)

[10]An expected long-term-return-on-assets rate significantly below the rate at which the obligation could be settled implies that settlement would be economically advantageous. [FAS87, ¶179]

[11]For example, those currently imposed by Section 415 of the Internal Revenue Code. [FAS87, ¶46, fn11]

b. Early retirement benefits
c. Death benefits
d. Disability benefits.

[FAS87, ¶47]

.144 Automatic benefit increases specified by the plan (for example, automatic cost-of-living increases) that are expected to occur shall be included in measurements of the projected, accumulated, and vested benefit obligations, and the service cost component required by this section. Also, retroactive plan amendments shall be included in the computation of the projected and accumulated benefit obligations once they have been contractually agreed to, even if some provisions take effect only in future periods. For example, if a plan amendment grants a higher benefit level for employees retiring after a future date, the higher benefit level shall be included in current-period measurements for employees expected to retire after that date. [FAS87, ¶48]

Measurement of Plan Assets

.145 For purposes of measuring the minimum liability required by the provisions of paragraph .130 and for purposes of the disclosures required by [FAS87, ¶49] paragraphs .150 and .150A, [FAS135, ¶4(p)] plan investments, whether equity or debt securities, real estate, or other, shall be measured at their fair value as of the measurement date. The fair value of an investment is the amount that the plan could reasonably expect to receive for it in a current sale between a willing buyer and a willing seller, that is, other than in a forced or liquidation sale. Fair value shall be measured by the market price if an active market exists for the investment. If no active market exists for an investment but such a market exists for similar investments, selling prices in that market may be helpful in estimating fair value. If a market price is not available, a forecast of expected cash flows may aid in estimating fair value, provided the expected cash flows are discounted at a current rate commensurate with the risk involved.[12] [FAS87, ¶49]

.146 For purposes of determining the expected return on plan assets and accounting for asset gains and losses pursuant to paragraphs .123 through .128, a market-related asset value, defined in paragraph .124, is used. [FAS87, ¶50]

.147 Plan assets used in plan operations (for example, buildings, equipment, furniture and fixtures, and leasehold improvements) shall be measured at cost less accumulated depreciation or amortization for all purposes. [FAS87, ¶51]

---

[12]For an indication of factors to be considered in determining the discount rate, refer to Section I69, "Interest: Imputation of an Interest Cost," paragraphs .106 and .107. If significant, the fair value of an investment shall reflect the brokerage commissions and other costs normally incurred in a sale. [FAS87, ¶49, fn12]

Measurement Dates

.148 The measurements of plan assets and obligations required by this section shall be as of the date of the financial statements or, if used consistently from year to year, as of a date not more than three months prior to that date. Requiring that the pension measurements be as of a particular date is not intended to require that all procedures be performed after that date. As with other financial statement items requiring estimates, much of the information can be prepared as of an earlier date and projected forward to account for subsequent events (for example, employee service). The additional minimum liability reported in interim financial statements shall be the same additional minimum liability (paragraph .130) recognized in the previous year-end statement of financial position, adjusted for subsequent accruals and contributions, unless measures of both the obligation and plan assets are available as of a more current date or a significant event occurs, such as a plan amendment, that would ordinarily call for such measurements. [FAS87, ¶52]

.149 Measurements of net periodic pension cost for both interim and annual financial statements shall be based on the assumptions used for the previous year-end measurements unless more recent measurements of both plan assets and obligations are available or a significant event occurs, such as a plan amendment, that would ordinarily call for such measurements. [FAS87, ¶53]

Disclosures

.150 An employer that sponsors one or more defined benefit pension plans shall provide the following information:[12a]

a. A reconciliation of beginning and ending balances of the benefit obligation[13] showing separately, if applicable, the effects during the period attributable to each of the following: service cost, interest cost, contributions by plan participants, actuarial gains

---

[12a]An employer is encouraged to provide disclosure of general descriptive information about the employer's benefit plans, including employee groups covered, type of benefit formula, **funding policy,** types of assets held, and significant nonbenefit liabilities, if any, if such a description would provide meaningful information, such as when the employer sponsors only a single plan. [FAS132, ¶53] [An employer is permitted to present] pension and other postretirement benefit disclosures in a parallel format in a single note to the financial statements. [FAS132, ¶61] [Refer to Illustration 6, Case One, for an example.]

[13]For defined benefit pension plans, the benefit obligation is the projected benefit obligation—the actuarial present value as of a date of all benefits attributed by the pension benefit formula to employee service rendered prior to that date. [FAS132, ¶5, fn2]

and losses, foreign currency exchange rate changes,[13a] benefits paid, plan amendments, business combinations, divestitures, curtailments, settlements, and special termination benefits

b. A reconciliation of beginning and ending balances of the fair value of plan assets showing separately, if applicable, the effects during the period attributable to each of the following: actual return on plan assets, foreign currency exchange rate changes,[13b] contributions by the employer, contributions by plan participants, benefits paid, business combinations, divestitures, and settlements

c. The funded status of the plans, the amounts not recognized in the statement of financial position, and the amounts recognized in the statement of financial position, including:
   (1) The amount of any unamortized prior service cost
   (2) The amount of any unrecognized net gain or loss (including asset gains and losses not yet reflected in market-related value)
   (3) The amount of any remaining unamortized, unrecognized net obligation or net asset existing at the initial date of application of this section
   (4) The net pension prepaid assets or accrued liabilities
   (5) Any intangible asset and the amount of accumulated other comprehensive income recognized pursuant to paragraph .131 of this section

d. The amount of net periodic benefit cost recognized, showing separately the service cost component, the interest cost component, the expected return on plan assets for the period, the amortization of the unrecognized transition obligation or transition asset, the amount of recognized gains and losses, the amount of prior service cost recognized, and the amount of gain or loss recognized due to a settlement or curtailment

e. The amount included within other comprehensive income for the period arising from a change in the additional minimum pension liability recognized pursuant to paragraph .131 of this section

f. On a weighted-average basis, the following assumptions used in the accounting for the plans: assumed discount rate, rate of compensation increase (for pay-related plans), and expected long-term rate of return on plan assets

g. If applicable, the amounts and types of securities of the employer and related parties included in plan assets, the approximate amount of future annual benefits of plan participants covered by insurance contracts issued by the employer or related parties, and any significant transactions between the employer or related parties and the plan during the period

---

[13a]The effects of foreign currency exchange rate changes that are to be disclosed are those applicable to plans of a foreign operation whose functional currency is not the reporting currency pursuant to Section F60, "Foreign Currency Translation." [FAS132, ¶5, fn3]

[13b]Refer to footnote 13a. [FAS132, ¶5, fn4]

h. If applicable, any alternative amortization method used to amortize prior service amounts or unrecognized net gains and losses pursuant to paragraphs .120 and .127 of this section
i. If applicable, any substantive commitment, such as past practice or a history of regular benefit increases, used as the basis for accounting for the benefit obligation
j. If applicable, the cost of providing special or contractual termination benefits recognized during the period and a description of the nature of the event
k. An explanation of any significant change in the benefit obligation or plan assets not otherwise apparent in the other disclosures required by this section.

Amounts related to the employer's results of operations shall be disclosed for each period[13c] for which an income statement is presented. Amounts related to the employer's statement of financial position shall be disclosed for each balance sheet presented. [FAS132, ¶5]

Reduced Disclosure Requirements for Nonpublic Entities

.150A A nonpublic entity[13d] may elect to disclose the following for its pension plans in lieu of the disclosures required by paragraph .150 of this section:[13e]

a. The benefit obligation, fair value of plan assets, and funded status of the plan
b. Employer contributions, participant contributions, and benefits paid
c. The amounts recognized in the statement of financial position, including the net pension prepaid assets or accrued liabilities and any intangible asset and the amount of accumulated other comprehensive income recognized pursuant to paragraph .131 of this section
d. The amount of net periodic benefit cost recognized and the amount included within other comprehensive income arising from a change in the minimum pension liability recognized pursuant to paragraph .131 of this section

[13c]Restatement of disclosures for earlier periods provided for comparative purposes is required unless the information is not readily available, in which case the notes to the financial statements shall include all available information and a description of the information not available. [FAS132, ¶15]

13d A nonpublic entity is any entity other than one (a) whose debt or equity securities trade in a public market either on a stock exchange (domestic or foreign) or in the over-the-counter market, including securities quoted only locally or regionally, (b) that makes a filing with a regulatory agency in preparation for the sale of any class of debt or equity securities in a public market, or (c) that is controlled by an entity covered by (a) or (b). [FAS132, ¶8, fn5]

[13e]Even though this section permits reduced disclosures for nonpublic entities, the incremental information required by paragraph .150 improves understanding and, therefore, those entities are encouraged to disclose that information. [FAS132, ¶59]

e. On a weighted-average basis, the following assumptions used in the accounting for the plans: assumed discount rate, rate of compensation increase (for pay-related plans), and expected long-term rate of return on plan assets
f. If applicable, the amounts and types of securities of the employer and related parties included in plan assets, the approximate amount of future annual benefits of plan participants covered by insurance contracts issued by the employer or related parties, and any significant transactions between the employer or related parties and the plan during the period
g. The nature and effect of significant nonroutine events, such as amendments, combinations, divestitures, curtailments, and settlements.

[FAS132, ¶8]

.151 [Editorial deletion, 2/98.]

Employers with Two or More Plans

.152 An employer that sponsors two or more separate defined benefit pension plans shall determine net periodic pension cost, liabilities, and assets by separately applying the provisions of this section to each plan. In particular, unless an employer clearly has a right to use the assets of one plan to pay benefits of another, a liability required to be recognized pursuant to paragraph .129 or .130 for one plan shall not be reduced or eliminated because another plan has assets in excess of its accumulated benefit obligation or because the employer has prepaid pension cost related to another plan. [FAS87, ¶55]

.153 The disclosures required by this section may be aggregated for all of an employer's defined benefit pension plans or may be disaggregated in groups if that is considered to provide the most useful information or is otherwise required by paragraph .153A. Disclosures about pension plans with assets in excess of the accumulated benefit obligation generally may be aggregated with disclosures about pension plans with accumulated benefit obligations in excess of assets. However, if those disclosures are combined, an employer shall disclose the aggregate benefit obligation and aggregate fair value of plan assets for pension plans with benefit obligations in excess of plan assets. Disclosure of amounts recognized in the statement of financial position shall present prepaid benefit costs and accrued benefit liabilities separately. [FAS132, ¶6]

.153A An employer may combine disclosures about pension plans outside the United States with those for U.S. plans unless the benefit obligations of the plans outside the United States are significant relative to the total benefit obligation and those plans use significantly different assumptions. [FAS132, ¶7]

Annuity Contracts

.154 An annuity contract is a contract in which an insurance company[14] unconditionally undertakes a legal obligation to provide specified benefits to specific individuals in return for a fixed consideration or premium. An annuity contract is irrevocable and involves the transfer of significant risk from the employer to the insurance company. Some annuity contracts **(participating annuity contracts)** provide that the purchaser (either the plan or the employer) may participate in the experience of the insurance company. Under those contracts, the insurance company ordinarily pays dividends to the purchaser. If the substance of a participating contract is such that the employer remains subject to all or most of the risks and rewards associated with the benefit obligation covered and the assets transferred to the insurance company, that contract is not an annuity contract for purposes of this section. [FAS87, ¶57] [Refer also to paragraph .158.]

.155 To the extent that benefits currently earned are covered by annuity contracts, the cost of those benefits shall be the cost of purchasing the contracts, except as provided in paragraph .158. That is, if all the benefits attributed by the plan's benefit formula to service in the current period are covered by **nonparticipating annuity contracts,** the cost of the contracts determines the service cost component of net pension cost for that period. [FAS87, ¶58]

.156 Benefits provided by the pension benefit formula beyond benefits provided by annuity contracts (for example, benefits related to future compensation levels) shall be accounted for according to the provisions of this section applicable to plans not involving insurance contracts. [FAS87, ¶59]

.157 Benefits covered by annuity contracts shall be excluded from the projected benefit obligation and the accumulated benefit obligation. Except as provided in paragraph .158, annuity contracts shall be excluded from plan assets. [FAS87, ¶60]

.158 Some annuity contracts provide that the purchaser (either the plan or the employer) may participate in the experience of the insurance company. Under those contracts, the insurance company ordinarily pays dividends to the purchaser, the effect of which is to reduce the cost of the plan. The purchase price of a participating annuity

[14]If the insurance company does business primarily with the employer and related parties (a **captive insurer**), or if there is any reasonable doubt that the insurance company will meet its obligations under the contract, the contract is not an annuity contract for purposes of paragraphs .101 through .170 of this section. Some contracts provide for a refund of premiums if an employee for whom an annuity is purchased does not render sufficient service for the benefit to vest under the terms of the plan. Such a provision shall not by itself preclude a contract from being treated as an annuity contract for purposes of this section. [FAS87, ¶57, fn14]

contract ordinarily is higher than the price of an equivalent contract without **participation rights.** The difference is the cost of the participation right. The cost of the participation right shall be recognized at the date of purchase as an asset. In subsequent periods, the participation right shall be measured at its fair value if the contract is such that fair value is reasonably estimable. Otherwise, the participation right shall be measured at its amortized cost (not in excess of its net realizable value), and the cost shall be amortized systematically over the expected dividend period under the contract. [FAS87, ¶61]

Other Contracts with Insurance Companies

.159 Insurance contracts that are in substance equivalent to the purchase of annuities shall be accounted for as such. Other contracts with insurance companies shall be accounted for as investments and measured at fair value. For some contracts, the best available evidence of fair value may be contract value. If a contract has a determinable cash surrender value or conversion value, that is presumed to be its fair value. [FAS87, ¶62]

Defined Contribution Plans

.160 For purposes of this section, a defined contribution pension plan is a plan that provides pension benefits in return for services rendered, provides an individual account for each participant, and has terms that specify how contributions to the individual's account are to be determined rather than the amount of pension benefits the individual is to receive. Under a defined contribution plan, the pension benefits a participant will receive depend only on the amount contributed to the participant's account, the returns earned on investments of those contributions, and forfeitures of other participants' benefits that may be allocated to the participant's account. [FAS87, ¶63]

.161 To the extent that a plan's defined contributions to an individual's account are to be made for periods in which that individual renders services, the net pension cost for a period shall be the contribution called for in that period. If a plan calls for contributions for periods after an individual retires or terminates, the estimated cost shall be accrued during the employee's service period. [FAS87, ¶64] [Refer to paragraph .1001 for an EITF Issue that provides interpretive guidance on this paragraph.]

.162 An employer shall disclose the amount of cost recognized for defined contribution pension plans during the period separately from the amount of cost recognized for defined benefit plans. The disclosures shall include a description of the nature and effect of any significant changes during the period affecting comparability, such as a change in the rate of employer contributions, a business combination, or a divestiture. [FAS132, ¶9]

.163 A pension plan having characteristics of both a defined benefit plan and a defined contribution plan requires careful analysis. If the *substance* of the plan is to provide a defined benefit, as may be the case with some "target benefit" plans, the accounting [FAS87, ¶66] requirements shall be determined in accordance with the provisions of this section applicable to a defined benefit plan and the disclosure requirements shall be determined in accordance with the provisions of paragraphs .150 and .150A. [FAS135, ¶4(p)]

Multiemployer Plans

.164 For purposes of this section, a **multiemployer plan** is a pension plan to which two or more unrelated employers contribute, usually pursuant to one or more collective-bargaining agreements. A characteristic of multiemployer plans is that assets contributed by one participating employer may be used to provide benefits to employees of other participating employers since assets contributed by an employer are not segregated in a separate account or restricted to provide benefits only to employees of that employer. A multiemployer plan usually is administered by a board of trustees composed of management and labor representatives and may also be referred to as a "joint trust" or "union" plan. Generally, many employers participate in a multiemployer plan, and an employer may participate in more than one plan. The employers participating in multiemployer plans usually have a common industry bond, but for some plans the employers are in different industries, and the labor union may be their only common bond. Some multiemployer plans do not involve a union. For example, local chapters of a not-for-profit organization may participate in a plan established by the related national organization. [FAS87, ¶67]

.165 An employer participating in a multiemployer plan shall recognize as net pension cost the required contribution for the period and shall recognize as a liability any contributions due and unpaid. [FAS87, ¶68] [Refer to paragraph .1001 for an EITF Issue that provides interpretive guidance on this paragraph.]

.166 An employer shall disclose the amount of contributions to multiemployer plans during the period. An employer may disclose total contributions to multiemployer plans without disaggregating the amounts attributable to pensions and other postretirement benefits. The disclosures shall include a description of the nature and effect of any changes affecting comparability, such as a change in the rate of employer contributions, a business combination, or a divestiture. [FAS132, ¶10]

.167 In some situations, withdrawal from a multiemployer plan may result in an employer's having an obligation to the plan for a portion of its unfunded benefit obligations. If withdrawal under circumstances that would give rise to an obligation is either probable or reasonably possible, the provisions of Section C59, "Contingencies," shall apply. [FAS87, ¶70 and FAS132, ¶11]

Multiple-Employer Plans

.168 Some pension plans to which two or more unrelated employers contribute are not multiemployer plans[, but are **multiple-employer plans**]. Rather, they are in substance aggregations of single-employer plans combined to allow participating employers to pool their assets for investment purposes and to reduce the costs of plan administration. Those plans ordinarily do not involve collective-bargaining agreements. They may also have features that allow participating employers to have different benefit formulas, with the employer's contributions to the plan based on the benefit formula selected by the employer. Such plans shall be considered single-employer plans rather than multiemployer plans for purposes of this section, and each employer's accounting shall be based on its respective interest in the plan. [FAS87, ¶71]

Non-U.S. Pension Plans

.169 This section includes no special provisions applicable to pension arrangements outside the United States. To the extent that those arrangements are in substance similar to pension plans in the United States, they are subject to the provisions of this section for purposes of preparing financial statements in accordance with accounting principles generally accepted in the United States. The substance of an arrangement is determined by the nature of the obligation and by the terms or conditions that define the amount of benefits to be paid, not by whether (or how) a plan is funded, whether benefits are payable at intervals or as a single amount, or whether the benefits are required by law or custom or are provided under a plan the employer has elected to sponsor. [FAS87, ¶72]

.170 It is customary or required in some countries to provide benefits in the event of a voluntary or involuntary severance of employment (also called termination indemnities). If such an arrangement is in substance a pension plan (for example, if the benefits are paid for virtually all terminations), it is subject to the provisions of this section. [FAS87, ¶73] [Refer to paragraph .185.]

Settlements and Curtailments of Pension Plans and Termination Benefits

.171 Paragraphs .172 through .188 address an employer's accounting for a **settlement** or a curtailment of its defined benefit pension plan and for termination benefits. [FAS88, ¶1] [No] other events [have been identified that do] not [involve] settlement of obligation[s] or curtailment[s] of plan[s that should result] in recognition of prior service cost [(paragraphs .118 through .122)] and unrecognized net gain or loss [(paragraphs .123 through .128)]. [FAS88, ¶45]

.172 Examples of transactions that constitute a settlement include (a) making lump-sum cash payments to plan participants in exchange for their rights to receive specified pension benefits and (b) purchasing nonparticipating annuity contracts to cover vested benefits. [FAS88, ¶3] A transaction that does not meet all of the criteria of [a settlement as defined in] paragraph .457 does not constitute a settlement for purposes of this section. For example, investing in a portfolio of high-quality fixed-income securities with principal and interest payment dates similar to the estimated payment dates of benefits may avoid or minimize certain risks. However, that does not constitute a settlement because the investment decision can be reversed and such a strategy does not relieve the employer (or the plan) of primary responsibility for a pension obligation nor does it eliminate significant risks related to the obligation. [FAS88, ¶4]

.173 Curtailments include:

a. Termination of employees' services earlier than expected, which may or may not involve closing a facility or discontinuing a [FAS88, ¶6] component of an entity [FAS144, ¶C11(a)]
b. Termination or **suspension** of a plan so that employees do not earn additional defined benefits for future services. In the latter situation, future service may be counted toward vesting of benefits accumulated based on past service. [FAS88, ¶6]

.174 A [plan] settlement and a curtailment may occur separately or together. If benefits to be accumulated in future periods are reduced (for example, because half of a work force is dismissed or a plant is closed) but the plan remains in existence and continues to pay benefits, to invest assets, and to receive contributions, a curtailment has occurred but not a settlement. If an employer purchases nonparticipating annuity contracts for vested benefits and continues to provide defined benefits for future service, either in the same plan or in a successor plan, a settlement has occurred but not a curtailment. If a plan is terminated (that is, the obligation is settled and the plan ceases to exist) and not replaced by a successor defined benefit plan, both a settlement and a curtailment have occurred (whether or not the employees continue to work for the employer). [FAS88, ¶7]

.175 [Deleted 8/01 because of FASB Statement 144, *Accounting for the Impairment or Disposal of Long-Lived Assets.*]

.176 [A determination] as to the proper sequence of events to follow in measuring the effects of a settlement and a curtailment that are to be recognized at the same time is arbitrary. [A]n employer should consistently apply the same sequence of events in determining the effects of all settlements and curtailments that are to be recognized at the same time. [FAS88, ¶47]

Accounting for Settlement of the Pension Obligation

.177 For purposes of paragraphs .171 through .188, the maximum gain or loss subject to recognition in earnings when a pension obligation is settled is the unrecognized net gain or loss defined in paragraph .123 of this section plus any remaining unrecognized net asset existing at the date of initial application of this section.[15] That maximum amount includes any gain or loss first measured at the time of settlement. The maximum amount shall be recognized in earnings if the entire projected benefit obligation is settled. If only part of the projected benefit obligation is settled, the employer shall recognize in earnings a pro rata portion of the maximum amount equal to the percentage reduction in the projected benefit obligation. [FAS88, ¶9]

.178 An *annuity contract* is a contract in which an insurance company[16] unconditionally undertakes a legal obligation to provide specified benefits to specific individuals in return for a fixed consideration or premium. An annuity contract is irrevocable and involves the transfer of significant risk from the employer to the insurance company. Some annuity contracts (participating annuity contracts) provide that the purchaser (either the plan or the employer) may participate in the experience of the insurance company. Under those contracts, the insurance company ordinarily pays dividends to the purchaser. If the substance of a participating annuity contract is such that the employer remains subject to all or most of the risks and rewards associated with the benefit obligation covered or the assets transferred to the insurance company, the purchase of the contract does not constitute a settlement. [FAS88, ¶5]

---

[15]At the time of initial application of this section an employer may have an unrecognized net asset [refer to footnote 3. T]he portion of such an unrecognized net asset remaining unamortized at the date of a subsequent settlement or curtailment shall be treated as an unrecognized net gain and shall be combined with the unrecognized net gain or loss arising subsequent to transition to this section before applying the provisions of this paragraph and paragraph .183. [FAS88, ¶21]

[16]If the insurance company is controlled by the employer, or if there is any reasonable doubt that the insurance company will meet its obligations under the contract, the purchase of the contract does not constitute a settlement for purposes of paragraphs .171 through .188. [FAS88, ¶5, fn1]

.179 If the purchase of a participating annuity contract constitutes a settlement, the maximum gain (but not the maximum loss) shall be reduced by the cost of the participation right before determining the amount to be recognized in earnings. [FAS88, ¶10]

.180 It is difficult to determine the extent to which a participating contract exposes the purchaser to the risk of unfavorable experience, which would be reflected in lower than expected future dividends. Under some annuity contracts described as participating the purchaser might remain subject to all or most of the same risks and rewards related to future experience that would have existed had the contract not been purchased. Some participating contracts may require or permit payment of additional premiums if experience is unfavorable. If a participating contract requires or permits payment of additional premiums because of experience losses, or if the substance of the contract is such that the purchaser retains all or most of the related risks and rewards, the purchase of that contract does not constitute a settlement. [FAS88, ¶34]

.181 If the cost of all settlements[17] in a year is less than or equal to the sum of the service cost and interest cost components of net periodic pension cost for the plan for the year, gain or loss recognition is permitted but not required for those settlements. However, the accounting policy adopted shall be applied consistently from year to year. [FAS88, ¶11]

Accounting for a Plan Curtailment

.182 The unrecognized prior service cost associated with years of service no longer expected to be rendered as the result of a curtailment is a loss. For example, if a curtailment eliminates half of the estimated remaining future years of service of those who were employed at the date of a prior plan amendment and were expected to receive benefits under the plan, then the loss associated with the curtailment is half of the remaining unrecognized prior service cost related to that plan amendment. For purposes of applying the provisions of this paragraph, unrecognized prior service cost includes the cost of retroactive

[17]For the following types of settlements, the cost of the settlement is:

a. For a cash settlement, the amount of cash paid to employees
b. For a settlement using nonparticipating annuity contracts, the cost of the contracts
c. For a settlement using participating annuity contracts, the cost of the contracts less the amount attributed to participation rights. (Refer to paragraph .158 of this section.)

[FAS88, ¶11, fn3]

plan amendments (refer to paragraphs .118 and .119) and any remaining unrecognized net obligation existing at the date of initial application of this section.[18] [FAS88, ¶12]

.183 The projected benefit obligation may be decreased (a gain) or increased (a loss) by a curtailment.[19]

a. To the extent that such a gain exceeds any unrecognized net loss (or the entire gain, if an unrecognized net gain exists), it is a *curtailment gain.*
b. To the extent that such a loss exceeds any unrecognized net gain (or the entire loss, if an unrecognized net loss exists), it is a *curtailment loss.*

For purposes of applying the provisions of this paragraph, any remaining unrecognized net asset existing at the date of initial application of this section shall be treated as an unrecognized net gain and shall be combined with the unrecognized net gain or loss arising subsequent to transition to this section. [FAS88, ¶13]

.184 If the sum of the effects identified in paragraphs .182 and .183 is a net loss, it shall be recognized in earnings when it is probable that a curtailment will occur and the effects described are reasonably estimable. If the sum of those effects is a net gain, it shall be recognized in earnings when the related employees terminate or the plan suspension or amendment is adopted. [FAS88, ¶14]

Termination Benefits

.185 An employer may provide benefits to employees in connection with their termination of employment. They may be either *special termination benefits* offered only for a short period of time or *contractual termination benefits* required by the terms of a plan only if a specified event, such as a plant closing, occurs. An employer that offers special termination benefits to employees shall recognize a liability and a loss when the employees accept the offer and the amount can be reasonably estimated. An employer that provides contractual termination benefits shall recognize a liability and a loss when it is probable that employees will be entitled to benefits and the amount can be reasonably estimated. Termination benefits may take various forms including lump-sum payments, periodic future payments, or both. They may be paid directly from an employer's assets, an existing pension plan, a new employee benefit plan, or a combination of those means.

[18]At the time of initial application of this section, an employer may have an unrecognized net obligation [refer to footnote 3. T]he portion of such an unrecognized net obligation remaining unamortized at the date of a subsequent curtailment shall be treated as unrecognized prior service cost before applying the provisions of [this] paragraph. [FAS88, ¶21]

[19]Increases in the projected benefit obligation that reflect termination benefits are excluded from the scope of this paragraph. (Refer to paragraph .185 of this section.) [FAS88, ¶13, fn4]

The cost of termination benefits recognized as a liability and a loss shall include the amount of any lump-sum payments and the present value of any expected future payments. A situation involving termination benefits may also involve a curtailment to be accounted for under paragraphs .182 through .184. [FAS88, ¶15]

.186 [Deleted 8/01 because of Statement 144.]

Disclosure and Presentation

.187 [An employer that has a settlement or curtailment of its defined benefit pension plan or has termination benefits as described in paragraphs .171 through .188, should consider the impact of a settlement or curtailment on the disclosures required in] paragraphs .150(a), .150(b), .150(d), .150(j), and .150A(g) of this section. [FAS132, ¶13] When gains or losses recognized under paragraphs .177, .179, .182, .183, and .185 of this section [meet] the criteria of Section I17, "Income Statement Presentation: Extraordinary Items," those gains or losses should be accounted for as extraordinary items. For many enterprises those gains or losses generally do not result from the type of unusual and infrequently occurring event or transaction required by Section I17 to be reported as an extraordinary item. [FAS88, ¶48]

Asset Reversions

.188 Certain employers have settled significant portions of their pension obligations as part of transactions in which plan assets in excess of obligations reverted to the employer (asset reversion transactions). Consistent with prior standards, an employer that previously entered into an asset reversion transaction and continued to provide defined benefits recognized a credit on its statement of financial position for the amount withdrawn instead of recognizing a gain at the time of the withdrawal. Net periodic pension costs of subsequent periods were then reduced by amortization of the deferred gain (that is, the amount withdrawn). An employer that entered into such a transaction before the effective date of this section shall recognize a gain as the cumulative effect of a change in accounting principle at the time of initial application of this section. The amount of gain recognized shall be the lesser of:

a. The unamortized amount related to the asset reversion
b. Any unrecognized net asset for the plan (or the successor plan) existing at the time of transition [see footnote 3].

[FAS88, ¶20]

Illustrations

.189 Pages 34230 through 34261 contain illustrations of the following requirements of this section:

Illustration 1—Delayed Recognition and Reconciliation of Funded Status

This section provides for delayed recognition of the effects of a number of types of events that change the measures of the projected benefit obligation and the fair value of plan assets. Those events include retroactive plan amendments and gains and losses. Gains and losses as defined in this section include the effects of changes in assumptions.

This section also requires disclosure of a reconciliation of the funded status of a plan to the net pension liability or asset recognized in the employer's financial statements. This illustration shows how that reconciliation provides information about items that have not been recognized due to delayed recognition. The illustration starts with an assumed funded status at the date of initial application of this section and shows how a series of events that change the obligation or the plan assets are reflected in the reconciliation. (Throughout this illustration the fair value of plan assets exceeds the accumulated benefit obligation and, therefore, no recognition of an additional minimum liability is required.)

Case 1—Company T at Transition

The reconciliation as of the date of initial application of this section is as follows:

Projected benefit obligation	$(10,000)
Plan assets at fair value	6,500
Funded status	(3,500)
Unrecognized net (gain) or loss	0
Unrecognized prior service cost	0
Unrecognized net obligation or (net asset) at date of initial application	3,500
(Accrued)/prepaid pension cost	$ 0

The unrecognized net gain or loss and the unrecognized prior service cost are both initially zero by definition. The unrecognized net obligation or asset at transition is defined in paragraph .114 as the difference between the funded status and the accrued or prepaid pension cost already recognized. If, as in this case, the past contributions were equal to amounts recognized as net pension cost in past periods, there is no recognized accrued or prepaid pension cost in the statement of financial position and, therefore, the unrecognized net obligation or asset at transition is equal to the funded status.

Case 2—Past Contributions Lower by $400

If Company T had not made a contribution of $400 for the last year before the date of initial application but had recognized the same net periodic pension cost as in Case 1, the situation would be as follows:

Projected benefit obligation	$(10,000)
Plan assets at fair value	6,100
Funded status	(3,900)
Unrecognized net (gain) or loss	0
Unrecognized prior service cost	0
Unrecognized net obligation or (net asset) at date of initial application	3,500
(Accrued)/prepaid pension cost	$ (400)

The unrecognized net obligation at transition is unchanged. It is the amount of the projected benefit obligation not yet recognized in net periodic pension cost and is not directly affected by funding decisions.

Case 3—Past Contributions Greater by $800

If, instead, the employer had made a contribution in excess of net periodic pension cost of $800, but the company had recognized the same net periodic pension cost as in Case 1, the reconciliation would be as follows:

Projected benefit obligation	$(10,000)
Plan assets at fair value	7,300
Funded status	(2,700)
Unrecognized net (gain) or loss	0
Unrecognized prior service cost	0
Unrecognized net obligation or (net asset) at date of initial application	3,500
(Accrued)/prepaid pension cost	$ 800

After Initial Application

At any date after initial application, any change in the projected benefit obligation or the plan assets (other than contributions and benefit payments) either is unrecognized or has been included in net pension cost for some period. Contributions decrease the accrued pension cost or increase the prepaid pension cost, and benefit payments reduce the obligation and the plan assets equally. Thus, all changes in either the obligation or the assets are reflected in the reconciliation. Using Case 1 above as the starting point, the following reconciliations illustrate the effect of various events that change either the projected benefit obligation or the plan assets.

Case 4—Fair Value of Assets Increases by $400

	Before	After
Projected benefit obligation	$(10,000)	$(10,000)
Plan assets at fair value	6,500	6,900
Funded status	(3,500)	(3,100)
Unrecognized net (gain) or loss	0	(400)
Unrecognized prior service cost	0	0
Unrecognized net obligation or (net asset) at date of initial application	3,500	3,500
(Accrued)/prepaid pension cost	$ 0	$ 0

Case 5—Increase in Discount Rate Reduces Obligation by $900

	Before	After
Projected benefit obligation	$(10,000)	$(9,100)
Plan assets at fair value	6,500	6,500
Funded status	(3,500)	(2,600)
Unrecognized net (gain) or loss	0	(900)
Unrecognized prior service cost	0	0
Unrecognized net obligation or (net asset) at date of initial application	3,500	3,500
(Accrued)/prepaid pension cost	$ 0	$ 0

Case 6—Plan Amendment Increases the Obligation by $1,500

	Before	After
Projected benefit obligation	$(10,000)	$(11,500)
Plan assets at fair value	6,500	6,500
Funded status	(3,500)	(5,000)
Unrecognized net (gain) or loss	0	0
Unrecognized prior service cost	0	1,500
Unrecognized net obligation or (net asset) at date of initial application	3,500	3,500
(Accrued)/prepaid pension cost	$ 0	$ 0

Case 7—Employer Accrues Net Pension Cost

Net pension cost includes:

Service cost	$ 600
Interest cost	1,000
Amortization of initial unrecognized net obligation	233
Return on assets	(650)
	$1,183

No contribution is made.

	Before	**After**
Projected benefit obligation	$(10,000)	$(11,600)
Plan assets at fair value	6,500	7,150
Funded status	(3,500)	(4,450)
Unrecognized net (gain) or loss	0	0
Unrecognized prior service cost	0	0
Unrecognized net obligation or (net asset) at date of initial application	3,500	3,267
(Accrued)/prepaid pension cost	$ 0	$ (1,183)

Illustration 2—Transition

Case 1

As of December 31, 1985, the projected benefit obligation and plan assets of a noncontributory defined benefit plan sponsored by Company A were:

Projected benefit obligation	$(1,500,000)
Plan assets at fair value	1,200,000
Initial unfunded obligation	$ (300,000)

Company A elected to apply the provisions of this section for its financial statements for the year ending December 31, 1986. At December 31, 1985, no prepaid or accrued pension cost had been recognized in Company A's statement of financial position (that is, all amounts accrued as net periodic pension cost had been contributed to the plan). The average remaining service period of active plan participants expected to receive benefits was estimated to be 16 years at the date of transition. In this situation the initial unrecognized net obligation (and loss or cost) of $300,000 is to be amortized (recognized as a component of net periodic pension cost) on a straight-line basis over the average remaining service period of 16 years [refer to footnote 3] as follows:

Year	Beginning-of-Year Balance	Amortization[a]	End-of-Year Balance
1986	300,000	18,750	281,250
1987	281,250	18,750	262,500
1988	262,500	18,750	243,750
1989	243,750	18,750	225,000
1990	225,000	18,750	206,250
1991	206,250	18,750	187,500
1992	187,500	18,750	168,750
1993	168,750	18,750	150,000
1994	150,000	18,750	131,250
1995	131,250	18,750	112,500
1996	112,500	18,750	93,750
1997	93,750	18,750	75,000
1998	75,000	18,750	56,250
1999	56,250	18,750	37,500
2000	37,500	18,750	18,750
2001	18,750	18,750	0

[a]300,000/16 = 18,750.

Case 2

As of December 31, 1985, the projected benefit obligation and plan assets of a noncontributory defined benefit plan sponsored by Company B were:

Projected benefit obligation	$(1,400,000)
Plan assets at fair value	1,600,000
Initial overfunded obligation	$ 200,000

Company B elected to apply the provisions of this section for its financial statements for the year ending December 31, 1986. In previous periods, Company B's plan was deemed to be fully funded for tax purposes, and the company decided not to make contributions that would not have been currently tax deductible. As a result, contributions were less than net pension cost for those periods, and the company had recognized unfunded accrued pension cost (a liability) of $150,000 at December 31, 1985.

The unrecognized net asset at transition defined in [footnote 3] consists of amounts previously charged to net pension cost in excess of the projected benefit obligation. Amounts charged to net pension cost in past periods include amounts contributed (plan assets) and amounts unfunded. In this case, at December 31, 1985 those amounts were:

Plan assets in excess of obligation	$200,000
Unfunded accrued pension cost	150,000
Unrecognized net asset	$350,000

The average remaining service period of active plan participants expected to receive benefits was estimated to be 10 years at the date of transition. In this situation, the initial unrecognized net asset of $350,000 may be amortized on a straight-line basis over either 10 years or 15 years [refer to footnote 3]. That amortization will result in an annual credit to net periodic pension cost of either $35,000 or $23,333.

Illustration 3—Amortization of Unrecognized Prior Service Cost

Case 1—Assigning Equal Amounts to Future Years of Service

Determination of Expected Future Years of Service

The amortization of unrecognized prior service cost defined in paragraph .119 is based on the expected future years of service of participants active at the date of the amendment who are expected to receive benefits under the plan. Calculation of the expected future years of service considers population decrements based on the actuarial assumptions and is not weighted for benefits or compensation. Each expected future service year is assigned an equal share of the initially determined prior service cost. The portion of prior service cost to be recognized in each of the future years is determined by the service years rendered in that year.

The following chart illustrates the calculation of the expected future years of service for the defined benefit plan of Company E. At the date of the amendment (January 1, 19X2), the company has 100 employees who are expected to receive benefits under the plan. Five percent of that group (5 employees) are expected to leave (either retire or quit) in each of the next 20 years. Employees hired after that date do not affect the amortization. Initial estimates of expected future years of service related to each amendment are subsequently adjusted only for a curtailment.

Determination of Expected Years of Service

Service Years Rendered in Each Year

Individuals	Future Service Years	Year 1	2	3	4	5	6	7	8	9	10	11	12	13	14	15	16	17	18	19	20
A1-A5	5	5																			
B1-B5	10	5	5																		
C1-C5	15	5	5	5																	
D1-D5	20	5	5	5	5																
E1-E5	25	5	5	5	5	5															
F1-F5	30	5	5	5	5	5	5														
G1-G5	35	5	5	5	5	5	5	5													
H1-H5	40	5	5	5	5	5	5	5	5												
I1-I5	45	5	5	5	5	5	5	5	5	5											
J1-J5	50	5	5	5	5	5	5	5	5	5	5										
K1-K5	55	5	5	5	5	5	5	5	5	5	5	5									
L1-L5	60	5	5	5	5	5	5	5	5	5	5	5	5								
M1-M5	65	5	5	5	5	5	5	5	5	5	5	5	5	5							
N1-N5	70	5	5	5	5	5	5	5	5	5	5	5	5	5	5						
O1-O5	75	5	5	5	5	5	5	5	5	5	5	5	5	5	5	5					
P1-P5	80	5	5	5	5	5	5	5	5	5	5	5	5	5	5	5	5				
Q1-Q5	85	5	5	5	5	5	5	5	5	5	5	5	5	5	5	5	5	5			
R1-R5	90	5	5	5	5	5	5	5	5	5	5	5	5	5	5	5	5	5	5		
S1-S5	95	5	5	5	5	5	5	5	5	5	5	5	5	5	5	5	5	5	5	5	
T1-T5	100	5	5	5	5	5	5	5	5	5	5	5	5	5	5	5	5	5	5	5	5
	1,050																				
Service Years Rendered		100	95	90	85	80	75	70	65	60	55	50	45	40	35	30	25	20	15	10	5
Amortization Fraction		100	95	90	85	80	75	70	65	60	55	50	45	40	35	30	25	20	15	10	5
		1,050	1,050	1,050	1,050	1,050	1,050	1,050	1,050	1,050	1,050	1,050	1,050	1,050	1,050	1,050	1,050	1,050	1,050	1,050	1,050

Amortization of Unrecognized Prior Service Cost

On January 1, 19X2, Company E granted retroactive credit for prior service pursuant to a plan amendment. This amendment generated unrecognized prior service cost of $750,000. The amortization of the unrecognized prior service cost resulting from the plan amendment is based on the expected future years of service of active participants as discussed in the previous paragraph.

Amortization of Unrecognized Prior Service Cost

Year	Beginning-of-Year Balance	Amortization Rate	Amortization	End-of-Year Balance
19X2	750,000	100/1050	71,429	678,571
19X3	678,571	95/1050	67,857	610,714
19X4	610,714	90/1050	64,286	546,428
19X5	546,428	85/1050	60,714	485,714
19X6	485,714	80/1050	57,143	428,571
19X7	428,571	75/1050	53,571	375,000
19X8	375,000	70/1050	50,000	325,000
19X9	325,000	65/1050	46,429	278,571
19Y0	278,571	60/1050	42,857	235,714
19Y1	235,714	55/1050	39,286	196,428
19Y2	196,428	50/1050	35,714	160,714
19Y3	160,714	45/1050	32,143	128,571
19Y4	128,571	40/1050	28,571	100,000
19Y5	100,000	35/1050	25,000	75,000
19Y6	75,000	30/1050	21,429	53,571
19Y7	53,571	25/1050	17,857	35,714
19Y8	35,714	20/1050	14,286	21,428
19Y9	21,428	15/1050	10,714	10,714
19Z0	10,714	10/1050	7,143	3,571
19Z1	3,571	5/1050	3,571	0

Case 2—Using Straight-Line Amortization over Average Remaining Service Period

Determination of Expected Future Years of Service

To reduce the complexity and detail of the computations shown in Illustration 3, Case 1, alternative amortization approaches that recognize the cost of retroactive amendments more quickly may be consistently used (paragraph .120). For example, a straight-line amortization of the cost over the average remaining service period of employees expected to receive benefits under the plan is acceptable.

If Company E (Case 1) had elected to use straight-line amortization over the average remaining service period of employees expected to receive benefits (1,050 future service years/100 employees = 10.5 years), the amortization would have been as follows:

Amortization of Unrecognized Prior Service Cost

Year	Beginning-of-Year Balance	Amortization[a]	End-of-Year Balance
19X2	750,000	71,429	678,571
19X3	678,571	71,429	607,142
19X4	607,142	71,429	535,713
19X5	535,713	71,429	464,284
19X6	464,284	71,429	392,855
19X7	392,855	71,429	321,426
19X8	321,426	71,429	249,997
19X9	249,997	71,429	178,568
19Y0	178,568	71,429	107,139
19Y1	107,139	71,429	35,710
19Y2	35,710	35,710	0

[a]750,000/10.5 = 71,429.

Illustration 4—Accounting for Gains and Losses and Timing of Measurements

The following shows the funded status of Company I's pension plan at December 31, 1986 and its assumptions and expected components of net periodic pension cost for the following year (all amounts are in thousands):

DECEMBER 1986—INITIAL SITUATION

Assumptions:	
Discount rate	10.00%
Expected long-term rate of return on plan assets	10.00%
Average remaining service	10 years

	Actual 12/31/86	For 1987	Projected 12/31/87
Projected benefit obligation	$(1,000)		$(1,060)
Plan assets at fair value	800		880
Funded status	(200)		(180)
Unrecognized net obligation existing at January 1, 1987	200		180
Unrecognized prior service cost	0		0
Unrecognized net (gain) or loss	0		0
(Accrued)/prepaid	$ 0		$ 0
Service cost component		$ 60[a]	
Interest cost component		100	
Expected return on assets		(80)	

Amortization of:	
Unrecognized net obligation existing at January 1, 1987	20
Unrecognized prior service cost	0
Unrecognized net (gain) or loss	0
Net cost	$100
Contribution	$100
Benefits paid	$100

Company I elected to apply the provisions of this section as of January 1, 1987 rather than as of an earlier date. Also, the company elected to measure pension-related amounts as of year-end. Alternatively, the company could have chosen to make the measurements as of another date not earlier than September 30. (Throughout this illustration it is assumed that the fair value of plan assets exceeds the accumulated benefit obligation and, therefore, no recognition of an additional minimum liability is required. For simplicity, all contributions and benefit payments are assumed to occur on the last day of the year.)

[a]Throughout this illustration the service cost component is assumed as an input rather than calculated as part of the illustration.

1987—LIABILITY LOSS

When Company I's plan assets and obligations were measured at December 31, 1987, the amount of the projected benefit obligation was not equal to the expected amount. Because the discount rate had declined to 9 percent and for various other reasons not specifically identified, the projected benefit obligation was higher than had been projected (a loss had occurred). The results were as follows:

Assumptions:		
Discount rate	10.00%	9.00%
Expected long-term rate of return on plan assets	10.00%	10.00%
Average remaining service	10 years	10 years

	Actual 12/31/86	For 1987	Projected 12/31/87	Actual 12/31/87	For 1988	Projected 12/31/88
Projected benefit obligation	$(1,000)		$(1,060)	$(1,200)		$(1,266)[b]
Plan assets at fair value	800		880	880		968[c]
Funded status	(200)		(180)	(320)		(298)
Unrecognized net obligation existing at January 1, 1987	200		180	180		160
Unrecognized prior service cost	0		0	0		0
Unrecognized net (gain) or loss	0		0	140		138
(Accrued)/prepaid	$ 0		$ 0	$ 0		$ 0
Service cost component		$ 60			$ 72	
Interest cost component		100			108	
Expected return on assets		(80)			(88)	

Market-related value of assets	$ 800		$ 800	
Actual return on assets—(increase)/decrease			(80)	
Amortization of:				
Unrecognized net obligation existing at January 1, 1987		20		20
Unrecognized prior service cost		0		0
Unrecognized net (gain) or loss		0[d]		2[d]
Net cost		$100		$114
Contribution		$100		$114
Benefits paid		$100		$114

---

[b](Actual projected benefit obligation at 12/31/87) + (service component) + (interest component) – (benefits paid).

[c](Actual plan assets at 12/31/87) + (expected return on assets) + (contributions) – (benefits paid).

[d]Paragraph .126 provides that net periodic pension cost may be based on unrecognized net gain or loss as of the beginning of the period. In the year of transition (1987) the beginning balance of unrecognized net gain or loss is zero by definition. The minimum amortization of unrecognized net gain or loss is calculated as follows:

	1987	1988
Unrecognized net (gain) or loss at 1/1	$ 0	$ 140
Plus asset gain or less asset loss not yet in market-related value of assets at 1/1—(fair value of plan assets) – (market-related value of plan assets)	0	0
Unrecognized net (gain) or loss subject to amortization	0	140
Corridor = 10% of the greater of projected benefit obligation or market-related value of assets at 1/1	100	120
Unrecognized net (gain) or loss outside corridor	0	20
× 1/average remaining service	0.10	0.10
Amortization	$ 0	$ 2

[e-f][Deleted 2/99 because of FASB Statement 135, *Rescission of FASB Statement No. 75 and Technical Corrections.*]

1988—ASSET GAIN

When Company I's plan assets and obligations were measured at December 31, 1988, the amount of plan assets was not equal to the expected amount because of market performance better than the expected or assumed 10 percent. The results were as follows:

Assumptions:		
Discount rate	9.00%	9.00%
Expected long-term rate of return on plan assets	10.00%	10.00%
Average remaining service	10 years	10 years

	Actual 12/31/87	For 1988	Projected 12/31/88	Actual 12/31/88	For 1989	Projected 12/31/89
Projected benefit obligation	$(1,200)		$(1,266)	$(1,266)		$(1,345)
Plan assets at fair value	880		968	1,068		1,167
Funded status	(320)		(298)	(198)		(178)
Unrecognized net obligation existing at January 1, 1987	180		160	160		140
Unrecognized prior service cost	0		0	0		0
Unrecognized net (gain) or loss	140		138	38		38
(Accrued)/prepaid	$ 0		$ 0	$ 0		$ 0
Service cost component		$ 72			$ 76	
Interest cost component		108			114	
Expected return on assets		(88)			(99)[g]	
Market-related value of assets	$ 880			$ 988[h]		
Actual return on assets—(increase)/decrease	(80)			(188)		

Amortization of:		
Unrecognized net obligation existing at January 1, 1987	20	20
Unrecognized prior service cost	0	0
Unrecognized net (gain) or loss	2[i]	0[i]
Net cost	$114	$ 111
Contribution	$114	$ 111
Benefits paid	$114	$ 111

[g]Expected return on plan assets = (expected long-term rate of return on plan assets) × (market-related value of plan assets). If contributions occurred other than at the end of the year, market-related value would consider those amounts.

[h]Market-related asset values may be calculated in a variety of ways. This example uses an approach that adds in 20% of each of the last five years' gains and losses. The only objective of the market-related calculation is to reduce the volatility of net pension cost.

Market-related value of assets at 1/1	$ 880
Expected return on assets	88
Contributions	114
Benefits paid	(114)
20% of last five years' asset gains and (losses)	20
Market-related value of assets at 12/31	$ 988

[i]Amortization of unrecognized net gain or loss is calculated as follows:

	1988	1989
Unrecognized net (gain) or loss at 1/1	$ 140	$ 38
Plus asset gain or less asset loss not yet in market-related value of assets at 1/1—(fair value of plan assets) – (market-related value of plan assets)	0	80
Unrecognized net (gain) or loss subject to amortization	140	118
Corridor = 10% of the greater of projected benefit obligation or market-related value of assets at 1/1	120	127
Unrecognized net (gain) or loss outside corridor	20	0
× 1/average remaining service	0.10	0.10
Amortization	$ 2	$ 0

[j][Deleted 2/99 because of Statement 135.]

1989—ASSET LOSS AND LIABILITY GAIN

When Company I's plan assets and obligations were measured at December 31, 1989, both an asset loss and a liability gain were discovered.

Assumptions:		
Discount rate	9.00%	9.25%
Expected long-term rate of return on plan assets	10.00%	10.00%
Average remaining service	10 years	10 years

	Actual 12/31/88	For 1989	Projected 12/31/89	Actual 12/31/89	For 1990	Projected 12/31/90
Projected benefit obligation	$(1,266)		$(1,345)	$(1,320)		$(1,409)
Plan assets at fair value	1,068		1,167	1,097		1,206
Funded status	(198)		(178)	(223)		(203)
Unrecognized net obligation existing at January 1, 1987	160		140	140		120
Unrecognized prior service cost	0		0	0		0
Unrecognized net (gain) or loss	38		38	83		83
(Accrued)/prepaid	$ 0		$ 0	$ 0		$ 0
Service cost component		$ 76			$ 79	
Interest cost component		114			122	
Expected return on assets		(99)			(109)	
Market-related value of assets	$ 988			$ 1,093[k]		
Actual return on assets—(increase)/decrease	(188)			(29)		

Amortization of:		
Unrecognized net obligation existing at January 1, 1987	20	20
Unrecognized prior service cost	0	0
Unrecognized net (gain) or loss	0[l]	0[l]
Net cost	$111	$ 112
Contribution	$111	$ 112
Benefits paid	$111	$ 112

---

[k]Market-related asset values may be calculated in a variety of ways. This example uses an approach that adds in 20% of each of the last five years' gains and losses. The only objective of the market-related calculation is to reduce the volatility of net pension cost.

Market-related value of assets at 1/1	$ 988
Expected return on assets	99
Contributions	111
Benefits paid	(111)
20% of last five years' asset gains and (losses) = .20(100 – 70)	6
Market-related value of assets at 12/31	$1,093

[l]Amortization of unrecognized net gain or loss is calculated as follows:

	1989	1990
Unrecognized net (gain) or loss at 1/1	$ 38	$ 83
Plus asset gain or less asset loss not yet in market-related value of assets at 1/1—(fair value of plan assets) – (market-related value of plan assets)	80	4
Unrecognized net (gain) or loss subject to amortization	118	87
Corridor = 10% of the greater of projected benefit obligation or market-related value of assets at 1/1	127	132
Unrecognized net (gain) or loss outside corridor	0	0
× 1/average remaining service	0.10	0.10
Amortization	$ 0	$ 0

[m][Deleted 2/99 because of Statement 135.]

Illustration 5—Recognition of Pension Liability, Including Minimum Liability

Case 1—Minimum Liability Less Than Unrecognized Prior Service Cost

Company K elected to apply the provisions of this section, including those requiring recognition of minimum liability, for its 1986 financial statements. The funded status of its plan for the years 1988 through 1991 is shown below.

	As of December 31,			
	1988	**1989**	**1990**	**1991**
		(in thousands)		
FUNDED STATUS—COMPANY K				
Assets and obligations:				
Accumulated benefit obligation	$(1,254)	$(1,628)	$(1,616)	$(1,554)
Plan assets at fair value	1,165	1,505	1,622	1,517
Unfunded accumulated benefits	$ (89)	$ (123)		$ (37)
Overfunded accumulated benefits			$ 6	
Projected benefit obligation	$(1,879)	$(2,442)	$(2,424)	$(2,331)
Plan assets at fair value	1,165	1,505	1,622	1,517
Items not yet recognized in earnings:				
Unrecognized net obligation (net asset) at January 1, 1986	280	260	240	220
Unrecognized prior service cost	715	1,314	1,172	1,039
Unrecognized net gain	(251)	(557)	(460)	(476)
(Accrued)/prepaid pension cost	$ 30	$ 80	$ 150	$ (31)

	As of December 31,			
	1988	**1989**	**1990**	**1991**
	(in thousands)			
DETERMINATION OF AMOUNTS TO BE RECOGNIZED				
(Accrued)/prepaid pension cost at beginning of year	$ 0	$ 30	$ 80	$ 150
Net periodic pension cost	(304)	(335)	(397)	(361)
Contribution	334	385	467	180
(Accrued)/prepaid pension cost at end of year	$ 30	$ 80	$ 150	$ (31)
Required minimum liability (unfunded accumulated benefits)	$ (89)	$ (123)	$ 0	$ (37)
Adjustment required to reflect minimum liability:				
Additional liability[a]	$ (119)	$ (84)	$ 203	$ (6)
Intangible asset (not to exceed unrecognized prior service cost)	$ 119	$ 84	$ (203)	$ 6
Balance of additional liability	$ (119)	$ (203)	$ 0	$ (6)
Balance of intangible asset	$ 119	$ 203	$ 0	$ 6

[a]This amount is equal to unfunded accumulated benefits, plus prepaid (or minus accrued) pension cost, minus the previous balance. For financial statement presentation, the additional liability is combined with the (accrued)/prepaid pension cost.

Journal Entries

The journal entries required to reflect the accounting for the company's pension plan for the years 1988 through 1991 are as follows (in thousands):

Year 1988

Journal Entry 1

Net periodic pension cost	304	
Accrued/prepaid pension cost		304
To record net pension cost for the period (paragraph .129)		

Journal Entry 2

Accrued/prepaid pension cost	334	
Cash		334
To record contribution (paragraph .129)		

Journal Entry 3

Intangible asset	119	
Additional liability		119
To record an additional liability to reflect the required minimum liability (For financial statement presentation, the additional liability account balance is combined with the accrued/prepaid pension cost account balance. Since prepaid pension cost of $30 has been recognized, an additional liability of $119 is needed to reflect the required minimum liability of $89 [equal to unfunded accumulated benefits]. Because the additional liability is less than unrecognized prior service cost, an intangible asset also is recognized.) (paragraphs .130 and .131)		

Year 1989

Journal Entry 1

Net periodic pension cost	335	
Accrued/prepaid pension cost		335
To record net pension cost for the period (paragraph .129)		

Journal Entry 2

Accrued/prepaid pension cost	385	
Cash		385
To record contribution (paragraph .129)		

Journal Entry 3

Intangible asset	84	
Additional liability		84
To adjust the additional liability to reflect the required minimum liability (For financial statement presentation, the additional liability account balance is combined with the accrued/prepaid pension cost account balance. The required minimum liability is determined independently of any prior years' amounts. Since unfunded accumulated benefits are $123 and a prepaid pension cost of $80 has been recognized, the amount of the additional liability is $203 or an increase of $84 from the previous period. Because the balance of the additional liability is less than unrecognized prior service cost, an intangible asset also is recognized.) (paragraphs .130 and .131)		

Year 1990

Journal Entry 1

Net periodic pension cost	397	
Accrued/prepaid pension cost		397
To record net pension cost for the period (paragraph .129)		

Journal Entry 2

Accrued/prepaid pension cost	467	
Cash		467
To record contribution (paragraph .129)		

Journal Entry 3

Additional liability	203	
Intangible asset		203
To reverse additional liability no longer required (Since plan assets exceed accumulated benefits, no additional liability is necessary.) (paragraph .132)		

Year 1991

Journal Entry 1

Net periodic pension cost	361	
Accrued/prepaid pension cost		361
To record net pension cost for the period (paragraph .129)		

Journal Entry 2

Accrued/prepaid pension cost	180	
Cash		180
To record contribution (paragraph .129)		

Journal Entry 3

Intangible asset	6	
Additional liability		6
To record an additional liability to reflect the required minimum liability amount (For financial statement presentation, the additional liability account balance is combined with the accrued/prepaid pension cost account balance. Since unfunded accumulated benefits of $37 exceed unfunded accrued pension cost of $31, recognition of an additional liability of $6 is necessary. Because the balance of additional liability is less than unrecognized prior service cost, an intangible asset also is recognized.) (paragraphs .130 and .131)		

Case 2—Minimum Liability in Excess of Unrecognized Prior Service Cost

Company L elected to apply the provisions of this section, including those requiring recognition of minimum liability, for its 1986 financial statements. The funded status of its plan for the years 1988 and 1989 is shown below.

	As of December 31,	
	1988	**1989**
	(in thousands)	
FUNDED STATUS—COMPANY L		
Assets and obligations:		
Accumulated benefit obligation	$(1,270)	$(1,290)
Plan assets at fair value	1,200	1,304
Unfunded accumulated benefits	$ (70)	
Overfunded accumulated benefits		$ 14
Projected benefit obligation	$(1,720)	$(1,807)
Plan assets at fair value	1,200	1,304
Items not yet recognized in earnings:		
Unrecognized prior service cost	92	86
Unrecognized net loss	486	497
(Accrued)/prepaid pension cost	$ 58	$ 80
DETERMINATION OF AMOUNTS TO BE RECOGNIZED		
(Accrued)/prepaid pension cost at beginning of year	$ 0	$ 58
Net periodic pension cost	(141)	(144)
Contribution	199	166
(Accrued)/prepaid pension cost at end of year	$ 58	$ 80
Required minimum liability (unfunded accumulated benefits)	$ 70	$ 0
Adjustment required to reflect minimum liability:		
Additional liability[a]	$ (128)	$ 128
Intangible asset (not to exceed unrecognized prior service cost)	$ 92	$ (92)
Charge to equity (excess of additional pension liability over unrecognized prior service cost)	$ 36	$ (36)
Balance of additional liability	$ (128)	$ 0
Balance of intangible asset	$ 92	$ 0
Balance of equity account	$ 36	$ 0

[a]This amount is equal to unfunded accumulated benefits, plus prepaid (or minus accrued) pension cost, minus the previous balance. For financial statement presentation, the additional liability is combined with the (accrued)/prepaid pension cost.

Journal Entries

The journal entries required to reflect the accounting for the company's pension plan for the years 1988 and 1989 are as follows (in thousands):

Year 1988

Journal Entry 1

Net periodic pension cost	141	
Accrued/prepaid pension cost		141
To record net pension cost for the period (paragraph .129)		

Journal Entry 2

Accrued/prepaid pension cost	199	
Cash		199
To record contribution (paragraph .129)		

Journal Entry 3

Excess of additional pension liability over unrecognized prior service cost	36	
Intangible asset	92	
Additional liability		128

To record an additional liability to reflect the required minimum liability (For financial statement presentation, the additional liability account balance is combined with the accrued/prepaid pension cost account balance. Since prepaid pension cost of $58 has been recognized, an additional liability of $128 is needed to reflect the required minimum liability of $70 [equal to unfunded accumulated benefits]. Because the additional liability is greater than unrecognized prior service cost, an intangible asset is recognized for the amount of additional liability up to the amount of unrecognized prior service cost, and equity is charged for the excess of the additional liability over unrecognized prior service cost.) (paragraphs .130 and .131)

Year 1989

Journal Entry 1

Net periodic pension cost	144	
Accrued/prepaid pension cost		144
To record net pension cost for the period (paragraph .129)		

Journal Entry 2

Accrued/prepaid pension cost	166	
Cash		166
To record contribution (paragraph .129)		

Journal Entry 3

Additional liability	128	
Excess of additional pension liability over unrecognized prior service cost		36
Intangible asset		92
To reverse additional liability no longer required (Since plan assets exceed accumulated benefits, no additional liability is necessary.) (paragraph .132)		

Illustration 6—Disclosure Requirements

The following cases provide examples that illustrate pension disclosures. [Companies that have pension and other postretirement benefit plans may also elect to present the required disclosures for their plans] in a parallel format in a single note to the financial statements. [Case 1 illustrates this type of disclosure.] The items presented in these examples have been included for illustrative purposes. However, items may be combined if individually immaterial. [FAS132, ¶61]

Case 1—Disclosures about Pension Plans

The following illustrates the 20X2 financial statement disclosures for an employer (Company A) with multiple defined benefit pension plans and other postretirement benefit plans. There is no additional minimum pension liability required to be recognized. During 20X2, the employer had an acquisition and made amendments to the plans.

	Pension Benefits		Other Benefits	
	20X2	**20X1**	**20X2**	**20X1**
Change in benefit obligation				
Benefit obligation at beginning of year	$1,266	$1,200	$ 738	$ 700
Service cost	76	72	36	32
Interest cost	114	108	65	63
Plan participants' contributions			20	13
Amendments	120		75	
Actuarial gain	(25)		(24)	
Acquisition	900		600	
Benefits paid	(125)	(114)	(90)	(70)
Benefit obligation at end of year	2,326	1,266	1,420	738
Change in plan assets				
Fair value of plan assets at beginning of year	1,068	880	206	87
Actual return on plan assets	29	188	(3)	24
Acquisition	1,000		25	
Employer contribution	75	114	171	152
Plan participants' contributions			20	13
Benefits paid	(125)	(114)	(90)	(70)
Fair value of plan assets at end of year	2,047	1,068	329	206
Funded status	(279)	(198)	(1,091)	(532)
Unrecognized net actuarial loss	83	38	59	60
Unrecognized prior service cost	260	160	585	540
Prepaid (accrued) benefit cost	$ 64	$ 0	$ (447)	$ 68

	Pension Benefits		Other Benefits	
	20X2	20X1	20X2	20X1
Weighted-average assumptions as of December 31				
Discount rate	9.25%	9.00%	9.00%	9.00%
Expected return on plan assets	10.00	10.00	10.00	10.00
Rate of compensation increase	5.00	5.00		

For measurement purposes, a 10 percent annual rate of increase in the per capita cost of covered health care benefits was assumed for 20X3. The rate was assumed to decrease gradually to 4 percent for 20X9 and remain at that level thereafter.

	Pension Benefits		Other Benefits	
	20X2	20X1	20X2	20X1
Components of net periodic benefit cost				
Service cost	$ 76	$ 72	$ 36	$ 32
Interest cost	114	108	65	63
Expected return on plan assets	(107)	(88)	(21)	(9)
Amortization of prior service cost	20	20	30	30
Recognized net actuarial loss	8	2	1	1
Net periodic benefit cost	$ 111	$ 114	$ 111	$ 117

Company A acquired FV Industries on December 31, 20X2, including its pension plans. The company's plans were amended on December 31, 20X2, to establish parity with the benefits provided by FV Industries.

The company has multiple nonpension postretirement benefit plans. The health care plans are contributory, with participants' contributions adjusted annually; the life insurance plans are noncontributory. The accounting for the health care plans anticipates future cost-sharing changes to the written plan that are consistent with the company's expressed intent to increase retiree contributions each year by 50 percent of the excess of the expected general inflation rate over 6 percent. On December 31, 20X2, the company amended its postretirement health care plans to provide long-term care coverage.

Assumed health care cost trend rates have a significant effect on the amounts reported for the health care plans. A one-percentage-point change in assumed health care cost trend rates would have the following effects:

	1-Percentage-Point Increase	1-Percentage-Point Decrease
Effect on total of service and interest cost components	$ 22	$ (20)
Effect on postretirement benefit obligation	173	(156)

[FAS132, ¶62]

Case 2—Disclosures for an Employer That Recognizes a Minimum Liability

The following illustrates the 20X2 financial statement disclosures if an employer (Company B) has multiple benefit plans including one pension plan for which the employer must recognize an additional minimum liability in accordance with the provisions of paragraph .130 of this section. As of December 31, 20X2, the assumptions are as follows:

- The accrued pension benefit cost for the underfunded plan is $89.
- The minimum liability is $153; thus, the additional minimum liability is $64. The additional minimum liability was $53 in the prior year.
- The total unrecognized [FAS132, ¶63] prior service cost [FAS135, ¶4(y)] for the underfunded plan is $50.
- The entry to record the change in the additional minimum liability for the period is:

Other comprehensive income	14	
Intangible asset		3
Accrued pension benefit cost		11

	Pension Benefits	
	20X2	**20X1**
Change in benefit obligation		
Benefit obligation at beginning of year	$1,266	$1,200
Service cost	76	72
Interest cost	114	108
Amendments	(20)	
Actuarial gain	(25)	
Benefits paid	(125)	(114)
Benefit obligation at end of year	1,286	1,266
Change in plan assets		
Fair value of plan assets at beginning of year	1,156	968
Actual return on plan assets	29	188
Employer contribution	139	114
Benefits paid	(125)	(114)
Fair value of plan assets at end of year	1,199	1,156
Funded status	(87)	(110)
Unrecognized actuarial loss	83	38
Unrecognized prior service cost	170	225
Net amount recognized	$ 166	$ 153

	Pension Benefits	
	20X2	**20X1**
Amounts recognized in the statement of financial position consist of:		
Prepaid benefit cost	$ 255	$ 227
Accrued benefit liability	(153)	(127)
Intangible asset	50	53
Accumulated other comprehensive income	14	
Net amount recognized	$ 166	$ 153

	Pension Benefits	
	20X2	**20X1**
Weighted-average assumptions as of December 31		
Discount rate	9.25%	9.00%
Expected return on plan assets	10.00	10.00
Rate of compensation increase	5.00	5.00

	Pension Benefits	
	20X2	**20X1**
Components of net periodic benefit cost		
Service cost	$ 76	$ 72
Interest cost	114	108
Expected return on plan assets	(116)	(97)
Amortization of prior service cost	35	35
Recognized actuarial loss	17	11
Net periodic benefit cost	$ 126	$129

The projected benefit obligation, accumulated benefit obligation, and fair value of plan assets for the pension plan with accumulated benefit obligations in excess of plan assets were $263, $237, and $84, respectively, as of December 31, 20X2, and $247, $222, and $95, respectively, as of December 31, 20X1.

[FAS132, ¶63]

Case 3—Alternative Disclosure for a Nonpublic Entity

The following illustrates the 20X2 financial statement disclosures that could be provided by Company A if it were a nonpublic entity.

	Pension Benefits	
	20X2	**20X1**
Benefit obligation at December 31	$2,326	$1,266
Fair value of plan assets at December 31	2,047	1,068
Funded status	$ (279)	$ (198)
Prepaid (accrued) benefit cost recognized in the statement of financial position	$ 64	$ 0

	Pension Benefits	
	20X2	**20X1**
Weighted-average assumptions as of December 31		
Discount rate	9.25%	9.00%
Expected return on plan assets	10.00	10.00
Rate of compensation increase	5.00	5.00

	Pension Benefits	
	20X2	**20X1**
Benefit cost	$111	$114
Employer contribution	75	114
Benefits paid	125	114

The company acquired FV Industries on December 31, 20X2, increasing the pension benefit obligation by $900 and pension plan assets by $1,000. Amendments during the year to the company's plans increased the pension benefit obligation by $120. [FAS132, ¶64]

Illustration 7—Accounting for a Business Combination

The following example illustrates how the liability (or asset) recognized by the acquiring firm at the date of a business combination would be reduced in years subsequent to the date of the business combination.

Company R purchased Company S on January 1, 19X2. Company S sponsors a single-employer defined benefit pension plan. The reconciliation of funded status of the Company S plan before and after the combination was as follows (in thousands):

	Precombination	Postcombination
Pension benefit obligation	$(1,000)	$(1,000)
Plan assets at fair value	500	500
Unrecognized loss	200	0
Unrecognized prior service cost	300	0
Liability recognized in the statement of financial position—unfunded accrued pension cost	$ 0	$ (500)

In subsequent periods, net periodic pension cost would not include any amortization of either the unrecognized prior service cost or the unrecognized loss existing at the date of the combination. However, the funding of the plan is not directly affected by a business combination. Whatever the basis of funding, it will, over time, reflect the past amendments and losses that underlie those amounts. As they are reflected in the funding process, contributions will, in some periods, exceed the net pension cost, and that will reduce the liability (unfunded accrued pension cost) recognized at the date of acquisition. [FAS87, ¶261]

.190 Pages 34262 through 34279 contain separate illustrations of the following requirements of this section:

Illustration 1—Accounting for a Plan Termination without a Replacement Defined Benefit Plan

Company A sponsored a final-pay noncontributory defined benefit plan. On November 16, 19X3, the employer terminated the plan, settled the accumulated benefit obligation of $1,500,000 (nonvested benefits became vested upon termination of the plan) by purchasing nonparticipating annuity contracts, and withdrew excess assets. Defined benefits were not provided under any successor plan. The plan ceased to exist as an entity.

As a result, Company A recognized a gain of $900,000, determined as follows:

	Company A (in thousands)		
	Before Termination	**Effect of Termination**	**After Termination**
Assets and obligations:			
Accumulated benefit obligation	$(1,500)	$ 1,500[a]	$0
Effects of projected future compensation levels	(400)	400[b]	0
Projected benefit obligation	(1,900)	1,900	0
Plan assets at fair value	2,100	(1,500)[a]	
		(600)[c]	0
Items not yet recognized in earnings:			
Unrecognized net asset at transition[d,e]	(200)	200	0
Unrecognized net gain subsequent to transition[e]	(300)	300	0
(Accrued)/prepaid pension cost on the statement of financial position	$ (300)	$ 300	$0

[a]The accumulated benefits of $1,500 were settled by using an equivalent amount of plan assets to purchase nonparticipating annuity contracts.

[b]The effects of projected future compensation levels ceased to be an obligation of the plan or the employer due to the termination of all plan participants. Under paragraph .183 of this section, the gain (that is, the decrease in the projected benefit obligation) resulting from the curtailment is first offset against any existing unrecognized net loss. Because the previously unrecognized amount in this case was a gain ($200 unrecognized net asset at transition plus $300 unrecognized net gain subsequent to transition), the $400 gain from the curtailment was recognized.

[c]Plan assets, in excess of the amount used to settle the pension benefits, were withdrawn from the plan.

[d]An unrecognized net asset at transition is treated as an unrecognized net gain for purposes of this section [refer to footnote 15].

[e]A pro rata amount of the maximum gain (paragraph .177), which includes the unrecognized net gain subsequent to transition ($300) and the unamortized net asset from transition ($200), is recognized due to settlement. The projected benefit obligation was reduced from $1,500 to $0 (the curtailment initially reduced the projected benefit obligation from $1,900 to $1,500 as described in footnote b), a reduction of 100 percent. Accordingly, the entire unrecognized net gain of $500 ($300 + $200) was recognized.

The journal entry required to reflect the accounting for the plan termination was:

Cash	600	
Accrued/prepaid pension cost	300	
Gain from plan termination		900

The gain from the plan termination without a replacement defined benefit plan was composed of the following:

Gain from curtailment	$400
Gain from settlement	500
Total gain	$900

Illustration 2—Accounting for a Settlement of a Pension Obligation

The following examples illustrate the accounting for a settlement of a pension obligation in three specific situations. The first example (Company B) had an unrecognized net obligation at the date of transition to this section, and the second and third examples (Company C and Company D) each had unrecognized net assets at the date of transition. Each company settled a portion of the obligation subsequent to transition to this section. Company B had a retroactive plan amendment after transition; Company C and Company D did not.

Example 2A—Projected Benefit Obligation Exceeds Plan Assets

Company B sponsors a final-pay noncontributory defined benefit plan. On December 31, 19X3, the plan settled the vested benefit portion ($1,300,000) of the projected benefit obligation through the purchase of nonparticipating annuity contracts.

As a result, Company B recognized a gain of $195,000, determined as follows:

	Company B (in thousands)		
	Before Settlement	**Effect of Settlement**	**After Settlement**
Assets and obligations:			
Vested benefit obligation	$(1,300)	$ 1,300[a]	$ 0
Nonvested benefits	(200)		(200)
Accumulated benefit obligation	(1,500)	1,300	(200)
Effects of projected future compensation levels	(500)		(500)
Projected benefit obligation	(2,000)	1,300	(700)
Plan assets at fair value	1,400	(1,300)[a]	100
Items not yet recognized in earnings:			
Unrecognized net obligation at transition[b]	650		650
Unrecognized prior service cost from amendment subsequent to transition	150		150
Unrecognized net gain subsequent to transition[c]	(300)	195	(105)
(Accrued)/prepaid pension cost on the statement of financial position	$ (100)	$ 195	$ 95

[a]The vested benefits of $1,300 were settled by using plan assets to purchase nonparticipating annuity contracts.

[b]An unrecognized net obligation at transition is treated as unrecognized prior service cost and therefore is not affected by settlement of the obligation [refer to footnote 15].

[c]A pro rata portion of the maximum gain (paragraph .177), the unrecognized net gain subsequent to transition, is recognized due to settlement. The projected benefit obligation was reduced from $2,000 to $700, a reduction of 65 percent. Accordingly, 65 percent of the maximum gain of $300, a gain of $195, was recognized. The journal entry required to reflect the accounting for the plan settlement was:

Accrued/prepaid pension cost	195	
Gain from settlement		195

Example 2B—Plan Assets Exceed the Projected Benefit Obligation

Company C sponsors a final-pay noncontributory defined benefit plan. On December 31, 19X3, the plan settled the vested benefit portion ($1,300,000) of the projected benefit obligation through the purchase of nonparticipating annuity contracts.

As a result, Company C recognized a gain of $325,000, determined as follows:

	Company C (in thousands)		
	Before Settlement	Effect of Settlement	After Settlement
Assets and obligations:			
Vested benefit obligation	$(1,300)	$ 1,300[a]	$ 0
Nonvested benefits	(200)		(200)
Accumulated benefit obligation	(1,500)	1,300	(200)
Effects of projected future compensation levels	(500)		(500)
Projected benefit obligation	(2,000)	1,300	(700)
Plan assets at fair value	2,100	(1,300)[a]	800
Items not yet recognized in earnings:			
Unrecognized net asset at transition[b,c]	(200)	130	(70)
Unrecognized net gain subsequent to transition[c]	(300)	195	(105)
(Accrued)/prepaid pension cost on the statement of financial position	$ (400)	$ 325	$ (75)

[a]The vested benefits of $1,300 were settled by using plan assets to purchase nonparticipating annuity contracts.

[b]An unrecognized net asset at transition is treated as an unrecognized net gain for purposes of this section [refer to footnote 15].

[c]A pro rata amount of the maximum gain (paragraph .177), which includes the unrecognized net gain subsequent to transition ($300) and the unamortized net asset from transition ($200), is recognized due to settlement. The projected benefit obligation was reduced from $2,000 to $700, a reduction of 65 percent. Accordingly, 65 percent of the maximum gain of $500 ($300 + $200), a gain of $325, was recognized. The journal entry required to reflect the accounting for the plan settlement was:

Accrued/prepaid pension cost	325	
Gain from settlement		325

Example 2C—Plan Assets Exceed the Projected Benefit Obligation and a Participating Annuity Contract Is Purchased to Settle Benefits

Company D sponsors a final-pay noncontributory defined benefit plan. On December 31, 19X3, the plan settled the vested benefit portion ($1,300,000) of the projected benefit obligation through the purchase of a participating annuity contract at a cost of $1,430,000. The plan could have purchased a nonparticipating contract covering the same benefits for $1,300,000. The participation features of the contract warranted a conclusion that its purchase constituted a settlement.

As a result, Company D recognized a gain of $240,000 (rounded), determined as follows:

	Company D (in thousands)		
	Before Settlement	Effect of Settlement	After Settlement
Assets and obligations:			
Vested benefit obligation	$(1,300)	$ 1,300[a]	$ 0
Nonvested benefits	(200)		(200)
Accumulated benefit obligation	(1,500)	1,300	(200)
Effects of projected future compensation levels	(500)		(500)
Projected benefit obligation	(2,000)	1,300	(700)
Plan assets at fair value:			
Participation right		130[a]	130
Other plan assets	2,100	(1,430)[a]	670
Items not yet recognized in earnings:			
Unrecognized net asset at transition[b,c]	(200)	130[d]	(70)
Unrecognized net gain subsequent to transition[c]	(300)	110[d]	(190)
(Accrued)/prepaid pension cost on the statement of financial position	$ (400)	$ 240	$(160)

[a]The vested benefits of $1,300 were settled by using $1,430 of plan assets to purchase a participating annuity contract. However, a nonparticipating contract covering the same benefits could have been purchased for $1,300. The plan paid the additional $130 to obtain the participation right.

[b]An unrecognized net asset at transition is treated as an unrecognized net gain for purposes of this section [refer to footnote 15].

[c]A pro rata amount of the maximum gain (paragraph .177), which includes the unrecognized net gain subsequent to transition ($300) and the unamortized net asset from transition ($200), was recognized due to settlement. However, any gain on a settlement that uses a participating annuity contract shall be computed by first reducing the maximum gain by the cost of the participation right [$200 + ($300 – $130) = $370]. The projected benefit obligation was reduced from $2,000 to $700, a reduction of 65 percent. Accordingly, a gain of $240 (rounded) was recognized (.65 × $370). The journal entry required to reflect the accounting for the plan settlement was:

Accrued/prepaid pension cost	240	
Gain from settlement		240

[d]The amount of gain from settlement was allocated as follows (rounded):

Unrecognized net asset at transition (.65 × $200)	$130
Unrecognized net gain subsequent to transition [.65 × ($300 – $130)]	110
	$240

Illustration 3—Accounting for a Plan Curtailment

The following examples illustrate the accounting for a curtailment in two specific situations. The first example (Company E) had an unrecognized net obligation at the date of transition to this section and a retroactive plan amendment after transition. The second example (Company F) had an unrecognized net asset at the date of transition. Both companies curtailed their plans subsequent to transition to this section.

Example 3A—Disposal of a Component—Projected Benefit Obligation Exceeds Plan Assets

Company E sponsors a final-pay noncontributory defined benefit plan. On January 1, 1988 (one year after transition) the company had a retroactive plan amendment resulting in $800,000 of prior service cost. On December 31, 1989, the management of Company E committed itself to a formal plan to dispose of a [FAS88, ¶57] component of the entity. [FAS144, ¶C11(c)] In connection with the disposal, the number of employees accumulating benefits under the plan would be reduced significantly. The portion of the projected benefit obligation based on the expected future compensation levels of the terminated employees was $90,000, and nonvested benefits of the terminated employees amounted to $20,000. The plan also had an unrecognized net obligation at the date of transition to this section that is treated as unrecognized prior service cost for purposes of applying this section. The remaining expected future years of service associated with those employees present at the date of transition was reduced by 30 percent due to the termination of employees. Accordingly, 30 percent of the unrecognized net obligation remaining unamortized at December 31, 1989 was a loss which amounted to $120,000.

The unrecognized prior service cost (which relates to the plan amendment of January 1, 1988) associated with the previously expected years of service of the terminated employees that will not be rendered was a loss which amounted to $160,000.

The sum of the effects resulting from the plan curtailment was a loss of $170,000, determined as follows:

	Company E (in thousands)		
	Before Curtailment	Effect of Curtailment	After Curtailment
Assets and obligations:			
Vested benefit obligation	$(1,300)		$(1,300)
Nonvested benefits	(200)	$ 20	(180)
Accumulated benefit obligation	(1,500)	20	(1,480)
Effects of projected future compensation levels	(500)	90	(410)
Projected benefit obligation	(2,000)	110[a]	(1,890)
Plan assets at fair value	1,400		1,400
Items not yet recognized in earnings:			
Unrecognized net obligation at transition[b]	400	(120)[b]	280
Unrecognized prior service cost resulting from plan amendment[c]	651	(160)[c]	491
Unrecognized net gain subsequent to transition	(151)		(151)
(Accrued)/prepaid pension cost on the statement of financial position	$ 300	$ (170)	$ 130

[a]Under paragraph .183 of this section, the gain (that is, the decrease in the projected benefit obligation) resulting from the curtailment is first offset against any existing unrecognized net loss. Because the previously unrecognized amount in this case was a gain ($151 unrecognized net gain subsequent to transition), the $110 gain from the curtailment was recognized.

[b]Because the plan had an unrecognized net obligation at the date of transition to this section [refer to footnote 3], the unrecognized amount is treated as prior service cost for purposes of applying this section. The remaining expected future years of service associated with those employees present at the date of transition was reduced by 30 percent due to the termination of employees. Accordingly, 30 percent of the unrecognized net obligation remaining unamortized at the date of the curtailment was recognized which amounted to $120.

[c]The unrecognized prior service cost (which related to the plan amendment of January 1, 1988) associated with the previously expected years of service of the terminated employees that will not be rendered was $160.

[d][Deleted 8/01 because of Statement 144.]

Example 3B—Plan Assets Exceed the Projected Benefit Obligation

Company F sponsors a final-pay noncontributory defined benefit plan. On July 27, 1990, the management of Company F decided to reduce significantly the operations of a line of business products. Although the decision did not result in closing down any facilities, it required the termination of a significant number of employees. The termination of employees [will take] place on November 1, 1990.

The portion of the projected benefit obligation based on expected future compensation levels of the terminated employees was $90,000, and the portion of nonvested benefits related to the terminated employees was $20,000.

As a result, Company F recognized a gain of $110,000 on November 1, 1990,* determined as follows:

*Under paragraph .184 of this section, if the sum of the effects resulting from the curtailment is a net loss, it is to be recognized when it is probable that the curtailment will occur and the effects are reasonably estimable. If the sum of those effects is a net gain, it [shall] be recognized when the related employees terminate. Company F estimated at July 27, 1990 that a net curtailment gain would result. Accordingly, the gain was recognized on the date employees terminated (November 1, 1990) and *was based on plan assets and obligations measured as of that date.*

	Company F (in thousands) As of November 1, 1990		
	Before Realization of Curtailment Gain	**Effect of Curtailment**	**After Realization of Curtailment Gain**
Assets and obligations:			
Vested benefit obligation	$(1,300)		$(1,300)
Nonvested benefits	(300)	$ 20	(280)
Accumulated benefit obligation	(1,600)	20	(1,580)
Effects of projected future compensation levels	(400)	90	(310)
Projected benefit obligation	(2,000)	110[a]	(1,890)
Plan assets at fair value	2,100		2,100
Items not yet recognized in earnings:			
Unrecognized net asset at transition[a]	(200)	0[a]	(200)
Unrecognized net loss subsequent to transition	100	0[a]	100
(Accrued)/prepaid pension cost on the statement of financial position	$ 0	$110	$ 110

[a]Under paragraph .183 of this section, the curtailment gain (that is, the decrease in the projected benefit obligation) is first offset against any existing unrecognized net loss. The unrecognized net asset from transition is treated as an unrecognized net gain [refer to footnote 15]. Thus the net amount of previously unrecognized gain or loss was a gain of $100 (unrecognized net loss of $100 plus the remaining unrecognized net asset from transition of $200). Because the previously unrecognized net amount was a gain, the $110 gain from curtailment was recognized.

If the previously existing unrecognized net amount had been a loss including the unrecognized net asset at transition and that loss exceeded the curtailment gain, the curtailment gain would have been offset, and no gain would have been recognized.

The journal entry required to reflect the accounting for the plan curtailment was:

Accrued/prepaid pension cost	110	
Gain from curtailment		110

Illustration 4—Calculation of Unrecognized Prior Service Cost Associated with Services of Terminated Employees

Company S sponsors a final-pay noncontributory defined benefit plan. On January 1, 19X3, the company had a retroactive plan amendment resulting in prior service cost of $800,000.

The unrecognized prior service cost that results from the plan amendment is amortized based on the expected future years of service of participants active as of January 1, 19X3 who are expected to receive benefits under the plan.

As of January 1, 19X3, the company had 100 employees who were expected to receive benefits under the plan. Based on the assumption that 5 percent of that group (5 employees) leaves (either quits or retires) in each of the next 20 years, the expected future years of service amounted to 1,050.

The amount of prior service cost associated with each expected future year of service is $762 ($800,000 ÷ 1,050). Exhibit A illustrates the originally expected expiration of the anticipated service years.

On December 31, 19X5, Company S terminated 25 employees active at the date of the plan amendment. Immediately prior to the curtailment, 765 expected future years of service remained (1,050 less 285 years of service rendered in the previous 3 years). The curtailment reduced the total expected future years of service at December 31, 19X5 from 765 to 555 (210) as illustrated in Exhibit B. Therefore, Company S will recognize $160,020 ($762 × 210) of prior service cost in conjunction with the curtailment.

Exhibit A

Determination of Expected Years of Service Rendered in Each Year before Curtailment

Individuals	Future Service Years	Year X3	X4	X5	X6	X7	X8	X9	Y0	Y1	Y2	Y3	Y4	Y5	Y6	Y7	Y8	Y9	Z0	Z1	Z2
A1-A5	5	5																			
B1-B5	10	5	5																		
C1-C5	15	5	5	5																	
D1-D5	20	5	5	5	5																
E1-E5	25	5	5	5	5	5															
F1-F5	30	5	5	5	5	5	5														
G1-G5	35	5	5	5	5	5	5	5													
H1-H5	40	5	5	5	5	5	5	5	5												
I1-I5	45	5	5	5	5	5	5	5	5	5											
J1-J5	50	5	5	5	5	5	5	5	5	5	5										
K1-K5	55	5	5	5	5	5	5	5	5	5	5	5									
L1-L5	60	5	5	5	5	5	5	5	5	5	5	5	5								
M1-M5	65	5	5	5	5	5	5	5	5	5	5	5	5	5							
N1-N5	70	5	5	5	5	5	5	5	5	5	5	5	5	5	5						
O1-O5	75	5	5	5	5	5	5	5	5	5	5	5	5	5	5	5					
P1-P5	80	5	5	5	5	5	5	5	5	5	5	5	5	5	5	5	5				
Q1-Q5	85	5	5	5	5	5	5	5	5	5	5	5	5	5	5	5	5	5			
R1-R5	90	5	5	5	5	5	5	5	5	5	5	5	5	5	5	5	5	5	5		
S1-S5	95	5	5	5	5	5	5	5	5	5	5	5	5	5	5	5	5	5	5	5	
T1-T5	100	5	5	5	5	5	5	5	5	5	5	5	5	5	5	5	5	5	5	5	5
	1,050																				
Service years rendered		100	95	90	85	80	75	70	65	60	55	50	45	40	35	30	25	20	15	10	5
Amortization fraction		100	95	90	85	80	75	70	65	60	55	50	45	40	35	30	25	20	15	10	5
		1,050	1,050	1,050	1,050	1,050	1,050	1,050	1,050	1,050	1,050	1,050	1,050	1,050	1,050	1,050	1,050	1,050	1,050	1,050	1,050
Expected future years of service remaining at year-end		950	855	765	680	600	525	455	390	330	275	225	180	140	105	75	50	30	15	5	0

Prior service cost	$800,000
Total expected future years of service	1,050
Amortization amount per each year of service	$762

Exhibit B

Determination of Expected Years of Service Rendered in Each Year after Curtailment

	Year																			
Individuals	**X3**	**X4**	**X5**	**X6**	**X7**	**X8**	**X9**	**Y0**	**Y1**	**Y2**	**Y3**	**Y4**	**Y5**	**Y6**	**Y7**	**Y8**	**Y9**	**Z0**	**Z1**	**Z2**
A1-A5	5																			
B1-B5	5	5																		
C1-C5	5	5	5																	
D1-D5*	5	5	5																	
E1-E5	5	5	5	5	5															
F1-F5	5	5	5	5	5	5														
G1-G5	5	5	5	5	5	5	5													
H1-H5*	5	5	5																	
I1-I5	5	5	5	5	5	5	5	5	5											
J1-J5	5	5	5	5	5	5	5	5	5	5										
K1-K5	5	5	5	5	5	5	5	5	5	5	5									
L1-L5*	5	5	5																	
M1-M5	5	5	5	5	5	5	5	5	5	5	5	5	5							
N1-N5	5	5	5	5	5	5	5	5	5	5	5	5	5	5						
O1-O5*	5	5	5																	
P1-P5	5	5	5	5	5	5	5	5	5	5	5	5	5	5	5	5				
Q1-Q5	5	5	5	5	5	5	5	5	5	5	5	5	5	5	5	5	5			
R1-R5*	5	5	5																	
S1-S5	5	5	5	5	5	5	5	5	5	5	5	5	5	5	5	5	5	5	5	
T1-T5	5	5	5	5	5	5	5	5	5	5	5	5	5	5	5	5	5	5	5	5
Service years rendered	100	95	90	60	60	55	50	45	45	40	35	30	30	25	20	20	15	10	10	5
Adjustment for termination			210																	
Total	100	95	300	60	60	55	50	45	45	40	35	30	30	25	20	20	15	10	10	5
Amortization fraction	100	95	300	60	60	55	50	45	45	40	35	30	30	25	20	20	15	10	10	5
	1,050	1,050	1,050	1,050	1,050	1,050	1,050	1,050	1,050	1,050	1,050	1,050	1,050	1,050	1,050	1,050	1,050	1,050	1,050	1,050
Expected future years of service remaining at year-end	950	855	555	495	435	380	330	285	240	200	165	135	105	80	60	40	25	15	5	0

*Terminated group of employees.

Illustration 5—Accounting for a Plan Curtailment When Termination Benefits Are Offered to Employees

Company G sponsors a final-pay noncontributory defined benefit plan. The company had an unrecognized net obligation at the date of transition to this section and did not have a retroactive plan amendment after that date. On May 11, 19X5, the company offered for a short period of time (until June 30, 19X5) special benefits to its employees in connection with their voluntary termination of employment (special termination benefits). The special termination benefit was a lump-sum payment to be made upon termination, payable in addition to the employee's regular plan benefits. The special termination benefit was paid directly from the employer's assets rather than from the plan assets.

On June 30, 15 percent of the employees accepted the offer. The amount of the special termination benefit payment was $125,000.

The portion of the projected benefit obligation based on the expected future compensation levels of the terminated employees amounted to $100,000, and all the employees terminated were fully vested in their accumulated benefits. The portion of the unrecognized net obligation at transition associated with the years of service no longer expected from the terminated employees was $150,000.

As a result, Company G recognized a loss of $175,000 that includes the cost of the special termination benefits and the loss* from the curtailment determined as follows:

*Under paragraph .184 of this section, if the sum of the effects resulting from the curtailment is a net loss, it is to be recognized when it is probable that the curtailment will occur and the effects are reasonably estimable. In this example, the effects resulting from the curtailment were not reasonably estimable until June 30, 19X5, the acceptance date for the offer of special termination benefits.

	Company G (in thousands)		
	Before Curtailment	**Effect of Curtailment**	**After Curtailment**
Assets and obligations:			
Vested benefit obligation	$(1,300)		$(1,300)
Nonvested benefits	(200)		(200)
Accumulated benefit obligation	(1,500)		(1,500)
Effects of projected future compensation levels	(500)	$ 100	(400)
Projected benefit obligation	(2,000)	100[a]	(1,900)
Plan assets at fair value	1,400		1,400
Items not yet recognized in earnings:			
Unrecognized net obligation at transition[b]	800	(150)	650
Unrecognized net gain subsequent to transition	(300)		(300)
(Accrued)/prepaid pension cost on the statement of financial position	$ (100)	$ (50)	$ (150)
Loss on curtailment		$ 50	
Cost of special termination benefits (lump-sum payments to terminated employees)		125	
Total loss		$ 175[c]	

[a]Under paragraph .183 of this section, the curtailment gain (that is, the decrease in the projected benefit obligation) is first offset against any existing unrecognized net loss. Since the previously unrecognized amount was a gain ($300 unrecognized net gain subsequent to transition), the $100 gain from the curtailment was recognized.

[b]An unrecognized net obligation at the date of transition to this section is treated as unrecognized prior service cost for purposes of applying this section. The portion of unrecognized prior service cost associated with the years of service no longer expected from the terminated employees ($150) was recognized.

[c]The loss Company G recognized was $175, which includes the cost of the special termination benefits of $125, the gain related to salary progression of $100 and the recognition of prior service cost of $150. The journal entry required to reflect the accounting for this event was:

Loss on employee terminations	175	
Accrued/prepaid pension cost		50
Liability for termination benefits		125

If the company had paid the termination benefits from the pension plan (by amending the plan and using plan assets), the same loss would have been recognized, but $175 would have been credited to the accrued pension cost liability.

Illustration 6—Transition for an Employer That Completed an Asset Reversion Prior to the Initial Application of This Section

Company H sponsors a final-pay noncontributory defined benefit pension plan. On September 9, 1981, the company settled a portion of its pension obligation through the purchase of annuity contracts and withdrew excess assets. The company continued to provide defined benefits to its employees. No gain was recognized on the transaction, and Company H recognized a credit in its statement of financial position equal to the amount of cash withdrawn. For financial reporting purposes, that amount was grouped with accrued or prepaid pension cost. In subsequent periods the amount of the reversion (a deferred gain) was amortized as a reduction of net periodic pension cost. The company had no other past differences between net periodic pension cost and amounts contributed and, therefore, had recognized no other accrued or prepaid pension cost.

As of January 1, 1985, the time of initial application of this section, the unamortized amount of the reversion gain was $287,000. Company H's transition to this section would be accomplished as follows:

		Company H (in thousands) **Computation of Unrecognized Net Asset**
Projected benefit obligation		$ (800)
Plan assets at fair value	$950	
Accrued pension cost on the statement of financial position	287	1,237
Unrecognized net asset		$ 437

	Company H (in thousands)		
	Before Recognition of Reversion Gain	**Effect of Recognition of Reversion Gain**	**After Recognition of Reversion Gain**
Assets and obligations:			
Projected benefit obligation	$(800)		$(800)
Plan assets at fair value	950		950
Item not yet recognized in earnings:			
Unrecognized net asset at transition	(437)	$287[a]	(150)
(Accrued)/prepaid pension cost on the statement of financial position	$(287)	$287[a]	$ 0

[FAS88, ¶57]

[a]Under paragraph .188 of this section, an employer that completed an asset reversion prior to the effective date of this section should recognize a gain as the cumulative effect of a change in accounting principle at the time of initial application of this section.

The gain recognized by Company H amounts to $287, which is the lesser of the unamortized amount of the reversion gain ($287) and the unrecognized net asset from transition ($437). The journal entry required to reflect the accounting as of January 1, 1985 was:

Accrued/prepaid pension cost	287	
Cumulative effect of a change in accounting principle		287

[Note: Additional guidance with respect to implementing Section P16 is presented in two FASB publications: *A Guide to Implementation of Statement 87 on Employers' Accounting for Pensions: Questions and Answers,* which addresses 107 questions, and *A Guide to Implementation of Statement 88 on Employers' Accounting for Settlements and Curtailments of Defined Benefit Pension Plans and for Termination Benefits: Questions and Answers,* which addresses 70 other questions. Both publications were written by FASB staff members Joan Lordi Amble and Jules M. Cassel, and are available from the Order Department, Financial Accounting Standards Board, 401 Merritt 7, P.O. Box 5116, Norwalk, CT 06856-5116, telephone (203) 847-0700.]

Glossary

.401 **Accumulated benefit obligation.** The actuarial present value of benefits (whether vested or nonvested) attributed by the pension benefit formula to employee service rendered before a specified date and based on employee service and compensation (if applicable) prior to that date. The accumulated benefit obligation differs from the projected benefit obligation in that it includes no assumption about future compensation levels. For plans with flat-benefit or non-pay-related pension benefit formulas, the accumulated benefit obligation and the projected benefit obligation are the same. [FAS87, ¶264]

.402 **Actual return on plan assets component (of net periodic pension cost).** The difference between fair value of plan assets at the end of the period and the fair value at the beginning of the period, adjusted for contributions and payments of benefits during the period. [FAS87, ¶264]

.403 **Actuarial present value.** The value, as of a specified date, of an amount or series of amounts payable or receivable thereafter, with each amount adjusted to reflect (a) the time value of money (through discounts for interest) and (b) the probability of payment (by means of decrements for events such as death, disability, withdrawal, or retirement) between the specified date and the expected date of payment. [FAS87, ¶264]

.404 **Allocated contract.** A contract with an insurance company under which payments to the insurance company are currently used to purchase immediate or deferred annuities for individual participants. See also **Annuity contract.** [FAS87, ¶264]

.405 **Amortization.** Usually refers to the process of reducing a recognized liability systematically by recognizing revenues or reducing a recognized asset systematically by recognizing expenses or costs. In pension accounting, amortization is also used to refer to the systematic recognition in net pension cost over several periods of previously *unrecognized* amounts, including unrecognized prior service cost and unrecognized net gain or loss. [FAS87, ¶264]

.406 **Annuity contract.** A contract in which an insurance company unconditionally undertakes a legal obligation to provide specified pension benefits to specific individuals in return for a fixed consideration or premium. An annuity contract is irrevocable and involves the transfer of significant risk from the employer to the insurance company. Annuity contracts are also called allocated contracts. [FAS87, ¶264] [I]f there is any reasonable doubt that the insurance company will meet its obligation under the contract, the contract is not an annuity [contract] for purposes of this section. [In addition,] if the insurance company does business primarily with the employer and related parties (a captive insurer), the contract is not an annuity contract for purposes of paragraphs .154

through .158. [FAS87, ¶57, fn14] If the insurance company is controlled by the employer, the purchase of the contract does not constitute a settlement for purposes of [applying paragraphs .178 through .181]. [FAS88, ¶5, fn1] Some annuity contracts (participating annuity contracts) provide that the purchaser (either the plan or the employer) may participate in the experience of the insurance company. Under those contracts, the insurance company ordinarily pays dividends to the purchaser. If the substance of a participating annuity contract is such that the employer remains subject to all or most of the risks and rewards associated with the benefit obligation covered or the assets transferred to the insurance company, that contract is not an annuity contract for purposes of this section [FAS87, ¶57] [and] the purchase of the contract does not constitute a settlement. [FAS88, ¶5]

.407 **Assumptions.** Estimates of the occurrence of future events affecting pension costs, such as mortality, withdrawal, disablement and retirement, changes in compensation and national pension benefits, and discount rates to reflect the time value of money. [FAS87, ¶264]

.408 **Attribution.** The process of assigning pension benefits or cost to periods of employee service. [FAS87, ¶264]

.409 **Benefit formula.** See **Pension benefit formula.** [FAS87, ¶264]

.410 **Benefits.** Payments to which participants may be entitled under a pension plan, including pension benefits, death benefits, and benefits due on termination of employment. [FAS87, ¶264]

.411 **Benefit/years-of-service approach.** Under this approach, an equal portion of the total estimated benefit is attributed to each year of service. The actuarial present value of the benefits is derived after the benefits are attributed to the periods. [FAS87, ¶264]

.412 **Captive [insurer].** An insurance company that does business primarily with related entities. [FAS87, ¶264]

.413 **Career-average-pay formula (Career-average-pay plan).** A benefit formula that bases benefits on the employee's compensation over the entire period of service with the employer. A career-average-pay plan is a plan with such a formula. [FAS87, ¶264]

.414 **Contributory plan.** A pension plan under which employees contribute part of the cost. In some contributory plans, employees wishing to be covered must contribute; in other contributory plans, employee contributions result in increased benefits. [FAS87, ¶264]

.415 **Curtailment.** See **Plan curtailment.** [FAS87, ¶264]

.416 **Defined benefit pension plan.** A pension plan that defines an amount of pension benefit to be provided, usually as a function of one or more factors such as age, years of service, or compensation. Any pension plan that is not a defined contribution pension plan is, for purposes of this section, a defined benefit pension plan. [FAS87, ¶264]

.417 **Defined contribution pension plan.** A plan that provides pension benefits in return for services rendered, provides an individual account for each participant, and specifies how contributions to the individual's account are to be determined instead of specifying the amount of benefits the individual is to receive. Under a defined contribution pension plan, the benefits a participant will receive depend solely on the amount contributed to the participant's account, the returns earned on investments of those contributions, and forfeitures of other participants' benefits that may be allocated to such participant's account. [FAS87, ¶264]

.418 **Discount rate.** The interest rate used to adjust for the time value of money. See also **Actuarial present value.** [FAS87, ¶264]

.419 **Expected long-term rate of return on plan assets.** An assumption as to the rate of return on plan assets reflecting the average rate of earnings expected on the funds invested or to be invested to provide for the benefits included in the projected benefit obligation. [FAS87, ¶264]

.420 **Expected return on plan assets.** An amount calculated as a basis for determining the extent of delayed recognition of the effects of changes in the fair value of assets. The expected return on plan assets is determined based on the expected long-term rate of return on plan assets and the market-related value of plan assets. [FAS87, ¶264]

.421 **Explicit approach to assumptions.** An approach under which each significant assumption used reflects the best estimate of the plan's future experience solely with respect to that assumption. [FAS87, ¶264]

.422 **Fair value.** The amount that a pension plan could reasonably expect to receive for an investment in a current sale between a willing buyer and a willing seller, that is, other than in a forced or liquidation sale. [FAS87, ¶264]

.423 **Final-pay formula (Final-pay plan).** A benefit formula that bases benefits on the employee's compensation over a specified number of years near the end of the employee's service period or on the employee's highest compensation periods. For example, a plan might provide annual pension benefits equal to 1 percent of the employee's average salary for the last five years (or the highest consecutive five years) for each year of service. A final-pay plan is a plan with such a formula. [FAS87, ¶264]

.424 **Flat-benefit formula (Flat-benefit plan).** A benefit formula that bases benefits on a fixed amount per year of service, such as $20 of monthly retirement income for each year of credited service. A flat-benefit plan is a plan with such a formula. [FAS87, ¶264]

.425 **Fund.** Used as a verb, to pay over to a funding agency (as to fund future pension benefits or to fund pension cost). Used as a noun, assets accumulated in the hands of a funding agency for the purpose of meeting pension benefits when they become due. [FAS87, ¶264]

.426 **Funding policy.** The program regarding the amounts and timing of contributions by the employer(s), participants, and any other sources (for example, state subsidies or federal grants) to provide the benefits a pension plan specifies. [FAS87, ¶264]

.427 **Gain or loss.** A change in the value of either the projected benefit obligation or the plan assets resulting from experience different from that assumed or from a change in an actuarial assumption. See also **Unrecognized net gain or loss.** [FAS87, ¶264]

.428 **Gain or loss (component of net periodic pension cost).** The sum of (a) the difference between the actual return on plan assets and the expected return on plan assets and (b) the amortization of the unrecognized net gain or loss from previous periods. The gain or loss component is the net effect of delayed recognition of gains and losses (the net change in the unrecognized net gain or loss) except that it does not include changes in the projected benefit obligation occurring during the period and deferred for later recognition. [FAS87, ¶264]

.429 **Interest cost component (of net periodic pension cost).** The increase in the projected benefit obligation due to passage of time. [FAS87, ¶264]

.430 **Interest rate.** See **Discount rate.** [FAS87, ¶264]

.431 **Loss.** See **Gain or loss.** [FAS87, ¶264]

.432 **Market-related value of plan assets.** A balance used to calculate the expected return on plan assets. Market-related value can be either fair market value or a calculated value that recognizes changes in fair value in a systematic and rational manner over not more than five years. Different ways of calculating market-related value may be used for different classes of assets, but the manner of determining market-related value shall be applied consistently from year to year for each asset class. [FAS87, ¶264]

.433 **Measurement date.** The date as of which plan assets and obligations are measured. [FAS87, ¶264]

.434 **Mortality rate.** The proportion of the number of deaths in a specified group to the number living at the beginning of the period in which the deaths occur. Actuaries use mortality tables, which show death rates for each age, in estimating the amount of pension benefits that will become payable. [FAS87, ¶264]

.435 **Multiemployer plan.** A pension plan to which two or more unrelated employers contribute, usually pursuant to one or more collective-bargaining agreements. A characteristic of multiemployer plans is that assets contributed by one participating employer may be used to provide benefits to employees of other participating employers since assets contributed by an employer are not segregated in a separate account or restricted to provide benefits only to employees of that employer. A multiemployer plan is usually administered by a board of trustees composed of management and labor representatives and may also be referred to as a "joint trust" or "union" plan. Generally, many employers participate in a multiemployer plan, and an employer may participate in more than one plan. The employers participating in multiemployer plans usually have a common industry bond, but for some plans the employers are in different industries and the labor union may be their only common bond. [FAS87, ¶264]

.436 **Multiple-employer plan.** A pension plan maintained by more than one employer but not treated as a multiemployer plan. Multiple-employer plans are not as prevalent as single-employer and multiemployer plans, but some of the ones that do exist are large and involve many employers. Multiple-employer plans are generally not collectively bargained and are intended to allow participating employers, commonly in the same industry, to pool their assets for investment purposes and reduce the costs of plan administration. A multiple-employer plan maintains separate accounts for each employer so that contributions provide benefits only for employees of the contributing employer. Some multiple-employer plans have features that allow participating employers to have different benefit formulas, with the employer's contributions to the plan based on the benefit formula selected by the employer. [FAS87, ¶264]

.437 **Net periodic pension cost.** The amount recognized in an employer's financial statements as the cost of a pension plan for a period. Components of net periodic pension cost are service cost, interest cost, actual return on plan assets, gain or loss, amortization of unrecognized prior service cost, and amortization of the unrecognized net obligation or asset existing at the date of initial application of this section. This section uses the term *net periodic pension cost* instead of *net pension expense* because part of the cost recognized in a period may be capitalized along with other costs as part of an asset such as inventory. [FAS87, ¶264]

.438 **Nonparticipating annuity contract.** An annuity contract that does not provide for the purchaser to participate in the investment performance or in other experience of the insurance company. See also **Annuity contract.** [FAS87, ¶264]

.439 **Participant.** Any employee or former employee, or any member or former member of a trade or other employee association, or the beneficiaries of those individuals, for whom there are pension plan benefits. [FAS87, ¶264]

.440 **Participating annuity contract.** An annuity contract that provides for the purchaser to participate in the investment performance and possibly other experience (for example, mortality experience) of the insurance company. [FAS87, ¶264]

.441 **Participation right.** A purchaser's right under a participating contract to receive future dividends or retroactive rate credits from the insurance company. [FAS87, ¶264]

.442 **Pension benefit formula (plan's benefit formula or benefit formula).** The basis for determining payments to which participants may be entitled under a pension plan. Pension benefit formulas usually refer to the employee's service or compensation or both. [FAS87, ¶264]

.443 **Pension benefits.** Periodic (usually monthly) payments made pursuant to the terms of the pension plan to a person who has retired from employment or to that person's beneficiary. [FAS87, ¶264]

.444 **Plan amendment.** A change in the terms of an existing plan or the initiation of a new plan. A plan amendment may increase benefits, including those attributed to years of service already rendered. See also **Retroactive benefits.** [FAS87, ¶264]

.445 **Plan assets.** Assets—usually stocks, bonds, and other investments—that have been segregated and restricted (usually in a trust) to provide benefits. Plan assets include amounts contributed by the employer (and by employees for a contributory plan) and amounts earned from investing the contributions, less benefits paid. Plan assets cannot ordinarily be withdrawn by the employer except in certain circumstances when a plan has assets in excess of obligations and the employer has taken certain steps to satisfy existing obligations. For purposes of this section, assets not segregated in a trust or otherwise effectively restricted so that they cannot be used by the employer for other purposes are not plan assets even though it may be intended that such assets be used to provide pensions. Amounts accrued by the employer as net periodic pension cost but not yet paid to the plan are not plan assets for purposes of this section. Securities of the employer held by the plan are includable in plan assets provided they are transferable. If a plan has liabilities other than for benefits, those nonbenefit obligations may be considered as reductions of plan assets for purposes of this section. [FAS87, ¶264]

.446 **Plan assets available for benefits.** See **Plan assets.** [FAS87, ¶264]

.447 **Plan curtailment.** An event that significantly reduces the expected years of future service of present employees or eliminates for a significant number of employees the accrual of defined benefits for some or all of their future services. [FAS87, ¶264] Curtailments include:

a. Termination of employees' services earlier than expected, which may or may not involve closing a facility or discontinuing a [FAS88, ¶6] component of an entity [FAS144, ¶C11(a)]
b. Termination or suspension of a plan so that employees do not earn additional defined benefits for future services. In the latter situation, future service may be counted toward vesting of benefits accumulated based on past service. [FAS88, ¶6]

.448 **Plan's benefit formula.** See **Pension benefit formula.** [FAS87, ¶264]

.449 **Plan termination.** An event in which the pension plan ceases to exist and all benefits are settled by purchase of annuities or other means. The plan may or may not be replaced by another plan. A plan termination with a replacement plan may or may not be in substance a plan termination for accounting purposes. [FAS87, ¶264]

.450 **Prepaid pension cost.** Cumulative employer contributions in excess of accrued net pension cost. [FAS87, ¶264]

.451 **Prior service cost.** The cost of retroactive benefits granted in a plan amendment. See also **Unrecognized prior service cost.** [FAS87, ¶264]

.452 **Projected benefit obligation.** The actuarial present value as of a date of all benefits attributed by the pension benefit formula to employee service rendered prior to that date. The projected benefit obligation is measured using assumptions as to future compensation levels if the pension benefit formula is based on those future compensation levels (pay-related, final-pay, final-average-pay, or career-average-pay plans). [FAS87, ¶264]

.453 **Retroactive benefits.** Benefits granted in a plan amendment (or initiation) that are attributed by the pension benefit formula to employee services rendered in periods prior to the amendment. The cost of the retroactive benefits is referred to as prior service cost. [FAS87, ¶264]

.454 **Return on plan assets.** See **Actual return on plan assets component** and **Expected return on plan assets.** [FAS87, ¶264]

.455 **Service.** Employment taken into consideration under a pension plan. Years of employment before the inception of a plan constitute an employee's past service; years thereafter are classified in relation to the particular actuarial valuation being made or discussed. Years of employment (including past service) prior to the date of a particular valuation constitute prior service; years of employment following the date of the valuation constitute future service; a year of employment adjacent to the date of valuation, or in which such date falls, constitutes current service. [FAS87, ¶264]

.456 **Service cost component (of net periodic pension cost).** The actuarial present value of benefits attributed by the pension benefit formula to employee services rendered by employees during that period. The service cost component is a portion of the projected benefit obligation and is unaffected by the funded status of the plan. [FAS87, ¶264]

.457 **Settlement.** A transaction that (a) is an irrevocable action, (b) relieves the employer (or the plan) of primary responsibility for a pension benefit obligation, and (c) eliminates significant risks related to the obligation and the assets used to effect the settlement. Examples of transactions that constitute a settlement include (a) making lump-sum cash payments to plan participants in exchange for their rights to receive specified pension benefits and (b) purchasing nonparticipating annuity contracts to cover vested benefits. [FAS88, ¶3]

.458 **Single-employer plan.** A pension plan that is maintained by one employer. The term also may be used to describe a plan that is maintained by related parties such as a parent and its subsidiaries. [FAS87, ¶264]

.459 **Suspension.** An event in which the pension plan is frozen and no further benefits accrue. Future service may continue to be the basis for vesting of nonvested benefits existing at the date of suspension. The plan may still hold assets, pay benefits already accrued, and receive additional employer contributions for any unfunded benefits. Employees may or may not continue working for the employer. [FAS87, ¶264]

.460 **Turnover.** Termination of employment for a reason other than death or retirement. [FAS87, ¶264]

.461 **Unfunded accrued pension cost.** Cumulative net pension cost accrued in excess of the employer's contributions. [FAS87, ¶264]

.462 **Unfunded accumulated benefit obligation.** The excess of the accumulated benefit obligation over plan assets. [FAS87, ¶264]

.463 **Unrecognized net gain or loss.** The cumulative net gain or loss that has not been recognized as a part of net periodic pension cost. See **Gain or loss.** [FAS87, ¶264]

.464 **Unrecognized prior service cost.** That portion of prior service cost that has not been recognized as a part of net periodic pension cost. [FAS87, ¶264]

.465 **Vested benefit obligation.** The actuarial present value of vested benefits. [FAS87, ¶264]

.466 **Vested benefits.** Benefits for which the employee's right to receive a present or future pension benefit is no longer contingent on remaining in the service of the employer. (Other conditions, such as inadequacy of the pension fund, may prevent the employee from receiving the vested benefit.) Under graded vesting, the initial vested right may be to receive in the future a stated percentage of a pension based on the number of years of accumulated credited service; thereafter, the percentage may increase with the number of years of service or of age until the right to receive the entire benefit has vested. [FAS87, ¶264]

Supplemental Guidance: Emerging Issues Task Force (EITF) Issues

.1000 [Listed below are EITF Issues that provide supplemental guidance for this section. These Issues are grouped by subject matter and may be either interpretive of or related by topic to the guidance in this section.

Business Combinations

EITF Issue No. 84-35, "Business Combinations: Sale of Duplicate Facilities and Accrual of Liabilities"

EITF Issue No. 95-14, "Recognition of Liabilities in Anticipation of a Business Combination"

EITF Issue No. 96-5, "Recognition of Liabilities for Contractual Termination Benefits or Changing Benefit Plan Assumptions in Anticipation of a Business Combination"

Other

EITF Issue No. 86-27, "Measurement of Excess Contributions to a Defined Contribution Plan or Employee Stock Ownership Plan"

EITF Issue No. 88-1, "Determination of Vested Benefit Obligation for a Defined Benefit Pension Plan"

EITF Issue No. 90-3, "Accounting for Employers' Obligations for Future Contributions to a Multiemployer Pension Plan"

EITF Issue No. 91-7, "Accounting for Pension Benefits Paid by Employers after Insurance Companies Fail to Provide Annuity Benefits"

EITF Issue No. 94-3, "Liability Recognition for Certain Employee Termination Benefits and Other Costs to Exit an Activity (including Certain Costs Incurred in a Restructuring)"

EITF Topic No. D-27, "Accounting for the Transfer of Excess Pension Assets to a Retiree Health Care Benefits Account"

EITF Topic No. D-36, "Selection of Discount Rates Used for Measuring Defined Benefit Pension Obligations and Obligations of Postretirement Benefit Plans Other Than Pensions"

EITF Topic No. D-92, "The Effect of FASB Statement No. 135 on the Measurement and Recognition of Net Periodic Benefit Cost under FASB Statements No. 87 and No. 106"]

.1001 [Listed below are those EITF Issues that provide interpretive guidance on specific material in this section.

Paragraphs .118 through .122 (FAS 87, ¶24-28)—EITF Issue No. 91-7
Paragraph .138, fn9(b) (FAS 106, ¶186)—EITF Topic No. D-36
Paragraph .140 (FAS 87, ¶198)—EITF Topic No. D-36
Paragraph .161 (FAS 87, ¶64)—EITF Issue No. 86-27
Paragraph .165 (FAS 87, ¶68)—EITF Issue No. 90-3]

(The next page is 34851.)

POSTEMPLOYMENT BENEFITS SECTION P32

Sources: FASB Statement 112; FASB Statement 123

[**Note:** A list of Issues discussed by the Emerging Issues Task Force (EITF) that provide supplemental guidance for this section is presented in paragraph .1000.]

Summary

This section presents standards for employers' accounting for postemployment benefits provided to former or inactive employees, including their beneficiaries and covered dependents, after employment but before retirement. Postemployment benefits may be paid as the result of a disability, layoff, death, or other event and may be provided in cash or in kind. If an obligation is not accrued only because the amount cannot be reasonably estimated, the financial statements shall disclose that fact.

Scope

.101 This section applies to all types of **postemployment benefits** provided to former or **inactive employees,** their beneficiaries, and covered dependents after employment but before retirement, except as noted in paragraph .102. Benefits may be provided in cash or in kind and may be paid as a result of a disability, layoff, death, or other event. Benefits may be paid immediately upon cessation of active employment or over a specified period of time. Employees' rights to benefits may accumulate or vest as they render service. [FAS112, ¶4]

.102 This section does not apply to:

a. Postemployment benefits provided through a pension or postretirement benefit plan (Sections P16, "Pensions," and P40, "Postretirement Benefits Other Than Pensions," specify the accounting for those costs.)
b. Individual deferred compensation arrangements that are addressed by Section C38, "Compensation to Employees: Deferred Compensation Agreements"
c. Special or contractual termination benefits covered by Sections P16 and P40
d. Stock compensation plans that are addressed by [FAS112, ¶5] Section C36, "Compensation: Stock-Based." [FAS123, ¶391]

Accounting for Postemployment Benefits

.103 Postemployment benefits that are within the scope of this section and that meet the conditions in paragraph .104 of Section C44, "Compensation to Employees: Paid Absences," shall be accounted for in accordance with [the provisions of] that section. Postemployment benefits that do not meet the conditions of paragraph .104 of Section C44, shall be accounted for in accordance with [the provisions of] paragraph .105 of Section C59, "Contingencies," [FAS112, ¶6] which requires recognition of a loss contingency when it is probable that an asset has been impaired or a liability has been incurred and the amount of loss can be reasonably estimated.[1] [FAS112, ¶21]

.104 [This section does not] provide guidance on how to measure an employer's postemployment benefit obligation. Sections P16 and P40 discuss measurement issues extensively. To the extent that similar issues apply to postemployment benefit plans, employers may refer to those sections for guidance in measuring their obligations in compliance with the requirements of this section. [In addition, this section does not] provide explicit guidance on discounting. As a result, the use of discounting in measuring postemployment benefit obligations [is] permitted but not required. [FAS111, ¶23]

Disclosures

.105 If an obligation for postemployment benefits is not accrued in accordance with Sections C44 or C59 only because the amount cannot be reasonably estimated, the financial statements shall disclose that fact. [FAS112, ¶7]

[1]For example, an employer may provide any former employee on permanent disability with continued medical insurance coverage until that employee meets the requirements for participation in the employer's postretirement medical plan. If the level of benefits provided is the same for any disabled employee regardless of years of service, the cost of those benefits should be recognized when the event causing a permanent disability occurs and a reasonable estimate can be made as specified by Section C59. [FAS112, ¶22]

Glossary

.401 **Inactive employees.** Employees who are not currently rendering service to the employer and who have not been terminated. They include those who have been laid off and those on disability leave, regardless of whether they are expected to return to active status. [FAS112, ¶1]

.402 **Postemployment benefits.** Benefits provided to former and inactive employees after employment but before retirement. Postemployment benefits include, but are not limited to, salary continuation, supplemental unemployment benefits, severance benefits, disability-related benefits (including workers' compensation), job training and counseling, and continuation of benefits such as health care benefits and life insurance coverage. [FAS112, ¶1]

Supplemental Guidance: Emerging Issues Task Force (EITF) Issues

.1000 [Listed below is an EITF Issue that provides supplemental guidance for this section. This Issue is related by topic to the guidance in this section.

EITF Issue No. 96-5, "Recognition of Liabilities for Contractual Termination Benefits or Changing Benefit Plan Assumptions in Anticipation of a Business Combination"]

(The next page is 35011.)

POSTRETIREMENT BENEFITS OTHER THAN PENSIONS

SECTION P40

Sources: FASB Statement 88; FASB Statement 106; FASB Statement 112; FASB Statement 132; FASB Statement 135; FASB Statement 144

[**Note:** A list of Issues discussed by the Emerging Issues Task Force (EITF) that provide supplemental guidance for this section is presented in paragraph .1000.]

Summary

This section presents standards for employers' accounting for postretirement benefits other than pensions (hereinafter referred to as postretirement benefits). Although it applies to all forms of postretirement benefits, this section focuses principally on postretirement health care benefits. This section requires accrual, during the years that the employee renders the necessary service, of the expected cost of providing those benefits to an employee and the employee's beneficiaries and covered dependents.

An employer's practice of providing postretirement benefits to selected employees under individual contracts, with specific terms determined on an individual-by-individual basis, does not constitute a postretirement benefit plan under this section. The accounting for those contracts is presented in Section C38, "Compensation to Employees: Deferred Compensation Agreements."

The accounting in this section is similar, in many respects, to the accounting for pensions as presented in Section P16, "Pension Costs." In applying accrual accounting to postretirement benefits, three fundamental aspects of pension accounting are adopted: delayed recognition of certain events, reporting net cost, and offsetting liabilities and related assets.

Delayed recognition means that certain changes in the obligation for postretirement benefits, including those changes arising as a result of a plan initiation or amendment, and certain changes in the value of plan assets set aside to meet that obligation are not recognized as they occur. Rather, those changes are recognized systematically over future periods. All changes in the obligation and plan assets ultimately are recognized unless they are first reduced by other changes. The changes that have been identified and quantified but not yet recognized in the employer's financial statements as components of net periodic postretirement benefit cost and as a liability or asset are disclosed.

Net cost means that the recognized consequences of events and transactions affecting a postretirement benefit plan are reported as a single amount in the employer's financial statements. That single amount includes at least three types of events or transactions that might otherwise be reported separately. Those events or transactions—exchanging a promise of deferred compensation in the form of postretirement benefits for employee service, the interest cost arising from the passage of time until those benefits are paid, and the returns from the investment of plan assets—are included as components of net periodic postretirement benefit cost.

Offsetting means that plan assets restricted for the payment of postretirement benefits offset the accumulated postretirement benefit obligation in determining amounts recognized in the employer's statement of financial position and that the return on those plan assets offsets postretirement benefit cost in the employer's statement of income. That offsetting is reflected even though the obligation has not been settled, the investment of the plan assets may be largely controlled by the employer, and substantial risks and rewards associated with both the obligation and the plan assets are borne by the employer.

This section requires that the accounting for postretirement benefits reflect the terms of the exchange transaction that takes place between an employer that provides postretirement benefits and the employees who render services in exchange for those benefits. Generally the extant written plan provides the best evidence of that exchange transaction. However, in some situations, an employer's cost-sharing policy or a past practice of regular increases in certain monetary benefits may indicate that the substantive plan—the plan as understood by the parties to the exchange transaction—differs from the extant written plan. The substantive plan is the basis for the accounting.

This section requires that an employer's obligation for postretirement benefits expected to be provided to or for an employee be fully accrued by the date that employee attains full eligibility for all of the benefits expected to be received by that employee, any beneficiaries, and covered dependents (the full eligibility date), even if the employee is expected to render additional service beyond that date. That accounting reflects the fact that at the full eligibility date the employee has provided all of the service necessary to earn the right to receive all of the benefits that employee is expected to receive under the plan.

The beginning of the attribution (accrual) period is the employee's date of hire unless the plan only grants credit for service from a later date, in which case benefits are generally attributed from the beginning of that credited service period. An equal amount of the expected postretirement benefit obligation is attributed to each year of service in the attribution period unless the plan attributes a disproportionate share of the expected benefits to employees' early years of service.

The disclosures required by this section may be presented separately or may be presented in a combined format with the disclosures required in Section P16 in a single note to the financial statements. This section permits reduced disclosure for nonpublic entities.

.101 This section establishes standards of financial accounting and reporting for an employer that offers **postretirement benefits other than pensions** (hereinafter referred to as **postretirement benefits**) to its employees.[1] [FAS106, ¶1]

Scope

.102 This section applies to *all* postretirement benefits expected to be provided by an employer[2] to current and former employees (including **retirees,** disabled employees,[3] and other former employees who are expected to receive postretirement benefits), their beneficiaries, and covered dependents, pursuant to the terms of an employer's undertaking to provide those **benefits.** Postretirement benefits include, but are not limited to,

---

[1]The accounting for benefits paid after employment but before retirement (for example, layoff benefits) is [FAS106, ¶1, fn2] [covered in Section P32, "Postemployment Benefits."] That section applies to all types of postemployment benefits provided to former or inactive employees, their beneficiaries, and covered dependents after employment but before retirement. [FAS112, ¶4]

[2]For some rate-regulated enterprises, [the provisions of] Section Re6, "Regulated Operations," may require that the difference between **net periodic postretirement benefit cost** as defined in this section and amounts of postretirement benefit cost considered for rate-making purposes be recognized as an asset or a liability created by the actions of the regulator. Those actions of the regulator change the timing of recognition of net periodic postretirement benefit cost as an expense; they do not otherwise affect the requirements of this section. [FAS106, ¶364]

[3]Health and other welfare benefits expected to be provided to employees deemed to be on a disability retirement are within the scope of this section. [FAS106, ¶136] The determination of disability benefits to be accrued pursuant to this section is based on the terms of the **postretirement benefit plan** defining when a disabled employee is entitled to postretirement benefits. [FAS106, ¶6, fn4] For example, the provisions of the postretirement health care plan may provide postretirement health care coverage after a disabled employee attains a specified number of years of credited service (which may include credit for periods after the employee is disabled), with a separate disability plan that provides health benefits prior to that date. Or, the postretirement health care plan may have special provisions for disabled employees that entitle them to benefit coverage under the postretirement benefit plan at a date earlier than that coverage would commence for other employees who are not disabled. [FAS106, ¶137] [Refer to the illustrations in paragraphs .218 through .220.]

postretirement health care;[4] life insurance provided outside a pension plan to retirees; and other welfare benefits such as tuition assistance, day care, legal services, and housing subsidies provided after retirement. Often those benefits are in the form of a reimbursement to plan participants or direct payment to providers for the cost of specified services as the need for those services arises, but they may also include benefits payable as a lump sum, such as death benefits. This section also applies to **settlement** of all or a part of an employer's **accumulated postretirement benefit obligation** or **curtailment** of a postretirement benefit plan and to an employer that provides postretirement benefits as part of a special **termination benefits** offer. [FAS106, ¶6]

.103 For the purposes of this section, a postretirement benefit plan is an arrangement that is mutually understood by an employer and its employees, whereby an employer undertakes to provide its current and former employees with benefits after they retire in exchange for the employees' services over a specified period of time, upon attaining a specified age while in service, or both. Benefits may commence immediately upon termination of service or may be deferred until retired employees attain a specified age. [FAS106, ¶7]

.104 An employer's practice of providing postretirement benefits may take a variety of forms and the obligation may or may not be funded. This section applies to any arrangement that is in substance a postretirement benefit plan, regardless of its form or the means or timing of its funding. This section applies both to written plans and to unwritten plans whose existence is discernible either from a practice of paying postretirement benefits or from oral representations made to current or former employees. Absent evidence to the contrary, it shall be presumed that an employer that has provided postretirement benefits in the past or is currently promising those benefits to employees will continue to provide those future benefits. [FAS106, ¶8]

.105 This section applies to deferred compensation contracts with individual employees if those contracts, taken together, are equivalent to a **plan** that provides postretirement benefits. It does not apply to an employer's practice of providing postretirement benefits to selected employees under individual contracts with specific terms determined on an individual-by-individual basis. Those contracts shall be accounted for individually, following the terms of the contract. To the extent the contract does not attribute the benefits to individual years of service, the expected future benefits shall be accrued over the

[4]Postretirement health care benefits are likely to be the most significant in terms of cost and prevalence, and certain of the issues that arise in measuring those benefits are unique. Therefore, much of the language of this section focuses on postretirement health care plans. Nevertheless, this section applies equally to all postretirement benefits. [FAS106, ¶6, fn5]

period of service required to be rendered in exchange for the benefits. (Refer to Section C38, "Compensation to Employees: Deferred Compensation Agreements," paragraph .101A.) [FAS106, ¶9]

.106 A postretirement benefit plan may be part of a larger plan or arrangement that provides benefits currently to active employees as well as to retirees. In those circumstances, the promise to provide benefits to present and future retirees under the plan shall be segregated from the promise to provide benefits currently to active employees and shall be accounted for in accordance with the provisions of this section. [FAS106, ¶10]

.107 This section does not apply to pension or life insurance benefits provided through a pension plan. The accounting for those benefits is set forth in Section P16, "Pension Costs."[5] [FAS106, ¶11]

Use of Reasonable Approximations

.108 This section is intended to specify accounting objectives and results rather than computational means of obtaining those results. If estimates, averages, or computational shortcuts can reduce the cost of applying this section, their use is appropriate, provided the results are reasonably expected not to be materially different from the results of a detailed application. [FAS106, ¶15]

Single-Employer Defined Benefit Postretirement Plans

.109 This section primarily focuses on an employer's accounting for a **single-employer plan** that defines the postretirement benefits to be provided to retirees. For purposes of this section, a **defined benefit postretirement plan** is one that defines the postretirement benefits in terms of (a) monetary amounts (for example, $100,000 of life insurance) or (b) benefit coverage to be provided (for example, up to $200 per day for hospitalization, 80 percent of the cost of specified surgical procedures, and so forth). (Specified monetary amounts and benefit coverage are hereinafter collectively referred to as *benefits.*) [FAS106, ¶16]

[5]Two Special Reports prepared by the FASB staff, *A Guide to Implementation of Statement 87 on Employers' Accounting for Pensions,* and *A Guide to Implementation of Statement 88 on Employers' Accounting for Settlements and Curtailments of Defined Benefit Pension Plans and for Termination Benefits,* provide accounting guidance on implementation questions raised in connection with Statements 87 and 88. Many of the provisions in this section are the same as or are similar to the provisions of Statements 87 and 88. Consequently, the guidánce provided in those Special Reports should be useful in understanding and implementing many of the provisions of this section. [FAS106, ¶11, fn6]

.110 In some cases, an employer may limit its obligation through an individual or an aggregate "cap" on the employer's cost or benefit obligation. For example, an employer may elect to limit its annual postretirement benefit obligation for each retired plan participant to a maximum of $5,000. Or, an employer may elect to limit its share of the aggregate cost of covered postretirement health care benefits for a period to an amount determined based on an average per capita cost per retired plan participant. Plans of that nature are considered to be defined benefit postretirement plans. Paragraphs .269 through .275 illustrate measurement considerations for defined-dollar capped plans. [FAS106, ¶17]

.111 A postretirement benefit is part of the compensation paid to an employee for services rendered. In a defined benefit plan, the employer promises to provide, in addition to current wages and benefits, future benefits during retirement. Generally, the amount of those benefits depends on the **benefit formula** (that may include factors such as the number of years of service rendered or the employee's compensation before retirement or termination), the longevity of the retiree and any beneficiaries and covered dependents, and the incidence of events requiring benefit payments (for example, illnesses affecting the amount of health care required). In most cases, services are rendered over a number of years before an employee retires and begins to receive benefits or is entitled to receive benefits as a need arises. Even though the services rendered by the employee are complete and the employee has retired, the total amount of benefits the employer has promised and the cost to the employer of the services rendered are not precisely determinable but can be estimated using the plan's benefit formula and estimates of the effects of relevant future events. [FAS106, ¶18]

Basic Elements of Accounting for Postretirement Benefits

.112 Any method of accounting that recognizes the cost of postretirement benefits over employee service periods (before the payment of benefits to retirees) must deal with two factors that stem from the nature of the arrangement. First, estimates or **assumptions** must be made about the future events that will determine the amount and timing of the benefit payments. Second, an **attribution** approach that assigns benefits and the cost of those benefits to individual years of service must be selected. [FAS106, ¶19]

.113 The **expected postretirement benefit obligation** for an employee is the **actuarial present value** as of a particular date of the postretirement benefits expected to be paid by the employer's plan to or for the employee, the employee's beneficiaries, and any covered dependents pursuant to the terms of the plan. Measurement of the expected postretirement benefit obligation is based on the expected amount and timing of future benefits, taking into consideration the expected future cost of providing the benefits and the extent to which those costs are shared by the employer, the employee (including consideration of contributions required during the employee's active service period and following retirement, deductibles, coinsurance provisions, and so forth), or others (such as through governmental programs). [FAS106, ¶20]

.114 The accumulated postretirement benefit obligation[6] as of a particular date is the actuarial present value of all future benefits attributed to an employee's service rendered to that date pursuant to paragraphs .138 and .139 and .147 through .150, assuming the plan continues in effect and that all assumptions about future events are fulfilled. Prior to the date on which an employee attains **full eligibility** for the benefits that employee is expected to earn under the terms of the postretirement benefit plan (the **full eligibility date**), the accumulated postretirement benefit obligation for an employee is a portion of the expected postretirement benefit obligation. On and after the full eligibility date, the accumulated postretirement benefit obligation and the expected postretirement benefit obligation for an employee are the same. Determination of the full eligibility date is affected by plan terms that provide incremental benefits expected to be received by or on behalf of an employee for additional years of service, unless those incremental benefits are trivial. Determination of the full eligibility date is not affected by plan terms that define when benefit payments commence or by an employee's current **dependency status.** (Paragraphs .209 through .220 illustrate determination of the full eligibility date.) [FAS106, ¶21]

.115 Net periodic postretirement benefit cost[7] comprises several components that reflect different aspects of the employer's financial arrangements. The **service cost** component of net periodic postretirement benefit cost is the actuarial present value of benefits attributed to services rendered by employees during the period (the portion of the expected postretirement benefit obligation attributed to service in the period). The service cost component is the same for an unfunded plan, a plan with minimal funding, and a well-funded plan. The other components of net periodic postretirement benefit cost are **interest cost**[8] (interest on the accumulated postretirement benefit obligation, which is a discounted amount), **actual return on plan assets, amortization** of **unrecognized prior service cost,** amortization of the **transition obligation** or **transition asset,** and the **gain or loss component.** [FAS106, ¶22]

---

[6]The accumulated postretirement benefit obligation generally reflects a ratable allocation of expected future benefits to employee service already rendered in the attribution period; the accumulated benefit obligation under Section P16 generally reflects the future benefits allocated to employee service in accordance with the benefit formula. In addition, unlike Section P16, this section implicitly considers salary progression in the measurement of the accumulated postretirement benefit obligation of a pay-related plan. [FAS106, ¶21, fn7] Thus, the accumulated postretirement benefit obligation disclosed pursuant to this section is defined in terms notionally more comparable to the projected benefit obligation under Section P16. [FAS106, ¶168]

[7]This section uses the term *net periodic postretirement cost* rather than *net postretirement benefit expense* because part of the cost recognized in a period may be capitalized along with other costs as part of an asset such as inventory. [FAS106, ¶5, fn3]

[8]The interest cost component of postretirement benefit cost shall not be considered interest for purposes of applying Section I67, "Interest: Capitalization of Interest Costs." [FAS106, ¶22, fn8]

Measurement of Cost and Obligations

Accounting for the Substantive Plan

.116 An objective of this section is that the accounting reflect the terms of the exchange transaction that takes place between an employer that provides postretirement benefits and the employees who render services in exchange for those benefits, as those terms are understood by both parties to the transaction. Generally, the extant written plan provides the best evidence of the terms of that exchange transaction. However, in some situations, an employer's **cost-sharing** policy, as evidenced by past practice or by communication of intended changes to a plan's cost-sharing provisions (refer to paragraphs .117 and .118), or a past practice of regular increases in certain monetary benefits (refer to paragraph .119) may indicate that the **substantive plan**—the plan as understood by the parties to the exchange transaction—differs from the extant written plan. The substantive plan shall be the basis for the accounting. [FAS106, ¶23]

.117 Except as provided in paragraph .118, an employer's cost-sharing policy, as evidenced by the following past practice or communication, shall constitute the cost-sharing provisions of the substantive plan if either of the following conditions exist. Otherwise, the extant written plan shall be considered to be the substantive plan.

a. The employer has a past practice[9] of (1) maintaining a consistent level of cost sharing between the employer and its retirees through changes in deductibles, coinsurance provisions, retiree contributions, or some combination of those changes or (2) consistently increasing or reducing the employer's share of the cost of the covered benefits through changes in retired or **active plan participants**' contributions toward their retiree health care benefits, deductibles, coinsurance provisions, out-of-pocket limitations, and so forth, in accordance with the employer's established cost-sharing policy
b. The employer has the ability, and has communicated to affected **plan participants** its intent, to institute different cost-sharing provisions at a specified time or when certain conditions exist (for example, when health care cost increases exceed a certain level).

[FAS106, ¶24]

.118 An employer's past practice of maintaining a consistent level of cost sharing with its retirees or consistently increasing or reducing its share of the cost of providing the covered benefits shall not constitute provisions of the substantive plan if accompanied

[9]A past practice would be indicated when the nature of the change and duration of the past practice are sufficient to warrant a presumption that it is understood by the plan participants. [FAS106, ¶176]

by identifiable offsetting changes in other benefits or compensation[10] or if the employer incurred significant costs, such as work stoppages, to effect that cost-sharing policy.[11] Similarly, an employer's communication of its intent to institute cost-sharing provisions that differ from the extant written plan or the past cost-sharing practice shall not constitute provisions of the substantive plan (a) if the plan participants would be unwilling to accept the change without adverse consequences to the employer's operations or (b) if other modifications of the plan, such as the level of benefit coverage, or providing offsetting changes in other benefits, such as pension benefits, would be required to gain plan participants' acceptance of the change to the cost-sharing arrangement. [FAS106, ¶25]

.119 A past practice of regular increases in postretirement benefits defined in terms of monetary amounts may indicate that the employer has a present commitment to make future *improvements* to the plan and that the plan will provide monetary benefits attributable to prior service that are greater than the monetary benefits defined by the extant written plan. In those situations, the substantive commitment to increase those benefits shall be the basis for the accounting. Changes in the benefits, other than benefits defined in terms of monetary amounts, covered by a postretirement health care plan or by other postretirement benefit plans shall not be anticipated. [FAS106, ¶26]

.120 Contributions expected to be received from active employees toward the cost of their postretirement benefits and from retired plan participants are treated similarly for purposes of measuring an employer's expected postretirement benefit obligation. That obligation is measured as the actuarial present value of the benefits expected to be provided under the plan, reduced by the actuarial present value of contributions expected to be received from the plan participants during their remaining active service and post-retirement periods. In determining the amount of the contributions expected to be received from those participants toward the cost of their postretirement benefits, consider-

[10]For example, a past practice of increasing retiree contributions annually based on a specified index or formula may appear to indicate that the substantive plan includes a determinable indexing of the retirees' annual contributions to the plan. However, if that past practice of increasing retiree contributions is accompanied by identifiable offsetting changes in other benefits or compensation, those offsetting changes would indicate that the substantive plan incorporates only the *current* cost-sharing provisions. Therefore, future increases or reductions of those cost-sharing provisions shall not be incorporated in measuring the expected postretirement benefit obligation. [FAS106, ¶25, fn9]

[11]By definition, an employer does not have the unilateral right to change a collectively bargained plan. Therefore, if the postretirement benefits are the subject of collective bargaining, the extant written plan shall be the substantive plan unless the employer can demonstrate its ability to maintain (a) a consistent level of cost sharing or (b) a consistent practice of increasing or reducing its share of the cost of the covered benefits in past negotiations without making offsetting changes in other benefits or compensation of the affected plan participants or by incurring other significant costs to maintain that cost-sharing arrangement. [FAS106, ¶25, fn10]

ation is given to any related substantive plan provisions, such as an employer's past practice of consistently increasing or reducing the contribution rates as described in paragraphs .117 and .118. An obligation to return contributions received from employees who do not attain eligibility for postretirement benefits and, if applicable, any interest accrued on those contributions shall be recognized as a component of an employer's postretirement benefit obligation. [FAS106, ¶27]

.121 Automatic benefit changes[12] specified by the plan that are expected to occur shall be included in measurements of the expected and accumulated postretirement benefit obligations and the service cost component of net periodic postretirement benefit cost. Also, **plan amendments** shall be included in the computation of the expected and accumulated postretirement benefit obligations once they have been contractually agreed to, even if some provisions take effect only in future periods. For example, if a plan amendment grants a different benefit level for employees retiring after a future date, that increased or reduced benefit level shall be included in current-period measurements for employees expected to retire after that date. [FAS106, ¶28]

Assumptions

.122 This section requires the use of **explicit assumptions,** each of which individually represents the best estimate of a particular future event, to measure the expected postretirement benefit obligation.[13] A portion of that expected postretirement benefit obligation is attributed to each period of an employee's service associated with earning the postretirement benefits, and that amount is accrued as service cost for that period. [FAS106, ¶29]

.123 The service cost component of postretirement benefit cost, any **prior service cost,** and the accumulated postretirement benefit obligation are measured using actuarial assumptions and present value techniques to calculate the actuarial present value of the expected future benefits attributed to periods of employee service. Each assumption used shall reflect the best estimate solely with respect to that individual assumption. All assumptions shall presume that the plan will continue in effect in the absence of evi-

[12]For purposes of this section, a plan that promises to provide retirees a benefit in kind, such as health care benefits, rather than a defined dollar amount of benefit, is considered to be a plan that specifies automatic benefit changes. (The assumed rate of change in the future cost of providing health care benefits, the assumed health care cost trend rate, is discussed in paragraph .134.) Because automatic benefit changes are not conditional on employees rendering additional years of service, the full eligibility date is not affected by those changes. A benefit in kind includes the direct rendering of services, the payment directly to others who provide the services, or the reimbursement of the retiree's payment for those services. [FAS106, ¶28, fn11]

[13]Measurement of an employer's postretirement benefit obligation is based on the current plan participants (a "closed group" approach). [FAS106, ¶183]

dence that it will not continue. Principal actuarial assumptions include the time value of money **(discount rates);** participation rates (for **contributory plans**); retirement age; factors affecting the amount and timing of future benefit payments, which for **postretirement health care benefits** consider past and present **per capita claims cost by age, health care cost trend rates, Medicare reimbursement rates,** and so forth; salary progression (for **pay-related plans**); and the probability of payment (turnover, dependency status, mortality, and so forth). [FAS106, ¶30]

.124 Many of the other assumptions used in postretirement benefit measurements also are similar to assumptions used in pension measurements, but the sensitivity of the measures to changes in the assumptions may be more significant. For example, the turnover assumption may have a more significant effect for postretirement benefits than for pension benefits because, in many cases, eligibility for postretirement benefits is an all-or-nothing proposition, while most pension plans provide reduced benefits for relatively short periods of service. The dependency status assumption also may have a more significant effect on postretirement benefit measurements than on pension measurements. Plan provisions that entitle an employee's spouse and other dependents to health care and other welfare benefits may substantially increase an employer's cost and obligation for postretirement benefits. [FAS106, ¶194]

.125 Postretirement benefit measurements are more sensitive to assumptions about retirement ages and the probability of retiring at each age than are pension measurements. For example, employer-provided postretirement health care benefits are significantly more expensive before Medicare coverage begins than after. Many pension arrangements provide for an actuarially reduced pension benefit for employees retiring before the normal retirement age; however, for an employee retiring early, there typically is no reduction in the postretirement benefit levels, and those benefits will be paid over a longer period of time and at a higher annual cost to the employer than if the employee retired at the normal retirement age. Similarly, postretirement benefit measurements are more sensitive than pension measurements to the life expectancy assumption. In particular, health care benefits are sensitive to that assumption because health care costs generally increase with age. [FAS106, ¶195]

.126 Assumed discount rates shall reflect the time value of money as of the **measurement date** in determining the present value of future cash outflows currently expected to be required to satisfy the postretirement benefit obligation. In making that assumption, employers shall look to rates of return on high-quality fixed income investments currently available whose cash flows match the timing and amount of expected benefit payments.[14] If settlement of the obligation with third-party insurers is possible (for example, the purchase of nonparticipating life insurance contracts to provide death benefits), the interest rates inherent in the amount at which the postretirement benefit obligation could be settled are relevant in determining the assumed discount rates. Assumed discount rates are used in measurements of the expected and accumulated postretirement benefit obligations and the service cost and interest cost components of net periodic postretirement benefit cost. [FAS106, ¶31]

.127 The **expected long-term rate of return on plan assets** shall reflect the average rate of earnings expected on the existing assets that qualify as **plan assets** and contributions to the plan expected to be made during the period. In estimating that rate, appropriate consideration shall be given to the returns being earned on the plan assets currently invested and the rates of return expected to be available for reinvestment. If the return on plan assets is taxable to the trust or other fund under the plan, the expected long-term rate of return shall be reduced to reflect the related income taxes expected to be paid under existing law. The expected long-term rate of return on plan assets is used with the **market-related value of plan assets** to compute the **expected return on plan assets.** (Refer to paragraph .152.) There is no assumption of an expected long-term rate of return on plan assets for plans that are unfunded or that have no assets that qualify as plan assets pursuant to this section. [FAS106, ¶32]

.128 The service cost component of net periodic postretirement benefit cost and the expected and accumulated postretirement benefit obligations shall reflect future compensation levels to the extent the postretirement benefit formula defines the benefits wholly or partially as a function of future compensation levels.[15] For pay-related plans, as-

[14]The objective of selecting assumed discount rates is to measure the single amount that, if invested at the measurement date in a portfolio of high-quality debt instruments, would provide the necessary future cash flows to pay the accumulated benefits when due. Notionally, that single amount, the accumulated postretirement benefit obligation, would equal the current market value of a portfolio of high-quality zero coupon bonds whose maturity dates and amounts would be the same as the timing and amount of the expected future benefit payments. Because cash inflows would equal cash outflows in timing and amount, there would be no reinvestment risk in the yields to maturity of the portfolio. However, in other than a zero coupon portfolio, such as a portfolio of long-term debt instruments that pay semiannual interest payments or whose maturities do not extend far enough into the future to meet expected benefit payments, the assumed discount rates (the yield to maturity) need to incorporate expected reinvestment rates available in the future. Those rates should be extrapolated from the existing yield curve at the measurement date. Assumed discount rates should be reevaluated at each measurement date. If the general level of interest rates rises or declines, the assumed discount rates should change in a similar manner. [FAS106, ¶186] [Refer to paragraph .1001 for an EITF Issue that provides interpretive guidance on this footnote.]

[15]For pay-related plans, salary progression is included in measuring the expected postretirement benefit obligation. For example, a postretirement health care plan may define the deductible amount or copayment, or a postretirement life insurance plan may define the amount of death benefit, based on the employee's average or final level of annual compensation. [FAS106, ¶33, fn12]

sumed compensation levels shall reflect the best estimate of the actual future compensation levels of the individual employees involved, including future changes attributed to general price levels, productivity, seniority, promotion, and other factors. All assumptions shall be consistent to the extent that each reflects expectations about the same future economic conditions, such as future rates of inflation. Measuring service cost and the expected and accumulated postretirement benefit obligations based on estimated future compensation levels entails considering any indirect effects, such as benefit limitations, that would affect benefits provided by the plan.[16] [FAS106, ¶33]

Assumptions Unique to Postretirement Health Care Benefits

.129 Measurement of an employer's postretirement health care obligation requires the use of several assumptions unique to health care benefits. Most significantly, it includes several assumptions about factors that will affect the amount and timing of future benefit payments for postretirement health care. Those factors include consideration of historical per capita claims cost by age, health care cost trend rates (for plans that provide a benefit in kind), and medical coverage to be paid by governmental authorities and other providers of health care benefits. [FAS106, ¶34]

.130 In principle, an employer's share of the expected future postretirement health care cost for a plan participant is developed by reducing the **assumed per capita claims cost** at each age at which the plan participant is expected to receive benefits under the plan by (a) the effects of coverage by Medicare and other providers of health care benefits, and (b) the effects of the cost-sharing provisions of the plan (deductibles, copayment provisions, out-of-pocket limitations, caps on the limits of the employer-provided payments, and retiree contributions).[17] The resulting amount represents the assumed **net incurred claims cost** at each age at which the plan participant is expected to receive benefits under the plan. If contributions are required to be paid by active plan participants toward

[16]For example, a plan may define the maximum benefit to be provided under the plan (a fixed cap). In measuring the expected postretirement benefit obligation under that plan, the projected benefit payments would be limited to that cap. For a plan that automatically adjusts the maximum benefit to be provided under the plan for the effects of inflation (an adjustable cap), the expected postretirement benefit obligation would be measured based on adjustments to that cap consistent with the assumed inflation rate reflected in other inflation-related assumptions. [FAS106, ¶33, fn13]

[17]In some cases, retiree contributions are established based on the average per capita cost of benefit coverage under an employer's health care plan that provides coverage to both active employees and retirees. However, the medical cost of the retirees may cause the average per capita cost of benefit coverage under the plan to be higher than it would be if only active employees were covered by the plan. In that case, the employer has a postretirement benefit obligation for the portion of the expected future cost of the retiree health care benefits that are not recovered through retiree contributions, Medicare, or other providers of health care benefits. [FAS106, ¶35, fn14]

their postretirement health care benefits, the actuarial present value of the plan participants' future contributions reduces the actuarial present value of the aggregate assumed net incurred claims costs. [FAS106, ¶35]

.131 The assumed per capita claims cost by age is the annual per capita cost, for periods after the measurement date, of providing the postretirement health care benefits covered by the plan from the earliest age at which an individual could begin to receive benefits under the plan through the remainder of the individual's life or the covered period, if shorter. The assumed per capita claims cost shall be the best estimate of the expected future cost of the benefits covered by the plan.[18] It may be appropriate to consider other factors in addition to age, such as sex and geographical location, in developing the assumed per capita claims cost. [FAS106, ¶36]

.132 Past and present claims data for the plan, such as a historical pattern of gross claims by age (claims curve), shall be used in developing the current per capita claims cost to the extent that those data are considered to be indicative of the current cost of providing the benefits covered by the plan. Those current claims data shall be adjusted by the assumed health care cost trend rate. The resulting assumed per capita claims cost by age, together with the **plan demographics,** determines the amount and timing of expected future **gross eligible charges.** [FAS106, ¶37]

.133 In the absence of sufficiently reliable plan data about the current cost of the benefits covered by the plan, the current per capita claims cost shall be based, entirely or in part, on the claims information of other employers to the extent those costs are indicative of the current cost of providing the benefits covered by the plan. For example, the current per capita claims cost may be based on the claims experience of other employers [FAS106, ¶38] in the same industry or geographical location [FAS106, ¶197] derived from information in data files developed by insurance companies, actuarial firms, or employee benefits consulting firms. [FAS106, ¶38] National or regional statistics about claims cost patterns also may provide information that may be used for developing the per capita claims cost by age. [FAS106, ¶197] The current per capita claims cost developed on those bases shall be adjusted to best reflect the terms of the employer's plan and the plan demographics. For example, the information shall be adjusted, as necessary, for differing demographics, such as the age and sex of plan participants, health care utilization patterns by men and women at various ages, and the expected geographical location of retirees and their dependents, and for significant differences between the nature and types of benefits covered by the employer's plan and those encompassed by the underlying data. [FAS106, ¶38]

---

[18] If significant, the internal and external costs directly associated with administering the postretirement benefit plan also shall be accrued as a component of assumed per capita claims cost. [FAS106, ¶36, fn15]

.134 The assumption about health care cost trend rates represents the expected annual rates of change in the cost of health care benefits currently provided by the postretirement benefit plan, due to factors other than changes in the demographics of the plan participants, for each year from the measurement date until the end of the period in which benefits are expected to be paid. Past and current health care cost trends shall be used in developing an employer's assumed health care cost trend rates, which implicitly consider estimates of health care inflation, changes in health care utilization or delivery patterns, technological advances, and changes in the health status of plan participants.[19] Differing services, such as hospital care and dental care, may require the use of different health care cost trend rates. It is appropriate for that assumption to reflect changes in health care cost trend rates over time. For example, the health care cost trend rates may be assumed to continue at the present level for the near term, or increase for a period of time, and then grade down over time to an estimated health care cost trend rate ultimately expected to prevail. [FAS106, ¶39]

.135 Certain medical claims may be covered by governmental programs under existing law or by other providers of health care benefits.[20] Benefit coverage by those governmental programs shall be assumed to continue as provided by the present law and by other providers pursuant to their present plans. Presently enacted changes in the law or amendments of the plans of other health care providers that take effect in future periods and that will affect the future level of their benefit coverage shall be considered in current-period measurements for benefits expected to be provided in those future periods. Future changes in laws concerning medical costs covered by governmental programs and future changes in the plans of other providers shall not be anticipated. [FAS106, ¶40]

.136 In some cases, determining the assumed per capita claims cost by age as described in paragraphs .131 through .133 may not be practical because credible historical information about the gross per capita cost of covered benefits may not be available or determinable to satisfy the stated measurement approach. However, credible historical information about **incurred claims costs** may be available. In those cases, an alternative method of developing the assumed per capita claims cost may be used provided the method results in a measure that is the best estimate of the expected future cost of the benefits covered by the plan. For example, the assumed health care cost trend rates may be

[19]An assumption about changes in the health status of plan participants considers, for example, the probability that certain claims costs will be incurred based on expectations of future events, such as the likelihood that some retirees will incur claims requiring technology currently being developed or that historical claims experience for certain medical needs may be reduced as a result of participation in a wellness program. [FAS106, ¶39, fn16]

[20]For example, a retiree's spouse also may be covered by the spouse's present (or former) employer's health care plan. In that case, the spouse's employer (or former employer) may provide either primary or secondary postretirement health care benefits to the retiree's spouse or dependents. [FAS106, ¶40, fn17]

determined by adjusting the expected change in the employer's share of per capita incurred claims cost by age by a factor that reflects the effects of the plan's cost-sharing provisions. However, an approach that projects net incurred claims costs using unadjusted assumed health care cost trend rates would implicitly assume changes in the plan's cost-sharing provisions at those assumed rates and, therefore, is not acceptable unless the plan's cost-sharing provisions are indexed in that manner or the substantive plan (refer to paragraphs .117 through .119) operates in that manner. [FAS106, ¶41]

.137 Assumed discount rates include an inflationary element that reflects the expected general rate of inflation. Assumed compensation levels include consideration of future changes attributable to general price levels. Similarly, assumed health care cost trend rates include an element that reflects expected general rates of inflation for the economy overall and an element that reflects price changes of health care costs in particular. To the extent that those assumptions consider similar inflationary effects, the assumptions about those effects shall be consistent. [FAS106, ¶42]

Attribution [21]

.138 An equal amount of the expected postretirement benefit obligation for an employee generally shall be attributed to each year of service in the **attribution period** (a benefit/years-of-service approach). However, some plans may have benefit formulas that attribute a disproportionate share of the expected postretirement benefit obligation to employees' early years of service. For that type of plan, the expected postretirement benefit obligation shall be attributed in accordance with the plan's benefit formula. [FAS106, ¶43] [Refer to illustrations in paragraphs .223 and .224.]

.139 The beginning of the attribution period generally shall be the date of hire. However, if the plan's benefit formula grants credit only for service from a later date and that **credited service period** is not nominal in relation to employees' total years of service prior to their full eligibility dates, the expected postretirement benefit obligation shall be attributed from the beginning of that credited service period. In all cases, the end of the

[21] Attribution is the process of assigning the expected cost of benefits to periods of employee service. The general objective is to assign to each year of service the cost of benefits earned or assumed to have been earned in that year. [FAS106, ¶200]

attribution period[22] shall be the full eligibility date.[23] (Paragraphs .221 through .224 illustrate the attribution provisions of this section.) [FAS106, ¶44]

Recognition of Net Periodic Postretirement Benefit Cost

.140 As with other forms of deferred compensation, the cost of providing postretirement benefits shall be attributed to the periods of employee service rendered in exchange for those future benefits pursuant to the terms of the plan. That cost notionally represents the change in the **unfunded accumulated postretirement benefit obligation** for the period, ignoring employer contributions to the plan, plan settlements, and payments made by the employer directly to retirees. However, changes in that unfunded obligation that arise from experience gains and losses and the effects of changes in assumptions may be recognized as a component of net periodic postretirement benefit cost on a delayed basis. In addition, the effects of a plan initiation or amendment generally are recognized on a delayed basis. [FAS106, ¶45]

.141 The following components shall be included in the net postretirement benefit cost recognized for a period by an employer sponsoring a defined benefit postretirement plan:

a. Service cost (refer to paragraph .142)
b. Interest cost (refer to paragraph .143)
c. Actual return on plan assets, if any (refer to paragraph .144)
d. Amortization of unrecognized prior service cost, if any (refer to paragraphs .145 through .150)
e. **Gain or loss** (including the effects of changes in assumptions) to the extent recognized (refer to paragraphs .151 through .157)

[22]Accrual of an obligation over the period of employee service rendered in exchange for that benefit is applicable to all forms of compensation. [FAS106, ¶135]

[23]For postretirement benefit plans that are pay-related or that otherwise index benefits during employees' service periods to their retirement date, the full eligibility date and retirement date generally will be the same. The attribution period for those benefits will differ from the attribution period for a similarly defined pension benefit with a capped credited service period. [FAS106, ¶227]

f. Amortization of the unrecognized obligation or asset existing at the date of initial application of this section,[24] hereinafter referred to as the **unrecognized transition obligation**[25] or **unrecognized transition asset.** [There is a constraint on delayed recognition of a transition obligation. (Refer to paragraphs .200 and .201.)]

[FAS106, ¶46]

Service Cost

.142 The service cost component recognized in a period shall be determined as the portion of the expected postretirement benefit obligation attributed to employee service during that period. The measurement of the service cost component requires identification of the substantive plan and the use of assumptions and an attribution method, which are discussed in paragraphs .116 through .139. [FAS106, ¶47]

Interest Cost

.143 The interest cost component recognized in a period shall be determined as the increase in the accumulated postretirement benefit obligation to recognize the effects of the passage of time. Measuring the accumulated postretirement benefit obligation as a present value requires accrual of an interest cost at rates equal to the assumed discount rates. [FAS106, ¶48]

Actual Return on Plan Assets

.144 For a funded plan, the actual return on plan assets shall be determined based on the **fair value** of plan assets (refer to paragraphs .160 and .161) at the beginning and end of the period, adjusted for contributions and benefit payments. If the fund holding the plan

---

[24]For a defined benefit plan, an employer shall determine as of the measurement date (paragraph .167) for the beginning of the fiscal year in which this section is first applied (the transition date), the amounts of (a) the accumulated postretirement benefit obligation and (b) the fair value of plan assets plus any recognized accrued postretirement benefit cost or less any recognized prepaid postretirement benefit cost. The difference between those two amounts, whether it represents a transition obligation or a transition asset, may be recognized either immediately in net income of the period of the change as the effect of a change in accounting principle, or on a delayed basis as a component of net periodic postretirement benefit cost. [FAS106, ¶110]

[25]Amortization of the unrecognized transition obligation or asset will be adjusted prospectively to recognize the effects of (a) a negative plan amendment pursuant to paragraph .150, (b) a constraint on immediate recognition of a net gain or loss pursuant to paragraph .155, (c) settlement accounting pursuant to paragraphs .184 and .185, (d) plan curtailment accounting pursuant to paragraphs .189 through .191, and (e) a constraint on delayed recognition of the unrecognized transition obligation pursuant to paragraph .200. [FAS106, ¶46, fn18]

assets is a taxable enterprise,[26] the actual return on plan assets shall reflect the tax expense or benefit for the period determined in accordance with generally accepted accounting principles. Otherwise, no provision for taxes shall be included in the actual return on plan assets. [FAS106, ¶49]

Prior Service Cost

.145 Plan amendments (including initiation of a plan) may include provisions that attribute the increase or reduction in benefits to employee service rendered in prior periods or only to employee service to be rendered in future periods. For purposes of measuring the accumulated postretirement benefit obligation, the effect of a plan amendment on a plan participant's expected postretirement benefit obligation shall be attributed to each year of service in that plan participant's attribution period, including years of service already rendered by that plan participant, in accordance with the attribution of the expected postretirement benefit obligation to years of service as discussed in paragraphs .138 and .139. [FAS106, ¶50] If an employer amends the benefits to be provided by the plan, the effect of the amendment is recognized immediately in measuring the employer's expected and accumulated postretirement benefit obligations, even if the effective date of the change in benefits is delayed until a specified date in the future. [FAS106, ¶174] If a plan is initiated that grants benefits solely in exchange for employee service after the date of the plan initiation or a future date, no portion of the expected postretirement benefit obligation is attributed to prior service periods because, in that case, the credited service period for the current employees who are expected to receive benefits under the plan begins at the date of the plan initiation or the future date. [FAS106, ¶50]

.146 Plan amendments that improve benefits are granted with the expectation that the employer will realize economic benefits in future periods. Consequently, except as discussed in paragraph .149, this section does not permit the cost of benefit improvements (that is, prior service cost) to be included in net periodic postretirement benefit cost entirely in the year of the amendment. Rather, paragraph .147 provides for recognition of prior service cost arising from benefit improvements during the remaining years of serv-

[26]Unlike most pension plans, the return on postretirement benefit plan assets may be subject to income tax because of the lack of tax-exempt vehicles for funding those benefits. At present, even if postretirement benefit plan assets are restricted and segregated within a trust, the income generated by those assets generally is taxable. If the plan has taxable income, the assessed tax will reduce the returns available for payment of benefits or reinvestment. When the trust or other entity holding the plan assets is taxed as a separate entity on the return on *plan assets* (as defined herein), the expected long-term rate of return should be determined by giving consideration to anticipated income taxes under enacted tax law. However, if the tax on income generated by plan assets is not a liability of the plan, but of the employer, the expected long-term rate of return should not anticipate a tax on those earnings, because that tax will be reflected in the employer's accounting for income taxes. [FAS106, ¶295]

ice to the full eligibility dates of those plan participants active at the date of the plan amendment. (Refer to paragraph .150 for plan amendments that reduce benefits.) [FAS106, ¶51]

.147 The cost of benefit improvements (including improved benefits that are granted to **fully eligible plan participants**) is the increase in the accumulated postretirement benefit obligation as a result of the plan amendment, measured at the date of the amendment. Except as specified in the next sentence and in paragraphs .148 and .149, that prior service cost shall be amortized by assigning an equal amount to each remaining year of service to the full eligibility date of each plan participant active at the date of the amendment who was not yet fully eligible for benefits at that date. If all or almost all of a plan's participants are fully eligible for benefits, the prior service cost shall be amortized based on the remaining life expectancy of those plan participants rather than on the remaining years of service to the full eligibility dates of the active plan participants. [FAS106, ¶52]

.148 To reduce the complexity and detail of the computations required, consistent use of an alternative amortization approach that more rapidly reduces unrecognized prior service cost is permitted. For example, a straight-line amortization of the cost over the average remaining years of service to full eligibility for benefits of the active plan participants is acceptable. [FAS106, ¶53]

.149 In some situations, a history of regular plan amendments and other evidence may indicate that the period during which the employer expects to realize economic benefits from an amendment that grants increased benefits is shorter than the remaining years of service to full eligibility for benefits of the active plan participants. Identification of those situations requires an assessment of the individual circumstances of the particular plan. In those circumstances, the amortization of prior service cost shall be accelerated to reflect the more rapid expiration of the employer's economic benefits and to recognize the cost in the periods benefited. [FAS106, ¶54]

.150 A plan amendment can reduce, rather than increase, the accumulated postretirement benefit obligation. A reduction in that obligation shall be used first to reduce any existing unrecognized prior service cost, then to reduce any remaining unrecognized transition obligation. The excess, if any, shall be amortized on the same basis as specified in paragraph .147 for prior service cost. Immediate recognition of the excess is not permitted. [FAS106, ¶55]

Gains and Losses

.151 Gains and losses are changes in the amount of either the accumulated postretirement benefit obligation or plan assets resulting from experience different from that assumed or from changes in assumptions. This section generally does not distinguish between those sources of gains and losses. Gains and losses include amounts that have been realized, for example, by the sale of a security, as well as amounts that are unrealized. Because gains and losses may reflect refinements in estimates as well as real changes in economic values and because some gains in one period may be offset by losses in another or vice versa, this section does not require recognition of gains and losses as components of net postretirement benefit cost in the period in which they arise, except as described in paragraph .156. (Gain and loss recognition in accounting for settlements and curtailments is addressed in paragraphs .182 through .191.) [FAS106, ¶56]

.152 The expected return on plan assets shall be determined based on the expected long-term rate of return on plan assets (refer to paragraph .127) and the market-related value of plan assets. The market-related value of plan assets shall be either fair value or a calculated value that recognizes changes in fair value in a systematic and rational manner over not more than five years. Different methods of calculating market-related value may be used for different classes of assets (for example, an employer might use fair value for bonds and a five-year-moving-average value for equities), but the manner of determining market-related value shall be applied consistently from year to year for each class of plan assets. [FAS106, ¶57]

.153 Plan asset gains and losses are differences between the actual return on plan assets during a period and the expected return on plan assets for that period. Plan asset gains and losses include both (a) changes reflected in the market-related value of plan assets and (b) changes not yet reflected in the market-related value of plan assets (that is, the difference between the fair value and the market-related value of plan assets). Plan asset gains and losses not yet reflected in market-related value are not required to be amortized under paragraphs .154 and .155. [FAS106, ¶58]

.154 As a minimum, amortization of an **unrecognized net gain or loss** (excluding plan asset gains and losses not yet reflected in market-related value) shall be included as a component of net postretirement benefit cost for a year if, as of the beginning of the year, that unrecognized net gain or loss exceeds 10 percent of the greater of the accumulated postretirement benefit obligation or the market-related value of plan assets. If amortization is required, the minimum amortization[27] shall be that excess divided by the average remaining service period of active plan participants. If all or almost all of a plan's participants are inactive, the average remaining life expectancy of the inactive participants shall be used instead of the average remaining service period. [FAS106, ¶59]

[27]The amortization must always reduce the beginning-of-the-year balance. Amortization of an unrecognized net gain results in a decrease in net periodic postretirement benefit cost; amortization of an unrecognized net loss results in an increase in net periodic postretirement benefit cost. [FAS106, ¶59, fn19]

.155 Any systematic method of amortization of unrecognized gains and losses may be used in place of the minimum amortization specified in paragraph .154 provided that (a) the minimum amortization is recognized in any period in which it is greater (reduces the unrecognized amount by more) than the amount that would be recognized under the method used, (b) the method is applied consistently, (c) the method is applied similarly to both gains and losses, and (d) the method used is disclosed. If an enterprise uses a method of consistently recognizing gains and losses immediately, any gain that does not offset a loss previously recognized in income pursuant to this paragraph shall first offset any unrecognized transition obligation; any loss that does not offset a gain previously recognized in income pursuant to this paragraph shall first offset any unrecognized transition asset. [FAS106, ¶60]

.156 In some situations, an employer may forgive a retrospective adjustment of the current or past years' cost-sharing provisions of the plan as they relate to benefit costs *already incurred* by retirees[28] or may otherwise deviate from the provisions of the substantive plan to increase or decrease the employer's share of the benefit costs *incurred in the current or past periods.* The effect of a decision to temporarily deviate from the substantive plan shall be immediately recognized as a loss or gain. [FAS106, ¶61]

.157 The gain or loss component of net periodic postretirement benefit cost shall consist of (a) the difference between the actual return on plan assets and the expected return on plan assets, (b) any gain or loss immediately recognized or the amortization of the unrecognized net gain or loss from previous periods, and (c) any amount immediately recognized as a gain or loss pursuant to paragraph .156. [FAS106, ¶62]

Measurement of Plan Assets

.158 Plan assets are assets—usually stocks, bonds, and other investments (except certain **insurance contracts** as noted in paragraph .162)—that have been segregated and restricted (usually in a trust) to be used for postretirement benefits. [FAS106, ¶63] Whether certain funding vehicles can be restricted solely for the provision of postretirement benefits, as opposed to funding both active employees' and retirees' benefits (and therefore,

[28]For example, the terms of a substantive postretirement health care plan may provide that any shortfall resulting from current year benefit payments in excess of the employer's stated share of incurred claims cost and retiree contributions for that year is to be recovered from increased retiree contributions in the subsequent year. The employer may subsequently determine that increasing retiree contributions for the shortfall in the prior year would be onerous and make a decision to bear the cost of the shortfall for that year. The employer's decision to bear the shortfall represents a change in intent and the resulting loss shall be recognized immediately. Future decisions by the employer to continue to bear the shortfall suggest an amendment of the substantive plan that shall be accounted for as described in paragraphs .145 through .150. [FAS106, ¶61, fn20]

qualify as plan assets) is subject to legal, not accounting, interpretation. [FAS106, ¶308] The amount of plan assets includes amounts contributed by the employer, and by plan participants for a contributory plan, and amounts earned from investing the contributions, less benefits, income taxes, and other expenses incurred. Plan assets ordinarily cannot be withdrawn by the employer except under certain circumstances when a plan has assets in excess of obligations and the employer has taken certain steps to satisfy existing obligations. Securities of the employer held by the plan are includable in plan assets provided they are transferable. [FAS106, ¶63] [Refer to paragraph .1001 for an EITF Issue that provides interpretive guidance on this paragraph.]

.159 Assets not segregated in a trust, or otherwise effectively restricted, so that they cannot be used by the employer for other purposes are not plan assets for purposes of this section, even though the employer may intend that those assets be used to provide postretirement benefits. Those assets shall be accounted for in the same manner as other employer assets of a similar nature and with similar restrictions. Amounts accrued by the employer but not yet paid to the plan are not plan assets for purposes of this section. [FAS106, ¶64]

.160 For purposes of the disclosures required by [FAS106, ¶65] paragraphs .169 and .169A, [FAS135, ¶4(r)] plan investments, whether equity or debt securities, real estate, or other, shall be measured at their fair value as of the measurement date. The fair value of an investment is the amount that the plan could reasonably expect to receive for it in a current sale between a willing buyer and a willing seller, that is, other than in a forced or liquidation sale. Fair value shall be measured by the market price if an active market exists for the investment. If no active market exists for an investment but an active market exists for similar investments, selling prices in that market may be helpful in estimating fair value. If a market price is not available, a forecast of expected cash flows may aid in estimating fair value, provided the expected cash flows are discounted at a current rate commensurate with the risk involved.[29] (Refer to paragraph .166.) [FAS106, ¶65]

.161 Plan assets used in plan operations (for example, buildings, equipment, furniture and fixtures, and leasehold improvements) shall be measured at cost less accumulated depreciation or amortization for all purposes. [FAS106, ¶66]

Insurance Contracts

.162 For purposes of this section, an insurance contract is defined as a contract in which an insurance company unconditionally undertakes a legal obligation to provide specified

[29]For an indication of factors to be considered in determining the discount rate, refer to Section I69, "Interest: Imputation of an Interest Cost," paragraphs .106 and .107. If significant, the fair value of an investment shall reflect the brokerage commissions and other costs normally incurred in a sale. [FAS106, ¶65, fn21]

benefits to specific individuals in return for a fixed consideration or premium; an insurance contract is irrevocable and involves the transfer of significant risk from the employer (or the plan) to the insurance company.[30] Benefits covered by insurance contracts shall be excluded from the accumulated postretirement benefit obligation. Insurance contracts shall be excluded from plan assets, except as provided in paragraph .164 for the cost of **participation rights.** [FAS106, ¶67]

.163 Some insurance contracts **(participating insurance contracts)** provide that the purchaser (either the plan or the employer) may participate in the [FAS106, ¶68] investment performance or [FAS106, ¶367] experience of the insurance company. Under those contracts, [FAS106, ¶68] if the insurance company has favorable experience, [FAS106, ¶367] the insurance company ordinarily pays dividends to the purchaser, the effect of which is to reduce the cost of the plan. [FAS106, ¶68] For example, if the insurance company's investment return is better than anticipated, or perhaps if actual experience related to mortality or other assumptions is favorable, the purchaser will receive dividends that reduce the cost of the contract. [FAS106, ¶367] If the participating insurance contract causes the employer to remain subject to all or most of the risks and rewards associated with the benefit obligation covered or the assets transferred to the insurance company, that contract is not an insurance contract for purposes of this section, and the purchase of that contract does not constitute a settlement pursuant to paragraphs .182 through .187. [FAS106, ¶68]

.164 The purchase price of a participating insurance contract ordinarily is higher than the price of an equivalent contract without a participation right. The difference is the cost of the participation right. The cost of the participation right shall be recognized at the date of purchase as an asset. In subsequent periods, the participation right shall be measured at its fair value if the contract is such that fair value is reasonably estimable. Otherwise the participation right shall be measured at its amortized cost (not in excess of its net realizable value), and the cost shall be amortized systematically over the expected dividend period under the contract. [FAS106, ¶69]

.165 To the extent that insurance contracts are purchased during the period to cover postretirement benefits attributed to service in the current period (such as life insurance benefits), the cost of those benefits shall be the cost of purchasing the coverage under the contracts, except as provided in paragraph .164 for the cost of a participation right. If all the postretirement benefits attributed to service in the current period are covered by

---

[30]If the insurance company providing the contract does business primarily with the employer and related parties (a **captive insurer**) or if there is any reasonable doubt that the insurance company will meet its obligations under the contract, the contract is not an insurance contract for purposes of this section. [FAS106, ¶67, fn22]

nonparticipating insurance contracts purchased during that period, the cost of the contracts determines the service cost component of net postretirement benefit cost for that period. Benefits attributed to current service in excess of benefits provided by nonparticipating insurance contracts purchased during the current period shall be accounted for according to the provisions of this section applicable to plans not involving insurance contracts. [FAS106, ¶70]

.166 Other contracts with insurance companies may not meet the definition of an insurance contract because the insurance company does not unconditionally undertake a legal obligation to provide specified benefits to specified individuals. Those contracts shall be accounted for as investments and measured at fair value. If a contract has a determinable cash surrender value or conversion value, that is presumed to be its fair value. For some contracts, the best available estimate of fair value may be contract value. [FAS106, ¶71]

Measurement Date

.167 The measurements of *plan assets and obligations* required by this section shall be as of the date of the financial statements or, if used consistently from year to year, as of a date not more than three months prior to that date. Even though the postretirement benefit measurements are required as of a particular date, all procedures are not required to be performed after that date. As with other financial statement items requiring estimates, much of the information can be prepared as of an earlier date and projected forward to account for subsequent events (for example, employee service). [FAS106, ¶72]

.168 Measurements of *net periodic postretirement benefit cost* for both interim and annual financial statements generally shall be based on the assumptions at the beginning of the year (assumptions used for the previous year-end measurements of plan assets and obligations) unless more recent measurements of both plan assets and the accumulated postretirement benefit obligation are available. For example, if a significant event occurs, such as a plan amendment, settlement, or curtailment, that ordinarily would call for remeasurement, the assumptions used for those later measurements shall be used to remeasure net periodic postretirement benefit cost from the date of the event to the year-end measurement date. [FAS106, ¶73]

Disclosures

.169 An employer that sponsors one or more defined benefit postretirement plans shall provide the following information:[30a]

a. A reconciliation of beginning and ending balances of the benefit obligation[31] showing separately, if applicable, the effects during the period attributable to each of the following: service cost, interest cost, contributions by plan participants, actuarial gains and losses, foreign currency exchange rate changes,[31a] benefits paid, plan amendments, business combinations, divestitures, curtailments, settlements, and special termination benefits
b. A reconciliation of beginning and ending balances of the fair value of plan assets showing separately, if applicable, the effects during the period attributable to each of the following: actual return on plan assets, foreign currency exchange rate changes,[31b] contributions by the employer, contributions by plan participants, benefits paid, business combinations, divestitures, and settlements
c. The funded status of the plans, the amounts not recognized in the statement of financial position, and the amounts recognized in the statement of financial position, including:
   (1) The amount of any unamortized prior service cost
   (2) The amount of any unrecognized net gain or loss (including asset gains and losses not yet reflected in market-related value)
   (3) The amount of any remaining unamortized, unrecognized net obligation or net asset existing at the initial date of application of this section or
   (4) The net postretirement benefit prepaid assets or accrued liabilities
d. The amount of net periodic benefit cost recognized, showing separately the service cost component, the interest cost component, the expected return on plan assets for the period, the amortization of the unrecognized transition obligation or transition asset,

---

[30a]An employer is encouraged to provide disclosure of general descriptive information about the employer's benefit plans, including employee groups covered, type of benefit formula, funding policy, types of assets held, and significant nonbenefit liabilities, if any, if such a description would provide meaningful information, such as when the employer sponsors only a single plan. [FAS132, ¶53] [An employer is permitted to present] pension [as required by Section P16] and other postretirement benefit disclosures in a parallel format in a single note to the financial statements. [FAS132, ¶61] [Refer to Illustration 6, Case One, of Section P16 for an example.]

[31]For defined benefit postretirement plans, the benefit obligation is the accumulated postretirement benefit obligation—the actuarial present value of benefits attributed to employee service rendered to a particular date. [FAS132, ¶5, fn2]

[31a]The effects of foreign currency exchange rate changes that are to be disclosed are those applicable to plans of a foreign operation whose functional currency is not the reporting currency pursuant to Section F60, "Foreign Currency Translation." [FAS132, ¶5, fn3]

[31b]Refer to footnote 31a. [FAS132, ¶5, fn4]

the amount of recognized gains and losses, the amount of prior service cost recognized, and the amount of gain or loss recognized due to a settlement or curtailment

e. On a weighted-average basis, the following assumptions used in the accounting for the plans: assumed discount rate, rate of compensation increase (for pay-related plans), and expected long-term rate of return on plan assets
f. The assumed health care cost trend rate(s) for the next year used to measure the expected cost of benefits covered by the plan (gross eligible charges) and a general description of the direction and pattern of change in the assumed trend rates thereafter, together with the ultimate trend rate(s) and when that rate is expected to be achieved
g. The effect of a one-percentage-point increase and the effect of a one-percentage-point decrease in the assumed health care cost trend rates on (1) the aggregate of the service and interest cost components of net periodic postretirement health care benefit cost and (2) the accumulated postretirement benefit obligation for health care benefits[32] (For purposes of this disclosure, all other assumptions shall be held constant, and the effects shall be measured based on the substantive plan that is the basis for the accounting.)
h. If applicable, the amounts and types of securities of the employer and related parties included in plan assets, the approximate amount of future annual benefits of plan participants covered by insurance contracts issued by the employer or related parties, and any significant transactions between the employer or related parties and the plan during the period
i. If applicable, any alternative amortization method used to amortize prior service amounts or unrecognized net gains and losses pursuant to paragraphs .148 and .155 of this section
j. If applicable, any substantive commitment, such as past practice or a history of regular benefit increases, used as the basis for accounting for the benefit obligation
k. If applicable, the cost of providing special or contractual termination benefits recognized during the period and a description of the nature of the event
l. An explanation of any significant change in the benefit obligation or plan assets not otherwise apparent in the other disclosures required by this section.

Amounts related to the employer's results of operations shall be disclosed for each period[32a] for which an income statement is presented. Amounts related to the employer's statement of financial position shall be disclosed for each balance sheet presented. [FAS132, ¶5]

[32]Measuring the sensitivity of the accumulated postretirement benefit obligation and the combined service and interest cost components to a change in the assumed health care cost trend rates requires remeasuring the accumulated postretirement benefit obligation as of the beginning and end of the year. [FAS106, ¶354]

[32a]Restatement of disclosures for earlier periods provided for comparative purposes is required unless the information is not readily available, in which case the notes to the financial statements shall include all available information and a description of the information not available. [FAS132, ¶15]

Reduced Disclosure Requirements for Nonpublic Entities

.169A A nonpublic entity[32b] may elect to disclose the following for its postretirement benefit plans in lieu of the disclosures required by paragraph .169:[32c]

a. The benefit obligation, fair value of plan assets, and funded status of the plan
b. Employer contributions, participant contributions, and benefits paid
c. The amounts recognized in the statement of financial position, including the net postretirement benefit prepaid assets or accrued liabilities
d. On a weighted-average basis, the following assumptions used in the accounting for the plans: assumed discount rate, rate of compensation increase (for pay-related plans), and expected long-term rate of return on plan assets
e. The assumed health care cost trend rate(s) for the next year used to measure the expected cost of benefits covered by the plan (gross eligible charges) and a general description of the direction and pattern of change in the assumed trend rates thereafter, together with the ultimate trend rate(s) and when that rate is expected to be achieved
f. If applicable, the amounts and types of securities of the employer and related parties included in plan assets, the approximate amount of future annual benefits of plan participants covered by insurance contracts issued by the employer or related parties, and any significant transactions between the employer or related parties and the plan during the period
g. The nature and effect of significant nonroutine events, such as amendments, combinations, divestitures, curtailments, and settlements.

[FAS132, ¶8]

Employers with Two or More Plans

.170 Postretirement benefits offered by an employer may vary in nature and may be provided to different groups of employees. As discussed in paragraph .171, in some cases an employer may aggregate data from unfunded plans for measurement purposes in lieu of performing separate measurements for each unfunded plan (including plans whose designated assets are not appropriately segregated and restricted and thus have no plan assets as that term is used in this section). Net periodic postretirement benefit cost, the accumulated postretirement benefit obligation, and plan assets shall be determined for

[32b]A nonpublic entity is any entity other than one (a) whose debt or equity securities trade in a public market either on a stock exchange (domestic or foreign) or in the over-the-counter market, including securities quoted only locally or regionally, (b) that makes a filing with a regulatory agency in preparation for the sale of any class of debt or equity securities in a public market, or (c) that is controlled by an entity covered by (a) or (b). [FAS132, ¶8, fn5]

[32c]Even though this section permits reduced disclosures for nonpublic entities, the incremental information required by paragraph .169 improves understanding and, therefore, those entities are encouraged to disclose that information. [FAS132, ¶59]

each separately measured plan or aggregation of plans by applying the provisions of this section to each such plan or aggregation of plans. [FAS106, ¶75]

.171 The data from all unfunded postretirement health care plans may be aggregated for measurement purposes if those plans provide different benefits to the same group of employees. [FAS106, ¶76] For example, an employer may have separate medical care, dental care, and eye care plans that provide benefit coverage to all retirees of the company. Similarly, an employer may combine two or more unfunded plans [if those plans] provide the same benefits to different groups of plan participants. For example, an employer may have identical postretirement medical care plans at each of its operating locations. This section permits combining plans in those situations because the differences in the plans are not substantive. Combining information in those cases results in combined measurements for accounting and disclosure purposes. [FAS106, ¶357] Data from other unfunded postretirement welfare benefit plans may be aggregated for measurement purposes in similar circumstances, such as when an employer has a variety of welfare benefit plans that provide benefits to the same group of employees. However, a plan that has plan assets (as defined herein) shall not be aggregated with other plans but shall be measured separately. [FAS106, ¶76]

.172 The disclosures required by this section may be aggregated for all of an employer's defined benefit postretirement plans or may be disaggregated in groups if that is considered to provide the most useful information or is otherwise required by paragraph .173. Disclosures about postretirement plans with assets in excess of the accumulated benefit obligation generally may be aggregated with disclosures about postretirement plans with accumulated benefit obligations in excess of assets. However, if those disclosures are combined, an employer shall disclose the aggregate benefit obligation and aggregate fair value of plan assets for plans with benefit obligations in excess of plan assets. Disclosure of amounts recognized in the statement of financial position shall present prepaid benefit costs and accrued benefit liabilities separately. [FAS132, ¶6]

.173 An employer may combine disclosures about postretirement benefit plans outside the United States with those for U.S. plans unless the benefit obligations of the plans outside the United States are significant relative to the total benefit obligation and those plans use significantly different assumptions. [FAS132, ¶7]

Multiemployer Plans

.174 For purposes of this section, a **multiemployer plan** is a postretirement benefit plan to which two or more unrelated employers contribute, usually pursuant to one or more collective-bargaining agreements. A characteristic of multiemployer plans is that assets contributed by one participating employer may be used to provide benefits to employees of other participating employers since assets contributed by an employer are not segregated in a separate account or restricted to provide benefits only to employees of that employer. [FAS106, ¶79]

.175 A multiemployer plan usually is administered by a board of trustees composed of management and labor representatives and may also be referred to as a "joint trust" or "union plan." Generally, many employers participate in a multiemployer plan, and an employer may participate in more than one plan. The employers participating in multiemployer plans usually have a common industry bond, but for some plans the employers are in different industries, and the labor union may be their only common bond. Some multiemployer plans do not involve a union. For example, local chapters of a not-for-profit organization may participate in a plan established by the related national organization. [FAS106, ¶80]

.176 In a multiemployer setting, eligibility for benefits is defined by the plan; retired employees continue to receive benefits whether or not their former employers continue to contribute to the plan. On the other hand, plan participants not yet eligible for benefits may lose accumulated postretirement benefits if their current or former employer withdraws from a plan unless they take or have a job with other employers who participate in the plan. While the plan may have the option of cancelling the accrued service credits that apply toward the required service, within the bargaining unit, of plan participants who were employed by a withdrawing employer and who become or are employed by another participating employer, that rarely occurs because of the difficulty of matching employees to specific employers. For example, in certain industries, an employee may work for more than one employer in a single day and different employers on different days, making it difficult to associate any portion of that employee's past service with a specific employer. [FAS106, ¶377]

.177 An employer participating in a multiemployer plan shall recognize as net postretirement benefit cost the required contribution for the period, which shall include both cash and the fair market value of noncash contributions, and shall recognize as a liability any unpaid contributions required for the period. [FAS106, ¶81]

.178 An employer shall disclose the amount of contributions to multiemployer plans during the period. An employer may disclose total contributions to multiemployer plans without disaggregating the amounts attributable to pensions and other postretirement benefits. The disclosures shall include a description of the nature and effect of any changes affecting comparability, such as a change in the rate of employer contributions, a business combination, or a divestiture. [FAS132, ¶10]

.179 In some situations, withdrawal from a multiemployer plan may result in an employer's having an obligation to the plan for a portion of the plan's unfunded accumulated postretirement benefit obligation. If it is either probable or reasonably possible that (a) an employer would withdraw from the plan under circumstances that would give rise to an obligation or (b) an employer's contribution to the fund would be increased during the remainder of the contract period to make up a shortfall in the funds necessary to maintain the negotiated level of benefit coverage (a "maintenance of benefits" clause), the employer shall apply the provisions of Section C59, "Contingencies." [FAS106, ¶83 and FAS132, ¶11]

Multiple-Employer Plans

.180 Some postretirement benefit plans to which two or more unrelated employers contribute are not multiemployer plans. Rather, those **multiple-employer plans** are in substance aggregations of single-employer plans, combined to allow participating employers to pool plan assets for investment purposes or to reduce the costs of plan administration. Those plans ordinarily do not involve collective-bargaining agreements. They may also have features that allow participating employers to have different benefit formulas, with the employer's contributions to the plan based on the benefit formula selected by the employer. Those plans shall be considered single-employer plans rather than multiemployer plans for purposes of this section, and each employer's accounting shall be based on its respective interest in the plan. [FAS106, ¶84]

Postretirement Benefit Plans outside the United States

.181 Except for [the date this section must be applied], this section includes no special provisions applicable to postretirement benefit arrangements outside the United States. Those arrangements are subject to the provisions of this section for purposes of preparing financial statements in accordance with accounting principles generally accepted in the United States. The applicability of this section to those arrangements is determined by the nature of the obligation and by the terms or conditions that define the amount of benefits to be paid, not by whether or how a plan is funded, whether benefits are payable at intervals or as a single amount, or whether the benefits are required by law or custom or are provided under a plan the employer has elected to sponsor. [FAS106, ¶85]

Accounting for Settlement of a Postretirement Benefit Obligation

.182 For purposes of this section, a settlement is defined as a transaction that (a) is an irrevocable action, (b) relieves the employer (or the plan) of primary responsibility for a postretirement benefit obligation, and (c) eliminates significant risks related to the obligation and the assets used to effect the settlement.[33] Examples of transactions that constitute a settlement include making lump-sum cash payments to plan participants in exchange for their rights to receive specified postretirement benefits and purchasing long-term nonparticipating insurance contracts for the accumulated postretirement benefit obligation for some or all of the plan participants. [FAS106, ¶90]

.183 A transaction that does not meet the three criteria of paragraph .182 does not constitute a settlement for purposes of this section. For example, investing in a portfolio of high-quality fixed-income securities with principal and interest payment dates similar to the estimated payment dates of benefits may avoid or minimize certain risks. However, that investment decision does not constitute a settlement because that decision can be reversed, and investing in that portfolio does not relieve the employer (or the plan) of primary responsibility for a postretirement benefit obligation nor does it eliminate significant risks related to that obligation. [FAS106, ¶91]

.184 For purposes of this section, the maximum gain or loss subject to recognition in income when a postretirement benefit obligation is settled is the unrecognized net gain or loss defined in paragraphs .151 through .155 plus any remaining unrecognized transition asset. That maximum gain or loss includes any gain or loss resulting from remeasurements of plan assets and the accumulated postretirement benefit obligation at the time of settlement. [FAS106, ¶92]

.185 If the entire accumulated postretirement benefit obligation is settled and the maximum amount subject to recognition is a gain, the settlement gain shall first reduce any remaining unrecognized transition obligation;[34] any excess gain shall be recognized in income.[35] If the entire accumulated postretirement benefit obligation is settled and the maximum amount subject to recognition is a loss, the maximum settlement loss shall be recognized in income. If only part of the accumulated postretirement benefit obligation is settled, the employer shall recognize in income the excess of the pro rata portion (equal to the percentage reduction in the accumulated postretirement benefit obligation) of the maximum settlement gain over any remaining unrecognized transition obligation or a pro rata portion of the maximum settlement loss. [FAS106, ¶93]

---

[33]If an insurance contract is purchased from an insurance company controlled by the employer, the purchase of the contract does not constitute a settlement. [FAS106, ¶90, fn24]

[34]As discussed in paragraph .200, in measuring the gain or loss subject to recognition in income when a postretirement benefit obligation is settled, it shall first be determined whether recognition of an additional amount of any unrecognized transition obligation is required. [FAS106, ¶93, fn25]

[35]Because the plan is the unit of accounting, the determination of the effects of a settlement considers only the unrecognized net gain or loss and unrecognized transition obligation or asset related to the plan for which all or a portion of the accumulated postretirement benefit obligation is being settled. [FAS106, ¶93, fn26]

.186 If the purchase of a participating insurance contract constitutes a settlement (refer to paragraphs .162 and .182), the maximum gain (but not the maximum loss) shall be reduced by the cost of the participation right before determining the amount to be recognized in income. [FAS106, ¶94]

.187 If the cost of all settlements[36] in a year is less than or equal to the sum of the service cost and interest cost components of net postretirement benefit cost for the plan for the year, gain or loss recognition is permitted but not required for those settlements. However, the accounting policy adopted shall be applied consistently from year to year. [FAS106, ¶95]

Accounting for a Plan Curtailment

.188 For purposes of this section, a curtailment is an event that significantly reduces the expected years of future service of active plan participants or eliminates the accrual of defined benefits for some or all of the future services of a significant number of active plan participants. Curtailments include:

a. Termination of employees' services earlier than expected, which may or may not involve closing a facility or discontinuing a [FAS106, ¶96] component of an entity [FAS144, ¶C12(a)]
b. Termination or suspension of a plan so that employees do not earn additional benefits for future service. In the latter situation, future service may be counted toward eligibility for benefits accumulated based on past service. [FAS106, ¶96]

.189 The unrecognized prior service cost associated with the portion of the future years of service that had been expected to be rendered, but as a result of a curtailment are no longer expected to be rendered, is a loss. For purposes of measuring the effect of a curtailment, unrecognized prior service cost includes the cost of plan amendments and any remaining unrecognized transition obligation. For example, a curtailment may result from the termination of a significant number of employees who were plan participants at the

---

[36]For the following types of settlements, the cost of the settlement is:

a. For a cash settlement, the amount of cash paid to plan participants
b. For a settlement using nonparticipating insurance contracts, the cost of the contracts
c. For a settlement using participating insurance contracts, the cost of the contracts less the amount attributed to participation rights. (Refer to paragraphs .163 and .164.)

[FAS106, ¶95, fn27]

date of a prior plan amendment.[37] The loss associated with that curtailment is measured as (a) the portion of the remaining unrecognized prior service cost related to that (and any prior) plan amendment attributable to the previously expected remaining future years of service of the employees who were terminated and (b) the portion of the remaining unrecognized transition obligation attributable to the previously expected remaining future years of service of the terminated employees who were plan participants at the date of transition. [FAS106, ¶97]

.190 The accumulated postretirement benefit obligation may be decreased (a gain) or increased (a loss) by a curtailment.[38] That (gain) loss shall reduce any unrecognized net loss (gain).

a. To the extent that such a gain exceeds any unrecognized net loss (or the entire gain, if an unrecognized net gain exists), it is a curtailment gain.
b. To the extent that such a loss exceeds any unrecognized net gain (or the entire loss, if an unrecognized net loss exists), it is a curtailment loss.

For purposes of applying the provisions of this paragraph, any remaining unrecognized transition asset shall be treated as an unrecognized net gain and shall be combined with the unrecognized net gain or loss arising subsequent to transition to this section. [FAS106, ¶98]

.191 If the sum of the effects identified in paragraphs .189 and .190 is a net loss, it shall be recognized in income when it is probable that a curtailment will occur and the net effect is reasonably estimable. If the sum of those effects is a net gain, it shall be recognized in income when the related employees terminate or the plan suspension or amendment is adopted. [FAS106, ¶99]

[37] A curtailment also may result from terminating the accrual of additional benefits for the future services of a significant number of employees. The loss in that situation is (a) a proportionate amount of the remaining unrecognized prior service cost based on the portion of the remaining expected years of service in the amortization period that originally was attributable to those employees who were plan participants at the date of the plan amendment and whose future accrual of benefits has been terminated and (b) a proportionate amount of the remaining unrecognized transition obligation based on the portion of the remaining years of service of all participants active at the date of transition that originally was attributable to the remaining expected future years of service of the employees whose future accrual of benefits has been terminated. [FAS106, ¶97, fn28]

[38] Increases in the accumulated postretirement benefit obligation that reflect termination benefits are excluded from the scope of this paragraph. (Refer to paragraphs .193 and .194.) [FAS106, ¶98, fn29]

Relationship of Settlements and Curtailments to Other Events

.192 A settlement and a curtailment may occur separately or together. If benefits expected to be paid in future periods are eliminated for some plan participants (for example, because a significant portion of the work force is dismissed or a plant is closed) but the plan remains in existence and continues to pay benefits, to invest assets, and to receive contributions, a curtailment has occurred but not a settlement. If an employer purchases nonparticipating insurance contracts for the accumulated postretirement benefit obligation and continues to provide defined benefits for future service, either in the same plan or in a successor plan, a settlement has occurred but not a curtailment. If a **plan termination** occurs (that is, the obligation is settled and the plan ceases to exist) and the plan is not replaced by a successor defined benefit plan, both a settlement and a curtailment have occurred (whether or not the employees continue to work for the employer). [FAS106, ¶100]

Measurement of the Effects of Termination Benefits

.193 Postretirement benefits offered as special or contractual termination benefits shall be recognized in accordance with paragraph .185 of Section P16.[39] That is, an employer that offers special termination benefits to employees shall recognize a liability and a loss when the employees accept the offer and the amount can be reasonably estimated. An employer that provides contractual termination benefits shall recognize a liability and a loss when it is probable that employees will be entitled to benefits and the amount can be reasonably estimated. A situation involving special or contractual termination benefits may also result in a curtailment to be accounted for under paragraphs .188 through .191 of this section. [FAS106, ¶101]

.194 The liability and loss recognized for employees who accept an offer of special termination benefits to be provided by a postretirement benefit plan shall be the difference between (a) the accumulated postretirement benefit obligation for those employees, assuming that those employees (active plan participants) not yet fully eligible for benefits

[39]An employer may provide benefits to employees in connection with their termination of employment. They may be either *special termination benefits* offered only for a short period of time or *contractual termination benefits* required by the terms of a plan only if a specified event, such as a plant closing occurs. An employer that offers special termination benefits to employees shall recognize a liability and a loss when the employees accept the offer and the amount can be reasonably estimated. An employer that provides contractual termination benefits shall recognize a liability and a loss when it is probable that employees will be entitled to benefits and the amount can be reasonably estimated. [FAS88, ¶15] Section P16 therefore applies to other benefits in addition to pensions. [This section reiterates] the applicability of Section P16, since practice may have been to exclude postretirement health care costs from the measurement of termination benefits. [FAS106, ¶333]

would terminate at their full eligibility date and that fully eligible plan participants would retire immediately, without considering any special termination benefits and (b) the accumulated postretirement benefit obligation as measured in (a) adjusted to reflect the special termination benefits. [FAS106, ¶102]

Disposal of a Segment

.195 [Deleted 8/01 because of FASB Statement 144, *Accounting for the Impairment or Disposal of Long-Lived Assets.*]

Defined Contribution Plans

.196 For purposes of this section, a **defined contribution postretirement plan** is a plan that provides postretirement benefits in return for services rendered, provides *an individual account* for each participant, and has terms that specify how contributions to the individual's account are to be determined rather than the amount of postretirement benefits the individual is to receive.[40] Under a defined contribution plan, the postretirement benefits a plan participant will receive are limited to the amount contributed to the plan participant's account, the returns earned on investments of those contributions, and forfeitures of other plan participants' benefits that may be allocated to the plan participant's account. [FAS106, ¶104] The employer's present obligation under the terms of [a defined contribution] plan is fully satisfied when the contribution for the period is made, provided that costs (defined contributions) are not being deferred and recognized in periods after the related service period of the individual to whose account the contributions are to be made. [FAS106, ¶382]

.197 To the extent a plan's defined contributions to an individual's account are to be made for periods in which that individual renders services, the net postretirement benefit cost for a period shall be the contribution called for in that period. If a plan calls for contributions for periods after an individual retires or terminates, the estimated cost shall be accrued during the employee's service period. [FAS106, ¶105] [Refer to paragraph .1001 for an EITF Issue that provides interpretive guidance on this paragraph.]

---

[40]For example, an employer may establish individual postretirement health care accounts for each employee, each year contributing a specified amount to each active employee's account. The balance in each employee's account may be used by that employee after the employee's retirement to purchase health care insurance or for other health care benefits. Rather than providing for defined health care benefits, the employer is providing a defined amount of money that may be used by retirees toward the payment of their health care costs. [FAS106, ¶104, fn30]

.198 An employer shall disclose the amount of cost recognized for defined contribution postretirement benefit plans during the period separately from the amount of cost recognized for defined benefit plans. The disclosures shall include a description of the nature and effect of any significant changes during the period affecting comparability, such as a change in the rate of employer contributions, a business combination, or a divestiture. [FAS132, ¶9]

.199 A postretirement benefit plan having characteristics of both a defined benefit plan and a defined contribution plan requires careful analysis. If the *substance* of the plan is to provide a defined benefit, as may be the case with some "target benefit" plans, the accounting [FAS106, ¶107] requirements shall be determined in accordance with the provisions of this section applicable to a defined benefit plan and the disclosure requirements shall be determined in accordance with the provisions of paragraphs .169 and .169A. [FAS135, ¶4(r)]

Amortization of Transition Obligation

.200 Amortization of the transition obligation shall be accelerated if the cumulative benefit payments subsequent to the transition date to all plan participants exceed the cumulative postretirement benefit cost accrued subsequent to the transition date. In that situation, an additional amount of the unrecognized transition obligation shall be recognized equal to the excess cumulative benefit payments. For purposes of applying this provision, cumulative benefit payments shall be reduced by any plan assets or any recognized accrued postretirement benefit obligation at the transition date. Payments made pursuant to a settlement, as discussed in paragraphs .182 through .186, shall be included in the determination of cumulative benefit payments made subsequent to the transition date. [FAS106, ¶112]

.201 If at the measurement date for the beginning of an employer's fiscal year it is expected that additional recognition of any remaining unrecognized transition obligation will be required pursuant to paragraph .200, amortization of the transition obligation for interim reporting purposes shall be based on the amount expected to be amortized for the year, except for the effects of applying paragraph .200 for any settlement required to be accounted for pursuant to paragraphs .182 through .186. Those effects shall be recognized when the related settlement is recognized. The effects of changes during the year in the initial assessment of whether additional recognition of the unrecognized transition obligation will be required for the year shall be recognized over the remainder of the year. The amount of the unrecognized transition obligation to be recognized for a year shall be finally determined at the measurement date for the end of the year based on the constraints on delayed recognition discussed in paragraph .200; any difference between the amortization of the transition obligation recognized during interim periods and the amount required to be recognized for the year shall be recognized immediately. [FAS106, ¶113]

Application of Standards in Paragraphs .101 through .201 to Specific Aspects of Accounting for Postretirement Benefits Other Than Pensions

.202 Paragraphs .205 through .308 provide additional discussion and examples that illustrate the application of certain requirements of this section to specific aspects of employers' accounting for postretirement benefits other than pensions. [FAS106, ¶391]

CONTENTS

Introduction

.203 The illustrations are referenced to the applicable paragraph(s) of this section where appropriate. Certain illustrations have been included to facilitate the understanding and application of certain provisions of this section that apply in specific circumstances that may not be encountered frequently by employers. The fact patterns shown may not be representative of actual situations but are presented only to illustrate those requirements. [FAS106, ¶391]

.204 Throughout these illustrations the accumulated postretirement benefit obligation and service cost are assumed as inputs rather than calculated based on some underlying population. For simplicity, benefit payments are assumed to be made at the end of the year, service cost is assumed to include interest on the portion of the expected postretirement benefit obligation attributed to the current year, and interest cost is based on the accumulated postretirement benefit obligation as of the beginning of the year. For unfunded plans, benefits are assumed to be paid directly by the employer and are reflected as a reduction in the accrued postretirement benefit cost. In many of the cases, application of the underlying concepts has been simplified by focusing on a single employee for purposes of illustration. In practice, the determination of the full eligibility date and the measurement of postretirement benefit cost and obligation are based on employee groups and consider various possible retirement dates and the probabilities associated with retirement at each of those dates. [FAS106, ¶392]

Illustration 1—Illustration of Terms

Case 1A—Expected Postretirement Benefit Obligation and Accumulated Postretirement Benefit Obligation

.205 This section uses two terms to describe certain measures of the obligation to provide postretirement benefits: *expected postretirement benefit obligation* and *accumulated postretirement benefit obligation.* The expected postretirement benefit obligation for an employee is the actuarial present value as of a measurement date of the postretirement benefits expected to be paid to or for the employee, the employee's beneficiaries, and any covered dependents. Prior to the date on which an employee attains full eligibility for the benefits that employee is expected to earn under the terms of the postretirement benefit plan (the full eligibility date), the accumulated postretirement benefit obligation for an employee is a portion of the expected postretirement benefit obligation. On and after the full eligibility date, the accumulated postretirement benefit obligation and the expected postretirement benefit obligation for an employee are the same. (Refer to paragraphs .113 and .114.) The following example illustrates the notion of the expected postretirement benefit obligation and the relationship between that obligation and the accumulated postretirement benefit obligation at various dates. [FAS106, ¶393]

.206 Company A's plan provides postretirement health care benefits to all employees who render at least 10 years of service and attain age 55 while in service. A 50-year-old employee, hired January 1, 19V3 at age 30 and eligible for benefits upon attaining age 55, is expected to terminate employment at age 62 and is expected to live to age 77. A discount rate of 8 percent is assumed.

At December 31, 19X2, Company A estimates the expected amount and timing of benefit payments for that employee as follows:

Age	Expected Future Claims	Present Value at Age 50	53	55
63	$ 2,796	$1,028	$1,295	$1,511
64	3,093	1,052	1,326	1,547
65	856	270	339	396
66	947	276	348	406
67	1,051	284	357	417
68	1,161	291	366	427
69	1,282	297	374	436
70	1,425	306	385	449
71	1,577	313	394	460
72	1,744	321	404	471
73	1,934	329	415	484
74	2,137	337	424	495
75	2,367	346	435	508
76	2,620	354	446	520
77	3,899	488	615	717
	$28,889	$6,292	$7,923	$9,244

[FAS106, ¶394]

.207 The expected and accumulated postretirement benefit obligations at December 31, 19X2 (age 50) are $6,292 and $5,034 (20/25 of $6,292), respectively. An equal amount of the expected postretirement benefit obligation is attributed to each year of service from the employee's date of hire to the employee's full eligibility date (age 55) (paragraphs .138 and .139). Therefore, when the employee is age 50, the accumulated postretirement benefit obligation is measured as 20/25 of the expected postretirement benefit obligation, as the employee has rendered 20 years of the 25-year credited service period. Refer to Case 1B (paragraphs .209 through .220) for additional illustrations on the full eligibility date and Case 1C (paragraphs .221 through .224) for additional illustrations on attribution. [FAS106, ¶395]

.208 Assuming no changes in health care costs or other circumstances, the accumulated postretirement benefit obligation at December 31, 19X5 (age 53) is $7,289 (23/25 of $7,923). At the end of the employee's 25th year of service and thereafter, the expected postretirement benefit obligation and the accumulated postretirement benefit obligation are equal. In this example, at December 31, 19X7, when the employee is 55 and fully eligible for benefits, the accumulated and expected postretirement benefit obligations are $9,244. At the end of the 26th year of service (December 31, 19X8) when the employee is 56, those obligations are $9,984 ($9,244 plus interest at 8 percent for 1 year). [FAS106, ¶396]

Case 1B—Full Eligibility Date

.209 The *full eligibility date* (paragraph .114) is the date at which an employee has rendered all of the service necessary to have earned the right to receive all of the benefits expected to be received by that employee under the terms of the postretirement benefit plan. Therefore, the present value of all of the benefits expected to be received by or on behalf of an employee is attributed to the employee's credited service period, which ends at the full eligibility date. Determination of an employee's full eligibility date is affected by plan terms that provide incremental benefits expected to be received by the employee for additional years of service, unless those incremental benefits are trivial. Determination of the full eligibility date is *not* affected by an employee's current dependency status or by plan terms that define when benefit payments commence. The following examples (paragraphs .210 through .220) are presented to assist in understanding the full eligibility date. [FAS106, ¶397]

Plans That Provide Incremental Benefits for Additional Years of Service

Graded benefit formula

.210 Some plans have benefit formulas that define different benefits for different years of service. To illustrate, assume a plan in which the percentage of postretirement health care coverage to be provided by an employer is defined by groups of years of service. The plan provides 20 percent postretirement health care coverage for 10 years of service after age 35, 50 percent for 20 years of service after age 35, 70 percent for 25 years of service after age 35, and 100 percent for 30 years of service after age 35. The full eligibility date for an employee who was hired at age 35 and is expected to retire at age 62 is at age 60. At that date the employee has rendered 25 years of service after age 35 and is eligible to receive a benefit of 70 percent health care coverage after retirement. The employee receives no additional benefits for the last two years of service. [FAS106, ¶398]

Pay-related plans

.211 Some plans may base the amount of benefits or level of benefit coverage on employees' compensation, for example, as a percentage of their final pay. To the extent the plan's postretirement benefit formula defines benefits wholly or partially as a function of future compensation (that is, the plan provides incremental benefits for additional years of service when it is assumed that final pay will increase), determination of the full eligibility date for an employee is affected by those additional years of service the employee is expected to render (paragraph .114). In addition, measurements of the postretirement benefit obligation and service cost reflect the best estimate of employees' future compensation levels (paragraph .128). [FAS106, ¶399]

.212 For example, assume a plan provides life insurance benefits to employees who render 20 years of service and attain age 55 while in service; the benefit is equal to 20 percent of final pay. A 55-year-old employee, who currently earns a salary of $90,000, has worked 22 years for the company. The employee is expected to retire at age 60 and is expected to be earning $120,000 at that time. The employee is eligible for life insurance coverage under the plan at age 55, when the employee has met the age and service requirements. However, because the employee's salary continues to increase each year, the employee is not *fully eligible* for benefits until age 60 when the employee retires because the employee earns an incremental benefit for each additional year of service beyond age 55. That is, the employee earns an additional benefit equal to 20 percent of the increase in salary each year from age 55 to retirement at age 60 for service during each of those years. [FAS106, ¶400]

Spousal coverage

.213 Some postretirement benefit plans provide spousal or dependent coverage or both if the employee works a specified number of years beyond the date at which the employee attains eligibility for single coverage. For example, a postretirement health care plan provides single coverage to employees who work 10 years and attain age 50 while in service; the plan provides coverage for dependents if the employee works 20 years and attains age 60 while in service. Because the additional 10 years of service may provide an incremental benefit to employees, for employees expected to satisfy the age and service requirements and to have covered dependents during the period following the employee's retirement, their full eligibility date is the date at which they have both rendered 20 years of service and attained age 60 while in service. For employees not expected to have covered dependents after their retirement or who are not expected to render at least 20 years of service or attain age 60 while in service, or both, their full eligibility date is the date at which they have both rendered 10 years of service and attained age 50 while in service. [FAS106, ¶401]

Single Plan Provides Health Care and Life Insurance Benefits

.214 Some postretirement benefit plans may have different eligibility requirements for different types of benefits. For example, assume a plan provides a postretirement death benefit of $100,000 to employees who render 20 or more years of service. Fifty percent health care coverage is provided to eligible employees who render 10 years of service, 70 percent coverage to those who render 20 years of service, and 100 percent coverage to those who render 30 years of service. Employees are eligible for the health care and death benefits if they attain age 55 while in service. [FAS106, ¶402]

.215 The full eligibility date for an individual hired at age 30 and expected to terminate employment at age 62 is the date on which that employee has rendered 30 years of service and attained age 55 while in service (age 60 in this example). At that date the employee is eligible for all of the benefits expected to be paid to or on behalf of that employee under the postretirement benefit plan ($100,000 death benefits and 100 percent health care coverage). The full eligibility date for an employee hired at age 37 and expected to retire at age 62 is the date on which that employee has rendered 20 years of service and attained age 55 while in service (age 57 in this example). At that date the employee is eligible for all of the benefits expected to be paid to or on behalf of that employee under the postretirement benefit plan ($100,000 death benefits and 70 percent health care coverage). [FAS106, ¶403]

Plans That Provide Benefits Based on Status at Date of Termination

.216 Some postretirement benefit plans provide coverage for the spouse to whom an employee is married when the employee terminates service; that is, the marital status of an employee upon termination of employment determines whether single or spousal coverage is to be provided. In measuring the expected postretirement benefit obligation, consideration is given to factors such as when benefit coverage will commence, who will receive benefits (employee and any covered dependents), and the expected need for and utilization of benefit coverage. However, determination of an employee's full eligibility date is not affected by plan terms that define when payments commence or by an employee's current marital (or dependent) status (paragraph .114). [FAS106, ¶404]

.217 For example, assume a plan provides postretirement health care coverage to employees who render at least 10 years of service and attain age 55 while in service; health care coverage also is provided to employees' spouses at the date of the employees' retirement. A 55-year-old employee is single, has worked for the company for 30 years, and is expected to marry at age 59 and to retire at age 62. Although the employee is entitled to spousal coverage only if married at retirement, at age 55 the employee has earned the right to spousal coverage. The probability that the employee will be married when the employee retires is included in the actuarial assumptions developed to measure the expected postretirement benefit obligation for that plan participant. The full eligibility date (age 55 in this example) is not affected by that measurement assumption. [FAS106, ¶405]

Postretirement Benefits to Be Received by Disabled Plan Participants

.218 Some plans provide postretirement benefits to disabled employees. For example, Company B provides disability income and health care benefits to employees who become disabled while in service and have rendered 10 or more years of service. Retiree health care benefits are provided to employees who render 20 or more years of service and attain age 55 while in service. Employees receiving disability benefits continue to accrue "credit" toward their eligibility for retiree health care benefits. Under this plan, an employee hired at age 25, who becomes permanently disabled at age 40, is entitled to receive retiree health care benefits commencing at age 55 (in addition to any disability income benefits commencing at age 40) because that employee worked for Company B for more than 10 years before becoming disabled. Under the terms of the plan the employee is given credit for working to age 55 even though no actual service is rendered by the employee after the disabling event occurs. [FAS106, ¶406]

.219 Because the employee is permanently disabled, the full eligibility date is accelerated to recognize the shorter period of service required to be rendered in exchange for the retiree health care benefits—in this case the full eligibility date is age 40, the date of the disabling event. For a similar employee who is temporarily disabled at age 40 but returns to work and attains age 55 while in service, the full eligibility date is age 55. Company B's expected postretirement benefit health care obligation for the permanently disabled employee is based on the employee's expected health care costs commencing at age 55 and is attributed ratably to that employee's active service to age 40. [FAS106, ¶407]

.220 Only some employees become and remain disabled. Therefore, in measuring the expected postretirement benefit obligation and in determining the attribution period for plan participants expected to become disabled, the probability and timing of a disabling event is considered in determining whether employees are likely to become disabled and whether they will be entitled to receive postretirement benefits. [FAS106, ¶408]

Case 1C—Attribution

Attribution Period

.221 Paragraph .139 states that the beginning of the *attribution period* shall be the date of hire unless the plan's benefit formula grants credit only for service from a later date, in which case benefits generally shall be attributed from the beginning of that credited service period. For example, for a plan that provides benefit coverage to employees who render 30 or more years of service or who render at least 10 years of service and attain age 55 while in service, without specifying when the credited service period begins, the expected postretirement benefit obligation is attributed to service from the date of hire to the earlier of the date at which a plan participant has rendered 30 years of service or has rendered 10 years of service and attained age 55 while in service. However, for a plan that provides benefit coverage to employees who render at least 20 years of service after age 35, the expected postretirement benefit obligation is attributed to a plan participant's first 20 years of service after attaining age 35 or after the date of hire, if later than age 35. [FAS106, ¶409]

.222 For a plan with a benefit formula that attributes benefits to a credited service period that is nominal in relation to employees' total years of service prior to their full eligibility dates, an equal amount of the expected postretirement benefit obligation for an employee is attributed to each year of that employee's service from date of hire to date of full eligibility for benefits. For example, a plan with a benefit formula that defines 100 percent benefit coverage for service for the year in which employees attain age 60 has a 1-year credited service period. If plan participants are expected to have rendered an average of 20 years of service at age 60, the credited service period is nominal in relation to their total years of service prior to their full eligibility dates. In that case, the service cost is recognized from date of hire to age 60. [FAS106, ¶410]

Attribution Pattern

.223 For all plans, except those that "frontload" benefits, the expected postretirement benefit obligation is attributed ratably to each year of service in the attribution period (paragraph .138). That is, an equal amount of the expected postretirement benefit obligation is attributed to each year of service from the employee's date of hire or beginning of the credited service period, if later, to the employee's full eligibility date unless (a) the credited service period is nominal relative to the total years of service prior to the full eligibility date (paragraph .222) or (b) the benefit formula frontloads benefits (paragraph .224). [FAS106, ¶411]

Frontloaded plans

.224 Some plans may have a benefit formula that defines benefits in terms of specific periods of service to be rendered in exchange for those benefits but attributes all or a disproportionate share of the expected postretirement benefit obligation to employees' early years of service in the credited service period. An example would be a life insurance plan that provides postretirement death benefits of $250,000 for 10 years of service after age 45 and $5,000 of additional death benefits for each year of service thereafter up to age 65 (maximum benefit of $300,000). For plans that frontload the benefit, the expected postretirement benefit obligation is attributed to employee service in accordance with the plan's benefit formula (paragraph .138). In this example, the actuarial present value of a $25,000 death benefit is attributed to each of the first 10 years of service after age 45, and the actuarial present value of an additional $5,000 death benefit is attributed to each year of service thereafter up to age 65. [FAS106, ¶412]

Illustration 2—Delayed Recognition and Reconciliation of Funded Status

.225 Pursuant to the provisions of this section, the recognition of certain changes affecting measurement of the accumulated postretirement benefit obligation or the fair value of plan assets may be delayed. Those changes include plan amendments (paragraph .146) and gains and losses due to experience different from that assumed or from changes in assumptions (paragraph .151). Information about the effect of the changes that have been afforded delayed recognition is provided through disclosure of the reconciliation of the funded status of a plan to the accrued or prepaid postretirement benefit cost recognized in the employer's statement of financial position (paragraph .169(c)). The following cases (2A through 2E, paragraphs .226 through .237) show how events that change the accumulated postretirement benefit obligation are reflected in that reconciliation. [FAS106, ¶417]

Case 2A—Unrecognized Obligation at Date of Transition

.226 For an unfunded plan with an accumulated postretirement benefit obligation of $600,000 at the date of transition (January 1, 19X3), the reconciliation of the funded status of the plan with the amount shown in the statement of financial position as of that date is as follows:

Accumulated postretirement benefit obligation	$(600,000)[a]
Plan assets at fair value	0
Funded status	(600,000)
Transition obligation at January 1, 19X3	600,000
(Accrued)/prepaid postretirement benefit cost	$ 0

[a]The actuarial present value of the obligation for fully eligible plan participants' expected postretirement benefits and the portion of the expected postretirement benefit obligation for other active plan participants attributed to service to December 31, 19X2. For example, assume a plan provides benefits to employees who render at least 20 years of service after age 35. For employees age 45 with 10 years of service at December 31, 19X2, the accumulated postretirement benefit obligation is 50% of the expected postretirement benefit obligation for those employees. For employees age 55 or older who have rendered 20 or more years of service at December 31, 19X2 and retirees (collectively referred to as fully eligible plan participants), the accumulated postretirement benefit obligation is the full amount of the expected postretirement benefit obligation for those employees.

[FAS106, ¶418]

.227 The transition obligation or asset is the difference between (a) the accumulated postretirement benefit obligation and (b) the fair value of plan assets plus any recognized accrued postretirement benefit cost or less any recognized prepaid postretirement benefit cost at the date of transition (paragraph .141, footnote 24). If, as in this case, advance contributions were not made and postretirement benefit cost was not accrued in prior periods, there is no accrued or prepaid postretirement benefit cost recognized in the statement of financial position, and, therefore, the transition obligation is equal to the unfunded status ($600,000). [FAS106, ¶419]

Unrecognized Amounts after Date of Transition

.228 After the date of transition, any change in the accumulated postretirement benefit obligation or the plan assets (other than contributions and benefit payments) either is unrecognized, due to the delayed recognition provisions of this section, or is included in net periodic postretirement benefit cost. Contributions by the employer increase plan assets and decrease the accrued postretirement benefit cost or increase the prepaid postretirement benefit cost, subject to the provision of paragraph .200 requiring recognition of an additional amount of the unrecognized transition obligation in certain situations. All changes in the accumulated postretirement benefit obligation and plan assets are reflected in the reconciliation. Using Case 2A as the starting point, the following reconciliations (Cases 2B through 2E [paragraphs .229 through .237]) illustrate the effect of changes in assumptions or changes in the plan on measurement of the accumulated postretirement benefit obligation. [FAS106, ¶420]

Case 2B—Employer Accrual of Net Periodic Postretirement Benefit Cost

.229 Benefit payments of $42,000 are made at the end of 19X3. Changes in accrued postretirement benefit cost, accumulated postretirement benefit obligation, and unrecognized transition obligation in 19X3 are summarized as follows:

	Accrued Postretirement Benefit Cost	Accumulated Postretirement Benefit Obligation	Unrecognized Transition Obligation
Beginning of year	$ 0	$(600,000)	$600,000
Recognition of components of net periodic postretirement benefit cost:			
Service cost	(32,000)	(32,000)	
Interest cost[a]	(48,000)	(48,000)	
Amortization of transition obligation[b]	(30,000)		(30,000)
	(110,000)	(80,000)	(30,000)
Benefit payments	42,000	42,000	
Net change	(68,000)	(38,000)	(30,000)
End of year	$ (68,000)	$(638,000)	$570,000

[a]Assumed discount rate of 8% applied to the accumulated postretirement benefit obligation at the beginning of the year.

[b]The transition obligation of $600,000 is amortized on a straight-line basis over 20 years. Illustration 3 (paragraphs .239 through .245) illustrates the constraint on delayed recognition of the transition obligation pursuant to paragraph .200.

[FAS106, ¶421]

.230 The funded status of the plan at January 1, 19X3 and December 31, 19X3 is reconciled with the amount shown in the statement of financial position at those dates as follows:

	1/1/X3	**Net Change**	**12/31/X3**
Accumulated postretirement benefit obligation	$(600,000)	$(38,000)	$(638,000)
Plan assets at fair value	0		0
Funded status	(600,000)	(38,000)	(638,000)
Unrecognized transition obligation	600,000	(30,000)	570,000
Accrued postretirement benefit cost	$ 0	$(68,000)	$ (68,000)

[FAS106, ¶422]

Case 2C—Plan Amendment That Increases Benefits

.231 The plan is amended on January 2, 19X4, resulting in a $90,000 increase in the accumulated postretirement benefit obligation. The effects of plan amendments are reflected immediately in measurement of the accumulated postretirement benefit obligation; however, the effects of the amendment are not recognized immediately in the financial statements, but rather are recognized on a delayed basis (paragraph .147). [FAS106, ¶423]

.232 Benefit payments of $39,000 are made at the end of 19X4. Changes in accrued postretirement benefit cost, accumulated postretirement benefit obligation, unrecognized transition obligation, and unrecognized prior service cost in 19X4 are summarized as follows:

	Accrued Postretirement Benefit Cost	Accumulated Postretirement Benefit Obligation	Unrecognized Transition Obligation	Unrecognized Prior Service Cost
Beginning of year	$ (68,000)	$(638,000)	$570,000	$ 0
Plan amendment		(90,000)		90,000
Recognition of components of net periodic postretirement benefit cost:				
Service cost	(30,000)	(30,000)		
Interest cost[a]	(58,240)	(58,240)		
Amortization of transition obligation	(30,000)		(30,000)	
Amortization of prior service cost[b]	(9,000)			(9,000)
	(127,240)	(178,240)	(30,000)	81,000
Benefit payments	39,000	39,000		
Net change	(88,240)	(139,240)	(30,000)	81,000
End of year	$(156,240)	$(777,240)	$540,000	$81,000

[a]Assumed discount rate of 8% applied to the accumulated postretirement benefit obligation at the beginning of the year and to the increase in that obligation for the unrecognized prior service cost at the date of the plan amendment [($638,000 × 8%) + ($90,000 × 8%)].

[b]As permitted by paragraph .148, prior service cost of $90,000 is amortized on a straight-line basis over the average remaining years of service to *full eligibility* for benefits of the active plan participants (10 years in this example).

[FAS106, ¶424]

.233 The funded status of the plan at December 31, 19X3 and 19X4 is reconciled with amount shown in the statement of financial position at those dates as follows:

	12/31/X3	Net Change	12/31/X4
Accumulated postretirement benefit obligation	$(638,000)	$(139,240)	$(777,240)
Plan assets at fair value	0		0
Funded status	(638,000)	(139,240)	(777,240)
Unrecognized prior service cost	0	81,000	81,000
Unrecognized transition obligation	570,000	(30,000)	540,000
Accrued postretirement benefit cost	$ (68,000)	$ (88,240)	$(156,240)

[FAS106, ¶425]

Case 2D—Negative Plan Amendment

.234 The plan is amended on January 4, 19X5, resulting in a $99,000 reduction in the accumulated postretirement benefit obligation. As with a plan amendment that increases benefits, the effect of a negative plan amendment (an amendment that decreases benefits) is reflected immediately in the measurement of the accumulated postretirement benefit obligation. The effects of the negative plan amendment are recognized by first reducing any existing unrecognized prior service cost and then any existing unrecognized transition obligation; the remainder is recognized in the financial statements on a delayed basis. [FAS106, ¶426]

.235 Benefit payments in 19X5 are $40,000. Changes in accrued postretirement benefit cost, accumulated postretirement benefit obligation, unrecognized transition obligation, and unrecognized prior service cost in 19X5 are summarized as follows:

	Accrued Postretirement Benefit Cost	Accumulated Postretirement Benefit Obligation	Unrecognized Transition Obligation	Unrecognized Prior Service Cost
Beginning of year	$(156,240)	$(777,240)	$540,000	$ 81,000
Plan amendment[a]		99,000	(18,000)	(81,000)
Recognition of components of net periodic postretirement benefit cost:				
Service cost	(30,000)	(30,000)		
Interest cost[b]	(54,259)	(54,259)		
Amortization of transition obligation[c]	(29,000)		(29,000)	
Amortization of prior service cost	0			0
	(113,259)	14,741	(47,000)	(81,000)
Benefit payments	40,000	40,000		
Net change	(73,259)	54,741	(47,000)	(81,000)
End of year	$(229,499)	$(722,499)	$493,000	$ 0

[a]Paragraph .150 requires that the effects of a plan amendment that reduces the accumulated postretirement benefit obligation be used first to reduce any existing unrecognized prior service cost, then any unrecognized transition obligation. Any remaining effects are recognized on a delayed basis over the remaining years of service to full eligibility for those plan participants who were active at the date of the amendment. If all or almost all of the plan participants were fully eligible at that date, the remaining effects should be recognized over the remaining life expectancy of those plan participants.

[b]Assumed discount rate of 8% applied to the accumulated postretirement benefit obligation at the beginning of the year and to the decrease in that obligation at the date of the plan amendment [($777,240 × 8%) – ($99,000 × 8%)].

[c]Unrecognized transition obligation of $522,000 ($540,000 – $18,000) is amortized on a straight-line basis over the 18 years remaining in the transition period.

[FAS106, ¶427]

.236 The funded status of the plan at December 31, 19X4 and 19X5 is reconciled with the amount shown in the statement of financial position at those dates as follows:

	12/31/X4	Net Change	12/31/X5
Accumulated postretirement benefit obligation	$(777,240)	$ 54,741	$(722,499)
Plan assets at fair value	0		0
Funded status	(777,240)	54,741	(722,499)
Unrecognized prior service cost	81,000	(81,000)	0
Unrecognized transition obligation	540,000	(47,000)	493,000
Accrued postretirement benefit cost	$(156,240)	$(73,259)	$(229,499)

[FAS106, ¶428]

Case 2E—Change in Assumption

.237 The assumed health care cost trend rates are changed at December 31, 19X5, resulting in a $55,000 increase in the accumulated postretirement benefit obligation. The net loss that results from a change in the health care cost trend rates assumption is reflected immediately in the measurement of the accumulated postretirement benefit obligation. However, as with most other gains and losses, the effect of a change in assumption may be recognized in the financial statements either immediately or on a delayed basis, as long as the recognition method is applied consistently.

	Before Change	Net Loss	After Change
Accumulated postretirement benefit obligation	$(722,499)	$(55,000)	$(777,499)
Plan assets at fair value	0		0
Funded status	(722,499)	(55,000)	(777,499)
Unrecognized net loss[a]	0	55,000	55,000
Unrecognized transition obligation	493,000		493,000
Accrued postretirement benefit cost	$(229,499)	$ 0	$(229,499)

[a]This section generally does not require recognition of gains and losses in the period in which they arise (paragraphs .151 through .156). However, at a minimum, amortization of an unrecognized net gain or loss is required to be recognized as a component of net periodic postretirement benefit cost for a year if, as of the beginning of the year, the unrecognized net gain or loss exceeds 10% of the greater of the accumulated postretirement benefit obligation or the market-related value of plan assets. Applications of those provisions are included in Illustration 5 (paragraphs .252 through .267).

[FAS106, ¶429]

Illustration 3—Constraint on Delayed Recognition of Transition Obligation

.238 [As indicated in paragraph .200] phasing in recognition of a transition obligation should not result in less rapid recognition than would have resulted under pay-as-you-go accounting. That is, after the transition date, the cumulative postretirement benefit cost accrued should not be less than cumulative benefit payments. Paragraphs .239 through .245 illustrate a situation in which recognition of the transition obligation is accelerated as a result of that constraint. [FAS106, ¶430]

.239 At December 31, 19X2, the accumulated (and unrecognized) postretirement benefit obligation and plan assets of a defined benefit postretirement plan sponsored by Company D [were] as follows:

Accumulated postretirement benefit obligation	$(255,000)
Plan assets at fair value	0
Transition obligation	$(255,000)

[FAS106, ¶435]

.240 Company D adopts [the provisions of] this section for the year beginning January 1, 19X3. At December 31, 19X2, Company D [had] no prepaid or accrued postretirement benefit cost. Company D [elected] to amortize the transition obligation over the average remaining service period of active plan participants at the date of transition—17 years. [FAS106, ¶436]

.241 Benefit payments in 19X3 are $45,000. Changes in accrued postretirement benefit cost, accumulated postretirement benefit obligation, and unrecognized transition obligation in 19X3 are summarized as follows:

	Accrued Postretirement Benefit Cost	Accumulated Postretirement Benefit Obligation	Unrecognized Transition Obligation
Beginning of year	$ 0	$(255,000)	$255,000
Recognition of components of net periodic postretirement benefit cost:			
Service cost	(30,000)	(30,000)	
Interest cost[a]	(20,400)	(20,400)	
Amortization of transition obligation[b]	(15,000)		(15,000)
	(65,400)	(50,400)	(15,000)
Benefit payments	45,000	45,000	
Net change	(20,400)	(5,400)	(15,000)
End of year	$(20,400)	$(260,400)	$240,000

[a]An 8% discount rate is assumed.

[b]$255,000 ÷ 17 years = $15,000 per year.

[FAS106, ¶437]

.242 In 19X4, benefit payments increase to $95,000 and service cost increases to $35,000. Changes in accrued postretirement benefit cost, accumulated postretirement benefit obligation, and unrecognized transition obligation in 19X4 are summarized as follows:

	Accrued Postretirement Benefit Cost	Accumulated Postretirement Benefit Obligation	Unrecognized Transition Obligation
Beginning of year	$(20,400)	$(260,400)	$240,000
Recognition of components of net periodic postretirement benefit cost:			
Service cost	(35,000)	(35,000)	
Interest cost	(20,832)	(20,832)	
Amortization of transition obligation[c]	(18,768)		(18,768)
	(74,600)	(55,832)	(18,768)
Benefit payments	95,000	95,000	
Net change	20,400	39,168	(18,768)
End of year	$ 0	$(221,232)	$221,232

[c]Amortization of the transition obligation in 19X4 includes straight-line amortization of $15,000 plus additional recognition of $3,768. The additional recognition is required because in 19X4 cumulative benefit payments subsequent to the January 1, 19X3 transition date exceed cumulative postretirement benefit cost accrued subsequent to that date (paragraph .200). The additional transition obligation required to be recognized ($3,768) is determined as follows:

	19X3	19X4
Benefit payments:		
1/1/X3 to beginning of current year		$ 45,000
Current year	$45,000	95,000
Cumulative 1/1/X3 to end of current year	$45,000	$140,000
Postretirement benefit cost recognized:		
1/1/X3 to beginning of current year		$ 65,400
Current year prior to recognition of any additional amount pursuant to paragraph .200	$65,400	70,832
Cumulative 1/1/X3 to end of current year before applying paragraph .200 constraint	65,400	136,232
Additional amount required to be recognized pursuant to paragraph .200	0	3,768
Cumulative 1/1/X3 to end of current year	$65,400	$140,000

[FAS106, ¶439]

.243 The objective of the constraint on delayed recognition of the transition obligation (paragraph .200) is to preclude slower recognition of postretirement benefit cost (as a result of applying the delayed recognition provisions of this section) than would have resulted under pay-as-you-go accounting for costs. An indication that the constraint may apply is the existence of a prepaid postretirement benefit cost after the date of transition for an enterprise that prior to the application of this section was on a pay-as-you-go basis of accounting for other postretirement benefits. For example, in paragraph .242, if the employer had not recognized the additional $3,768 of transition obligation, the employer would have had a prepaid postretirement benefit cost equal to that amount. [FAS106, ¶440]

.244 The funded status of the plan at December 31, 19X3 and 19X4 is reconciled with the amount shown in the statement of financial position at those dates as follows:

	12/31/X3	Net Change	12/31/X4
Accumulated postretirement benefit obligation	$(260,400)	$ 39,168	$(221,232)
Plan assets at fair value	0		0
Funded status	(260,400)	39,168	(221,232)
Unrecognized transition obligation	240,000	(18,768)	221,232[d]
Accrued postretirement benefit cost	$ (20,400)	$ 20,400	$ 0

[d]In 19X5, the straight-line amortization of the unrecognized transition obligation will be $14,749 ($221,232 ÷ 15 years remaining in the transition period).

[FAS106, ¶441]

.245 Paragraph .201 states that if at the measurement date for the beginning of an employer's fiscal year it is expected that additional recognition of any remaining unrecognized transition obligation will be required pursuant to paragraph .200, amortization of the transition obligation for interim reporting purposes shall be based on the amount expected to be amortized for the year, except for the effects of applying the constraint in paragraph .200 for any settlement required to be accounted for pursuant to paragraphs .182 through .186. Those effects shall be recognized when the related settlement is recognized. The effects of changes during the year in the initial assessment of whether additional recognition of the unrecognized transition obligation will be required for the year shall be recognized over the remainder of the year. The amount of the unrecognized transition obligation to be recognized for a year shall be finally determined at the end of the year (or the measurement date, if earlier) based on the constraints on delayed recognition discussed in paragraph .200; any difference between the amortization of the transition obligation recognized during interim periods and the amount required to be recognized for the year shall be recognized immediately. [FAS106, ¶442]

Illustration 4—Plan Amendments and Prior Service Cost

.246 This section requires that, at a minimum, prior service cost arising from a plan initiation or plan amendment be recognized by assigning an equal amount of the prior service cost to each remaining year of service to the full eligibility date of each plan participant active at the date of the plan initiation or amendment (paragraph .147). Consistent use of an alternative amortization method that more rapidly reduces the unrecognized prior service cost is permitted (paragraph .148). [FAS106, ¶449]

.247 Company H has a postretirement benefit plan that provides benefits to employees who render at least 20 years of service after age 35. On January 2, 19X4, Company H amends its postretirement benefit plan to increase the lifetime cap on benefits provided, resulting in unrecognized prior service cost of $750,000 (the increase in the accumulated postretirement benefit obligation as a result of the plan amendment). Amortization of that unrecognized prior service cost is illustrated in Cases 4A and 4B (paragraphs .248 through .251). [FAS106, ¶450]

Case 4A—Equal Amount Assigned to Each Future Year of Service to Full Eligibility Date

.248 The determination of the amortization of prior service cost is based on remaining years of service prior to the full eligibility date of each plan participant active at the date of the amendment but not yet fully eligible for benefits. (Refer to paragraph .453 for the definition of plan participant.) Future years of service of active employees who are not plan participants are excluded. Each remaining year of service prior to the full eligibility date of each active plan participant not yet fully eligible for benefits is assigned an equal share of the prior service cost (paragraph .147). Thus, the portion of prior service cost to be recognized in each of those future years is weighted based on the number of those plan participants expected to render service in each of those future years. [FAS106, ¶451]

.249 At the date of the amendment (January 2, 19X4), Company H has 165 employees of whom 15 are fully eligible for benefits, 10 are under age 35, and 40 are expected to terminate before becoming eligible for any benefits. Because the 10 employees under age 35 have not met the age requirements to participate in the plan (only service after age 35 is credited) and 40 employees are not expected to receive benefits under the plan, those 50 employees are not considered to be plan participants and, therefore, are excluded from the calculation. The 15 fully eligible plan participants also are excluded from the calculation because they do not have to render any additional service to earn the added benefits. The remaining 100 employees have not yet earned the full amount of the benefits they are expected to earn under the plan. Those employees are expected to become fully eligible for those benefits over the next 20 years. Their remaining years of service to full eligibility for benefits is the basis for amortization of the prior service cost. [FAS106, ¶452]

.250 The following schedules illustrate the calculation of the expected remaining years of service prior to full eligibility (Schedule 1) and the amortization schedule for recognizing the prior service cost (Schedule 2). Employees hired after the date of the plan amendment or who attain age 35 after the date of the plan amendment do not affect the amortization nor do revised estimates of remaining years of service, except those due to a curtailment.

Schedule 1—Determination of Expected Remaining Years of Service Prior to Full Eligibility as of January 2, 19X4

Indiv.	Remaining Years of Service Prior to Full Elig.	Year 19X4	19X5	19X6	19X7	19X8	19X9	19Y0	19Y1	19Y2	19Y3	19Y4	19Y5	19Y6	19Y7	19Y8	19Y9	19Z0	19Z1	19Z2	19Z3	Total Remaining Years of Service Prior to Full Elig.
A1-A4	1	4																				4
B1-B6	2	6	6																			12
C1-C5	3	5	5	5																		15
D1-D5	4	5	5	5	5																	20
E1-E7	5	7	7	7	7	7																35
F1-F5	6	5	5	5	5	5	5															30
G1-G9	7	9	9	9	9	9	9	9														63
H1-H7	8	7	7	7	7	7	7	7	7													56
I1-I5	9	5	5	5	5	5	5	5	5	5												45
J1-J5	10	5	5	5	5	5	5	5	5	5	5											50
K1-K4	11	4	4	4	4	4	4	4	4	4	4	4										44
L1-L8	12	8	8	8	8	8	8	8	8	8	8	8	8									96
M1-M8	13	8	8	8	8	8	8	8	8	8	8	8	8	8								104
N1-N5	14	5	5	5	5	5	5	5	5	5	5	5	5	5	5							70
O1-O4	15	4	4	4	4	4	4	4	4	4	4	4	4	4	4	4						60
P1-P3	16	3	3	3	3	3	3	3	3	3	3	3	3	3	3	3	3					48
Q1-Q4	17	4	4	4	5	4	4	4	4	4	4	4	4	4	4	4	4	4				68
R1-R3	18	3	3	3	3	3	3	3	3	3	3	3	3	3	3	3	3	3	3			54
S1-S2	19	2	2	2	2	2	2	2	2	2	2	2	2	2	2	2	2	2	2	2		38
T1	20	1	1	1	1	1	1	1	1	1	1	1	1	1	1	1	1	1	1	1	1	20
Service years rendered		100	96	90	85	80	73	68	59	52	47	42	38	30	22	17	13	10	6	3	1	932
Amortization fraction		$\frac{100}{932}$	$\frac{96}{932}$	$\frac{90}{932}$	$\frac{85}{932}$	$\frac{80}{932}$	$\frac{73}{932}$	$\frac{68}{932}$	$\frac{59}{932}$	$\frac{52}{932}$	$\frac{47}{932}$	$\frac{42}{932}$	$\frac{38}{932}$	$\frac{30}{932}$	$\frac{22}{932}$	$\frac{17}{932}$	$\frac{13}{932}$	$\frac{10}{932}$	$\frac{6}{932}$	$\frac{3}{932}$	$\frac{1}{932}$	

Note: To determine total remaining service years prior to full eligibility, consideration is given to the remaining number of years of service to the full eligibility date of each plan participant or group of plan participants active at the date of the plan amendment who is not yet fully eligible for benefits. For example, in 19X4, individuals A1-A4 meet the company's age and service requirements for full eligibility for the benefits they are expected to receive under the plan. Although it may be expected that those employees will work beyond 19X4, benefits are not attributed to years of service beyond their full eligibility date (paragraph .114). Refer to Case 4B, paragraph .251, for less complex amortization approaches.

Schedule 2—Amortization of Unrecognized Prior Service Cost

Year	Beginning-of-Year Balance	Amortization Rate	Amortization	End-of-Year Balance
19X4	$750,000	100/932	$80,472	$669,528
19X5	669,528	96/932	77,253	592,275
19X6	592,275	90/932	72,425	519,850
19X7	519,850	85/932	68,401	451,449
19X8	451,449	80/932	64,378	387,071
19X9	387,071	73/932	58,745	328,326
19Y0	328,326	68/932	54,721	273,605
19Y1	273,605	59/932	47,479	226,126
19Y2	226,126	52/932	41,845	184,281
19Y3	184,281	47/932	37,822	146,459
19Y4	146,459	42/932	33,798	112,661
19Y5	112,661	38/932	30,579	82,082
19Y6	82,082	30/932	24,142	57,940
19Y7	57,940	22/932	17,704	40,236
19Y8	40,236	17/932	13,680	26,556
19Y9	26,556	13/932	10,461	16,095
19Z0	16,095	10/932	8,047	8,048
19Z1	8,048	6/932	4,828	3,220
19Z2	3,220	3/932	2,414	806
19Z3	806	1/932	806	0

[FAS106, ¶453]

Case 4B—Straight-Line Amortization over Average Remaining Years of Service to Full Eligibility Date

.251 To reduce the complexity and detail of the computations shown in Case 4A (paragraph .250, Schedules 1 and 2), alternative amortization approaches that recognize prior service cost related to plan amendments more rapidly may be applied if used consistently (paragraph .148). For example, if Company H (Case 4A) elects to use straight-line amortization of prior service cost over the average remaining years of service prior to full eligibility for benefits of the active plan participants (932 future service years ÷ 100 employees = 9.32 years), the amortization would be as follows:

Year	Beginning-of-Year Balance	Amortization	End-of-Year Balance
19X4	$750,000	$80,472[a]	$669,528
19X5	669,528	80,472	589,056
19X6	589,056	80,472	508,584
19X7	508,584	80,472	428,112
19X8	428,112	80,472	347,640
19X9	347,640	80,472	267,168
19Y0	267,168	80,472	186,696
19Y1	186,696	80,472	106,224
19Y2	106,224	80,472	25,752
19Y3	25,752	25,752	0

[a]$750,000 ÷ 9.32 years = $80,472.

Note: Under this approach, the first year's amortization is the same as the first year's amortization under the weighted remaining years of service method illustrated in Case 4A (paragraph .250, Schedule 2). Thereafter, the amortization pattern will differ.

[FAS106, ¶454]

Illustration 5—Accounting for Gains and Losses and Timing of Measurements

.252 Gains and losses are changes in the amount of the accumulated postretirement benefit obligation or plan assets resulting from experience different from that assumed or changes in assumptions (paragraph .151). This illustration demonstrates the effects of gains and losses in accounting for postretirement benefits for Company I from 19X3 to 19X5. Case 5A (paragraphs .254 through .258) illustrates the accounting for a loss resulting from changes in assumptions in measuring the accumulated postretirement benefit obligation. Case 5B (paragraphs .259 through .261) illustrates the effect of a gain when the return on plan assets exceeds projections. Case 5C (paragraphs .262 through .264) illustrates the accounting in a year when both gains and losses are experienced. [FAS106, ¶455]

.253 Company I adopts [the provisions of] this section for the fiscal year beginning January 1, 19X3 and elects a December 31 measurement date (date at which the accumulated postretirement benefit obligation and plan assets are measured). Alternatively, as discussed in paragraph .167, the company could choose a measurement date not earlier than September 30. The company's accumulated postretirement benefit obligation on December 31, 19X2 is $6,000,000, and the plan is unfunded. Beginning in 19X3, and unless otherwise noted, the company funds at the end of each year an amount equal to the benefits paid that year plus the service cost and interest cost for that year. For illustrative purposes, the following assumptions are used to project changes in the accumulated postretirement benefit obligation and plan assets during the period 19X3 through 19X5:

	19X3	**19X4**	**19X5**
Discount rate	9.5%	9.0%	9.0%
Expected long-term rate of return on plan assets		10.0%	10.0%
Average remaining years of service of active plan participants	12	12	12

[FAS106, ¶456]

Case 5A—Loss on Obligation

.254 The reconciliation of the funded status of Company I's postretirement benefit plan with the amount shown in the statement of financial position at the date of transition (January 1, 19X3) follows:

	Actual 1/1/X3
Accumulated postretirement benefit obligation	$(6,000,000)
Plan assets at fair value	0
Funded status	(6,000,000)
Unrecognized transition obligation	6,000,000
(Accrued)/prepaid postretirement benefit cost	$ 0

[FAS106, ¶457]

.255 Company I elects to amortize the unrecognized transition obligation over a 20-year period rather than the average remaining service period of active plan participants at the date of transition (12 years). Projected changes in prepaid postretirement benefit cost, accumulated postretirement benefit obligation, unrecognized transition obligation, and plan assets in 19X3 are summarized as follows:

	Prepaid Postretirement Benefit Cost	Accumulated Postretirement Benefit Obligation	Unrecognized Transition Obligation	Plan Assets
Beginning of year	$ 0	$(6,000,000)	$6,000,000	$ 0
Recognition of components of net periodic postretirement benefit cost:				
Service cost	(300,000)	(300,000)		
Interest cost	(570,000)	(570,000)		
Amortization of transition obligation	(300,000)		(300,000)	
	(1,170,000)	(870,000)	(300,000)	
Assets contributed to plan	1,500,000			1,500,000
Benefit payments from plan		630,000		(630,000)
Net change	330,000	(240,000)	(300,000)	870,000
End of year—projected	$ 330,000	$(6,240,000)	$5,700,000	$ 870,000

[FAS106, ¶458]

.256 When Company I's plan assets and obligations are measured at December 31, 19X3, the accumulated postretirement benefit obligation is $760,000 greater than had been projected (a loss occurs) because the discount rate declined to 9 percent and for various other reasons not specifically identified. Company I elects to amortize amounts in excess of the "corridor" over the average remaining service period of active plan participants.[41] [FAS106, ¶459]

[41] Paragraph .154 states that, at a minimum, amortization of an unrecognized net gain or loss is included as a component of net periodic postretirement benefit cost if, as of the beginning of the year, that unrecognized net gain or loss exceeds 10 percent of the greater of the accumulated postretirement benefit obligation or market-related value of plan assets. As used herein, *amounts in excess of the corridor* refers to the portion of the unrecognized net gain or loss in excess of the greater of those defined amounts. [FAS106, ¶459, fna]

.257 The change in the funded status of the plan at December 31, 19X3 from amounts projected and the reconciliation of the funded status of the plan with the amount shown in the statement of financial position at that date follow:

	Projected 12/31/X3	Net Loss	Actual 12/31/X3
Accumulated postretirement benefit obligation	$(6,240,000)	$(760,000)	$(7,000,000)
Plan assets at fair value	870,000		870,000
Funded status	(5,370,000)	(760,000)	(6,130,000)
Unrecognized net loss		760,000	760,000
Unrecognized transition obligation	5,700,000		5,700,000
Prepaid postretirement benefit cost	$ 330,000	$ 0	$ 330,000

[FAS106, ¶460]

.258 In addition to the funded status reconciliation, the 19X3 financial statements include the following disclosure of the components of net periodic postretirement benefit cost (as required by [FAS106, ¶461] paragraph .169(d)): [FAS135, ¶4(r)]

Service cost	$ 300,000
Interest cost	570,000
Amortization of transition obligation	300,000
Net periodic postretirement benefit cost	$1,170,000

[FAS106, ¶461]

Case 5B—Gain on Assets

.259 Changes in prepaid postretirement benefit cost, accumulated postretirement benefit obligation, unrecognized transition obligation, unrecognized net loss, and plan assets are projected at the beginning of the year. That projection serves as the basis for interim accounting until a subsequent event occurs requiring remeasurement. The projection at the beginning of 19X4 follows:

	Prepaid Postretirement Benefit Cost	Accumulated Postretirement Benefit Obligation	Unrecognized Transition Obligation	Unrecognized Net Loss	Plan Assets
Beginning of year	$ 330,000	$(7,000,000)	$5,700,000	$760,000	$ 870,000
Recognition of components of net periodic postretirement benefit cost:					
Service cost	(320,000)	(320,000)			
Interest cost	(630,000)	(630,000)			
Amortization of transition obligation	(300,000)		(300,000)		
Amortization of unrecognized net loss[a]	(5,000)			(5,000)	
Expected return on plan assets[b]	87,000				87,000
	(1,168,000)	(950,000)	(300,000)	(5,000)	87,000
Assets contributed to plan	1,650,000				1,650,000
Benefit payments from plan		700,000			(700,000)
Net change	482,000	(250,000)	(300,000)	(5,000)	1,037,000
End of year—projected	$ 812,000	$(7,250,000)	$5,400,000	$755,000	$1,907,000

[a]Refer to Schedule 2 (paragraph .266) for computation.

[b]Refer to Schedule 1 (paragraph .265) for computation.

[FAS106, ¶462]

.260 When Company I's plan assets and obligations are measured at December 31, 19X4, the fair value of the plan assets is $150,000 greater than expected (an experience gain) because market performance was better than the 10 percent return that was assumed. The change in the funded status of the plan at December 31, 19X4 from amounts projected and the reconciliation of the funded status of the plan with the amount shown in the statement of financial position at that date follow:

	Projected 12/31/X4	**Net Gain**	**Actual 12/31/X4**
Accumulated postretirement benefit obligation	$(7,250,000)		$(7,250,000)
Plan assets at fair value	1,907,000	$ 150,000[c]	2,057,000
Funded status	(5,343,000)	150,000	(5,193,000)
Unrecognized net (gain) or loss	755,000	(150,000)	605,000
Unrecognized transition obligation	5,400,000		5,400,000
Prepaid postretirement benefit cost	$ 812,000	$ 0	$ 812,000

[c]Refer to Schedule 1 (paragraph .265) for computation.

[FAS106, ¶463]

.261 The 19X4 financial statements include the following disclosure of the components of net periodic postretirement benefit cost:

Service cost	$ 320,000
Interest cost	630,000
Expected return on plan assets	(87,000)
Amortization of transition obligation	300,000
Recognized net actuarial loss	5,000
Net periodic postretirement benefit cost	$1,168,000

[FAS135, ¶4(r)]

Case 5C—Loss on Assets and Gain on Obligation

.262 Projected changes in prepaid postretirement benefit cost, accumulated postretirement benefit obligation, unrecognized transition obligation, unrecognized net loss, and plan assets for 19X5 are summarized as follows:

	Prepaid Postretirement Benefit Cost	Accumulated Postretirement Benefit Obligation	Unrecognized Transition Obligation	Unrecognized Net Loss	Plan Assets
Beginning of year	$ 812,000	$(7,250,000)	$5,400,000	$605,000	$2,057,000
Recognition of components of net periodic postretirement benefit cost:					
Service cost	(360,000)	(360,000)			
Interest cost	(652,500)	(652,500)			
Amortization of transition obligation	(300,000)		(300,000)		
Amortization of unrecognized net loss[a]	0			0	
Expected return on plan assets[b]	193,700				193,700
	(1,118,800)	(1,012,500)	(300,000)	0	193,700
Assets contributed to plan	1,912,500				1,912,500
Benefit payments from plan		900,000			(900,000)
Net change	793,700	(112,500)	(300,000)	0	1,206,200
End of year—projected	$ 1,605,700	$(7,362,500)	$5,100,000	$605,000	$3,263,200

[a]Refer to Schedule 2 (paragraph .266) for computation.

[b]Refer to Schedule 1 (paragraph .265) for computation.

[FAS106, ¶465]

.263 When Company I's plan assets and obligations are measured at December 31, 19X5, both an asset loss of $220,360 and a liability gain of $237,260 are determined. The change in the funded status of the plan at December 31, 19X5 from amounts projected and the reconciliation of the funded status of the plan with the amount shown in the statement of financial position at that date follow:

	Projected 12/31/X5	Net Gain/Loss	Actual 12/31/X5
Accumulated postretirement benefit obligation	$(7,362,500)	$ 237,260	$(7,125,240)
Plan assets at fair value	3,263,200	(220,360)[c]	3,042,840
Funded status	(4,099,300)	16,900	(4,082,400)
Unrecognized net (gain) or loss	605,000	(16,900)	588,100
Unrecognized transition obligation	5,100,000		5,100,000
Prepaid postretirement benefit cost	$ 1,605,700	$ 0	$ 1,605,700

[c]Refer to Schedule 1 (paragraph .265) for computation.

[FAS106, ¶466]

.264 The 19X5 financial statements include the following disclosure of the components of net periodic postretirement benefit cost:

Service cost	$ 360,000
Interest cost	652,500
Expected return on plan assets	(193,700)
Amortization of transition obligation	300,000
Net periodic postretirement benefit cost	$1,118,800

[FAS135, ¶4(r)]

Supporting Schedules

Schedule 1—Plan Assets

.265 This section requires use of an assumption about the long-term rate of return on plan assets and a market-related value of plan assets to calculate the expected return on plan assets. If the fund holding plan assets is a taxable entity, the expected long-term rate of return on plan assets is net of estimated income taxes, and the nonbenefit liability for accrued income taxes reduces plan assets. This section defines market-related asset value as either fair value or a calculated value that recognizes changes in fair value in a systematic and rational manner over not more than five years (paragraph .152). This schedule reflects the calculation of market-related value, the fair value of plan assets, the actual return on plan assets, and the deferred asset gain or loss for the year (the difference between actual and expected return on plan assets included in the net amortization and deferral component of net periodic postretirement benefit cost).

	19X3	19X4	19X5
Expected long-term rate of return on plan assets		10.0%	10.0%
Beginning balance, market-related value[a]	$ 0	$ 870,000	$1,937,000
Contributions to plan (end of year)	1,500,000	1,650,000	1,912,500
Benefits paid by plan	(630,000)	(700,000)	(900,000)
Expected return on plan assets		87,000	193,700
	870,000	1,907,000	3,143,200
20% of each of last 5 years' asset gains (losses)		30,000	(14,072)
Ending balance, market-related value	$ 870,000	$1,937,000	$3,129,128
Beginning balance, fair value of plan assets	$ 0	$ 870,000	$2,057,000
Contributions to plan	1,500,000	1,650,000	1,912,500
Benefits paid	(630,000)	(700,000)	(900,000)
Actual return (loss) on plan assets[b]	0	237,000	(26,660)
Ending balance, fair value of plan assets	$ 870,000	$2,057,000	$3,042,840
Deferred asset gain (loss) for year[c]	$ 0	$ 150,000	$ (220,360)
Gain (loss) not included in ending balance market-related value[d]	$ 0	$ 120,000	$ (86,288)

[a]This example uses an approach that adds in 20% of each of the last 5 years' gains or losses.

[b]Refer to Schedule 3 (paragraph .267) for computation.

[c](Actual return on plan assets) – (expected return on plan assets).

[d](Ending balance, fair value of plan assets) – (ending balance, market-related value of plan assets).

[FAS106, ¶468]

Schedule 2—Test for Amortization of Unrecognized Net Gain or Loss

.266 This section generally does not require recognition of any of the gain or loss in the period in which it arises and permits a minimum amortization of an unrecognized net gain or loss whereby the net amount in excess of the "corridor" is amortized over the average remaining service period of active plan participants (paragraph .154 and paragraph .256, footnote 41). That allows a reasonable opportunity for gains and losses to offset each other without affecting net periodic postretirement benefit cost.

	19X3	19X4	19X5
10% of beginning balance of accumulated postretirement benefit obligation	$600,000	$700,000	$725,000
10% of beginning balance of market-related value of plan assets[e]	$ 0	$ 87,000	$193,700
Greater of the above	$600,000	$700,000	$725,000
Unrecognized net (gain) loss at beginning of year		$760,000	$605,000
Asset gain (loss) not included in beginning balance of market-related value[f]		0	120,000
Amount subject to amortization		$760,000	$725,000
Amount in excess of the corridor subject to amortization		$ 60,000	$ 0
Divided by average remaining service period (years)		12	
Required amortization		$ 5,000	

[e]Refer to Schedule 1 (paragraph .265) for calculation of market-related value of plan assets.

[f]Refer to Schedule 1 (paragraph .265) for calculation of gain or loss not included in prior year's ending balance market-related value.

[FAS106, ¶469]

Schedule 3—Determination of Actual Return or Loss on Plan Assets

.267 The determination of the actual return or loss on plan assets component of net periodic postretirement benefit cost is as follows:

	19X3	19X4	19X5
Plan assets at fair value, beginning of year	$ 0	$ 870,000	$ 2,057,000
Plus: assets contributed to plan	1,500,000	1,650,000	1,912,500
Less: benefit payments from plan	(630,000)	(700,000)	(900,000)
	870,000	1,820,000	3,069,500
Less: plan assets at fair value, end of year	(870,000)	(2,057,000)	(3,042,840)
Actual (return) loss on plan assets	$ 0	$ (237,000)	$ 26,660

[FAS106, ¶470]

.268 [Deleted 2/99 because of FASB Statement 135, *Rescission of FASB Statement No. 75 and Technical Corrections.*]

Illustration 6—Defined-Dollar Capped Plans

.269 The following cases (6A and 6B, paragraphs .270 through .275) demonstrate the operation of defined-dollar capped plans and the possible effect of the "cap" on projecting costs for purposes of measuring the accumulated postretirement benefit obligation and net periodic postretirement benefit cost. The examples are simplified and illustrate only one aspect of the measurement process (paragraph .110 and paragraph .128, footnote 16). [FAS106, ¶472]

Case 6A—Dollar Cap Defined on Individual Coverage

.270 Company J sponsors a postretirement health care plan for its salaried employees. The plan has an annual limitation (a "cap") on the dollar amount of the employer's share of the cost of covered benefits incurred by a plan participant. The retiree is responsible, therefore, for the amount by which the cost of the benefit coverage under the plan incurred during a year exceeds that cap. The company adjusts the cap annually for the effects of inflation. For 19X3, the cap is $1,500; the inflation adjustment in 19X4 and 19X5 is assumed to be 4 percent. The employer's health care cost trend rate assumption is 13 percent for 19X4 and 12 percent for 19X5. [FAS106, ¶473]

.271 The employer's projected cost of providing benefit coverage in 19X3 through 19X5 for a 67-year-old retiree follows. Similar projections are made for each age at which a plan participant is expected to receive benefits under the plan. In this example, the incurred claims cost exceeds the cap on the employer's share of the cost in each year.

	Expected Cost for 67-Year-Old Retiree		
	19X3	**19X4**	**19X5**
Gross eligible charges	$3,065	$ 3,463	$ 3,879
Medicare[a]	(890)	(1,003)	(1,125)
Deductible/coinsurance	(325)	(340)	(355)
Incurred claims cost	$1,850	$ 2,120	$ 2,399
Annual cap on employer's cost	$1,500	$ 1,560	$ 1,622
Employer's share of incurred claims cost	$1,500	$ 1,560	$ 1,622
Retiree's share of gross eligible charges[b]	$ 675	$ 900	$ 1,132

[a]The change in Medicare reflects the portion of the gross eligible charges for which Medicare is responsible under enacted Medicare legislation.

[b]Deductible/coinsurance plus share of incurred claims: 19X3—[$325 + ($1,850 – $1,500)]; 19X4—[$340 + ($2,120 – $1,560)]; 19X5—[$355 + ($2,399 – $1,622)].

[FAS106, ¶474]

.272 If, based on the health care cost trend rate assumptions, the employer's share of costs for each plan participant is not expected to be less than the cap in the future, Company J could measure its expected postretirement benefit obligation by projecting the annual cap. However, if per capita claims data for some plan participants or estimates of the health care cost trend rate indicate that in the future the employer's share of the incurred claims cost will be less than the cap for at least some plan participants, the employer's obligation is to be measured as described in paragraphs .129 through .137. [FAS106, ¶475]

Case 6B—Dollar Cap Defined in the Aggregate for the Retiree Group

.273 Company K sponsors a contributory postretirement health care plan for its hourly employees. The plan has an annual limitation (a "cap") on the dollar amount of the employer's share of the cost of covered benefits incurred by the retiree group as a whole. The Company agrees to bear annual costs equal to a specified dollar amount ($1,500 in 19X3) multiplied by the number of retired plan participants (the employer contribution); participating retirees are required to contribute a stated amount each year ($1,000 in 19X3). The cap on the employer's share of annual costs and the retirees' contribution rates are increased 5 percent annually. The shortfall in a year (the amount by which incurred claims cost exceed the combined employer and retiree contributions) is initially borne by the employer but is passed back to retirees in the subsequent year through supplemental retiree contributions for that year (a retrospective adjustment). [FAS106, ¶476]

.274 The employer projects the aggregate cost of benefits expected to be paid to current plan participants (40 retirees) in each future period as follows:

	19X3	19X4	19X5
Gross eligible charges	$160,000	$215,000	$197,000
Medicare	(46,500)	(62,350)	(57,300)
Deductible/coinsurance	(20,750)	(27,440)	(24,700)
Incurred claims cost	$ 92,750	$125,210	$115,000
Retiree contributions[a]	$ 40,000	$ 42,000	$ 44,080
Maximum employer contribution[b]	60,000	63,000	66,160
	$100,000	$105,000	$110,240
Shortfall (to be recovered by additional retiree contributions in subsequent year)		$ 20,210	$ 4,760
Supplemental contribution from retirees due to shortfall in prior year			$ 20,210

[a]Per retiree: 19X3—$1,000; 19X4—$1,050; 19X5—$1,102.

[b]Per retiree: 19X3—$1,500; 19X4—$1,575; 19X5—$1,654.

[FAS106, ¶477]

.275 If, as in this example, retirees absorb the entire shortfall in annual contributions and if there is a projected shortfall for all future years, the employer could measure its expected postretirement benefit obligation by projecting its annual contribution (contribution rate × expected number of retirees = expected obligation for the year). [FAS106, ¶478]

Illustration 7—Disclosure Requirements

.276 The following cases provide examples that illustrate postretirement benefit disclosures. The items presented in these examples [relate solely to postretirement benefit plans and] have been included for illustrative purposes [only]. However, items may be combined if individually immaterial. [Companies that have pension and other postretirement benefit plans may also elect to present the required disclosures for their plans] in a parallel format in a single note to the financial statements. [For an example of this type of disclosure refer to Illustration 6, Case 1 of Section P16. That example presents the same postretirement benefits disclosure as Case 7A in paragraph .277 below combined with the relevant pension disclosures.] [FAS132, ¶61]

Case 7A—Disclosures about Postretirement Benefit Plans

.277 The following illustrates the 20X2 financial statement disclosures for an employer (Company A) with multiple postretirement benefit plans. During 20X2, the employer had an acquisition and made amendments to the plans.

	Postretirement Benefits	
	20X2	**20X1**
Change in benefit obligation		
Benefit obligation at beginning of year	$ 738	$ 700
Service cost	36	32
Interest cost	65	63
Plan participants' contributions	20	13
Amendments	75	
Actuarial gain	(24)	
Acquisition	600	
Benefits paid	(90)	(70)
Benefit obligation at end of year	1,420	738
Change in plan assets		
Fair value of plan assets at beginning of year	206	87
Actual return on plan assets	(3)	24
Acquisition	25	
Employer contribution	171	152
Plan participants' contributions	20	13
Benefits paid	(90)	(70)
Fair value of plan assets at end of year	329	206
Funded status	(1,091)	(532)
Unrecognized net actuarial loss	59	60
Unrecognized prior service cost	585	540
Prepaid (accrued) benefit cost	$ (447)	$ 68

	Postretirement Benefits	
	20X2	20X1
Weighted-average assumptions as of December 31		
Discount rate	9.00%	9.00%
Expected return on plan assets	10.00	10.00

For measurement purposes, a 10 percent annual rate of increase in the per capita cost of covered health care benefits was assumed for 20X3. The rate was assumed to decrease gradually to 4 percent for 20X9 and remain at that level thereafter.

	Postretirement Benefits	
	20X2	20X1
Components of net periodic benefit cost		
Service cost	$ 36	$ 32
Interest cost	65	63
Expected return on plan assets	(21)	(9)
Amortization of prior service cost	30	30
Recognized net actuarial loss	1	1
Net periodic benefit cost	$111	$117

Company A acquired FV Industries on December 31, 20X2, including its postretirement benefit plans. The company's plans were amended on December 31, 20X2, to establish parity with the benefits provided by FV Industries.

The company has multiple nonpension postretirement benefit plans. The health care plans are contributory, with participants' contributions adjusted annually; the life insurance plans are noncontributory. The accounting for the health care plans anticipates future cost-sharing changes to the written plan that are consistent with the company's expressed intent to increase retiree contributions each year by 50 percent of the excess of the expected general inflation rate over 6 percent. On December 31, 20X2, the company amended its postretirement health care plans to provide long-term care coverage.

Assumed health care cost trend rates have a significant effect on the amounts reported for the health care plans. A one-percentage-point change in assumed health care cost trend rates would have the following effects:

	1-Percentage-Point Increase	1-Percentage-Point Decrease
Effect on total of service and interest cost components	$ 22	$ (20)
Effect on postretirement benefit obligation	173	(156)

[FAS132, ¶62]

Case 7B—Alternative Disclosure for a Nonpublic Entity

.278 The following illustrates the 20X2 financial statement disclosures that could be provided by Company A if it were a nonpublic entity.

	Postretirement Benefits	
	20X2	**20X1**
Benefit obligation at December 31	$ 1,420	$ 738
Fair value of plan assets at December 31	329	206
Funded status	$(1,091)	$ (532)
Prepaid (accrued) benefit cost recognized in the statement of financial position	$ (447)	$ 68

	Postretirement Benefits	
	20X2	**20X1**
Weighted-average assumptions as of December 31		
Discount rate	9.00%	9.00%
Expected return on plan assets	10.00	10.00

For measurement purposes, a 10 percent annual rate of increase in the per capita cost of covered health care benefits was assumed for 20X3. The rate was assumed to decrease gradually to 4 percent for 20X9 and remain at that level thereafter.

	Postretirement Benefits	
	20X2	**20X1**
Benefit cost	$111	$117
Employer contribution	171	152
Plan participants' contributions	20	13
Benefits paid	90	70

The company acquired FV Industries on December 31, 20X2, increasing the postretirement benefit obligation by $600 and related plan assets by $25. Amendments during the year to the company's plans increased the postretirement benefit obligation by $75. [FAS132, ¶64]

279-.280 [Deleted 2/98 because of FASB Statement 132, *Employers' Disclosures about Pensions and Other Postretirement Benefits*.]

Illustration 8—Accounting for Settlements

.281 This section provides for delayed recognition of the effects of a plan initiation or a plan amendment, the transition obligation or transition asset, and gains or losses arising in the ordinary course of operations. In certain circumstances, however, recognition of some or all of those previously delayed amounts is appropriate. Settlements are events that may require income or expense recognition of certain previously unrecognized amounts and adjustments to liabilities or assets recognized in the employer's statement of financial position. The settlement of all or part of the accumulated postretirement benefit obligation is the event that requires recognition of all or part of a previously unrecognized net gain or loss and unrecognized transition asset. A settlement also may accelerate recognition of a transition obligation under the constraint in paragraph .200 (paragraphs .184 and .185). The following cases (8A through 8C, paragraphs .282 through .292) illustrate the accounting for settlements in various circumstances. [FAS106, ¶484]

Case 8A—Settlement When an Unrecognized Transition Obligation Exists

.282 Company L sponsors a postretirement life insurance plan. On January 1, 19X3, the company adopts [the provisions of] this section; prior to that date it accounted for postretirement benefits on a pay-as-you-go (cash) basis. On December 31, 19X4, Company L settles the accumulated postretirement benefit obligation for its current retirees ($70,000) through the purchase of nonparticipating life insurance contracts. [FAS106, ¶485]

.283 In accounting for the settlement, Company L must determine whether recognition of an additional amount of any unrecognized transition obligation is required pursuant to the constraint on delayed recognition of the transition obligation (paragraphs .200 and .201). At December 31, 19X4, the cumulative postretirement benefit cost accrued subsequent to the date of transition exceeds the cumulative benefit payments subsequent to that date (including payments made pursuant to the settlement) in this example; thus, the constraint on delayed recognition of the transition obligation is not operative. The results of the settlement are as follows:

	December 31, 19X4		
	Before Settlement	**Settlement**	**After Settlement**
Accumulated postretirement benefit obligation	$(257,000)	$ 70,000	$(187,000)
Plan assets at fair value	73,000	(70,000)[a]	3,000
Funded status	(184,000)	0	(184,000)
Unrecognized net gain	(44,575)	12,124[a]	(32,451)
Unrecognized prior service cost	33,000		33,000
Unrecognized transition obligation	195,000	(12,124)[a]	182,876
Accrued postretirement benefit cost	$ (575)	$ 0	$ (575)

[a]The maximum settlement gain subject to recognition is the unrecognized net gain subsequent to transition plus any unrecognized transition asset ($44,575 + $0 = $44,575) (paragraph .184). If, as in this case, only part of the accumulated postretirement benefit obligation is settled, a pro rata portion of the maximum gain based on the relationship of the accumulated postretirement benefit obligation settled to the total accumulated postretirement benefit obligation ($70,000 ÷ $257,000 or 27.2%) is subject to recognition. That amount ($44,575 × 27.2% = $12,124) must first reduce any unrecognized transition obligation; any excess is recognized in income in the current period (paragraph .185). In this case, the settlement gain is entirely offset against the unrecognized transition obligation.

[FAS106, ¶486]

Case 8B—Settlement When an Unrecognized Transition Asset Exists

.284 Company M sponsors a postretirement life insurance plan. On January 2, 19X5, Company M settles the accumulated postretirement benefit obligation for its current retirees ($200,000) through the purchase of nonparticipating life insurance contracts. [FAS106, ¶487]

.285 Pursuant to paragraphs .184 and .185, a settlement gain of $78,506 is recognized, determined as follows:

	January 2, 19X5		
	Before Settlement	Settlement	After Settlement
Accumulated postretirement benefit obligation	$(257,000)	$ 200,000	$ (57,000)
Plan assets at fair value	350,900	(200,000)	150,900
Funded status	93,900	0	93,900
Unrecognized net gain	(44,575)	34,679[a]	(9,896)
Unrecognized prior service cost	33,000		33,000
Unrecognized transition asset	(56,333)	43,827[a]	(12,506)
Prepaid postretirement benefit cost	$ 25,992	$ 78,506	$104,498

[a]The maximum settlement gain is measured as the unrecognized net gain subsequent to transition plus the unrecognized transition asset ($44,575 + $56,333 = $100,908) (paragraph .184). Since only a portion of the accumulated postretirement benefit obligation is settled, a pro rata portion of the maximum gain based on the relationship of the accumulated postretirement benefit obligation settled to the total accumulated postretirement benefit obligation ($200,000 ÷ $257,000 or 77.8%) is subject to recognition. That amount ($100,908 × 77.8% = $78,506) must first reduce any unrecognized transition obligation ($0); any excess is recognized in income in the current period (paragraph .185). In this case, the entire settlement gain of $78,506 is recognized in income. The transition constraint of paragraph .200 that requires additional recognition of a *transition obligation* in certain circumstances is not applicable because there is an unrecognized *transition asset.*

[FAS106, ¶488]

Case 8C—Effect of Mid-Year Settlement on Transition Constraint

.286 A settlement is an event that requires remeasurement of the accumulated postretirement benefit obligation prior to the settlement. This case illustrates the accounting for a settlement of part of the accumulated postretirement benefit obligation that occurs mid-year and the interaction between that event and other provisions of the section, such as the constraint on delayed recognition of the transition obligation. [FAS106, ¶489]

.287 Company N adopts [the provisions of] this section for the fiscal year beginning January 1, 19X3 and elects a year-end (December 31) measurement date. At the date of transition, the company's accumulated postretirement benefit obligation for its postretirement life insurance plan is $6,000,000, and there are no plan assets. In 19X3, the company establishes a policy of funding at the end of each year an amount equal to the benefits paid during the year plus the service and interest cost for the year. Benefits are paid at the end of each year and in 19X3 are $630,000, which is less than the net periodic postretirement benefit cost accrued for the year ($1,170,000); thus, no additional transition obligation is recognized pursuant to paragraph .200. Company N elects to amortize net unrecognized gains and losses in excess of the "corridor" over the average remaining service period of plan participants (paragraph .154 and paragraph .256, footnote 41). [FAS106, ¶490]

.288 At the beginning of 19X4, Company N projects the life insurance benefits expected to be paid in 19X4 to retirees' beneficiaries to determine whether recognition of an additional amount of the unrecognized transition obligation will be required (paragraph .201). Although Company N is considering settling a portion of the accumulated postretirement benefit obligation, the effects of the settlement are not included in the projection because plan settlements are not anticipated for measurement or recognition prior to their occurrence. The projection indicates that no additional amount is required to be recognized. On June 30, 19X4, Company N contributes additional funds ($1,430,000) and settles a portion ($1,900,000) of the accumulated postretirement benefit obligation for its current retirees through the purchase of nonparticipating life insurance contracts. [FAS106, ¶491]

.289 The changes in the funded status of the plan during the first six months of the year and a reconciliation of the funded status of the plan with the amount shown in the statement of financial position immediately prior to the settlement are as follows:

	Actual 12/31/X3	Six Months Postretirement Benefit Cost	Assets Contributed to Plan	Effects of Remeasurement Immediately before Settlement	Before Settlement 6/30/X4
Accumulated postretirement benefit obligation	$(6,600,000)	$(457,000)[a]		$ 420,000[b]	$(6,637,000)
Plan assets at fair value	870,000	43,500[c]	$1,430,000	0[b]	2,343,500
Funded status	(5,730,000)	(413,500)	1,430,000	420,000	(4,293,500)
Unrecognized net (gain) or loss	360,000	0		(420,000)[b]	(60,000)
Unrecognized transition obligation	5,700,000	(150,000)			5,550,000
Prepaid postretirement benefit cost	$ 330,000	$(563,500)	$1,430,000	$ 0	$ 1,196,500[d]

[a]Represents 6 months' service cost of $160,000 and interest cost of $297,000 on the accumulated postretirement benefit obligation for 19X4, assuming a 9% discount rate.

[b]A gain results from the remeasurement of the accumulated postretirement benefit obligation immediately prior to the settlement as a result of a change in the assumed discount rates based on the interest rates inherent in the price at which the accumulated postretirement benefit obligation for the retirees will be settled. No gain or loss results from remeasurement of plan assets.

[c]Represents 6 months' return on plan assets, assuming a 10% return.

[d]Because there is a settlement (treated as a benefit payment) and a prepaid asset exists as a result of providing the funds to effect that settlement, the constraint on delayed recognition of the transition obligation pursuant to paragraph .200 may be applicable. The test to determine whether additional recognition is necessary should be done based on amounts for the full year (paragraph .291).

[FAS106, ¶492]

.290 In accounting for a settlement, an employer must determine whether recognition of an additional amount of any unrecognized transition obligation is required pursuant to the constraint on delayed recognition (paragraph .200). Any additional transition obligation required to be recognized as a result of a settlement is recognized when the related settlement is recognized (paragraph .201) as illustrated in the following table. Detailed calculations are presented in paragraph .291.

	June 30, 19X4			
	Before Settlement	Settlement	Recognition of Transition Obligation	After Settlement
Accumulated postretirement benefit obligation	$(6,637,000)	$ 1,900,000		$(4,737,000)
Plan assets at fair value	2,343,500	(1,900,000)		443,500
Funded status	(4,293,500)	0		(4,293,500)
Unrecognized net (gain) or loss	(60,000)	17,160[e]		(42,840)
Unrecognized transition obligation	5,550,000	(17,160)[e]	$(718,822)	4,814,018
Prepaid postretirement benefit cost	$ 1,196,500	$ 0	$(718,822)	$ 477,678

[e]The maximum settlement gain subject to recognition is the unrecognized net gain subsequent to transition plus any unrecognized transition asset ($60,000 + $0 = $60,000). If, as in this case, only part of the accumulated postretirement benefit obligation is settled, a pro rata portion of the maximum gain based on the relationship of the accumulated postretirement benefit obligation settled to the total accumulated postretirement benefit obligation ($1,900,000 ÷ $6,637,000 or 28.6%) is subject to recognition. That amount ($60,000 × 28.6% = $17,160) must first reduce any unrecognized transition obligation (paragraph .185); any excess is recognized. In this situation, the settlement gain is entirely offset against the unrecognized transition obligation.

[FAS106, ¶493]

.291 When a settlement occurs in the middle of the year, as in this example, the additional transition obligation to be recognized, if any, pursuant to the constraint in paragraph .200 is determined based on projected amounts for the full year. In this case, at June 30, 19X4, cumulative benefit payments from the date of transition (January 1, 19X3) to December 31, 19X4 are projected to exceed cumulative postretirement benefit cost accrued for that same period as illustrated in the following table. The additional transition obligation to be recognized is the amount by which cumulative benefit payments exceed cost accrued, or $718,822.

	Projected 12/31/X4
Benefit payments:	
1/1/X3 to beginning of 19X4	$ 630,000
19X4 excluding settlement	410,000
Settlement	1,900,000
Cumulative benefit payments	2,940,000
Postretirement benefit cost recognized:	
1/1/X3 to beginning of 19X4	$1,170,000
19X4	1,051,178[f]
Cumulative cost recognized	2,221,178
Benefit payments in excess of cost recognized	$ 718,822

[f]$563,500 for period 1/1/X4 through 6/30/X4 plus $487,678 for period 7/1/X4 through 12/31/X4. The net postretirement benefit cost of $487,678 recognized in the second half of 19X4 (paragraph .292) includes amortization ($130,108) of the unrecognized transition obligation that remains after recognizing an additional portion ($718,822) of the unrecognized transition obligation pursuant to paragraph .200. Because determination of the additional portion of the transition obligation to be recognized and the transition obligation amortized in the second half of 19X4 are interrelated, those amounts are determined in a single computation that is intended to result in unrecognized transition obligation at the end of the year that appropriately reflects the constraint of paragraph .200.

[FAS106, ¶494]

.292 After the settlement, net periodic postretirement benefit cost for the remainder of the year is remeasured. The projected funded status of the plan reconciled to the projected amounts to be shown in the statement of financial position follows:

	After Settlement 6/30/X4	Six Months Postretirement Benefit Cost	Benefit Payments	Assets Contributed to Plan	Projected 12/31/X4
Accumulated postretirement benefit obligation	$(4,737,000)	$(379,745)[g]	$ 410,000		$(4,706,745)
Plan assets at fair value	443,500	22,175[h]	(410,000)	$1,246,745	1,302,420
Funded status	(4,293,500)	(357,570)	0	1,246,745	(3,404,325)
Unrecognized net gain	(42,840)	0			(42,840)
Unrecognized transition obligation	4,814,018	(130,108)[i]			4,683,910
(Accrued)/prepaid postretirement cost	$ 477,678	$(487,678)	$ 0	$1,246,745	$ 1,236,745

[g]Represents 6 months' service cost of $150,000 and interest cost of $229,745 on the accumulated postretirement benefit obligation, assuming a 9.7% discount rate.

[h]Represents 6 months' return on plan assets, assuming a 10% return.

[i]Unrecognized transition obligation at 6/30/X4 of $4,814,018 ÷ 18.5 years remaining in amortization period = $260,217; half-year amortization = $130,108.

[FAS106, ¶495]

Illustration 9—Accounting for Curtailments

.293 This section provides for delayed recognition of the effects of a plan initiation or a plan amendment, the transition obligation or transition asset, and gains or losses arising in the ordinary course of operations. In certain circumstances, however, recognition of some or all of those previously delayed amounts is appropriate. Curtailments are events that may require income or expense recognition of certain previously unrecognized amounts and adjustments to liabilities or assets recognized in the employer's statement of financial position. [FAS106, ¶496]

.294 A curtailment is an event that significantly reduces the expected years of future service of active plan participants or eliminates the accrual of defined benefits for some or all of the future services of a significant number of active plan participants. Such a reduction or elimination raises doubt about the continued existence of the future economic benefits of prior plan amendments. Therefore, an appropriate portion of the remaining unrecognized prior service cost should be recognized when it is probable that a curtailment will occur, the effects are reasonably estimable, and the estimated effects of the curtailment are a net loss. When the estimated effects of a curtailment are a net gain, the gain should be recognized in income when the related employees terminate or the plan suspension or amendment is adopted (paragraphs .189 through .191). For purposes of measuring those effects, any remaining unrecognized transition obligation is treated as unrecognized prior service cost. The following cases (9A and 9B, paragraphs .295 through .298) illustrate the accounting for curtailments. [FAS106, ¶497]

Case 9A—Curtailment When an Unrecognized Gain and an Unrecognized Transition Obligation Exist

.295 Company P sponsors a postretirement benefit plan. On October 29, 19X4, Company P decides to reduce its operations by terminating a significant number of employees effective December 31, 19X4. On October 29, 19X4, it is expected that a curtailment gain will result from the termination. A consequence of the curtailment is a significant reduction in the number of employees accumulating benefits under the plan. The *remaining years of expected service* associated with those terminated employees who were plan participants at the date of transition is 22 percent of the remaining years of service of all plan participants at the date of transition. The *remaining years of service prior to full eligibility* associated with those terminated employees who were plan participants at the date of a prior plan amendment is 18 percent of the remaining years of service of all plan participants at the date of that plan amendment. [FAS106, ¶498]

.296 The sum of the effects of the plan curtailment is a gain of $5,160 that should be recognized in income when the related employees terminate (paragraph .191). That gain is determined as follows:

	December 31, 19X4		
	Before Curtailment	Curtailment	After Curtailment
Accumulated postretirement benefit obligation	$(257,000)	$ 54,000[a]	$(203,000)
Plan assets at fair value	73,000		73,000
Funded status	(184,000)	54,000	(130,000)
Unrecognized net gain	(44,575)		(44,575)
Unrecognized prior service cost	33,000	(5,940)[a]	27,060
Unrecognized transition obligation	195,000	(42,900)[a]	152,100
(Accrued)/prepaid postretirement benefit cost	$ (575)	$ 5,160	$ 4,585

[a]The effect of the curtailment consists of two components:

1. The unrecognized transition obligation and unrecognized prior service cost associated with remaining years of service no longer expected to be rendered—measured as 22% (reduction in the remaining years of expected service associated with those terminated employees who were plan participants at the date of transition) of the unrecognized transition obligation of $195,000 ($42,900) and 18% (reduction in the remaining years of service prior to full eligibility for benefits associated with those terminated employees who were plan participants at the date of a prior plan amendment) of the unrecognized prior service cost of $33,000 related to that amendment ($5,940) (paragraph .189)
2. The gain from the decrease in the accumulated postretirement benefit obligation of $54,000 (due to the termination of employees whose accumulated benefits were not vested under the plan) in excess of the unrecognized net loss of $0, or $54,000 (paragraph .190(a)).

[FAS106, ¶499]

Case 9B—Curtailment Related to a Disposal of a Portion of the Business and an Unrecognized Loss and Unrecognized Transition Obligation Exist

.297 Company R sponsors a postretirement benefit plan. On December 31, 19X4, Company R sells a portion of its business at a gain of $100,000 before considering the effect of the related curtailment of its postretirement benefit plan. In connection with the sale, the number of employees accumulating benefits under the plan is significantly reduced; thus, a curtailment occurs. The *remaining years of expected service* associated with the terminated employees who were plan participants at the date of transition is 22 percent of the remaining years of service of all plan participants at the date of transition. The *remaining years of service prior to full eligibility* associated with the terminated employees who were plan participants at the date of that prior plan amendment is 18 percent of the remaining years of service of all plan participants at the date of that plan amendment. [FAS106, ¶500]

.298 The sum of the effects of the plan curtailment is a loss of $36,265 that should be recognized with the gain of $100,000 associated with Company R's sale of a portion of its business. The loss is determined as follows:

	December 31, 19X4		
	Before Curtailment	Curtailment	After Curtailment
Accumulated postretirement benefit obligation	$(343,000)	$ 54,000[a]	$(289,000)
Plan assets at fair value	73,000		73,000
Funded status	(270,000)	54,000	(216,000)
Unrecognized net loss	41,425	(41,425)[a]	0
Unrecognized prior service cost	33,000	(5,940)[a]	27,060
Unrecognized transition obligation	195,000	(42,900)[a]	152,100
Accrued postretirement benefit cost	$ (575)	$(36,265)	$ (36,840)

[a]The effect of the curtailment consists of two components:

1. The unrecognized transition obligation and unrecognized prior service cost associated with remaining years of service no longer expected to be rendered—measured as 22% (reduction in the remaining years of expected service associated with those terminated employees who were plan participants at the date of transition) of the unrecognized transition obligation of $195,000 ($42,900) and 18% (reduction in the remaining years of service prior to full eligibility for benefits associated with those terminated employees who were plan participants at the date of a prior plan amendment) of the unrecognized prior service cost of $33,000 related to that amendment ($5,940) (paragraph .189)
2. The gain from the decrease in the accumulated postretirement benefit obligation of $54,000 (due to the termination of employees whose accumulated benefits were not vested under the plan) in excess of the unrecognized net loss of $41,425, or $12,575 (paragraph .190(a)).

[FAS106, ¶501]

Illustration 10—Accounting for a Partial Settlement and a Full Curtailment That Occur as a Direct Result of a Sale of a Line of Business

.299 Company S sells a line of business on December 31, 19X4; prior to that date, the company had no formal plan for disposal of those operations. Company S has a separate postretirement benefit plan that provides health care benefits to retirees of the division that is sold. In connection with that sale, (a) all of the employees of that division are terminated by Company S resulting in no further accumulation of benefits under the postretirement benefit plan (a full curtailment), (b) most of the terminated employees are hired by the acquiring company (some terminated employees fully eligible for benefits elect to retire immediately), (c) an accumulated postretirement benefit obligation of $80,000 for postretirement benefits related to the hired employees is assumed by the acquiring company (a partial settlement, since the obligation for current retirees is retained by Company S), and (d) plan assets of $100,000, representing $80,000 for the settlement of the accumulated postretirement benefit obligation and $20,000 as an excess contribution, are transferred from the plan to the acquiring company. A $300,000 gain from the sale is calculated before considering the related effects on the plan. [FAS106, ¶502]

.300 The employer's accounting policy is to determine the effects of a curtailment before determining the effects of a settlement when both events occur simultaneously. Pursuant to paragraph .189, the unrecognized prior service cost associated with the portion of the future years of service that had been expected to be rendered, but as a result of a curtailment are no longer expected to be rendered, is a loss. When a full curtailment occurs, the entire remaining unrecognized prior service cost and unrecognized transition obligation is a loss because there are no future years of service to be rendered. [FAS106, ¶503]

.301 The net loss from the curtailment is $228,000, which is recognized with the $300,000 gain resulting from the disposal of the division. The effect of the curtailment is determined as follows:

	December 31, 19X4		
	Before Curtailment	**Curtailment-Related Effects Resulting from Sale**	**After Curtailment**
Accumulated postretirement benefit obligation	$(257,000)	$ (10,000)[a]	$(267,000)
Plan assets at fair value	110,000		110,000
Funded status	(147,000)	(10,000)	(157,000)
Unrecognized net gain	(49,575)	10,000[a]	(39,575)
Unrecognized prior service cost	33,000	(33,000)[b]	0
Unrecognized transition obligation	195,000	(195,000)[c]	0
(Accrued)/prepaid postretirement benefit cost	$ 31,425	$(228,000)	$(196,575)

[a]The increase in the accumulated postretirement benefit obligation as a result of the fully eligible employees retiring earlier than expected is a loss of $10,000. That loss reduces the unrecognized net gain of $49,575; any excess (none in this case) would be recognized as the effect of a curtailment (paragraph .190).

[b]Measured as 100% (reduction in the remaining years of service prior to full eligibility for benefits associated with those terminated employees who were plan participants at the date of a prior plan amendment) of the unrecognized prior service cost of $33,000 related to that amendment (paragraph .189).

[c]Measured as 100% (reduction in the remaining years of expected service associated with those terminated employees who were plan participants at the date of transition) of the unrecognized transition obligation of $195,000 (paragraph .189).

[FAS106, ¶504]

.302 The $8,128 loss related to the settlement and transfer of plan assets that is recognized with the gain from the sale is determined as follows:

	December 31, 19X4		
	After Curtailment	**Settlement and Transfer of Plan Assets**	**After Settlement**
Accumulated postretirement benefit obligation	$(267,000)	$ 80,000[d]	$(187,000)
Plan assets at fair value	110,000	(100,000)[d]	10,000
Funded status	(157,000)	(20,000)	(177,000)
Unrecognized net gain	(39,575)	11,872[e]	(27,703)
Unrecognized prior service cost	0		0
Unrecognized transition obligation	0		0
Accrued postretirement benefit cost	$(196,575)	$ (8,128)	$(204,703)

[d]The accumulated postretirement benefit obligation for the employees hired by the purchaser is determined to be $80,000 and is settled when Company S transfers plan assets of an equal amount to the purchaser. In connection with the purchase agreement, Company S transfers an additional $20,000 of plan assets.

[e]Represents a pro rata amount of the maximum gain based on the relationship of the accumulated postretirement benefit obligation settled to the total accumulated postretirement benefit obligation ($80,000 ÷ $267,000 or 30%). The maximum gain is measured as the unrecognized net gain subsequent to transition plus any unrecognized transition asset ($39,575 + $0 = $39,575). The settlement gain is, therefore, 30% of $39,575, or $11,872; recognition of that gain is subject to first reducing any remaining unrecognized transition obligation. As there is no remaining unrecognized transition obligation (the remainder was recognized in connection with the curtailment), the gain of $11,872 is recognized together with the excess $20,000 transfer of plan assets as part of the net gain from the sale (paragraphs .184 and .185).

[FAS106, ¶505]

.303 The sum of the effects related to postretirement benefits resulting from the sale is a loss of $236,128, the components of which are as follows:

Curtailment loss (paragraph .301)	$228,000
Settlement gain and loss from transfer of plan assets (paragraph .302)	8,128
Effects of sale	$236,128

[FAS106, ¶506]

Illustration 11—Accounting for the Effects of an Offer of Special Termination Benefits

.304 The measurement of the effects of an offer of special termination benefits pursuant to paragraphs .193 and .194 and the accounting for the related curtailment are illustrated in the following paragraphs. [FAS106, ¶507]

.305 On January 16, 19X5, Company T offers for a short period of time (until January 30, 19X5) special benefits to its employees who elect voluntary termination of employment during that period (special termination benefits). As part of the offer, employees who voluntarily terminate will be credited with an additional five years of service and five years of age to determine eligibility for postretirement health care benefits. Employees are normally eligible for those benefits upon attaining age 55 and rendering at least 20 years of service. [FAS106, ¶508]

.306 On January 30, 19X5, employees representing 18 percent of the work force accept the offer of special termination benefits. For those employees, the accumulated postretirement benefit obligation attributed to prior service periods based on their previously expected retirement dates (without consideration of the special offer) is $280,000. If those employees were assumed to terminate (retire) immediately upon attaining full eligibility for benefits (age 55 with 20 years of service), the accumulated postretirement benefit obligation for those employees would be $450,000. The accumulated postretirement benefit obligation for those employees after they accept the offer of the special termination benefits (full eligibility date accelerated, benefit coverage begins immediately) is $630,000. [FAS106, ¶509]

.307 The *remaining years of expected service* associated with the terminated employees who were plan participants at the date of transition is 24 percent of the remaining years of service of all plan participants at the date of transition. In addition, the portion of the unrecognized prior service cost arising from a prior plan amendment associated with the *remaining years of service prior to full eligibility* that are no longer expected to be rendered by the terminated employees is $25,000. [FAS106, ¶510]

.308 Pursuant to paragraph .191, if the sum of the effects resulting from a curtailment is a net loss, it shall be recognized in income when it is probable that a curtailment will occur and the effects are reasonably estimable. In this illustration, the effects resulting from the curtailment are not reasonably estimable until January 30, 19X5, the acceptance date of the offer of special termination benefits. Consequently, at January 30, 19X5, the employer recognizes a loss of $453,400 that includes the cost of the special termination benefits ($180,000) and the net loss from the curtailment ($273,400) determined as follows:

	January 30, 19X5			
	Before Employee Terminations	**Special Termination Benefits**	**Effect of Curtailment**	**After Employee Terminations**
Accumulated postretirement benefit obligation:				
Employees accepting offer	$(280,000)	$(180,000)[a]	$(170,000)[b]	$ (630,000)
Other employees	(633,000)			(633,000)
	(913,000)	(180,000)	(170,000)	(1,263,000)
Plan assets at fair value	141,000			141,000
Funded status	(772,000)	(180,000)	(170,000)	(1,122,000)
Unrecognized net gain	(88,000)		88,000[b]	0
Unrecognized prior service cost	148,500		(25,000)[c]	123,500
Unrecognized transition obligation	693,333		(166,400)[c]	526,933
Accrued postretirement benefit cost	$ (18,167)	$(180,000)	$(273,400)	$ (471,567)

[a]The loss from acceptance of the special termination benefits is $180,000 ($450,000 – $630,000), representing the difference between (1) the accumulated postretirement benefit obligation measured assuming that active plan participants not yet fully eligible for benefits would terminate employment at their full eligibility date and that fully eligible plan participants would retire immediately and (2) the accumulated postretirement benefit obligation reflecting the special termination benefits (paragraph .194).

[b]The increase in the accumulated postretirement benefit obligation as a result of the employees (fully eligible plan participants and other active plan participants not yet fully eligible for benefits) retiring at a date earlier than expected is a loss of $170,000 ($280,000 – $450,000). That amount is reduced by the unrecognized net gain of $88,000 (paragraph .190(b)) as part of the accounting for the curtailment.

[c]Additional effects of the curtailment are (1) the reduction of $25,000 in the unrecognized prior service cost (arising from a prior plan amendment) associated with the remaining years of service prior to full eligibility that are no longer expected to be rendered by the terminated employees and (2) the reduction of $166,400 in the unrecognized transition obligation associated with remaining years of service no longer expected to be rendered—measured as 24% (reduction in the remaining years of expected service associated with those employees affected by the early retirement who were plan participants at the date of transition) of the unrecognized transition obligation of $693,333 (paragraph .189).

[FAS106, ¶511]

[**Note:** Additional guidance with respect to implementing Section P40 is presented in FASB publication: *A Guide to Implementation of Statement 106 on Employers' Accounting for Postretirement Benefits Other Than Pensions: Questions and Answers.* The publication addresses 64 questions and was written by FASB staff members, Kenneth E. Dakdduk and Jules M. Cassel. This publication is available from the Order Department, Financial Accounting Standards Board, 401 Merritt 7, P.O. Box 5116, Norwalk, CT 06856-5116, telephone (203) 847-0700.]

Glossary

.401 **Accumulated postretirement benefit obligation.** The actuarial present value of benefits attributed to employee service rendered to a particular date. Prior to an employee's full eligibility date, the accumulated postretirement benefit obligation as of a particular date for an employee is the portion of the expected postretirement benefit obligation attributed to that employee's service rendered to that date; on and after the full eligibility date, the accumulated and expected postretirement benefit obligations for an employee are the same. [FAS106, ¶518]

.402 **Active plan participant.** Any active employee who has rendered service during the credited service period and is expected to receive benefits, including benefits to or for any beneficiaries and covered dependents, under the postretirement benefit plan. Also refer to **Plan participant.** [FAS106, ¶518]

.403 **Actual return on plan assets (component of net periodic postretirement benefit cost).** The change in the fair value of the plan's assets for a period including the decrease due to expenses incurred during the period (such as income tax expense incurred by the fund, if applicable), adjusted for contributions and benefit payments during the period. [FAS106, ¶518]

.404 **Actuarial present value.** The value, as of a specified date, of an amount or series of amounts payable or receivable thereafter, with each amount adjusted to reflect (a) the time value of money (through discounts for interest) and (b) the probability of payment (for example, by means of decrements for events such as death, disability, or withdrawal) between the specified date and the expected date of payment. [FAS106, ¶518]

.405 **Amortization.** Usually refers to the process of reducing a recognized liability systematically by recognizing revenues or of reducing a recognized asset systematically by recognizing expenses or costs. In accounting for postretirement benefits, amortization is also used to refer to the systematic recognition in net periodic postretirement benefit cost over several periods of previously *unrecognized* amounts, including unrecognized prior service cost, unrecognized net gain or loss, and any unrecognized transition obligation or asset. [FAS106, ¶518]

.406 **Assumed per capita claims cost (by age).** The annual per capita cost, for periods after the measurement date, of providing the postretirement health care benefits covered by the plan from the earliest age at which an individual could begin to receive benefits under the plan through the remainder of the individual's life or the covered period, if shorter. To determine the assumed per capita claims cost, the per capita claims cost by age based on historical claims costs is adjusted for assumed health care cost trend rates.

The resulting assumed per capita claims cost by age reflects expected future costs and is applied with the plan demographics to determine the amount and timing of future gross eligible charges. Also refer to **Gross eligible charges** and **Per capita claims cost by age.** [FAS106, ¶518]

.407 **Assumptions.** Estimates of the occurrence of future events affecting postretirement benefit costs, such as turnover, retirement age, mortality, dependency status, per capita claims costs by age, health care cost trend rates, levels of Medicare and other health care providers' reimbursements, and discount rates to reflect the time value of money. [FAS106, ¶518]

.408 **Attribution.** The process of assigning postretirement benefit cost to periods of employee service. [FAS106, ¶518]

.409 **Attribution period.** The period of an employee's service to which the expected postretirement benefit obligation for that employee is assigned. The beginning of the attribution period is the employee's date of hire unless the plan's benefit formula grants credit only for service from a later date, in which case the beginning of the attribution period is generally the beginning of that credited service period. The end of the attribution period is the full eligibility date. Within the attribution period, an equal amount of the expected postretirement benefit obligation is attributed to each year of service unless the plan's benefit formula attributes a disproportionate share of the expected postretirement benefit obligation to employees' early years of service. In that case, benefits are attributed in accordance with the plan's benefit formula. Also refer to **Credited service period.** [FAS106, ¶518]

.410 **Benefit formula.** The basis for determining benefits to which participants may be entitled under a postretirement benefit plan. A plan's benefit formula specifies the years of service to be rendered, age to be attained while in service, or a combination of both that must be met for an employee to be eligible to receive benefits under the plan. A plan's benefit formula may also define the beginning of the credited service period and the benefits earned for specific periods of service. [FAS106, ¶518]

.411 **Benefits.** The monetary or in-kind benefits or benefit coverage to which participants may be entitled under a postretirement benefit plan, including health care benefits, life insurance not provided through a pension plan, and legal, educational, and advisory services. [FAS106, ¶518]

.412 **Captive insurer.** An insurance company that does business primarily with related entities. [FAS106, ¶518]

.413 **Contributory plan.** A plan under which retirees or active employees contribute part of the cost. In some contributory plans, retirees or active employees wishing to be covered must contribute; in other contributory plans, participants' contributions result in increased benefits. [FAS106, ¶518]

.414 **Cost-sharing (provisions of the plan).** The provisions of the postretirement benefit plan that describe how the costs of the covered benefits are to be shared between the employer and the plan participants. Cost-sharing provisions describe retired and active plan participants' contributions toward their postretirement health care benefits, deductibles, coinsurance, out-of-pocket limitations on participant costs, caps on employer costs, and so forth. [FAS106, ¶518]

.415 **Credited service period.** Employee service period for which benefits are earned pursuant to the terms of the plan. The beginning of the credited service period may be the date of hire or a later date. For example, a plan may provide benefits only for service rendered after a specified age. Service beyond the end of the credited service period does not earn any additional benefits under the plan. Also refer to **Attribution period.** [FAS106, ¶518]

.416 **Curtailment (of a postretirement benefit plan).** An event that significantly reduces the expected years of future service of active plan participants or eliminates the accrual of defined benefits for some or all of the future services of a significant number of active plan participants. [FAS106, ¶518]

.417 **Defined benefit postretirement plan.** A plan that defines postretirement benefits in terms of monetary amounts (for example, $100,000 of life insurance) or benefit coverage to be provided (for example, up to $200 per day for hospitalization, 80 percent of the cost of specified surgical procedures, and so forth). Any postretirement benefit plan that is not a defined contribution postretirement plan is, for purposes of this section, a defined benefit postretirement plan. [FAS106, ¶518]

.418 **Defined contribution postretirement plan.** A plan that provides postretirement benefits in return for services rendered, provides an individual account for each plan participant, and specifies how contributions to the individual's account are to be determined rather than specifies the amount of benefits the individual is to receive. Under a defined contribution postretirement plan, the benefits a plan participant will receive depend solely on the amount contributed to the plan participant's account, the returns earned on investments of those contributions, and the forfeitures of other plan participants' benefits that may be allocated to that plan participant's account. [FAS106, ¶518]

.419 **Dependency status.** The status of a current or former employee having dependents (for example, a spouse or other relatives) who are expected to receive benefits under a postretirement benefit plan that provides dependent coverage. [FAS106, ¶518]

.420 **Discount rates.** The rates used to reflect the time value of money. Discount rates are used in determining the present value as of the measurement date of future cash flows currently expected to be required to satisfy the postretirement benefit obligation. Also refer to **Actuarial present value.** [FAS106, ¶518]

.421 **Expected long-term rate of return on plan assets.** An assumption about the rate of return on plan assets reflecting the average rate of earnings expected on existing plan assets and expected contributions to the plan during the period. [FAS106, ¶518]

.422 **Expected postretirement benefit obligation.** The actuarial present value as of a particular date of the benefits expected to be paid to or for an employee, the employee's beneficiaries, and any covered dependents pursuant to the terms of the postretirement benefit plan. [FAS106, ¶518]

.423 **Expected return on plan assets.** An amount calculated as a basis for determining the extent of delayed recognition of the effects of changes in the fair value of plan assets. The expected return on plan assets is determined based on the expected long-term rate of return on plan assets and the market-related value of plan assets. [FAS106, ¶518]

.424 **Explicit (approach to) assumptions.** An approach under which each significant assumption used reflects the best estimate of the plan's future experience solely with respect to that assumption. [FAS106, ¶518]

.425 **Fair value.** The amount that a plan could reasonably expect to receive for an investment in a current sale between a willing buyer and a willing seller, that is, other than a forced or liquidation sale. [FAS106, ¶518]

.426 **Full eligibility (for benefits).** The status of an employee having reached the employee's full eligibility date. Full eligibility for benefits is achieved by meeting specified age, service, or age and service requirements of the postretirement benefit plan. Also refer to **Full eligibility date.** [FAS106, ¶518]

.427 **Full eligibility date.** The date at which an employee has rendered all of the service necessary to have earned the right to receive all of the benefits expected to be received by that employee (including any beneficiaries and dependents expected to receive benefits). Determination of the full eligibility date is affected by plan terms that provide incremental benefits expected to be received by or on behalf of an employee for additional years of service, unless those incremental benefits are trivial. Determination of the full eligibility date is *not* affected by plan terms that define when benefit payments commence or by an employee's current dependency status. [FAS106, ¶518]

.428 **Fully eligible plan participants.** Collectively, that group of former employees (including retirees) and active employees who have rendered service to or beyond their full eligibility date and who are expected to receive benefits under the plan, including benefits to their beneficiaries and covered dependents. [FAS106, ¶518]

.429 **Funding policy.** The program regarding the amounts and timing of contributions by the employer(s), plan participants, and any other sources to provide the benefits a postretirement benefit plan specifies. [FAS106, ¶518]

.430 **Gain or loss.** A change in the value of either the accumulated postretirement benefit obligation or the plan assets resulting from experience different from that assumed or from a change in an actuarial assumption, or the consequence of a decision to temporarily deviate from the substantive plan. Also refer to **Unrecognized net gain or loss.** [FAS106, ¶518]

.431 **Gain or loss component (of net periodic postretirement benefit cost).** The sum of (a) the difference between the actual return on plan assets and the expected return on plan assets, (b) any gain or loss immediately recognized or the amortization of the unrecognized net gain or loss from previous periods, and (c) any amount immediately recognized as a gain or loss pursuant to a decision to temporarily deviate from the substantive plan. The gain or loss component is generally the net effect of delayed recognition of gains and losses (the net change in the unrecognized net gain or loss) except that it does not include changes in the accumulated postretirement benefit obligation occurring during the period and deferred for later recognition. [FAS106, ¶518]

.432 **Gross eligible charges.** The cost of providing the postretirement health care benefits covered by the plan to a plan participant, before adjusting for expected reimbursements from Medicare and other providers of health care benefits and for the effects of the cost-sharing provisions of the plan. [FAS106, ¶518]

.433 **Health care cost trend rates.** An assumption about the annual rate(s) of change in the cost of health care benefits currently provided by the postretirement benefit plan, due to factors other than changes in the composition of the plan population by age and dependency status, for each year from the measurement date until the end of the period in which benefits are expected to be paid. The health care cost trend rates implicitly consider estimates of health care inflation, changes in health care utilization or delivery patterns, technological advances, and changes in the health status of the plan participants. Differing types of services, such as hospital care and dental care, may have different trend rates. [FAS106, ¶518]

.434 **Incurred claims cost (by age).** The cost of providing the postretirement health care benefits covered by the plan to a plan participant, after adjusting for reimbursements from Medicare and other providers of health care benefits and for deductibles, coinsurance provisions, and other specific claims costs borne by the retiree. Also refer to **Net incurred claims cost (by age).** [FAS106, ¶518]

.435 **Insurance contract.** A contract in which an insurance company unconditionally undertakes a legal obligation to provide specified benefits to specific individuals in return for a fixed consideration or premium. An insurance contract is irrevocable and involves the transfer of significant risk from the employer (or the plan) to the insurance company. If the insurance company providing the contract is a captive insurer, or if there is any reasonable doubt that the insurance company will meet its obligations under the contract, the contract is not an insurance contract for purposes of this section. [FAS106, ¶518]

.436 **Interest cost (component of net periodic postretirement benefit cost).** The accrual of interest on the accumulated postretirement benefit obligation due to the passage of time. [FAS106, ¶518]

.437 **Market-related value of plan assets.** A balance used to calculate the expected return on plan assets. Market-related value can be either fair value or a calculated value that recognizes changes in fair value in a systematic and rational manner over not more than five years. Different methods of calculating market-related value may be used for different classes of plan assets, but the manner of determining market-related value shall be applied consistently from year to year for each class of plan asset. [FAS106, ¶518]

.438 **Measurement date.** The date of the financial statements or, if used consistently from year to year, a date not more than three months prior to that date, as of which plan assets and obligations are measured. [FAS106, ¶518]

.439 **Medicare reimbursement rates.** The health care cost reimbursements expected to be received by retirees through Medicare as mandated by currently enacted legislation. Medicare reimbursement rates vary by the type of benefits provided. [FAS106, ¶518]

.440 **Multiemployer plan.** A postretirement benefit plan to which two or more unrelated employers contribute, usually pursuant to one or more collective-bargaining agreements. A characteristic of multiemployer plans is that assets contributed by one participating employer may be used to provide benefits to employees of other participating employers since assets contributed by an employer are not segregated in a separate account or restricted to provide benefits only to employees of that employer. A multiemployer plan is usually administered by a board of trustees composed of management and labor representatives and may also be referred to as a "joint trust" or "union plan." Generally, many employers participate in a multiemployer plan, and an employer may participate in more than one plan. The employers participating in multiemployer plans usually have a common industry bond, but for some plans the employers are in different industries and the labor union may be their only common bond. [FAS106, ¶518]

.441 **Multiple-employer plan.** A postretirement benefit plan maintained by more than one employer but not treated as a multiemployer plan. Multiple-employer plans are generally not collectively bargained and are intended to allow participating employers, commonly in the same industry, to pool their plan assets for investment purposes and to reduce the cost of plan administration. A multiple-employer plan maintains separate accounts for each employer so that contributions provide benefits only for employees of the contributing employer. Multiple-employer plans may have features that allow participating employers to have different benefit formulas, with the employer's contributions to the plan based on the benefit formula selected by the employer. [FAS106, ¶518]

.442 **Net incurred claims cost (by age).** The employer's share of the cost of providing the postretirement health care benefits covered by the plan to a plan participant; incurred claims cost net of retiree contributions. Also refer to **Incurred claims cost (by age).** [FAS106, ¶518]

.443 **Net periodic postretirement benefit cost.** The amount recognized in an employer's financial statements as the cost of a postretirement benefit plan for a period. Components of net periodic postretirement benefit cost include service cost, interest cost, actual return on plan assets, gain or loss, amortization of unrecognized prior service cost, and amortization of the unrecognized transition obligation or asset. [FAS106, ¶518]

.444 **Nonparticipating insurance contract.** An insurance contract that does not provide for the purchaser to participate in the investment performance or in other experience of the insurance company. Also refer to **Insurance contract.** [FAS106, ¶518]

.445 **Participating insurance contract.** An insurance contract that provides for the purchaser to participate in the investment performance and possibly other experience (for example, morbidity experience) of the insurance company. Also refer to **Insurance contract.** [FAS106, ¶518]

.446 **Participation right.** A purchaser's right under a participating insurance contract to receive future dividends or retroactive rate credits from the insurance company. [FAS106, ¶518]

.447 **Pay-related plan.** A plan that has a benefit formula that bases benefits or benefit coverage on compensation, such as a final-pay or career-average-pay plan. [FAS106, ¶518]

.448 **Per capita claims cost by age.** The current cost of providing postretirement health care benefits for one year at each age from the youngest age to the oldest age at which plan participants are expected to receive benefits under the plan. Also refer to **Assumed per capita claims cost (by age).** [FAS106, ¶518]

.449 **Plan.** An arrangement that is mutually understood by an employer and its employees, whereby an employer undertakes to provide its employees with benefits after they retire in exchange for their services over a specified period of time, upon attaining a specified age while in service, or a combination of both. A plan may be written or it may be implied by a well-defined, although perhaps unwritten, practice of paying postretirement benefits or from oral representations made to current or former employees. Also refer to **Substantive plan.** [FAS106, ¶518]

.450 **Plan amendment.** A change in the existing terms of a plan. A plan amendment may increase or decrease benefits, including those attributed to years of service already rendered. [FAS106, ¶518]

.451 **Plan assets.** Assets—usually stocks, bonds, and other investments—that have been segregated and restricted (usually in a trust) to provide for postretirement benefits. The amount of plan assets includes amounts contributed by the employer (and by plan participants for a contributory plan) and amounts earned from investing the contributions, less benefits, income taxes, and other expenses incurred. Plan assets ordinarily cannot be withdrawn by the employer except under certain circumstances when a plan has assets in excess of obligations and the employer has taken certain steps to satisfy existing obligations. Assets not segregated in a trust, or otherwise effectively restricted, so that they cannot be used by the employer for other purposes are not plan assets, even though it may be intended that those assets be used to provide postretirement benefits. Amounts accrued by the employer as net periodic postretirement benefit cost but not yet paid to the plan are not plan assets. Securities of the employer held by the plan are includable in plan assets provided they are transferable. If a plan has liabilities other than for benefits, those nonbenefit obligations are considered as reductions of plan assets. [FAS106, ¶518] [Refer to paragraph .1001 for an EITF Issue that provides interpretive guidance on this paragraph.]

.452 **Plan demographics.** The characteristics of the plan population including geographical distribution, age, sex, and marital status. [FAS106, ¶518]

.453 **Plan participant.** Any employee or former employee who has rendered service in the credited service period *and is expected to receive employer-provided benefits* under the postretirement benefit plan, including benefits to or for any beneficiaries and covered dependents. Also refer to **Active plan participant.** [FAS106, ¶518]

.454 **Plan termination.** An event in which the postretirement benefit plan ceases to exist and all benefits are settled by the purchase of insurance contracts or by other means. The plan may or may not be replaced by another plan. A plan termination with a replacement plan may or may not be in substance a plan termination for accounting purposes. [FAS106, ¶518]

.455 **Postretirement benefit plan.** Refer to **Plan.** [FAS106, ¶518]

.456 **Postretirement benefits.** All forms of benefits, other than retirement income, provided by an employer to retirees. Those benefits may be defined in terms of specified benefits, such as health care, tuition assistance, or legal services, that are provided to retirees as the need for those benefits arises, such as certain health care benefits, or they may be defined in terms of monetary amounts that become payable on the occurrence of a specified event, such as life insurance benefits. [FAS106, ¶518]

.457 **Postretirement benefits other than pensions.** Refer to **Postretirement benefits.** [FAS106, ¶518]

.458 **Postretirement health care benefits.** A form of postretirement benefit provided by an employer to retirees for defined health care services or coverage of defined health care costs, such as hospital and medical coverage, dental benefits, and eye care. [FAS106, ¶518]

.459 **Prior service cost.** The cost of benefit improvements attributable to plan participants' prior service pursuant to a plan amendment or a plan initiation that provides benefits in exchange for plan participants' prior service. Also refer to **Unrecognized prior service cost.** [FAS106, ¶518]

.460 **Retirees.** Collectively, that group of plan participants that includes retired employees, their beneficiaries, and covered dependents. [FAS106, ¶518]

.461 **Service cost component (of net periodic postretirement benefit cost).** The portion of the expected postretirement benefit obligation attributed to employee service during a period. [FAS106, ¶518]

.462 **Settlement (of a postretirement benefit plan).** An irrevocable action that relieves the employer (or the plan) of primary responsibility for a postretirement benefit obligation and eliminates significant risks related to the obligation and the assets used to effect the settlement. Examples of transactions that constitute a settlement include (a) making lump-sum cash payments to plan participants in exchange for their rights to receive specified postretirement benefits and (b) purchasing nonparticipating insurance contracts for the accumulated postretirement benefit obligation for some or all of the plan participants. [FAS106, ¶518]

.463 **Single-employer plan.** A postretirement benefit plan that is maintained by one employer. The term also may be used to describe a plan that is maintained by related parties such as a parent and its subsidiaries. [FAS106, ¶518]

.464 **Substantive plan.** The terms of the postretirement benefit plan as understood by an employer that provides postretirement benefits and the employees who render services in exchange for those benefits. The substantive plan is the basis for the accounting for that exchange transaction. In some situations an employer's cost-sharing policy, as evidenced by past practice or by communication of intended changes to a plan's cost-sharing provisions, or a past practice of regular increases in certain monetary benefits may indicate that the substantive plan differs from the extant written plan. [FAS106, ¶518]

.465 **Termination benefits.** Benefits provided by an employer to employees in connection with their termination of employment. They may be either special termination benefits offered only for a short period of time or contractual benefits required by the terms of a plan only if a specified event, such as a plant closing, occurs. [FAS106, ¶518]

.466 **Transition asset.** The unrecognized amount, as of the date this section is initially applied, of (a) the fair value of plan assets plus any recognized accrued postretirement benefit cost or less any recognized prepaid postretirement benefit cost in excess of (b) the accumulated postretirement benefit obligation. [FAS106, ¶518]

.467 **Transition obligation.** The unrecognized amount, as of the date this section is initially applied, of (a) the accumulated postretirement benefit obligation in excess of (b) the fair value of plan assets plus any recognized accrued postretirement benefit cost or less any recognized prepaid postretirement benefit cost. [FAS106, ¶518]

.468 **Unfunded accumulated postretirement benefit obligation.** The accumulated postretirement benefit obligation in excess of the fair value of plan assets. [FAS106, ¶518]

.469 **Unrecognized net gain or loss.** The cumulative net gain or loss that has not been recognized as a part of net periodic postretirement benefit cost or as a part of the accounting for the effects of a settlement or a curtailment. Also refer to **Gain or loss.** [FAS106, ¶518]

.470 **Unrecognized prior service cost.** The portion of prior service cost that has not been recognized as a part of net periodic postretirement benefit cost, as a reduction of the effects of a negative plan amendment, or as a part of the accounting for the effects of a curtailment. [FAS106, ¶518]

.471 **Unrecognized transition asset.** The portion of the transition asset that has not been recognized either immediately as the effect of a change in accounting or on a delayed basis as a part of net periodic postretirement benefit cost, as an offset to certain losses, or as a part of accounting for the effects of a settlement or a curtailment. [FAS106, ¶518]

.472 **Unrecognized transition obligation.** The portion of the transition obligation that has not been recognized either immediately as the effect of a change in accounting or on a delayed basis as a part of net periodic postretirement benefit cost, as an offset to certain gains, or as a part of accounting for the effects of a settlement or a curtailment. [FAS106, ¶518]

Supplemental Guidance: Emerging Issues Task Force (EITF) Issues

.1000 [Listed below are EITF Issues that provide supplemental guidance for this section. These Issues are grouped by subject matter and may be either interpretive of or related by topic to the guidance in this section.

Business Combinations: Restructuring

EITF Issue No. 84-35, "Business Combinations: Sale of Duplicate Facilities and Accrual of Liabilities"
EITF Issue No. 96-5, "Recognition of Liabilities for Contractual Termination Benefits or Changing Benefit Plan Assumptions in Anticipation of a Business Combination"

Other

EITF Issue No. 86-27, "Measurement of Excess Contributions to a Defined Contribution Plan or Employee Stock Ownership Plan"
EITF Issue No. 88-23, "Lump-Sum Payments under Union Contracts"
EITF Issue No. 92-12, "Accounting for OPEB Costs by Rate-Regulated Enterprises"
EITF Issue No. 92-13, "Accounting for Estimated Payments in Connection with the Coal Industry Retiree Health Benefit Act of 1992"
EITF Issue No. 93-3, "Plan Assets under FASB Statement No. 106"
EITF Topic No. D-27, "Accounting for the Transfer of Excess Pension Assets to a Retiree Health Care Benefits Account"
EITF Topic No. D-36, "Selection of Discount Rates Used for Measuring Defined Benefit Pension Obligations and Obligations of Postretirement Benefit Plans Other Than Pensions"
EITF Topic No. D-92, "The Effect of FASB Statement No. 135 on the Measurement and Recognition of Net Periodic Benefit Cost under FASB Statements No. 87 and No. 106"]

.1001 [Listed below are those EITF Issues that provide interpretive guidance on specific material in this section.

Paragraph .126, fn14 (FAS 106, ¶186)—EITF Topic No. D-36
Paragraph .158 (FAS 106, ¶308)—EITF Issue No. 93-3
Paragraph .197 (FAS 106, ¶105)—EITF Topic No. 86-27
Paragraph .451 (FAS 106, ¶518)—EITF Issue No. 93-3]

(The next page is 37647.)

QUASI REORGANIZATIONS SECTION Q15

Sources: ARB 43, Chapter 7A; ARB 46; FASB Statement 109

Summary

If an enterprise elects to restate the carrying values of the balance sheet amounts to fair value as part of a quasi reorganization or corporate readjustment, the offsetting adjustment shall be charged to retained earnings. If the adjustment exceeds the balance in the retained earnings account, any difference shall be charged to additional paid-in capital. A new retained earnings account shall be established at the effective date of such readjustment, and the effective date generally shall be disclosed for a period of 10 years.

.101 [As noted in] Section A31, "Additional Paid-In Capital," additional paid-in capital, however created, shall not be used to relieve the income account of the current or future years of charges that otherwise would be made against income. This rule might be subject to the exception that if, upon reorganization, a reorganized enterprise would be relieved of charges that would be made against income if the existing enterprise were continued, it might be regarded as permissible to accomplish the same result without reorganization provided the facts were as fully revealed to and the action as formally approved by the shareholders as in reorganization. [ARB43, ch7A, ¶1]

.102 Readjustments of the kind mentioned in the [above] exception to the rule fall in the category of what are called *quasi reorganizations*. This section does not deal with the general question of quasi reorganizations, but only with cases in which the exception permitted [in paragraph .101] is availed of by an enterprise. Hereinafter, such cases are referred to as *readjustments*. [ARB43, ch7A, ¶2]

.103 [This section provides guidance on the accounting during and after a readjustment. It does not address any] other types of readjustments, such as correcting erroneous credits made to additional paid-in capital in the past. [ARB43, ch7A, ¶12]

Accounting for a Readjustment

.104 An enterprise [that] elects to restate its assets, capital stock, additional paid-in capital, and retained earnings through a readjustment and thus avail itself of permission to relieve its future income account or retained earnings of charges that would otherwise be made against it shall make a clear report to its shareholders of the restatements proposed to be made, and obtain their formal consent. It shall present a fair balance sheet as at the date of the readjustment, in which the adjustment of carrying amounts is reasonably complete, in order that there may be no continuation of the circumstances that justify charges to additional paid-in capital. [ARB43, ch7A, ¶3]

.105 Assets shall be carried forward as of the date of readjustment at fair and not unduly conservative amounts, determined with due regard for the accounting to be employed by the enterprise thereafter. If the fair value of any asset is not readily determinable a conservative estimate may be made, but in that case the amount shall be described as an estimate and any material difference arising through realization or otherwise and not attributable to events occurring or circumstances arising after that date shall not be carried to income or retained earnings. [ARB43, ch7A, ¶4]

.106 If potential losses or charges are known to have arisen prior to the date of readjustment but the amounts thereof are then indeterminate, provision may properly be made to cover the maximum *probable* losses or charges. [Section C59, "Contingencies," contains more detailed guidance for accounting for contingent losses.] If the amounts provided are subsequently found to have been excessive or insufficient, the differences shall not be carried to retained earnings nor used to offset losses or gains originating after the readjustment, but shall be carried to additional paid-in capital. [ARB43, ch7A, ¶5]

.107 When the amounts to be written off in a readjustment have been determined, they shall be charged first against retained earnings to the full extent of such retained earnings; any balance shall then be charged against additional paid-in capital. An enterprise that has subsidiaries shall apply this rule in such a way that no consolidated retained earnings survive a readjustment in which any part of losses has been charged to additional paid-in capital. [ARB43, ch7A, ¶6]

.108 If the retained earnings of any subsidiaries cannot be applied against the losses before resort is had to additional paid-in capital, the parent company's interest in such retained earnings shall be regarded as capitalized by the readjustment just as retained earnings at the date of acquisition are capitalized, so far as the parent is concerned. [ARB43, ch7A, ¶7] [The parent company's accounting for its investments in subsidiaries is discussed in Section C51, "Consolidation."]

.109 The effective date of the readjustment, from which the income of the enterprise is thereafter determined, shall be as near as practicable to the date on which formal consent of the stockholders is given, and shall ordinarily not be prior to the close of the last completed fiscal year. [ARB43, ch7A, ¶8]

Accounting after a Readjustment

.110 When the readjustment has been completed, the enterprise's accounting shall be substantially similar to that appropriate for a new enterprise. [ARB43, ch7A, ¶9]

.111 After such a readjustment retained earnings previously accumulated cannot properly be carried forward under that title. A new retained earnings account shall be established, dated to show that it runs from the effective date of the readjustment, and this dating shall be disclosed in financial statements until such time as the effective date is no longer deemed to possess any special significance. [ARB43, ch7A, ¶10] The dating of retained earnings following a quasi reorganization would rarely, if ever, be of significance after a period of 10 years and there may be exceptional circumstances in which the discontinuance of the dating of retained earnings could be justified at the conclusion of a period less than 10 years. [ARB46, ¶2]

.112 Additional paid-in capital originating in such a readjustment is restricted in the same manner as that of a new enterprise; charges against it shall be only those that may properly be made against the initial additional paid-in capital of a new enterprise. [ARB43, ch7A, ¶11]

Accounting for a Tax Benefit

.113 The tax benefits of deductible temporary differences and carryforwards as of the date of a quasi reorganization as defined and contemplated in this section ordinarily are reported as a direct addition to contributed capital if the tax benefits are recognized in subsequent years. The only exception is for enterprises that have previously both adopted [the provisions of] FASB Statement 96, *Accounting for Income Taxes,* and effected a quasi reorganization that involves only the elimination of a deficit in retained earnings by a concurrent reduction in contributed capital prior to adopting [the provisions of] Section I27, "Income Taxes." For those enterprises, subsequent recognition of the tax benefit of prior deductible temporary differences and carryforwards is included in income and reported as required by paragraph .136 of Section I27 (without regard to the referenced exceptions) and then reclassified from retained earnings to contributed capital. Those enterprises shall disclose (a) the date of the quasi reorganization, (b) the manner of reporting the tax benefits and that it differs from present accounting requirements for other enterprises and (c) the effect of those tax benefits on income from continuing operations, income before extraordinary items, and on net income (and on related per share amounts). [FAS109, ¶39]

(The next page is 38295.)

Remeasurement

[illegible]

[illegible]

[illegible]

[illegible]

REAL ESTATE SECTION R10

Sources: FASB Statement 66; FASB Statement 67; FASB Statement 98; FASB Statement 140; FASB Statement 144; FASB Interpretation 43

[**Note:** A list of Issues discussed by the Emerging Issues Task Force (EITF) that provide supplemental guidance for this section is presented in paragraph .1000.]

Summary

The accounting for certain real estate transactions is covered in Sections Re1, "Real Estate: Sales," and Re2, "Real Estate: Accounting for Costs and Initial Rental Operations of Real Estate Projects."

Sections Re1 and Re2 relate to enterprises in the real estate industry that are frequently involved in highly complex transactions. This section includes the contents of each of the above two sections that are pertinent to occasional real estate transactions of those enterprises in other than the real estate industry. This section describes which of the above two sections is pertinent to a particular situation.

.101 Section Re1, "Real Estate: Sales," [presents] standards for recognition of profit on all real estate sales transactions [FAS66, ¶1] (including real estate with property improvements and integral equipment) [FIN43, ¶2] without regard to the nature of the seller's business. [FAS66, ¶1]

.101A The terms *property improvements* and *integral equipment* as they are used in Section Re1 refer to any physical structure or equipment attached to the real estate that cannot be removed and used separately without incurring significant cost. Examples include an office building, a manufacturing facility, a power plant, and a refinery. [FIN43, ¶2]

.101B The sale of timberlands or farms (that is, land with trees or crops attached to it) is viewed as being similar to the sale of land with property improvements or integral equipment and thus subject to the provisions of Section Re1. [However,] natural assets such as those that have been *extracted from* the land (for example, oil, gas,[a] coal, and gold)

---

[a]In accordance with Section Oi5, "Oil and Gas Producing Activities," *mineral interests in properties* include fee ownership or a lease, concession, or other interest representing the right to extract oil or gas subject to such terms as may be imposed by the conveyance of that interest. Mineral interests in properties also include royalty interests, production payments payable in oil or gas, and other nonoperating mineral interests in properties operated by others. [FIN43, ¶14, fn3]

are substantially different and are, thus, not subject to the provisions of Section Re1. Similarly, sales of timber or corn, wheat, or any other harvested crop (that is, anything that will have been detached from the land by the time it reaches the buyer) would not be subject to the provisions of Section Re1. [FIN43, ¶14]

.101C The provisions of Section Re1 do not apply to transactions that involve the following:

a. The sale of only property improvements or integral equipment without a concurrent (or contemplated) sale of the underlying land[b]
b. The sale of the stock or net assets of a subsidiary or a segment of a business if the assets of that subsidiary or that segment, as applicable, contain real estate, unless the transaction is, in substance,[c] the sale of real estate
c. The sale of securities that are accounted for in accordance with Section I80, "Investments: Debt and Equity Securities."[d]

[FIN43, ¶3]

.102 Although Section Re1 applies to all sales of real estate, many of the extensive provisions were developed over several years to deal with complex transactions that are

[b]Except for sales of property improvements or integral equipment with the concurrent lease (whether explicit or implicit in the transaction) of the underlying land to the buyer. Those transactions should be accounted for in accordance with paragraphs .138 and .139 of Section Re1 [paragraphs .141 and .142 of this section]. In addition, sales of property improvements or integral equipment subject to an existing lease of the underlying land are also subject to the provisions of Section Re1. [FIN43, ¶3, fn1]

[c]Determining whether a transaction is in substance the sale of real estate requires judgment. In making that determination, one should consider the nature of the entire real estate component being sold (that is, the land plus the property improvements and integral equipment), and not the land only. Further, that determination should not consider whether the operations in which the assets are involved are traditional or nontraditional real estate activities. For example, if a ski resort is sold and the lodge and ski lifts are considered to be affixed to the land (that is, they cannot be removed and used separately without incurring significant cost), then it would appear that the sale is in substance the sale of real estate and that the entire transaction would be subject to the provisions of Section Re1. Transactions involving the sale of underlying land (or the sale of the property improvements or integral equipment subject to a lease of the underlying land) should not be bifurcated into a real estate component (the sale of the underlying land) and a non-real-estate component (the sale of the lodge and lifts) for purposes of determining profit recognition on the transaction. [FIN43, ¶25]

[d]Sales of those types of securities are addressed by [FIN43, ¶3, fn2] Section F39, "Financial Instruments: Transfers." [FAS140, ¶355]

frequently encountered in enterprises that specialize in real estate transactions [and, therefore, the accounting requirements are contained within Section Re1]. The decision tree [in paragraph .178 highlights] the major provisions of this section and will help a user identify criteria that determine when and how profit is recognized. Those accounting for relatively simple real estate sales transactions will need to apply only limited portions of Section Re1. [Those requirements are reproduced in paragraphs .106 through .178 of this section.] The general requirements for recognizing all of the profit on a nonretail land sale at the date of sale are set forth in paragraphs .106 through .108, and are highlighted on the decision tree in paragraph .178. Paragraphs .109 through .177 elaborate on those general provisions. [FAS66, ¶2]

.103 Section Re2, "Real Estate: Accounting for Costs and Initial Rental Operations of Real Estate Projects," [presents] accounting and reporting standards for acquisition, development, construction, selling, and rental costs associated with real estate projects. It also provides guidance for the accounting for initial rental operations and criteria for determining when the status of a rental project changes from nonoperating to operating. [FAS67, ¶1]

.104 Section Re2 does not apply to:

a. Real estate developed by an enterprise for use in its own operations,[1] other than for sale or rental.
b. "Initial direct costs" of sales-type, operating, and other types of leases, which are defined in Section L10, "Leases," paragraph .411. The accounting for initial direct costs is prescribed in Section L10.
c. Costs directly related to manufacturing, merchandising, or service activities as distinguished from real estate activities.

Paragraphs .120 through .123 of Section Re2 do not apply to real estate rental activity in which the predominant rental period is less than one month. [FAS67, ¶2]

.105 [Deleted 11/92 because of FASB Statement 111, *Rescission of FASB Statement No. 32 and Technical Corrections.*]

[1]In this context, "real estate developed by an enterprise for use in its own operations" includes real estate developed by a member of a consolidated group for use in the operations of another member of the group (for example, a manufacturing facility developed by a subsidiary for use in its parent's operations) when the property is reported in the group's consolidated financial statements. However, such property is not "real estate developed for use in the enterprise's operations" when reported in the separate financial statements of the entity that developed it. [FAS67, ¶2, fn1]

Real Estate Sales Other Than Retail Land Sales

Recognition of Profit by the Full Accrual Method

.106 Profit shall be recognized in full when real estate is sold, provided (a) the profit is determinable, that is, the collectibility of the sales price is reasonably assured or the amount that will not be collectible can be estimated, and (b) the earnings process is virtually complete, that is, the seller is not obliged to perform significant activities after the sale to earn the profit. Unless both conditions exist, recognition of all or part of the profit shall be postponed. Recognition of all of the profit at the time of sale or at some later date when both conditions exist is referred to as the *full accrual method* in this section. [FAS66, ¶3] [Refer to paragraph .1001 for an EITF Issue that provides interpretive guidance on paragraphs .106 and .107.]

.107 In accounting for sales of real estate, collectibility of the sales price is demonstrated by the buyer's commitment to pay, which in turn is supported by substantial initial and continuing investments that give the buyer a stake in the property sufficient that the risk of loss through default motivates the buyer to honor its obligation to the seller. Collectibility shall also be assessed by considering factors such as the credit standing of the buyer, age and location of the property, and adequacy of cash flow from the property. [FAS66, ¶4]

.108 Profit on real estate sales transactions[2] shall not be recognized by the full accrual method until all of the following criteria are met:

a. A sale is consummated (refer to paragraph .109).
b. The buyer's initial and continuing investments are adequate to demonstrate a commitment to pay for the property (refer to paragraphs .111 through .119).
c. The seller's receivable is not subject to future subordination (refer to paragraph .120).
d. The seller has transferred to the buyer the usual risks and rewards of ownership in a transaction that is in substance a sale and does not have a substantial continuing involvement with the property (refer to paragraph .121).

Paragraphs .122 through .146 describe appropriate accounting if the above criteria are not met. [FAS66, ¶5] [Refer to paragraph .1001 for EITF Issues that provide interpretive guidance on this paragraph.]

---

[2] Profit on a sale of a partial interest in real estate shall be subject to the same criteria for profit recognition as a sale of a whole interest. [FAS66, ¶5, fn1]

Consummation of a Sale

.109 A sale shall not be considered consummated until (a) the parties are bound by the terms of a contract, (b) all consideration has been exchanged, (c) any permanent financing for which the seller is responsible has been arranged, and (d) all conditions[3] precedent to closing have been performed. Usually, those four conditions are met at the time of closing or after closing, not when an agreement to sell is signed or at a preclosing. [FAS66, ¶6] [Refer to paragraph .1001 for an EITF Issue that provides interpretive guidance on this paragraph.]

Buyer's Initial and Continuing Investment

.110 "Sales value" shall be determined by:

a. Adding to the stated sales price the proceeds from the issuance of a real estate option that is exercised and other payments that are in substance additional sales proceeds. These nominally may be management fees, points, or prepaid interest or fees that are required to be maintained in an advance status and applied against the amounts due to the seller at a later date.
b. Subtracting from the sale price a discount to reduce the receivable to its present value and by the net present value of services that the seller commits to perform without compensation or by the net present value of the services in excess of the compensation that will be received. Paragraph .134 specifies appropriate accounting if services are to be provided by the seller without compensation or at less than prevailing rates.

[FAS66, ¶7]

.111 Adequacy of a buyer's initial investment shall be measured by (a) its composition (refer to paragraphs .112 and .113) and (b) its size compared with the sales value of the property (refer to paragraph .114). [FAS66, ¶8]

.112 The buyer's initial investment shall include only: (a) cash paid as a down payment, (b) the buyer's notes supported by irrevocable letters of credit from an independent established lending institution,[4] (c) payments by the buyer to third parties to reduce existing indebtedness on the property, and (d) other amounts paid by the buyer that are part of the sales value. Other consideration received by the seller, including other notes of the

---

[3]Paragraph .123 provides an exception to this requirement if the seller is constructing office buildings, condominiums, shopping centers, or similar structures. [FAS66, ¶6, fn2]

[4]An "independent established lending institution" is an unrelated institution such as a commercial bank unaffiliated with the seller. [FAS66, ¶9, fn3]

buyer, shall be included as part of the buyer's initial investment only when that consideration is sold or otherwise converted to cash without recourse to the seller. [FAS66, ¶9] [Refer to paragraph .1001 for EITF Issues that provide interpretive guidance on this paragraph.]

.113 The initial investment shall not include:

a. Payments by the buyer to third parties for improvements to the property
b. A permanent loan commitment by an independent third party to replace a loan made by the seller
c. Any funds that have been or will be loaned, refunded, or directly or indirectly provided to the buyer by the seller or loans guaranteed or collateralized by the seller for the buyer[5]

[FAS66, ¶10] [Refer to paragraph .1001 for EITF Issues that provide interpretive guidance on this paragraph.]

.114 The buyer's initial investment shall be adequate to demonstrate the buyer's commitment to pay for the property and shall indicate a reasonable likelihood that the seller will collect the receivable. Lending practices of independent established lending institutions provide a reasonable basis for assessing the collectibility of receivables from buyers of real estate. Therefore, to qualify, the initial investment shall be equal to at least a major part of the difference between usual loan limits and the sales value of the property. Guidance on minimum initial investments is provided in paragraphs .147 and .148. [FAS66, ¶11] [Refer to paragraph .1001 for EITF Issues that provide interpretive guidance on this paragraph.]

.115 The buyer's continuing investment in a real estate transaction shall not qualify unless the buyer is contractually required to pay each year on its total debt for the purchase price of the property an amount at least equal to the level annual payment that would be needed to pay that debt and interest on the unpaid balance over no more than (a) 20 years for debt for land and (b) the customary amortization term of a first mortgage loan by an independent established lending institution for other real estate. For this purpose, contractually required payments by the buyer on its debt shall be in the forms specified in paragraph .112 as acceptable for an initial investment. Except as indicated in the following sentence, funds to be provided directly or indirectly by the seller (refer to paragraph .113(c)) shall be subtracted from the buyer's contractually required payments in

[5]As an example, if unimproved land is sold for $100,000, with a down payment of $50,000 in cash, and the seller plans to loan the buyer $35,000 at some future date, the initial investment is $50,000 minus $35,000, or $15,000. [FAS66, ¶10, fn4]

determining whether the initial and continuing investments are adequate. If a future loan on normal terms from an established lending institution bears a fair market interest rate and the proceeds of the loan are conditional on use for specified development of or construction on the property, the loan need not be subtracted in determining the buyer's investment. [FAS66, ¶12] [Refer to paragraph .1001 for an EITF Issue that provides interpretive guidance on this paragraph.]

Release Provisions

.116 An agreement to sell property (usually land) may provide that part or all of the property may be released from liens securing related debt by payment of a release price or that payments by the buyer may be assigned first to released property. If either of those conditions is present, a buyer's initial investment shall be sufficient both to pay release prices on property released at the date of sale and to constitute an adequate initial investment on property not released or not subject to release at that time in order to meet the criterion of an adequate initial investment for the property as a whole. [FAS66, ¶13]

.117 If the release conditions described in paragraph .116 are present, the buyer's investment shall be sufficient, after the released property is paid for, to constitute an adequate continuing investment on property not released in order to meet the criterion of an adequate continuing investment for the property as a whole (refer to paragraph .115). [FAS66, ¶14]

.118 If the amounts applied to unreleased portions do not meet the initial and continuing-investment criteria as applied to the sales value of those unreleased portions, profit shall be recognized on each released portion when it meets the criteria in paragraph .108 as if each release were a separate sale. [FAS66, ¶15]

.119 Tests of adequacy of a buyer's initial and continuing investments described in paragraphs .111 through .118 shall be applied cumulatively when the sale is consummated and annually afterward. If the initial investment exceeds the minimum prescribed, the excess shall be applied toward the required annual increases in the buyer's investment. [FAS66, ¶16]

Future Subordination

.120 The seller's receivable shall not be subject to future subordination. This restriction shall not apply if (a) a receivable is subordinate to a first mortgage on the property existing at the time of sale or (b) a future loan, including an existing permanent loan commitment, is provided for by the terms of the sale and the proceeds of the loan will be applied first to the payment of the seller's receivable. [FAS66, ¶17]

Continuing Involvement without Transfer of Risks and Rewards

.121 If a seller is involved with a property after it is sold in any way that results in retention of substantial risks or rewards of ownership, except as indicated in paragraph .146, the absence-of-continuing-involvement criterion has not been met. Forms of involvement that result in retention of substantial risks or rewards by the seller, and accounting therefor, are described in paragraphs .128 through .145. [FAS66, ¶18]

Recognition of Profit When the Full Accrual Method Is Not Appropriate

.122 If a real estate sales transaction does not satisfy the criteria in paragraphs .106 through .121 for recognition of profit by the full accrual method, the transaction shall be accounted for as specified in the following paragraphs. [FAS66, ¶19]

Sale Not Consummated

.123 The deposit method of accounting described in paragraphs .159 through .161 shall be used until a sale has been consummated (refer to paragraph .109). "Consummation" usually requires that all conditions precedent to closing have been performed, including that the building be certified for occupancy. However, because of the length of the construction period of office buildings, apartments, condominiums, shopping centers, and similar structures, such sales and the related income may be recognized during the process of construction, subject to the criteria in paragraphs .144 and .145, even though a certificate of occupancy, which is a condition precedent to closing, has not been obtained. [FAS66, ¶20]

.124 If the net carrying amount of the property exceeds the sum of the deposit received, the fair value of the unrecorded note receivable, and the debt assumed by the buyer, the seller shall recognize the loss at the date the agreement to sell is signed.[6] If a buyer defaults, or if circumstances after the transaction indicate that it is probable the buyer will default and the property will revert to the seller, the seller shall evaluate whether the circumstances indicate a decline in the value of the property for which an allowance for loss should be provided. [FAS66, ¶21]

Initial or Continuing Investments Do Not Qualify

.125 If the buyer's initial investment does not meet the criteria specified in paragraphs .111 through .114 for recognition of profit by the full accrual method and if re-

[6]Section Re2, "Real Estate: Accounting for Costs and Initial Rental Operations of Real Estate Projects," paragraph .124, specifies the accounting for property that is substantially completed and that is to be sold. [FAS144, ¶C30]

covery of the cost of the property is reasonably assured if the buyer defaults, the installment method described in paragraphs .150 through .155 shall be used. If recovery of the cost of the property is not reasonably assured if the buyer defaults or if cost has already been recovered and collection of additional amounts is uncertain, the cost recovery method (described in paragraphs .156 through .158) or the deposit method (described in paragraphs .159 through .161) shall be used. The cost recovery method may be used to account for sales of real estate for which the installment method would be appropriate. [FAS66, ¶22]

.126 If the initial investment meets the criteria in paragraphs .111 through .114 but the continuing investment by the buyer does *not* meet the criteria in paragraphs .115 and .119, the seller shall recognize profit by the reduced profit method described in paragraphs .162 and .163 at the time of sale if payments by the buyer each year will at least cover both of the following:

a. The interest and principal amortization on the maximum first mortgage loan that could be obtained on the property
b. Interest, at an appropriate rate,[7] on the excess of the aggregate actual debt on the property over such a maximum first mortgage loan

If the criteria specified in this paragraph for use of the reduced profit method are not met, the seller may recognize profit by the installment method (refer to paragraphs .150 through .155) or the cost recovery method (refer to paragraphs .156 through .158). [FAS66, ¶23]

Receivable Subject to Future Subordination

.127 If the seller's receivable is subject to future subordination as described in paragraph .120, profit shall be recognized by the cost recovery method (refer to paragraphs .156 through .158). [FAS66, ¶24]

Continuing Involvement without Transfer of Risks and Rewards

.128 If the seller has some continuing involvement with the property and does not transfer substantially all of the risks and rewards of ownership, profit shall be recognized by a method determined by the nature and extent of the seller's continuing involvement. Generally, profit shall be recognized at the time of sale if the amount of the seller's loss of profit because of continued involvement with the property is limited by the terms of the sales contract. The profit recognized shall be reduced by the maximum exposure to loss.

[7]Section I69, "Interest: Imputation of an Interest Cost," paragraphs .106 and .107, provide criteria for selecting an appropriate rate for present-value calculations. [FAS66, ¶23, fn6]

Paragraphs .129 through .146 describe some common forms of continuing involvement and specify appropriate accounting if those forms of involvement are present. If the seller has some other form of continuing involvement with the property, the transaction shall be accounted for according to the nature of the involvement. [FAS66, ¶25]

.129 *The seller has an obligation to repurchase the property, or the terms of the transaction allow the buyer to compel the seller or give an option*[8] *to the seller to repurchase the property.* The transaction shall be accounted for as a financing, leasing, or profit-sharing arrangement rather than as a sale. [FAS66, ¶26] [Refer to paragraph .1001 for an EITF Issue that provides interpretive guidance on this paragraph.]

.130 *The seller is a general partner in a limited partnership that acquires an interest in the property sold (or has an extended, noncancelable management contract requiring similar obligations) and holds a receivable from the buyer for a significant*[9] *part of the sales price.* The transaction shall be accounted for as a financing, leasing, or profit-sharing arrangement. [FAS66, ¶27]

.131 *The seller guarantees*[10] *the return of the buyer's investment or a return on that investment for a limited or extended period.* For example, the seller guarantees cash flows, subsidies, or net tax benefits. If the seller guarantees return of the buyer's investment or if the seller guarantees a return on the investment for an extended period, the transaction shall be accounted for as a financing, leasing, or profit-sharing arrangement. If the guarantee of a return on the investment is for a limited period, the deposit method shall be used until operations of the property cover all operating expenses, debt service, and contractual payments. At that time, profit shall be recognized on the basis of performance of the services required, as illustrated in paragraphs .171 through .175. [FAS66, ¶28]

---

[8]A right of first refusal based on a bona fide offer by a third party ordinarily is not an obligation or an option to repurchase. [FAS66, ¶26, fn7]

[9]For this purpose, a significant receivable is a receivable in excess of 15 percent of the maximum first-lien financing that could be obtained from an independent established lending institution for the property. It would include:

a. A construction loan made or to be made by the seller to the extent that it exceeds the minimum funding commitment for permanent financing from a third party that the seller will not be liable for
b. An all-inclusive or wraparound receivable held by the seller to the extent that it exceeds prior-lien financing for which the seller has no personal liability
c. Other funds provided or to be provided directly or indirectly by the seller to the buyer
d. The present value of a land lease when the seller is the lessor (refer to paragraph .142, footnote 16).

[FAS66, ¶27, fn8]

[10]Guarantees by the seller may be limited to a specified period of time. [FAS66, ¶28, fn9]

.132 *The seller is required to initiate or support operations or continue to operate the property at its own risk, or may be presumed to have such a risk, for an extended period, for a specified limited period, or until a specified level of operations has been obtained, for example, until rentals of a property are sufficient to cover operating expenses and debt service.* If support is required or presumed to be required[11] for an *extended* period of time, the transaction shall be accounted for as a financing, leasing, or profit-sharing arrangement. If support is required or presumed to be required for a *limited* time, profit on the sale shall be recognized on the basis of performance of the services required. Performance of those services shall be measured by the costs incurred and to be incurred over the period during which the services are performed. Profit shall begin to be recognized when there is reasonable assurance that future rent receipts will cover operating expenses and debt service including payments due the seller under the terms of the transaction. Reasonable assurance that rentals will be adequate would be indicated by objective information regarding occupancy levels and rental rates in the immediate area. In assessing whether rentals will be adequate to justify recognition of profit, total estimated future rent receipts of the property shall be reduced by one-third as a reasonable safety factor unless the amount so computed is less than the rents to be received from signed leases. In this event, the rents from signed leases shall be substituted for the computed amount. Application of this method is illustrated in paragraphs .171 through .176. [FAS66, ¶29]

.133 If the sales contract does not stipulate the period during which the seller is obligated to support operations of the property, support shall be presumed for at least two years from the time of initial rental unless actual rental operations cover operating expenses, debt service, and other contractual commitments before that time. If the seller is contractually obligated for a longer time, profit recognition shall continue on the basis of performance until the obligation expires. Calculation of profits on the basis of performance of services is illustrated in paragraphs .171 through .176. [FAS66, ¶30]

.134 If the sales contract requires the seller to provide management services relating to the property after the sale without compensation or at compensation less than prevailing rates for the service required (refer to paragraph .110) or on terms not usual for the services to be rendered (refer to paragraph .132, footnote 11(d)), compensation shall be im-

[11] Support shall be presumed to be required if: (a) a seller obtains an interest as a general partner in a limited partnership that acquires an interest in the property sold; (b) a seller retains an equity interest in the property, such as an undivided interest or an equity interest in a joint venture that holds an interest in the property; (c) a seller holds a receivable from a buyer for a significant part of the sales price and collection of the receivable depends on the operation of the property; or (d) a seller agrees to manage the property for the buyer on terms not usual for the services to be rendered, and the agreement is not terminable by either the seller or the buyer. [FAS66, ¶29, fn10]

puted when the sale is recognized and shall be recognized in income as the services are performed over the term of the management contract. [FAS66, ¶31]

.135 *The transaction is merely an option to purchase the property.* For example, undeveloped land may be "sold" under terms that call for a very small initial investment by the buyer (substantially less than the percentages specified in paragraph .148) and postponement of additional payments until the buyer obtains zoning changes or building permits or other contingencies specified in the sales agreement are satisfactorily resolved. Proceeds from the issuance of the option by a property owner shall be accounted for as a deposit (refer to paragraphs .159 through .161). Profit shall not be recognized until the option either expires or is exercised. When an option to purchase real estate is sold by an option holder,[12] the seller of the option shall recognize income by the cost recovery method (refer to paragraphs .156 through .158) to the extent nonrefundable cash proceeds exceed the seller's cost of the option if the buyer's initial and continuing investments are not adequate for profit recognition by the full accrual method (refer to paragraphs .110 through .119). [FAS66, ¶32]

.136 *The seller has made a partial sale.* A sale is a partial sale if the seller retains an equity interest in the property or has an equity interest in the buyer. Profit (the difference between the sales value and the proportionate cost of the partial interest sold) shall be recognized at the date of sale if:

a. The buyer is independent of the seller.
b. Collection of the sales price is reasonably assured (refer to paragraph .107).
c. The seller will not be required to support the operations of the property or its related obligations to an extent greater than its proportionate interest.

[FAS66, ¶33]

.137 If the buyer is not independent of the seller, for example, if the seller holds or acquires an equity interest in the buyer, the seller shall recognize the part of the profit proportionate to the outside interests in the buyer at the date of sale. If the seller controls the buyer, no profit on the sale shall be recognized until it is realized from transactions with outside parties through sale or operations of the property. [FAS66, ¶34]

---

[12] When an option to purchase real estate is sold by an option holder, the sales value includes the exercise price of the option and the sales price of the option. For example, if the option is sold for $150,000 ($50,000 cash and a $100,000 note) and the exercise price is $500,000, the sales value is $650,000. [FAS66, ¶32, fn11]

.138 If collection of the sales price is not reasonably assured, the cost recovery or installment method of recognizing profit shall be used. [FAS66, ¶35]

.139 If the seller is required to support the operations of the property after the sale, the accounting shall be based on the nature of the support obligation. For example, the seller may retain an interest in the property sold and the buyer may receive preferences as to profits, cash flows, return on investment, and so forth. If the transaction is in substance a sale, the seller shall recognize profit to the extent that proceeds from the sale, including receivables from the buyer, exceed all of the seller's costs related to the entire property. Other examples of support obligations are described in paragraphs .132 through .134. [FAS66, ¶36]

.140 If individual units in condominium projects[13] or time-sharing interests are being sold separately and all the following criteria are met, profit shall be recognized by the percentage-of-completion method on the sale of individual units or interests:

a. Construction is beyond a preliminary stage.[14]
b. The buyer is committed to the extent of being unable to require a refund except for nondelivery of the unit or interest.[15]
c. Sufficient units have already been sold to assure that the entire property will not revert to rental property. In determining whether this condition has been met, the seller shall consider the requirements of state laws, the condominium or time-sharing contract, and the terms of the financing agreements.
d. Sales prices are collectible (refer to paragraph .107).
e. Aggregate sales proceeds and costs can be reasonably estimated. Consideration shall be given to sales volume, trends of unit prices, demand for the units including seasonal factors, developer's experience, geographical location, and environmental factors.

[13]A condominium project may be a building, a group of buildings, or a complete project. [FAS66, ¶37, fn12]

[14]Construction is not beyond a preliminary stage if engineering and design work, execution of construction contracts, site clearance and preparation, excavation, and completion of the building foundation are incomplete. [FAS66, ¶37, fn13]

[15]The buyer may be able to require a refund, for example, if a minimum status of completion of the project is required by state law and that status has not been attained; if state law requires that a "Declaration of Condominium" be filed and it has not been filed, except that in some states the filing of the declaration is a routine matter and the lack of such filing may not make the sales contract voidable; if the sales contract provides that permanent financing at an acceptable cost must be available to the buyer at the time of closing and it is not available; or if the condominium units must be registered with either the Office of Interstate Land Sales Registration of the Department of Housing and Urban Development or the Securities and Exchange Commission, and they are not so registered. [FAS66, ¶37, fn14]

If any of the above criteria is not met, proceeds shall be accounted for as deposits until the criteria are met. [FAS66, ¶37]

.141 *The seller sells property improvements*[15a] *and leases the underlying land to the buyer of the improvements.* In these circumstances, the transactions are interdependent and it is impracticable to distinguish between profits on the sale of the improvements and profits under the related lease. The transaction shall be accounted for as a lease of both the land and improvements if the term of the land lease to the buyer from the seller of the improvements either (a) does not cover substantially all of the economic life of the property improvements, thus strongly implying that the transaction is in substance a lease of both land and improvements, or (b) is not for a substantial period, for example, 20 years. [FAS66, ¶38]

.142 If the land lease described in paragraph .138 covers substantially all of the economic life of the improvements and extends for at least 20 years, the profit to be recognized on the sale of the improvements at the time of sale shall be (a) the present value of the rental payments[16] not in excess of the seller's cost of the land plus (b) the sales value of the improvements minus (c) the carrying value of the improvements and the land. Profit on (1) the buyer's rental payments on the land in excess of the seller's cost of the land and (2) the rent to be received on the land after the maturity of the primary indebtedness on the improvements or other customary amortization term shall be recognized when the land is sold or the rents in excess of the seller's cost of the land are accrued under the lease. Calculations of profit in those circumstances are illustrated in paragraphs .169 and .170. [FAS66, ¶39]

.143 *The sale of the property is accompanied by a leaseback to the seller of all or any part of the property for all or part of its remaining economic life.* Real estate sale-leaseback transactions shall be accounted for in accordance with Section L10, paragraphs .130A through .130M and .160A through .160M. [FAS98, ¶23]

.144 *The sales contract or an accompanying agreement requires the seller to develop the property in the future, to construct facilities on the land, or to provide off-site improvements or amenities.* The seller is involved with future development or construction work if the buyer is unable to pay amounts due for that work or has the right under

[15a]*Property improvements* include both property improvements and integral equipment ([as described in] paragraph .101A of Section Re1 and this section). [FIN43, ¶4]

[16]The present value of the specified rental payments is the present value of the lease payments specified in the lease over the term of the primary indebtedness, if any, on the improvements, or over the customary amortization term of primary debt instruments on the type of improvements involved. The present value is computed at an interest rate appropriate for (a) primary debt if the lease is not subordinated or (b) secondary debt if the lease is subordinated to loans with prior liens. [FAS66, ¶39, fn15]

the terms of the arrangement to defer payment until the work is done. If future costs of development can be reasonably estimated at the time of sale, profit allocable to (a) performance before the sale of the land and (b) the sale of the land shall be recognized when the sale of the land meets the criteria in paragraph .108. Profit allocable to performance after the sale shall be recognized by the percentage-of-completion method as development and construction proceed, provided that cost and profit can be reasonably estimated from the seller's previous experience. [FAS66, ¶41]

.145 The profit shall be allocated to the sale of the land and the later development or construction work on the basis of estimated costs of each activity; the same rate of profit shall be attributed to each activity. No profit shall be recognized at the time of sale if future costs of development cannot be reasonably estimated at that time. [FAS66, ¶42]

.146 *The seller will participate in future profit from the property without risk of loss (such as participation in operating profits or residual values without further obligation).* If the transaction otherwise qualifies for recognition of profit by the full accrual method, the transfer of risks and rewards of ownership and absence of continuing involvement criterion shall be considered met. The contingent future profits shall be recognized when they are realized.[17] All the costs of the sale shall be recognized at the time of sale; none shall be deferred to periods when the contingent profits are recognized. [FAS66, ¶43]

Minimum Initial Investments

.147 Minimum initial investment requirements for sales, other than retail land sales, that are to be accounted for by the full accrual method are specified in paragraph .114. The table of minimum initial investments in paragraph .148 is based on usual loan limits for various types of properties. However, lenders' appraisals of specific properties may differ. Therefore, if a recently placed permanent loan or firm permanent loan commitment for maximum financing of the property exists with an independent established lending institution, the minimum initial investment should be whichever of the following is greater:

a. The minimum percentage of the sales value (refer to paragraph .110) of the property specified in paragraph .148
b. The lesser of:
   (1) The amount of the sales value of the property in excess of 115 percent of the amount of a newly placed permanent loan or firm permanent loan commitment from a primary lender that is an independent established lending institution
   (2) Twenty-five percent of the sales value

[FAS66, ¶53] [Refer to paragraph .1001 for an EITF Issue that provides interpretive guidance on this paragraph.]

[17] Section C59, "Contingencies," paragraph .118, addresses accounting for gain contingencies. [FAS66, ¶43, fn16]

.148 This table does not cover every type of real estate property. To evaluate initial investments on other types of property, enterprises may make analogies to the types of properties specified, or the risks of a particular property can be related to the risks of the properties specified. Use of this table is illustrated in paragraphs .164 through .170.

	Minimum Initial Investment Expressed as a Percentage of Sales Value
Land	
Held for commercial, industrial, or residential development to commence within two years after sale	20
Held for commercial, industrial, or residential development to commence after two years	25
Commercial and Industrial Property[17a]	
Office and industrial buildings, shopping centers, and so forth:	
Properties subject to lease on a long-term lease basis to parties with satisfactory credit rating; cash flow currently sufficient to service all indebtedness	10
Single-tenancy properties sold to a buyer with a satisfactory credit rating	15
All other	20
Other income-producing properties (hotels, motels, marinas, mobile home parks, and so forth):	
Cash flow currently sufficient to service all indebtedness	15
Start-up situations or current deficiencies in cash flow	25

[17a]Although operating facilities such as manufacturing facilities, power plants, and refineries are not specified [here], those types of operating facilities meet the description of an *industrial property.* The Appraisal Institute provides the following definition of *industrial property:*

> Land and/or improvements that can be adapted for industrial use; a combination of land, improvements, and machinery integrated into a functioning unit to assemble, process, and manufacture products from raw materials or fabricated parts; factories that render service, e.g., laundries, dry cleaners, storage warehouses, or those that produce natural resources, e.g., oil wells. [*The Dictionary of Real Estate Appraisal,* 1993]

[FIN43, ¶13]

	Minimum Initial Investment Expressed as a Percentage of Sales Value
Multifamily Residential Property	
Primary residence:	
Cash flow currently sufficient to service all indebtedness	10
Start-up situations or current deficiencies in cash flow	15
Secondary or recreational residence:	
Cash flow currently sufficient to service all indebtedness	15
Start-up situations or current deficiencies in cash flow	25
Single-Family Residential Property (including condominium or cooperative housing)	
Primary residence of the buyer	5*
Secondary or recreational residence	10*

[FAS66, ¶54] [Refer to paragraph .1001 for EITF Issues that provide interpretive guidance on this paragraph.]

*If collectibility of the remaining portion of the sales price cannot be supported by reliable evidence of collection experience, the minimum initial investment shall be at least 60 percent of the difference between the sales value and the financing available from loans guaranteed by regulatory bodies such as the Federal Housing Authority (FHA) or the Veterans Administration (VA), or from independent, established lending institutions. This 60-percent test applies when independent first-mortgage financing is not utilized and the seller takes a receivable from the buyer for the difference between the sales value and the initial investment. If independent first-mortgage financing is utilized, the adequacy of the initial investment on sales of single-family residential property should be determined in accordance with paragraph .147. [FAS66, ¶54, fn(a)]

Description of Certain Methods of Accounting for Real Estate Sales Transactions

.149 Paragraphs .150 through .163 describe several of the methods of profit recognition that are provided for by this section. [FAS66, ¶55]

Installment Method

.150 The installment method apportions each cash receipt and principal payment by the buyer on debt assumed between cost recovered and profit. The apportionment is in the same ratio as total cost and total profit bear to the sales value. The calculation is illustrated in paragraph .177. [FAS66, ¶56]

.151 If the stated interest rate is equal to or less than an appropriate interest rate, it is acceptable not to reduce the receivable to its present value. This ordinarily results in reducing profit recognized in the earlier years. [FAS66, ¶57]

.152 Under the installment method, the receivable less profits not recognized does not exceed what the property value would have been if the property had not been sold. [FAS66, ¶58]

.153 The income statement, or related footnotes, for the period including the date of sale presents the sales value, the gross profit that has not yet been recognized, and the total cost of the sale. Revenue and cost of sales (or gross profit) are presented as separate items on the income statement or are disclosed in the footnotes when profit is recognized as earned. This presentation is illustrated [for a retail land sale transaction] in paragraph .194 [of Re1, "Real Estate: Sales."] [FAS66, ¶59]

.154 Paragraph [.173 of Section Re1, "Real Estate: Sales"[18]] describes accounting for obligations for future improvement costs under the percentage-of-completion method. That description applies as well to accounting for those obligations under the installment method. [FAS66, ¶60]

---

[18]If there is an obligation for future improvement costs that is recognized under the percentage-of-completion method:

a. Estimates are based on costs generally expected in the construction industry locally.
b. Unrecoverable costs of off-site improvements, utilities, and amenities are provided for. In determining the amount of unrecoverable costs, estimates of amounts to be recovered from future sale of the improvements, utilities, and amenities are discounted to present value as of the date the net unrecoverable costs are recognized.

[FAS66, ¶75]

.155 If after adoption of the installment method the transaction meets the requirements for the full accrual method (specified in paragraphs .106 through .121) of recognizing profit for real estate sales other than retail land sales, the seller may then change to the full accrual method. The remaining profit that was not recognized is recognized in income at that time. [FAS66, ¶61]

Cost Recovery Method

.156 Under the cost recovery method, no profit is recognized until cash payments by the buyer, including principal and interest on debt due to the seller and on existing debt assumed by the buyer, exceed the seller's cost of the property sold.[19] The receivable less profits not recognized, if any, does not exceed what the depreciated property value would have been if the property had not been sold. [FAS66, ¶62]

.157 The income statement for the period including the date of sale presents the sales value, the gross profit that has not yet been recognized, and the total cost of the sale. Gross profit not yet recognized is offset against the related receivable on the balance sheet. Principal collections reduce the related receivable, and interest collections on such receivables increase the unrecognized gross profit on the balance sheet. Gross profit is presented as a separate item of revenue on the income statement when it is recognized as earned. [FAS66, ¶63]

.158 If, after the adoption of the cost recovery method, the transaction meets the requirements for the full accrual method (specified in paragraphs .106 through .121), the seller may then change to the full accrual method. The remaining profit that was not recognized is recognized in income at that time. [FAS66, ¶64]

Deposit Method

.159 Under the deposit method, the seller does not recognize any profit, does not record notes receivable, continues to report in its financial statements the property and the related existing debt even if it has been assumed by the buyer, and discloses that those items are subject to a sales contract. The seller continues to charge depreciation to expense as a period cost for the property for which deposits have been received [FAS66, ¶65] unless the property has been classified as held for sale in accordance with paragraph .107 of Section D60, "Disposal of Long-Lived Assets." [FAS144, ¶C9] Cash received from the buyer, including the initial investment and subsequent collections of principal and interest, is reported as a deposit on the contract except that, for sales that are not retail land sales,

[19]For an all-inclusive or "wraparound" receivable held by the seller, interest collected is recognized as income to the extent of, and as an appropriate offset to, interest expense on prior-lien financing for which the seller remains responsible. [FAS66, ¶62, fn23]

portions of cash received that are designated by the contract as interest and are not subject to refund offset carrying charges (property taxes and interest on existing debt) on the property. Interest collected that is subject to refund and is included in the deposit account before a sale is consummated is accounted for as part of the buyer's initial investment (refer to paragraph .110) at the time the sale is consummated. [FAS66, ¶65]

.160 When a contract is canceled without a refund, deposits forfeited are recognized as income. [FAS66, ¶66]

.161 The seller's balance sheet presents nonrecourse debt assumed by the buyer among the liabilities; the debt assumed is not offset against the related property. The seller reports the buyer's principal payments on mortgage debt assumed as additional deposits with corresponding reductions of the carrying amount of the mortgage debt. [FAS66, ¶67]

Reduced-Profit Method

.162 A reduced profit is determined by discounting the receivable from the buyer to the present value of the lowest level of annual payments required by the sales contract over the maximum period specified in paragraph .112 and excluding requirements to pay lump sums. The present value is calculated using an appropriate interest rate,[20] but not less than the rate stated in the sales contract. This method permits profit to be recognized from level payments on the buyer's debt over the maximum term established in paragraph .115 and postpones recognition of other profits until lump sum or other payments are made. [FAS66, ¶68]

.163 To illustrate, assume a sale of land that cost the seller $800,000 and is being sold for $1,000,000 with the following financing:

Buyer's initial investment	$ 250,000
First mortgage note payable to an independent lending institution (Terms—15 percent interest payable annually over 20 years: $79,881 per year including principal and interest)	500,000
Second mortgage note payable to seller (Terms—12 percent interest payable annually over 25 years: $31,875 per year including principal and interest)	250,000
Total selling price	$1,000,000

The amortization term of the second mortgage (25 years) exceeds the term permitted by paragraph .112 (20 years for sales of land). It is assumed that the payments by the buyer each year will meet the requirement in paragraph .123, that the reduced-profit method is to be applied, and that the market interest rate is 16 percent.

[20] Section I69, paragraphs .106 and .107, provide criteria for selecting an appropriate rate for present-value calculations. [FAS66, ¶68, fn24]

The present value of \$31,875 per year for 20 years at a market rate of 16 percent is \$31,875 × 5.92884 = \$188,982.

The profit to be recognized at the time of sale is reduced by the difference between the face amount of the seller's receivable (\$250,000) and the reduced amount (\$188,982), or \$61,018. The profit recognized at the time of sale is \$1,000,000 (sales price) minus \$800,000 (cost) minus \$61,018, or \$138,982. Additional profit of \$61,018 is recognized as the second mortgage payments are received in years 21 through 25. [FAS66, ¶69]

Exhibit I

Illustration of Effect of Land Lease—New Multifamily Residential Property

.164 Land improvements may be sold and concurrently the land under the improvements may be leased to the buyer of the improvements. [FAS66, ¶77]

.165 This exhibit illustrates the effect of loans issued in connection with long-term land leases on evaluations of the adequacy of a buyer's initial investment if improvements on the land are sold separately. In addition, it demonstrates the limit that a lease places on profit recognition if the leased land is owned by the seller of the improvements, making the lease of land and sale of improvements interdependent transactions. [FAS66, ¶78]

.166 The calculations are illustrated for four different circumstances: two examples with a primary land lease and two with a subordinated land lease. [FAS66, ¶79]

.167 Primary Land Lease: Land Owned by Third Party Lessor—Nonqualifying

Assumptions:

Sales price of improvements	\$875,000
Represented by proceeds of:	
Cash down payment	\$125,000
Loan by insurance company: lien on leasehold improvements, 28-year term, 8½%, payable in equal monthly installments of principal and interest	657,000
Note received by seller from buyer: 12-year term, 9½%, payable in equal monthly installments of principal and interest	93,000
	\$875,000

Land lease for 99 years @ \$19,000/year, net, payable monthly in advance

Cost of constructing improvements—\$750,000

No continuing involvement by seller

Computations:

Present value of 336 monthly payments on land lease of \$1,583.33 discounted at 8½% (interest rate on loan from insurance company): \$1,583.33 + (\$1,583.33 × 127.9071)	\$ 204,000
Loan from insurance company	657,000
Equivalent primary debt	861,000
Note receivable from buyer	93,000
Total debt or equivalent	954,000
Down payment	125,000
Sales value	\$1,079,000

Because 15% of the sales value of the improvements is \$161,850, the initial investment of \$125,000 (about 12% of adjusted sales value) is inadequate to recognize profit on the sale of improvements. The second test is therefore irrelevant. [FAS66, ¶80]

.168 Primary Land Lease: Land Owned by Third-Party Lessor—Qualifying

Assumptions:

Sales price of improvements	\$875,000
Represented by proceeds of:	
Cash down payment	\$165,000
Loan by insurance company: lien on leasehold improvements, 28-year term, 8½%, payable in equal monthly installments of principal and interest	657,000
Note received by seller from buyer: 12-year term, 9½%, payable in equal monthly installments of principal and interest	53,000
	\$875,000

Land lease for 99 years @ \$17,880/year, net, payable monthly in advance

Cost of constructing improvements—\$750,000

No continuing involvement by seller

Computations:

Present value of 336 monthly payments on land lease of $1,490 discounted at 8½% (interest rate on loan from insurance company):	
$1,490 + ($1,490 × 127.9071)	$ 192,000
Loan from insurance company	657,000
Equivalent primary debt	849,000
Note receivable from buyer	53,000
Total debt or equivalent	902,000
Down payment	165,000
Sales value	$1,067,000

Because 15% of the sales value of the improvements is $160,050, the initial investment of $165,000 (15% of the sales value) is adequate to recognize profit on the sale of improvements. However, the second test must also be applied.

The initial investment required by the second test is:

Sales value	$1,067,000
115% of $849,000 (loan from primary lender)	976,350
	$ 90,650

The initial investment of $165,000 exceeds the amount required, so recognition of profit on sale of improvements is appropriate. The second test may alternatively be applied as the ratio of total debt or equivalent to the equivalent primary debt: $902,000/$849,000 = 106%. Because 106% is less than 115%, the initial investment exceeds the difference between the sales value of the property and 115% of the equivalent primary debt.

Profit recognition:

Sales price of improvements	$875,000
Less: Cost of improvements	750,000
Profit recognized at time of sale	$125,000

[FAS66, ¶81]

.169 Subordinated Land Lease: Land Owned by Seller—Qualifying

Assumptions:

Sales price of improvements	$ 914,000
Represented by proceeds of:	
Cash down payment	$ 154,000
Loan by insurance company: first lien on the fee or on subordinated leasehold, 28-year term, 8¼%, payable in equal monthly installments of principal and interest	760,000
	$ 914,000

Land lease for 99 years @ $11,580/year, net, payable monthly in advance,
and 5% of gross rents
Cost of land—$200,000
Cost of constructing improvements—$750,000
No continuing involvement by seller

Computations:

Present value of 336 monthly payments on land lease at $965 discounted at 12% (imputed interest for a second lien receivable): $965 + ($965 × 96.432696)	$ 94,000
Loan from insurance company (primary debt)	760,000
Total debt or equivalent	854,000
Down payment	154,000
Sales value	$1,008,000

The initial investment ($154,000) is more than 15% of the sales value. (15% × $1,008,000 = $151,200).

The initial investment is also larger than the excess of the sales value over 115% of the primary debt.

Sales value	$1,008,000
115% of $760,000	874,000
Excess of sales value over 115% of debt	$ 134,000

Therefore, the initial investment of $154,000 is adequate, and recognizing profit on the sale of the improvements is appropriate.

Profit recognition:

Sales value		$1,008,000
Less: Cost of improvements	$750,000	
Cost of land	200,000	950,000
Profit recognized at time of sale		$ 58,000

The effect of including the present value of the lease is to reduce profit recognized by $106,000: $94,000 (present value of the land lease) – $200,000 (cost of land). [FAS66, ¶82]

.170 Subordinated Land Lease: Land Owned by Seller—Nonqualifying

Assumptions:

Sales price of improvements	$ 875,000
Represented by proceeds of:	
Cash down payment	$ 132,000
Loan by insurance company: first lien on the fee or on subordinated leasehold, 28-year term, 8¼%, payable in equal monthly installments of principal and interest	743,000
	$ 875,000

Land lease for 99 years @ $19,332/year, net, payable monthly in advance
Cost of land—$200,000
Cost of improvements—$750,000
No continuing involvement by seller

Computations:

Present value of 336 monthly payments on land lease of $1,611 discounted at 12% (imputed interest for a second lien receivable): $1,611 + ($1,611 × 96.432696)	$ 157,000
Loan from insurance company (primary debt)	743,000
Total debt or equivalent	900,000
Down payment	132,000
Sales value	$1,032,000

The initial investment ($132,000) is less than 15% of the sales value (15% × $1,032,000 = $154,800), and therefore is inadequate to recognize profit on sale of improvements. Profit recognized at time of sale should not exceed that recognizable under the installment method as if the subordinated lease were an installment receivable.

Profit recognition on installment method:

Sales value		$1,032,000
Less: Cost of improvements	$750,000	
Cost of land	200,000	950,000
Anticipated profit on sale of improvements		$ 82,000

Cash received or to be received by the seller, other than the proceeds of the primary loan, is:

Down payment	$132,000
Present value of land lease payments	157,000
	$289,000

The percentage of profit in each collection is therefore:

$$\frac{\$\ 82{,}000}{\$289{,}000} = 28.37\%$$

Profit recognizable in the period of sale is 28.37% of the down payment of $132,000, or $37,450. The remaining profit of $44,550 will be recognized at the rate of 28.37% of the portion of each lease payment that is equivalent to a reduction of principal on a loan of $157,000 for 28 years at 12%.

The effect of including the present value of the lease in the sales value of the improvements is to reduce the profit recognized on the improvements by $43,000: $157,000 (present value of the land lease) – $200,000 (cost of the land). [FAS66, ¶83]

Exhibit II

Illustration of Profit Recognition—Sale of Property with Construction and Support Obligations by Seller

.171 This exhibit illustrates the method of accounting required for a sale of property in which the seller is obligated to construct multifamily units and in which cash flow deficits are anticipated. The example applies to obligations of the seller specified in paragraphs .131 through .133. [FAS66, ¶84]

.172 Assumptions:

a. Company X develops and sells multifamily residential projects. The Company performs directly all developmental activities, including initial planning, site acquisition, obtaining of financing, and physical construction of the project.

b. During the year ended December 31, 19X1 the Company began a project of 100 units. The project was planned and substantial activity had been performed in 19X1 but physical construction had not started as of December 31, 19X1. However, all contracts had been let, and the Company had obtained construction financing.

c. On December 31, 19X1, the Company sold the project to a limited partnership syndication (fully formed) in which it is the sole general partner:

Sales value	$1,100,000
Represented by proceeds of:	
Cash down payment	$ 165,000
Permanent financing assumed by the buyer, consisting of a 28-year 8½% fully amortizing first mortgage loan by a conventional lender, payable in equal monthly payments of principal and interest to maturity	825,000
Second mortgage note received by the Company payable in equal monthly installments including interest at 9½% over 12 years	110,000
	$1,100,000

d. The closing occurred on December 31, 19X1 and included delivery or performance of the following:

(1) The Company delivered to the buyer a legal title to the land and all existing improvements.

(2) The Company delivered to the buyer a firm commitment from an outside lender for permanent financing, and the buyer assumed permanent financing formerly in the name of the Company.

(3) The Company received from the buyer $165,000 cash and a second mortgage note for $110,000.

(4) The Company signed a contract to deliver the completed project for a single price of $1,100,000.

e. Costs incurred by the Company and total costs estimated to complete the project, as of December 31, 19X1, were:

	Costs to Date	Estimated Costs to Complete	Total Estimated Costs
Land	$117,000		$117,000
Feasibility, zoning, architectural	35,000		35,000
Finance and other	85,000	$ 10,000	95,000
Site improvements		20,000	20,000
Building construction		571,000	571,000
Total	$237,000	$601,000	$838,000

f. The Company has completed an extensive market research and feasibility study analyzing its cost estimates, the rent-up incubation period, and subsequent rent levels. The initial rent-up will commence in 19X2. Accordingly, a support period of two years is presumed for 19X3 and 19X4.
g. Based on its market analysis, the projected results are as follows:

	19X2	**19X3**	**19X4**
Rental expense	$ 37,000	$ 58,000	$ 58,000
Debt service	93,000	93,000	93,000
Total	130,000	151,000	151,000
Rental revenue	(75,000)	(150,000)	(180,000)*
Anticipated net deficit (surplus) in cash flow	55,000	1,000	(29,000)
Safety factor of ⅓ of rental revenue	25,000	50,000	60,000
Adjusted anticipated net deficit in cash flow	$ 80,000	$ 51,000	$ 31,000

*$180,000 equals 95% of gross scheduled rents.

h. Initial cost estimates by the Company on previous projects have never varied from final costs by more than one-half of one % of total costs. [FAS66, ¶85]

.173 Calculations of Profit to Be Recognized:

Schedules A and B (refer to paragraphs .174 and .175) illustrate calculations of profit to be recognized in the period of sale, in the period of construction, and in each period in which the seller will support operations (19X2-19X4). The following features should be noted:

a. The percentage of estimated total profit to be recognized each period is determined by the ratio of gross costs incurred to the end of the period to total estimated gross costs of the project, including gross costs during the period of support of operations. (Construction costs should be included even if construction is performed by parties other than the seller.)
b. The estimated total profit that is the basis of the calculation in each period (that is, the profit to which the percentage in (a) is applied) is determined by adding the sales value and two-thirds of the projected revenue during the period of support of operations and deducting the estimated total costs of the project, including costs of operating the property and debt service.
   (1) Actual amounts of revenue and costs are substituted for estimated amounts in the calculation as the actual amounts are known. However, in this illustration, remain-

ing estimates of future revenue and expense are not changed because of actual results even though experience might indicate that projections of future amounts should be revised.

(2) Projected and actual revenues in the calculation should exclude amounts that accrue to the buyer, for example, revenue in excess of the sum of operating expenses and debt service.

(3) One-third of projected revenue should be excluded from the estimate of profit to provide a margin of safety (refer to paragraph .172(g)). Actual results incorporated in the calculation need not be reduced by a safety factor.

(4) The calculation illustrated should be applied only if objective information is available regarding occupancy levels and rental rates for similar property in the immediate area. This will provide reasonable assurance that rent revenue from the project will be sufficient to cover operating expenses and debt service, including payments due to the seller under the terms of the transaction. Unless that evidence is available, no profit should be recognized on the transaction until rent revenue actually reaches levels that assure coverage of those costs.

c. Schedule A shows calculation of profit to be recognized each period on the assumption that actual revenue and costs are the same as those projected in paragraph .172(g) *adjusted* for the safety margin of one-third of revenue.

d. Schedule B shows calculation of profit to be recognized each period on the assumption that actual revenue and costs are the same as those projected in paragraph .172(g) *before* adjustment for safety margin.

e. Schedule C illustrates the calculation of estimated future rent receipts by adjustment for a safety margin.

[FAS66, ¶86]

.174 **Schedule A**

Example of Profit Calculation

(assuming actual rental revenue equals *adjusted* projection)

Revenues	
Sales value	$1,100,000
Adjusted—projected rental revenue*	
19X2	50,000
19X3	100,000
19X4	120,000
	1,370,000

*Two-thirds of projected revenue during periods of support of operations; this can also be calculated as projected rental expenses plus projected debt service less projected deficit cash flow. [FAS66, ¶87, fn29]

Costs	
Total estimated costs of project (paragraph .172(e))	838,000
Estimated rental expenses and debt service	
19X2	130,000
19X3	151,000
19X4	151,000
	1,270,000
Total projected profit	$ 100,000

Profit to be recognized:

$$\frac{\text{Cost to date}}{\text{Total costs}} \times \text{projected profit}$$

Profit recognized in period of sale:

$$\frac{\$\ 237{,}000}{1{,}270{,}000} \times \$100{,}000 = \$18{,}661$$

Total profit to date	$ 18,661
Less profit previously reported	0
Current profit recognition	$ 18,661

Profit recognized in period of construction:

$$\frac{\$\ 838{,}000}{1{,}270{,}000} \times \$100{,}000 = \$65{,}984$$

Total profit to date	$ 65,984
Less profit previously recognized	18,661
Current profit recognition	$ 47,323

Profit recognized during support period (19X2):

$$\frac{\$\ 968{,}000}{1{,}270{,}000} \times \$100{,}000 = \$76{,}221$$

Total profit to date	$ 76,221
Less profit previously recognized	65,984
Current profit recognition	$ 10,237

Profit recognized during support period (19X3):

$$\frac{\$1{,}119{,}000}{1{,}270{,}000} \times \$100{,}000 = \$88{,}110$$

Total profit to date	$ 88,110
Less profit previously recognized	76,221
Current profit recognition	$ 11,889

Profit recognized during support period (19X4):

$$\frac{\$1{,}270{,}000}{1{,}270{,}000} \times \$100{,}000 = \$100{,}000$$

Total profit to date	$100,000
Less profit previously recognized	88,110
Current profit recognition	$ 11,890

[FAS66, ¶87]

.175 **Schedule B**

Example of Profit Calculation
(assuming actual rental revenue equals *unadjusted* projection)
(in thousands)

	Profit Recognized in Period of Sale	**Profit Recognized in Period of Construction**	**Profit Recognized during Support Period 19X2**	**19X3**	**19X4**
Revenues					
Sales value	$1,100	$1,100	$1,100	$1,100	$1,100
Adjusted—projected rental revenue*					
19X2	50	50	75†	75†	75†
19X3	100	100	100	150†	150†
19X4	120	120	120	150‡	151§
	1,370	1,370	1,395	1,475	1,476
Costs					
Same as Schedule A	1,270	1,270	1,270	1,270	1,270
Total projected profit	$ 100	$ 100	$ 125	$ 205	$ 206

---

*Two-thirds of projected revenue during periods of support of operation; this can also be calculated as projected rental expenses plus projected debt service less projected deficit cash flow.

†Actual rental revenue.

‡Actual rental revenue excluding amounts not needed to meet cash flow requirements of the property.

§Because the property has attained a level of occupancy in excess of the original adjusted projection, and there is no reason to believe that such occupancy level cannot be sustained, the projected 19X4 rental revenue should be adjusted to 19X3 actual rental revenue.

Profit to be recognized:

$$\frac{\text{Cost to date}}{\text{Total costs}} \times \text{projected profit}$$

Profit recognized in period of sale:

$$\frac{\$\ 237{,}000}{1{,}270{,}000} \times \$100{,}000 = \$18{,}661$$

Total profit to date	$ 18,661
Less profit previously reported	0
Current profit recognition	$ 18,661

Profit recognized in period of construction:

$$\frac{\$\ 838{,}000}{1{,}270{,}000} \times \$100{,}000 = \$65{,}984$$

Total profit to date	$ 65,984
Less profit previously reported	18,661
Current profit recognition	$ 47,323

Profit recognized during support period (19X2):

$$\frac{\$\ 968{,}000}{1{,}270{,}000} \times \$125{,}000 = \$95{,}276$$

Total profit to date	$ 95,276
Less profit previously reported	65,984
Current profit recognition	$ 29,292

Profit recognized during support period (19X3):

$$\frac{\$1{,}119{,}000}{1{,}270{,}000} \times \$205{,}000 = \$180{,}626$$

Total profit to date	$180,626
Less profit previously reported	95,276
Current profit recognition	$ 85,350

Profit recognized during support period (19X4):

$$\frac{\$1{,}270{,}000}{1{,}270{,}000} \times \$206{,}000 = \$206{,}000$$

Total profit to date	$206,000
Less profit previously reported	180,626
Current profit recognition	$ 25,374

[FAS66, ¶88]

.176 **Schedule C**

Calculation of Adjusted Projected Rental Revenue

Assume an office building under development is sold together with an agreement to support operations of the property for three years. The projected annual rent roll is $1,000,000 of which $350,000 is supported by signed lease agreements. The projected rental revenue for the first year of operation is $600,000; the second year $750,000; and the third year $1,000,000. At the time of sale, the amounts to be included in the calculation would be as follows:

Year	Projected Rental Revenue	Safety Factor (33⅓%)	Adjusted Projected Rental Revenue
1	$ 600,000	$200,000	$400,000
2	750,000	250,000	500,000
3	1,000,000	333,333	666,667

If at the time of sale there were signed lease agreements for $450,000, then the $450,000 would be used in year 1 because it is greater than the adjusted projected rental revenue. The adjusted projected rental revenue for years 2 and 3 would remain $500,000 and $666,667, respectively. [FAS66, ¶89]

Exhibit III

Illustration of Profit Recognition—Installment Method, with Debt Assumed by Buyer

.177 Assumptions:

Cash down payment	$ 150,000
Second mortgage payable by buyer to seller (10-year amortization of principal plus interest)	350,000
Total cash to be received by seller	500,000
First mortgage assumed by buyer (20-year amortization of principal plus interest)	500,000
Total sales price and sales value	1,000,000
Cost	600,000
Total profit	$ 400,000

The initial investment is assumed to be inadequate for full profit recognition, and the installment method of accounting is assumed to be appropriate. It is also assumed that, after the down payment, the buyer pays $25,000 of principal on the first mortgage and $35,000 of principal on the second mortgage.

Profit recognition: Under the installment method, profit recognition attributable to the down payment is $60,000, representing 40% ($400,000/$1,000,000) of $150,000.

Profit recognition attributable to the principal payments by the buyer on the first and second mortgages is $24,000, representing 40% of $60,000 ($25,000 + $35,000).

[FAS66, ¶90]

Decision Tree

.178 The following decision tree [is] intended to provide an overview of the major provisions in this section that relate to the accounting for sales of real estate. It should not be used without further reference to the section. The highlighted boxes describe the general requirements for recognizing all of the profit on a sale of real estate other than a retail land sale at the date of sale. [FAS66, ¶123]

SALES OF REAL ESTATE OTHER THAN RETAIL LAND SALES

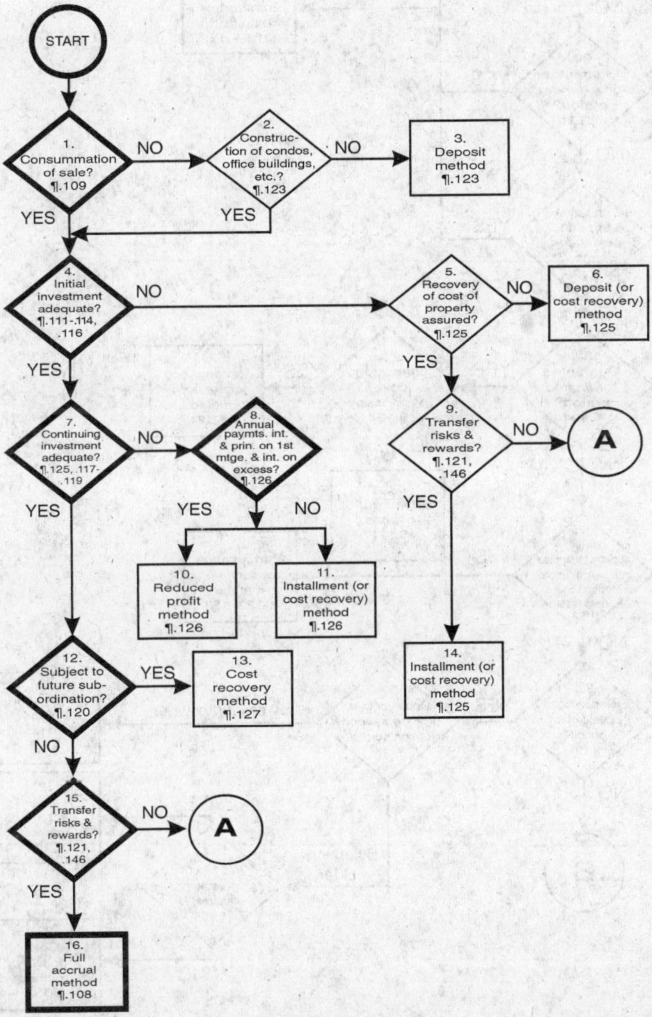

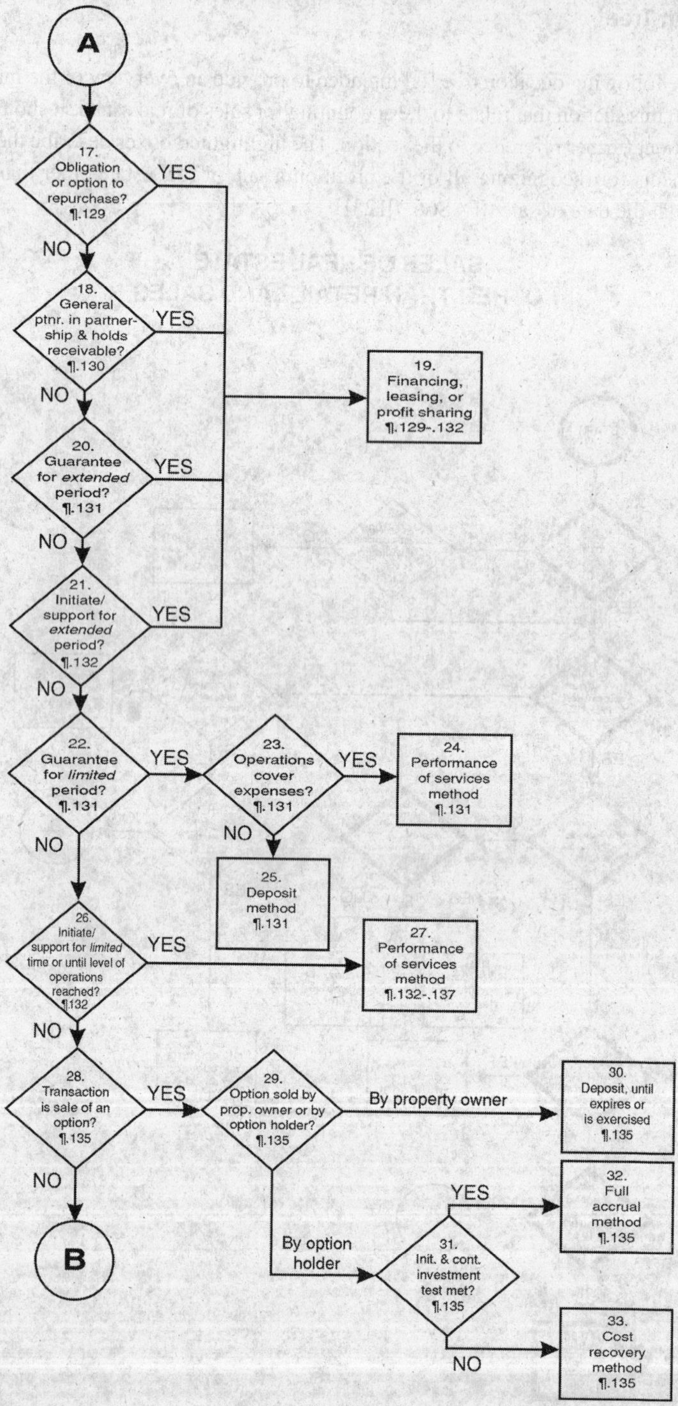
A
17. Obligation or option to repurchase? ¶.129
YES
NO
18. General ptnr. in partnership & holds receivable? ¶.130
YES
NO
19. Financing, leasing, or profit sharing ¶.129-.132
20. Guarantee for *extended* period? ¶.131
YES
NO
21. Initiate/ support for *extended* period? ¶.132
YES
NO
22. Guarantee for *limited* period? ¶.131
YES
NO
23. Operations cover expenses? ¶.131
YES
NO
24. Performance of services method ¶.131
25. Deposit method ¶.131
26. Initiate/ support for *limited* time or until level of operations reached? ¶.132
YES
NO
27. Performance of services method ¶.132-.137
28. Transaction is sale of an option? ¶.135
YES
NO
29. Option sold by prop. owner or by option holder? ¶.135
By property owner
By option holder
30. Deposit, until expires or is exercised ¶.135
31. Init. & cont. investment test met? ¶.135
YES
NO
32. Full accrual method ¶.135
33. Cost recovery method ¶.135
B

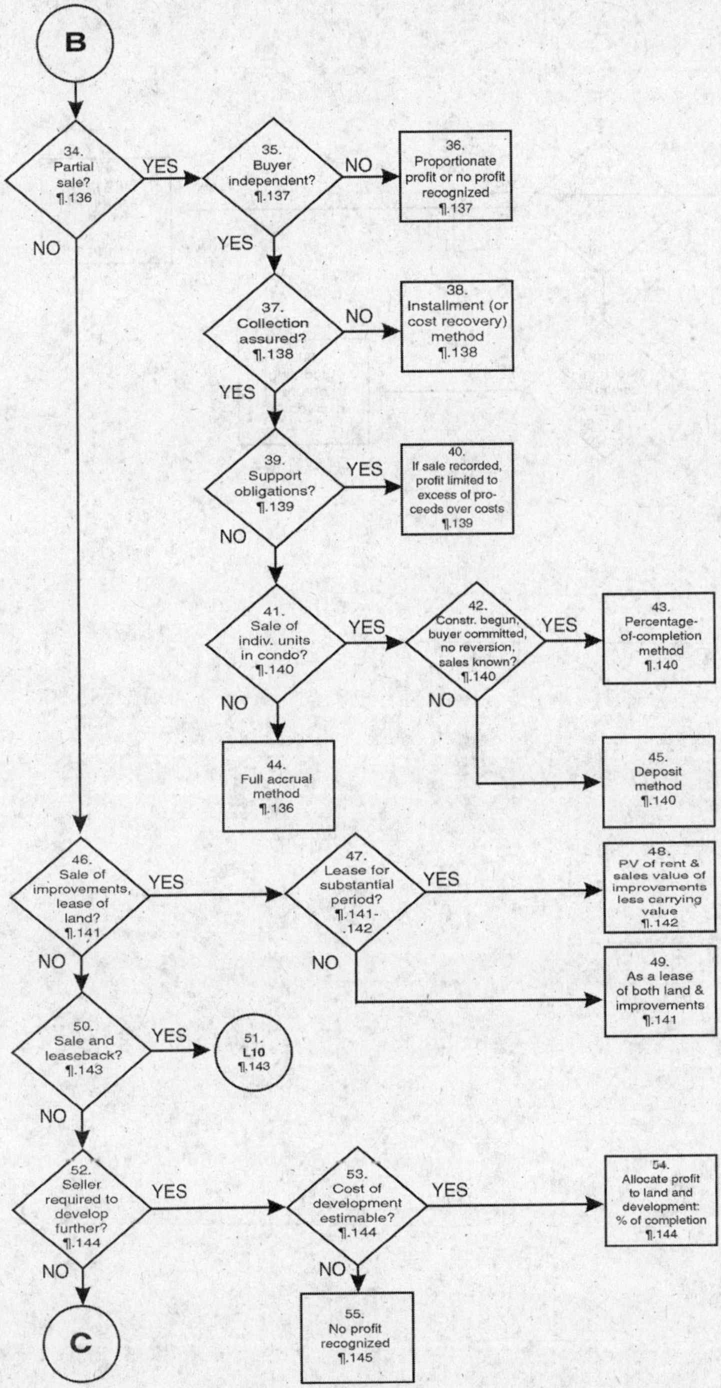
B
34. Partial sale? ¶.136
YES
NO
35. Buyer independent? ¶.137
NO
YES
36. Proportionate profit or no profit recognized ¶.137
37. Collection assured? ¶.138
NO
YES
38. Installment (or cost recovery) method ¶.138
39. Support obligations? ¶.139
YES
NO
40. If sale recorded, profit limited to excess of proceeds over costs ¶.139
41. Sale of indiv. units in condo? ¶.140
YES
NO
42. Constr. begun, buyer committed, no reversion, sales known? ¶.140
YES
NO
43. Percentage-of-completion method ¶.140
44. Full accrual method ¶.136
45. Deposit method ¶.140
46. Sale of improvements, lease of land? ¶.141
YES
NO
47. Lease for substantial period? ¶.141-.142
YES
NO
48. PV of rent & sales value of improvements less carrying value ¶.142
49. As a lease of both land & improvements ¶.141
50. Sale and leaseback? ¶.143
YES
NO
51. L10 ¶.143
52. Seller required to develop further? ¶.144
YES
NO
53. Cost of development estimable? ¶.144
YES
NO
54. Allocate profit to land and development: % of completion ¶.144
55. No profit recognized ¶.145
C

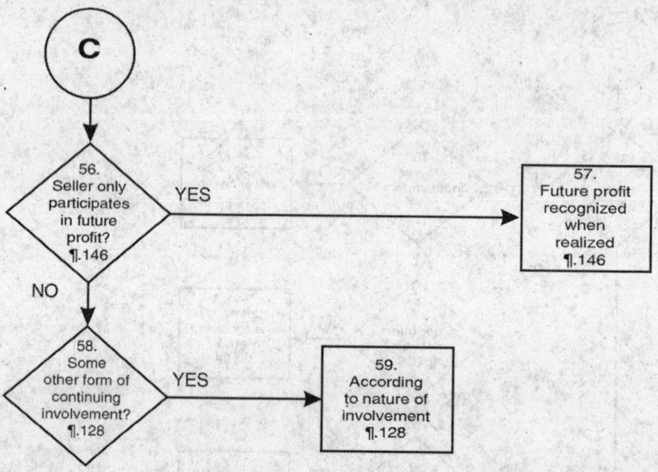
C
56.
Seller only
participates
in future
profit?
¶.146
YES
57.
Future profit
recognized
when
realized
¶.146
NO
58.
Some
other form of
continuing
involvement?
¶.128
YES
59.
According
to nature of
involvement
¶.128

Supplemental Guidance: Emerging Issues Task Force (EITF) Issues

.1000 [Listed below are EITF Issues that provide supplemental guidance for this section. These Issues are grouped by subject matter and may be either interpretive of or related by topic to the guidance in this section.

Revenue Recognition

EITF Issue No. 84-17, "Profit Recognition on Sales of Real Estate with Graduated Payment Mortgages or Insured Mortgages"
EITF Issue No. 86-6, "Antispeculation Clauses in Real Estate Sales Contracts"
EITF Issue No. 86-7, "Recognition by Homebuilders of Profit from Sales of Land and Related Construction Contracts"
EITF Issue No. 87-9, "Profit Recognition on Sales of Real Estate with Insured Mortgages or Surety Bonds"
EITF Issue No. 88-12, "Transfer of Ownership Interest as Part of Down Payment under FASB Statement No. 66"

Sale-Leaseback Transactions

EITF Issue No. 84-37, "Sale-Leaseback Transaction with Repurchase Option"
EITF Issue No. 85-27, "Recognition of Receipts from Made-Up Rental Shortfalls"
EITF Issue No. 86-17, "Deferred Profit on Sale-Leaseback Transaction with Lessee Guarantee of Residual Value"
EITF Issue No. 88-21, "Accounting for the Sale of Property Subject to the Seller's Preexisting Lease"
EITF Issue No. 00-11, "Lessors' Evaluation of Whether Leases of Certain Integral Equipment Meet the Ownership Transfer Requirements of FASB Statement No. 13"
EITF Issue No. 00-13, "Determining Whether Equipment Is 'Integral Equipment' Subject to FASB Statements No. 66 and No. 98"

Special-Purpose Entities (SPEs)

EITF Issue No. 96-21, "Implementation Issues in Accounting for Leasing Transactions involving Special-Purpose Entities"
EITF Issue No. 97-1, "Implementation Issues in Accounting for Lease Transactions, including Those involving Special Purpose Entities"

Other

EITF Issue No. 88-14, "Settlement of Fees with Extra Units to a General Partner in a Master Limited Partnership"
EITF Issue No. 88-24, "Effect of Various Forms of Financing under FASB Statement No. 66"
EITF Issue No. 89-14, "Valuation of Repossessed Real Estate"
EITF Issue No. 98-8, " Accounting for Transfers of Investments That Are in Substance Real Estate"
EITF Issue No. 01-2, "Interpretations of APB Opinion No. 29"]

.1001 [Listed below are those EITF Issues that provide interpretive guidance on specific material in this section.

Paragraphs .106 and .107 (FAS 66, ¶3-4)—EITF Issue No. 88-24
Paragraph .108 (FAS 66, ¶5)—EITF Issues No. 86-7 and 88-24
Paragraph .109 (FAS 66, ¶6)—EITF Issue No. 88-24
Paragraph .112 (FAS 66, ¶9)—EITF Issues No. 87-9, 88-12, 88-24, and 01-2
Paragraph .113 (FAS 66, ¶10)—EITF Issues No. 87-9, 88-12, and 88-24
Paragraph .114 (FAS 66, ¶11)—EITF Issues No. 87-9 and 88-12
Paragraph .115 (FAS 66, ¶12)—EITF Issue No. 84-17
Paragraph .129 (FAS 66, ¶26)—EITF Issue No. 86-6
Paragraph .147 (FAS 66, ¶53)—EITF Issue No. 87-9
Paragraph .148 (FAS 66, ¶54)—EITF Issues No. 87-9 and 88-12]

(The next page is 38345.)

RELATED PARTIES — SECTION R36

Sources: ARB 43, Chapter 1A; FASB Statement 57; FASB Statement 109

[**Note:** A list of Issues discussed by the Emerging Issues Task Force (EITF) that provide supplemental guidance for this section is presented in paragraph .1000.]

Summary

Financial statements shall include disclosures of material related party transactions, other than compensation arrangements, expense allowances, and other similar items in the ordinary course of business. The nature of certain common control relationships shall be disclosed if the nature of those relationships could significantly affect the reporting enterprise. The reporting of certain related party transactions is specified in other sections.

Introduction

.101 Examples of transactions between **related parties** include transactions between (a) a parent company and its subsidiaries; (b) subsidiaries of a common parent; (c) an enterprise and trusts for the benefit of employees, such as pension and profit-sharing trusts that are managed by or under the trusteeship of the enterprise's **management;** (d) an enterprise and its **principal owners,** management, or members of their **immediate families;** and (e) **affiliates.** Transactions between related parties commonly occur in the normal course of business. Some examples of common types of transactions with related parties are: sales, purchases, and transfers of realty and personal property; services received or furnished, for example, accounting, management, engineering, and legal services; use of property and equipment by lease or otherwise; borrowings and lendings; guarantees; maintenance of bank balances as compensating balances for the benefit of another; intercompany billings based on allocations of common costs; and filings of consolidated tax returns. Transactions between related parties are considered to be related party transactions even though they may not be given accounting recognition. For example, an enterprise may receive services from a related party without charge and not record receipt of the services. [FAS57, ¶1]

Disclosures

.102 Financial statements shall include disclosures of material related party transactions, other than compensation arrangements, expense allowances, and other similar items in the ordinary course of business. However, disclosure of transactions that are eliminated in the preparation of consolidated or combined financial statements is not required in those statements.[1] The disclosures shall include:[2]

a. The nature of the relationship(s) involved
b. A description of the transactions, including transactions to which no amounts or nominal amounts were ascribed, for each of the periods for which income statements are presented, and such other information deemed necessary to an understanding of the effects of the transactions on the financial statements
c. The dollar amounts of transactions for each of the periods for which income statements are presented and the effects of any change in the method of establishing the terms from that used in the preceding period
d. Amounts due from or to related parties as of the date of each balance sheet presented and, if not otherwise apparent, the terms and manner of settlement [FAS57, ¶2]
e. The information required by paragraph .149 of Section I27, "Income Taxes." [FAS109, ¶288(s)]

.103 Transactions involving related parties cannot be presumed to be carried out on an arm's-length basis, as the requisite conditions of competitive, free-market dealings may not exist. Representations about transactions with related parties, if made, shall not imply that the related party transactions were consummated on terms equivalent to those that prevail in arm's-length transactions unless such representations can be substantiated. [FAS57, ¶3]

.104 If the reporting enterprise and one or more other enterprises are under common ownership or management **control** and the existence of that control could result in operating results or financial position of the reporting enterprise significantly different from

---

[1]The requirements of this section are applicable to separate financial statements of each or combined groups of each of the following: a parent company, a subsidiary, a corporate joint venture, or a 50-percent-or-less owned investee. However, it is not necessary to duplicate disclosures in a set of separate financial statements that is presented in the financial report of another enterprise (the primary reporting enterprise) if those separate financial statements also are consolidated or combined in a complete set of financial statements and both sets of financial statements are presented in the same financial report. [FAS57, ¶2, fn2]

[2]In some cases, aggregation of similar transactions by type of related party may be appropriate. Sometimes, the effect of the relationship between the parties may be so pervasive that disclosure of the relationship alone will be sufficient. If necessary to the understanding of the relationship, the name of the related party should be disclosed. [FAS57, ¶2, fn3]

those that would have been obtained if the enterprises were autonomous, the nature of the control relationship shall be disclosed even though there are no transactions between the enterprises. [FAS57, ¶4]

.105 Notes or accounts receivable due from officers, employees, or affiliated enterprises shall be shown separately and not included under a general heading, such as notes receivable or accounts receivable. [ARB43, ch1A, ¶5]

Reporting of Certain Related Party Transactions

.106 [The reporting of certain related party transactions is specified in other sections. Inclusion of subsidiaries in consolidated financial statements is discussed in Section C51, "Consolidation," paragraphs .102 and .103, and Section I82, "Investments: Equity Method." The reporting of leases between related parties is discussed in Section L10, "Leases," paragraphs .125 through .127. Certain transfers and exchanges between enterprises under common control are discussed in Section N35, "Nonmonetary Transactions," paragraph .110. The reporting of substitution or addition of debtors in troubled debt restructurings involving related parties is specified in Section D22, "Debt: Restructurings," paragraph .138.]

Glossary

.401 **Affiliate.** A party that, directly or indirectly through one or more intermediaries, controls, is controlled by, or is under common control with an enterprise. [FAS57, ¶24(a)]

.402 **Control.** The possession, direct or indirect, of the power to direct or cause the direction of the management and policies of an enterprise through ownership, by contract, or otherwise. [FAS57, ¶24(b)]

.403 **Immediate family.** Family members whom a principal owner or a member of management might control or influence or by whom they might be controlled or influenced because of the family relationship. [FAS57, ¶24(c)]

.404 **Management.** Persons who are responsible for achieving the objectives of the enterprise and who have the authority to establish policies and make decisions by which those objectives are to be pursued. Management normally includes members of the board of directors, the chief executive officer, chief operating officer, vice presidents in charge of principal business functions (such as sales, administration, or finance), and other persons who perform similar policymaking functions. Persons without formal titles also may be members of management. [FAS57, ¶24(d)]

.405 **Principal owners.** Owners of record or known beneficial owners of more than 10 percent of the voting interests of the enterprise. [FAS57, ¶24(e)]

.406 **Related parties.** Affiliates of the enterprise; entities for which investments are accounted for by the equity method by the enterprise; trusts for the benefit of employees, such as pension and profit-sharing trusts that are managed by or under the trusteeship of management; principal owners of the enterprise; its management; members of the immediate families of principal owners of the enterprise and its management; and other parties with which the enterprise may deal if one party controls or can significantly influence the management or operating policies of the other to an extent that one of the transacting parties might be prevented from fully pursuing its own separate interests. Another party also is a related party if it can significantly influence the management or operating policies of the transacting parties or if it has an ownership interest in one of the transacting parties and can significantly influence the other to an extent that one or more of the transacting parties might be prevented from fully pursuing its own separate interests. [FAS57, ¶24(f)]

Supplemental Guidance: Emerging Issues Task Force (EITF) Issues

.1000 [Listed below is an EITF Issue that provides supplemental guidance for this section. This Issue is related by topic to the guidance in this section.

EITF Issue No. 85-1, "Classifying Notes Received for Capital Stock"]

(The next page is 38847.)

RESEARCH AND DEVELOPMENT SECTION R50

Sources: FASB Statement 2; FASB Statement 86; FASB Statement 142; FASB Interpretation 6

[**Note:** A list of Issues discussed by the Emerging Issues Task Force (EITF) that provide supplemental guidance for this section is presented in paragraph .1000.]

Summary

Research and development costs shall be charged to expense when incurred. Disclosure in the financial statements is required for the total research and development costs charged to expense in each period for which an income statement is presented.

Scope

.101 This section specifies:

a. Those activities that shall be identified as research and development for financial accounting and reporting purposes
b. The elements of costs that shall be identified with research and development activities
c. The accounting for research and development costs
d. The financial statement disclosures related to research and development costs.

[FAS2, ¶1]

.102 Accounting for the costs of research and development activities conducted for others under a contractual arrangement is a part of accounting for contracts in general [(refer to Sections Co4, "Contractor Accounting: Construction-Type Contracts," and Co5, "Contractor Accounting: Government Contracts")] and is beyond the scope of this section. Indirect costs that are specifically reimbursable under the terms of a contract are also excluded. [FAS2, ¶2] [Refer to Section Co2, "Computer Software to Be Sold, Leased, or Otherwise Marketed," for the accounting and reporting of research and development costs related thereto The accounting and reporting for certain other software costs are addressed in paragraphs .113 through .119.]

.103 This section does not apply to activities that are unique to enterprises in the extractive industries, such as prospecting, acquisition of mineral rights, exploration, drilling, mining, and related mineral development. It does apply, however, to research and development activities of enterprises in the extractive industries that are comparable in nature to research and development activities of other enterprises, such as development or improvement of processes and techniques including those employed in exploration, drilling, and extraction. [FAS2, ¶3]

Activities Constituting Research and Development

.104 For purposes of this section, **research** and **development** are defined as follows:

a. *Research* is planned search or critical investigation aimed at discovery of new knowledge with the hope that such knowledge will be useful in developing a new product or service (hereinafter *product*) or a new process or technique (hereinafter *process*) or in bringing about a significant improvement to an existing product or process.
b. *Development* is the translation of research findings or other knowledge into a plan or design for a new product or process or for a significant improvement to an existing product or process whether intended for sale or use. It includes the conceptual formulation, design, and testing of product alternatives, construction of prototypes, and operation of pilot plants. It does not include routine or periodic alterations to existing products, production lines, manufacturing processes, and other ongoing operations, even though those alterations may represent improvements, and it does not include market research or market-testing activities.

[FAS2, ¶8]

.105 A process [(refer to paragraph .104(a))] may be a system whose output is to be sold, leased, or otherwise marketed to others. A process also may be used internally as a part of a manufacturing activity or a service activity where the service itself is marketed. A process may be intended to achieve cost reductions as opposed to revenue generation. Paragraph .104(b), however, specifically excludes from research and development activities "market research or market-testing activities." [It is intended] that the acquisition, development, or improvement of a process by an enterprise for use in its selling or administrative activities be excluded from the definition of research and development activities. [FIN6, ¶4]

.106 [Examples of activities that typically would be included in research and development activities and those that typically would be excluded are presented in paragraphs .111 and .112, respectively. Application of this section to costs incurred to obtain or develop computer software is presented in paragraphs .113 through .119.]

Elements of Costs to Be Identified with Research and Development Activities

.107 Elements of costs shall be identified with research and development activities as follows:

a. *Materials, equipment, and facilities.* The costs of materials (whether from the enterprise's normal inventory or acquired specially for research and development activities) and equipment or facilities that are acquired or constructed for research and development activities and that have alternative future uses (in research and development projects or otherwise) shall be capitalized as tangible assets when acquired or constructed. The cost of such materials consumed in research and development activities and the depreciation of such equipment or facilities used in those activities are research and development costs. However, the costs of materials, equipment, or facilities that are acquired or constructed for a particular research and development project and that have no alternative future uses (in other research and development projects or otherwise) and therefore no separate economic values are research and development costs at the time the costs are incurred.
b. *Personnel.* Salaries, wages, and other related costs of personnel engaged in research and development activities shall be included in research and development costs. [FAS2, ¶11]
c. *Intangible assets purchased from others.* The costs of intangible assets that are purchased from others for use in research and development activities and that have alternative future uses (in research and development projects or otherwise) shall be accounted for in accordance with Section G40, "Goodwill and Other Intangible Assets." [FAS142, ¶D3] The amortization of those intangible assets used in research and development activities is a research and development cost. However, the costs of intangibles that are purchased from others for a particular research and development project and that have no alternative future uses (in other research and development projects or otherwise) and therefore no separate economic values are research and development costs at the time the costs are incurred.[2]
d. *Contract services.* The costs of services performed by others in connection with the research and development activities of an enterprise, including research and development conducted by others [on] behalf of the enterprise, shall be included in research and development costs.
e. *Indirect costs.* Research and development costs shall include a reasonable allocation of indirect costs. However, general and administrative costs that are not clearly

---

[[1]Editorial deletion, 6/01.]

[2]Paragraph .107(c) is not intended to alter the conclusions in Section B51, "Business Combinations," regarding allocation of cost to assets acquired in a business combination. [FAS2, ¶34]

related to research and development activities shall not be included as research and development costs. [FAS2, ¶11]

Accounting for Research and Development Costs

.108 All research and development costs encompassed by this section shall be charged to expense when incurred. [FAS2, ¶12]

Disclosure

.109 Disclosure shall be made in the financial statements of the total research and development costs charged to expense in each period for which an income statement is presented. [FAS2, ¶13]

.110 [Deleted 12/82 because of FASB Statement 71, *Accounting for the Effects of Certain Types of Regulation.*]

Examples

.111 The following are examples of activities that typically would be included in research and development in accordance with paragraph .104 (unless conducted for others under a contractual arrangement—refer to paragraph .102):

a. Laboratory research aimed at discovery of new knowledge
b. Searching for applications of new research findings or other knowledge
c. Conceptual formulation and design of possible product or process alternatives
d. Testing in search for or evaluation of product or process alternatives
e. Modification of the formulation or design of a product or process
f. Design, construction, and testing of preproduction prototypes and models
g. Design of tools, jigs, molds, and dies involving new technology
h. Design, construction, and operation of a pilot plant that is not of a scale economically feasible to the enterprise for commercial production
i. Engineering activity required to advance the design of a product to the point that it meets specific functional and economic requirements and is ready for manufacture.

[FAS2, ¶9]

.112 The following are examples of activities that typically would be excluded from research and development in accordance with paragraph .104:

a. Engineering follow-through in an early phase of commercial production

b. Quality control during commercial production including routine testing of products
c. Trouble-shooting in connection with breakdowns during commercial production
d. Routine, ongoing efforts to refine, enrich, or otherwise improve upon the qualities of an existing product
e. Adaptation of an existing capability to a particular requirement or customer's need as part of a continuing commercial activity
f. Seasonal or other periodic design changes to existing products
g. Routine design of tools, jigs, molds, and dies
h. Activity, including design and construction engineering, related to the construction, relocation, rearrangement, or start-up of facilities or equipment other than (1) pilot plants (refer to paragraph .111(h)) and (2) facilities or equipment whose sole use is for a particular research and development project (refer to paragraph .107(a))
i. Legal work in connection with patent applications or litigation and the sale or licensing of patents.

[FAS2, ¶10]

Computer Software

.113 Computer software is developed for many and diverse uses. Accordingly, in each case the nature of the activity for which the software is being developed should be considered in relation to the guidelines in paragraphs .104, .111, and .112 to determine whether software costs should be included or excluded. [FAS2, ¶31]

Purchase or Lease of Software

.114 Costs incurred to purchase or lease computer software developed by others are not research and development costs unless the software is for use in research and development activities. [FIN6, ¶5] The phrase "for use in research and development activities" includes tools used to facilitate research and development or components of a product or process that are undergoing research and development activities. [FAS86, ¶50]

Internal Development of Software

.115 An enterprise may undertake development of computer software internally for its own use. The software may be intended, for example, to be used in the research and development activities of the enterprise or as a part of a newly developed or significantly improved product or process. [FIN6, ¶6]

.116 [Deleted 8/85 because of FASB Statement 86, *Accounting for the Costs of Computer Software to Be Sold, Leased, or Otherwise Marketed.*]

.117 Costs incurred by an enterprise in developing computer software internally for use in its research and development activities are research and development costs and, therefore, shall be charged to expense when incurred.[3] This includes costs incurred during all phases of software development because all of those costs are incurred in a research and development activity. [FIN6, ¶8]

.118 [Deleted 8/85 because of FASB Statement 86, *Accounting for the Costs of Computer Software to Be Sold, Leased, or Otherwise Marketed.*]

.119 To the extent that the acquisition, development, or improvement of a process by an enterprise for use in its selling or administrative activities includes costs for computer software, those costs are not research and development costs.[4] Examples of the excluded costs of software are those incurred for development by an airline of a computerized reservation system or for development of a general management information system. [FIN6, ¶4]

[3]The alternative future-use test does not apply to the internal development of computer software; paragraph .107(c) applies only to intangibles *purchased from others.* [FIN6, ¶8, fn2]

[4]Accounting for the costs of [development of software for an enterprise's own use] is not currently [considered] a significant problem and, therefore, [has not been included in Section Co2, "Computer Software to Be Sold, Leased, or Otherwise Marketed."] The majority of companies expense all costs of developing software for internal use, and [it has not been concluded] that this predominant practice is improper. Also, Section Co2 clarifies activities that are research and development activities and establishes a high capitalization threshold that is likely to be applied to costs incurred in developing software for internal use as well as for sale or lease to others. [FAS86, ¶26]

Glossary

.401 **Development.** Translation of research findings or other knowledge into a plan or design for a new product or process or for a significant improvement to an existing product or process, whether intended for sale or use. It includes the conceptual formulation, design, and testing of product alternatives, construction of prototypes, and operation of pilot plants. It does not include routine or periodic alterations to existing products, production lines, manufacturing processes, and other ongoing operations even though those alterations may represent improvements and it does not include market research or market-testing activities. [FAS2, ¶8]

.402 **Research.** Planned search or critical investigation aimed at discovery of new knowledge with the hope that such knowledge will be useful in developing a new product or service (hereinafter *product*) or a new process or technique (hereinafter *process*) or in bringing about a significant improvement to an existing product or process. [FAS2, ¶8]

Supplemental Guidance

.501-.502 [Deleted 8/85 because of FASB Statement 86, *Accounting for the Costs of Computer Software to Be Sold, Leased, or Otherwise Marketed.*]

Supplemental Guidance: Emerging Issues Task Force (EITF) Issues

.1000 [Listed below are EITF Issues that provide supplemental guidance for this section. These Issues are related by topic to the guidance in this section.

EITF Issue No. 86-14, "Purchased Research and Development Projects in a Business Combination"
EITF Issue No. 99-5, "Accounting for Pre-Production Costs Related to Long-Term Supply Arrangements"
EITF Issue No. 00-20, "Accounting for Costs Incurred to Acquire or Originate Information for Database Content and Other Collections of Information"]

(The next page is 38887.)

RESEARCH AND DEVELOPMENT ARRANGEMENTS

SECTION R55

Sources: FASB Statement 68; FASB Statement 141; FASB Statement 142; FASB Technical Bulletin 84-1

[**Note:** A list of Issues discussed by the Emerging Issues Task Force (EITF) that provide supplemental guidance for this section is presented in paragraph .1000.]

Summary

This section specifies how an enterprise should account for its obligation under an arrangement for the funding of its research and development by others. The enterprise must determine whether it is obligated only to perform contractual research and development for others, or is otherwise obligated. To the extent that the enterprise is obligated to repay the other parties, it records a liability and charges research and development costs to expense as incurred.

Scope

.101 This section [presents] standards of financial accounting and reporting for an enterprise that is a party to a research and development arrangement[1] through which it can obtain the results of research and development funded partially or entirely by others. It applies whether the research and development is performed by the enterprise, the funding parties, or a third party. Although the limited-partnership form of arrangement is used for illustrative purposes in this section, this section also applies for other forms. This section does not address reporting of government-sponsored research and development. [FAS68, ¶3]

Accounting and Reporting

.102 An enterprise shall determine the nature of the obligation it incurs when it enters into an arrangement with other parties who fund its research and development. The factors discussed in paragraphs .103 through .109 and other factors that may be present and relevant to a particular arrangement shall be considered when determining the nature of the enterprise's obligation. [FAS68, ¶4]

---

[1]The legal structure of a research and development arrangement may take a variety of forms and often is influenced by federal and state income tax and securities regulations. An enterprise might have an equity interest in the arrangement, or its legal involvement might be only contractual (for example, a contract to provide services and an option to acquire the results of the research and development). [FAS68, ¶2]

Obligation Is a Liability to Repay the Other Parties

.103 If the enterprise is obligated to repay any of the funds provided by the other parties regardless of the outcome of the research and development, the enterprise shall estimate and recognize that liability. This requirement applies whether the enterprise may settle the liability by paying cash, by issuing securities, or by some other means. [FAS68, ¶5]

.104 To conclude that a liability does not exist, the transfer of the financial risk involved with research and development from the enterprise to the other parties must be substantive and genuine. To the extent that the enterprise is committed to repay any of the funds provided by the other parties regardless of the outcome of the research and development, all or part of the risk has not been transferred. The following are some examples in which the enterprise is committed to repay:

a. The enterprise guarantees, or has a contractual commitment that assures, repayment of the funds provided by the other parties regardless of the outcome of the research and development.
b. The other parties can require the enterprise to purchase their interest in the research and development regardless of the outcome.
c. The other parties automatically will receive debt or equity securities of the enterprise upon termination or completion of the research and development regardless of the outcome.

[FAS68, ¶6]

.105 Even though the written agreements or contracts under the arrangement do not require the enterprise to repay any of the funds provided by the other parties, surrounding conditions might indicate that the enterprise is likely to bear the risk of failure of the research and development. If those conditions suggest that it is probable[2] that the enterprise will repay any of the funds regardless of the outcome of the research and development, there is a presumption that the enterprise has an obligation to repay the other parties. That presumption can be overcome only by substantial evidence to the contrary. [FAS68, ¶7]

.106 Examples of conditions leading to the presumption that the enterprise will repay the other parties include the following:

a. The enterprise has indicated an intent to repay all or a portion of the funds provided regardless of the outcome of the research and development.

[2] *Probable* is used here consistent with its use in Section C59, "Contingencies," to mean that repayment is likely. [FAS68, ¶7, fn1]

b. The enterprise would suffer a severe economic penalty if it failed to repay any of the funds provided to it regardless of the outcome of the research and development. An economic penalty is considered "severe" if in the normal course of business an enterprise would probably choose to pay the other parties rather than incur the penalty. For example, an enterprise might purchase the partnership's interest in the research and development if the enterprise had provided the partnership with proprietary basic technology necessary for the enterprise's ongoing operations without retaining a way to recover that technology, or prevent it from being transferred to another party, except by purchasing the partnership's interest.

c. A significant related party[3] relationship between the enterprise and the parties funding the research and development exists at the time the enterprise enters into the arrangement.

d. The enterprise has essentially completed the project before entering into the arrangement.

[FAS68, ¶8]

.107 An enterprise that incurs a liability to repay the other parties shall charge the research and development costs to expense as incurred. The amount of funds provided by the other parties might exceed the enterprise's liability. That might be the case, for example, if license agreements or partial buy-out provisions permit the enterprise to use the results of the research and development or to reacquire certain basic technology or other assets for an amount that is less than the funds provided. Those agreements or provisions might limit the extent to which the enterprise is economically compelled to buy out the other parties regardless of the outcome. In those situations, the liability to repay the other parties might be limited to a specified price for licensing the results or for purchasing a partial interest in the results. If the enterprise's liability is less than the funds provided, the enterprise shall charge its portion of the research and development costs to expense in the same manner as the liability is incurred. For example, the liability might arise as the initial funds are expended, or the liability might arise on a pro rata basis. [FAS68, ¶9]

[3]Related parties are defined in Section R36, "Related Parties." [FAS68, ¶8, fn2] Although transactions between related parties commonly occur in the normal course of business, the conditions of competitive free-market dealings between independent parties may not exist. Accordingly, the enterprise might be influenced by considerations other than those that would exist in arm's-length transactions with unrelated parties. This is particularly true if the related parties can directly or indirectly influence the enterprise's decision whether or not to acquire the results of the research and development. However, the enterprise's obligation should not be accounted for as a liability just because the enterprise is the general partner. [FAS68, ¶32]

Obligation Is to Perform Contractual Services

.108 To the extent that the financial risk associated with the research and development has been transferred because repayment of any of the funds provided by the other parties depends *solely* on the results of the research and development having future economic benefit, the enterprise shall account for its obligation as a contract to perform research and development for others. [FAS68, ¶10]

.109 If the enterprise's obligation is to perform research and development for others and the enterprise subsequently decides to exercise an option to purchase the other parties' interests in the research and development arrangement or to obtain the exclusive rights to the results of the research and development, the nature of those results and their future use shall determine the accounting for the purchase transaction.[4] [FAS68, ¶11]

Loan or Advance to the Other Parties

.110 If repayment to the enterprise of any loan or advance by the enterprise to the other parties depends solely on the results of the research and development having future economic benefit, the loan or advance shall be accounted for as costs incurred by the enterprise. The costs shall be charged to research and development expense unless the loan or advance to the other parties can be identified as relating to some other activity, for example, marketing or advertising, in which case the costs shall be accounted for according to their nature. [FAS68, ¶12]

Issuance of Warrants or Similar Instruments

.111 If warrants or similar instruments are issued in connection with the arrangement, the enterprise shall report a portion of the proceeds to be provided by the other parties as paid-in capital. The amount so reported shall be the fair value of the instruments at the date of the arrangement. [FAS68, ¶13]

[4]Section B51, "Business Combinations," paragraph .145 states: ". . . the accounting for the cost of an item to be used in research and development activities is the same under paragraphs .107 and .108 of Section R50, 'Research and Development,' whether the item is purchased singly, or as part of a group of assets, or as part of an entire enterprise in a business combination." [FAS68, ¶11, fn3] The accounting for other recognized intangible assets acquired by the enterprise is specified in Section G40, "Goodwill and Other Intangible Assets." [FAS142, ¶D7]

Disclosures

.112 An enterprise that under the provisions of this section accounts for its obligation under a research and development arrangement as a contract to perform research and development for others shall disclose[5] the following:[6]

a. The terms of significant agreements under the research and development arrangement (including royalty arrangements, purchase provisions, license agreements, and commitments to provide additional funding) as of the date of each balance sheet presented
b. The amount of compensation earned and costs incurred under such contracts for each period for which an income statement is presented.

[FAS68, ¶14]

---

[5] Section R36 specifies additional disclosure requirements for related party transactions and certain control relationships. [FAS68, ¶14, fn4]

[6] An enterprise that is a party to more than one research and development arrangement need not separately disclose each arrangement unless separate disclosure is necessary to understand the effects on the financial statements. Aggregation of similar arrangements by type may be appropriate. [FAS68, ¶14, fn5]

Supplemental Guidance

Accounting for Stock Issued to Acquire the Results of a Research and Development Arrangement

.501 *Question*—How should an enterprise account for stock issued to acquire the results of a research and development arrangement? [FTB84-1, ¶1]

.502 *Background*—[An] enterprise [that is a party to a research and development arrangement] usually has an option either to purchase the [other parties'] interest in or to obtain the exclusive rights to the entire results of the research and development in return for a lump sum payment or royalty payments to the [other parties]. Some arrangements contain a provision that permits the enterprise to acquire complete ownership of the results for a specified amount of the enterprise's stock or cash at some future time. In some of those purchase agreements, the [other parties have] the option to receive either the enterprise's stock or cash;in others, the enterprise makes the decision. Sometimes, warrants or similar instrumens to purchase the enterprise's stock are issued in connection with the arrangement. [FTB84-1, ¶2]

.503 *Response*—When an enterprise that is or was a party to a research and development arrangement acquires the results of the research and development arrangement in exchange for cash, common stock of the enterprise, or other consideration, the transaction is a purchase of tangible or intangible assets resulting from the activities of the research and development arrangement. Although such a transaction is not a business combination, [FTB84-1, ¶6] paragraphs .103 through .105 of Section B51, "Business Combinations," [FAS141, ¶E23] describe the general principles that apply in recording the purchase of such an asset. [FTB84-1, ¶6]

.504 Accordingly, when an enterprise that is or was a party to a research and development arrangement exchanges stock for the results of the research and development arrangement, whether pursuant to the exercise of warrants or similar instruments issued in connection with the arrangement or otherwise, the enterprise should record the stock issued at its fair value, or at the fair value of consideration received, whichever is more clearly evident. The transaction should be accounted for in this manner whether the enterprise exchanges stock for the results of the research and development arrangement, for rights to use the results, or for ownership interests in the arrangement or a successor to the arrangement. The fair value should be determined as of the date the enterprise exercises its option to acquire the results of the research and development arrangement. [FTB84-1, ¶7]

Supplemental Guidance: Emerging Issues Task Force (EITF) Issues

.1000 [Listed below is an EITF Issue that provides supplemental guidance for this section. This Issue is related by topic to the guidance in this section.

EITF Issue No. 99-16, "Accounting for Transactions with Elements of Research and Development Arrangements"]

(The next page is 39567.)

Sources: ARB 43, Chapter 1A; ARB 51; FASB Statement 5

Summary

Preacquisition retained earnings or deficit of a purchased subsidiary shall not be included in consolidated retained earnings. Dividends declared from the preacquisition retained earnings of a subsidiary shall not be credited to income of the parent company.

Appropriation of retained earnings shall be shown within stockholders' equity. Costs or losses shall not be charged to an appropriation of retained earnings and no part of an appropriation shall be transferred to income.

.101 The retained earnings or deficit of a purchased subsidiary at the date of acquisition by the parent shall not be included in consolidated retained earnings. [ARB51, ¶9]

.102 [No dividend declared out of the retained earnings of a subsidiary created prior to acquisition shall] be credited to the income account of the parent company. [ARB43, ch1A, ¶3]

.103 [If] a portion of retained earnings [is] "appropriated" for loss contingencies, the appropriation of retained earnings [shall be] shown within the stockholders' equity section of the balance sheet and be clearly identified as an appropriation of retained earnings. Costs or losses shall not be charged to an appropriation of retained earnings, and no part of the appropriation shall be transferred to income. [FAS5, ¶15]

.104 [Section Q15, "Quasi Reorganizations," provides guidance on the treatment of retained earnings in quasi reorganizations.]

(The next page is 39747.)

[[1]Editorial deletion, 6/01.]

Sources: ARB 43, Chapter 1A; APB Opinion 10; FASB Statement 48; FASB Statement 111; FASB Technical Bulletin 90-1

[**Note:** A list of Issues discussed by the Emerging Issues Task Force (EITF) that provide supplemental guidance for this section is presented in paragraph .1000.]

Summary

Profit ordinarily shall be recognized at the time a sale in the ordinary course of business is effected. Accordingly, revenues ordinarily shall be recognized at the time a transaction is completed, with appropriate provision for uncollectible accounts. The installment method of recognizing revenue is not acceptable unless collection of the sale price is not reasonably assured.

Revenue from sales transactions in which the buyer has a right to return the product shall be recognized at time of sale only if specified conditions are met. If those conditions are not met, revenue recognition is postponed; if they are met, sales revenue and cost of sales shall be reported in the income statement and shall be reduced to reflect estimated returns. Expected costs or losses relating to sales returns also shall be accrued.

Revenue from the sale of separately priced extended warranty and product maintenance contracts should be deferred and generally recognized in income on a straight-line basis. Costs that are directly related to the acquisition of those contracts are deferred and charged to expense in proportion to the revenue recognized. All other costs are charged to expense as incurred.

Profit and Revenue Recognition

.101 Profit is realized when a sale in the ordinary course of business is effected, unless the circumstances are such that the collection of the sale price is not reasonably assured. [ARB43, ch1A, ¶1] [Accordingly,] revenues shall ordinarily be [recognized] at the time a transaction is completed, with appropriate provision for uncollectible accounts. [APB10, ¶12] In the absence of the circumstances referred to above or other specific guidance, such as in Sections R10, "Real Estate," or Re1, "Real Estate: Sales," the installment method is not acceptable. [FAS111, ¶8(a)] An exception to the general [principle] may be made with respect to inventories in industries, such as [the] packing-house industry, in which, owing to the impossibility of determining costs, it is a trade custom to [account for] inventories at net selling prices, which may exceed cost. [ARB43, ch1A, ¶1]

.102 Unrealized profit shall not be credited to income of the enterprise either directly or indirectly, by charging against such unrealized profits amounts that ordinarily would be charged against income. [ARB43, ch1A, ¶1]

Installment Method of Accounting

.103 The installment method of recognizing revenue is not acceptable unless the circumstances[1] are such that the collection of the sale price is not reasonably assured. [APB10, ¶12]

Other Guidance on Revenue Recognition

.104 [Refer to Sections Co4, "Contractor Accounting: Construction-Type Contracts," and Co5, "Contractor Accounting: Government Contracts," for principles regarding accounting for profits on contracts. In addition, refer to Sections Fr3, "Franchising: Accounting by Franchisors," and L20, "Lending Activities," for accounting principles on recognition of franchisor and loan fee revenue.]

Revenue Recognition When Right of Return Exists

Applicability and Scope

.105 Paragraphs .107 through .109 specify criteria for recognizing revenue on a sale in which a product may be returned, whether as a matter of contract or as a matter of existing practice, either by the ultimate customer or by a party who resells the product to others. The product may be returned for a refund of the purchase price, for a credit applied to amounts owed or to be owed for other purchases, or in exchange for other products. The purchase price or credit may include amounts related to incidental services, such as installation. [FAS48, ¶3]

[1] There are exceptional cases in which receivables are collectible over an extended period and, because of the terms of the transactions or other conditions, there is no reasonable basis for estimating the degree of collectibility. When those circumstances exist, and as long as they exist, either the installment method or the cost-recovery method of accounting may be used. (Under the cost-recovery method, equal amounts of revenue and expense are recognized as collections are made until all costs have been recovered, postponing any recognition of profit until that time.) [APB10, ¶12, fn8]

.106 Paragraphs .107 through .109 do not apply to [the following]:

a. Accounting for revenue in service industries if part or all of the service revenue may be returned under cancellation privileges granted to the buyer
b. Transactions involving real estate or leases
c. Sales transactions in which a customer may return defective goods, such as under warranty provisions.

[FAS48, ¶4]

Criteria for Recognizing Revenue When Right of Return Exists

.107 If an enterprise sells its product but gives the buyer the right to return the product, revenue from the sales transaction shall be recognized at time of sale only if *all* of the following conditions are met:

a. The seller's price to the buyer is substantially fixed or determinable at the date of sale.
b. The buyer has paid the seller, or the buyer is obligated to pay the seller and the obligation is not contingent on resale of the product.[2]
c. The buyer's obligation to the seller would not be changed in the event of theft or physical destruction or damage of the product.
d. The buyer acquiring the product for resale has economic substance apart from that provided by the seller.[3]
e. The seller does not have significant obligations for future performance to directly bring about resale of the product by the buyer.
f. The amount of future returns[4] can be reasonably estimated (refer to paragraph .109).[5]

---

[2]This condition is met if the buyer pays the seller at time of sale or if the buyer does not pay at time of sale but is obligated to pay at a specified date or dates if, however, the buyer does not pay at time of sale and the buyer's obligation to pay is contractually or implicitly excused until the buyer resells the product, then the condition is not met. [FAS48, ¶22]

[3]This condition relates primarily to buyers that exist "on paper," that is, buyers that have little or no physical facilities or employees. It prevents enterprises from recognizing sales revenue on transactions with parties that the sellers have established primarily for the purpose of recognizing such sales revenue. [FAS48, ¶6, fn2]

[4]Exchanges by ultimate customers of one item for another of the same kind, quality, and price (for example, one color or size for another) are not considered returns for purposes of this section. [FAS48, ¶6, fn3]

[[5]Because] detailed record keeping for returns for each product line might be costly in some cases, reasonable aggregations and approximations of product returns [are permitted]. [FAS48, ¶20]

Sales revenue and cost of sales that are not recognized at time of sale because the foregoing conditions are not met shall be recognized either when the return privilege has substantially expired or if those conditions subsequently are met, whichever occurs first. [FAS48, ¶6]

.108 If sales revenue is recognized because the conditions of paragraph .107 are met, any costs or losses that may be expected in connection with any returns shall be accrued in accordance with Section C59, "Contingencies." Sales revenue and cost of sales reported in the income statement shall be reduced to reflect estimated returns. [FAS48, ¶7]

.109 The ability to make a reasonable estimate of the amount of future returns depends on many factors and circumstances that will vary from one case to the next. However, the following factors may impair the ability to make a reasonable estimate:

a. The susceptibility of the product to significant external factors, such as technological obsolesence or changes in demand
b. Relatively long periods in which a particular product may be returned
c. Absence of historical experience with similar types of sales of similar products, or inability to apply such experience because of changing circumstances, for example, changes in the selling enterprise's marketing policies or relationships with its customers
d. Absence of a large volume of relatively homogeneous transactions.

The existence of one or more of the above factors, in light of the significance of other factors, may not be sufficient to prevent making a reasonable estimate; likewise, other factors may preclude a reasonable estimate. [FAS48, ¶8]

Supplemental Guidance

Accounting for Separately Priced Extended Warranty and Product Maintenance Contracts

.501 *Question*—How should revenue and costs from a separately priced extended warranty[501] or product maintenance contract be recognized? [FTB90-1, ¶1]

.502 *Background*—An *extended warranty* is an agreement to provide warranty protection in addition to the scope of coverage of the manufacturer's original warranty, if any, or to extend the period of coverage provided by the manufacturer's original warranty. A *product maintenance contract* is an agreement to perform certain agreed-upon services to maintain a product for a specified period of time. The terms of the contract may take different forms, such as an agreement to periodically perform a particular service a specified number of times over a specified period of time, or an agreement to perform a particular service as the need arises over the term of the contract. Some contracts may provide both extended warranty coverage and product maintenance services. A contract is *separately priced* if the customer has the option to purchase the services provided under the contract for an expressly stated amount separate from the price of the product. [FTB90-1, ¶2]

.503 *Response*—Revenue from separately priced extended warranty and product maintenance contracts should be deferred and recognized in income on a straight-line basis over the contract period except in those circumstances in which sufficient historical evidence indicates that the costs of performing services under the contract are incurred on other than a straight-line basis. In those circumstances, revenue should be recognized over the contract period in proportion to the costs expected to be incurred in performing services under the contract.[502] [FTB90-1, ¶3]

[501]Warranties are explicitly included within the scope of Section C59, [which] addresses warranty obligations that are incurred in connection with the sale of the product, that is, obligations that are not separately priced or sold but are included in the sale of the product. [FTB90-1, ¶8]

[502]The pattern of cost incurrence may vary depending on characteristics of the product or may be a function of the coverage provided under the contract. [For example,] when the coverage under the contract varies, such as those situations in which the period of the extended warranty partially overlaps the period of the product's original warranty, or the extended warranty contains a graduating deductible, costs of providing services under the contract may vary proportionate to that coverage. [FTB90-1, ¶9]

.504 Costs that are directly related to the acquisition of a contract and that would have not been incurred but for the acquisition of that contract (incremental direct acquisition costs)[503] should be deferred and charged to expense in proportion to the revenue recognized. All other costs, such as costs of services performed under the contract, general and administrative expenses, advertising expenses, and costs associated with the negotiation of a contract that is not consummated, should be charged to expense as incurred. [FTB90-1, ¶4]

.505 A loss should be recognized on extended warranty or product maintenance contracts if the sum of expected costs of providing services under the contracts and unamortized acquisition costs exceeds related unearned revenue. Extended warranty or product maintenance contracts should be grouped in a consistent manner to determine if a loss exists. A loss should be recognized first by charging any unamortized acquisition costs to expense. If the loss is greater than the unamortized acquisition costs, a liability should be recognized for the excess. [FTB90-1, ¶5]

[503]Acquisition costs should be identified consistent with guidance in paragraph .105 of Section L20, which defines acquisition costs in terms of incremental direct costs. [FTB90-1, ¶12]

Supplemental Guidance: Emerging Issues Task Force (EITF) Issues

.1000 [Listed below are EITF Issues that provide supplemental guidance for this section. These Issues are grouped by subject matter and are related by topic to the guidance in this section.

Long-Term Power Contracts

EITF Issue No. 91-6, "Revenue Recognition of Long-Term Power Sales Contracts"
EITF Issue No. 96-17, "Revenue Recognition under Long-Term Power Sales Contracts That Contain both Fixed and Variable Pricing Terms"

Other

EITF Issue No. 84-15, "Grantor Trusts Consolidation"
EITF Issue No. 85-9, "Revenue Recognition on Options to Purchase Stock of Another Entity"
EITF Issue No. 85-24, "Distribution Fees by Distributors of Mutual Funds That Do Not Have a Front-End Sales Charge"
EITF Issue No. 87-10, "Revenue Recognition by Television 'Barter' Syndicators"
EITF Issue No. 90-22, "Accounting for Gas-Balancing Arrangements"
EITF Issue No. 91-9, "Revenue and Expense Recognition for Freight Services in Process"
EITF Issue No. 95-1, "Revenue Recognition on Sales with a Guaranteed Minimum Resale Value"
EITF Issue No. 95-4, "Revenue Recognition on Equipment Sold and Subsequently Repurchased Subject to an Operating Lease"
EITF Issue No. 99-19, "Reporting Revenue Gross as a Principal versus Net as an Agent"
EITF Issue No. 00-10, "Accounting for Shipping and Handling Fees and Costs"
EITF Issue No. 00-21, "Accounting for Revenue Arrangements with Multiple Deliverables"
EITF Issue No. 00-22, "Accounting for 'Points' and Certain Other Time-Based or Volume-Based Sales Incentive Offers, and Offers for Free Products or Services to Be Delivered in the Future"
EITF Issue No. 00-24, "Revenue Recognition: Sales Arrangements That Include Specified-Price Trade-in Rights"
EITF Issue No. 01-3, "Accounting in a Purchase Business Combination for Deferred Revenue of an Acquiree"
EITF Issue No. 01-4, "Accounting for Sales of Fractional Interests in Equipment"
EITF Issue No. 01-9, "Accounting for Consideration Given by a Vendor to a Customer (Including a Reseller of the Vendor's Products)"
EITF Issue No. 01-14, "Income Statement Characterization of Reimbursements Received for 'Out-of-Pocket' Expenses Incurred"

EITF Topic No. D-85, "Application of Certain Transition Provisions in SEC Staff Accounting Bulletin No. 101"
EITF Topic No. D-96, "Accounting for Management Fees Based on a Formula"]

(The next page is 41729.)

SEGMENT DISCLOSURES AND RELATED INFORMATION

SECTION S30

Sources: FASB Statement 131; FASB Statement 135; FASB Technical Bulletin 79-4; FASB Technical Bulletin 79-5

[**Note:** A list of Issues discussed by the Emerging Issues Task Force (EITF) that provide supplemental guidance for this section is presented in paragraph .1000.]

Summary

This section presents standards for the way that public business enterprises report information about operating segments in annual financial statements and requires that those enterprises report selected information about operating segments in interim financial reports issued to shareholders. It also presents standards for related disclosures about products and services, geographic areas, and major customers. This section does not apply to nonpublic business enterprises or to not-for-profit organizations.

This section requires that a public business enterprise report financial and descriptive information about its reportable operating segments. Operating segments are components of an enterprise about which separate financial information is available that is evaluated regularly by the chief operating decision maker in deciding how to allocate resources and in assessing performance. Generally, financial information is required to be reported on the basis that it is used internally for evaluating segment performance and deciding how to allocate resources to segments.

This section requires that a public business enterprise report a measure of segment profit or loss, certain specific revenue and expense items, and segment assets. It requires reconciliations of total segment revenues, total segment profit or loss, total segment assets, and other amounts disclosed for segments to corresponding amounts in the enterprise's general-purpose financial statements. It requires that all public business enterprises report information about the revenues derived from the enterprise's products or services (or groups of similar products and services), about the countries in which the enterprise earns revenues and holds assets, and about major customers regardless of whether that information is used in making operating decisions. However, this section does not require an enterprise to report information that is not prepared for internal use if reporting it would be impracticable.

This section also requires that a public business enterprise report descriptive information about the way that the operating segments were determined, the products and services provided by the operating segments, differences between the measurements used in reporting segment information and those used in the enterprise's general-purpose financial statements, and changes in the measurement of segment amounts from period to period.

Introduction and Scope

.101 This section requires that public business enterprises[1] report certain information about operating segments in complete sets of financial statements of the enterprise and in condensed financial statements of interim periods. It also requires that public business enterprises report certain information about their products and services, the geographic areas in which they operate, and their major customers. [FAS131, ¶1]

.102 The objective of requiring disclosures about segments of an enterprise and related information is to provide information about the different types of business activities in which an enterprise engages and the different economic environments in which it operates to help users of financial statements:

a. Better understand the enterprise's performance
b. Better assess its prospects for future net cash flows
c. Make more informed judgments about the enterprise as a whole.

That objective is consistent with the objectives of general-purpose financial reporting. [FAS131, ¶3]

.103 An enterprise might meet that objective by providing complete sets of financial statements that are disaggregated in several different ways, for example, by products and services, by geography, by legal entity, or by type of customer. However, it is not feasible to provide all of that information in every set of financial statements. This section requires that general-purpose financial statements include selected information reported on a single basis of segmentation. The method [used in this section] for determining what information to report is referred to as the management approach. The management approach is based on the way that management organizes the segments within the enterprise for making operating decisions and assessing performance. Consequently, the seg-

---

[1]For convenience, the term *enterprise* is used throughout this section to mean public business enterprise unless otherwise stated. [FAS131, ¶1, fn1]

ments are evident from the structure of the enterprise's internal organization, and financial statement preparers should be able to provide the required information in a cost-effective and timely manner. [FAS131, ¶4]

.104 The management approach facilitates consistent descriptions of an enterprise in its annual report and various other published information. It focuses on financial information that an enterprise's decision makers use to make decisions about the enterprise's operating matters. The components that management establishes for that purpose are called *operating segments*. [FAS131, ¶5]

.105 This section requires that an enterprise report a measure of segment profit or loss and certain items included in determining segment profit or loss, segment assets, and certain related items. It does not require that an enterprise report segment cash flow. However, paragraphs .126 and .127 require that an enterprise report certain items that may provide an indication of the cash-generating ability or cash requirements of an enterprise's operating segments. [FAS131, ¶6]

.106 To provide some comparability between enterprises, this section requires that an enterprise report certain information about the revenues that it derives from each of its products and services (or groups of similar products and services) and about the countries in which it earns revenues and holds assets, regardless of how the enterprise is organized. As a consequence, some enterprises are likely to be required to provide limited information that may not be used for making operating decisions and assessing performance. [FAS131, ¶7]

.107 Nothing in this section is intended to discourage an enterprise from reporting additional information specific to that enterprise or to a particular line of business that may contribute to an understanding of the enterprise. [FAS131, ¶8]

.108 This section applies to public business enterprises. Public business enterprises are those business enterprises that have issued debt or equity securities that are traded in a public market (a domestic or foreign stock exchange or an over-the-counter market, including local or regional markets), that are required to file financial statements with the Securities and Exchange Commission, or that provide financial statements for the purpose of issuing any class of securities in a public market. This section does not apply to parent enterprises, subsidiaries, joint ventures, or investees accounted for by the equity method if those enterprises' "separate company" statements also are consolidated or combined in a complete set of financial statements and both the separate company statements and the consolidated or combined statements are included in the same financial report. However, this section does apply to those enterprises if they are public enterprises and their financial statements are issued separately. This section also does not apply to not-for-profit organizations or to nonpublic enterprises. Entities other than public business enterprises are encouraged to provide the disclosures described in this section. [FAS131, ¶9]

Operating Segments

Definition

.109 An *operating segment* is a component of an enterprise:

a. That engages in business activities from which it may earn revenues and incur expenses (including revenues and expenses relating to transactions with other components of the same enterprise),[2]
b. Whose operating results are regularly reviewed by the enterprise's chief operating decision maker to make decisions about resources to be allocated to the segment and assess its performance, and
c. For which discrete financial information is available.

An operating segment may engage in business activities for which it has yet to earn revenues, for example, start-up operations may be operating segments before earning revenues. [FAS131, ¶10]

.110 Not every part of an enterprise is necessarily an operating segment or part of an operating segment. For example, a corporate headquarters or certain functional departments may not earn revenues or may earn revenues that are only incidental to the activities of the enterprise and would not be operating segments. For purposes of this section, an enterprise's pension and other postretirement benefit plans are not considered operating segments. [FAS131, ¶11]

.111 The term *chief operating decision maker* identifies a function, not necessarily a manager with a specific title. That function is to allocate resources to and assess the performance of the segments of an enterprise. Often the chief operating decision maker of an enterprise is its chief executive officer or chief operating officer, but it may be a group consisting of, for example, the enterprise's president, executive vice presidents, and others. [FAS131, ¶12]

---

[2]The definition of an operating segment should include components of an enterprise that sell primarily or exclusively to other operating segments of the enterprise if the enterprise is managed that way. Information about the components engaged in each stage of production is particularly important for understanding vertically integrated enterprises in certain businesses, for example, oil and gas enterprises. [FAS131, ¶79]

.112 For many enterprises, the three characteristics of operating segments described in paragraph .109 clearly identify a single set of operating segments. However, an enterprise may produce reports in which its business activities are presented in a variety of different ways. If the chief operating decision maker uses more than one set of segment information, other factors may identify a single set of components as constituting an enterprise's operating segments, including the nature of the business activities of each component, the existence of managers responsible for them, and information presented to the board of directors. [FAS131, ¶13]

.113 Generally, an operating segment has a *segment manager* who is directly accountable to and maintains regular contact with the chief operating decision maker to discuss operating activities, financial results, forecasts, or plans for the segment. The term segment manager identifies a function, not necessarily a manager with a specific title. The chief operating decision maker also may be the segment manager for certain operating segments. A single manager may be the segment manager for more than one operating segment. If the characteristics in paragraph .109 apply to more than one set of components of an organization but there is only one set for which segment managers are held responsible, that set of components constitutes the operating segments. [FAS131, ¶14]

.114 The characteristics in paragraph .109 may apply to two or more overlapping sets of components for which managers are held responsible. That structure is sometimes referred to as a matrix form of organization. For example, in some enterprises, certain managers are responsible for different product and service lines worldwide, while other managers are responsible for specific geographic areas. The chief operating decision maker regularly reviews the operating results of both sets of components, and financial information is available for both. In that situation, the components based on products and services would constitute the operating segments. [FAS131, ¶15]

Reportable Segments

.115 An enterprise shall report separately information about each operating segment that (a) has been identified in accordance with paragraphs .109 through .114 or that results from aggregating two or more of those segments in accordance with paragraph .116 and (b) exceeds the quantitative thresholds in paragraph .117. Paragraphs .118 through .123 specify other situations in which separate information about an operating segment shall be reported. Exhibit 145A [presents] a diagram that illustrates how to apply the main provisions in this section for identifying reportable operating segments. [FAS131, ¶16]

Aggregation Criteria

.116 Operating segments often exhibit similar long-term financial performance if they have similar economic characteristics. For example, similar long-term average gross margins for two operating segments would be expected if their economic characteristics were similar. Two or more operating segments may be aggregated into a single operating segment if aggregation is consistent with the objective and basic principles of this section, if the segments have similar economic characteristics, and if the segments are similar in each of the following areas:

a. The nature of the products and services
b. The nature of the production processes
c. The type or class of customer for their products and services
d. The methods used to distribute their products or provide their services
e. If applicable, the nature of the regulatory environment, for example, banking, insurance, or public utilities.

[FAS131, ¶17] [Refer to paragraph .1001 for an EITF Issue that provides interpretive guidance on this paragraph.]

Quantitative Thresholds

.117 An enterprise shall report separately information about an operating segment that meets any of the following quantitative thresholds:

a. Its reported revenue, including both sales to external customers and intersegment sales or transfers, is 10 percent or more of the combined revenue, internal and external, of all operating segments.
b. The absolute amount of its reported profit or loss is 10 percent or more of the greater, in absolute amount, of (1) the combined reported profit of all operating segments that did not report a loss or (2) the combined reported loss of all operating segments that did report a loss.
c. Its assets are 10 percent or more of the combined assets of all operating segments. [FAS131, ¶18]

Operating segments that do not meet any of the quantitative thresholds may be considered reportable, and separately disclosed, if management believes that information about the segment would be useful to readers of the financial statements.[3] [FAS135, ¶4(x)]

.118 An enterprise may combine information about operating segments that do not meet the quantitative thresholds with information about other operating segments that do not meet the quantitative thresholds to produce a reportable segment only if the operating segments share a majority of the aggregation criteria listed in paragraph .116. [FAS131, ¶19]

.119 If total of external revenue reported by operating segments constitutes less than 75 percent of total consolidated revenue, additional operating segments shall be identified as reportable segments (even if they do not meet the criteria in paragraph .117) until at least 75 percent of total consolidated revenue is included in reportable segments. [FAS131, ¶20]

.120 Information about other business activities and operating segments that are not reportable shall be combined and disclosed in an "all other" category separate from other reconciling items in the reconciliations required by paragraph .131. The sources of the revenue included in the "all other" category shall be described. [FAS131, ¶21]

.121 If management judges an operating segment identified as a reportable segment in the immediately preceding period to be of continuing significance, information about that segment shall continue to be reported separately in the current period even if it no longer meets the criteria for reportability in paragraph .117. [FAS131, ¶22]

.122 If an operating segment is identified as a reportable segment in the current period due to the quantitative thresholds, prior-period segment data presented for comparative purposes shall be restated to reflect the newly reportable segment as a separate segment even if that segment did not satisfy the criteria for reportability in paragraph .117 in the prior period unless it is impracticable to do so. For purposes of this section, information is impracticable to present if the necessary information is not available and the cost to develop it would be excessive. [FAS131, ¶23]

.123 There may be a practical limit to the number of reportable segments that an enterprise separately discloses beyond which segment information may become overly detailed. Although no precise limit has been determined, as the number of segments that are reportable in accordance with paragraphs .117 through .122 increases above 10, the enterprise should consider whether a practical limit has been reached. [FAS131, ¶24]

---

[3]Enterprises are encouraged to report information about segments that do not meet the quantitative thresholds if management believes that it is material. Those who are familiar with the particular circumstances of each enterprise must decide what constitutes *material*. [FAS131, ¶78]

Disclosures

.124 An enterprise shall disclose the following [FAS131, ¶25] for each period for which an income statement is presented: [FAS135, ¶4(x)]

a. General information as described in paragraph .125
b. Information about reported segment profit or loss, including certain revenues and expenses included in reported segment profit or loss, segment assets, and the basis of measurement, as described in paragraphs .126 through .130
c. Reconciliations of the totals of segment revenues, reported profit or loss, assets, and other significant items to corresponding enterprise amounts as described in paragraph .131
d. Interim period information as described in paragraph .132. [FAS131, ¶25]

However, reconciliations of balance sheet amounts for reportable segments to consolidated balance sheet amounts are required only for each year for which a balance sheet is presented. [FAS135, ¶4(x)] Previously reported information for prior periods shall be restated as described in paragraphs .133 and .134. [FAS131, ¶25]

General Information

.125 An enterprise shall disclose the following general information:

a. Factors used to identify the enterprise's reportable segments, including the basis of organization (for example, whether management has chosen to organize the enterprise around differences in products and services, geographic areas, regulatory environments, or a combination of factors and whether operating segments have been aggregated)
b. Types of products and services from which each reportable segment derives its revenues.

[FAS131, ¶26]

Information about Profit or Loss and Assets

.126 An enterprise shall report a measure of profit or loss and total assets for each reportable segment. An enterprise also shall disclose the following about each reportable segment if the specified amounts are [(a)] included in the measure of segment profit or loss reviewed by the chief operating decision maker [FAS131, ¶27] or (b) are otherwise regularly provided to the chief operating decision maker, even if not included in that measure of segment profit or loss: [FAS135, ¶4(x)]

a. Revenues from external customers
b. Revenues from transactions with other operating segments of the same enterprise
c. Interest revenue
d. Interest expense
e. Depreciation, depletion, and amortization expense
f. Unusual items as described in paragraph .101 of Section I22, "Income Statement Presentation: Unusual or Infrequent Items"
g. Equity in the net income of investees accounted for by the equity method
h. Income tax expense or benefit
i. Extraordinary items
j. Significant noncash items other than depreciation, depletion, and amortization expense.

An enterprise shall report interest revenue separately from interest expense for each reportable segment unless a majority of the segment's revenues are from interest and the chief operating decision maker relies primarily on net interest revenue to assess the performance of the segment and make decisions about resources to be allocated to the segment. In that situation, an enterprise may report that segment's interest revenue net of its interest expense and disclose that it has done so.[4] [FAS131, ¶27] [Refer to paragraph .1001 for an EITF Issue that provides interpretive guidance on paragraphs .126 and .127.]

.127 An enterprise shall disclose the following about each reportable segment if the specified amounts [(a)] are included in the determination of segment assets reviewed by the chief operating decision maker [FAS131, ¶28] or (b) are otherwise regularly provided to the chief operating decision maker, even if not included in the determination of segment assets: [FAS135, ¶4(x)]

a. The amount of investment in equity method investees
b. Total expenditures for additions to long-lived assets other than financial instruments, long-term customer relationships of a financial institution, mortgage and other servicing rights, deferred policy acquisition costs, and deferred tax assets.

[FAS131, ¶28]

[4]Information about interest is most important if a single segment comprises a mix of financial and nonfinancial operations. If a segment is primarily a financial operation, interest revenue probably constitutes most of segment revenues and interest expense will constitute most of the difference between reported segment revenues and reported segment profit or loss. If the segment has no financial operations or only immaterial financial operations, no information about interest is required. [FAS131, ¶95]

Measurement

.128 The amount of each segment item reported shall be the measure reported to the chief operating decision maker for purposes of making decisions about allocating resources to the segment and assessing its performance.[5] Adjustments and eliminations made in preparing an enterprise's general-purpose financial statements and allocations of revenues, expenses, and gains or losses shall be included in determining reported segment profit or loss only if they are included in the measure of the segment's profit or loss that is used by the chief operating decision maker. Similarly, only those assets that are included in the measure of the segment's assets that is used by the chief operating decision maker shall be reported for that segment.[6] If amounts are allocated to reported segment profit or loss or assets, those amounts shall be allocated on a reasonable basis.[7] [FAS131, ¶29]

.129 If the chief operating decision maker uses only one measure of a segment's profit or loss and only one measure of a segment's assets in assessing segment performance and deciding how to allocate resources, segment profit or loss and assets shall be reported at those measures. If the chief operating decision maker uses more than one measure of a segment's profit or loss and more than one measure of a segment's assets, the reported measures shall be those that management believes are determined in

---

[5]Segment information [is] not required to be provided in accordance with the same generally accepted accounting principles used to prepare the consolidated financial statements for several reasons. Preparing segment information in accordance with the generally accepted accounting principles used at the consolidated level would be difficult because some generally accepted accounting principles are not intended to apply at a segment level. Examples include allocation of the cost of an acquisition to individual assets and liabilities of a subsidiary using the purchase method of accounting, accounting for the cost of enterprise-wide employee benefit plans, accounting for income taxes in an enterprise that files a consolidated income tax return, and accounting for inventory on a last-in, first-out basis if the pools include items in more than one segment. In addition, there are no generally accepted accounting principles for allocating joint costs, jointly used assets, or jointly incurred liabilities to segments or for pricing intersegment transfers. [FAS131, ¶84]

[6]For example, an enterprise that accounts for inventory using a specialized valuation method for internal purposes should not be required to restate inventory amounts for each segment, and an enterprise that accounts for pension expense only on a consolidated basis should not be required to allocate pension expense to each operating segment. [FAS131, ¶81]

[7]Expenses incurred at the consolidated level could be allocated to segments in a variety of ways that could be considered "reasonable." For example, an enterprise could use either the number of employees in each segment or the segment's total salary expense in relation to the consolidated amounts as a basis for allocating pension expense to segments. Those two approaches to allocation could result in significantly different measures of segment profit or loss. However, both the number of employees and the total salary expense might be reasonable bases on which to allocate total pension expense. In contrast, it would not seem reasonable for an enterprise to allocate pension expense to a segment that had no employees eligible for the pension plan. [FAS131, ¶88]

accordance with the measurement principles most consistent with those used in measuring the corresponding amounts in the enterprise's consolidated financial statements. [FAS131, ¶30]

.130 An enterprise shall provide an explanation of the measurements of segment profit or loss and segment assets for each reportable segment. At a minimum, an enterprise shall disclose the following:

a. The basis of accounting for any transactions between reportable segments.
b. The nature of any differences between the measurements of the reportable segments' profits or losses and the enterprise's consolidated income before income taxes, extraordinary items, discontinued operations, and the cumulative effect of changes in accounting principles (if not apparent from the reconciliations described in paragraph .131). Those differences could include accounting policies and policies for allocation of centrally incurred costs that are necessary for an understanding of the reported segment information.
c. The nature of any differences between the measurements of the reportable segments' assets and the enterprise's consolidated assets (if not apparent from the reconciliations described in paragraph .131). Those differences could include accounting policies and policies for allocation of jointly used assets that are necessary for an understanding of the reported segment information.
d. The nature of any changes from prior periods in the measurement methods used to determine reported segment profit or loss and the effect, if any, of those changes on the measure of segment profit or loss.
e. The nature and effect of any asymmetrical allocations to segments. For example, an enterprise might allocate depreciation expense to a segment without allocating the related depreciable assets to that segment.

[FAS131, ¶31]

Reconciliations

.131 An enterprise shall provide reconciliations of all of the following:

a. The total of the reportable segments' revenues to the enterprise's consolidated revenues.
b. The total of the reportable segments' measures of profit or loss to the enterprise's consolidated income before income taxes, extraordinary items, discontinued operations, and the cumulative effect of changes in accounting principles. However, if an enterprise allocates items such as income taxes and extraordinary items to segments,

the enterprise may choose to reconcile the total of the segments' measures of profit or loss to consolidated income after those items.

c. The total of the reportable segments' assets to the enterprise's consolidated assets.
d. The total of the reportable segments' amounts for every other significant item of information disclosed to the corresponding consolidated amount. For example, an enterprise may choose to disclose liabilities for its reportable segments, in which case the enterprise would reconcile the total of reportable segments' liabilities for each segment to the enterprise's consolidated liabilities if the segment liabilities are significant.

All significant reconciling items shall be separately identified and described. For example, the amount of each significant adjustment to reconcile accounting methods used in determining segment profit or loss to the enterprise's consolidated amounts shall be separately identified and described. [FAS131, ¶32]

Interim Period Information

.132 An enterprise shall disclose the following about each reportable segment in condensed financial statements of interim periods:

a. Revenues from external customers
b. Intersegment revenues
c. A measure of segment profit or loss
d. Total assets for which there has been a material change from the amount disclosed in the last annual report
e. A description of differences from the last annual report in the basis of segmentation or in the basis of measurement of segment profit or loss
f. A reconciliation of the total of the reportable segments' measures of profit or loss to the enterprise's consolidated income before income taxes, extraordinary items, discontinued operations, and the cumulative effect of changes in accounting principles. However, if an enterprise allocates items such as income taxes and extraordinary items to segments, the enterprise may choose to reconcile the total of the segments' measures of profit or loss to consolidated income after those items. Significant reconciling items shall be separately identified and described in that reconciliation.

[FAS131, ¶33]

Restatement of Previously Reported Information

.133 If an enterprise changes the structure of its internal organization in a manner that causes the composition of its reportable segments to change, the corresponding information for earlier periods, including interim periods, shall be restated unless it is impracticable to do so. Accordingly, an enterprise shall restate those individual items of disclosure that it can practicably restate but need not restate those individual items, if any, that it cannot practicably restate. Following a change in the composition of its reportable segments, an enterprise shall disclose whether it has restated the corresponding items of segment information for earlier periods. [FAS131, ¶34]

.134 If an enterprise has changed the structure of its internal organization in a manner that causes the composition of its reportable segments to change and if segment information for earlier periods, including interim periods, is not restated to reflect the change, the enterprise shall disclose in the year in which the change occurs segment information for the current period under both the old basis and the new basis of segmentation unless it is impracticable to do so. [FAS131, ¶35]

Enterprise-Wide Disclosures

.135 Paragraphs .136 through .138 apply to all enterprises subject to this section including those enterprises that have a single reportable segment. Some enterprises' business activities are not organized on the basis of differences in related products and services or differences in geographic areas of operations. That is, an enterprise's segments may report revenues from a broad range of essentially different products and services, or more than one of its reportable segments may provide essentially the same products and services. Similarly, an enterprise's segments may hold assets in different geographic areas and report revenues from customers in different geographic areas, or more than one of its segments may operate in the same geographic area. Information required by paragraphs .136 through .138 need be provided only if it is not provided as part of the reportable operating segment information required by this section. [FAS131, ¶36]

Information about Products and Services

.136 An enterprise shall report the revenues from external customers for each product and service or each group of similar products and services unless it is impracticable to do so. The amounts of revenues reported shall be based on the financial information used to produce the enterprise's general-purpose financial statements. If providing the information is impracticable, that fact shall be disclosed. [FAS131, ¶37]

Information about Geographic Areas

.137 An enterprise shall report the following geographic information unless it is impracticable to do so:

a. Revenues from external customers (1) attributed to the enterprise's country of domicile and (2) attributed to all foreign countries in total from which the enterprise derives revenues. If revenues from external customers attributed to an individual foreign country are material, those revenues shall be disclosed separately. An enterprise shall disclose the basis for attributing revenues from external customers to individual countries.
b. Long-lived assets other than financial instruments, long-term customer relationships of a financial institution, mortgage and other servicing rights, deferred policy acquisition costs, and deferred tax assets (1) located in the enterprise's country of domicile and (2) located in all foreign countries in total in which the enterprise holds assets. If assets in an individual foreign country are material, those assets shall be disclosed separately.

The amounts reported shall be based on the financial information that is used to produce the general-purpose financial statements. If providing the geographic information is impracticable, that fact shall be disclosed. An enterprise may wish to provide, in addition to the information required by this paragraph, subtotals of geographic information about groups of countries. [FAS131, ¶38]

Information about Major Customers

.138 An enterprise shall provide information about the extent of its reliance on its major customers. If revenues from transactions with a single external customer amount to 10 percent or more of an enterprise's revenues, the enterprise shall disclose that fact, the total amount of revenues from each such customer, and the identity of the segment or segments reporting the revenues. The enterprise need not disclose the identity of a major customer or the amount of revenues that each segment reports from that customer. For purposes of this section, a group of entities known to a reporting enterprise to be under common control shall be considered as a single customer, and the federal government, a state government, a local government (for example, a county or municipality), or a foreign government each shall be considered as a single customer. [FAS131, ¶39]

Illustrative Guidance

.139 Paragraphs .140 through .145 provide specific examples that illustrate the disclosures that are required by this section and provides a diagram for identifying reportable operating segments. The formats in the illustrations are not requirements. [Enterprises are] encouraged [to use] a format that provides the information in the most understandable manner in the specific circumstances. The following illustrations are for a single hypothetical enterprise referred to as Diversified Company. [FAS131, ¶121]

.140 Exhibit 140A is an illustration of the disclosure of descriptive information about an enterprise's reportable segments. (References to paragraphs in which the relevant requirements appear are given in parentheses.) [FAS131, ¶122]

Exhibit 140A

Diversified Company
Disclosures about Reportable Segments

Description of the types of products and services from which each reportable segment derives its revenues (paragraph .125(b))

Diversified Company has five reportable segments: auto parts, motor vessels, software, electronics, and finance. The auto parts segment produces replacement parts for sale to auto parts retailers. The motor vessels segment produces small motor vessels to serve the offshore oil industry and similar businesses. The software segment produces application software for sale to computer manufacturers and retailers. The electronics segment produces integrated circuits and related products for sale to computer manufacturers. The finance segment is responsible for portions of the company's financial operations including financing customer purchases of products from other segments and real estate lending operations in several states.

Measurement of segment profit or loss and segment assets (paragraph .130)

The accounting policies of the segments are the same as those described in the summary of significant accounting policies except that pension expense for each segment is recognized and measured on the basis of cash payments to the pension plan. Diversified Company evaluates performance based on profit or loss from operations before income taxes not including nonrecurring gains and losses and foreign exchange gains and losses.

Diversified Company accounts for intersegment sales and transfers as if the sales or transfers were to third parties, that is, at current market prices.

Factors management used to identify the enterprise's reportable segments (paragraph .125(a))

Diversified Company's reportable segments are strategic business units that offer different products and services. They are managed separately because each business requires different technology and marketing strategies. Most of the businesses were acquired as a unit, and the management at the time of the acquisition was retained.

[FAS131, ¶122]

.141 Exhibit 141A illustrates a suggested format for presenting information about reported segment profit or loss and segment assets (paragraphs .126 and .127). The same type of information is required for each year for which [FAS131, ¶123] an income statement [FAS135, ¶4(x)] is presented. Diversified Company does not allocate income taxes or unusual items to segments. In addition, not all segments have significant noncash items other than depreciation and amortization in reported profit or loss. The amounts in this exhibit are assumed to be the amounts in reports used by the chief operating decision maker. [FAS131, ¶123]

Exhibit 141A

Diversified Company
Disclosure of Reported Segment Profit or Loss, and Segment Assets

	Auto Parts	Motor Vessels	Software	Electronics	Finance	All Other	Totals
Revenues from external customers	$3,000	$5,000	$9,500	$12,000	$ 5,000	$1,000[a]	$35,500
Intersegment revenues	—	—	3,000	1,500	—	—	4,500
Interest revenue	450	800	1,000	1,500	—	—	3,750
Interest expense	350	600	700	1,100	—	—	2,750
Net interest revenue[b]	—	—	—	—	1,000	—	1,000
Depreciation and amortization	200	100	50	1,500	1,100	—	2,950
Segment profit	200	70	900	2,300	500	100	4,070
Other significant noncash items:							
Cost in excess of billings on long-term contracts	—	200	—	—	—	—	200
Segment assets	2,000	5,000	3,000	12,000	57,000	2,000	81,000
Expenditures for segment assets	300	700	500	800	600	—	2,900

[a]Revenue from segments below the quantitative thresholds are attributable to four operating segments of Diversified Company. Those segments include a small real estate business, an electronics equipment rental business, a software consulting practice, and a warehouse leasing operation. None of those segments has ever met any of the quantitative thresholds for determining reportable segments.

[b]The finance segment derives a majority of its revenue from interest. In addition, management primarily relies on net interest revenue, not the gross revenue and expense amounts, in managing that segment. Therefore, as permitted by paragraph .126, only the net amount is disclosed.

[FAS131, ¶123]

.142 Exhibit 142A [presents] illustrations of reconciliations of reportable segment revenues, profit or loss, and assets, to the enterprise's consolidated totals (paragraphs .131(a), .131(b), and .131(c)). Reconciliations also are required to be shown for every other significant item of information disclosed (paragraph .131(d)). For example, if Diversified Company disclosed segment liabilities, they are required to be reconciled to total consolidated liabilities. The enterprise's financial statements are assumed not to include discontinued operations or the cumulative effect of a change in accounting principles. As discussed in Exhibit 140A, the enterprise recognizes and measures pension expense of its segments based on cash payments to the pension plan, and it does not allocate certain items to its segments. [FAS131, ¶124]

Exhibit 142A

Diversified Company
Reconciliations of Reportable Segment Revenues, Profit or Loss, and Assets

Revenues	
Total revenues for reportable segments	$39,000
Other revenues	1,000
Elimination of intersegment revenues	(4,500)
Total consolidated revenues	$35,500
Profit or Loss	
Total profit or loss for reportable segments	$ 3,970
Other profit or loss	100
Elimination of intersegment profits	(500)
Unallocated amounts:	
Litigation settlement received	500
Other corporate expenses	(750)
Adjustment to pension expense in consolidation	(250)
Income before income taxes and extraordinary items	$ 3,070
Assets	
Total assets for reportable segments	$79,000
Other assets	2,000
Elimination of receivables from corporate headquarters	(1,000)
Goodwill not allocated to segments	4,000
Other unallocated amounts	1,000
Consolidated total	$85,000

Other Significant Items

	Segment Totals	Adjustments	Consolidated Totals
Interest revenue	$3,750	$ 75	$3,825
Interest expense	2,750	(50)	2,700
Net interest revenue (finance segment only)	1,000	—	1,000
Expenditures for assets	2,900	1,000	3,900
Depreciation and amortization	2,950	—	2,950
Cost in excess of billing on long-term contracts	200	—	200

The reconciling item to adjust expenditures for assets is the amount of expenses incurred for the corporate headquarters building, which is not included in segment information. None of the other adjustments are significant. [FAS131, ¶124]

.143 Exhibit 143A illustrates the geographic information required by paragraph .137. (Because Diversified Company's segments are based on differences in products and services, no additional disclosures of revenue information about products and services are required (paragraph .136)). [FAS131, ¶125]

Exhibit 143A

Diversified Company
Disclosure of Geographic Information

	Revenues[a]	Long-Lived Assets
United States	$19,000	$11,000
Canada	4,200	—
Taiwan	3,400	6,500
Japan	2,900	3,500
Other foreign countries	6,000	3,000
Total	$35,500	$24,000

[a]Revenues are attributed to countries based on location of customer.

[FAS131, ¶125]

.144 Exhibit 144A [presents] an illustration of the information about major customers required by paragraph .138. Neither the identity of the customer nor the amount of revenues for each operating segment is required. [FAS131, ¶126]

Exhibit 144A

Diversified Company
Disclosure about Major Customers

Revenues from one customer of Diversified Company's software and electronics segments represents approximately $5,000 of the company's consolidated revenues.

[FAS131, ¶126]

Diagram for Identifying Reportable Operating Segments

.145 The diagram in Exhibit 145A illustrates how to apply the main provisions for identifying reportable operating segments as defined in this section. The diagram is a visual supplement to the written standards section. It should not be interpreted to alter any requirements of this section nor should it be considered a substitute for the requirements. [FAS131, ¶127]

[**Note:** Additional guidance with respect to implementing Section S30 is presented in FASB Highlights, "Segment Information: Guidance on Applying Statement 131," in FASB *Status Report,* December 31, 1998. This article addresses 23 questions and was written by FASB staff member Noreen A. McPartland. This publication is available from the Order Department, Financial Accounting Standards Board, 401 Merritt 7, P.O. Box 5116, Norwalk, CT 06856-5116, telephone (203) 847-0700.]

Exhibit 145A

Diagram for Identifying Reportable Operating Segments

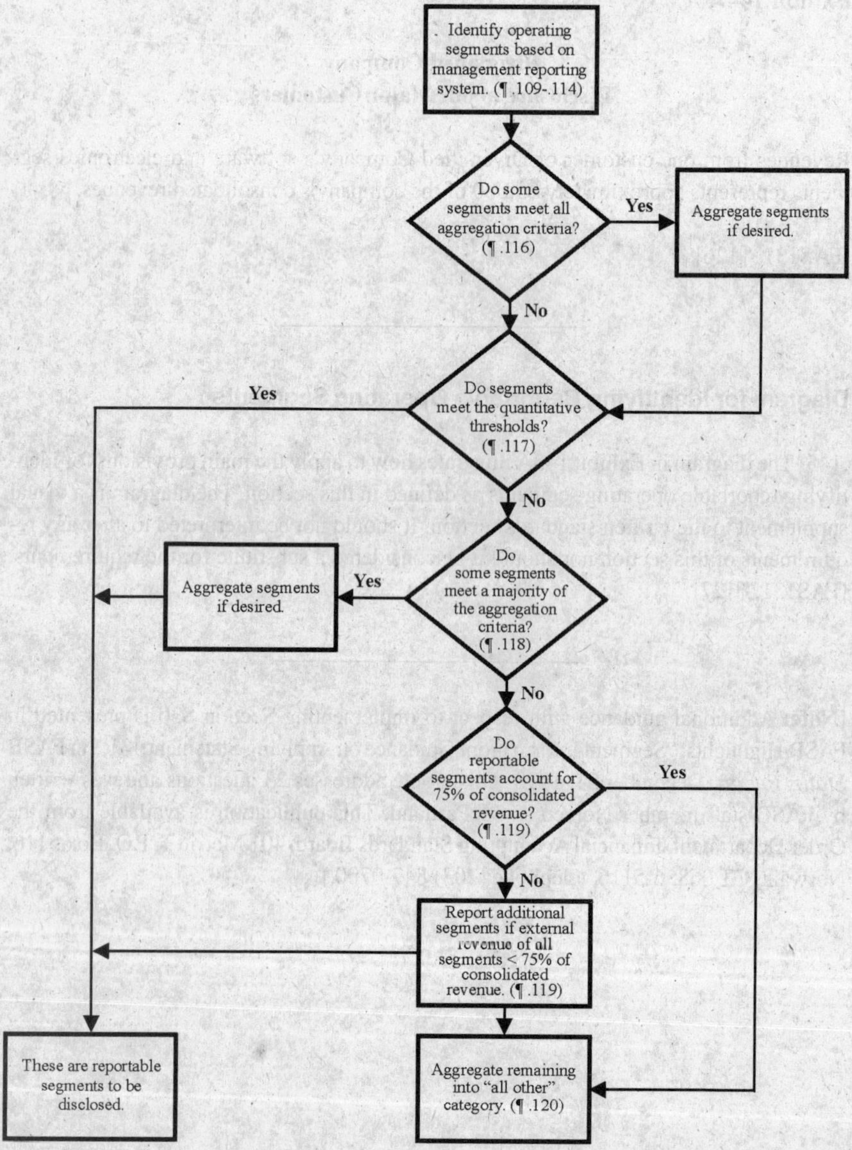

Supplemental Guidance

Segment Reporting of Puerto Rican Operations

.501 *Question*—Are Puerto Rican operations and operations related to other areas under U.S. sovereignty or some type of American jurisdiction, such as the Virgin Islands and American Samoa, to be considered *foreign* operations and thus subject to the disclosure requirements of [FTB79-4, ¶1] paragraph .137 of this section. [FAS131, ¶135(a)]

.502 *Response*—The degree of interrelationship between the United States and Puerto Rico (as well as non-self-governing U.S. territories such as the Virgin Islands and American Samoa) is such that Puerto Rican operations of U.S. enterprises should be considered domestic operations. Factors such as proximity, economic affinity, and similarities in business environments also indicate this classification for the Puerto Rican operations of U.S. enterprises. This section does not prohibit additional disclosures about Puerto Rican operations that might be useful in analyzing and understanding an enterprise's financial statements. [FTB79-4, ¶3]

Customers of Health Care Facilities

.503 *Question*—Would an insuring entity (such as Blue Cross) be considered a *customer* of a health care facility as that term is defined in [FTB79-5, ¶1] paragraph .138 of this section? [FAS131, ¶136]

.504 *Response*—An insuring entity should not be considered the *customer* of a health care facility as that term is used in this section. The fact that an insuring entity is a paying agent for the patient does not make the insuring entity the customer of the health care facility because the insuring entity does not decide which services to purchase and from which health care facility to purchase the services. The latter two factors are important in determining the customer. [FTB79-5, ¶3]

Supplemental Guidance: Emerging Issues Task Force (EITF) Issues

.1000 [Listed below is an EITF Issue that provides supplemental guidance for this section. This Issue is interpretive of the guidance in this section.

EITF Topic No. D-70, "Questions Related to the Implementation of FASB Statement No. 131"]

.1001 [Listed below is an EITF Issue that provides interpretive guidance on specific material in this section.

Paragraph .117 (FAS 131, ¶18)—EITF Topic No. D-70
Paragraphs .126 and .127 (FAS 131, ¶27-28)—EITF Topic No. D-70]

(The next page is 42687.)

TAXES: REAL AND PERSONAL PROPERTY TAXES

SECTION T10

Source: ARB 43, Chapter 10A

Summary

Real and personal property taxes are generally accrued on the taxpayer's books during the fiscal period of the taxing authority for which the taxes are levied.

Background Information

.101 In practice, real and personal property taxes have been charged against the income of various periods, as indicated below:

a. Year in which paid (cash basis)
b. Year ending on assessment (or lien) date
c. Year beginning on assessment (or lien) date
d. Calendar or fiscal year of taxpayer prior to assessment (or lien) date
e. Calendar or fiscal year of taxpayer including assessment (or lien) date
f. Calendar or fiscal year of taxpayer prior to payment date
g. Fiscal year of governing body levying the tax
h. Year appearing on tax bill.

[ARB43, ch10A, ¶10]

.102 Some of these periods may coincide, as when the fiscal year of the taxing body and that of the taxpayer are the same. The charge to income is sometimes made in full at one time, sometimes ratably on a monthly basis, and sometimes on the basis of prior estimates adjusted during or after the period. [ARB43, ch10A, ¶11]

.103 The various periods mentioned represent varying degrees of conservatism in accrual accounting. Some justification may be found for each usage, but all the circumstances relating to a particular tax must be considered before a satisfactory conclusion is reached. [ARB43, ch10A, ¶12]

.104 Consistency of application from year to year is the important consideration and selection of any of the periods mentioned is a matter for individual judgment. [ARB43, ch10A, ¶13]

Basis Considered Most Acceptable

.105 Generally, the most acceptable basis of providing for property taxes is monthly accrual on the taxpayer's books during the fiscal period of the taxing authority for which the taxes are levied. The books will then show, at any closing date, the appropriate accrual or prepayment. [ARB43, ch10A, ¶14]

Treatment in Financial Statements

Balance Sheet

.106 An accrued liability for real and personal property taxes, whether estimated or definitely known, shall be included among the current liabilities. If estimates are subject to a substantial measure of uncertainty, the liability shall be described as estimated. [ARB43, ch10A, ¶16]

Income Statement

.107 While it is sometimes proper to capitalize in property accounts the amount of real estate taxes applicable to property that is being developed for use or sale, these taxes are generally regarded as an expense of doing business. They may be (a) charged to operating expenses; (b) shown as a separate deduction from income; or (c) distributed among the several accounts to which they are deemed to apply, such as factory overhead, rental income, and selling or general expenses. [ARB43, ch10A, ¶17]

.108 In condensed income statements appearing in published reports, the amounts of real and personal property taxes, however charged in the accounts, are rarely shown separately. They are frequently combined with other taxes but not with taxes on income. [ARB43, ch10A, ¶18]

(The next page is 41703.)

VALUATION: USE OF VALUATION ALLOWANCES

SECTION V18

Source: APB Opinion 12

Summary

Valuation allowances are items that reduce or increase the carrying amount of an asset or a liability. For purposes of financial statement presentation, valuation allowances shall be deducted from or added to the assets or liabilities to which they relate.

.101 [A **valuation allowance** is described in paragraphs 34 and 43 of FASB Concepts Statement No. 6, *Elements of Financial Statements,* as a separate item that reduces or increases the carrying amount of an asset or a liability. For example, an estimate of uncollectible amounts reduces receivables to the amount expected to be collected, or a premium on a bond receivable increases the receivable to its cost or present value. Concepts Statement 6 concludes that valuation allowances are part of the related assets or liabilities and are neither assets nor liabilities in their own right.]

.102 [For purposes of financial statement presentation,] accumulated allowances for depreciation and depletion and asset valuation allowances for losses such as those on receivables and investments [APB12, ¶2] shall be deducted from the assets or groups of assets to which the allowances relate, with appropriate disclosure. [APB12, ¶3]

.103 [Specific requirements and guidance applicable to valuation allowances are included in this text in the sections that address the assets to which they relate. For example, the valuation allowance for receivables is discussed in Section C59, "Contingencies," paragraphs .128 and .129, and Section D22, "Debt: Restructurings," footnote 6, and the valuation allowance for mortgage loans is discussed in Section Mo4, "Mortgage Banking Activities," paragraph .105.]

Glossary

.401 **Valuation allowance.** A separate item that reduces or increases the carrying amount of an asset or a liability. Valuation allowances are part of the related assets or liabilities and are neither assets nor liabilities in their own right. [Concepts Statement 6, ¶34 & 43]

(Refer to Volume II of the *Current Text* for the appendixes.)

(This page intentionally left blank.)

(This page intentionally left blank.)

Topical Index

INTRODUCTION TO THE TOPICAL INDEX

The topical index includes references to documents contained in the *Original Pronouncements* volumes, all sections of the *Current Text* volumes, matters discussed by the FASB Emerging Issues Task Force (EITF), and supplemental guidance published by the FASB in the form of question-and-answer *Highlights* and Special Reports.

Original Pronouncements References

For *Original Pronouncements,* the topical index generally excludes references to introductory paragraphs and those paragraphs that provide background information or bases for conclusions. However, if those paragraphs facilitate an understanding of an accounting standard, they are referenced. Superseded paragraphs and pronouncements are not indexed except for those superseded pronouncements with significantly delayed effective dates. The related pronouncements are also retained in the text but shaded to alert the reader that the material has been superseded. The effective date and transition paragraphs are also not indexed, but the effective dates of all pronouncements are listed in Appendix C.

Current Text References

The topical index provides references to specific paragraphs of all sections of the *Current Text.* It also includes references to all sections that have been superseded by pronouncements with significantly delayed effective dates; those superseded sections are presented in Appendix E of the *Current Text.*

EITF Issue References

References to Issues discussed by the FASB Emerging Issues Task Force (through the March 20–21, 2002 meeting) also are included in the topical index. Issues that have been either nullified or resolved by a subsequent pronouncement, superseded by another Issue, deemed no longer technically helpful, or codified in another Issue are not referenced in the topical index. Appendix D presents a listing of all Issues discussed to date and their current status. Those matters are summarized by issue number in a separate publication, *EITF Abstracts.*

Other References

Also included in the topical index are references to supplemental guidance published by the FASB in the following documents:

- FASB *Highlights,* "Computer Software: Guidance on Applying Statement 86," February 1986 (Q&A.86)
- FASB Special Report, *A Guide to Implementation of Statement 87 on Employers' Accounting for Pensions: Questions and Answers* (Q&A.87)
- FASB Special Report, *A Guide to Implementation of Statement 88 on Employers' Accounting for Settlements and Curtailments of Defined Benefit Pension Plans and for Termination Benefits: Questions and Answers* (Q&A.88)
- FASB Special Report, *A Guide to Implementation of Statement 91 on Accounting for Nonrefundable Fees and Costs Associated with Originating or Acquiring Loans and Initial Direct Costs of Leases: Questions and Answers* (Q&A.91)
- FASB Special Report, *A Guide to Implementation of Statement 106 on Employers' Accounting for Postretirement Benefits Other Than Pensions: Questions and Answers* (Q&A.106)
- FASB Special Report, *A Guide to Implementation of Statement 109 on Accounting for Income Taxes: Questions and Answers* (Q&A.109)
- FASB *Viewpoints,* "Accounting for Reinsurance: Questions and Answers about Statement 113," FASB *Status Report,* February 26, 1993 (Q&A.113) [**Note:** For the convenience of the user, this article is reproduced in Topic No. D-34 of *EITF Abstracts.*]
- FASB *Viewpoints,* "Application of FASB Statements 5 and 114 to a Loan Portfolio," April 12, 1999 (Q&A.114) [**Note:** For the convenience of the user, this article is reproduced in Topic No. D-80 of *EITF Abstracts.*]
- FASB Special Report, *A Guide to Implementation of Statement 115 on Accounting for Certain Investments in Debt and Equity Securities: Questions and Answers* (Q&A.115)
- FASB *Highlights,* "Time for a Change—Implementing FASB Statements 116 and 117," January 1995 (Q&A.116/117)
- FASB Special Report, *A Guide to Implementation of Statement 125 on Accounting for Transfers and Servicing of Financial Assets and Extinguishments of Liabilities: Questions and Answers* (third edition) (Q&A.125)
- FASB *Highlights,* "Segment Information: Guidance on Applying Statement 131," FASB *Status Report,* December 31, 1998 (Q&A.131)
- FASB Special Report, *A Guide to Implementation of Statement 140 on Accounting for Transfers and Servicing of Financial Assets and Extinguishments of Liabilities: Questions and Answers* (Q&A.140)

Organization of the Topical Index

References in the topical index are made to the source documents in the following manner:

- *Current Text*—to the CT section and paragraph number
- *Original Pronouncements*—to the document and paragraph number
- EITF Issues—to the issue number or to Appendix D in *EITF Abstracts*
- Supplemental guidance—to the *Highlights* or FASB Special Report by the applicable FAS number and question number.

An example follows:

	OP	CT	EITF/Other
LENDING ACTIVITIES			
Commitment Fees and Costs	FAS91, ¶8-10	L20.107-109	EITF.85-20 Q&A.91 #25-29

The reference FAS91, ¶8-10 indicates paragraphs 8 through 10 of FASB Statement No. 91, *Accounting for Nonrefundable Fees and Costs Associated with Originating or Acquiring Loans and Initial Direct Costs of Leases.* L20.107-109 indicates paragraphs .107 through .109 of the *Current Text* Section L20, "Lending Activities." The reference to EITF.85-20 indicates EITF Issue No. 85-20, "Recognition of Fees for Guaranteeing a Loan." Q&A.91 #25-29 refers to questions 25 through 29 of the FASB Special Report, *A Guide to Implementation of Statement 91 on Accounting for Nonrefundable Fees and Costs Associated with Originating or Acquiring Loans and Initial Direct Costs of Leases: Questions and Answers.*

Multiple references on an individual topic are listed in alphabetical and numerical order and there is not necessarily a direct relationship between references listed on the same line.

Order Information on Source Material

Copies of *EITF Abstracts,* EITF Issue Summary packages and related meeting minutes, and the FASB *Highlights, Viewpoints,* and Special Reports listed above can be obtained from the FASB Order Department. The *Original Pronouncements* loose-leaf service also may be obtained from the FASB. In addition, for non-AICPA members, the *Current Text* loose-leaf service may be obtained from the FASB. For information call 1-800-748-0659.

AICPA members may obtain copies of the annual bound volumes of the *Original Pronouncements* and *Current Text,* as well as the *Current Text* loose-leaf service, from the

American Institute of Certified Public Accountants. Members who wish to order copies of these publications should call the AICPA at 1-888-777-7077.

Non-AICPA members may obtain copies of the annual bound volumes of the *Original Pronouncements* and *Current Text* from John Wiley & Sons, Inc. Call 800-225-5945; outside the United States call 732-469-4400.

FAS–FASB Statements　FIN–FASB Interpretations　FTB–FASB Technical Bulletins
APB–APB Opinions　AIN–AICPA Interpretations　ARB–Accounting Research Bulletins
CON–FASB Concepts　EITF–EITF Issues　Q&A–FASB Special Reports

See "Terminology" for references to defined terms presented in various accounting pronouncements.

See the Introduction to the Topical Index for details on the use of this index.

FAS–FASB Statements · FIN–FASB Interpretations · FTB–FASB Technical Bulletins
APB–APB Opinions · AIN–AICPA Interpretations · ARB–Accounting Research Bulletins
CON–FASB Concepts · EITF–EITF Issues · Q&A–FASB Special Reports

See "Terminology" for references to defined terms presented in various accounting pronouncements.

See the Introduction to the Topical Index for details on the use of this index.

See "Terminology" for references to defined terms presented in various accounting pronouncements.

See the Introduction to the Topical Index for details on the use of this index.

FAS–FASB Statements FIN–FASB Interpretations FTB–FASB Technical Bulletins
APB–APB Opinions AIN–AICPA Interpretations ARB–Accounting Research Bulletins
CON–FASB Concepts EITF–EITF Issues Q&A–FASB Special Reports

See "Terminology" for references to defined terms presented in various accounting pronouncements.
See the Introduction to the Topical Index for details on the use of this index.

FAS–FASB Statements　FIN–FASB Interpretations　FTB–FASB Technical Bulletins
APB–APB Opinions　AIN–AICPA Interpretations　ARB–Accounting Research Bulletins
CON–FASB Concepts　EITF–EITF Issues　Q&A–FASB Special Reports

See "Terminology" for references to defined terms presented in various accounting pronouncements.
See the Introduction to the Topical Index for details on the use of this index.

FAS–FASB Statements
APB–APB Opinions
CON–FASB Concepts
FIN–FASB Interpretations
AIN–AICPA Interpretations
EITF–EITF Issues
FTB–FASB Technical Bulletins
ARB–Accounting Research Bulletins
Q&A–FASB Special Reports

FAS–FASB Statements
APB–APB Opinions
CON–FASB Concepts
FIN–FASB Interpretations
AIN–AICPA Interpretations
EITF–EITF Issues
FTB–FASB Technical Bulletins
ARB–Accounting Research Bulletins
Q&A–FASB Special Reports

See "Terminology" for references to defined terms presented in various accounting pronouncements.
See the Introduction to the Topical Index for details on the use of this index.

FAS–FASB Statements | FIN–FASB Interpretations | FTB–FASB Technical Bulletins
APB–APB Opinions | AIN–AICPA Interpretations | ARB–Accounting Research Bulletins
CON–FASB Concepts | EITF–EITF Issues | Q&A–FASB Special Reports

	Original Pronouncements	Current Text	EITF and Other
BANKING AND THRIFT INDUSTRIES—continued			
See Financial Instruments: Transfers (FAS 125)			
See Financial Instruments: Transfers (FAS 140)			
See Impairment: Loans			
See Lending Activities			
See Liabilities: Extinguishments			
See Mortgage Banking Activities			
See Savings and Loan Associations			
Accounting for Individual Credit Card Acquisitions			EITF.93-1
Accounting Issues Related to the Deposit Insurance Funds Act of 1996			EITF.D-57
Acquisition of a Banking or Thrift Institution	FAS72, ¶2-12	B51.146-155	
	FAS141, ¶E11	G40.155-159	
	FAS141, ¶E20	Bt7.102-106	
	FAS142, ¶D9	Bt7.108-115	
	FAS142, ¶D11		
	FIN9, ¶1		
	FIN9, ¶4-5		
	FIN9, ¶7-8		
. . Amortization of Goodwill			EITF.85-42
. . Amortization of Goodwill for Business Combinations Initiated Prior to the Effective Date of Statement 72			EITF.89-19
. . Amortization of Unidentifiable Intangible Assets			EITF.85-8
			EITF.D-100
. . FSLIC-Assisted Acquisitions of Thrifts			EITF.88-19
. . Goodwill			EITF.85-42
. . Identifiable Intangible Assets	FAS72, ¶4	Bt7.106	EITF.85-42
	FIN9, ¶8		
. . Net-Spread Method	FAS72, ¶2	B51.146	
	FIN9, ¶1-4	Bt7.103	
. . Recognized Intangible Assets	FAS72,¶4	B51.149	EITF.85-42
	FAS141, ¶E11	Bt7.106	
	FAS141, ¶E20		
	FAS142, ¶D9		
	FAS142, ¶D11		
	FIN9, ¶8		
. . Regulatory-Assisted Acquisitions of Thrifts			EITF.88-19
. . Regulatory-Assisted Combinations	FAS72, ¶3	B51.151-155	
	FAS72, ¶8-11	Bt7.111-115	
	FAS141, ¶E11		
. . Sale of Assets of Acquired Banking or Thrift Institution	FAS72, ¶7	Bt7.110	

See "Terminology" for references to defined terms presented in various accounting pronouncements.
See the Introduction to the Topical Index for details on the use of this index.

FAS–FASB Statements FIN–FASB Interpretations FTB–FASB Technical Bulletins
APB–APB Opinions AIN–AICPA Interpretations ARB–Accounting Research Bulletins
CON–FASB Concepts EITF–EITF Issues Q&A–FASB Special Reports

See "Terminology" for references to defined terms presented in various accounting pronouncements.
See the Introduction to the Topical Index for details on the use of this index.

FAS–FASB Statements FIN–FASB Interpretations FTB–FASB Technical Bulletins
APB–APB Opinions AIN–AICPA Interpretations ARB–Accounting Research Bulletins
CON–FASB Concepts EITF–EITF Issues Q&A–FASB Special Reports

See "Terminology" for references to defined terms presented in various accounting pronouncements.
See the Introduction to the Topical Index for details on the use of this index.

FAS–FASB Statements
APB–APB Opinions
CON–FASB Concepts
FIN–FASB Interpretations
AIN–AICPA Interpretations
EITF–EITF Issues
FTB–FASB Technical Bulletins
ARB–Accounting Research Bulletins
Q&A–FASB Special Reports

See "Terminology" for references to defined terms presented in various accounting pronouncements.
See the Introduction to the Topical Index for details on the use of this index.

FAS–FASB Statements FIN–FASB Interpretations FTB–FASB Technical Bulletins
APB–APB Opinions AIN–AICPA Interpretations ARB–Accounting Research Bulletins
CON–FASB Concepts EITF–EITF Issues Q&A–FASB Special Reports

See "Terminology" for references to defined terms presented in various accounting pronouncements.
See the Introduction to the Topical Index for details on the use of this index.

FAS–FASB Statements | FIN–FASB Interpretations | FTB–FASB Technical Bulletins
APB–APB Opinions | AIN–AICPA Interpretations | ARB–Accounting Research Bulletins
CON–FASB Concepts | EITF–EITF Issues | Q&A–FASB Special Reports

See "Terminology" for references to defined terms presented in various accounting pronouncements.
See the Introduction to the Topical Index for details on the use of this index.

FAS–FASB Statements FIN–FASB Interpretations FTB–FASB Technical Bulletins
APB–APB Opinions AIN–AICPA Interpretations ARB–Accounting Research Bulletins
CON–FASB Concepts EITF–EITF Issues Q&A–FASB Special Reports

See "Terminology" for references to defined terms presented in various accounting pronouncements.
See the Introduction to the Topical Index for details on the use of this Index.

FAS–FASB Statements FIN–FASB Interpretations FTB–FASB Technical Bulletins
APB–APB Opinions AIN–AICPA Interpretations ARB–Accounting Research Bulletins
CON–FASB Concepts EITF–EITF Issues Q&A–FASB Special Reports

See "Terminology" for references to defined terms presented in various accounting pronouncements.
See the Introduction to the Topical Index for details on the use of this index.

See "Terminology" for references to defined terms presented in various accounting pronouncements.
See the Introduction to the Topical Index for details on the use of this index.

FAS–FASB Statements FIN–FASB Interpretations FTB–FASB Technical Bulletins
APB–APB Opinions AIN–AICPA Interpretations ARB–Accounting Research Bulletins
CON–FASB Concepts EITF–EITF Issues Q&A–FASB Special Reports

See "Terminology" for references to defined terms presented in various accounting pronouncements.

See the Introduction to the Topical Index for details on the use of this index.

See "Terminology" for references to defined terms presented in various accounting pronouncements.

See the Introduction to the Topical Index for details on the use of this index.

FAS–FASB Statements FIN–FASB Interpretations FTB–FASB Technical Bulletins
APB–APB Opinions AIN–AICPA Interpretations ARB–Accounting Research Bulletins
CON–FASB Concepts EITF–EITF Issues Q&A–FASB Special Reports

See "Terminology" for references to defined terms presented in various accounting pronouncements.

See the Introduction to the Topical Index for details on the use of this index.

FAS–FASB Statements FIN–FASB Interpretations FTB–FASB Technical Bulletins
APB–APB Opinions AIN–AICPA Interpretations ARB–Accounting Research Bulletins
CON–FASB Concepts EITF–EITF Issues Q&A–FASB Special Reports

See "Terminology" for references to defined terms presented in various accounting pronouncements.

See the Introduction to the Topical Index for details on the use of this index.

FAS–FASB Statements FIN–FASB Interpretations FTB–FASB Technical Bulletins
APB–APB Opinions AIN–AICPA Interpretations ARB–Accounting Research Bulletins
CON–FASB Concepts EITF–EITF Issues Q&A–FASB Special Reports

See "Terminology" for references to defined terms presented in various accounting pronouncements.

See the Introduction to the Topical Index for details on the use of this index.

See "Terminology" for references to defined terms presented in various accounting pronouncements.

See the Introduction to the Topical Index for details on the use of this index.

FAS–FASB Statements | FIN–FASB Interpretations | FTB–FASB Technical Bulletins
APB–APB Opinions | AIN–AICPA Interpretations | ARB–Accounting Research Bulletins
CON–FASB Concepts | EITF–EITF Issues | Q&A–FASB Special Reports

See "Terminology" for references to defined terms presented in various accounting pronouncements.

See the Introduction to the Topical Index for details on the use of this index.

FAS–FASB Statements FIN–FASB Interpretations FTB–FASB Technical Bulletins
APB–APB Opinions AIN–AICPA Interpretations ARB–Accounting Research Bulletins
CON–FASB Concepts EITF–EITF Issues Q&A–FASB Special Reports

See "Terminology" for references to defined terms presented in various accounting pronouncements.

See the Introduction to the Topical Index for details on the use of this index.

FAS–FASB Statements FIN–FASB Interpretations FTB–FASB Technical Bulletins
APB–APB Opinions AIN–AICPA Interpretations ARB–Accounting Research Bulletins
CON–FASB Concepts EITF–EITF Issues Q&A–FASB Special Reports

See "Terminology" for references to defined terms presented in various accounting pronouncements.

See the Introduction to the Topical Index for details on the use of this index.

FAS–FASB Statements FIN–FASB Interpretations FTB–FASB Technical Bulletins
APB–APB Opinions AIN–AICPA Interpretations ARB–Accounting Research Bulletins
CON–FASB Concepts EITF–EITF Issues Q&A–FASB Special Reports

See "Terminology" for references to defined terms presented in various accounting pronouncements.
See the Introduction to the Topical Index for details on the use of this index.

FAS–FASB Statements FIN–FASB Interpretations FTB–FASB Technical Bulletins
APB–APB Opinions AIN–AICPA Interpretations ARB–Accounting Research Bulletins
CON–FASB Concepts EITF–EITF Issues Q&A–FASB Special Reports

See "Terminology" for references to defined terms presented in various accounting pronouncements.

See the Introduction to the Topical Index for details on the use of this index.

FAS–FASB Statements
APB–APB Opinions
CON–FASB Concepts
FIN–FASB Interpretations
AIN–AICPA Interpretations
EITF–EITF Issues
FTB–FASB Technical Bulletins
ARB–Accounting Research Bulletins
Q&A–FASB Special Reports

See "Terminology" for references to defined terms presented in various accounting pronouncements.
See the Introduction to the Topical Index for details on the use of this index.

FAS–FASB Statements FIN–FASB Interpretations FTB–FASB Technical Bulletins
APB–APB Opinions AIN–AICPA Interpretations ARB–Accounting Research Bulletins
CON–FASB Concepts EITF–EITF Issues Q&A–FASB Special Reports

See "Terminology" for references to defined terms presented in various accounting pronouncements.
See the Introduction to the Topical Index for details on the use of this index.

FAS–FASB Statements FIN–FASB Interpretations FTB–FASB Technical Bulletins
APB–APB Opinions AIN–AICPA Interpretations ARB–Accounting Research Bulletins
CON–FASB Concepts EITF–EITF Issues Q&A–FASB Special Reports

See "Terminology" for references to defined terms presented in various accounting pronouncements.

See the Introduction to the Topical Index for details on the use of this index.

See "Terminology" for references to defined terms presented in various accounting pronouncements.
See the Introduction to the Topical Index for details on the use of this index.

FAS–FASB Statements
APB–APB Opinions
CON–FASB Concepts
FIN–FASB Interpretations
AIN–AICPA Interpretations
EITF–EITF Issues
FTB–FASB Technical Bulletins
ARB–Accounting Research Bulletins
Q&A–FASB Special Reports

See "Terminology" for references to defined terms presented in various accounting pronouncements.
See the Introduction to the Topical Index for details on the use of this index.

FAS–FASB Statements | FIN–FASB Interpretations | FTB–FASB Technical Bulletins
APB–APB Opinions | AIN–AICPA Interpretations | ARB–Accounting Research Bulletins
CON–FASB Concepts | EITF–EITF Issues | Q&A–FASB Special Reports

See "Terminology" for references to defined terms presented in various accounting pronouncements.
See the Introduction to the Topical Index for details on the use of this index.

See "Terminology" for references to defined terms presented in various accounting pronouncements.
See the Introduction to the Topical Index for details on the use of this index.

FAS–FASB Statements | FIN–FASB Interpretations | FTB–FASB Technical Bulletins
APB–APB Opinions | AIN–AICPA Interpretations | ARB–Accounting Research Bulletins
CON–FASB Concepts | EITF–EITF Issues | Q&A–FASB Special Reports

See "Terminology" for references to defined terms presented in various accounting pronouncements.

See the Introduction to the Topical Index for details on the use of this index.

FAS–FASB Statements | FIN–FASB Interpretations | FTB–FASB Technical Bulletins
APB–APB Opinions | AIN–AICPA Interpretations | ARB–Accounting Research Bulletins
CON–FASB Concepts | EITF–EITF Issues | Q&A–FASB Special Reports

See "Terminology" for references to defined terms presented in various accounting pronouncements.
See the Introduction to the Topical Index for details on the use of this index.

FAS–FASB Statements | FIN–FASB Interpretations | FTB–FASB Technical Bulletins
APB–APB Opinions | AIN–AICPA Interpretations | ARB–Accounting Research Bulletins
CON–FASB Concepts | EITF–EITF Issues | Q&A–FASB Special Reports

See "Terminology" for references to defined terms presented in various accounting pronouncements.

See the Introduction to the Topical Index for details on the use of this index.

FAS–FASB Statements FIN–FASB Interpretations FTB–FASB Technical Bulletins
APB–APB Opinions AIN–AICPA Interpretations ARB–Accounting Research Bulletins
CON–FASB Concepts EITF–EITF Issues Q&A–FASB Special Reports

See "Terminology" for references to defined terms presented in various accounting pronouncements.

See the Introduction to the Topical Index for details on the use of this index.

FAS–FASB Statements FIN–FASB Interpretations FTB–FASB Technical Bulletins
APB–APB Opinions AIN–AICPA Interpretations ARB–Accounting Research Bulletins
CON–FASB Concepts EITF–EITF Issues Q&A–FASB Special Reports

See "Terminology" for references to defined terms presented in various accounting pronouncements.

See the Introduction to the Topical Index for details on the use of this index.

FAS–FASB Statements FIN–FASB Interpretations FTB–FASB Technical Bulletins
APB–APB Opinions AIN–AICPA Interpretations ARB–Accounting Research Bulletins
CON–FASB Concepts EITF–EITF Issues Q&A–FASB Special Reports

See "Terminology" for references to defined terms presented in various accounting pronouncements.
See the Introduction to the Topical Index for details on the use of this index.

FAS–FASB Statements　FIN–FASB Interpretations　FTB–FASB Technical Bulletins
APB–APB Opinions　AIN–AICPA Interpretations　ARB–Accounting Research Bulletins
CON–FASB Concepts　EITF–EITF Issues　Q&A–FASB Special Reports

Note: The Q&A 114 text is reproduced in *EITF Abstracts* as Topic No. D-80.

See "Terminology" for references to defined terms presented in various accounting pronouncements.

See the Introduction to the Topical Index for details on the use of this index.

Note: The Q&A 113 text is reproduced in *EITF Abstracts* as Topic No. D-34 and the Q&A 114 text is reproduced in *EITF Abstracts* as Topic No. D-80.

FAS–FASB Statements FIN–FASB Interpretations FTB–FASB Technical Bulletins
APB–APB Opinions AIN–AICPA Interpretations ARB–Accounting Research Bulletins
CON–FASB Concepts EITF–EITF Issues Q&A–FASB Special Reports

See "Terminology" for references to defined terms presented in various accounting pronouncements.
See the Introduction to the Topical Index for details on the use of this index.

Note: The Q&A 114 text is reproduced in *EITF Abstracts* as Topic No. D-80.

FAS–FASB Statements   FIN–FASB Interpretations   FTB–FASB Technical Bulletins
APB–APB Opinions   AIN–AICPA Interpretations   ARB–Accounting Research Bulletins
CON–FASB Concepts   EITF–EITF Issues   Q&A–FASB Special Reports

See "Terminology" for references to defined terms presented in various accounting pronouncements.
See the Introduction to the Topical Index for details on the use of this index.

FAS–FASB Statements FIN–FASB Interpretations FTB–FASB Technical Bulletins
APB–APB Opinions AIN–AICPA Interpretations ARB–Accounting Research Bulletins
CON–FASB Concepts EITF–EITF Issues Q&A–FASB Special Reports

See "Terminology" for references to defined terms presented in various accounting pronouncements.
See the Introduction to the Topical Index for details on the use of this index.

See “Terminology” for references to defined terms presented in various accounting pronouncements.

See the Introduction to the Topical Index for details on the use of this index.

See "Terminology" for references to defined terms presented in various accounting pronouncements.
See the Introduction to the Topical Index for details on the use of this index.

	Original Pronouncements	Current Text	EITF and Other

FAS–FASB Statements
APB–APB Opinions
CON–FASB Concepts
FIN–FASB Interpretations
AIN–AICPA Interpretations
EITF–EITF Issues
FTB–FASB Technical Bulletins
ARB–Accounting Research Bulletins
Q&A–FASB Special Reports

FAS–FASB Statements | FIN–FASB Interpretations | FTB–FASB Technical Bulletins
APB–APB Opinions | AIN–AICPA Interpretations | ARB–Accounting Research Bulletins
CON–FASB Concepts | EITF–EITF Issues | Q&A–FASB Special Reports

See "Terminology" for references to defined terms presented in various accounting pronouncements.
See the Introduction to the Topical Index for details on the use of this index.

FAS–FASB Statements | FIN–FASB Interpretations | FTB–FASB Technical Bulletins
APB–APB Opinions | AIN–AICPA Interpretations | ARB–Accounting Research Bulletins
CON–FASB Concepts | EITF–EITF Issues | Q&A–FASB Special Reports

See "Terminology" for references to defined terms presented in various accounting pronouncements.

See the Introduction to the Topical Index for details on the use of this index.

FAS–FASB Statements
APB–APB Opinions
CON–FASB Concepts
FIN–FASB Interpretations
AIN–AICPA Interpretations
EITF–EITF Issues
FTB–FASB Technical Bulletins
ARB–Accounting Research Bulletins
Q&A–FASB Special Reports

See "Terminology" for references to defined terms presented in various accounting pronouncements.

See the Introduction to the Topical Index for details on the use of this index.

FAS–FASB Statements
APB–APB Opinions
CON–FASB Concepts
FIN–FASB Interpretations
AIN–AICPA Interpretations
EITF–EITF Issues
FTB–FASB Technical Bulletins
ARB–Accounting Research Bulletins
Q&A–FASB Special Reports

See "Terminology" for references to defined terms presented in various accounting pronouncements.

See the Introduction to the Topical Index for details on the use of this index.

FAS–FASB Statements FIN–FASB Interpretations FTB–FASB Technical Bulletins
APB–APB Opinions AIN–AICPA Interpretations ARB–Accounting Research Bulletins
CON–FASB Concepts EITF–EITF Issues Q&A–FASB Special Reports

See "Terminology" for references to defined terms presented in various accounting pronouncements.
See the Introduction to the Topical Index for details on the use of this index.

FAS–FASB Statements
APB–APB Opinions
CON–FASB Concepts
FIN–FASB Interpretations
AIN–AICPA Interpretations
EITF–EITF Issues
FTB–FASB Technical Bulletins
ARB–Accounting Research Bulletins
Q&A–FASB Special Reports

See "Terminology" for references to defined terms presented in various accounting pronouncements.
See the Introduction to the Topical Index for details on the use of this index.

FAS–FASB Statements FIN–FASB Interpretations FTB–FASB Technical Bulletins
APB–APB Opinions AIN–AICPA Interpretations ARB–Accounting Research Bulletins
CON–FASB Concepts EITF–EITF Issues Q&A–FASB Special Reports

See "Terminology" for references to defined terms presented in various accounting pronouncements.
See the Introduction to the Topical Index for details on the use of this index.

FAS–FASB Statements FIN–FASB Interpretations FTB–FASB Technical Bulletins
APB–APB Opinions AIN–AICPA Interpretations ARB–Accounting Research Bulletins
CON–FASB Concepts EITF–EITF Issues Q&A–FASB Special Reports

See "Terminology" for references to defined terms presented in various accounting pronouncements.
See the Introduction to the Topical Index for details on the use of this index.

FAS–FASB Statements FIN–FASB Interpretations FTB–FASB Technical Bulletins
APB–APB Opinions AIN–AICPA Interpretations ARB–Accounting Research Bulletins
CON–FASB Concepts EITF–EITF Issues Q&A–FASB Special Reports

See "Terminology" for references to defined terms presented in various accounting pronouncements.

See the Introduction to the Topical Index for details on the use of this index.

See "Terminology" for references to defined terms presented in various accounting pronouncements.
See the Introduction to the Topical Index for details on the use of this index.

FAS–FASB Statements | FIN–FASB Interpretations | FTB–FASB Technical Bulletins
APB–APB Opinions | AIN–AICPA Interpretations | ARB–Accounting Research Bulletins
CON–FASB Concepts | EITF–EITF Issues | Q&A–FASB Special Reports

See "Terminology" for references to defined terms presented in various accounting pronouncements.

See the Introduction to the Topical Index for details on the use of this index.

FAS–FASB Statements FIN–FASB Interpretations FTB–FASB Technical Bulletins
APB–APB Opinions AIN–AICPA Interpretations ARB–Accounting Research Bulletins
CON–FASB Concepts EITF–EITF Issues Q&A–FASB Special Reports

See "Terminology" for references to defined terms presented in various accounting pronouncements.
See the Introduction to the Topical Index for details on the use of this index.

Note: The Q&A 113 text is reproduced in *EITF Abstracts* as Topic No. D-34 and the Q&A 114 text is reproduced in *EITF Abstracts* as Topic No. D-80.

See "Terminology" for references to defined terms presented in various accounting pronouncements.

See the Introduction to the Topical Index for details on the use of this index.

Note: The Q&A 113 text is reproduced in *EITF Abstracts* as Topic No. D-34.

FAS–FASB Statements | FIN–FASB Interpretations | FTB–FASB Technical Bulletins
APB–APB Opinions | AIN–AICPA Interpretations | ARB–Accounting Research Bulletins
CON–FASB Concepts | EITF–EITF Issues | Q&A–FASB Special Reports

See "Terminology" for references to defined terms presented in various accounting pronouncements.

See the Introduction to the Topical Index for details on the use of this index.

FAS–FASB Statements | FIN–FASB Interpretations | FTB–FASB Technical Bulletins
APB–APB Opinions | AIN–AICPA Interpretations | ARB–Accounting Research Bulletins
CON–FASB Concepts | EITF–EITF Issues | Q&A–FASB Special Reports

See "Terminology" for references to defined terms presented in various accounting pronouncements.

See the Introduction to the Topical Index for details on the use of this index.

FAS–FASB Statements	FIN–FASB Interpretations	FTB–FASB Technical Bulletins
APB–APB Opinions	AIN–AICPA Interpretations	ARB–Accounting Research Bulletins
CON–FASB Concepts	EITF–EITF Issues	Q&A–FASB Special Reports

See "Terminology" for references to defined terms presented in various accounting pronouncements.
See the Introduction to the Topical Index for details on the use of this index.

FAS–FASB Statements | FIN–FASB Interpretations | FTB–FASB Technical Bulletins
APB–APB Opinions | AIN–AICPA Interpretations | ARB–Accounting Research Bulletins
CON–FASB Concepts | EITF–EITF Issues | Q&A–FASB Special Reports

See "Terminology" for references to defined terms presented in various accounting pronouncements.
See the Introduction to the Topical Index for details on the use of this index.

FAS–FASB Statements　FIN–FASB Interpretations　FTB–FASB Technical Bulletins
APB–APB Opinions　AIN–AICPA Interpretations　ARB–Accounting Research Bulletins
CON–FASB Concepts　EITF–EITF Issues　Q&A–FASB Special Reports

See "Terminology" for references to defined terms presented in various accounting pronouncements.
See the Introduction to the Topical Index for details on the use of this index.

FAS–FASB Statements FIN–FASB Interpretations FTB–FASB Technical Bulletins
APB–APB Opinions AIN–AICPA Interpretations ARB–Accounting Research Bulletins
CON–FASB Concepts EITF–EITF Issues Q&A–FASB Special Reports

See "Terminology" for references to defined terms presented in various accounting pronouncements.
See the Introduction to the Topical Index for details on the use of this index.

FAS–FASB Statements FIN–FASB Interpretations FTB–FASB Technical Bulletins
APB–APB Opinions AIN–AICPA Interpretations ARB–Accounting Research Bulletins
CON–FASB Concepts EITF–EITF Issues Q&A–FASB Special Reports

See "Terminology" for references to defined terms presented in various accounting pronouncements.

See the Introduction to the Topical Index for details on the use of this index.

See "Terminology" for references to defined terms presented in various accounting pronouncements.
See the Introduction to the Topical Index for details on the use of this index.

See "Terminology" for references to defined terms presented in various accounting pronouncements.

See the Introduction to the Topical Index for details on the use of this index.

See "Terminology" for references to defined terms presented in various accounting pronouncements.

See the Introduction to the Topical Index for details on the use of this index.

FAS–FASB Statements | FIN–FASB Interpretations | FTB–FASB Technical Bulletins
APB–APB Opinions | AIN–AICPA Interpretations | ARB–Accounting Research Bulletins
CON–FASB Concepts | EITF–EITF Issues | Q&A–FASB Special Reports

See "Terminology" for references to defined terms presented in various accounting pronouncements.

See the Introduction to the Topical Index for details on the use of this index.

FAS–FASB Statements FIN–FASB Interpretations FTB–FASB Technical Bulletins
APB–APB Opinions AIN–AICPA Interpretations ARB–Accounting Research Bulletins
CON–FASB Concepts EITF–EITF Issues Q&A–FASB Special Reports

See "Terminology" for references to defined terms presented in various accounting pronouncements.
See the Introduction to the Topical Index for details on the use of this index.

FAS–FASB Statements   FIN–FASB Interpretations   FTB–FASB Technical Bulletins
APB–APB Opinions   AIN–AICPA Interpretations   ARB–Accounting Research Bulletins
CON–FASB Concepts   EITF–EITF Issues   Q&A–FASB Special Reports

See "Terminology" for references to defined terms presented in various accounting pronouncements.

See the Introduction to the Topical Index for details on the use of this index.

FAS–FASB Statements
APB–APB Opinions
CON–FASB Concepts
FIN–FASB Interpretations
AIN–AICPA Interpretations
EITF–EITF Issues
FTB–FASB Technical Bulletins
ARB–Accounting Research Bulletins
Q&A–FASB Special Reports

See "Terminology" for references to defined terms presented in various accounting pronouncements.

See the Introduction to the Topical Index for details on the use of this index.

FAS–FASB Statements
APB–APB Opinions
CON–FASB Concepts
FIN–FASB Interpretations
AIN–AICPA Interpretations
EITF–EITF Issues
FTB–FASB Technical Bulletins
ARB–Accounting Research Bulletins
Q&A–FASB Special Reports

See "Terminology" for references to defined terms presented in various accounting pronouncements.

See the Introduction to the Topical Index for details on the use of this index.

See "Terminology" for references to defined terms presented in various accounting pronouncements.
See the Introduction to the Topical Index for details on the use of this index.

FAS–FASB Statements FIN–FASB Interpretations FTB–FASB Technical Bulletins
APB–APB Opinions AIN–AICPA Interpretations ARB–Accounting Research Bulletins
CON–FASB Concepts EITF–EITF Issues Q&A–FASB Special Reports

See "Terminology" for references to defined terms presented in various accounting pronouncements.

See the Introduction to the Topical Index for details on the use of this index.

See "Terminology" for references to defined terms presented in various accounting pronouncements.

See the Introduction to the Topical Index for details on the use of this index.

FAS–FASB Statements FIN–FASB Interpretations FTB–FASB Technical Bulletins
APB–APB Opinions AIN–AICPA Interpretations ARB–Accounting Research Bulletins
CON–FASB Concepts EITF–EITF Issues Q&A–FASB Special Reports

See "Terminology" for references to defined terms presented in various accounting pronouncements.

See the Introduction to the Topical Index for details on the use of this index.

FAS–FASB Statements
APB–APB Opinions
CON–FASB Concepts
FIN–FASB Interpretations
AIN–AICPA Interpretations
EITF–EITF Issues
FTB–FASB Technical Bulletins
ARB–Accounting Research Bulletins
Q&A–FASB Special Reports

See "Terminology" for references to defined terms presented in various accounting pronouncements.

See the Introduction to the Topical Index for details on the use of this index.

See "Terminology" for references to defined terms presented in various accounting pronouncements.
See the Introduction to the Topical Index for details on the use of this index.

FAS–FASB Statements FIN–FASB Interpretations FTB–FASB Technical Bulletins
APB–APB Opinions AIN–AICPA Interpretations ARB–Accounting Research Bulletins
CON–FASB Concepts EITF–EITF Issues Q&A–FASB Special Reports

See "Terminology" for references to defined terms presented in various accounting pronouncements.
See the Introduction to the Topical Index for details on the use of this index.

FAS–FASB Statements
APB–APB Opinions
CON–FASB Concepts
FIN–FASB Interpretations
AIN–AICPA Interpretations
EITF–EITF Issues
FTB–FASB Technical Bulletins
ARB–Accounting Research Bulletins
Q&A–FASB Special Reports

See "Terminology" for references to defined terms presented in various accounting pronouncements.
See the Introduction to the Topical Index for details on the use of this index.

FAS–FASB Statements FIN–FASB Interpretations FTB–FASB Technical Bulletins
APB–APB Opinions AIN–AICPA Interpretations ARB–Accounting Research Bulletins
CON–FASB Concepts EITF–EITF Issues Q&A–FASB Special Reports

See “Terminology” for references to defined terms presented in various accounting pronouncements.

See the Introduction to the Topical Index for details on the use of this index.

See "Terminology" for references to defined terms presented in various accounting pronouncements.

See the Introduction to the Topical Index for details on the use of this index.

See "Terminology" for references to defined terms presented in various accounting pronouncements.
See the Introduction to the Topical Index for details on the use of this index.

FAS–FASB Statements FIN–FASB Interpretations FTB–FASB Technical Bulletins
APB–APB Opinions AIN–AICPA Interpretations ARB–Accounting Research Bulletins
CON–FASB Concepts EITF–EITF Issues Q&A–FASB Special Reports

See "Terminology" for references to defined terms presented in various accounting pronouncements.
See the Introduction to the Topical Index for details on the use of this index.

FAS–FASB Statements FIN–FASB Interpretations FTB–FASB Technical Bulletins
APB–APB Opinions AIN–AICPA Interpretations ARB–Accounting Research Bulletins
CON–FASB Concepts EITF–EITF Issues Q&A–FASB Special Reports

Note: The Q&A 114 text is reproduced in *EITF Abstracts* as Topic No. D-80.

See "Terminology" for references to defined terms presented in various accounting pronouncements.

See the Introduction to the Topical Index for details on the use of this index.

Note: The Q&A 114 text is reproduced in *EITF Abstracts* as Topic No. D-80.

FAS–FASB Statements FIN–FASB Interpretations FTB–FASB Technical Bulletins
APB–APB Opinions AIN–AICPA Interpretations ARB–Accounting Research Bulletins
CON–FASB Concepts EITF–EITF Issues Q&A–FASB Special Reports

See "Terminology" for references to defined terms presented in various accounting pronouncements.

See the Introduction to the Topical Index for details on the use of this index.

FAS–FASB Statements FIN–FASB Interpretations FTB–FASB Technical Bulletins
APB–APB Opinions AIN–AICPA Interpretations ARB–Accounting Research Bulletins
CON–FASB Concepts EITF–EITF Issues Q&A–FASB Special Reports

See "Terminology" for references to defined terms presented in various accounting pronouncements.

See the Introduction to the Topical Index for details on the use of this index.

FAS–FASB Statements FIN–FASB Interpretations FTB–FASB Technical Bulletins
APB–APB Opinions AIN–AICPA Interpretations ARB–Accounting Research Bulletins
CON–FASB Concepts EITF–EITF Issues Q&A–FASB Special Reports

See "Terminology" for references to defined terms presented in various accounting pronouncements.
See the Introduction to the Topical Index for details on the use of this index.

FAS–FASB Statements FIN–FASB Interpretations FTB–FASB Technical Bulletins
APB–APB Opinions AIN–AICPA Interpretations ARB–Accounting Research Bulletins
CON–FASB Concepts EITF–EITF Issues Q&A–FASB Special Reports

See "Terminology" for references to defined terms presented in various accounting pronouncements.
See the Introduction to the Topical Index for details on the use of this index.

FAS–FASB Statements | FIN–FASB Interpretations | FTB–FASB Technical Bulletins
APB–APB Opinions | AIN–AICPA Interpretations | ARB–Accounting Research Bulletins
CON–FASB Concepts | EITF–EITF Issues | Q&A–FASB Special Reports

See "Terminology" for references to defined terms presented in various accounting pronouncements.
See the Introduction to the Topical Index for details on the use of this index.

FAS–FASB Statements FIN–FASB Interpretations FTB–FASB Technical Bulletins
APB–APB Opinions AIN–AICPA Interpretations ARB–Accounting Research Bulletins
CON–FASB Concepts EITF–EITF Issues Q&A–FASB Special Reports

See "Terminology" for references to defined terms presented in various accounting pronouncements.

See the Introduction to the Topical Index for details on the use of this index.

FAS–FASB Statements
APB–APB Opinions
CON–FASB Concepts
FIN–FASB Interpretations
AIN–AICPA Interpretations
EITF–EITF Issues
FTB–FASB Technical Bulletins
ARB–Accounting Research Bulletins
Q&A–FASB Special Reports

See "Terminology" for references to defined terms presented in various accounting pronouncements.
See the Introduction to the Topical Index for details on the use of this index.

FAS–FASB Statements FIN–FASB Interpretations FTB–FASB Technical Bulletins
APB–APB Opinions AIN–AICPA Interpretations ARB–Accounting Research Bulletins
CON–FASB Concepts EITF–EITF Issues Q&A–FASB Special Reports

See "Terminology" for references to defined terms presented in various accounting pronouncements.
See the Introduction to the Topical Index for details on the use of this index.

See "Terminology" for references to defined terms presented in various accounting pronouncements.
See the Introduction to the Topical Index for details on the use of this index.

FAS–FASB Statements FIN–FASB Interpretations FTB–FASB Technical Bulletins
APB–APB Opinions AIN–AICPA Interpretations ARB–Accounting Research Bulletins
CON–FASB Concepts EITF–EITF Issues Q&A–FASB Special Reports

See "Terminology" for references to defined terms presented in various accounting pronouncements.
See the Introduction to the Topical Index for details on the use of this index.

FAS–FASB Statements; FIN–FASB Interpretations; FTB–FASB Technical Bulletins
APB–APB Opinions; AIN–AICPA Interpretations; ARB–Accounting Research Bulletins
CON–FASB Concepts; EITF–EITF Issues; Q&A–FASB Special Reports

See "Terminology" for references to defined terms presented in various accounting pronouncements.
See the Introduction to the Topical Index for details on the use of this index.

FAS–FASB Statements | FIN–FASB Interpretations | FTB–FASB Technical Bulletins
APB–APB Opinions | AIN–AICPA Interpretations | ARB–Accounting Research Bulletins
CON–FASB Concepts | EITF–EITF Issues | Q&A–FASB Special Reports

See "Terminology" for references to defined terms presented in various accounting pronouncements.

See the Introduction to the Topical Index for details on the use of this index.

Note: The Q&A 113 text is reproduced in *EITF Abstracts* as Topic No. D-34.

FAS–FASB Statements
APB–APB Opinions
CON–FASB Concepts
FIN–FASB Interpretations
AIN–AICPA Interpretations
EITF–EITF Issues
FTB–FASB Technical Bulletins
ARB–Accounting Research Bulletins
Q&A–FASB Special Reports

Note: The Q&A 113 text is reproduced in *EITF Abstracts* as Topic No. D-34.

See "Terminology" for references to defined terms presented in various accounting pronouncements.

See the Introduction to the Topical Index for details on the use of this index.

Note: The Q&A 113 text is reproduced in *EITF Abstracts* as Topic No. D-34.

FAS–FASB Statements FIN–FASB Interpretations FTB–FASB Technical Bulletins
APB–APB Opinions AIN–AICPA Interpretations ARB–Accounting Research Bulletins
CON–FASB Concepts EITF–EITF Issues Q&A–FASB Special Reports

Note: The Q&A 113 text is reproduced in *EITF Abstracts* as Topic No. D-34.

See "Terminology" for references to defined terms presented in various accounting pronouncements.

See the Introduction to the Topical Index for details on the use of this index.

FAS–FASB Statements FIN–FASB Interpretations FTB–FASB Technical Bulletins
APB–APB Opinions AIN–AICPA Interpretations ARB–Accounting Research Bulletins
CON–FASB Concepts EITF–EITF Issues Q&A–FASB Special Reports

See "Terminology" for references to defined terms presented in various accounting pronouncements.

See the Introduction to the Topical Index for details on the use of this index.

See "Terminology" for references to defined terms presented in various accounting pronouncements.
See the Introduction to the Topical Index for details on the use of this index.

FAS–FASB Statements | FIN–FASB Interpretations | FTB–FASB Technical Bulletins
APB–APB Opinions | AIN–AICPA Interpretations | ARB–Accounting Research Bulletins
CON–FASB Concepts | EITF–EITF Issues | Q&A–FASB Special Reports

See "Terminology" for references to defined terms presented in various accounting pronouncements.
See the Introduction to the Topical Index for details on the use of this index.

FAS–FASB Statements | FIN–FASB Interpretations | FTB–FASB Technical Bulletins
APB–APB Opinions | AIN–AICPA Interpretations | ARB–Accounting Research Bulletins
CON–FASB Concepts | EITF–EITF Issues | Q&A–FASB Special Reports

See "Terminology" for references to defined terms presented in various accounting pronouncements.
See the Introduction to the Topical Index for details on the use of this index.

See "Terminology" for references to defined terms presented in various accounting pronouncements.

See the Introduction to the Topical Index for details on the use of this index.

See "Terminology" for references to defined terms presented in various accounting pronouncements.

See the Introduction to the Topical Index for details on the use of this index.

FAS–FASB Statements FIN–FASB Interpretations FTB–FASB Technical Bulletins
APB–APB Opinions AIN–AICPA Interpretations ARB–Accounting Research Bulletins
CON–FASB Concepts EITF–EITF Issues Q&A–FASB Special Reports

See "Terminology" for references to defined terms presented in various accounting pronouncements.

See the Introduction to the Topical Index for details on the use of this index.

FAS–FASB Statements FIN–FASB Interpretations FTB–FASB Technical Bulletins
APB–APB Opinions AIN–AICPA Interpretations ARB–Accounting Research Bulletins
CON–FASB Concepts EITF–EITF Issues Q&A–FASB Special Reports

See "Terminology" for references to defined terms presented in various accounting pronouncements.
See the Introduction to the Topical Index for details on the use of this index.

FAS–FASB Statements FIN–FASB Interpretations FTB–FASB Technical Bulletins
APB–APB Opinions AIN–AICPA Interpretations ARB–Accounting Research Bulletins
CON–FASB Concepts EITF–EITF Issues Q&A–FASB Special Reports

See "Terminology" for references to defined terms presented in various accounting pronouncements.

See the Introduction to the Topical Index for details on the use of this index.

FAS–FASB Statements FIN–FASB Interpretations FTB–FASB Technical Bulletins
APB–APB Opinions AIN–AICPA Interpretations ARB–Accounting Research Bulletins
CON–FASB Concepts EITF–EITF Issues Q&A–FASB Special Reports

See "Terminology" for references to defined terms presented in various accounting pronouncements.
See the Introduction to the Topical Index for details on the use of this index.

FAS–FASB Statements FIN–FASB Interpretations FTB–FASB Technical Bulletins
APB–APB Opinions AIN–AICPA Interpretations ARB–Accounting Research Bulletins
CON–FASB Concepts EITF–EITF Issues Q&A–FASB Special Reports

See "Terminology" for references to defined terms presented in various accounting pronouncements.

See the Introduction to the Topical Index for details on the use of this index.

FAS–FASB Statements FIN–FASB Interpretations FTB–FASB Technical Bulletins
APB–APB Opinions AIN–AICPA Interpretations ARB–Accounting Research Bulletins
CON–FASB Concepts EITF–EITF Issues Q&A–FASB Special Reports

See "Terminology" for references to defined terms presented in various accounting pronouncements.
See the Introduction to the Topical Index for details on the use of this index.

FAS–FASB Statements
APB–APB Opinions
CON–FASB Concepts
FIN–FASB Interpretations
AIN–AICPA Interpretations
EITF–EITF Issues
FTB–FASB Technical Bulletins
ARB–Accounting Research Bulletins
Q&A–FASB Special Reports

FAS–FASB Statements FIN–FASB Interpretations FTB–FASB Technical Bulletins
APB–APB Opinions AIN–AICPA Interpretations ARB–Accounting Research Bulletins
CON–FASB Concepts EITF–EITF Issues Q&A–FASB Special Reports

FAS–FASB Statements FIN–FASB Interpretations FTB–FASB Technical Bulletins
APB–APB Opinions AIN–AICPA Interpretations ARB–Accounting Research Bulletins
CON–FASB Concepts EITF–EITF Issues Q&A–FASB Special Reports

See "Terminology" for references to defined terms presented in various accounting pronouncements.

See the Introduction to the Topical Index for details on the use of this index.

FAS–FASB Statements FIN–FASB Interpretations FTB–FASB Technical Bulletins
APB–APB Opinions AIN–AICPA Interpretations ARB–Accounting Research Bulletins
CON–FASB Concepts EITF–EITF Issues Q&A–FASB Special Reports

	Original Pronouncements	Current Text	EITF and Other
LEASES—continued			
Direct Financing Leases—continued			
. . Offsetting Nonrecourse Debt with Lease Receivables	FAS135, ¶5	B10.101A-101B	
	FIN39, ¶5-7		
	FTB88-1, ¶16-17	B10.107	
	FTB88-1, ¶21-22	L10.542-545	
. . Penalty for Failure to Renew Lease	FAS13, ¶18	L10.114	
. . Sale of Leased Property	FAS140, ¶352	L10.116	
. . Sale or Assignment of Lease Receivable with Recourse	FAS140, ¶352	L10.116	
. . Subleases	FAS13, ¶36-37	L10.132-135	
	FAS13, ¶39		
	FAS145, ¶9		
. . Termination	FAS13, ¶18	L10.114	
. . Unearned Income	FAS98, ¶22	L10.114	
Discontinued Operations			
. . Subleases	FIN27, ¶2	L10.135	
Double-Dip Tax Leases			EITF.89-20
Economic Life			
. . Criteria for Classifying Leases	FAS13, ¶7	L10.103	
Equipment			
. . Determining Whether Equipment Is "Integral Equipment"			EITF.00-13
. . Revenue Recognition on Equipment Sold and Subsequently Repurchased Subject to an Operating Lease			EITF.95-4
. . Sales of Fractional Interests in Equipment			EITF.01-4
. . Sales with a Guaranteed Minimum Resale Value			EITF.95-1
Estimates			
. . Change in Estimates	FAS13, ¶9	L10.105	
. . Executory Costs	FAS13, ¶8	L10.104	
	FAS13, ¶10	L10.106	
. . Lease Term	FAS98, ¶22	L10.414	
. . Leveraged Leases	FAS13, ¶46	L10.148-148B	
	FAS109, ¶256-258		
. . Residual Value	FAS13, ¶5	L10.113-114	
	FAS13, ¶17-18	L10.148	
	FAS13, ¶46	L10.407	
		L10.422	
Executory Costs			
. . Allocation between Land and Buildings	FAS13, ¶26	L10.122	
. . Capital Leases	FAS13, ¶7	L10.103	
. . Consideration in Calculation of Deferred Profit in a Sale-Leaseback Transaction			EITF.89-16
. . Direct Financing Leases	FAS98, ¶22	L10.114	
. . Estimation	FAS13, ¶8	L10.104	
	FAS13, ¶10	L10.106	

See "Terminology" for references to defined terms presented in various accounting pronouncements.

See the Introduction to the Topical Index for details on the use of this index.

See "Terminology" for references to defined terms presented in various accounting pronouncements.
See the Introduction to the Topical Index for details on the use of this index.

See "Terminology" for references to defined terms presented in various accounting pronouncements.
See the Introduction to the Topical Index for details on the use of this index.

FAS–FASB Statements | FIN–FASB Interpretations | FTB–FASB Technical Bulletins
APB–APB Opinions | AIN–AICPA Interpretations | ARB–Accounting Research Bulletins
CON–FASB Concepts | EITF–EITF Issues | Q&A–FASB Special Reports

See "Terminology" for references to defined terms presented in various accounting pronouncements.
See the Introduction to the Topical Index for details on the use of this index.

FAS–FASB Statements | FIN–FASB Interpretations | FTB–FASB Technical Bulletins
APB–APB Opinions | AIN–AICPA Interpretations | ARB–Accounting Research Bulletins
CON–FASB Concepts | EITF–EITF Issues | Q&A–FASB Special Reports

See "Terminology" for references to defined terms presented in various accounting pronouncements.

See the Introduction to the Topical Index for details on the use of this index.

FAS–FASB Statements FIN–FASB Interpretations FTB–FASB Technical Bulletins
APB–APB Opinions AIN–AICPA Interpretations ARB–Accounting Research Bulletins
CON–FASB Concepts EITF–EITF Issues Q&A–FASB Special Reports

See "Terminology" for references to defined terms presented in various accounting pronouncements.

See the Introduction to the Topical Index for details on the use of this index.

FAS–FASB Statements | FIN–FASB Interpretations | FTB–FASB Technical Bulletins
APB–APB Opinions | AIN–AICPA Interpretations | ARB–Accounting Research Bulletins
CON–FASB Concepts | EITF–EITF Issues | Q&A–FASB Special Reports

See "Terminology" for references to defined terms presented in various accounting pronouncements.

See the Introduction to the Topical Index for details on the use of this index.

See "Terminology" for references to defined terms presented in various accounting pronouncements.
See the Introduction to the Topical Index for details on the use of this index.

FAS–FASB Statements FIN–FASB Interpretations FTB–FASB Technical Bulletins
APB–APB Opinions AIN–AICPA Interpretations ARB–Accounting Research Bulletins
CON–FASB Concepts EITF–EITF Issues Q&A–FASB Special Reports

See "Terminology" for references to defined terms presented in various accounting pronouncements.
See the Introduction to the Topical Index for details on the use of this index.

FAS–FASB Statements
APB–APB Opinions
CON–FASB Concepts
FIN–FASB Interpretations
AIN–AICPA Interpretations
EITF–EITF Issues
FTB–FASB Technical Bulletins
ARB–Accounting Research Bulletins
Q&A–FASB Special Reports

See "Terminology" for references to defined terms presented in various accounting pronouncements.

See the Introduction to the Topical Index for details on the use of this index.

FAS–FASB Statements; FIN–FASB Interpretations; FTB–FASB Technical Bulletins
APB–APB Opinions; AIN–AICPA Interpretations; ARB–Accounting Research Bulletins
CON–FASB Concepts; EITF–EITF Issues; Q&A–FASB Special Reports

See "Terminology" for references to defined terms presented in various accounting pronouncements.
See the Introduction to the Topical Index for details on the use of this index.

FAS–FASB Statements FIN–FASB Interpretations FTB–FASB Technical Bulletins
APB–APB Opinions AIN–AICPA Interpretations ARB–Accounting Research Bulletins
CON–FASB Concepts EITF–EITF Issues Q&A–FASB Special Reports

See "Terminology" for references to defined terms presented in various accounting pronouncements.

See the Introduction to the Topical Index for details on the use of this index.

FAS–FASB Statements | FIN–FASB Interpretations | FTB–FASB Technical Bulletins
APB–APB Opinions | AIN–AICPA Interpretations | ARB–Accounting Research Bulletins
CON–FASB Concepts | EITF–EITF Issues | Q&A–FASB Special Reports

See "Terminology" for references to defined terms presented in various accounting pronouncements.

See the Introduction to the Topical Index for details on the use of this index.

FAS–FASB Statements FIN–FASB Interpretations FTB–FASB Technical Bulletins
APB–APB Opinions AIN–AICPA Interpretations ARB–Accounting Research Bulletins
CON–FASB Concepts EITF–EITF Issues Q&A–FASB Special Reports

See "Terminology" for references to defined terms presented in various accounting pronouncements.
See the Introduction to the Topical Index for details on the use of this index.

See "Terminology" for references to defined terms presented in various accounting pronouncements.

See the Introduction to the Topical Index for details on the use of this index.

FAS–FASB Statements FIN–FASB Interpretations FTB–FASB Technical Bulletins
APB–APB Opinions AIN–AICPA Interpretations ARB–Accounting Research Bulletins
CON–FASB Concepts EITF–EITF Issues Q&A–FASB Special Reports

See "Terminology" for references to defined terms presented in various accounting pronouncements.

See the Introduction to the Topical Index for details on the use of this index.

FAS–FASB Statements FIN–FASB Interpretations FTB–FASB Technical Bulletins
APB–APB Opinions AIN–AICPA Interpretations ARB–Accounting Research Bulletins
CON–FASB Concepts EITF–EITF Issues Q&A–FASB Special Reports

See "Terminology" for references to defined terms presented in various accounting pronouncements.

See the Introduction to the Topical Index for details on the use of this index.

See "Terminology" for references to defined terms presented in various accounting pronouncements.
See the Introduction to the Topical Index for details on the use of this index.

See "Terminology" for references to defined terms presented in various accounting pronouncements.

See the Introduction to the Topical Index for details on the use of this index.

FAS–FASB Statements FIN–FASB Interpretations FTB–FASB Technical Bulletins
APB–APB Opinions AIN–AICPA Interpretations ARB–Accounting Research Bulletins
CON–FASB Concepts EITF–EITF Issues Q&A–FASB Special Reports

See "Terminology" for references to defined terms presented in various accounting pronouncements.

See the Introduction to the Topical Index for details on the use of this index.

See "Terminology" for references to defined terms presented in various accounting pronouncements.

See the Introduction to the Topical Index for details on the use of this index.

FAS–FASB Statements FIN–FASB Interpretations FTB–FASB Technical Bulletins
APB–APB Opinions AIN–AICPA Interpretations ARB–Accounting Research Bulletins
CON–FASB Concepts EITF–EITF Issues Q&A–FASB Special Reports

See "Terminology" for references to defined terms presented in various accounting pronouncements.

See the Introduction to the Topical Index for details on the use of this index.

FAS–FASB Statements FIN–FASB Interpretations FTB–FASB Technical Bulletins
APB–APB Opinions AIN–AICPA Interpretations ARB–Accounting Research Bulletins
CON–FASB Concepts EITF–EITF Issues Q&A–FASB Special Reports

See "Terminology" for references to defined terms presented in various accounting pronouncements.

See the Introduction to the Topical Index for details on the use of this index.

See "Terminology" for references to defined terms presented in various accounting pronouncements.
See the Introduction to the Topical Index for details on the use of this index.

FAS–FASB Statements | FIN–FASB Interpretations | FTB–FASB Technical Bulletins
APB–APB Opinions | AIN–AICPA Interpretations | ARB–Accounting Research Bulletins
CON–FASB Concepts | EITF–EITF Issues | Q&A–FASB Special Reports

See "Terminology" for references to defined terms presented in various accounting pronouncements.
See the Introduction to the Topical Index for details on the use of this index.

FAS–FASB Statements | FIN–FASB Interpretations | FTB–FASB Technical Bulletins
APB–APB Opinions | AIN–AICPA Interpretations | ARB–Accounting Research Bulletins
CON–FASB Concepts | EITF–EITF Issues | Q&A–FASB Special Reports

See "Terminology" for references to defined terms presented in various accounting pronouncements.

See the Introduction to the Topical Index for details on the use of this index.

FAS–FASB Statements | FIN–FASB Interpretations | FTB–FASB Technical Bulletins
APB–APB Opinions | AIN–AICPA Interpretations | ARB–Accounting Research Bulletins
CON–FASB Concepts | EITF–EITF Issues | Q&A–FASB Special Reports

See "Terminology" for references to defined terms presented in various accounting pronouncements.

See the Introduction to the Topical Index for details on the use of this index.

FAS–FASB Statements | FIN–FASB Interpretations | FTB–FASB Technical Bulletins
APB–APB Opinions | AIN–AICPA Interpretations | ARB–Accounting Research Bulletins
CON–FASB Concepts | EITF–EITF Issues | Q&A–FASB Special Reports

See "Terminology" for references to defined terms presented in various accounting pronouncements.
See the Introduction to the Topical Index for details on the use of this index.

FAS–FASB Statements FIN–FASB Interpretations FTB–FASB Technical Bulletins
APB–APB Opinions AIN–AICPA Interpretations ARB–Accounting Research Bulletins
CON–FASB Concepts EITF–EITF Issues Q&A–FASB Special Reports

See "Terminology" for references to defined terms presented in various accounting pronouncements.
See the Introduction to the Topical Index for details on the use of this index.

FAS–FASB Statements
APB–APB Opinions
CON–FASB Concepts
FIN–FASB Interpretations
AIN–AICPA Interpretations
EITF–EITF Issues
FTB–FASB Technical Bulletins
ARB–Accounting Research Bulletins
Q&A–FASB Special Reports

See "Terminology" for references to defined terms presented in various accounting pronouncements.
See the Introduction to the Topical Index for details on the use of this index.

See "Terminology" for references to defined terms presented in various accounting pronouncements.

See the Introduction to the Topical Index for details on the use of this index.

FAS–FASB Statements FIN–FASB Interpretations FTB–FASB Technical Bulletins
APB–APB Opinions AIN–AICPA Interpretations ARB–Accounting Research Bulletins
CON–FASB Concepts EITF–EITF Issues Q&A–FASB Special Reports

See "Terminology" for references to defined terms presented in various accounting pronouncements.

See the Introduction to the Topical Index for details on the use of this index.

FAS–FASB Statements | FIN–FASB Interpretations | FTB–FASB Technical Bulletins
APB–APB Opinions | AIN–AICPA Interpretations | ARB–Accounting Research Bulletins
CON–FASB Concepts | EITF–EITF Issues | Q&A–FASB Special Reports

See "Terminology" for references to defined terms presented in various accounting pronouncements.
See the Introduction to the Topical Index for details on the use of this index.

FAS–FASB Statements FIN–FASB Interpretations FTB–FASB Technical Bulletins
APB–APB Opinions AIN–AICPA Interpretations ARB–Accounting Research Bulletins
CON–FASB Concepts EITF–EITF Issues Q&A–FASB Special Reports

See "Terminology" for references to defined terms presented in various accounting pronouncements.
See the Introduction to the Topical Index for details on the use of this index.

See "Terminology" for references to defined terms presented in various accounting pronouncements.
See the Introduction to the Topical Index for details on the use of this index.

FAS–FASB Statements FIN–FASB Interpretations FTB–FASB Technical Bulletins
APB–APB Opinions AIN–AICPA Interpretations ARB–Accounting Research Bulletins
CON–FASB Concepts EITF–EITF Issues Q&A–FASB Special Reports

See "Terminology" for references to defined terms presented in various accounting pronouncements.
See the Introduction to the Topical Index for details on the use of this index.

FAS–FASB Statements FIN–FASB Interpretations FTB–FASB Technical Bulletins
APB–APB Opinions AIN–AICPA Interpretations ARB–Accounting Research Bulletins
CON–FASB Concepts EITF–EITF Issues Q&A–FASB Special Reports

See "Terminology" for references to defined terms presented in various accounting pronouncements.
See the Introduction to the Topical Index for details on the use of this index.

FAS–FASB Statements FIN–FASB Interpretations FTB–FASB Technical Bulletins
APB–APB Opinions AIN–AICPA Interpretations ARB–Accounting Research Bulletins
CON–FASB Concepts EITF–EITF Issues Q&A–FASB Special Reports

See "Terminology" for references to defined terms presented in various accounting pronouncements.
See the Introduction to the Topical Index for details on the use of this index.

FAS–FASB Statements | FIN–FASB Interpretations | FTB–FASB Technical Bulletins
APB–APB Opinions | AIN–AICPA Interpretations | ARB–Accounting Research Bulletins
CON–FASB Concepts | EITF–EITF Issues | Q&A–FASB Special Reports

See "Terminology" for references to defined terms presented in various accounting pronouncements.

See the Introduction to the Topical Index for details on the use of this index.

FAS–FASB Statements FIN–FASB Interpretations FTB–FASB Technical Bulletins
APB–APB Opinions AIN–AICPA Interpretations ARB–Accounting Research Bulletins
CON–FASB Concepts EITF–EITF Issues Q&A–FASB Special Reports

See "Terminology" for references to defined terms presented in various accounting pronouncements.

See the Introduction to the Topical Index for details on the use of this index.

See "Terminology" for references to defined terms presented in various accounting pronouncements.
See the Introduction to the Topical Index for details on the use of this index.

FAS–FASB Statements FIN–FASB Interpretations FTB–FASB Technical Bulletins
APB–APB Opinions AIN–AICPA Interpretations ARB–Accounting Research Bulletins
CON–FASB Concepts EITF–EITF Issues Q&A–FASB Special Reports

See "Terminology" for references to defined terms presented in various accounting pronouncements.
See the Introduction to the Topical Index for details on the use of this index.

See "Terminology" for references to defined terms presented in various accounting pronouncements.

See the Introduction to the Topical Index for details on the use of this index.

FAS–FASB Statements FIN–FASB Interpretations FTB–FASB Technical Bulletins
APB–APB Opinions AIN–AICPA Interpretations ARB–Accounting Research Bulletins
CON–FASB Concepts EITF–EITF Issues Q&A–FASB Special Reports

See "Terminology" for references to defined terms presented in various accounting pronouncements.
See the Introduction to the Topical Index for details on the use of this index.

FAS–FASB Statements FIN–FASB Interpretations FTB–FASB Technical Bulletins
APB–APB Opinions AIN–AICPA Interpretations ARB–Accounting Research Bulletins
CON–FASB Concepts EITF–EITF Issues Q&A–FASB Special Reports

See "Terminology" for references to defined terms presented in various accounting pronouncements.

See the Introduction to the Topical Index for details on the use of this index.

FAS–FASB Statements FIN–FASB Interpretations FTB–FASB Technical Bulletins
APB–APB Opinions AIN–AICPA Interpretations ARB–Accounting Research Bulletins
CON–FASB Concepts EITF–EITF Issues Q&A–FASB Special Reports

	Original Pronouncements	Current Text	EITF and Other
QUALITATIVE CHARACTERISTICS			
Choice between Accounting Methods	CON2, ¶6-20		
Comparability	CON2, ¶111-122		
Conservatism	CON2, ¶91-97		
Costs and Benefits	CON2, ¶133-144		
Decision Making	CON2, ¶36-39		
Exposure Draft Comments and Responses	CON2, ¶152-160		
Glossary	CON2, Glossary		
Hierarchy of Accounting Qualities	CON2, ¶32-45		
Materiality	CON2, ¶123-132		
Nature of Accounting Choices	CON2, ¶6-20		
Neutrality	CON2, ¶98-110		
Recognition Criteria Derived from	CON5, ¶61		
Relation to Elements of Financial Statements	CON6, ¶9-19		
Relation to Objectives of Financial Reporting	CON2, ¶21-26		
Relation to Recognition, Measurement, and Display	CON6, ¶23		
Relation to Role of Decision Making	CON2, ¶27-31		
Relative Importance and Trade-offs	CON2, ¶42-45		
Relevance	CON2, ¶46-57		
Reliability	CON2, ¶58-97		
Representational Faithfulness	CON2, ¶63-80		
Timeliness	CON2, ¶56-57		
Understandability	CON2, ¶40-41		
Verifiability	CON2, ¶81-89		
QUARTERLY FINANCIAL STATEMENTS			
See Interim Financial Reporting			
QUASI REORGANIZATIONS			
See Capital Stock: Capital Transactions			
See Debt: Restructurings			
See Disclosure			
See Income Taxes			
Readjustments	ARB43, Ch.7A, ¶2-3	Q15.102	
		Q15.104	
. . Accounting after, Additional Paid-in Capital	ARB43, Ch.7A, ¶11	Q15.112	
. . Accounting after, Retained Earnings	ARB43, Ch.7A, ¶10	Q15.111	
	ARB46, ¶2		
. . Accounting after, Similar to New Enterprise	ARB43, Ch.7A, ¶9	Q15.110	
. . Charge to Retained Earnings, Additional Paid-in Capital	ARB43, Ch.7A, ¶6	Q15.107	
. . Effective Date of Readjustment	ARB43, Ch.7A, ¶8	Q15.109	
. . Fair Value of Assets Carried Forward	ARB43, Ch.7A, ¶4	Q15.105	
. . Losses, Provision for	ARB43, Ch.7A, ¶5	Q15.106	
. . Retained Earnings of Subsidiaries	ARB43, Ch.7A, ¶7	Q15.108	

FAS–FASB Statements FIN–FASB Interpretations FTB–FASB Technical Bulletins
APB–APB Opinions AIN–AICPA Interpretations ARB–Accounting Research Bulletins
CON–FASB Concepts EITF–EITF Issues Q&A–FASB Special Reports

See "Terminology" for references to defined terms presented in various accounting pronouncements.
See the Introduction to the Topical Index for details on the use of this index.

FAS–FASB Statements | FIN–FASB Interpretations | FTB–FASB Technical Bulletins
APB–APB Opinions | AIN–AICPA Interpretations | ARB–Accounting Research Bulletins
CON–FASB Concepts | EITF–EITF Issues | Q&A–FASB Special Reports

See "Terminology" for references to defined terms presented in various accounting pronouncements.

See the Introduction to the Topical Index for details on the use of this index.

FAS–FASB Statements FIN–FASB Interpretations FTB–FASB Technical Bulletins
APB–APB Opinions AIN–AICPA Interpretations ARB–Accounting Research Bulletins
CON–FASB Concepts EITF–EITF Issues Q&A–FASB Special Reports

See "Terminology" for references to defined terms presented in various accounting pronouncements.

See the Introduction to the Topical Index for details on the use of this index.

FAS–FASB Statements | FIN–FASB Interpretations | FTB–FASB Technical Bulletins
APB–APB Opinions | AIN–AICPA Interpretations | ARB–Accounting Research Bulletins
CON–FASB Concepts | EITF–EITF Issues | Q&A–FASB Special Reports

See "Terminology" for references to defined terms presented in various accounting pronouncements.
See the Introduction to the Topical Index for details on the use of this index.

FAS–FASB Statements FIN–FASB Interpretations FTB–FASB Technical Bulletins
APB–APB Opinions AIN–AICPA Interpretations ARB–Accounting Research Bulletins
CON–FASB Concepts EITF–EITF Issues Q&A–FASB Special Reports

See "Terminology" for references to defined terms presented in various accounting pronouncements.

See the Introduction to the Topical Index for details on the use of this index.

FAS–FASB Statements
APB–APB Opinions
CON–FASB Concepts
FIN–FASB Interpretations
AIN–AICPA Interpretations
EITF–EITF Issues
FTB–FASB Technical Bulletins
ARB–Accounting Research Bulletins
Q&A–FASB Special Reports

See "Terminology" for references to defined terms presented in various accounting pronouncements.
See the Introduction to the Topical Index for details on the use of this index.

	Original Pronouncements	Current Text	EITF and Other

See "Terminology" for references to defined terms presented in various accounting pronouncements.
See the Introduction to the Topical Index for details on the use of this index.

FAS–FASB Statements
APB–APB Opinions
CON–FASB Concepts
FIN–FASB Interpretations
AIN–AICPA Interpretations
EITF–EITF Issues
FTB–FASB Technical Bulletins
ARB–Accounting Research Bulletins
Q&A–FASB Special Reports

See "Terminology" for references to defined terms presented in various accounting pronouncements.

See the Introduction to the Topical Index for details on the use of this index.

FAS–FASB Statements FIN–FASB Interpretations FTB–FASB Technical Bulletins
APB–APB Opinions AIN–AICPA Interpretations ARB–Accounting Research Bulletins
CON–FASB Concepts EITF–EITF Issues Q&A–FASB Special Reports

See "Terminology" for references to defined terms presented in various accounting pronouncements.

See the Introduction to the Topical Index for details on the use of this index.

FAS–FASB Statements   FIN–FASB Interpretations   FTB–FASB Technical Bulletins
APB–APB Opinions   AIN–AICPA Interpretations   ARB–Accounting Research Bulletins
CON–FASB Concepts   EITF–EITF Issues   Q&A–FASB Special Reports

See "Terminology" for references to defined terms presented in various accounting pronouncements.
See the Introduction to the Topical Index for details on the use of this index.

FAS–FASB Statements | FIN–FASB Interpretations | FTB–FASB Technical Bulletins
APB–APB Opinions | AIN–AICPA Interpretations | ARB–Accounting Research Bulletins
CON–FASB Concepts | EITF–EITF Issues | Q&A–FASB Special Reports

See "Terminology" for references to defined terms presented in various accounting pronouncements.
See the Introduction to the Topical Index for details on the use of this index.

See "Terminology" for references to defined terms presented in various accounting pronouncements.

See the Introduction to the Topical Index for details on the use of this index.

FAS–FASB Statements FIN–FASB Interpretations FTB–FASB Technical Bulletins
APB–APB Opinions AIN–AICPA Interpretations ARB–Accounting Research Bulletins
CON–FASB Concepts EITF–EITF Issues Q&A–FASB Special Reports

See "Terminology" for references to defined terms presented in various accounting pronouncements.

See the Introduction to the Topical Index for details on the use of this index.

FAS–FASB Statements | FIN–FASB Interpretations | FTB–FASB Technical Bulletins
APB–APB Opinions | AIN–AICPA Interpretations | ARB–Accounting Research Bulletins
CON–FASB Concepts | EITF–EITF Issues | Q&A–FASB Special Reports

See "Terminology" for references to defined terms presented in various accounting pronouncements.

See the Introduction to the Topical Index for details on the use of this index.

FAS–FASB Statements | FIN–FASB Interpretations | FTB–FASB Technical Bulletins
APB–APB Opinions | AIN–AICPA Interpretations | ARB–Accounting Research Bulletins
CON–FASB Concepts | EITF–EITF Issues | Q&A–FASB Special Reports

See "Terminology" for references to defined terms presented in various accounting pronouncements.
See the Introduction to the Topical Index for details on the use of this index.

FAS–FASB Statements FIN–FASB Interpretations FTB–FASB Technical Bulletins
APB–APB Opinions AIN–AICPA Interpretations ARB–Accounting Research Bulletins
CON–FASB Concepts EITF–EITF Issues Q&A–FASB Special Reports

See "Terminology" for references to defined terms presented in various accounting pronouncements.

See the Introduction to the Topical Index for details on the use of this index.

FAS–FASB Statements FIN–FASB Interpretations FTB–FASB Technical Bulletins
APB–APB Opinions AIN–AICPA Interpretations ARB–Accounting Research Bulletins
CON–FASB Concepts EITF–EITF Issues Q&A–FASB Special Reports

See "Terminology" for references to defined terms presented in various accounting pronouncements.
See the Introduction to the Topical Index for details on the use of this index.

FAS–FASB Statements FIN–FASB Interpretations FTB–FASB Technical Bulletins
APB–APB Opinions AIN–AICPA Interpretations ARB–Accounting Research Bulletins
CON–FASB Concepts EITF–EITF Issues Q&A–FASB Special Reports

See "Terminology" for references to defined terms presented in various accounting pronouncements.

See the Introduction to the Topical Index for details on the use of this index.

FAS–FASB Statements | FIN–FASB Interpretations | FTB–FASB Technical Bulletins
APB–APB Opinions | AIN–AICPA Interpretations | ARB–Accounting Research Bulletins
CON–FASB Concepts | EITF–EITF Issues | Q&A–FASB Special Reports

See "Terminology" for references to defined terms presented in various accounting pronouncements.

See the Introduction to the Topical Index for details on the use of this index.

FAS–FASB Statements FIN–FASB Interpretations FTB–FASB Technical Bulletins
APB–APB Opinions AIN–AICPA Interpretations ARB–Accounting Research Bulletins
CON–FASB Concepts EITF–EITF Issues Q&A–FASB Special Reports

See "Terminology" for references to defined terms presented in various accounting pronouncements.
See the Introduction to the Topical Index for details on the use of this index.

FAS–FASB Statements FIN–FASB Interpretations FTB–FASB Technical Bulletins
APB–APB Opinions AIN–AICPA Interpretations ARB–Accounting Research Bulletins
CON–FASB Concepts EITF–EITF Issues Q&A–FASB Special Reports

See "Terminology" for references to defined terms presented in various accounting pronouncements.

See the Introduction to the Topical Index for details on the use of this index.

FAS–FASB Statements FIN–FASB Interpretations FTB–FASB Technical Bulletins
APB–APB Opinions AIN–AICPA Interpretations ARB–Accounting Research Bulletins
CON–FASB Concepts EITF–EITF Issues Q&A–FASB Special Reports

See "Terminology" for references to defined terms presented in various accounting pronouncements.
See the Introduction to the Topical Index for details on the use of this index.

FAS–FASB Statements | FIN–FASB Interpretations | FTB–FASB Technical Bulletins
APB–APB Opinions | AIN–AICPA Interpretations | ARB–Accounting Research Bulletins
CON–FASB Concepts | EITF–EITF Issues | Q&A–FASB Special Reports

See "Terminology" for references to defined terms presented in various accounting pronouncements.
See the Introduction to the Topical Index for details on the use of this index.

FAS–FASB Statements FIN–FASB Interpretations FTB–FASB Technical Bulletins
APB–APB Opinions AIN–AICPA Interpretations ARB–Accounting Research Bulletins
CON–FASB Concepts EITF–EITF Issues Q&A–FASB Special Reports

See "Terminology" for references to defined terms presented in various accounting pronouncements.
See the Introduction to the Topical Index for details on the use of this index.

FAS–FASB Statements FIN–FASB Interpretations FTB–FASB Technical Bulletins
APB–APB Opinions AIN–AICPA Interpretations ARB–Accounting Research Bulletins
CON–FASB Concepts EITF–EITF Issues Q&A–FASB Special Reports

See "Terminology" for references to defined terms presented in various accounting pronouncements.
See the Introduction to the Topical Index for details on the use of this index.

FAS–FASB Statements FIN–FASB Interpretations FTB–FASB Technical Bulletins
APB–APB Opinions AIN–AICPA Interpretations ARB–Accounting Research Bulletins
CON–FASB Concepts EITF–EITF Issues Q&A–FASB Special Reports

See "Terminology" for references to defined terms presented in various accounting pronouncements.
See the Introduction to the Topical Index for details on the use of this index.

FAS–FASB Statements | FIN–FASB Interpretations | FTB–FASB Technical Bulletins
APB–APB Opinions | AIN–AICPA Interpretations | ARB–Accounting Research Bulletins
CON–FASB Concepts | EITF–EITF Issues | Q&A–FASB Special Reports

See "Terminology" for references to defined terms presented in various accounting pronouncements.

See the Introduction to the Topical Index for details on the use of this index.

See "Terminology" for references to defined terms presented in various accounting pronouncements.
See the Introduction to the Topical Index for details on the use of this index.

FAS–FASB Statements | FIN–FASB Interpretations | FTB–FASB Technical Bulletins
APB–APB Opinions | AIN–AICPA Interpretations | ARB–Accounting Research Bulletins
CON–FASB Concepts | EITF–EITF Issues | Q&A–FASB Special Reports

---

See "Terminology" for references to defined terms presented in various accounting pronouncements.
See the Introduction to the Topical Index for details on the use of this index.

FAS–FASB Statements FIN–FASB Interpretations FTB–FASB Technical Bulletins
APB–APB Opinions AIN–AICPA Interpretations ARB–Accounting Research Bulletins
CON–FASB Concepts EITF–EITF Issues Q&A–FASB Special Reports

See "Terminology" for references to defined terms presented in various accounting pronouncements.
See the Introduction to the Topical Index for details on the use of this index.

FAS–FASB Statements | FIN–FASB Interpretations | FTB–FASB Technical Bulletins
APB–APB Opinions | AIN–AICPA Interpretations | ARB–Accounting Research Bulletins
CON–FASB Concepts | EITF–EITF Issues | Q&A–FASB Special Reports

See "Terminology" for references to defined terms presented in various accounting pronouncements.
See the Introduction to the Topical Index for details on the use of this index.

FAS–FASB Statements FIN–FASB Interpretations FTB–FASB Technical Bulletins
APB–APB Opinions AIN–AICPA Interpretations ARB–Accounting Research Bulletins
CON–FASB Concepts EITF–EITF Issues Q&A–FASB Special Reports

See "Terminology" for references to defined terms presented in various accounting pronouncements.
See the Introduction to the Topical Index for details on the use of this index.

FAS–FASB Statements | FIN–FASB Interpretations | FTB–FASB Technical Bulletins
APB–APB Opinions | AIN–AICPA Interpretations | ARB–Accounting Research Bulletins
CON–FASB Concepts | EITF–EITF Issues | Q&A–FASB Special Reports

See "Terminology" for references to defined terms presented in various accounting pronouncements.
See the Introduction to the Topical Index for details on the use of this index.

FAS–FASB Statements | FIN–FASB Interpretations | FTB–FASB Technical Bulletins
APB–APB Opinions | AIN–AICPA Interpretations | ARB–Accounting Research Bulletins
CON–FASB Concepts | EITF–EITF Issues | Q&A–FASB Special Reports

See "Terminology" for references to defined terms presented in various accounting pronouncements.
See the Introduction to the Topical Index for details on the use of this index.

FAS–FASB Statements FIN–FASB Interpretations FTB–FASB Technical Bulletins
APB–APB Opinions AIN–AICPA Interpretations ARB–Accounting Research Bulletins
CON–FASB Concepts EITF–EITF Issues Q&A–FASB Special Reports

See "Terminology" for references to defined terms presented in various accounting pronouncements.

See the Introduction to the Topical Index for details on the use of this index.

See "Terminology" for references to defined terms presented in various accounting pronouncements.

See the Introduction to the Topical Index for details on the use of this index.

FAS–FASB Statements FIN–FASB Interpretations FTB–FASB Technical Bulletins
APB–APB Opinions AIN–AICPA Interpretations ARB–Accounting Research Bulletins
CON–FASB Concepts EITF–EITF Issues Q&A–FASB Special Reports

See "Terminology" for references to defined terms presented in various accounting pronouncements.
See the Introduction to the Topical Index for details on the use of this index.

FAS–FASB Statements | FIN–FASB Interpretations | FTB–FASB Technical Bulletins
APB–APB Opinions | AIN–AICPA Interpretations | ARB–Accounting Research Bulletins
CON–FASB Concepts | EITF–EITF Issues | Q&A–FASB Special Reports

See "Terminology" for references to defined terms presented in various accounting pronouncements.
See the Introduction to the Topical Index for details on the use of this index.

FAS–FASB Statements FIN–FASB Interpretations FTB–FASB Technical Bulletins
APB–APB Opinions AIN–AICPA Interpretations ARB–Accounting Research Bulletins
CON–FASB Concepts EITF–EITF Issues Q&A–FASB Special Reports